A Noble Company

This book begins with an utterly conventional school photograph. Four ranks of young Wykehamists gaze back at the camera. In the middle of the seated second row sits Malcolm Robertson, affectionately known as the 'Bobber', the housemaster of Hopper's. It is the early summer of 1938. The young men around him were part of that generation of whom many went straight to war instead of to university. The Bobber, an indefatigable correspondent, would keep in touch with them wherever they were in the world, and they would write back to a father figure who had never ceased to encourage them …

The Second World War … would see Wykehamists spread across the world in almost every imaginable theatre of war and military outfit. They served in rifle regiments, the Foot Guards, the Royal Artillery, the Royal Tank Regiment, there was a sprinkling of cavalrymen and sappers, and of course a number joined the Royal Navy, Fleet Air Arm, and the RAF … Their letters, mostly back to the Bobber, bring to life much of this strange new reality they faced. It is also striking to find how strongly the poetic tradition of the First World War lived on …

[Other] letters in which families try to cope with their loss are deeply moving … Altogether twelve Wykehamists, five in the Scots Guards alone, landed on the Anzio beachhead in January 1944. Half of them were killed.

Shaun Hullis must be congratulated on an extraordinary achievement. His background research is deeply impressive, to say nothing of the profusion of maps and photographs he has assembled.

Antony Beevor

A Noble Company

Bobber's Boys at War
1939–1945

Shaun Hullis

SPL

First published in Great Britain in 2024 by
Sunnyside Publications Ltd
in conjunction with Pen & Sword

ISBN 978 1 39907 877 1

A CIP catalogue record for this book is
available from the British Library

Typeset by Mac Style
Printed in the UK by Short Run Press Limited, EX2 7LW.

For a complete list of Pen & Sword titles please contact

PEN & SWORD BOOKS LIMITED
47 Church Street, Barnsley, South Yorkshire, S70 2AS, England
E-mail: enquiries@pen-and-sword.co.uk
Website: www.pen-and-sword.co.uk
or
PEN AND SWORD BOOKS
1950 Lawrence Rd, Havertown, PA 19083, USA
E-mail: uspen-and-sword@casematepublishers.com
Website: www.penandswordbooks.com

For Gabrielle, Benedict, & Aemilia

It would be easy for some young man chancing upon this book to feel that the life and work of these men must have been a glorious venture, an end in itself, and one which all men must achieve in order to satisfy an appetite for adventure, excitement and suspense. To him I would say this:

That when war comes to a country there is only one course for its people to take, and that is to fight as hard as they can until it is won … or lost.

That it is necessary for the sacrifice, the unselfish and continuing effort and the heroism of deliberate courage to be recorded so that it cannot ever be forgotten.

That the strain, discomfort and boredom which are the three predominant factors in modern warfare cannot be brought into their true perspective in a book of this kind, or it would be so long and dull that nobody would read it.

That there is no glory to be had out of war that cannot be had out of some greater and more creative enterprise.

That nothing will ever compensate us for the men we have lost, not even the way so many of them died. They were ready to die because they wanted to save their children and their children's children from future wars. The least and the most that any of us can do is to devote ourselves to finding a complete and lasting peace, and then to maintaining it with all our energy.

When you have finished this book, please turn back and read these few sentences again.

Scott, P., *The Battle of the Narrow Seas* (Country Life, 1945)

Contents

Foreword

Lieutenant General Sir Hew Pike KCB, DSO, MBE

'With my best wishes to you and love to Miss Bobber'. These words are a constant refrain in the letters making up this unique tribute to Malcolm Robertson and to his sister, Sheila. Equally constant are the reflections by young men of their gratitude for their years in Hopper's and the debt that they owe to the Bobber as their Housemaster, as well as to Miss Bobber, 'which we can never really repay' as one puts it.

> Feelings, too, of unremembered pleasure: such …
> As have no slight or trivial influence
> On that best portion of a good man's life,
> His little, nameless, unremembered acts
> Of kindness and of love.

In normal times, expressions of pride in schooldays are more likely to be voiced amongst older generations at dinners and reunions. But these were not normal times. These young men and their families found themselves swept up in great events. Consequently, this book is transformed into an intensely human story of young lives set against a tapestry of famous campaigns that are now a part of the nation's pantheon. Confronting what has been described by one wartime commander, the then Brigadier Shan Hackett, as 'the unlimited liability clause in the military contract', these boys sensed a premature urge to think back on their years with the Bobber.

Of remembrance, it has been written, 'A nation is not merely a place where we happen to be. A nation is a narrative of which we are a part. Society is a contract between the dead, the living, and those not yet born. Without a strong sense of duty between the generations, we would never make the sacrifice necessary to a future we may not live to see. We must make space to hear the call across the years of those who have died.' The Hopperites in that 1938 House photograph all recognised that their duty lay in what one described as 'beastly departures' and in what many would have felt to be anything but their natural environment, as they confronted the realities of military life. 'I'm a very indifferent soldier', confesses one in a letter to the Bobber – almost certainly wrongly!

It comes down to the letters, doesn't it? They consistently embrace colourful descriptive writing, honesty, humour, nostalgia, sincerity, courage, compassion, understanding – even an occasional venture into Latin from OFLAG IX, *pace* Dons' Common Room! How would they all have ever got by without such determined correspondence? Without its massive mailbag, this book would be little more than another chronology of important but well known events. The letters transfigure it into something altogether different. With the Bobber's heartfelt urge to write and stay in touch, he creates a family within a network of families, as he exchanges letters with his young charges, and as devoted parents write to him about their own lives and their sons, and about the fortunes of other Hopperite families, with their sons also at war. Malcolm Robertson becomes 'the stone in the midst of all', a comfort and confessor to many and a light to lighten anxieties, fears, even despair.

As Hopperites on our way 'up to books', some of us would occasionally cast a glance to left or right and nod respectfully to a forebear as we hurried through War Cloister. Such courteous instincts no doubt still prevail. We salute those who gave their lives, and all those who served their country, as we enjoy the pages of this extraordinary book. Many congratulations must therefore go to Shaun Hullis for a truly heroic endeavour, as well as to Richard Walker for his tireless research and legwork. And our special love and thanks are surely owed, this day and every day, to the Bobber and to Miss Bobber.

> Then hold your head up all the more,
> This tide
> And every tide;
> Because he was the son you bore,
> And gave to that wind blowing, and that tide!

Hew Pike
('I' 1956–60)

Preface

I was crossing Winchester College's Chamber Court with a colleague one afternoon in 2012 when we were accosted by the College Archivist, Suzanne Foster, who enquired in passing where we were off to.

'Well', I said, 'if you play your cards right you may well be on the receiving end of an interview we're on our way to record with a D-Day veteran.'

By way of background, Michael Wallis (a don and former CO of the School's CCF) and I were about to head off to North Hampshire to meet Brigadier Sir John ('Nick') Somerville, featured in this book.

Suzanne was intrigued, as she had literally just come from reading some wartime letters from an Old Hopperite to 'the Bobber'.

'Who are you meeting?' she asked.

It was none other than Nick Somerville himself, of course, who happened to be the very author of those letters! Our combined astonishment at this coincidence paled into insignificance compared to the sheer delight, tinged with some inevitable emotion, displayed by both Nick and his wife when we revealed that the School had retained this long-forgotten correspondence. As you might imagine, copies of the letters are now a highly-valued part of their family archive.

The chain of events goes on ... I was invited to 'take Preces' (evening assembly for a reading and prayer) in Hopper's (my old House in the mid-sixties), the Housemaster explaining that the boys were getting a little bored with the same old deliveries in Mugging Hall every evening: 'You've got about seven minutes, David, but it's entirely up to you what you read to them.'

By coincidence, my allotted evening was just three days after Remembrance Day 2012, and I decided that the modern-day pupil might like to hear what their fellow Hopperite had felt in his somewhat less comfortable surroundings some seventy years earlier, so I read them extracts from Nick's letters to the Bobber. Suffice it to say that, according to the Housemaster, one could have heard a pin drop, such was their fascination with Nick's very personal correspondence, which I ended with the following closing lines from his letter, written on July 13th 1944:

> Well, I'm afraid that I must stop now as the shells are starting to come over and I shall have to get into a slit-trench soon. Back again now after a short and sweet little stonc, some of which landed pretty close – luckily no casualties. Give my love to Miss Robertson and I hope the House is doing well. From Nick

I don't mind admitting that those seven minutes and the way the boys related to them are high on my list of valued memories from my ten years working at Winchester College.

David Fellowes ('I' 1963–67)

Acknowledgements

This independently published book owes a lot to many people. Service Records have come from different branches of the Ministry of Defence, as well as historical accounts held by individual regiments, the Navy, and the Royal Air Force. The National Archives at Kew have provided further valuable information.

Importantly, the boys' families have been both supportive and conscientious in seeking out material relevant to the book's focus: letters, diaries, unpublished memoirs, and photographs – many of them only seen previously by very few people – as well as obituaries and eulogies. Newspaper cuttings, souvenirs, memorabilia, and medals, kept safe and stored away all these years, have been retrieved from their boxes in attics. To all those who put in the time and effort to dust off those boxes and unearth this precious material relating to their husband, brother, father, uncle, or cousin, we are hugely grateful for your contribution. Many of us connected to the boys are likely to discover things about them which we did not know previously, in the case of both those who survived and those who died.

The record contained within this book could never have been so comprehensive and interesting without the dedication and hard work of Winchester College staff, past and present. The retention and archiving of the boys' letters to the Bobber have allowed that correspondence to be the treasure trove awaiting wider readership, eighty years later. We have had access to obituaries in *The Trusty Servant* (alumni magazine), as well as many other avenues of research which have provided valuable information. Suzanne Foster has been unstinting in her efforts, and ever available to contribute additional background for the book. We are indebted to her, as well as to the School more widely for its support and for its faith in the project's potential.

David Fellowes has been centre stage in his support and encouragement right from the start. It was he, with his steady hand, who steered the course to Shaun Hullis, whom he secured as our splendid author. Michael Wallis has been there to read the draft text and make helpful suggestions. Thank you both.

The Commissioning Editor, Henry Wilson, believed in this book from an early stage. He has been ever patient and flexible throughout the process of its production, as has George Chamier with his editing of the text. Our thanks go to them and their colleagues at Pen and Sword.

Introduction

Sunnyside House, Winchester College, 1938.

The above photograph still hangs on walls in several homes, a memento passed down by fathers to their sons or daughters. In other homes, it sits in boxes of letters and souvenirs from the family's past. And in others it has been lost or, its significance not appreciated, thrown away. In its faded monochrome, it is not hard to see it as a distant irrelevance. But many boys in this photograph became the fathers of children still living; the last survivors died less than a decade ago; and their lives were lived in colour.

However, one huge gulf does separate us from these boys. Less than two years after this photograph was taken, Europe was plunged into another shattering war, and almost every boy pictured served in some capacity. The Second World War took the place which university usually fills for school-leavers, and in some cases left our subjects permanently scarred physically or mentally; but those who made it through the war went on to live full and rich lives which lasted far longer than their war years. The war may have shaped them, but in most cases it did not define them. Nevertheless, it was an experience which few of us today can comprehend, and which none of the boys can have anticipated.

Later in this account we will read poems which one of them wrote during the war; here he reminds us of the difficulty of interpreting what those involved in the war wrote of their experiences, either at the time or later. He also sums up how these young men felt when the call to arms came:

> I came from an upper middle class background. I was by no means a natural soldier, and had there not been a war I would not have dreamt of becoming one. But that was my fate, and I was expected to become an officer, and became one. It was profoundly important to me that I should carry out my duties as best I could, though they might be alien and terrifying.
>
> I do not claim that I had a profound insight into the experiences I was undergoing. I do not even claim that an honest account of what I felt at the time is given. But

> these poems and pieces of prose are what I chose to write. Rather than expressing real feelings they can be evasions of real feeling, because evasion was necessary to enable me to face my life.
>
> That is the kind of person I was, and this is what I wrote.[1]

We should also remember that service takes many different forms. Our subjects became infantrymen, tank crew, artillerymen, engineers, signallers, pilots, aircrew, seamen – but not all saw combat (although the nature of the conflict meant that even civilians were at risk of the war coming to them). There were other roles which were just as important but wholly unglamorous: one of our subjects conducted research which improved military diving equipment; another administered large swathes of Africa. Whatever their task, their war effort centred on people, and people need to be looked after:

> The thing to remember about it all is that the Army probably never had a more naturally inefficient soldier than me. I think people realised that it was no good putting me in charge of other people's lives. Luckily, I mainly filled an administrative role. It is very important to keep things organised in a war. Troops have to be kept happy, and watered, and fed, and clothed, and looked after. If they get ill, they have to know that there's a doctor who they can go to. If they've got fears about the dentist at home trying to sleep with their wives, a chap needs to be able to get leave for them to sort those things out. These are the problems that everybody had. That is what an officer is for.[2]

Once committed to doing their duty, whatever it might be, to the best of their ability, the young men found themselves embroiled in a war which rapidly became global and all-consuming, as is neatly explained by a contemporary:

> The war of 1939–1945, unlike that of 1914–1918 in Flanders, was one of range and movement, presenting the participants from day to day with a kaleidoscopic variety of fresh faces, odd locations, and unfamiliar activities … I was totally absorbed, like every other Platoon Commander, in the business in hand and the prospects of survival for myself and my men. For the rest of the time, as a temporary soldier with no long-term career aspirations, I had as my main aim, when not occupied with training or regimental chores, to derive as much interest and amusement as possible with my companions of the moment from our unusual circumstances and surroundings.[3]

The truth of this statement about 'range and movement' is evident in the travels of our subjects: between them they saw active service in, over, or off Algeria, Australia, Belgium, Burma, Canada, the Caribbean, Egypt, the Faroes, France, Germany, Greece, India, Iran, Iraq, Italy, Kenya, Lebanon, Libya, the Netherlands, Norway, Palestine, Panama, Singapore, South Africa, Southern Rhodesia, Syria, Thailand, Transjordan, Tunisia, and the United States of America. They traversed the Arctic, North and South Atlantic, North and South Pacific, and Indian Oceans; only the great Southern Ocean eluded them.

* * *

Sunnyside, from the garden to the rear; a photograph taken around 1938 by John Kennedy, one of our subjects. As a visiting tutor there between 2004 and 2008, I can testify that its aspect has not changed significantly.

This is not a book about school life, but about lives connected by a school – and not just by a school, but by one boarding house amongst the many at Winchester College. That house was Sunnyside, also known as Hopper's (and later as Turner's). A boarding housemaster is a hugely influential figure in a schoolboy's life, and those who spent their formative years in Hopper's with Malcolm Robertson[4] and his sister Sheila between 1920 and their retirement in 1943 owed them a life-long debt. A close friend wrote:

> Together they created to a remarkable degree the life and atmosphere of a family, in which everyone was made to feel that he mattered, none suffered to imagine that he mattered too much, and all learnt to take their part in the hospitality which the housemaster and his sister delighted to offer. Above all it was the least gifted, the diffident, the potential misfit that profited most from their affectionate understanding. No kinder hearts or shrewder heads ever combined to help the lame dog over the stile.[5]

Nick Somerville, who arrived in September 1936, described life at Hopper's in his memoirs:[6]

Somerville.

> Hopper's … was run by Malcolm Robertson, affectionately known by everyone as 'The Bobber', who had learned much about humanity from his experiences in the trench warfare of the Great War. His sister – 'Miss Bobber' – did all the housekeeping, read Dickens to the Juniors on Sunday evening, and, although she was a spinster, like so many of her wartime generation, did her best to be a mother to new arrivals. As a New Man I was given a 'Tee Jay' to look after [me] and teach me all the Win.Coll. 'Notions'. These were special names for people, places, and activities. There were upwards of a hundred special words which

Victorious Hopper's XI, Turner Pot (Senior Inter-House Cricket Cup) 1936.

Back row (L to R): Arthur Majendie, Nigel Weir, Gerry Rickman, Sam Clayton, Hew Tompson. Middle row (L to R): Willie Whitelaw, Mike Sinclair, David Wilson, Michael Osmond, Bill Cliff Hodges. Front row: John Pinney, John Sinclair.

Of the twelve 'Hopperites' in this photograph, five died in the Second World War, & two others spent over three years in Japanese captivity. Between them they earned an MC, a DFC, & a DSO.

became a Wykehamical language. My TJ was David Kemp, who was a clever Exhibitioner and who later became a distinguished QC. He was very patient and thankfully got me through my oral exam six weeks later.[7]

Life at Winchester was well organised and strict. We were fortunate to have Willie Whitelaw – the future Viscount and Deputy Prime Minister to Margaret Thatcher – as Head of House when I joined. He controlled prefects' duties with fairness and understanding, and established a very happy regime.

Still, we all rose at 0615hrs, fell into an ice-cold hip-bath, dressed in time for tea and biscuits, before walking the ten-minute journey 'up to books' (i.e. our class room) for 'morning lines' at 0730hrs. Then into Chapel for morning prayers, back up to house for breakfast at 0830hrs, and back 'up to books' again for lessons from 0915 to 1245hrs. After lunch every day was given to sport and exercise, and on Monday, Tuesday, Thursday, and Friday we had lessons from 1515 to 1745hrs. Tea or supper was at 1800hrs and Prep from 1900–2100hrs. At 2100hrs Bobber talked to the House and said prayers ('Preces'). He then said goodnight to each man.[8]

Robertson had the personal touch which made him an excellent housemaster; Whitelaw, for example, considered him one of the formative influences on his life:

> I began for the first time in my life to develop a little confidence in myself. I owed much of this to a remarkable housemaster, Major Robertson, always known as 'Bobber'. He had the largest feet I have ever seen and was in many ways an eccentric. He understood boys, though, and he took a special interest in each one of us.[9]

One of the youngest of our subjects, Graham Mackrill, only arrived in the House in April 1938. He had been at Bramcote Preparatory School in Scarborough with another of our subjects – Robert Holtby – and when he passed the entrance examination in March 1938, Robertson wrote to him there:

> I am glad you did well enough, after all the interruptions, to take JP1: very creditable! I think I sent you this card once before [a photograph of Sunnyside, with hand-written annotations 'Our Drawing Room' and 'Your Dormitory'], but you may like to show your friends where you are going to! R. Holtby wasn't quite so good – JP2. Give my greetings, and congratulations, to Mr Pidcock. See you on April 29th! Yours, Malcolm Robertson.[10]

* * *

But when Robertson sat down for the Hopper's house photograph a few months later, in the summer of 1938, the shades of hundreds of his Marlborough contemporaries and Winchester College colleagues and pupils must have seemed very close. Twenty years before, he had witnessed some of their deaths personally. He was sure that it was about to happen again – Czechoslovakia had mobilized its forces on May 19th in response to German provocations over the Sudetenland. Robertson's only uncertainty was which of his charges would die this time around.[11]

I

'Covered with France from head to foot'

The Bobber's War, 1914–1918

The British Empire had last declared war on Germany on August 4th 1914, when Robertson was thirty-one years old and had been teaching at Winchester College almost continuously since September 1905. With a decade of experience in the College Officer Training Corps, his thoughts turned to how best he might serve his country. The New Armies being raised from volunteers across the nation needed officers, and the OTC contingents of the public schools were designed to provide them. The Winchester OTC rapidly organized a camp at Tidworth for 500 Cadets from (amongst others) Bradfield, Charterhouse, Clifton, Eton, Harrow, Marlborough, Rugby, Sherborne, and Winchester, which ran from August 31st to September 16th:[1]

> The early stages of the war found most of us in a great perplexity. We wanted to help, we were almost ashamed to appear in public without uniform, but we were not quite sure what to do. The happy idea of a camp at Tidworth Pennings solved all our difficulties: it gave us something to do, it gave most of us a uniform to wear, and it gave us an opportunity of seeing what others meant to do, with the result that Kitchener's New Army should benefit by a good number of officers …
>
> Our best thanks are due to the two Winchester dons who gallantly put up so many tents so that not one of them blew down … The morning was taken up with drill, judging distances, or semaphore, and later on with attack and defence schemes or digging trenches … Occasionally also we took part in night work.
>
> Such was our serious work. The lighter moments also call for comment … Captain Robertson kept our money, managed sing-song, and sold picture post-cards among his other activities …
>
> One very satisfactory result was that the War Office recognised the efficiency of the seventeen-day camp by granting commissions to practically all of those who applied for them.

At the end of the camp, Robertson took a commission in a Kitchener battalion. Strangely, it was a Yorkshire unit – 9th (Service) Battalion, The Duke of Wellington's (West Riding) Regiment. 9DWR, raised in Halifax in September, immediately came south to join 17th (Northern) Division in Dorset, being headquartered in the Masonic Hall at Wimborne. The commanding officer of 9DWR was a Wykehamist, Lieutenant Colonel Frederick Arthur Hayden DSO,[2] at fifty-three still capable of active command.

One wonders whether Hayden specifically requested help from Winchester's OTC. He certainly needed it. His Adjutant, Captain Miller, had only just returned from India, and the infant battalion was in chaos. No uniforms were at first available; blankets were in short supply; the unit had only a few old and inert rifles. Although the troops were issued with Lee-Enfield rifles (with ammunition!) before the end of the year, it was not until March 1915 that they received their full quota of rifles and webbing. Robertson's organizational skills, as displayed in the August camp, must have been a godsend to the harassed Adjutant.[3]

Robertson also brought four former pupils with him to 9DWR, where their recent OTC experience was useful: they were Frederick 'Cully' Cullinan, Alan Ferguson, Maurice Savory, and Thomas 'Jugs' Weatherby. As a result, Robertson's Winchester nickname – 'The Bobber' – stuck to him, and when a younger unrelated Robertson joined the unit, the two were distinguished as 'Young Bobber' and 'T'Owd Bobber'.

Three of the five Wykehamists were dead by March 1917, and when Cullinan followed in 1923, only T'Owd Bobber remained.

* * *

After 9DWR arrived in Wimborne, Weatherby wrote to his former housemaster at Winchester, Revd John Trant Bramston:[4]

> Dear Trant,
> I have just seen the new *Wykehamist* and Podge's appeal for money for motor ambulances, so here are a few pounds from the Wykehamists in this Regiment. My cheque is for Cullinan as well as myself …
>
> We were at camp at Wool and we only moved here last Monday after spending three months under canvas. The last few weeks were very trying, either very wet or very cold. It was a great inducement to get up when one heard one's servant breaking ice outside for you to wash in. Most of the men are in public halls in the town, and the remainder billeted in private houses. All the officers have been made honorary members of the Club and we all mess together there but sleep in houses in the town. Four of us – Bobber, Savory, Alan [Ferguson], and myself live with an Oriental lady, or should I say a lady who has lived all her life in Turkey, and with the town surveyor; quite a good house, but unluckily no bath. As you probably know, our Colonel, Hayden, is a Wykehamist – he was in College the same time as Dad was in the house.
>
> I suppose I may say that I am getting on quite well. I have been appointed second-in-command to a company and if we get any machine-guns I have been promised the command of them. About a fortnight ago Bobber and I went over and called at the Pippin's home near Moreton;[5] but they were all away. Colonel Parke has gone to India in command of a brigade, and Mrs Parke has gone with him – but we had a very jolly tea with the two little girls, aged ten and seven. Poor Pippin the Bairn's death must be a great blow. I hear that he was recommended for a VC and see that Robert Baird is wounded; if you have any letters from the front from him I should like to see them.[6]

* * *

A French company (Réunies de Nancy – Editions du 'Crl. des Flandres') published a postcard in 1915 which showed Parke's original roadside grave being tended by two young French girls. The caption read: 'Little French girls keep green the memory of brave Englishmen dead on the field of honour.' (Copyright holder unknown)

Robertson was a regular attender at 9DWR reunions in the 1930s, and when asked to speak – as he often was – he recalled their training at Wimborne and Bovington:

> Major Robertson … awakened memories of early days. 'The Bobber' recalled that when he joined the Battalion on its formation he and the other members did not speak the same language![7] He described his arrival at Bovington and being given a half-raw rabbit's leg for tea by Captain Miller (who was the life and soul of the 9th in early days);[8] on asking, 'Where's the Mess, and what time is dinner?' he was told, 'There is no Mess, and you've had your dinner!'… 'A' Company, after being held up as the model company of the 9th Battalion, broke and chased a rabbit at Wimborne one field day.[9] He elicited the fact that there were about twenty present who had made the original sixteen-mile march under him, the only officer, for a 'battle' at Lulworth …[10]

With his OTC experience, Robertson was immediately commissioned Captain[11] and took over 'D' Company, assisted by Lieutenant Maurice Savory. Robertson was an unlikely soldier – short-sighted, extremely tall, and with enormous (size 16) feet – but all the evidence suggests that he was an excellent and respected officer.

* * *

9th BATTALION AT WIMBORNE, 1914.

Top row:—H. M. Woodhead, E. S. Walsh, M. W. Clarke, J. A. Benjamin, D. H. Fletcher, T. Weatherby, M. J. Savory, F. J. F. Cullinan, J. W. Robertson, J. E. Raphael, L. Wray Fox.
Second row:—E. A. Berrisford, Capt. P. R. Simner, Capt. M. Robertson, Capt. N. W. Fraser, D.S.O., Major Beresford Johnstone, Lt.-Col. F. A. Hayden, D.S.O., Capt. and Adjt. A. E. de'l. Miller, Major Watts, Capt. Wannell, A. M. Davis,.
Third row:—H. Giles, J. Hawkes, L. de Pinto, A. Ferguson, H. McColl.

HQ 'D' Company, 9DWR, Wimborne 1914

Back Row (L–R) CSM Riles; Pte Swales (Company Clerk); Pte Leonard (Company Storeman); CQMS Mulhall

Front Row (L–R) Lt Savory; Capt Robertson; 2Lt Knight

(Mulhall collection, reprinted in The Iron Duke, *1981.)*

Weatherby.

9DWR had not even gone overseas when, early in May 1915, the first of Bobber's boys died. Weatherby went down with 'spotted fever' (meningococcal meningitis) and died in the Alexandra Military Hospital, Cosham, on Saturday, May 8th. Ferguson wrote to Bramston shortly afterwards:

> As you can imagine, his death has been a very great blow to me. For three or four years now he has been a very great friend of mine. The first night of the war I met him in London, and we decided to join some regiment together. For a long time it seemed as though it would be impossible, but eventually we did manage it. But apparently we were never meant to see service together, and I can only be thankful that I have at any rate been able to train with him for five or six months.[12]

Weatherby's funeral was held the following Tuesday in his home village of Lindfield; Robertson and the others acted as pall-bearers, and their wreath read: 'From the four friends who knew him at Winchester and in his Regiment'.[13]

None of the others would receive so grand a military funeral.

* * *

Robertson left no memoir of his war service, but he is mentioned in many sources, not least the diary and letters of Lieutenant Jack W. Russell ('C' Company), which Robertson edited for publication from October 1927:[14]

> By permission of his parents, I am making a selection of passages from the diary and letters which Jack Russell sent to them between July 15th 1915, when the Battalion went to the front, and July 7th 1916, when he was killed at the head of his Company in an attack on the 'Quadrangle Support Trench' near Contalmaison.[15]

All comments in the diary which state 'MR' are Robertson's.

From this and other sources, we can reconstruct some of Robertson's experiences – as a Company Commander in the trenches in the Ypres Salient and on the Somme; as a Brigade Bombing Officer and Assistant Staff Captain in 52 Infantry Brigade (he was awarded the Military Cross for his services in these roles); and finally as a Company Commander in an Officer Cadet Battalion at Pirbright, the ideal job for a skilled instructor with front-line experience (and for which Robertson earned his OBE).

* * *

9DWR moved to Winchester from Bovington at the end of May 1915 and remained there until July 15th. That day, the Battalion entrained for Folkestone, whence it sailed to Boulogne. Within a fortnight, 9DWR had reached the front line, each company sending a platoon forward to spend twenty-four hours in the trenches near Vlamertinghe, a couple of miles west of Ypres. 9DWR took over its own trenches on August 2nd, came out on the 14th, and went forwards again on the 18th. Russell recorded these early experiences and the Winchester officers' part in them:

August 24th 1915
At about 1000hrs I met Savory, and, wanting something to do, offered to take him out along a disused trench which runs outside our barbed wire, to see a supposed German sniper's post ... We had to crawl on hands and knees, in many places absolutely flat; in one spot it was only half a foot deep with thick barbed wire close over it ... I have two tears in my shirt about two feet long, and three in my breeches. Savory followed, and used some language on me for having enticed him along such a place!

August 30th 1915
At 0950hrs went off with Capt. Robertson ('The Bobber') and four Sergeants to inspect some third and fourth line trenches (Vierstraat line). Wandered about them for 1½ hours, taking notes; met Captain Wannell coming down the side of a hedge with Sergeant Riles, picking blackberries. We set to work ourselves and found them really luscious! ... I have failed to tame any of the cats which hang round all the redoubts here!

September 2nd 1915
Ferguson dropped in, and we all determined we would not mind if the war was over tomorrow, but that it was infinitely better out here than training at Bovington!

September 5th 1915
Went along to IC 'D' Company in 'W' Redoubt to try and get some 'eggs' from them [*these were the first Mills bombs, one dozen, received by our Battalion. MR*]. Found Savory and the Bobber, who needed a lot of persuading! During the argument I drank lemonade, and in the end they decided to go shares with me; so I put six nice little eggs in a sandbag and then, since it was raining, spent half an hour in Bobber's dugout, looking at Punch and eating peppermint creams ... After tea, we left the reserve dugouts for the trenches. I carried my big cat [*he had 'tamed' one by now. MR*] in one sandbag and bombs in another. Fletcher carried the kitten. We had great fun going up the communication trench with the cat swearing and scrabbling inside the bag, while we floundered knee-deep in sludge.

Three days later, Cullinan wrote to Trant Bramston as follows:[16]

I was indeed glad to get your letter this morning. If there are things we look forward to out here, it is the mail from Home. Our trench postman brings the letters into the trench about midnight.

We moved into these fire trenches yesterday. It has been a wet week, and the mud and water was in consequence very bad in the trenches. But thanks be! Today has been gloriously fine and sunny and we have, to a certain extent, been able to dry ourselves and our surroundings.

I am writing this in my dugout in the fire trench. The time is just after midnight and I am taking the 2100–0200hrs watch. Every few minutes I have to go along the trench to see that all is well. The night is always more lively as regards rifle fire than the day.

The Germans have splendid lights, which they send up, lighting up the whole place. We have some too, of course, but not so good.

Poor Trant! You must indeed have a hard time looking through the 'lists' each day. You know we are much better off out here – we have no time to think on such things. I had a great pleasure in seeing Max the other day – it is hard on him to have lost all his friends in that Hooge affair – but he has had a wonderful experience in coming through it all right.

Well, I think that this life is teaching me one thing anyhow – that we must have been made for something better. I expect you came to that conclusion many years ago.

Only think whom I met the other day when out riding with the Bobber – but Grey-Edwards, very well and in great form too! We met him midst the ruins of what is perhaps the most famous town on the Western Front. Alan [Ferguson], who is flourishing, tells me he saw Baird the other day – now an almighty 'Knut' on somebody's staff! Oh! And have you seen Alan's gazette in the paper? I am so glad he has been made a Lieutenant, and so will you be!

The pipes have not yet arrived, but no doubt will come by today's mail – I am ever so grateful to you, Trant, for sending them. Would you like to send me some literature? I have the *Oxford Book of English Verse* with me but would like a collection of short stories – or some'ut of the sort. You know I am a wild reader – and even out here feel the want of it greatly. I say wild because I have no method – but wander around! However, you know my tastes by now – how I enjoyed the books you lent me at Hursley!

You ask after Bobber and I give my old answer – he is a schoolmaster, not a soldier. He carries on, but worries himself to death – and yet is still (unofficially) his kindly old self… .

Ever yours
Fred Cully

At around this time, Robertson sent a letter which was printed in *The Wykehamist* in November:[17]

A FRIEND IN NEED.

It was by a mistake that it ever came to Flanders. A year ago today, when its owner took the plunge from civilisation and entered the wilds of Dorsetshire with a motley horde of patriots, it was left, with other insignia, books, and relics, in a snug corner of College Street. Perhaps it ought to have been handed over with the other paraphernalia with which the perplexed substitute is asked to grapple, but it was not College property; it cost, in fact, no less than eighteen pence by private contract, and such things are not lightly parted with. During November's mud and February's winds I often thought if not of it, yet of all to which it once admitted me. The thoughts were mixed, I will confess; there were many days when it was good to be out and about in sun and air from 0600hrs till dusk, afoot or on horseback. But there were other days when the heart yearned for the familiar prison-bars, and the easy access to Culture in its better sense, and the evening stroll with an intimate friend, surrounded by venerable walls and trees. It was not till later that it became associated with these and kindred ideas, for it rested peacefully out of sight and out of mind, and it was only by a fluke that it came forth again to take its chance on active service.

The ways of Army Administration, like those of Providence, are impenetrable. Just when we were expecting to depart from our Dorset haunts – now a very grateful and comforting memory to most of us – for the tracts of Salisbury Plain, and when the very orders for the march thither were issued and anxiously perused, there came as an afterthought, it seemed, a suggestion that it might be a good thing for the Division to spend a few weeks in Hampshire. So to Hampshire on foot and with many bitter-sweet experiences by the way, we came. It was not the county we had known: Oliver's Battery could hardly be discerned amid a veritable fungus-growth of shanties, suggestive of Mafeking, or some back-veldt dorp: there were no orchids to be found on Shawford Down, or birds in Hursley gorse; even Morn Hill seemed to be no longer (as recently) the exclusive pleasaunce of Saturday golfers and funeral parties; and the road to 'Winton' – a sore puzzle to my Yorkshire friends till a kindly brigade order gave the synonym – was now irrefutably the worst and most unpleasant road in England! Still, we were not deterred, and away in the valley we found what we had left, and dallied there as long as duty allowed.

And so it came about that in mid-June, when the strawberries were ripe and the smell of hay was sweet, it was withdrawn from its hiding-place, and passed again into my pocket with a knife of fifteen years' service and a much-thinned purse! It came into use not in daytime so much, for then all might wander in and out at will, but in the evening, when bidden to the Informator's good cheer (and how many in khaki know what that means!), or when the last light lingered in Meads, or when a hail from Kingsgate Street met a welcoming invite to a yarn from the indispensable and familiar figure who burns late oil in Orderly Room – then its kindly offices were called upon once more, and not in vain.

Then came a day long waited and wished for by others than us – for it was the day of what we still called Eton Match. Perhaps Fate was kinder than we thought in giving us only two hours to watch the game, and grasp hurried hands of friends, old and young. There remained the weirdest impression of mixed feelings and bustle, crowned by one peaceful half-hour in that hospitable meadow house, where many a warrior, young or old, has learnt his work or told his tale. Then the triumphal march to the station (for with such men and such good spirits it was nothing less) and the train. I dragged out a handful of coppers to buy some papers, and among them it once more.

From that moment it became a friend, a companion, a fetish, if you will. It has been four times in the firing line, and been used to open lids, or hammer tacks, or to illustrate the making of a tourniquet. It has eased a safety-catch or a hand-guard; it opens *Punch* weekly and *The Wykehamist* when it comes (time of publication uncertain). Some day – who knows? – it may turn a bullet. I showed it to one who also had the right to carry it, the day before the fight at Hooge, when we were peacefully exchanging gossip some miles in rear.

It went with me to a certain rest camp, where three Wykehamists fed me, and I saw some faces familiar at the Depot or at Tidworth Pennings. I took it to a ruined city of ill-omened name, where, riding with one of the youngest captains Winchester has produced, we met a figure which arrested our attention – an aeronaut, who did not deny the soft impeachment that he was (unsuccessfully) bent on finding a little loot: and he, too, was a Wykehamist, true to the sporting tradition of his house and native land! More power to his elbow – or his wings!

After a long and trying spell of front trenches, I seized a fine September day to ride over to a beautiful cemetery outside a chateau park under a wooded hill. There sleeps a true son of Wykeham whose voice only just over a year ago was ringing through School at Medal Speaking, and through Meads on the next morning's parade. He lies among his men; and there was another grave near by of one with whom – strange irony – I read much German once. There were a few weeds among the flowers on their graves, and it was with the first thing that came to my hand that I removed them. To my fancy it seemed to do the work lovingly and well, and in future when I clutch it in night watches, or ease the sodden envelopes of letters to be censored – those letters fuller than a dozen novels of human suffering and hopefulness, and unselfishness, and mirth – it will be dearer to me and more intimate than ever.

And after all this, what is 'it'? you may ask. Only a key of Commoner Gate; but by it, I remember my friends, and by it I hope to enter Civilisation again some day, when the tyranny is over past.

Russell's diary reveals the conditions in which he and Robertson lived:

September 20th 1915
Went to 'D' Company's quarters; had a bath in Captain Robertson's canvas bath, and played cut-throat bridge with Doggy and Alan Ferguson. Managed to screw another four francs out of them!

October 22nd 1915
Marched at 1300hrs to our present abode, arriving 1800hrs. The men are sleeping fifteen to a tent, which helps to keep them warm. Potts, Captain Robertson, Savory, and I are sharing a tent. After coffee and bread and jam, we turned in and slept somewhat restlessly – chilly, and the ground jolly hard after our soft mattresses!

October 27th 1915
Had to get up at 0645hrs. Savory, Walsh, Cully, and myself had to parade with one hundred men for some inspection. Eventually only twenty-five men and one officer were wanted, so being junior I got let in ... When we were jolly fed up with standing about, the King suddenly came along, taking the salute of each unit ... Then tramped back to the Battalion, which had moved into the huts we first occupied on arrival in Belgium (Canada Huts). At 1600hrs started for the theatre with Potts, old Bobber, Benjy, Giles, and Knight. We walked about a mile and then jumped a lorry ... The show is called 'The Fancies'. The actors are some officers, including one of the RAMC, who goes up with an ambulance to the trenches every night after the performance, and two quite pretty [*sic. MR*] French girls (Lanoline and Grisoline)! We got in good time into our seats, stalls, which Bobber had booked in advance ... The show was roaringly funny – all comic songs and a jolly good assortment of dresses, kilts, old fishermen, dress-suits, etc. One of the girls sang 'Gilbert the Filbert' and the other songs in pigeon English ('You'd naver berlieve me' etc.). Caught another 'bus' back to within three-quarters of a mile of camp, and straight to bed after good big slices of cake.

October 27th 1915
We packed up for the trenches … Had a jolly tedious march and got settled into our new quarters at 2300hrs [*'Sanctuary' – or as the men called it, 'Sanitary' – Wood. MR*]. It is quite a peaceful spot except when an attack is on; it is Hades then, as shells burst in from left and right, front and back. At present the Boche only shells when he sees people moving, so we have to keep quiet in day-time. I am in a dugout with Savory, since some of 'D' Company are with us. We are toppingly comfortable.

November 9th 1915
Being relieved tonight, so had an easy day. Went with Savory to see the Bobber and Ferguson. Played bridge till tea. Bobber and I won, but I'm afraid he found my calls somewhat rash! After tea we settled down to wait till the relieving 'Scotties' came in; got awfully bored, tried to read, ate cake, failed to boil some water, betted on how long our candle would last. Pitch dark and raining in torrents, so we had a cheery trudge to look forward to. First party of Jocks came in at 2130hrs, so we got ready to move; 2200hrs, still waiting; 2230hrs, decided the others must have got lost; 2330hrs, still waiting. The doctor and I had a glorious laugh at a poor Jock who tumbled face-first into a muddy ditch five feet deep; some real Scotch swearing! 2345hrs, we found the Scotch officers' kit bags dumped in a shell hole full of water; midnight, still waiting. At last found four Scotch officers, mud up to their eyes, and wishing there was 'whusky' in the dugout. 0100hrs we moved off, CSM Green and I bringing up the rear. We stumbled along two miles of communication trench, then slipped and flopped over two miles of muddy open ground; finally arrived in camp with 'D' Company at 0600hrs, when it was daylight.

[*Note: if I remember right, this was part of the remnants of 9th Division coming away from Loos. They were full of new hands, and had been 'paid out' on the way … This accounts for the bad relief. Our guides were not to blame! I myself lifted at least six incapables out of the trench that night. MR*]

November 12th 1915
0900hrs Wannell, Cully, Ferguson, and myself on digging fatigue; everything horribly muddy and raining hard … At 2200hrs Danby came in to try and give us a nightmare about the trenches we are going into … According to his tale the trenches are up to the waist in sludge, one long series of crump-holes; parapets and parados all tumbled down; arms and legs 'without any meat on them' sticking out all over the place; the Hun only fifteen yards away! A cheerful account, terribly exaggerated probably … [*This description of the Hooge trenches was not very far wide of the mark! MR*]

November 20th 1915
Changed our billets to some dugouts about two miles away, while the other three companies [including Robertson's 'D' Company] went up into the trenches [at Hooge]. Dugout with Wannell and Potts only fair – rats, and not rain-proof. Had to carry rations up to the trenches – impossible to describe them – mud, debris, dead bodies if you care to dig for them. There is a crater thirty yards in diameter and about sixty feet deep, said to have more than five hundred dead in it … The front trenches are as near the abomination of desolation as you could want.

December 8th 1915
At 1700hrs 'D' Company relieved us, and by 1800hrs I was settled into my new quarters (the 'Culvert'), about a hundred yards behind the support line. Later Ferguson came down to share my dugout. We felt jolly cold and scarcely slept at all … Squelched back to my dugout and found it leaking all round. With thorough delight we heard two naval officers pass on the way up to the firing line, which they have been sent out to inspect, as being about the worst trenches on the whole front. We go over the open at night, as the communication trench is fully waist deep in mud in places. Wannell gave their guide strict instructions to take them straight up the trench (they had nice blue suits and white collars and nice long sheepskin overcoats). Hearsay that on leaving the front line these officers said they did not know how men could live in such conditions.

Robertson also wrote about the visit of these two naval officers that night:

It was early in December 1915 that a party of naval officers were sent to visit the trenches, with a view to lecturing afterwards to their ships' companies on the discomforts and excitements of trench life. So there came one awful night of wet and misery to 'D' Company of the 9th Battalion, two officers, one of whom was Midshipman L.R.D. Helm of the *Iron Duke*. We were holding the front line at Hooge, C6 and 7, if my memory is correct, next the Crater and including the 'Fish-hook', completely water-logged, only some twenty-five yards from the Hun. Among the Company officers at the time were Lieutenants M.J. Savory and A. Ferguson, who afterwards so gallantly defended Trenches 88 and 89 near Houplines against the German raid to capture our first Stokes Mortar, and Lieutenant H.H. McColl, a notorious fire-eater, who won the first MC in the Brigade, and after being two or three times wounded with the Battalion, joined a bombing squadron of the RAF 'for a rest'. This latter, in particular, undertook the education of our naval friends, and provided the material which was a few days later worked up into a lecture delivered before Admiral Jellicoe and the officers and men of the *Iron Duke*. I met one of them afterwards who told me it was a great success, and very lurid. Helm was first brought up the communication trench (which we seldom used) through water up to his arm-pits, trotted round the Company front through two or three feet of water, and out to the 'Fish-hook' post to throw a bomb at Fritz, though I sternly forbade McColl to take him on a raid! He left us finally complete with 'blighty', for McColl threw him as a souvenir a chunk of a shell that had just burst near us, in catching which he cut two fingers pretty deeply. I believe his hand was still bandaged when he gave his lecture.

The cheering effect of this visit was immense. I remember a Sergeant (Duffy, I think, of No.14 Platoon) saying:

'Well, goodnight, Sir, and give our respects to the Navy,'

and the reply:

'If the Navy could see this place, it would send its respects to you; I've seen more water tonight than I ever saw on the sea!'

Shortly afterwards, at Christmas, when we were again in the same line, I received a card, which I have before me as I write. Outside is the *Duke*'s crest, and inside printed: 'God rest ye merrie gentlemen, let nothing you dismay', and in MS: 'To Captain Robertson, and the three other officers of 'D' Company. To wish you as quiet, dry, warm, and comfortable a Christmas as is possible.' This card was passed greedily from hand to hand through the men of the Company, and was followed by others in 1916, when we were near Ginchy, and in 1917 when I was no longer in France.[18]

Capt F.A. Potts gave an account of the ghastly Christmas experienced by 9DWR, which began with a disastrous move up to the trenches:

Sunday December 19th 1915 was a tragic night, not only for the Territorial battalions of the Duke of Wellington's, against whom were launched the gas clouds in which the deadly phosgene was used for the first time, but also for the 9th, who were spared the gas (except for tear-gas shells), but had to move up to battle positions through the Menin Gate and the Sallyport, ringed round with fire by the German guns, and lost heavily. It may be true, in the words of the GOC Division, that, after this evening's entertainment 'the Dukes were stamping their feet and asking to be led against the Germans' – any rate, when they moved up for that nervous period, the last tour before going back for rest, the Battalion were in a chastened mood, hardly suitable for the season.[19]

9DWR's move forward in support had cost them over a hundred men, with four officers wounded (including the new CO and Captain Miller), and the 'A' Company Commander killed. Russell was on leave at the time but commented:

Poor old Inchley was killed; awful bad luck – he leaves a wife and two kiddies. It makes one feel an awful slacker to have missed it.

Inchley's local newspaper report on his death included the following precis of a letter of condolence which Robertson sent to the bereaved wife:

Captain Malcolm Robertson, after narrating how Lieutenant Inchley was killed, assured the widow that the whole Battalion was full of sorrow in her bereavement, and could only hope that the knowledge that her husband did his duty calmly and bravely to the end would bring her some comfort. His loss to the Battalion was greatly felt, for his value had just become known.[20]

Potts records how 9DWR spent December 25th 1915:

Christmas Day dawned gloomily but peacefully over Hooge and the Bellewarde Lake ... Through the short day [9DWR] could only feed in imagination on the Christmas fare awaiting them in the huts behind Vlamertinghe. Eventually 51 Brigade arrived to relieve, full of good cheer but cursing their lot, and the Duke's filed down the Menin Road to the Cavalry Barracks in Ypres, where they got rid of their 'gum boots, thigh' like gigantic Christmas stockings, and resumed their ankle boots if they had not been 'blown up by shell fire' in the trenches. The cookers drawn up in the court of the barracks sent them on their way with a much needed pick-me-up of rum and tea. But it was not until the small hours of Boxing Day that the last detachments of exhausted men crawled into camp and lay down on the hut floors, almost too tired to think of food.[21]

In an article in *The Wykehamist* written a year later, Robertson recalled his feelings on returning from the line that day:

> We had just come out of the trenches at Christmas in a particularly bad sector of the line, and were covered with France from head to foot, and dazed as men are dazed this winter with the exposure and the misery of it all. I found some letters waiting for me at my billet, and opened them eagerly as one who welcomes a coastline after long days at sea and gains touch with a drier world. Some of the usual letters were there. Then I opened rather a larger one and took out a little blue book, from which fell a small printed paper: 'Winchester, 1916 … We do not forget you for one day.' And underneath some initials we know well. I turned to the book. It was freezing outside, and that photograph of Winnall came in rather well, I thought. Soon we thawed, and then on to the summer ones, which almost breathed the warmth of a river-valley. That valley I could see at every season of the year: could almost smell the rushes, hear the hive of summer above the brawling of its streams, or feel the October veils of mist when sea-weary gulls make it their home. Far away outside I heard some men cheering at an impromptu concert: the cheers seemed to echo through me like the good roar at Sixes. The dark spaces of my billet became the dusky soul-tenanted corners of Cloisters – only I missed the single austere figure sitting there. Behind all the photographs there seemed to be a purpose: the little book was an anthology of Winchester, indeed of Wykehamists I knew. Of that life each salient part was represented. I was invited to hang round the fountain once more with 'Saul' or the 'Epilogue' on my lips, while I watched the goldfish that neither memorize nor recite (I put the first ones into the pool myself, but they have long since died); to traverse that very slippery plank alongside of Logic after a breathless rush down Hills; to wait for the ball to come out of 'ropes'; to lie under the ilex trees amid a mass of blue campanula flowers and let reason and fancy hold their eternal debate; to see the soft glow of light in Chamber Court on dark Sunday evenings when a light rain falls. There was a great and communicative strength in that Christmas token of love and trust from Winchester. I know that others have felt it, too, and are as grateful as I.[22]

He took the trouble to send a letter to the Mayor of Keighley, which was printed in the *Yorkshire Evening Post* under the heading 'Men of whom Keighley is Proud':[23]

> Captain Malcolm Robertson, commanding 'D' Company, 9th West Riding Regiment, says: 'Of five DCMs awarded to the Battalion to date, four have gone to men from your town in my Company: Sergt. Pearson, Lance-Corporal Rossall, Private W. Bridgewater, and Private J. Brogan. Sergeant A. O'Neill, now my Company Sergeant-Major, who is largely responsible for the good work done by my Company, is also, I understand, a Keighley man; also Sergeant Jackson. I don't know Yorkshire much, but if we get through to the end I shall want to see the town which has produced many plucky fellows. I need only add that your men much appreciated the kind way that their friends at home remembered them at Christmas.'

Throughout January 1916, 9DWR were out of the line resting, training, and carrying out fatigue tasks at Eperlecques, near St Omer. There was one highlight, not recorded in the war diary, which Russell considered worthy of mention:

> January 4th 1916
> The GOC Sir Douglas Haig came round and shook hands with the few officers he happened to see. Bobber and Ferguson both shook paws and were told we were 'grand fellows', probably because of the '19th' show.

Robertson still commanded 'D' Company, but on January 24th went on a course, as we discover from Russell's diary: 'The big and "old" Bobber has left us to go to some bombing school; bad luck on him and us.'

During this rest period, Cullinan wrote to Bramston; the letter is undated and with no more helpful heading than 'BEF', but internal evidence puts it in January 1916:

> We are all more or less well here, those who are left of us. The Bobber is doleful as usual, and talks of leaving the Battalion. Alan has his back up about something, but is otherwise in good form.[24]

On February 5th, 9DWR returned to the Ypres Salient and occupied trenches at St Eloi. Potts recorded their adventures:

> On our left, only a mile or so away, [was] a long, low embankment largely made of clay thrown up when the Ypres–Comines Canal was made. This was the so-called 'Bluff,' a name given because it ended abruptly in a steep slope in front of the German lines, of which it gave an admirable view. Now it was covered with bushes and trees, many of them firs, and looked jolly enough in the winter sunlight. Our first days at St Eloi were uneventful …
>
> But after we had been in for a week and were expecting our first relief, early one fine afternoon a heavy bombardment began, so far as we were concerned of such a scattered nature that practically no casualties were caused … The bombardment was heaviest on the Bluff, where great fountains spouting earth and trees seemed to have opened. Later we learnt that on the other side of the canal a German attack had been launched and part of the Bluff taken … That night, and almost every night for a week, we watched sudden bombardments on the Bluff itself, wreathed in white smoke clouds, revealed by orange flashes, while giant tea-trays were banged all round. These heralded night attacks, made by various units of our Division, and all we learned were unsuccessful.[25]

After what 52 Brigade's report described as a 'disastrous delay', the first counter-attack on the night of February 14th failed, degenerating into a drawn-out hand-grenade exchange in the darkness. A second counter-attack on the evening of the 15th also failed. Robertson was one of the few people to come out well in 52 Brigade's report:

> During these operations, the grenade supply to both 51 and 52 Brigades was carried out by the 52 Brigade. The Bomb Store was inconveniently situated for supplying 10th Lancashire Fusiliers. The advanced store at VOORMEZEELE necessitated large carrying parties for 1½ miles over heavy country. As soon as the lorries arrived at the Divisional Store, at H.29 central, they were sent up to 51 Brigade Headquarters, and to the 10th Lancashire Fusiliers' Dump on the Lille Road. This worked well under the supervision of Captain Robertson, 9th West Riding Regiment.[26]

Robertson had evidently by then returned to 'D' Company; Cullinan was running 'C', as Russell recorded:

> Cully is doing toppingly as OC, and fairly pulling the Company together. We are a terribly young lot: 'Cully' aged twenty; Culling just nineteen; Maxwell-Stuart nineteen; and myself nineteen – also a new sub, Pickles, age about thirty.

Potts described 9DWR's next moves:

> We were all agreed that it could only be a question of a day or two before we were withdrawn from our own safe spot and sent on just such another murderous errand as the rest, but when it was told that 3rd Division had relieved our Brigade on the other side of the canal, our cowardly hopes of release rose high. Shortly after we were at last relieved and marched back to Reninghelst. But after only one day's absence from the trenches, orders to relieve 165 Brigade of 3rd Division were given out, and the dawn of a miserable February day found us endeavouring to find our positions in somewhat impromptu trenches (the old support trenches) on the Bluff and in its neighbourhood.
>
> The days that followed were full of excitements and casualties … Our own artillery, we thought, was a great deal too prodigal with their 9-inch shells, which made the most horrible gaps in our own defences. Snow fell … At last we left the Bluff, but only to side-step a few hundred yards to the right, in front of one of the most famous spots of the war, Hill 60 … We had hardly had time to settle down in our new trenches before most unpleasant preparations began to be made.[27]

An attack was being readied by 165 Brigade to the right flank of 9DWR, and commenced on Thursday, March 2nd. Russell described the events vividly:

> At 0430hrs we all 'stood to'. We were on the left flank of the attacking battalion, but had strict orders not to 'go over' with the Gordons; 'C' Company had the 'post of honour' next them. Suddenly rapid fire started, then bombs, then our guns, hell-for-leather. As it grew light we could see the Jocks going forward in small squads, and some Germans running forward holding their hands up. Then old Cunningham took some of our Battalion bombers along a trench and captured eighteen Boche. Then other prisoners started to go along our trench towards HQ. They were in a terrible state, trembling from head to foot, shifty eyes, expecting to receive blows, a lot with blood-stained bandages on, all murmuring 'Mercy, camerade.' Poor beggars, they were shattered wrecks … like panic-stricken sheep.
>
> We then consolidated the recaptured trench. I stood over one badly wounded German and tried to look sympathetic … Cully, Bobber, and others highly amused at the idea of my 'looking sympathetic'!

But within hours of 165 Brigade's attack, 9DWR underwent one of its worst experiences of the war so far. Russell's account continues:

> About 0900hrs the Germans started to strafe us, and gave us absolute hell for an hour and a half. We simply crouched at the bottom of the trench and shuddered; some awful

> sights. Suddenly a green flare went up. Cully fairly rose to the occasion, rallied the Company toppingly, and got all the bays manned. But the counter-attack came against the Scotties, who drove them back easily and took more prisoners. During a slight lull for an hour after this we got down some bread and marmalade and hot tea. Then the Hun artillery started again, not so intensely as before, but we all began to cringe, and it was the longest day any of us had spent. At 1500hrs we got a message we were going to be relieved – pretty thankful!

That message was delivered by 12642 Private Arthur Sunley, who recorded his memories of that day:[28]

> I think all the artillery on the Western Front was concentrated on this small frontage; the earth shook as if an earthquake was in being, as if all Hades had been let loose, shells just skimming over the frail dug-outs that had been made in the side of the trench … One landed on a dug-out and Sergeant Haigh, who was in charge of the HQ Orderlies, was instantly killed. Hearing another shout for help, I went around a corner of a trench and with the assistance of Corporal Williamson (Signals) from Huddersfield district (Holmfirth, I believe) carried out a wounded Orderly, poor old Tom Healey from Ilkley – but unfortunately he was mortally wounded … Hearing another cry for help, we went back to the same trench where another chap was buried up to his waist; after struggling an hour we managed to release him. With assistance from a Signaller named Snow, we were carrying him to a dressing station when I placed my foot on another man … It proved to be Corporal Williamson, who had previously assisted me with Healey; he was dead.
>
> I was then detailed to proceed to Railhead for a new draft from England – poor chaps, what a baptism … I arrived at 'B' Company HQ with two thirds of them; I don't know what happened to the other fellows … This was about 2300hrs. Some of the chaps were weeping from sheer exhaustion; it was enough to unnerve the bravest of men – straight from England in to one of the fiercest bombardments it was possible to experience …
>
> The Battalion casualties were very heavy, three Company Sergeant Majors being killed. I was in conversation with Sergeant Major Liversedge from Meltham – a splendid fellow – a few minutes before he was killed. Being sent with a message to Battalion HQ Durham Light Infantry, after an exciting run through shell fire, eventually arrived, but their HQ was like a Field Ambulance Dressing Station – full of wounded men.
>
> On returning through the front line, I met Lieutenant Potts (smiling as usual) who gave me some German souvenirs which had been taken from prisoners, to hand to HQ. Proceeding through a communication trench I came across one of our orderlies (Private Taylor) badly wounded in the face: his eye was hanging down his cheek. Someone was attending to him, so I carried on to the Battalion HQ. There were only four of the Battalion Orderlies left, which necessitated a constant running about with messages. Thus, having just delivered one, you were sent post haste with another. I felt quite bucked to take the last message, which read 'Hang on like Hell; we shall be relieved tonight', sent by Captain and Adjutant S. Danby.
>
> I was quite elated taking this message to the front line; the different receptions of the message by the Company Commanders were rather striking. Captain P.R. Simner ('A' Company), gave a light cheer and said, 'Notify all the boys as you go round.' Captain

> Robertson ('D' Company) was also cheerfully excited. Captain Cullinan ('C' Company), was in a dugout with other officers and they all cheered to the echo. Captain Benjamin ('B' Company) looked at the message and remarked, 'Oh, is that so, Sunley?' and looked disappointed he was going out – although inwardly, he was pleased as everyone else. The Battalion was very fortunate in their Company Commanders; no battalion could have wished for better officers or finer gentlemen.

9DWR moved out at dusk, but were caught in another heavy bombardment and suffered further casualties before they reached safety. Russell again recorded his impressions of the day and its aftermath:

> The day wore slowly to a close; put some more food down us at 1700hrs. At last in late evening we started for home. When a mile clear of the trenches we had casualties again, including dear old Maxwell-Stuart, who was killed by a whizz-bang. God, it's dreadful; he was such a top-hole fellow, only joined our Company lately, but we had come to know each other awfully well in our midnight watches – 2300hrs to 0300hrs is a wonderful time for learning to know a fellow.
>
> Friday, March 3rd 1916
> We got back to camp somehow at 0800hrs, done to the world but tremendously thankful to be out of it. We lost 150 men out of less than five hundred, and two officers killed, the longest and worst twenty-four hours I ever spent. I found everyone in camp (near Reninghelst) thought I was dead; the rumour had got round somehow. I convinced people I was not a ghost by eating a hearty brekker which old Bobber had most kindly got ready for us. He had kept 'open house' going since midnight, feeding all the officers as they straggled in at various hours. I got straight down to it after brekker and slept till 1930hrs, then, after supper with 'D' Company officers, slept again till 0900hrs. When Cunningham and I woke up (March 4th) we started singing and shouting out of pure *joie de vivre.* We were really bucked to be alive, though for the first few hours, after all the shelling, we kept ducking at the whistling of the wind in the trees! Bath in Reninghelst, then to officers' club with Cully, Savory, and Mallinson to have tea with the old Bobber. At 1800hrs we all went to old Stuart's funeral; as I said, he was a top-hole fellow.

Robertson added a proud note to his edited version of Russell's diary:

> The history of 17th Division, which fails in several places to do justice to the 9th Dukes, entirely omits any mention of the Battalion staying in this extra day after the Brigade was relieved, and earning the high praise and special thanks of 76 Brigade and of the GOC 3rd Division.

Cullinan was awarded the Military Cross for his actions on March 2nd, his citation reading:

> For conspicuous good work during operations. He kept his men well in hand, and sent in information of great value. He displayed great power of leadership.[29]

Robertson now relinquished command of 'D' Company, handing his men over to Savory and moving to the staff of 52 Brigade as Brigade Bombing Officer. The following month, his old Company came under attack. Russell's diary describes the action, in which Savory was wounded twice:

> We were in the thick of it on April 26th. 'C' Company in reserve had no casualties, but 'D' caught it very badly; Savory and Mallinson were both wounded. The stunt started about 1700hrs. Savory did awfully well; he was early wounded by shrapnel in the shoulder, but hung on to his job. While going up a battered trench, he suddenly met a German raiding party. The leader fired and hit him through the lung. Savory fired back and knocked the Boche out – some nerve after his two wounds. Mallinson had a gash right across his jaw and bled profusely. He was bound up and put in a dugout, having fainted, but was next seen with a man's rifle at a bombing stop, where he stolidly did sentry for three hours, till Benjy [Captain Benjamin, OC 'B' Company] came along from the right and ordered him back; even then he flatly refused at first. Benjy himself did splendidly and helped to reorganise the right of 'D' (who lost forty-six men) as well as keeping 'B' well in hand. He deserves some decoration if ever man did. Ferguson did well too; he and young Stuart were badly shaken by the three hours bombardment, and couldn't sleep for the first two nights in our cellars; they kept seeing great columns of earth going sky-high. Another message of praise and thanks in Brigade orders. We relieved 'D' Company – their trenches were an abomination of desolation. We stayed on all night trying to get things ship-shape. There were some beastly sights, including the Hun shot by Savory, a brutish looking devil (about sixteen stone) with close-cropped head, and foul little pig-eyes and yellow skin. He was an Iron Cross man, but he did look a beast.

The Iron Cross belonging to this German was sent to Savory by the special wish of the Brigadier and is now in the collection of the Regimental Museum. When it was presented in 1980, the medal had with it a manuscript note from Robertson:

> This Iron Cross was taken off the dead body of an enormous German officer, shot by Captain Maurice Savory (OC 'D' Company 9th Duke of Wellington's) on 26th April 1916. The Germans wanted to get one of the first Stokes Mortars taken into the line, and after a three-hour bombardment, during which MJS was wounded slightly but refused to leave the Company, they raided trenches 88 and 89 (next the Lys, in front of Armentières), held by 'D' Company. Maurice, though shot first and badly wounded, killed the leader and hit two other Germans, and – ably supported by Lieuts Alan Ferguson and E. Mallinson – repelled the raid and saved the gun. 'D' Company had forty-six men (out of about eighty) killed and wounded.

Robertson was upset by the casualties among his former charges, and we know that he wrote to at least one widow, the wife of Private John Philip Ireland:

> I just want to add a few words of sympathy from his old Company Commander on the death of your husband. He was a fine, well-trained, soldier, and was always of the greatest use in the Company. He was last seen alive helping a stretcher-bearer (who was also killed) to bring in wounded during a terrible bombardment. The Company did

> splendidly, and every man was a hero who stuck it, for they drove the Germans back. It will be a terrible blow to you and your family, but you may still be proud of a good husband for the way he did his duty.[30]

* * *

Robertson now watched 9DWR from the Brigade staff, and disappears from our sources. We do, however, have his summary of events over the next couple of months, as his coda to Russell's diary:

> The diary … describes the last fortnight in trenches and the three days' march back from Armentières to the Houlle and Moulle area, where the Division was trained for the Somme. In summer weather, with good billets, bathing and good cheer, it was, perhaps, the happiest time we ever had. The Battalion left Armentières at midnight on May 16th–17th, and got into billets at Moulle, near St Omer, on the 19th where 'a glorious time, though rather hard work' ensued.

During that happy and glorious time, Cullinan again sent news to Bramston: 'Alan is flourishing in health and spirits, though sometimes pretending otherwise. The Bobber is in his usual form; Savory as you have heard I suppose is in England wounded – "well out of it", as we say here.'[31]

The fun soon ended, however, as Robertson's commentary on Russell's letter proves:

> Late in June we went up to the Somme, via Morlancourt on July 2nd, up to Fricourt on the 3rd, and on to Shelter Trench and Bottom Wood. On the morning of July 7th, in the third of three hopeless attacks by 52 Brigade ordered by the Corps (back at Heilly) on Quadrangle Support Trench, Jack was killed at the head of his beloved 'C' Company, as he would have wished. His last entry, on July 2nd, at Morlancourt, ends on his characteristic note of cheerfulness. Surely no officer was ever better loved by all ranks of a battalion, and no spirit ever passed more bravely and gaily into the Great Beyond. His body was never recovered.

The Brigadier was appalled at the conditions in which his men made their attacks near Mametz Wood, and his description of the carnage tells us what Robertson witnessed:

> In the old No Man's Land the bodies of our men were to be seen just as they fell, in every conceivable attitude; some prone, others huddled up in a crouching position, or kneeling in the act of firing, all stark and rigid like so many wax-work figures; in the captured German trenches the dead in places were literally piled up in heaps, friend and foe mixed up in an inextricable mess where hand-to-hand fighting had taken place.[32]

Ferguson.

One of those killed had been Ferguson.[33]

* * *

On July 10th, Cullinan wrote to his former housemaster from his hospital bed in London; the handwriting is shaky and some of the pencilled words have been gone over repeatedly to make them clearer. Wounded on July 4th, Cullinan had been brought back from France to the Queen Alexandra Military Hospital in Millbank.[34] News of his arrival there had reached Revd Bramston, who had immediately written to ask whether he might visit.

> My dear Trant,
> Come up on Wednesday – best time 1400hrs. I am going on well and will be able to be up and out. Your news re Alan is a horrible shock to me – I was laid out by the same shell and more or less unconscious when they carried him away on a stretcher and after that I never heard what actually happened. He and I were very close friends during the last few months. Morley too – it is horrible – I will await your coming eagerly.
> Fred Cully[35]

* * *

On August 1st 1916, British troops took the Pommiers Redoubt, halfway between Mametz and Montauban. One wit erected the board seen below, which Robertson then 'liberated' and after the war presented to the Winchester OTC.[36]

* * *

One of the most powerful letters which I have encountered in the Winchester College archives was written by Cullinan in November 1916, describing to Bramston in graphic terms the conditions which 9DWR endured on the Somme that winter.

> Just a line to let you know how we are going on. I've been in hospital for a week with general collapse, but am fairly fit again now and will be off back to my Battalion tomorrow. We have had a hell of a time down here. No one at home can conceive, even in the remotest way, what the conditions are like out here now – pushing in the winter. Last winter was nothing compared to this – the mud, the continual and intense shelling, and the fearful difficulties of transport. We have had six days in the advanced trenches in two spells of three days, and it has knocked us out. To give you a small idea of what the mud is like up there, you will find it hard to believe that one man in my Company

was stuck in the mud for three days and three nights, under intense shell-fire. When we got him out, he died of exhaustion. This is only one case of several. We have had a lot of trench feet and enough casualties to go on with. Seven more of our officers gone under, and there may have been more since. The trenches are all hastily dug of course, and filled with mud and corpses – no dugout or cover from the weather of any kind. Oh, it is very choice I can tell you – 'Hell with the lid off' one of my men called it. Iron rations, nothing else, all the time, and no possible chance of making a fire and getting a hot drink. The Boche is frightfully 'windy' and puts up intense barrage fire on the smallest excuse, and he seems to have unlimited guns and shells.

Well, well, this is very dispiriting, isn't it. But then I think my heart and spirit have been altogether broken by the conditions and difficulties. A month with you now, Trant, in peaceful Winton is the highest conception of Heaven for me at the minute. God must be dead, Trant, to let this go on – Man was not made to stand it.[37]

* * *

Savory had missed the Somme, owing to his wound in April, and it was not until January 1917 that he returned to 9DWR, 'to the intense joy of his old Company'.[38]

Savory.

The joy was as short-lived as its source. When 'D' Company came out of the trenches at Sailly Saillisel on the night of February 1st, eleven men were killed or wounded by enemy shell-fire. Savory was one of them. He died of his wounds on February 3rd.[39]

* * *

It may have been coincidence, but Robertson's posting back to England came on February 2nd:

> February 2nd 1917
> Battalion proceed to Camp 108 [Bronfay]; arrived at about 1400hrs. Captain ROBERTSON appointed Assistant Commandant 17th Division School.[40]

> February 1917
> Wastage from Causes Other than Battle Casualties: Captain M. Robertson (to England Duty).[41]

He served for the rest of the war on the staff of 19th Officer Cadet Battalion, Pirbright. In March 1917 came the news that he had been Mentioned in Dispatches;[42] in June, he was one of those awarded a Military Cross in the King's Birthday Honours list.[43] Many of the awards on this list were not for any specific incident (no citation exists for Robertson's) but for continued excellent leadership by officers too junior in rank to receive a DSO. In fact, *The Iron Duke* several times incorrectly stated that Robertson held a DSO. Perhaps he had been recommended for one.

* * *

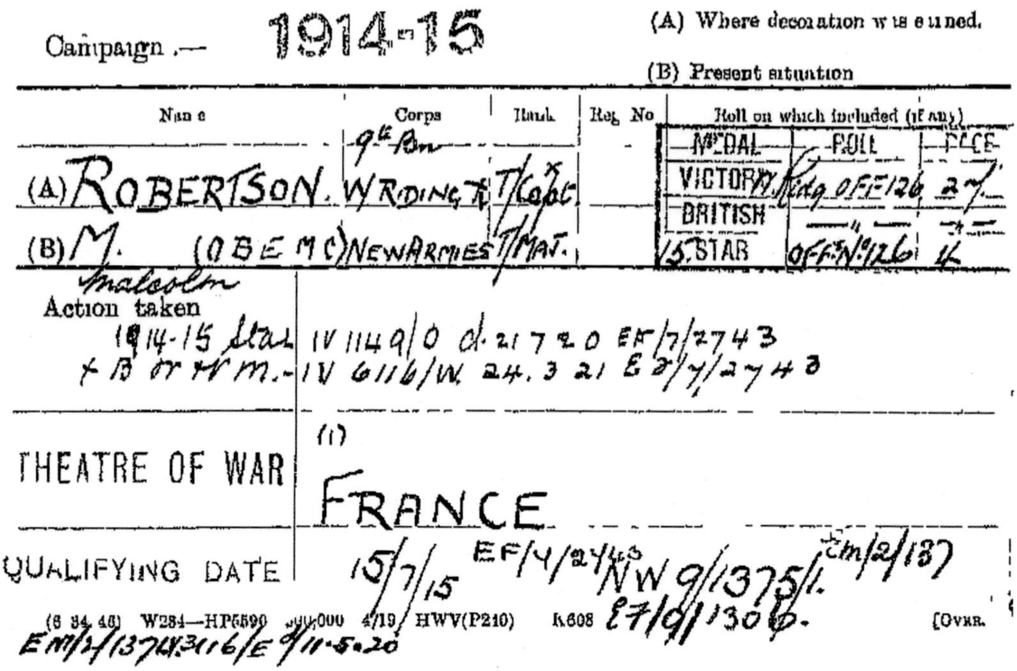

Campaign .— 1914-15

(A) Where decoration was earned.

(B) Present situation

Name	Corps	Rank	Reg. No	Roll on which included (if any)		
	9th Bn			MEDAL	ROLL	PAGE
(A) ROBERTSON.	W RIDING R.	T/Capt		VICTORY	Kg. OF E/126	27
(B) M. Malcolm (OBE MC)	NEW ARMIES	T/Maj.		BRITISH	"	"
				15 STAR	OF F. N° 126	16

Action taken
1914-15 Star IV 1149/0 d. 21720 EF/7/2743
+ B or V M. - IV 6116/W. 24.3.21 E 7/7/2743

THEATRE OF WAR (1) FRANCE

QUALIFYING DATE 15/7/15 EF/4/2443 NW 9/1375/1. em/2/187

(6 34 46) W234—HP5590 ...000 4/19 HWV(P210) K608 27/9/1306. [Over.

EM/2/1374/3116/E 4/11.5.20

Robertson returned to Winchester College after the war, his final award being an OBE for his work with the Officer Cadets. He took command of the Winchester OTC in July 1919,[44] and became increasingly involved with the 9DWR Old Comrades' Association, travelling north to attend their annual dinners repeatedly from 1929 until the last in March 1939, at which he said that 'the dinner was one of the year's functions which he put before all others.'[45]

His first letter to *The Iron Duke* appeared in November 1925:

> We have received the following news of old officers of the 9th Battalion from Major M. Robertson DSO, himself an old officer of the 9th. He is a master at Winchester College, and has just retired from the OTC after completing nineteen years' service, and having commanded it for six years. 'It may interest many who have made inquiries about Captain Miller MC, who was the life and soul of the 9th in early days, to know that he is flourishing in Kenya Colony … Captain Cullinan MC, after surviving the war, was killed in the disastrous Yokohama earthquake … Captain McColl is now a Forestry Officer in Burmah, married, and the father of a son called "Bonzo" because he is so ugly. Failing the old game, he now hunts tigers, and sent me lately a letter from a native complaining that "tigers had lately been very rude" in his district. I expect they will get a Mills bomb or two among them if they are not careful.'

Robertson, now the last survivor of the five Wykehamists who had joined 9DWR in September 1914, had written Cullinan's obituary in *The Wykehamist*, ending with the words:

> One could think of him there as a bit of good crystalline rock, that stands firm-anchored on a slope of shifting stones, leaving an occasional raw place on the hand that rubs against it, but never a speck of dirt, and whispering in the ears of those who hesitate the challenge of the upward way. He is gone, but what he gave is still ours and his.[46]

* * *

In 1920, Robertson took over as housemaster of Hopper's. Two years later, he oversaw the dedication of the house war memorial, in Grubbing Hall. He would spend every day of the next twenty-one years being able to see the name of his friend Maurice Savory as he ate.

II

Why Worry?

July 1938–June 1940

There is a life in peace and strife
which everyone must live;
we give our best and go to rest
when we've no more to give.

For when the heart has done its part
and can no longer beat,
with love and hope beyond our scope,
we may admit defeat.

There is a death, Elizabeth,
for which we all must wait;
and men and war can do no more
than try to change the date –

(Nigel Weir, September 1939)

When the house photograph was taken in the summer of 1938, Robertson's fears were becoming more and more real. In 1937 Neville Chamberlain had taken over as Prime Minister, pursuing a dual policy of appeasement and re-armament; Britain needed time to prepare itself if it was to take a stand against Fascism. As Chamberlain set out for Munich in September 1938, the whole House of Commons cheered him to the rafters. But the Munich Crisis finally made it clear to all – including Chamberlain – that war with Germany was inevitable. Britain braced itself for a conflict for which it was not yet ready. On September 25th, Hugh Rose[1] wrote from Sunnyside to his parents:

> The Bobber is very well and full of the international situation. He can speak of little else and has been saying for the last three days that either Hitler will have to climb down or war within twenty-four hours. Tomorrow we are going to be fitted for gas masks and five from each house have been appointed to assemble them in event of mobilization. At last someone is getting a move on.[2]

In Winchester College Football, the big match of the season was & is 'Fifteens', played between the tribes known as 'OTH' & 'Commoners'. A long tradition of colourful team lists ('Hot Rolls') produced this beauty in 1938, on which several of our subjects appear. (Winchester College Archives)

Hopper's had an outstanding junior cross-country running team in 1938, which won Beloe Pot in the Junior Steeplechase. In the back row, from left, we see Charles Duffin (Scots Guards, armoured battalion), David Martyn (Coldstream Guards, armoured battalion), Nick Somerville (South Wales Borderers) and Mike Hirst (Royal Armoured Corps). The front row (from left) includes John McArthur (Royal Navy), Pat Metcalfe (Royal Armoured Corps), and Michael Elliott-Binns (Royal Artillery). One of the seven pictured died in the war. (Winchester College Archives; edited by dansteele.net)

* * *

Of the boys in the 1938 house photograph, a quarter had left school by the time that war broke out including, on July 26th 1938, almost immediately after the photograph, James Clerk-Rattray,[3] Angus Grant,[4] Gerry Rickman,[5] and Hew Tompson.[6] On the night before, they attended their farewell 'Domum' Dinner, at which the guest of honour was a certain Dr T.S. Eliot.

Clerk-Rattray.

Grant.

Rickman.

Tompson.

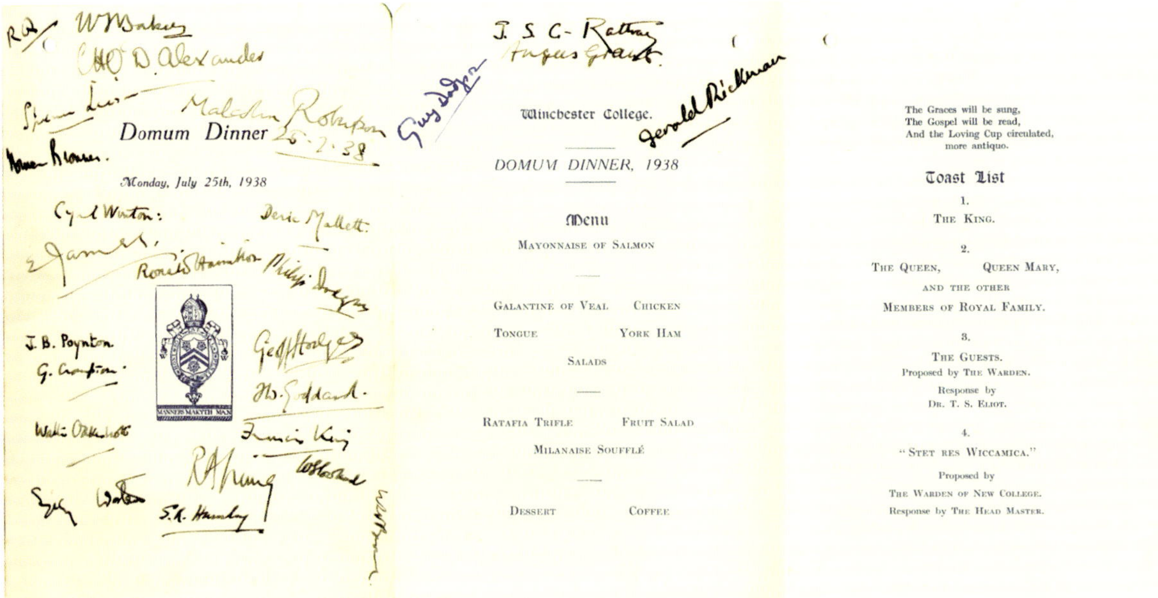
Domum Dinner

Monday, July 25th, 1938

Winchester College.

DOMUM DINNER, 1938

Menu

MAYONNAISE OF SALMON

GALANTINE OF VEAL CHICKEN

TONGUE YORK HAM

SALADS

RATAFIA TRIFLE FRUIT SALAD

MILANAISE SOUFFLÉ

DESSERT COFFEE

The Graces will be sung,
The Gospel will be read,
And the Loving Cup circulated,
more antiquo.

Toast List

1.
THE KING.

2.
THE QUEEN, QUEEN MARY,
AND THE OTHER
MEMBERS OF ROYAL FAMILY.

3.
THE GUESTS.
Proposed by THE WARDEN.
Response by
DR. T. S. ELIOT.

4.
"STET RES WICCAMICA."
Proposed by
THE WARDEN OF NEW COLLEGE.
Response by THE HEAD MASTER.

Leaving Hopper's was not the end of a boy's relationship with Robertson, as Willie Whitelaw recalled many years later:

> This remarkable man's real legacy to those in his charge was that he cared for us in after life. All those who were in his house must have experienced those extraordinary letters, totally illegible and written all round every page. They pursued us wherever we went, right through the war and indeed thereafter until his death. In my case they continued long enough for him to give me his strong views on various political events at the start of my political career. If Major Robertson had lived longer I would certainly have received some stern and critical comments on my ministerial responsibilities. Many of them would undoubtedly have been justified, and I would have paid attention to all of them, such is the trust inspired by a really understanding schoolmaster.[7]

The next to leave Hopper's, on December 20th 1938, was Rickman's cousin Guy Dodgson;[8] three more departed on April 4th 1939 (John Boyd,[9] Charles Murray,[10] and John Pinney);[11] and on August 1st, just in time for the outbreak of war, Dick Simpkin,[12] and John Sinclair.[13]

Dodgson.

Boyd.

Murray.

Pinney.

Simpkin.

Sinclair.

Gerry Rickman's father had been a superb battalion commander during the First World War, twice earning a DSO. His son went straight from Winchester into the Regular Army, learning the profession of arms at the Royal Military College (RMC), Sandhurst, and gaining his commission as 2nd Lieutenant 95580, Royal Northumberland Fusiliers, in July 1939.[14]

Hew Tompson had become a Commoner Prefect by the time that he left, and had gained some success at cricket and gymnastics. A 'late developer', according to Robertson, he had 'no flair for mathematics' (as he was the first to admit); however, he managed to pass into Sandhurst and took a commission in the Royal Artillery.

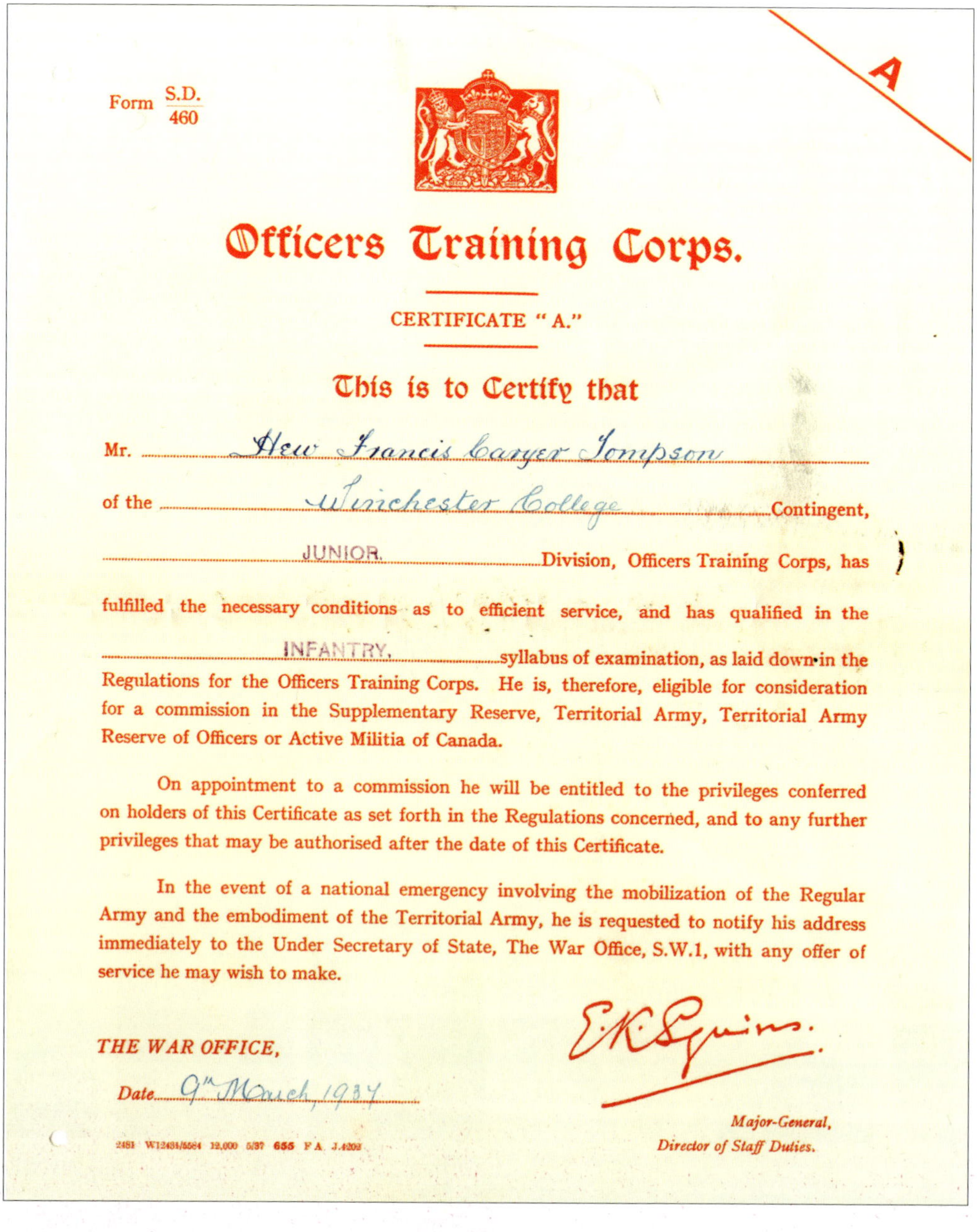

Form S.D./460

A

Officers Training Corps.

CERTIFICATE "A."

This is to Certify that

Mr. Hew Francis Carver Tompson

of the Winchester College Contingent,

JUNIOR Division, Officers Training Corps, has fulfilled the necessary conditions as to efficient service, and has qualified in the INFANTRY syllabus of examination, as laid down in the Regulations for the Officers Training Corps. He is, therefore, eligible for consideration for a commission in the Supplementary Reserve, Territorial Army, Territorial Army Reserve of Officers or Active Militia of Canada.

On appointment to a commission he will be entitled to the privileges conferred on holders of this Certificate as set forth in the Regulations concerned, and to any further privileges that may be authorised after the date of this Certificate.

In the event of a national emergency involving the mobilization of the Regular Army and the embodiment of the Territorial Army, he is requested to notify his address immediately to the Under Secretary of State, The War Office, S.W.1, with any offer of service he may wish to make.

THE WAR OFFICE,

Date 9th March, 1937

E.K. Squires.

Major-General,
Director of Staff Duties.

2481 W12431/5564 12,000 5/37 655 F.A. J.4202

Angus Grant, who had fenced for the School and was a keen musician, spent a year studying languages in France and Switzerland; on March 11th 1939, however, he was commissioned as a 2nd Lieutenant into a Territorial Army unit, the Lovat Scouts,[15] which his father had commanded from 1928 to 1932, and in which his older brother (also a Hopperite) was serving. The Lovat Scouts were

> a family Regiment in more ways than one. In 1939 there were approximately a hundred, including eleven officers, who were sons of former Scouts. Each Squadron teemed with brothers, uncles, nephews and cousins.[16]

In July 1939 Grant started work for the Blue Funnel Line.[17] It was to be a short-lived career.

Grant (wearing spectacles) with fellow officers of the Lovat Scouts, 1939. (Grant family collection; edited by dansteele.net)

Joining Grant in the Lovat Scouts was Charles Murray. He had signed up for the Territorial Army straight after leaving Winchester in April, being commissioned into the Seaforth Highlanders before transferring to the Lovat Scouts a year later.[18]

Others followed the university route, overwhelmingly to Cambridge and Oxford. James Clerk-Rattray commenced his studies at Trinity College, Cambridge, in 1938, although he also signed up with a Territorial Yeomanry unit, the Scottish Horse, in January 1939.[19]

Guy Dodgson's next stop was also Cambridge (Magdalene College), where he started in 1939. John Pinney, however, preferred Oxford; he studied French and German at Christ Church for a year, and built on his sporting successes at Winchester by representing Oxford in athletics in 1940.

James Boyd spent some months in France after leaving Winchester, falling in love with French culture and the songs and singers of the time – especially Charles Trenet. He went up to St Andrews to study English and Modern Languages, contributing to the university magazine under the pseudonym 'Don Juan'. But when war broke out, he left university to enlist.[20]

Hopper's 'Glee Club' (house musicians), 1939; their housemaster's 'private side' of Sunnyside can be seen in the background.
Front row (L to R): John Sinclair (Scots Guards), Richard Simpkin (Royal Tank Regiment), Bruce Fortune (Black Watch), 'Mi' Edmunds (Oxford & Bucks Light Infantry), 'Dan' Somerville (Royal Artillery).
Back row (L to R): Horace Barlow, Christopher Pringle (Fleet Air Arm), Guy Richardson (Fleet Air Arm), Christopher Sheepshanks (Rifle Brigade), Martin Monier-Williams. Three died; one was captured; and another was severely wounded. (Winchester College Archives)

After leaving Winchester at the start of August 1939, Dick Simpkin and John Sinclair joined Clerk-Rattray at Trinity College, Cambridge. Sinclair and his two elder brothers had between them covered ten years in Hopper's, and were considered to have made a great contribution to the life of the House and School, according to Robertson leaving happy memories and being a source of great pride to their many friends. At Winchester Sinclair had been a Senior Prefect, a good golfer and fencer, a plucky cross-country runner, and a sound debater. Robertson stated that he had a keen and balanced mind, and with his attractive manner might have had a very successful career at the Bar. He attested into the Suffolk Regiment in Cambridge on October 14th 1939, but was immediately transferred to the Army Reserve to allow him to complete his degree.

OATH TO BE TAKEN BY RECRUIT ON ATTESTATION.

I.....John Henry Lund Sinclair.....swear by Almighty God that I will be faithful and bear true allegiance to His Majesty King George the Sixth, His Heirs, and Successors, and that I will, as in duty bound, honestly and faithfully defend His Majesty, His Heirs, and Successors, in Person, Crown, and Dignity against all enemies, and will observe and obey all orders of His Majesty, His Heirs and Successors, and of the Generals and Officers set over me.

His recruiting officer noted that Sinclair was just a shade over 5′10″ in height, weighed 142lbs, and had a 35½″ chest; he had an appendix scar from an operation in 1931 and a birthmark over the lower end of his left lumbar region. His dark hair and complexion were accompanied by grey-green eyes. At the end of his year at Cambridge, he took a Second in French before being posted to the Sandhurst OCTU on November 15th 1940. Whilst he was there, a note was added to his file: 'Military Conduct: Very Good'.

* * *

Dick Simpkin possibly regretted leaving Hopper's more than most. His father, Sir Oswald Simpkin KCB CBE, had been Warden of Winchester College (Chairman of the Governing Body) until shortly before his death.[21] Sir Oswald's mother had died in 1888, when he was eight, and his father in 1895. He had been taken in by his uncle and aunt, George and Ethel ('Occy') Coller, who had three children, but only their daughter – Evelyn – had survived childhood. In 1920, Evelyn and Oswald had married, despite the fifteen-year age gap between them. Their only child, Dick Simpkin, was born in April 1921. Evelyn seems not to have been very close to her son, but in a letter written in January 1945 he stated that 'I owe everything, from the fact that I survived as a baby onwards, to Occy.'[22]

Simpkin had been sent to boarding school at the age of eight, but was very unhappy there and moved to live with Occy at Twyford, where he was educated until he went to board at Winchester. There, in the family environment fostered by Robertson and his sister Sheila, he had found some peace. Letters from the pair of them followed him home when he heard the news of his father's death on May 31st 1936, and show how deeply they cared about their young charges:

Richard Simpkin's section of twenty on the Duke of York's Camp, Southwold, 1938. His report on the camp appeared in The Wykehamist *in October 1938.* (Simpkin family collection)

My dear Richard,

Yes, I knew, but was asked not to tell you till Arthur Ley [Simpkin's legal guardian] came. My instinct was to tell you myself and try to help you face it, but my hands were tied. I'm not a person who likes pretending, as you know.

You will be brave, and I think thankful that your good father is spared further suffering, and a life that was becoming no life to a man of his ability and energy. You must stay till Tuesday, if they want you, but my advice to you is to come back to ordinary routine life as soon as you can – it depends when the funeral is, I expect. All here know now, and send you their sympathy, and will try to help you when you come back. I am glad you will have Arthur Ley; he and I will have to share your father's part towards you. Do all you can to help your mother and Granny, and give them both our sympathy. They must rest now.

Be brave, and think of other people, not yourself too much.

You will find that old and happy memories of your father will be uppermost later, and that he will be much nearer to you, if you are worthy of him, than you think possible now.

Matron is seeing to your things. You can count on Sheila's and my help and interest.

Yours affectionately,

MR[23]

My dear Richard,
There were people in the Hall so I could not say much to you. You know how grieved I am and how much I have felt for you these last days of anxiety. You will be able to help in so many ways. I am glad you got home so quickly. With my love,
Yours affectionately
Sheila M Robertson[24]

In the summer of 1938, after the House photograph, Simpkin attended the Duke of York's Camp in Southwold. The camps had been founded after the First World War by the Duke of York, who had unexpectedly become King George VI in 1936; they aimed to bring together boys from different social backgrounds, and ran until the start of the Second World War. Even after his accession, King George often visited, and although Simpkin did not mention it in his report for the school magazine, the King was rowed ashore from the Royal Yacht (*Victoria & Albert*) on August 2nd 1938.

After leaving Sunnyside, Simpkin spent three terms at Trinity, studying Mechanical Science.[25] But in the changed circumstances, extra-curricular activities took on new importance. He had proved himself an excellent shot whilst at Winchester, and now served with the Cambridge University OTC, gaining his 'Certificate B' and serving with their unit of the Local Defence Volunteers (Home Guard).[26]

* * *

Duncan McMurtrie[27] and his family were on holiday when war was declared on September 3rd 1939, as his younger brother Anthony recalled:

We used to have our family holidays down at Thurlestone in South Devon. We didn't have any money as a family, so that was the most economical thing to do; it took most of the day to drive down and we parked in a field which was literally not more than 250 yards from the beach down in one direction; in the other direction there was a farm where we used to collect milk, butter, eggs, and cream. Each morning I was designated to do the walk and collect the dairy produce, and my father, who was a lawyer, had all his official correspondence forwarded to this farm. So there was a great bundle to pick up each day as well. He kept an eye on things while he was away, put it that way.

The great joy of Thurlestone for most of us was a choice of three beaches nearby. There was a rock with a big hole right through the middle, which was a local landmark, and we could leave our caravan, just walk across one or two fields, and everywhere was the edge of the coast – walking down on to the beach was lovely.

We went there, I suppose for at least five years in succession, up until 1939. Then it all came to an end. We were sitting in the caravan one afternoon – my two brothers Duncan, Peter, and me, and my mother presiding. We had Devonshire splits – which are delicious bread rolls – Devonshire cream, and strawberry jam. Suddenly the door of the caravan opened and my father said to my mother, with a rather worried look on his face,

'He's gone,' and she said to him, 'Who's gone?'

The steward of the Golf Club, who was a reservist for the Royal Marines, had apparently just been called back to active service. We thought this was extremely ominous, because it was September 2nd, the day after the Germans had invaded Poland; and after a family conference we decided it would be sensible to go home.

So my father and us three boys went down to the beach and collected our canoe, a faltboat (rubber skin stretched over a bamboo-type framework), and we had a quick dip in the sea in the moonlight. Then we picked up the canoe and came back to the caravan. My mother had been packing up the caravan and dismantling the tent where Duncan and Peter slept; I slept in the caravan with my parents. Shortly before midnight we left Devon, on a long drive – 350 miles I guess. My mother drove the whole way, I think, through Basingstoke and Slough and all the way towards Hitchin; we lived near a village called St Ippolyts. She was a pretty good driver.

We had a nice breakfast, the five of us. We sat downstairs in the sitting room and relaxed, turned on the radio, and all of a sudden we heard Neville Chamberlain saying, 'And I have to tell you that this country is now at war with Germany.'

It didn't come as a huge surprise, but nevertheless was a real shock. My mother, who was a pretty strong person, having driven an ambulance in the First World War and having also played hockey for England – so she was no pushover – just suddenly fainted. She was standing up, and fell over in a dead faint, six feet down on to the carpet, stretched out in front of us. Because she had undoubtedly had a premonition that one if not two of her three sons would somehow be caught up in the war. She'd had this earlier experience in the First World War, when her brother Gilbert had been killed at the Battle of the Aisne in 1914, aged twenty, while she had been at school. So it all rather came home to her, and she confessed to us that it was a total shock, a total surprise. We'd never seen her like that before.

That's my memory of the declaration of war, which will always remain with me, I suppose.[28]

'Dan' Somerville also remembered the outbreak of war:[29]

When the news was announced that we were at war in 1939, I was in Ireland at the last of those great pre-war parties with all the family there. My great-aunt Hildergard opened up Glenbarrahane, and we all packed in. It was the last time the house was full of people.

All I knew about the war was that a ruthless dictator was on top and that he could do more or less what he liked. Clearly he had to be got rid of. I could never understand why the Americans took so long to come in. My parents' outlook on the war was very much conditioned by what they had experienced in World War One. My Godmother (with whom my mother was very close) had lost her only son in the Great War, and my mother had lost her first sweetheart in that war, and for both my parents it was, 'Oh no, here we are again; what good is there in Germans?' and 'The only good German is a dead one.' This was, I thought, a shocking thing to believe.[30]

* * *

Two more boys left Hopper's at the end of the term: Horace Barlow,[31] and Guy Richardson. Barlow – the great-grandson of Charles Darwin – was one of only two boys in the 1938 photograph who did not serve in the armed forces during the war, though he did serve his country in other important ways. In a 2010 interview, Barlow described his early life thus:

Barlow.

> My father was not a scientist at all. He read Classics at Oxford and became a senior civil servant, and was a wise old bird who knew how to get round corners everywhere. My mother was a Darwin – grandchild of Charles, and very keenly interested both in Charles Darwin himself and in Darwinism, all her life. She, like most females of that age, never went to university, but she did quite a lot of scientific work … and she was a very good botanist and knew the names of all the plants and tried to teach them to me, without any luck whatever, I'm afraid. But she did teach me about Darwinism, which was obviously always in her mind; she would often point out interesting little botanical details that had evolutionary significance, and I think I learnt a lot from her, and that was my first stroke of luck. The other one was being sent to Winchester, which was a school where the scientific teaching was very good. And that meant that it had a lot of very good science students there, so I learned there what a lot of people only learn when they come up to university: namely that they are really not quite top of the barrel, so to speak, in the things they think they're good at. Because I was in more or less the same vintage as Freeman Dyson and James Lighthill, and several others who far outshone me in my mathematical and physical abilities.

Barlow joined Trinity College, Cambridge in January 1940; on his ninetieth birthday in 2012 he made a speech there – soon after a long hospital stay with a life-threatening illness – in which he modestly summed up his early career as follows:

> I have been here at Trinity, on, and off, for seventy-two years. Thank you for putting up with me so long.
>
> I originally planned to come up in 1939 to read the hard, Physics, version of the NST, but I switched to Medical Sciences for two sound, but not very courageous, reasons. The first reason was that, with the onset of war, the government recognised that there was going to be a shortage of doctors, so they exempted from call-up almost anyone who could switch to Medicine. This made switching from Physics to Medicine almost a patriotic duty for me, but there was also a special reason I favoured it. I was coming up from Winchester where, through some accident of illness among staff and students in the school, I had, for a brief period, been taught Mathematics in the same class as Freeman Dyson and James Lighthill, even though those two were both at least a year further advanced in Maths than I, and well over a year younger. The concept of a whole, uniformly brilliant, flock of mature Dyson-Lighthills for me to compete with at Cambridge was obviously completely implausible, but frankly it occupied my mind and terrified me. Even though my Maths had been good enough to help gain me a place at Winchester, I felt that a slightly lower standard of competition might suit me better.
>
> So I came up in January 1940, having switched both date and subject only a few weeks earlier… . The switch had two major effects on my career. First, though curtailed, the wartime medical course allowed time for Part 2 lectures given by William Rushton

> on the Physiology of Vision, and he inspired my own life-long interest in it. It was the start of a long period of fruitful discoveries which radically changed the field of human sensory perception… .
>
> A second advantage to me from my switch to Medicine was that the Rockefeller Foundation instituted a number of scholarships for British medical students to study at US medical schools, feeling that their education might be suffering from wartime interference. I was fortunate enough to be awarded one of these at Harvard Medical School, but through time-table problems, I lost almost a year before I could join the Harvard course.
>
> Fortune favoured me again, and I spent a fascinating year [1943–1944] helping to show why divers went down and failed to come up. It turned out to be that the troubles resulted from failure to remove carbon dioxide fast enough in the modified submarine escape equipment used by the divers. Fairly straightforward modifications partially averted the problem before the end of the war.

Guy Richardson, in common with seven of the eleven other leavers thus far, was the son of an officer;[32] his older brother Jim had also passed through Hopper's during Robertson's tenure.[33] Like Simpkin, Richardson was an excellent shot, captaining the team at Bisley in 1938-1939; he was also President of the Winchester rowing VIII.

Bruce Fortune & Guy Richardson, Morning Hills, 1937. (Rose family collection)

* * *

Britain had learned from the scramble of volunteers in August 1914, when the system had been unable to cope with the huge numbers of applicants and many potential officers had gone into the ranks, where their leadership qualities had often been squandered. Nor did the government yet know to what desperate straits it would be reduced over the next year. On the outbreak of war, experienced soldiers and reservists had been recalled to the colours, and the Territorial Army had been mobilized – but there was no sense that large numbers of new officers would urgently be required. Instructions had gone out to eighteen- and nineteen-year-old boys itching to join up that they should register their willingness to serve and then await call-up to an Officer Cadet Training Unit (OCTU), as a notice in *The Wykehamist* explained:

> They will best serve by waiting in patience and carrying on with their School or University work, developing to the full such special qualifications for service as they possess and getting themselves into first-rate physical condition. After sufficient numbers have been sent direct to OCTUs to satisfy immediate requirements, all further vacancies in those Units will be given only to those serving in Other Rank Training Units, i.e., in the ranks, as was the intention under the Military Training Act of last summer that constituted the Militia. Men called up in their age-group who have had previous military experience in the OTC will be able then to turn it to account; and if in their service in the ranks they show military capacity and promise, they are likely to be spotted at once and drafted for training for commissioned rank. Special educational qualifications in any branch should be valuable.[34]

* * *

At Winchester, the first term of the war began, as planned, on September 22nd 1939, several weeks later than would be usual in modern times. A year previously, there had been the panic of Munich; now Poland had fallen, not only to the German forces which had invaded on September 1st, but also to Russian troops who had moved in from the east on September 17th. The day before Winchester's term began, the Germans announced that all Jews in Poland were to be concentrated into ghettoes.

It was immediately clear that school life was not going to be the same. Many of the teaching staff had disappeared, some never to return.[35] The Somerville brothers returned to Hopper's to find a strange mixture of normality and utter strangeness, as 'Dan' explained:

> We found that the whole school was being put on a war footing. Bobber was deeply upset that all of us were going to have to survive another war. I remember that a lot of us went to dig up a nearby golf course at Hockley to plant potatoes, and strange pill-boxes and anti-tank obstacles appeared on the streets.[36]

Those beginning their studies at Oxford or Cambridge in 1939 found that the universities had instituted the 'War Degree', a truncated one-year course which nevertheless conferred an Oxford or Cambridge degree. The atmosphere of the universities was otherwise largely unchanged by the onset of war. Western Europe had not yet experienced *Blitzkrieg* (a term actually invented by the *New York Times* rather than the Nazis), and there was a sense of unreality about the whole period, the 'Phoney War', so brilliantly satirized by Evelyn Waugh in *Put Out More Flags.* The British Expeditionary Force which had been sent to France, just as in 1914, was by now in position along the Belgian frontier. However, on October 14th a German U-boat penetrated the Royal Navy's principal anchorage at Scapa Flow and sank the battleship HMS *Royal Oak.* Two days later, German bombers attacked British warships in the Firth of Forth.

But the war for the most part continued quietly, with little obvious impact on life in mainland Britain. There were German raiders at sea, and German aircraft continued to make isolated raids on the north of the country, but the main threat was technologically-advanced magnetic mines sown in British home waters. On November 21st one severely damaged a new cruiser, HMS *Belfast*, and on December 4th the equally modern battleship HMS *Nelson* suffered the same fate. Two Wykehamists would earn the George Cross or George Medal for defusing such mines.

* * *

It had been decided that on the outbreak of war, distinctions between Regular, Territorial, Special Reserve, and Temporary commissions – largely meaningless and unnecessarily complicated in wartime – would be done away with, and all officers would be granted emergency commissions into the Regular Army. The old structures of officer training were swept away. Until the outbreak of war, RMC Sandhurst had operated like an exclusive boarding school: the parents of its students – 'Gentlemen Cadets' – had paid the Army to turn their sons into officers. Tuition fees, boarding fees, books, equipment, and uniforms had all to be paid for; there had been an entrance examination, with a published order of merit and scholarships and bursaries for the academically gifted or sons of officers.

On the outbreak of war, Sandhurst officially 'closed', though its buildings remained in use: the Gentlemen Cadets there were either given commissions straight away or remained on the Sandhurst site, where they joined either the cavalry or infantry OCTU. The infantry training wing was given the title 161 OCTU, and the cavalry (in reality, armour) became 101 OCTU. Artillery and engineer officers had traditionally been trained at RMA Woolwich, which also closed for the duration, several OCTUs being opened in various locations around the country. All potential Army officers would first receive some basic training as ordinary soldiers before proceeding to OCTU if considered 'officer material'. The Royal Air Force and Royal Navy adopted a similar system, but wartime officers were commissioned into the RAF Volunteer Reserve (RAFVR) and RN Volunteer Reserve (RNVR) respectively.

* * *

The winter of 1939 to 1940 was the coldest since 1894, with a temperature of -18°C recorded in Buxton in January 1940; both the Thames and Southampton Docks froze over. The BEF in France shivered in inadequate accommodation and winter clothing, but faced little danger from the enemy. Some indication of the quietness of the Western Front can be gauged from the fact that the first British infantryman to be killed in action in the Second World War died on December 9th, three months into the conflict. Between September and December 1939, 4,130 people had died in road accidents in Great Britain, whilst the armed forces had lost 2,511 dead.

Several boys in Hopper's had relatives with the BEF: on January 19th 1940, Gavin Younger joined the house, a week after his father Harry (also a Hopperite) had gone to France with 1st Lothians and Border Yeomanry.[37]

> Dear Bobber,
> I write to say how sorry I am that I am not able to bring Gavin to Sunnyside for his first half … We crossed over here on the 11th and are making our way up by degrees to our appointed place. Please give my love to Gavin and tell him I am in France if he does not already know. We kept our move over here very secret and they may not have heard at home that I am with the BEF. I leave him with every confidence in your care and hope that he will add his contribution to Sunnyside and Win.Coll… .
> P.S. Intense cold here and very poor billets for the men, but we are moving along and may do better in the next place.[38]

One of those in the 1938 photograph – Bruce Fortune[39] – had a Wykehamist father with an exalted role in the BEF: Major General Sir Victor Morven Fortune was commanding 51st (Highland) Division near the German border.[40] And when 2nd Battalion, Grenadier Guards went out to France in 1939, it took with it Lieutenant Geoffrey Gwyer, the half-brother of John Kennedy, one of the other boys in the 1938 photograph.[41]

* * *

It was only at sea that the war seemed to be prosecuted with any vigour, and on December 13th the British cruisers *Exeter* and *Ajax* and the New Zealand cruiser *Achilles* intercepted the German pocket-battleship *Admiral Graf Spee* off the River Plate in South America, crippling the enemy vessel and forcing her captain to scuttle his warship four days later.

Despite the bitter cold, food rationing began in earnest in January 1940, when ration books were first issued; the weekly allowance for each person was four ounces of bacon or ham, four ounces of butter, and twelve ounces of sugar. Meat rationing began in March: each person was allowed 1s 10d worth of meat a week. In 'E' house, the butter ration was placed on a plate on each table, and as they awaited the end of grace the boys all kept their knives poised over the butter to make sure that not an instant was lost in getting their fair share. On one occasion, a pupil of the day recalled, he and his companions slammed down their knives so quickly and simultaneously that the butter dish disintegrated.[42] Another commented that the food at Winchester, which had always been 'undistinguished but edible', now became even more monotonous: 'Woolton Pie (with carrots and spuds) was a main dish. School food was good preparation for five years in the Army.'[43]

* * *

The Phoney War continued. The harsh winter had led to a shortage of coal, which in turn led to the cancellation of many passenger train services. An IRA bombing campaign that winter had caused explosions at Euston Station and in Oxford Street, which had done more damage in London than anything which the Germans had yet achieved. But on March 18th, Mussolini and Hitler met in the Brenner Pass, where Mussolini committed the still-neutral Italy to joining in the war on Germany's side at an as-yet-unspecified 'decisive hour'.

On March 2nd the war came close to Winchester for the first time. Off the Isle of Wight, the British merchant vessel *Domala* was bombed by German aircraft and beached in flames in the Solent; she had been sailing from Antwerp with 143 British Indian subjects on board. Among her crew was 22-year-old Wykehamist Hugh Morgan; he was one of over a hundred people to be killed in the attack, and the first Wykehamist to die in the Second World War.[44] No one now remembers the *Domala;* much worse was to happen over the next three months, let alone the next five years.

* * *

As it became clear that the war was going to be long and bitter, those still at school began to take the OTC a bit more seriously, and the training at Winchester became more immediate and relevant:

> I learned my infantry battle-drills in Meads: how to strip a Bren-gun, and how to fire a 2-inch mortar (in theory, of course). We did night manoeuvres in khaki battledress with the Home Guard on occasional night patrols, and of course arms drill and 'field days' against Marlborough and suchlike. So we all had excellent preliminary training before the real thing.[45]

The OTC opened an Air Training Corps section, which taught aircraft recognition, and volunteers from among the senior boys spent part of their nights on an official rota, watching out for fires and hostile aircraft.

But despite the fact that the country was at war – or perhaps *because* it was at war – the boys' own parochial concerns seemed of overriding interest. As yet there was no sense that the national way of life or even national existence were under serious threat. As one said, 'I never felt there was any danger of our being over-run and defeated.'[46]

* * *

Edmunds.

The first school term of 1940 – Common Time – ended on April 2nd, and with it the school careers of four of our subjects: Michael Edmunds,[47] Bruce Fortune, Hugh Rose, and 'Dan' Somerville. Unlike the other three, Fortune did not go on to university, but after a summer partly spent on a Forest Camp with Guy Richardson, joined the Army in August.

'Mi' Edmunds was a high-flier, a keen and useful violinist and pianist who had won the German Translation Prize. He had a quick mind, was fond of arguing, and would have done well at Christ Church, Oxford, but only stayed there one term. He gained experience, before going to OCTU, in the Home Guard at Banbury and in the family brewing business (of which he was made a director at twenty-one). Robertson felt sure that Edmunds had ability and gifts which would qualify him, after the war, either for business or for public service.

Christopher Somerville was known to his family as 'Dan', though he signed some of his letters 'Charlie'.[48] He was a keen fencer (representing the school from 1937 to 1940), and went on to New College, Oxford to take a War Degree in English:

Dan Somerville.

I missed the early part of the war because I was at Oxford. By the time I was due to be called up I was no longer eighteen – I was twenty. So I think you can't really say it affected my teenage years at all. I wasn't called up until I had got my so-called university degree. I say 'so-called' because my qualification was only part of way to a full degree, and awarded after only four terms' work – it was all the university would give until the war was over, because anybody doing that sort of work was not doing war work. You were doing something that was connected with your future life – if you had one. Of course, none of us knew how much of a future we were going to have. You just took life as it came.

There were masses of girls around, but you were not allowed to invite any girl to your room after 1630hrs. Nor were you yourself to stay out after midnight. And if you did stay out, there were known places where you could climb in, to dodge the Dean's displeasure and a fine. If you were going to have to climb in, it was best if you weren't too drunk at the time! So you could see girls a bit, but I didn't want to get myself to get into any entanglement. There was a war on; none of us knew whether we'd have a future, and it seemed sensible to leave that sort of thing alone. None of us had any idea how long the war was going to go on for. I think we knew that we were not going to give in. We had Churchill at the helm, and the one thing that Churchill was not going to do was give up. Although his judgement of events and people was bad on the whole, he exemplified the British Bulldog spirit, and I think we knew that we were going to win in the end. It was a very hairy time before we did, for sure.

When I finished my degree, I thought that there would only be one term until I was called up. So I went back in October 1941 and had the eight weeks of the Michaelmas term in Oxford. This extra term with my tutor, David Cecil, was very valuable; we did what we liked, and he opened my eyes to a great deal. He believed

> that if you didn't like certain authors the fault was with you, not with them. It was always possible to enlarge one's taste if you took the trouble. As a writer I do not think his style has ever been bettered, and most of what I have learnt and is not innate in me, I learned from him.[49]

Robertson later stated that on arriving in Sunnyside Hugh Rose had suffered from diffidence which it had cost him many an effort to conquer, and that he was 'remembered at Winchester for his loyalty and old-world courtesy, as a good linguist and hard worker, and as a persistent runner who helped his life-long friend and almost-brother, Bruce Fortune, to bring athletic honours to their House.'

Rose went on to Magdalene College, Cambridge, where after four terms he took good Seconds in French and German in the first part of the Tripos. The Master of Magdalene later wrote to Robertson as follows:

Rose.

> We were all very fond of him, and he was an example of that gentle and high character which we have found in so many of our Wykehamists. I shall always remember his kindly smile as he greeted me in the courts, and I felt his influence in the College was entirely for good and much more effective than that of those who were more demonstrative.[50]

So many sources mention Rose's smile that it must have been striking indeed. He was still smiling when he died.

* * *

Neither the British nor the French had any conception of the storm which was about to break. Indeed, on April 4th Chamberlain announced in a speech that Hitler had 'missed the bus' militarily, and could not hope to win. By now, the RAF had dropped sixty-five million leaflets over Germany, a waste of aircraft, paper, and, more importantly, trained aircrew. But the war was about to become a great deal more serious – and Gerry Rickman was just in time for it. He would have the dubious distinction of being the first of those pictured in 1938 to go into action, and the last to finish the war.

* * *

2nd Lieutenant Rickman had been with his Battalion – 2nd Royal Northumberland Fusiliers (2RNF) – when war was declared, but a week later, had been sent with a group of other officers to the Regimental Depot to help to train the new intake. 2RNF had disembarked in Cherbourg on October 2nd, and had spent most of the winter in Turcoing on the Franco-Belgian border, where the unit had busied itself building defences along the frontier and visiting France's vaunted Maginot Line. By the beginning of April, 2RNF had its orders in case of a German attack on Belgium. The British 'Plan D' was to advance into Belgium and hold the line of the River Dyle. 2RNF would initially be employed securing the BEF's routes behind its advance – traffic control and the protection of key locations and infrastructure, including Brussels airfield.

On April 6th, Rickman re-appeared in the Battalion war diary: 'Information received that 2nd Lieutenant G. Rickman would be attached to the Battalion for three months from the Infantry Base Depot. 2nd Lieutenant P. Bulman to go in exchange.'[51]

He reported for duty in Turcoing on April 9th at 1500hrs. Earlier that day, German forces had invaded Norway, installing the Norwegian Fascist Vidkun Quisling as their puppet in place of King Haakon. At the same time, they invaded Denmark, thus securing their grip on the Baltic Sea. Fierce naval battles took place in Norwegian waters between British and German vessels over the following week, and on April 14th British troops landed to support Norwegian forces. For a while it seemed that the German invasion might not only be halted but even driven back, but by the beginning of May the evacuation of British troops had begun, a pattern to become familiar across the globe in the years to follow: Dunkirk, Greece, Crete, Malaya, Singapore, Tobruk, Burma – two years of humiliating retreat and bungling, interspersed with many a false dawn of victory. Flushed with his success in Norway, at the beginning of May Hitler authorized an attack on Belgium, Holland, and France. His intention was to feint into Belgium, which he knew would draw the BEF forward into that country; he would then launch an armoured strike through the Ardennes, side-stepping the Maginot Line, and thrust for the Channel coast, splitting the British and French forces apart.

On May 7th, Chamberlain faced angry opponents in the House of Commons, dissatisfied with his conduct of the war and in particular the Norwegian debacle. He narrowly survived the vote, but then on May 10th came the shattering news of the German attack. Chamberlain resigned, and on Monday, May 13th Churchill made his first appearance in the House of Commons as Prime Minister in a new coalition government. Already the French were being out-fought, and great gaps were being torn in their lines; Churchill, at least, appreciated the seriousness of the situation, and declared that 'I have nothing to offer but blood, toil, tears, and sweat.'

The following day, the War Office announced the formation of the Local Defence Volunteers (better known as the Home Guard), to be made up of males between the ages of seventeen and sixty-five. School and university OTCs were of course ideally placed to supply young men, experienced staff, and weapons for this organization.

* * *

When the Germans invaded Belgium on May 10th, the British carried out 'Plan D' exactly as they had practised – and exactly as Hitler wanted. 2RNF entered Belgium at 0615hrs on May 11th and took up their allotted sector and role around Merchtem. Rickman had joined 'D' Company as a Platoon Commander on April 11th, and so was with his unit during the advance and the five days during which it protected lines of communication. One of 2RNF's major roles was to clear the roads of refugees so that military traffic could be kept flowing. On May 15th, 2RNF recorded that

> the Corps Commander had stopped 2nd Lieutenant Rickman and asked who was doing traffic control, and on hearing the answer had replied that it was being done very well. Quiet night; no alarms, etc. The refugees were on the move the whole night.

Elsewhere, however, defeat was in the air. The Dutch surrendered on May 15th, after bombers flattened the centre of Rotterdam. The French were in disarray, the inhabitants of Paris fleeing south in their thousands, and their Premier telephoned Churchill that day to announce that 'We are beaten; we have lost the battle.' As May 16th dawned it was clear that the BEF would have to pull back from its advanced line in Belgium, now in terrible danger of being outflanked. At 1800hrs 2RNF withdrew to Kirxken, west of the Dendre Canal.

* * *

The future was uncertain, and sending one's sons off to boarding school – especially one near the south coast – was an act of faith when the world was collapsing. Nevertheless, parents trusted Robertson, as John Kennedy's father showed in a letter on May 16th:

> Dear Robertson,
> Just a line to say I place John under you *in loco parentis* – he can be employed in any way – watching for parachutes etc – on the land – I consider all education at present times of secondary importance – the whole thing is to make use of all manpower and thousands of younger boys than he is were in the trenches last war – Consider him your son –
> This needs no answer – I think you will understand what I am getting at – you need not refer to me – you have my full authority –
> My wife fully agrees.
> C.F. Kennedy[52]

* * *

German forces entered Brussels on May 17th, and on May 18th 2RNF retired behind the line of the River Escaut. It was not easy; traffic management had collapsed, and the roads were solid with refugees. 'D' Company arrived after five hours on the move, only to be told that the Battalion had been allocated the wrong position and would have to redeploy. By 2200hrs their HQ had reached Ooteghem, tasked with supporting the brigades of 4th Division along the river. But it was so dark that proper positions had to wait until morning.

* * *

The first Hopperite to die on active service in the Second World War was Major Jack Battye, who was accidentally shot in India on May 19th whilst commanding 2/22 Mountain Battery, Royal Artillery.[53]

* * *

On the afternoon of May 19th, Rickman's Company occupied positions to support 4th Division's reserve line, held by 12 Infantry Brigade. The plan had originally been for three machine-gun battalions to assist in the defence, but the other two battalions had been pulled back into reserve, leaving 2RNF to do the job alone.

> All these orders were given verbally and were not confirmed in writing, as the enemy is expected on the line R. ESCAUT at dawn tomorrow, and speed is essential.[54]

Around 0800hrs on May 20th the Germans did indeed catch up with the BEF on the Escaut, and began to push hard against the defences. 'D' Company had been due to move up into the line to assist 11 Infantry Brigade, but instead were held on the reserve line until the situation was clear; when the Germans managed to force a bridge-head across the section of river defended by 44th Division on May 21st, 'D' Company became the defensive left flank of the reserve line. It was time to retreat again.

* * *

Grant and Murray, meanwhile, had been mobilized along with the rest of the Lovat Scouts in 1939, their role being reconnaissance and close protection duties. Grant was serving as a Second Lieutenant in 1 Troop of 'A' Squadron; his brother was the regimental Gas Officer. The Regiment formed part of 9th (Highland) Division until March 1940, when they joined the Mounted Cavalry Division in Nottinghamshire. It was clear that no one quite knew what to do with the unit. On April 22nd, however, the Lovat Scouts lost the ponies with which they had trained, and began to re-train in a dismounted role. Bizarrely, they were now allocated as garrison troops on the remote Danish-controlled Faroe Islands – in the North Atlantic, between Norway and Iceland – which the Lovat Scouts were to protect from an expected German invasion.

On May 22nd they embarked at Glasgow on the *Ulster Prince,* which sailed the next day and moored in the port of Thorshavn on the morning of May 25th 1940, in thick fog. The war diary recorded that 'as the ship came alongside the pier with the pipers playing, crowds of people, including hundreds of children, came down from the town to look on, and remained there all day.'[55]

Grant and Murray were to spend the best part of two years on garrison duty in the Faroes. 'A' Squadron was billeted in Thorshavn at first, but after a month the three squadrons began to rotate through positions at other points, especially the magnificent natural harbour of Skaalefjord. There were continual patrols and cross-country marches, as well as vigorous training in marksmanship and observation. But the real action was elsewhere.

* * *

By May 20th German armour was racing for the Channel coast, with some tanks already at the mouth of the Somme, and it became clear that the only hope for the BEF was to head for the port of Dunkirk for evacuation. And so, on the night of May 22nd, 4th Division retreated across the border back into France, and occupied the defences which had been created over the winter near Turcoing – indeed, 'C' Company of 2RNF set up its Vickers guns in the very positions which it had constructed. The longer they could hold this line, the better a chance the BEF had of getting away. 2RNF had not suffered much so far, or seen much action, and it was hard for the men to understand the gravity of the situation; it seemed to them that they had abandoned perfectly good positions for no obvious reason. Most of their information came from German propaganda leaflets, which included useful maps of the general progress of the campaign. They remained in their positions until May 26th.

* * *

On May 23rd a brigade of British troops landed at Calais – so tantalizingly close to home – where, after several days of desperate close-quarters fighting, four Wykehamists lay dead and three had been captured (two of them wounded); elsewhere in France, two more Wykehamists were killed on May 23rd alone. Several of the dead and captured at Calais were members of 2KRRC, including Hopperite Mike Sinclair, brother of John Sinclair. One of those fatally wounded was Lieutenant Colonel Chandos Hoskyns of 1RB, who succumbed to his wounds in hospital in Winchester in June and was buried in the town. The commanding officer of the Calais garrison, Brigadier Claude Nicholson, also a Wykehamist, later died as a prisoner of war.

* * *

Back in Winchester, a tragic loss hit Hopper's just before midnight on May 25th, as Mike Sinclair went into captivity in Calais and Grant and Murray landed in the Faroes. David Eccles, one of the other boys in the 1938 house photograph, had fallen ill the previous night after treatment for a boil on his neck, and septicaemia killed him. The shock of losing a fellow pupil, a friend, in such a close community as a boarding house cannot be overstated – this was not death in the abstract, in some corner of a foreign field. Robertson almost certainly penned Eccles' obituary in *The Wykehamist*:

> He had won his way by solid work … and had been accepted for entry at Magdalen in October (having passed also part of his Science Prelims with a view to the Honour School of Agriculture) and for the regimental list of the Coldstream Guards. He was second Prefect of his house, its keen Platoon Commander and cricket captain, and, as a magnificently stout-hearted Fives player, had twice won Watney Cup. He showed throughout his school days the loyalty and robust common-sense he learnt in his beautiful home, where he had early shouldered responsibilities. He not only knew what should be done in garden, field, or wood, but could do a man's job with the best – the sure way to the respect and affection which were his on every side, both there and here. His many friends of all standings will cherish the memory of a singularly honest worker and good comrade, and offer his parents heartfelt sympathy in their loss.[56]

* * *

Now the pace of retreat hastened. On May 27th, 2RNF moved back behind the Yser Canal, just north of Ypres; Rickman and 'D' Company held the centre of the Battalion's line, at Elverdinghe, and were dug in by nightfall. The Germans arrived on the eastern side that evening, but did not press home an attack. The following morning, Belgium surrendered. Metcalfe wrote to his parents from Hopper's that day:

> You said there was lots of news from the BBC; there is certainly plenty of that now – too much, in fact. The Germans seem to be getting it all their own way. And with the news this morning that Belgium had surrendered, it looks as if the BEF are in for a really nasty time. Still, John [his brother] is not there yet and perhaps by the time his ten days' leave is up there will no longer be a BEF in France. People are really getting anxious here about parachutists, and I hope the Local Defence Volunteers get properly trained to deal with them if they come.[57]

2RNF had a quiet day, with some shelling, but in the late afternoon there was confusion which could have had dire repercussions. The infantry sharing the line with 2RNF received orders to withdraw four hundred yards to allow an artillery bombardment of the enemy-held bank of the canal – but the order did not reach the machine-gunners. As the infantry retired, the rumour spread that the Germans had crossed the canal in force, and the result was that the temporary and limited withdrawal just kept going. As the infantry went, they picked up 2RNF's reserves:

> Orders were also given by the infantry commanders concerned to 2nd Lieutenant G. Rickman and Platoon Sergeant Major Blackburn to withdraw their platoons. On receipt of this information, Battalion HQ turned out all available personnel … and advanced to the line of the Canal. No enemy were found to be near the Canal.[58]

2RNF withdrew again that night, this time to a line which was not behind a waterway, from Poperinghe to Woesten. They were only there for a day, moving late on May 29th to the final defensive line which they would hold, that of the Bergues-Furnes Canal.

The Battalion's war now hotted up; the Germans were pursuing closely, and traffic choked the narrow roads. Around Rickman the vehicles of the BEF were going up in smoke, as had most of 2RNF's paperwork that afternoon. The war diary described the evening as a 'most depressing drive'. 2RNF nonetheless reached the canal line in the small hours of May 30th, and were lucky enough to have a quiet day. Hell broke loose on May 31st, however. Having received orders for withdrawal to the evacuation beaches that morning, Rickman and his comrades began destroying personal kit and any equipment which was not needed; the Battalion's inessential personnel had already been evacuated. But at around 1530hrs, the Germans made determined attempts to break the line, with heavy shelling. Once again, the infantry retired, and 2RNF tried to remedy the situation:

> Apparently, at some time before this the enemy had put in an attack. It is hard to say where and when, but the infantry gave way and came streaming back past Battalion HQ,

> some without rifles or equipment. As many as possible were collected and ordered back to the line. 'C' and 'D' companies remained in position or were ordered to withdraw by officers in these two rifle battalions. Several posts had their guns knocked out of action after expending their ammunition.
>
> What actually happened is hard to say, but 'C' Company when mustered in the evening had four guns workable left, and 'D' Company consisted of Captain Pratt and eight Other Ranks.

Rickman's Company Commander had been wounded in the head, which would have left Rickman in charge had the Battalion been able to find him. It was not a good moment to have become separated – 50th Division, which 2RNF had been supporting, was ordered to the coast that night, and the fighting troops were to move to Bray Dunes. Advance parties of 2RNF set out at 1930hrs, and Battalion HQ moved off with the remnants of 'C' and 'D' companies at midnight. By noon on June 1st 2RNF had gathered six officers and just over 150 Other Ranks – a fraction of its established strength – with 'A' and 'B' companies completely adrift. Rickman was also still missing. The shattered Battalion was re-organized as ordinary infantry in case a counter-attack was needed to cover the evacuation – only to be told half an hour later that they must head for Dunkirk immediately to be picked up by ship. They set out straight away, having destroyed their few remaining vehicles and machine-guns, and keeping only personal weapons. It was an eight-mile march to the Mole at Dunkirk, but they were there by 1730hrs and at 2100hrs boarded a destroyer bound for England. Behind them, what was left of 2RNF was scattered and leaderless.

'A' and 'B' companies arrived at Bray Dunes at 0400hrs on June 1st, but had no further instructions. At 1700hrs a panic caused them to be deployed to stop a rumoured German attack, but by 2145hrs they were on their way to Malo-les-Bains, about a mile from the Dunkirk Mole. Shell-fire caused fourteen casualties along the way. On reaching the Mole, they found that the last boat had left for the night, so 'A' Company and half of 'B' acquired boats of their own and set off for home. The remainder – a forlorn party of 'B' Company – were evacuated by destroyer on the night of June 2nd. But where was Rickman?

On arrival in England, evacuated troops were disarmed and dispersed around a number of reception camps, no matter what their unit. Thus members of 2RNF initially found themselves in Aldershot, Bordon, Camberley, Cardiff, Harwich, Leicester, Mytchett, Pontefract, and Tweseldown. From there, they were sent back to their parent formations; all the machine-gun battalions ended up in Paignton, but moved to Bridestowe on June 5th. The war diary recorded that 'parties of the Battalion still continued to drift in at all hours of the day and night'.[59]

On June 6th, 2RNF's war diary showed 168 Other Ranks and three officers as 'Missing', one of whom was Rickman. But by the following afternoon Rickman had re-joined the Battalion. Where he had been, and how he had escaped from Dunkirk, is not known.

* * *

Although Rickman could rejoice that he had made it back, there had been a heavy human cost to the BEF; for example, from Hopper's, James Graham had been killed in action in a rearguard action at Cassel in Belgium on May 30th.[60]

Another Hopperite who was taken off the beaches was Geoffrey Gwyer.[61] Robertson wrote that he did 'fine work' during the retreat from Brussels to Dunkirk, and then on the beaches themselves, and was recommended for a higher award than the mention in dispatches which he in fact received. Gwyer was very badly wounded in the last stages of the evacuation:

> To those who saw him helpless with his shattered leg for over six months in Epsom Hospital, it was a miracle that he ever walked, let alone served, again. But his pluck and cheeriness were then, as always, indomitable; by 1941 he was instructing at Windsor.[62]

How John Kennedy felt on seeing his half-brother in such circumstances is not recorded. Nor do we know what David Middleditch thought when he heard the news that his cousin, Captain John Middleditch, had been wounded whilst serving as a Captain with the Green Howards.[63]

John Pinney, too, must have felt anxiety for his older brother Bernard, who had just overlapped with the start of Robertson's tenure in Hopper's.[64] Bernard was now a Major in the Royal Artillery, commanding 12 Battery, 6th Anti-Aircraft Regiment, at Dunkirk. He was awarded the Military Cross for his actions there:

> Throughout whole operation was untiring in fighting his guns and inspiring and organising his Battery and its Section Commanders. This officer was continually under shell fire and performed fine work after the destruction of his guns.[65]

Christopher Pringle would have been greatly relieved when he found that his older brother, Major Michael Pringle RASC – not a Wykehamist – had been safely evacuated from Dunkirk.

* * *

By the time that the evacuation from Dunkirk ended on the night of June 3rd, 338,000 men (including around 120,000 French and Belgians) had been taken off. Of over 800 vessels involved, some 240 had been destroyed. And the British Expeditionary Force had left behind it 2,472 guns, 84,427 vehicles, and 660,000 tons of ammunition and stores – not to mention 11,000 dead and 41,000 missing, presumed captured.[66]

Covering the evacuation had been the fighter aircraft of the RAF, over a hundred of which had been lost in the process. One of them was flown by Hopperite Pilot Officer Nigel Weir, well known to most of the boys in the 1938 photograph. He had left Winchester in 1937, and, having served with the Oxford University Air Squadron, was commissioned into the RAFVR in September 1939. He was posted to fly Hurricanes with 145 Squadron on May 12th 1940, and his first combat report dates from June 1st, the day before his twenty-first birthday. His sortie with 'B' Flight to cover the evacuation beaches north of Dunkirk was eventful:[67]

> I left Manston at 1100hrs in a composite formation of thirty-nine fighters, of which about twelve were French Bloch 152s. Near Dunkirk this formation sighted and attacked a large number of enemy aircraft.

Weir estimated that when they encountered the Germans at 1130hrs there were over seventy Messerschmitts, all fighters (single-seater Bf109s and twin-engine Bf110s); the 110s were at around 6,000ft with the 109s above them.

> I was in the leading section … to the north of our formation, and flying east, when we saw, a thousand feet below us, thirty 110s flying west at around six thousand feet. Our section dived and attacked the rear machine, but before he came into my sights I noticed that the enemy aircraft had formed a circle … I therefore cut across the circle, hoping that their packed formation would prevent them firing at me. When I was about half-way across, one enemy aircraft opened fire on me with his rear gun, and as I ducked one other machine came into my sights. I opened fire on a beam attack and blew his nose off and part of his port engine: he stood up on his tail, and my Section Leader saw him crash into the sea.
>
> I dived out and climbed to join the Hurricanes, but the first machine I met turned out to be a 109. I pulled my machine into a very steep climb and gave him a short burst in his belly. I saw my tracers enter his fuselage, but he did not catch fire, although he ceased climbing and started to fall.
>
> At this point some shots came past me very close, followed by a Hurricane zooming, so I kicked on rudder and skidded, as a result of which I began to spin. I pulled out of spin at about a thousand feet, and went well out to sea before climbing again. On my return the Germans were disappearing fast, and our formation was standing home.

Weir claimed a 110 confirmed killed, and a 109 'possible' – though it is more likely that this was only damaged.

On June 4th, in the House of Commons, Churchill made perhaps his most famous speech:

> Even though large tracts of Europe and many old and famous states have fallen, or may fall, into the grip of the Gestapo and all the odious apparatus of Nazi rule, we shall not flag or fail. We shall go on to the end; we shall fight in France; we shall fight on the seas and oceans; we shall fight with growing confidence and growing strength in the air; we shall defend our island, whatever the cost may be; we shall fight on the beaches; we shall fight on the landing grounds; we shall fight in the fields and in the streets; we shall fight in the hills; we shall never surrender. And even if, which I do not for a moment believe, this island or a large part of it were subjugated and starving, then our Empire beyond the seas, armed and guarded by the British Fleet, would carry on the struggle, until, in God's good time, the New World, with all its power and might, steps forth to the rescue and the liberation of the old.[68]

* * *

Metcalfe reported to his parents how Winchester was responding to the news of Dunkirk:

> Here the casualties are just beginning to appear. Nearly all the relations of men in the House, and the Old Wykehamists I know, have returned unhurt or only slightly wounded. Winchester is full of soldiers from France – French and Belgian as well as from the BEF. Meanwhile we are beginning to do something about the parachutists. Nearly all the OTC rifles have been taken to equip the Local Defence Volunteers, and a post is being set up from where we can watch all the College grounds during the night. In fact, this evening I am going out there; four of us watch in relays and there is always supposed to be someone watching the whole time.[69]

* * *

It is often forgotten that the Dunkirk evacuation was not the end of the war in France, which continued until France's surrender on June 22nd. Large numbers of British troops remained in the country. Guy Richardson's brother Jim did not even reach France until May 23rd; disembarking at Cherbourg, 2RTR went into action near Abbeville on the 27th. From then the unit retreated gradually to the Seine and beyond, eventually being evacuated from Brest and Cherbourg on June 16th.

Bruce Fortune was very conscious of the continued fighting, because his father was leading 51st Highland Division in support of French attempts to hold the line of the Somme. However, the Germans crossed on June 5th, forcing Fortune's Division back towards the coast and eventual capture at St Valery-en-Caux. It was there that the

Fortune's disgust is clearly visible in this German photograph taken shortly after 51st Division's surrender. The German officer at left, to whom he had surrendered, is, of course, Rommel. (IWM RML342; edited by DB Colour)

second Hopperite loss of the war occurred, when Gavin Younger's father was killed in a 'friendly fire' incident.[70] For a long time Harry Younger's sons, wife, and elderly mother clung to the hope that he was a prisoner of war – the wait for definite news was hugely distressing.

III

'Sacrifice won't make this world a better place, but willing sacrifice will'

June–December 1940

The shocking collapse of France in six weeks after the German attack had changed the entire tenor of Britain's approach to the conflict. The country stood alone and seemingly defenceless, the parlous nature of her defences obvious even to the meanest intelligence. As head boy Tony Pawson noted, there was a feeling that everyone needed to do more to help the nation in its hour of need:

The rather self-conscious Hopper's 'Bather Cup' squad in the spring of 1940, after their success in the OTC drill competition. All of them feature in this narrative: of the six in the second (seated) row, only two lived to see the end of the war. (back row) Finch, Herbert, McMurtrie, McArthur, Hill. (standing) Huggins, Pringle, Somerville J., Kennedy, Metcalfe, Hirst, Brooke, Middleditch. (seated) Duffin, Eccles, Fortune, Rose, Edmunds, Sheepshanks. (front row) Mackrill, Walker.

> The School had already planted potatoes in an area of Hockley, which had been ploughed up for them, and special volunteers gave up their half-rems [half days] to learn farming under the guidance of the Sparsholt Institute. Owing, however, to the many reverses suffered during the term, and the state of crisis which existed, it was felt that our war effort was insufficient. In the last fortnight, therefore, cricket was abandoned and the School took to digging. Large portions were dug up in Kingsgate Park by the nets, the fives courts, Fishcroft (far end), Furley's wall, and the bank along Romans Road cricket pitch. Trenches were also dug at Bar End to prevent the landing of hostile aircraft, and a shelter was dug for the hospital. In addition, volunteers painted all the windows in the div. rooms, science building, old and new Mill, and Quirister Palace. At the end of the term, three harvest and one lumber camps were organised by Mr Lucas. About thirty men, or less, went to each.[1]

* * *

On July 16th, Hitler officially announced to his armed forces his intention to invade Britain. The Battle of Britain had begun on July 10th with a series of air battles over the Channel, as German aircraft attacked British coastal shipping and tried to wear down the RAF. The fighting swirled inland into the skies over Winchester. Nigel Weir's next combat report was filed on July 18th, after a successful engagement twenty miles south of Bognor Regis, beginning at 1300hrs.[2]

> 'B' Flight was ordered to patrol base at angels ten [code for 10,000ft]. Shortly after take-off we received vector 240, angels ten. In order to be able to see bandits against the cloud layer at that height, we climbed a further 2,000ft. I was flying No.2 in Blue Section, and sighted an aircraft flying south over the sea; it was 10,000ft below, and I kept an eye on it while telling the controller to inform Blue Leader. As these attempts failed I went into the lead and dived down, pulling out to the right when nearly in range to allow Blue Leader to open fire. I opened fire simultaneously from the quarter, closing in to an astern attack when Blue Leader broke away. I followed the enemy into thin cloud, which he reached after evasive tactics of the most violent kind. Several large panels of metal came off him, and I finally broke away just in time to avoid collision.

Weir stated that he had fired one burst, lasting fifteen seconds, at the enemy aircraft – a Heinkel He111 bomber – from a range of 300 yards 'closing to point-blank range'. His combat report was, it seems, too literary for the authorities, and swathes of it were crossed out.

> ~~The enemy was in a bad way, but far from finished. Unfortunately for him, he still had to receive the attention of Blue 3 and Green Section, while his rear gunners were both out of action~~. Green Section sent him diving into the sea, where he at once vanished, leaving one live member of the crew in the water. This man was still swimming when we left. ~~I suggested that one of the many Walruses flying in the vicinity might come and collect him while we were still there to mark the spot, but none had arrived by the time we left~~. Returned to base and landed at 1329hrs.[3]

Weir had thus shared in another confirmed kill. Four days later, on July 22nd, he took off at 0620hrs and saw combat 20 miles south of Selsey Bill. The action began at 0700hrs at 15,000ft, and ended at sea level.[4]

> We had been vectored back from Beachy Head to Selsey Bill, where sundry bandits were alleged to be flying around. I sighted one a long way south of us, flying south, but by that time the Blue Section leader had begun to dive on a Dornier Do17 a few thousand feet below us, heading south. Green Section left us, and as Blue Section dived flat out the Dornier dived east. Blue Leader silenced the rear-gunner and damaged the starboard engine. As soon as he broke away I, as Blue 2, opened fire from above at three hundred yards, aiming ahead of the pilot. After a time, seeing he was still flying on, I transferred my fire to the starboard engine, which caught fire just after I broke away.

Weir estimated that he had fired from ranges of 300 yards down to about 50 yards, in one continuous burst of seventeen seconds. When he broke away his guns were empty: he had fired 330 rounds from each gun, a total of over 2,600 bullets.

> Blue 3 attacked, and the Dornier finally landed in the sea. We signalled a motor boat to rescue the crew, and when this had been done we all returned to base, leaving the rubber dinghy on the sea.

Weir landed at 0735hrs.Once again, he had shared in a confirmed kill.

* * *

Nick Somerville recalled this period vividly:

> These were exciting times; the daily news was of huge proportions; Winston Churchill's speeches stirred us all; and the whole House was pulling together under the Bobber's emotional involvement with us all.[5]

Cloister Time – the summer term – ended on July 30th 1940, and with it the next three boys left: David Kemp, Roger Rigby, and Christopher Sheepshanks.[6] Kemp we have already encountered shepherding Nick Somerville through his early days in Hopper's; he was planning to move on to Cambridge.

Rigby.

Rigby, who had shown a talent for art, had decided to leave Winchester a year early in order to fit in university before joining the forces. He went on to Magdalene College, Cambridge,[7] where he combined his academic studies with preparation to join the Royal Armoured Corps. In his memoirs he later recalled the somewhat strange way in which he signed on with 23rd Hussars: it reads like something out of Evelyn Waugh's *Men at Arms.*

At Cambridge all undergraduates had to do a half day each week of military training. We had all been members of our school Corps and had passed the Army Certificate 'A' examination. At the end of our year at Cambridge we passed Army Certificate 'B'. This qualified us to go straight to an OCTU instead of spending time in the ranks before selection. I wanted to go into tanks, so I did my Army training in the Cambridge University armoured squadron.

One day I was introduced to a Grenadier Guards Captain. I never discovered quite what his job was. He seemed to be operating quite independently and without any precise brief – a sort of talent-scout. He also seemed to be very well-off. He had a car with a generous allowance of petrol, and owned a racehorse, a filly called Ferle. He suggested to me that it might be a good idea to join one of the newly-formed tank regiments, which were looking for officers. The one he favoured was 23rd Hussars. He knew the new Colonel of this Regiment – Roscoe Harvey, a celebrated pre-war amateur steeplechase rider – and could introduce me to him. I agreed to this proposal.

The Captain then asked me to go with him to watch his filly run in the Oaks. The Derby and the Oaks were run on the spring course at Newmarket during the war, because Epsom was in a dangerous area from the point of view of bombing. The Captain arranged for me to meet Colonel Harvey by the paddock before a particular race.

As a fairly impoverished student, I suspected that this excursion to Newmarket might give rise to embarrassing expenditure. So before we set off in the Captain's car I went to the pawnbroker in Magdalene Street and pawned my wrist watch for £3.

We had a good day's racing. I was introduced to Colonel Harvey, who said that provided I passed out of the OCTU with a good report, he would take me into 23rd Hussars. Guided by the Grenadier Captain, I placed some bets. I won several pounds. So that evening I went back and got my watch back from the pawnbroker and went away feeling quite rich.[8]

After taking his War Degree in 1941, Rigby marked time in Manchester before starting his Army training:

A lot has happened since I last stayed at Sunnyside. From that time till I was called up I had about two months, which I spent in Manchester. I had a job as chauffeur for a relative who makes steel in large quantities; when I was not driving him I worked in the garage at his works, where there are fourteen cars of all types, and what I learnt about cars has stood me in good stead since. I used to lunch in the board room at the works, and that was most interesting since there were men who came from all sides of the steel trade; experts from Woolwich Arsenal and leading trade unionists, American magnates and English works managers. The conversation always revolved round the war and steel, but it was most instructive.[9]

* * *

Sheepshanks spent his next year at Corpus Christi, Oxford. Although he had always, according to Robertson, fallen just short of being a Scholar, he was a very keen cricketer, having also developed an enthusiasm for playing the French Horn. He seems to have

Sheepshanks.

had a well developed sense of humour, since Robertson added that Sheepshanks' 'considerable and not unhumorous talent for 'grousing' and 'sporting baulks' [starting false rumours] sometimes drew the salutary fire of his friends, but those who knew his principles and saw him brave the discomforts of a Harvest Camp knew that he could face facts and would not fail.'

* * *

In the skies, the war still raged, and Weir was in the thick of the action. On August 8th 1940 a large battle took place over the British convoy CW9 – code-named 'Peewit' – off the Isle of Wight. It was a bright sunny day when 145 Squadron were scrambled from Westhampnett, near Tangmere to help to protect the convoy from Ju87 Stuka dive-bombers escorted by 109s. By the time that the RAF fighters arrived, the Stukas were low on fuel and ammunition, and the 109s covered their withdrawal. At around 0900hrs the Hurricanes of 145 Squadron approached unobserved out of the sun and went in to attack the rear Ju87s five miles south-south-west of the Needles. Weir was again flying as part of Blue Section in 'B' Flight and recalled: 'We were ordered to reinforce 'A' Flight over a convoy, as many bandits were approaching. About a minute before we arrived, we saw 'A' Flight engaged with the fighter screen.'[10]

Weir estimated enemy numbers at over eighty, comprising sixty Stukas and twenty-five fighters: the fighters he called 109s and He113s – the latter aircraft type had not, in fact, gone into German front-line service, though the Germans pretended that it had. The enemy were spread out from 4,000ft up to about 12,000ft.

> As we arrived, the first of numerous waves of bombers swept past. Green Section went after them. Blue Section followed, and I was rather left behind. During the dive, three 109s crossed in front of me, and one peeled off onto the tail of Blue 3. I changed direction slightly, fired, and followed him down.

Weir had set his sights at 300 yards.

> Although my burst was short he began to smoke and dived straight into the sea. After this I could see no aircraft for a minute, and finally saw the second wave of Ju87s passing on my right. I went after them and found one Hurricane already firing from astern. It shot one down. I picked the right-hand aircraft (there were nine or ten) and fired with no effect, but as none of them had returned my fire I closed to about twenty yards and gave him a short burst from below. He at once gave out white smoke and broke away from his squadron. I followed him as he dived towards the ships, dropping back, as I had throttled back sharply. He dropped his bombs, very wide, and I caught up with him and fired again till he fell into the sea.
>
> After this I joined Green 2 in pursuit of a straggler, fired a two-second burst from about 250 yards, and then ran out of ammunition. Green 2 subsequently brought this one down. I returned to base to re-arm at about 0930hrs.

Two of 145's Hurricanes had failed to return,[11] but after re-arming, the remaining pilots took off at lunch-time and again became embroiled in the convoy battle. Weir's second combat report of the day read as follows:

> We had climbed after twenty-six He111s and Bf110s, but as they were far above us we were unable to catch them. We returned to shore at Dungeness and were then told that the convoy south of the Isle of Wight was being attacked. The Squadron streamed back west, Blue Section being at the rear, since it had been in front before. We headed well south of the convoy, hoping to cut off the bombers' retreat, for we could not hope to reach the convoy in time.

At 1245hrs his flight encountered twenty-four 110s some thirty miles south of the Isle of Wight.

> About fifteen or twenty miles south of the convoy we found two squadrons of 110s, about five miles apart, flying round in defensive circles low down (at about 2,000ft). There were only three of us, and we circled round at 12,000ft for a long time wondering how best to attack, and asking for help. We were split up, watching for other possible attackers, and just keeping note of where each member of the Section was.
>
> After about ten minutes, I had decided on the manner of attack I should adopt, and was about to dive when a 109 flew across in front of me – a decoy, I think. I pulled round to get on his tail, and we flew round in circles till I was just gaining a position from which I could fire. At this point he dived steeply – almost vertically. I went after him, but could not get closer than five hundred yards, so I opened fire straight down onto his tail, and when I was sure he was hit I pulled out and continued towards the 110s, where he had tried to lead me. My flight Commander, Blue 1, saw him dive straight into the sea, as he was not then engaged himself. He and Blue 3 attacked later.
>
> At about five hundred yards I opened fire on one of the 110s of the approaching side of the ring, allowing six to eight lengths deflection, and after a short burst began to pull out. One came up to meet me, but as I was doing over 500mph I could not pull my sights on to him. I fired a short burst behind him to put him off, and then flashed over the rear-gunner quite low but quite safe, with a relative speed of about 700mph.
>
> After this I made off towards the convoy, in case it should be attacked again. There were no enemy aircraft there, but one had crashed and sunk, leaving a patch of vivid, blue-green smoke to mark the spot. One could see it for miles.

The Germans sent yet more aircraft to destroy 'Peewit' before nightfall. 145 Squadron, who had again landed to refuel and re-arm, were again scrambled at 1630hrs to meet the threat. Outnumbered two to one, Weir and his comrades were forced to engage the German escorts, leaving the Stukas free to carry out their attacks. The convoy suffered terribly, and the RAF lost thirteen aircraft defending it, as well as five damaged – Weir's Hurricane was one of them, and he had to make a forced landing.[12] For the loss of sixteen aircraft shot down and eighteen damaged, the Germans had sunk all but four of the twenty-three ships in 'Peewit'.

Weir had claimed three 'kills' that day: two 109s and a Stuka. Of these, however, only the second 109 had been witnessed, so his tally was one 'confirmed' and two 'unconfirmed' victories. For this fine work – and his earlier kills over Dunkirk – Weir would be awarded the DFC (dated August 30th 1940) and promoted to Flying Officer (dated September 5th 1940). But after the loss of five pilots in one day – and two more a few days later – 145 Squadron were in no condition to carry on fighting. On August 14th they moved north for a rest.

* * *

Fortune.

On the same day, Bruce Fortune joined the Army. His name was really John Fortune, but he was always known by his middle name instead. As we have seen, he had gained his colours for athletics whilst in Hopper's. After leaving, he was one of the most frequent correspondents amongst Robertson's former charges, and will play a prominent role in this narrative. The day before joining up, he had written to Robertson from the family home in Kirkcudbrightshire:

> We have just heard that my father's address in Germany is Camp *Oflag* VIIC Germany. I believe I promised to let you know. As yet we have heard nothing from him but it will take a long time to come through. Guy [Richardson] and I had a lovely time in Essex and thoroughly enjoyed ourselves. We were billeted on a nice but extraordinary family, who insisted on feeding us till we nearly burst. We only paid 25/- a week and our wages came to just under £2 so we managed to make both ends meet. To begin with we were cutting pit props, but when the Army commandeered all our wood we were put on to cutting and sharpening stakes for fortification purposes. We saw quite a bit of the Army as Royal Engineers transports were frequently coming up into the wood to be loaded. They infrequently got stuck and we had to dig them out. However they were a cheery lot and we got a lot of fun out of them. I believe this particular RE Company was fortifying a long stretch of river and our stakes were being used to make tank traps, etc. We certainly gave them some good bits of timber which ought to stop the largest German tank.
>
> Guy and I started more or less as ordinary workmen but we were soon promoted almost to the rank of under foreman. The foreman, not being very good at his office work, called upon us to help him and we spent a large part of our time sending away green and yellow forms in triplicate and doing other odd jobs for him, such as checking each load of stakes as it went out.
>
> It was all really most interesting, and what with the hard work it was really worth while, and much better than that stuffy old office at Perth.
>
> I go to Perth to join up tomorrow – so the next time you see me I shall probably be in uniform.
>
> Have just had a few days leave, fixing things up – no grouse, but we had some quite sporting days' shooting nevertheless.[13]

Robertson's closeness to the Fortune family is confirmed by the letter which he received from Bruce's sister Jean at around this time:

My dear Major Robertson,
Thank you so much for your letter – and for so kindly giving me a reference again. I started in the Ambulance today – and it's much better than sitting in an office. We have got Daddy's address, which I thought you might like.

Prisoner of War Post (no stamp)
KRIEGSGEFANGENEN Post.
Major Gen. V.W. Fortune CB, DSO
British Prisoner of War
Oflag No. VIIC/H
Germany

I don't think Mummy has actually heard – but two officers have escaped and got back. Yes, it was very hard luck on the Highland Division and no one quite knows how much Bruce and I miss Daddy – he has been such a wonderful father, and always did so much for us that now we have the feeling that there is no one behind us; however, it is a lovely thought that he will come back one day.[14]

It was typical of Robertson that he wrote to General Fortune in Germany immediately; his letter arrived quite quickly, as Lady Fortune reported in November:

Victor received your letter of August 18th and was very pleased and told me to thank you post-haste. Thanks awfully for writing him … Victor says they are treating them as well as they can and now they are getting their food parcels they seem quite happy. My best love to Sheila.[15]

* * *

A heavy burden rested on Robertson's shoulders: not only the responsibility of looking after the boys in his house, but the reliance which so many parents and relatives placed on him, and the emotional burdens which they shared, sure that he would understand better than most. He wrote to them all, and they all wrote to him. When Harry Younger's death was confirmed late in August, his widow Anna told Robertson the news:

Dear Major Robertson,
I am so grateful for both your letters – I have kept a spark of hope going, but here is the story. I had a letter from a Major Rennie of the Black Watch. He says that Harry and Mike Ansell were going to escape after St Valery and they lay up in a barn hoping to get away. They were found by some British soldiers who mistook them for Germans and shot them. Mike was wounded in the eye and Harry killed … I just keep it at the bottom of my heart that a miracle could happen, but I have tried hard to face Rennie's letter and how it is really true. I feel I can only bear it if one feels it was right for him and he offered himself so unreservedly I feel somehow one ought to be glad not sorry that he has so fulfilled himself. Now life seems to be impossible without him. I can think of lots of times when bad news never really got him down – he could always turn his mind to something inspiring, and with his example I must try to do the same. After all, sacrifice won't make this world a better place, but willing sacrifice will – and just as he was willing to die, so I must gladly give up my happiness. I do believe he will

influence his children still – perhaps even more than if he had lived … I am so glad to think you will be there to help Gavin… [16]

Soon enough, Anna Younger was calling Robertson 'Dear Bobber'. Lady Fortune was already on 'Dear Bobber' terms by October 1940 and signed her delightfully chatty letters to him with the nickname 'Evergreen'.

Dear Bobber,
Herewith the wee book you wanted. We loved your letter and Bruce very pleased to hear all about some of his friends. I have today seen him and his friend (a lad called Wingate-Gray whose father is a gunner – he was at Wellington) off to Dunbar so they are over the worst of their discomfort and my word it is that. It's perfectly marvellous how that Class live – they were the only two who undressed and there was never any hot water and they don't now even issue them with mugs just two dixies however it has not done them any harm and Bruce looks quite well on it and grown a lot. Jean is not very happy in the air raids – the house opposite her was set on fire and also next door they had no water or gas – cooked their breakfast on candles and boiled the kettle on an upturned electric iron. I should think there will be an awful epidemic of Typhoid or something soon in London with the water all smashed up. We are moderately peaceful here. Things drone about at night sometimes and we hear guns in the distance…. I am going to sheet this house up for the winter at the end of next month as it's too lonely in the dark cold days. I'm delighted there is to be no winter time as I've only been given 42 gallons of Petrol for my light against 100 last year and we need not get up in the morning but must be up at 1600hrs.

I've only had one letter from Victor through Germany – and two through Portugal: so not much doing yet although we are led to believe the Red X parcels are getting there. They are at Salzburg and all say the country is lovely – and food seems to be the one thing they all ask for. I am told meals are 0700hrs Tea – 1100hrs Soup and Potatoes –1600hrs Tea – 1900hrs Soup and Potatoes. One loaf every five days and our prisoners get fed on the fat of the land. There are 1,200 officers in the camp and they have started a sort of university and all study something. I have a nephew who has taken up German, French Agriculture, and Wines. Victor has sent for books on trees and shrubs – He lives in a cell with another old man as he says it's quieter than in the more crowded rooms upstairs – which have lovely views over mountains and trees. They have two windows but cannot see out. I should think he will go mad all winter in a cell but I quite understand wanting to be quiet as the young and noise does rather worry at his age. I've got Lord Galloway to complain to the House and get him moved if possible – where will this all end – how and where? and the more states Hitler annexes the less likely they are to get food – it's awful. You and Sheila seem to be being your usual kind selves to everyone. The Sinclair is in Victor's camp. Love to Sheila.

Yours ever,
Evergreen

I sold 14 sheep and only got £23 – everything is controlled so no money to be made.[17]

* * *

Kemp.

The war changed people's perspectives, especially those of the young. When he had left Winchester in July, Kemp had planned to go up to Cambridge. Instead, he joined the Army, as he told Robertson in September:[18]

> The posts here are slow anyway, but since the raids have started they are quite paralytic and I only got your letter dated the 11th yesterday. As you know, at the beginning of the holidays I intended going to Cambridge rather than being called up at nineteen; however, I thought that I might as well ask Jack Parr[19] for particulars of the Rifle Brigade scheme. This seemed so promising that after a long discussion with my father I decided to have a shot at it, with the proviso that if it was not going to start soon I should go to Cambridge. I had some correspondence with Jack Parr and Moore Gwyn of the Rifle Depot, the upshot of which was that I am now on their list and liable to be called up for training any moment now. I am afraid I always had a slight prejudice against going up to the Varsity with its half-way life, neither purely military nor purely ordinary, and a fear that I might make the worst of both worlds. Now that there is no risk of my being left in the air doing nothing and perhaps wasting all the winter in idleness, as I might have done, had I desired to be called up at nineteen but not under the Rifle Depot scheme, I think the chief objection to not going to the Varsity is removed. There remains your other point – that I would lose touch with my Classics – and here I am afraid you are right; though I make a point of reading Classical authors regularly, my composition etc. must inevitably be a little rusty when I next try my hand at them. I do wish you to understand that I have not come to this decision without much thought, but that in the end I was convinced that this would be better. I am not a military person by any means, and I will need all the training that I can get.
>
> While I am here I do a certain amount of LDV work and on our last exercise at night we had a lot of excitement; a German bomber came over and dropped a Molotov Bread-basket which scattered incendiary bombs all round us; we put out five in the Hotel grounds alone and afterwards fought a baby forest fire, beating it with branches until after midnight. I expect you have had your share of these things too.

Kemp was commissioned into the Rifle Brigade as 2nd Lieutenant 184646 on April 26th 1941.[20]

* * *

Although Robertson knew Hopperites from before his time as housemaster, the first of his personal charges to die in the war was Arthur Townsend, who had left in 1934. On September 29th 1940 Townsend was night-flying in a Harvard trainer when it came down at Kidlington in Oxfordshire, killing him.[21]

But the first Hopperite whose loss really struck the collective consciousness of the 1938 photograph boys was Nigel Weir. 145 Squadron returned to active duty on October 9th, after the official end of the Battle of Britain. On November 7th, Weir's Hurricane I (serial P2770) went missing over the sea near Ventnor during combat with a 109. Weir was posted 'missing in action', and in May 1941 this was changed to 'missing, presumed killed in action'. With no grave but the sea, he is commemorated in Panel 6 of the Runnymede Memorial.[22]

Weir's Hopperite contemporary Bill Cliff Hodges wrote to Robertson a month later, from active service in Scotland:

> The tragic news about Nigel Weir the other day really brought the War home to me again and made one long to do one's bit, especially after waiting so long. Did you hear what happened to Michael Sinclair? As yet I've had no news about him.[23]

Nick Somerville remembered Weir for the rest of his days:

> Many of our predecessors in the house had gone to war in France – at Dunkirk and Calais, and Nigel Weir, who I knew well, had been shot down and killed flying a fighter in the air battle. I said a prayer for him and others quietly in War Cloister, and the memory comes back to me whenever I go there.

Hopperite Duncan McMurtrie soon afterwards wrote a poem inspired by Weir; it formed the first of three linked poems entitled 'RAF' and carrying a prologue of lines from Cecil Day-Lewis' pre-war poem *A Time to Dance:*

But the fierce updraught of their spirit
Forced them to the stars.

The second stanza of McMurtrie's poem seems certain to refer to Weir:

We sing of who were great,
  Spirits like snow-line spruce,
Arrayed in their evergreen glory,
  As swift as hawks in flight,
So strong who asked no truce,
  They paid our bill for warring.
Straight into Fate's gun-sights
  On eagles' wings they flew,
Knowing and doing their duty;
  Until the gods of life
Took them to life anew
  In the hour of their beauty.

We sing of some who had
  The skylark power of song,
Aglow with their golden adventure;
  Of some who made us glad
With words and who were strong
  To reach our heart's warm centre;

Those who explored all art,
   And crystallized desires,
Touched with the coals of creation;
   All whose reckless hearts
Were dynamos to fire
   Them to the heights of passion.

Some were great lovers, some could dream.
   All were young and live,
Flushed with a sunrise splendour.
   As owl's sight their eyes were keen;
They loved their land and gave
   Their heart-blood to defend her.
Souls which were like pure ice,
   Clean-cut and bright and clear,
Alight with their glacier flashes.
   Their name will never die,
Wreathing in the smoky air
   Far above their ashes.

The Wykehamist[24] later published the following poem by Tim Corsellis:[25]

In Memoriam A.N.C.W.

I knew Nigel Weir
Slightly so
He stood upright and still
With an uncertain smile playing
Swaying across his lips.
Straight he stood as a poker,
His neck ran into his head
And his chin was close to his throat.
When he spoke
His words came kindly, softly clear
Lisping but meticulously formed
Each syllable was of kindness.

I knew Nigel Weir.
Sometimes he spoke to me
When I was scarcely nice to know,
Spoke kindly and wisely.
The man was polite –
Oh, ugly word, polite –
Where others did not care.
He and I fenced each other,
His was the greater grace,

His foot was swifter sure,
His hands knew more.

I knew Nigel Weir.
Even saw his soul
In his few verses
More able and more lively
Than my own wild words.
He and I felt together
But he always excelled
In his feelings, his actions,
And his pliant expression.

I read his poems
But only once
I wondered
At Nigel Weir
Until I saw him
Moving about the Spitfires;
Remembered his swift arms
And his sensitive eyes;
And I pitied the German sons
And I pitied his troubled soul.

I knew Nigel Weir
And the strange contradiction
Of his coarse, hard hands.
Heard he had won him a victim,
Envied his arm and
Pitied his mind.
Then I took to the sky
And forgot the man Weir.

Periodically I saw his brother.
And he died
With the frustration
Of a ribbon for valour
Sewn on his chest.
Cruel, mean joke,
This jeering compensation.

I remembered the words of another,
  'Just as the flower of life seemed set to bloom
  And as the sun had pierced a frigid sky
  You chose the solemn unrelenting tomb;
  You chose to die.'

I joined them to your name, Nigel –
Strange that this should be the first time
I've ever called you 'Nigel'.

I knew Nigel Weir
Vaguely so.
He was always one step ahead of me
And he was of greater promise.
  O world, it's Weir that's dead.

Corsellis was himself killed on active service in the Air Transport Auxiliary in 1941.

* * *

Bruce Fortune was by now at 165 OCTU in Dunbar with John Boyd:

> Thank you for your letter. I was sorry to hear about Nigel Weir and had no idea he had been killed.
>
> I came on here to Dunbar just over six weeks ago and still officially have ten more weeks before the completion of my course. There is a rumour that we are being pushed through in three months instead of four, but I don't think it is a true one. But it is a known fact that the next company which comes here on the 20th of this month is only going to be here for three months. They have discovered that the last month of the four month course does little to improve your fighting efficiency as an officer, and might well be dispensed with, especially as at present they are crying out for officers. So with luck I ought to be an officer by the middle of February.
>
> I enjoyed my ten weeks in the Black Watch and it was well worth the experience. All except five of the potential officers of my lot came on here – the other five are waiting to go on to an OCTU in India at Bangalore, prior to joining the Indian Army. They have twice been on embarkation leave [leave granted before deploying overseas] but have not yet gone. They do very little soldiering and spend most of their days in the Perth canteens or having interviews with selection boards. I think they regard it as an easier way of getting into the Indian Army than coming to Dunbar and getting posted from here.
>
> The discipline in this OCTU is rigid and you have to watch your step as the whole town seems to be full of spies who report on your progress as a budding officer from time to time! We take it in turns to be Platoon and Company Commanders etc., and generally run the whole show ourselves. Each platoon has a Platoon Sergeant Instructor who is supposed to look after things – but they do very little and we hardly ever see them except for weapon training. Quite a lot of our officers here are ex-schoolmasters – some are quite tolerable – the others are not. We personally have a queer young fellow from the Warwickshire Regiment who is very unsociable and now and again for no apparent reason starts off in a flow of dirty language. He is in charge of his platoon and whenever we march anywhere, he insists on walking at least 100 yards in front or to the rear of the platoon, without saying a word to anyone.

We do a certain amount of MT which consists of learning to drive trucks and motorcycles. We are also taught a large amount of maintenance and towards the end of our course we drive as a convoy – to Edinburgh and back. Such things as this are the only enlightening moments we are allowed in our course; for life here after ten weeks is extremely dull and Dunbar has no amusements of any kind. There are no concerts or entertainments, although a few weeks ago we had the Polish Choir down here. There is one decent cinema and we have a Cadets Club to which we can go. These are the only forms of recreation we have, so you can see after a bit we get what is called extremely 'browned off'. There are no societies of any description and absolutely no *esprit de corps* at all. We are also cursed with a number of ex-CSMs and QMSs etc who have come to be officers. Some of them are extremely old and offensive and we don't get on too well with them. On the other hand there are several very nice old soldiers who realise that they are on the same level as everyone else and muck in with the rest. We are getting a week's leave over Christmas and I hope to go down to Bengairn, in the neighbourhood of which a certain battalion of the Duke of Wellingtons is believed to be stationed!

I have heard several times from David Kemp who I expect comes to visit you quite often. I hope he gets to a decent OCTU and does not land up in a place like Bulford.

I hope the House is flourishing still, and as yet has not been troubled by any bombs. I sympathise with you about the warnings, as the siren is perpetually sounding here at night, but the Army does not take any notice of warnings and refuses to act till the bombs start dropping, so we just stay in bed.[26]

* * *

The following day, Boyd turned to Robertson for advice as to which regiment he should opt for. The decision would have fateful consequences.[27]

Boyd.

I was called up to this OCTU on the 27th September, and so have only another month to go before I pass out. As you may know, Bruce Fortune is also here – not in the same company as myself, as he came the month after I did.

The life here is really very good fun, although quite hard. However, I was in good training after a month or so of being a navvy before I came here.

I expect you know pretty well what happens here already, so I won't give you a very detailed account. We are now well on in our three months of 'collective training', and very interesting it is, especially for one who has not been in the Initial Training Cadre. The first month of recruit training in 'A' Company was rather boring at times even for me, and must have been much worse for those who had already done some time in the ranks. However, the work now is much more interesting, and it seems that in this new warfare the job of Platoon Commanders is going to be far more responsible and interesting than ever before.

We are thinking now about what regiments we are going to try and get into after we leave here, and I would like very much if you could give me some advice about this. You may remember that I asked you a long time ago for a testimonial for the Intelligence

Service. At that time, and until about a week ago, I thought that one joined a regiment and was then seconded to the Intelligence; but an officer from the War Office came here about a week ago, and told us that we had to join the Intelligence Corps in the first place. We had an interview, and I was told that my French was good, but that my German would need improvement, and that they might be able to use me in Intelligence. I was also told to put down Intelligence as my first choice of regiment.

In the meantime, however, my aunt Mrs William Boyd, mother of Nigel Boyd, had been making great efforts to get me into the Black Watch, which was the regiment that I wanted to join. She had even written to a kind General whose name I am afraid I have forgotten, and he had applied to the War Office for me. I only heard about all this after I had had the Intelligence interview.

I wonder if you could give me some advice about this. It would seem rather ungrateful not to try and get into the Black Watch, which I should prefer to any other regiment, after all these people have made such an effort for me. However, if I should be more use in the Intelligence I feel I should go into it. There is also the consideration that the having been in the Intelligence would probably be of more use to me after the war, especially as I have decided to try and get into the Civil Service if I am not too old when the war stops! I feel, though, that this consideration should come last.

I am awfully sorry to bother you about this complicated problem, especially at a time when you must be very busy, but I should very much like to have your advice about it. I should perhaps mention that I was told by one of the officers that as I had been Company Commander for a week, I would have quite a good chance of getting into the regiment that I put down as my first choice anyway.

I enjoyed being Company Commander thoroughly, as it was quite a new experience for me to be responsible for so many people. We had quite a Wykehamist week as Bruce [Fortune] was in command of his platoon that week. I was succeeded by another Wykehamist, Flower[28] of Trants, who left, I think, in 1926!

How are things going with you under these new conditions? I hope you have not been having too many bombs, and that everything goes on much as usual. I find it hard to imagine anything disturbing the routine of life at Winchester.

* * *

Angus Grant was still cooling his heels in the Faroes, as he told Robertson in a letter written the same day as Boyd's:

Grant.

I apologise, by way of a start, for not writing to you for twelve months. However I hope you will forgive me and even write me a note when you have time, as I should very much like to know what has become of Hopperites of my year. As you probably know we started the war on horseback at Beauly where we were for six months. We were then near Newark on Trent for about one month, during which time we lost the horses. For the last seven months we have been on a windy island as you have probably heard from Charles, who did not come with us (I mean C. Murray) owing to being ill when we moved from England. As you can imagine after the summer months had gone, we got rather bored with the place and hoped to be sent somewhere more worthy of a Lovat Scout. However we understand that soldiers at home are even more bored with their lot, so we shouldn't really grumble …

We get quite a bit of fishing here, both trout and sea-trout – no rivers big enough for salmon. There is not much else in the way of sport as we know it – a few hares and snipe. The natives' chief sport is hunting whales, which really is good fun. (You will find a description of this in the end of John Buchan's *Island of Sheep*. He stayed here for a few days holiday and describes the people and country accurately).

When the whales are sighted, word goes round and the whole population takes to its boats armed with spears and javelins and they try to drive them ashore at the head of a *fjord*, where there is generally a beach. If they are successful in this, it is quite an easy matter to kill the whales on shore, but it sometimes happens that they have to kill them in the water, which is more exciting. Boats are apt to be overturned and soon the sea becomes red.

The people are decent folk and our men get on well with them and are often entertained to meals etc. At present of course there is far more money than usual coming into the pockets of the natives, with the result that they sometimes get above themselves. For instance yesterday we were rather amused because the fellows unloading our ship went on strike. But it didn't take long to find a man in the regiment who works a winch for a living in Glasgow, and soon our fatigue party was simply throwing cases of 'Maconochie' and bags of flour ashore. It was very amusing to watch the strikers' sulky faces as they realized that we could unload the ship just as well, if not better, than they themselves.

The rain is our real trouble, and the wind also – They make training rather difficult and much of it has to be done indoors. It is also very difficult getting around from one island to another and not only difficult, but for most of us an unpleasant and painful proceeding, as few of us are good sailors. There are not quite 30,000 people, the largest town having 4,000. There are most of modern conveniences to be found – electric light, gymnasium, a limited drainage system, a few houses with baths, cinema both civilian and NAAFI. So we have made the troops very comfortable – every man has a spring bed and mattress. Against these advantages, the draw-backs are very little leave (most of us have not been home for a year) and not many new faces to see. Personally, I don't mind much about leave or about 'new faces', but I should like to go to Egypt or somewhere where there is a modicum of likelihood of hearing a shot let off in anger.

The islands are about sixty miles from top to bottom and are made of basalt. Walking is very steep, the highest point being about 3000ft. The old houses are curiously built with roofs of turf – green grass – on birch bark, all of which had to be imported as there are no trees on the island.

This letter is I am afraid a very patchy affair but it may give you some idea of the life of comfort and ease in which we are living! Tell me about old Hopperites, present Hopperites, dons, and bombs. (What are Ridgway, Hamilton, James, Cowland, etc., doing?)[29]

Men of the Lovat Scouts training on the Faroes, July 20th 1941. (IWM H10569)

* * *

McMurtrie.

According to Robertson, Duncan McMurtrie, who had come to Hopper's from Pinewood School, was always keen on 'good literature, the countryside, gardening (he made an excellent job of House Agriculture), and other things beyond the ken of some of his more ordinary contemporaries. To them he was perhaps a bit of a freak – the fact was that he was a good deal of a poet and wrote verse of real promise and some vision: he also had ambition and great power of concentrated work, which might have carried him a long way.' On December 14th, McMurtrie wrote a dedicatory foreword to a collection of his poetry which he gave to his family. This would later form the core of *The Diary of a Heart*, published by the Oxford University Press in 1951.

> To my Mother and Father and to my brothers Peter and Anthony I have dedicated my poems, for I wished to dedicate them to my home and it was they who made my home mean so much to me; it was a sure refuge to which I could turn in times of trouble.

To any who should read these poems I would give this apology and excuse for any faults. The poems were written in moments of passion, and afterwards when I could never recapture that passion, I did not find it possible to change them without spoiling them.

They were written in times of sorrow and they reflect that sorrow; but let no one think because so few reflect joy that my life was joyless. I have never been able to write poetry when I was happy, but when I was sad I could not help it. That is why most of these poems reflect sorrow; but in them the sorrow expressed is not always the real one. Sometimes it is, but sometimes I have felt sad and written about something sad rather than about my real sorrow.

Some of my views and thoughts I now consider morbid or sordid or merely stupid; but I have included them because I intend this book to be something into which I may look in my later years and in which I may recapture some of those moments which now seem so precious, but which I know will die. So I have called it *The Diary of a Heart.*

IV

'When will this ---- war end?'

December 17th 1940–May 1941

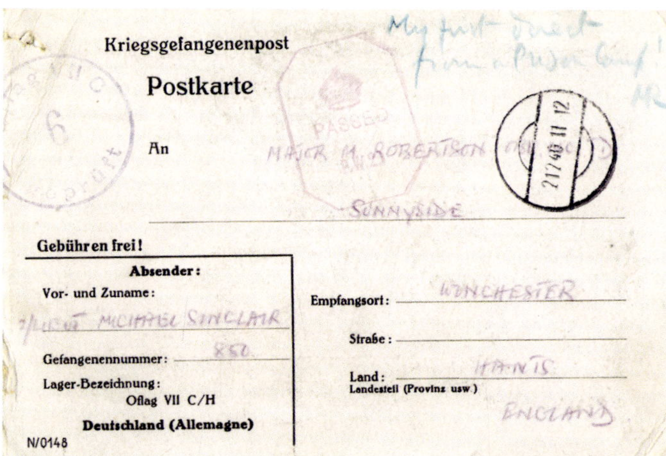

Kriegsgefangenenpost

Postkarte

An MAJOR M. ROBERTSON

SUNNYSIDE

Gebühren frei!

Absender:

Vor- und Zuname: 2/LIEUT MICHAEL SINCLAIR

Gefangenennummer: 850

Lager-Bezeichnung: Oflag VII C/H

Deutschland (Allemagne)

Empfangsort: WINCHESTER

Straße:

Land: HANTS

Landesteil (Provinz usw.)

ENGLAND

N/0148

Four more of our subjects left Hopper's on December 17th 1940: Charles Duffin, Michael Hirst, John Huggins, and John Kennedy.

Duffin.

Hirst.

Huggins.

Kennedy.

Duffin was good at languages, with prizes for French and for German Speech, and went on to Trinity College, Cambridge, with an exhibition. He would take a Second in Modern Languages before joining the Scots Guards.[1] We will see much of him later.

Hirst was also a linguist (he had won the German prize), and like Duffin decided to take a War Degree, but in his case at Oxford. We are fortunate in that he recorded his memories, albeit many years later:[2]

> I have written this so that the family should have some record of my service in the 1939–1945 war. It was neither very dangerous nor exciting, and sometimes very boring, but it was often interesting or funny, and very occasionally frightening.
>
> On leaving Winchester, in 1941 I went to Oriel College, Oxford, to study Modern Languages (French and German). I was allowed to defer call-up by being 'attested' – I was formally in the Army, but could complete the short war-time degree course. Part of the conditions was that I served in the University Senior Training Corps (STC), which prepared me for OCTU without the need for basic training. So I was attested into the Royal Artillery as 1127222 Gunner Hirst M.J. and did my artillery training with the STC; wooden-wheeled 18-pounders initially, and, when those were needed for the defence of Britain after Dunkirk, French '75s' of 1914–1918 vintage but with rubber tyres!

* * *

1st Viscount Malvern, Lady Malvern, and their son John Huggins, May 3rd 1935, by Bassano. (Huggins family, also NPG x151320)

John Huggins decided not to go to university, but joined the RAF for pilot training.[3] He was the son of the Prime Minister of Southern Rhodesia, Godfrey Huggins (later 1st Viscount Malvern),[4] a far-sighted leader who had foreseen the need for a huge expansion of flying training if there were to be another global war. One only has to look at the losses of Bomber Command in the Second World War – over 55,000 aircrew – to realize that training personnel on this scale would have been impossible in the skies of the United Kingdom; we have already encountered one Hopperite killed in flying training in 1940. After the fall of France in 1940, the Empire Air Training Scheme was set up, with pilots training in Canada, South Africa, and Rhodesia. The United States also offered flying training facilities (as we shall see), and by the end of the war 220,000 aircrew had been trained for the Commonwealth war effort. The scheme freed up British flying instructors for operational duties, put the trainees in less stressful environments (no enemy aircraft gate-crashing training flights or bombing airfields), and guaranteed better weather. All of this speeded up the training process and had a measurable impact on the course of the war.

Godfrey Huggins was a prime mover in the whole scheme. As early as 1934, Southern Rhodesia had offered to provide facilities for flying training for the RAF. Huggins specifically asked for a senior RAF officer to come out to investigate the viability of such a scheme, and in 1936 the Southern Rhodesia Air Unit was approved; the idea was that a small nucleus of personnel would be trained there, who would then train more pilots, who would then set up Elementary Flying Training Schools and Service Flying Training Schools. By 1938 the scheme was in action, and on a visit to London in July 1939 Huggins proposed that it be expanded on a wartime footing. By December 1939 facilities existed ready to train both Rhodesian and British pilots; Huggins undertook that his government would meet the full construction costs of the scheme – projected at £947,000 (some £37,250,000 in modern terms) – as well as 20 per cent of the annual running costs.

The first EFTS to open anywhere in the Empire Air Training Scheme was Belvedere, in Southern Rhodesia, on May 25th 1940; SFTS Cranborne followed in July. Rhodesia was now planning to produce 1,768 pilots a year, as well as other aircrew. Rhodesian pilots would be channelled initially to 237 (Rhodesia) Squadron RAF.

One of the first graduates of the scheme to join 237 Squadron was the Prime Minister's own son, John.

* * *

John Kennedy also joined the RAF, and was also trained overseas. He had come to Hopper's from Aysgarth School, and returned to teach there for a short spell while awaiting his RAFVR call-up. At Winchester, Kennedy had been a prefect and a Gold Medallist for 'Gymna'. An active member of the committee of the Natural History Society, he owed his keen love of nature to his half-brother Geoffrey, and to his Yorkshire home.

On his mother's side, Kennedy was from a Hopperite family: Constance Frances Monckton had married Cyril Gwyer ('I' 1900–1902), who died in 1918 serving with the Grenadier Guards; her brother-in-law, Charles Percy Gwyer ('I' 1896–1900) had also been killed in action, at Gallipoli in 1915. She also lost her own two brothers in that war. Geoffrey Gwyer was her son from that marriage. After her husband's death, Constance remarried, living at Welburn Manor, Kirbymoorside, Yorkshire, with her new husband Colonel Charles Fraser Kennedy. John Kennedy was their only son. After her losses in the First World War, Constance did not deserve to lose both her sons in the Second – but she did. No Winchester family suffered more in the two world wars; no woman gave more than she.

Kennedy wrote to Robertson early in March to let him know how his application for the RAF was going:

> I enlisted in the RAF the other day and went through my first 'medical' then and there. Apparently they seemed pleased with me, as the CO when he interviewed me said I had a very good chance of getting in and that there was nothing wrong with my physique. I am now waiting to go to Cardington near Bedford for my other exams. I thought that if it was still during the term when I go, I might go on down and look you up, as I should like to see you all again …
>
> My father's operation was a great success and he … will soon be taking up his Home Guard post again and relieving me of being Acting OC of 'C' Company!!, which I have been finding heavy work!![5]

* * *

During 1940, Britain had been concentrating on survival; in 1941, its forces were still concentrated at home, with operations in the Mediterranean and the Near East being the main focus. The British official history of this period states that between January and July 1941 more than 144,000 troops arrived in Egypt from the United Kingdom alone. This period saw many of the Hopper's boys in training and then shipping out for war. Of course, Murray and Grant had already been deployed to the Faroes, and though the danger there was slight, anxious mothers and fathers felt their sons' absence acutely. This letter from Murray's father – written in January 1941 – is typical of many:

> My dear Bobber,
> I meant to write to you at Christmas time, but as Charles was then in the offing I got news of you from time to time. Now he has gone overseas! While life seems to be much busier, and more full of incident, than mine was in the last war, I always have the feeling that one ought to be doing more …
>
> Please give your sister our love – we often talk and think of you both and – whatever may become of Charles – I shall never cease to be grateful for your taking him at Sunnyside and for those years he had there.[6]

* * *

Between February 6th and 7th 1941, the Battle of Beda Fomm in Libya crowned Operation Compass, Wavell's successful advance west from the Egyptian frontier. Beda Fomm, alas, is not part of our story, but in this brilliant action alone, the small British 'Combeforce' captured 25,000 Italian soldiers, 107 tanks, and 93 artillery pieces.[7] Amongst the many Wykehamists at Beda Fomm were two older brothers of our subjects: John Sinclair's brother Christopher, serving in 2RB, and Guy Richardson's brother Jim, a Squadron Commander in 2RTR.[8] Lieutenant Roy Farran, of 3rd Hussars, knew Richardson well, and in his memoirs described what he witnessed:

> Jim Richardson, a Squadron Leader of 2nd Tanks, takes all the honours for the battle. Putting his eight cruiser tanks around a pimple-shaped mound on which stood the mosque of Beda Fomm, he broke up wave after wave of Italian tanks. The M-13s were coming in along the line of the road in batches of thirty, but each time their attack met disaster when they encountered the cruisers around the mosque. Their crews were brave enough, but their tactics were almost too crude to be sane …
>
> The battle went on all day, until the Pimple by the mosque was littered with burning tanks … Once we went up to the Pimple to take over some prisoners from Jim Richardson during a lull in the battle. He was smiling, strong and confident, from the turret of his cruiser, and he told us not to waste time in picking out the best pairs of binoculars, but to hurry the prisoners back to the rear before another attack developed.[9]

The Italian army surrendered shortly after dawn on February 8th. 2RTR alone took over 15,000 prisoners. Over a hundred M-13s were found in front of 2RTR's positions, at least forty-eight of them destroyed by fire from the cruiser tanks. 2RTR had lost three men killed and four wounded in the whole battle. For his actions, 'handling his Squadron in a brilliant manner', Richardson was awarded the DSO. When Robertson heard the news, he was delighted, and wrote to the family:

> My dear Mrs Richardson (and 'Father'),
>
> Well done Jim! His DSO in yesterday's *Times* is a great source of pride to us, and also, no doubt, to you his parents. I trust he came through unwounded, and will continue to have luck, as well as show merit. In the last war, I always reckoned a subaltern's (even if acting Major) DSO was the best decoration there was, and I expect it is so still … Nor again have we had one word of Guy, except that he was to join at Gosport in January [1941], and hoped he might get over some day. If he ever got there, I fear he may have had lively – and unpleasant! – times, especially of late.
>
> These are anxious days for mothers (and wives), and even for such as us who have the welfare of scores of good boys at heart. When they acquit themselves as Jim has done (and you saw Humphrey Woods got an MC, and Christopher Sinclair a 'mention'; his Colonel (Renton) was in the same list as Jim) we feel cheered and well-rewarded.
>
> Mrs Fortune writes from Aberdalgie, Perth, sorry for Victor transferred to Poland (Mike Sinclair is with him) and full of pride in Bruce, already making his mark after a warm welcome to the 1st Battalion of his father's old regiment.
>
> We carry on here under many difficulties. David Kemp (Guy's rowing friend) has just turned up from Tidworth, commissioned in the Rifle Brigade a fortnight ago. We still have grateful memories of [illegible] his cheese – a really generous gift!!
>
> Yrs ever
>
> Bobber[10]

* * *

Nick Somerville.

Winchester suffered a number of air raids, largely due to being close to Southampton. As Head of House, I had to plan a roster for fire-watching at night in case of incendiary bombs landing and starting a fire. I also had to make a diagram of all the plumbing pipes and stopcocks in the house so that we would know how to handle damage and leaks to the plumbing.[11]

Such precautions as described by Nick Somerville seem almost laughable to us now, but in late 1940 and early 1941 German bombing was a genuine and widespread threat, which did not discriminate between serviceman and civilian; two Hopperites of an earlier generation were to die in early 1941 as the result of such enemy attacks. Shortly before term began in January, Francis Burlton – roughly the same age as Robertson – was killed by a bomb in Bow Street, London.[12] What happened is described by another civilian who was caught by the same bomb:

My dad, sister, and me used to go down Holborn tube station to shelter with our bedding each night … One of the bosses of Elder and Fyffes, the Shipping Offices opposite where we lived, saw us tramping with our bedding and … said, 'Why don't you shelter here? It's a wonderfully built shelter; cost a lot of money …' It was wonderful to leave our bedding there. But on January 11th 1941 it got a direct hit. My mum, sister, and me were dug out of the debris, but my dad was one of the twenty-eight killed. It was a Saturday night, but the building burned till the Tuesday afternoon.[13]

'Dan' Somerville dealt with some of the consequences of bombing in the capital at the tail end of 1940:

Late in November 1940 I went and stayed with my Great Uncle Jack and did some war work in London. I was paired up with a girl who could drive, as I couldn't in those days. She and I went round together in a van, and we salvaged furniture from bombed-out houses and took it to a central depot. We unloaded it where it was used to provide extra furniture to people who'd been bombed out of their house and had no furniture and had to live somehow. She drove, and I moved the heavy stuff. Once, we made a mistake, and we cleared furniture out of a house which we thought had been bombed – but it hadn't; it had always been like that! The woman who owned the house came back, caught us clearing all the furniture out of her house, and was not best pleased!

I was in London for about two months. I was one of the few people who was taking exercise by running around Kensington Palace Gardens and Hyde Park. I didn't meet a single other jogger in those days. There was an enormous pile of metal objects of every kind in Hyde Park, where Rotten Row is. It was a huge great pile – it was a couple of hundred yards long and 20–30 feet high. Full of everything. They said they were going to melt them down to make guns and things. My Great Uncle Jack gave them two metal Chinese gods, pretty hideous things that he'd picked up in his travels in the Far East. Whenever he went for his walk along Rotten Row he could see these gods grinning at him out of the heap. He thought they were going to be immediately used for guns, but they didn't use them for years.[14]

John Kennedy experienced a German raid even in rural Yorkshire, when bombs fell on his family home in Kirbymoorside on the night of March 3rd:

> The other night we had a great excitement. We were sitting in the drawing-room at about 2020hrs when we heard a bomb go off very close, so we all went out of the front door to see what was to be seen. The planes seemed right overhead, so we decided we had better go under cover. Just then we heard a queer 'swishy' noise and suddenly incendiaries began dropping all round Welburn. They lit up the whole place just like day, and exploded after about two minutes, and the whole of our lawn was covered with them. I rushed for my LDV steel-helmet and we all rushed out to the stack-yard which joins our back yard. There were about five in the stack-yard and one rick was on fire. My mother took a mat out of the front hall and put one out with it. We soon got a chain of buckets on to the rick and had it under control before the raiders returned. The local Auxiliary Fire Service rolled up and gave the stack a final 'sowsting'. Suddenly someone saw the squash court on fire, and it appeared that two had fallen on it – but we soon put them out. One fell through the roof of the cottage which is attached to our house, but luckily bounced outside off a stone slab!! One hit 'The Hall' – which is now an Orthopaedic Hospital – above the front door, and did no damage. A stick, on which they came, landed just outside our drawing-room window. But no house caught fire, which was very lucky. They say about five hundred were dropped, and all within ¼-mile of our house.[15]

Nowhere was safe; soon afterwards, on April 22nd, 67-year-old Hopperite Harry Thomson was killed by a German bomb which fell on Torquay.[16] The irony was that he was in the town because his home in Southsea had already been bombed:

The scene after the bombing of Mixbury in Lower Warberry Road, Torquay on April 22nd 1941. (Torquay Herald Express)[17]

His house was wrecked, and then he joined up with some cousins at Torquay. One day a 'plane was returning, injured, and to lighten its cargo dropped a bomb just over their house. He, the maid serving tea, and two of the cousin's children were killed instantly, and the rest injured, but not seriously, and they made a good recovery: but Harry's death was a great blow to the family.[18]

Graham Mackrill.

Another area which suffered heavy attack from the air in 1940 to 1941 was the Yorkshire port of Hull. This was home to three of Robertson's boys: Ian Mackrill (who had left in 1937); Graham Mackrill (one of our subjects);[19] and David Mackrill (who arrived at Sunnyside in 1941). Ian Mackrill had an exciting career in the war, serving with 'Phantom' (the GHQ Liaison Regiment), who sped around the battlefront gathering information and passing it straight to high command.[20]

Their father contacted Robertson early in May 1941, in a chatty letter which shows that his office suffered at least twice in air raids.[21]

Dear Robertson …
I have had an extreme dose of work to tackle since my office was bombed on January 20th. Fortunately the works were intact except for bad roof damage and some flood. I am just seeing a little daylight and getting put right, although I lost a lot of office equipment, etc.; however, what pleases me most was no one was killed or hurt. The rest I can take in.

David is looking forward to joining his brother at Sunnyside next half; they enjoyed this holiday and had some trout fishing. Ian had forty-eight hours leave last Thursday and Friday he had to go from Colchester to see Colonel Ramsden (an Old Wykehamist) of the Green Howards at Richmond (Yorkshire); he arrived home at 0230hrs and went off to Richmond by car at 1000hrs. Called and saw his brother at Bolton Abbey and they both went to Richmond; he came back here at 2100hrs and travelled to London next morning with Graham and myself …

With remembrances to you and your sister.

Yours ever
Henry W. Mackrill

May 8th: We had an awful 'Blitz' last night in the City; much damage to property. I got my windows blown in and roof damage at the office and works.

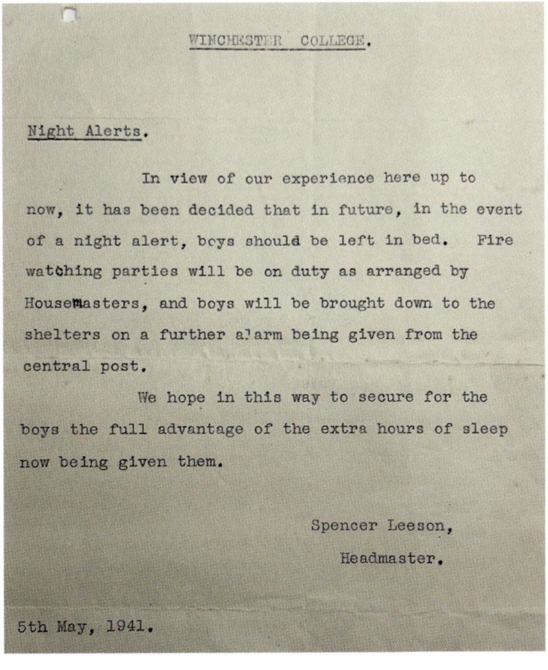

WINCHESTER COLLEGE.

Night Alerts.

In view of our experience here up to now, it has been decided that in future, in the event of a night alert, boys should be left in bed. Fire watching parties will be on duty as arranged by Housemasters, and boys will be brought down to the shelters on a further alarm being given from the central post.

We hope in this way to secure for the boys the full advantage of the extra hours of sleep now being given them.

Spencer Leeson,
Headmaster.

5th May, 1941.

* * *

Simpkin.

The bombing transformed Dick Simpkin's life in ways which could never have been predicted.[22]

In September 1940, he was staying in his grandmother's flat in the Dolphin Square complex in Pimlico, and volunteered as an ambulance driver at London County Council Ambulance Station 44, in the underground garage.[23] Guy Richardson, who also lived in Dolphin Square, had volunteered as an ambulance driver in July. One of their fellow drivers was 27-year-old Barbara Grant Johnson, who felt 'a frisson of excitement' when she saw the handsome young Simpkin for the first time during an 'Alert' in September.[24] The attraction was immediate, mutual, and intense.[25]

Ambulance workers and other volunteer personnel were by no means safe. On the night of September 22nd, a raid and reports of unexploded bombs led large numbers of residents and teams from the Heavy Rescue Service to take shelter underground in Dolphin Square. Just after 2300hrs a bomb crashed through into the shelter under Hawkins House, where it exploded. Luckily, the Heavy Rescue Teams were close at hand; despite the darkness, dust, and risk of explosions from broken gas pipes, they quickly moved in along the one passage into the shelter. Nearly sixty residents were brought out, swamping the First Aid post. Three weeks later, on October 15th, Ambulance Station 44 took a direct hit which destroyed over 150 vehicles and started a fire; all that was left of Occy Coller's Rolls Royce was the 'Spirit of Ecstasy' from the bonnet. Another bomb hit elsewhere in the complex, destroying Richardson's flat. At 0230hrs the ramp down to the garage was hit, killing one of their colleagues.

Barbara and Simpkin were already talking of marriage. Occy had met Barbara quite soon into her relationship with Simpkin, and was broadly supportive. By October Simpkin was suggesting that his mother should be informed, since she would need to give her permission for his marriage: he would not be twenty-one until April 1942. But the matter became urgent when Simpkin was called up for service in the Army;[26] on October 22nd he received orders to report to 102 OCTU, Royal Armoured Corps, at Alma Barracks, Aldershot, on November 7th. Simpkin handed in his ambulance uniform, armband, staff pass, and helmet on October 31st; Barbara signed the receipt.

Early in November, the couple drove to Norfolk, where they collected Occy, and then on to Keswick in the Lake District, to meet Simpkin's mother. They then drove back south, staying in Retford on the night before Simpkin reported to his OCTU. Back in London, Barbara wrote to Simpkin repeatedly, describing in one letter how she had watched, from the top of the *campanile* of Westminster Cathedral, as the Thames turned red in the light of the flames. She went to visit him in Aldershot on the weekend of December 2nd, and they decided to announce their engagement at Christmas.

However, within days Simpkin's mother wrote to him stating that she would not consent under any circumstances to their marriage before he was twenty-one; that she refused in any way to recognise their engagement (although she did concede that, if she considered the circumstances suitable, she would consent to an engagement six months before he came of age); and that she would cut his allowance to the barest minimum for his personal requirements from January 1941. It was the beginning of a brutal clash which would eventually destroy Simpkin's relationships with his mother and grandmother.

The age-gap between the couple, and Barbara's active Catholicism, should not have mattered, but they did – though not to Simpkin, who was preparing to convert. He wrote to Barbara about the challenges which they faced:

> Apart, we can make nothing of our lives but drag through them uninspired and achieving nothing. Together, we are strong and can live in a faith that is given to few … No one ever gained anything from shrinking away from the world … If one of us should be killed, our personality will live on in the other in a very true and eternal sense, and our children will not be handicapped.[27]

He also wrote to his mother:

> I am very sorry about the way you feel about myself and Barbara, but I do understand your point of view and realise that it is the normal one. Although we cannot announce our engagement, I'm sure you'll see that your decision has not changed our feelings in the least. I'm also certain that we can stand up to this or any other test. It's simply that it seems to us unnecessary to wait, and that the strain of waiting is bound to tell on us both, especially in times like these. As for attempting some clandestine form of marriage, this is abhorrent to us both – so you need have no fears in this direction. It is your consent that we want, and nothing would be better than to hear that you have re-considered your decision.[28]

The couple spent Christmas 1940 together in Bournemouth, and the beginning of 1941 saw frantic activity as they sought to change Lady Evelyn's mind. Simpkin passed out from his OCTU in February, and Barbara travelled to Winchester to be vetted by the family doctor, who was opposed to the marriage. Since Simpkin had kept Robertson in the picture, Barbara visited him as well. Robertson and his sister took a carefully neutral but not discouraging position in the matter. Barbara's final interview was with the family solicitor, John Venning, whose good opinion of her seems to have tipped the balance. Evelyn withdrew her veto in March.

Simpkin spent his post-commissioning leave at Occy's house, 'Wildwood', in Norfolk, where Barbara joined him. On March 13th he reported to his regiment in East Grinstead, but preparations for the wedding were in full swing. One last hurdle remained, and at 0830hrs on Wednesday, April 2nd, in the crypt of Westminster Cathedral, Simpkin was formally received into the Catholic Church. In the same magnificent building, two hours later, he and Barbara were married in a Nuptial Mass. The witnesses were Occy and Venning. Simpkin's mother was not present.

* * *

Term had ended at Winchester on April 1st 1941, and with it Patrick Metcalfe's time in Robertson's care. Metcalfe was the younger son of Aubrey Metcalfe, who served

Richard and Barbara Simpkin, April 1941.
(Simpkin family collection; edited by dansteele.net)

Richard Simpkin, April 1941.
(Simpkin family collection; edited by dansteele.net)

Metcalfe.

as India's Foreign Secretary from 1936 to 1939, before being appointed Governor of Baluchistan, on the North-West Frontier, until he retired in 1943.[29] Aubrey Metcalfe's grandson Julian later encountered persistent rumours that Patrick was one of the many alleged illegitimate sons of Edward, Prince of Wales, who became Edward VIII in January 1936 until his abdication in December the same year. Pat certainly bore a strong resemblance to Edward, and he was indeed conceived during Edward's visit to India in 1922, while Aubrey Metcalfe was acting as his ADC. That the Prince of Wales would have been the sort of man to take advantage of a subordinate's wife is confirmed by his Private Secretary, Alan Lascelles, who recorded in his diaries that Edward seduced the wife of a District Officer whilst on a visit to Africa. Despite all of this, the rumours have been scotched conclusively by DNA testing.

Pat Metcalfe was born in England, but his early life was spent in India until – like so many sons of empire – he was sent off to boarding school at the age of eight. Most of his school holidays were spent in England, with relatives, given the length of sea voyages to India. He came to Hopper's in 1935 and proved quite proficient as an athlete, helping his house to win the Taylor Cup (inter-house athletics) and Beloe Cup (Junior Steeplechase) in 1938. He was a rower, winning the Burne Cup (for senior rowing IVs) in 1939, and rowing in the school VIII in 1940. He was also part of a team which took the Bather Cup, second prize in the OTC's inter-House drill competition. His older brother John, also a Hopperite, was already in the Army with the Coldstream Guards.[30]

Less than two months after leaving Winchester, Metcalfe joined the Royal Scots – though he would spend very little time with them. As early as June it was clear that he was going to be commissioned, and that he would be joining the Indian Army. His Commanding Officer commented that his

> military conduct during his 348 days with the Colours was very good. The rapidity with which he became commissioned is proof of his qualities.[31]

* * *

By late April, Bruce Fortune had been in the Army for over seven months, and his mother wrote to Robertson to keep him up to date:

> Dear Bobber …
> I went north and spent two weekends with Bruce and he was very well and so keen and everyone likes him. There are lots of old hands who served with his father who are nice to him, and Bruce thinks he is in the only Regiment and the only Battalion of same in the Army, and funnily enough in his father's old Company, so all is rosy at present.
> We went and spent a Sunday at Kilravock. Hugh [Rose] was very well and very nice. The old man's practically bed-ridden and rather pathetic.
> I heard today that Victor had been moved to *Stalag* XXI.D – rather a shame; he was so happy in his last camp and they all loved him. Your letters were of real interest in the camp. All the Old Wykehamists got together and discussed the affairs of the old school. So do go on writing to them …
> When will this – - – - war end?
> Yours,
> 'Evergreen'
> Rather withered with affairs of the state.[32]

* * *

As Greece fell to the Germans in April 1941, Simpkin was on honeymoon with Barbara. It is clear from Occy's letters that he expected soon to be going overseas:

> Dear Major Robertson,
> It is the great wish of Richard and myself that you should treat the fishing on the Meon as your own, going when you can or when you wish – I cannot give it up at present – and as Richard said, it is our link with Winchester and his happy days there. He and his wife came for two nights this last weekend – it was sad parting with them – and so sad for them to have to part so soon – but Richard is so brave and calm – and I am so happy with regard to their marriage and if God wills he should come back safely – I

> am sure it will be a happy one – he joins his troops today … I shall not see him again. Barbara hopes soon to get a job and she will always be able to come here for holidays etc. Soon I hope to go to my daughter's for a little time – Sheila has kindly asked me to come and see you – and I hope to later on – I will write to her soon … Please give her my love – yours always very sincerely,
>
> Ethel Coller.[33]

Simpkin reported to 53rd Training Regiment, Royal Armoured Corps at Tidworth, but was immediately sent on embarkation leave, which he and Barbara spent in the Lake District. On reporting for duty again, Simpkin received the usual dose of inoculations, but fell ill after his typhoid jab; he went off on leave again, this time 'sick leave', recuperating at Occy's Norfolk home ('Herondyke', a converted boathouse), with Barbara by his side. His reaction to the inoculation had been so severe that he was offered the chance to stay in England for instructional duties. It is clear that his decision to go overseas had not been an easy one:

> Sometimes I wonder if I was right to come, when I had the chance of pulling a fast one, and staying. But what I feel is that we were playing for safety in doing as we did, running no risks with the one thing too precious to be exposed to danger – our conscience and our mutual respect … I feel that had I been in a stronger state of mind and body, I'd have had a desire for an instructional job. But I was so weak that this was the only thing we could do to set me on my feet. What hurts is that you should have to pay for my weakness … It is your strength that keeps me going, the fact that you, my wonderful wife, pulled me together when I was on the verge of going completely to pieces. I know how much it cost you; thank you my love.[34]

Simpkin rejoined his regiment on May 30th, reached his embarkation port on May 31st, and the next day boarded a ship bound for the Middle East. He would not return to Barbara for four years. His grandmother wrote to Robertson again:

> I was so pleased to have your letter this morning – thank you very much for writing – Richard has gone overseas – he left for an embarkation port on the night of the 31st of May – we of course have no idea when he sailed or where he has gone – he had been ill a month – reported for duty on the morning of the 30th of May – and was told he had to leave the next day – they left me on the 29th – it was a great shock to us all – and I fear I am not a bit reasonable about it – and full of anxiety and fear night and day – he received your kind present the morning he left me – and as I am sure you will understand had not time to write – his wife is now at Barton – and is I believe looking for a job – I am so very glad the fishing is giving you and your friends so much pleasure, and if Richard knew he would be as glad as I am – it is much the best thing for you to arrange with Mr Arnold when he should go! I think you have arranged that well!! – I am bringing it on – hoping some day Richard may fish there again – I should love to see you and Sheila – but at present I can't make myself come to Winchester – so much happiness lies there – and much sorrow – but when I feel I can come I will write at once – I shall remain here until the end of the month – then I must go back to Barton

to see how Barbara is getting on – and what she has arranged to do – and then come back here – I am sure you and Sheila must be very tired with house manning difficulties and with catering etc. – please give her my very best love …[35]

* * *

Fortune had been commissioned into the Black Watch as a 2nd Lieutenant 172294 on February 15th 1941.[36] By the beginning of May he had joined 1st Battalion (1BW), as he informed Robertson:

I have been meaning to write you for some time, but what with schemes etc. I have had to put it off till now. I am at present on 48 hours leave and am spending it here with my Mama…. I hope to get seven days leave at the end of May, so if I may I think I will come and see you as I hope to be down in London … I haven't been over the Border for nearly a year, so a trip South will not do me any harm.

I have changed my occupation since I last wrote, having now taken over temporarily the command of our Carrier Platoon, and now prance into battle with Bren carriers – and motor-cyclists. It's quite fun and if there is any scrapping to be done in the early stage of battle, you get it. The only thing is that the Carrier Platoon in itself has a greater fire-power than the whole of the rest of the Battalion and the responsibility is something tremendous. Also, being in command of the Battalion recce group, the Carrier Platoon officer generally stops all the CO's rockets – and being very junior, he generally gets other people's shares of the raspberries that fly around. However, I am surviving the strain …[37]

This war is a funny one. It looks as though we may end up on the plains of Palestine after all, and dear old mad Colonel Rose will be right! I hope not. I saw him the other day looking rather like a cherub wrapped up in his dressing gown and sitting by the fire.

Well I must away and catch a train back to Leith – I leave at 1245hrs and arrive at 0620hrs in time for reveille![38]

Boyd, too, had joined a Scottish unit, though not the Black Watch: instead, he was serving as 2nd Lieutenant 165710 with 1st Battalion, The King's Own Scottish Borderers (1KOSB), on a course at the V Corps School, as he explained to Robertson in May.

How glad I am that you advised me not to join the Intelligence. Your letter arrived just after I had been accepted, and I was afraid for a time that I might not be able to get out of it. However I did, and I am very thankful for it.

As you see, I did not get into the Black Watch, but was posted instead to my own county regiment, which is really much more suitable. Also I have been lucky enough to get into the 1st Battalion, which is – to put it mildly – a really first-class fighting unit.

Life is, as you no doubt know, very strenuous down here, especially at this school where we get up at 0630hrs to do PT before breakfast. However, I have never been so fit in my life, and am enjoying it thoroughly.

I was on leave about a week ago and met Alastair Thorburn[39] who is a Regular in our 4th Battalion and was also home on leave. He is very fit and in excellent form and sent you his love. I also met Bill [Cliff] Hodges[40] up in Edinburgh when I was there. He sees a lot of Alastair as he is with their brigade. James Gammell[41] who was in Phil's, is Adjutant of this School, and is an acting or temporary Captain – I think he must be very temporary as he has to take two of his pips down when he moves out of the area.

I wonder if I could come over and see you, as I have a week-end leave on Saturday 21st May. If I could possibly come for the weekend I should very much like to, but please tell me if this is not possible, as I know you must be having a most awfully difficult time with rations and bombing.[42]

V

'Bodies all over the deck at night – and I dare not even look in the lifeboats!'

June–November 1941

By the summer of 1941, Britain's catalogue of wartime disasters had lengthened. The focus of the nation's efforts was now the war in North Africa, which would be fought back and forth across the desert several times between 1940 and 1943. First, the Italians had moved east from Libya into Egypt; then the British had driven them back into Libya and past Benghazi; but Wavell's brilliant successes, leaving his troops poised to sweep through to Tripoli, were rendered futile by the need to support Greece against Italian and German aggression; evacuation of Commonwealth forces from Greece in April was followed by the loss of Crete late in May. The world was stunned by the news of the sinking of HMS *Hood* on May 24th, only partly compensated for by the destruction of the *Bismarck* on the 27th. The fall of Greece and Crete, together with the grievous naval losses suffered in evacuating Commonwealth forces, had focused Britain's attention on its weakness in the eastern Mediterranean. The Vichy French held Syria, and there were fears of a German invasion through Turkey, threatening not only Egypt but the oil pipeline from Persia and Iraq into Palestine and Jordan. Even Cyprus was considered a likely target for a German airborne invasion. For the time being, it was in the Mediterranean and its environs that our subjects would begin to see battle.

* * *

From the day that Dick Simpkin embarked for the Middle East he wrote to Barbara daily, until he reached his unit in the field, at which time he started to write every third day. Regular letters also went to Occy, occasional letters to his mother, and a few to Robertson.[1] The letter-heads show that Simpkin sailed on a Cunard-White Star Line vessel, and this makes it probable that he sailed as part of convoy WS9A on either RMS *Franconia* or RMS *Samaria*.[2] His first letter to Robertson was dated June 10th and contained belated thanks for a wedding present:

> Thanks so much for your letter and for the book. I should have written before, but things have been so muddled and involved that I thought I'd wait until I got on the boat, with ample leisure. Incidentally, I seem to remember your sending me down to Wells to order ten copies of George Blore, with the comment – 'It may not be much good,

but it'll do very well for wedding presents!' Seriously, though, it's a delightful thing to have – an anthology from an unusual point of view.

I expect my grandmother will have written to you, and told you of how uncertain everything was – I took very unkindly to a typhoid injection – and that I nearly missed the boat. I hope as the summer goes on she may come down and stay with you. My going has been a great shock to her, but she's stood up to it with all her usual courage. But she's had too many shocks in the last few years. Of course, quite frankly, it was a very hard blow for us. But we've been so terribly lucky in everything, really, and I suppose fighting is what soldiers are for. But it's not easy to be calm about it, especially when there are so many people who would sell their souls to get out there. Still, there it is. Barbara's been simply splendid about it – of course waiting is far the hardest part. She is going to get a job – may have got one by now – and I hope she'll get an interesting one. I'm sure if she's down Winchester way she'll look you up. What does give me very great pleasure is that she has met my mother, and they get on very well ...

Perhaps it won't be very long before I see you again – anyway, optimism's the only way to keep sane nowadays.[3]

The convoy reached Freetown on June 18th, setting sail again on June 20th. After rounding the Cape, the *Franconia* and *Samaria* put in to Durban for a four-day layover on July 4th; the convoy then sailed as far as Aden before splitting up and making for Egyptian ports. What follows is a digest of Simpkin's letters to Barbara *en route;* we start with his description of how a junior officer spent his day on board ship:

After breakfast, usually up on deck for a while to have game of shovel-board. Then mug up Arabic for an hour or so until 1000hrs, when we have our first hour's Arabic lesson. Sometimes we have boat drill in the morning, but this is less frequent now we know where to go. Then I read on deck (*Pickwick Papers* – light modern novels are no use to me) till lunch at 1215hrs, then coffee and the afternoon on deck, reading or wandering around. I find serious reading impossible, except for Catholic books in small doses ... The ship's library has a pretty poor collection of fiction ... I've been soaking myself in detective stories; I feel more and more convinced that the detective story form is the best type of modern light fiction. It's a theme which offers infinite variations, and some mental exercise.

I've been censoring some men's letters today. It's amazing what good letters they write, and, for the most part, how discreet they are. But what I do deplore is a lot of officers sitting round a table reading out to each other choice selections. Would you believe it!

There's normally someone playing the piano in the lounge during tea, and I stay there till the second Arabic lesson at 1700hrs. Then wash and brush up for dinner at 1815hrs. Typical menu: *hors d'oeuvres,* soup, salmon, duck, pears Hélène, real fresh fruit. Then we deck for a while and down for coffee, the odd drink perhaps, and a game of chess. I play chess a certain amount ... but very badly. I find I can't concentrate. But to look at the board brings back very fond memories.

I usually go up on deck for a while about 2130hrs, then come down and write to you; then up on deck till about midnight if it's a nice night, and to bed about 0100hrs. Read for a bit, prayers, and sleep ... The days are long but the time passes.

There were female nurses on board, and Simpkin reported, 'Bodies all over the deck at night – and I dare not even look in the lifeboats!'

What becomes clear from his letters is how full of insecurity Simpkin was:

> I hate the Army too much to feel able to settle down in it ... Things would be so much easier if there was someone I knew well enough to be at ease with. But of course I'm always at my worst in a Mess, and I do find this way of life a terrific strain. I've felt very low and sad today. Everyone's specially hearty tonight, and singing loudly in the next room. To be on one's guard (tho' what against – heaven knows) the whole time is a terrific strain. I think it's because I feel inferior to the other people my own age, and frightened of them. I'm sure that's the explanation. It's a silly feeling, but if one has it, as I always have, it makes things very tiring. I can put up a show all right, but it does cost a lot. I've still got the same symptoms, terrified of other people and so on, and I have to fight these down the whole time. Heaven knows what I'll be like when I get some men under me. But I think I'm strong enough to keep steady as long as I'm fit and well-occupied. I took an elementary [Arabic] class the other day! You know there's something about teaching that fascinates me, even when I'm only one jump ahead of the people I'm teaching. It's the one time I feel really sure of myself, oddly enough. You know, I used to have an absolute terror of speaking, even getting up and saying poetry in a class at school, but I cured this by making a rule that I would speak in every debate there was at school and this cured me completely ...
>
> I've still got this terror of meeting and talking to other people. I suppose it comes from a complete loathing and mistrust of the Army, and most of all I find that I cannot look at people to whom I'm talking. I can look anyone in the eyes on purpose, so to speak, but I find that if I'm just talking to someone I suddenly realise that I'm looking in a quite different direction. In many ways I wish I could revert to the ranks. I would do it like a shot were it not that, as things are, I can keep in touch with you better and stand a better chance of getting home quickly afterwards.

It was a huge comfort to him that there was an admirable Catholic chaplain on the ship – his new faith sustained him through his worries:

> I get up just after 0700hrs, and go to Mass and Holy Communion at 0730hrs... I went twice to Mass today. I prayed very hard for you this morning. To hear our names coupled in the last prayer after the Mass was very wonderful, darling ... Every afternoon I say the Rosary right through. I feel that if I get really intimate with it, it will be a tremendous help to me when things get difficult ...
>
> I feel very low ... I've decided to have a talk with Father Barber tomorrow ... My mind is going all to bits and I'm determined to do something about it ... I'm afraid I was very depressed last night. The Veganin I took didn't make me sleep and had the most amazing effect on me ... It was what I imagine drugged dreams must be like – but I'd quite recovered by morning. In future I'll stick to straight aspirin...
>
> I feel better today. I prayed very hard for strength and it was given me. I asked for the right answer and I was given it. I decided this morning not to talk to Father Barber about myself, because that would be an admission of defeat ... I promise you that if things are too difficult to face, I will talk to a priest.

I went to confession tonight, so I'll be starting off with a clean sheet anyway … The Catholic 'club' which happens every night in Father Barber's cabin had its last meeting tonight. I have seldom seen a man work so hard. We were streaming out into the passages all round. They're a good set of chaps – it's a great relief to put officialdom to one side and relax in a completely unmilitary atmosphere … My own view is that it should be possible to meet as Catholics on an absolutely equal basis, and this does in fact work very well.

As the long voyage ended, the rising temperatures began to cause Simpkin trouble and he suffered from 'prickly heat': 'It's really hot for the first time … The sweat is literally pouring off … quite unlike anything I'd ever imagine.'

There was a delay to disembarking in Egypt, but after several days Simpkin boarded an overnight train to Abbassia, near Cairo: 'A big garrison town – but I hope we'll be able to get to our own units quite soon and get on with the job. It's like Tidworth, but a hundred times more so, and the Mess at the RAC Depot is chiefly cavalry – excellent food, etc., but rather expensive.'[4]

By the next day, like so many new arrivals, he was struck down with 'gyppy tummy'. So began an intensely dull month as he awaited posting to a battalion.

* * *

Three more Hopperites emerged at the end of July into the bleakness of a Britain struggling to see how the war could be won: Michael Elliott-Binns, David Middleditch, and Christopher Pringle.

Elliott-Binns.

Middleditch.

Pringle.

Pringle was a musician and a rower whilst at Winchester, and on leaving went on to Manchester University to study Economics, his family home being in the city.[5] Middleditch was a talented historian – he won the Vere Herbert Smith Prize for the subject – and went up to Trinity College, Cambridge with a Kitchener Scholarship.[6] Robertson had called in favours to ensure that Middleditch would go to Trinity, as shown by a letter from a Wykehamist tutor there, Patrick Duff:[7]

I have no authority to accept David Middleditch without submitting his name to the Admissions Committee, but, considering how problematical all prophecy is nowadays,

I think you can reasonably tell the Kitchener people he is coming here. His father was before my time, but the name is of course familiar. If you will get the enclosed form filled up, I will bring the application before the next meeting of the Committee, not yet fixed … Harry Edwards, home on leave between the Field Security and an OCTU, is enthusiastic about Winchester and about you.[8]

* * *

Michael Elliott-Binns would later write with great candour and sensitivity about his time at Winchester, at Cambridge, and in the Army.[9] His published works make clear the close affection to which male friendship can lead, but give the lie to the modern assumption that deep attachment must of necessity have a sexual component.

My prep school was on the whole a miserable experience, probably the worst period of my life. My refuge and consolation was reading, and I found myself writing poetry. I was clever and went on to Winchester, where I was happy. When I had finished my prep I used to write long imaginative poems, bad imitations of Shelley and Keats.

Then one evening my life changed. I slipped in beside another boy in his cubicle and found him with his face transfigured, writing poetry. I read what he was writing and resolved from that moment onwards to write as he wrote and to follow and love him …

I related only to other boys in the dimension of life that made me write poetry. There was attraction, but the idea of homosexual relations never arose. I was deeply moral and would no more consider that than robbing a bank or seducing a girl.[10]

The boy whom Elliott-Binns had so admired was Duncan McMurtrie. Their friendship shaped Elliott-Binns' entire life.

Elliott-Binns won the Leslie Hunter Prize for an essay in Classical Archaeology before becoming a classical Scholar at St John's College, Cambridge.

* * *

On August 4th, Simpkin wrote that he was hoping to pull strings to get the posting he wanted, by contacting Guy Richardson's brother:

If I can get in touch with Jim Richardson, it might be a great help, as I believe he's on the staff now and very highly thought of.

The welcome news that he was to join 4th Battalion, Royal Tank Regiment (4RTR), reached Simpkin on August 21st:

I'm glad, because life here was becoming pretty intolerable. Life in the desert is at any rate hard and healthy, and I think a period with a unit is a necessary preliminary to any sort of job out here. It's a very good battalion – it's a good job and I'm lucky to have a day to prepare things and get ready generally. At any rate I'll be able to save some money … I'm afraid I shall have to leave most of my books behind but I shall try to take a few.

Since April 13th 1941, when Rommel's troops had reached the Egyptian frontier, the port of Tobruk had been under siege. In late September, 4RTR moved by sea from Mersa Matruh into the Tobruk perimeter. Plans were afoot to relieve the town, and Simpkin would be heavily involved.

* * *

Tompson.

At around the same time, Hew Tompson was just about to set out for the Middle East. At Sandhurst, Tompson had volunteered for the Royal Artillery, and after training at Larkhill with 110 OCTU had been posted to 78 (Duke of Lancaster's Yeomanry) Medium Regiment, where, Robertson later recorded, he made many friends and won golden opinions. Formed in April 1940, by September the unit was at Pontypridd in South Wales. But in June 1941 Tompson was posted to 11 (Honourable Artillery Company) Regiment, RHA, equipped with the superlative 25-pounder gun which was to become the standard British field-piece of the war, its use brought to devastating perfection by the Royal Artillery.[11]

> I have just been posted to this Regiment. I only hope I shall be able to hold it down, having got this far. Armitage (College)[12] is with me, and we thought we might get down for Eton Match, only we neither of us knew the date. I wonder if you would be kind enough to let me know, as well as all the news from Sunnyside. We have had some lovely days here and the country is looking perfectly glorious, particularly Sussex with its beech trees. I've never see anything so beautiful as the spring this year.
>
> The gunnery we do here is rather different to what I have been used to during the last eighteen months, and incidentally, being so much quicker, a lot of the slightly 'embarrassing' mathematics is dispensed with![13]

Tompson was promoted Lieutenant at the beginning of August 1941,[14] as Simpkin languished at Abbassia, and wrote to his mother on August 10th with important news:

> Darling Mummeye …
> We have now been definitely told that we are going abroad and as next of kin I am allowed to tell you but it mustn't go on. Whether I shall go with them or not I don't know, as I have been given a specialist's job and have not so far been on any course or had any instruction in it except what I have picked up here. I am going to see the Colonel either today or tomorrow and find out exactly where I stand. If I am going I hope to be on leave some time within the next month, which I know is going to make things very awkward for you; unfortunately I can't really use the telephone to talk about it … I shall have to bring a lot of my kit, etc., home in any case, and if you like I will bring my bed back, only it's rather large and low! There is also poor old Ted to think of; he's been rather ill lately; poisoned I think by trying to eat a hedgehog (dead some days!). Anyway, he is a little better today …
> Best love, your very loving
> Hew[15]

11 RHA would be travelling to Egypt to become part of 1 Support Group of 1st Armoured Division.[16] However, it was a while before they departed. Tompson managed to snatch some time at home in mid-September, after which he wrote to his mother, letting slip that he was travelling northwards to his port of embarkation:

> I don't suppose we shall, any of us, ever forget that famous day (and night) which I spent at home; it was lucky that we didn't realise at the time what agony it was going to be, or it would have spoilt a perfectly wonderful day, indeed worthy of my last day at home.
>
> One expects and gets so much from one's parents that it is very difficult to sit down and thank you for anything in particular when I realise that everything that I have had or done in the world has been given by you. And what a lot I've had; the best of everything in fact.
>
> I do wish that it didn't take beastly departures to make us realise quite how much we do owe… Do please remember that as far as your children are concerned, they couldn't have asked for better parents, and I shall be happy if I do half as well for my children as you have done for yours.
>
> We left at 0830hrs … The trip here was lovely and it was so noticeable that the further North we went the nicer the people became, I think only because there are so much fewer troops.
>
> We are living in the most appalling discomfort, but I hope this won't last too long.
>
> My address from now on is: HFC Tompson, 11th (HAC) Regiment RHA, c/o Army Post Office 1515. I doubt if I will get your letters for months but they will find me eventually… Take care of yourself. I will write again if I can.
>
> your loving
> Hew
>
> P.S. This may never reach you but it's having a good try.
>
> P.P.S. I haven't lost my luggage yet![17]

Five days later, he wrote a cryptic letter to say that he was taking ship at Liverpool:

> You remember the building that my great-grandfather designed? I saw it this morning, looking just the same. Take care of yourself. My love to you all. I will write as soon as I can. We must just live for the end.[18]

* * *

There was a war on, and Robertson knew his duty – to prepare his charges as best he could for what life might throw at them. Typical of him is the letter which he wrote to Mackrill on Sunday, September 14th 1941, discussing the School Certificate examinations (the 1941 equivalent of modern GCSEs):[19]

Mackrill.

> My dear Graham,
>
> I hope the news of Certificate, which I only got last night, hasn't reached you before this! All our Sunnyside chaps got through, Lewin

with four and Holtby with five 'Credits' and some passes, and at the other end Gray with five 'Very Goods' and four 'Credits', ranging from Greek to Additional Maths! You also did very well, with the following result:

2 Very Good – Latin (!from what I remember of it!) and Elementary Maths.

5 Credits- English Language, English Literature, Scripture, French, and Drawing.

2 Passes- History and Science.

Don't let anyone think you are a great wiz, because the standard isn't very high, and if you get a swelled head I shall soon find something to 'rub your nose in'! But you won't, and I'm pleased that you did your stuff and put up a thoroughly sound all-round performance. Now you can start getting educated and really learn something … (McArthur, by the way, got six 'Credits' and a 'Pass' in Science.)

I heard from Edmond Holtby[20] that you and Robert had been a help, but not many people come up to his standard of work! He is a whole-hearted whole-timer, I fancy.

Thank your father for his letter. So glad he and his escaped the worst of the last Blitz.

Well done – now you must go into training to become a prefect later on – before I leave, perhaps. I'm very anxious to bequeath a really sound and loyal house to my (unknown) successor, and you and others may be and should be the chaps to help (and you would do!). Yours ever, MR.

You left no holiday address on my special paper, so I must post this to Hull.

Love to Ian. Time he wrote again!

* * *

By coincidence, Tompson would be travelling on the RMS *Samaria,* probably the same ship which Simpkin had taken to Egypt. On September 29th he was afloat but still allowed to write home:

> I am now 'aboard' and confined to it for good. It is really very comfortable and the amount of food we eat is almost indecent. Butter *ad lib,* and God knows what else … Our departure from dry land was very depressing, standing for hours in pouring rain with a leaking roof, and when they were hauling my luggage on board they very nearly dropped it into the sea, sponge-bag and all.
>
> I don't think we are going to have a particularly slack time. I see a good many training programmes being drawn up, but I dare say it will get fairly monotonous doing nothing but read and feel sick. There is something about the rumbling on even a stationary boat that makes you feel fairly ill, and the heat is simply terrific.[21]

The *Samaria* set off from Liverpool the following day to join convoy WS12 as it assembled off the Clyde. The convoy started its voyage to the Middle East on October 1st,[22] and Tompson wrote a letter home the following day:

> We are now three days out and God knows where we are; it has been frightfully rough and nearly everybody has collapsed, but oddly enough not me, which is very surprising, but is simply hasn't affected me in the very slightest. It's interesting to see the heartiest type of louts collapsing first on a boat, isn't it? They are so impossible when well!

Cigarettes here are 1/8 per fifty, Champagne is 7/6 per bottle, and beer 4d per pint, so we are steadily moving back to a peacetime standard of living, which is a pity but pleasant. I think of you all and wish I could be with you again and bring some of the mass of butter with me.

So far we have had no trouble except for one air-raid warning, this afternoon, which, in the tradition of all I have ever witnessed, came to nothing! We hear no news of any kind at all; wirelesses are not allowed.

There is absolutely nothing to do on board except read, but we are very comfortable, unlike the men, who live in the most deplorable conditions like so many cattle, there being so many on board. They have nowhere to sit at all except on the decks, which are terribly crowded, and what's worse is the appalling stuffiness and smell five decks down where they eat, sleep and somehow have their being. Their food is excellent, which is something. The conditions unfortunately encourage the attitude of 'damn you Jack, I'm all right' except that damn isn't the word they use. This is a pity, as it might be the same in real trouble – but I doubt it somehow, as they are all in surprisingly high spirits.[23]

WS12 reached Freetown on October 14th and left in the early afternoon of the 19th. The troops were not allowed ashore, however. The convoy's next stop would be Cape Town or Durban, different portions stopping in different ports. The *Samaria* crossed the equator on October 22nd, as Tompson's Neptune certificate shows.

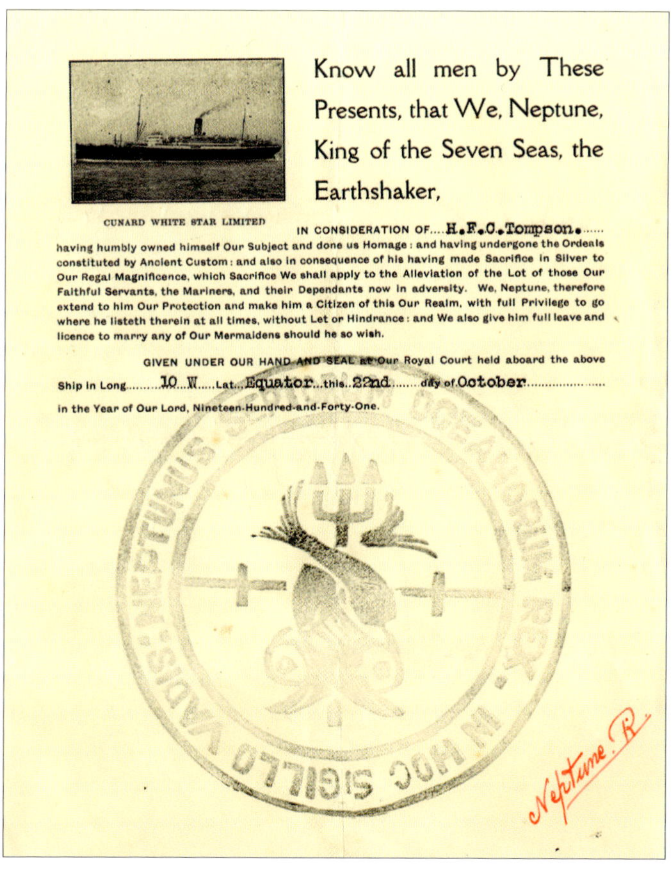
Know all men by These Presents, that We, Neptune, King of the Seven Seas, the Earthshaker,

CUNARD WHITE STAR LIMITED

IN CONSIDERATION OF....H.F.C.Tompson......
having humbly owned himself Our Subject and done us Homage: and having undergone the Ordeals constituted by Ancient Custom: and also in consequence of his having made Sacrifice in Silver to Our Regal Magnificence, which Sacrifice We shall apply to the Alleviation of the Lot of those Our Faithful Servants, the Mariners, and their Dependants now in adversity. We, Neptune, therefore extend to him Our Protection and make him a Citizen of this Our Realm, with full Privilege to go where he listeth therein at all times, without Let or Hindrance: and We also give him full leave and licence to marry any of Our Mermaidens should he so wish.

GIVEN UNDER OUR HAND AND SEAL at Our Royal Court held aboard the above Ship in Long.........10 W.....Lat...Equator...this..22nd........day of October....................... in the Year of Our Lord, Nineteen-Hundred-and-Forty-One.

Neptune R.

He wrote:

> We crossed the line the other day and went through the usual ceremony, rather a savage one when run entirely by soldiers, but still great fun and a change. The men loved it because almost all the officers were half drowned and covered with some awful white paste. I must say I was surprised that not a soul was hurt, except for one cut on the back of the head.
>
> We spent a week in port; it was terribly hot and we very soon got tired of the niggers[24] who seemed to know no English except the very worst form of filth which I hope they didn't learn from the missionaries![25]

An eagerly-anticipated run ashore took place in Durban, which Tompson and his companions reached on November 3rd.[26] Tompson wrote about the visit at length as a break from the monotony of life on the troop-ship. And what a break it was; Durban was well known for welcoming troops in transit.

> We had the most incredible time in Durban, where we stopped for a week. As we stepped off the boat we were whisked up by large cars and driven all over the place, given dinners, taken to all sorts of parties. They really were wonderfully kind to us ….
>
> I spent two of the days in the sea; it was boiling hot and the surf-riding was great fun. I got very badly sunburnt on the last day and could hardly move the next day. It was also rather nice seeing the whole town ablaze with light every night.
>
> I met an old Wykehamist wandering round the town one afternoon, a big man in sugar; he drove me all over his vast plantations and we went round a sugar mill; it was very interesting, and the Mauritian chemist and rather odd population was very Hollywood. We had a large old Wykehamist dinner; people flocked in from miles around.[27]

This Old Wykehamist dinner in Durban was described in the following letter to *The Wykehamist*:[28]

> During the recent visit of this convoy to a certain port, an Old Wykehamist dinner was held at the Cumberland Hotel. 'Domum' was sung, and followed by the traditional hot, in which College and the younger generation of 'C' defeated 'A' and 'I'. The only 'baker' we could obtain came off a sofa, and was two feet square and harder than most – an excuse which 'A' and 'I' put forward for their defeat. The excuse was not accepted. The following were present at the dinner:
>
> G. Keble Moberly C, 1884–87
> G.S. Moberly C, 1910–14
> R.E.E. Christian C, 1902–05
> P.H. Duranty A, 1894–97
> J.D. Eggar A, 1930–35
> H.F.C. Tompson I, 1933–38
> J.L.F. Armitage Coll. 1933–37
> I am, Sir, yours, etc.,
> J.L.F. Armitage, Lieut., RHA
> 11th Regt., Royal Horse Artillery
> November 11th 1941

Tompson's letter continues:

> One day, with a flourish of trumpets, we trooped off to see the Valley of a Thousand Hills, the trippers' delight; however, it was so misty with rain that I could only see about three of them and so we came away rather disappointed.
>
> The English in Durban are rather rich (2/- income tax) (and slightly common!) and I think slightly unpatriotic in their general attitude. They were terribly kind, and I know very keen for us to win the war, but except for being very charming to us they do nothing whatever. If they were South Africans one could understand it, but I am talking about the large number of people who went there after Munich. The Native is also treated in rather an odd way; he is just dirt, and one is hardly allowed to ask him the way without going to prison!
>
> It is becoming very hot again, and therefore very difficult to take exercise unless you get up very early. But we are all pretty well in a rut of routine now, and I can read morse and semaphore like lightning …
>
> We have just heard about the *Ark Royal*; what a pity, but she has had a good run for her money. Our Padre – such a nice man – had two brothers on her, and was very worried till we heard that there were only 18 casualties.[29]

As the voyage neared its close, Tompson was one of those who attended a joint HAC-RAF dinner aboard the *Samaria* on Sunday, 16th November.

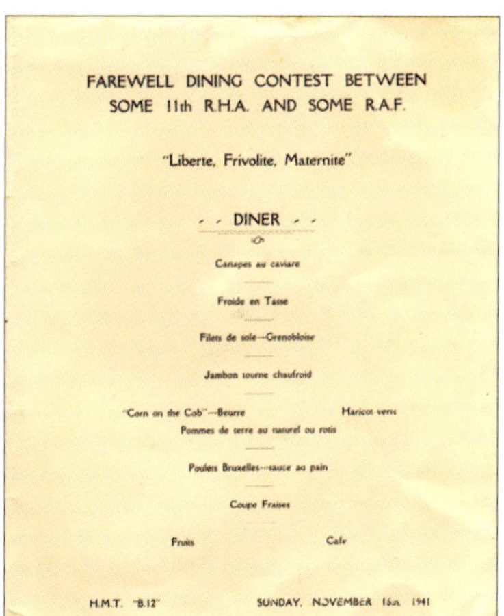

FAREWELL DINING CONTEST BETWEEN
SOME 11th R.H.A. AND SOME R.A.F.

"Liberte, Frivolite, Maternite"

DINER

Canapes au caviare

Froide en Tasse

Filets de sole—Grenobloise

Jambon tourne chaufroid

"Corn on the Cob"—Beurre   Haricot verts
Pommes de terre au naturel ou rotis

Poulets Bruxelles—sauce au pain

Coupe Fraises

Fruits   Cafe

H.M.T. "B.12"   SUNDAY, NOVEMBER 16th 1941

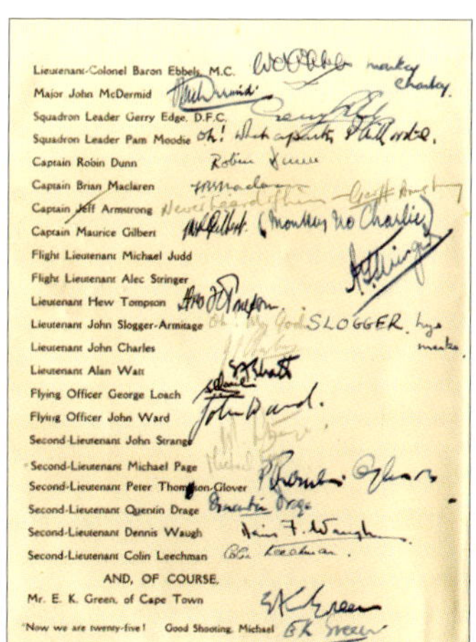

Lieutenant-Colonel Baron Ebbels, M.C.
Major John McDermid
Squadron Leader Gerry Edge, D.F.C.
Squadron Leader Pam Moodie
Captain Robin Dunn
Captain Brian Maclaren
Captain Jeff Armstrong
Captain Maurice Gilbert
Flight Lieutenant Michael Judd
Flight Lieutenant Alec Stringer
Lieutenant Hew Tompson
Lieutenant John Slogger-Armitage
Lieutenant John Charles
Lieutenant Alan Watt
Flying Officer George Loach
Flying Officer John Ward
Second-Lieutenant John Strange
Second-Lieutenant Michael Page
Second-Lieutenant Peter Thompson-Glover
Second-Lieutenant Quentin Drage
Second-Lieutenant Dennis Waugh
Second-Lieutenant Colin Leechman
AND, OF COURSE,
Mr. E. K. Green, of Cape Town

"Now we are twenty-five!   Good Shooting, Michael

VI

'A two-pounder shot went straight through the German and nicked the armour by the small of my back'

November–December 1941

The war in North Africa was one in which logistics played a vital role. Everything which an army required to fight – food, fuel, ammunition, water – had to be brought with it. The further that an army advanced, the more strained became its supply lines. The two major ports on the North African shore were Tripoli, for the Italians and Germans, and Alexandria, for the British and their allied contingents. Between these major ports lay smaller ones – Benghazi, Tobruk, and Mersa Matruh – control of which governed the whole conduct of the campaign.

The desert was a peculiar environment, where there were few civilians and little chance of living off the land; armies had to have motorized transport and were thus dependent on their supply of petrol. The further from base they drove, the less and less fuel reached the front line – especially for the British, whose petrol still travelled in impractical, flimsy four-gallon tins, which split and leaked at the slightest provocation. Thus it was as though the British and German-Italian armies were on elastic: the British elastic seemed to reach full stretch westwards at Benghazi, and the Axis elastic looked as though it might just stretch eastwards as far as Alexandria.

In March and April 1941, German troops had arrived in North Africa and forced the British back to the Egyptian border – but Commonwealth forces had managed to fortify the port of Tobruk and to hold it against everything which the Axis forces could throw at them in terms of air power and ground assault. The Royal Navy ran tremendous risks maintaining the supply line to Tobruk, whilst 75 miles to the east, British land forces planned their counter-offensives. These aimed to raise the siege, to drive Rommel's troops back to Benghazi, and then, it was hoped, out of North Africa entirely. Operation Brevity in May 1941 had enjoyed limited success; but Operation Battleaxe in June had been a failure, and had led to Wavell being relieved of command and being replaced by Auchinleck. Commonwealth troops in Egypt had now been designated the Eighth Army and prepared for a third – and, they hoped, decisive – attack into Libya: Operation Crusader.

The plan of Crusader was to drive across the Libyan frontier – known as 'The Wire' – well to the south of the main German concentrations, and then to hook northwards across the German and Italian lines of communication. The enemy would then have to retire from the Egyptian border and, it was hoped, abandon the siege of Tobruk.

It would be impossible to tell the story of Operation Crusader and the ensuing to-and-fro of battles in anything but a full-length history; November 1941 saw an immensely complex series of armoured clashes, during which great heroism was displayed on both sides. John Pinney's older brother, Bernard, one of Robertson's former charges, was recommended for a Victoria Cross; Simpkin was another of those decorated for his courage.

* * *

Bernard Pinney was in command of 'J' Battery, 3rd Royal Horse Artillery, which he had joined in the late summer after recovering from a wound received in the Syrian campaign. He had written to Robertson on September 3rd:

> It is just a year since Rosemary and I lunched with you, and since then I have been at London, Wolverhampton, and Aden in anti-aircraft, and then 1st Field Regiment, getting fairly mildly shot in the foot by a bullet from a distant machine-gun, and now, after nearly two months in hospital and convalescing, am in the above Battery, for the second time, as I was once a Subaltern in it.
>
> You will be interested to hear that I saw quite a lot of Robert [Pinney] in Cairo – he had been in the country a month or two and was still a reinforcement at a Base Camp not far out. He seemed on the whole unchanged, except for having lost his youthful insubordination! It is rather sad finding him as a Lance Corporal without any good chance of becoming an officer or a Senior NCO, and living in a tent with men who could barely read or write. He was quite philosophic about it and seemed to me to be doing his menial job and hoping peace would come as soon as possible.
>
> The above may not be quite fair on him, as he was pathetically keen to get away from the Base Depot, and get started in a fighting unit. I hope to spend a leave with him in three or four months' time at Luxor or somewhere where everyone met is not a soldier.
>
> I hope you were told of the arrival of Betsy Anne Pinney at Racedown on June 8th. I am terribly glad she has arrived without trouble and naturally long to see her.
>
> There are many Wykehamists about here, but I have met no Hopperites – Bill Leggatt, Douglas Packard, Ransome all G1s and hence Lieutenant Colonels (I still prefer the satisfying seclusion of regimental soldiering).
>
> When will the next peacetime Eton Match be? Winchester in a peaceful June is a cool and pleasant memory in this barren spot.
>
> P.S. Other New Zealanders tell me that, had Robert tried at all, he could – without any difficulty – have stayed in New Zealand, as a farmer with two children was high up on the Exemption List. He always was a philanthropic ass.[1]

Robertson pencilled at the bottom, 'My last letter from Bernard'.

* * *

As Crusader began at first light on November 18th, the Germans had been about to launch another of their attempts to break into Tobruk; but by the end of November 19th, 7 Armoured Brigade had reached the airfield at Sidi Rezegh, some two miles south-east of Ed Duda – which was itself less than six miles from the Tobruk perimeter. Italian and German forces launched a counter-attack the following day, and it came as a shock to them when, on the morning of November 21st, the Matilda II tanks of 4RTR, alongside those of 'D' Squadron 7RTR, broke out from their positions around Tobruk. The garrison's role in the coming battle was not to be a passive one; the Matildas had orders to press forwards towards Ed Duda to the south-east, and to link up with XXX Corps.

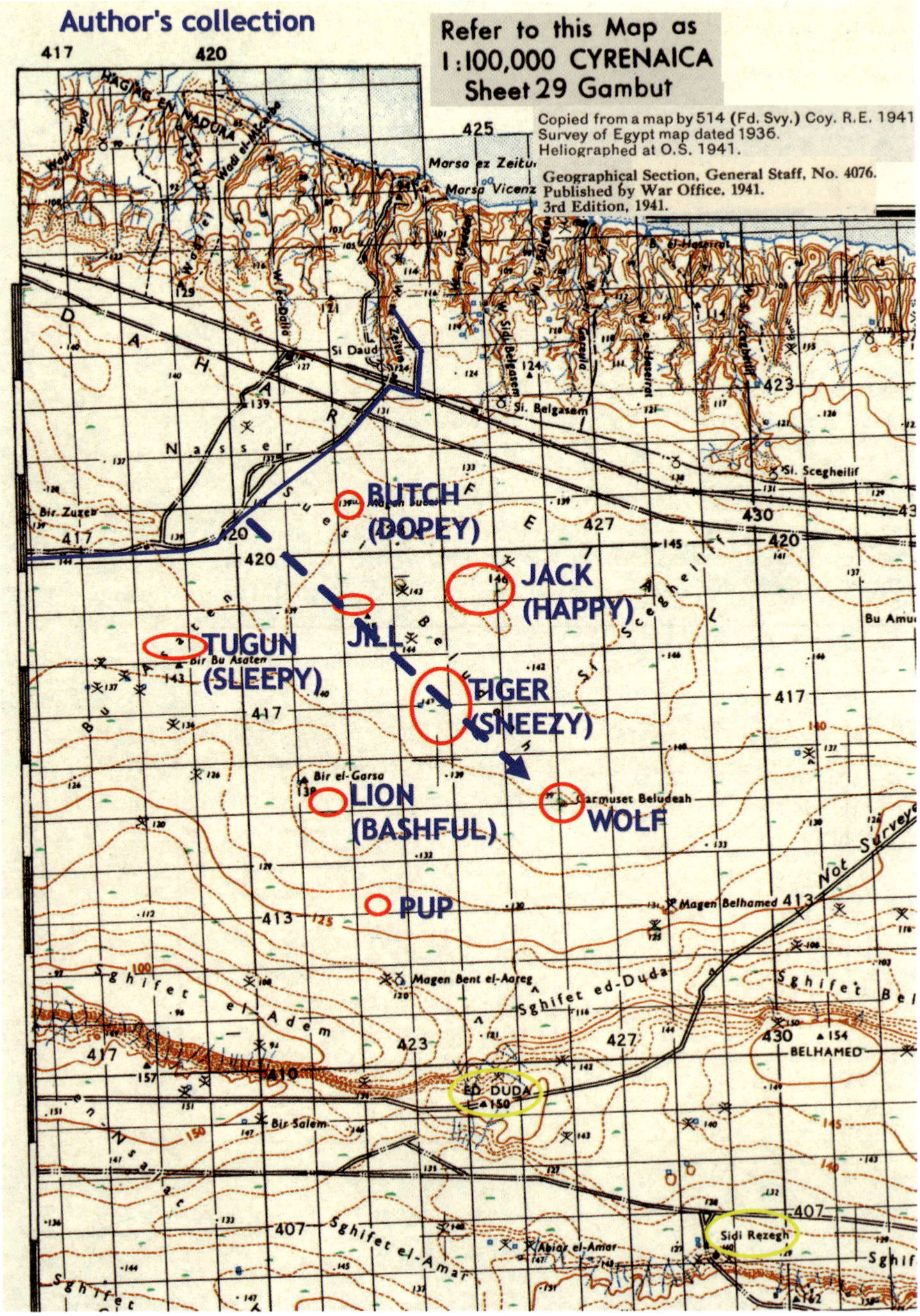

As far as the Tobruk garrison was aware, five strong Italian positions – code-named BUTCH/DOPEY, JACK/HAPPY, JILL, TIGER/SNEEZY and TUGUN/SLEEPY – barred the way to Ed Duda; in fact, Axis forces held a much more continuous line than anticipated, which caused problems, and the defenders included large numbers of Germans. These strongpoints were to be attacked by infantry, with 4RTR and 'D' Squadron, 7RTR in support. There is no one consistent version of what happened that day, but it appears that 'D'/7RTR and its accompanying infantry overran BUTCH at around 0630hrs, though the attackers failed to seize TUGUN; 'B'/4RTR, in reserve, then attacked TUGUN. Shortly afterwards, at around 0715hrs, 2nd Black Watch suffered heavy casualties breaking in to JILL, but, together with 4RTR then pressed on to TIGER, which had been secured by 1015hrs, with JACK also falling to infantry assisted by 4RTR. By 1545hrs, TUGUN was also in the hands of the Tobruk garrison, who had now opened a salient driving towards Ed Duda and the relief forces. Simpkin had been in the thick of the fight, and his war had almost come to an abrupt end before it had fairly started, as he later recalled in one of the few memories of the war which he set down on paper:

> My first moment of action was when I was marker tank in the Tobruk breakout, and a very brave German jumped on my back flaps armed with a Molotov cocktail and a crowbar. We had a doubly lucky escape. My Troop Corporal was covering, but his gunner pressed the wrong button and a two-pounder shot went straight through the German and nicked the armour by the small of my back. The tank being a diesel one, we managed to get the engine fire out. I must admit that ever since then I've suffered a certain amount of 'infantry terror'.[2]

An official account of Simpkin's actions that day gives a bit more detail of what he was up to at the time of this incident:

> On November 21st 1941, 2nd Lieutenant Simpkin was commanding his Troop of tanks. He had to lead the Squadron in a flank movement at speed and find a gap through the rear defences and enter the objective. He did this with consummate dash and skill.[3]

The plan had been to push on to Ed Duda at 1430hrs, but this was unachievable. Although over 1,000 Axis and German troops had surrendered, other German units made repeated counter-attacks throughout the day. The Tobruk garrison's 32 Army Tank Brigade had started the day with 158 tanks, of which only 40 were now serviceable; 2nd Black Watch had lost 79 dead and 197 wounded out of the 612 men who had begun the day. And so on November 22nd the break-out corridor remained static, whilst fighting raged around Sidi Rezegh, the garrison working to secure the eastern flank of the salient ready for another advance.

* * *

As Simpkin had been attacking on November 21st, Bernard Pinney had been defending Sidi Rezegh. When Crusader began, the three troops of Pinney's 'J' Battery each had four 2-pounder anti-tank guns mounted on new three-ton Chevrolet trucks; the guns could be dismounted for use, or fired from the back of the trucks, which were known as 'portees'. The 2-pounders had a maximum effective range of no more than 800 yards, far less than the weapons of the German tanks which they were supposed to destroy.

By the evening of November 20th Pinney's guns were at Sidi Rezegh, which was under attack from 15th and 21st *Panzer* Divisions. The fight for the airfield would decide the battle: whoever held the escarpment at Sidi Rezegh dominated the plain before Tobruk.

At around 1030hrs on November 21st, around sixty Mark III and IV tanks of 21st *Panzer* Division attacked from the east. As the German tanks came on, they were countered by Pinney's 2-pounders, 'C' Troop engaging them first from the portees. Two guns were lost, but at least four *panzers* were knocked out, and by 1330hrs the Germans had withdrawn. However, they came on again later, their advance being heralded by Stuka attacks and severe shelling. Nearby, 2RB's headquarters party watched as the two remaining guns of 'A' Troop, commanded by Lieutenant Ward Gunn, tried to fend off the attack:

> There were three weapons capable of taking on the enemy tanks – two 2-pounders on their unarmoured portees under Ward Gunn (3rd RHA), and one Bofors anti-aircraft gun commanded by Pat McSwiney. These three engaged the enemy as best they could, outranged and unarmoured as they were.[4]

The German tanks made directly for 'A' Troop, firing high explosive to disable the portees and kill the gun crews. Ward Gunn nevertheless drove around his guns encouraging their crews. Among those watching was Wykehamist Captain Tom Bird,[5] himself a very courageous man who finished the war with a DSO, MC and bar – as well as witnessing two Victoria Cross actions.

> The small party around the blazing pick-ups watched these three guns firing away at the enemy; watched the crews, completely undaunted, picked off one by one. The enemy gave everything they had: machine-gun fire from the tanks and the supporting infantry, mortars, shells from the Mark IVs and the field guns. One 2-pounder was destroyed; the Bofors gun was set on fire.[6]

Sergeant Finagin of 'J'/3RHA also witnessed the fight:

> The second attack came in from the south-east and soon the whole of his Troop were banging away. 'A' Troop's action that afternoon will never die in my memories. They fought magnificently and to the last man; all across their frontage at a short distance of two to three hundred yards lay many tanks broken and burning. The gunners were buried three hours later where they had fallen.[7]

Three of the four portees were set on fire, and the gun crew of the last all killed or wounded.

> The driver, not unnaturally, began to drive it out of the battle. Ward Gunn, at Battalion HQ, was joined at that moment by Bernard Pinney ... He said to Ward: 'Go and stop that blighter', and even then it seemed hard to be so described for driving a useless gun and dead crew out of action.[8]

Ward Gunn ran over and stopped the driver, and the pair dragged the dead from the portee. They then got the gun back into action, with Pinney serving as their loader. 2RB did not dare to watch:

> No one could gauge the effect of this fire, because to look over the edge of a slit trench was suicidal ... The Germans concentrated their fire on the burning vehicles of Battalion HQ and the one remaining gun. But at least the two nearest enemy tanks were blazing.
>
> In a matter of seconds the portee was on fire, the off-side front wheel had been hit, and the tyre was blazing; two boxes of ammunition held in brackets behind the passenger seat were also in flames. Pinney took the Pyrene fire extinguisher and got the fire in the tyre under control; but the ammunition boxes continued to burn. Ward Gunn, who had kept on firing throughout, was hit in the forehead and killed instantly. Pinney pushed his body out of the way and went on firing until further hits made the gun unusable. He drove away unscathed.[9]

Tom Bird saw the whole action and acted as a witness for the VC recommendations which followed. He wrote: 'I should not have thought it possible to carry on under such heavy fire and remain so calm and unconcerned as Bernard.'

Pinney still tried to do more. Back at Battery HQ, he gave orders to get a damaged portee back into action.

> What followed was not easy to perform, but the situation was serious. The new detachment were of necessity given the task of preparing their gun for action, and therefore, to remove from it the remains of their predecessors. The stern and urgent needs of battle were paramount, and in utter silence they made ready for their contribution and complied with the order: 'You men get these men's bodies scraped off the gun and get it back into action as quickly as possible.'[10]

The Germans did not press home their attack, but tried again later in the day. Their resolve had taken a severe knock, however, and they withdrew as soon as they encountered resistance from what remained of Pinney's battery. That night, Brigadier 'Jock' Campbell, commanding the Support Group, visited Pinney and the survivors. Campbell had himself performed actions that day which would result in a VC, but he told Pinney that he and his men had changed the entire course of the day's action.

Pinney was recommended for the VC, but was instead mentioned in dispatches. He would have been well content that the VC went posthumously to Ward Gunn, although he did not live to hear the news – he was killed the next morning, at the age of thirty-eight.

> After leaguering for the night, 'C' Troop awoke to find a German tank leaguer about 3,000–4,000 yards away. This was instantly engaged by 60th Field Regiment and the Troop, and, after some delay, by our own tanks. The enemy did not stay, but withdrew. At about 0730hrs Major Pinney took another gun and portee up to 'C' Troop. By then the firing had died down. At about 0745hrs it was noticed that he was missing, and a search of the area resulted in the discovery of his body. He had been killed by a small shell splinter at the base of the skull.[11]

Pinney's mother broke the news to Robertson in a brief letter on Boxing Day:

> My dear Bobber and Sheila,
> You must be one of the first to know Bernard has earned the right to be one of your honoured dead. The news only reached us this morning though the date given is November 22nd 'Middle East' – in the Libyan Battle we expect – soon after it began, leading his 'J' Battery RHA …
> Your friend,
> Hester Pinney[12]

* * *

Soon after the accompanying photograph overleaf was taken, a message arrived from the King's Dragoon Guards that two of their armoured cars had broken down back near the Tobruk perimeter, and that German artillery was using them for target practice. Gardner set out with Gearing, each in a Matilda tank, to see what could be done to help. Gardner found that only one armoured car now survived, and ordered Gearing to distract the enemy while he attempted to tow it to safety. He did not succeed; enemy fire wounded him in the leg, killed his loader, and severed the tow-rope. By now, only one man from the armoured car crews survived, Lieutenant Beame (who had lost his legs). Gardner somehow got Beame on to the rear decking of his Matilda – being wounded in the arm as he did so – and managed to get his two tanks back to safety. For this, Gardner was awarded the Victoria Cross.

However, Rommel had counter-attacked that day, and it seemed as though Operation Crusader was about to end in ignominious defeat. By nightfall on November 24th, Allied vehicles were streaming back towards Egypt. Only the personal intervention of General Auchinleck, Commander-in-Chief of Middle East Forces, prevented collapse.

Meanwhile, 2nd New Zealand Division had been pushing tentatively along the escarpment towards Ed Duda, and launched night attacks in the Sidi Rezegh area on November 25th. 32 Army Tank Brigade also attacked. 2nd Leicesters and 'D'/7RTR attacked near BUTCH to secure the salient's base and flank, whilst Simpkin again became embroiled in fierce action. His medal citation is terse:

> On another occasion he was ordered to act as Battalion Reconnaissance Officer in the unexpected absence of that officer. He took bearings and led the Battalion with great skill into the attack on WOLF, in the night, fighting his Troop with great dash and determination.[13]

This well-known photograph was taken on November 23rd, as Simpkin was taking a break beside a Matilda (named 'Defiance'); with Simpkin are Captain Pip Gardner MC (left), Major A.G. Roberts (commanding 'C'/4RTR), & 2nd Lieutenant Paul Gearing (right). (IWM E 6804; edited by DB Colour)

WOLF was the last enemy position between Tobruk and Ed Duda and was held by Italians of the *Bologna* Division, who had already proven tenacious in defence. 2nd York & Lancasters attacked, with 4RTR in support. As the attack went in, the infantry suffered heavy casualties, and four Matildas from 'A'/4RTR struck mines, but 'B'/4RTR broke in from the flank. By 2230hrs most of the position was in British hands, and at first light 'C'/4RTR helped to clear the rest of WOLF. The attack had captured 200 prisoners (including the commanding officer of the *Bologna* Division), two of the feared German 88mm guns, and twelve Italian 37mm guns. It was now time, at last, to seize Ed Duda, and at 1146hrs on November 26th the attack began, spearheaded by 1RTR and 4RTR. Despite severe losses, and ferocious counter-attacks, the Tobruk break-out force had secured its objective by 1700hrs. Physical contact was made with the New Zealanders at 1830hrs, 230 days after the siege of Tobruk had begun.

But the fighting was still far from over. The corridor which now linked Tobruk to Ed Duda was long and narrow, the forces which had created it down to fewer than fifty battered tanks and tiny numbers of exhausted infantry, and the Axis forces were determined to annihilate 2nd New Zealand Division around Sidi Rezegh. Three of Rommel's divisions were launched into the attack: 15th and 21st *Panzer*, and the tanks of the Italian *Ariete*. On November 29th, 15th *Panzer* Division nearly overran Ed Duda. Simpkin was one of those who stopped them:

> Again at Ed Duda on 29th November this officer took part in a counter-attack on the enemy when his tank ran on to a mine-field hastily laid by the enemy. He was unable to extricate his tank for some hours, but remained with his crew, fighting with the utmost determination for five hours before towing operations could be carried out. His tank was penetrated, and he and his gunner were wounded.[14]

At first light on December 4th Rommel made one last attempt to drive the Tobruk garrison from Ed Duda – but failed. Shortly afterwards, reduced to a mere forty tanks, *Panzerarmee Afrika* admitted defeat, abandoned the siege of Tobruk, and began a retreat which took them back to where they had started, beyond Benghazi. It was the first time that a German army had been defeated in the Second World War.

The cost had been high. 4RTR and 'D'/7RTR had suffered casualties of eighty-five officers and men; Simpkin's commanding officer, Lieutenant Colonel Walter O'Carroll DSO, was at the end of his tether, having been concealing that he was suffering from tuberculosis. Nevertheless, O'Carroll took the time to write medal recommendations, including one putting Simpkin forward for an MC. The quotations about Simpkin's conduct above are drawn from that citation, which was received by Brigade on December 13th. The commanding officer of 32 Army Tank Brigade, Brigadier Willison, annotated the citation with a hand-written 'Strongly recommended. I saw him at Ed Duda.'

The document passed on to Division within twenty-four hours, being signed by Major General Scobie, commanding Tobruk Fortress. Lieutenant General Ritchie – who had taken over Eighth Army in the middle of the fighting – approved the award on December 23rd. The final signature was Auchinleck's.

* * *

Grant and Murray were having a much less exciting time on the Faroes. From the spring of 1941, the occasional attack by German aircraft – usually on shipping – had relieved the monotony, and Angus Grant commented on one such raid in a letter written on December 7th 1941:

> Life is much the same as when I wrote to you a year ago – at present we are struggling with winter gales, which appear to be unusually severe this winter. What with huts blowing down, mines coming ashore, and getting the rations, etc., round the islands, we have our hands fairly full. The men, however, are getting pretty handy at 'living on the country' – in fact it is quite a popular game as it means they get coffee and eggs from the locals, for which His Majesty will eventually have to stump up.
>
> The men are in fairly good heart in spite of our twenty months spent out here, but we hope and pray that the Madhouse at Whitehall will let us off with two years. We

have occasional aeroplanes over, but they don't do much harm – they prefer attacking Faroese smacks, to tell the truth. However, recently we have had hardly any, as I dare say they find 'the German Ocean' rather unkind in December.

Did you hear about the diary belonging to a Hun pilot whose aeroplane crashed into one of the hills here? He had been all over the east coast of Scotland and on one occasion over Fort William, where he dropped bombs the effect of which he was not able to see owing to mist. The diary was about the only thing we found, as his bombs must have exploded when he crashed. The Corporal sent up to investigate reported that all he could find was 'One diary, some twisted MGs and other metal, and about 200lbs of meat!'

The locals are extraordinarily good to the men and to ourselves, and this says a lot for the men's behaviour after twenty months of garrison work. The only trouble with them (the locals) is drink – they'll do anything for a bottle of whisky or methylated spirits. The other day a small boat with about ten fishermen on board arrived back in the evening from a fishing expedition in various stages of illness. They had picked up a barrel of something in the sea and tasted it. One of them had the bright idea that there was a possibility of getting drunk, so they drank it on the off-chance. This they did successfully, but got a bit more than they bargained for, as the liquid turned out to be wood spirit. Two of them died and two have gone blind. I don't know if this very macabre story will serve as material for speeches in debating society on Total Prohibition!

ENSA have just started sending up parties here (they might almost have managed this before we had spent 1½ years here). The first one was taken aback slightly by the West Coasters' method of expressing their approval – a sort of clucking noise from the back of the throat!

I don't know if I told you that Willie Gammell was posted to us about six months ago. He was in Phil's (?) shortly after the last war and says he finished his time in your div. He's a real good fellow and a great reinforcement to the Wykehamist or rather Wykehamical elements among us. He is at present doing ADC to his brother, who commands some Division, but he is to return shortly I hope.

If and when you have time, I should be very interested to hear what Hopperites, especially those of my own year, are up to.[15]

* * *

Convoy WS12 had stopped off at Aden on November 28th, and the *Samaria* docked at Port Tewfik in Egypt on December 5th. And so it was that when Tompson wrote home on December 7th – the day of the Japanese attack on Pearl Harbor – he had finally reached the war.

I am afraid this will be very untidy indeed as it is written by doubtful candlelight; I feel so unhappy that I won't be with you for Christmas, this year, anyway; but if this should reach you about that time remember that I shall be thinking of you. I hope you have got anyhow some of the letters I have written, because if you haven't it will be a little discouraging for one who as you know was never at any time a good letter-writer.

We have been now to so many odd places that I feel I know quite a lot about these native people; they still treat us all like tourists and 'do' you right and left. I do feel the more I see of them the more I look forward to coming home; and you can rest assured that however great our income tax becomes, I will not be driven to living abroad for nine months in the year!

I seem to have everything I need, which is a great comfort. I have also got a camp table like William's which has been invaluable on the voyage and I feel sure will continue to be. I can't tell you how wonderfully they have all behaved, the men in particular. Living honestly under unforgivable conditions and filthy food, they have kept clean and happy, which 'makes you marvel'. I simply can't think why the Government let these shipping companies blatantly make money out of the troops, but they must have made a fortune out of us alone. The sailors themselves are very nice, but below decks there is a nest of stewards – head, chief, and ordinary – who are nothing but shits. I can't tell you just how bloody they were to us all.

They seem to have done a great deal of messing about with the clocks lately so that it begins to get dark at about 1430hrs and light at the same time in the morning (slightly exaggerated) … I met John [Armitage], who was at Winchester with me, and we played a lot of bridge together and is now, I hope, a lifelong friend; it's maddening to me to think of all the people I knew and disliked when there, that I have met since and really liked; him, for instance.[16]

* * *

Hugh Rose was by now at 165 OCTU in Dunbar, and described his training vividly to his sisters Elizabeth and Madeleine in a letter written on December 9th:[17]

We had a fearsome week after I saw you, and this week's training may be as bad … We got generally chased by everyone last week. By the Drill Sergeant for being lazy on parade – or rather, not smart enough. And also there was a great row because we appeared to be slack about cleaning and dusting our rooms, so as a result we had to do a double lot of scrubbing during the week …

I thought we were in for a fearful week, but so far it hasn't been too bad. I started off yesterday poorly, by having another bilious attack in the small hours of the morning. Also we had a gas test, when one has to be gassed for two minutes with a gas which irritates the nose or throat and is supposed to give you mental depression. However, it wasn't half as bad as people made out, and I must have a fairly iron constitution, for I didn't feel any marked untoward effects except that one sneezed continuously for a quarter of an hour on emerging. In the afternoon we were meant to give little talks on our lectures, and of course I haven't looked at my notes much yet, but luckily I didn't have to perform.

Today we had a map-reading test, which meant a pleasant walk across the hills, for we weren't allowed to travel on roads.

* * *

Fortune had been having a spot of bother, as he informed Robertson on December 10th:

Thank you so much for 'Libyan Sands' and for your letter – which are both very informative. You ask for a bulletin – well here is the truth, which I gather from your and other people's letters, has become distorted.

It all occurred on exercise on the 'Black Isle'. We had been fighting all day and just completed the battle and were on our way home. It was by this time dark – and when I say dark it really was pitch black, and visibility was nil. On the road near Fortrose I unfortunately met with an accident. I was on a motor-bike and came round a corner and before I knew where I was had hit one of my own blasted Bren Carriers which was foolishly standing in the middle of the road with no lights. Its lights had fused, but instead of getting off the road, it remained on the main thoroughfare and plumb in the centre of it. Luckily I was not going more than about 15mph, but I struck the carrier with my right leg on the near-side track and was flung headlong into the ditch. The motor-bike did not suffer – neither did the carrier. But my right leg was far from whole.

However, they picked me up and put me in a truck and brought me in here at great speed, where they soon had me under anaesthetic and were patching up the damage. Luckily there was nothing broken, and the only major damage was two rather large and unsightly gashes in my leg – one just below the knee and the other further down across the shin. The former luckily missed the actual knee and the latter was right through to the bone – but no further. They put the whole thing in plaster and kept it there for sixteen days. The day before yesterday they took it out, and both wounds seem to have healed remarkably well – though when I shall be able to use my leg again I don't know. The whole thing was very lucky as owing to the metal content and size of the thing I hit, the damage might have been very much worse.

I hope to have some of the stitches out today.

My mother was up here for a few days but has now gone home – she was in great form and behaved rather like Florence Nightingale, going round the whole ward doing things for people. My locker, where I was supposed to keep my belongings, is needless to say full of food, etc., collected by the 'Evergreen'!

I hope our lot in Libya are doing well. Hugh Rose is, I believe, getting on all right at Dunbar, though he says his slowness of movement has become noted throughout his company! He is, incidentally, in the same company as I was and lives in the same hotel. I expect you have heard from him.

I have in the bed next to me an Australian, forty-nine years old, who broke his pelvis in a car smash. A very good chap and keeps us all amused. He has been in the same position for six weeks and consequently is getting rather 'browned off', all done up in plaster from his chest down to his left toe. He tells me he was bombed in Liverpool and was buried and suffers slightly from claustrophobia, and the plaster on his chest has a consequent ill effect on him. He wakes in the middle of the night and feels he is buried again and suffocating and very nearly tears the plaster off him. Still he is very cheerful, and that is the main thing.

On my other side is an RAF Pilot Officer who crashed a Defiant – breaking some small bone in his neck. He also is all in plaster from head to waist. But he manages to get up and wheel himself about in a chair. The rest of the inmates of my ward are nearly all suffering from rotten stomachs – and are dieting hard, with one appendix, one who has just had his left kidney removed, one who came in with a bit of Bakelite

> in his torso from a bomb which exploded while he was giving a demonstration. We are a motley crew, but all quite cheerful.
>
> I hope to be out of here in the next ten days or so, though how long it is going to take me to walk goodness knows. I hope not long. The only complication will be if my knee gives trouble.[18]

The hole in Fortune's knee was still visible fifty years later.

* * *

Duncan McMurtrie left Sunnyside a term later than Elliott-Binns, on December 16th, and joined his friend in Cambridge, where he had won a Classical Exhibition to Trinity Hall. His younger brother Anthony summed up Duncan's character as follows:

> He had very wide interests: butterflies, birds, charting a lake, fishing (there's a photograph of him as a boy holding a fishing rod in Scotland), art. My mother had a horse, and a pony for her boys, and Duncan went riding with her around the countryside around the farms or cross-country hacking. He invented the expression 'Beside, Beside' – meaning to ride alongside each other – which she thought was lovely. He just enjoyed hacking around the countryside as a child – no serious competitions or anything like that.
>
> Very often he'd spend quite a long time – I would almost say 'locked away' – in his bedroom, thinking or writing, or most likely writing. He didn't sit downstairs with our parents and go chatting away about nothing. He was busy doing things upstairs in his room, but he was not introverted. He didn't agree with everything everybody said. He liked a good argument. He did argue with authority figures, including my father. I think it was unspoken that after the war he would go into the law. If he had, he would have done extremely well, but I don't think he would have found life at all easy; because he was so clever, he would have found life very frustrating, I think.
>
> Between leaving school and going to Cambridge, I suppose there were maybe two or three months. So he joined the Home Guard. We had a unit up in the village, which is a ten minute walk, and he used to go walking up there in the evening with our gardener, who was another member of the Home Guard. They had a lovely time together playing soldiers in the village hall, a bit like 'Dad's Army' really – but it didn't last very long, because he then quite quickly went up to Cambridge.
>
> When he was at Cambridge, he was with his great friend Michael Elliott-Binns. They were very, very close – only emotionally; you could almost say blood brothers. Nothing more than that. After the war, Michael came to see us at our house, the Grange. He was an unusual man, a very unusual man, actually. He came to lunch. Quite charming. But sadly he didn't live very long after that.[19]

* * *

Along with McMurtrie, three other Hopperites left in December1941: Henry Brooke, Michael Finch, and Arthur Herbert.

Brooke.

Finch.

Herbert.

Finch went to take a War Degree in Classics at Corpus Christi, Oxford.[20] Henry Brooke was the son of a wine merchant, but his Anglo-Irish family had long-established military connections, to the extent that they had been labelled the 'Fighting Brookes'.[21] The most famous of his relatives was the great Field Marshal Lord Alanbrooke, Churchill's Chief of the Imperial General Staff – the professional head of Britain's armed forces for much of the Second World War. Henry Brooke would show himself made of the same stuff. He did not go to university on leaving; nor did Arthur Herbert, to start with.[22]

Herbert's mother, Marjorie, was the sister of the Alan Ferguson with whom Robertson had joined 9DWR, and who had been killed in action on the Somme in 1916; one can imagine how close an eye Robertson kept on his dead friend's nephew. Herbert had, in fact, already joined the Army by the time that he left Sunnyside; taking advantage of the half day every Wednesday, he had travelled down to Southampton on November 5th 1941 and enlisted in the Royal Corps of Signals. His attestation form stated that this young man appeared to be seventeen years and ten months old, with a fresh complexion, brown eyes, and fair hair. He stood 5′ 9″ tall, weighed in at 124½lbs, and had a chest size (expanded) of 33½ inches. He was assessed as in A1 physical condition, and immediately released back to school.

* * *

On December 14th, two days before Brooke, Finch, Herbert, and McMurtrie left Robertson's care, Rigby wrote to his former housemaster about how his officer training was going at Blackdown.

Rigby.

> I was called up and came straight to this OCTU. It is rightly considered to be about the most efficient OCTU in the area. I have had two months here and the first six weeks were pretty good hell! Most people who come here have already had at least a year's service and have been NCOs. They are also much older men. Even these chaps say that this is the worst place they have been to, so you can imagine what it was like for me at first, who did not even know how to make an Army bed feel comfortable.
>
> However, all that is past, and, now we have got down to our technical training, life is becoming most amusing. A very small portion of our time is spent in lectures; mostly we do practical training: driving (tanks, motor-bikes, cars), all sorts of gunnery, and wireless. When these technical courses are over we have six weeks collective training,

Christmas card to MR from J.A.C. Richardson, December 1941. (Winchester College Archives)

mostly TEWTs; and then having passed innumerable exams we should get commissioned some time at the beginning of April. When I say 'we', I mean the troop of thirty or so of which I am one, and in which I stay till the end of the six months here. I have managed to get home for a couple of week-ends and I think we will get six days at Christmas, when I hope all the family will reunite.[23]

Pinney.

John Pinney, Bernard's younger brother, had left Sunnyside in April 1939 and started a degree in French and German at Christ Church, Oxford. This he had abandoned in 1940, joining the Royal Fusiliers before taking a commission. But his commission was unusual; he was placed on the General List, which provided a home for specialists who were not going to be posted to specific regiments or corps. It was almost certainly his languages which sent 180513 Officer Cadet John Pinney direct from his OCTU to be a 2nd Lieutenant 'without Army pay and allowance' on March 15th 1941.[24] In fact, he had been attached to the Colonial Service and posted to Kenya. On January 11th 1942, in a letter to his parents, he responded to the death of his brother:[25]

Many thanks for a letter from Mama and diary received yesterday (dated October 27th). Other than the sad cable about Bernard, these are the only letters I have received for some while. Perhaps the mail ships have been singled out each time.

How you must miss Bernard, where all around you reminds you of him – his home, his horse, and all his goods and chattels. It's bad enough here where his photo, a letter, and his memory are what one remembers him by.

I have just put in a strongly worded application to go and do some soldiering, backed by a letter from the District Commissioner. I wonder if it will move the colossi of the Secretariat.

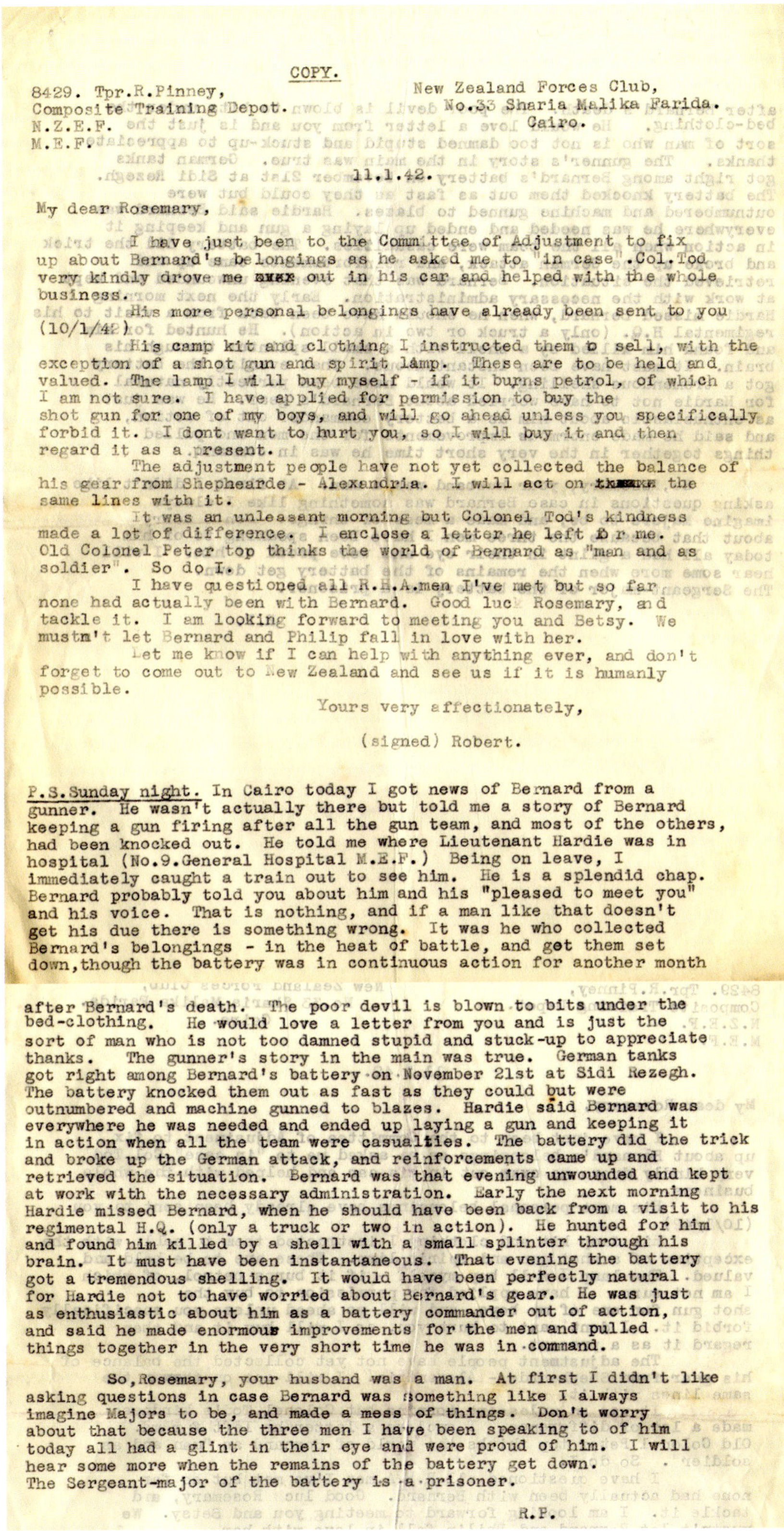

COPY.

8429. Tpr.R.Pinney,
Composite Training Depot.
N.Z.E.F.
M.E.F.

New Zealand Forces Club,
No.33 Sharia Malika Farida.
Cairo.

11.1.42.

My dear Rosemary,

I have just been to the Committee of Adjustment to fix up about Bernard's belongings as he asked me to "in case".Col.Tod very kindly drove me xxxx out in his car and helped with the whole business.

His more personal belongings have already been sent to you (10/1/42)

His camp kit and clothing I instructed them to sell, with the exception of a shot gun and spirit lamp. These are to be held and valued. The lamp I will buy myself - if it burns petrol, of which I am not sure. I have applied for permission to buy the shot gun for one of my boys, and will go ahead unless you specifically forbid it. I dont want to hurt you, so I will buy it and then regard it as a present.

The adjustment people have not yet collected the balance of his gear from Shephearde - Alexandria. I will act on thxxxx the same lines with it.

It was an unleasant morning but Colonel Tod's kindness made a lot of difference. I enclose a letter he left for me. Old Colonel Peter top thinks the world of Bernard as "man and as soldier". So do I.

I have questioned all R.H.A.men I've met but so far none had actually been with Bernard. Good luck Rosemary, and tackle it. I am looking forward to meeting you and Betsy. We mustn't let Bernard and Philip fall in love with her.

Let me know if I can help with anything ever, and don't forget to come out to New Zealand and see us if it is humanly possible.

Yours very affectionately,

(signed) Robert.

P.S.Sunday night. In Cairo today I got news of Bernard from a gunner. He wasn't actually there but told me a story of Bernard keeping a gun firing after all the gun team, and most of the others, had been knocked out. He told me where Lieutenant Hardie was in hospital (No.9.General Hospital M.E.F.) Being on leave, I immediately caught a train out to see him. He is a splendid chap. Bernard probably told you about him and his "pleased to meet you" and his voice. That is nothing, and if a man like that doesn't get his due there is something wrong. It was he who collected Bernard's belongings - in the heat of battle, and get them set down,though the battery was in continuous action for another month after Bernard's death. The poor devil is blown to bits under the bed-clothing. He would love a letter from you and is just the sort of man who is not too damned stupid and stuck-up to appreciate thanks. The gunner's story in the main was true. German tanks got right among Bernard's battery on November 21st at Sidi Rezegh. The battery knocked them out as fast as they could but were outnumbered and machine gunned to blazes. Hardie said Bernard was everywhere he was needed and ended up laying a gun and keeping it in action when all the team were casualties. The battery did the trick and broke up the German attack, and reinforcements came up and retrieved the situation. Bernard was that evening unwounded and kept at work with the necessary administration. Early the next morning Hardie missed Bernard, when he should have been back from a visit to his regimental H.Q. (only a truck or two in action). He hunted for him and found him killed by a shell with a small splinter through his brain. It must have been instantaneous. That evening the battery got a tremendous shelling. It would have been perfectly natural for Hardie not to have worried about Bernard's gear. He was just as enthusiastic about him as a battery commander out of action, and said he made enormous improvements for the men and pulled things together in the very short time he was in command.

So,Rosemary, your husband was a man. At first I didn't like asking questions in case Bernard was something like I always imagine Majors to be, and made a mess of things. Don't worry about that because the three men I have been speaking to of him today all had a glint in their eye and were proud of him. I will hear some more when the remains of the battery get down. The Sergeant-major of the battery is a prisoner.

R.P.

VII

'The grimness of life is beyond words'

January–July 1942

Tompson.

Commonwealth troops had followed the retreating *Panzerarmee Afrika* through Cyrenaica during December 1941, until, early in January 1942, the enemy reached the line from which they had started, near Agedabia and El Agheila on the eastern shores of the Gulf of Sirte. The battered units which had spearheaded Operation Crusader were withdrawn, and the inexperienced 1st Armoured Division took over the task of holding the front line. Auchinleck expected a pause in operations whilst both sides regrouped, and he started to build up supplies ready for a renewed offensive in February. 1st Armoured Division took over at the front, but made the mistake of spreading its units too thinly across the desert, using the model of all-arms 'Jock Columns' operating independently with penny-packets of infantry, artillery, anti-tank guns, and anti-aircraft guns. Hew Tompson was to suffer the consequences.

On January 14th 1942, 11RHA's war diary recorded its dispersal into 'Baron' column, named after Tompson's commanding officer – Lieutenant Colonel W.A. Ebbels MC – whose nickname was 'Baron'.[1] The following day, 'James' Column was formed, under the command of Lieutenant Colonel 'Jimmy' Bosvile, yet another Wykehamist.[2] These *ad hoc* battlegroups moved out on January 16th to take over the front line from 7th Armoured Division:

> January 18th, 0600hrs
> BARON Column took over from LINDON Column (7 Support Group) and at first light advanced ten miles and occupied OP and gun positions, from which enemy positions were kept under observation and all targets that presented themselves engaged. Column withdrew at dusk…
>
> January 19th, 0600hrs
> BARON Column again advanced ten miles, but nothing eventful reported all day.
>
> January 20th
> BARON and JAMES columns continued patrol and OP activities in area west of BETTAFUL… Visibility all day poor owing to slight sand storm. Exceptionally quiet day, with very little enemy movement seen.[3]

In a Western, someone would at this point have said, 'It's quiet; too quiet.'

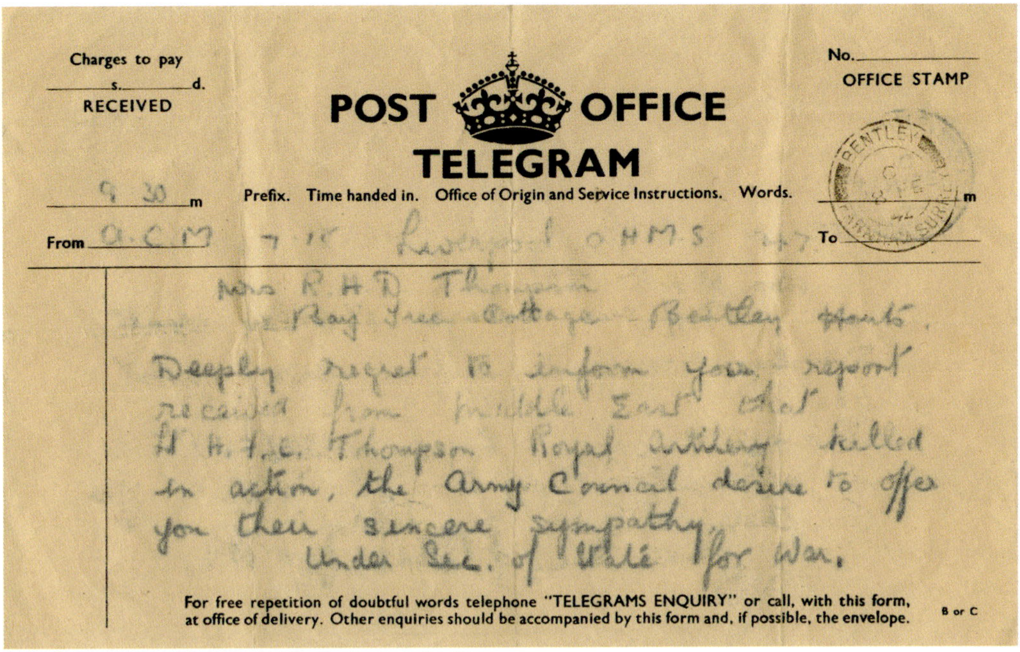
Charges to pay
s. d.
RECEIVED

POST OFFICE
TELEGRAM

No.
OFFICE STAMP
BENTLEY 8 FE 42

9.30 m   Prefix. Time handed in. Office of Origin and Service Instructions. Words.
From O.C.M 7.K Liverpool OHMS 47   To

Mrs R.H.D Thompson
Bay Tree Cottage Bentley Hants.
Deeply regret to inform you report
received from Middle East that
Lt H.J.C. Thompson Royal Artillery killed
in action, the Army Council desire to offer
you their sincere sympathy.
Under Sec. of State for War.

For free repetition of doubtful words telephone "TELEGRAMS ENQUIRY" or call, with this form, at office of delivery. Other enquiries should be accompanied by this form and, if possible, the envelope.   B or C

The dreaded telegram reached Tompson's mother on the morning of February 8th. She broke the news to Robertson in what he described as a 'brave letter', written the very next day:

> Dear Major Robertson,
> I feel I must write our truly sad news to you – I cannot let you see it in the paper – we heard yesterday morning that Hew had been killed in action in Libya – You have been such a true friend to him and indeed to us all, and I feel that you and your sister will realise almost more than anyone just how awful it is – Indeed, there is just nothing to be said, but I did want you both to know – We did know that his Regiment, 11th (HAC) RHA was in the thick of it in Libya.
> I do hope you are both well.
> Yours ever
> Bridget Tompson[4]

As usual, Robertson replied immediately, and Mrs Tompson replied equally swiftly:

> My dear Major Robertson,
> So very many thanks for your letter – I am so grateful for it and for the one you sent me which you had from Hew. I have had no particulars; I heard from the War Office yesterday that there were no particulars that could be given, not even a date – I do not know in which month it happened. Our last letter was dated January 7th and I know mails have been in from Libya as late as January 14th, so it may have been between those two dates. We have one or two great friends in Cairo and I may eventually know

more and will let you know. Hew went abroad on September 29th and we had only had two letters since he arrived, a great many written on the voyage, and the cable to tell of his arrival – I am so glad you saw him and were pleased with him the last time he came to Winchester with Penelope – He did develop very much and there was much of his Father in him –

Indeed we were all so sorry to hear of Bernard Pinney's death; he was a delightful person and is a real and serious loss to the Regiment and indeed the Army – My son-in-law William Pike was a great friend of his and we knew him so well when he was at the Shop.[5]

The grimness of life is beyond words – and the news as bad as possible – What is going to become of us all?[6]

On the day on which she wrote this letter, Singapore fell to the Japanese, and Rickman went into captivity.

* * *

11RHA's war diary records that the pages covering January 1st to 20th were deliberately destroyed on the 23rd to 'avoid [them] falling into enemy hands', but the above extracts suggest that a copy had already been made. Certainly, a full diary survives for January 21st, the day on which the Germans smashed brutally into the dispersed British columns in the El Agheila area, their counter-attack as usual coming much sooner and more vigorously than anticipated. The Germans had been reinforced by sea, and now had the advantage of shorter supply lines. Their advance on Egypt would not stop until nine guns of 11RHA halted the *panzers* on Ruweisat Ridge, near Alamein, on July 2nd – the turning point of Britain's whole war. But that is another story.

0730hrs
Advance of BARON Column to normal OP and gun positions. The move forward from night leaguer area (B8262) was observed by enemy and our troops were shelled. The shelling, though heavy (approximately four 10.5cm guns) was ineffective and wild.

0830hrs
OPs established.

0930hrs
OPs report 40 enemy tanks and MT advancing. General order given for withdrawal. This was carried out by bounds… Enemy column divided in two, one moving up each flank. Everything went smoothly for about 15 miles, though several tractors and Bofors guns were lost in soft sand. At B9565 a wide sand dune belt was encountered. 'E' Battery had already taken up position covering this. BARON Column withdrew past CHARLES Column ('E' Battery) but many vehicles got hopelessly bogged in the sand. As a result, 'A' Battery lost six guns. 'E' Battery engaged tanks over open sights and then withdrew, losing three guns stuck in sand. Meanwhile JAMES Column ('B'

Battery) on left were being attacked and suffered equally, losing three guns. 'B' Battery Commander Major Linton also became missing about this time.

On clearing sand, withdrawal continued while enemy refuelled. Heavy dive-bombing attack at 1130hrs in which Lt H.F.C. Tompson was severely wounded and later died.[7]

Three days later, 'Slogger' Armitage was also mortally wounded in action. He had indeed proved, in Tompson's words, 'a lifelong friend'.

* * *

With no inkling of what the fighting in North Africa had in store for him that year, Hugh Rose wrote to his sister Madeleine ('Madey') from Dunbar on January 28th; it was her birthday.

I hope the coming year will be a very happy one, but I'll also add successful, because I'm sure it will be.

I have done nothing at all exciting since returning to Dunbar. We live under the shadow of daily threats and scares of extra drills and even getting chucked out. I thought we had passed that stage, but they seem to have revived the idea, I suppose to brace us up. Anyhow, the main point is that we sweat and toil the whole time in constant peril of some dire fate befalling us.

The weather has been somewhat beastlier than before. We have had snow, which meant we had to suffer the ignominy of being snowballed on the march by kids of five or six with no hope of retaliation or stopping them ... The roads, too, have been glassy, and in hobnails it is a great strain keeping on one's feet. I have fallen smack on my back more times than I like to remember, and I still feel sore.

One day, too, we had an endurance test, which involved running mostly, and clambering over rocks, up cliffs, and sliding down on back or seat (it was beyond one's control to decide which) and also we had to wade in the sea to get round one point in the cliffs. Wow, was it icy! However, this is all in the day's fun.

What gets me most annoyed and weary is sitting up late at nights cleaning stuff for Drill Parades. And one is inclined to relapse into that stupid and dazy state which I am sure you have experienced when one ploughs through the day's work with one idea – to wriggle worn-out between the blankets in the evening with a vague feeling that anyhow you are one day nearer better times.[8]

* * *

Details of Tompson's death began to filter through to his family from those who had been with him on his last day:

My dear Mrs Tompson,
Just a line to send you my very deepest sympathy over Hew. I know he must be a terrible loss to you; he is a great loss to the Regiment as a whole and to us in particular. I thought you might like to know that I do not think he suffered at all; he was badly

hit in a dive bombing attack, and I tried to get him back to an ambulance in my car, but he unfortunately died on the way without ever really regaining consciousness. He was buried by Colonel A. Bond, Senior Chaplain, HQ Middle East Force, who said he would write to you.

I was Second in Command of the Regiment at the time, and I expect you have heard from his Battery Commander …

Again with deepest sympathy.

Yours sincerely,

J.H. Benson[9]

Dear Mrs Tompson,

You will, I know, have heard the tragic news of Hew long before this reaches you, but although letters are small consolation at such a time, I am writing to say how deeply we all feel his loss and feel for you. I would have written sooner but for regulations forbidding mentioning casualties at the time of their occurrence.

He was killed by a bomb during a dive-bombing attack on a part of his Battery on the afternoon of January 21st. I saw him very shortly afterwards and he looked very peaceful and had obviously suffered no pain. He was buried in the desert after dark that night. Our padre was not available – but Major Benson found the Deputy Assistant Chaplain General – B.K. Bond – who read the service. A rough cross with his name and particulars were erected on the grave.

The nation can ill afford to lose such a splendid type of officer as Hew was. Beloved by his men – as well as by his brother officers – he was always keen and cheerful and very efficient. His loss is indeed a great one – not only to his nearest and dearest, but also to the Regiment and the Army as a whole.

My wife and I were particularly fond of him, and she I know will be terribly grieved by the news. It seems quite impossible to express to you how deeply we all feel for you – but it may be some small help to know that, although you have not met us, you are very much in our thoughts and have our very deepest sympathy in the loss of such a splendid, gallant son.

Yours very sincerely,

Wilfred Ebbels[10]

Interspersed with the expressions of sympathy were letters from Tompson himself, which continued to arrive despite the death of their author. The grave mentioned in the letter above was lost, just as was Bernard Pinney's, and never since located – and so Tompson and Pinney are commemorated on the Alamein Memorial.

The many kindly-intentioned letters of condolence could not be ignored, but the writing of replies to – in many cases – strangers made stressful demands on Mrs Tompson. Two letters written three days apart – one to the Headmaster of Winchester, and another to her son-in-law – show the contrast between the public and private faces which the bereaved wore:

Dear Mr Leeson,

Thank you so very much for writing to me. I am so grateful for your letter and for all you say in it – I do not know if you will remember how my husband's whole soul was in Hew's future; I hope it is not wrong of me to feel thankful he has been spared this, because now he will surely understand more of the meaning and purpose of all this suffering which we find so hard to fathom, or to face – At present I feel as if life had lost all point and purpose, but I know this is wrong and it will pass.

Hew did so well after he joined his Regiment; it was so comforting to see all the endless trouble that was taken over him at Winchester bearing fruit in every kind of way.

Thank you again so much for writing …[11]

I have written to so many people, and still have a pile of letters before me that I feel I can never answer and must – and I have never written to you, who are so far the most important person possible to whom I want to write –

Thank you more than I can say for your cable; you don't know what it was to get that lovely loving message, impossible for me to try and explain, nor can I possibly begin to say anything about it at all, and therefore you are easy to write to, because I know you understand this and there are so many letters in which one has to say something and just can't – to almost complete strangers like the Headmaster of Winchester – There is something so utterly stunning about a loss such as ours, impossible to explain – perhaps it is merciful to feel like this, though I never thought for one moment that Hew would get through, did you?

Jock Whiteley sent a cable from Cairo to say he had found out all particulars for us and had written them. I suppose we shall hear in about two months time. There is something terribly inhuman and grim about this utter lack of news. The Casualty Office could not even tell me the month.[12]

Robertson, however, seems not to have counted as a stranger. Mrs Tompson visited him in early October, and wrote soon afterwards:

It was lovely seeing you and your sister last week – I found lunch with my cousin more terribly trying than I would have imagined possible, and this may have partly been caused by the awful contrast with my visit to you! I quite wished I could have come to see you both after I had seen her – just to restore my balance.[13]

Another message of condolence came from HM King George VI.

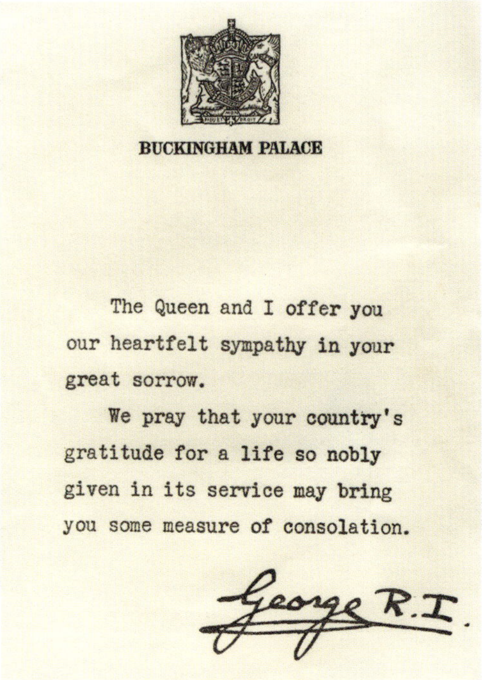
BUCKINGHAM PALACE

The Queen and I offer you our heartfelt sympathy in your great sorrow.

We pray that your country's gratitude for a life so nobly given in its service may bring you some measure of consolation.

George R.I.

* * *

Reeling from the loss of Cyrenaica, Britain was about to reach one of its lowest points in the entire war. The Japanese attack on Pearl Harbor on December 7th 1941 had been followed by a rapid series of disasters for the British in the Far East. Japanese troops overran Hong Kong swiftly, and poured into Burma and Malaya; the capital ships *Repulse* and *Prince of Wales* were sunk by Japanese aircraft. The fall of Singapore in February 1942 – the greatest British surrender in history – was the crowning humiliation.

Wavell, the greatest Wykehamist of the century, had been making every effort to blunt the enemy advance with the limited resources at his disposal. He had been intimately involved with the war as Commander-in-Chief, Middle East, a post which he had held from February 1940 until mid-1941, when Churchill had relieved him of it; in July 1941 he had become Commander-in-Chief, India. On January 1st 1942, at American request, Wavell was additionally appointed Supreme Commander of American-British-Dutch-Australian Command (ABDACOM), tasked with holding Burma, Malaya, Singapore, Sumatra, Java, Borneo, the Philippines, the Celebes, New Guinea, and Australia. If Wavell's forces had been as extensive as his geographical command, the plan might have had some merit. He did what he could with what he had. On January 7th he established ABDACOM headquarters in Singapore, moving it to Java on the 18th. But Allied resistance crumbled across the whole front, and Wavell resigned as Supreme Commander on February 25th, by which time there was no ABDACOM left to command. The final ABDA forces were destroyed in the Battle of the Java Sea in March.

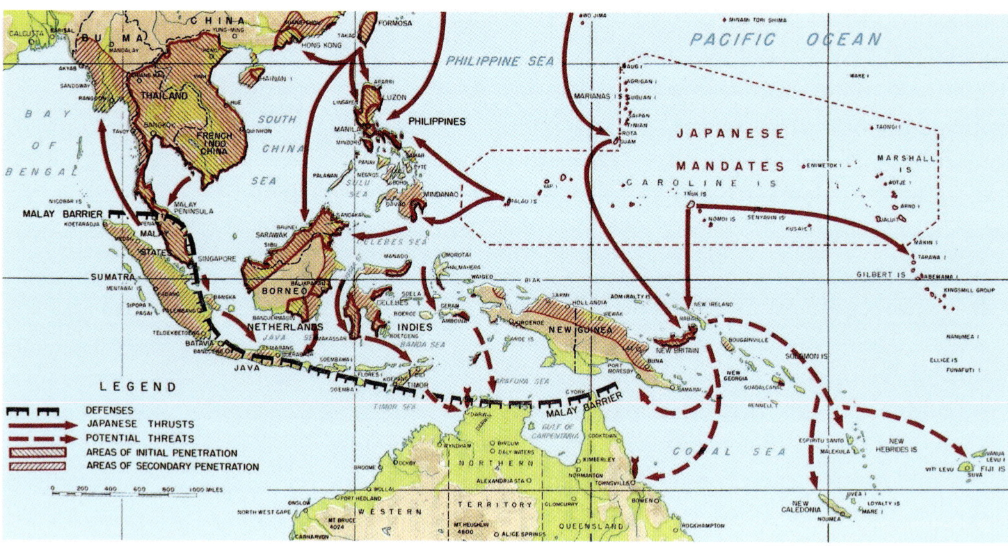

* * *

The first of our subjects to arrive in the Far East had been Pat Metcalfe, back in the autumn of 1941. Having completed his training as an Officer Cadet at the Mhow OCTU in India, he wrote to Robertson early in February 1942 from the Fighting Vehicles School at Ahmednagar, where all training associated with armour was conducted.

Thank you very much for your letter, giving me all the latest from Winchester; it was a great joy to receive it. It arrived last week just before I left Mhow, having finished 4½ months there. Now I have come here to learn about a tank for the next three months. But if you find time, to write another letter, would you address it, please, c/o my father, The Residency, Baluchistan, India, as by the time it comes, I expect I shall have left this place.

We left Mhow last Friday, amid great rejoicing, having learned practically nil there, and arrived here yesterday, Saturday, so I still know very little about this place. We are stuck right out in the hills, miles from anywhere, but I think, at any rate, the course is interesting, and we get four days' break in the middle, so time should pass fairly quickly. There are about seventy cadets in all here, divided up into squads of eight, each under a Corporal or Sergeant, and for the first six weeks do 'Driving and Maintenance', and then go on to 'Gunnery'. Meanwhile they do treat us as future officers and not as school-boys!

Last we heard of John, he was off to join the Battalion, so he may be anywhere now.[14]

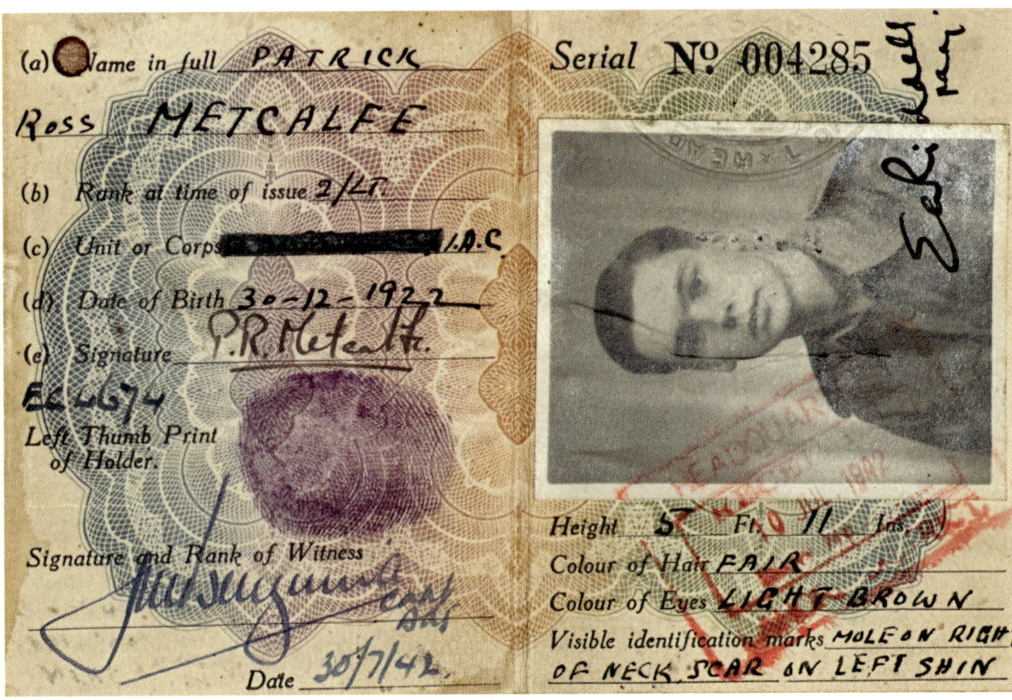

(a) Name in full PATRICK
ROSS METCALFE
(b) Rank at time of issue 2/LT.
(c) Unit or Corps [redacted] I.A.C
(d) Date of Birth 30-12-1922
(e) Signature P.R. Metcalfe.
EC6674
Left Thumb Print of Holder.
Signature and Rank of Witness
Date 30/7/42.

Serial No. 004285

Height 5 Ft. 11 Ins.
Colour of Hair FAIR
Colour of Eyes LIGHT BROWN
Visible identification marks MOLE ON RIGHT OF NECK SCAR ON LEFT SHIN

Metcalfe's older brother John – who had left Hopper's in 1937 – had joined the Coldstream Guards in 1940, and was in fact in North Africa with 3rd Battalion. By the end of the summer, he would be a prisoner of war.

Metcalfe would over time successfully complete three courses at the Fighting Vehicles School: Driving, Maintenance, and Armament (March 23rd to May 2nd 1942); Driving and Maintenance on the Stuart tank (November 21st 1942), and Stuart tank Armament (undated).

Tank crewmen of 7th Light Cavalry – with which Hirst would later serve – on their Stuart III (M3A1) tank, 1944. This picture was probably taken at Imphal. It was on vehicles such as these that Metcalfe trained at the Fighting Vehicles School. (National Army Museum 1981-11-72-8; unknown colourizer)

Rigby, who also later served in Stuarts, described them as follows in his memoirs:

> We had sixteen General Stuart Mark IIs, an American light tank: twenty-three tonnes each. They had a 37mm gun in the turret, co-axially mounted with a Browning machine-gun. You could mount another Browning on the outside of the turret for firing at low-flying aircraft. We carried 27,000 rounds of Browning ammo in belts, with one in three bullets being tracer, so you could see where you were firing. We had 125 rounds for the 37mm, mostly AP (armour piercing) but also HE (high explosive) and a few rounds of canister. The ammo was stored nose-down in rubber slots in a ring round the base of the turret. You could tell which was which when you were loading the guns, as the end of the brass shell cases had colour marks to tell you which kind of projectile to load. It was a four-man tank: driver, wireless operator, gunner, and crew commander. The crew commander was also the loader. We also carried a smoke discharger, a Very light pistol, some hand-grenades, and pistol ammunition.
>
> The Stuart had a seven-cylinder radial Continental aero engine running on high-octane fuel, developing 650 brake horse power. It would go at 45mph in fifth gear. When we were on long marches, we could start out with two jettisonable tanks of extra petrol strapped on top of the engine compartment; they connected to the fuel tanks. When the petrol in the extra tanks had been used up, you pulled a lever inside the turret and they simply rolled over the side and were left behind.

It had very reliable rubber tracks. If we wanted to climb steeply, or if it was muddy, we could fix metal bars called grousers across the tracks; then we could climb more or less anything.[15]

* * *

Rickman had been the next to arrive in the Far East, reaching Bombay in January 1942. By then he was a Captain in 9th Royal Northumberland Fusiliers, a machine-gun battalion in 18th Division. He seldom talked about his wartime experiences, but when in 1989 his grand-daughter Jessica asked him for help with a school project, he wrote a short account for her. Most of it was news even to his daughters.

Rickman.

A three month sea journey – from October 1941 to January 1942 – took some 20,000 British troops (including me) from Liverpool to Singapore, calling in *en route* at Halifax (Canada), Port of Spain (British West Indies), Capetown (South Africa), Mombasa (East Africa), and Bombay (India). We joined the garrison of Singapore only a fortnight before the island fell to the Japanese on their drive southwards towards Australia. As a professional soldier (I was a Captain in a machine-gun infantry regiment) I was attuned to the thought of possibly being wounded or even, at worst, killed – but one never contemplated the possibility of being captured by the enemy.[16]

However, Rickman and fellow Hopperite Sam Clayton were two of the 80,000 British, Indian, Australian, and local troops who went into Japanese captivity at Singapore.

On February 15th 1942 I was captured by renegade turncoat Sikh soldiers, who, unknown to us, had deserted to the Japanese in the middle of the battle, thinking, by so doing, that they could defeat the British, then the Imperial rulers of their country, India. At the early age of twenty-two, I therefore became a prisoner-of-war. It was three and a half years before I regained my liberty. Only by experiencing the loss of freedom can you really understand what the word 'liberty' means. Throughout these years of imprisonment, the worst thing was not being able to determine the length of one's sentence and date of release. The first six months were spent in Changi PoW camp, on the north-east corner of Singapore Island.[17]

On his release in 1945, Rickman reported that 'at Changi, in March 1942, all officers from the highest to the lowest in rank were forced to take down their badges of rank and made to wear one star or pip on the left breast. This is directly contrary to Geneva convention for the treatment of PoWs.'[18] It seems somewhat odd that Rickman selected this specific breach of protocol for comment when the Japanese did far worse things to officers than simply attack their status.

As always, Robertson was in touch with the family, and in April received the following from Rickman's anxious mother, Muriel. Despite her own misery and uncertainty about

Rickman's fate, she appreciated that Robertson, too, had an emotional investment in his former pupils.

> Dear Major Robertson,
> I am very grateful for your letter. One's friends can help one so much to keep a stiff upper lip. I am only one of many thousands just now who are tormented by anxiety as the result of the colossal tragedy of Singapore, to which Gerry went in the ill-fated 18th Division, which only arrived three days before it fell. He sailed at only a few days' notice in October and after a journey of three months disembarked at Bombay – and they were stationed about a hundred miles away – and I have just one letter from there – full of pleasure and interest in such a new and different kind of life – Since when I have had no news beyond the War Office telegram which knocked me sideways – as I never knew they had left Bombay.
>
> Whatever else I may lose, nothing can rob me of the happiness I got from being able to give him his time as a Wykehamist – and I know that if he is a prisoner of war his thoughts will return there over and over again. He was doing so well as an officer, and his men would have done anything for him – and he for them.
>
> My heart has never ceased aching for Mrs Tompson – to whom please give my love. The murder of the boys you have taught and cared for must hit you very hard too.[19]

* * *

The disaster of Singapore distracted the public from the dangers of the Japanese thrust through Burma towards India, but Wavell was well aware of the threat and returned to his role in India. A year later, in June 1943, he was appointed Viceroy, and shortly afterwards ennobled as Viscount Wavell of Cyrenaica and Winchester. He took over from Lord Linlithgow as Viceroy in October 1943.

The Japanese would continue to press towards and into India even as late as 1944, being stopped at Imphal and Kohima in some of the bitterest fighting of the war. Many Wykehamists were involved in these brutal actions and the brilliant campaigns by Field Marshal Bill Slim which pushed them out of Burma by the end of May 1945. Dodgson, Fortune, Herbert, Hirst, Metcalfe, Rigby, and Dan Somerville all served under these two outstanding commanders.

* * *

Simpkin's MC was 'gazetted' on February 24th 1942,[20] and on the same date he wrote to Robertson:

> Thank you so much for your postcard, which I received today, and for your congratulations. Actually, my wound was very slight, and I came straight out of hospital and back to duty after a couple of days. I hope all goes well with you in spite of catering problems. I'm so sorry your sister has been ill and has missed her holiday. I saw Jim Richardson about a month ago, and went sailing with him a couple of times.[21] I wonder how Guy

[Richardson]'s getting on – last I heard he'd had malaria – I imagine he's due home fairly soon now …[22]

* * *

Henry Brooke had joined the Royal Armoured Corps as a Trooper, receiving his basic training at Bovington, as he explained in a letter to Robertson in February:[23]

Brooke.

I am very sorry I haven't written before, but they certainly seem to find enough work for you here to keep you busy from the time you wake up at 0600hrs till the time you go to bed. The first five weeks were pretty hectic, while we were still on the square. That is to say we were doing general military training. At the end of the five weeks the troop is passed off the square in front of the CO. Then your specialized training starts: five weeks Driving and Maintenance, five weeks Gunnery, four weeks Wireless, and four weeks Collective Training, when all that you have learnt is put into practice. The courses are very well run, and the NCOs are excellent. But our training is terribly concentrated, doing in six months what should take about two years, so that by the time you have worked up your notes, and cleaned and polished your equipment, there is not much time to yourself.

But I am enjoying myself here immensely. The whole Regiment except the staff are between 18 and 19½, and everybody is pretty keen to get to a service unit. The lines of the 58th are pretty small for the number of troops here, and more are coming in, but space seems to be found for them. The food here is absolutely excellent; we have a professional caterer to look after the cookhouse. We have cocoa and cake at 1100hrs and supper as well as tea in the evening. We have a CO's parade every week, and there is a great deal of stress laid on smart turn-out. I am afraid Sheepshanks wouldn't like it here, as everything in the barrack room has to be dressed by the right: beds, boots, blankets – but you get so used to it it comes naturally.

Since this Regiment is unique in the Army we get dozens of generals coming to inspect us. Once they had three generals in two days; each time the Regiment has to turn out on a general's parade. I get a week's leave in a month's time so I will come and visit you one day if I may. Christopher Foot ('G')[24] is the only other Wykehamist besides us four. But I have met the brother of the Brookes in 'F'.

I do hope the house is flourishing and that it will decorate the sand-grouse before the end of the half.[25]

* * *

By contrast with Mrs Tompson's experiences, Angus Grant's parents heard of his death on the day it happened, March 18th 1942. Amazingly, despite the shock, they wrote to Robertson immediately:

My dear Malcolm,
I know that you and Sheila will be sad to hear that Angus was taken suddenly ill in the Faroes – where he had been with the Scouts nearly two years – and died this afternoon; acute kidney trouble. He was a good lad, not brainy but full of character and was very well reported on both from above and below him. I have always felt that you two were largely responsible for turning him out so well. That is why I want to thank you again, now that he has finished his job not without credit. It is a bit shattering, but Margery, who is taking it splendidly, and I get comfort in the feeling that both we and Angus himself are in a noble company in these times.

I hope that you are both well. If I know you, you will both be overworking yourselves grossly.

Iain and his wife are still in the West: he instructing the Army in hill-craft. She is a dear and we are lucky to have such a daughter-in-law. There isn't any use in wishing one was younger, but in these brave times, it is a bit irksome to command a Home Guard Company covering 1000 square miles.

Our love to you both
Yours ever
Iain Grant[26]

Grant had been twenty-one years old, a popular officer, whose death was described in the history of the Lovat Scouts as 'a tragic loss to his many friends … Angus was one of the finest and most popular troop leaders in the Regiment'.[27] His conscientious thoroughness and gentle courtesy had apparently endeared him to his brother officers and men; he was 'a first rate troop leader, an enthusiast for the pipes, a student of Gaelic, a lover of Highland hills and glens, and one for whom nothing was too much trouble'.

* * *

This photograph, from Ellemi Rubeksen's albums, shows several Faroes girls & British servicemen. Ellemi is at left with the mixing bowl. (Fuggle family collection)

In January 2023, out of the blue, Grant's nephew Johnnie received a letter from the son of a wartime RAF wireless operator who had been stationed on the Faroes in 1943. Kenneth Fuggle married one of the islanders, Ellen Marie 'Ellemi' Rubeksen, the daughter of the harbourmaster in Thorshavn (capital of the Faroes, in the south-east of the island of Strymoy). Ellemi was a dental nurse, aged twenty-two, the youngest of four children, and lived with her parents at 32 Torsgota. Fuggle asked her three times to marry him before she accepted, and he later said that he knew that he was not her first love.[28]

Among Ellemi's effects when she died, aged fifty-seven, in 1978, was an album including photographs of life in wartime Thorshavn. There are snaps of smiling girls with soldiers and airmen; of a Lovat Scouts piper; of the Lovat Scouts patrolling the mountains; and of Nissen huts in the bleak countryside.

Prominent among the images is a portrait photograph of Grant, labelled 'Anges' Grant (Ellemi was always told at school that she would not be any good at English). Ellemi can only have received such a formal portrait from Grant or his family. But the most striking sequence consists of eleven photographs of Grant's funeral.

With the photographs are a few scrappy informal letters in Grant's handwriting.

My dear Elemi [*sic*],
Would you care to come to a small party over here at 2100hrs on Saturday evening (April 26th)? You told me you had friends in Gote,[29] or better still why not stay with the Haraldsens here? I hope that you could manage to come. I think I could arrange to get you by car to or from Gote, from Fuglefjord. Do your best.
Yours,
Angus Grant[30]

My dear Ellemi,
I have seen very little of you recently, apart from waving to you across the street occasionally. However, can you put that state of affairs right by coming on Saturday (28th) to a small party for officers at the [Hotel] Foroyar?
Perhaps you could write me another of those charming letters saying if you can come.
Yours ever,
Angus
P.S. I would call for you at about 2130hrs on Saturday evening, if you find you can come.[31]

My dear Ellemi,
A very happy Christmas to you and I hope you will have a good holiday. Let me know if you will be in Ostero in the next few weeks – Sandy Fraser and I could get up a small party if you were over here.
Are my wife's teeth ready yet? If not, I think you are a very slow worker. I expect you are too busy playing Bob all day, instead of working.
If these gloves are too small, will you tell me. I do not think you will be able to get your enormous hands into them! I am afraid they will not quite arrive on Christmas Day as they have been very slow in Fuglefjord knitting them.
Wishing you a very Happy New Year from
Angus Grant[32]

My dear Ellemi,
A very late invitation I am afraid! Can you come to a small party tonight at 2130hrs at the club? Sorry to be so late about inviting you. Let me know if you can come – I shall be at Hotel Forayar between 1830hrs and 1900hrs so perhaps you could telephone me there. I am on duty tonight and shall be a little late coming to the party. However, I shall be there by 2145hrs.
Yours,
Angus[33]

These utterly trivial notes are very strange things for Ellemi to have kept unless she valued them above their apparent worth; taken with the evidence of the portrait photograph, and the funeral sequence (photographed for the most part from a window overlooking the procession), it seems probable that Ellemi Rubeksen and Angus Grant were in love. But for the war, their paths would never have intersected. Perhaps, given time, they might have married. But it was not to be. Unlike Tompson and Pinney, Angus Grant received a full military funeral; he guards the Faroes still, from grave 138 of the Torshavn Cemetery.[34]

Ellemi Rubeksen's sequence of pictures showing Grant's funeral. First, his coffin is carried down the steps of what is now Torshavn Cathedral; the coffin is then carried along Bryggjubakki (the houses in the view have not changed much, though the gardens opposite are much more luxuriant); the coffin is loaded on to a Bedford MWD utility vehicle; the procession forms up & winds its way through to the cemetery; & a Lovat Scouts piper plays a lament. The photograph of Grant's grave is more modern.

At least one more of Robertson's charges would find love because of the war – happily, this was to have a more cheerful sequel.

* * *

A few days after Grant's funeral, Murray wrote to Robertson from the Faroes:

Murray.

> Excuse the ink but I can't find any other just now.
>
> You will have heard about poor Angus by the time you get this. He died after a very short illness on Thursday. We are all very sad about it and he will be a very great loss to the Regiment, for he was one of the keenest and best fellows we've got. He was buried out here on Saturday. I shall miss him a lot as we've been together since we went to Win. Coll.
>
> I've just returned from two months in the UK on a course and I was able to get a good long leave. I got quite a lot of shooting and it did a lot to make me recover from the effect of a year in these islands!! I wonder how much longer they will leave us here. I only hope that it isn't for the duration, as it does become rather a strain on us all living in the same small messes all the time. I had the best part of six weeks entirely on my

> own before I went home. However, one does read a lot of books, but never has enough. I have one a month sent to me from home so manage to read one good book occasionally as well as a multitude of sixpenny detective stories. I read Nigel Weir's poems recently and some of them aren't at all bad; in fact, very good.[35]

* * *

Bernard Pinney's father wrote to Robertson in March, when he and his wife had digested their grief.

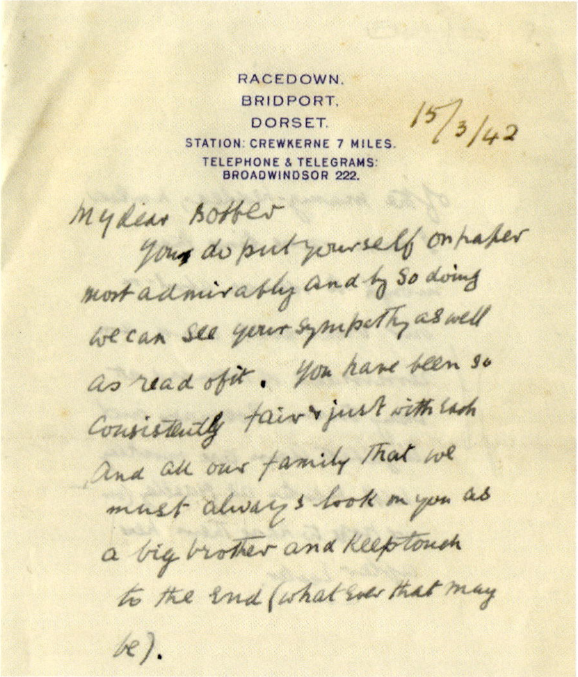

RACEDOWN.
BRIDPORT.
DORSET.
STATION: CREWKERNE 7 MILES.
TELEPHONE & TELEGRAMS:
BROADWINDSOR 222.

15/3/42

My dear Bobber

Your do put yourself on paper most admirably and by so doing we can see your sympathy as well as read of it. You have been so consistently fair & just with each and all our family that we must always look on you as a big brother and keep touch to the end (what ever that may be).

* * *

John McArthur and Nick Somerville left Hopper's on March 31st 1942.[36] Somerville had been busy during his last year at Winchester:

McArthur.

Nick Somerville.

> I was fortunate to be made Head of House and one of three Sergeant Majors in the OTC. Naturally our work in the Corps took on much more relevance, and I became a qualified drill and weapon training instructor.
>
> I was also fortunate in being in Dr Eric James' Sixth Form science class. Knowing that I was not going to university, but straight into the Army, he suggested that I write an elementary book on wireless. He also suggested, rather to my horror, that for Chemistry I should study the role of carbon rings in the chemistry of scent. He knew I

had no sisters, and had made arrangements for me to do some study and work in Boots Laboratory in Winchester, which was full of beautiful young girls!

Looking back on my last year at Winchester, I learned far more from the experience of learning how to run things than from my classroom studies. In April 1942 I joined the Army. Being under the age of eighteen when I had enlisted in Belfast whilst still at school, I was posted to the 70th Young Soldiers Battalion of The Royal Welch Fusiliers, much to my annoyance – but my recruit training was to be done at Brecon in No.21 ITC (Infantry Training Centre) at Dering Lines Camp.

For his part, McArthur enlisted in the Royal Navy. Neither he nor Somerville could have anticipated the circumstances in which they would next meet.

* * *

Rigby had just completed his officer training, being commissioned into 23rd Hussars as 2nd Lieutenant 232700 on April 18th 1942.[37] 23rd Hussars were a new creation, one of several tank units formed as Britain's need for armour increased.

Rigby.

I passed out of 102 OCTU at Blackdown in Surrey, as a 2nd Lieutenant in the 23rd Hussars. I was just about the proudest young man in the British Empire that day. I was wearing my brand new cavalry-twill service dress. My Sam Browne belt was lovingly polished, my buttons shone, and I was on the way home to Durford Wood for some leave. As I left the barracks to walk down to Deepcut to get the bus, a Lance Corporal in the Scottish Horse was coming up the road on the opposite side. As he drew near he threw me a salute, the first I ever received, and the best.

I was given a few days' leave and then told to join the Regiment, but the problem was that nobody seemed to know where they were. They had been training in the North Yorkshire Moors near Whitby, but they and the whole of 11th Armoured Division had moved from there.

This is where my brother John came in handy. He was then a Major working in the War Office in Whitehall in an office called QM4. It was responsible for troop movements. I went to London and had lunch with John. We went to his office, which was four floors underground. He fairly soon found out that 23rd Hussars were moving to a new training area on the Sussex Downs, and RHQ was to be at Plumpton racecourse near Lewes. So, on the appointed day, I donned my nice new uniform and set off by train from Petersfield, changed at Havant, and arrived at Brighton in time for lunch.

Brighton was being attacked intermittently by hit-and-run German fighters, coming over from France at very low level and lining themselves up on one of the streets running into the town from the sea-front. They fired their machine-guns, swooped over the rooftops, circled around, and made off back to France. These were nuisance raids of no serious military significance, but two Royal Marines had been killed at the railway station shortly before my arrival, and one or two small bombs had done some damage. I found a nice small restaurant in a street leading back from the sea. The old waiter who looked after me was very protective. When I was going, he volunteered to go out into the street first, to check if a fighter was coming.

> I got the train round to Plumpton, and there, sure enough, were all the headquarters vehicles of 23rd Hussars. RHQ had just been established in the grand-stand. I was well received by Colonel Harvey. He didn't want to talk about the war, but took me out by the finishing straight of the race-course and told me in detail how he had won a pre-war steeplechase there. I thought, what a strange war. Here we are, preparing to fight the best modern army in the world, and all the Colonel is interested in is horses.[38]

Rigby was assigned to 'C' Squadron, and shortly thereafter replied to Robertson, who had written to congratulate him on his commission.

> Thank you very much for your kind note; yes it was the 17th [April], and it seems an extremely long time ago, so much has happened since then.
>
> The address at the top is really no guide and my home address is still the one to write to. Actually, Regimental HQ is at the race course but the squadrons are outside. My Squadron Mess is an old country house not far from Lewes, with a lovely prospect of downland to the south; there could hardly be a better place to spend the spring in.
>
> There is one Old Wykehamist in the Regiment, Bill Shebbeare, late of Chawker's, who is our Captain and Adjutant – very rightly; he is one of the nicest officers in the Regiment, and on the whole they are a good lot, most of them having come either from the 10th Hussars or the Inniskillings. My special duty is the charge of all the squadron transport and all the echelon personnel, about sixty-two all told; I find it rather an handful to start off with.
>
> On the 28th I am going to Bovington (near Wareham) for a seven week course of wireless. I believe that week-end leaves are fairly frequent down there, so there may be a chance of getting to Winchester some time this half.
>
> When I was at Blackdown I got up to Cambridge once or twice and looked up David Middleditch. He seemed to be getting a lot of enjoyment out of life up there; and who wouldn't![39]

Robertson forwarded Rigby's letters to Rigby's sister Margaret, who was serving with the ATS in Wales. Her reply is preserved in the Winchester archives:[40]

> Thank you so much for sending on Roger's letters to me. As they contain the first news which I have received from him since he went to Plumpton, I was very pleased to see them and to hear that he seems to be enjoying life as a 2nd Lieutenant.
>
> Actually, I have never known Roger to be unhappy in any situation of his own choosing, and I think that he will get on well in the Army, as he seems so keen, and, his battalion being a new and go-ahead one, he won't have much chance to get 'browned off'!
>
> It seems years since Roger was at Winchester. I don't think I have visited the town at all since he left and I can't imagine it or the school being brought into this war. Wars and dictators seem of so very little consequence when one is living among ancient buildings which have seen so many other fighting leaders come and go, and I am sure that Winchester's atmosphere can be little changed.
>
> I hope that you and your sister and Sunnyside are flourishing and will continue to flourish in spite of Hitler.

* * *

On May 4th, Robertson lost another: Squadron Leader Fred Hollins AFC, whose middle name was Undecimus ('No.11'); he was one of twelve children. Hollins – who had left Hopper's in 1930 – was serving with 228 Squadron, operating Sunderland flying boats on anti-submarine patrols. A Sunderland on a transit flight from Oban to Lochboisdale, piloted by Flying Officer Briscoe, crashed on landing and was completely wrecked. Two of the fourteen men on board were killed, one of them Hollins.[41] On hearing the news, Robertson re-read a letter which Hollins had written in June 1941 and scrawled on it, 'My last from Fred, whom everyone loved!'

In September, Robertson received a letter from Trinity College, Cambridge:

> I hope you'll write something to *The Times* about Fred Hollins. I never knew him really well, but he was surely one of the most attractive personalities to be lost yet in this war, and it's intolerable that he should be commemorated only by the dead Who's Who recital of facts in today's (or was it yesterday's?) *Times*. I am surprised that some brother officer shouldn't have written long ago. I saw much more of Jack and Frank, but Fred had more charm than all the rest of that nicest of families.[42]

Robertson took on the challenge, and sent Hollins' obituary to *The Times*, in which it was published on October 5th 1942:

> **SQUADRON LEADER F. U. HOLLINS**
>
> M. R. writes: —
>
> Squadron Leader Frederick Undecimus Hollins, A.F.C., R.A.F.V.R., recently announced to have been killed on active service last May, was surely one of the most attractive and vivid personalities to be lost yet in this war. I knew him intimately during and after his six years at Winchester, where he and five brothers (there is another in the Navy and five sisters) covered in "Sunnyside" an almost unbroken spell of 22 years. Humphrey, the eldest, was outstanding in his generation; senior Co-Prae, scholar elect of Balliol, winner of the English Speech, of sterling character and great charm, he was killed serving in The Sherwood Foresters in Second Ypres just 27 years before the death of his youngest brother Fred, who was curiously like him in many ways. Fred played the violin and sang tenor well. He worked hard and successfully during the present war gaining rapid promotion and winning the A.F.C. In 1939 he married Daphne Jackson and had a daughter. His group commander wrote: "He served under me in two squadrons and I had a high opinion of his capabilities and leadership. We mourn the loss of a fine officer and a splendid mess-mate."

Robertson added in Hollins' Winchester obituary that 'there was about Fred "a deal of Ariel, just a streak of Puck".'[43]

Unusually, Robertson did not hear back from Hollins' widow, Daphne, when he wrote his letter of sympathy. But in 1945, she finally replied, her grief clearly still raw despite the passage of years:

I feel covered with shame to learn that you never received an answer to the letter you wrote at Fred's death. I'm afraid I was too dazed and bowled over at the time to deal with anything, so another sister of mine answered my letters that needed an answer – very weak and feeble of me I admit, but I had Sarah to look after and I tried to thrust all grief into the background. Apparently my sister missed out your letter, which must have seemed very ungrateful. I meant, too, to write to you after you'd put that charming obituary notice in *The Times*, but I funked it. I'd driven the horror deep and tried to keep it buried, which was a mistake. Even now I can't talk about Fred, except to complete strangers, which is odd.

My only brother was killed in Italy a year after Fred.

I've been living with my family off and on, but have now a small cottage here and have at last been able to unpack my wedding presents!

Sarah is a good companion and full of fun – I think you'd like her.[44]

* * *

In Singapore, Rickman had been a prisoner for just under three months when the Japanese put him and his men to work. Rickman's liberation questionnaire states that he worked at Keppel Harbour from May 6th until November 3rd 1942, under the command of Major H.S. Flower, of his own Battalion. Wherever possible, Commonwealth troops wanted to work in their original units, but the Japanese tried hard to break their old ties and to undermine existing command structures.

During this period, I supervised my own troops, working as stevedores in Keppel Harbour (the civilian harbour in Singapore town).[45]

This tallies with the account of Sergeant Govan Easton of 9RNF:[46]

May 2nd 1942
Most of the Battalion marched to Singapore to be based in Godown 23 on Keppel Harbour. We became dock labourers. Now we began to experience hard labour for long hours.

The prisoners were well aware by now of the arbitrary brutality of their captors, and so it was a brave man who took any risks. Nevertheless, according to his liberation questionnaire, Rickman and his men did just that:

Sabotage
Did you do any sabotage or destruction of enemy factory plant, war material, communications, etc., while employed in working parties or during escape?
Keppel Harbour Docks – we removed many parts of vehicles and trucks being loaded into the holds of Jap ships bound for Burma and Japan. We stole anything we could from stationary cars. We punctured cans of oil and lubricants in loading, breaking them by bumping them down with the winches whenever possible. One Japanese cargo ship bound for Rangoon from Singapore had to put back into Singapore with a

burnt-out hold. The Japs laid the blame on us. It was more probably an accident than done intentionally.

* * *

Nick Somerville wrote to Peter Walker from Brecon on Sunday, May 24th 1942. The British Army's massive expansion from a small, professional force in 1939 into a thoroughly professional citizen army in 1944-1945 meant that young leaders such as our subjects had to work with men and women whose childhoods and upbringings were very different from their own.

My Dear Peter,
Sorry I haven't written before, but this first week has been pretty busy. I live in a barrack room hut with twenty other chaps, all under nineteen and a good many who have given a wrong age and are only seventeen. We are a mixed bag. Some are miners' sons, some come from the slums of Birmingham, others have lived on a Welsh farm miles from any civilization; we have a half-caste Spaniard, and a boy who has been in the Merchant Navy for five years, joining as a cabin boy when he was thirteen. He has been torpedoed twice and so decided to chuck it and join the Army. The language is quite appalling and one has to put up with the incredible crudity and coarseness of their jokes. But underneath this they are extraordinarily good chaps and I am glad to say that so far there have been no quarrels and we have all enjoyed it. To begin with it was a great adventure and we were all in it together and there was no distinction between us. They called me Paddy and I called them Harry or Bert and we got on famously. It was only the other day that they discovered who my father was and that I was going in for a commission, and I am thankful to say that it hasn't made the slightest difference.

We have a first class lot of NCOs and don't see much of the officers. Work has been hard, eight periods a day, but I have done most of it before so that it is far easier for me. What I like about this Platoon is that it is so desperately keen. They are all volunteers and with the enthusiasm of youth want to be as smart as possible. They even ask each other questions in the barrack room at night and march up and down trying to get their drill right. Everyone is happy and cheerful and there is no comparison between us and the dim old buffers in the Intelligence Corps who have the next hut to us. They are always grousing and saying why the hell can't it stop raining or why can't we have another blanket.

We do two months here and then get a week's leave, when we come back and do one of those assault courses with sticks of gelignite and the 69 hand-grenade which makes a fearful noise and does no damage. Yesterday they had an accident with a sticky-bomb and one man was killed and seven injured. What makes one windy is that you cannot trust some of these people with a lethal weapon...

We had some very strenuous bayonet fighting on Wednesday and they have given us P14s, which is bloody. However, they say that all Recruits must use these as there are not enough SMLEs to go round. I loathe them because they are so clumsy and heavy.

I wish I had someone like you to talk to here. They are a different type of friend altogether.[47]

* * *

Duffin.

By the end of May 1942, Duffin was two-thirds of the way through his officer training at the Sandhurst OCTU:

> Last week a scheme carried me far enough south to see a chalk stream once more – full of rising fish – which of course reminded me of the mayfly on the Meon … and then it struck me it was just about time I wrote.
>
> As you know I've had 4½ out of my six months here now and we are at last the senior troop of the squadron – but, though one is ashamed to admit it, quite the worst troop the squadron has. It really makes me awfully annoyed, for as individuals we are a very good crowd indeed, but when we get together a sort of a blanket of apathy settles on us and effectively snuffs out any enthusiasm we may have in us so that the whole troop is inert and incredibly mediocre. (I often wish I was back in that platoon with Bruce Fortune and David Eccles which managed to collar Bather Pot – quite a different spirit, though we were only playing at soldiers then).
>
> The reason of course is that we are all 'browned off'. The teaching here is all one could desire and the instructors know their job, but everything is so impersonal that it's almost dis-encouraging. I think they ought to pat us on the back more – it makes all the difference in the world.
>
> Of course we have all sorts of types in our strength of twenty-five. The people from the universities have the most enthusiasm in them, but just can't see eye to eye with the training methods they use here, and are too young to come to the point and lead the rest – while these people are mostly old soldiers who are full of experience and know how to handle chaps but are too bloody idle to take a ball on themselves and do it – so there we are! The Squadron Leader suggested to me yesterday that I should be made Troop Leader for a whole month instead of the usual week and try and instill some enthusiasm into the troop – of course I'm quite willing to have a shot, but if it does happen I'm afraid I won't exactly be too optimistic.
>
> We do take ourselves seriously, don't we!?! Actually I think we are slowly going uphill now – we have finished our technical courses and are now on collective training which offers much more scope to the individual – and we seem to be taking the RMC Athla [athletics], which comes off next Saturday, pretty keenly.
>
> I'm sure I could easily be chucked out of this place for such a mutinous letter!
>
> There are only two old Wykehamists here besides myself. One is Powell of 'A' and the other Llewellyn-Smith of 'D', whom I'm just getting to know. He is much older than me – like most people here now! Hugh Rose is near here somewhere, but like a fool I lost the letter he wrote me and I can't remember his address – infuriating, when one knows he is only some five miles away!
>
> Last week a troop passed out with much pomp and ceremony and I was the Brigadier's orderly. I walked about with a huge silver baton which had Gerry Rickman's name on it, among scores of other previous orderlies. Also I've been Acting Squadron Leader this week, which meant that I wore two pips on my arm and commanded some seventy-odd fellow cadets.
>
> I'm starting to get my uniform now. It takes ages. I hope they let me have Blues.

The Sinclairs are still at Camberley Court and I'm seeing them – and I hope John – tonight. Very bad luck on Michael [Sinclair] being recaptured.

I really must stop now and try, with a superhuman effort, to write my half-yearly letter to my grandmother![48]

* * *

The morale of Allied forces in North Africa was now at its lowest ebb. In constant retreat since January 21st, they were about to make a stand at Gazala, near Tobruk. Between late January and May 1942, following their withdrawal from Agedabia, the British had been busy creating the 'Gazala Line', a series of brigade-strength defensive 'boxes' running from Gazala south into the desert. However, the 'boxes' were too widely separated to provide mutual support. There was no real confidence in higher command, and although individual units would fight with great courage they were often left exposed by the unannounced retreat of the troops around them. Nor could the Eighth Army take comfort from Allied progress in other theatres of war; the first half of 1942 had seen the war effort reach its nadir. In the Atlantic, U-Boats were strangling Britain's supply lines. The Russians were still reeling from the previous summer's German invasion.

Simpkin and his comrades in 4RTR were among the last to fall victim to the Allies' losing streak. Since mid-February, the Battalion had been in Egypt, re-equipping with Valentine tanks.[49] In the Simpkin family's collection is this photograph of the officers of the Battalion, dated March 6th 1942.

The last of the Valentines arrived on April 12th, as 4RTR prepared to re-enter the battle zone. Simpkin took the time to write to Robertson on May 21st:

Not much news for you I'm afraid. I'm in hospital at the moment with 'desert sores' – languishing in bed and feeling perfectly fit and rather fed up. I've had a very interesting time the last few months … I certainly am lucky to be in the battalion I'm in – I wouldn't change it for anything. I had my twenty-first birthday party in Alex, but tho' it was a good enough party, it remained a poor celebration so far from home.

We have the news on about six times a day here, and one gets rather tired of it … I expect Barbara's got a job by now – but mail is so patchy that we can't keep up to date with anyone's movements. I hope I'm not writing this too small for you. Airgraphs seem about the only reasonably quick and reliable means of communication.[50]

Soon afterwards, 4RTR rushed forwards by rail, and on May 27th received orders to move to El Adem immediately, where they became embroiled in fierce fighting. That same day, Jim Richardson had a narrow escape. He was now with HQ 7th Armoured Division, which was deployed to cover the open southern flank. But the speed of the German advance was such that at about 0830hrs that morning they overran the HQ. Peter Vaux, a staff officer who was present, later described what happened. One of his close colleagues aboard their Armoured Command Vehicle was yet another Wykehamist, Captain Donald Reid, with whom Vaux [51]

shared a peculiar edifice we had erected from Italian groundsheets and wireless aerials which we called 'The Chateau', where we slept and kept our personal belongings; to this I retired at about 0400hrs on the 27th, after doing duty for the first half of the night on the main, positional control on ACV1. Donald took over for the rest of the night …

About 0800hrs, Donald came running to the Chateau, calling out, 'Wake up! The RAF report three hundred tanks and a thousand vehicles south of Bir Hacheim, and we're moving in ten minutes.'

There was no time to pack up the Chateau, as I had to run to my own ACV2, where my crew were already tightening the camouflage and the big aerial. This steel monster contained all our intelligence paraphernalia, including the maps and charts of the enemy, and two large No.9 radios with separate receivers and transmitters. All around us was a sense of orderly confusion as some forty or fifty vehicles prepared to move.

ACV1 had the blue flag up for an immediate move, but was quite unable to do so itself, as the wheels churned uselessly trying to heave its fourteen tons out of the hole which had been dug for it. Only when another ACV gave it a tow did it become mobile. By that time, and as we moved off to the west, shells were falling amongst us, and Grant tanks of 4 Armoured Brigade were withdrawing through our column. Our own protective troop of light tanks had been sent off to the south and was in action many miles away.

As we steamed away at best speed, the northerly breeze sent a wall of dust from our wheels billowing out to the right. I was sitting on the roof of the ACV while the others were below sorting our maps and radio headsets, when suddenly there was a rattling of machine-guns and thudding of 20mm cannon, and a column of German armoured cars and half-tracks dashed through the concealing dust and were amongst us, firing in all directions. A number of vehicles stopped, clearly hit, and amongst these was ACV1, from which I saw some figures jump a moment before it burst into flames.

Reid and Richardson were both on board ACV1 at the time. Reid takes up the story:

> Loud gunfire was heard, and the ACV was hit, the driver sitting behind me being killed, and myself slightly wounded, by flying metal. I opened the door and told the General that vehicles all round were in flames, and that a German tank had its guns trained on us some one hundred yards away. We quickly piled out on to the ground and set light to our codes and any other documents we could lay our hands on. Meanwhile the battle swept on and over us, and we saw that our small protective unit of armoured cars had been wiped out.

General Messervy,[52] Lieutenant Colonel 'Pete' Pyman, Richardson, Reid, and three Other Ranks had escaped from the vehicle. Luckily, the Germans were unaware of the nature of the unit which they had overrun.

> We cut off the General's badges, and when the Germans came up I was attended to by one of their doctors, who remarked that the man next door to me looked rather old for war. I replied that he was my batman – but it was of course the General, minus his badges of rank. We were then told to pile into captured British vehicles with other prisoners, and instead of going back westwards, we joined the German columns moving east.

The prisoners were treated well, being given water, oranges, and chocolate by their captors. However, after nine hours in captivity, Messervy, Reid, and Richardson escaped:

> Our truck was driven by a young German, and we discussed the possibility of knocking him on the head at an appropriate moment, taking over the vehicle, and attempting to escape. At this point the whole column came under heavy artillery fire, and in the smoke and confusion we stopped and the driver flung himself flat on the ground. This was our chance, and we scattered. The last time I saw the General he was running hard, weaving all the time, whilst a German fired at him with a Schmeisser. My driver/batman and I leapt into a handy slit trench and feigned dead to passing enemy troops.
>
> Night fell, and the battle had moved on east, so we decided to walk in the same direction and to hide up later. We found a jerry-can, filled it with water from the radiator of a destroyed vehicle, and walked for several hours by the stars. Before dawn came we stumbled on an old well, and decided to make it our hiding place for the next few hours, until we could see the state of play. Soon after first light we saw some vehicles a mile or so away, approaching in our direction. They turned out to be a troop of the Royals, and on learning who we were, they sent us back, where we shortly joined up with the rest of the HQ staff and learned of their story since leaving us the day before.

Roy Farran of 3rd Hussars, who had seen Richardson in action at Beda Fomm, was now attached to the HQ:

> The General gave me command of a small composite force, whose duty it would be to protect the HQ from a similar surprise. It was a large command for a subaltern – ten armoured cars of mixed varieties, eight Bofors guns, a 2-pounder portee, and a tank. Aptly, Jim Richardson (of Beda Fomm fame, who was now G2) christened it 'Frigforce'.[53]

Jim Richardson (right) with General Messervy after their successful escape. (Copyright holder unknown; from Forty, G., *Desert Rats at War*)

* * *

Back in England with 23rd Hussars, Rigby's life was suddenly thrown into turmoil, as he recalled in his memoirs:

> In May 1942 a number of young tank officers were whisked away from their regiments in England and sent to India to help train and officer the Indian Armoured Corps. I was one of that number.[54]

It is interesting that his first action on hearing the news on May 28th was to write a letter to Robertson:[55]

> All my plans have been changed, I am not going to Bovington; I am not staying with the Regiment; I am not staying in England. My embarkation leave, has in fact already started, and very shortly I go to India.

> This being so, I must get over and see you soon, before it is too late. I could manage to get to Winchester any day from Tuesday 2nd – Friday 5th [June] inclusive, I can't unfortunately manage any days next weekend, I mean Saturday or Sunday. There is a bus that would get me to Winchester late in the morning of any of those days.
>
> Possibly there is a school match or some other function on one of these days. Perhaps you could suggest the best to come on. I always look forward to revisiting Winchester.

That he succeeded in visiting is evident from the paean of praise for Winchester in his next letter:[56]

> I am most grateful to you and your sister for your hospitality; I don't think I have ever appreciated Winchester so much before. I suppose this was partly because I knew I wouldn't see it again for a long, long time. The cricket in the sun, somebody casting a line, Chapel clock striking, fencing in Meads, and all the old faces, make up a picture I shall not forget.

* * *

On June 5th 4RTR took the lead in an attack on the Aslagh ridge conducted by 5th Indian Division. However, they suffered a drubbing from German tanks and anti-tank guns working together skilfully, and lost twenty tanks. As the Gazala line collapsed, 4RTR and their old partners 7RTR retired within the former perimeter of Tobruk. When the Afrika Korps broke through the defences on June 20th, the two RTR units counter-attacked, but after a battle lasting over eight hours they were destroyed. The Tobruk garrison received orders to surrender early the following morning – though 2nd Battalion, Cameron Highlanders, and a few tanks fought on for some time afterwards; over two hundred men of 3rd Battalion, Coldstream Guards also broke out of the perimeter and escaped successfully. But John Metcalfe, who was serving with 3rd Coldstream, did not make it; he went into the bag, along with Simpkin and over 30,000 other troops.[57]

Simpkin did not write about the fall of Tobruk – one of the bitterest humiliations of the desert war, and second in size only to Singapore as a Commonwealth capitulation. However, in a questionnaire which he completed on his eventual release,[58] when asked whether he had received any training in how to behave if captured, he replied tersely that a Major Salter had given him instruction on escape and evasion in April 1942. Simpkin certainly put this to good use; he dated his capture at Tobruk to June 24th, three days after the surrender, and explained that on the night of June 23rd – along with two other RTR officers and a driver from 25 Field Regiment RA – he had sneaked past the guards around a vehicle park near Tobruk, stolen a lorry, and headed east. However, the whole party was recaptured by Italian artillerymen in the area of Fort Capuzzo before the night was out.[59]

* * *

Robertson kept in touch with as many Wykehamists as he could; and not only them, but their anxious families as well. Some of his correspondence, as we have seen, concerned Fortune's father, who had been captured in June 1940. General Fortune was not the only Wykehamist to be a prisoner of war. By the middle of 1942, several Hopperites and their relatives were also in captivity. Those captured during the fall of France in 1940 were held in Germany; all those who were captured in North Africa were held at first in Italian camps; most unfortunate of all were those who were captured by the Japanese. In the course of the war, Hopper's had representatives in all three: John Sinclair's brother Mike was one of the six Hopperites in German hands, Simpkin amongst the four who began their captivity in Italian camps, and Rickman one of three who were prisoners of the Japanese.

To put these figures into perspective, seventeen Wykehamists fell into Japanese hands during the war, most of them in the space of four months (December 1941–March 1942) in the invasions of Hong Kong, Singapore, Java, and Sumatra. Of these, two were murdered by their captors, one committed suicide, and one suffered permanent damage to his sight.

Thirty-three Wykehamists were originally held in Italy. Although Italian camps were far harder to escape from than German ones, the armistice in September 1943 created a window of opportunity for the prisoners to reach Allied lines or Switzerland; five of them made it, another being killed whilst assisting the Italian partisans. One prisoner was repatriated on grounds of ill health. The other twenty-six were rounded up after the Armistice and spent the rest of the war in German camps. None died in captivity.

A further fifty-five Wykehamists were captured by the Germans, most of them in 1940 but a steady trickle thereafter (the last being captured in April 1945 and released after four days). One – 'Slogger' Armitage – died of his wounds immediately after capture; Jim Richardson and Donald Reid, of course, only spent nine hours in German hands before escaping; two others escaped during the fall of France in 1940, though one of them was killed by a French air raid just after he reached Gibraltar; one escaped after being captured at Saint-Nazaire in 1942. One Wykehamist prisoner committed suicide, and three were repatriated owing to ill health. John Pendlebury was captured during the fall of Crete in May 1941 and executed. Mike Sinclair was shot and killed whilst trying to escape from *Oflag* IVc Colditz in September 1944; he and his great Wykehamist partner in crime, Gris Davies-Scourfield, had by then spent a great deal of time on the run in occupied Europe.

Setting Armitage aside, a Wykehamist's chances of dying in captivity were zero whilst held by the Italians, roughly one in twenty-five when held by the Germans, but just over one in six if in Japanese hands.

There was one further Wykehamist prisoner of war, the poet and SOE operative Frank Thompson, who was captured by the Bulgarians in 1944. His execution followed swiftly.

* * *

General Fortune did not sit and repine in captivity. For one thing, he encouraged escape at every opportunity, seeing it as a valuable tool in the fight to maintain the prisoners' spirits. In 1946, he wrote that

> when an escaping enterprise was in course of preparation in a camp a very large number of officers were employed in organising and in making plans, although possibly the enterprise only aimed at getting two or three of them out of the camp. What is perhaps not generally known is that the mere fact of the plan being in course of preparation within the camp had a very important effect on morale; although a good many officers might have very little to do with it, they knew it was going on. For this reason I am very glad to be able to say a word of appreciation to all those who not only took every opportunity to escape themselves, but also to those who, unable to take part in the escape, were only too willing always to help with the plans, and render that close co-operation at vital moments, without which those who were going out would never have had a chance.
>
> I know that all those who were in command of camps – they were known as SBOs (Senior British Officers) in *Oflags* and 'Men of Confidence' in *Stalags* – would be glad to join with me in thanking those who were in any way responsible for escaping enterprises. Their efforts helped materially to keep the morale of the various camps so high.[60]

In February 1942, a group of RAF personnel arrived at Spangenberg Castle, in use as *Oflag* IXA/H:

> The Major General came up, looking firm, imperturbable, and rather friendly – even to junior officers. After welcoming us, telling us that there were already two hundred and fifty or so British Army officers there, and going into some administrative matters, he got down to more secret things. Firstly, there was escape. This was something which it was our duty to carry out, but there were certain rules. Escape must be discussed with him or his Committee, before attempted – unless, of course, a perfect and unexpected chance revealed itself. Moreover, we were not to go breaking into various rooms not used by POWs at present, because this might only stir up the Germans unnecessarily, who might then come upon various illicit activities which were always in progress. Secondly, there was the wireless, a precious asset. But it could never be referred to as such, and the news read out to us from the BBC bulletins was not to be discussed. Germans might hear. If the wireless had to be referred to, it was the 'Canary'.[61]

General Fortune continued to serve his men as best he could. As the most senior British officer held by the Germans, at every opportunity he tried to persuade his captors to treat his men better. When Robertson received a letter from Lady Fortune in June 1942, he pencilled the note: 'Very characteristic of V.F., who took great trouble for all ranks'. It opened as follows:

> Dear Bobber,
> Victor writes me 'Could you get the Bobber to phone Sir John Shelly Rollo at Arlington that 1509175 Pte J. Lansley RA, son of his head carter, who has lost a leg, is here and very well and much appreciated Sir John's message to him.'[62]

Fortune's fellow prisoners found him an inspiration:

> The arrival of Major General Fortune [at Laufen] had made a great difference to almost everybody in the camp. 'The General' was an inspiring personality, completely unwavering at all times and lending some of his own overbrimming confidence to those of us who had become slack physically and war-weary in mind. The General provided all officers with an epic example of how it should be possible to lead the life of a prisoner-of-war without loss of dignity and self-respect. He did for us what Winston Churchill did for the people of Britain.[63]

Whilst the Germans were legally allowed to put Other Ranks to work, officers were exempt. The main battle for them, therefore, was against boredom. In the winter of 1942–1943, General Fortune asked the Royal Caledonian Curling Club to send polished granite curling stones to Spangenberg. When these arrived, by way of Switzerland, the prisoners flooded the castle's dry moat, so that when it froze they were able to go curling.

* * *

On May 1st 1942, a new pupil joined Hopper's; the stability of the Robertsons' environment would be important for a boy whose mother had died five years previously and whose father was a busy army officer – in the boy's own words 'a loving but distant father, who focused on army life'.[64] The boy's name was David Montgomery, and he was the only son of the commanding officer of South Eastern Command, the relatively unknown Lieutenant General Bernard Law Montgomery.[65]

B.L. Montgomery and his son David. (IWM ZZZ 7687D)

* * *

The Axis forces were now pushing hard against the Allies in North Africa, whose line had begun to stabilize around the small Egyptian coastal village of El Alamein, where there was a natural defensive position some sixty-five miles from Alexandria. Rommel had a penchant for launching attacks around the southern (desert) end of British defensive lines; but at Alamein, the south end of the line was secured by the Qattara Depression, an area of sand below sea-level which was impassable to large forces of vehicles. The narrowness of the gap between the sea and the Qattara Depression – only forty miles – limited the enemy's options for an attack. When, on July 2nd, 11RHA halted the German advance, it marked the moment when the balance of the war at last tipped decisively in the Allies' favour.[66] But there were many sadnesses still to come.

On July 8th, Jim Richardson took command of a Jock Column – a combined arms force of Stuart light tanks from 'A'/6RTR, a troop of 25-pounders from 2RHA, and a troop of anti-tank guns – with orders to support 9th Australian Division, in position around El Alamein itself. At 0900hrs on July 9th, Richardson set out with 'A'/6RTR to rendezvous with the rest of his new command, but twenty-four hours later the 6RTR war diary recorded: 'Reports from Australian Field Ambulance that Major J.A.C. Richardson had been wounded and was on D1 list'.[67]

Richardson's force had reached El Daba at 0255hrs. What happened next was witnessed by Wykehamist Lieutenant Christopher Seton-Watson, who was then serving with the detachment of 2RHA which formed part of Richardson's column:[68]

> We spent the night in leaguer not far from the sea, just north of the main road and in front of the Australian guns. Australian infantry attack at 0330hrs; huge barrage. Our column dispersed at 0530hrs. Shortly afterwards Jim Richardson, Bill, and I were standing around, awaiting orders, when a stray 105mm shell dropped right beside us. Jim was seriously injured, and died of his wounds next day.[69]

Richardson's career up to his untimely death at twenty-six suggests that he would have been marked out for high promotion in the Army; as well as his DSO, he had been mentioned in dispatches. His obituarist in *The Times* wrote of him that

> the personal losses sustained in war are grievous. Among them are losses of even greater significance, as when one of the generation on whom the future depends and who has proved his quality is taken. Such was Major J.A.C. (Jim) Richardson. A member of a happy and devoted family, and endowed with exceptional looks, charm, ability, and strength of character, he had already proved his quality in war and was marked down for a career of distinguished service … So passes a great gentleman and a brilliant young soldier, whom none who knew him will forget, and whose influence and example will remain an inspiration. He will fill a worthy place in Valhalla.
>
> 'So he passed over, and all the trumpets sounded for him on the other side.'

* * *

During Elliott-Binns' time at Cambridge in 1942, his focus remained his friendship with McMurtrie:

Elliott-Binns.

> Cambridge at this time was a transitional place, meaning little compared to Winchester. Two aspects of my life in Cambridge were important. One was my continuing relationship with Duncan. We both went on to Cambridge for the year allowed to us, and until I joined the Army on my nineteenth birthday Duncan was the major influence in my life.
>
> The other aspect was my training for war. Because of a chance encounter I joined the Field Artillery Officer Training Unit, not the infantry. It was expected of me that I should become an officer. I don't think I could have been an effective infantry officer, but I was an effective gunner officer, though by no means a conventional one.

Duncan McMurtrie had left Hopper's for Trinity Hall, Cambridge, on winning a Classical Exhibition in December 1941. He was young enough to stay for five terms, and his family hoped that he would do so and take the first part of the Law Tripos. But after doing well in 'Mays' he went down in June 1942.[70]

* * *

Duffin was commissioned into the Scots Guards as 2nd Lieutenant 240007 on July 17th.[71] He had done rather well at Sandhurst, as he told Robertson soon afterwards:

> Here I am in the most sumptuous Mess you've ever seen – five-course dinners – four-course lunches – everything done for you, etc., etc. – All the same, most of the younger officers are incredibly vain and stupid – the sort that slur their 'Rs' and pronounce them as 'Ws' on purpose! I get very annoyed with them.
>
> I passed out 'A' at RMC and managed to get the Belt of Honour for the most outstanding Cadet!!! – I think most thanks are due to Jock Parr – it's nice to have that behind one![72]

He soon joined 3rd (Armoured) Battalion, Scots Guards, in Codford on Salisbury Plain. This made it easy for him to visit Winchester, as he did in the autumn of 1942; he wrote a thank-you letter from the Guards Club during a break from a course:

> Thank you and Sheila most awfully for such a pleasant week-end. As usual I was treated like a king and I really don't know how you manage to do it – especially when inconsiderate fellows like myself go ringing up at the last possible moment.
>
> I had the usual dreadful journey back – was left waiting for a whole hour at Romsey – and when eventually we set off for home from Salisbury in a truck we didn't get far as the driver had forgotten to fill it with water and it almost blew up! When we did eventually struggle in, a storm burst upon us – we reached the Mess soaked, where I found I was Picquet Officer for the next day – entailing a rise before Reveille. I retired

cursing to my room to find the whole of it under an inch of water! Never mind, not all the waters of Codford could damp the warmth of a welcome at Sunnyside.

I've come up here for the week-end from a gunnery school on rather a lovely part of the Dorset coast. I'm only there for a week. The Mess is enormous, but very garish and chromium-plated, and most of its inhabitants seem to bear all its main characteristics. Yesterday it made me wild to be able to look out of the window and see the sea and then turn round and see rows of individuals frowsting behind papers in a fuggy room, so I put on my mac. and went for a huge walk along the top of the cliffs. There was a terrific gale blowing and it was all most impressive. If I'd been Wordsworth or somebody I would have written a sonnet on the spot, but being myself, I somehow didn't!!

I came up the Itchen Valley in the train yesterday and was delighted to find Winchester in brilliant sunlight. One gets a very good view of Chapel out of the train – not to mention Sunnyside, of course.[73]

* * *

Nick Somerville had earned promotion to Lance Corporal by the time that he wrote to Walker again; though still in Brecon, he was now in 21st ITC's potential NCOs Cadre. From a military family, Somerville was disappointed by the low standards of some of his fellow trainees.

It makes such a difference to have someone to talk to. I miss it terribly here. The usual topic of conversation is women and dirty jokes, which makes me feel rather depressed sometimes. You can have too much of that … This course ends on August 8th, so I rather doubt my being able to see you. However, if I can get a week-end or something after the 30th I will certainly let you know and we might be able to fix something in London. I long to talk to someone and hear some decent music. Everything here is rather shallow. People seem to live from day to day and don't worry about the war, even though their friends are being cut up in Libya. It makes me quite wild sometimes when they don't even know that Tobruk has fallen, etc., etc. They amble down the streets as though they were still civvies with nothing better to do. I sincerely hope they get hold of the fighting spirit, because if these soldiers were to go into action they wouldn't stand it for a minute. They don't seem to give a damn for the Army. I suppose that will always be the case with conscripts.

Every officer should go through the ranks and if possible a Cadre. I have learned all sorts of things which I would not otherwise know about, the little things which the men appreciate. I am learning how to teach, using the simplest possible words, so that the men can understand. Some of them cannot read or write, and they have no adjectives except 'bloody' or 'fucking'.[74]

* * *

Guy Richardson was at home in Fleet when the bad news about his brother arrived on July 18th. The Robertsons saw the announcement in the newspaper on July 21st, and wrote letters of condolence immediately. Sheila's anguished note to 'Nan' (as Richardson's mother was known) shows her grief plainly:

Dearest Nan,
How can I write to you – but you do know what I feel about you – and Jim. You have all been so much in my thoughts and I am so glad you have had Guy and Peggy and Alec within hail in this crushing blow – He had done so well, and we were all so proud of him. I do so grieve for him. I was always so fond of Jim and he was nice and kind to me always. I will write again – you have been such a faithful friend always. I do feel for you and such tension you have had. It is so hard for Peggy and Guy – and all these young things. They are wonderful.[75]

Guy Richardson.

Robertson's letter was more sedate but none the less heartfelt:

My dear Mrs Richardson,
I looked at my *Times* ten minutes ago, and saw your news: and our hearts are sore for you, though full of pride. Jim was a soldier every inch and all the way, and death in action must with him, as with Bernard Pinney and others of our fine 'regulars', [have] been part of his contract. It was always clear that he wanted to be where the fighting was, and he had part of his reward in that DSO with its grand citation ...[76]

Nan Richardson replied the following day:[77]

We – Guy and I – had a telegram on Saturday morning, telling us officially that Jim had been wounded on July 10th and was on the dangerously ill list, and telephoned Alec at the War Office. Then on Sunday Alec came down to tell us (Peggy too) that Jim had died of his wounds the same day. I feel so grateful that he did not have to suffer long. We heard later that he was wounded in the chest, and I picture him leading his tanks into action, standing up, inspiring his men to the end, and I feel so gratefully proud of having been his mother.

We must try to be brave now, as he would wish, and also to be worthy of such a magnificent son.

We had two airgraphs from Jim dated June 17th, saying he had been sent as Second-in-Command of 6th Battalion Tank Regiment four days previously, owing to the loss of officers, and that the Battalion had gone back to rest early in July. Alec says that apparently two Squadrons were ready for action again and Jim took them up – I see on that day our armoured troops moved forward. So perhaps he was going forward with the line, even a little way, when he was wounded. You have so many magnificent young men that have given all they had in this Crusade against Evil and although they have not been spared to see it through, never the less each one and all of their sacrifices must surely be part of the ultimate victory.

Guy went off to RN Air Station Arbroath, Scotland. He is Sub-Lieutenant (A) RNVR now. He has been so splendid over this and such a help to the rest of us with his courage and outlook, as he feels the loss of Jim as keenly as we all do.

Thank you again so much for your thoughts and for all your share of making Jim's character what it was.

Yours ever,
Agnes Richardson

Her husband later wrote to Robertson as follows:[78]

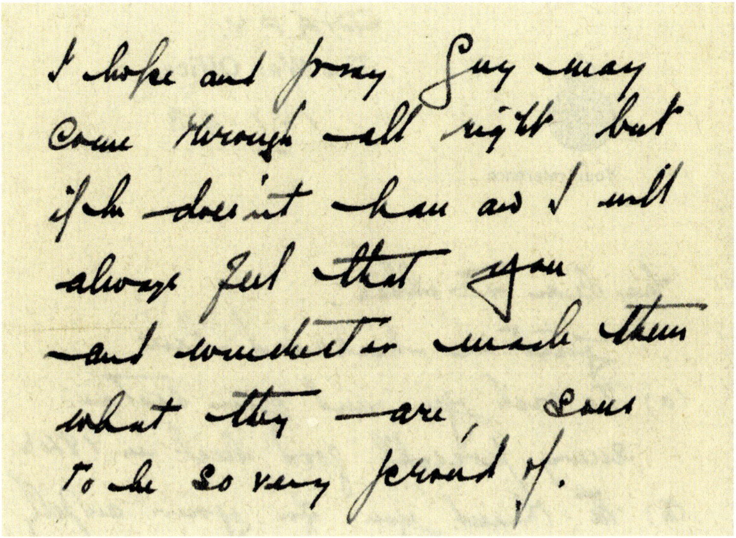

I hope and pray Guy may
come through all right but
if he doesn't Nan and I will
always feel that you
and Winchester made them
what they are, sons
to be so very proud of.

VIII

'I feel his loss very much, as he was always rather like a younger brother to me'

July–December 1942

I cannot say that I am impressed by the fact that it is the triumph of morality we are fighting for. For that we must make gigantic efforts as soon as the last shot is fired. It seems to be impossible while the show is on.

(Hugh Rose, September 20th 1942)

On July 28th 1942, four more of our subjects moved on from Hopper's: Crispin Hill,[1] Robin Lewin,[2] David Martyn,[3] and Peter Walker.[4]

Hill.

Lewin.

Martyn.

Walker.

Hill was the son of the Headmaster of Aldro School near Godalming, and as well as being an excellent shot (he was in the Shooting VIII in his final year), Robertson noted that he was a carpenter and an electrician – thus explaining his Heath Harrison grant for engineering, with which he joined Brasenose College, Oxford. He spent two years at Oxford before taking a commission in the RNVR.

Lewin was from a military family, and although his father (a retired Major General) had been a Gunner, Lewin was to go into the infantry; like so many Wykehamists, he joined one of the rifle regiments, the King's Royal Rifle Corps. Instead of going to university, he went straight into the Army.

As for Martyn, he was a Hopperite through-and-through; not only had his maternal uncle been in the house, but he was the cousin of Christopher, Mike, and John Sinclair. His own younger brother, Peter, was also a Wykehamist, though not a Hopperite.[5] Robertson wrote that Martyn, who would join the Coldstream Guards, left from Sixth Book 1(b) as a Senior Prefect with a fine record. He won a prize for French Speech, was 'mentioned' for the German and Spanish Prizes, and won the Hundred Yards, Quarter Mile, and Long Jump, as his contribution to Taylor Cup. He found himself completely during his last year, and did and cared much for his House.

By the time that he signed up for the Army on August 7th 1942, Martyn stood 6′½″ tall, weighed 150lbs, had a 38″ chest, and boasted a birthmark inside his right arm. His complexion was listed as 'fresh', his eyes as grey-blue, and his hair as light brown. The Army assessed Martyn's languages as follows:

(6.) (a) Foreign Languages (state dialects where necessary and degree of proficiency, *i.e.*, " fluent," " good," or " fair ")	Special Qualifications: Speak	Read	Write
French	Good	Good	Good
German	Good	Good	Good
Spanish	Fair	Fair	Fair

Martyn attended the Guards Armoured Training Wing from October 10th 1942 for pre-OCTU training, and started his course at 100 OCTU – the RAC OCTU – at Sandhurst on December 12th.

Walker had been noteworthy as a runner, musician, and prefect whilst in Hopper's, and when he left went up to New College, Oxford. Like Martyn, he was destined for service in tanks. In Walker's case, his particulars on enlistment in Oxford on November 17th 1942 were 5′10½″ tall; weight 167lbs; chest 40″; complexion 'fresh'; eyes blue; hair brown.

* * *

By August 1942, the Axis advance in North Africa had been brought to a standstill. However, after a visit to Cairo, Churchill decided that a fresh approach was needed. He replaced Auchinleck, who had stabilized the Alamein line and halted the German advance; General Sir Harold Alexander took over as Commander-in-Chief, Middle East Command, whilst Lieutenant General William 'Strafer' Gott was given command of Eighth Army. But Gott was killed as he flew to Cairo on August 7th, and the CIGS, Alanbrooke, convinced Churchill that Montgomery was the man for the job.

The following day, Montgomery penned a brief note to Robertson:[6]

My dear Robertson,
I have been ordered to Egypt very suddenly, and have placed David in entire charge of:
Major T. Reynolds, Amesbury School, Hindhead. Tel: Hindhead 432.
Will you in future send everything to Major Reynolds; school bills, reports, all communications, in fact everything.
I have not been able to see David.
In great haste,
Yrs sincerely,
B.L. Montgomery

Beneath Mongomery's signature Robertson added a pencilled comment (as he often did when receiving letters): 'I believe in him, and never did in Auchinleck!'

As events showed, Robertson's trust was not misplaced. For the first time, an Allied commander was being allocated resources sufficient for the task ahead of him. In the desert war so far the rules had been relatively simple: the two sides had formed lines stretching southwards into the desert from the fixed point of the Mediterranean coastline. The coast was a flank which could not be turned; neither side had the amphibious capability to transport significant forces around the northern end of the enemy line. Attacks, therefore, had traditionally involved hooking around the southern end of the enemy front. At Alamein the opposing lines were very short, and the southern end of the front was secured by the Qattara Depression. The Germans, now on the defensive, had made their line strongest in the north; here the minefields were densest. Everything seemed to suggest that Montgomery should take the usual course of action and punch at the southern end of the German line. But Montgomery wanted to strike a knock-out blow and drive the Germans back as quickly as he could. To do so, he needed to use the only decent road, along the coast. His attack, therefore, would be against the enemy's strongest positions, in the north, which he hoped to gradually crumble away before bursting through and racing westwards into Libya. Attacking in the north would be unexpected, and even more so if the enemy could be convinced that the real attack was to come in the south.

This is no place for a detailed description of all of the complicated battles at Alamein; instead, we must focus on our subjects' role in what lay ahead.

* * *

Hugh Rose had been commissioned into the Black Watch in March,[7] and found himself in 1st Battalion, the same unit as Bruce Fortune. Rose's father had served in the same Battalion, and General Fortune had once commanded it. 1BW were in 154 Brigade of the reconstituted 51st (Highland) Division, which sailed from the Clyde on June 20th 1942, travelling around the Cape and calling at Cape Town on July 18th. On the day that they sailed, Fortune's mother wrote to Robertson:

Rose.

> The Highlanders are away, sad to say and wonderful. Why have some of the old prewar Regiments not gone, and these trainee ones go? It's suicide; it's just they know the Scotch will fight …
>
> Best love to you both. I ache for my Brucie.[8]

Rose described their travels in a letter to Robertson:

> It seems a long time since I spent a very pleasant day in Winchester sometime in May, which I believe was the last you saw or heard of me. After that it was really a restless time wondering how many more days one had in the old home country and trying to

make the best of it. I went to Town twice and once to Cambridge for a few hours only, owing to the trains, and did not really meet anyone I wanted to at all. So I was really almost glad to get embarked and away from the tension.

Our voyage lasted eight weeks and I must say I really enjoyed it. We never had any rough weather, and we were excellently fed. One thinks with longing out here in the arid scorching desert waste, of all the iced drinks it was possible to get then at the bar.

We were pretty cramped for sleeping space. I shared a cabin just larger than a Third sleeper, with my Company Commander (a Major) and the two other Platoon Commanders of 'B' Company. The men slept on mess decks and it was stifling hot at night owing to black-out, though a number would sleep on deck. They kept very cheerful the whole time and we had plenty of parades, lectures, competitions, etc., to alleviate the boredom … On the boat I was able to keep myself in practice at one of the things I did at Cambridge. Connected with Mr Mansel and Mr McIntosh and at which Charlie Duffin was pretty good [i.e. French]. I made quite a few friends thereby, though rather toward the end of the trip, which was a pity …

At Cape Town, by the way, we had a marvellous three days. We were allowed ashore from about 1400hrs to midnight and everyone was lavish with their entertainment to us. Unfortunately the shops were shut two days as it was a weekend.[9]

The convoy arrived in Suez on August 14th and the troops began the process of acclimatization and desert training. The heat was intense, making it difficult to maintain personal hygiene, and disease soon spread. One of those afflicted was Fortune, as Rose informed Robertson in September:

We seem to have got through the unpleasant experience of acclimatisation with all the gastric chills, etc., it involves, and very few went off to hospital with the more serious complaints of dysentery or enteric. If they once go 'down the line' it means they are struck off our strength and we do not see them again.

I thought for a while we had lost Bruce when I heard he was in Hospital with the old trouble. (At the OTC camps he never could stand the heat and flies either). However I was overjoyed to see him back a week ago with a defiant curl to his black moustache, which has now surpassed itself and is now of the David Niven type instead of a Clark Gable which is all he could raise before. His stomach anyway is behaving better which makes life sweeter and is the main thing … He had a day in Cairo but as he had only just come out of hospital was not well disposed to enjoy it … Nigel Noble, the other Wykehamist,[10] has been ill, but he may come back too.[11]

Fortune himself had written to Robertson a few days before:

Thank you so much for your postcard. It came amongst the first batch of mail we have received. We arrived out here as the grouse came into season and have been sweating in this infernal desert ever since. Still it is not as bad as it might be, and in some ways is a good healthy open air life.

I saw Popham of 'A', Dawson Bates of 'B', Asquith of 'H', and Merrick of 'K' the other day. Just arrived out here and after three days up into the line. Hugh is very well

> and sends his love … Nigel Noble is away in hospital with tummy trouble. I really did mean to come down and see you all before we went – but we got whisked off so quickly. Give my love to Sheila. It will be a sorrowful day when you both leave Sunnyside.[12]

* * *

On the same day, some 2,000 miles away, in the somewhat less unhealthy environs of Queen's Gate Gardens in South Kensington, 2665309 Guardsman Recruit Martyn also sat down to write a letter to Robertson. Like Fortune, he had recently been in hospital, suffering the effects of exposure to rather different elements.

> I am at home to-day on a day pass, which is a welcome change. We have only got another fortnight to do at Caterham before we go on to the Guards Armoured Training Wing, and if we get the four or five days in between that we are hoping for I thought I would come down and see you then; but I will let you know later. It is great fun at the Depot now, and the rush seems just a matter of course, and once you've got used to it everything goes very easily. We passed out on our second inspection on Friday and are now polishing ourselves up and trying to turn from Recruits into Guardsmen! We have a Company Commander's inspection next week and a final one by the Commandant the week after.
>
> I should have liked to see John McA[rthur] before he went. Does he go to sea almost at once? I don't suppose he arrived in Winchester yesterday if he said he was going to, or did he?
>
> I spent a very restful five days, a week or two back, in hospital which was rather dull, especially as I felt quite well after 24 hours, but I developed a 'febrile chill' with a temperature of 104.5 after a night operation spent in a trench with thunder, lightning, and rain – and no enemy – and was therefore hastily removed by ambulance! They can deal with very little at the depot and any case like that is bound to go to hospital, which takes so long.
>
> I can't remember what Nick [Somerville]'s programme was like at Brecon; it seemed pretty excessive as far as I can remember but I can't compare it with ours. We get two or three drills a day, four PTs a week, and the rest W/T, lectures on Gas, Tactics, and Map Reading. Reveille 0630hrs and Lights Out at 2200hrs. It's not very strenuous really. Our last parade ends at 1600hrs, and we clean our kit till 1715hrs, or more if we want it…
>
> Please remember me to Miss Robertson and the 'chaps' as P.M.W[alker] would have it, and I hope you all have a good term.[13]

* * *

Out in the desert, Rose had not bumped into as many Wykehamists as Fortune, but he had met one who trumped Fortune's:

> By the way, I shook hands with and saluted one Old Wykehamist who was in College, had a son in Freddie's, and was in my father's regiment. He is a wonderful figure of a man, and one could almost sense his dynamic personality. (Guessed who?)[14]

As a Platoon Commander in 'B' Company, Rose had a great responsibility, which he clearly took seriously. 12 Platoon was something of a hotch-potch, and in such circumstances his role and that of the Platoon Sergeant were crucial:

> I have had many worries with my Platoon. You might remember it only formed when I took over in May out of a Depot draft (of eight months training in the average), old stagers of two years in 'B' Company, and drafts from other regiments and battalions. We were getting on OK until my Platoon Sergeant, a first-class keen NCO, got ill and had to be left in Hospital at Cape Town.
>
> Since then, Section Commanders have had their private enmities and rivalries. They are inclined to side with the men in their complaints, and on the whole cause me much extra trouble in chasing them to keep them up to the mark.[15]

1BW were preparing for a role in Montgomery's planned offensive. They needed to become accustomed to desert hardships as quickly as possible.

> Since we arrived we have toured this country quite thoroughly, pitching and striking camps almost the same day … We have been getting progressively more wild and woolly every new billet – or rather spot of desert – we have encamped in. At first we had limitless water, if one walked 200 yards to a tap, and showers within ¾ mile. Also a first-rate canteen or canteens (if one walked on, they were approximately one to every two miles); also cinemas, where I'm told one could see fairly ancient films of thriller or romance interest, but which relieved the monotony for the ordinary soldier. Further on, we had to fetch Canteen supplies in a company truck, and one went to showers once a week to a place ten miles off in transport. Now we only see water in two- or four-gallon petrol tins and are strictly rationed. And being miles from anywhere, one three-ton vehicle makes one journey per week to the Bulk NAAFI for canteen supplies. Tinned food is excellent out here. I think our cooked rations originate in tins. I had some delicious tinned potatoes the other evening. When lucky we get tinned peaches, pears, and pineapples, the latter, the most popular, being cheapest, costing just about 10d – but having nothing else to spend money on, the Jocks soon make them disappear. Beer is Australian or Canadian and very heady and none too popular …
>
> I fully appreciate now the effect of some of Saint-Beuve's poems which create the atmosphere of somnolence and languor caused by the extreme heat of Oriental countries. Mr McIntosh will know the ones I mean in 'Nine French Poets'. That is one of the things I miss – that one is entirely out of touch with anything literary. I unfortunately only took a couple of my favourite books with me and those appear to have been lost, as I have a whole kit-bag which has failed to turn up. Now we rarely see a newspaper and then it is several days old. I spent a couple of most enjoyable days with a unit coming from a part of the world where you did some teaching before the last war, Bobber [South Africa]. They were better off, in that they have more transport than us, and so got the day's papers and were able to cart about with them books, wirelesses, chairs, tables, tents, and other amenities which help to make life more pleasant in the midst of barren desolation.[16]

In early September the Highland Division moved off towards the front line and began training for the attack. Plans for the Second Battle of El Alamein were being carefully worked out, and 51st Division's objectives were already known. The attack was to involve an advance by infantry towards enemy entrenchments under cover of an artillery barrage. Training was carried out with a high degree of realism. Nevertheless, Rose did manage to find some pleasure in the 'barren desolation' – particularly his beloved birds:

> I have bathed three times in the sea – wonderfully refreshing and the brilliant ultramarine after the sandy grey-green of the desert was a pleasant sight for the eyes. I have just seen a swallow scudding past. I often wondered where they went in the winter months. One sees things which are a mixture between wagtails and fieldfares. Also I believe I saw the descendants of those birds [Sand Grouse] which ornamented the end of Grubbing Hall one time when 'Pots' were scarce and came to stay as a sort of mascot. On the banks of the Nile I saw lots of hoopoe. Do you remember the sensation caused when you saw one in Water Meads several years ago, Bobber? I seem to remember the *Hampshire Chronicle* was humming with the news.[17]

* * *

In the front line at El Alamein, the *Panzerarmee Afrika* made one last attempt to break through to Alexandria. At the Battle of Alam Halfa, Montgomery's forces compelled the attackers to retreat with crippling losses. By September 5th it was clear that the Axis campaign in North Africa could go no further, although it would not be until May 1943 that it ended once and for all. As the dust settled over the mangled remains of tanks and their crews, the two sides continued to harass one another. On September 8th a German air attack killed Hopperite Major the Hon. Henry Browne, of 1st Battalion, Rifle Brigade – in Robertson's words, 'a fine soldier and a leader of men'.[18]

* * *

> Well, Bobber, I wish I could see the general situation with more clarity, but I don't believe anyone can. This war has produced more shocks and setbacks than one cares to think of, with people living in a state of apathy, wishful-thinking, and false security in the meantime. I certainly hope and think that we shall have this show finished out here before next spring. One can merely hope and wait, and beyond that adopt a fatalist attitude.[19]

On October 17th, a month after writing the above, Rose wrote his Christmas cards *(below)* so as to be in good time, given the vagaries of the wartime post.[20] He knew that soon he would be in action.

Unusually for the desert, Montgomery had scheduled a night attack, to take place on 23rd/24th October 1942. His infantry were to advance first, enabling engineers to clear anti-tank mines behind them and thus allowing tanks to pass through to smash the Axis forces. The infantry would advance behind an artillery barrage which would move forwards in front of them as they advanced. If the infantry moved too quickly, they would walk into their own side's shell-fire; too slowly, and the barrage would move ahead, giving

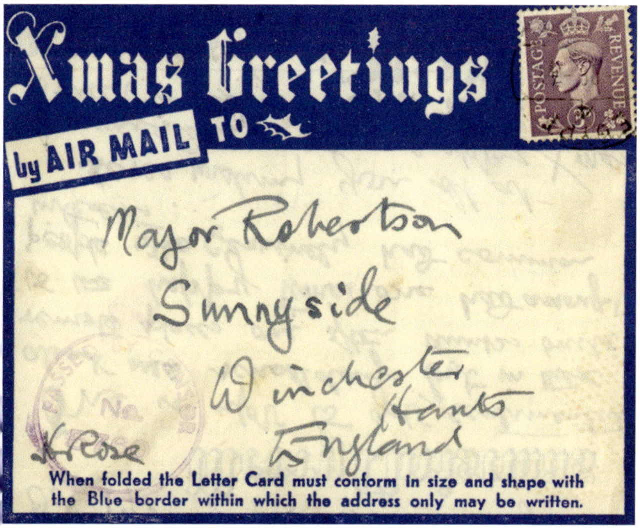

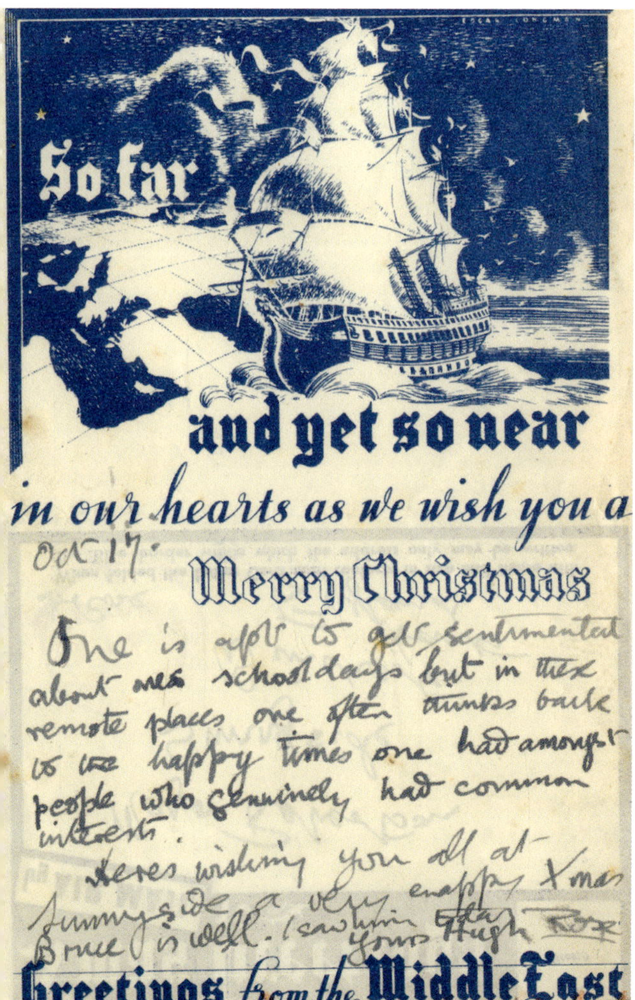

the enemy time to recover. These were First World War methods, but tried and tested ones, supported by the best artillery in the world.

In the 1½-mile frontage assigned to the Highland Division, 1BW were to be in the northernmost (right-hand) lane of the four allocated to 154 Brigade, putting them essentially in the centre of the Division's advance. Having crossed the start line they would attack through German positions code-named LEVEN, COMRIE, and DOLLAR, which would bring them to the 'Green Line'; from there they would push on to a large enemy position code-named KILLIN, on the 'Red Line'; then through CRIEFF and PERTH to the 'Black Line'. On the final 'Blue' line was a large objective called STIRLING, nearly four miles west of their start line.

On the night of 22nd/23rd October, the men of 51st Division moved up to their start line and concealed themselves ready for the attack. At 2140hrs on the 23rd, the biggest artillery bombardment yet fired in the desert war crashed into the air, gun flashes splitting the skies, the shells invisible but terrifyingly audible in their flight. And so it began.

Led by its pipers, 1BW advanced in perfect order as far as the Green Line, keeping up close behind the artillery barrage. The unit encountered little opposition. 'B' and 'C' Companies then made for the Red Line, in front of which lay KILLIN. This they overran, but as they consolidated they were struck by artillery fire – possibly their own – and suffered heavy casualties. Nevertheless, 'A' and 'D' companies then advanced through them towards the 'Black Line', 1BW's intended objective. 'A' Company fell foul of a dense anti-personnel minefield, laced with 500lb bombs and covered by heavy machine-guns. Despite this, they almost made it to the 'Black Line'. To their right, 'D' Company stormed a large enemy strongpoint, but were unable to make further progress owing to fire from positions on their right flank. The commanding officer of 154 Brigade, Brigadier Houldsworth, wrote: 'Thanks to the leading of Hugh and his brother officers, the 42nd advanced dead straight and with never a falter through three miles of German defences.'[21]

Casualties in the Battalion had been heavy. Fortune had come through unscathed, although the Carrier Platoon (of which he was second-in-command) spent the night ferrying ammunition forwards to the rifle companies. Fortune did not often refer to his first battle, but later recalled that driving through the imperfectly-marked British minefields, as well as the imperfectly-cleared German ones, made the task very difficult. Fortune's superior, Captain Ian Molteno, was badly wounded when his carrier triggered a mine, losing an eye and being out of action until February 1945. The following morning, the Carrier Platoon was disbanded and Fortune was transferred to replace a casualty in a rifle company. Fortune reported to his new Company Commander, Major Charles Osborne, who was shaving in a slit trench, using the body of a dead German as a table for his shaving kit. Fortune remembered thinking, 'This man is mad.' That was the least of his problems; he was in the middle of a vast battle, taking command of men whom he hardly knew, and had neither trained nor fought with.[22] He had also lost friends in the attack – among them Rose, who had not been so lucky. Robertson learned the news from Rose's father in the following letter:[23]

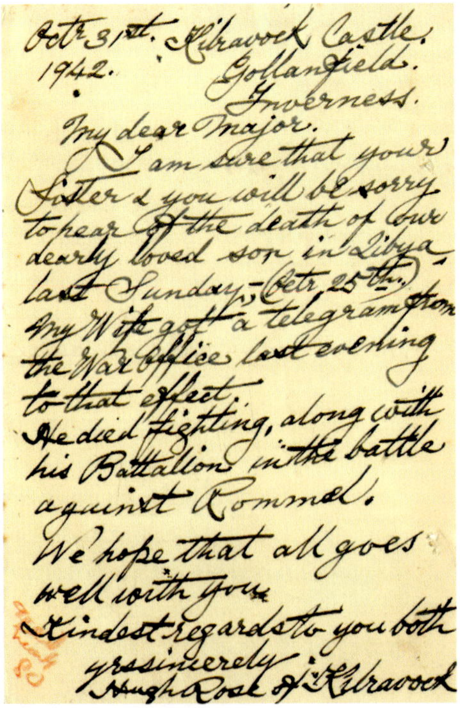
Octr 31st. Kilravock Castle.
1942. Gollanfield.
Inverness.

My dear Major.
I am sure that your Sister & you will be sorry to hear of the death of our dearly loved son in Libya last Sunday – Octr 25th.
My Wife got a telegram from the War Office last evening to that effect.
He died fighting, along with his Battalion in the battle against Rommel.
We hope that all goes well with you.
Kindest regards to you both
yrs sincerely
Hugh Rose of Kilravock

Fortune's mother, who knew the Rose family well, visited Kilravock when she heard the news and wrote to Robertson shortly afterwards:

> Dear Bobber,
> How nice of you to send me the letters. Hugh was rather pathetic [in the proper sense of 'arousing pity owing to vulnerability'] and poor dear he is saved further worries. His old father said, 'I always knew I should never see him again, but now I shall see him sooner than I expected.' Rather sweet, and once again today we have been commiserating the useless sacrifice of our many friends 24, 25 and 26 years ago, and let's hope it won't be repeated after this war. I hope there is not some awful trap in this show. They are so clever, I shall not be happy till they are all in the Bag …
> Bruce will feel Hugh's death awfully. They were so pleased to go out together, and Hugh was always so faithful to Bruce.[24]

Robertson scrawled sadly at the bottom: 'Bruce Fortune and Hugh Rose were like brothers.'

Alas, Hugh Rose had no brothers of his own. He had been born in 1921, when his father was already fifty-eight years old. Colonel Rose had only married in October the previous year, and his joy in at last having a son and heir is evident in the accompanying photograph, taken three weeks and one day after the birth. His son was to become the twenty-sixth chief of the Clan Rose and to inherit the seat of the Rose Clan, Kilravock Castle. All these dreams were shattered in the instant of Hugh's death at Alamein. Colonel Rose died in February 1946, aged eighty-two, and Kilravock passed to his daughter, (Anna) Elizabeth Rose. She never married, and left Kilravock to a Christian trust. As of 2023, the Castle stands empty and disused. The Rose line only continued through the younger sister, Madeleine, but some of the family's records and memorabilia are still in the hands of Rose's close relatives, John and Joanna Baird. As they point out, this sad sequel indicates the impact which Hugh Rose's death had and still has on the wider family.

In a letter to Robertson written exactly a month after Rose's death, Fortune explained exactly what had happened.

> We have had a scrap and I am glad to say came out on top. Our Jocks did their stuff in great style and I am sure it would have done my father all the good in the world to have seen and heard them. I wish he could have been here to lead them – they still remember him, a lot of them – in fact I saw a [Bren-gun] carrier the other day bearing the name 'Victor Fortune'. St Valery has now been avenged I am sure – what the future holds we cannot tell. At present the Axis seems to have received a shaking in this theatre of the war. But Rommel isn't rubbed off as easily as all that, and we expect further opposition.
>
> Poor Hughie Rose was killed the first night of the push. He received a machine-gun bullet in the neck while leading his Platoon on to our final objective. Those who saw him said he was doing splendidly and was supremely happy when he died. I hope his old father does not take it too hard. I feel his loss very much, as he was always rather like a younger brother to me.[25]

A Hopperite who bumped into Fortune in India in 1945 passed on the following in a letter to Robertson: 'He told me about poor Hugh Rose. He said he saw him after he was killed. He had only a little bit of shrapnel in the neck. He still had his crook in his hand and a broad grin on his face.'[26]

Rose's death gets a specific mention in the superlative *The Black Watch & the King's Enemies*:

> The Colonel was congratulating little Hughie Rose of Kilravock, as he found him on his objective with his Platoon, when Rose was struck in the neck and killed instantly. He was the youngest officer in the Battalion, the only son of a father with a great record in the Regiment, and the last of his direct line.[27]

Lt Hugh Rose.

Rose, who died a month short of his twenty-first birthday, had been the seventh male of his family in a century to die overseas in the service of his country.[28] Robertson later wrote that 'no one who knew him was surprised to hear that he went "dead straight" in the spirit of his family motto, "Constant and True".'

News of Rose's death had reached his parents swiftly – within the week – but only a week after that, Rose's Christmas airgram to Robertson reached its destination; earlier than anticipated, but far too late.

A remarkable letter survives in the Winchester archives from Donald Scott, a pupil then in his last term. Scott was one of the outstanding players of Winchester College Football at the time, but on September 23rd the sport had claimed the life of his brother, Malcolm. With his own grief still fresh, and his own Army service imminent, Scott sat down and wrote the following on November 5th:

> Dear Major Robertson,
> The Old Wykehamists in the 1st Battalion of the Black Watch have often been in my thoughts lately, and it came as a great shock when I saw the death of Rose in the papers this morning.
> It must be a great loss to his fellow officers, but even more to you and your sister and his parents. You both have my deepest sympathy, for I know what he must have meant to you. I shall never forget those few hours I had with him last half when he came over from Aldershot. He told me all about the Black Watch and his Battalion, and made me wish even more to get into it eventually. He was so cheerful then that it is hard to believe he is no more, but I am sure he met his fate with that same pleasant smile which he always had.
> These words are but cold comfort, but I hope you do not mind me taking the liberty in writing to you.
> Yours very sincerely
> Donald[29]

Rose's father received a letter from his son's Platoon which was written in mid-November, and passed a copy on to Robertson. It is hard to know how common such letters were, but they illustrate the close bonds between a 'good' officer and his men. Given the rocky relationship with his Platoon which Rose had described in his last letter, he must have done something right by the time that they went into action.

> Dear Sir,
> We all realise the great loss you sustained when your son, our late Platoon Commander, was killed in action, and we humbly offer our heartfelt sympathy to you and his relatives.
> From the time he joined the 42nd early in the year he had shown dash and spirit, much admired by the men. To the last, 2nd Lt. Rose proved himself a man, eager, like us all, to get this job done, a job which deprived him of a life which would, we are sure, have played its part as nobly in the future as it has done in the past.
> It is, we trust, a comfort to you to know that your son suffered very little; also to know that his Platoon laid him out at rest that same morning, sadly aware that it had lost one of the best.
> All the time we knew Mr Rose, he acquitted himself admirably, both as a soldier and a gentleman. He was ever thoughtful of the men's comforts, and all complaints he dealt with satisfactorily. His strong sense of duty is reflected many, many times o'er.
> Please accept then, this, 12 Platoon's humble token in respect to the late 2nd Lt. Rose, and may God comfort you in your bereavement.
> Yours in deepest sympathy
> NCOs and men of No12 Platoon[30]

The war in North Africa swept on, driving Axis forces back through Libya and eventually to total defeat in Tunisia. On November 8th 1942, in Operation Torch, Allied troops landed in Algeria, amongst them many Wykehamists. Fortune's letter to Robertson that month concluded:

The weather is getting colder and I expect we will soon be in battledress. We see quite a lot of European birds about – all in the process of migration – also now and again of course we bump into an odd gazelle. How they manage to exist on the sparse vegetation is a wonder. Still I suppose in wartime they supplement their diet with a good amount of 'bully' and biscuit which the Army leaves about.

Well, Bobber, I hope you and Miss Bobber have a very good Christmas and New Year. We hope to be back some time in 1943![31]

* * *

Duncan McMurtrie had come very near winning the Belt of Honour at the Sandhurst OCTU, and was commissioned as a 2nd Lieutenant into the Scots Guards on December 4th 1942.[32]

Shortly after being commissioned, McMurtrie wrote to Robertson:

At home at last for a week's leave before reporting to the Regiment. The OCTU was a very stiff course, but worth it for the result! I got an 'A' in the grading. There were only thirteen for the course, and mine, I was told, was the fourth. I am taking this opportunity of writing a few overdue letters. I had no time at all during the OCTU. We were only too glad to sleep for any respite over five minutes!

When I go to Pirbright I shall be on the direct line to Winchester. I may be able to run down and see you again … I expect that you and Miss Robertson must be looking forward with somewhat mixed feelings to July. But quite honestly I don't suppose that you and Winchester will ever be completely separated. The rest to come must seem welcome; you both certainly deserve it … But I shall see you again before you finally leave Sunnyside.

My new uniform still seems a little strange. But I am very glad indeed that I am in the Scots Guards.[33]

Robertson wrote that 'it was a great day for him when he was brought down to help judge Drill Cup in 1943, and those who had known him as an impulsive and rather easily-rattled little boy in early days were impressed by his growth and poise.'

* * *

December 18th 1942 was the last day of term, and Robertson knew that this would be his final Christmas in Hopper's; his retirement as housemaster from the end of August 1943 had already been announced. For Holtby, too, the day was an ending – in his case, to a school career which had begun unpromisingly. His father, a Hopperite himself, had written to Robertson in November 1940:

Dear Bobber,
I am glad our lad is at long last beginning to find himself. It is good to hear he is interested; apathy and indifference is so terribly difficult to fight against …
Edmond[34]

Holtby's career at Winchester ended with him being Captain of Fencing, a trumpeter, bugler, and French horn player, a Sergeant in the OTC, and even a Bombing Instructor with the Home Guard. Perhaps he had received coaching in the latter skill from Robertson. As a farmer's son, he could have applied for exemption from military service, but his father was supportive of Holtby's desire to join up:

We have mixed feelings about him serving … being our only son. But I want him to do as his instinct dictates. Personally, if he does serve and come through, it will put something into him which nothing else in civil life will. The young farmer who can be done without and who sees himself reserved, is not a very distinguished member of society.

I do not know precisely what are Mary's views on the subject but mine – after due consideration – are that he is right to do his share. And he may like the life so well as to stick to it.[35]

Also on December 18th, Robertson forwarded a copy of the school magazine, *The Wykehamist*,[36] to Hew Tompson's mother. That edition included a supplement giving short obituary notices of Winchester's war dead so far. Tompson's name was there, alongside sixty others, including that of his friend 'Slogger' Armitage, and that of Angus Grant.

Robertson's accompanying letter was grim but redolent with the care which he put into commemorating his boys.

> My dear Mrs Tompson,
> This sad 'Xmas card' (of which you no doubt already have a copy) brings you and the daughters our joint good wishes for as happy a Xmas and New Year as may be. I hope you will like the short account of Hew, but you will see, from the number, alas! involved, that we had to condense; and we also agreed not to compete, as it were, in praise, and to try to make what we wrote ring true. There must be mistakes, and probably omissions which parents will regret: but they all have fuller and more intimate letters or notices than can be printed in a supplement of this kind. One of the reasons that people always, I hope, trust my 'characters' of the living is that I always indicate any weakness as well as make the most of any strength. In writing of Hew, Henry Browne, Fred Hollins, even Bernard Pinney, I could not forget old anxieties or write as if they had never existed. But I think their friends will value the human touch and the restraint from adulation, which so easily rings false.
>
> You and friends of the House will like to know that our successors here with effect from late August meet with our full approval – Marcus Hampton[37] and his bright and able young wife (and boy of two). He is an old Clifton and Cambridge man, played county cricket (albeit for Worcestershire), and has run Scouts, School shop and grounds, and other things here most efficiently and with general approval. We shall get a home ourselves either in his house or in that of his mother who recently died. His twin (and only brother), the youngest Captain in the Navy, was killed on the bridge of his cruiser off Crete,[38] and it broke the old mother's heart, though she never gave way.
>
> Yours ever sincerely,
> Malcolm Robertson.
>
> I thought you'd like Hew's father mentioned. I could never forget his love of the boy and his anxiety for him.[39]

HEW FRANCIS CARYER TOMPSON (I, 1933-38), born February 19, 1920, was killed in action in Libya on January 21, 1942, during a dive-bombing attack on the R.H.A. Battery to which he had been posted some months before leaving England the previous autumn. His Colonel wrote of him as "always keen and cheerful and very efficient." This would have been a great satisfaction to his father, Major-General R. H. D. Tompson (I, 1893-97), a distinguished Gunner and Staff Officer, to whom just before his own death (accelerated by over-work for the Defence of London) Hew's inability to pass into Woolwich had been a disappointment. The fact was he was a late developer and had no flair for Mathematics: but he left as a Co. Prae., had some success at cricket and gymna, and managed to pass into the R.M.C. There he had the chance to volunteer for the R.A., and after training at Larkhill was posted to the 78th (D. of L. Y.) Medium Regt., where he made many friends and won golden opinions. He "got his jacket" in June, and was promoted Lieutenant in August 1941, and from many letters it is clear that he "found himself" on active service and was a valuable Officer and good comrade.

IX

'Nothing short of death will prevent me coming back to England like greased lightning'

July 10th 1941–February 9th 1943

A flying instructor in Southern Rhodesia shows a student pilot where he must & must not put his feet when climbing into the cockpit of a De Havilland Tiger Moth for his first flying lesson. (IWM CRH 115)

We must backtrack a little, as far as the summer of 1941, for we have lost sight of some of our subjects. John Huggins was nineteen years, five months, and fifteen days old when, on July 10th 1941, he boarded an aeroplane for the first time: de Havilland Tiger Moth R4913, of 25 Elementary Flying Training School, at Belvedere, Salisbury, in Southern Rhodesia. The aircraft was flown by his instructor, Sergeant Foster, who over the next few days demonstrated to Huggins the cockpit layout, effects of controls in straight and level flight, climbing, gliding, medium

Huggins.

turns, taking off into the wind, approaches, and landing. Luckily, Huggins' family still possess his flying log books, enabling us to view his progress. Gradually the flights grew longer, the manoeuvres more complicated, and Huggins' use of the controls more confident. On July 24th he practised spinning, and the following day was assessed by Pilot Officer Leslie on his readiness for a solo; a second assessment was conducted by Flying Officer Loat on July 26th. Amazing as it may seem, this young man was trusted to fly Tiger Moth T7675 solo for twenty-five minutes on July 28th, after only thirteen hours' tuition. But the Tiger Moth was a simple and sedate aircraft, and being flown in fine weather conditions; it would be a long time before Huggins was ready to graduate as a pilot. The following month, still on Tiger Moths, he moved on to emergency procedures such as abandoning an aircraft or conducting a forced landing, before performing his first aerobatics on August 16th.

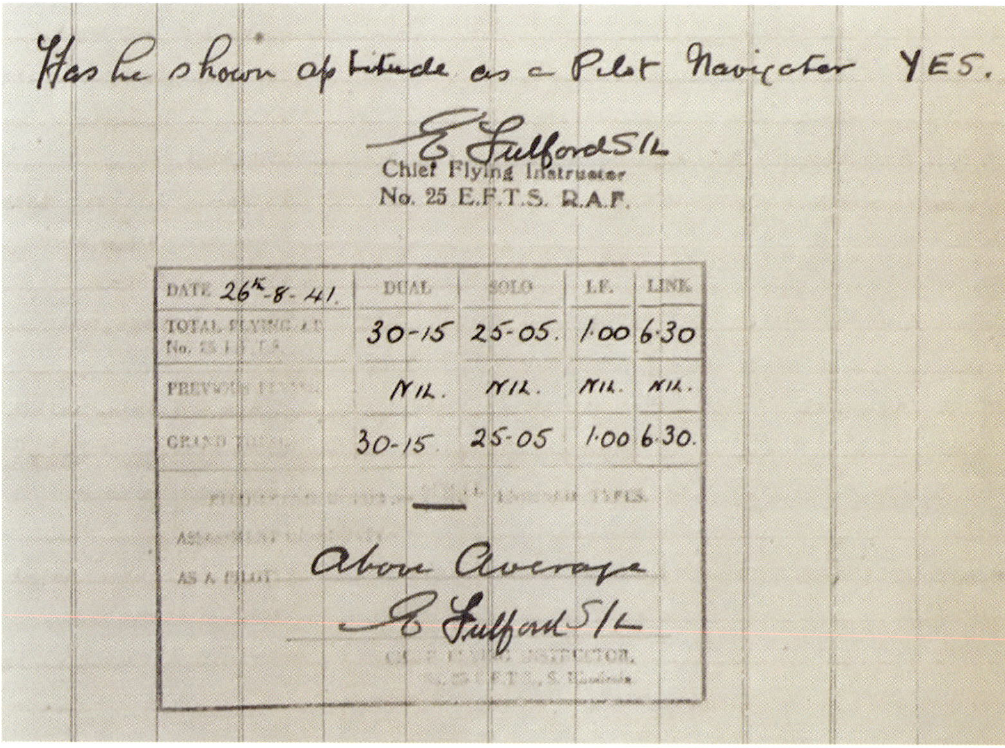

Has he shown aptitude as a Pilot Navigator YES.

E. Fulford S/L
Chief Flying Instructor
No. 25 E.F.T.S. R.A.F.

DATE 26th-8-41.	DUAL	SOLO	I.F.	LINK
TOTAL FLYING AT No. 25 E.F.T.S.	30-15	25-05.	1.00	6.30
PREVIOUS FLYING	NIL.	NIL.	NIL.	NIL.
GRAND TOTAL	30-15	25-05	1.00	6.30.

AS A PILOT Above Average

E. Fulford S/L

Huggins then progressed to Harvard trainers at 20 Service Flying Training School at Cranborne. These were monoplanes, faster than a Tiger Moth, with an enclosed cockpit and a retractable undercarriage – a much tougher proposition for a budding pilot.

Instructors, trainees, & Harvards, at 20 SFTS, Cranborne, in January 1943. (IWM TR1263; the original is in colour)

* * *

Dan Somerville.

'Dan' Somerville was now commencing his own, very much earthbound, training in the Royal Artillery. In his memoirs he wrote of this period as follows:

> I had received my call-up papers, and had been asked if I wanted to go in as a Private instead of straight to officer training. I said yes, as I wanted to know what it was like to be a Private with no responsibilities, so I had some idea what they had to put up with.
>
> I started in the Army in November 1941, and had two months in Bulford Camp on Salisbury Plain learning what soldiers do. I had nothing much with me but the military kit which they issued us with, and this was laid out daily, neat and tidy for inspection, on our simple bed in the barrack room. Three rules they told us when we joined:
>
> 1. If it moves, salute it.
> 2. If it doesn't move, pick it up.
> 3. If you can't pick it up, paint it.
>
> In other words, once you are in the Army you might be ordered to do anything, but when ordered to do something you do it. You don't say, 'But, Sir, what a bloody silly thing.' You don't say that once you have accepted military discipline.[1]

Somerville sent a letter to Robertson in late November from Bulford, where he was in the Potential Officers Training Squad of 4th Field Training Regiment. He signed himself 'Charlie' Somerville.[2]

> Everyone in this barracks, and nearly everyone in this Potential Officers Squad, is a University man, which was more than I expected. It's a help in some ways, as one doesn't run much risk of getting one's things pinched and there are some interesting people to talk to; on the other hand, it makes it more difficult to get to know the other chaps.
>
> It occurred to me that you might like to know something about my recent metamorphosis, and I have (for once) a little leisure, so here goes. Not that much of this will be news to you … I expect you know Bulford pretty well, as it was a going concern in the last war and is not so far from Winchester. My first sight of it was not calculated to stir the blood. It was raining and there was a pretty fair wind blowing. Bulford seemed to be an enormous mass of corrugated huts of various shapes and sizes; it looked very gloomy. However, things looked a bit better when we had a look at our barracks, one of the rare brick buildings that Bulford boasts, and consequently very much warmer than the rest …
>
> We work pretty long hours – up at 0600hrs, and finish at 1715hrs, when we get the rest of the day to ourselves. There's plenty to do; marching drill; gun drill; miniature range; lectures; PT – all fill up the time most effectively. As a rule you don't feel like doing much after parades are over. Discipline is pretty strict here; the NCOs are a good lot, but they keep you up to the mark – a good thing, you will say. The officers too seem to know their stuff, which was more than I expected of some of them; in fact I've learned quite a lot during the past week. They do things different in the Army to those thrust down us by the STC gun drill, and that sort of stuff is not much like the work we used to do on our old 18-pounders; though it is a help having done some of the drill before.

A month later, on Christmas Day, Brigadier Somerville penned a letter to Robertson about his boys:

> My dear Bobber,
>
> A line to thank you for Nick's report and for the nice things you said about him. I am very proud to hear that he does the job for you. He is in great form and I think likes the responsibility and is very proud of the House. I sent him off the other day with some of my chaps to see an anti-tank gun shoot, and to his great joy he was allowed to fire the gun. He has also had a run round with my signal section. Not much else in the military way Xmas week, but after we come back from my leave home I hope there will be a scheme for him to go out on.
>
> Dan has been given one of eleven Lance Corporal stripes, 'acting, provisional, without pay', which is I think a good mark, and he must be getting down to things, as I gather there are about fifty of them awaiting OCTU. He is very proud.
>
> I wish we could get going in the East. These infernal Japs seem to be able to anchor ships off any coast they like and nobody interferes. Our slowness off the mark as usual.
>
> All good luck for 1942.
>
> Yours, Desmond[3]

In 'Dan' Somerville's memoirs he sounds less proud of his stripes than his father suggests: 'I was made Lance-Corporal before my time ran out there – I was looking after prisoners, German and our own people. I didn't know the hell what I was going to get or where I was going to be sent.'

As it happened, it was Catterick, where Somerville joined 123 OCTU for six months.

* * *

By Christmas Eve 1941 Huggins had been assessed as 'Average' on the Harvard and ready to gain his wings, which were back-dated to November 4th. His commission as Pilot Officer 80269 was dated January 2nd 1942.[4]

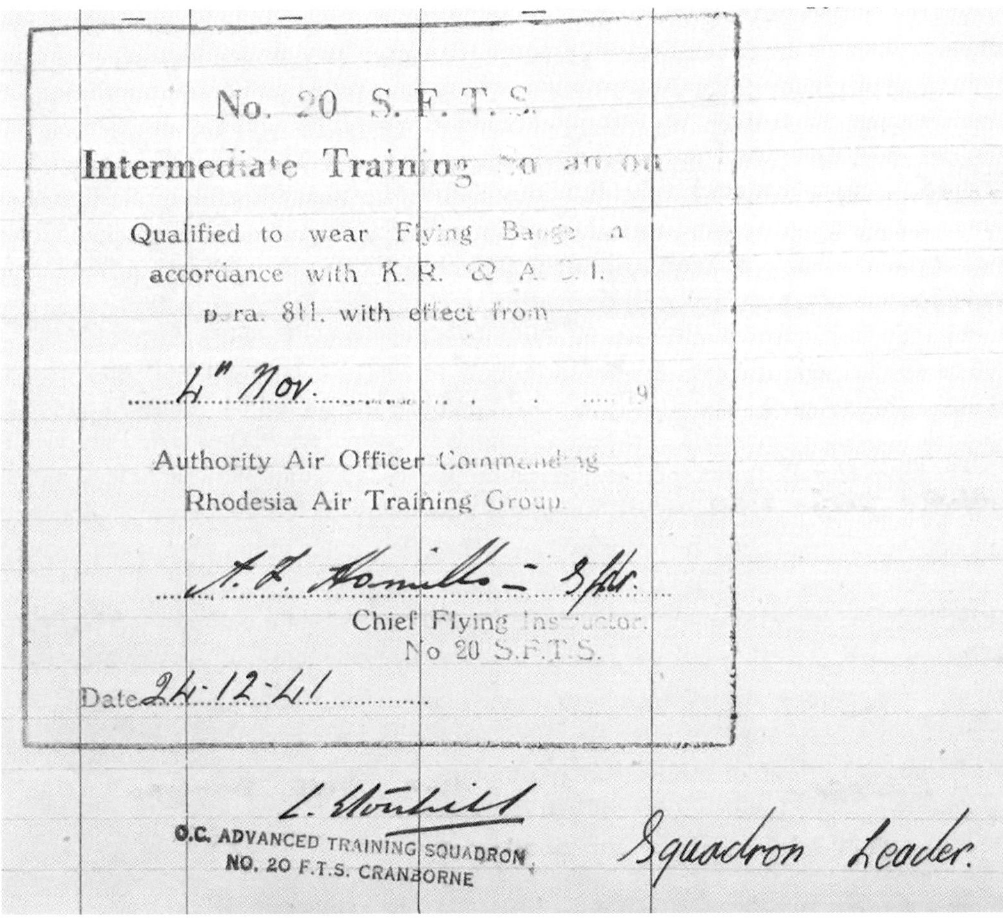
No. 20 S.F.T.S.
Intermediate Training Squadron
Qualified to wear Flying Badge in accordance with K.R. & A.C.I. para. 811. with effect from
4th Nov. 19
Authority Air Officer Commanding Rhodesia Air Training Group.
S/Ldr.
Chief Flying Instructor. No 20 S.F.T.S.
Date 24-12-41

O.C. ADVANCED TRAINING SQUADRON NO. 20 F.T.S. CRANBORNE
Squadron Leader.

His father wrote proudly to Robertson two days later:[5]

> Dear Robertson,
> John went off on the 2nd, very happy and excited with a grin from ear to ear. He did very well and received good reports all through, and is rated a very good pilot. He obtained a commission and for the most part made steady friends … Unfortunately his chief

friend, a thoroughly fine character, has gone to Coastal Command school and John is going to Army Co-operation operational school Mid East; he applied for that because he said they fly Hurricanes, have guns, bombs and cameras, and that appealed to him. I am sure he will do well if he survives, and in regard to that he has changed his mind and wants to go in for Medicine so if I have anything left to sell and he survives I hope he may yet go to Oriel …

John does not like the Rhodesians but he will get over that – all colonials brag and are somewhat immature for their age and inclined to think that being a nuisance to others is funny. Unless they give us a chance to survive as an independent unit I do not want my boys to live here …

Huggins himself wrote shortly afterwards:[6]

Here we are at the end of our training and waiting for a boat to take us somewhere or other … We get out after lunch every day until 0600hrs the following morning.

Among twelve others I have been given a commission and am now a Pilot Officer. We all managed to get through the big 'wings' exam and there were no more setbacks. With another fellow from England I am going to Army Co-operation. I decided to do this as there is a chance of more interesting work in that kind of squadron. Nowadays most of the fighter pilots seem to carry out instruction by radio and hope they are guided to the enemy planes. In Army co-op there is much more individual work and a chance of doing things on one's own.

I left young Hanbury in Rhodesia.[7] His lot are three weeks behind ours and he will be in his last fortnight now. We finished our flying on January 2nd. He is also flying single-engined planes – Harvards – and will probably go to a fighter Squadron …

If you write in the near future best address will be: c/o RAF HQ Middle East. We will all be controlled from there and that is the most satisfactory place for letters.

* * *

Shortly before Huggins qualified, on December 14th 1941, Guy Richardson wrote to Robertson from Trinidad. He had crossed the Atlantic for training at HMS *Goshawk* (Royal Naval Air Station Piarco), ten miles from Port of Spain. The base housed the Fleet Air Arm's No.1 Observer School, which comprised several training squadrons equipped with Fairey Albacore biplanes, Supermarine Walruses, and Grumman Goose amphibians.

Guy Richardson.

We are having a very interesting time out here – the hours are a bit stiff – 0430hrs to 1300hrs, and now search and patrols on two afternoons a week. There is also extra mugging, which we usually do after supper. Since I have been here I have averaged about six hours sleep per twenty-four hours. That may sound a good deal to you, but I am afraid I am only just getting used to such a strenuous life…. I think some good-natured fairy must be looking after my fate, as the work and this life in general suits me down to the ground. I am glad to hear that McArthur is doing 'Y' Scheme. He should get on pretty well at it.

I wonder when I shall see England next. It should have been quite soon, but now that things are blowing up a bit I expect they will find better places for us to go.

I wonder if the Japanese movements round the Aleutian Islands are to try and draw the Canadians back from England, so that the Boche can have a smack at us next spring without facing numerically superior forces – I wouldn't be surprised. That is only 'JP2' conjecture,[8] but it would serve them a double purpose.

We hope to go for a drive through the sugar, cacao, and other plantations this evening if the weather behaves itself. I am greatly looking forward to it as I have seen practically nothing of that part of the island.

I was fool enough to pick up malaria a little time ago, but I am fit and flourishing again now. It is a beastly thing to recover from. I had the actual fever for a little over a fortnight and found that it needed a further week to put me back in sorts again.

I was pleased to see in the papers today that Bob Crisp, a great friend of my brother's, had won the DSO for fighting in the desert – they were in the same battalion.[9]

Robertson made a note on this letter:

Guy Richardson in Trinidad, on return from which he was torpedoed, lost all kit, and was rescued from an open boat.

No trace of this sinking and rescue can be found in Richardson's service record, family archives, or official records. It remains one of those puzzles which I hope one day to solve.

* * *

Having finished his training on armoured fighting vehicles, Metcalfe was commissioned into 45th Indian Cavalry as 2nd Lieutenant 363896. On June 21st 1942, shortly after his arrival at his Regiment, which was equipped with Stuart light tanks, Metcalfe again wrote to Robertson, describing his move from Meerut to Nira:[10]

Metcalfe.

I have just finished a 1400 mile road-trip across half of India. The Regiment has just moved, and I went with the road party. It was great fun and I thoroughly enjoyed it, although it got extremely hot round about Delhi. Still, I saw a lot of new places and people, which I would not have seen from the train. Here we are stuck in camp for an indefinite time. It is quite nice and cool now that the monsoon has broken, but rather muddy, as well as being forty miles from Poona with only rather a shaky train service connecting, so we don't see much life!

* * *

Rigby reached India in August 1942. It was a difficult time, with the British on the back foot in both the Far East and Middle East.

> I disembarked from the SS *Orion* in Bombay two days after Mahatma Gandhi and Pandit Nehru had been arrested and imprisoned. They and the Congress Party had been stirring up civil disobedience against the government. The country was in turmoil. We were told to move about in Bombay in parties of no less than four, and all carrying pistols. We went by train to Lucknow to join the new Indian Armoured Corps recruit school. All the way up in the train, the bridges were guarded by troops. When we arrived at Lucknow station after dark on the second day of the journey, we were met by lorries with an escort of thirty riflemen to convey us to the Officers' Mess.[11]

Rigby.

It is evident from his memoirs that Rigby was a brilliant raconteur, and of all his stories the following is perhaps worthiest of quotation in full:

> After I had been there a few days I was ordered to take a tin box containing secret codes and deliver it to an officer in a place called Gorakhpur. To get there I had to travel on a metre-gauge railway. It was excessively hot. I was allotted a first class compartment to myself. My bearer, Hira Lal, was in a compartment at the end of the carriage with any other servants of the first class passengers. Hira Lal had brought tiffin (a picnic lunch). This consisted of some sandwiches and a banana. I had these on a small table in front of the window.
>
> At about lunch time the train stopped at a busy station. There were crowds of people on the platform. This was where two white nurses had been lynched a few days before, so I had the door locked and the screens down on the side of the carriage facing the platform. On the other side I had the screens up and the window open so as to get some air. I was reclining on the bed, my pistol on my thigh, snoozing in the heat and contemplating eating my lunch. Suddenly there was a noise. Someone was actually in the compartment with me. I awoke, grabbed my pistol and was just in time to see a huge grey ape – a langur. It was on the table. With one long thin arm it grabbed the top of the open window, with the other it grabbed my banana, and with extraordinary agility it swung itself out of the window and on to the carriage roof where, together with its tribe, it ate my lunch.
>
> I was kindly welcomed at Gorakhpur by the Scottish officer to whom I had to deliver the codes. He lived in a comfortable house with a garden tended by his Scottish wife ... He invited me to dine and stay the night. I think he and his wife were lonely in that remote place where there were almost no other Europeans.
>
> As the sun was setting we walked in their garden. I looked up to the north, and there rising quite high in the sky above the familiar heat haze of the plains was a pure white apparition. I could not make out what it was. I asked. It was Everest and its surrounding peaks. A wonderful, wonderful, vision, never to be forgotten.
>
> When I got back next day to Lucknow I met one of my fellow officers who had also been sent off to take secret codes to another station. He had gone to Almora, a small hill station in the Himalayan foothills. The only people in the depot were some old soldiers, some sick ones, the soldiers' wives and families, one or two elderly officers, and the wives of the English officers who were away with the regiment.

My friend handed over his tin trunk full of codes, and was then taken to the Officers' Club, where he could have a meal and a room before returning to Lucknow next day. My friend got a beer, sat on the verandah to admire the view, read the magazines, and enjoy the blessedly cool climate in that elevated place.

Four white women arrived in their shorts to play tennis. After their game they came up to the bar for a drink. It was then that for the first time they saw my friend. They called for the poker dice. Indian club barmen always had sets of poker dice handy. It was common practice to have a drink and play poker dice to decide who would pay. The loser paid, of course.

The girls played the poker, but then the winner came over to my friend and said, 'I won you.'

His journey with the codes ended rather more animatedly than mine had done.[12]

Later in the year, Rigby scribbled a cramped airgraph to Robertson with news of his movements:[13]

I hope this miniature is legible. It brings best wishes to all for a better New Year. Since my arrival in the August heat I have had a most interesting life, starting in Lucknow, continuing with short visits to Bombay and other towns further north, and now I am settled at Poona for a few weeks learning some tactics. At one time I was Quartermaster for 1800 Indian warriors of all tribes and faiths; a most absorbing task.

The cold weather here is delightful, like a warm English spring, day after day the same. Except for the prevalence of uniforms and the rise in prices India is still very pre-war, rather too much, I fear. I hope young Montgomery will emulate his father; that was a fortunate appointment.

I still remember our last walk in Meads in spring and hope to repeat it one day soon.

The need for training for the Indian Armoured Corps had resulted in the opening of an armoured-car school at Ferozepur in the Punjab, and a tank school in a large area of jungle some twenty miles south of Jhansi, near a village called Babina. Rigby arrived with the first of the staff at Babina later in 1942. He was made Training Adjutant and promoted to Captain, still aged only twenty – 'It just goes to show how woefully few officers in the Indian Army knew anything about tanks at that time.'[14]

* * *

'Dan' Somerville had been gazetted as 2nd Lieutenant 237556, with effect from July 4th 1942[15] and was posted to Northern Ireland to join 145 (Berkshire Yeomanry) Field Regiment RA, then part of 61st Infantry Division.[16]

Your letter I enjoyed so much that I sent it on to Nick and hope he has preserved it. There was nothing at all libellous in it (except in a general way) so it would be quite safe to keep it!

Here we seem to have settled down for the winter, which is now approaching in all its accustomed severity. We are seven miles from any town, so it won't be very easy to keep ourselves and the men occupied. Libraries and language courses help a bit (though I don't think our NCOs have much to learn as far as language goes!). I am now trying to get hold of two foils and a mask, which is all the equipment I need to start a small number of enthusiasts on fencing. Would you tell Holtby or some member of the gymna staff that I am prepared to pay anything up to 15/- apiece for foils and mask; that I don't care how old or dilapidated the equipment is; that I am prepared to pay postage and cash; in short, that I am ready to commit any number of crimes in the calendar in order to procure them.

Did I tell you that I met Rae,[17] late of Toye's, at HQRA on a divisional scheme? I saw him for a few moments only, and then pushed off on my motor-bike and haven't seen him since. I don't think I told you that I now ride a motor-bike with great speed and fury; in fact I'm told I look quite impressive as long as I have the whole road to myself. When something else comes along it's not so easy. I had a dreadful time once trying to pass a convoy three miles long.

Great news of Bruce and Hugh. I hope all goes well with them. Have you any news of Guy Richardson, or of his address, or the address of Peter Frewen ('E')[18] who was a crony of mine at New College and whom I saw once or twice at Bulford?[19]

Somerville's 'crony' Peter Frewen had less than six months left to live; and by the time that Somerville wrote this letter, Hugh Rose had been dead for a week.

* * *

As 1942 went on, the Japanese began to move their prisoners from Singapore to construct a railway linking Thailand with Burma. Rickman was one of them.

Rickman.

The second period was spent in Siam (Thailand, as it is called today) building the railway from Ban Pong (west of Bangkok) to the Three Pagodas Pass (the Siam/Burma border – 345 kilometres in length) – and onward to Rangoon. These reflections mostly concern life in Siam, building the railway, the aim of which was to transport Japanese men and materials to support their forward armies deep into Burma, fighting our Fourteenth Army.

This extract from a nominal roll maintained by his Battalion suggests that Rickman left 'over land' (OVL) – namely, by train to Thailand – on November 7th 1942:[20]

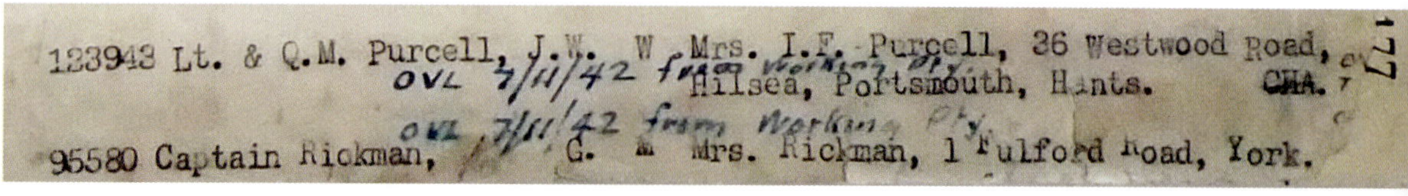
123943 Lt. & Q.M. Purcell, J. W. W Mrs. I. F. Purcell, 36 Westwood Road,
OVL 7/11/42 from Working Pty
Hilsea, Portsmouth, Hants. CHA.
OVL 7/11/42 from Working Pty
95580 Captain Rickman, G. M. Mrs. Rickman, 1 Fulford Road, York.

Six trainloads of 650 prisoners of war, known as 'Letter Parties' Q-P-O-N-M-L, and collectively forming Work Group IV under Lieutenant Colonel Douglas Rhys Thomas, were sent off from Singapore between November 1st and 6th, so it seems probable that this was the group with which Rickman travelled. Certainly, Sergeant Easton – who had been at Keppel Harbour at the same time as Rickman – records that his group left in this move:

> November 7th
> By train, twenty per truck, to Thailand. The journey actually took until December 1st, when we arrived in Ban Pong. On to Kanchanaburi, and then we marched, or walked, across the bridge over the River Kwai and so to Wan Lung. Days and nights of toil lay ahead.[21]

Japanese nomenclature and prison camp names are hugely confusing, but essentially Work Group IV was responsible for an area of the railway between Wang Pho and Kinsaiyok, with its headquarters and hospital at Tha Sao (known to the prisoners as Tarsao or Tarsau). Rickman's liberation questionnaire states that he arrived on the railway on December 4th.

> We worked under Japanese railway engineers and were administered by Japanese PoW staff, many of whom were Koreans … Our days started at 0600hrs and finished twelve to fourteen hours later at 1600–2000hrs. In the monsoon season it bucketed down with rain, and we were constantly drenched. Marching to and from work in the morass of mud was extremely unpleasant, especially for those barefoot. It was also very tiring to men with no energy, owing to an insufficiency of food.

* * *

The war in the Far East claimed its first Hopperite the day before Rickman reached the Death Railway. Clephan Bell had left Hopper's nearly twenty years previously but had nevertheless been one of Robertson's boys. When war came, after being rejected on age and medical grounds for flying, he had volunteered for an RAF medical unit, and went as Aircraftsman Second Class (AC2) to Singapore in June 1941. In mid-February 1942 he cabled that he had escaped to Java, escorting the wounded. Then his mother and sister experienced a weary and anxious period of waiting until December 1943, when they heard the bare fact that he had died in Japanese hands, on December 3rd 1942, at the age of thirty-seven. Robertson wrote that it was 'almost a relief to his friends to know that one so gentle, friendly, and cultured, did not have to endure that last year of distress'.

Bell's story deserves to be better known: the short version is that when the Japanese discovered that he had been an actor in civilian life they tortured him into broadcasting for them from the Tanah Abang radio station in Batavia. Bell then committed suicide by slashing his wrists. His lonely death earned him a posthumous mention in dispatches after the war. Whether or where the Japanese buried his body is unknown.

* * *

9RNF moved from camp to camp as the demands of railway construction and maintenance required. Although Rickman recorded only that he had been in 'approx twenty-five camps' between December 4th 1942 and August 16th 1945, Sergeant Easton provided slightly more detail.

> March 5th 1943
> Many members of the Battalion returned to Non Pladuck, the base camp for the railway.
>
> April 22nd 1943
> Left Non Pladuck; based at Wampo. We had become track layers. We laid sleepers, rails, and hammered in the spikes. Great speedo. From here on the Battalion would never come together again as a unit.

Rickman's account of conditions in captivity, despite its lightness of touch, makes for humbling reading, and I make no apology for quoting it almost unabridged.

> The first problem encountered was the change of diet from the European (meat, potatoes, and bread) to the Asiatic (based on rice and vegetables). One's liver and kidneys could not cope with the absorption of all the extra water the rice turned into. Until one slowly acclimatised, one had awful pains in the stomach and lower back, and continual diarrhoea. So hungry did one get that, on occasions, some even ate dog, kitten, snake, and rat. Some of them were surprisingly tasty, in fact! So far as I am aware there was no cannibalism.
>
> Under these conditions, with the starvation diet we were on, a big weight loss was inevitable. My young and previously fit lean frame (6′1″ tall) shed 5¾ stone (80½lbs) – from 12 stone (168lbs) to 6¼ stone (87½lbs). In fact, when I was released I was only about half the weight I started at.
>
> Can you imagine what life was like with no hot baths for 3½ years (we washed in the River Kwai, and doubtless we all smelt the same), no electricity (we had candles and coconut-oil lamps), no clothes replacements (you had to carry all your own possessions on your own back when marching from camp to camp), no newspapers of any kind, no drugs (in meaningful quantities), no regular communication home (we were allowed one printed post-card annually), and no female company?
>
> 'Informal' is the best description for our clothing. I retained a few pieces of my original uniform for wear on high days and holidays (one day a month!). More usual were a black loin-cloth made of umbrella material, wooden clogs with toe-straps made from bits of bicycle-tyre, and a hat made from banana leaves – very smart really!
>
> I had a spoon and fork to eat with, but no plate. However, as we were captured next door to the Ford Motor works, I picked up a hub-cap of a Ford car. This made a super plate, and I used it for the next 3½ years. I drank from a white enamelled mug, and took my Army water bottle into captivity. Before every meal we were trained to dunk all our eating and drinking utensils into boiling water. This precaution removed any infection which flies (the main carriers of disease) had deposited on them. This was vital, especially in the cholera camps we passed through. In Thailand, the cholera epidemic was quite appalling. In one of the camps we were in, 232 out of a total of 400 men died in a single month.

There were few, if any, drugs available, and the Red Cross only very seldom were allowed to send them in to us. One of our medical officers took out his own appendix in a lonely up-country camp, using a torch, a mirror, a hurricane lamp, a razor blade, medical stitching kit, and no anaesthetic – and he lived! Had he not operated, he would not have survived. No one else could do it for him.

Diseases such as malaria, dysentery, and jaundice, together with vitamin deficiency diseases such as beri-beri, jungle ulcers, and the natural mental stress of daily survival, affected nearly everyone. The mosquito caused us the biggest hazard, giving us all malaria, which tended to recur every month. Scorpions gave one an immensely painful sting. Centipedes, about six inches long, and large furry black spiders were unpleasant, and bedbugs came out of the bamboo at night and over-bloated themselves on our blood. Many types of deer abounded, as well as wild cats and other members of that family. Many animals one heard more frequently than saw. Huge lizards skittered about, and snakes slithered this way and that, but didn't bite unless you trod on them. Many of us, through necessity, walked barefoot, but few were ever bitten. Elephants were used for moving trees and the wooden poles for bridge building. The bright green jungle-clad mountains and other landscape scenes were quite out of this world, if only one had had the time to enjoy them, but there was no time for pondering. Had one had a camera (strictly forbidden) one could have got marvellous shots of superb butterflies, moths, and monkeys a-swinging.

Naturally there was no such thing as a water closet available – nor was there any loo paper. Our solution was to follow the normal Asiatic traditions. Sixteen-foot trenches were dug, up to fifteen–twenty yards long. Bamboo poles were laid from front to rear over these trenches. Gaps one foot wide were left uncovered, every three feet. Flapped lids, also made of bamboo, were made to cover the gaps, with a hinge (created from rushes) making the gaps closeable when not in use. These trenches accommodated fifteen–twenty men squatting at the same time. There was no screen between individuals. In spite of the proximity of one's neighbours, one soon lost any embarrassment and modesty one might have begun with! It was all a bit noisy (mainly due to our diet) but there was nearly always a good deal of laughter! In spite of the hinged lids, flies still got down to the darkened depths of the trenches and laid their eggs there. In due course these turned into maggots, and the whole trench bottom became a sea of seething maggots. Instead of paper, each prisoner took a small bottle of water to the loo for his personal use. One took a little time to acquire the skill, and one had to wash one's hands scrupulously afterwards, but the system worked … In most of the larger camps, officers and men had separate latrine trenches. Sometimes it was possible to erect reed screens around them to give a little privacy.

The difference between day and night-time temperatures was immense, and there were certain seasons and places where sleep at night was well-nigh impossible under the rice sacks we used instead of blankets.

Rickman clearly took pride in the way in which he and his companions rose to the challenges of their new existence:

When faced with what might seem insoluble problems, man can be very ingenious – commensurate often with the risks which are deemed to be acceptable. The advantage we had was that our officers and men were drawn from all walks of life. Few were regular or professional soldiers like myself. How, for instance, do you get clothes clean without soap? One of us burnt some bamboo and collected the ash, which was put into a four-gallon drum of water, into which dirty clothes had been placed. If one built a fire and put the drum on to it and brought it to the boil, the dirt, through the action of the wood-ash, boiled clean. Prisoners used a similar four-gallon petrol drum for brewing an alcoholic drink, using a yeast tablet, rotting bananas, brown sugar, and water.

Thanks be to Buddha and every other deity for the marvellous multi-purpose bamboo ... It was used for everything: hut construction, furniture manufacture, bed slatting, containers for liquids and solids, scoops, medical instruments, bed-pans, and also for the manufacture of false limbs for amputees.

By June 1943, confirmation had at last reached home that Rickman was a prisoner of war. As usual, Robertson wrote to the family, and received this reply:

Dear Major Robertson,
Thank you so much for your kind words of congratulation and encouragement. I am terrified of those filthy Japs. If Gerry's cheerfulness can prevail, then it will have proved a valuable asset, not only to himself but to his fellow captives. What a fate for a real soldier – War Office says that no more definite address came through from one of the Malay Camps. It is too much to hope that Clayton and Gerry would be together. They must just have overlapped in the House. I hope you are enjoying the freedom from wartime worries and responsibilities as Housemaster – but I dare say fresh ones will crop up!

Meantime good luck and my best wishes.
Yours sincerely,
Muriel Philbrick[22]

In fact, Rickman and Clayton *were* together, for at least some of the time, as Clayton explained in a post-war letter:

At one period I saw quite a lot of Gerry, as we were in the same camp; from his men I learnt that he showed up splendidly under conditions which required a higher courage and unselfishness than even war demands, where many men, brave in battle, broke down. I also saw a good deal of Henry Lewin, who was in 'F'.[23]

* * *

The next arrival in India was Guy Dodgson, who had been commissioned into the Royal Engineers as Second Lieutenant 201726 in August 1941.[24] By the end of 1942 he was in India with 219 Field Park Company RE,[25] and wrote a lively letter to Robertson:[26]

Dodgson.

Just a line to let you know what has happened to me. I had a good trip out here on a very comfortable boat with three days shore leave in South Africa ... Three days was a very short time and I'm afraid I met too nice a girl there – a Colonel's daughter from Brighton. At least so she said, and I quite believe it. I was with another subaltern whom I'd known for the last year, and he paired off with the Colonel's daughter's friend – who was niece of the Chief of Police of the town – so we dropped right into society right away and had a wonderful time. Lovely bathing, of course; huge rollers, which were most exciting, especially when my 'Bird' (as I seem to remember you calling one of my girlfriends before) went and fainted in the water and went clean out so that I had to do artificial respiration!

Anyhow, then we arrived here, and I've never ceased to be amazed and revolted. My friend and I were lucky enough to get posted together to British troops instead of the usual Sappers and Miners, which are native. We are all under canvas, and tho' quite warm by day it is really pretty chilly at night. Four blankets. We are lulled asleep by jackals and natives banging drums. So you see that tho' the address says 'Base', actually it's far from it. We're six miles from the nearest town, which is 100% Indian except for a couple of cinemas and a soldiers' and officers' club. The latter is a pretty one-eyed place and has a dance every Saturday night with about one female per ten officers. I've been doing quite a lot of touring about and have seen quite a lot – enough in fact – of the Indian roads. They aren't so good, and the dust is shocking. Actually, tho', I've got out here at the best time, during the cool season – so I shall get a chance of getting used to the heat. Life on the whole is much too easy except for spasms.

At the moment I am on a battle course. This morning we had to crawl seventy yards, chest on the ground, bullets over our heads. Everyone's exhaustion at the end, my – the finish of any race wasn't in it; it just about lays you out ... We had a very fine Christmas; plenty to eat and a certain amount to drink, tho' shockingly expensive. I had four pints of beer, the first ale since landing, at 3/5 a pint! Wicked.

* * *

Kennedy.

John Kennedy was just about to start his own flying training. He probably began at the little-known RAF Regent's Park, home to No.1 Air Crew Receiving Centre and consisting of Lord's cricket ground, the restaurant of London Zoo and some blocks of flats nearby. Sir Roger du Boulay (who had left Winchester College in 1940 and flew Hurricanes over Burma) remained cynical about why the flats were used:

> We actually lived in one of those big blocks of flats north of Regent's Park .... The reason for that was that an Air Commodore owned all these properties north of the Park ... and funnily enough when the war came they were all commandeered at very high rents by the Royal Air Force.[27]

The facility had opened on June 14th 1941, its location chosen partly because of its proximity to railway stations, enabling personnel to be brought in and out easily as the RAF expanded massively. Potential aircrew had their basic medical check-ups in their local area, and then reported to Lord's. There they were allocated to Flights and received their initial kitting. Their two or three weeks of basic training included an induction to service life, a more rigorous medical examination, and aptitude tests designed to stream recruits towards the right specialism. Potential aircrew wore a white band on their forage caps to distinguish them from those destined for ground trades. Conditions were spartan, but for those used to boarding schools not so unfamiliar: eight-man rooms containing nothing but 'biscuits' (square mattresses like sofa cushions, to be assembled into beds); blankets for bedding; meals in the zoo restaurant eaten at high speed after queuing for an eternity. And the training was the same as for recruits the world over: drill, laying out kit in a precise order for inspection, and polishing things in places where no one would ever see the shine.[28]

After six weeks at RAF Regent's Park, recruits went on to Initial Training Wings elsewhere. But for Kennedy there came an abrupt change of scene. Like Huggins, he was to be trained overseas; unlike Huggins, his training was to take place in Canada and the United States.

* * *

The entry of the United States into the war in December 1941 had changed a great many things, but even before Pearl Harbor the Americans had been stretching the definition of neutrality. One method by which they had helped the British was the 'Arnold Scheme', named after American General 'Hap' Arnold. As early as June 1941, the United States Army Air Corps had agreed to train 4,000 RAF pilots alongside its own trainees. Every five weeks, a new set of potential pilots arrived in the US to be sent to flying schools across the country.

Six British Flying Training Schools (BFTS) were set up, in Florida, Texas, Arizona, California, and Oklahoma. 'Primary' flying training took place on the Stearman PT-17 biplane, with experienced civilian instructors; the course lasted some nine or ten weeks and involved sixty hours of flying. By the end of this period, the trainees had gone solo. They then progressed to 'basic' flying training, another ten or so weeks, including seventy hours on the Vultee BT-13 Valiant monoplane with military instructors – some of them RAF pilots. Then came 'advanced' flying training on North American AT-6 Harvards. The scheme was not as successful as had been originally hoped, with half of the trainees failing (or being killed in accidents). But the aim of training 4,000 pilots had been achieved by 1943: of 7,885 trainees, 4,493 passed. Of these, some 600 stayed on in America for a year to act as instructors, and when they returned to England often carried out the same role in flying schools there.

* * *

Kennedy's first letter to Robertson from Canada was written in Ottawa on February 18th 1942, three days after the fall of Singapore.[29] His letters to Robertson are striking in their constant reference to birds and other wildlife; as Robertson later wrote, 'He seemed always to be closely akin to nature, and like [his half brother] Geoffrey Gwyer to know no fear.' Indeed, there are photographs of Kennedy, as a child, holding a pet owl and red squirrel (not at the same time).

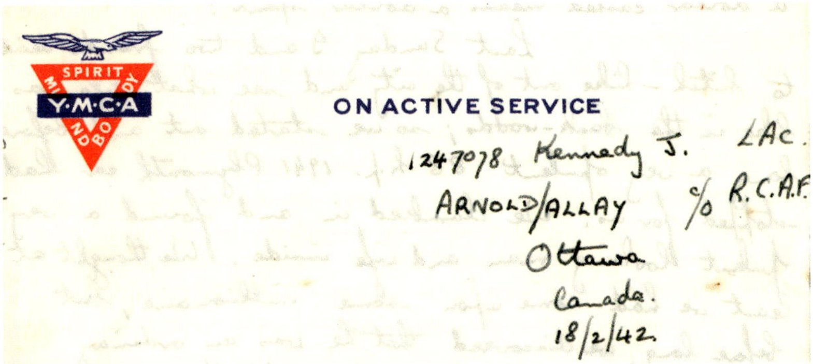
SPIRIT
Y·M·C·A
MIND
BODY
ON ACTIVE SERVICE
1247078 Kennedy J. LAc.
ARNOLD/ALLAY c/o R.C.A.F.
Ottawa
Canada.
18/2/42.

As you will have observed from my address, I have reached 'the promised land' at last, but am a mere bird of passage here in New Brunswick waiting to migrate to the warmer reaches of the Southern States. After a few very cold days in Manchester, we set sail on a long and tedious trip across the water. The first few days were very rough and, as was to be expected, most of us succumbed to *'le mal de mer'*. The usual discomforts accompanying lack of space and sleeping in hammocks did little to cure one's illness, and it was only after the fifth day that I came to life again properly. We didn't see many birds of interest, except for one or two very small black and white gulls, which I think were Little Auks, right in the very middle of the Atlantic – amazing.

We have been here in Moncton just over two weeks and are expecting to start our training any day now, in or around Alabama. The people are very hospitable and one receives many invitations out to meals. The shops are full of food and a dollar cashed means a dollar spent!

Last Sunday I and two friends decided to hitch-hike out of the city and see what life was like in the back-woods; so we started out and before long a very opulent 88hp 1941 Plymouth car had stopped for us. We clambered in and found a very opulent-looking man and wife inside. We thought at least we had come upon some millionaire, but before long we discovered that he was an ordinary fireman off one of the local trains! However, upon hearing what we intended to do, he offered to take us to his father-in-law's farm and show us round the woods himself. We drove through Salisbury, which is the centre of the silver-fox farming, and eventually arrived at the house. He had to park the car on the road and we then walked about ¼-mile across country to get to the place. One had to cross the Petitcodiac river, which was frozen up, and apparently in summer they use a boat; but what happens when the ice just isn't bearing, I don't know! After a simple meal, we sallied forth into the forest armed with a .22 rifle.

The walking was very unpleasant, as every other step one took one's foot would break through the crust on the top of the snow and one would drop about two feet down into it. We tracked white rabbits, foxes, deer, red squirrels, and other small animals, and saw where porcupines had nibbled all the bark off young trees, but unfortunately did not see any, nor any lynxes, which are in the district. Moose and bears are to be found there, but the latter are still hibernating. We saw some kind of a woodpecker, which was very large and pied (not unlike our Greater Spotted) and flew within a few yards of us without any fear. We also saw some 'chickadees', which were very like our Marsh-tits and came within three feet of us.

We were then given another meal and they finally ran us back to the camp in their car. Next Sunday we are thinking of trying to see a Red Indian settlement about sixty miles away from here; but it may be rather difficult, as there are only about five main roads open in the district – and they are several inches deep in fine ice!

The weather out here is very pleasant, and usually a very warm, clear sun shines from a very blue, clear sky. However, it can be cold and we have had an occasional fall of snow.

There is no black-out over here at all and it is just the same as in the days of peace – the only reminder of war being the sirens, which are fitted to trains to warn traffic at the level-crossings, instead of having gates.

Gray from Freddie's is here, but otherwise Winchester is not represented, except for me.

Moncton is noted for being the best place to see the tidal bore on the Petitcodiac, which has been known to have been about five foot high and comes up the river twice a day – a phenomenon caused, apparently by the combination of the high tides in the Bay of Fundy and the formation of the rock at the mouth of the river. However, at this time of year the river is full of loose ice and the bore is hardly visible.

The city is named after General Moncton, who – I don't know if you knew – was a direct ancestor of my mother's … All going well I should be back in England next October most probably, and will look forward to seeing you and your sister again then.

* * *

Huggins had been posted to 237 (Rhodesia) Squadron RAF, who were then stationed at Mosul in Iraq. But before he could become operational, he needed to learn how to fly modern fighter aircraft, such as the Hawker Hurricanes with which 237 were equipped. This required attendance at an Operational Conversion Unit, and so in February 1942 he began his advanced training at 74 OTU in Palestine, as can be seen in the page overleaf from his log-book.[30] His first flights there were in Miles Magister I trainers R1954 and P6379, which were two-seat open-cockpit monoplanes – they have been described as less demanding for a trainee than the Tiger Moth, and an absolute joy to fly despite their top speed of just over 130mph. Hurricanes, however, had a top speed of 340mph, which made them a different proposition; furthermore, there were no two-seat versions, so one's first flight in a Hurricane was also perforce one's first solo. Luckily, Hurricanes were considered very easy to land. Huggins' first solo in a Hurricane I (Z4025) came on February 27th, and lasted for an hour.[31] It must have been an extraordinary thrill to be in charge of something so powerful and to know that he might soon enough fly one in combat. In fact, he would never fire his guns in anger.

Huggins needed to learn the ropes of Army co-operation flying, and so his flights in March were all geared to that end; he flew a variety of Hurricanes (and the odd Magister) on flights of up to two hours. Lessons included several each on Tactical Reconnaissance, Navigation, Photographic Reconnaissance, Artillery Reconnaissance, Mail Delivery and T-Panel, and Rail Reconnaissance. On March 27th, in Hurricane Z7013, he had his longest flight of the month – 2¼ hours – and the excitement of live-firing his eight .303-inch Browning machine-guns. On the same day, he flew again in a different aircraft to carry out aerobatics. His last flight of the month was a two-hour oxygen climb, getting used

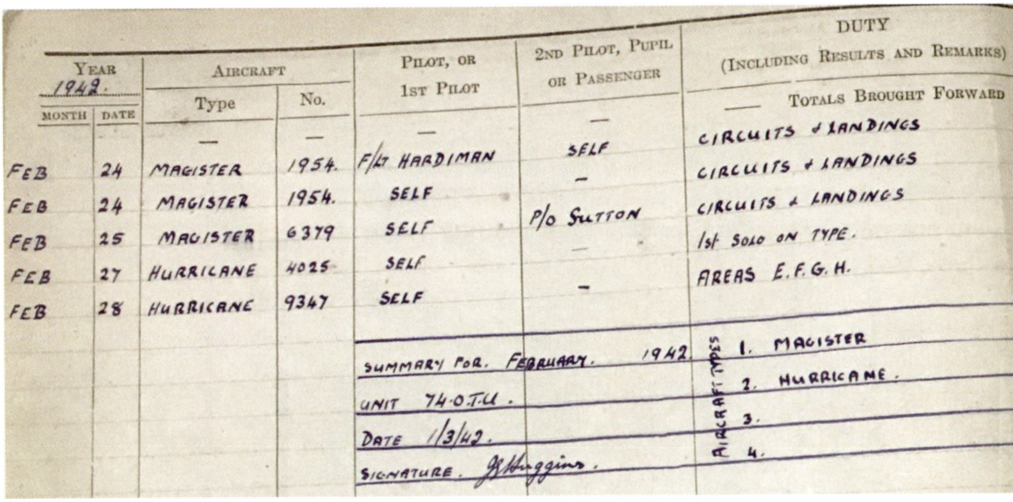

YEAR 1942. MONTH	DATE	AIRCRAFT Type	No.	PILOT, OR 1ST PILOT	2ND PILOT, PUPIL OR PASSENGER	DUTY (INCLUDING RESULTS AND REMARKS)
		—	—	—	—	TOTALS BROUGHT FORWARD
FEB	24	MAGISTER	1954.	F/Lt HARDIMAN	SELF	CIRCUITS & LANDINGS
FEB	24	MAGISTER	1954.	SELF	—	CIRCUITS & LANDINGS
FEB	25	MAGISTER	6379	SELF	P/O SUTTON	CIRCUITS & LANDINGS
FEB	27	HURRICANE	4025	SELF	—	1st SOLO ON TYPE.
FEB	28	HURRICANE	9347	SELF	—	AREAS E.F.G.H.

SUMMARY FOR. FEBRUARY. 1942.
UNIT 74 O.T.U.
DATE 1/3/42.
SIGNATURE. JHuggins.

AIRCRAFT TYPES
1. MAGISTER
2. HURRICANE.
3.
4.

to flying at high altitude. By the end of the month Huggins had over two hundred hours of flying under his belt, in four different types of aircraft. He was ready for operations, and set out for Iraq and 237 Squadron.

* * *

Herbert.

Arthur Herbert had enlisted in November 1941, but did not start his training until April 7th 1942, when he reported for duty and was assigned to 3 Holding Battalion; however, three days later he proceeded to Oxford University for No.4 Potential Officers' Course. He was admitted to New College on what was sometimes referred to as the 'Army Course'. These short courses were arranged by the three armed services to provide basic training in technical trades – such as signals – and the trainees mingled with the undergraduates. Officially speaking, the trainees *were* undergraduates, and matriculated into the University, though their courses were only six months long. There were courses for RAF, Royal Navy, and Royal Corps of Signals trainees. One of those who attended Oxford for such a course was the future actor Richard Burton, a beneficiary of the greater social mobility which these courses promoted (Burton attended Exeter College in the second half of 1944 on the RAF course). As well as some undemanding lectures and academic work, the potential officers took part in military activities (they wore military uniform three days a week and gowns for the rest of the time).

It may seem perverse of the armed forces to have sent potential officers to university instead of feeding them straight into the OCTU system, but it was felt that seeing a bit of life – however untypical – before service would make them better officers. *The Times*, for example, opined in an editorial that the Army, Navy, and Air Force must

> recruit trained minds in a variety and in numbers quite as great as the universities are able to supply. They need men of many highly specialized scientific requirements … but

> they need also men who have profited by that rapid enlargement of mental horizons which is the first gift that a university confers.[32]

What is even more surprising is that the Navy and RAF allowed their trainees total freedom of choice of subject – two thirds of the RAF candidates studied arts subjects (Burton, for example, took English Literature and stunned audiences with his performances for OUDS). The Army's Signallers, however, had to study scientific subjects.

* * *

By April 1942, Kennedy had moved from Canada to the southern states of America, where he began flying training at Tuscaloosa, in Alabama:[33]

> As you will observe from my address I am now enjoying the warm sun of the Southern States, in contrast to the snow in Canada. I was a month in Georgia, near Albany, on an acclimatization course. It was over 80°F in the shade and the countryside was very sandy and barren. One was not allowed into the grass at all as rattle-snakes are very numerous there. This was a bore as I was not able to see much of the wild life. Nevertheless I saw a lot of buzzards, loggerhead shrikes, and bright red cardinals. Where I am at present, in Alabama, we get marvellous birds, ranging from humming-birds to cow-birds and blue-birds. The butterflies and moths are as large as tits and again are marvellous. I often think what a hey-day Charles Duffin would have if he were here.
>
> This aerodrome is run by civilians, except for a skeleton US Army Air Corps Staff, and the quarters are very comfortable. The food of course is marvellous, ranging from strawberries and ice cream to hamburgers or steaks, etc. The discipline is very strict, and one has to make one's bed in exactly the right way with 45° turns at the corners, and one's clothes have to be folded and placed in exactly the right part of one's locker. The flying instruction is believed to be literally the best in the world, as all the instructors have flown for several thousands of hours each before. Every manoeuvre one does has to be done precisely and exactly correct, so that if one does a medium turn to the right or left one has to turn exactly 90° or 180° not 89°, 91°, 179°, or 181°. When one does a spin one has to do two complete spins and then come out of it in exactly the same direction as one went into it in. We also have a good few ground subjects such as meteorology, airplane structures and propellers, engines, theory of flight, etc. We are examined in these every week and the questions take the form of 'quizzes' when one has to say if the statement is true or false. One usually stands a 50-50 chance of guessing it right, if one doesn't know it.
>
> Tuscaloosa is a very interesting town and is teetotal, so when we have a day off we go into Birmingham, which is one of the largest cities of the South and where the RAF is little seen – and so offered unbounded hospitality. It is quite safe to go there with an empty purse, as one can be certain one will have a good time. One night I went to a dance at the broadcasting station and had my picture, a ghastly one, in the paper with the rest of our party.
>
> Last Saturday I tried my hand at a game of golf on the local course. Luckily I was playing quite well considering I had not played for several months.

There is the University of Alabama here in the town and there are about 5,000 men and girls in it. I went and heard a talk given by Dorothy Thompson there about two weeks ago, which was fairly good but I didn't agree with all her ideas, by a long way.[34]

I have also seen numerous films since I have been out here, some very good. I was even dragged into *Target for Tonight* when I was in Georgia!

We play a certain amount of American sports here including base-ball, volley-ball, basket-ball, and badminton. But I don't think they compare at all favourably with British games.

In the Kennedy family collection is a hand-written poem which he composed in June 1942, entitled *Human Discontent*; it is roughly contemporary with the image below of Kennedy in his American uniform.

When God evolved the human form
To live on earth a human life,
Did He foresee the day to come
When, moulded by the cast of strife,
That form should lose all piety?
Misguide itself, forget its love?
And in the face of godless brutes
Become a mechanism pure?
When steeped in greedy, gory deeds,
Imbibe a sacrilegious word,
And make itself a worthless sage –
The pilot of a martial bord.
Would man aspire to be the lord
Of all the sky within his ken?
Deny the gods their ancient rights
Of hurling thunderbolts at men?
But now the time has come when he
Becomes a fiendish, ferric strain
With artificial arms and legs
And wireless-operated brain.
Perhaps mankind has won its goal
By challenging its Maker's art –
Creating automatic men
To carry on the human's part.

* * *

Huggins reached Mosul on April 14th and reported for duty.[35] Three days later, he was in the air again in Hurricane Z4855, as 237 ran him through his paces; by the end of April he had flown around the local area, practised flying in formation, and conducted two air-to-ground shoots in one day. On May 1st he flew two sorties of 'shadow firing', a practice intended to improve air-to-ground gunnery; a pilot would fire at the shadow cast by his own or an accompanying aircraft. But something went wrong on the second flight, when Huggins recorded 'Forced Landing' in his log book. It cannot have been a serious prang; Huggins flew the Hurricane involved again in late June, and Z4855 was still flying in 1945. Huggins himself was back in the air on May 2nd, taking a week off between May 8th and 14th.

Hurricanes of 237 (Rhodesia) Squadron RAF at Mosul, May 12th 1942. (IWM E 11721)

On May 24th, when he did no flying, Huggins wrote to Robertson for the first time since joining 237:[36]

> You mentioned in your letter that McArthur was in for the Navy and then added some initials; were they anything to do with the Marines, as they were always being mentioned by him?
>
> Since last writing it has grown rather warmer. Occasionally it still manages to rain, though where the moisture comes from round here is hard to see. These attempts at rain are usually preceded by very warm still days, but after the attempt we have anything up to three days reasonable weather. The main snag from our point of view is that our aeroplane engines, being made for European temperatures, usually get damned hot even in process of taxying out prior to take off. In the air it is damned hot with an engine in front of you and the air itself at about 80°F.
>
> This letter is making slow progress as about every three lines a sandfly, a beast of minute proportions but colossal biting and itching power, starts feeding off my meagre frame. Then if it isn't a fly it's the cat, which insists that I give it a drink of water all day and all night! What a life!
>
> The Squadron has quite an assortment of pets. The most recent acquisitions to the Mess are a baby fox and a multi-coloured lamb. The colours are put there by the owner when he is tight and next morning he cannot understand the change in the colour scheme.

Your nephew must be having quite a time if he is still in Malta. That little island is certainly putting up a magnificent show – a miniature battle of Britain really. It must be quite a drain on the Luftwaffe's reserves as lately they have been losing 40–50 planes a month. I suppose Malta is a big source of worry for German supplies to Libya.

So Mexico has decided to declare war on Germany! There cannot be many countries left now who are not at war with someone or other. Bigger and better shambles after the war, all these nations and politics mixed up in a nice big fiasco. What about Ireland! Will they cease to be so small-minded and realize that it is more than the survival of the British Isles that is involved in this war. The same applies to those ludicrous people in South Africa. I think I shall go and live on a real South Sea island after the war until all these stupid politicians have finished making a mess of the world. They will do that if given the fraction of a chance.

The following month began with more of the same practice, but on June 10th 'C' Flight moved to Kermanshah in Iran, and Huggins was one of those who made the transfer. He did not record any flying that day in his log book, but he was in the air on June 15th and recorded cross-country flights from Kermanshah on June 26th and 29th. By now the heat was becoming insufferable, the main body at Mosul recording a temperature of 115°F in the shade, the highest June temperature in Mosul for eighteen years.

* * *

By contrast, John Sinclair's brother Mike was in the cooler – prisoner-of-war slang for solitary confinement. He was a serial escaper, and clearly, to judge from this postcard to Robertson on June 21st, wholly unrepentant.[37]

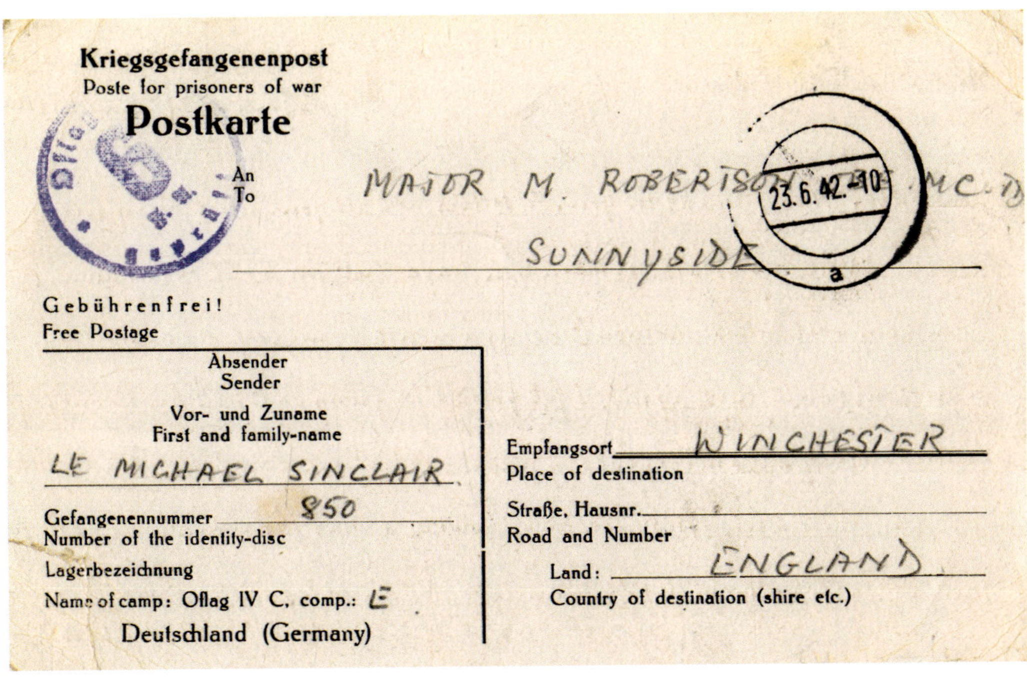
Kriegsgefangenenpost
Poste for prisoners of war
Postkarte

An
To

MAJOR M. ROBERTSON M.C.
SUNNYSIDE

23.6.42.-10

Gebührenfrei!
Free Postage

Absender
Sender

Vor- und Zuname
First and family-name
Lt MICHAEL SINCLAIR

Gefangenennummer 850
Number of the identity-disc

Lagerbezeichnung
Name of camp: Oflag IV C, comp.: E
Deutschland (Germany)

Empfangsort WINCHESTER
Place of destination

Straße, Hausnr.
Road and Number

Land: ENGLAND
Country of destination (shire etc.)

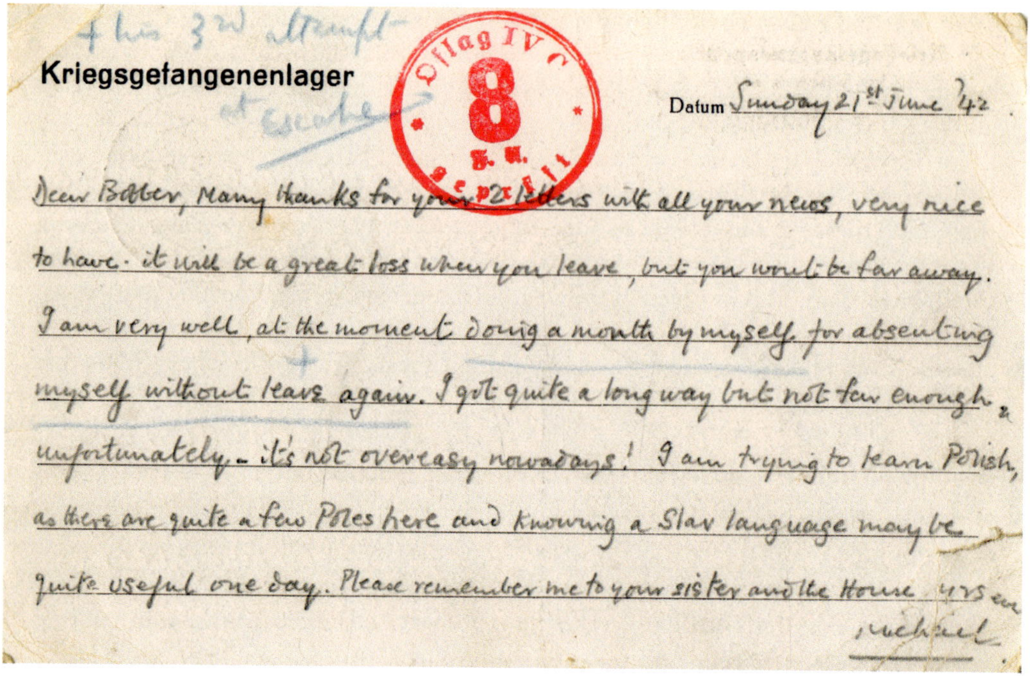

+ his 3rd attempt at escape

Kriegsgefangenenlager

Oflag IV C 8 Geprüft

Datum Sunday 21st June '42

Dear Bobber, Many thanks for your letters with all your news, very nice to have. it will be a great loss when you leave, but you won't be far away. I am very well, at the moment doing a month by myself for absenting myself without leave again. I got quite a long way but not far enough, unfortunately – it's not over easy nowadays! I am trying to learn Polish, as there are quite a few Poles here and knowing a Slav language may be quite useful one day. Please remember me to your sister and the House. Yrs ever

Michael

* * *

In July, Huggins flew on only one day. He was posted 'supernumerary, non-effective, sick' on July 20th, and in a letter from Huggins' mother to Robertson, we discover that his sickness was malaria, and that his sick leave was spent far from the wastes of Iran:

> Dear Major Robertson,
> I am glad the photo of John arrived safely. It is a good likeness of him, although it makes him look somewhat older. He has had malaria since being in Iraq but is fit and well again. In his last letter he had had sick leave which he spent at Tel Aviv and the result of his Board was that he was fit to fly again.
>
> Yes, John seems to have settled down and is happy in his world of flying. He has been given responsible things to do which he enjoyed doing. We have had letters from people who have come in contact with him up there, all of which speak well of him. He has evidently decided to go in for the medical profession after all, so my husband has sent him some medical books to help him in the meantime …
>
> With kindest regards to both.
> Yours Sincerely,
> Blanche E. Huggins[38]

* * *

Kennedy, meanwhile, was still in training in America, as his mother told Robertson in July:[39]

Dear Major Robertson,
Funnily enough I have been thinking of writing to you several times lately and telling you what news I had of the boys. Yes! John is still in USA. His present address is – Gunter Field, Montgomery, Alabama. He was due back in September, but said if he got his wings and commission he would be kept as an Instructor for another three or four months or more – we imagine this has happened, as he wrote he wasn't coming back in September and won't be back till after Xmas sometime – but haven't heard that he has got his 'wings'. He writes very happily but longs for home – he will have told you all about it in his letters. He is so sweet – the way he has sent all of us parcels of things: chocolate, cigarettes, stockings, etc. He thinks of everyone.

Geoffrey has gone East again. We don't know where to but it was 'tropical kit'. He really has made a wonderful recovery from his wound and only if one knows about it you notice a small limp now and again ... Geoffrey's address is 6th Battalion, c/o APO 1915. Do write him a line if you have a moment.

Constance Kennedy

Kennedy was gazetted Pilot Officer in October 1942[40] but, as his mother had surmised, was retained as an instructor – and for much longer than he would have liked.

* * *

Herbert had by now finished at New College, and went on to 148 Training Brigade. By this stage of the war (September 1942), the standard of potential Army officers was so variable that it was decided to send all of them on a basic course at Wrotham Camp, halfway between Sevenoaks and Gillingham. There, where the village of Vigo now stands, 10,000 trainees at a time experienced their pre-OCTU training at the hands of 148 Training Brigade. On arrival, trainees were screened to determine how much of the full eight-week course they required before progressing to their specialist OCTU. Instruction covered fieldcraft, tactics, navigation, drill, and weapons-handling (the Camp had an assault course, rifle range, mortar range, and grenade range). Nick

237 Squadron fitters working on the engine of a Hurricane in Iran in May 1942. (IWM E11720; edited by dansteele.net)

Somerville also spent time at Wrotham, attached to 'A' Company of 4th Battalion, Royal Berkshire Regiment. Another of our subjects known to have passed through was Robin Lewin, who Somerville reported had 'arrived apparently knowing nothing about his weapons, and has gone on a six-week basic infantry course'.

* * *

Having returned to 237 in Iran on September 11th, four days later Huggins was part of a ground party which left Kermanshah for Abadan Island in the south-west of the country. Abadan has the unenviable reputation of being one of the hottest inhabited places on earth, allegedly recording a high of 188.1°F in 1967. Huggins spent just over three weeks there, according to his log-book, and arrived back by air on October 9th – missing the visit of Lord Trenchard to Kermanshah by one day.

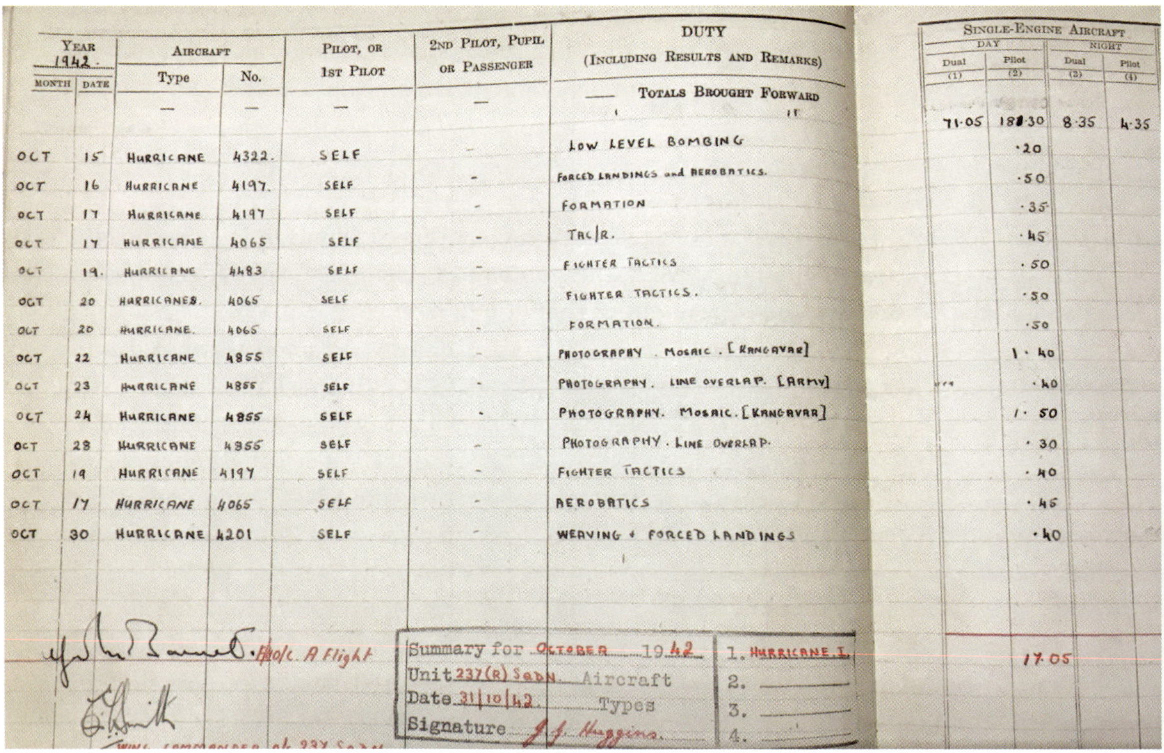

Year 1942 Month	Date	Aircraft Type	Aircraft No.	Pilot, or 1st Pilot	2nd Pilot, Pupil or Passenger	Duty (Including Results and Remarks)	Single-Engine Aircraft Day Dual (1)	Day Pilot (2)	Night Dual (3)	Night Pilot (4)
		—	—	—	—	— Totals Brought Forward	71·05	18[illegible]·30	8·35	4·35
OCT	15	HURRICANE	4322.	SELF	-	LOW LEVEL BOMBING		·20		
OCT	16	HURRICANE	4197.	SELF	-	FORCED LANDINGS and AEROBATICS.		·50		
OCT	17	HURRICANE	4197	SELF	-	FORMATION		·35		
OCT	17	HURRICANE	4065	SELF	-	TAC/R.		·45		
OCT	19.	HURRICANE	4483	SELF	-	FIGHTER TACTICS		·50		
OCT	20	HURRICANES.	4065	SELF	-	FIGHTER TACTICS.		·50		
OCT	20	HURRICANE.	4065	SELF	-	FORMATION.		·50		
OCT	22	HURRICANE	4855	SELF	-	PHOTOGRAPHY. MOSAIC. [KANGAVAR]		1·40		
OCT	23	HURRICANE	4855	SELF	-	PHOTOGRAPHY. LINE OVERLAP. [ARMY]		·40		
OCT	24	HURRICANE	4855	SELF	-	PHOTOGRAPHY. MOSAIC. [KANGAVAR]		1·50		
OCT	28	HURRICANE	4855	SELF	-	PHOTOGRAPHY. LINE OVERLAP.		·30		
OCT	19	HURRICANE	4197	SELF	-	FIGHTER TACTICS		·40		
OCT	17	HURRICANE	4065	SELF	-	AEROBATICS		·45		
OCT	30	HURRICANE	4201	SELF	-	WEAVING + FORCED LANDINGS		·40		
								17·05		

O/C. A Flight

Summary for OCTOBER 1942 | 1. HURRICANE I.
Unit 237(R) SQDN. | Aircraft | 2.
Date 31/10/42. | Types | 3.
Signature J. J. Huggins. | 4.

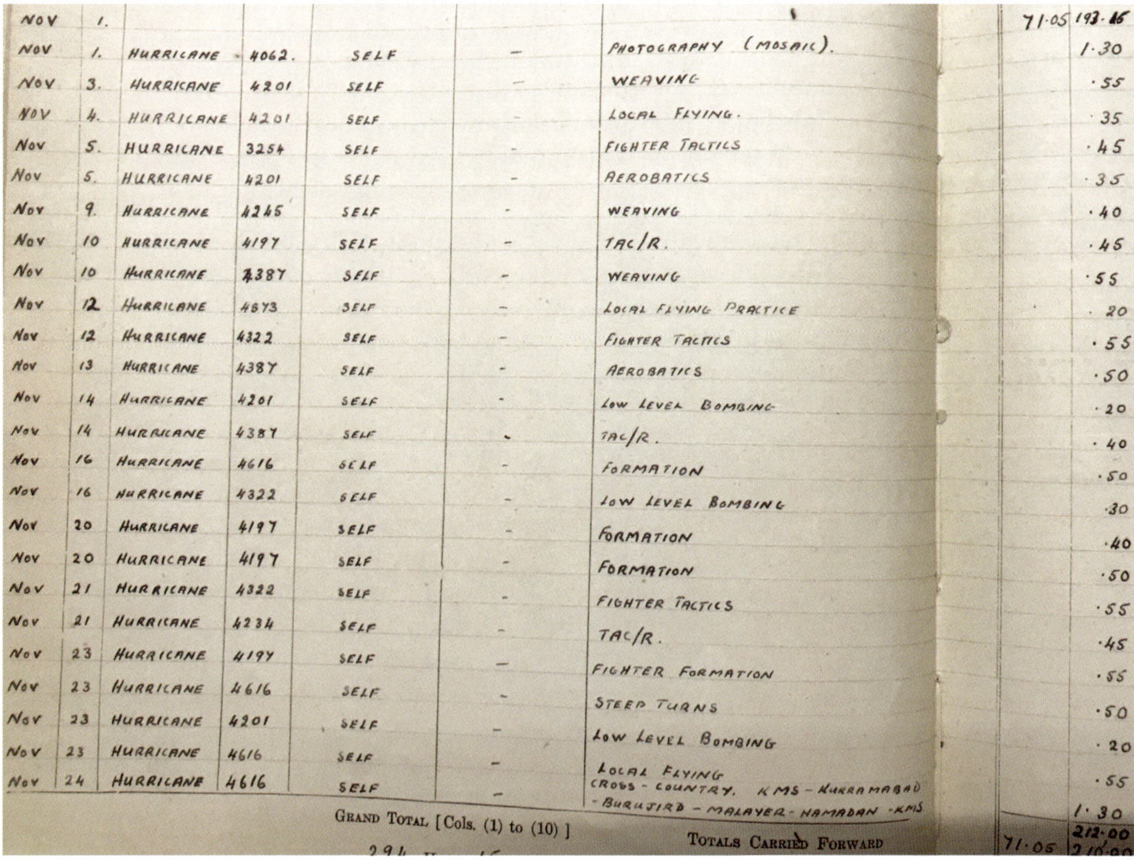

NOV	1.						71·05	193·45
NOV	1.	HURRICANE	4062.	SELF	–	PHOTOGRAPHY (MOSAIC).		1·30
NOV	3.	HURRICANE	4201	SELF	–	WEAVING		·55
NOV	4.	HURRICANE	4201	SELF	–	LOCAL FLYING.		·35
NOV	5.	HURRICANE	3254	SELF	–	FIGHTER TACTICS		·45
NOV	5.	HURRICANE	4201	SELF	–	AEROBATICS		·35
NOV	9.	HURRICANE	4245	SELF	–	WEAVING		·40
NOV	10	HURRICANE	4197	SELF	–	TAC/R.		·45
NOV	10	HURRICANE	4387	SELF	–	WEAVING		·55
NOV	12	HURRICANE	4673	SELF	–	LOCAL FLYING PRACTICE		·20
NOV	12	HURRICANE	4322	SELF	–	FIGHTER TACTICS		·55
NOV	13	HURRICANE	4387	SELF	–	AEROBATICS		·50
NOV	14	HURRICANE	4201	SELF	–	LOW LEVEL BOMBING		·20
NOV	14	HURRICANE	4387	SELF	–	TAC/R.		·40
NOV	16	HURRICANE	4616	SELF	–	FORMATION		·50
NOV	16	HURRICANE	4322	SELF	–	LOW LEVEL BOMBING		·30
NOV	20	HURRICANE	4197	SELF	–	FORMATION		·40
NOV	20	HURRICANE	4197	SELF	–	FORMATION		·50
NOV	21	HURRICANE	4322	SELF	–	FIGHTER TACTICS		·55
NOV	21	HURRICANE	4234	SELF	–	TAC/R.		·45
NOV	23	HURRICANE	4197	SELF	–	FIGHTER FORMATION		·55
NOV	23	HURRICANE	4616	SELF	–	STEEP TURNS		·50
NOV	23	HURRICANE	4201	SELF	–	LOW LEVEL BOMBING		·20
NOV	23	HURRICANE	4616	SELF	–	LOCAL FLYING		·55
NOV	24	HURRICANE	4616	SELF	–	CROSS-COUNTRY. KMS – KURRAMABAD – BURUJIRD – MALAYER – HAMADAN – KMS		1·30
				GRAND TOTAL [Cols. (1) to (10)] 29[illegible]		TOTALS CARRIED FORWARD	71·05	212·00

* * *

Pringle.

Chris Pringle, meanwhile, had just joined the Royal Navy, and was destined for the Fleet Air Arm. By this stage of the war it was apparent that aircraft carriers were the most important of warships, both in the Pacific against Japan and in the Atlantic against U-boats. As Ordinary Seaman FX585707, Pringle reported on October 20th to HMS *Royal Arthur,* a rather grand title for the former Butlin's holiday camp at Ingoldmells near Skegness. HMS *Royal Arthur* trained 'hostilities-only' signallers, wireless telegraphists, and coding personnel. Pringle served there until November 26th. His next posting was HMS *Shrapnel,* a name concealing the more prosaic South West Essex Technical College in Walthamstow, where courses in wireless and radar were conducted. Pringle would remain there until April 3rd 1943.

* * *

On November 11th 1942, a year after attesting in Southampton, Herbert finally reached 150 OCTU, which gave Royal Corps of Signals officer cadets their final training before

Edmunds.

commissioning. Much further away was 'Mi' Edmunds, who had left Hopper's in 1940. With effect from March 1st 1941, he had been gazetted a 2nd Lieutenant in the Oxfordshire & Buckinghamshire Light Infantry, the regiment in which his father served in both world wars.[41] After a time with 70th (Young Soldiers) Battalion near his father in Northern Ireland, and a posting to a glider-borne battalion, for which his slight physique was unsuited, he had joined 7th Battalion (7OBLI), in 56th Infantry Division. 7OBLI would come to have an outstanding fighting record, and Edmunds served with it in Persia, Iraq, Sicily, Italy, and Egypt. By November 17th 1942 he was with Persia-Iraq Command (PAIFORCE), as he told Robertson in one of his only surviving letters:

> It's a long time since I last wrote, during which time I have come a long way. We are in the Iraq-Persia Command now, though I may not say where we are stationed. I was glad to leave England, as soldiering there seems so unprofitable – just a long wait for something which may never come. We all enjoyed the voyage out here – almost as good as a peace-time cruise, except for the blackout. I'm only allowed to tell you of one place through which we passed, and that is Baghdad; it did not impress me at all favourably – a city not so much of a thousand and one nights as of a million and one smells. Fortunately we were not there very long. It is very wet here now, and will be very cold shortly, so we haven't, as we had hoped, escaped English winter weather![42]

* * *

HMS Forester, *1942.* (IWM FL9830)

McArthur.

Like Pringle, John McArthur was also now in the Royal Navy, and already playing an active role. After leaving school in 1942 he enlisted as a rating, and after his training was posted to HMS *Forester* (H74), an F-class destroyer which had entered service in March 1935. The vessel had seen a lot of action and in May 1942 had suffered serious damage whilst returning from Murmansk. This kept her out of action until October 1942, McArthur having arrived aboard in September. She then accompanied 8th Destroyer Flotilla at Scapa Flow for Russian convoy escort duties. On November 19th *Forester* joined two cruisers covering inbound Arctic convoy QP15, west of Bear Island; she stayed with them until November 25th. On December 26th 1942, McArthur's vessel sailed from Akureyri in Iceland as part of the destroyer screen around the battleship HMS *Anson* and cruiser HMS *Cumberland*, covering the rear of Convoy JW51B as far as Bear Island. This was to prevent any attack by heavy German ships approaching from the south – a very real threat at the time – and to be ready to prevent German vessels from breaking out into the North Atlantic. The weather was atrocious, with Force 9 gales worsening to Force 12 at some points, but that did not prevent the German *Hipper* and *Lutzow* from setting out with six destroyer escorts to destroy the convoy. Although *Forester* remained on that task until December 30th, the Germans did not attack the convoy until the following day, resulting in the Battle of the Barents Sea. The German flotilla was beaten off by determined attacks from the outnumbered escorts, and all fourteen merchant ships reached Russia safely. Hitler was furious at the poor performance of his fleet and came close to scrapping all Germany's surface warships; the head of the *Kriegsmarine*, Admiral Raeder, resigned. Raeder's replacement was Admiral Dönitz, who would briefly succeed Hitler as Führer in 1945.

* * *

On December 14th 1942, Huggins returned to Kermanshah to collect an aircraft, flying it back to Kirkuk (where 237 were now stationed) three days later. The ORB's last reference of 1942 to Huggins comes on December 31st, when it records his promotion to Flying Officer with effect from October 1st.

His family's archives contain several wartime pictures of him in uniform, and although it is not easy to date them it is likely that Huggins had by now – like so many young warriors wishing to look older – grown his moustache. Huge responsibility and expectations rested on the shoulders of our subjects, but they were little more than teenagers, often commanding men older and more experienced than themselves. Anything which helped them feel more mature must have made their task easier.

* * *

Somewhat less mobile – though not for want of trying – was Mike Sinclair, by now just finishing another month in solitary confinement for yet another escape attempt (his fourth). As previously, he wrote to Robertson from his cell.[43]

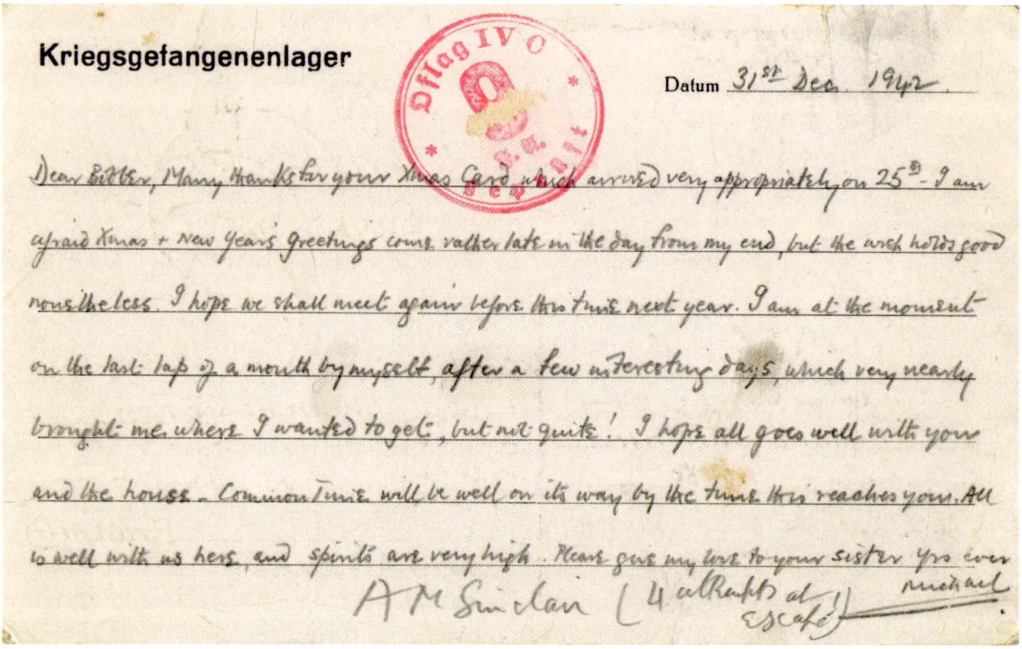

Kriegsgefangenenlager

Oflag IV C

Datum 31st Dec. 1942.

Dear Bitter, Many thanks for your Xmas Card which arrived very appropriately on 25th – I am afraid Xmas + New Years greetings come rather late in the day from my end, but the wish holds good nonetheless. I hope we shall meet again before this time next year. I am at the moment on the last lap of a month by myself, after a few interesting days, which very nearly brought me where I wanted to get, but not quite! I hope all goes well with you and the house – Common Time will be well on its way by the time this reaches you. All is well with us here, and spirits are very high. Please give my love to your sister. Yrs ever Michael

A M Sinclair (4 attempts at escape!)

* * *

By January 7th 1943, HMS *Forester* was conducting anti-submarine training off Scapa Flow, but the following day, she headed for the Kola Inlet to join the escort of returning convoy RA52, arriving on January 14th. While she was at sea, Robertson received a letter from McArthur's parents:

> Dear Mr Robertson,
> How kind of you to write and enquire about old John – I got a letter today, he's been (from hints given) in this last Russian Convoy, and expects to come on leave and maybe go to the King Alfred to train for his commission; he got forty-eight hours' leave about December 12th, and luckily we were in London and how we did enjoy it! He's huge, both ways, and very fit – delighted in Iceland fiords and the scenery.
>
> In his letter today, he said he'd met Herbert (A.P.H.'s son) and they'd had a delightful chat – where, I don't know! He said the cold had been intense but he loved every moment and his Ordinary Seamen were the very best and it was an honour to be with them, a different tale to his time at Collingwood, when he had those Borstal Boys to manage. It's all been good for him tho'.
>
> I am sad to think you are both leaving, but it's as well to spend a bit of one's life on one's own, and – what a relief from those awful parents!

I miss coming to Winchester very much and loved my time always there; one felt as if war was far away.

To go back to John, he did go off at a moment's notice and I know mentioned to me how guilty he felt not seeing you again. His address is O/Sea. J.C. McA. P/JX321428 HMS 'Forester' c/o G.P.O. London.

Where is David Martyn? I wonder if your sister realises she has a huge painting I bought in Winchester hanging in one of your bed-rooms. Ages ago I got David Martyn to try and get Lavery [?] to send it, but he had no wood, then I wrote to Robert Holtby, but I expect he couldn't manage it – so do you mind if I leave it with you and if I can get down from London, one day, I'll bring it back and see you both at same time!

Every good wish for 1943.

Yours sincerely,

M. McArthur[44]

Convoy RA52 reached Loch Ewe safely on February 8th. It had been McArthur's last voyage as a seaman; he now left *Forester* to embark upon his officer training.

At HMS *King Alfred* in May, a confidential report on Ordinary Seaman McArthur assessed him as 'a well-disciplined youngster who is on the way to becoming a good officer. Keen, conscientious – though not very intelligent.'[45]

Instead of being posted to a sea-going vessel, McArthur's next appointment was in Dartmouth for a six-week course on small landing-craft. The course was run from the Royal Naval College, the usual occupants having been moved to Eaton Hall in Cheshire; the establishment became HMS *Effingham* for the rest of the war. His course report in July 1943 was positive: 'A very pleasant type of officer. Keen and efficient with plenty of "go". Very reliable. Should become a good leader.'[46]

McArthur's naval future was to lie in Combined Operations.

* * *

Mackrill was also destined for the Navy, though at the time he was busily preparing himself to take over as senior prefect in Sunnyside. The war was not far away, though:

> We did have a few bombs on Winchester in daylight on February 9th. They destroyed a few houses and killed eight people. It was just a hit-and-run raid.[47]

Mackrill.

Mackrill gave more information in his diary for 1943, which includes a wealth of detail about life at Winchester at the time:

> German Dornier 217 bomber swooped over the house at lunch time and dropped some bombs near Odeon. A few children were killed. (Six killed and fifteen injured.) Ellis Cup v Trant's; we won 5-3.[48]

* * *

In late January 1943, 237 moved from Kirkuk via Transjordan and Palestine to El Daba in Egypt. Huggins wrote to Robertson during the move:

> Many thanks for your air letter of December 28th. An improved means of correspondence in many ways. I am unable to reply the same way as I am *pro: temp:* in transit, and, paper supplies being as they are, we can only obtain our rations of air letters, airgraphs, etc, at our units …
>
> I met Ronnie Hamilton a few days ago. Unfortunately he was in a hurry and I was unable to see him again as my travels took me elsewhere. Also met (by sight) Proud of 'B' House. He naturally did not recognise me, as our only encounters at Winchester were in Junior Canvas (is the name right?). This is not as popular a place for OWs as Cairo, and I don't blame them. A **** country; no excitement and nowhere to go. Oh yes, I forgot to mention Toddy Hanbury of 'K' House was through here a few days back. He is doing the same job as I am, Army co-op, but like myself has no particular love for the Middle East version of that kind of work. My hopes of getting into photographic reconnaissance are still high, but patience is needed as all transfers are necessarily a lengthy affair. I think they have to be approved by London!
>
> One young officer the same age as myself, also here in transit, comes from Marlborough. Time is heavy on our hands and we while away many afternoons talking about cricket matches, the future of public schools, etc. It is pleasant to meet someone from England who 'speaks the same language' and knows the same places. Having saved up enough money to pay my passage to England from Rhodesia, once the war is over and I am twenty-one, nothing short of death will prevent me coming back to England like greased lightning. Medicine still to the fore.
>
> News *non est.*[49]

Huggins did not stay with 237 for long after their arrival at El Daba. His posting to photographic reconnaissance had come through, and on February 9th 1943 he left the Squadron for 2 Photographic Reconnaissance Unit (PRU).[50] Life was about to become considerably more exciting.

X

'I stopped one in Tripolitania'

January–May 1943

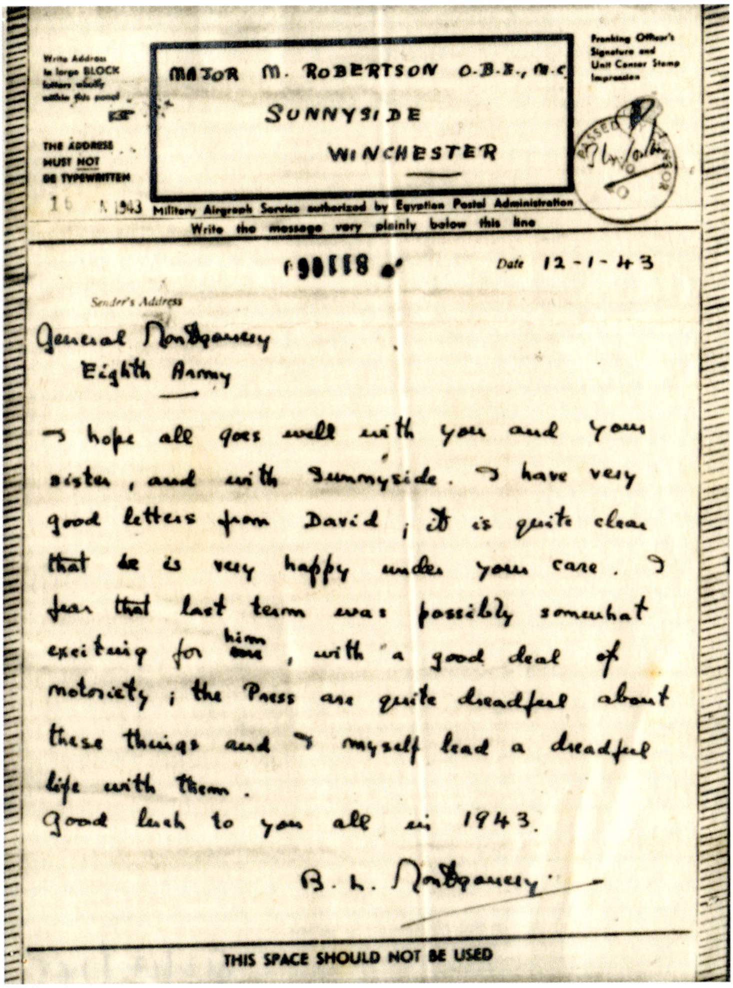

Write Address in large BLOCK letters wholly within this panel

THE ADDRESS MUST NOT BE TYPEWRITTEN

MAJOR M. ROBERTSON O.B.E., M.C.
SUNNYSIDE
WINCHESTER

Franking Officer's Signature and Unit Censor Stamp Impression

PASSED BY CENSOR

16 1943 Military Airgraph Service authorized by Egyptian Postal Administration

Write the message very plainly below this line

Date 12-1-43

Sender's Address

General Montgomery
Eighth Army

I hope all goes well with you and your sister, and with Sunnyside. I have very good letters from David; it is quite clear that he is very happy under your care. I fear that last term was possibly somewhat exciting for him, with a good deal of notoriety; the Press are quite dreadful about these things and I myself lead a dreadful life with them.
Good luck to you all in 1943.

B. L. Montgomery

THIS SPACE SHOULD NOT BE USED

By mid January 1943, Eighth Army was pursuing the retreating Axis forces through Libya, and had reached the area of Homs, west of the Gulf of Sirte and a few miles beyond the great Roman ruins of Leptis Magna. It was as far as the British had ever reached in North Africa, and Tripoli lay within their grasp. It was vital to capture this port intact so that supplies could continue to support the offensive.

Fortune.

Since Alamein, Fortune had served continuously in a rifle company as a Platoon Commander. When the breakthrough at Alamein had begun in November, he and his comrades had driven through the carnage of a British tank unit which had been annihilated whilst advancing westwards, the rising sun behind them, straight towards German anti-tank guns. One of the dead in the husks of 3rd Hussars' tanks was Fortune's brother-in-law, Alan Dawes, who had tried just days before to visit Fortune, but had missed him.

On Fortune's seventieth birthday in 1991, his son Johnnie presented him with a rare copy of a wartime collection of poetry written by soldiers who had fought in the Western Desert. Fortune wrote to thank him, saying that it was a subject which was never far from his thoughts; indeed, he said, he thought of it every day. A year or so later, he shared his memories with his son.[1]

Fortune recalled how 1BW advanced in 3-ton trucks across the desert, using sun compasses as they cut across the base of the bulge of Cyrenaica through Agedabia towards Mersa Brega. Fortune's truck, crewed by an Indian driver from the RASC, broke down, and he was left behind. As he tried to catch up with the Battalion he came upon an encampment of trucks which turned out to be Montgomery's Advanced HQ. Although there was no sign of Montgomery himself, Fortune and his men were fed and entertained by his charming staff officers. The next morning, he and his men located and rejoined their Battalion.

The advance began, as usual, to peter out because of a lack of supplies, especially fuel, but 1BW reached Mersa Brega and took over from troops of 7th Armoured Division. Danger was ever present, mostly in the form of mines and booby-traps, at which the Germans were expert; they laid them liberally as a delaying tactic. One of Fortune's memories was of a patrol from 7BW being 'written off' when it opened the door to a house, which immediately exploded. Often the Germans left a small rear party whose job it was to prime the mines, their positions marked by jerry cans to warn passers-by. As the last German left, he would remove the cans. Once Fortune rounded a corner of a road to see Germans in the act of removing the cans prior to withdrawal.

The one which terrified the infantry most was the 'S' mine – Fortune considered it a great threat, their worst fear. The 'S' mine *(Schrapnellmine)* was an horrific anti-personnel weapon which could be set off by a trip-wire or by sensitive hair-triggers on its top. Then the main body of the weapon sprang into the air and exploded at about waist height, sending a spray of ball-bearings and shrapnel in all directions. These mines were intended to injure, not to kill outright, and the terrible wounds which they inflicted made them one of the most feared weapons which the Germans produced. Not knowing where they could safely put their feet struck at the troops' morale. In Italy, men were on one occasion killed when a cat triggered an 'S' mine.

The men responsible for clearing such weapons were the Royal Engineers, whom Fortune described as 'the best' and 'fearless'. One Sapper was attached to each infantry platoon, to give advice and share expertise. When Fortune's men were assigned to clear a mined obstacle and were very uneasy, his Sapper said, 'It's okay, Sir; I know what to do. I'll brief the men.' They cleared the mines using their bayonets, and suffered no casualties.

When Fortune's father had surrendered 51st Division at St Valery in 1940, it had been re-formed with any available men. Thus it was that Fortune's Platoon of the Black Watch (The Royal Highlanders) was for the most part made up not of Scots, but of Yorkshiremen, whom Fortune considered more intelligent than the average, especially the NCOs. Fortune's first action as a Platoon Commander came when he was ordered to patrol ahead at night. It is always funny what people remember; Fortune's abiding memory fifty years later was that although his men had been given suede 'desert boots' with crepe soles so that their progress would be quiet, one man with big feet was unable to get into them. As he crashed along in the rear in his ammunition boots, they heard ahead of them a German artillery battery coming into action; it fired a salvo and withdrew.

Three months in the front line had changed Fortune irrevocably and made him a professional:

> The Germans and Italians each had distinctive smells. The Germans used *ersatz* soap which smelt horrible; an indescribable smell. The Italians had a more fragrant, scented smell. The positions of each nationality smelt of their soap. In the night, approaching a position, one could always tell whether it was occupied by Italians or Germans. The Germans were very good, but the Italians didn't have their heart in it. In Egypt, it seemed like they felt, 'Why are we here?' As the battle moved west into Cyrenaica [an Italian colony] their resolve stiffened a little. They fought dirty.

Fortune's professionalism and courage now faced their sternest test. As 154 Brigade advanced from Homs on January 19th 1943, it came up against a *djebel* (hill) about four miles to the west, topped by a fort, which controlled the road along which any advance on Tripoli must travel:

> It was obvious that our position was completely dominated by the feature known as EDINBURGH CASTLE to the north-west of HOMS. During the night January 19th/20th the Battalion sent forward a patrol which reported that this position was held by the enemy.[2]

As Fortune remembered it, night patrols from the other battalions provided contradictory reports as to whether there was an enemy presence on the hill. When day broke, Lieutenant Colonel Roper-Caldbeck, commanding 1BW, decided to delay action until he had confirmation of the situation:

> At first light two more patrols were sent out, one on the RIGHT towards EDINBURGH CASTLE and the other up the WADI ZAIDAN on our LEFT. This latter reported back at about 1100hrs with the information that it had dislodged a small party of enemy and that the WADI was now clear for a distance of about two miles. At 0830hrs

> Battalion HQ was heavily shelled by the enemy's 210mm guns. His shelling and sniping throughout the morning was very active and accurate.[3]

Fortune was placed in charge of the EDINBURGH CASTLE patrol, given his experience of reconnaissance when commanding the Carrier Platoon. Fortune took Sergeant Baddeley and one section of men along a covered route until he was able to observe enemy in strength on the position: not only did he see infantry and machine-guns, but two of the dreaded 88mm anti-tank guns, protected by an extensive anti-tank ditch. None of this was visible from the plain.

Montgomery was desperate to reach Tripoli, because if he did not take the port he would have to withdraw. He badgered the commanding officer of 51st Division, General Wimberley, to press onwards. At around 1030hrs, Wimberley directed that an immediate company-strength attack, with support from tanks, should be made on EDINBURGH CASTLE.

Fortune was on his way back to make his report when, to his horror, he saw the British armour advancing with men of 1BW forming up behind. As the enemy opened fire, Fortune realized that to return by the safe, covered, route would take too long. He therefore decided to cut across open ground straight to the tanks.

Setting off at a run towards the leading Valentine, with the idea of using its radio to inform Roper-Caldbeck of the danger, it concerned him, momentarily, that his men might think that he was running away; but he could not worry about that. When he looked back, his men, led by Sergeant Baddeley, were walking. The men did not like turning their backs on the enemy or want to be seen 'running away' and they kept looking back at the Germans. Fortune yelled at them to follow him at the double, and they immediately complied.

As Fortune reached the tank he should have used the infantry liaison phone on the back, which would have enabled him to talk to the tank commander from relative safety. Fortune was unable to recall why he did not do so; sometimes he stated that the phone had been broken, but he also admitted that in his excitement he may simply have forgotten. Instead, he yelled up at the tank commander, who was standing in the turret, trying to communicate above the noise of the gun-fire. His men took shelter under a bank behind him. As Fortune pointed to the enemy with his left arm, gun in hand, a burst of machine-gun fire caught him from the left. One bullet passed through his left forearm, and another through his abdomen, nicking his lung and exiting through his liver.

Fortune fell back amongst his men. Baddeley opened his shirt to check the wound, and Fortune recalled that one of his Jocks, seeing the entry and exit wounds, exclaimed, 'Jings, he's fair riddled!' Fortune did not find this comforting, though he claimed that it looked worse than it was. A Jeep was brought forward to evacuate him, and as Fortune was lifted onto the bonnet someone grabbed his injured arm and he cried out in pain. The Jeep withdrew under fire, with Fortune being held down on the bonnet, and raced to the Regimental Aid Post, the first stage of treatment for the wounded. Roper-Caldbeck, a great admirer of General Fortune and aghast at what had just occurred, was present and told the doctor, 'For God's sake, don't let Bruce die!'

Fortune was transferred very quickly to a Field Surgical Unit, since the British Army was working on the principle that the interval between wounding and primary surgery should be no more than eight hours. The greatest danger to the casualty was loss of blood leading to low blood pressure, which in turn would lead to shock and increased risk of death. Traditional blood transfusions were complicated by different blood types and storing 'live' blood on the battlefield. Instead, surgeons were by now using blood plasma – the clear sticky liquid which carries red cells, white cells, and platelets. Removing these from the plasma did away with the compatibility issue, and plasma could be dried for easy transportation and storage. The surgeons simply added water to make the plasma ready for use.

The two innovations of forward surgery and blood plasma transfusions saved Fortune's life. His wife, Sue, later recorded in her memoirs his account of his treatment:

> Bruce told me of that day and how lucky he was in many ways; that he was picked up so quickly, that there was a hospital at the forward base, a brilliant Australian surgeon in attendance (whom he would have dearly liked to meet to say 'thank you'), and the presence of the newly formed Field Blood Transfusion Units. He had been shot through arm, base of left lung, and the liver … He always made light of this. Once, when asked what part he played in the action at Homs, he replied, 'By doing something very stupid'.[4]

However, there was nearly a disaster when a transfusion was being administered by way of a blood vessel in his foot. The orderly inserted it incorrectly, and the blood began to build up under the skin. His complaints about discomfort were ignored until an enormous blood-filled 'balloon' was discovered on his instep. The transfusion was therefore not reaching his bloodstream, and he could also have lost his foot. Luckily, the error had been detected in time.

Once Fortune's condition had stabilized, he was sent by ambulance to Tripoli, which had by then fallen without a fight. He described the journey as 'purgatory. I think the ambulances were designed to kill us. They had absolutely no springs.'

From there he was flown in an antiquated Bristol Bombay transport back to Tobruk, where he was transferred to a hospital train and thence to 92nd General Hospital.[5] Lady Fortune wrote a delightful letter to Robertson on March 16th with news of her son's progress:

> Dear Bobber,
> Bruce is getting on very well. He has been flown and in a hospital train for three days and nights and eventually arrived near Cairo as that is where 92nd General Hospital is. He writes very cheerily and loves the Doctor. The food is good and plenty of amusement. When he gets up he is now allowed to turn over, so very pleased and seems to be much better. Wimberley wrote his wife that it was 'just touch and go' and his Brigadier wrote me he was not out of danger on February 11th, so he has been pretty bad; however, it's all over now. It will be six months before he is fit to go back.
>
> I thought you would like to read the enclosed and add the little MC to your list. He seems to have put up a good show and Victor will be awfully pleased. Will you please

return this to me – it's one of my most valuable possessions and I should not like it lost. Won't Victor be pleased. I'm so excited – have felt quite sick ever since.

Whisky needed.

Yours ever, and hope the term is ending well.

Love to Sheila.

Yours,

Eleanor

I bought this paper as I thought it would cheer up friends. Pre war, very expensive, and very vulgar.[6]

Inevitably, Fortune himself wrote to Robertson.[7]

How very sorry I am that I haven't written for such a long time. I have just received your post card of November 26th 1942. It has pursued me across many miles of desert only to find me sitting like a fossil in a Middle East hospital. Still it was very welcome indeed, and I was so glad to hear of your musical party. It must have been a great show, and the thought of it brings back many memories of Sunnyside.

You will probably have heard that I stopped one in Tripolitania. Rather unpleasant, but might have been worse. Also very annoying as we were just on the last lap to Tripoli. Still, I eventually found myself in hospital in that fair city. It was a marvellous place with a veranda to every ward and very comfortable beds. It was very light, having quantities of glass panelling which used to rattle like anything when the Tripoli barrage started up, which it did pretty frequently. We were however destined for further back, and after a few days were evacuated by air and then by hospital train back here.

This hospital is not one of the best as far as luxury goes, but still we have been without it (luxury) for so long, that it doesn't seem to matter. My wounds are healing well, although I still have an obstinate lung. After more or less recovering here, I think they will send us to South Africa to convalesce, which should be fun. I had a cousin in Durban, but unfortunately she has now gone home, on return of her husband to UK to ME.

Well, enough about myself. Gilbert Talbot of 'A' House blew in to see me yesterday. He has just come down from Tunisia to be Jumbo Wilson's ADC. A very good job I should think.[8] The young Rooper of 'F' House was in here with jaundice. He is still as tired as ever – now in 3rd Coldstreams. I believe Broderick of 'A' is in his lot. I

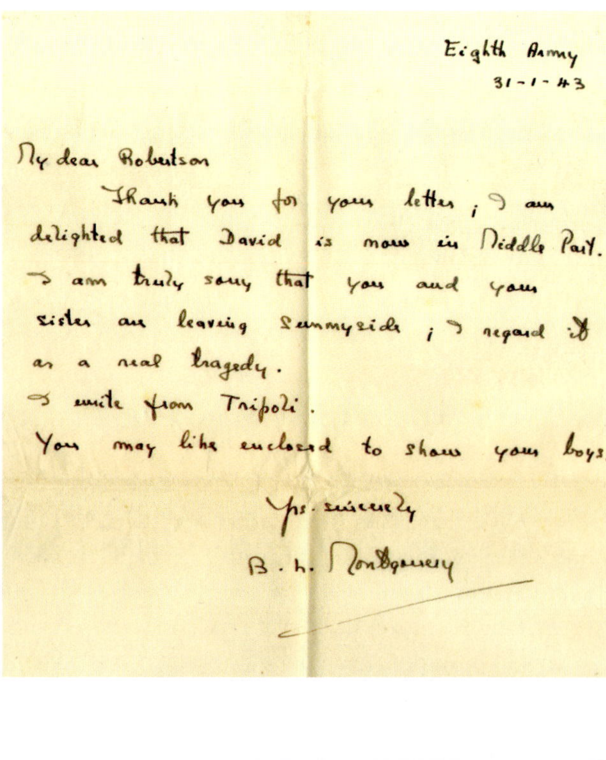
Eighth Army
31-1-43

My dear Robertson

Thank you for your letter; I am delighted that David is now in Middle Part.
I am truly sorry that you and your sister are leaving Sunnyside; I regard it as a real tragedy.
I write from Tripoli.
You may like enclosed to show your boys.

Yrs. sincerely
B. L. Montgomery

bumped into Popham ('A') in 60th twice in my travels in the desert. At one time, we were both engaged in making an airfield. The landing ground looked much worse when we had finished than at the beginning of our operations. We both agreed it was a waste of time! I have not seen the inimitable Sheepshanks yet. Had an airgraph from Pat Metcalfe in 45th Cavalry, POONA, on receipt of your letter to me and Athla programme sent on to him. Said he was a bit bored and getting very wet in the Monsoon.

Well, Bobber, we had a good chase out here while it lasted. The HD is still going strong. Our chaps had a good rabbit shoot at Mareth, so I believe.

* * *

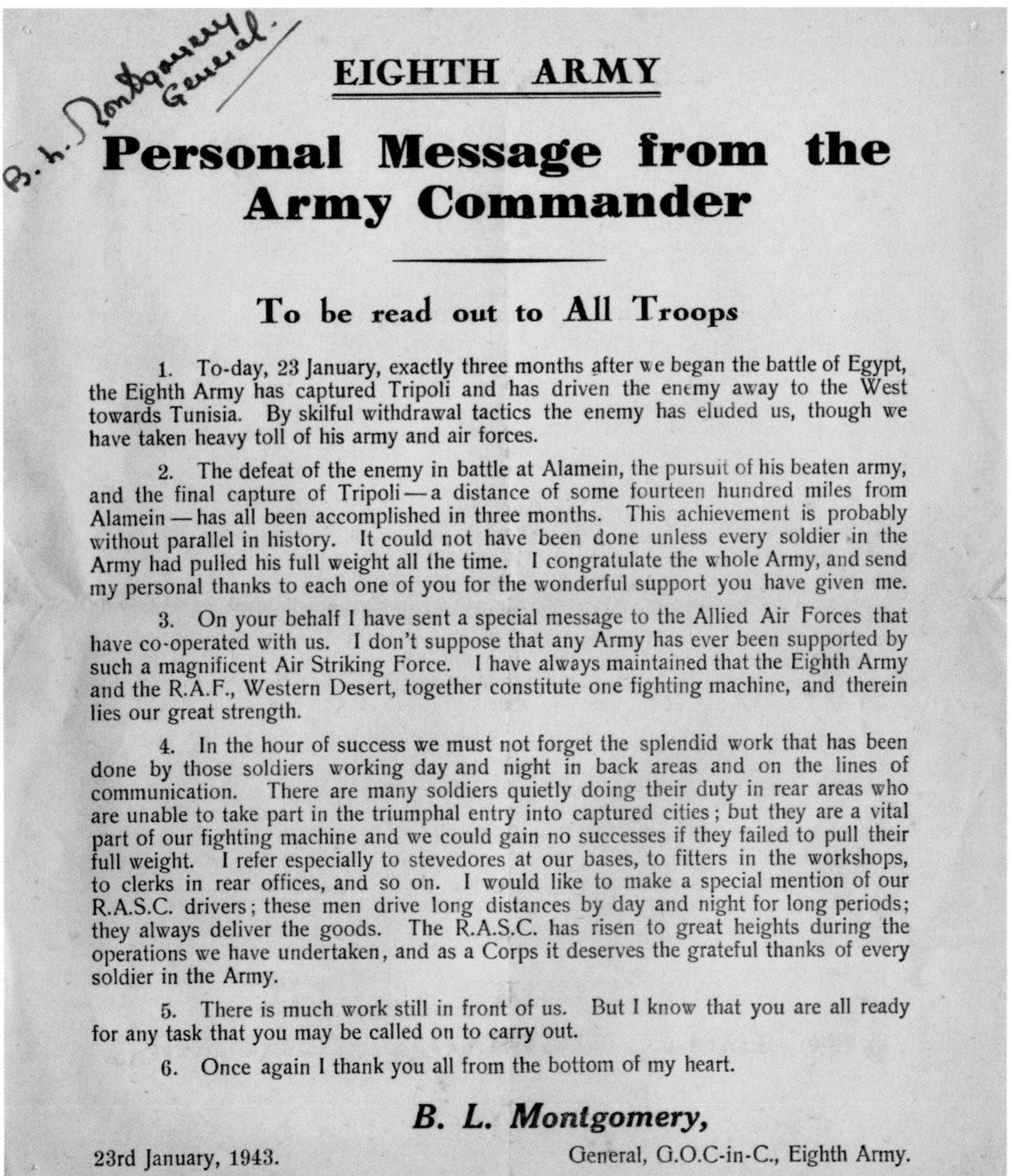

B. L. Montgomery General.

EIGHTH ARMY

Personal Message from the Army Commander

To be read out to All Troops

1. To-day, 23 January, exactly three months after we began the battle of Egypt, the Eighth Army has captured Tripoli and has driven the enemy away to the West towards Tunisia. By skilful withdrawal tactics the enemy has eluded us, though we have taken heavy toll of his army and air forces.

2. The defeat of the enemy in battle at Alamein, the pursuit of his beaten army, and the final capture of Tripoli — a distance of some fourteen hundred miles from Alamein — has all been accomplished in three months. This achievement is probably without parallel in history. It could not have been done unless every soldier in the Army had pulled his full weight all the time. I congratulate the whole Army, and send my personal thanks to each one of you for the wonderful support you have given me.

3. On your behalf I have sent a special message to the Allied Air Forces that have co-operated with us. I don't suppose that any Army has ever been supported by such a magnificent Air Striking Force. I have always maintained that the Eighth Army and the R.A.F., Western Desert, together constitute one fighting machine, and therein lies our great strength.

4. In the hour of success we must not forget the splendid work that has been done by those soldiers working day and night in back areas and on the lines of communication. There are many soldiers quietly doing their duty in rear areas who are unable to take part in the triumphal entry into captured cities; but they are a vital part of our fighting machine and we could gain no successes if they failed to pull their full weight. I refer especially to stevedores at our bases, to fitters in the workshops, to clerks in rear offices, and so on. I would like to make a special mention of our R.A.S.C. drivers; these men drive long distances by day and night for long periods; they always deliver the goods. The R.A.S.C. has risen to great heights during the operations we have undertaken, and as a Corps it deserves the grateful thanks of every soldier in the Army.

5. There is much work still in front of us. But I know that you are all ready for any task that you may be called on to carry out.

6. Once again I thank you all from the bottom of my heart.

B. L. Montgomery,

23rd January, 1943. General, G.O.C-in-C., Eighth Army.

Roper-Caldbeck had recommended Fortune for an 'immediate' Military Cross after the action in which he was wounded. The citation differs in several important respects from the account given above, and since it even gets the date of the action incorrect, Fortune's own account has been preferred:

> On January 19th 1943, at HOMS, Lieutenant Fortune was ordered to lead a daylight patrol forward to establish definitely whether the enemy were holding a certain feature. From the outset, this patrol had to move in full view of the enemy, over extremely open ground. Soon after he set out, his patrol came under machine-gun fire, but Lieutenant Fortune managed to work his way forward to within some 500 yards of the enemy positions. From here he was able to gain much valuable information and located the existence of an anti-tank ditch, two machine-guns, and two anti-tank guns. Having extricated his patrol in an extremely able manner, this officer was on his way back when his party again came under very heavy machine-gun fire. At this point, some of our tanks, moving forward to recce the same positions, came in sight. Telling his patrol to keep under cover, Lieutenant Fortune ran under heavy fire to warn the tank commander of the presence of the tank ditch and the anti-tank guns. In doing this, he was very severely wounded. Although in great pain, he continued under fire until he reached the leading tank and had warned its commander. Although he then collapsed, his chief thought whilst his own men were extricating him was for their safety.
>
> Recommended for MC (Immediate) by W. Roper Caldbeck, Lieutenant Colonel commanding 1st Battalion The Black Watch (RHR)
>
> Recommended for MC: B.L. Montgomery GOC Eighth Army[9]

* * *

Middleditch.

It is all too easy, in retrospect, to see that the war had by this stage been won, and to focus on the Normandy landings in 1944 as the inevitable next step on the road to Berlin (and the Burma campaign of 1945 as a far-off, irrelevant appendix). But although many Hopperites had seen action, and some had become casualties or prisoners of war, most of our subjects were still in training, and the end of the war seemed a long way off.

Like most of our subjects, David Middleditch wrote regularly to keep Robertson updated. He had 'enlisted' – registering his willingness to join the Army – in November 1941, before going up to Cambridge, and had been 'embodied' (put into uniform) on August 20th 1942. As usual, he had served in the ranks before proceeding to 100 OCTU (Sandhurst) in mid-October 1942:

> I have been here just over a fortnight and am enjoying it enormously. Sandhurst is certainly a great improvement over Blackdown.
>
> Thank you for your postcard. I was so sorry to hear about Scott; it's an awful thing to have happened.
>
> This place is full of OWs, but I believe some of them were down at Winchester the other day so no doubt you have heard all about them. I see quite a lot of Michael Hirst

and Henry Brooke who are at present in the Driving and Maintenance Wing. I am still ploughing along at General Military Training, entirely infantry work but not bad fun, with lots of marching, night compass work, map reading, weapon pit digging, etc. – all very open air and healthy. This culminates in a week at a battle school in Wales, where I believe Michael Hirst got on very well and compared extremely favourably with the more town-bred section of his troop.

My troop consists of men going to the Reconnaissance Corps which provides reconnaissance for infantry divisions, and RAC men going to armoured car regiments which do the same thing for the armoured division, and includes two professional footballers, two amateur jockeys, and five Canadians, very good tough chaps with no frills on them.

Sandhurst seems extremely well run, as was Blackdown, and Prior-Palmer the Commandant seems a pretty good chap. He's got a most resolute chin anyway! There's still a good deal of ceremonial, a band, the Adjutant on a white horse etc., but I find it a most welcome change from ordinary work and although we have a servant (1 to 14 officer cadets) they don't carry personal spit and polish to such lengths as at Blackdown.

I should very much like to get down to Winchester if I ever get an opportunity and I know Michael [Hirst] wants to as well. We are going to find if bus and train services make this at all possible.

Please give my best regards to Miss Robertson. The longer I'm in the Army the more I miss Sunnyside food, 'Bobber Concerts', and being read to in the drawing room.[10]

* * *

Ahead of Middleditch in the training pipeline was Michael Elliott-Binns, who had been completing his training at Catterick. In February 1943, he told Robertson about his experiences:

Elliott-Binns.

I am afraid it is a scandalously long time since I wrote to you last. I think it was just after I went down from Cambridge. Quite a lot of water has flowed under my bridge since then, as it has under most people's. Perhaps I had better start by giving my life history first and getting the 'I' part of the letter over.

I spent a very pleasant month or so working on the land and walking and reading a bit and writing a bit of poetry, in other words my old life of a gentleman of leisure, and then on August 14th received my papers ordering me to go to Wrotham – about which I expect you have heard – on August 17th, my birthday, which I hope is a good omen. It was rather a wrench going off, but the time was so short I was gone before I knew it, and I was very cheered to meet lots of people I knew on the station. I spent a rather idyllic fortnight there driving trucks and doing a bit of motor-cycling and going to the big towns at weekends, the last bit of southern civilisation I have met with.

Then I was sent off to Catterick a fortnight before my time, and I have just completed my five months there. On the whole I have definitely enjoyed it. My Troop consists almost entirely of old undergraduates and mostly clever ones, so it has really been like Cambridge over again. At first we did pretty badly, but after a time we adapted ourselves to Catterick and I think Catterick adapted itself to us and we left more or less in a hail of bouquets and went off to a Firing Camp in Wales, where it rained most of the time but in spite of it we got a very excellent report. But I have got absolutely used to rain and bad conditions thanks to Battle Camp, where we got an exceptionally hard time. I was very grateful for Steeplechases and what exercise I did take at Winchester, and I think I really did pretty well. At least I was one of the eight people who managed to climb Helvellyn, which the camp was quite near, in full equipment without dropping out for a rest.

I think that will do for Catterick, which looking back was one of the pleasantest and most amusing times of my life. I am now on my second leave; my first was at Christmas, waiting to join my Regiment. I have been posted to 170th Field Regiment, Riverside, Halkirk, Caithness. I could hardly have a longer journey inside Britain, but the last part through the Highlands ought to be very fine. All I have seen of Scotland so far was a couple of wonderful days at Edinburgh for my brother's wedding.

I am now having a very quiet and pleasant leave with just my parents home. I need a rest, as I have had not a single day off for nearly a month, and that the month where all the hard work and hard living comes.

I hope I will get another couple of months in England – hope, because although I may be all right technically, I still don't know anything really about the Army and don't feel fit to go out and fight till I get some more experience.

That will be enough autobiography.

I have not come across many Old Wykehamists. Anthony Hill waved to me from a column of infantry at Wrotham and I have met three or four at Catterick. . . . I heard that Herbert was at the Signals OCTU but I never saw him.

If you could spare me the time for a post-card I should be very grateful. I have heard nothing from anybody for quite a time. I know it is very hard for us to write judging by myself, not that I have not the time, but after a day's work the inclination to do nothing is very great. I have not even heard from Duncan [McMurtrie]. . . .

I apologise for the blots.

I feel very Wiccamical at the moment. I have just finished Macdonell's 'England, their England', which ends up on the top of St Catherine's Hill after a visit to Winchester. It made me feel rather sentimental and regretful for the days when my most serious problems were how to get off cricket and how to do as little work as possible in Toyetime.

I hope things are going well with the house, as they always do, and particularly with the people who left about the same time as I did. As I am so near to going into action, in all probability, it seems quite likely that some of them have already.

Finally my best wishes to everybody, particularly you and Miss Bobber,

Yours

Michael Elliott-Binns

alias 'Old Binns', which always makes me feel as if I was about ninety-six and sitting in the back room of a pub leaning on a stick.[11]

* * *

At around the same time as Elliott-Binns, Middleditch wrote to Robertson again whilst on a weekend's leave:

I'm afraid it's a long time since I wrote last. I'm just about to start the last course here, 'collective training', which is tactics and work in the armoured cars themselves and should be great fun. It lasts seven weeks and I'm due to pass out about March 26th. I've been accepted for the XII Lancers but it's a bit of a toss up whether one is actually posted to them; but as they're abroad I think I will be in the end. They were, with XI Hussars, the first mechanised regiment and are, I believe, a very good crowd… .

There are lots of OWs here. Old Majendie is an officer, and when Lord Louis Mountbatten took the salute at a passing out parade, the other day, I'm pretty sure that I saw young Majendie in the background wearing Commando uniform. My ex-Squadron Leader was a Beloeite called Gregory-Hood. He was a Grenadier Guardsman and too affected to go down at all well. At any rate I don't think it quite the thing to return one's Sergeant-Major's salute left-handed in front of the Squadron!

Michael Hirst and Henry Brooke seem very well and will be passing out within a few weeks. I also see David Martyn occasionally, tho' he is in the Old Building and I have been moved to the New.[12]

* * *

Rigby.

Rigby and Metcalfe realized early in 1943 how close they were to one another geographically, Rigby being on the staff of the Fighting Vehicles School at Ahmednagar. Both wrote to Robertson in the space of a fortnight. Rigby was first off the mark, at the end of January.[13]

I have just had word from Pat Metcalfe, who is not far from Ahmednagar where I am at the moment. He tells me he met Lieutenant Colonel Ridgeway the other day. I was very sorry to hear, through Pat, of Hugh Rose's death. Such things are hardly credible.

I have been moved about a bit out here, and have met a good deal of different types. I don't think I could have tolerated pre-war India. People who have been in England for the last three years would not believe it possible that the English civilian population of India could be so indolent and complacent.

The cold weather has been pleasant, but all too short. I long for an English climate. I hope all is well with you and your sister. These airgraphs are so short they only serve to bridge the gap till our next meeting.

Metcalfe.

On February 13th 1943 – almost exactly a year since Rickman had been captured – Metcalfe contacted Robertson, hinting that he might go to the front in the near future.[14]

Thank you very much for your post-card of November 30th, which came a week or so ago; the latest I have heard from you was in an Air Mail Letter Card sent to Roger Rigby, with whom I have just got in touch, and who sent it on to me. I was up in Delhi on a few days' leave early in January and met Robin Ridgway[15] – now a Lieutenant Colonel! – who told me Roger was out here and gave me his address. He, apparently, is at one of the Training Centres teaching Tank Driving and Maintenance; rather a dull job, I should think.

I was very sorry to hear of Hugh Rose's death in Libya; I think John [Metcalfe] was really very lucky not to be in it. He seems to be fairly happy in the few letters from him that have got through.

Here we are very busy teaching our boys to drive, and shoot out of, tanks; and though our new address, which you see at the top of this, does not mean anything yet, we hope it may do some time soon; meanwhile we are very occupied with schemes, etc., all day and every day. Thank goodness the Sikhs, in which Squadron I am, are fairly intelligent and quick to pick up things, and make very good mechanics …

Here we are really quite comfortable in brick huts – we even have electric light – and if it was not getting rather hot and very dusty, it would really be a very pleasant spot. The atmosphere is completely peace-time, except that we are working rather harder than the Indian Army ever did in peace-time!

I hope Winchester is still bomb-free and everyone well there.

* * *

Michael Hirst had completed his Oxford degree in 1942 (gaining a Third), and immediately went to the Royal Armoured Corps Pre-OCTU at Blackdown in Hampshire. He served a couple of months there – as he put it in his memoirs, mainly 'bull, drill, and general military training'. He had mixed feelings about his time at Blackdown:

Hirst.

One Warrant Officer at Blackdown whom I remember with affection was a Welsh Guardsman who always said, 'S-i-i-ing your words of command' – and it certainly worked. The brightest spot was the Salvation Army canteen (doughnuts and coffee); the darkest our Troop Sergeant Major, a Guardsman who bullied us all the time. The survivors of our Troop finally made it to RAC OCTU at Sandhurst, and as we were marched in to replace the troop which was passing out that day, we were delighted by our TSM being blasted by 'Shagger' Brand, the redoubtable RSM at Sandhurst, who, thinking the TSM too familiar (and doubtless being aware of his reputation), deliberately in front of us said, 'You stand at attention when you are speaking to me, Troop Sergeant Major.' The RSM was fierce but fair, and we all respected him.

Sandhurst was also better than Blackdown in terms of the syllabus:

Sandhurst had lovely old buildings and beautiful grounds, having been a Military College since Victorian times. We dined with all the pomp and ceremony of an Officers' Mess, while life was rather like a Public School, with fixed class times for each subject. We started with General Military Training, then Driving and Maintenance (D&M), Wireless, and finally Tactics. There was always controversy between the D&M and Wireless Wings about which way electricity flows … D&M insisted that it flowed from Positive to Negative, but when you went to the Wireless Wing they would say, 'We don't care what they told you in D&M, in this Wing electricity flows from Negative to Positive.' Though we were under a lot of pressure, the atmosphere was much more pleasant than at Blackdown, though the standard of drill and turnout was very high and demanding.

A typical example of exchanges on the parade ground, in front of the whole Sandhurst OCTU. A fly had caused me to wriggle my nose:

Adjutant: 'There is movement in the rear rank of 9 Troop, S'art Major!'

RSM: 'Take that Officer Cadet's name, Sergeant.'

Staff Sergeant marches up to me and halts smartly six inches in front of me and yells, 'What is your name, SIR?' (with great emphasis on the last word).

Self: 'Officer Cadet Hirst, Staff.'

Staff Sergeant (at top of his voice): 'Officer Cadet Hirst idle and inattentive, Sir.'

Hirst was, by his own admission, not a natural soldier. He states in his memoirs that there was a distinct possibility that he would be RTU'd (adjudged unsuitable to be an officer and 'Returned to Unit') because of what he described as

my generally sloppy military performance. Once I was tank commander on manoeuvres (we took turns at various positions in the crew). We had Guards Armoured Division drivers as part of the permanent staff, and they would do exactly as they were told, neither more nor less. The wireless set in the tank had a three-way switch, so that one could talk either to the other tanks in the Troop, or to Squadron HQ, or to the crew on intercom. I realised that we were heading straight for a swamp and ordered, 'Driver, Left'. Unfortunately, I was on to the rest of the Troop and not to the driver. My commands became ever more frantic, and the rest of the Cadets were killing themselves laughing as they knew what was happening. Eventually we finished up completely bogged. Two more tanks got bogged trying to tow it out, but meanwhile we Cadets had all left to go back to do Military Law.

The permanent staff must have hated us on such occasions, but on the whole they were very helpful. We had a mutually satisfactory arrangement with our PT instructor: we walked instead of 'doubling' when no officers were in sight, and he got a silver cigarette case at the end of the course. In our Morse exam, our instructor keyed slower and slower until we all got it right and passed.

It was touch and go when it was our Troop's turn to go to North Wales to do some infantry field work. We climbed Snowdon, did an assault crossing of a lake, and on the last day had a 'treasure hunt'. We were split into groups of three; both my mates, though 'townies', had done a lot of bush-walking. We were given a map reference to go to, which turned out to be the top of a mountain, Glyder Fach. We decided to go up a ridge, while all the rest opted to go up a gully. The 'Tigers' – two instructors and a rather self-opinionated Cadet whom none of us liked – had gone ahead to lay the clues. When we reached the top of the mountain, all was shrouded in mist, and to our horror there was only one very damp clue left. Obviously all the others had got there first, taken their clue, and gone. RTU loomed large, but there was nothing else to do than go on with the next leg. This was to a place called Pwll Du, a deserted farmhouse in the middle of a flat and dreary moor. More disaster; no clues there at all! Not knowing what to do next, we decided to eat our rations.

While we were doing this, the Tigers turned up, very surprised and mortified to see us. We had been ahead of everyone all the time, and the clue which we found on Glyder Fach was from the previous week's course. They gave us the next clue and rather airily told us to go ahead; they would catch us up. They didn't, and we arrived back at our billets at Penmaenmawr on the coast in time for a good feed in town, before joining the others after they got back for our regular evening meal. This saved our bacon as far as RTU was concerned.

We all eventually passed out in a ceremony which involved the graduating Cadets marching up the steps into the Old Building, followed by the Adjutant on his grey horse, while the new intake arrived as we had done a few months before. We had the usual celebrations. Spirits were hard to get, but I bought a half bottle of rum from the pub at Slaidburn. No one else drank it, so I was rather the worse for wear …

* * *

John Kennedy, meanwhile, was trapped in the United States as a flying instructor, though desperate to serve on operations. He too wrote to Robertson in mid-February 1943, his frustration plain to see.

I am at present instructing down here in Mississippi, hemmed in on all sides by nothing but cotton. It is a very poor part of the country and the population is well over half black. As a result life gets very monotonous and little goes on in the way of social entertainment. However, I succeeded in getting eleven days off for Christmas and went up to New York. There, as you may imagine, I had the time of my life, though it cost me a fortune. The train journey took over forty hours each way and I could not get a sleeper, but the discomfort was well worth while. I went to a huge selection of the night-clubs, saw several very good shows, went to a large debutante dance, a Spanish cocktail party, several other dances, etc., went up the Empire State Building, and did a hundred and one other things. I was welcomed from my return by five dense students, whom I am still trying to get through the course here. I'm afraid I was never made for an instructor and when I hear of my friends, with whom I was trained, flying Spitfires – my boon – it makes my blood boil. But as far as I know there is no way of getting out of this instructing.

The news sounds very good at present and everyone is very optimistic on this side of the water. I am very sorry to hear that you and your sister leave at the end of Cloister Time; going back to Sunnyside, whenever that may be, won't be the same without your being there.[16]

Kennedy's letter to Robertson was dispatched by the American V-Mail system (short for Victory Mail). Using a technique developed by the British, standard letter-forms were given free of charge to service personnel, and then photographed on to microfilm before being printed at their destination. The resultant saving in weight more than compensated for the labour-intensive process.

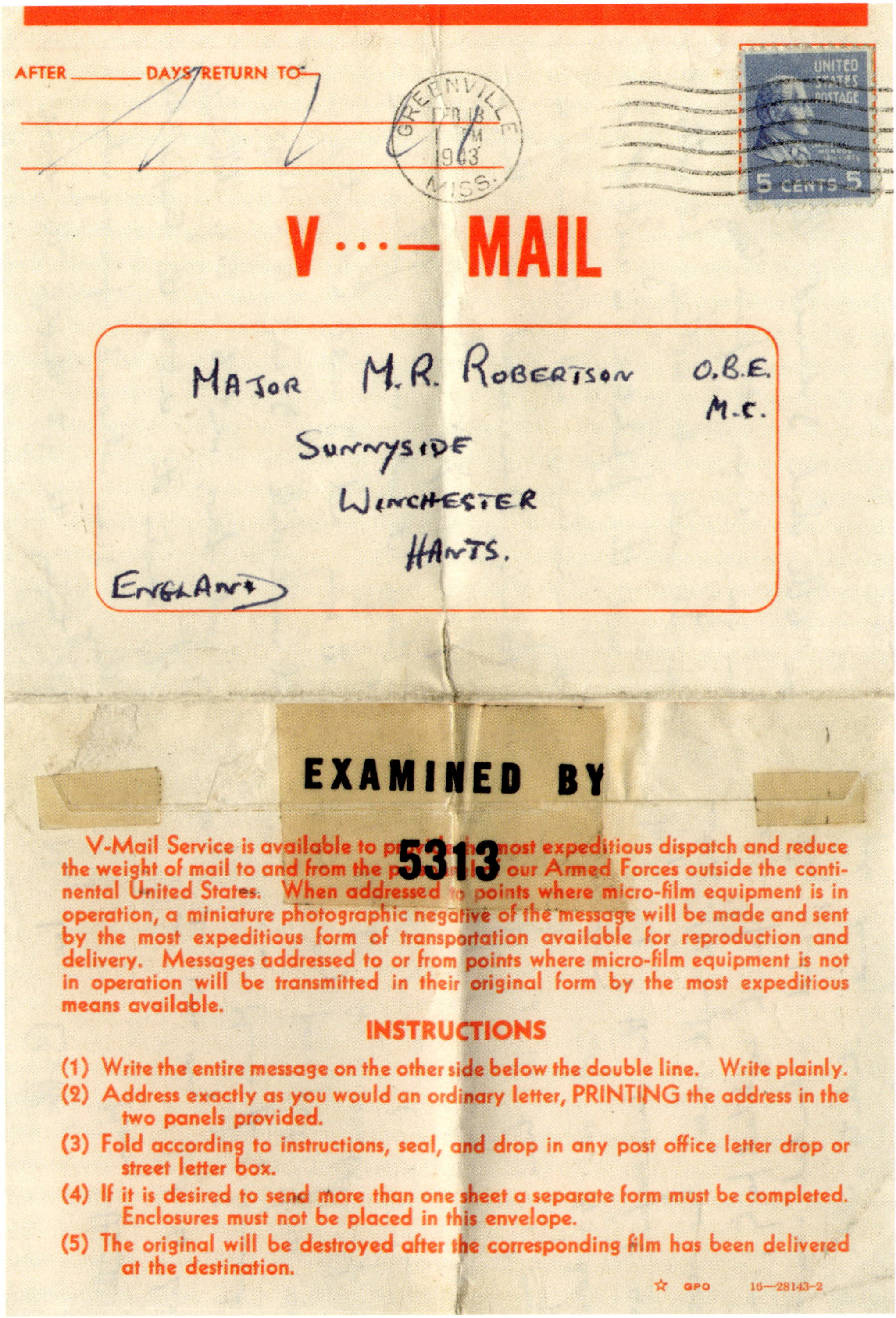

AFTER ______ DAYS RETURN TO

GREENVILLE FEB 18 1 PM 1943 MISS.

UNITED STATES POSTAGE

5 CENTS 5

V···— MAIL

MAJOR M.R. ROBERTSON O.B.E. M.C.

SUNNYSIDE

WINCHESTER

HANTS.

ENGLAND

EXAMINED BY

5313

V-Mail Service is available to provide the most expeditious dispatch and reduce the weight of mail to and from the personnel of our Armed Forces outside the continental United States. When addressed to points where micro-film equipment is in operation, a miniature photographic negative of the message will be made and sent by the most expeditious form of transportation available for reproduction and delivery. Messages addressed to or from points where micro-film equipment is not in operation will be transmitted in their original form by the most expeditious means available.

INSTRUCTIONS

(1) Write the entire message on the other side below the double line. Write plainly.

(2) Address exactly as you would an ordinary letter, PRINTING the address in the two panels provided.

(3) Fold according to instructions, seal, and drop in any post office letter drop or street letter box.

(4) If it is desired to send more than one sheet a separate form must be completed. Enclosures must not be placed in this envelope.

(5) The original will be destroyed after the corresponding film has been delivered at the destination.

☆ GPO 16—28143-2

In this undated & battered picture taken at Greenville Army Flying School, Mississippi, a wonderfully casual Kennedy (second left) stands in front of a Harvard trainer, with, one assumes, his 'five dense students, whom I am still trying to get through the course here'. (Kennedy family collection; edited by dansteele.net)

* * *

Bad news continued to flood in to Robertson from all sides, Fortune's survival and his MC being among the few bright spots. In February, Hopperite Squadron Leader 'Cam' Crichton-Miller was killed when the Halifax bomber in which he flying was shot down over occupied France.[17] As a meteorological officer, Crichton-Miller was not aircrew and had no need to be on a combat mission, but had wanted to see the practical consequences of his weather forecasts. His widow was pregnant with their first child. Few things can be more poignant than the death notice which appeared in *The Times* in June:

Crichton-Miller. On June 12th 1943, after an operation, Anne Margot Campbell, baby daughter of Sheila and Campbell Crichton-Miller (reported killed in action February 1943), aged four days.

* * *

Hirst was commissioned into the Yorkshire Hussars on February 20th 1943.[18]

To understand why I joined the Yorkshire Hussars, a little background is necessary. My father, Colonel C.J. Hirst MC, TD, served in the Yorkshire Dragoons in the 1914–1918 war in France, and commanded it in peacetime from 1926 to 1931. I knew that the Yorkshire Dragoons had gone to the Middle East with horses, and understood that they were to be mechanised and become artillery. However, half-way through my time at Oxford, I was told that the Yorkshire Dragoons now were tanks, so I switched to the Royal Armoured Corps. Because of censorship, there were more rumours than hard facts. Later on, when I had nearly completed my training at Sandhurst, I learned that the Yorkshire Dragoons had in fact become Motorised Infantry. As I had already been trained as a tank officer, I applied for a commission in the Yorkshire Hussars, the Yorkshire Dragoons' sister regiment, and was accepted by their Honorary Colonel, Lord Grimethorpe. However, this did not mean that one necessarily ever got to the Regiment, as you will see!

There I was, with one pip on each shoulder and a shiny Yorkshire Hussars badge on my cap; 264517 2nd Lieutenant Hirst M.J., but still a long away from my Regiment, which I presumed to be in the Middle East.

New recruits and young officers, after their initial training at depots and schools, had to go to a training regiment before they went on active service. These consisted of infantry battalions, given an RAC number but retaining their former title. So I was sent to 109 RAC, the 1/6th Lancashire Fusiliers (XXth of Foot; we knew them as the 'Double Cross' when no original Lancashire Fusiliers officer was in hearing). We were stationed at Welbeck Abbey, the seat of the Duke of Portland, where as a little boy I had gone to visit my father at the annual camp of the Yorkshire Dragoons. There I had enjoyed the sight of the CO, my father, with his head bandaged, and the former CO, Tommy Thompson, with his arm in a sling, after racing each other over the Mess tent and sliding down the other side, after a rather hectic guest night!

I enjoyed my time with the Lancashire Fusiliers. We learned a lot about managing men, preparing us for posting to a service regiment. The Officers' Mess was in the servants' quarters, a separate wing from the huge main house. The riding school was the Regimental office, and the men were in huts.

A previous Duke of Portland had had underground tunnels built so that he could be driven unseen in his carriage through the park all the way to the railway station at Worksop. The trouble with these tunnels was that the tanks had a habit of falling through the roof.

Our Squadron's tanks were initially parked facing outwards on the edge of a big grove of trees, with various tents inside as armoury, stores, fitters' workshop, guard tent, and so on. One very windy day, I was taking my Troop in weapons-cleaning. We were going to use the guard tent, but I changed my mind and took them to the armoury tent instead. At the height of the storm a huge limb from an oak tree fell on the guard tent, killing two men. One was crushed as he lay on his bed, and the guard commander as he sat at a table, reading. A tragic accident, which would have been much worse if we all had been there. As a result, concrete hard-standings were built for the tanks elsewhere.

Many of the men were pretty hard-bitten and there was much grumbling at a lot of unnecessary 'spit and polish', especially when we had to make our tanks nice and shiny by applying a mixture of petrol and oil. This was more than usually stupid; it nullified the camouflage, it collected dust, and it had to be washed off with more petrol; all this wasted fuel which had to be imported through the U-boat blockade at tragic cost of ships and lives. The men were fully justified in their comment, 'fucking sailors' blood'.

Of course, all the good tanks were needed for active service, not training. Our tanks were mainly worn-out Valentines – and later Churchills in the same state. The best of the latter in my troop would do four miles per gallon, the worst ½ a mile per gallon. When we changed tanks, we had to take the Valentines to Ollerton station to put them on railway flat trucks. My tank had very little steering and went straight over the top of a roundabout on the way. Then, when loaded, it was two inches off-centre, and while correcting this it stuck in reverse gear and nearly finished up on the main line with an express train coming.

I and two of my best friends, Eric Clarke and John Power, who both went to Xth Hussars, used regularly to go to Worksop, where we were hospitably entertained by the Ward Jones family: he was high up in United Steel, and we were very fond of his daughters.[19]

* * *

Sheepshanks.

After his spell at Corpus Christi, Oxford, Sheepshanks had been commissioned into the Rifle Brigade in February 1942[20] and gazetted Lieutenant on October 1st. By then he had nearly reached his unit, 7th Battalion (7RB), who were preparing for battle at El Alamein. Robertson stated that Sheepshanks' service in 7RB 'broadened and strengthened him, without abating his old loves and loyalties. He felt that he had great happiness to repay, and it is clear by all accounts that he had become a good officer.'

The *Rifle Brigade Chronicle* stated that he 'arrived in Egypt at a critical time, and like all young officers was determined to join a battalion as soon as possible, and that was characteristic of him.'

He caught up with 7RB on October 31st, and 'proved himself, during the last few days of the battle, to be a thoroughly reliable officer. No matter what work was to be done, he was always cheerful and confident. Early in 1943, he took over the command of a platoon of anti-tank guns.'

He was – as usual in Rifle Brigade or KRRC units – one of several Wykehamists with the Battalion: 7RB also included Major Kenneth Hicks,[21] Lieutenant Dick Adams,[22] and his younger brother, 2nd Lieutenant William Adams.[23] David Kemp would join them at a later stage.

Sheepshanks wrote to Robertson in February and March 1943:

Once again, let me say how desperately sorry I am that you should be leaving Sunnyside. I feel that I owe more to you and the House you created than I can ever say. I had all my manifold faults and shortcomings mercilessly pinned down, and I feel whatever small success I have ever achieved has been due – together with my family life at home – to the excellent training I received in Sunnyside. I value the five years I spent with you more highly than most things. My father has always got great delight from my being at Sunnyside, and I venture to think the enjoyment was not undeserved on the whole. I must have been a terrible fusser and nuisance …

I knew Colonel 'Squeak' Purdon[24] was a Wykehamist but hadn't remembered that you knew him. I suppose you will also know Kenneth Hicks who was about contemporary with Colonel Purdon. I thought Colonel Squeak was quite one of the most charming people I have ever met, and if I see him again and get the chance to speak to him I'll certainly pass on your message to him.

I have at the moment with me Hugh Butler[25] who used to be in Freddie's in my time. He is the most delightful person and wishes to be remembered to you very much. I heard the other day that Gilbert Talbot was all right and well.

At the present I am not awfully overworked, but have enough work to do to keep me interested and amused. I read a good deal and still worship at the shrine of the immortal Pickwick with Sam Weller, Tony Weller, and the red-nosed man in close attendance. It is a source of never-failing amusement and newly-discovered joy every time one opens the cover.

I live in perfect comfort with the protection of one of those excellent institutions called bivouacs. My bed fits in beautifully and just gives my nose about six inches clearance between it and the roof when in bed. Getting in is rather a complicated ritual which calls for a certain amount of contortionism if one is to get in without knocking the shelter over, but once in one can view the oddities of the weather with a certain amount of equanimity. It is quite a pleasant sensation lying in bed covered with warm clothes, mackintoshes, and ground sheets, and hearing the rain pattering on the roof. Admittedly I view gales and heavy rain with marked disapproval and even more the ugly necessity of having to rouse oneself and dress, wash, and shave in a sharpish morning wind.

As I think I told you before, the flowers here are perfectly beautiful and are far too varied for a layman like myself to describe. We get a lot of yellow daisies (large) and poppies, and a perfect host of the Clarkia variety. Also the other day I came across a perfectly ordinary garden pea flower without a pod. Birds abound, but I am not an ornithologist so I cannot elaborate, but feel sure you would enjoy them all.

I saw Bill Cliff-Hodges [*sic*] the other day, though not to talk to,[26] and have met James Clerk-Rattray on a course.

All my love to you and your sister, and apologies for this dreadful scrawl.[27]

I hope you are well and will forgive my rather slow method of writing this but at this moment I haven't anything quicker available by me at the moment. I haven't written for a bit but really haven't a great deal of interest to say. I'm well and comfortable and really enjoying myself quite a lot.

Life is really just as I told you before. The food is still excellent and we are able to get eggs now and then. The method of getting eggs is very entertaining though I expect that other people have told you what it's like. Nearly every native out here from the oldest to the youngest (aged usually from eighty to about five and all very dirty) has eggs and is willing to offer them for sale by barter. They all manage to speak a sort of pidgeon English mixed with their own tongue and a few words of Italian. The method is to hail a 'Wog' and then each side tries to make the best bargain it can with its opponent. Certain fixed standards are usually applicable, *viz* commodities of exchange are tea, sugar, cigarettes, and biscuits. I was told the other day that flour is good if one has any to spare. Money's not usually accepted, but the only time I did use it, a perfectly frightful young fellow sold me 25 for 50 piastres (about 10/-) which I'd won at bridge the night before. The whole lot were bad! Unfortunately I never managed to find the fellow again to make him see reason and refund my money, but I had an amusing time trying to reason with him while he was on a donkey. He of course said he'd never seen me before but wouldn't dream in any way of selling bad eggs. These people out here do make me laugh as they are so funny and lazy. One can often see the sign 'Party at Work' and all you actually see is a party of 'Wogs' doing no work of any description but mainly sitting down or maybe leaning on a shovel. Another very good sight is the way the 'Wog' gets about. If they do have a car (usually fast) they overload it till the springs practically touch the ground and then drive it as fast as they possibly can without any mercy at all. There are frequently as many as eight in one two-seater, usually yelling a bit to encourage the driver. I have also seen one man riding a motorbike pulling behind him a trailer-load of seven creatures. Humbler modes of transport are camels and donkeys, invariably overloaded, and it is almost ludicrous to see a huge fat man on a tiny little donkey that can't stand more than two feet high. We had to warn one of them off a place where he was in imminent danger of going up on some scattered mines, of which there must be quite a number.

As I think I told you in a former letter the flowers out here are simply marvellous. There seems to be no limit to the variety of flowers and colours. I'm not much of a botanist but can appreciate the general effect a bit. There are yellow daisies, a small sort of ground lilac, anemones, a queer sort of clover, conical in shape, and innumerable small flowers of a varying mixture of colours, usually some sort of blue or mauve, with accompanying reds, golds, and white. I can't describe them more accurately I'm afraid, which is a pity for I know you like to have a more accurate description.

I've met fairly frequently out to dinner in a mess or some other place an awfully nice person called Anthony Sturt who has a slow way of speaking but can't make out whether it is he that you mention.[28] Christopher Sinclair is not with us but I expect you hear fairly frequently from him via his parents. I told you I'd met James Clerk-Rattray, who is one of the most complete Guardsmen I have ever met now.

P.S. Sorry for this awful scrawl but I hope it'll pass. C.[29]

Although the campaign in North Africa was heading towards a successful conclusion, there was much bitter fighting for First and Eighth Armies in the deserts and mountains of Tunisia which claimed the lives of several more Hopperites. Defensive victories by Eighth Army at Medenine and First Army at Kasserine had crippled the German forces in Tunisia, who had lost so many tanks that they would never again be able to launch an offensive. Their supply routes were under regular and effective attack by Allied submarines and aircraft operating from Malta. On March 9th, the day after his defeat at Medenine, Rommel had handed over command of his troops to his colleague von Arnim and left North Africa, never to return. Victory for the Allies was now only a matter of time. However, ahead of Eighth Army still lay the as yet untouched German defences of the Mareth Line.

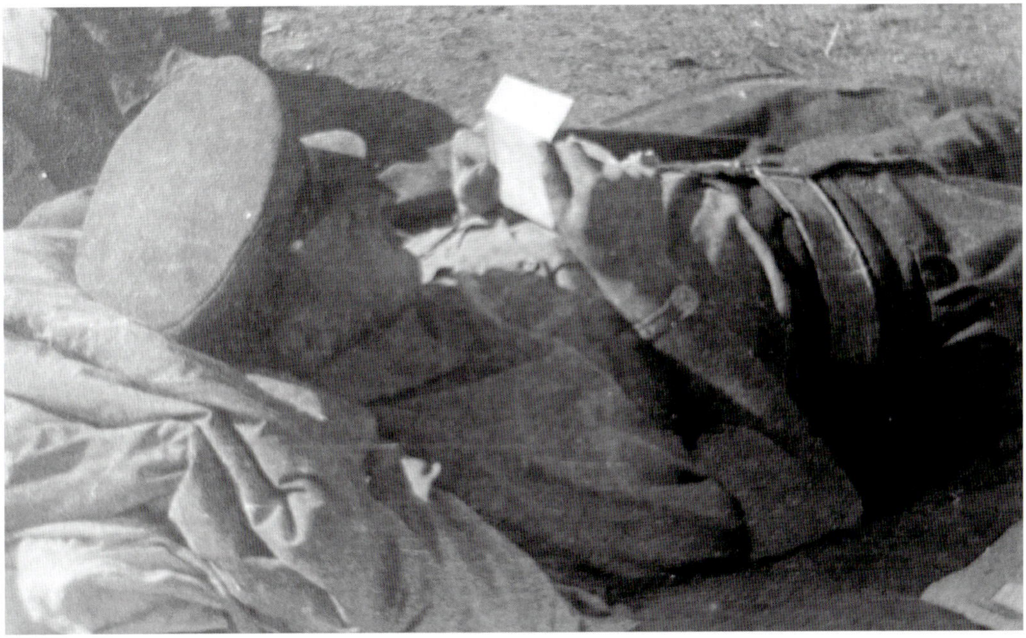

Geoffrey Gwyer in the desert during the war. (Kennedy family collection)

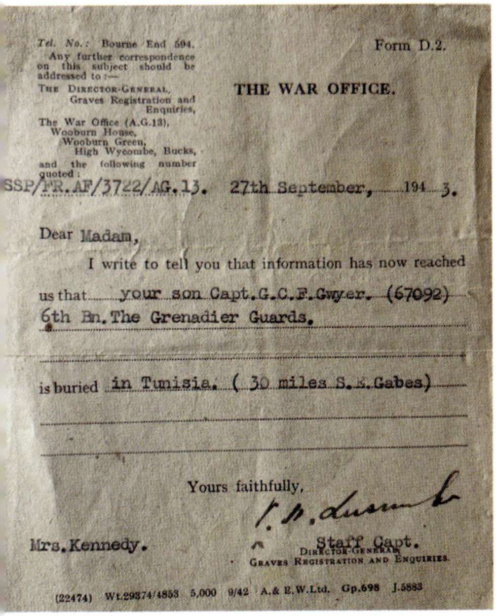

Tel. No.: Bourne End 594.
Any further correspondence on this subject should be addressed to:—
THE DIRECTOR-GENERAL, Graves Registration and Enquiries,
The War Office (A.G.13), Wooburn House, Wooburn Green, High Wycombe, Bucks,
and the following number quoted:

Form D.2.

THE WAR OFFICE.

SSP/FR.AF/3722/AG.13. 27th September, 1943.

Dear Madam,

I write to tell you that information has now reached us that your son Capt. G.C.F. Gwyer. (67092) 6th Bn. The Grenadier Guards.

is buried in Tunisia. (30 miles S.E. Gabes)

Yours faithfully,

Staff Capt.
Director-General,
Graves Registration and Enquiries.

Mrs. Kennedy.

(22474) Wt.29374/4853 5,000 9/42 A.& E.W.Ltd. Gp.698 J.5883

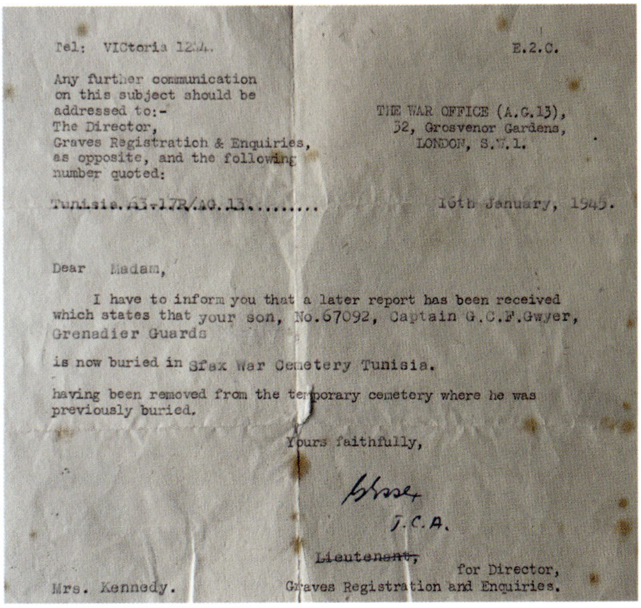

Tel: VICtoria 1234.

E.2.C.

Any further communication on this subject should be addressed to:-
The Director,
Graves Registratioh & Enquiries,
as opposite, and the following number quoted:

THE WAR OFFICE (A.G.13),
32, Grosvenor Gardens,
LONDON, S.W.1.

Tunisia. A3.17R/AG.13......... 16th January, 1945.

Dear Madam,

I have to inform you that a later report has been received which states that your son, No.67092, Captain G.C.F.Gwyer, Grenadier Guards

is now buried in Sfax War Cemetery Tunisia.

having been removed from the temporary cemetery where he was previously buried.

Yours faithfully,

J.C.A.

~~Lieutenant,~~
for Director,
Graves Registration and Enquiries.

Mrs. Kennedy.

After three months in reserve after El Alamein, 7RB and the other units of 1st Armoured Division went into the front line in southern Tunisia on March 15th 1943. Two days later, Geoffrey Gwyer, the half-brother of John Kennedy, was killed in action at the Horseshoe, in the Wadi Zeuss, as Eighth Army tried to break the Mareth Line.[30]

Kennedy wrote to Robertson in April 1943:

> You will, of course, have heard about Geoffrey's death, which I expect came as much a blow to you almost as it did to me and my family. I thought after Dunkirk that he had had his share of bad luck, but I suppose it just doesn't work that way. I am afraid my mother will have taken it very hard, as she lost a husband, two brothers, and a brother-in-law in the last war, and I think that is anyone's share of the nightmares of war – let alone this, on top of it all.

As it was to turn out, this was not the final nightmare which Constance Kennedy would have to face in this war. For now, though, Kennedy's letter went on:

> Geoffrey was always a perfect brother to me and my sisters, and was always very kind and generous to us. He was always very popular with people who knew him, too, and I think the main reason for this was the fact that he seldom got down-hearted but always made the best of everything that came his way. However, I feel that if it had to be, he would have preferred it no other way than on the battlefield.[31]
>
> I have been very inactive – socially – lately as I have been very busy finishing off one more 'class' of cadets. However, I did get time off to fly over to Dallas, Texas, which was interesting. I didn't have time to go out and see the cattle-ranches and so on, as they are further west and I had very little time as it was.[32]

His promotion to Flying Officer came on April 9th,[33] but this was small consolation for being so far from the action and for the death of his half-brother.

* * *

On March 19th, Montgomery launched Operation Pugilist, an attempt to break through the Mareth Line defences frontally. By March 22nd, however, the British attackers had been forced to admit defeat after heavy losses in both the main attack and subsidiary operations. The Mareth Line was proving to be a serious obstacle – but it was more vulnerable than the enemy supposed. Its western flank was secured by the Matmata Hills, beyond which lay a broad tract of waterless desert, long considered impassable for vehicles. However, the Long Range Desert Group had discovered a practicable route through this area, some sixty miles to the west, where a gap between the Djebel Melab and Djebel Tebaga hills – the Tebaga Gap – led into the rear of the Axis position. If an outflanking force could pass over the Matmata range and across the desert, the Mareth Line could be attacked from the rear. At the same time as attacking the Mareth Line frontally, Montgomery had sent the New Zealand Division on a long forced march round the enemy's western flank. With the defeat of the frontal attacks on the Mareth Line, this 'left hook' now became the main axis of attack.

The New Zealanders attacked at Tebaga on March 21st but encountered stiff resistance from two German divisions. Montgomery therefore committed 1st Armoured Division to the offensive. On leaving their positions at Medenine on March 23rd, 7RB faced a journey of 160 miles across some truly terrible going; they drove continuously for forty-eight hours, without a halt to sleep. At lunchtime on March 26th 7RB halted south-east of El Hamma, only to be told that they would be in action very shortly.

> There was just time to 'brew up', wash off some of the worst of the dust, and make preparations for this new battle in strange and unreconnoitred surroundings ... During the afternoon the hot, south-easterly wind was still blowing, bringing with it, on this day, a swarm of locusts.[34]

At 1600hrs the New Zealanders attacked with massive artillery support and punched a hole through the German front, into which 1st Armoured Division now poured. 7RB followed the armour as it advanced into the darkness, illuminated by explosions, muzzle-flashes, and the glare of burning vehicles.

> It was a miserable night's march, without contact with the enemy but consisting of innumerable starts and stops, bumps and jerks, as drivers of the armoured brigade's echelon vehicles in front fell asleep or drove into slit-trenches or failed to follow the tail-light of the truck in front.[35]

At dawn the next day, 7RB were five miles short of El Hamma, and German resistance was stiffening as the defenders clung to their ground with the help of numerous anti-tank guns.

> The day was static, with a small amount of aircraft activity, and with the Khamsin [hot wind] and dust at its most intense peak of intolerability.[36]

But by the end of March 27th the Germans had been pushed into the hills six miles north of the town, and 7RB continued the pursuit as far as El Hamma. The enemy were holding the last line of hills between the British and the coastal plain; these protected the end of the new German line at Wadi Akarit, against which Eighth Army were now pushing. At 1400hrs on March 31st the Commander of 7 Motor Brigade – Wykehamist Brigadier Jimmy Bosvile – ordered his three battalions each to attempt to seize one of the four possible routes through these hills, so that the remainder of 1st Armoured Division could pass through at first light. He allocated 7RB the most westerly pass, between Djebel Hadoudi and Djebel Zemlet el Beida, with its spur Djebel Djerouala.

The easiest approach was northwards around the east end of the salt lake to a road junction at Oglat Telmam. Once this was secure, 'B' Company was to advance north-west to seize Djebel Djeroula; then 'A' Company would take the western end of Djebel Zemlet el Beida, allowing 'C' and 'D' companies to storm the pass between that hill and Djebel Hadoudi. All this, however, would be preceded by a seven-mile approach over

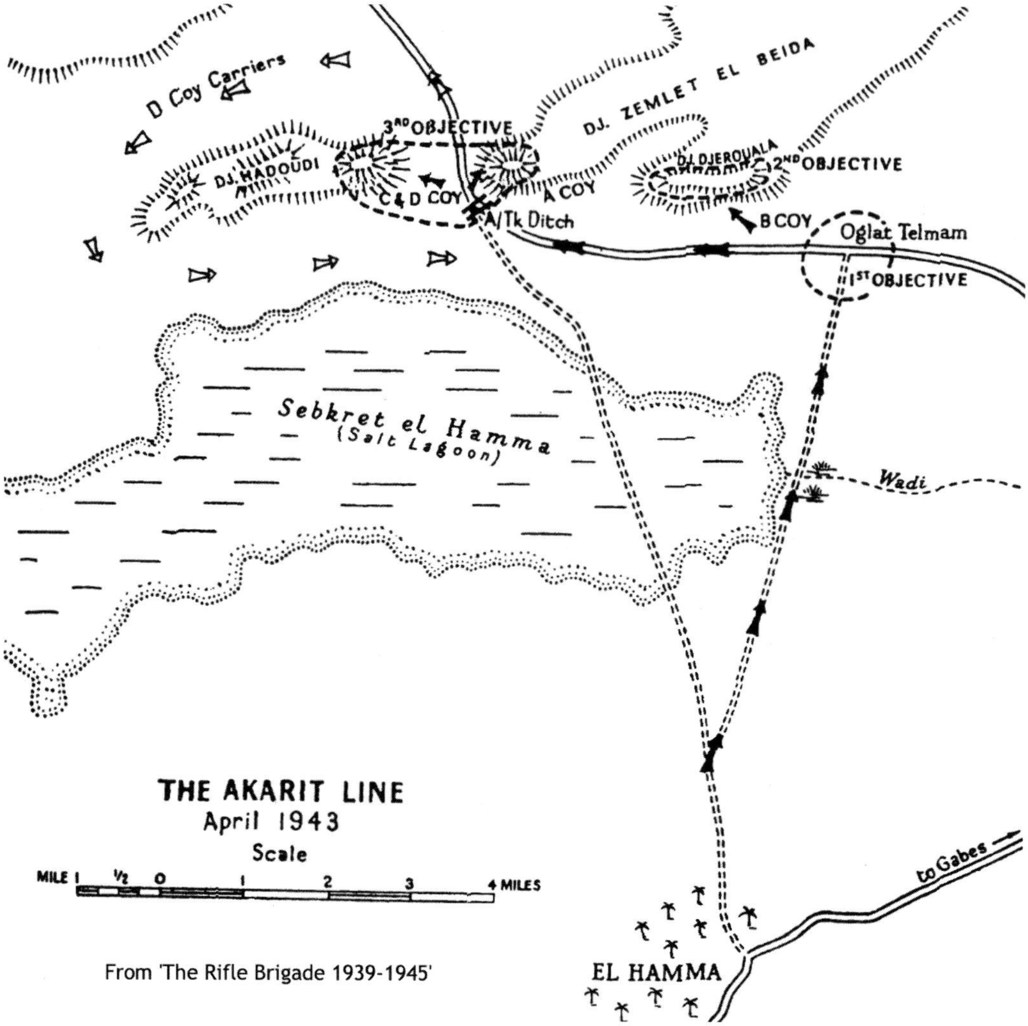

From 'The Rifle Brigade 1939-1945'

open ground to Oglat Telmam and would carry the Battalion out of range of its usual supporting artillery; the support of a medium artillery regiment was promised instead, which was less satisfactory, since although the 5.5-inch guns had longer range and delivered a heavier shell than the usual 25-pounders, they had a much slower rate of fire.

As 7RB moved up for the attack, 'D' Company took the lead, but encountered mines on the track to Oglat Telmam. By 0100hrs on April 1st, however, 'B' Company had captured its objective, taking prisoner fifteen Italian soldiers of the *Pistoia* Division. 'A' Company then went forwards. In the darkness, however, the unit went astray, although it signalled success at 0415hrs. But when 'D' Company moved into the pass at 0500hrs, it found an anti-tank ditch, strongly defended by the enemy. Undeterred, 'D' Company fixed swords[37] and charged as dawn broke, capturing the pass, fifty prisoners, four machine-guns, and two anti-tank guns. Wykehamist Hew Butler's four 6-pounder anti-tank guns of 'C' Company were then brought up to secure the position against armoured counter-attack.

Now, however, things began to go seriously wrong. 'A' Company, which should have been in position to cover 'D', had in fact occupied the wrong feature, and the enemy still controlled Point 180, which overlooked 'D' Company's positions. 'A' Company never received its fresh orders to clear the hills to the west of the pass.

> As dawn broke at 0530hrs on April 1st, everybody had high hopes that 2 Armoured Brigade would exploit our success with the minimum of delay. However, the golden opportunity was let slip, and we grimly held on to our positions from 0530hrs until 1000hrs under direct observation from the hills around us by enemy artillery and mortar OPs, who lost no time in making life extremely uncomfortable. To add insult to injury, the medium regiment which should have been in call at first light had moved out of call during the night, and the two RHA OP officers informed the CO at 0900hrs, in response to his somewhat irate demand for artillery support, that their guns were out of range.[38]

'C' and 'D' companies suffered badly as they waited in vain for the other two companies to catch up and for the armour to arrive to exploit their gains. Unknown to the Riflemen, however, higher command had decided that the attempt to 'bounce' the Wadi Akarit line had failed, and that 7RB should be withdrawn. It had all been for nothing, as their commanding officer later reflected:

> The position was hopeless, and we were withdrawn, much the worse for wear and very bitter that so much wasted effort, which could have paid a wonderful dividend had its initial success been taken advantage of, had been utterly wasted.[39]

7RB had suffered incredibly heavy losses for one battalion: 14 officers and 141 men killed, wounded, and missing. There was a Wykehamist in each category. Dick Adams was one of those who had been wounded, severely enough to keep him away from the Battalion for months, missing the whole conclusion of the campaign in Tunisia. Hew Butler had been wounded and taken prisoner. And Sheepshanks had died, at the age of twenty-one, of the wounds which he received.[40]

Robertson wrote to Sheepshanks' parents immediately on hearing the news, and on April 14th Sir Thomas replied:[41]

> My dear Bobber,
> You, better than most, will know that this has hit us pretty hard, but contrary to my first days' thoughts, letters do bring comfort, especially from old and valued friends who knew him, and in particular your letter and Livingstone's have and always will mean very much to us.
>
> Today I feel – what I didn't five days ago – that that old quotation 'Tis better to have loved and lost etc.' is true. He gave us 21 years of true happiness and we must be and are deeply grateful, even though fate has taken him away just when he was developing into something rather fine. You know how he repaid us for all our efforts – or rather after us you know best since no one except Beth and me can know what a loving and devoted son he was. And again only Beth and I are left to know what we and he owe to you and Miss Robertson.

First, five years of unbroken happiness at Sunnyside in a community of which I don't believe one would find the equal elsewhere. His loyalty to and affection for you and the House was touching and was indeed an easy target always for a leg-pull.

Second, the foundation of a character which to a father's eye at any rate was developing into something fine: courage, enthusiasm, and a readiness to fight and overcome difficulties.

Third, a real and unaffected passion for music. It meant an enormous amount to him and brought him more happiness almost than anything. His year at Corpus continued the process you started. As you say, the Army was not his line to begin with, but once again he fought and won and I sincerely believe that he was really happy with his Battalion. I haven't yet heard from the War Office, but the news came in a letter from his CO – one Darling.[42]

He was killed on March 31st but I have not details. The CO described him as 'a first-class officer and showed great powers of leadership and command. In action he was gallant and brave and at all times showed a complete disregard for his personal safety. He is a great loss to the Regiment as an officer and an individual.' This may be the conventional letter of a CO but anyhow I take it as genuine.

The one thing I cannot bring myself to do at the moment is to re-read C.'s letters home, but in one of the last we got he said, according to the best of my recollection and I have it pretty well right I am sure, 'It is sad to think of Sunnyside without the Bobber. It can never be quite the same. I can never repay all I owe to him and Miss Robertson.' Well, he has done his best now, poor boy.

He was rather reserved, but just before he went abroad he made a tremendous effort and told me how grateful he was to us for sending him to Winchester. It was I who ought to be grateful because I loved his five years with you as much as he did – not the less because he had difficulties to overcome and I took pride in watching him do it.

You may like to know what Livingstone wrote. He said 'as you know C. was an admirable member of the College and I for one shall never forget his delightfully generous, loyal, vivid nature – one of the best types that England produces and that other countries, whatever their virtues, don't produce. One pictures him naturally as a member of a victorious army and I suppose that is where he fell. I often think of those lines of Simonides on the dead at Thermopylae: "Their fate was far famed, their fortune noble; instead of lamentation they have memory; instead of pity, praise."'

I thought I remembered my Greek Epigrams a little but I can't recollect the one he mentions and should like to get hold of the original Greek.[43]

If I have got to be content with memories, at least they are happy and proud memories. But for other people's sake I do pray that this may all stop before the casualties on his Long Roll begin to compare with those on mine.

I know you will forgive me unburdening myself like this to you, but it is a relief to talk about him to one who knew him. One day I will try and come down to Winchester for the day, but I must give time an opportunity to do its work first.

Poor Beth, as you will guess, is pretty shattered – you know what a mother she was! – but she bears up very bravely.

Yours ever

Tom Sheepshanks

* * *

As 'Dan' Somerville explained to Robertson in March, he was now in Buckinghamshire, a pleasant change at least from Northern Ireland. His Regiment was based near Beaconsfield and had just completed Exercise SPARTAN (March 4th to 12th), arguably the largest military exercise ever held in this country, as the troops in Britain began to gear themselves up for the liberation of occupied Europe.

Dan Somerville.

> I met Nick in London on the 20th, and he told me that you were leaving Sunnyside at the end of Common Time, not Cloister Time as I had supposed ... I don't want to say anything elaborate, but just want to express my sorrow at the fact that you are leaving at last, and my satisfaction at the thought that you will still be at Winchester, and only about two hundred yards from College.
>
> In a recent Battalion report after an exercise this sentence was written. 'The CO, after a certain period, retired from active command, but his influence continued to be felt.' I hope the parallel turns out to be a good one!
>
> We are not now as far away from you as before, and thank goodness we have got clear of the awful weather we used to have. Here it is really very nice, bright sun, decent village country, and a large and comfortable house surrounded by an apple orchard, which promises well. Billets are very good, and most units are quite content.
>
> I was out on a big scheme a short while ago, and must have ridden close on eight hundred miles on my motor-bike. On one epic night march I spent nine hours in the saddle, and had almost to be helped off at the end of it. Fortunately the weather was perfect; very cold and dark at night, but dry and that is the main thing where large exercises are concerned, as you probably know. I fell off three or four times, mostly through running into vehicles without lights, but escaped with superficial bumps, cuts, and bruises. Even the motor-bike managed to pull itself together sufficiently to get me home![44]

* * *

Middleditch was commissioned into XII Royal Lancers as a 2nd Lieutenant on March 27th 1943, but was immediately posted to 161 Regiment RAC, which had until the previous year been an infantry unit, 12th Battalion, Yorkshire Regiment (Green Howards). No sooner had he settled in with them than he was posted yet again, as he told Robertson on May 1st:

> Apologies for not having written for so long. As you can see from the above address I've been moved from the Green Howards. I spent about three weeks with them at Trowbridge. It was quite fun but there was very little to do. My Squadron Leader was a great friend of my father's, and my Sergeant had known him in India, so I was very lucky in that respect. I was then suddenly [on April 22nd 1943] transferred to 27th Lancers at Cambridge. We are up here for ten days shooting on the ranges, and are under canvas, finding it rather cold but quite fun. A lot of my friends are still up at Cambridge, so I have a very good time there, and also have an interesting job with my own vehicles and my own men to train.

Funnily enough both my COs were Freddyites and contemporary with John [Middleditch, his late cousin] – also, former 12th Lancers. I expect you remember them, 'Kate' Savill[45] and Horsbrugh-Porter. Both are very good Colonels, but I think the 27th live in pretty good fear of Colonel Porter.

There's been no news of getting out to the 12th yet, but I'm still hoping. However I wouldn't mind staying on with the 27th who are a very good lot …[46]

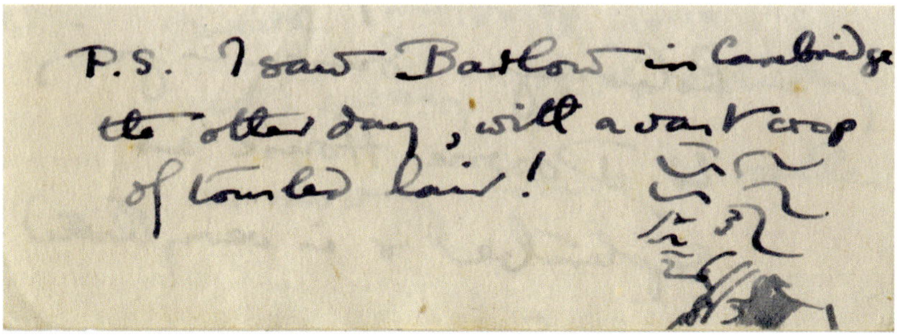
P.S. I saw Barlow in Cambridge the other day, with a vast crop of tousled hair!

Middleditch's sketch of Barlow, taken from the above letter.

* * *

The bad news did not stop. On April 26th, Lieutenant Colonel Lawrence Younger (who had left Hopper's just before Robertson's tenure began) was killed by shell-fire near Djebel Kournine.[47] Robertson, who had now moved out of Sunnyside preparatory to his retirement, wrote on the same day to the last of our subjects who was still in Hopper's, Mackrill. His letter sets out many of the values which he considered important, and in many ways speaks to the young prefect as an equal.

My dear Graham,
I was going to write to you anyhow, having returned from my lovely week's holiday with F.W.G. [Frederick Walter Goddard] and family in Cornwall, and now I have your beautiful post-card to thank for! I think that coast deserves a better name than 'Worms Head'! I suppose some foul Biologist christened it that!![48] So glad you went and had good weather, and learned a good deal.

Yes, the worst of the move is over, but we are far from straight, and visitors and callers began before even the furniture was in, let alone in position! There is a great deal more to do – some urgent (I've not yet handed over papers, etc., to Marcus Hampton, though I've seen him three times as problems crop up), and the rest can be done at leisure. My study and the garage are choc-a-bloc at present, but I've just cleared my table for writing, though I can't find a lot of my paper. The Hamptons really began moving into Sunnyside four days earlier than we originally intended, and it made it impossible for Sheila and me to clear up a lot of our business in peace. However, with good will on both sides, we've done marvels, and we shall have more leisure than they do to do some things gradually later on. SMR simply must get a holiday soon. We have only one helper here – having left all our food and servants for them and you at Sunnyside (!) – and SMR is doing half the housework as well as all the preserving at present.

By the way, I spoke to Duff (about entry for Darwin and Gray at Trinity) and asked him to confirm, which he does, that it is still all right for you to go up in October. He says yes, and that they have some vacancies reserved in the Labs. So it is up to you to take advantage of that and I do hope you will make work for Higher Certificate the first charge on your time. We shall all look rather fools if you [illegible] it up and can't take advantage of your chance at Cambridge. Possibly you will later after all come back to the idea of being a doctor, or doing research work of some kind.

I do hope you'll do your best to keep up the standard all round in the House. Letter after letter we get bears witness to the fact that there is something different, and something better, about many of our traditions. Distinguished parents, brother dons, College servants, all say the same. All the small things I've so often worried you about tell cumulatively – tidiness and absence of litter in Hall and galleries, walking about smartly (you and Inglis aren't two of the best!), whole and clean hats, absence of wanton damage, politeness to servants (and of course to visitors), and a dozen other things, and fundamentally, of course, a religion which enters into and affects one's daily conduct and relations with other human beings. One needs time, as you know, for prayer and contemplation, but in my opinion the ultimate test of religion is that it makes a man behave decently: so many 'professional holy-men' are often unscrupulous and prejudiced and devoid of Christian sympathy and humility.

You are a bit easy-going for a Senior Prefect and will have to take a pull on yourself about punctuality and keeping the other prefects up to their job. I hope WMH will still give them their individual jobs. I'm sure it is a good plan. But in the end the Senior Prefect must be responsible for good order and discipline, which are the foundation of everything. Many a Hopperite who used to get the rough side of my tongue (? in fact, my shoe!) has written to bless me for it since.

Well, there's a lot more. Mr Hampton will have his own ideas about some things and I can't and shan't try to interfere. But I'm quite sure that a lot of things we ordered and established after a long struggle (in some cases) are worth preserving! Come and talk to me swiftly if you are in any difficulty. Love to Ian (if now on leave) and greetings to your parents, and good luck!

Yours ever,
'Bobber'[49]

Three days later, yet another Hopperite – Guy Wilson – perished in an aeroplane crash at Barnstaple in Devon.[50]

* * *

Fortune was still in hospital in Egypt in May. By this stage, it is clear that he was walking, as he had visited Cairo.

By now you will have relinquished your command at Sunnyside. A sad day for everyone. But I am sure your hospitality will be just the same in your new home. I have not met many Wykehamists out here lately, as I have been unable to get around much. I bumped into that rather strange individual Fullerton-Carnegie of 'K' who was in a nerve hospital

> next door to my last one. He was looking very fit and as far as I could see his nerves were flourishing too.
>
> My wounds have now completely recovered and I was sent here with the idea of going to South Africa, but I seem to have recovered so quickly that there seems to be some doubt as to whether they will now send me to the Union. This is annoying in a way, as I will be graded 'B' at the highest for four months or so and will spend the time hanging around down here at the Base. And, if I have to hang around, to be quite honest, I would rather do it in South Africa with a fishing rod in my hand, than in this God-forsaken country where the chances of complete recovery seem to be remote.
>
> I have just returned from 48 hours in Cairo – and 48 hours was quite enough. In my present condition I was quite unable to keep up with the pace. The great city was very full, and prices had soared to fantastic heights, thanks to the Yanks, who are all quite prepared to pay anything for everything.
>
> Our chaps received quite a knock the other day. Very few of my friends left on their feet I gather. Still they all performed miracles. Had a cable from my father in Geneva – all very well.[51]

Robertson noted, apropos Fortune's Cairo jaunt, 'Silly. This did him in.'

Instead of 'hanging around', Fortune was transferred to South Africa by hospital ship. Many of his companions on board were tuberculosis or lung cases, whose survival was in the balance. Fortune was probably regarded in the same light; shortly before his death – many years later – a shadow was found on his lung, which he believed to be scar tissue from the old wound. South Africa offered them all a better chance of recovery. However, they had first to get there; Fortune recalled that patients were buried at sea all the way down the Red Sea. He himself was not out of danger, and he contracted a very severe fever. This did, however, at least secure him a cabin on his own with air conditioning.

* * *

Brooke.

Henry Brooke was late to the party in Tunisia, only joining 16th/5th Lancers on May 3rd after three weeks on a troop-ship. The final battle of the North African campaign was about to begin. The Eighth Army from Egypt and the First Army from Algeria had between them squeezed the Germans and Italians into a smaller and smaller pocket of North Africa until, on May 12th 1943, the southern shores of the Mediterranean were swept clear of Axis forces. It was a worse defeat for the Axis powers than Stalingrad; 230,000 German and Italian troops were captured. On May 13th, General Alexander sent his famous signal to the Prime Minister:

> Sir, it is my duty to report that the Tunisian Campaign is over. All enemy resistance has ceased. We are masters of the North African shores.

But Brooke and five other newly-joined officers had been 'left out of battle', remaining to the rear in case of casualties – of which there were a number.

> I am very sorry I haven't written to you before, but I've either been too lazy or, when I have decided to do it, something else crops up. We spent a very pleasant month after it was over on the beach just north of BOU FICHA. The sand and flies were pretty bad, but it was lovely being able to swim every day. But since then we have moved and are now inland living on the side of a hill covered in olives. The dust is very bad and it is very hot but we have got used to it by now. There's plenty of fruit – melons, grapes, etc. – and unlimited eggs. We can get to the sea to bathe once a week. I am enjoying it all very much. We have several OWs with us: C. Foot ('G'), P. Gore ('A'),[52] and our Colonel.[53] The Rifle Brigades who are with us are swarming with them; eleven in all I think.[54]

During this period, a tank driver called Sam Knowles joined 16th/5th Lancers, and was posted to Brooke's Troop in 'B' Squadron. In 2016, Knowles published his memoirs, to which Brooke wrote the foreword. Knowles described his arrival as follows:

> I was allocated to 2nd Troop, commanded by Lieutenant H.A.G. Brooke who was, in the fullness of time, destined to become Colonel of the Regiment. For the present, however, he commanded a tank troop almost devoid of the essential ingredients of actual tanks, since at that time the Squadron only had one tank – a Sherman – to call its own. Gradually, replacement tanks were received and we were able to commence work on them to make them ready for action.[55]

They had plenty of time: 16th/5th Lancers were not to see action again until January 1944.

XI

'A very pleasant level-headed officer. Plays most games well'

Interlude, 1943

On July 22nd 1942, Guy Richardson reported for duty with 769 Squadron, Fleet Air Arm, at HMS *Condor* in Arbroath. From there, and the nearby HMS *Peewit,* he was to practise deck landings preparatory to joining an aircraft carrier. At this time, the aircraft which carried observers were the Fairey Swordfish and Albacore biplanes, dependable but uninspiring mounts. He went on leave – his training complete – on November 22nd 1942, with the following endorsement to his personnel file:

Richardson.

> General conduct: satisfactory.
> Of temperate habit.
> Professional ability: average.
> Zeal & energy: above average.
> Power of command: average.
> Judgment: above average.
> Reliability: average.
> A very good type of junior officer who should do well with increasing experience. Keen and loyal and a good messmate.
> Capt. R.M. Taylor

Richardson was now on embarkation leave; he was going to cross the Atlantic again, and on December 1st he went on to the books of HMS *Asbury.* This innocuous name concealed the identities of the Berkley Carteret and Montery Hotels in Asbury Park, New Jersey. It was here that newly-arrived RN personnel were quartered before being posted to new, American-built ships, or back to RN vessels which had come to the USA for repair.

Richardson – promoted Temporary Sub Lieutenant (A) on December 3rd – was being sent overseas with over a hundred other personnel to set up 850 Naval Air Squadron. This squadron was being raised at the American naval base at Quonset Point, on Narragansett Bay in North Kingstown, Rhode Island. The squadron was to be embarked on the Lend-Lease escort carrier HMS *Pursuer* and equipped with twelve Curtiss Seamew aircraft. The Seamew was a complete failure as a combat aircraft (it was nicknamed the 'Sea Cow' by its crews), and Richardson was very fortunate not to go into combat aboard one. His

destination had in fact changed: he was being posted instead to 832 Naval Air Squadron, with effect from December 31st 1942.[1]

The puzzle was that, as far as Richardson knew, 832 Squadron was serving on HMS *Victorious*, a modern aircraft carrier based with the Home Fleet in Scotland. Commissioned in 1941, she had gained an enviable reputation in the pursuit of the *Bismarck*, on Arctic and Malta convoys (Operation Pedestal), and in Operation Torch, the Allied landings in Algeria.

* * *

In late October 1942, during the Battle of the Santa Cruz Islands in the Pacific, America had lost two of its three fleet aircraft carriers; USS *Hornet* had been sunk and USS *Enterprise* damaged beyond quick repair. These losses left the USN with only one purpose-built carrier in the entire Pacific, the USS *Saratoga*. That the Americans then begged the British to send help should be better known.

It must have been a great surprise to Richardson to find *Victorious* in dry dock at the Norfolk Navy Yard, Virginia, where she arrived on December 31st. In great secrecy, she had left Greenock on December 20th to cross the Atlantic and join the United States Navy.

Before she could join the US Pacific fleet, *Victorious* required modifications: Talk-between-Ship radios; new radar and plotting equipment; and a new homing system to enable aircraft to find their way back to the carrier. Thirty-five USN personnel joined the ship's company to make all this new equipment work, and for ease of supply the crew of *Victorious* received USN uniforms.

On January 1st 1943, 832 Squadron flew its Albacores off the ship and parked them at Norfolk Naval Air Station. In their place they took over sixteen brand-new Avenger torpedo-bombers, all bearing USN white star markings. Soon enough, all *Victorious*' thirty-six Wildcat fighters (known as Martlets in British service) also changed to

American markings (though all *Victorious*' aircraft bore a small White Ensign on the tail). Richardson and his new crewmates had to adapt rapidly to the unfamiliar Avenger, a radical change from their Albacores (and a great improvement). Typically, the British had decided to give the type a different name in Fleet Air Arm service, and so Richardson would go into battle in a 'Tarpon'.[2]

British aircrew and maintenance ratings get to grips with their new Tarpons in 1943. (IWM A21391)

As well as mastering a new aircraft, the pilots also had to learn the USN's rules for deck landings and take-offs, which were different to Fleet Air Arm procedures – sometimes, in fact, the complete opposite. Then they practised these on dry land, before graduating to the real thing on the deck of the USS *Charger*. All this had to be accomplished in just one month, for *Victorious* left Norfolk on February 3rd 1943, Pacific-bound. Richardson wrote to his mother that day, as she told Robertson in March: 'I heard from Guy last week, written on February 3rd, still in USA. He had met Brian MacCaw, who had landed nearby for repairs to his plane, some time ago. Guy says he is in "great fettle", but of course can't tell us much.'[3]

Richardson's crew and the rest of the British airmen flew as often as they could during the week-long transit to the Panama Canal – not without risk, since two Wildcats were lost along the way. As they headed south, attempts were made to maintain secrecy, and *Victorious* received the radio code-name *Robin*. One day, when challenged by a US

THE TIMES

THROUGH THE PANAMA CANAL

The aircraft-carrier H.M.S. Victorious being manoeuvred through a lock of the Panama Canal with only a few feet to spare on either side. She was lent by Great Britain at that time to the U.S. Navy for use in the Pacific theatre of operations.

warship, *Victorious* gave her identity as USS *Robin* – and the name stuck. So, nearly, did *Victorious*, as she transited the canal. Despite the removal of various masts, derricks, and even projecting gun sponsons, she was a very tight fit, and one lock gate took off the submarine lookout post on her port side. Whilst all her bits and pieces were replaced, the crew had two days' shore leave in Panama City before departure on February 18th.

It was not until much later that images of her voyage were released for publication, one appearing in *The Times* on October 23rd. Richardson kept a copy.

* * *

USS *Robin* was bound for Pearl Harbor, and *en route* her airmen and flight-deck crews rehearsed the drills which were a matter of life and death. Two hundred and forty landings were conducted during this part of the voyage, an average of around five per aircraft, and there were five accidents. The problem was that the Avenger was a far different aircraft to what had been envisaged by the designers of British aircraft carriers. It was also designed for American systems, so that, for example, its arrester-hook was too small to consistently catch the thicker British arrester wires.

This photograph, from USN archives, shows an Avenger of 832 Squadron aboard an aircraft carrier. Because the aircraft bears British markings, and the carrier deck is not an American (wooden) one, this must date from 1944/45, aboard HMS Illustrious. (US Navy National Museum of Naval Aviation 1996.253.1733)

One of Richardson's comrades on 832 Squadron – pilot John Fay – later explained the difficulties which the Avenger crews faced, and described the deck accident in which the entire three-man crew of an Avenger died on February 26th:

> With the experience which the Squadron had now acquired, it was apparent that the ship in its present condition was not really suitable for landing Avengers safely. These were, after all, the largest and heaviest aircraft ever landed on a British deck. With a maximum setting on the arrester wire hydraulic system, the wires would still pull out

for a considerable way. This meant that if an aircraft caught any wire forward of the fourth, it would go into the crash barriers. Our flight-deck personnel were becoming skilled at lowering the barriers as soon as the aircraft had caught an arrester wire, and in this way had saved many aircraft from damage. To a certain extent we were living in a fools' paradise, thinking that with the combined skills of the batsman, pilots, and barrier operators, everything would be all right until we reached Pearl, where suitable modifications could be carried out.

I took over the watch just as some Avengers were landing on. I heard Commander Price shout, 'Good God!' I looked out on to the deck, and saw one of the worst sights of my life. The Avenger which had just landed was going up in a sheet of flame. I could just see the Pilot starting to get out of the cockpit. The aircraft had caught the first wire, but had rolled gently towards the port side of the ship. The port wheel had gone over the edge and had cut a pipe supplying petrol to the flight deck. The fuel had then ignited. The Observer had got out of the rear cockpit, but then tripped over a wire and fell into the flames. He had run along the deck trying to put the flames out, and had been taken into the Pilots' and Observers' Ready Room. The Pilot had got out all right but was badly burned.

In the meantime, the Air Gunner, also burned, had, unknown to anyone on deck, run down a companionway and gone straight to the nearby sick-bay. His disappearance caused me considerable worry, as Commander Flying sent me to find him and, as he was not to be seen anywhere, it was assumed that he was still in the blazing aircraft.

The fire raged. It was drawn into ventilators and smoke started to appear in various parts of the ship. It was a full hour before the fires were under control. I was not a little worried about the depth charges in the aircraft exploding, but they just melted and were ditched. Sadly, the Observer and Pilot died next day, and the Air Gunner the day after. It was a severe jolt for us, as we had not realized how much damage shock could do, and we had been told that they all had a chance.[4]

All three of the dead had been married men.[5]

Avenger flying from *Victorious/Robin* was stopped with immediate effect.

* * *

The USS *Robin* reached Pearl Harbor on March 4th, and all her aircraft flew to Ford Island for modifications and more training. The Avengers were fitted with larger arrester-hooks, better suited to British wires, and aboard ship the Americans added two more arrester-wires in front of the original four, so that there was more chance of the Avengers catching a wire on landing. There was also damage to repair from the Panama transit and the deck fire, and the dockyard took the opportunity to add more defensive weapons wherever they would fit. It appears that by the end of this refit, *Victorious/Robin* boasted sixteen 4.5-inch guns in eight futuristic-looking turrets, six turrets containing octuple 2-pounder 'pom-poms', twenty-one 40mm Bofors guns in single, twin, and quad mounts, and sixty-five 20mm Oerlikons in single mounts.

HMS Victorious *at Ford Island, Pearl Harbor, March 4th 1943.* (Richardson family collection; edited by dansteele.net)

The Fighter Direction Office – an innovation which no American carrier yet boasted – gained air-conditioning as well, whilst the ship itself was repainted in USN blue-grey so as to avoid confusion. Perhaps most important, however, was the installation of no fewer than three ice-cream-making machines and a Coca Cola machine.

Richardson wrote a brief note to his old housemaster from Hawaii on March 15th, though the censor blanked out the letter's origin and the only item of interest in its contents:

> I was very sorry to hear that you are retiring from the house at the end of Cloister Time. I know that the Hamptons will be the best possible replacements, but you and your wonderful sister will be missed a great deal.
>
> I came across [XXXXXXXXXXXXXX] the other day. He seemed to be in great form, although he did not seem to like his present job over much.
>
> Here's hoping that the House will turn up trumps for you before you leave.[6]

A further Avenger was lost on April 8th,[7] but exactly a month later, the *Robin* set out from Pearl Harbor with the battleship USS *North Carolina,* heading south-west for Noumea in New Caledonia, there to join USS *Saratoga.* Noumea was the USN's forward base for the defence of the islands of the southern Pacific and reminded some of *Victorious*' crew of Scapa Flow, but with a few more palm trees.

No sooner had USS *Robin* joined *Saratoga,* on May 17th, than there was a 'flap', and both carriers were immediately sent out with two battleships and seven destroyers to conduct a sweep of the Coral Sea, since a Japanese naval task force was on the move and could in theory be about to turn south to attack. The personnel of the two navies watched one another in eager rivalry; the British were impressed with the speed at which

Saratoga could take her aircraft on board (sixty landed in less than forty-five minutes), and although their own landings were quite quick, they were crestfallen when a Wildcat's guns accidentally fired on landing; three men were injured by ricochets, including the Navigating Officer.

As HMS *Victorious*, the British carrier had seen plenty of action and had operated with USN vessels before, but never yet under their command. Now, as the USS *Robin,* she had to adapt to American ways. It was quite reassuring to see how tightly the escorts protected the two carriers, with a close-protection battleship only a mile away. As the operation went on, the *Victorious/Robin* sent up daily patrols of Avengers to search for surface contacts or enemy submarines; her Wildcats also took to the air when requested by Admiral Ramsey on the *Saratoga.* But it was only during the return to Noumea that the two navies managed to start digging deeper into their Allies' strengths and weaknesses. The last two days of the voyage were spent in practising skills and drills, and when the task force reached Noumea on May 24th their new recruits learned an important lesson. British practice was to enter harbour in elegant line astern, in the order prescribed by the senior officer; the American way was to break formation a few miles offshore and make a mad dash for home, every ship for herself and the Devil take the hindmost. *Robin* was certainly not victorious on this occasion, but British carriers were built for speed, and only the destroyer escorts had any hope of beating her next time. That speed also had operational consequences; whilst the Americans turned their whole force into the wind when a carrier was conducting take-offs or landings, the *Robin* could pile on the speed, drop out of formation, conduct her launch or recovery, and then resume her place without everyone else having to follow suit.

HMS Victorious *from the air, wearing her USN paint-scheme & carrying Wildcat fighters in FAA & USN camouflage.* (Copyright holder unknown)

Throughout the last week of May and the first three weeks of June, the two carriers went out on exercise repeatedly in balmy weather conditions. On June 18th they conducted joint night-flying exercises, and on June 20th they swapped aircraft, *Saratoga*'s landing on *Robin* and vice-versa. The general conclusions reached by both sides were that the USN pilots were better trained than the British ones; that the FAA crews were better at torpedo attacks; that the Avenger was really just too big for the *Victorious*, having for example to be loaded so carefully on to her small lifts that it broke the rhythm of launching and landing-on; that the USN's dive-bombing aircraft were unstoppable even by the densest of flak when they had begun their dives; and that the *Victorious*' Fighter Direction Office and its procedures were far in advance of the USN's.

The upshot was a decision to play to the carriers' strengths; all sixty Wildcats would be embarked on the *Robin*, making her a fighter carrier, whilst 832 Squadron's sixteen Avengers would operate from the *Saratoga* along with the USN strike aircraft. The American aircrew were delighted; the USS *Robin* was the only ship in the fleet aboard which alcohol was served. Richardson and the rest of 832 would be going 'dry' for as long as they stayed on the *Saratoga* – which, as it turned out, was to be a whole month.

The aircrew of 832 Naval Air Squadron on board USS Saratoga, *June/July 1943. Richardson can clearly be seen in the back row, third from left.* (IWM A 19680)

The crew of HMS Victorious *dress the deck ready for leaving Noumea harbour on July 27th 1943; USS* Saratoga *lies in front of them.* (IWM A19653)

On June 27th, with 832 operating from its new home, Task Group 36.3 put out to sea to provide cover for landings on New Georgia in the Solomon Islands. Operating 300 miles from the island, in the Coral Sea, the two carriers were not to be directly involved, but to intervene if the Imperial Japanese Navy tried to attack the landing forces. This was not a passive role; the carriers sat at the centre of a 200-mile circle which was patrolled vigorously by their aircraft, looking for trouble. Whilst aboard *Saratoga*, 832 Squadron aircraft flew for a total of 381 hours, and made 153 deck landings. These figures were not achieved without cost, however: three Avengers were written off in accidents (one crashed on take-off, another on landing, and a third force-landed owing to failure of the oil system); one Avenger was damaged when its arrester-hook broke during landing. But no one was killed.

For twenty-eight days they steamed in search of the enemy; the *Robin* set new records for continuous operations by a British-built aircraft carrier, covering 12,233 miles at an average speed of over 18 knots. But there were no engagements with the enemy, and no calls for help from New Georgia. Only towards the end of the deployment did a patrolling Douglas Dauntless from *Saratoga* make contact with a Japanese 'Betty' reconnaissance bomber, which turned tail before the fighters could reach it.

832 Squadron returned to their mother ship on July 24th, the day before the carriers reached Noumea. No doubt there was a drink to celebrate. But the crisis had passed; the Americans no longer needed British carrier support; and on July 31st Richardson and his comrades paraded on deck to bid farewell to the *Saratoga* and Noumea. As the *Victorious* steamed away, *Saratoga*'s aircraft staged a low fly-by (what the British called 'beating up'), and the flight-deck was showered with souvenir pieces of metal when one passing Avenger's tailplane lost an argument with its companion's propeller.

* * *

Pringle.

Meanwhile, yet another Hopperite – also in the Fleet Air Arm – had crossed the Atlantic. On April 4th 1943, Christopher Pringle had joined HMS *Ariel,* in Warrington, Lancashire. *Ariel* was the appropriate-sounding home of the Air Radio and Air Mechanics Training Establishment. Pringle was promoted Radio Mechanic on June 25th and Leading Radio Mechanic the following day. He had received exciting news: he was being posted to the United States. On July 1st he arrived at the transit camp HMS *Waxwing* in Townhill, Dunfermline, where he awaited his turn to embark. His journey to New Jersey took a week, and he arrived on August 5th, being officially taken on the books of HMS *Asbury* on the following day.

On August 9th Pringle moved to RAF Moncton in New Brunswick, Canada. This was a personnel holding station which processed thousands of aircrew beginning training or transferring to new units. Pringle spent ten days there before moving to 2 Telegraphist Air Gunners School, RCAF Yarmouth, Nova Scotia, where there were over 180 training aircraft. He did not remain at Yarmouth for long, however, but was shipped back to

Moncton on August 27th 1943. As Pringle moved around, Richardson was crossing the Atlantic for the fourth time since the war had begun.

* * *

On August 9th, *Victorious* arrived in Pearl Harbor, where eight new American aircraft carriers lay ready for action. The British vessel dropped off its loaned American crewmen, took on eighty more as passengers, locked two Japanese prisoners in her cells, and set off for San Diego on August 12th. By August 26th she had bashed her way through the Panama Canal again, and on September 1st arrived back at Norfolk Navy Yard. The last vestiges of USS *Robin* disappeared as American communications equipment was removed, and by late September *Victorious* was in dry dock in Liverpool, undergoing a refit which kept her out of action until March 1944.

* * *

Victorious' aircraft had flown off before she reached Liverpool, and landed at RNAS Hatston – HMS *Sparrowhawk* – an airfield in Orkney near Scapa Flow which housed FAA Squadrons who were temporarily homeless. As part of his duties on relinquishing command, the Captain of *Victorious* completed reports on his officers, including Richardson:

> Professional ability: above average.
> Zeal & energy: above average.
> Power of command: above average.
> Judgment: above average.
> Reliability: above average.
> Above average for his age. Good in the air and on deck. Has shown great initiative while in charge of life-saving equipment in the Squadron. A very pleasant level-headed officer. Plays most games well.
> Captain Mackintosh.

XII

'You have seen two wars rather too intimately now'

May–December 1943

The end of the desert war in May 1943 had left the Allies with a difficult decision. The Americans favoured an invasion of North-West Europe as soon as possible, so as to please the Russians. The British wanted to harry the Italians until they broke, and to clear the Mediterranean of the enemy. For the time being, the British point of view had won, and plans had been put in train to invade Sicily and mainland Italy as soon as possible. If Italy could be knocked out of the war quickly, then Allied troops could be at the borders of Nazi Germany and Austria by Christmas 1943, threatening the very foundations of Hitler's empire. At the very least, the British suggested, the move would tie up substantial German forces and prevent them from interfering with Allied advances elsewhere. In fact, it would take the Allies until April 1945, in a slow and bitter struggle, to smash the German armies in Italy and to force their way to the Austrian border. No one expected it to take that long.

Meanwhile, in Britain troops were being assembled and trained for the landings in occupied France, which would, however, not occur for another year; and in India the priorities were to secure the frontier with Burma to prevent further Japanese advances, and to begin the process of taking Burma back. Our subjects were deeply involved in all three theatres.

* * *

Martyn.

David Martyn was just behind Hirst in his officer training. His commission as 2nd Lieutenant was gazetted with effect from June 5th 1943,[1] and it was a source of pride, but no surprise to his friends, that – with what Robertson described as 'his good brain, judgement, and physique' – he won the Belt of Honour at the Sandhurst OCTU. He was the third senior prefect from Hopper's to have earned this accolade, and Robertson was quick to send his congratulations, to which Martyn replied:

> Thank you very much indeed for your kind letter which came yesterday – I'm so glad the belt has completed a hat trick. I did think of that, as a matter of fact, on Friday [June 4th]. It was a great thrill winning it and with two of us it has put the Old Wykehamist total up a bit, which was already pretty high.
>
> We spent our last week at camp near Hindhead which brought to an end our tactical training with endless schemes – day and night – all over those commons. We ran the

camp more or less ourselves and Alan B. and I had quite a bit of paper work as well as tank work to deal with. However the weather was excellent and the tanks all kept going which was the main thing, and we did not have anything more than one or two minor accidents. It is usually there that these men get killed just as they are about to pass out, as you've probably seen. We had to organize schemes of our own and so on and were really quite busy to the end.

Then came passing out parade, which you say Uncle Sandy has told you about. A good speech by General Willoughby Norrie (whose signature I now have on my belt). We gave him quite a good parade, I think – still trained up from when His Majesty was down the time before.

I start duty next Wednesday with the Holding Battalion – in London – at Regents Park Barracks, and then should be ready to go with our armour whenever they choose to send us!

I saw Peter Walker at Eton last Saturday [June 5th 1943], looking for some friends at the 'Fourth' [Eton's annual celebration day]. He gets into uniform fairly soon, I gather. I keep trying to get hold of John McArthur, but we never seem to be able to be in the same place at the same time!

Thank you again so much for writing, and I am glad the belt 'fitted in' so well, so to speak![2]

Martyn reached the Holding Battalion on June 16th and was then posted to 1st (Armoured) Battalion, Coldstream Guards with effect from September 14th.

* * *

Dan Somerville.

'Dan' Somerville seemed set to be part of the leading edge of the invasion force. On June 14th, the commanding officer of 61st Division addressed his assembled officers to tell them that they were now one of the three Assault Divisions – those which would be the first ashore on D-Day. A fortnight later, Lieutenant Colonel Jackson sent the following memorandum to his three batteries of 145 (Berkshire Yeomanry) Field Regiment:

SECRET
To: OC 395, 396, 509 Batteries
From: RHQ
Subject: Training
All training from now on will be done with our new Assault role as a background. The men may be told that we are training as an Assault Division. No reference will be made to any higher formation to which we may or may not be allocated.
The essential features of the Assault training are:

(i) Toughness
(ii) Aggressiveness
(iii) To be completed at home both in the dark and in water.[3]

* * *

Kemp.

Training was of course not without its dangers; David Kemp almost came a cropper in the middle of June 1943. He had been commissioned into the Rifle Brigade on April 26th 1941 from 167 OCTU in Malvern. After service with 2nd Motor Training Battalion and 8RB, he was posted on May 6th 1943 as an instructor to 170 (Motor and Machine-Gun) OCTU in Newmarket. On June 18th, Kemp was instructing a soldier in how to fire the Type 68 anti-tank grenade, of the sort shown, from a discharger cup fitted to the end of a rifle. The grenade should have soared from the cup to its target, but it had been inserted back-to-front, with its warhead closest to the bullet being fired, and it travelled only a short distance before exploding. Fortunately, both Kemp and the trainee were behind sand-bags; unfortunately, Kemp's arm was poking out, and he took a large chunk of shrapnel through his wrist, breaking both bones. He was lucky enough to be sent straight to an excellent surgeon at 30 General Hospital, at Naburn in York, who reconstructed his wrist, which recovered its full range of movement.[4]

* * *

Lewin.

Robin Lewin was hot on Martyn's heels, his commission as 2nd Lieutenant 277430 in the King's Royal Rifle Corps being dated July 2nd 1943.[5] The KRRC was a popular regiment with Wykehamists; however, for a while Lewin's place in it seemed doubtful, as his father – a retired Major General – explained to Robertson a few months later:[6]

> My dear Bobber,
> Your card to Robin came this morn and is being forwarded to Strensall. He had a week's leave end of July and beginning of August and now says he will get no more for thirteen weeks. His future is in the melting pot. The 60th[7] are to lose some forty young officers to the Middlesex, Manchesters, and Northumberland Fusiliers; his Battalion – No1 Motor Training Battalion – is being broken up, and the 10th Battalion has gone to Strensall to take over. Every chance of Robin's being sent off, as 10th Battalion is full. He was on the verge of getting a regular commission but may cry off unless he is guaranteed 60th. At one moment he thought of trying for a transfer to the Scots Guards, but for the time being nothing can be done. I am making private enquiries into the matter, as it is rumoured that the

Adjutant General regards the 60th and Rifle Brigade as 'class' regiments and wants to break that; but I really don't know yet the facts …

Love to you two from us.
Yours ever,
Ernest Lewin

As luck would have it, Lewin stayed with the KRRC. How far any strings were pulled is unclear.

* * *

Robertson's retirement as housemaster was formally announced in *The Wykehamist* in June 1943.[8] Towards the end of the same issue there appeared the following, probably unique in the annals of prisoner-of-war history:

'Bobbae sororique excellentissimae salutem dant Wiccamici Priores.
Wiccamici ordinibus te Capti, Bobba, salutant,
Nec vero spatium nec compes impedit ulla.
Lugent, quod de sede tua descendis, alumni
Attamen, infixo propius te cordibus, aequant
Maerentes animos. Mox jam Deus optima rerum
Omnipotens donare velit gratamque quietem.'[9]

This message was recently received by Major M. Robertson and his sister from a prisoner of war camp in Germany.

The names were all written in the same handwriting as the Latin verses. They are given below:—

V.M. Fortune ('D' 1897–1901), N. Christopherson ('I' 1907–1913), M.P.D. Dewar ('K' 1920–1924), M.J.H. Wilson ('H' 1912–1916), D.E.G. Wilson ('H' 1920–1925), J.R. Johnston ('A' 1916–1921), J.W.M. Mansel ('B' 1922–1928), E.G.G. Lillingston ('K' 1906–1911), R. Wood ('I' 1923–1929), N.H. Kindersley ('E' 1914–1918), R.R. Blades ('I' 1925–1931), W.K.R. Murray ('D' 1917–1921), P.M. Greenwell ('G' 1928–1931), C.J. Odling ('A' 1909–1913), J.L. Pumphrey ('C' 1929–1934), G.D.Milne ('F' 1922–1926), R.M. Longstaff ('E' 1929–1934), F.A.V. Parker ('E' 1926–1931), H.F. Ford ('G' 1929–1934), M.C. Burn ('F' 1926–1931), J.R. Barrett ('A' 1931–1937), C. Nicholson ('G' 1912–1915), A.S. Robertson ('E' 1929–1934), A.M. Sinclair ('I' 1931–1936), M.L. Stevens ('B' 1932–1937), A.G.H. Bampfylde ('G' 1933–1938), J.R.K. Sinclair ('A' 1932–1937), P.A. Venables ('B' 1918–1922), D.F. Parkinson ('H'1934–1939), E.G.B. Davies-Scourfield ('B' 1932–1936).

More tangibly, a committee of seven of the two hundred Hopperites who had been in the Robertsons' charge wrote to all former denizens of Sunnyside inviting contributions to a retirement fund for them; it was hoped that some £500 might be raised and paid to them on July 1st 1943. We know that the Mackrills, for example, sent £15 (the family still have the begging letter); if the target was reached, it would be equivalent to around £18,000 today.

In July, General Fortune wrote to Robertson on a standard German postcard. It shows us that letters from Robertson were reaching him within two months.

Kriegsgefangenenpost

Geprüft 33 Oflag IX A/Z

Postkarte

17.7.43.18

PASSED P.W. 3038

An Major Malcolm Robertson OBE MC

Gebührenfrei!

Absender:
Vor- und Zuname: Major General V. M. Fortune
Gefangenennummer: 957
Lager-Bezeichnung:
Kriegsgef.-Offizierlager IX A/H
Deutschland (Allemagne)

Empfangsort: Winchester College
Straße: Winchester
Land: Hants
Landesteil (Provinz usw. England

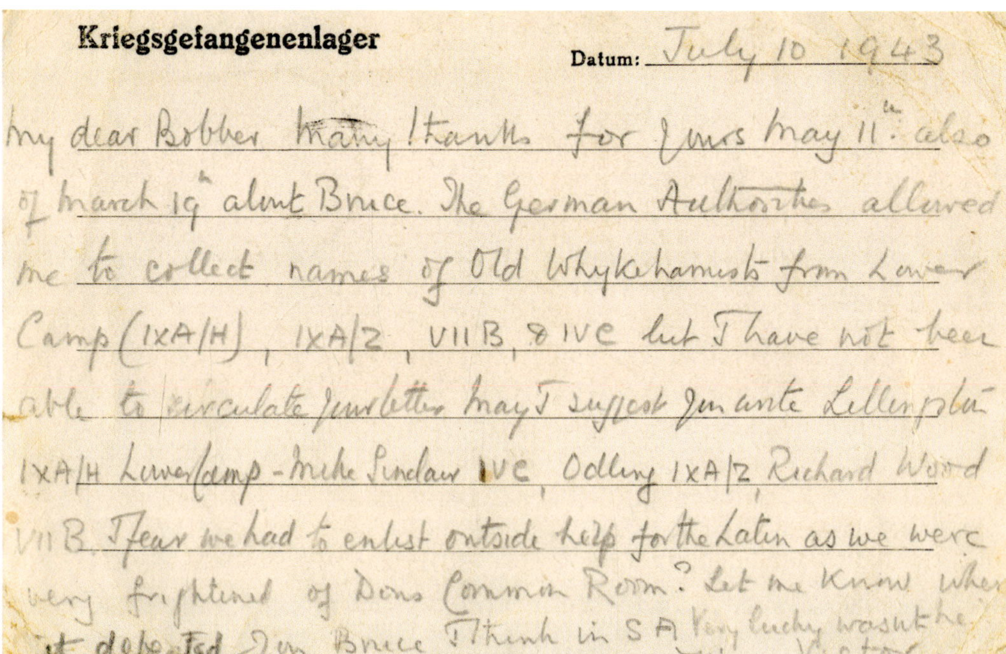

Kriegsgefangenenlager

Datum: July 10 1943

My dear Bobber Many thanks for yours May 11th also of March 19th about Bruce. The German Authorities allowed me to collect names of Old Wykehamists from Lower Camp (IXA/H), IXA/Z, VIIB, & IVC but I have not been able to circulate your letter may I suggest you write Letters plain IXA/H Lower Camp – Mike Sinclair IVC, Odling IXA/Z, Richard Wood VIIB. I fear we had to enlist outside help for the Latin as we were very frightened of Dons Common Room? Let me know where it defeated you. Bruce I think in SA Very lucky wasn't he. Yrs Victor

* * *

Mackrill.

On July 27th 1943, the last of our subjects left Hopper's. Graham Mackrill was the middle brother of three who passed through the House, and from his time in 'Bug Soc' preserved a life-long interest in nature, fishing, shooting, and conservation. His family still possess his butterfly nets and collection of moths. Montgomery visited Winchester late in May,[10] and lectured to the school on his campaigns in North Africa. He visited his son, spoke to Robertson about David's progress, and lunched at Sunnyside. Mackrill wrote to his parents about his meeting with the great man.

> I am rather pleased because a bit ago General Montgomery came down and we had him to lunch, and I was talking to him about the house and what I was going to do, and he suddenly said 'Well, when you want to get into the Gunners, just write to me and I'll fix it.' Jolly nice of him, and so now I am in a very strong position. He stayed with the Headmaster and talked to the school about the campaigns. Jolly interesting, and in addition we got an extra holiday (we hope) and I got his signature and this photograph, so I'm well off.

Mackrill kept Monty's autograph on his copy of *Infantry Section Leading 1938,* and the photograph to which he referred in this letter.

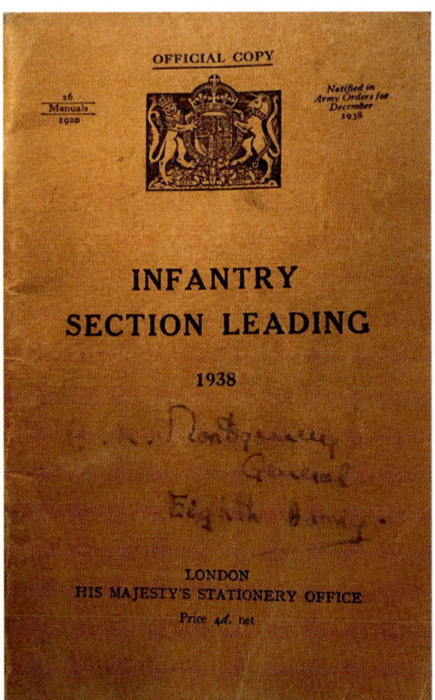

Mackrill did later write to Montgomery about it on the strength of their meeting; allegedly, Mackrill did not fancy all the walking involved in being an infantry soldier.[11]

* * *

Simpkin.

Despite his best efforts, Simpkin was still in Italian captivity. As we have seen, he had attempted to escape from Tobruk when it fell in June 1942, but had been captured. The initial stages of capture by the Italians were most unpleasant, their arrangements being wholly inadequate for the number of prisoners for whom they found themselves responsible. It was also perilous to travel from North Africa to Italy, given the scale of Allied attacks on Axis shipping. Nevertheless, Simpkin arrived in *Campo di Concentramento* PG75, Bari, in July 1942. It was a transit camp, and he moved on at the end of the month to PG21 at Chieti. That, however, provided him and his 4RTR friend Lieutenant Paul Gearing MC with an opportunity – the chance to jump from a moving train and to disappear into the night.[12] As their train passed Foggia on the night of July 31st, the two officers jumped clear and made their escape as best they could. It was hard to be on the run in Italy at that stage of the war; the Italians could spot a foreigner easily, and few were prepared to risk assisting the enemies of the Fascist regime. Simpkin and Gearing were recaptured by railway militiamen on August 4th while hiding in a goods truck in Pescara station.

On arriving at Chieti, Simpkin wrote to his family, who passed on his news to Robertson in late November – by which time it was out of date.[13]

> At last, a letter from Richard confirming his address – 2/Lieut R.E. Simpkin, 1 *Settore Concentramento*, PG21, PM 3300 Italy. I know he would love to hear from you – the letter was dated August 31st 1942. He writes cheerfully, is well – except for minor ailments – and seems to be looking after himself – he is longing for fresh clothes!

Simpkin and Gearing found that there was a great deal of tension between the Chieti camp authorities and the inmates at the time, and after a near riot and physical abuse of some inmates late in September, a selection of prisoners was transferred to other camps. Simpkin and Gearing, being known troublemakers ('*pericolosi*') were transferred on October 12th to PG5 Gavi, a forbidding castle in which the most troublesome of Allied prisoners were held. They would remain there, no matter how hard they tried, for almost exactly a year; Gavi was practically escape-proof, even more so than the infamous Colditz Castle, but Simpkin later recorded that on arrival he almost immediately joined a tunnelling attempt with Captain L.T. Murdoch (Royal Wiltshire Yeomanry) and others.[14] Tunnels were very hard to dig from the castle, which stood on a towering hill and was built on solid rock; the guards were also very alert.

Despite the difficult conditions, Simpkin told Barbara that 'life is really quite civilised in comparison with the last camp'.[15] Indeed, by January 1943 Simpkin reported that he was learning to play bridge – which he had studiously avoided in North Africa as his ignorance of the game stopped him being invited to spend time with people whom he did not like. In his letters to Barbara he included messages for Gearing's wife – and Gearing did the same for him.

The tunnel was discovered on December 6th 1942. Undeterred by this failure, Simpkin tried again, this time with Gearing, as well as Sub Lieutenant P.M. Bateman and others.

This tunnel was in turn discovered on September 3rd 1943, the day that British troops landed in mainland Italy.

After the Axis defeat in Tunisia, relations between Mussolini and King Victor Emmanuel of Italy had grown strained, and the King had begun to intrigue to take over the reins of power himself. Canadian, American and British troops had landed in Sicily on July 10th; on July 23rd the Fascist Grand Council had passed a motion of no confidence in Mussolini, who was sacked as Prime Minister and arrested. Mussolini's place as Prime Minister was taken by the distinguished soldier Marshal Pietro Badoglio, who had resigned from the Italian general staff after the Italian army's poor showing in Greece in 1940. The Italians now wished to leave the war; sadly for all concerned, the war was to come to them.

* * *

Rigby (at right, holding antler) after a successful hunt. (Rigby family collection)

Far away in India, Rigby enjoyed some memorable leaves, including several shooting trips. Another was a sailing trip on a reservoir in Bhopal, 100 miles from the tank school at Babina. Rigby and his commanding officer approached the British Resident (Bhopal was in one of the nominally independent Princely States).

> He was extremely helpful. He arranged for us to be lodged in Minto Hall, the state rest house, a huge mock Palladian white marble *palazzo,* complete with servants. The only down-side was that all the curtains were mauve. I enjoyed myself in these surroundings, so unlike the simple circumstances of life at Babina, where there was no electricity, sanitation was by a potty under the *charpoy* [bed] and a thunderbox on the back verandah, and somewhere a sweeper of course to deal with them.
>
> The Resident also arranged for us to borrow one of the Nawab's yachts plus its crew, so we could go sailing. We had some very nice sailing on the lake. There was enough wind, the crew were handy, and Peter enjoyed learning how to do it from me.[16]

His next leave – twenty-eight days in June 1943 – showed the global nature of this war, since there in the Himalayas he was mistaken for an escaped Italian prisoner of war.

> It was much-needed leave, as we suffered at the tank school in the terrific heat. Mike Errock and I decided to make an expedition to the princely Himalayan state of Chamba to try to shoot a red bear.[17] We borrowed a Cogswell and Harrison .375 express rifle and some ammunition from a fellow officer, went by train to Pathankot, and by taxi up to an old Hill station, Dalhousie. It was wonderfully cool up at 7,000 feet. The deodars gave out a scent which reminded me of Scotland.

Coming up the path towards us were two Chamba State Policemen armed with Lee-Enfield Rifles.

We walked for two days over the mountain and down to the little town of Chamba. The Prime Minister sold us a licence to shoot a limited number of game, including one red bear, in a particular 'block'. The State was divided into ninety blocks, the best of which were reserved for the Rajah. The one we obtained was known to be the home of some red bears. There was only one licence for each block each year, but in wartime there was almost no demand for licences. The plan was to trek for four days to our block, staying in rest houses *en route.* We would then climb the mountain and establish a base camp in a large tent. Mike Errock's bearer and most of the stores would stay there. We would then go on up to 12,000 feet with a two-man tent, and camp there on the red bear feeding grounds. We would be up there for two weeks.

We had to hire a state registered *shikari* (hunter) and his assistant, the *chhota* (little) *shikari.* The *shikari*'s job was to find the game and lead us in stalking it. The *chhota shikari* carried the rifle, skinned the carcases, and acted as watchman in case we ourselves were attacked by the bear. We needed nine ponies to carry all our food and gear from Chamba, and five pony men.

It was a great expedition in wonderful country. As there was only one rifle, we took it in turns to be the hunter. Mike shot the one red bear which our licence allowed, and I shot some Himalayan goral, a bit like mountain goats. I celebrated my twenty-first birthday at the rest house at Rakh by the roaring river Ravi. We opened our one tin of pineapple on that special occasion.

On our return journey to Chamba, Mike and I were walking along in advance of our slow-moving ponies and our men. Neither of us had shaved for the best part of three weeks. Mike was short, dark, and had a very scruffy, bristly black beard. We were wearing battledress trousers, slouchy felt hats, and on our feet a kind of *chapli* (leather sandal) that is made in Chamba.

Coming up the path toward us were two Chamba state policemen armed with Lee-Enfield rifles.

They promptly arrested us. We spoke Urdu; they spoke Punjabi. We tried to explain that we were officers on holiday, but they didn't believe it. In fact they didn't want to believe it. They thought and hoped that we were two Italian prisoners of war, escaping from the camp near Dehra Dun. There was a bounty of ten rupees a head to anyone who made a capture. These two policemen thought that they were on to a good thing. So we were arrested; we all sat on a wayside bench in the sun, and discussed the situation.

In due course our *shikari* and the rest of our caravan came along and established our credentials. The policemen, though disappointed, took it in good heart. We proceeded with them to the nearest wayside shop, where we all sat and drank *motia*, a particularly potent wine made from apricots.[18]

* * *

Michael Hirst left England in June 1943:

I was placed in draft RWWHF, bound I knew not where, with a mixed lot of officers and men from various arms of the service. After many delays, we sailed from Liverpool on the Polish passenger liner *Batory*, quite a good ship.[19] We had regular film shows. The officers were in canvas bunks in the saloons – reasonably comfortable, though crowded. The men were crammed on the various levels of the hold, in hammocks. The hatches were open in fine weather, but it was pretty stuffy, especially with people being sea-sick from the decks above.

Hirst.

Our convoy went round the north of Ireland, across the notorious Bay of Biscay in calm weather, into the Med., and eventually arrived at Algiers.[20] I do not remember when, if ever, we were told that our destination was North Africa. We did boat drill every day, putting on our life-jackets, which we always carried with us, and falling-in – in the Army sense! – at our boat stations in our drafts. While this was going on, the ship was being inspected to ensure that all accommodation was clean and tidy, hammocks stowed, and so on. If you were Orderly Officer that day, you went on this inspection with the Ship's Adjutant, Medical Officer, Sergeant-Major, and Ship's officers. Our only other duty was the censoring of mail. Some men understandably resented their letters being read, but if they had known how boring it was reading the same thing over and over again, they would have realised that we took not the slightest interest in their personal affairs. I do remember one officer starting to read bits out that amused him, but we soon shut him up.

The convoy was escorted by destroyers, which ranged round the fringes of the convoy like sheepdogs. The speed of the convoy was that of the slowest ship. There were no exciting incidents, thank God.

At Algiers, Hirst and his companions were trans-shipped and hurried eastwards:

Instead of disembarking, the troops from the whole convoy were put on to two ships, the SS *Cristobal* and the SS *Colon*; to move us further east along the North African coast, through an area where plenty of U-boats were lurking, speed had to be relied on for safety. As you can imagine, the ships were terribly crowded. We were all given cards; those with red had to be on deck all day, those with green *vice versa*. It was first come, first served, and we were very lucky to have a cabin and bathroom. Later arrivals were not so fortunate, and we had the amusing situation of a Brigadier sleeping in the passage and asking us Second Lieutenants if he could use our bathroom! We had more sense than to refuse!

We had two days and a night in Algiers harbour. Working flat-out, the galley could only produce two meals a day for everyone, though, being an American ship, much more elaborate and luxurious than what we were accustomed to. The men got chicken, unheard of in the British Army, while we had mackerel and cranberry sauce, my first taste of American cuisine. We had one boat drill in harbour, but by the time everyone below had struggled up on deck, and those on the top deck with boat stations on lower decks had struggled down, an hour and a half had passed and there would not have been many survivors out of the several thousands on board the two ships if we had been torpedoed.

We sailed on the second night and reached Philippeville, two hundred miles east of Algiers, safely by next morning. We marched five miles to our camp, a pretty place among the cork-oaks and with the sea below. Despite not being very fit after being cooped up in a troopship, my only trouble was a sore shoulder from a badly adjusted pack-strap. Transit camps were very boring places, with not much to do and being uncertain about what the next move would be. I considered 'the local wogs a moth-eaten lot in filthy rags'. But the main worry was that I was in the British North African Forces area, while the Yorkshire Hussars were in the Mediterranean Expeditionary Force.

After a short stay, we were put on a train for a three-day journey, the last seventy miles by truck, to Sousse in Tunisia via Constantine. The men were in cattle trucks, the officers in over-crowded carriages. My comment: 'French colonial railways are even more inefficient than their home ones.' To be fair, they had been through a German occupation, a blockade, and a major war. One engine broke down; the French driver showed me the inside of the furnace, with water squirting into the flames from the leaky boiler tubes. We stopped for anything from half-an-hour to six hours at every station, and we used to get hot water from the engine for washing and brewing tea at these numerous halts, at one of which we moved on without warning, leaving quite a few troops behind. However, they hitched a lift and soon caught up. At one stop we managed all to get a very welcome bathe in a deep but very smelly river.

We arrived at Sousse in early July, the camp in quite a pleasant spot in an olive grove by the sea. We were not doing much work, just waiting. I suppose the main excitement while we were there was the sound in the night of planes passing over our heads for the Allied invasion of Sicily. We all had bouts of diarrhoea ('Tunisian Tummy') while we were there, and I spent a very uncomfortable twenty-first birthday on the 'thunderbox'.

We had nice bathing in the sea, and I was wishing that I had a local bird book; I saw storks and wheatears and a funny kind of chaffinch out there. Our main food was bully beef and biscuits. However, my limited French was of some use in bargaining with the Arabs (whom I described in a letter as 'filthy') and buying eggs for the mess. Melons and lemons were the only fruits. Most of the local shops had been destroyed in the fighting.[21]

With the persistence of Odysseus seeking Ithaca, Hirst was determined to reach his unit. Many reinforcements felt this way – the loyalty to the regiment which even the newly-trained showed is a tribute to the system. Unfortunately, the Army did not always take these feelings into account, and as the manning crisis deepened in 1944 the ties to regiments were often ignored. Hirst did not let the Army stand in his way.

I still had one friend who had been at Sandhurst with me, Don Outhwaite, also bound for the Yorkshire Hussars, so we took every opportunity to move east, and eventually we were on our way again, this time by truck. Unfortunately, we had to leave all our heavy kit behind to go into store in Algiers, including my Leica camera, and in spite of much correspondence later, I never saw it again.

Our destination was Tripoli, which was in MEF; at least we were going to the same command as the Yorkshire Hussars. This was a very interesting trip, as we drove along the shores of the Gulf of Gabes, through the Monastir Gap and the Mareth Line. At Monastir we swam out to some islands, and I also noted that we got omelette sandwiches and ice-cream there, so we must have visited a French café.

At the beginning of August we arrived at a Tank Reinforcement Unit, where we actually did a bit of training. It was a few miles west of Tripoli, and we lived in bivouacs, which we deepened to give us a bit more headroom. Again we could swim in the Med., though the coast was a bit rocky. We were only there a few days before we moved to a bigger transit camp. We could go into Tripoli, where there were good cafes, shops full of ghastly souvenirs, and barbers.

As we had done some training at the last camp, the Commandant was under the impression that we had come there to do a course FROM the Yorkshire Hussars, and we did not disabuse him. He told us that there were two places on a Dakota going to Cairo, so off we went, bound for the RAC Base Depot at Abbassia. We had a quick but uncomfortable flight (no seats) stopping at El Adem, scene of a big tank battle, to refuel.

On arrival at Cairo West Airport we found out that the Yorkshire Hussars were in the desert just outside Cairo, near Giza. We knew if we went to the Base Depot, our chances of getting to the regiment were nil, so we hitched a ride to the Yorkshire Hussars, and luckily we were accepted. Regimental Part 3 Orders stated, 'The postings of 2nd Lts Hirst and Outhwaite, which have already taken place, are hereby confirmed.' This was at the end of August 1943.

* * *

After commissioning, Nick Somerville had returned to 21 ITC at Dering Lines, Brecon, to assist with recruit training. On August 28th he wrote another letter to Peter Walker. One of the biggest problems with Somerville as a correspondent is that he dated his letters erratically, most bearing a vague heading such as 'Sunday'. This one, at least, is firmly dated.

Nick Somerville.

I am due my second pip in October and I expect to get posted to a service battalion then. If not, I shall certainly apply for it. To tell you the truth, I am getting browned off with mucking about here. We have had a bit of fun, though; I went on an artillery scheme lasting five days, which was marvellous fun. I was representing a skeleton company of infantry. Most of the time I spent giving fire orders to the gunners over the wireless, and then watching the shells come over and land on the spot of land I had indicated …

I was out all last weekend for three days with my Platoon on an exercise. We covered sixty-eight miles and slept out. Of course, it had to rain during both nights, and we all got soaked – blankets, clothes, and everything. The second night we were able to get into a barn, but the first night we slept in a puddle of four or five inches' depth. Most uncomfortable, but it didn't do anybody any harm. We went on to fight two battles, which were pretty successful, though as usual a little chaotic.[22]

The chaos involved sneaking up behind an 'enemy' platoon of Home Guard and opening fire on them from fifty yards, before launching a bayonet charge which sent them running. The Home Guard complained.

We had some fun the other day up at Cwm Gwdi, which is our field firing range. We accidentally (?) shot three sheep. So we fleeced them, and skinned and gutted them, and ate them for supper. We put in a bit of bayonet practice on the heads and guts, which the lads enjoyed, and took the remainder back to camp. I reported the slaughter to the Claims Officer, but there has been a bit of a row about our fleecing them. However, I spun them a fairly good yarn which should go down all right …

I saw John McArthur in Bond Street not so long ago. He is a 'Snottie' [Midshipman] and going into Naval Commandos, at the moment training in Scotland. Most interesting about two convoys to Russia; said he was scared stiff. Pretty tough going in the fo'c'sle I should think.

Had a fearfully intellectual airgraph from McMurtrie, who was just going to Sicily. All about religion, death, etc., and very typical. He seems to have changed a bit, as he gets on with his brother officers.[23]

* * *

Hirst, having finally reached his Regiment, awaited action as the summer gave way to autumn:

When we arrived, 'A' Squadron, to which I had been assigned, was doing tank gunnery training away from the camp. We had old Crusader and Sherman tanks. The desert where we operated was flat and pebbly with occasional small rocky outcrops which looked higher than their one hundred feet. It was good to get away after two months in transit camps, and to get to know the other officers in the Squadron. We worked from 0700hrs to 1300hrs, and then from 1600hrs to 1800hrs. After we got back to the Regiment, I went into Cairo to replace the clothing that I had lost with my kit. Among other things, I had lost my camp bed, but by this time I was quite used to sleeping on the ground. Owing to the unorthodox way in which I had joined the Regiment, my pay only started arriving just before we left. Mess bills were fairly steep, so I did not see much of Shepheards Hotel and other bright lights of Cairo. From my letters, the only outing to that famous hotel was with the Padre, when we had Chicken Maryland and ice-cream. I was promoted to Lieutenant while in Egypt. This was automatic, six months after being commissioned.

I was pleased when I was temporarily given a troop while the Troop Leader was away. We did tactical training in our tanks, and, of course, vehicle maintenance was an on-going job. One of the things that I enjoyed most was taking the troop out in our trucks on map-reading exercises. This gave us a chance to see something of the country, including the very fertile Nile Delta which adjoined the deserts. I had a couple of very interesting visits to the famous step-pyramid of Sakkara.

My other excursion was to do a gas course at Dir Suneid, in what is now the Gaza Strip in Palestine. Though the course was not very exciting, it had the advantage of week-end leave in Palestine at either end. We travelled by train, crossing the Suez Canal at El Kantara, where I had a nice meal at the French Club. We spent one weekend in Tel Aviv, which I described rather unkindly as like a Jewish Blackpool, and one in Jerusalem, where, having done the right thing and seen the alleged Garden of the Tomb, we were so put off by the accompanying talk that we decided against visiting any more historic or religious sites and went on a spree, staying at the King David Hotel.

* * *

Middleditch also arrived in North Africa after the end of the campaign, having left Britain by sea on July 13th and reached XII Lancers (12RL) on August 11th.

Middleditch.

Thank you so much for your air letter card which arrived today. I've just received the *Wykehamist* including the Eton Match number, so I'm well provided with news. Very sorry to see that Peter Frewen was killed; one of the nicest Freddyites. I've met someone who knew him out here, who tells me that he was killed at Hammam Lif, just at the edge of the Cap Bon Peninsula, a place that I've visited. British North Africa Force seems sadly deficient of OWs; the only one I've met was the elder Evans and I didn't know who he was until afterwards! I see that Somerville got the Belt, a very well deserved one I'm sure. Is he in the South Wales Borderers?

I'm very fit and well at the moment and enjoying life very much. We're out a good deal and get some shooting in addition to normal work. The country is extremely pleasant, very highly cultivated but with very lovely mountains within easy reach. I continue to like the Regiment very much; I've a good Squadron Leader and the other subalterns are very nice on the whole.[24]

Despite the pleasantness of his companions and Algerian surroundings, Middleditch fell ill on December 15th, being admitted first to 183 Field Ambulance and then to 96 General Hospital at Guelma, where he remained over Christmas, being discharged on January 3rd 1944. It had been an anti-climactic start to his active service career.

* * *

There was disappointment, too, for 'Dan' Somerville. In June, he had been told that his unit would be attacking across the beaches of occupied France; in August, the men of 61st Division discovered that it would now be a Follow-Up Division, passing through the Assault Divisions and advancing inland. But in September came the news that they would not be joining the invasion at all; they had been assigned back to Home Forces. The Adjutant of 145 Field Regiment, then in Wootton Underwood, sent round a memorandum to break the news:[25]

To: OCs 395, 396, 509 Batteries.
Herewith extracts from Divisional Commander's speech for verbal communication to all ranks by Batteries.

'Owing to the present manpower situation, it has been necessary to transfer the Division from Second Army back to Home Forces. Our role and all training and preparations are to aim at a return to the continent of Europe at the earliest opportunity.

Owing to all your efforts, we have a very fine Divisional spirit, and that is something that should be cherished and improved by every means in our possession. Every one of us who is not smart and happy and does not show that he is proud of himself and of the Division whose sign he wears is doing harm not only to himself but to the reputation and potential fighting qualities of the Division.

Next week we go on a big exercise; let every individual do that little bit more than he thinks he can manage, to show the world what a good Division we are.'

It is perhaps relevant that one of 61st Division's nicknames was 'The Sixty-Worst'.

* * *

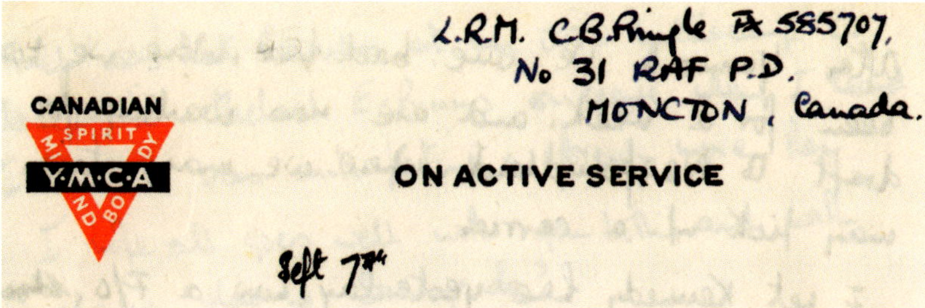

Pringle.

Kennedy.

By happenstance, Pringle met John Kennedy at Moncton on September 6th, as he told Robertson the next day:

> I came over here at the beginning of last month, and spent a few very pleasant days in New Jersey, at a place called Asbury Park, about forty-five miles south of New York. I managed to get a few hours in the city, and saw some of the sights, including the Empire State Building.
>
> From there we came up to Moncton, and spent a week here before being moved to Yarmouth in Nova Scotia. Here we found that we were not wanted, and that the draft was a mistake! So we spent a very enjoyable week sunbathing, strolling about the aerodrome, and walking in the country. Yarmouth is a charming place, right on the south-western tip of Nova Scotia. I saw some tuna fish whilst I was there, weighing just under 700lbs, and estimated value about $500. The country is somewhat mosquito-infested, as it is very low-lying. The only swift communication, apart from airplanes, is a single-track rail that runs to Halifax, the chief port, so the place is very isolated.
>
> After Yarmouth we came back here, where we have been for a week, and are now waiting for a draft to Newfoundland, where we may stay, or may pick up a carrier.
>
> I met Kennedy here yesterday, now a Flying Officer, awaiting draft back home. He has been out here for twenty-one months instructing and training. He seemed in very good form, and we had dinner together in Moncton. I hope to get a game of golf with him on the local thirteen-hole course later in the week. He has been in Moncton for 5½ weeks now, but it is such a large place that I never met him until yesterday. But the world is a small place! I have not seen any other Wykehamists since I joined up … .
>
> This is a very slack and enjoyable existence. We live on the fat of the land, eggs, milk, butter, chocolate, etc., unlimited, and above all, fruit. I get through about four oranges a day, and about three or four pints of milk! I feel rather guilty about it when I think of you all in England …
>
> I can't give you much news about OWs. The last I heard of Micky Finch was that he was at an OCTU battle-camp in Lancashire. Michael Elliott-Binns on leave when I heard. I think he was anticipating a foreign move then.

Pringle's move to Newfoundland did come quickly; a week later, he was posted to RNAS Argentia, known as HMS *Avalon III*. He would stay there until June 1944. Strangely, although in Canada, Argentia was US territory, having been ceded to the Americans in January 1941 in return for Lend-Lease convoy escorts. The airfield built there was used from August 1941 to protect convoys, but as small escort carriers took over these duties, Argentia became the home of reserve replacement aircraft for the carriers. Pringle was one of the personnel allocated to maintain the Swordfish biplanes stored at Argentia. It seems that these aircraft were never in fact used, and possibly the only excitement during Pringle's time there was when HMS *Tracker* was sent for repair after a stormy Atlantic crossing. For a month, starting on November 14th 1943, *Tracker*'s 816 Squadron was stationed ashore at Argentia. Since it had only three aircraft undamaged and fit for use, it is likely that Pringle had a busy time fixing what he could.

* * *

Sinclair.

McMurtrie.

Two other Hopperites cooling their heels in North Africa were John Sinclair and Duncan McMurtrie, both of them in 1st Battalion, Scots Guards (1SG). Sinclair was already a veteran, having disembarked in Algeria in March 1943 and gone into the line at Medjez-el-Bab later that month. Constant patrolling had led to casualties, and on April 3rd Sinclair had been wounded. By the end of the North African campaign, 1SG had been reduced to half strength, and it took a long time to reconstitute the Battalion. In August 1SG moved to Hammamet in north-east Tunisia, where it trained for three months. McMurtrie joined during this period, having written to Robertson that summer as he awaited posting to the Battalion.

> As you can see I am in North Africa at last, after being on three drafts! The heat is terrific, even for a luxury life, and as for Active Service – my God! The native villages smell, but there is some quite good wine and some fruit … Don't bother to answer this hasty note. You can have no idea how I envy you the cool of Meads and all that water …[26]

One of the few releases from the heat was bathing in the Mediterranean, and McMurtrie's anthology *The Diary of a Heart* includes a poem inspired by a near-drowning on such an occasion:

Mediterranean Rescue
This is the power of the sea –
Not grand and tyrannical mastery –
But offering playful waves, and the lure
Of surf wind-combed like ruflled hair.

So she wore her smile; but underneath
Cruelly, furtively, wantonly dragging,
Persuading, and panicking life; not clutching
But irresistibly coaxing the breath
From the body that answers no will.

So he would have gone, but we made
A chain of brown arms to connect the land
To his body; and the land's power flowed
Through the arms to the drowning man.

With a mocking suggestion of power
The waves broke the life-line through;
But in water our feet were on sand
And through our thighs we drew
Earth's gift of male strength, and we joined
And we brought him in to the shore.

The siren who had failed to beguile
Another Odysseus tight-lipped smiled
While we pumped the life she would take
Stroke by brown-armed piston stroke.
And the sea, with a Sphinx-smile, tossed her hair
Across the white bay at us who knew
The joy of the thing created, and we heard
Our masterpiece breathing there.

The areas where he was staying had been fought over in April and May, and this led him to set out his views on death in another poem, *Beyond Grief*:

This is for you, my Deadly Nightshade flower,
The gleam upon the knife-edge, or the thorn
That swings its last blossom to the dancing feet
Of birds upon it; this is all that puts
A certain beauty on the point of pain
And lets the thoughts find something beyond grief.

Tonight I walked where lately they have fought,
And deep among the mountains poised to break
Like waves upon the valley, there I knew
That soon again men will live those neurotic hours,
And I be with them in the tortured night
Strung on the taut nerve-string. And if so be

That I shall give my life – no; not give –
Accept the risk realized; no man does more,
But only thinks it worth his deed – if that be so,
Then I would have you read this, and take comfort here.
The rendezvous is easy; there is no pain
With the quick bullet for a go-between.

Comfort is rationed by the loss; but fill full
Your large glass with sunlight. Know what I

Tonight, among the desolation of the exploded guns
And cactus, knew. For what the momentary eye
Held and let drop, the mind knew was not
Meaningless, the actor's hollow death stage-mask.

Know that on the dust, where man's dust is,
He is not there. For one whose seeking eye
Drew in through the sordid flesh-crust and grew one
With olives and moving corn, and waves on a moonless night,
Grey movement breaking luminous from the wide
Grey formless sea-plain, he is more than flesh.

For being such I am as one who is journeyed far,
Who could not leave myself in the dead corpse of war.

In late October, after reaching 1SG, McMurtrie sent Robertson and his sister a series of four airgraphs, all written on the same date and intended to be read as a sequence.[27]

I have today received your printed letter. It was sat on by my brother, Peter. You remember Peter? He has left Marlborough; but he failed to get into the Fleet Air Arm on medical grounds. However an operation has put that to rights. Now he hopes to put in a year up at Cambridge and fish up some sort of a degree as a result, after the war, to serve as some qualification. Then he will go to the Fleet Air Arm. He beat me you know – getting six credits in School Certificate! When I received your letter I was surprised, since it was not running true to form. It ought to have been on a postcard. Postcards are always regarded as the form from you, aren't they?!! But anyway I was most pleased to hear from you. I received a charming letter from Francis King, who is now Adjutant of a fighter squadron in Ceylon. I wrote him a quarto of air-graphs earlier on. He told me about Robin Ridgway – good work. I also received a Roll and Register from home. A number of shocks in it – Christopher Sheepshanks, Hugh Rose, and many others. I suppose you will feel them deeply. You have seen two wars rather too intimately now. I will close and continue on another Air-Graph …

Here is my second Air-Graph. I sincerely hope you and Sheila are now recovered from your tiring early-war days, and are now settled down to a life of peace. I am glad to see that Winchester has not lost you, nor you Winchester. It always was a good combination. Please remember me to all the old firm – those who still remember an insignificant boy who just scraped an Exhibition in Classics. I will write to Eric James, James Mansell, and Jack Parr in the near future. Reading between the lines of Leeson's report in the Roll and Register, Winchester is yet what it was. A certain number of the hopes and regrets that make a public school; and some private griefs, that follow war. Keep it up, Bobber. Life for me is grand. I have never felt more in my element. A good Platoon, in a good Company, in a good Battalion. Life is hard, but good. Plenty of work, but in all earnestness I never minded a share in that. When I return I will certainly try to visit you. See if you'll recognise me. I eat now! And perhaps we'll drink a toast to Winchester, Sunnyside (never Turner's to me) and my happy days there, if mediocre days in the school.

McMurtrie (seated, fourth from left) with the men of 'a good Platoon, in a good Company, in a good Battalion', North Africa, late 1943. (McMurtrie family collection; edited by author)

Dear Miss Robertson,
I have just written a line or two to the Bobber. But I feel I owe you one and more too. I write separately since the space on these forms is so limited. But I always regard you and the Bobber and Sunnyside (not Turner's, please!) as one. I have many memories of those days; and believe me memories and letters play an important part of life out here. I have given the Bobber some news, so I will not repeat myself. Is Sunnyside still Sunnyside? Or has the old house moved completely to Culver Lodge? I hope to see you both again ere long. I reckon to be home by my 21st birthday – 'Where's that old Short Roll?' Is the Itchen where it was? I expect there have been many changes, in staff, in policy, and in school life. But I reckon they will not be so fundamental as many will think. The fundamental Winchester, not even two wars can change; nor even the years. I owe much there, and it is a debt that I shall gratefully remember. Maybe one day I shall be one of those lucky ones who have been able to repay it, at least in part.

This completes the quarto with a little more news. Do you remember Alan Brown? He paid you one or two visits with David Townsend, stretching back to 1933. He is a Fellow and Law Don of Worcester. He is in this Battalion and asks to be remembered to you. Anthony, my youngest brother, has just gone to Field House, Marlborough, from A1. I wonder if you ever visit Jenny's these days. You have heard, I expect, of Roddie McLeod's death in the 2nd Battalion. A very nice chap and a great pity. John

> Weir, I hear, is now Adjutant there. Archie Pearson you probably know is Regimental Adjutant. Ronnie Taylor, who is in the Grenadiers, is in this brigade. So is Pridham, in the Brigade Support Group. Jack Pym was killed in the Micks. My Company distinguished itself with one VC, three MMs, and four mentions in despatches, all in the last battle. Geoffrey Gwyer, of course, was killed earlier. We are suffering the start of the rainy season, and one Irish Guards Sergeant was washed away and drowned while walking along the main road. Wind and rain under canvas never was much fun. But I'm getting pretty good at improvising and roughing it. Oh yes – I am fit and well. Wishing you and Miss Robertson a happy and peaceful Christmas and New Year and hoping for a swift return to peace.

A week short of McMurtrie's twentieth birthday, he and Sinclair left North Africa, landing with 1SG at Taranto on December 7th. One of McMurtrie's last surviving poems from North Africa was penned shortly before departure:

Tunisia, 1943
What will this country give to take away,
What to remember? What can I relate
That made the absence worth the lonely day?
Or farther still, in distant frost-bound years,
Far-caged from now, when you perhaps have set
My leather chair before the evening fire,
And I, grey-haired, a little sadly turn
My life before its failing embers – what?
What through the window dim in the sunset then;
What precious to recapture from its dawn?
Perhaps, I think, when from tall Indian corn
A hidden music from dark Arab throats
Dropped on the running water, softly afloat,
As gentle as the bloom at petal-fall;
And days as blue as the wildflax flower,
And hour by hour, the swallows' homing call.

Within two months, both he and Sinclair would be dead.

* * *

In India, there was also a good deal of frustration involved for those eager for action. Metcalfe managed to visit his parents in Baluchistan in mid-September, as Wykehamist Major General Geoffrey Hind told Robertson, writing from Ziarat:

Metcalfe.

> Have seen a deal of the Metcalfes. John is in Italy, prisoner of war, present wherabouts doubtful. Hope he gets away. Pat was here last week. A Hindu Horseman. Now Armoured Corps. Developing well.[28]

For his part, Rigby had become bored of Bihasa, as he told Robertson in mid-November:

> Till recently my whole year has been spent at a large tank school in central India, where they made me a Captain and a training Adjutant. The work was creative, and for several months quite amusing. But when we got the place going, routine life became irksome, and I was glad to leave. Pat Metcalfe of the 45th has written once or twice, and I have heard a lot about him from a mutual acquaintance. If reports are true, he is no longer his old staid self, but carouses with the best of them. I don't know of any other OW out here, except our new Viceroy, but there must be several.
>
> I don't expect an answer to this, but at the same time I should love to hear your news and something of the school. I never see the casualty lists, but there must be many sad additions which I shall have to know one day.[29]

* * *

Dodgson.

Dodgson joined 2 Field Company RE at Tondebhavi, near Bangalore, on August 8th 1943, and took over 3 Section. However, big changes were afoot, and on September 25th he departed with an advance party to Nowgong, to which the entire Company had orders to move. It took Dodgson and his sixty Other Ranks until October 4th to arrive at their new camp at Bijawar, the main body catching up on October 12th. The OC rejoined them there from the Divisional Jungle Training Cadre, where he had received instruction in their new role. 70th Division was being split up, and its units becoming part of Orde Wingate's much expanded Special Force of Chindits; Dodgson and his comrades were to be part of Operation Thursday, the second Chindit expedition into Burma.

On November 1st, 2 Field Company conducted its first Long Range Penetration exercise, from which it returned four days later. Almost immediately, the Company was split up into so-called 'Commando' Troops, each attached to a different Column of 16 (British) Infantry Brigade, commanded by the legendary Bernard Fergusson DSO, a former ADC to Wavell.[30] 16 Brigade comprised nine Columns;[31] many of the personnel were artillerymen or reconnaissance troops re-purposed as infantry. Dodgson was in charge of the Commando Troop attached to 54 Column, made up of personnel from 45th Regiment, Reconnaissance Corps. He and his men joined their Column on November 7th. The column's war diary records his arrival, but calls him 'Lt G.H. Dobson'.

Most of the Chindits arrived at their operational areas by air; 16 Brigade, by contrast, were the only ones to walk the whole way, across some of the most difficult terrain on earth.

* * *

Rigby was also on the move, leaving his training role in the first week in November 1943, on being posted to an Indian tank regiment – 18th (King Edward's Own) Cavalry – on the North-West Frontier. The troublesome peoples along the border had not calmed down despite the far larger wars around the globe, and so forces had to be maintained there which could have been more usefully employed elsewhere. As a result, Rigby would spend the rest of the war in what was, in the grand scheme of things, a backwater. He made light of it when he wrote to Robertson to tell him of his move:

Rigby.

> A week ago I joined my new unit at Rawalpindi, a very pleasant cantonment. It is amusing to think that after so much training to fight the Germans and then the Japs, I should finally be opposed to a lot of dissatisfied tribesmen. However, tanks play a very large role here, and it will be interesting to learn how this unending war is fought.[32]

Rigby liked 18th Cavalry:

> The 18th Cavalry officers were a good bunch. Half were Indian, and half Irish, Scots, or English. The Colonel and Second-in-Command were both Indian. Lieutenant-Colonel Hira lal Atal was a Brahmin, a cousin of Pandit Nehru. The Second-in-Command, Mohammed Jousuf (always known as 'Joseph') was an Afridi from a village near Kohat in the North-West Frontier Province – a Muslim, of course.
>
> We even had a prince: Captain Gaekwar, alias the Gaekwar of Baroda. When he went on leave his own special train came to fetch him. He was, incidentally, not a particularly efficient soldier – rather a liability, in fact. It was not easy to find a job humble enough for his limited talents.
>
> Our full complement of officers was thirty-three. But since at any time there would be several away on courses (usually at the Fighting Vehicle School at Ahmednagar), several sick, and several on leave, there were probably about twenty members of the Mess present. The Colonel and the Second-in-Command were over forty years old, but the rest of us were much younger, the majority being under twenty-five. So we were a close-knit lot.[33]

However, Rigby was soon on the move again, and although he remained with 18th Cavalry he was in many respects being marooned on a desert island, the fort of Mir Ali in tribal territory in South Waziristan. There 'B' Squadron were on detached service. It was a difficult journey, though not without its highlights.

> I took an overnight train from Rawalpindi to Dera Ismail Khan, arriving at dawn. There one had to change to a train that went to Bannu. That was the last town in British India; the border of tribal territory was just outside, and from there to Mir Ali was about forty miles. I was given a room in the Officers' Club, and someone sent a message to 'B' Squadron to come and get me next day.[34]

It was November 17th 1943.

> That evening the Club Secretary asked if I would like to have a bottle of Guinness with my dinner. In 1943, any kind of imported alcohol was a great rarity in India. The Secretary said that he had managed to buy some cases of Guinness at an auction in Bombay. It was an extra strength export brew, which had been salvaged from a cargo boat torpedoed *en route* to Singapore. He could not guarantee that it didn't have salt-water contamination. I said I would try it.

It was a large bottle and the label was written in English and Chinese characters. There was absolutely nothing wrong with that Guinness. In fact it was a perfect accompaniment to the curry meal, and it sent me off to bed feeling no pain whatsoever.

Next day John Fraser, whom I was to replace, came down from Mir Ali in an armoured scout car to fetch me. 18th Cavalry, being an armoured regiment, could use the road in tribal territory in reasonable safety. But if I had been an officer in any of the other units, I would have had to wait in Bannu until the 'road open' day. Then I would have travelled up the line in a convoy with all the other reinforcements and stores for the troops in the garrisons all the way up to Razmak, which was the end of the road, and which had a division of troops as its garrison.

Shortly after leaving Bannu in our scout car, we came to a large sign by the roadside: YOU ARE ENTERING TRIBAL TERRITORY. MURDER IS LEGAL.

The most hazardous part of the road was the Shinki Tangi, a defile which winds through a mountain range. A river comes down through this valley and the military road crossed and re-crossed it on steel bridges. On the heights on either side were stone-built fortresses manned by piquets of infantry to guard the road. No doubt these guards were watching our solitary vehicle coming up from Bannu on a day when the road would otherwise have been entirely unused. If they were there, they were keeping well hidden behind the steel shutters protecting the ports in the walls through which they could shoot. I detected no movement.

As we came to the entrance to the pass John Fraser said that this was where we should sit down. The scout car had no turret, but it did have about half an inch of armour on its sides. The driver had a visor to see through. So we did sit, but of course it would have been comparatively easy for anyone on the hillsides to take a pot-shot at us.

The principal risk was that of ambush. A common trick was to roll some stones across the road. When a vehicle got to the stones and couldn't get past, it had to turn round. That in itself might not have been easy on a narrow mountain road above a gorge. If it did turn round, the ambushers would then roll stones across the road behind it, thus trapping its escape. If the crew got out to escape, they would be shot.[35]

* * *

Herbert.

2nd Lieutenant 273495 Arthur Herbert had been commissioned into the Royal Corps of Signals on April 28th 1943.[36] He had spent the rest of the year on courses: first came Vehicle Waterproofing at the Northern Ireland Vehicle Maintenance School (July 18th to 24th) and then No.11 Officers' Advanced Lines Course at Catterick (August 22nd to December 11th). As a new 2nd Lieutenant, it came as a great surprise when he was told that he was staying on at Catterick to become an instructor on the course which he had just completed – and that the post came with the acting rank of Captain, effective from December 11th. Unsurprisingly, he wrote to Robertson the very next day:[37]

Just a line to give you my news. I had intended to visit Winchester this weekend, as my course ended and I was due for leave. The Army, however, had other plans; so I am now here, as an instructor, on Army Technical Telephone Equipment. On account of this job, I am now a Captain!

I much enjoyed my time in London, and managed to get home at weekends, besides which Mother was in town on two occasions for a few days, so I had quite a gay time! I am getting a fortnight's leave on December 20th over Christmas, which will be nice.

* * *

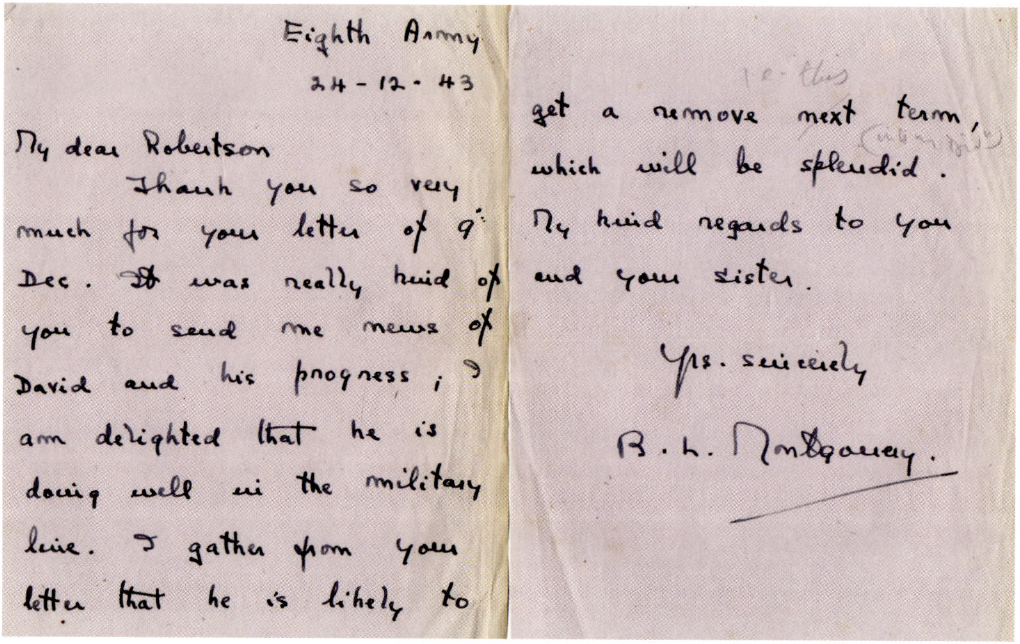

Eighth Army
24-12-43

My dear Robertson

Thank you so very much for your letter of 9th Dec. It was really kind of you to send me news of David and his progress; I am delighted that he is doing well in the military line. I gather from your letter that he is likely to get a remove next term, which will be splendid. My kind regards to you and your sister.

Yrs. sincerely

B. L. Montgomery.

* * *

The isolation of the garrison of Mir Ali was absolute, so Rigby was lucky in his companions.[38]

On arrival within the defences of Mir Ali, I was welcomed into 'B' Squadron. I had fallen among a bunch of life-long friends. We had six officers in Mir Ali, so the arrangement was that we shared an Officers' Mess with the two officers of a Mountain Battery, Major Ball and Lieutenant Box.

The Major was a bit of a rough diamond; however, he was an experienced gunner and we admired his Battery. Lieutenant Box was a small, quiet, bespectacled young man. But he was a mathematician, and was expert at working out ranges and trajectories, wind factors, fling, and the other mysteries of mountain gunnery. Their Battery had been in Eritrea in 1941. They had taken part in the assault on Keren, and were present when the Duke of Aosta had surrendered at Aruba Alagi. Major Ball had moved swiftly to loot the Duke's mess, and had 'liberated' his collection of 78rpm gramophone records and his gramophone. So in our little mess in Mir Ali, we could wind the handle, put on the needle, and listen to Italian opera, a big bonus in that spartan fort.

The officers of Mir Ali, Christmas Day 1943; Rigby standing second right. (Rigby family collection)

* * *

Fortune.

Bruce Fortune, as a fellow Black Watch officer, had been invited to become an ADC to Wavell, a post which he held until 1945. To be an ADC to an official as important as the Viceroy was an immensely prestigious role. Although Wavell arrived back in Delhi as Viceroy on October 19th 1943, Fortune did not get there until late December.

WRNS 3rd Officer Susan Mary Mackie,[39] however, arrived in India on the same day as Wavell, as a signals officer in Lord Mountbatten's Combined Operations HQ. She worked in the Secretariat Building, near the spectacular Viceroy's House designed by Lutyens, and would come to know the Wavells and their staff very well. Her first meeting with Fortune was on the day of his arrival, as she recorded in a letter home on December 28th 1943:

> I asked George [Cruikshank, one of Wavell's ADCs] to have a quiet dinner at the Mess – it was my sleeping day as I had been on duty all night. I retired thankfully to

bed with the lovely thought of a day's rest and quiet evening ahead. I was summoned to the telephone – it was George, who told me to cancel dinner and put on my party dress – the new ADC had arrived and we were all going out for dinner ... The Viceregal Packard came rolling up and out popped Felicity Wavell [the Viceroy's daughter] and another girl, followed by George, and Hugh Easton [another of Wavell's ADCs], and lastly a tall kilted figure – very good looking, dark-haired, with a moustache. I was introduced to the new ADC, Bruce Fortune ... We all went to the Piccadilly [Hotel]. I sat next to Bruce, who is rather quiet but very attractive, and very easy to talk to. He goes off on tour shortly with the Viceroy. We had a very jolly evening and danced a lot.[40]

XIII

'It was a dead man. His leg had been blown off at the knee, and the battledress trousers were still smoking'

June–December 1943

Huggins.

Huggins had achieved his heart's desire; flying photographic reconnaissance (PR) missions. For a pilot who had chosen Army co-operation because it would give him more freedom than flying conventional fighter missions, PR was the perfect next step. Huggins would be flying missions lasting four or five hours in a single-seater aircraft modified for long range and high altitude. Best of all, the type used for these missions was the Spitfire. However, there were drawbacks: the Spitfires used were unarmed, relying on altitude and speed to keep them out of trouble; they only had one engine, so any mechanical problems could be fatal. Five hundred pilots lost their lives flying PR missions during the war, making it the most dangerous posting in the RAF. Of those lost, over a quarter have no known grave.

As when he joined 237, Huggins required careful training before he would be ready to take on such a challenging role. Having left 237 Squadron, he waited in Cairo for his posting to convert from Hurricanes to Spitfires. During this period, his father, Sir Godfrey, arrived by flying boat to visit the Rhodesian pilots, and, of course, his son. He arrived on March 14th, and film footage exists in the Imperial War Museum archives of the pair in Mena, where Sir Godfrey stayed with the Australian politician Major Richard Casey DSO, MC, who had been appointed a member of the British War Cabinet and sent to Egypt as Minister-Resident for the Middle East.[1] There is also a photograph of father and son, taken on March 16th, of which the Huggins family possesses a copy.

On April 24th 1943, Huggins started at 74 OTU again, this time learning the ropes on Spitfires. It was June before he actually joined his new unit. Although Huggins had been posted from 237 Squadron to 2PRU, he actually joined them in their new guise as 680 Squadron, which formed in Egypt on February 1st 1943. After the Axis defeat in Tunisia, 680 moved to Landing Ground 219 (now Cairo airport) and Nicosia on Cyprus, reconnaissance efforts focusing on the eastern Mediterranean. Huggins joined the Squadron at LG219 on June 8th, and flew with them for the first time the following day. His flight appears both in his log-book and 680's Operations Records Book:

Huggins & his father meet in Cairo on March 16th 1943. (Huggins family collection; also IWM E23068)

> LG 219 1050hrs-1250hrs F/O J.G. HUGGINS carried out local photography in Spitfire BS363. Time: 2.00.[2]

> June 9 Spitfire – Self – Training PR Sortie – 2.00

For the first few days after that, his flying was limited to air tests, checking aircraft for serviceability before combat sorties. It also enabled Huggins to get to know the individual characteristics and foibles of the Spitfires which might carry him on missions.[3] On June 13th Huggins finally flew his first operational sortie, as he proudly noted in his log book, after nearly eight hours in the air:

> June 13 Spitfire AB310 Self – Base to Derna – 2.45
> June 13 Spitfire AB310 PR Peloponnese. Landed El Daba. 5.25 1st operational sortie.
> June 13 Spitfire AB310 El Daba to Base – .45.

> LG219 0650hrs-1745hrs F/O J.G. HUGGINS flew to Derna in Spitfire AB310 and from there carried out a PR of PELOPONESSUS, returning to Derna and then to base. Time: 8.55.[4]

A pattern of missions followed by air tests seems to have been usual. Huggins flew three such tests between June 16th and 18th.[5] From now until the end of the year he would specialize in overflights of Greece and the Aegean islands.

Huggins' next PR sortie was over the Piraeus (the port of Athens) and Maleme (an airfield in western Crete). To accomplish this he set out on June 20th for Derna, a three-hour flight in Spitfire BP908, which he had air-tested twice in the days preceding. The following day at 0800hrs, he took off from Derna in another PR.IV,[6] overflew his targets, landed at Mersa Matruh, and then returned to LG219. The flight lasted just over five hours, but was only 'partly successful'. Five days later, he set out again on the same pattern in the same Spitfire, flying to Derna at 1150hrs on June 26th, refuelling and taking off for a look at Argos and Hassani airfields. Argos was the last airfield from which RAF Hurricanes had operated in Greece in 1941 (Roald Dahl being amongst the pilots who were evacuated from there), and Hassani would later become the original Athens airport. From Athens, Huggins flew on to Mersa Matruh, where he stayed the night before flying back to LG219 on June 27th. He had spent a total of 5 hours 25 minutes in the air.[7] But missions were growing more dangerous; 680's monthly summary recorded that 'for the first time in 680 Squadron an aircraft was brought back with bullet holes in it'.[8]

On July 2nd Huggins flew Spitfire BP936 to Nicosia to join 'C' Flight, taking off from LG219 at 1400hrs and landing at 1545hrs. Even a simple ferry flight like this was potentially dangerous; that same month, Captain Main of the South African Air Force, serving with 680, baled out whilst making the same journey, and was drowned.[9]

* * *

Huggins' first sortie from Nicosia took place on July 11th, with a flight over the Greek islands of Patmos, Kos, and Rhodes, which were in Italian hands. He flew Spitfire PR.IV BR416, of which several photographs still exist.

Huggins' July 11th mission began at 0755hrs and went well, including photography of Maritza airfield on Rhodes, though low cloud prevented him from taking images of part of the coast of Kos. His aircraft was equipped with a single camera, cited in 680's

Spitfire PR.IV BR416 first flew in April 1942, & joined 2PRU later that year after a spell with 1PRU in England. She remained in front-line service until 1944, after which she was transferred to Huggins' old friend 74 OTU. There she was struck off charge in September 1945.

In these photographs she is seen at the beginning & end of her career in the Middle East. The two images in a light 'PR Pink' colour scheme were taken at Marble Arch airfield in Libya (the Italian fascist monument can be seen in the background). The aircraft's protective engine filter (an 'Aboukir' filter) can be clearly seen, as can the transparent blisters on the sides of the canopy which allowed the pilot a better view of what was beneath him. The chin of the PR.IV was also slightly deeper than the Spitfire V fighter from which it was derived, accommodating a bigger oil reserve for extended flights.[10]

The final image (below), in a darker ('PR Royal Blue') camouflage scheme & with the addition of fuselage code 'X', was taken at 74 OTU, Petah Tikva, in Palestine. A trainee is leaving the aircraft whilst a member of the ground crew is removing the film canister from a vertical F24 camera. (IWM CM 5762)

records as being a 36-inch. PR Spitfires could carry several different types of camera, which were remotely controlled by the pilot. Given the freezing conditions at the altitudes of 22,000–44,000ft from which photographs were usually taken, the cameras were kept functional and free from condensation by warm air fed from the engine. The F24 camera

weighed only 40lbs and could take a variety of lenses (3.25-inch, 5-inch, 8-inch, 14-inch, or 20-inch); depending on its mounting, it could take up to 125 photographs directly down from the aircraft ('vertical') or at a fixed angle to the sides ('oblique'). A typical fit might be three F24s in the aft fuselage, two vertical and one oblique. However, BR416 carried an F52 camera, which, although double the weight of an F24, had a longer focal length, making it ideal for high-altitude missions; five hundred images could be taken, using 5, 8, 14, 20, 36, or 40-inch lenses. Huggins landed at 1210hrs after a flight lasting over four hours.

As the Italians came under increasing pressure at home, it became vital to keep an eye on their forces in the Aegean, especially since Allied convoys carrying troops to Sicily were running from Alexandria. Huggins spent much of July and early August on such tasks, each flight lasting three hours or more.[11] On July 20th he covered Simi and Rhodes (including Maritza again); on July 23rd, Rhodes harbour and coastline south; on July 28th, August 4th and August 12th, the airfields of Effiarti (on the island of Scarpanto, as Karpathos was known), and Kattavia and Calato on Rhodes. But on August 9th, as Huggins flew a sortie to Rhodes, his single Rolls-Royce Merlin engine developed coolant trouble. The engines were cooled by liquid ethylene glycol, and if this leaked then the engine could catch fire or seize up. Glycol problems had been quite common in Merlin engines used in earlier models of Spitfire, and the PR.IVs which Huggins was flying were old. This time, he made it back safely (though the Spitfire which he flew on this sortie was destroyed in a crash on its return from a mission only a month later). On another mission, on August 20th, he conducted two runs over Rhodes, only for one of his cameras to fail.[12]

It appears that the Nicosia detachment took the weekend off in mid-August, as their operations book states:

> August 15th 1943, Platres
> 0300hrs Having taken off from the New Forest Park Hotel at 1800hrs, all pilots were badly whistled. 'C' Flight, always ahead of the game, saw the moon eclipsed.
>
> August 16th 1943, Nicosia
> 2200hrs This time the moon actually was eclipsed. Sicily entirely in Allied hands.
>
> August 21st 1943, Nicosia
> 1400hrs All pilots except this chronicler took off to pluck the pleasant plums of Platres.

But Huggins' time on Cyprus was drawing to an end. His replacement arrived on the following day, and on August 23rd, as 680's operations book recorded, 'F/O J. HUGGINS took off in Spitfire V EN264 for Kilo 8 after a month and a half on the island (also a time and a half).'

* * *

In Italy, Badoglio and the King had begun secret peace negotiations with the Allies, who completed their conquest of Sicily by August 17th. The new Italian government claimed in public that Italy would remain an ally of Germany, but the Germans were not fooled, and began to take precautions against an Italian defection. Field Marshal Kesselring had persuaded Hitler that the best policy to adopt in Italy was for the Germans to make a stand as far south as possible and to give ground only slowly. This turned out to be excellent advice.

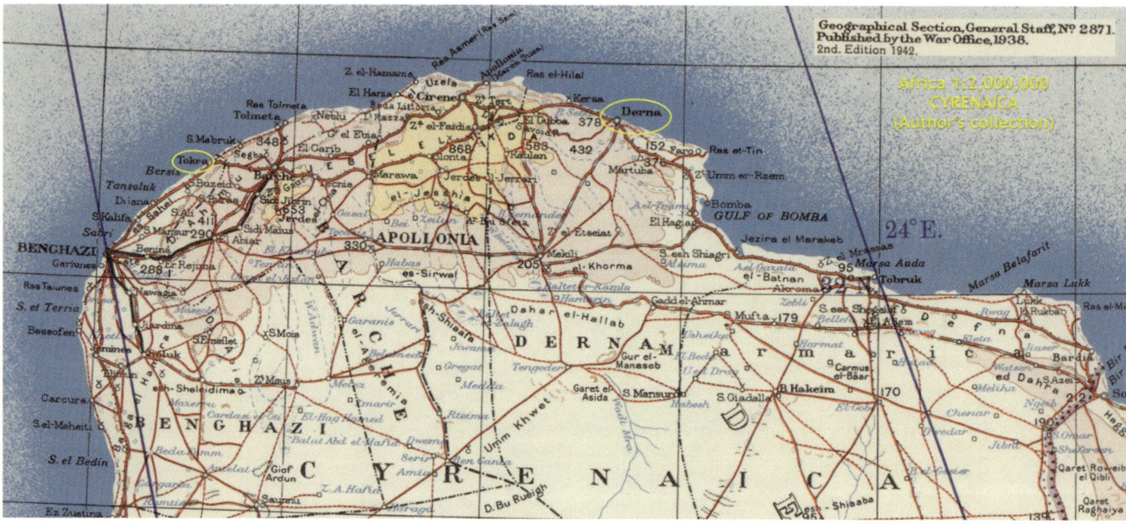

With the Allied focus in the Mediterranean now on mainland Italy, 680 Squadron's detachment at Derna in Libya prepared to move to a new airfield at Tocra, two hours flying time to the west. After shuttling back and forth several times, Huggins flew from Derna to Tocra on August 31st, which now became his base of operations.[13] 680 Squadron's diarist recorded the somewhat chaotic day:

> August 31st 1943, Derna
> 0815hrs F/O Lowe took off on an operation, but returned after thirty minutes flying, with trouble. The operation was cancelled, and he took off for Tocra, with F/Lt Tozer, F/O Westinghouse, F/O Huggins, and F/O Owen. Owing to the shortage of pilots, two aircraft were left at Derna, and F/O Westinghouse and F/O Walker returned by road and flew them to Tocra.
>
> The Main Party left Derna at 1200hrs, under the command of Captain Stanley. The intention was to leave at 1000hrs, and make Tocra in one day, but as usual everything went wrong. The party was two hours late, caused by the obstinacy of a certain aircraft to become airborne. All went well, until the convoy reached Wadi El Kuf, when it got inextricably involved with approximately two hundred vehicles.[14]

From Tocra, Huggins' missions would no longer cover the Greek islands, but the Greek mainland and Crete.

* * *

September 3rd 1943 was the fourth anniversary of Britain's declaration of war on Germany. That day, Huggins flew his first sortie from Tocra, photographing roads and railways in the northern Peloponnese; Simpkin's tunnel was discovered at Gavi; British troops came ashore on the toe of Italy; and the secret armistice between Italy and the Allies was officially signed.

The Allies made the armistice public on September 8th, but unfortunately did not give Badoglio the chance to warn the Italian armed forces. Individual commanders were forced to make decisions as to whether to remain loyal to their former allies the Germans, or to fight them. The lack of co-ordination meant that some Italian units were disarmed by the Germans and some even massacred; others simply evaporated as the personnel deserted and rushed back to their homes. Allied landings at Salerno, south of Naples, on September 9th met fierce German resistance; the King and Badoglio fled Rome and sought Allied protection as the Germans took over the city. On September 12th Mussolini was rescued by German forces, who then set him up as figurehead of a puppet Fascist government in the north of Italy. Badoglio's government formally declared war on Germany on October 13th. Italy was divided; its inhabitants now had to make the best they could of the terrible situation.[15] An Italian civil war had begun.

* * *

Simpkin.

British and Commonwealth prisoners in Italian camps had also had no prior warning of the armistice, and when the announcement came on the evening of September 8th, Senior British Officers in most camps informed their men that the British authorities had ordered prisoners of war to stay in their camps, hoping that Italy's collapse would be rapid and that the prisoners would be better off where they were. Unfortunately, the Germans moved rapidly to take over the camps, Gavi especially. When many inmates tried to hide, they were rooted out by German military police and put on trains bound for Germany. Although many jumped from the trains, Simpkin and Gearing found themselves in *Stalag* VIIA at Moosburg before the month was out – Simpkin sent a postcard from there on September 23rd – but were transferred by September 30th to *Oflag* IXA/Z at Rotenburg, a sub-camp of *Oflag* IXA/H (Spandenberg). An officer who was repatriated from Rotenburg in October wrote to Barbara on October 30th to say that 'I left RES looking very fit in Oflag IXA/Z, where things are quite bearable'.[16]

The following day, Simpkin wrote to Robertson:[17]

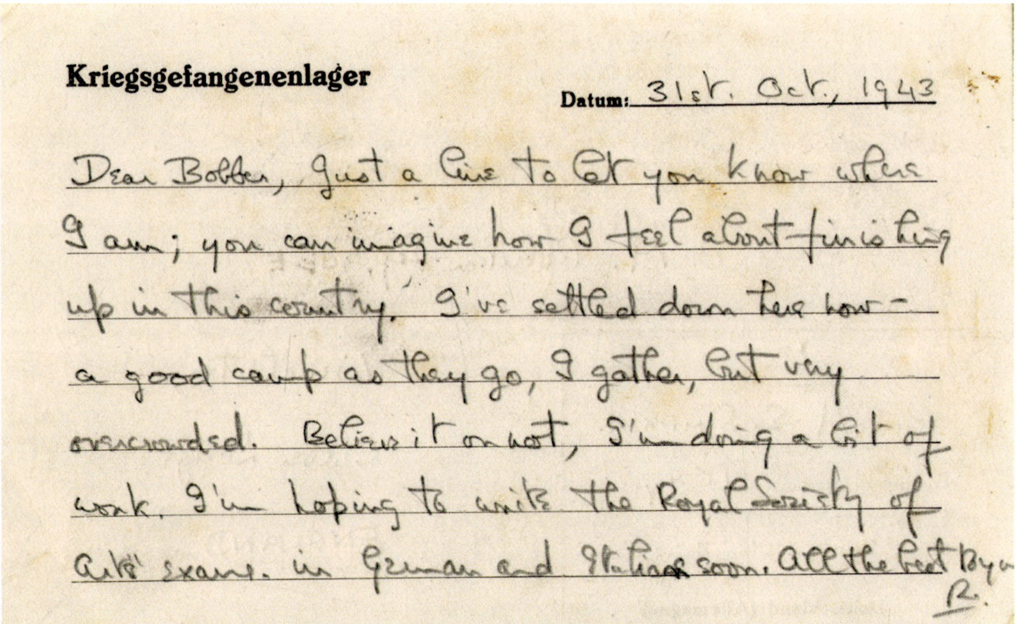

Kriegsgefangenenlager

Datum: 31st. Oct., 1943

Dear Bobber, just a line to let you know where I am; you can imagine how I feel about finishing up in this country. I've settled down here now – a good camp as they go, I gather, but very overcrowded. Believe it or not, I'm doing a bit of work. I'm hoping to write the Royal Society of Arts' exams. in German and Italian soon. All the best Bye

R.

Shortly thereafter, Simpkin's official prisoner-of-war identity card was issued.

Kr.-Gef. Offizierlager IX A
Hauptlager
Zweiglager

Ausgestellt: Rotenburg/Fulda
am -3. NOV. 1943

Kennkarte für Kriegsgefangene

Nur gültig für den Lagerbetrieb und in Verbindung mit der Erk.-Marke Nr. 1697

Dienstgrad: Oberleutnant
Name: Simpkin
Vorname: Richard

Lichtbild
-3. NOV. 1943
Kriegsgefangener
1697

Zur Beachtung!
Die Kennkarte dient als Ausweis der Krf. gegenüber den Organen der deutschen Lagerkommandantur. Sie ist wie die Erk.-Marke stets mitzuführen u. mit dieser auf Verlangen bei namentlichen Appells und beim Verlassen des Lagers vorzuweisen.
Verlust ist sofort zu melden.

Der Kommandant

* * *

When the American Fifth Army landed at Salerno on Thursday September 9th, it was a truly Allied effort; the British X Corps – 56th (London) Division, 46th Division, and 7th Armoured Division – landed at the northern end of the beach-head; the American VI Corps took the southern end. The objective was to take the vital port of Naples, as well as cutting off any German troops further south in Italy. Unfortunately, the Germans had decided not to hold the south and had several days' warning of the Allied landings (Operation Avalanche). The choice of landing beaches was also very obvious. The Germans had therefore placed 15th *Panzergrenadier* and 16th *Panzer* divisions in the landing area.

Edmunds.

56th Division were on the British right – six miles from the nearest American landings – and the right-hand brigade was 167 (London) Infantry Brigade. With them was 7th Battalion, Oxfordshire & Buckinghamshire Light Infantry, Michael Edmunds' unit. 7OBLI were to land forty minutes after the two assault battalions and push on to Eboli, whilst the others secured Battipaglia. This optimistic plan to advance twelve miles on the first day did not, of course, survive first contact with the enemy.

As the invasion fleet approached the Italian coast on the night of September 8th it came under constant attack from the air – which would result in extra work for Huggins and his colleagues in 680 Squadron. 167 Brigade reached its first objective ashore as planned, and 7OBLI were summoned in at 0445hrs on September 9th. As they pushed through a gap in the defensive barbed wire and formed up ready to advance, enemy 6-inch guns and machine-guns opened fire from the left flank. The range – 400 metres – was pretty much point-blank. The guns were silenced by a destroyer and 'C' Company, and 7OBLI advanced across marshy ground to take their objectives. The first German counter-attacks came in from the south at around 1000hrs, but the soft going prevented the enemy tanks and flame-throwers from over-running the infantry. In the afternoon the Battalion advanced to Santa Lucia, but came under heavy fire a mile beyond it. On September 10th the advance continued through Farina, but encountered strong opposition, and by dusk 7OBLI had withdrawn to their start point.

Clerk-Rattray.

Other units had also been attacking that day, among them 2nd Battalion, Scots Guards, in 201 Guards Brigade of 56th Division. Hopperite James Clerk-Rattray was one of at least four Wykehamists in 2SG then; although he seems to have been on detached service at the time of the landings, his Winchester contemporaries Captain John Weir – Nigel Weir's brother – and Lieutenant Roderick McLeod were both serving in 'F' Company. In 'Left Flank' Company (2SG's anti-tank specialists), Lieutenant John Stainton commanded a platoon of four 6-pounder guns. On the morning of September 10th, 2SG launched a daylight attack on a set of buildings known as the 'Tobacco Factory' (in fact, a tomato-processing plant), which commanded the German supply route along the coast. The complex and a neighbouring set of barracks were surrounded by iron railings 8ft high, and sub-divided into smaller strong-points with barbed wire.

As the attack began, a shell struck Battalion HQ and killed and wounded several officers, including the Adjutant. Left Flank Company cleared the barracks and a railway station to the south, and Right Flank Company and 'G' Company got across the railway line; but without artillery support they were unable to hold the ground taken, and by nightfall 2SG had withdrawn. Weir was appointed Adjutant, and thus left 'F' Company – which, in the light of the sequel, probably saved his life, for the time being.

* * *

In Libya, meanwhile, the PR.IV Spitfires of 680 Squadron were getting more and more tired. Cameras began to fail inexplicably, and air tests revealed engines running rough.[18] On September 10th came urgent orders to take daily photographs of all Axis airfields and landing grounds in Greece and Crete, to see whether there was a threat from that direction to convoys heading for Salerno. Allied shipping off the beaches was proving very vulnerable to guided 'Fritz X' bombs from German aircraft, and there was insufficient fighter cover to protect them. Instead of flights at intervals of three days to a week, Huggins was now flying almost daily missions:[19]

> September 10th 1943, Tocra
> 0800hrs Signal from Middle East. Sixteen aerodromes and landing grounds to be covered daily until further notice. A pleasant change after the slack period we have just had. F/Os Huggins and Owen off in the morning to cover Larissa, Argos, Maloi, and Agrinion, Araxos, and Kalamata respectively …
> BR432 Spitfire; F/O Huggins. PR 0700hrs–0745hrs to Derna. 0805hrs–1255hrs Larissa, Argos, H. and S., and Moloi landing grounds...
> All successful sorties. Bags of work for the Photo Section and Interpreters.

> September 11th 1943, Tocra
> Four more today. The same targets as yesterday. F/Lt Tozer, F/O Huggins off in the morning … All the trips were uneventful except F/O Huggins who was unable to cover Kalamata. 'Most Immediate' signal sent to Middle East to report that this aerodrome was not covered. No end of argument with ciphers over the 'Most Immediate' part of it.
> EN388 Spitfire; F/O Huggins. PR 0830hrs-1130hrs Tymbaki aerodrome, Kandia, Heraklion aerodrome, Kastelli Pediata aerodrome.

> September 12th 1943, Tocra
> Today is the third day in succession that all the Greek and Crete aerodromes and landing grounds and ports are to be covered … F/O Huggins was airborne at 1305hrs and covered Megara, Eleusis, Tatoi, Hassani, and Piraeus.
> BR432 Spitfire; F/O Huggins. PR 1535hrs–1715hrs Athens area. Run over Suda Bay and Maleme aerodrome.

* * *

A quiet day followed 7OBLI's failed advance on the 10th, but at 1800hrs on September 11th the enemy began a heavy bombardment of the beach-head, and at 2000hrs a major counter-attack rolled in under bright moonlight. 8th Royal Fusiliers, on the left flank of 167 Brigade, were driven back; 9th Royal Fusiliers had already been reduced to a mere 120 men in bitter fighting in Battipaglia; the full force of the German attack therefore fell on 7OBLI, which found itself threatened from three sides. With superb support from the artillery, the Battalion held its ground – around 500 German dead were subsequently found outside its positions.

* * *

As Edmunds and 7OBLI fought to save the beach-head on the night of September 11th, 2SG were making a second unsuccessful attempt to capture the Tobacco Factory. Without armoured support, and attacking across 300 metres of open moon-lit fields, they discovered the hard way that the enemy garrison had not withdrawn, as they had been told, but had been reinforced. Right Flank Company lost all its officers to intense machine-gun fire. 'G' Company broke into the compound but had to withdraw after close-quarters fighting among a confusing warren of buildings and barbed wire. 'F' Company crossed the railway embankment but – confronted by tanks as well as intense small-arms fire – was overrun, fewer than twelve men escaping capture. McLeod was one of those killed, as his Commanding Officer described:

> Roderick died very gallantly while charging an enemy machine-gun post during a night attack. He got to within a few yards of the objective, actually throwing his grenades, when he was killed instantly along with two of his men by a burst of machine-gun fire. We shall miss his charming personality more than I can say; his men will miss a trusted leader, and the Regiment has lost a most efficient and promising young officer.[20]

On Sunday September 12th, as darkness fell, the Guards withdrew.

* * *

7OBLI now moved to what they were promised was a quiet sector, at the north end of the perimeter, near Pontecagnano. The terrain here was much more broken, with hills rising to 1,300ft, and 7OBLI took up positions to block the valley of the Picentino River and the road which followed it to the coast. According to the Regimental records, the sector remained quiet for about half an hour after their arrival, at which point the area came under heavy attack from the air and on the ground. On September 15th, a fierce and intense attack fell upon the Battalion once again. By around 1600hrs some twenty tanks and large numbers of infantry were closing in on 7OBLI's positions. Although determined resistance stopped one German tank attack, elsewhere the defenders were forced to call down friendly artillery fire on their own positions to halt the enemy. The Germans were stopped but came on again at 1500hrs on September 16th – again, 7OBLI fought them to a standstill.

How great a part Edmunds played in this superb defence is unclear. What is known is that on September 16th he was admitted to 185 Field Ambulance, not wounded but having succumbed to illness – probably malaria. Over the course of the next week, the Commanding Officer, Adjutant, two Company Commanders, and many of the men were hospitalized with sickness. The Battalion's narrative states that

> this was a direct result of the Regiment's first week of fighting in the marshes around the beach-head, where, in spite of mepacrin tablets, mosquito veils, gloves and ointment, mosquitoes, considerably larger than any we had experienced in Bombay, Iraq, or the desert, had feasted on our blood and done their worst.

Edmunds would not return to his unit until early December (he was not present with them on November 28th, but was present by December 13th). He was fortunate – the Battalion suffered heavily once again on Monte Camino in November.

* * *

The pressure on Huggins and 680 Squadron now began to relent, as the Germans failed to contain the Salerno landings.

September 14th 1943, Tocra
Everyone pleased; the cover of all the aerodromes, etc., has been revised; only two sorties today. F/O Huggins took off at 0910hrs to cover Kandia, Heraklion, and Kastelli Pediata. Kastelli was under cloud again.
EN389 Spitfire; F/O Huggins. PR 0910hrs–1350hrs Crete, run over Heraklion aerodrome and Kandia Harbour.

September 18th 1943, Tocra
0830hrs Two aircraft off this morning, F/O Huggins for Crete and F/O Lomas for Athens and Piraeus.
EN389 Spitfire F/O Huggins. PR 0830hrs–1130hrs Tymbaki, Heraklion, and Kastelli aerodromes. Kandia Harbour.

Huggins had now flown seventeen operational missions. On September 20th he did no flying of any sort, but sat down and wrote a letter to Robertson:[21]

I received a copy of the Wykehamist Roll and saw the latest awards and information. I did not realize that Gerry Rickman had been in the Singapore fighting and is now reported missing. I think I told you that I met Helme and Rooper of 'F', in Cairo, and from them gathered the news of Bruce Fortune's MC and also being wounded.

How is 'I' house getting on under its new management? Well, I sincerely hope. I wonder if there is any semblance of the old hospitality at Hopper's Private Side that I remember so well. Somehow I think anyone would be hard put to rise to such standards. I would love the chance to come over to England and see all my Winchester friends again, now, while most of the dons I knew are still there. My hopes of getting to England for any length of time after the war are rather slender unless I inherit a fortune from somewhere.

Local news is very meagre. Out in the blue under canvas is an unexciting life. Flying is a forbidden topic in letters! The main consolation is that we are pretty healthy and have quite a lot to occupy our time. My Flight Commander, by name Tozer, is from Merchant Taylor's and was there when Spenser Leeson was headmaster. Quite amusing comparing our impressions of the same man …

War news is good. Let's hope it continues as such.

The following day, he took off from Tocra for a four-hour flight over the Athens area. There was good news that day, which appeared to be a success due partly to the squadron's efforts over the Dodecanese. – 'Quite a celebration in the Officers' Mess on hearing the news that we had occupied Leros and Kos, islands which are well known to all our pilots'.

However, 680 continued to have problems with their equipment, and morale was low because on September 16th one of their pilots had died suddenly from polio.[22] The whole detachment at Tocra had been put into quarantine for a fortnight from when his first symptoms had appeared.

The Gremlins seem to have been having the time of their lives with our cameras lately. The Photographic Officers have checked everything but still they are not always 100%.The Flight Commander ordered a Flight Photograph to be taken at 1730hrs this afternoon. After three months in the desert, slacks and black ties appeared. The personnel looked like a Base unit.[23]

The occupation of Leros and Kos was to prove a great error; the operations had been conducted on a shoestring, and the lack of Allied air cover gave the Germans the perfect opportunity to inflict an embarrassing defeat on the British and to take revenge on the Italian troops on the islands. It was quickly apparent that the Germans were building up their air forces in Greece and Crete, and 680 received orders to monitor the airfields there. At 0630hrs on September 23rd a high-priority signal from headquarters reached Tocra, urgently revising their intended objectives for the day. Five hours later, orders came to photograph Larissa aerodrome immediately. Huggins was the stand-by pilot. The signal arrived at 1130hrs; he was briefed at 1200hrs; he took off at 1240hrs.[24] His flight took him over Larissa, Lamia and the Bay of Navarino (Pylos), and he landed safely back at 1715hrs. On the 25th it was Athens and Piraeus, and two days later – the day on which the quarantine ended – Huggins returned for a visual survey of Larissa. A 'visual' survey was not standard practice, but if the weather was too poor for high-altitude camera runs, 680 pilots tended to do a low pass over the target in order to see for themselves what was going on. It was not a healthy thing to do in an unarmed aircraft in poor visibility, but the pilots did not want to come back with nothing.

Huggins' last flight of the month came on September 28th:

> Tocra
> 0800hrs Today started well; three signals with numerous corrupt groups arrived; bags of panic!!! Two sorties were off by 0800hrs, F/O Huggins covering Crete and P/O Ellison the Athens area. Fortunately, F/Lt Tozer arrived at Tocra from Base with all the 'Nat Gen' and was able to bring some order out of the chaos.

Huggins' mission involved photographic runs over Maleme and Kastelli airfields.[25] By now the Luftwaffe was making heavy raids on Leros and Kos preparatory to landings from the sea. It is not surprising to find that Huggins now flew his highest intensity of operations: between October 1st and October 11th he is reported to have flown ten operational sorties, coming under anti-aircraft fire on October 8th. Conditions were becoming very hazardous, as 680's monthly summary shows:

> This month we completed 196 sorties involving 683 hours of operational flying over a vast area of sea, from Tocra in Libya, and Nicosia in Cyprus as far afield as Salonika. We lost one aircraft when the pilot, F/O Hay, in attempting to break through a front of thick cloud, crashed near Kos, and was killed. A high tribute must be paid to the ground crews who kept the aircraft in such excellent condition. 'B' Flight at Tocra had to contend with fine, penetrating sand which can clog practically anything provided it is given the chance … 'B' Flight is 700 miles and 'C' Flight 500 miles away from base.
>
> The totals, individually and collectively, comprise a record for the Squadron, which has been operating for just over two years. Furthermore, we compiled the total flying in very poor weather, necessitating upon occasion low 'dicing' i.e. flying just under the cloud base, in poor conditions of visibility, in order to obtain vital visual reports, although this form of reconnaissance is not the policy of a PR squadron, operating in unarmed aircraft. The number of sorties encountering FLAK has been 300% greater than in any previous month … On the 8th, F/O Huggins observed flak over Piraeus.[26]

In these ten flights, Huggins took pictures of aerodromes in Crete and Greece (Agrinion, Araxos, Argos, Kandia, Eleusis, Hassani, Heraklion, Kastelli Pediata, Megara, Paramythia, Tatoi, and Yanina), as well as the harbours at Patras and Piraeus, and the island of Syros. He also photographed central Athens, Marathon, and the anchorage at Salamis, even conducting a sweep for German shipping off Crete.[27] It is interesting that the only aerial photograph of which Huggins kept a copy was taken on his mission over Piraeus on October 5th.

This intensity of operations was unsustainable. After a brief break, Huggins was back on operations on October 16th, with a sortie over Crete and the Cycladic islands. The next day, he photographed Piraeus for the final time, as well as the Cyclades.

* * *

PARTITO NAZIONALE FASCISTA

FEDERAZIONE DEI FASCI DI COMBATTIMENTO DI REGGIO CALABRIA

ASSOCIAZIONE NAZIONALE FASCISTA
ADDETTI ALLE AZIENDE IND. DELLO STATO

H.Q. Eighth Army
C.M.F.

Italy
29-9-43

N. .... di protocollo
Risposta al foglio N. ....
del ....
dell'Ufficio ....
OGGETTO

Dear Macknill

I have your letter of 3rd Sept and am glad you wrote to me. I am not quite clear as to your position, and you say "I have no wish to be a miner". Does that mean you have been directed by the Ministry of Labour to work in a coal mine until you are old enough to be a soldier?

Perhaps you will let me know the exact situation.

In any case you cannot join the R.H.A. direct. You have to join the Royal Artillery, and then you get sent to R.H.A. only if you are a very good officer indeed; it is a corps d'elite.

" VIVERE NON È NECESSARIO.
È NECESSARIO NAVIGARE "

Write to me again and explain exactly what is your present situation, and what it is you want to do.

Yrs. sincerely

B. L. Montgomery

Allied forces in mainland Italy moved forwards as quickly as the weather, terrain, and Germans allowed. Arguments still rage as to whether the Italian campaign was a waste of time and resources. When one visits Cassino and the other battlefields one can only marvel at the difficulty of fighting up the Italian peninsula, across the grain of the country, over river after river, each one dominated by hills and providing the defenders with every natural advantage. The Germans were lucky in that their commander, Kesselring, was superb in defence, even though his background was as a Luftwaffe officer; the Allies were unlucky in that theirs, Alexander, was always forced to attempt too much with too little. And both sides were unfortunate in that the Italian campaign was very much an infantryman's war, in which defenders and attackers alike suffered from the weather and the savagery of close-quarters fighting.

At this stage in the campaign, Montgomery was still in command of Eighth Army. He wrote to Graham Mackrill on September 29th, in response to a letter which Mackrill had written to him. Montgomery was always very thoughtful; he wrote his letter on captured Fascist notepaper – bound to appeal to a young fan – and addressed the envelope himself.[28]

A pencilled note, in different handwriting, beneath Montgomery's signature states: 'The present position is that youths born prior to 1 January 1926 are not at present eligible for enlistment with the Army on a duration of war engagement, but are only eligible for enlistment into the Army on a regular engagement.'

* * *

By early October, Clerk-Rattray and his fellow members of 2SG were on the line of the Volturno River, north of Naples. The Americans crossed the river on October 13th near Capua, and the following day 201 (Guards) Brigade received orders to follow and occupy the hills between Monte Grande and Bellona, which they achieved by the end of October 18th. The Brigade HQ war diary for the following day recorded what Clerk-Rattray was up to:

> Preparations were now being made to maintain the Brigade in the forthcoming assault on the towering heights above the village of Rochetta, the northern tip of the ridge. Orders were issued to requisition every able-bodied mule and horse. Lieutenant J.B. Clerk Rattray, Scots Guards, the Camp Commandant, an ex-cavalry officer, was put in charge of this task. The first conscripts included four stallions who proceeded to chase their attendants up trees and bit the OC Horse and Mule Transport.[29]

* * *

Huggins' last operational flight with 680 Squadron – and, as he could not have known, of the entire war – was on October 19th in a regular mount, the ageing Spitfire PR.IV EN388. At 0840hrs Huggins took off for Crete and the Cycladic islands for one final time, spending four and a half hours in the air to successfully complete his thirty-fifth mission. On October 22nd he flew himself from Tocra back to LG219 near Cairo.[30]

Unsurprisingly, he was assessed as medically unfit and did not fly again until May 1944. He was posted away from 680 Squadron on December 31st 1943, and joined Air HQ at El Adem.[31] He was then returned to Rhodesia to train other pilots. He had seen more than his fair share of action.

* * *

For a month – beginning on November 5th – 201 Guards Brigade were involved in the bitter battle for Monte Camino, which overlooked two avenues of advance towards Cassino, that to the east referred to as the Mignano Gap. Observers on these mountains could call down artillery fire on troops advancing on the plains, and it was difficult to mask movement or build-ups for attacks if the Germans held the high ground. Monte Camino actually has three major peaks – Camino (3,158ft), La Difensa (2,958ft), and Maggiore (1,673ft) – and Clerk-Rattray's mules would be of huge importance if these were to be taken and held, especially given that the Germans had prepared strong positions and the weather was turning bad.

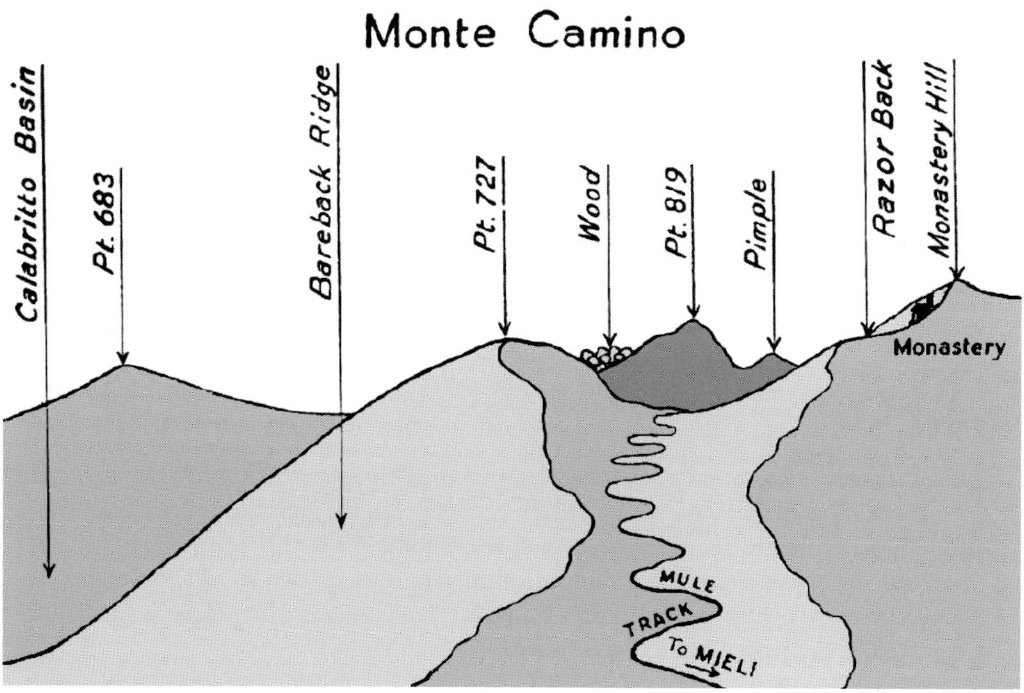

As 2nd Scots Guards advanced up Bare Arse ridge on November 7th, torrential rain was falling, reducing visibility to a matter of yards and making the climb even more arduous. The Germans counter-attacked 201 Brigade's footholds on Camino the following day, movement up the slopes becoming impossible in daylight. The foot of the mule track up which the British intended to bring supplies – at Mieli – came under shell-fire. When

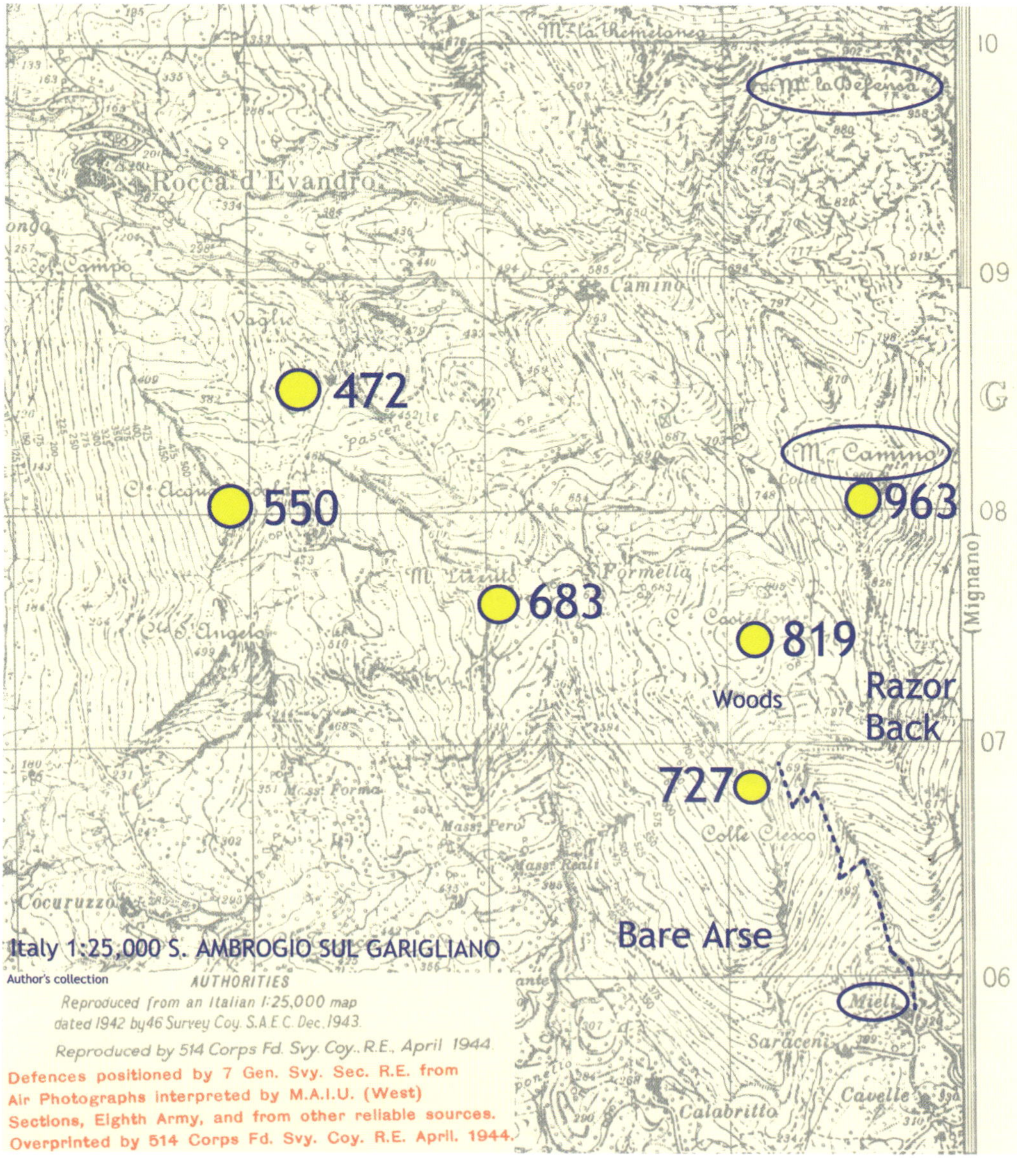

calm descended on the mountain around 2100hrs, the Grenadier Guards on Point 819 at last received food, water, and ammunition from a party of porters, sending their wounded down the long treacherous route to Mieli.

> On this day Lieutenant Clerk-Rattray showed that the mule track was negotiable by the simple expedient of taking a mule train up it until he came under fire near the top. It was thereafter known as the mule track.[32]
>
> Lieutenant Clerk-Rattray, Scots Guards, during the night attempted to reach the Grenadiers with rations on mules by the mule track. Near the top, however, the path was being swept by machine-gun fire, so he left the rations on the ground and returned.[33]

The Guards' positions were becoming less and less tenable. By the morning of November 9th, the Germans still held strong positions on the western flanks of Monastery Hill and Razor Back ridge, from which their machine-guns dominated Point 819 and the surrounding slopes. Point 819 itself was in their hands, though two weak companies of the Grenadier Guards and 'F' Company 2SG clung to its western side. Two reserve companies and the Grenadiers' headquarters were pinned down at Point 727.

> Bitter fighting continued all day round our three companies. The enemy, from the top of Point 819, was able to hurl stick grenades down among them. Movement of any sort was impossible as they were continually covered by snipers. The Germans made repeated efforts to rush them. They were compelled to lie low while the large numbers of automatic weapons gave these attacks covering fire. As soon as this covering fire lifted, they sprang up and fired every weapon they had into the assaulting German infantry. Several times a voice in good English called on them to surrender.[34]

Though it left a bitter taste, the decision was taken to abandon Camino for the time being, there being insufficient troops to do any more, and the weather becoming even worse. An orderly withdrawal took place on the night of November 14th, but 2SG found themselves in a muddy field without accommodation but with plenty of rain. Nevertheless, their war diary recorded that

> a tribute should be paid to those who organised and delivered supplies. A dump had been made in Sipicciano and another in Mieli and thence replenishments came by porters and mules along roads which were shelled frequently and accurately and were even troubled by distant Spandau fire. Except in the case of the Grenadiers on the first day, supplies always arrived at the top of the mule track.[35]

The attackers went back in on December 2nd, using two corps where 201 Guards Brigade had failed. By December 11th, Camino and its surroundings were in Allied hands.

* * *

Thomas.

News of another Hopperite casualty reached Robertson as 1943 gave way to 1944. Flying was still a hazardous undertaking, with powered flight slightly less than fifty years old. Although technology had advanced rapidly, much was still subject to chance – especially in bad weather. On Sunday, December 5th, Squadron Leader 'Mike' Thomas was piloting Short Sunderland flying boat W6103 '2-B' on a transit flight from Castle Archdale to Stranraer; the aircraft belonged to 423 Squadron, RCAF. At 1307hrs the Sunderland descended out of cloud at around 1,200ft straight into the side of Knocklayd, a mountain south of Ballycastle in Northern Ireland. Thomas attempted to pull up, but the Sunderland's belly hit the mountainside and flew to pieces; the engines separated from the wings and the Sunderland flipped on to its back. W6103 had travelled only a hundred yards from

The Short Sunderland III (W6103 2-B) in which Thomas was killed, moored in this image on Lough Erne. The aerials for 2-B's ASV Mk.II radar can be seen in a row of four projecting upwards from the aft fuselage, with the broadside array of aerials showing as two regular rows of four dots, the topmost running along the boundary between the upper surface camouflage & white sides. The IWM catalogue incorrectly states that Thomas was the Captain of the aircraft when it crashed. (IWM HU91910)

its point of impact, so the deceleration would have been abrupt. To make matters worse, the wreck then caught fire. Thomas was one of nine who died in the crash; there were seven survivors, including the aircraft's Captain, who, along with the Navigator, was held responsible for the crash. Thomas, who was still only twenty-five years old when he died, left a widow, Daphne, and a daughter, Fiona, less than a year old.[36]

* * *

Somewhat ironically, given his travels across the whole width of the Mediterranean to reach the Yorkshire Hussars, on December 12th Hirst found himself back in Britain.

The New Holland, *on which Hirst returned to Britain.* (Copyright holder unknown)

Early in November 1943, the Regiment was ordered to return to England, and we moved to an embarkation camp outside Alexandria. I returned with a convoy of trucks to pick up more stores, and nearly got into trouble as I very unwisely led our convoy past a slow-moving one of Basuto Pioneers (South African natives with white officers), much to the annoyance of the Major in charge of them. Back at our camp, I messed with a unit of Australian artillery. When playing volleyball at the embarkation camp, I badly sprained my left ankle, which still occasionally gives out.

Hirst.

We sailed on the Dutch liner *New Holland*, and had an uneventful voyage, landing at Gourock on the Clyde on December 12th. I had been the fifth and junior officer in a four-berth cabin, and when we reached the Clyde one of the others went ashore with an advance party, so I had a chance of a top bunk for the last night. Unfortunately, I had celebrated too well on Cyprus brandy, and fell out – so found it safer to remain on the deck.

* * *

Mackrill.

Despite having Monty's promise of help, on leaving Sunnyside Mackrill sought a commission in the the Royal Naval Volunteer Reserve – the 'Wavy Navy' as he always called it (owing to the undulating rank braid worn by RNVR officers). He applied under the 'Y' Scheme, by which boys still at school who had good qualifications and seemed sound officer material joined as Ratings, completed basic training, and then went on to officer training. The problem was that Mackrill had been wearing 'milk bottle bottom' glasses since he had been a small child, and might not pass the medical examination.

> He went on a train to his medical, and, knowing that he wouldn't be enrolled if he wore glasses, threw them out of the window. Luckily the Doctor, who was elderly, checked his good eye first, and then forgot to turn over the page of letters to be read. My father, trying to remember the letters, managed to pass with perfect vision … After the war, he went to his optician, and his sight had improved so much that he then only needed reading glasses from about the age of fifty. One good thing to have come out of the war![37]

Mackrill reported for duty at HMS *Ganges* – a shore base at Shotley, south of Ipswich – as an Ordinary Seaman in December 1943. *Ganges* was where 'Hostilities Only' new entrants undertook their initial training. Mackrill, who was accommodated in the Jellicoe Annexe across the road, wrote home once a week from December 16th 1943, and the following excerpts give a flavour of his time there:

> It seems to be a goodish spot over the road. When your day's work is over, there is billiards, a bar, flics four days a week, dances twice, and ENSA once a fortnight. Also music and play-reading. But though it sounds terrific there are a hell of a lot of us, and these places are limited in size. All seems to be going reasonably at present; lots

of square-bashing to come (foot and arms drill), which is pretty boring because I have done most of it at Win. Coll., but one or two things are different. We had to pass a swimming test this morning. I did a similar one at Win. Coll. By Gad it was a superb indoor swimming pool (INDOOR), all warmed. I thought it would be very cold, but it was wizard. I could have stayed in for hours. It was a similar one to the one at the Lansdowne, but bigger … I have found several Y Scheme men now, but there are few of them compared to the total number – most of them are none too good; lots of language. But you can soon pick out the ones who are any good.[38]

Now, a word about the chaps I have to live with. An incredible crowd of people. I have not come across one other public school chap in over six hundred people. Some swear so much that it ceases to mean anything. We had a talk the other day from the Padre on swearing and VD, but it seems to have had very little effect on most people.[39]

* * *

Michael Elliot-Binns, meanwhile, was not enjoying similar luxury. Instead, he endured the terrible conditions in the mountains south of Cassino during the winter of 1943 to 1944, serving with 71st (West Riding) Field Regiment, Royal Artillery, which fired to support the operations to capture Monte Camino.[40]

Elliott-Binns.

I was a supernumerary officer and had little to do, but I began to learn about war and saw my first dead men. The line was broken to the Battery Command Post. There was no Signaller easily available and another officer was on duty on the Troop position, so I went myself to mend it. I walked quickly along the ditch beside the railway bed, running my hand along the wire and climbing over piles of rubble and broken sleepers. My eye was on the wire, and I almost stepped on something before I noticed it. At first it looked like a heap of brown sacking. Then I saw it was a dead man. His leg had been blown off at the knee, and the battledress trousers were still smoking. I looked up and saw that there were half a dozen dead bodies lying in the road. I only noticed that their faces were very pale before I looked away. The line went right under the dead man, and I went on to the exchange for help. I felt slightly sick. They were the first dead men I had ever seen.[41]

It was winter, and conditions in the mountains could be bad. A week before Christmas I was sent to take charge of a communications post in a village high on a mountain looking down over enemy country. My men were Signallers and anti-tank gunners, who were used to carry provisions and ammunition to the infantry in the front line. For the first time I really had a job and related to men of my own …

One of my Signallers needed to love me, and I naturally responded. We were both very young, and he was good to look at. He had been a farm labourer in Herefordshire and his voice took me back to my beloved Devonshire village, which had been my last home. He showed me the photograph of his girl-friend whom he loved in England. Now he loved me and would be with me whenever he could be. I lived in an inner sanctum with the Signals Sergeant, and he joined us there. No-one seemed to mind, but rather to approve. Life was cold and grim, and our love was warming. It was my last experience of love of this kind, never expressed in physical terms, and was brief.

Elliott-Binns speaks eloquently in his works of his love for his fellow men. He is very clear that despite the depth of his affections, his use of the term is in no way sexual:

> It must be remembered that I am writing about the Thirties ... I was governed by the outlook and moral code of the time. The Sixties revolution, which broke traditional moulds and emphasised freedom, in particular sexual freedom, had not happened. The poems and narrative written here must be interpreted in the light of their own time, and understood as being written by someone brought up in that time, whose use of words is coloured by his upbringing.
>
> Love ... has no relationship of necessity with sexual love, though between particular people sexual love may be a dimension. I also use it in the social language of the day, though 'affection' would be a better word ... In those days love between those of opposite sexes, those of the same sex, was accepted just because there were no necessary physical implications. The social and moral rule was that full sexual relationships took place between those of the opposite sex who were married to each other. In other relationships, physical manifestations were limited and carefully controlled.

Christmas Day 1943 stuck in Elliott-Binns' memory:

> I had always spent Christmas at home, a Christmas of good food, wine, presents, chocolates, holly, all the usual trappings of an English Christmas. Last year it was different. I returned to the gun lines, taking with me a party including my Signaller. I spent most of the day coming down from the mountain, which was part of the front line at the time. We had kit to carry on our backs, the country was rough, and I was

without a map or any knowledge of the country, and I took a much longer route than was necessary. Yet I will always look back on that Christmas with pleasure. I had been working with these men for some days in bitter weather, cut off in a little world of our own. I think we had grown to like and trust one another. They never complained or lost heart. It was not a normal Christmas, but it was the Christmas of the manger, and in the middle of war it was a Christmas of peace and good will.

As we walked back across our mountain I found that my feelings were changed. Love was not just towards him but was towards the whole party of men, and my face shone to them, and they smiled back.

It was the beginning of Elliott-Binns' deep Christian faith.

OLD WYKEHAMIST NEWS

At Oflag IX, Germany, a special Carol Service was held during Christmas week. At this Service a " Carol in Captivity " was performed—the words by Major Maurice Wilson, Cameron Highlanders (H, 1912-16), and the music composed by Lieut.-Colonel Donald Frazer, 15th/19th Hussars. A copy of this carol was made especially for Winchester College and has just arrived from Major-General Victor Fortune, C.B., D.S.O. (D, 1897 - 1901), who is a prisoner of war in that camp.

The carol has been given to Moberly Librarian, who will arrange for it to be exhibited in the open cases. Not only will it be regarded by posterity as a valuable memorial of the Second German War, but it also bears witness to the invincible cheerfulness and courage of men who have now been nearly four years in captivity.

XIV

'One just must carry on'

Anzio, January–March 1944

By January 1944 the Allies had reached the Garigliano River and positions in front of the infamous Monte Cassino, which stands on the south-western side of the Apennine mountains running down the spine of Italy. Here the German Gustav Line lay behind the natural barriers of the Rapido, Liri, and Garigliano rivers; the line ran along a series of barren hills and mountains which provided the defenders with excellent observation and fields of fire. One of the mountains – Monte Cassino itself – was crowned by a famous Benedictine monastery which had stood there for centuries. As early as October 1943, the Germans had recognized the strategic importance of the monastery, which lay directly along the route from Naples to Rome, 100 miles or so to the north-west. The ridge upon which the monastery was located was the best defensive position south of Rome, and if the Allies wanted to make use of their armour, the Liri valley which Monte Cassino dominated was the only suitable route. German forces had taken over the area around the monastery, whereupon most of the monks had been evacuated to Rome; however, the Germans had not occupied the fortress-like monastery buildings themselves.

For four months – from mid-January until May 18th 1944 – the Allies would batter away at the German defences blocking their way northwards. Try as they might, they could not get through the Gustav Line. The battles around Cassino would cost the Allies over 50,000 casualties, and condemn them to a second winter of war in Italy.

* * *

Simpkin continued to languish in Rotenburg, from which he shared his news with Robertson on January 12th:

Simpkin.

> Thank you so much for your letter, which reached me this morning, you and your sister's good wishes, and particularly for all the interesting news. Unfortunately, owing to a misunderstanding of which you may have heard, I didn't see as much of Italy as I should have liked. A great pity, as one only gets one chance like that in a lifetime, and if one misses that, it is impossible for the majority to make further opportunities … I hadn't heard about Rufus' [Mike Sinclair's] latest effort, or about his brother's being wounded. I hope it was nothing serious. Guy Richardson certainly seems to get around. His father, too, is, I gather, now in the States. Other Wykehamists

> in this camp are: Tony Farquahar (Furley's c.1930), Colonel Young (Beloe's also c.1930) and J.R.K. Sinclair (Furley's up to about '38 – unfortunate end, as far as I remember). I'm sitting for the Royal Society of Arts Exams in German and Italian, if the course of the war permits. I would like to know just how much these Diplomas are worth, as the standard of papers I have seen does not appear exceedingly high.[1]

Unfortunately, though he may have been fit back in October 1943, in January 1944 he suffered a severe attack of septicaemia, necessitating ten days in hospital and treatment with primitive 'M&B' antibiotics.[2] After his recovery, he received his first letter from his mother since being taken prisoner two years previously.

* * *

Four days later, there occurred a death which struck the Hopperite community as forcefully as had that of Nigel Weir. Bill Cliff Hodges had left Hopper's only a year ahead of our subjects and was therefore well known to almost all of them. He had written long letters to Robertson throughout the war from 309 Battery of 78th (Lowland) Field Regiment RA; but only once a year, usually on December 18th – perhaps he had a note in his diary every year to 'Write to The Bobber'. He had even apologized when his 1941 letter had been late (dated January 4th 1942). Cliff Hodges had travelled to Egypt in the summer of 1942, where his guns had joined in the immense barrage at El Alamein at the end of October, though he was himself wounded in the leg by a shell-splinter. His usual December letter had again been delayed because he was in hospital with jaundice, but by December 26th 1942 he had been able to write:

> So far I am still all in one piece and intend to remain so, altho' my left leg is now a fraction heavier than my right as it carries a small bit of a Jerry shell.[3]

After this, the regular spacing of letters had broken down, and it was only May 1943 when Cliff Hodges next wrote – again, from a Cairo hospital.

> There's plenty of time for writing now, as you will see from the address – the result of an argument with a mine on the night of March 22nd. I had quite a few holes in quite a few places but they're all filled in now. My left eye is the only thing that's holding me back. I can see objects with it, but it only improves very slowly and I'll probably have to wear an eyeglass in the end. However, that will qualify me for immediate promotion to Brigadier![4]

In early December, as Clerk-Rattray and his comrades in 201 Brigade were taking Camino, Cliff Hodges (promoted Captain, not Brigadier) reached Italy, back with his Regiment despite his near-blinding. He returned to his usual schedule of letter-writing with a last airgraph to Robertson:

> The scenery is of course magnificent, especially on a sunny, frosty morning. Blue sky, snow down as far as the trees, mostly small oaks – all autumn tinted, little villages

> perched precariously on hillsides and sea-green, fast-flowing rivers. But mostly it rains, and everything is a sea of water and thick, sticky, mud. Crew and self are just back from five days on top of a 400ft hill and glad of the chance to get dry and clean. The other day we were more fortunate. Very poor people in a minute village entertained us most royally. Beds with sheets, stacks of macaroni, some poultry, pig, sheep, apples, local delicacies, and of course gallons of Vino! All poor stuff as of course Gerry likes good wine as much as anyone. We could hardly do a thing for ourselves except eat and a few other essential necessities.[5]

However, Cliff Hodges' next 'argument with a mine', near the Garigliano River south of Cassino on January 16th 1944, saw his luck run out. His obituary in *The Times* was composed by two (unnamed) Wykehamist friends:

> Bill was a born athlete. From his earliest years at St Edmunds he showed himself to be an outstanding player of all games, shining particularly on the football field. At Winchester he became one of the best Soccer players the school had ever known, being in the eleven for three years and leading the side in 1937; and he was a first class player of Winchester football, being Captain of OTH VI in 1936. At Cambridge he gained his Blue in 1938 and was asked to captain the university side for the following year. But it was in other directions his real interests lay; he was at his happiest in his appreciation of beautiful things, in music and painting, and most of all in his love of the country. Shooting and particularly fishing were the sports that he most enjoyed. His natural charm, gaiety of spirit, his gentleness, and his modesty won him a circle of devoted friends. To these qualities as he grew older were added an unselfishness and awareness of others.[6]

* * *

The day after Cliff Hodges' death, James Clerk-Rattray left 2SG and was posted to HQ 201 Guards Brigade. He would remain on the Brigade staff until March 13th 1944. Brooke had also by now reached Italy, from where he wrote to Robertson early in February 1944:[7]

Clerk-Rattray.

Brooke.

> In some ways it is a great improvement on North Africa. The country is much more like England and the surroundings are more pleasant. In North Africa we were on the bare hillside and except for olive trees there was nothing. We had a great Xmas; the whole Regiment went and stayed with a battalion of Grenadier Guards. It was a huge success. We are

now living in some half-shelled buildings – farmhouses and villas – but since it is the first time the Regiment has had a roof over its head for the last two and a half years it's a very pleasant change.

I went and caught malaria at the beginning of January (even though it wasn't the malaria season), so I have been in hospital for the last three or four weeks, and only got back to the Regiment last Monday and am still convalescing.

Recurring attacks of this malaria explained why Brooke had a reputation throughout his post-war career for explosive bursts of temper (one, famously but understandably, when a group of young officers secreted a live Swaledale ram in his wardrobe in the Officers' Mess at Catterick whilst he was playing cards). The letter continues:

The country here, as I expect you know, consists of a series of very high steep and rocky mountains with flat and highly cultivated plains between them. These plains are dotted with farmhouses, orchards, vineyards, and orange groves, and are cut by rivers, canals, and dykes. In fact the Devil's own country to fight across. And I take my hat off to the infantry at the way they've kept cracking away despite the cold and the mud. All the country which has been fought over is absolutely devastated. In some villages not even the walls of the houses are standing. The people are in a very bad way; homeless and starving. The last three weeks we haven't had a drop of rain and the weather has been beautiful. This is rather an exception to the normal weather at this time of year. So I do hope it'll keep like it.

We spent the first months up at Minturno doing purely an anti-tank role. We were then whisked up to Cassino to exploit the breakthrough up the Liri Valley after the New Zealanders had taken Cassino. This thank goodness never came off. And we spent a very pleasant month in a regimental harbour. We organized a villa at Positano for the officers and another at Amalfi for the chaps. Both these places are on the west coast near the Isle of Capri… .

The Germans out here are fighting like demons, holding on to every inch of ground to the last man. There's certainly no sign of a crack. Their morale is very high and they still think they're going to win the war! But they must be in rather a nasty position. Russians seem to be getting on well. I think this year should see Germany beaten and then we've got to deal with those savages the Japanese.

I do hope the house is doing all right under the new management. What is Nick Somerville doing? I saw Charles Duffin was married in the *Tatler* the other day.

The announcement of Duffin's marriage had appeared in the *Tatler & Bystander*'s 'Review of Weddings' on November 10th 1943. Both Kemp and Robertson had attended the wedding.

* * *

The Anzio landings on January 22nd 1944 were the Allies' attempt to break the impasse on the Gustav Line by threatening the Germans' lines of communication. A landing

THE TATLER AND BYSTANDER, NOVEMBER 10, 1943 183

Getting Married

The "Tatler and Bystander's" Review of Weddings

Tweddle — Ward

Alistair R. Scott Tweddle, son of Mr. and Mrs. David Tweddle, of Southdown, Cheam, married Pamela Charlotte Ward, only child of Mr. and Mrs. B. W. Kent Ward, of Edgbaston, and Estoril, Banstead, Surrey, at St. Andrew's Presbyterian Church, Cheam

Flint — Terry

Francis M. Russell Flint, R.N.V.R., only son of Mr. W. Russell Flint, R.A., P.R.W.S., and Mrs. Russell Flint, married Elizabeth Terry, only daughter of Dr. and Mrs. L. H. Terry, of The Lynch, Goodwick, Pembrokeshire, at Our Lady of Victories, Kensington

McKenzie — Platt

Lt./Cdr. Roderick F. McKenzie, R.N.V.R., son of Mr. and Mrs. R. D. McKenzie, of Wimbledon Park, S.W., and Mrs. Daphne Platt, widow of Major C. J. Platt, and daughter of Capt. and Mrs. W. H. Schroder, of Strathcarron, Ross-shire, were married quietly in London

Corbally — Tudsbery

T Major Patrick Corbally, The Royal Ulster Rifles, elder son of the late Capt. L. Corbally and Mrs. Corbally, of Avon Dasset, Warwickshire, married Diana Tudsbery, younger daughter of Colonel and Mrs. H. T. Tudsbery, of Lympstone, Devon, at Brompton Oratory

Alexander — Henderson

Edward Murray Mayne Alexander, of Red House, Bridge of Allan, Stirlingshire, and 63, Pont Street, S.W., and Mrs. Phyllis Irene Hazel Henderson, of 2, Lyall Street, S.W., were married at Chelsea Register Office

Roberts — Leslie

Lt. David Leslie Roberts, R.A., son of the late Sydney C. Roberts and Mrs. D. M. Greenfield, of Bromley, Kent, married Joan Mary Leslie, elder daughter of Brig. and Mrs. W. Leslie, of Penzance, Cornwall, at the King's Chapel of the Savoy

Davies — Madeley

Anthony I. O. Davies, son of the late D. O. Davies, of Las Palmas, Canary Islands, and Mrs. Helen Davies, married Gillian Hamilton Madeley, only child of Major and Mrs. G. H. Madeley, of Grey Gables, Truro, at St. Paul's, Knightsbridge

Duffin — Upton

Charles John Riddel Duffin, Scots Guards, son of Major and Mrs. C. G. Duffin, of Ardleevan, Dunmurry, Belfast, married Florence A. P. Upton, daughter of the late J. H. Upton and Mrs. Upton, of Barbon, Westmorland, and Dolphin Square, S.W., at Holy Trinity, Brompton

Dix Hamilton — Woodburn

Capt. Michael L. Dix Hamilton, The Lovat Scouts, son of the late Lt.-Col. and Mrs. S. Hamilton Dix, married Mabel (Brownie) Woodburn, daughter of Dr. W. Y. Woodburn and the late Lady Mabel Woodburn, and adopted daughter of Mr. and Mrs. Rupert Colomb, at Holy Trinity, Brompton

in strength south-west of Rome would, it was thought, prevent the Germans from reinforcing the Gustav Line in the face of Allied attempts to break through, and would also force them to abandon the Gustav Line as their communications were threatened. Owing to a lack of dynamic leadership, however, the advance at Anzio became bogged down and the Germans were able to contain it. Major John Weir MC was one of many who disapproved of the way in which the Anzio landings had been handled, as his great Winchester friend Tony Pawson later recalled:

> Only twice at Anzio did such an even-tempered man show anger. The first was at the pathetically incompetent early leadership of the American General John P. Lucas, who was only sacked after condemning them to extended suffering in the narrow confines of the beach-head. In his final letter home there was also a blast against the BBC for broadcasting that the war was nearly over, when it had not even come to its bloody climax. As he commented: 'It is hard enough to maintain everyone's morale under the terrible conditions here. Telling us the war is nearly over makes that doubly difficult, as it undermines the normal willingness to take necessary risks.'
>
> Nothing ever undermined his own willingness to do that.[8]

Twelve Wykehamists are known to have gone ashore in the Anzio beach-head between January and May 1944, with another landing during the break-out towards Rome.[9] Of these thirteen, six are still there, and a seventh was captured. A death rate of 46 per cent among Wykehamists makes Anzio the most dangerous place in which pupils of the school have ever served; two were even killed by the same shell. Of those who landed, a disproportionate five were from Hopper's – four from our 1938 house photograph – of whom two were killed. Those who speak of 'a generation lost' in the First World War should also look hard at casualty rates among young officers in Italy and Normandy in 1944.

* * *

Sinclair.

When 1SG landed on PETER YELLOW beach at 0230hrs on January 22nd 1944, the Battalion contained five Wykehamists, four of whom were to die at Anzio. David Scrymgeour Wedderburn was the commanding officer; John Weir was in charge of Right Flank Company, with John Sinclair as one of his Platoon Commanders; Anthony Tuke was responsible for the 6-pounder guns of the anti-tank Platoon; and Duncan McMurtrie was a Platoon Commander in 'B' Company – though at the time of the landing he was with the 'rear party' in Naples.

Tuke was the last of the 1SG Wykehamists ashore that morning, riding in at first light on a DUKW amphibious truck. 1SG dug slit trenches in the woods at the southern, Anzio, end of the key *Via Anziate,* spending the night of January 22nd in 'The Triangle', some three miles north of Anzio itself.

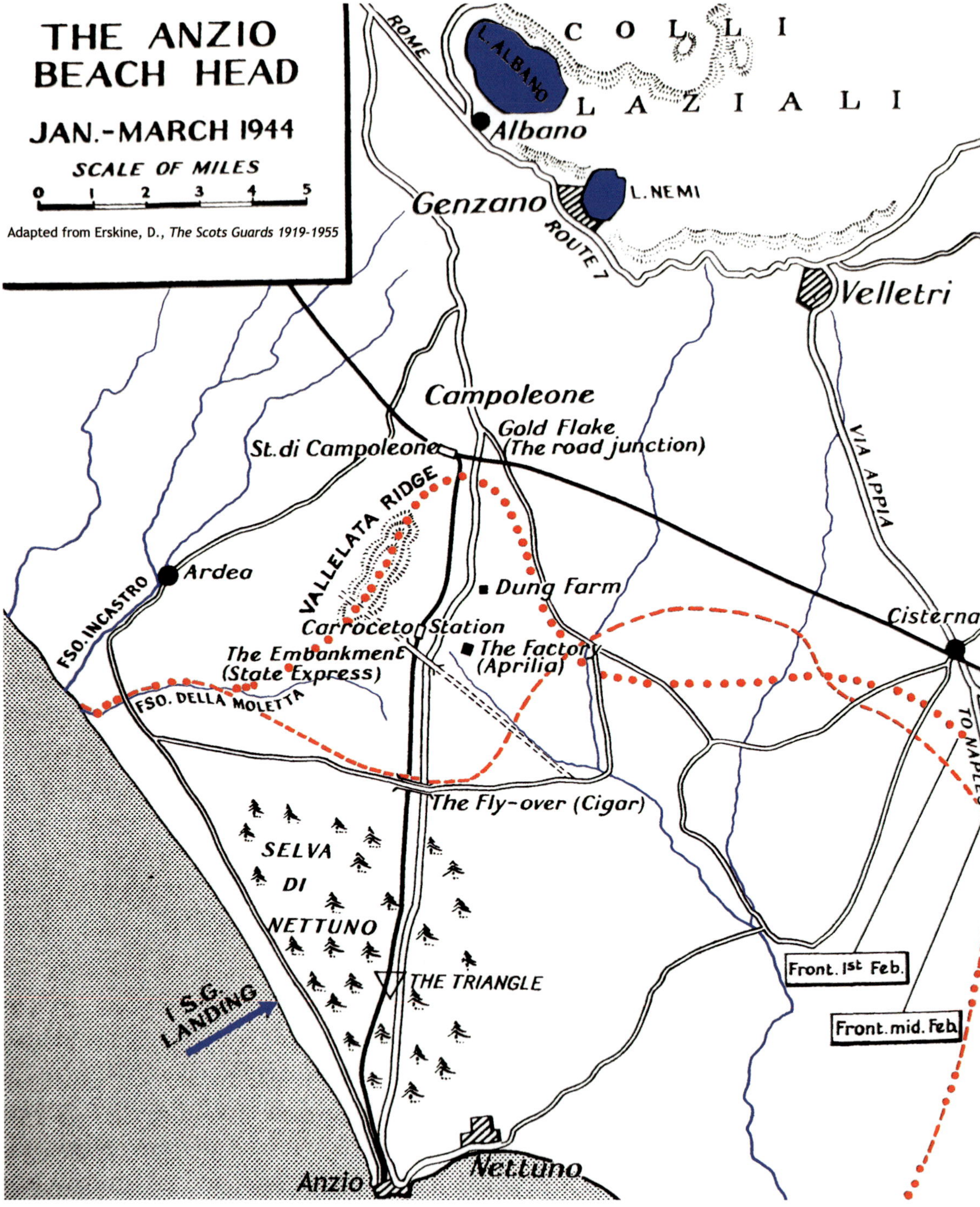

Although this will be in no way a full account of the Anzio fighting, it is as well to become familiar with the topography of the British sector before we follow the fortunes of our subjects. Roughly three miles further north along the *Via Anziate,* a smaller road crossed it on a bridge, with long embankments on either side. This was known to the British as

'The Flyover'. Three miles north of the Flyover was another bridge over the *Via Anziate*, this one intended for a railway track – again, there was a substantial embankment, known with stunning originality as 'The Embankment'. Just beyond the Embankment, ten miles inland on the *Via Anziate*, lay 'The Factory', as it was called by Allied troops, the dominant position and compact structure of which rendered it the principal strategic point on the beach-head. Before it was levelled by weeks of bombing and shelling, the Factory – actually a settlement called Aprilia – was a compact, geometrically laid out cluster of brick buildings, designed in 1936 to be a model for Fascist farm settlements. Located on a slight rise, it stood like a fortress dominating the surrounding countryside. The hamlet of Carroceto, located 500 yards to the south-west, was an equally important objective. Possession of the Factory and Carroceto would offer the enemy strong defensive positions to block the Allied advance, as well as assembly areas from which to launch further attacks.However, the objective for which 24 Guards Brigade was aiming was GOLD FLAKE, an intersection of roads and railways around Campoleone. Their attack went in at dawn on Tuesday, January 25th, and met very stiff resistance in the Factory area, although it was taken in the late afternoon.

The Factory, Anzio, looking inland towards the Alban Hills. (Copyright holder unknown; edited by author)

During a strong German counter-attack on January 26th, Tuke's 6-pounders destroyed two enemy tanks, but the next morning Scrymgeour-Wedderburn decided to take 1SG forward to occupy the buildings of an Agricultural School. These appear on maps as 'Dung Farm', although it seems that the actual word used by the troops was somewhat riper. The advance began at last light, Weir's Right Flank Company occupying Dung Farm itself without opposition, and by 0100hrs on Friday, January 28th, Battalion HQ was established there. A German counter-attack at 0600hrs was driven off by accurate shell-fire.

During the day on January 28th, Sinclair was tasked to lead a patrol west to a house on a nearby ridge. He encountered the enemy, engaged them in a brisk fire-fight, and then withdrew, lying up in a culvert until night fell and it was possible to return safely to the Battalion. No move was made on the following day, but on the night of January 29th 1SG advanced a mile northwards to Point 105, which was to be the start-line for an attack on Campoleone itself. After a ten-minute artillery barrage, the Battalion attacked at 2330hrs, 'B' and 'C' Companies meeting fierce resistance on the left. They retired and came at the enemy from the right, which had been cleared by Left Flank and Right Flank Companies.

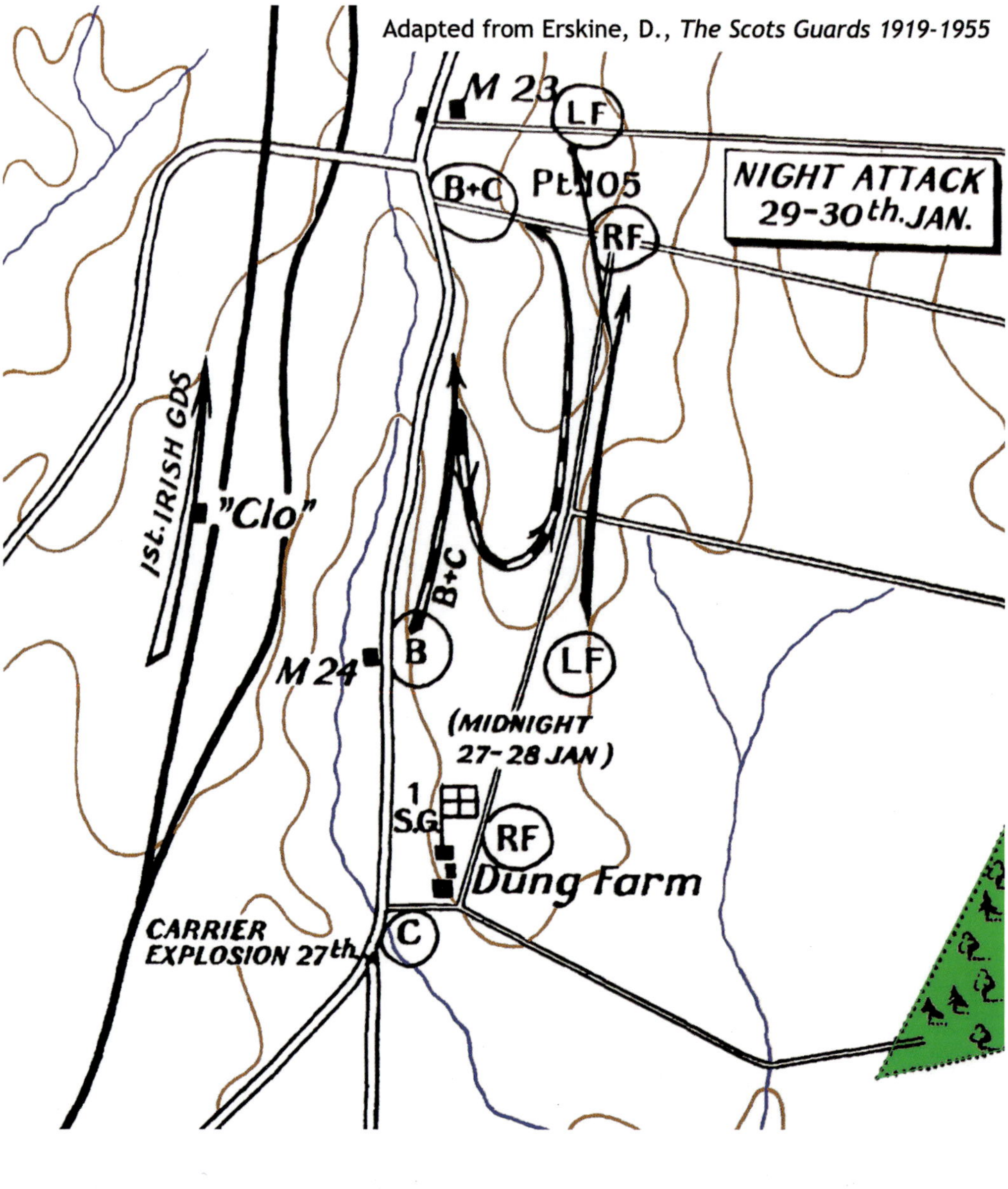

Despite the success of the night advance, a powerful German counter-attack with tanks overran Left Flank Company at around 0730hrs on January 30th. It had been an expensive attack. As a result of the casualties among officers, John Sinclair was promoted Captain.

That afternoon, other troops advanced to occupy the heights just south of Campoleone, and the next morning, British troops crossed the Rome-Cisterna railroad; but the gains could not be held, and this was to mark the furthest advance of the beach-head troops until the final breakthrough in May. Shell-fire was constant. It was clear that the troops could go no further, and that the Germans were planning a major counter-offensive. Barbed wire and mines appeared along the British front.

* * *

John Sinclair's brother, Mike, was still in German hands, and a week after the Anzio landings he wrote to Robertson again, though some of the letter was censored by his captors.[10]

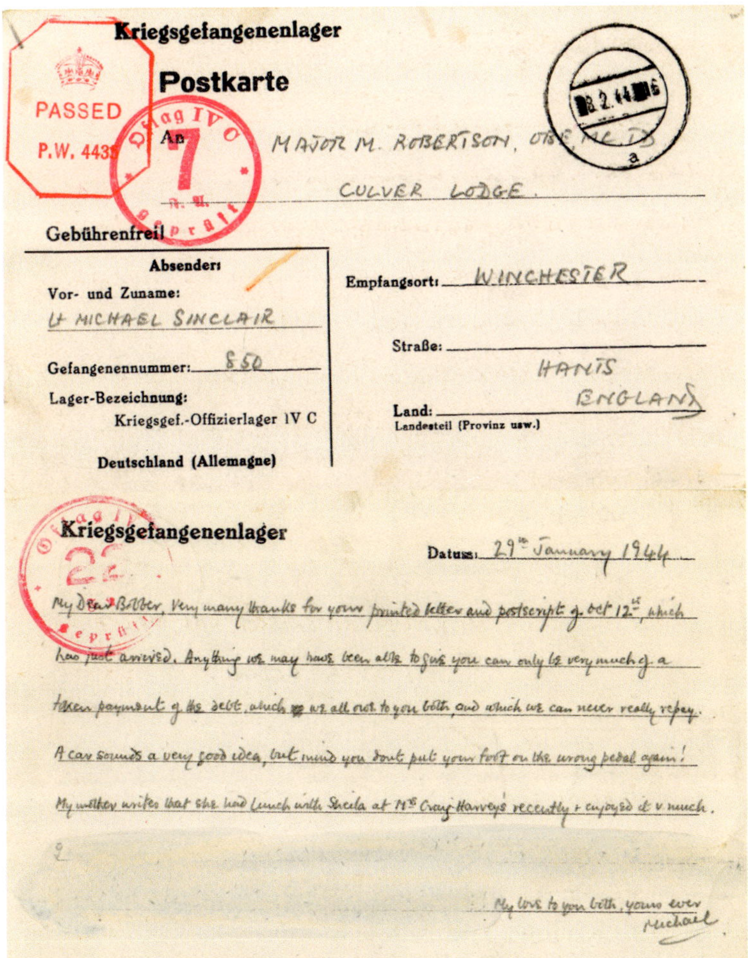

Kriegsgefangenenlager

PASSED P.W. 443

Oflag IV C 7 geprüft

Postkarte

An MAJOR M. ROBERTSON, OBE, MC, TD

CULVER LODGE.

Gebührenfrei!

Absender:

Vor- und Zuname: Lt MICHAEL SINCLAIR

Gefangenennummer: 850

Lager-Bezeichnung: Kriegsgef.-Offizierlager IV C

Deutschland (Allemagne)

Empfangsort: WINCHESTER

Straße:

HANTS

Land: ENGLAND

Landesteil (Provinz usw.)

Kriegsgefangenenlager

Datum: 29th January 1944

My dear Bobber, Very many thanks for your printed letter and postscript of Oct 12th, which has just arrived. Anything we may have been able to give you can only be very much of a token payment of the debt, which we all owe to you both, and which we can never really repay. A car sounds a very good idea, but mind you don't put your foot on the wrong pedal again! My mother writes that she had lunch with Sheila at Mrs Craig-Harvey's recently & enjoyed it v much.

My love to you both, yours ever
Michael

* * *

Elliott-Binns came ashore at Anzio on February 1st, and was posted to 29 Battery, 19th Field Regiment, as a Gun Position Officer. He arrived just one day before his great friend Duncan McMurtrie.

> Early in January 1944 I was withdrawn to Naples, and toward the end of the month I was in action on the Anzio Beach-head. I arrived among the first reinforcements. There seemed to be a shortage of gunner officers. On the deck of the boat that brought me from the bay of Naples to Anzio, a Scots Guards officer was sitting. He was going out to join his Battalion, and I asked him whether he had come across Duncan. He told me that Duncan was with the rear party and had not yet come out. We had been within a few hundred yards of each other and we had not known.[11]

Elliott-Binns.

One of the difficulties in writing a book of this nature is that letters home could not contain accounts of any fighting until a specified length of time had elapsed – and even then soldiers did not tend to give detailed narratives of their experiences, not least to spare their families anxiety. Despite regulations forbidding it, some kept diaries – like

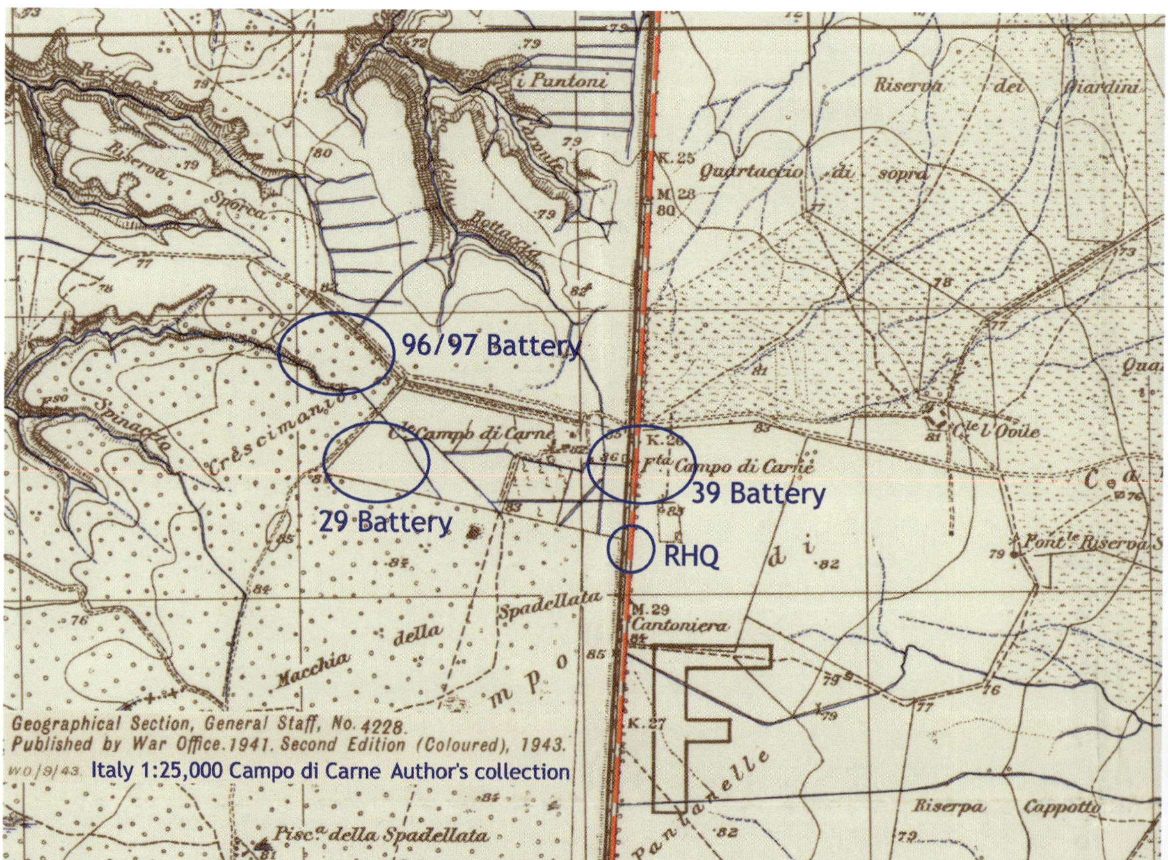

Arthur Herbert – but these were often light on detail. Most accounts which we have from our subjects are, therefore, written in hindsight, with all the flaws of memory which come with that process. But Elliott-Binns felt an urge to write while at Anzio, which he did in the form of short, undated, descriptive pieces of his experiences, conversations, and actions. Set down whilst he was in the beach-head, and transcribed for publication unaltered fifty years later, they are first-hand accounts from a sensitive and observant amateur soldier of what it was like to be in the forefront of battle.

> The divisional artillery were strung out along the front of a line of wood, but there was not quite room enough and I was put in charge of the right-hand Troop. The other Troops had some cover from a line of wood, but mine was exposed, and the Germans had gathered their forces and began to attack expecting to drive us back into the sea. I began by firing four guns with twenty-four gunners. Five days later, I was firing two guns with five gunners and the Sergeant Major. I have never heard of another artillery Troop in Italy that suffered such casualties through shell-fire.

Elliott-Binns' new Field Regiment was commanded by Wykehamist Lieutenant Colonel Anthony Hamilton OBE. The unit's war diary records the casualties which Elliott-Binns saw at first hand.

> February 1st
> In support of 24 Guards Brigade; heavy shelling, also bombing and machine-gunning by low-flying aircraft of Regimental area. 2 Other Ranks killed and 2 Other Ranks wounded.
>
> February 2nd
> 105mm harassed gun areas. Lieutenant Harrison wounded.
> RHQ advance party machine-gunned by FW190 on road to new position. Lieutenant E.A. Lassen wounded. Other Ranks 2 killed and 6 wounded.
>
> February 3rd
> Heavy and continuous shelling of gun areas. Direct hit on a gun of 39 Battery. Other Ranks 5 killed, 8 wounded. Enemy attack developed on 24 Guards Brigade positions. SOS and DF tasks fired.

* * *

From Nairobi, where he was on leave recovering from a mysterious illness, John Pinney wrote to Robertson on February 2nd 1944. In his letter, he described his duties in the frontier town of Mandera, an arid place in the very north-eastern corner of Kenya. Inhabited mostly by Somalis, it was very different from other districts where Pinney had worked, and very different from Anzio.[12]

Pinney.

> Mandera is a cluster of huts set down in a red sandy desert where vegetation is stunted thorn bush growing just above a man's height. In

> some places one can walk for three or four days with an average visibility of a hundred yards, so flat is the country …
>
> One's main job is the preservation of law and order along the Abyssinian frontier, for which there is a large and well armed Police force. Even though it is over two years since Ethiopia was conquered, there are still large quantities of arms and ammunition in the hands of the 'shifta', for which 'outlaw' is not (in the circumstances now prevalent in southern Ethiopia) an accurate translation. With these they make forays into British territory to pinch stock, with an occasional massacre thrown in. One of the roots of the trouble is the Pagan-Islamic feuds. The Shifta are mainly pagan, while their victims, the Somalis, are fanatical Mohamedans. For the last few months there has been a lull, owing to the drought, which has made raiding impossible.

* * *

The British advance northwards had been on a very narrow front, a finger some three miles deep and no more than one and one-half miles wide extending from the beach-head towards Campoleone. The flanks were very exposed. West of the *Via Anziate,* a maze of deep, brush-covered ravines offered the enemy concealed assembly areas from which they could infiltrate between the isolated strongpoints held by the British. East of the road the country was more open, but the railway embankment east of Campoleone offered covered assembly areas for German armour. If the Germans could pinch off the British units holding this salient (including 1SG), they would achieve the destruction of a sizeable portion of the Allied forces and at the same time open the way for further attacks down the *Via Anziate.*

The apex of the salient, just south of the railway at Campoleone, was held by 3 Brigade. On the western flank of the salient, echeloned to the south-west, was 24 Guards Brigade: 1st Irish Guards, 1SG, and 5th Grenadier Guards, with 2nd North Staffordshires attached. On the east flank of the salient, echeloned to the south-east, were 6th Gordons and 1st Loyal North Lancashire Regiment, with whom Wykehamist Major John Brownrigg was serving.

Late on the evening of February 3rd, enemy troops began to infiltrate between 1SG and the unit on their right. At 2330hrs, 6th Gordons came under attack. Enemy units also struck the positions at the tip of the salient. Shortly before midnight, the German artillery opened fire on the base of the salient. By dawn the enemy's intention was clear: a two-pronged assault from the west and east, aiming to capture the Factory-Carroceto area and thus to cut off the whole of 3 Brigade.

McMurtrie had arrived in the front line two days previously, joining 'B' Company as a Platoon Commander, and set out on patrol on the night of February 3rd. He was unfortunate in that his departure coincided with the onset of the German attack. McMurtrie was seriously wounded, and died shortly afterwards.[13]

McMurtrie.

* * *

Years before, in 1940, McMurtrie had mused on his own death in a poem included in *The Diary of a Heart:*

Death
I would not know my end,
  When I must die;
I would not wish to spend
  Last hours of misery.

But ere to my long home
  I take my way,
I know that I must climb
  The heights of ecstasy.

But I must go alone,
  For where I go
There is a beauty known
  That only few may know.

Only a few may live
  In that pure air;
But my whole life I'll give
  To be for a moment there.

For my life-blood will flow
  Warm in my veins;
And for a space I'll know
  What life and living means.

And then my heart's weak powers
  Will strain and give;
Man chokes his own life-fires
  When he has learned to live.

* * *

When the fighting subsided, McMurtrie's Company Commander, Captain Balfour, wrote to the family. His letter contains clear hints that casualties had been heavy.

> Dear Mrs McMurtrie,
> If this is a very poor effort, you must forgive me, but I find it very difficult to put on paper all the things I want to say. May I try on behalf of myself and the Company I command since John Tyldesley-Jones was killed [on January 27th], to tell you how deeply we feel for you in your bereavement and how sad we are to lose Duncan for ourselves. We had seen comparatively little of him lately, owing to his courses and going to hospital (with

malaria), but he had already endeared himself to the Company. He had only been in the line two days when he was killed out on patrol. He was out with one other man on a recce patrol and they ran into a German counter-attack just as they were going out. Those of us who are left will miss him very deeply.

With every sympathy,
Yours sincerely,
E. Balfour[14]

* * *

News of McMurtrie's death reached his family fairly swiftly. Sitting at his dining table in Hertfordshire in 2021, Duncan's younger brother Anthony recalled with absolute clarity the day in mid-February 1944 on which his mother told him the news:

> I absolutely hero-worshipped Duncan. I asked him for his autograph and used to polish his boots when he came home on leave. I remember that day as clearly as if it happened yesterday.
>
> At Marlborough we had central feeding, so there were something like five hundred boys all eating under one roof in a central feeding hall – and we also had the City of London School billeted on us, probably another four hundred boys, who had their meals at an earlier session. Anyway, I was having lunch, sitting with my friends on bench seats at long tables. And I looked up to see my housemaster bending over from the other side of the table.
>
> 'Hey, McMurtrie. I've got a very important telephone call coming this afternoon, but unfortunately I can't take it because I've got to go and play squash.'
>
> I thought this was a little strange.
>
> He said, 'Would you mind sitting in my study this afternoon and taking any message that comes through?'
>
> So I said, 'Yes, Sir, of course; yes.'
>
> Over I went to his study, which had a good selection of magazines – *The Field* and *Country Life* and a few other bits and bobs – and I was wading my way through these magazines when all of a sudden the telephone rang. So I lifted the handset and said, 'Hello, Mr Jennings' study.'
>
> And someone said, 'Hello', and he put the phone down.
>
> I thought, 'Oh my God, that's my father.' I recognized his voice. 'What on Earth is he doing, ringing me up here? What's going on?' So I couldn't work it out at all. I was very puzzled by this.
>
> And within ten minutes the door opened and in walked my mother and my housemaster. And she said, 'Darling, come, come and sit down,' and we sat on the sofa and she said, 'I'm terribly sorry to have to tell you that Duncan has been killed in Italy at Anzio. And I wanted to come down and tell you personally.'
>
> They worked it so that my housemaster took us down to his private house, where his wife laid on some tea for us. We had a cup of tea and a piece of cake, and then we got on the train at Marlborough, changing at Savernake. We got to Reading, and she was trying to get us a connection back to Paddington. Reading station was absolutely

jam-packed with troops, all with their packs on their backs and carrying kit-bags and rifles, and Lord knows what, and we could hardly move, there were so many – there were hundreds and hundreds of soldiers on Reading station. I can't imagine how we ever got as far as the barrier. But my mother pushed her way through the crowd to the barrier and leaned up to the ticket collector and whispered in his ear.

He said, 'This way, Madam; step this way. Stand back, you boys, stand back' – and we were suddenly through the barrier and on to the train to Paddington.

Eventually we arrived in Paddington, in the dark, in the blackout, trying to find her car, an Austin Seven. It had masks over the headlights, with just three or four slits in; because of the blackout side-lights were allowed, but headlights had to have this mask. She started to drive in the blackout through London, twenty-seven miles to St Ippolyts. Finally we got home. My father was waiting at the front door with the door open. My brother Peter was there; he'd been brought back from a local school where he'd been teaching on a temporary basis, having had a small operation. He went into the dining room for supper, and at that point, not until then, did my mother collapse and just sat on the floor and cried, and cried, and cried, and cried, and cried.

I've always thought, ever since then, what an incredibly brave performance it was on her part. It was really amazing what courage she summoned up in order to undertake that journey – not only the physical journey, but the emotional part. She was quite a tough woman, morally, physically, spiritually. She had driven an ambulance in the First World War for the British Red Cross, very near the front line – she told us that she had once eaten stewed cat – and in the early 1920s she played hockey for England, with some quite conspicuous success on their US tour, winning twelve matches out of twelve. She was quite determined that she was going to be the person who was going to tell me the bad news of Duncan's death, and to comfort me as required.

My father then had two nervous breakdowns. All he wanted to do was not to talk about Duncan; all my mother wanted to do was to talk about Duncan. He found it quite difficult. My mother persuaded our local GP, which in today's circumstances seems incredible, to drive her and my father up to a nursing home in North Wales, where he was – I suppose I could say 'detained' – for probably two weeks, and given treatment for his mental condition. He spent a lot of his time sending my mother telegrams – on average, two a day, sometimes three a day – saying, 'Let me out of here. I must come home.' I remember vividly my mother sitting down in front of the fireplace in the dining room, having just had breakfast, holding these telegrams in her hand. I was, I guess, sixteen, with my arms around her, trying to comfort her.

My other brother, Peter, unbelievably under the circumstances, had gone off to train in Canada with the Fleet Air Arm, which had the highest casualty rate of any of the Armed Services. So I was left on my tod to comfort and look after our mother, which was quite a challenge, as I recall. But we understood each other – we were really close – and it all worked out in the end. But it is quite vivid in my memory.

My mother and I visited Duncan's grave some years later. It was a trip organized by the British Legion for the relatives of the deceased. It wasn't a morbid occasion, more a reflective occasion. I know she found it very helpful to reconcile herself to the loss of her elder son. She was also greatly comforted by the thought that it was so beautifully maintained and the people were well remembered and due tribute had been paid to them. It was a comforting occasion for both of us, really. But my father didn't want to come, you know, because he'd had a second breakdown after the first one.

In St Ippolyts, there's a very old church, with one or two Roman bricks in the tower. The Chancel was more or less obscured from the congregation in the main part of the church by a fairly heavy rood screen, so my parents took it out, and moved it back to the access to the bell tower. It looks good there, and has the effect of opening up the Chancel to the congregation. They erected new choir stalls on both sides, and on the back end of the stalls, facing the altar, there's a small brass plaque saying that they were erected in memory of Duncan.

The other thing they did was to erect a sort of memorial, a sundial standing on top of a millstone, at the centre point of the kitchen garden, with paths running from it north, south, east, and west. Either side there were four rose beds which we planted up. That they also found comforting; not in any way morbid, but a pleasant memory, you know, something nice to look at.

QUOD ENIM IN ILLO AMABAM
NON PERIIT
OMNIA VINCIT AMOR

'For what I loved in him
has not died.
Love conquers everything.'

* * *

McMurtrie's father wrote to Robertson late in February:

My dear Robertson,
We thank you for your letter. Thank God he acquitted himself worthily leading a recce patrol in the very spearhead, when he ran into a heavy counter-attack and was seriously wounded. I judge he had just gone out and that they got him in, but our news is fragmentary and incomplete. The above is however correct as we received an air mail from his (recently appointed!) Company Commander Captain Eustace Balfour and saying that he had died of wounds. This was on February 2nd.

We are proud that he acquitted himself worthily in a cause which he (and we too) thought affected the whole future of the world. We will try to be worthy of his sacrifice and that of all his worthy brothers who have fallen in this war.

Yours was Duncan's second home and you saw as much or even more of him for some years than we did. You were dear to each other. You had a larger 'family' than us and we feel so very profoundly for you and your sister in this almost endless list of losses of your old house.

You, like us, did your best for Duncan. He had a happy life – we have nothing but happy memories. My wife is one of the really great women and is almost too wonderful. Peter and Anthony have been amazing. Peter never a tear. The worst of love and being such a united happy family is that it almost overpowers one.

You knew Duncan – his virtues and weaknesses. Well, he was dead keen to get into action – he never I think expected to come back – he fought the Medical Officers to get passed fit after malaria and jaundice (and he still wasn't 100%). He would have wished no better end. He was a keen soldier and knew no fear. He would have no regrets – so why should we?

I am in rather a selfish mood, however, having had my gall-bladder and a large stone removed which left me in a sorry state – i.e. reaction from shock.

You or I must tell Michael Binns, who is also out there. They were very great friends.

I have written at great length as you said you would like to hear any news we could give you.

You will not misunderstand if I quote from a letter of August 1943 from his Battalion Commander to a mutual friend. We are not repeating it to anyone but you.

'Duncan McMurtrie is a charming boy and an extremely efficient officer. He came out here to this Battalion with a good reputation and he is certainly living up to it. For one so young he is extremely serious at his job and stands no nonsense from anybody. In fact, I like him.'

Thank you for all you have done.

With our kindest regards to your sister and yourself.

Yrs,

Donald McMurtrie[15]

* * *

'You or I must tell Michael Binns. They were very great friends' – but that is not how Elliott-Binns discovered that his beloved friend was dead. He wrote:

Because I was frequently up at observation posts I shared the more dangerous and uncomfortable life of the infantry, and they had my admiration and devotion. I had one specially poignant reason for this devotion … While I had taken on what could be expected to be the rather unheroic option of a gunner officer, Duncan had joined the Scots Guards. As a child I feared going to school. Growing to be a man I feared having to fight. Duncan looked forward to it as fulfilment. He was not to know anything beyond. I survived this period of desperate fighting. My Winchester friend did not.

Some weeks later the Scots Guards, which, like all the Division's battalions, had suffered heavily, were out of the line resting. I met one of their officers and asked where Duncan was, so that I could go and see him. He told me that he had been killed a few days after landing on the beach-head. His body lay in the Anzio Military Cemetery, and all I could do was to go and weep for him there … an expedition of private grief … The graves consist of rows of little rectangles of parched earth, each with a white cross above it. They lie under the high wall of the civilian cemetery with its dark cypresses and shrine. On the other side you look over the roofs of Anzio to the sea. When you in England look at the sea, your minds go out to all the continents and islands spread over the globe which lie beyond it. It is different for us. Our hearts travel westward, through the Mediterranean, past the Straits of Gibraltar, over the great waves of the Bay of Biscay, to England. Somehow home seems much closer by the sea. I am glad that these men, some of whom I know, lie there. They seem to be buried on the doorstep of their home. I think I had just about completely forgotten life in England and my home … My friend … linked Anzio and England in a way that was real to me then.

While I was a soldier I wrote one poem only, that entitled 'Anzio Military Cemetery', where my Winchester friend, who was killed a couple of miles from me and whom I never saw since the day we left Cambridge together, was buried:

Outside the civilian cemetery
   With its cypresses and shrines
The pitiful rectangles of dust
   Are dressed in their military lines.

As I search for a name, the crosses
   Grow roots under my feet,
Branching out in innumerable
   Tendrils of private grief.

Death continually weaves his web
   Between the sun and our eyes,
And bars of sorrow shadow the face
   Of others as well as mine.

Silent and tall are the cypresses
   On the other side of the wall.
Perhaps in the depths of their dark hearts
   Hides the reason for it all.

I return through the woods. The sunlight
  Fumbles the top of the trees,
And I feel like searchlights the hostile eyes
  Ceaselessly sweeping the leaves.

And softly the sun goes down in gold,
  And softly the evening falls,
And the stars come out, my comfort,
  But they aren't any comfort at all.

Elliott-Binns returned to Cambridge after the war, and at first his poetry was all about McMurtrie.

I never met you after all.
Our interweaving threads were traced
Across the Mediterranean map,
And still fate cheated us with small
Discrepancies of time and place.
The bullet crossed, and your thread snapped,
Somewhere past Carroceto, where,
Distorted into symbols, farms
Crumble to attitudes of harm,
And death weighs down the air.

And my regret that in my shells'
Saunter or shriek above your head
No word of comfort might be said.
Nor could the bush of smoke unfold
Its insubstantial foliage,
Rising from seeds of iron, to tell
All that my tongue has left untold.
Nor craters on the lettered page
Of pockmarked countrysides indent
Some message to be permanent.

The watchers pace the towers above
The yearning of my starving city,
Their expectation all in vain
For glimpses of your drowning sail.
No more will your excess of love
Within my harbour-wall's embrace
Find haven from unsatisfied
Search of earth for resting place.
My heart for its renewal cries.
O pardon my self-pity.

It was part of the grieving process, a catharsis: Elliott-Binns wrote that he 'needed to face the past before I could fully turn my attention to my future'. The following is his last poem about his friend.

> Dust unto dust. The sons of Adam die.
> The autumn winds bear unresisting leaves,
> And horror's hold grows tight. Your wounds break raw
> Over my face. Blood on my lips.
> Blood out of bodies, water into ships,
> And earth turns on. O mountainous my grief.
> The granite rocks that heavenward I heave
> Splinter to rocks I fall on. Outward reach
> The blind hands, close on darkness, utter void.
> O mine my lost one, brother of my soul,
> Submissive heir, whose wounds succeed
> To legacies the spear-struck side bequeathed,
> The body broken, making others whole,
> Let me go down to find you, let me seek
> The vein's tide back to heart, not strive
> To force the drag of whirl-pools. Walls sweat drops,
> Pain's channel narrows, gathers to feet and hours,
> And darkness arches over. Poison draws
> Down tortured limbs remorselessly, and nerves
> Are tattered pennants streaming down the storm.
> The earth is stilled. Time's moment culminates
> To death and birth. Torn hands on trap-door heave.
> The body shudders, trembling on light's verge.

* * *

It is a measure of the man Robertson was that he wrote in February 1944 to Anthony McMurtrie as well as to Duncan's parents, even though Anthony was at Marlborough College and not a Wykehamist (though, of course, Robertson had also attended Marlborough). Anthony was amazed when his own reply to Robertson surfaced seventy years later:

> Dear Major Robertson,
> Thank-you very much for your nice letter. It was very nice of you to think of writing to me, even tho' we have never met, just because I was Duncan's younger brother.
>
> I have given Mr Jennings your message and he says that he expects and hopes to see you next Saturday.
>
> On viewing the situation, I agree with you that it is up to Peter and I (perhaps as I am still at school, more particularly me) to try our utmost to do well and to endeavour to fill so large a blank.
>
> You can have no idea how comforting it is to hear such a good reputation being revealed. In conclusion may I quote a piece about him out of a local paper, which makes

me feel prouder than I was before; it runs: 'He died the noblest death a man may die, fighting for God and right and Liberty; and such a death is immortality.'

Very many thanks for your advice.

Yours sincerely,

Anthony McMurtrie[16]

Duncan's mother wrote:

Dear Bobber,

Forgive the slip but you have been 'the Bobber' to us unofficially for so many years.

How kind and thoughtful to let us see Duncan's letter and poem – which I return. I had seen the latter before and some day I will send you extracts from some of his overseas mail to us as I know you will like to see how he evolved. Just at the moment I don't feel up to looking through such letters.

I am trying to carry on my Red Cross work, which daily increases in spite of a staff of seven, but I fear I am working very automatically and feel rather like a chicken running about after its head has been cut off. Still I feel one just must carry on until the job he gave his life for is well and truly completed.

Very sincerely yours,

Margaret McMurtrie[17]

* * *

At daybreak on February 4th, German infantry, supported by tanks and self-propelled guns, broke through the left flank of 1IG and reached the Campoleone–Nettuno railway, parallel to the *Via Anziate*. Later it became evident that the more serious threat was to the east flank. At 0725hrs at least six enemy tanks overran a company of 6th Gordons and established themselves on a small ridge just east of the main road. German infantry poured in behind the tanks, anti-tank guns were brought up, and additional tanks completed the isolation of 3 Brigade.

However, during the afternoon enemy attacks petered out in the face of stubborn British resistance, supported by accurate artillery fire. At 1600hrs, a counter-attack by fresh units inflicted heavy losses on the enemy, who were forced to fall back. However, 1st Division was now clearly on the defensive and its over-extended line was too exposed. Over 1,400 men had been killed, wounded or were missing; of those, more than 900 had been taken prisoner. 1st Division retired to a shorter, more defensible line about a mile north of Carroceto and the Factory.

The enemy had also suffered heavily, with some 500 killed and 300 captured. They undertook no large-scale attack for three days, but subjected every part of the beach-head to shelling from long-range guns as well as air attack. With his Troop of 29 Battery, Elliott-Binns experienced far worse than most artillery units:

The Germans had built up their forces, repulsed the Allied attacks with heavy losses, and went into the offensive themselves. It seemed virtually certain that the small Allied force would be driven into the sea. The infantry were withering away and the gunners had to fire continually to break up attacks. We were credited with saving the beach-head.

Inevitably, we became primary targets for the enemy artillery, and my Troop on the right was exposed. In five days I lost nineteen of my twenty-four gunners, but my command post was not hit. As the officer in charge it was necessary for me to walk round the position from gun-pit to gun-pit when I was not firing, while others could keep their heads down …

During that week I had an experience unlike that of any junior Gunner officer I have heard of. In open warfare, such as in the African desert, a troop could be over-run, but I have never heard of one suffering casualties of that kind through continual shelling. The consequences for me were psychologically overwhelming. I had fulfilled my childhood dream of becoming something of a school-boy hero, because I was still only twenty. My Troop and I had become fused together, and I stayed with them till I was demobilised. Near the end of the campaign, a senior Subaltern who had been wounded returned, and logically had to take over my position. My Troop Commander kept him at the wagon lines till the campaign was over. While it lasted, the Troop was mine. Everything except Anzio and my Troop that I adored had dropped away from me.

I was second-in-command of my Troop, but the second-in-command has authority over the gun position, while the Troop Commander is available for the responsible and dangerous job of manning observation posts with the infantry. At Anzio, my Troop lost seven officers senior to myself, two of them killed, a fantastic level of casualties. For much of the time I was holding both top jobs in my Troop and was commended for my work with the infantry. My men thought I should have had some kind of recognition, but I think to the Regimental authorities I was an inexplicable phenomenon, to be watched with mild apprehension. There was a sense in which I was fighting a different war to the one they were fighting. But my Troop, in spite of its casualties, did its work fast and effectively.

The war diary records:

February 4th
Gun areas harassed; one gun of 96/97 Battery hit. Other Ranks 1 killed, 2 wounded. 3 Other Ranks also wounded by shelling. Captain J.E. Aitchison RA killed by shell at 'F' Troop line maintenance post.

February 5th
Wagon-line area machine-gunned. Major R.S. Streatfeild MC, RA, and 4 Other Ranks wounded. Gun areas harassed intermittently. Direct hit on 39 Battery Command Post. Lieutenant A.F.C. Carpenter RA died of wounds, Lieutenant A.J. Alcock RA wounded, and 4 Other Ranks wounded. Captain L.A.J. Richardson RA wounded in OP.

February 7th
Owing to casualties to men, and guns out of action due to faulty packings, 'A' and 'B' Troops of 29 Battery were combined into a composite Troop … Major F.T. Mills RA and Captain B. Carlin RA and 3 Other Ranks missing.

February 8th
39 Field Battery shelled and one gun hit. Lieutenant G.E. Bartlett RA and 8 Other Ranks wounded. Lieutenant R.A. Crossland RA wounded in OP.

After the losses sustained in the fighting at Campoleone, the units of 1st Division were considerably below strength; fighting in rain, mud, and near-freezing temperatures, they had had very little rest since landing. West of the *Via Anziate,* Buonriposo Ridge was held by 2 North Staffs, 5 Grenadier Guards, and 1SG. The centre was held by 168 Brigade; 2 Brigade held the east flank.

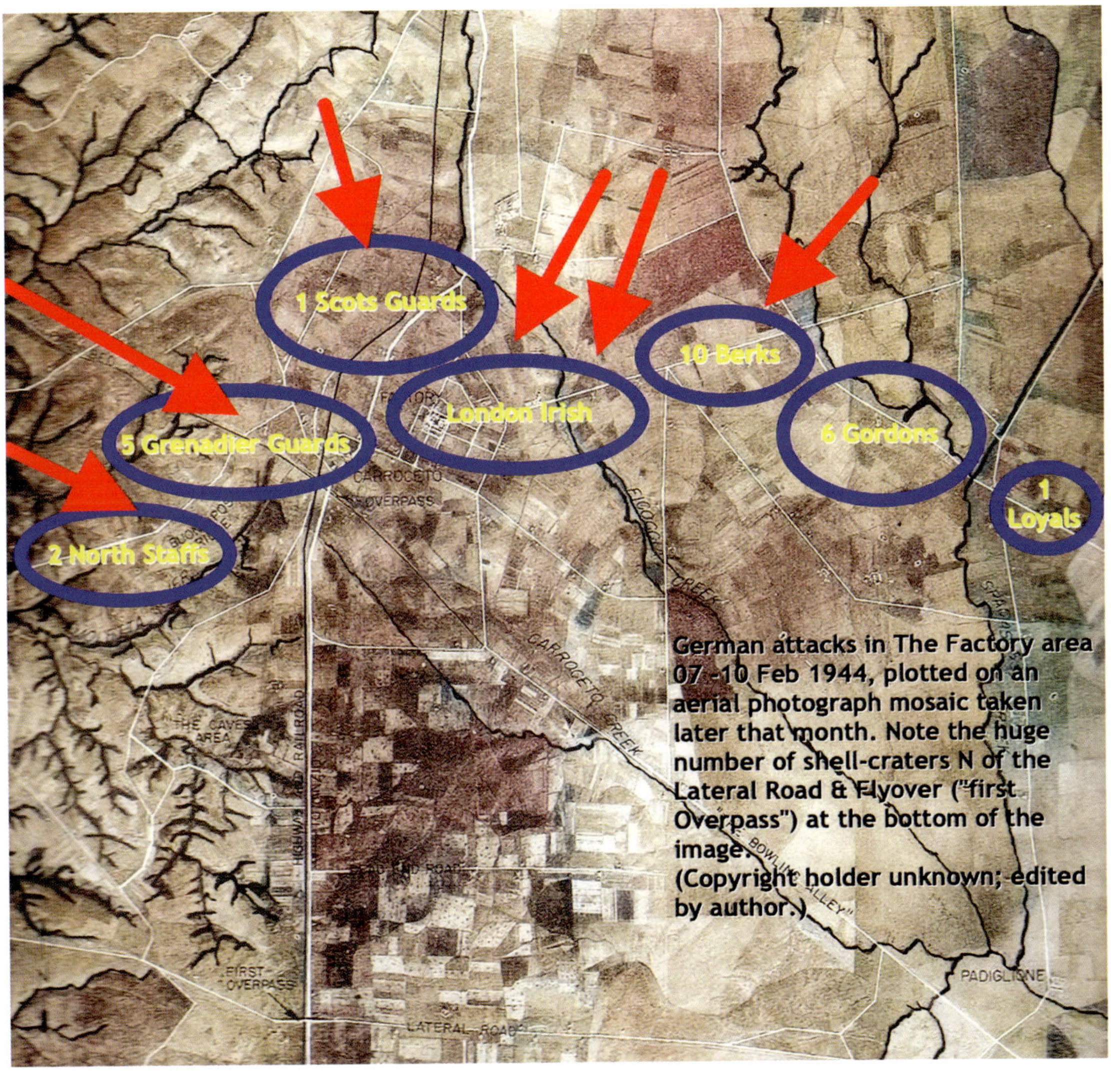

German attacks in The Factory area 07 -10 Feb 1944, plotted on an aerial photograph mosaic taken later that month. Note the huge number of shell-craters N of the Lateral Road & Flyover ("first Overpass") at the bottom of the image. (Copyright holder unknown; edited by author.)

On the night of February 7th/8th German units attacked from the east and west, converging on Carroceto and the Factory. By midnight the attack along the Buonriposo Ridge was general; slipping through the darkness and the many deep '*wadis*' west of the *Via Anziate,* small but heavily-armed groups of Germans hooked round behind the forward British units, cut communications, and set up strongpoints. Whenever the defenders ran low on ammunition, the main enemy force would attempt to overrun the position. It was in this fashion that 2 North Staffs were isolated and overwhelmed. Elliott-Binns was with them:

> I was sent up to an observation post with the forward infantry, an experience for which I had had no real preparation. It's queer the thoughts that come to one in the most trying situations. That evening I decided to deepen the trench I was going to watch from when it became light. I went up with one of my men and a pick and shovel. We set to work. The ground seemed to be solid rock, and each blow of the pick seemed to dislodge no more than a few grains of dust. We were just talking together about whether to give the job up, when without warning a German attack came in, a major attack, centred on 'my' battalion, which they overwhelmed. I do not know what their strength was, but they outnumbered us horribly, and it was no discredit to the infantry that they pushed us back. I was right forward and had a very sticky night of it. But every now and then, when things were at their worst, I kept thinking, 'Well, anyway, I won't have to carry on digging that damned slit trench. That's one comfort.' They captured my Battery Commander at headquarters. I managed to ditch my truck, which was hemmed in, and escape on foot with my three men and such equipment as we could carry, and arrived back at the gun position.

By 0130hrs the Germans were pushing forwards along the Buonriposo Ridge from 2 North Staffs' former positions, and 1SG were facing attacks from the north and south-west. Some enemy units managed to reach the *Via Anziate,* and all morning the Germans pushed hard towards Carroceto and the Factory. But as the day wore on, the Germans concentrated on digging in along the Buonriposo Ridge, giving 1SG valuable breathing space. Their war diary reported what happened next:

> 1400
> After MG and artillery fire, Right Flank send one platoon to mop up enemy at 865337 and take nineteen prisoners-of-war from I/725 *Grenadier* Regiment. Captain J.H.L. Sinclair killed on return – only casualty.[18]

The day after Sinclair's death, his batman, Guardsman Raeburn, wrote to Sinclair's parents:

> Dear Mr and Mrs Sinclair,
> I expect you will have already heard the very sad news about your son's death. Seeing that I was his batman I feel it is my duty to let you know something about his death. It happened yesterday morning, Tuesday February 8th, at 1100hrs; only two days before that he had been promoted to the rank of Captain.
>
> He went out yesterday morning with a Platoon of men to round up some Germans who had been causing us some trouble all the night before. He was very successful in the attack and succeeded in bringing in some twenty prisoners. He was killed by an enemy machine-gun when only a few yards from safety; later on in the day we got the machine-gunner who was responsible for his death.

It isn't easy for me to write this letter, as your son was far more to me than just an officer; he was a perfect gentleman. He was the one I went to if anything went wrong. Now that he has gone I seem to have no one out here with me; my life seems very empty.

I came out of the line last night to get your son's kit fixed up ready to send home. This I did today: the cigarette lighter, his wallet with some money and photographs, cigarette case, and Army book was handed to the Captain Quartermaster today. You should receive same in due course. I don't know whether he told you or not, but his wrist watch and personal revolver were lost early in the campaign.

Well, friends, on behalf of the boys in the Company we send our heartfelt sympathy for your great loss, as Captain Sinclair was greatly respected and admired by all.

Yours in deep sympathy,
Gdsm. Raeburn R.[19]

* * *

Simpkin's grandmother was still in regular communication with Robertson, who wrote to her with the news; she replied on February 24th:

Dear Major Robertson,
I am indeed grieved to hear of John Sinclair's death – I had not heard. I was very fond of him – and at one time saw a great deal of him and had such a nice long letter from him at Christmas and a card – Richard will be very sorry; he always asks for all his friends and for you and Sheila – I have just had a letter written December 26th and a card dated January 12th – in both he says he is very fit – oh dear, when will this awful war finish?[20]

* * *

Elliott-Binns was back in action very soon:

It's surprising how many animals you find up in the front line. The day following I watched the enemy lines from the upper floor of the farmhouse which was the battalion command post, I think as the only way of giving me something of a rest, as the enemy were too far away for me to see anything significant. After a time I looked down to rest my eyes. Below me I saw two oxen. One of them was flat on its side, obviously dead. The other was lying beside it munching a pile of hay. Every now and then it would turn to look at its companion. It seemed to be waiting for it to get up. I had been through quite a tough time those last few days, and I thought I was pretty hardened. But there was something about that sight which went right to my heart, and I said to myself out loud, 'It's a bloody war. It really is a bloody war.'

His jottings at Anzio are undated but give vivid snapshots of his experiences in the line alongside the infantry, as well as in the gun positions and in the rear areas – they contrast sharply with the stark entries in the Regimental war diary.

War is not a bit as one imagines. Only once have I felt that I was at war, the war of the cinema and books. I was crossing a mine-field with my Major. We were some 300 yards behind our forward positions. Suddenly a flare went up from the German lines. It hung intensely bright in the sky, and we went flat on our faces. I looked round and saw some barbed wire close by, silhouetted against the glare, so clearly that I could make out each spike. Just that, and the two bodies hunched on the ground, and a mortar bomb burst ahead of us as the landscape began to darken.

February 9th
Intermittent shelling of Battery areas. FW190s machine-gunned battery areas. 1 Other Rank wounded. Lieutenant J. Dawes RA and 1 Other Rank wounded at OP.

* * *

As German pressure built on February 9th, 1SG had taken the decision to withdraw Weir's Right Flank Company and 'C' Company closer to the railway bridge; but before they could move, the Germans launched a strong attack from the Factory.

February 10th, 0030hrs
Attack reaches Regimental Aid Post (867328). Captain J. Hamilton (Padre) and Captain G.S. Hodge (MO) taken prisoner. One tank reaches station and shoots it up. Lieutenant-Colonel D.S. Wedderburn leaves Battalion HQ to make tank-destroyers and Troop 46 RTR (in support) take decisive action …

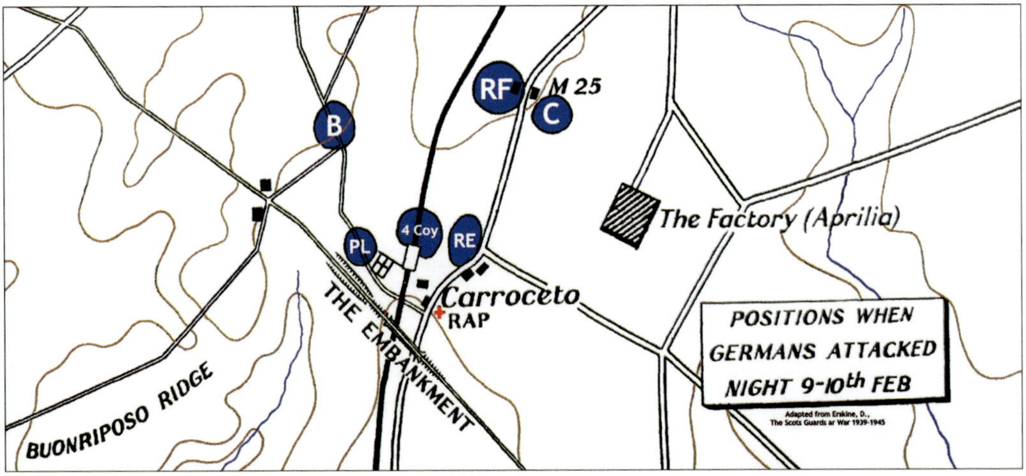

0400hrs
… and returns having met with little success.

Scrymgeour-Wedderburn was a superb Battalion Commander; he always wore a beret, never a helmet, and carried his deer-stalking stave as though he were merely out for a walk in the hills rather than leading hundreds of men into battle.

0430hrs
'C' Company ordered to withdraw behind railway bed embankment, Right Flank to 866331.

0500hrs
Move successfully completed …

0515hrs
Assumed that 'B' Company is over-run, touch having been lost for some time.

Back at the gun lines, 19 Field continued to respond to calls for assistance from the infantry. The Royal Artillery had by now developed sophisticated fire plans, some of which had specific code-names. A 'Mike' target was an emergency call for the fire of a whole Field Regiment (twenty-four guns) to be directed on one grid reference. An 'Uncle' target was a call for the fire of a division's three artillery regiments – seventy-two 25-pounders – to be unleashed on the specified co-ordinates immediately. In an emergency, a Forward Observation Officer like Elliott-Binns could on his own initiative summon an 'Uncle' fire mission by simply calling, 'Uncle Target' and the desired grid reference. Still more spectacular was a 'Victor' target, which involved the guns of an entire Army Corps – essentially, every gun in the Anzio beach-head. The nature of targets can suggest when the fighting was especially fierce: Elliott-Binns' Regiment were involved in 'Mike' and 'Uncle' fire missions on February 4th and 5th, an 'Uncle' on the 7th, two 'Victor' shoots on the 10th, an 'Uncle' on the 12th (which reconnaissance later suggested had killed 40–50 Germans), a 'Victor' on the 15th, three 'Victor' shoots on the 17th and again on the 18th, and the last 'Victor' of the month on February 28th.

February 10th
'Victor' targets fired on 'Factory' at 0520hrs and 1115 hrs. Captain B. Blunt RA killed at OP. 4 Other Ranks wounded.

1SG continued their dogged withdrawal to the safety of the embankment.

0700hrs
Sortie by tanks and tank-destroyers through bridge. Under cover of this diversion, 25 men of Right Flank and one Platoon 23 Field Company, Royal Engineers, withdraw behind embankment.

> 0830hrs
> Second sortie by tanks.
>
> Persistent shelling causes heavy casualties during the remainder of the day.
>
> 2100hrs
> Relief of 5th Grenadier Guards and 1SG by 1DWR commences.
>
> February 11th, 0300hrs
> Whole Battalion has arrived at 'A' Echelon. Battalion re-organized with one Rifle Company.

19 Field Regiment gave valuable support to the infantry despite German attempts to suppress their devastating fire.

> February 11th
> Anti-personnel bombs dropped in Regimental area during night. Mortaring and shelling of battery areas. 3 Other Ranks wounded. Captain R.V. Casebourne RA wounded in OP. 4 other Other Ranks wounded.
>
> February 12th
> Anti-personnel bombs dropped during night on RHQ area... Enemy propaganda leaflets scattered on 29 Field Battery position by shell. Harassing of battery areas by artillery and mortars continued.
>
> February 13th
> Anti-personnel bombs dropped on 29 Field Battery position. 29 Battery machine-gunned – 4 Other Ranks wounded.

* * *

At the Minturno on the Gustav Line, a further Allied offensive planned for the night of February 8th was called off as 56th Division was urgently needed at Anzio. Brooke and 16th/5th Lancers were therefore kept in place to hold the line. There was heavy shelling from time to time, some of which caused casualties, but there they stayed until the end of February – 'We spent the first months up at Minturno doing purely an anti-tank role.'[21]

* * *

Murray.

Meanwhile, in the Canadian Rocky Mountains, the Lovat Scouts were training for mountain warfare. Charles Murray's father wrote to Robertson on February 13th with his news:

> Charles has been asking for Winchester news once or twice recently from his temporary 'habitat' in Western Canada! ... I have no idea where the Scouts are off to next but they are now ready (I gather) to fight at

the 10,000ft level, by rope or ski, and longing to get on with the job. So far, Charles has only had one rock on his head which, being as hard as ever, resulted in only eight stitches being required and a nasty headache![22]

* * *

After a brief rest, 1SG were warned on February 13th to be prepared to go back into the line – which had by now been pushed back nearly as far as the Flyover. Their orders put them at one hour's notice to move, suggesting that the situation was very touch-and-go. They were not called upon immediately, however, and the next day they managed to assemble two Rifle Companies. They also received a visit from General Alexander,[23] who spoke to all the officers and senior NCOs. It was the prelude to a move forwards to the Flyover, where 1SG started to dig in and erect barbed wire at 0230 on February 15th.

The enemy meanwhile kept up the pressure on the British artillery positions:

February 14th
Slight harassing fire from 88mm on 'D' Troop 39 Battery.

February 15th
88mm harassed 'D' Troop 39 Battery again.

February 16th
Anti-personnel bombs dropped on battery areas during night and on RHQ in daylight. Major O.C.H. Burton RA wounded by spent bullet from enemy aircraft – later died of wounds. Regimental area harassed by enemy artillery – 5 Other Ranks wounded.

The Flyover, Anzio, from the Allied side. (Copyright holder unknown; edited by author)

A fresh German attack was expected, but before it arrived 1SG were relieved and went out of the line again.

The storm broke the next morning, February 18th. The Germans were less than a mile from the Allied gun lines in the Padiglione Woods, and once under the cover of those woods they would have freedom of movement to annihilate the beach-head. The Allied troops were exhausted. Only the Flyover and the positions along the embankments to either side of it stood between the Germans and victory. The key position was held by 1 Loyals.

At dawn, from the direction of 'Dead-End Road', the Germans attacked across open fields. The morning mist concealed their approach, and a platoon of 'B' Company, 1 Loyals, sheltering in waterlogged trenches from a hail of mortar rounds, was overrun by what eye-witnesses described as a wall of men throwing stick-grenades. At 0730hrs the German attack switched to Wykehamist Major John Brownrigg's 'A' Company, closest to the Flyover itself. Brownrigg was killed, but his Company held its positions.[24]

Over the next fourteen hours the Flyover was subjected to attacks by the equivalent of five brigades of infantry, supported by tanks. Most of those fifteen battalions focused their efforts on 1 Loyals. The divisional history later recorded that in the afternoon of February 18th

> waves of German infantry poured across the open ground below the Dead End Road, only to meet a veritable hail of artillery, mortar, and machine-gun fire. The enemy suffered appalling casualties, yet there appeared to be no limit to his resources in manpower, and whenever a German soldier fell, there always seemed to be another to take his place.[25]

Some of the attackers reached the 'Lateral Road' – the track which crossed the Flyover – and a small party even crossed the embankment and occupied a house south of the British line. The desperate fighting was hand-to-hand. But by 2130hrs there was evidence that the enemy was pulling back to reorganize.

* * *

At 0430hrs on February 19th the Germans made one last attempt to break through the Loyals at the Flyover, but artillery fire smashed the attack: 'February 19th. "Uncle" targets fired on attack on 1 Loyals position … Gun areas bombed – no damage.'

Two hours later, an Allied counter-attack pushed the Germans back a mile. The Flyover had held; the Germans were unable to mount another major attack in the three months following; and thus the beach-head had been saved. Just.

For that day, 1SG's war diary recorded only the laconic 'Strong attack on 1 Loyals held. Turning point in battle.'

After February 20th, the front remained static until May 1944. The fighting, however, continued. Anzio was not finished with Hopper's yet.

* * *

The artillery had played a huge role in breaking up the German attacks, and Elliott-Binns had been a busy man. Official records suggest that he was wounded on February 18th, but neither he nor the war diary make any reference to it.

> He lifted the tarpaulin for a moment, and I saw him. His head, shoulders and arms were silhouetted black against the canvas. I phoned back fire orders and waited breathlessly for the first round. Our own troops were desperately close and I was afraid it might fall short. There was a whistle, and a cloud of black smoke rose only a hundred yards from the target. A second later came the bang. My third round was almost a direct hit. I put down eight more and had the satisfaction of seeing bits of tarpaulin flying in the air. Then one man ran out of the trench and disappeared over the crest. Five minutes later stretcher bearers approached under a Red Cross. They removed two bodies and disappeared. For a moment I was triumphant, and then like cold water other thoughts came to me, and I shivered. It was the first time I looked upon men I had killed. A week later I heard that the enemy had dropped a mortar bomb on the trench where I had been, and killed two men.

> February 20th
> Anti-personnel bombs dropped in gun areas. Slight harassing fire on battery areas. 29 Battery Command Post received direct hit – Lieutenant O.M. Gould RA and 9 Other Ranks wounded.

> February 21st
> Gun areas harassed – 1 gun 29 Battery hit; slit trench 39 Battery hit – 4 Other Ranks killed. Lieutenant J.J.L. Bell RA wounded in OP.

> 'Hi, where are you going to? Are you an officer?' It was the Military Policeman outside the town of Anzio who was speaking. I didn't answer him. I was thinking. I thought of the ruined houses round the Flyover Bridge near which I had been the day before at an Observation Post. I thought of the MP who had given me cigarettes and an orange, when I went to him for help, dirty and unshaven, because my truck was blocked by a three-tonner slewed across the track, with the driver dead beside it. I thought of Duncan and the others lying very still a few hundred yards from us on the hill … The MP looked queerly at the strange-looking untidy officer who would not answer him. Didn't he understand English? 'Where are your badges of rank?' he said.

* * *

Finch.

Micky Finch had left Hopper's late in 1941 and taken his War Degree in Classics at Corpus Christi College, Oxford. After OCTU, in September 1943 he had been commissioned into the Suffolk Regiment,[26] but was now serving with 2/7th Queen's Royal Regiment (West Surrey). He had left England in January, arrived in Naples, joined his new Battalion on February 4th, been posted to 'A' Company on February 6th, and landed at Anzio at 0800hrs on February 18th.

Initially positioned as a counter-attack force south of the Flyover, 2/7th Queen's were soon given a much more perilous mission. North-west of the Flyover, an American unit – 2nd Battalion, 157th Infantry Regiment – had since February 16th been holding the '*wadis*', preventing the Germans from widening the scope of their major attack. Despite valiant resistance, 2/157th had been driven into a smaller and smaller perimeter centred on a natural fortress, a series of caves in a *wadi* wall. The Germans and Americans were intermingled, and on the night of the 18th the enemy were close enough to throw hand grenades into the cave containing the battalion command post. 2/157th called for artillery fire on their own position, which drove the enemy away sufficiently for supplies to be brought up. On the following night, a hundred wounded were evacuated. But 2/157th were exhausted and if their position – 'The Caves' – fell, the stand of 1 Loyals at the Flyover would have been in vain.

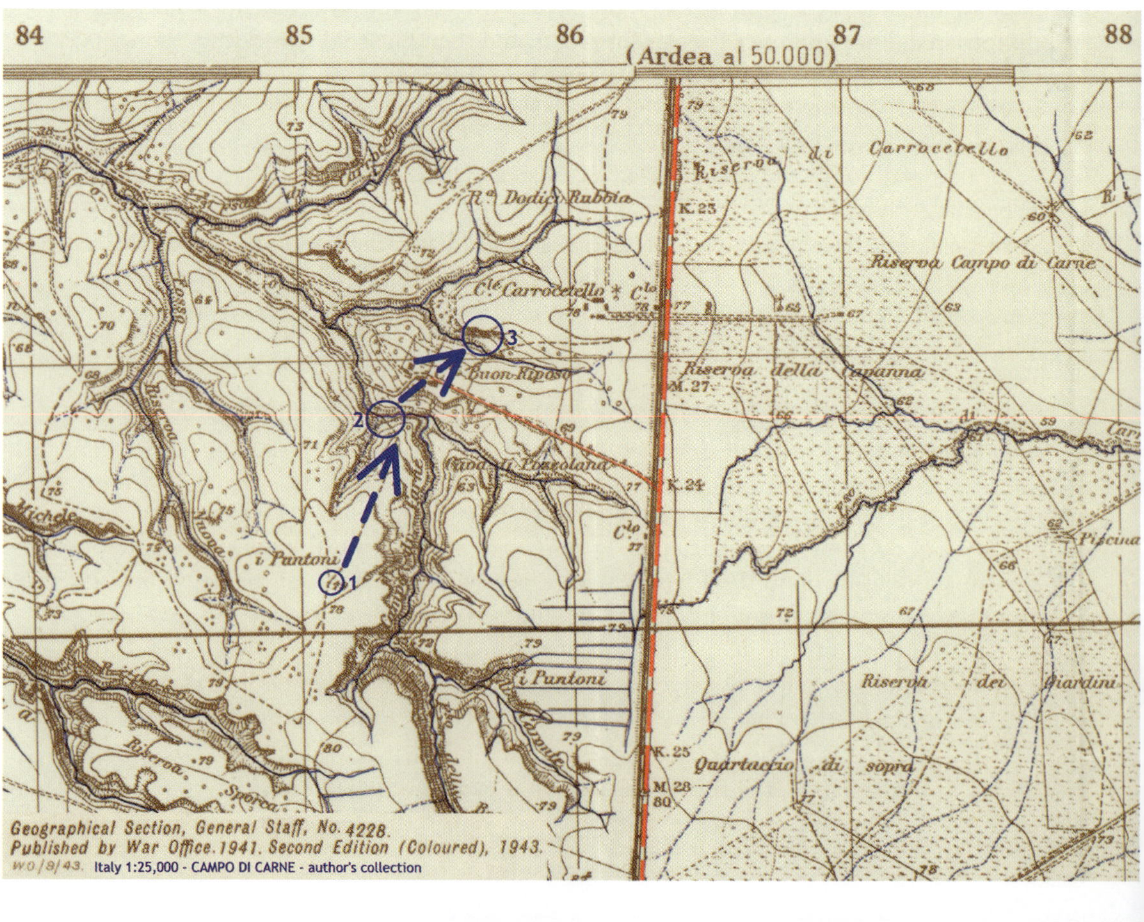

Italy 1:25,000 - CAMPO DI CARNE - author's collection

2/7th Queens had been selected to take over The Caves, and moved off at 1800hrs on February 21st. The war diary[27] describes their night in bald terms, but in sufficient detail for their movements to be plotted on the ground:

> 1930hrs
> 'D' and 'C' companies deployed to left and right respectively, area 851302 [area 1 on map] to secure wadi crossing at 853308 [area 2 on map].
>
> 2030hrs
> Crossing secure, 'B' and 'A' companies begin to pass through. Air raid in progress.

The Battalion history records, 'We ran into trouble from the start … Even to reach the positions involved considerable fighting.'[28]

> 2040hrs
> Whole load of anti-personnel bombs dropped on crossing. Fairly heavy casualties suffered, mainly amongst portering party who were bringing up the rear of the column, but including 'A' Company Commander (Lieutenant Heald) killed and 'D' Company Commander (Major Domoney) wounded.
>
> 'D' and 'A' companies push on and reach HQ of 2/157th, situated at 857311 in caves [area 3 on map], after overcoming some opposition. Four prisoners of war taken; identifications 3 and 5 companies 1027 *Panzer Grenadier* Reinforcement Battalion. 'B' Company pass through tunnel to take up their positions in area 857303. 'A' Company retained in HQ area for defence of the large number of cave entrances.

Owing to the trouble on the way in, 2/7th Queen's – already under strength – had suffered some seventy casualties and lacked supplies, ammunition, or heavy weapons. The latter problem was solved by taking over the Americans' weapons, but ammunition for these was low. 'D' Company moved east to bar approach from the *Via Anziate*; 'C' took up position to the south; and 'B' were to the north. The Battalion's official history is typically British in its leavening of gentle humour when describing the unimaginable chaos of the battle: 'In the caves we found many seriously wounded Americans, while huddled in the back galleries were about thirty Italian refugees – men, women, and children – and one large, very bad tempered pig.'

Although the Americans were keen to be gone, 'the situation everywhere was incredibly confused and we kept coming across Germans in all sorts of unexpected places'. 2/157th therefore sat tight for a further twenty-four hours.

Problems were multiplying. By 0500hrs on February 22nd it was clear that 'D' Company, closest to the road, had been over-run by the enemy. Although the day was quiet, and 2/157th managed to slip away that night, the Germans attacked 'C' Company at 0700hrs on February 23rd. Faced with flame-throwers and out of ammunition, the survivors of 'C' Company were forced to capitulate. 'B' Company were next, but instead of surrendering they managed to retire into the caves along with 'A' Company. The Germans kept the defenders away from the mouths of the caves by dropping hand grenades from above, and brought up three tanks to pound the entrances from only 200 yards away, 'making a great deal of noise which was increased by lusty protestations from the pig and the only slightly less discordant wailing of its owners'.

One wonders whether Finch was in the same cave as the pig.

The commanding officer – Lieutenant Colonel Baynes – dealt with the threat by calling down an 'Uncle' target on to his own position. By 1400hrs the German threat was considerably diminished, their only movement being stretcher-bearers rescuing the wounded.

> We had now had no food or water for nearly 24 hours, and the CO gave permission for half the emergency ration to be eaten. Those of us who had previously tried this obnoxious mixture – tasting like dessicated ammunition boots, sawdust, and dried mud – preferred to remain hungry. Those whose first experience of it this was were not long in hoping it would be their last.

At 1630hrs orders came to withdraw. The remnants of 2/7th Queen's awaited nightfall anxiously, troubled only by a German attempt to sneak in to the caves from the rear. The first party of fifteen set out at 1845hrs, immediately preceded by another 'Uncle' shoot on the area. When the Germans realized what was going on, 'all hell broke loose, and the parties had to split up in all directions. Suddenly there were Germans everywhere ...'

When Baynes reached safety late that night he found that from his entire Battalion he had a total of just three officers and seventeen men. In the space of three days, 2/7th Queen's had lost 362 men killed, wounded, and missing. Many of these had been taken prisoner, but how many was unknown.

Finch was one of those missing. After all his training, his fighting career had lasted a week.

* * *

Elliott-Binns wrote:

> I had been in the line with the infantry and was driving back in my Jeep to the guns. It was a misty night, and vehicles were hopelessly bogged down all along the narrow muddy track. As we were passing an Advanced Dressing Station an orderly called to us and asked if we would take two infantrymen who had fallen out from the march back to their transport. I managed to squeeze them in, one by the driver and the other at the back with me perched up beside him. He was a nice young fellow and easy to talk to. His voice – which was the only physical attribute I could tell – was pleasant. The Jeep was nosing its way forward, sometimes almost sticking in the mud, and twice it nearly overturned. Yet I felt extraordinarily happy and loving to all the world, particularly the infantryman happy beside me. I had my arm on his shoulder to support myself and the feel was comforting. Yet it was not just he himself personally. He had changed from a

normal pleasant acquaintance into a symbol of that body of men whom I honour and admire and pity more than any others, the British infantry.

* * *

The news that their son was missing reached Finch's father and mother on the evening of March 6th. As usual, on hearing of their loss, the parents immediately felt compelled to tell Robertson.

My dear Bobber,
I begin thus as Micky always called you this.

I am writing to tell you that last evening about 1900hrs we had a War Office telegram to say our Michael was missing since February 29th in Italy. We had had a letter from him during the morning written on February 13th. It was the fourth since he left early in January. It was full of news and his adventures. They had landed at Naples. I thought he would be in Sicily from the fact that oranges and lemons were growing – June-like days and January nights. However it was obvious from the letter of February 13th he was in the line. He was in the Suffolk Regiment and attached to 2/7th Battalion Queen's Royal Regiment.

We know no more. I will let you know if and when the Red Cross can help us. In the meantime we can but trust, hope, and wait.

Thank you so much for all that you and your sister did for him at Sunnyside. I am sure he's never let you down. He loved his Winchester life so much, and his mother and I are for ever grateful.

I do hope you are both well.
Our kindest regards.
Sincerely yours
Ernest Finch[29]

By the strangest of chances, on the same day that Sir Ernest Finch posted this letter he discovered that his son was alive and in German hands. He told Robertson the story in a letter a couple of weeks later:

My dear Bobber,
Thank you so much for your letter received this morning. Yes the miracle has happened! Michael is a prisoner of war. I am so sorry I didn't write before – my wife said she was going to write to your sister and tell her. It was extraordinary how we knew.

He was reported missing since February 29th – on March 6th at 1900hrs we got the War Office wire – Monday evening and Tuesday were grim. On Tuesday evening about 2330hrs – my wife had turned in with a sleeping draught – the telephone went – I was sitting alone, my life having gone so to speak full circle – Michael gone! My rooms and nursing home gone! Off the full staff and teaching this year! What's the use? I answered the phone, prepared to say I couldn't go out to see anyone when the voice in the vernacular said

'Is your name Finch?'

Yes.

'Avs yer anyone belonging yer called Lieutenant Michael Finch?'

Yes, my son. Why?

'Well, I just wanted to tell yer it were given out on Rome Radio at 11 o'clock that he's a prisoner of war, on his way to Germany; he says yer not to worry, he's all right and 'opes he'll be 'ome again soon. Goodnight!'

I had the sense to insist on the name and address – got the reply 'No, it's now't. Goodnight!' but insisted and got it. I woke up my wife to tell her – she, poor girl, thought it was just another dream.

The next day we went to the address, a clean wee house in the slums. The woman who was doing the kitchen said 'Oh, yes, it were our Norah; she'd never listened to Rome Radio before. The first was an officer from Liverpool, then one from Bolton, and then your son's name, and we thought it was a funny name, either Fitch or Finch! So our Norah, who likes reading telephone books' (I never met anyone else with this taste) 'looked it up and then went out to telephone. The first kiosk she came to was out of order. So she told us that she walked a full half mile to the next to telephone.'

It's all too wonderful. Two days later both War Office and British Red Cross confirmed, unasked, that the broadcast had come through.

'While there is no reason to doubt the accuracy of this report, yet it must be understood that Lieut M.H.A. Finch is still missing for official purposes, etc., etc.'

It will be weeks before we hear officially, I expect, but what a relief. I am sure it is Fifth Army front, from what he said, and in addition I met a chap by chance again from 2/7th QRR who left them a few weeks ago and he says that they were then outside Cassino. The War Office have written again to say he was missing on February 21st and not February 29th, but that doesn't matter now.

If my wife hasn't written to your sister, will you thank her for her letter – my wife has been very busy with domestic difficulties and an avalanche of letters.

I'll let you know as soon as I know anything official, and again so many thanks to you and your colleagues who have been asking about him.

Sincerely Yours,

Ernest Finch[30]

* * *

Nowhere in the Anzio bridgehead was safe.

A small patrol had gone out the night before and had met a strong German outpost. Only one man had got back untouched. That morning I was talking to the Company Commander, when a Private shoved his head into the dug-out and asked what he should do with the mail for the dead men. The Company Commander told him to bring them in to him. There was a telegram among the letters. He ripped it open and glanced at it, and after a few moments he handed it to me. 'It's from his wife,' he said. I took it from him and read, 'So glad to hear that you are still fit and well.'

February 23rd
1210hrs warning that Regimental area was to be shelled received from HQRA; information from VI Corps.
1210hrs Regimental area harassed by 88mm gun. Captain L.S. Giness RA wounded and 2 Other Ranks killed at OP.

February 24th
0600hrs Lieutenant-Colonel A.E.H. Hamilton OBE, RA, killed by direct hit on his dugout at 24 Guards Brigade HQ. Lieutenant-Colonel R.B. Greig RA took over command of Regiment.
Lieutenant B.O.B. Paterson wounded in OP.

'Puggins' Hamilton was the third Wykehamist to have been killed at Anzio in the space of three weeks. His father, a Hopperite, had been killed in action in 1916.[31]

* * *

On February 26th 1SG – now reduced to little more than company strength – were withdrawn to a rest area, where they heard the welcome news that they were to leave the beach-head. But on February 28th came the double blow for Winchester of a shell-burst which killed two more Wykehamists: Scrymgeour-Wedderburn and Weir. A shell landed, wounding a colleague, and as other officers ran to his aid two more shells struck trees close by. Detonated above ground, the shells sprayed fragments down in a lethal air-burst, killing Weir and four others instantly and fatally wounding Scrymgeour-Wedderburn.

Weir's death was a final blow to a family shattered by its losses in the war, as can be understood from a notice in *The Times* of April 26th 1944:

> A service will be held at the Church of the Holy Trinity, Shaftesbury, at 1215hrs on Monday, May 1st, in memory of Major John Weir MC, Scots Guards, recently killed in action, and of his father, Wing Commander A.G. Weir RAF, lost at sea on active service in April 1941, and of his elder brother, F/O Nigel Weir DFC, RAFVR, killed in action, November 1940.[32]

Scrymgeour-Wedderburn died of his wounds on March 1st, mourned by all. The commanding officer of 1st Irish Guards wrote to his family:

> The whole Division is absolutely miserable; the general and senior staff officers left the battle to pay their last respects when they buried him. He had done wonders for the Battalion; his own personal success was outstanding – it is so wicked to think he got over all these dangers to catch it back here.[33]

The two officers lie only a few yards apart in the Beach Head Cemetery at Anzio.

* * *

On the day of the fatal shelling, Robertson responded to a letter of sympathy from Peter Walker:[34]

> My dear Peter,
> Thank you for your warm and understanding letter about Duncan [McMurtrie]. His death, on top of John Sinclair's and Bill [Cliff] Hodges', has hit us very hard. We older people are more able to appreciate a 'difficult' boy than his equals ('aequales', I mean), and Duncan, with all his oddities, was a bit of a genius and had very fine qualities. Actually, I believe we two knew and understood him in some ways more than his own people, with whom he tended to scrap …
>
> All this is worse for me than last time when I was for half the war sharing the risks with lads nearer my own age – whom I knew too rather as brothers or pals than as 'children' in rather a special way. I have so often shared confidences about ambitions, troubles, friendships, yes, sins too – of which parents know little. I was backing Duncan to get a first at Cambridge, had he had full time to read Law, and he might have written really good poetry later; there was great feeling in much he did write. He was very highly strung, almost (Sheila and old Matron used to think) a little cracked at times, but the way he tackled Cert A and later the Guards shews what he could do – you didn't see the four airgraphs (service) he wrote us at Xmas, did you? Full of his gratitude to Winchester and us and his desire to 'repay the debt'. He has done that, poor lad. I've

sent them, with a poem of his, to his mother today. Nigel Lillingston was here yesterday, looking very smart in his Scots Greys uniform, but too modest to go into Chapel in it! Very pleased, as we are, with his Belt of Honour. He's the other type – simple and less perceptive, but utterly straight.

Walker had evidently written to the McMurtries on the same day as he wrote to Robertson, because Mr and Mrs McMurtrie also composed replies to his letter on February 28th:

Dear (Peter) Walker!
Indeed no stranger. Duncan spoke of you to me so often. He was a poor correspondent (even to us until he went abroad) but he certainly counted you as one of his closest friends. I think you must have acted as sharpening stones to each other, for I know he enjoyed having little 'tiffs' with you. Only real friends can disagree at times and remain friends.

You who knew him and his character so well, will like to know that he developed very rapidly once he joined the Regiment and some of what he called his serious letters to us from abroad showed that he had 'found' himself. His perspective, his humour, his poetry all fell into their right places.

We have naturally a great sorrow, but we have also besides pride, so many many happy memories, all so precious.

I hope one day that we shall meet you when we can smile at Duncan's little foibles, after all so little.

Thank you so very much for writing.
Yours very sincerely,
Margaret McMurtrie[35]

My Dear Peter Walker,
Of course I remember you and especially as one of my son Duncan's close friends. Thank you so much for writing. He told us much of his Winchester days and friends. He certainly did mature quickly and he developed his sense of humour considerably.

Merely as a matter of interest to you, we have received letters from Sandhurst OCTU, Pirbright, his Regiment, and Battalion, which make us proud indeed!

Duncan's poetry did mature and I will bear in mind your words about possible publication.

Frankly, Duncan was I am told a very efficient officer and died on recce patrol in the spearhead of the beach-head when he ran into a German counter-attack. He would have wished no better end and would have had (or rather, has) no regrets. He pushed hard to get there, as he had hardly recovered from malaria and jaundice.

You are no stranger, my boy, for we have a common tie of friendship.

Thank you again; it means so very much.
With all good wishes.
Yours very sincerely,
D.S.A. McMurtrie[36]

* * *

Elliott-Binns wrote:

> One of the few amenities at Anzio was a bath, a real porcelain bath with a plug. Of course, it was in a tent, and had no taps, but the attendant filled it with a canvas bucket. It was really a private bath belonging to the Reinforcement Camp, but I always got a good welcome from the attendant when I went down. He had been invalided out of one of the infantry battalions with bad feet, and he liked to talk to someone who could tell him what was happening up at the front, and a Gunner officer knew more than most. Once I did not get down to have a bath for a long time. I eventually managed it, and while the attendant was preparing the bath he looked round and said, 'You know, Sir, I thought you'd been killed.' It gave me quite a shock. Then I thought how easily it might be true. It seemed a queer job somehow, to fill baths for people and chat to them, when he quite expected never to see them alive again.

* * *

News of Cliff Hodges' death had by now reached Hopperites across the globe, and it spurred several to write to Robertson, as Charles Murray did on March 13th:[37]

> I was very sorry indeed to read about Bill Hodges in a back number of *The Times*. He was a delightful fellow and I used to see quite a lot of him in the north. We are having a very interesting and busy time out here and I've been round about a place called Jasper. The most wonderful scenery I've ever seen anywhere. It must be among the best in the world. I hope to go to Vancouver for a few days' leave next week which will be interesting. I hear that it's a fun place.

Mike Sinclair also wrote, but mostly about his own brother's death:[38]

Kriegsgefangenenpost

HSA you might like to see this. MR

Postkarte

Oflag IV C

PASSED P.W. 3249

An MAJOR. M. ROBERTSON O.B.E. M.C.

CULVER LODGE

05.4.44.-14

Gebührenfrei!

Absender:

Vor- und Zuname: Lt MICHAEL SINCLAIR

Gefangenennummer: 850

Lager-Bezeichnung: Kriegsgef.-Offizierlager IV C

Deutschland (Allemagne)

Empfangsort: WINCHESTER

Straße:

Land: HANTS

Landesteil (Provinz usw.)

ENGLAND

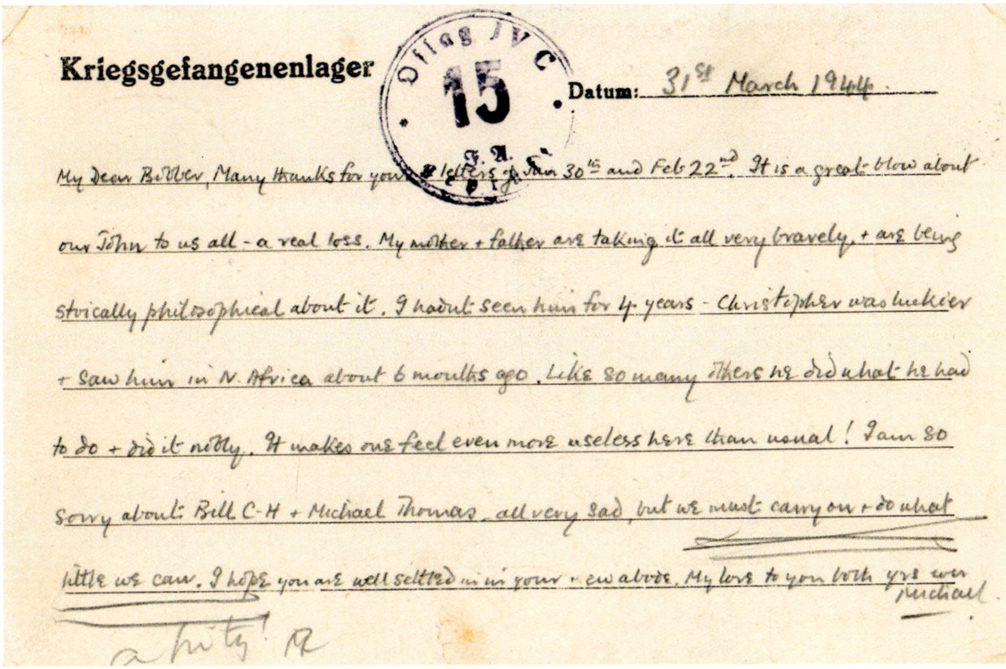

Kriegsgefangenenlager

Oflag IV C 15

Datum: 31st March 1944.

My Dear Bobber, Many thanks for your letters of Jan 30th and Feb 22nd. It is a great blow about our John to us all – a real loss. My mother + father are taking it all very bravely, + are being stoically philosophical about it. I hadn't seen him for 4 years – Christopher was luckier + saw him in N. Africa about 6 months ago. Like so many others he did what he had to do + did it nobly. It makes one feel even more useless here than usual! I am so sorry about Bill C-H + Michael Thomas – all very sad, but we must carry on + do what little we can. I hope you are well settled in in your new abode. My love to you both yrs ever Michael

a pity! R

Simpkin heard the news of John Sinclair's death from Robertson:

> Thanks very much for your letter of February 26th. I'm very sorry to hear John Sinclair has been killed. It will be an awful blow to his parents, and I'm afraid may knock his mother over completely … Thanks for your news of various people. I'm expecting my exams at the end of April, war events permitting.[39]

XV

'Comfort is unheard of in the jungle. No MT to carry your bedroll – everything you want, down to your nail-scissors & anti-louse powder, goes on your back. "Hannibal Eclipsed" is our motto. Maybe you saw it in the papers.'

India & Burma, January–May 1944

Captain Bruce Fortune MC, ADC to His Excellency the Viceroy of India, Viceroy's House, New Delhi, February 1944, by Cecil Beaton. (IWM IB 563)

In New Delhi, Susan Mackie had been smitten from the first by Bruce Fortune, and within weeks it became apparent that her interest was reciprocated. Her diary for January 11th 1944 records the first time that he invited her out for the evening:

> A note arrived in the office from Bruce asking me to come up to Viceroy's House for dinner with him and Hugh – he is leaving in a few days on tour with His Excellency. He says I am difficult to get hold of, but sadly as neither of us works regular hours it's a case of him on duty, or me. He sent a car for me at 1900hrs and we went first to a drinks party given by Pamela Humphreys [Wavell's eldest daughter], and after dinner went off to the Piccadilly. It really was a lovely evening. Bruce is so attractive and has such a wonderful smile.

Fortune was away with Wavell from January 18th to 29th, on what the Viceroy described as a 'strenuous but interesting' tour[1] of the United Provinces (administered by a Wykehamist),[2] Bombay, and Udaipur. They visited the Gurkha recruiting depot at Gorakphur, Lucknow, and Bombay, flying to Belgaum on the 25th, driving through Bijapur to Sholapur, and thence by train back to New Delhi. One of the officials they met – Michael Scott, ADC to the Governor of Bombay[3] – wrote to Robertson shortly afterwards:

> My dear Bobber,
> I thought you might like to know that Bruce Fortune has been here with the August Satrap whom he serves so well. He is looking fairly fit now; and he captivated every one by his modesty, charm, good looks, and good sense … . Bruce's mother might be glad of independent news of him if you chose to pass it on. I cannot very well write, not having met them.[4]

Back at Viceroy's House, Fortune continued to see a lot of Susan, who had just returned from a visit to Ceylon, where Mountbatten was setting up his headquarters.

> February 2nd
> Changed and went on night duty. A note was waiting for me from Bruce asking me to come up to see round the Viceregal Gardens. Having only been at Viceroy's House in the evening, I look forward to seeing them. I am on duty tomorrow afternoon but arranged to go out with him tomorrow evening.

> February 3rd
> Bed most of the day … Bruce called for me at 2015hrs and we went straight up to Viceroy's House – had dinner in his room; the table, laid for two, was drawn right up to the fire. It was heaven and we had a lovely dinner. He is rather shy, but so nice. Then went and danced at the Piccadilly and afterwards drove out to Safdar Jung. We climbed up the tower and saw the whole place under moonlight – it was very beautiful but very eerie as there are so many ruins around it. It was a lovely evening.

That day, in the Arakan region of Burma, the Japanese General Tanahashi launched an offensive, so confident of success that he left only one battalion as a reserve.

* * *

The Arakan peninsula had been the scene of a failed British offensive late in 1942, but now two Indian divisions had been tasked with pushing the Japanese out. This attack began well, but a strong Japanese position called the Razabil Fortress commanded the coastal road and prevented further progress, forcing the Allies to switch their main thrust to the Kalapanzin valley. This they were able to do because they had constructed a lateral road across the Mayu, a mountain range which split the Arakan peninsula from top to bottom. This vital road ran through the Ngakyedauk Pass (known to Allied soldiers as 'Okeydoke Pass').

The Japanese were about to launch two attacks of their own: the one in the Arakan, and another towards India itself, aiming to smash through the Allied lines at Imphal and Kohima. Tanahashi's target for his Arakan counter-stroke was along the Mayu to the Ngakyedauk Pass. He hoped to split the Allies, and to cut their lines of communication. In previous battles, such a situation had led to the rapid collapse of British and Indian troops, who had feared being isolated and destroyed.

Tanahashi's 6,000 troops made a lightning march of over thirty miles along the Mayu and, on February 6th, fell upon the administrative and supply units to the rear of the Allied front line. This position would become known as the 'Admin Box'. The Allied rear-echelon troops grabbed their weapons and fought for their lives, spurred on by what had happened to one of their field hospitals, where over eighty wounded and doctors had been bayoneted in cold blood.

What the Japanese did not appreciate was just how much the Allies had learned since 1942, and just how great were the resources upon which they could call in an emergency. Japanese courage and determination had carried them a long way in 1942; but they were no longer enough. Although they had cut the Allied supply lines, command of the air allowed supplies to be flown in instead. Wingate and his Chindits had already shown that it was possible to defeat the Japanese in the jungle and to survive on supplies from the air, and on a larger scale this was what the British did in the Battle of the Admin Box. Ten days' rations for 40,000 men had been prepared for just such an emergency, and although the siege of the Admin Box lasted for three weeks, at no point did the Allied troops crack as the Japanese had expected. Instead, the Japanese threw themselves into futile attacks on prepared positions, suffering crippling casualties and unable to live on the enemy's supplies which they had expected to fall into their hands.

The whole character of the war in the Far East had changed – air power was crucial in the Chindit expeditions, and it continued to dominate the Burma theatre. Although only infantry can occupy and hold ground, the Allied campaign to liberate Burma from the Japanese depended to a large extent on the British, Indian, and American air forces. Burma veterans like Wykehamist Sir Roger du Boulay – a Hurricane pilot – were full of praise for their commander, who had the vision and the determination to make this all happen: 'That was the turning-point; that was General Slim. Previously, whenever you were surrounded, you retreated. General Slim said no, stay there, and we'll supply you. That was Bill Slim.'[5]

* * *

Dodgson.

Dodgson was about to begin one of the most challenging tasks possible for a British soldier in the Second World War: a Chindit expedition into Japanese-held Burma. Operation Thursday began on Saturday, February 5th, when Brigadier Bernard Fergusson's 16 Brigade began its long-range penetration march into northern Burma, heading for the Japanese communications node at Indaw. Essentially, their march was pointless; the other Chindit brigades were flown in straight to their operating zones. Although the Brigade started its journey towards the crossing of the river Chindwin on February 5th, the tail end of the unit was as much as a week behind. To all intents and purposes, 16 Brigade clambered its 300 miles in single file. And Dodgson was at the tail end, since 45 and 54 Columns were the rearmost in the Brigade, and 54 was behind 45. Fergusson felt sorry for them:

> To be tail column of a long line of columns is misery; and to be in that position for a period of two months an abominable cruelty which I should have avoided inflicting could I possibly have done so. But to pass columns ahead of each other was impossible without loss of time ... Just as the men at the tail of a column are always bound to be the weariest, so also the fatigue endured by the last columns of a long line is far greater even than the fatigue of those who are blazing the trail. One is always striving to catch up, and one lacks also the exhilaration of knowing that you are seeing something new, something which the others have not seen.[6]

It took a full month for all nine Columns of 16 Brigade to get across the Chindwin, and the march in was a terrible experience. For a start, it rained all the way. The Brigade's route from Tagap Ga, south of Ledo – where the supply road to China began – lay through dense forest, and went across the grain of the country, meaning that the Chindits had to hack their vertiginous mule-tracks up ridges and then all the way down again for trivial gains of horizontal distance. Dodgson typically under-stated the difficulties when interviewed sixty years later by his great-nephew, William Jackson:

> I had the RE platoon, loaded mostly with explosive. We had eight mules to carry the explosives and a few other things. I went on, pitching camps and making bridges out of pre-fabricated materials; although there was one enormous bridge built out of local logs, I was not involved in that. Our initial job when we started marching was to dig steps up about 2000 ft up muddy clay and to revet them, to get the thing started. After that first hill one took devious routes up the others. When we started off on the hilly tracks and ridge paths, we either marched along the ridges or valleys, where you got a straight walk up the stream. On the hilly paths every now and again the mules missed their footing and fell over, and you then had to take the panniers off them and back to the path, and then the mule was dragged up. With 3,000 people walking in single file, when the mules fell the whole line was halted for half an hour to an hour because the whole column was jammed up.[7]

The thirty-five miles between Tagap Ga and Hkalak took Dodgson and his companions nine days to traverse. Fergusson's HQ was about half-way along the human snake, though he was constantly up and down the front end of the column, and he experienced the same conditions as Dodgson:

> This march was the heaviest imaginable. The rain was torrential and almost continuous; the gradients were often one in two; no single stretch of level going a hundred yards in length existed between Tagap Ga and Hkalak, and few thereafter ... The path had to be re-made, or the traverses rebuilt, two to three times during the passage of a column. The cold was intense, particularly at bivouacs over five thousand feet. The seventy pounds which men were carrying were greatly increased in weight due to saturation with water.[8]

Dodgson described his equipment and supplies as follows:

> Our weapons were basic; each man had a Lee Enfield rifle which had a magazine with ten rounds in it, with a bolt so you could only shoot one round at a time. We only had as much ammunition as we could carry, which was pretty limited, about 30–40 rounds, because one was already carrying rations and equipment.
>
> We were issued with American 'K' rations, which came in a cake-sized box. I used to swap my cigarettes for other people's chocolate, but they soon put an end to that because those who swapped their chocolate were going without part of their carefully calculated rations. We also had a gold sovereign, in case we needed to bribe anyone, and a capsule with a needle containing something to kill us if we were badly injured or captured.
>
> We were supplied by air. They dropped rations, clothes, and spare boots – the Indian boots were always falling to pieces, so one was dependent on the drops from the air. One opened up a clearing for the drop site, then one lit a fire so that the aircraft could see the smoke and know where to drop. There were means of indicating which units needed supplying, and these great bundles of stuff about the size of a bale of straw came down and would hopefully land in the clearing and not in the jungle, which would mean that it would probably get caught up in the trees and not fall to the floor.

Fergusson reported that the supply-drops were 'on the whole atrocious', and calculated that half of the supplies dropped fell down cliffs and were completely lost.

From the Chinese outpost at Hkalak, Dodgson and his companions ploughed on towards Lulum Nok, a journey which introduced a new complication – the enemy. Although most Japanese posts were along the Chindwin itself, there were rumours that they had troops in villages such as Gum Ga and Tekti, between 16 Brigade and the river. The cautious advance units placed booby-traps on paths to their flanks, to deter Japanese patrols from getting too close.

The journey from Hkalak to Lulum Nok took four days, and was somewhat less arduous – though these things are relative. There were 'only' two really steep hills, and biting flies called *polaungs* were replaced by leeches,

> which increased both in number and appetite. Out of one bivouac, beside a chilly stream, we were driven by fair weight of numbers to seek immunity on higher ground. We passed through several Naga villages, and learned from them that we were not, as

we had idly hoped, the first Europeans to come there: a party of five had visited them seven years before.[9]

Fergusson's matter-of-fact descriptions of the miseries of the march make it clear just how much Wingate was asking of 16 Brigade:

We were now on paths which Japanese patrols had occasionally used; and at one point we even found some fox-holes at the side of the track. Occasional heavy rainfalls held us up, as for much of the way the track coincided with the bed of various streams. The legend on the map 'Path follows bed' is common enough throughout Upper Burma, and to the initiated it means weary, heavy wading in depths varying from ankle-deep to waist-deep. The risks of foot-rot are very real unless discipline is strict, by which I mean the drying of socks and the compulsory massaging of feet in the evening, or whenever chance offers. Whether or not 'path follows bed' you must resign yourself to the knowledge that your feet will always be wet: if you are not travelling along a stream, you will be crossing them frequently. The wetting of your feet is the least part of it: it is the introduction of innumerable grains of sand between socks and feet, and between socks and boots, which makes life Hell …

When I looked across the Chindwin on the morning of February 29th … the spot where we were seemed nearly perfect. There was ample cover on both sides of the river. The bank on which we were was high, but there were plenty of places where mules could get down. At the foot of the bank was a broad beach, and on the opposite side, shingle jutted out at least six hundred yards. The actual width to be crossed cannot have exceeded three hundred, and the current was no more than a knot … The forests across the river were silent and mysterious; we were looking into the sun, and the shadows lay thick on the farther cliffs. I had sent warning orders some days before that gliders were to be loaded ready at Air Base, so that they could fly in with the river-crossing equipment on the receipt of the single code word 'Trip'.[10]

* * *

As the Battle of the Admin Box opened on February 6th, Susan made her postponed daylight visit to the Viceroy's Gardens:

Bruce collected me about 1530hrs and we went up to Viceroy's House. The day was rather dull, but nothing could spoil the beauty of the gardens … I saw through all the state rooms – dining room, ball room, and the Durbar Hall … Bruce put on all the lighting …

February 10th
Picked up by Bruce at 1315hrs; went straight to Viceroy's House; had lunch under a tree in the garden just outside the ADC room. Simply wonderful – all those gorgeous flowers and the fountains playing – it was hot and lovely. Went for a walk and sat for ages in the Round Garden … Bruce came to collect me at 2000hrs and we went out for dinner and danced; then out to see an old fort – how eerie it was – full moon shining

through broken parts of the great doorway – jackals running silently about; you could see their black forms in the shadows, and dogs were barking in the distance.

February 14th
Bruce phoned to ask if I was coming up this evening – followed by a note by a bearer whom I found hanging about outside my room! I collected those who were coming up with me to the cinema party, and we were called for at 1945hrs. There were huge fires in the reception rooms tonight – everything looked gorgeous as usual. Cecil Beaton was there; didn't think much of him. He posed quite a lot and was wearing an enormous mauve cravat. Didn't see much of Bruce – he was being very official with His Excellency. All presented again and then had supper. Chris, George, Bruce, and self got in a huddle and were broken up to be social with others! Saw *The Gentler Sex*; both Their Excellencies came. After the film we had drinks and eventually left about 2330hrs.

Beaton was – amongst other things – a celebrated fashion and portrait photographer, whose contribution to the war effort was a superb series of photographs from almost every theatre of the war. Amongst his many lovers (of both sexes) was Greta Garbo.[11] His diary recorded:

The pretentious buildings of the Viceroy's House and the Secretariat are of no known style. Made of tongue-coloured stone, which retains the dry heat of the day and throws it out angrily at dusk, they appear, at the far end of a processional drive, like a city built for an exhibition. They were designed for peace-time activities; few modern cities could be less practical or convenient for a war headquarters than the present capital. However, in an attempt to alleviate the overcrowding of Delhi, Lord Wavell has partitioned off the house to accommodate several large, separate households. One of the four wings now comprises the office of the Private Secretary to the Viceroy and his staff; another wing is occupied by the Commander-in-Chief, Eastern Fleet, with sixty naval officers; in another wing are Army officers. The Comptroller's house is taken over by officers of GHQ, while the Military Secretary's house is converted into a leave camp, as is most of the Viceroy's house at Simla. The Viceroy and his family insist on leading as simple a life as is possible in these awe-inspiring surroundings.[12]

Susan's diary shows that any good intentions which she had for an early night were usually scuppered by an urgent invitation from the Viceregal household and its entourage.

February 15th
We dined in the private dining room of the Imperial. The Maharaja of Jaipur was there … Gene [Markey] is very amusing and in spite of his numerous marriages to the 'stars' – at the moment it is Hedy Lamarr – he is extraordinarily nice … After dinner we all drove to George Merrill's house (FDR's personal representative here in Delhi), a funny little man. We all made rather a noisy entrance and were guided into a room, and there I found the whole of Viceroy ADC-erie. What fun it was … Bruce in pretty good form … We took George and Bruce home.

February 17th
Slept most of the day. Bruce came at around 1630hrs and we had tea in the garden in the sun. It was heavenly just lazing and listening to the gramophone. He left about 1830hrs, but came back at 2000hrs and we drove up to Viceroy's House. We had a wonderful dinner in his room. How I love the scarlet-liveried *khitmagars* [waiters] who dance attendance on us. We sat in front of a huge fire and drank old brandy. In the corner of the room was a huge bank of white jasmine. I loved the whole evening. How pleasant it is to be quiet for a change. He leaves tomorrow with His Excellency on tour to Madras and Central Provinces, and will be away for a whole fortnight – he comes back on March 2nd.

Beaton caught up with Wavell just before his departure and wrote:

Friday, February 18th
It takes a great person not to become affected by this regal ceremonial and continuous sycophantic deference. Lord Wavell has this quality of greatness: at worst he becomes bad-tempered, but this is understandable. After lunch I had a walk round the garden with Wavell. He said the Japs had suddenly attacked in Burma in great force. He couldn't imagine how such numbers hadn't been detected in spite of the fact that the Japs move at night, lie in wait all day, and need practically no communications. (They carry food for eight days on them.) Wavell thought it would take some considerable time before we were able to clear up the trouble in this part.

Beaton wrote a very astute assessment of Wavell's character later in his diaries:

Wavell has a genius for cutting through the façades, and seeing people as they really are, in spite of their shyness, their alibis, and their sometimes false presentation of themselves. As for him, although his personality is not particularly vivid or spell-binding, he is deeply impressive. He never tries to charm or hypnotize, but cannot help emanating integrity of mind, directness of purpose, and unaffected simplicity of style. Indians, who are always quick to note the dominant characteristics of Englishmen, are the first to appreciate the golden goodness of Wavell. They know that he is entirely devoid of malice, deceit, or guile, that he is eminently fair, and, above all things, sincere. To be complimented by him is a reward well worth while. For in his dry and somewhat melancholy voice, and talking quietly, without moving his lips, and in a tone that is deep and easy to listen to, he says nothing that is banal … This fine man is incapable of glib sentences … His thoughts are never ready-made, and his conversation is carefully chosen. Literature and poetry mean much to him … He is a taciturn man, and can be as silent in the Mess as on purely social occasions. But his silences are completely un-selfconscious. He has extraordinary powers of concentration: when he is thinking it is a full-time, absorbing occupation, and he is oblivious of the world. I have sometimes tried to interrupt his thoughts, and only succeeded in realizing how foolish was the attempt … Yet, if he is interested, he can become voluble … The Wavells have accepted me almost as one of their family, and my heart is full of gratitude and friendliness for each and all of the remarkable brood. But it is the father who is on a monumental scale: merely watching

> him be his simple, ordinary self has been an experience which, I hope, may have taught me a bit about greatness.

Fortune returned to New Delhi as planned on March 2nd, and Susan was excited:

> Bruce due back today from his tour with His Excellency. Early dinner and off to night duty. Wrote a note to welcome him back and to ask him to come to Akbar Road tomorrow, but no word yet. Perhaps they haven't got back ... He eventually rang about 2300hrs – they had just got back. Had a wonderful tour, and they shot six tigers!

When Susan was on night duty, Fortune often used to telephone her – one of his habits was playing classical gramophone records to her down the line.

> March 3rd
> Bruce came down to Akbar Road about 1600hrs and we all went to see the Qutab Minar, and had tea in the shadow of the ruins ... We climbed to the top and had a wonderful view ... Bruce has got my sunglasses; must remember to ask for them. He told me that some of the Black Watch were coming on leave from Burma and were staying at the Viceroy's House for a few days, and asked me to dine on the 7th.

* * *

Four thousand miles away as the crow flies, but much further by sea, convoy KMF29A left the Clyde on March 3rd, bound for Alexandria and Ceylon, and carrying no fewer than nine Squadrons of the Fleet Air Arm destined for the Eastern Fleet. Eight squadrons were on board the escort carriers HMS *Atheling* and HMS *Begum* (which Richardson would later come to know well).

The escort carrier HMS Begum. (Copyright holder unknown)

However, 832 Squadron – now equipped with twelve Avengers and four Wildcats – had been split across two dedicated aircraft transport ships, HMS *Engadine* and HMS *Athene*. Richardson had embarked on the *Engadine* the day before sailing, and would have been impressed by the size of the escort: two light cruisers, two sloops, and no fewer than eight frigates. He was less impressed by the *Engadine*; whilst *Begum* was hardly a thing of beauty, for sheer ugliness *Engadine* could scarcely be surpassed.

Richardson.

KMF29A arrived in Alexandria on March 17th, but did not tarry; *Begum* was through the Suez Canal by the end of the 19th. Aden was the convoy's last stop (on March 27th), at which point *Atheling*, *Athene*, *Begum*, and *Engadine* split off to join convoy AJ2, which sailed for Ceylon on March 28th and docked at Colombo on April 4th. 832 Squadron's aircraft and personnel disembarked and transferred to RNAS *Kutukurunda* (HMS *Ukussa*), a newly-established airfield which would rapidly become the biggest Royal Naval Air Station in the world, with over 3,000 personnel busily servicing as many as a hundred aircraft at a time. Richardson's stay there would be short; he was about to complete his near-circumnavigation of the globe.

HMS Engadine, *on which Richardson travelled to Ceylon.* (Copyright holder unknown)

* * *

The head of the 16 Brigade column had reached the Chindwin on February 29th, but Dodgson and the tail were days behind them, with 54 Column each day covering the same trail as 45 had traversed the day before. On March 2nd, 54 Column received a supply drop, but on March 3rd they faced an eight-mile journey, described in the war diary as 'very hard, ending with a bivuoac on a razor-like hill; it was extremely difficult to tether mules and to find a place to sleep.'[13]

The final stage of the journey to the Chindwin was, however, a shorter march – though it did take Dodgson on a 'path follows bed' knee-deep in water the whole way. 54 Column emerged on to the banks of the Chindwin at 1500hrs on March 4th. It was not their final destination, which was Indaw, some 200 miles further on. Wingate had wanted 16 Brigade to be there on March 5th; he had just flown in to discuss the situation with Fergusson. There was space on a sandbank for tiny American observation aircraft to land and evacuate the sick.

Although this Vultee L-5 Sentinel aircraft is in RAF service (with 194 Squadron, in Burma), it was aircraft like it (& L-1 Vigilants) belonging to the American 1st Air Commando which evacuated some 1,000 Chindits just in the first month of Operation Thursday. (Copyright holder unknown)

On March 5th, as 54 Column moved off uphill to keep up with the rest of the Brigade, Dodgson was put aboard one of these light aircraft and flown back to India. He was suffering from jaundice, but one suspects that the real cause of his illness was total exhaustion. There was no dishonour in it; no man who completed that journey had anything of which to be ashamed. On May 17th, Dodgson wrote to Robertson, reflecting on his experiences.[14]

> I seem to have got very out of touch with everything this last eight months, as I've had only just enough time and writing material to write home with. The whole time in the jungle, only a part of it in action, and I got jaundice in the middle of that and had to be evacuated, so have just had a very pleasant month in hospital and a month's sick leave in a hill station.
>
> I gather that Fourteenth Army has had a bit of publicity at home – it certainly deserves it. Comfort is unheard of in the jungle. No motor transport to carry your bedroll – everything you want down to your nail-scissors and anti-louse powder goes on your back. 'Hannibal Eclipsed' is our motto. Maybe you saw it in the papers… .
>
> I also see Bruce Fortune is ADC to Wavell – I must try and see him. Charles Duffin and Freddie Jackson married? What a life – it doesn't give us chaps out here a chance,

does it? Any girl is a beauty out here, and do they make the best of it – it would shake some of them to go back to England, and have to share a man instead. All round I think it's a terrible country this – and I never want to see it again, no matter what any Pukka *sahib* says! It brings out the worst and kills the best in any man.

Bill Cliff Hodges killed, I see; very sad – I'm afraid the casualties are piling up, aren't they – and will do so even more when this second front starts.

I wonder how life goes on in Winchester. As quiet and peacefully as ever I think. No bananas and meringues I suppose – but what compensation are they for not being at home? I've another four years to make my five or six before I'm due for repatriation!! Makes you laugh, doesn't it? The Yanks do eighteen months or two years and are then flown home.

I'm afraid I seem to be writing you a very morbid letter – but all the things that would be most interesting to you are as usual *verboten*.

* * *

In Delhi, Susan Mackie's thoughts were far more cheerful:

March 6th
Got up at 1600hrs and went into the garden to wait for Bruce, who came just after 1630hrs. It was very cool lying under the tree and we had a nice quiet tea. Later we went down to Connaught Circle to do some shopping. There were lots of Black Watch Jocks wandering about; it was wonderful to see the familiar kilt and red hackle.

March 7th
Today has been one of the most wonderful days. I have been thrilled beyond measure … Duty all afternoon … Bathed and changed; a car called … at 1945hrs to take us to Viceroy's House. Bruce met us at the door.

Susan's diary is supplemented by letters which she wrote at the time:

Bruce had everything so marvellously organised. He told me that we would have quite a walk before we got to the dining room – he was right. Along the long marble passage and up the wide staircase, we passed the State rooms; the vast halls were brilliantly lit… We came to the room we were going to dine in … The room was huge. The walls were blue and gold, and a great chandelier in the centre of the ceiling … We had an absolutely wonderful meal and equally wonderful wine. It was all quite hilarious … After coffee and liqueurs we had brandy, and just as that was being passed round I heard the old familiar and thrilling droning up of the pipes – my tummy turned over completely – and a red-kilted figure marched in playing 'Highland Laddie' – I could have wept with joy and sadness at the same time … He took his traditional dram from Brucie, saluted, and marched off. We were all from home, but thousands of miles away, and all a little homesick.

March 9th
Bed at 1015hrs and slept till 1230hrs … Was collected by Bruce and Douglas [Nicoll] at 1315hrs. Went down to the Imperial and sat on the terrace with a cool drink – it

> was a boiling day … Went out to the station in Old Delhi to see some of the Jocks off … Back to Viceroy's House and the swimming pool. Hugh Easton brought a hamper down and we had a picnic tea on the grass. It was so peaceful. Douglas goes back to the jungle tonight.

Mackie had known Nicoll since 1940; she would never see him again.[15] She next dined at Viceroy's House the following day.

> Bruce came out to meet me and escorted me out to the terrace where we were to dine. It was a wonderful setting and the night was so warm. At the far end of the terrace was a long table lit with three large candelabra and beautiful flowers down the centre. Everything softly lit; it was like a fairyland …
>
> There were seventeen of us; six Black Watch on leave from Burma, Bruce, myself, ADCs, and house party. We all sat and chatted while waiting for Their Excellencies to appear. The table plan was passed around and I saw that I had been put beside His Excellency – oh Lordy – but happily I saw Bruce was next to me. Shortly one of the ADCs said, 'Come on, chaps, into line.' The house party stood on one side and the guests on the other. Down the terrace, led by an ADC, came Their Excellencies …
>
> His Excellency is a poppet and it was quite easy to talk to him. I just prattled on. The only slightly alarming thing to start with was I was on his blind side and he would swing his head round in order to see you with his good eye!
>
> We left to go to the Hunt Ball about 2230hrs. The high spot of the evening was when two pipers appeared. The floor was cleared and three sets did an eightsome. Our set had four kilted Black Watch, including Bruce, who partnered me. I had such an amazing feeling of pride to be with them all. They all gave vent to the appropriate war-whoops – the din was wonderful.
>
> March 11th
> Sat in the sun, and had tea with Bruce, in the gardens. It was heavenly. Bruce has arranged a lunch party at the pool tomorrow, which should be wonderful … There is an Old Wykehamist dinner at Viceroy's House tonight; Wavell, Bruce, and Arthur Leveson were all at Winchester, and a few more were gathered in. Bruce rang me to tell me it was a great success. They dined on the terrace, sang Dulce Domum, had the piper, drank champagne, and all were a bit pixilated.

It was unfortunate that Wavell's own son, Archie John, was 'Continent' (Winchester slang for 'unwell' or 'in the sick-house'), and therefore unable to attend this gathering. Three months later he lost his left hand in action against the Japanese.

The following day was marked by a swimming party and lunch – which Susan described as 'swarming with Black Watch' – after which she and Fortune slept on cushions under a sun canopy before dancing on the grass and swimming again. Supper at the Viceroy's House followed. On March 14th, a huge thunderstorm caused a black-out during Susan's night duty, and she noted, 'Then the thunder started. I rang Bruce, I was so frightened.'

A notice of the dinner appeared in *The Wykehamist* in June 1944:[16]

To the Editor of the Wykehamist.

Dear Sir, On March 11th the Viceroy gave a Dinner at the Viceroy's House, New Delhi, at which thirty-one Old Wykehamists were present. The dinner table was laid in the Moghal Garden amongst dwarf orange trees. After dinner the Viceroy toasted the King-Emperor, and then called on the Monner to propose "Stet Res Wiccamica." The Black Watch piper, who had just been playing to us, and who was not a Wykehamist, inadvertently competed with the Monner for a moment, but the situation was restored. Later the junior man made quite a reasonable speech for a College man, and "Domum" was sung. We then resorted to the lawn not for a hot, nor to sing, but to talk. Present :

W. D. Monro ...	... COLL.	1886-93
The Viceroy ...	... COLL.	1896-1900
M. G. Hallett ...	... COLL.	1896-1902
O. K. Caroe ...	... E	1906-11
W. A. Lister ...	... C	1910-15
C. W. Armstrong ...	... D	1912-17
G. S. Johnston ...	... A	1913-18
H. R. Lenanton ...	... K	1914-19
R. L. Ferard ...	... D	1915-20
A. B. Phillpotts ...	... C	1915-20
E. H. W. Cobb ...	... COLL.	1916-20
L. A. Liddell ...	... A	1917-20
J. R. Carlisle-Taylor	... H	1916-21
A. Llewellyn Smith	... COLL.	1917-22
J. R. L. Tweed ...	... G	1918-22
A. J. P. Sellar ...	... H	1919-24
H. S. Stephenson ...	... C	1920-25
I. G. Robertson ...	... E	1920-25
A. E. Leveson ...	... D	1921-27
G. A. Haig	... D	1922-27
A. F. W. Humphrys	... D	1923-28
T. M. Horder ...	... COLL.	1923-29
J. N. Nicholson ...	... I	1924-29
P. H. M. Nelson ...	... B	1925-30
P. A. C. Don ...	... H	1927-32
G. L. L. Reynolds ...	... F	1928-33
S. C. G. Hallett ...	... COLL.	1932-37
H. W. G. Pawson	... B	1933-38
A. R. Reid	... C	1934-38
W. R. P. Ridgway ...	... Staff	1926-39
J. B. Fortune ...	... I	1934-39
G. W. Robinson ...	... COLL.	1934-39
Continent :		
A. J. A. Wavell ...	... E	1929-34

Yours sincerely,
A. F. W. HUMPHRYS,
Lieut.-Colonel

The Viceroy's House,
New Delhi.

March 21st
Bruce ... picked me up at 1300hrs. We went up to the House and then walked down to the pool. A *khitmagar* brought our lunch in a basket and we sat on cushions by the pool and ate it. They even had hot pancakes and potatoes in their jackets – ham and salad. We bathed and raced around on the grass for exercise. I got very burnt and my face was like a lobster. Dinner in Brucie's room, and home early.

March 28th
Heavenly day. Bruce called for me at 1000hrs, and we walked into town. Bank first, then bought up the town. It was a grand feeling. The day was so warm and I am so happy ... Finished up in Davico's and made pigs of ourselves on strawberries and cream. Went straight on duty.

* * *

Late in March, the Japanese launched the second and more dangerous of their two Burmese offensives, code-named 'U-Go', which aimed to occupy positions so strong that it would be impossible for the British to try to reconquer Burma from India. The Japanese attack led to the battles of Imphal and Kohima – separate, but strategically intertwined. The plain at Imphal was ideal terrain for the Allies to defend, but easy for the Japanese to cut off from the outside world. The nearest railhead was Dimapur, over 125 miles by road. Kohima lay on that road, and control of it would be hotly contested; the fighting which took place around Kohima was some of the fiercest anywhere in the entire war, and it was by no means a foregone conclusion that the Allies would be able to hold on to the area. On March 29th, the Japanese 15th Division cut the Imphal–Dimapur road at Kanglatongbi; on April 5th, their 31st Division laid siege to Kohima.

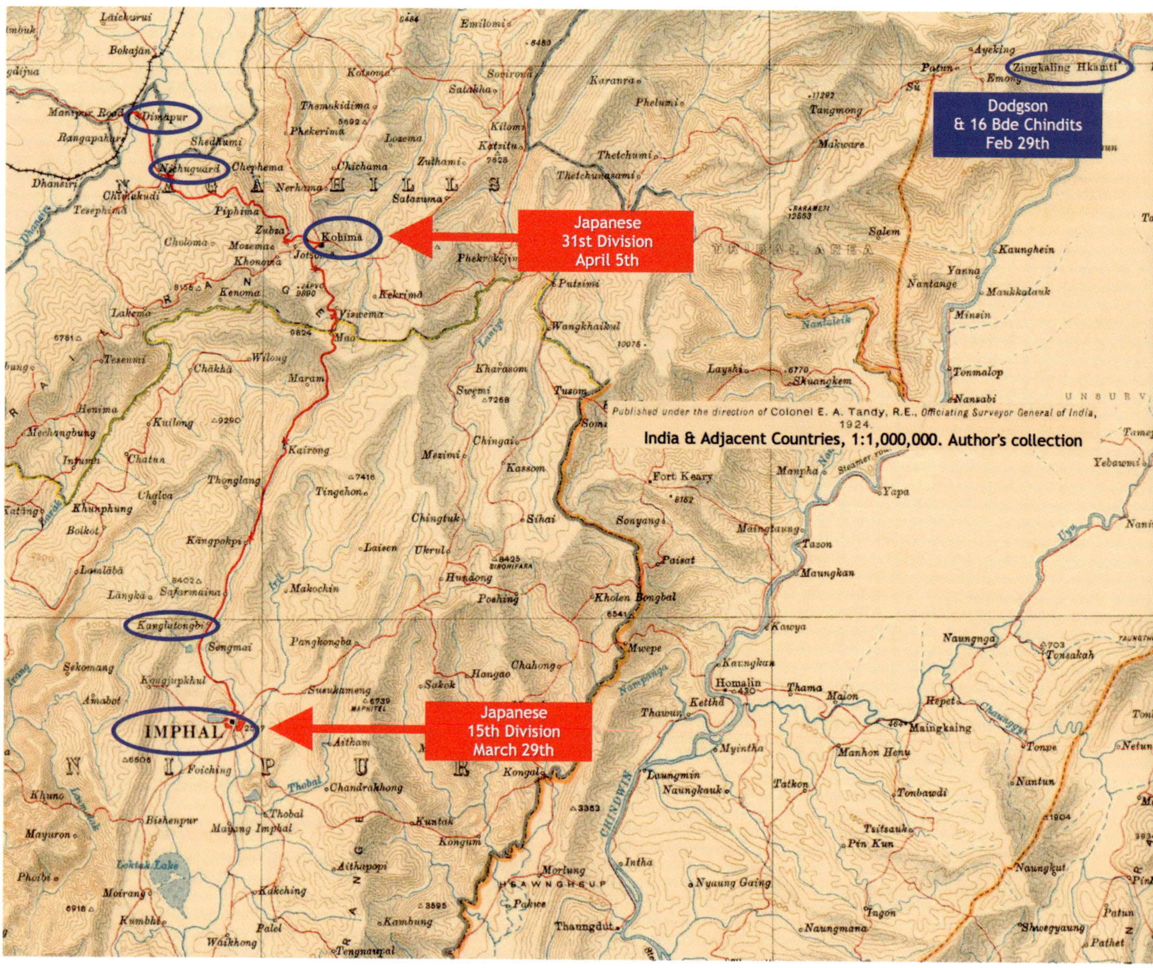

Published under the direction of Colonel E. A. Tandy, R.E., Officiating Surveyor General of India, 1924.
India & Adjacent Countries, 1:1,000,000. Author's collection

* * *

Lord Mountbatten and his staff were getting ready to move to Ceylon, and Susan had very little time left with Fortune.

April 1st
Early duty … Bruce collected me from the office … We had a lovely lunch by the pool … Later we went shopping, and I collected my new white and silver evening dress from Georgina. Back to House and had a swim – then drinks in the ADC room. What a heavenly feeling to have forty-eight hours leave before me. Dinner at the House, talked until after 2300hrs, then off to the Piccadilly and danced until 0100hrs.

Three days later, she and Fortune decided not to attend a crowded lunch party beside the swimming pool, but instead drove out of Delhi for a picnic in the countryside. They lunched under a tree and then lay in the shade until forced to move by a herd of cows. In the evening, they danced at the Gymkhana until, in Susan's words, 'we streamed – it was heaven'.

April 8th was Susan's leaving party: she and Fortune lunched by the pool, swam and lazed as usual, and then he took her up the dome of Viceroy's House, from which there were tremendous views. At her quarters, Susan prepared to receive guests:

Bruce arrived with the booze and mixed the most wizard rum cocktail … We drank busily until 2130hrs then piled into two cars and went off to the Piccadilly. What a happy party it was. I got slightly pixilated – I think – Still, I was gloriously happy. Joan, the angel, asked Hal to take them home and left Bruce and me. We got lost. It was a wonderful moonlight night – eventually finished up at the House. I got home after 0400hrs …

April 9th
It's not much good attempting to say anything of my heart and feelings of today. It was my last day in Delhi – six of the happiest months and great friendships – and I am going away from it all. Bruce has something that no one else has, and there has been an unspoken understanding between us that has been more than wonderful. I have been so very very happy. I woke this morning after three hours sleep and was up by 0930hrs … We went to church together and Bruce joined us. How happy I am when he is near, and how I want him to be …

The lump in my throat got bigger and bigger. Duty in the afternoon, but I could not concentrate much on work. Bruce wrote me a note and he feels the same. Got Flo to relieve me early in order to go to Evensong. Bruce collected me and we walked to the church in the glorious evening light – how peaceful it all was.

After the service we walked up to the House, while all the colours become diffused and magical. My last visit to Viceroy's House. We had a drink in the ADC room and played the Emperor Concerto once again. Outside the sun set and the trees grew black and silhouetted against the dark blue of the sky. We decided to have dinner before going to finish my packing, so we went through to his room where we dined, then sat and talked over a brandy. I didn't want to pack or go – Bruce insisted that he'd stay up and take me to the plane. We left at 2230hrs to go back, and he came and sat in my room while I finished my packing – how depressed and sad we were. Got finished and he took my case out to the car on the stroke of midnight. We drove back in the brilliant moonlight – the Vista looked mysterious. We finished our brandy and then walked round the gardens. They are quite magical by the strange cold light of the moon. The round garden with its huge pool looked magnificent – the great moon seemed to float in the water, and the flowers were shadowed blobs in the pale light. We wandered round until nearly 0230hrs and then went back and snoozed until nearly 0430hrs. First we walked round to the great steps of the Durbar Hall, regally climbed them, said 'Hello' to George V, and came down again. It is very sad saying goodbye to it all.

It was still dark when we left for the airport. We arrived to find the plane standing waiting – waiting to take me away 1500 miles from all my friends and Bruce. How strange and deserted the airport was – just that one plane waiting. I had my luggage weighed – then we just walked around. No signs of the Wrens who were coming with me and no telephone working to find out what had happened. We were supposed to take off at 0515hrs and it was nearly that time – so we kept walking. I don't know which of us felt more lost. We did not speak much, but were silently transmitting our agony to each other. I could not believe I was really going away. At last we heard that one car-load of Wrens was on its way. We went and sat in the car and waited. All the Wrens arrived and gradually went planewards. I was the last to go aboard. We hugged silently, and I turned and went up the steps. We took off as dawn was breaking.

* * *

Rigby was not so far from the war as it had at first seemed. Mir Ali was close to the village of Ipi, the original base of Mirza Ali Khan – otherwise known as the Faqir of Ipi – a thorn in the side of the British and later Pakistani governments for decades. In 1938 he had moved closer to the Afghan border, to Gorwekht, but continued his guerilla campaign against the British. He declared himself head of an independent state – Pashtunistan – and bizarrely had the support of the Nazis, who called him the 'Freedom Hero of Waziristan'. Early in 1941, the Faqir had demanded £12,500 a month from the Axis powers to continue to stir up trouble for the British. The Germans code-named their contacts with the Faqir Operation *Feuerfresser*, which was intended to lead to Operation Tiger in September 1941 – a general rising (*Grossaufstand*) along the North-West Frontier. The *Abwehr* department charged with this mission sent two agents to the Faqir in July 1941, but they were intercepted by Afghan troops south of Kabul, and one was killed in the ambush. The German plans ultimately came to nothing owing to their total failure to understand the local circumstances, their remoteness from the theatre, and the Faqir's complete lack of comprehension of the global context.

Nevertheless, one product of this liaison seems to have been the arrival in Gorwekht in late 1943 or early 1944 of two Italian mountain-guns, probably all the way from East Africa. They could be carried on camels, and intelligence suggested that the Faqir had some gunners able to use the weapons. Rigby was part of the British response:

> These guns were a threat because they could knock holes in the mud-walled forts of the Tochi Scouts (the local militia) and they could shell us in Mir Ali, which was only

defended by barbed wire and low stone walls. One day Peter Clarke, our Squadron Commander, had a call from the officer commanding the Tochi Scouts in Spinwam. The Scouts had a fort there by the crossing of a river, close to a large village. The Faqir of Ipi's guns had arrived and were in the hills on the opposite side of the river. The Tochis wanted us to come quickly and demonstrate for all to see – the Tochis, the tribesmen in the village, and the Faqir and his men – that they should not play war games in the presence of a squadron of modern tanks.

We kitted up our tanks in a hurry, and got to Spinwam, twenty miles away. The Tochis all came out to welcome us, and you could see all the villagers coming on to their rooftops. They knew that the Faqir's guns were in the hills ready for action.

The Tochi commanding officer asked us to put on an exhibition of mobility and speed. So we lined all our tanks across the wide, stony river valley, and simply charged at top speed up-stream. The shallow mountain streams and the rocky valley were no obstacle. We had an exhilarating drive.

We all went back to the fort where the Tochis put on a memorable feast of barbecued fat-tailed sheep and chapattis for all of us. Nothing more was heard thereabouts of the Faqir and his guns.[17]

Rigby's own sketch of the Stuart tanks haring up the valley bottom at Spinwam in a show of strength. (Rigby family collection)

* * *

Metcalfe.

Metcalfe's Regiment – 45th Cavalry – was part of the Allied response to the 'U-Go' offensive, and the Stuart tanks of 'A' Squadron took up positions on the Dimapur–Kohima road at Nichuguard on April 10th. 'C' Squadron joined them on the 22nd, but 'B' Squadron was still at Ranchi, 700 miles to the west by road. At this stage, Metcalfe was with 'B', and so a long way from the action. His comrades did extremely good work, clearing the road to Kohima and parking some of their tanks in the famous District Commissioner's Bungalow – scene of some of the fiercest fighting on any front in the war – on April 30th.

* * *

In Ceylon, Susan had started work on April 13th. A letter from Fortune arrived the same day, and she wrote: 'I feel very lost … He is as miserable as I am …'

The letters kept coming, generally arriving two days after they were written, thanks to the frequent flights between Delhi and Kandy; one written on the 14th, another on the 15th. One fat missive told Susan that Fortune was going on another tour with Wavell, starting on May 2nd. His letter describing his trip reached her on May 17th:

> We had a great trip to Sikkim, and it was terrific to get up into the hills and be able to feel cold for once in a while. To get there we more or less made history in more ways than one. To begin with, we only took fifteen hours, Delhi to Gangtok – no one has ever done it in a day before – and then our diverse modes of transport couldn't have been more different. Leaping out of a high-powered aircraft, we leaped onto a collection of elephants, which trumpeted loudly and bore us across a nearby river, which unfortunately was in flood. No one knew whether elephants could swim! It was eventually decided that even if they couldn't they might always cheat by having one foot on the bottom!
>
> We then motored though tea plantations for miles and miles and eventually entered a large valley or gorge, up which we motored in a tortuous, and in places precarious, road. This valley of the Tista river is so deep that although we were climbing constantly, it still remained muggy and hot, and the dust from our rather *kutcha* [makeshift] cars was worse than the Western Desert. At last we started to get into the hill country, and you could see the change of features of the local populace. They began to look more Asiatic, and from the scraggy Indian you began to see tough little men, with thick calves and cheerful Mongolian faces, clad very often in their one piece jerkin and kilt, with a huge kukri dangling from their belt. As it grew dark we passed through several villages, and it was grand to smell the reek of a real good log fire again and to see the cosy log huts these people live in.
>
> We arrived in Gangtok quite late at night and got our first sniff of mountain air. The people are so charming, always smiling, and dress in gorgeous robes – some of them – and always seem pleased to see you.
>
> Our stay was just like one long pantomime. We went to one official function which terminated with a cabaret show. The Bhutan warriors were the highlight of the

performance – these sturdy little hill-men, dressed in a garb which must be something like the dress of the ancient Scots, perform wild leaps and turns in perfect time with one another, and with the grace of trained ballet dancers. Their music is a bit painful – but rather adds to the riot of fun. Tibetan dancers did their stuff, and the local people – Lepchas – did a barn dance, rushing round amongst some hay, which they had strewn on the ground, kneading it with their feet, and yelling at one another to go faster. Finally, in a state of exhaustion, they fall in a heap and call it a day. Finally the local school-children sang 'Land of Hope and Glory', which gave the party a more sober atmosphere – and we all went home …

We managed to get to the Tibetan frontier – 17,000 feet – my, did my head ache. We made it on foot and ponies, but at one stage we almost had to carry the ponies! We reached the pass leading into Tibet in a roaring hailstorm – so, feeling a bit browned off, as they say, we found a small cave in which we took shelter. Someone produced a bottle of brandy and some tea, and we had a rousing party, watched by some grinning Tibetans, who thought it was a great joke. It was lovely up there – the snow, rhododendrons, swift-running stream, and waterfall – I didn't want to come back, but one has to.[18]

* * *

Mackrill.

When Mackrill had left Hopper's in July 1943 and joined the Royal Navy, he had done so just as the Navy was changing its officer selection procedures, since the number and quality of temporary officers were woefully low. When McArthur had joined, potential officers had been selected from the ranks of new recruits, sent to sea on an operational vessel for at least two months (McArthur had done his sea time on HMS *Forester*), and then put before the Admiralty Selection Board. The Board was looking for signs of personal cleanliness and turnout, the ability to speak clearly, above-average intelligence, and intangibles such as personality and an officer-like attitude. However, the varied experience and competence of those who then went on HMS *King Alfred* for officer training had made it hard to run courses.

Quite sensibly, the Navy decided instead to identify potential officers as before, but to give them extra training to a higher standard during their initial courses. These potential officers would then be sent on board dedicated training ships for five weeks, giving them all a common experience and standard of training, before going before the Selection Board. The course on board ship aimed to accustom trainees to life in a Royal Navy warship, as well as to complete their understanding of the contents of the *Seaman's Pocket Book,* which had been introduced in June 1943. It included information vital for a civilian learning to be a sailor: a glossary of sea terms, and the basics of safety, navigation, steering, rigging, anchors, cables, and boat-work. A 'miscellaneous' section included such useful information as how to sling and fold a hammock.

The new system was in place by the autumn of 1943, and was revised in January 1944 in the light of experience – just in time for Mackrill to be a beneficiary. Thus, after his initial training at HMS *Ganges,* he went to a training ship instead of straight to HMS *King Alfred.* The most obvious change was an increase in time on board ship from five to seven weeks, since the trainees had struggled to get used to life on board a warship at the same time as learning the ropes, cables, and hawsers.

Mackrill was trained on the light cruiser HMS *Dauntless* in March and April 1944, operating out of Rosyth in the Firth of Forth. *Dauntless* had been on active service from the start of the war, both in the Far East and the Indian Ocean, having taken part for example in the Allied landings on Madagascar in 1942. By 1943 she was thoroughly obsolete,[19] and so had been relegated to be one of the three training ships for potential officers. *Dauntless* had accommodation for 180 trainees, who arrived in batches of twenty or so every week.

HMS Dauntless. (IWM FL 5375)

Mackrill and his companions formed a Division, under a Royal Navy Lieutenant and a Petty Officer who stayed with them for the whole period. A Division messed together, and trainees in their first weeks aboard received extra rations of bread and milk to make up for the voracious appetites which they developed. The potential officers spent time getting used to life on board, learning the necessary procedures and words of command as they progressed through the quarter-deck, the main and fore-top, the forecastle, and general supervisory duties.

After their initial period on board, they worked from 0600hrs until 0900hrs daily before five one-hour instructional periods. There were daily semaphore, Aldis-lamp, and flag-hoisting lessons; every day at evening quarters they practised drills such as lowering and hoisting boats, and action and emergency stations. In most weeks there would be a bigger drill such as a night exercise involving the firing of star-shell, simple

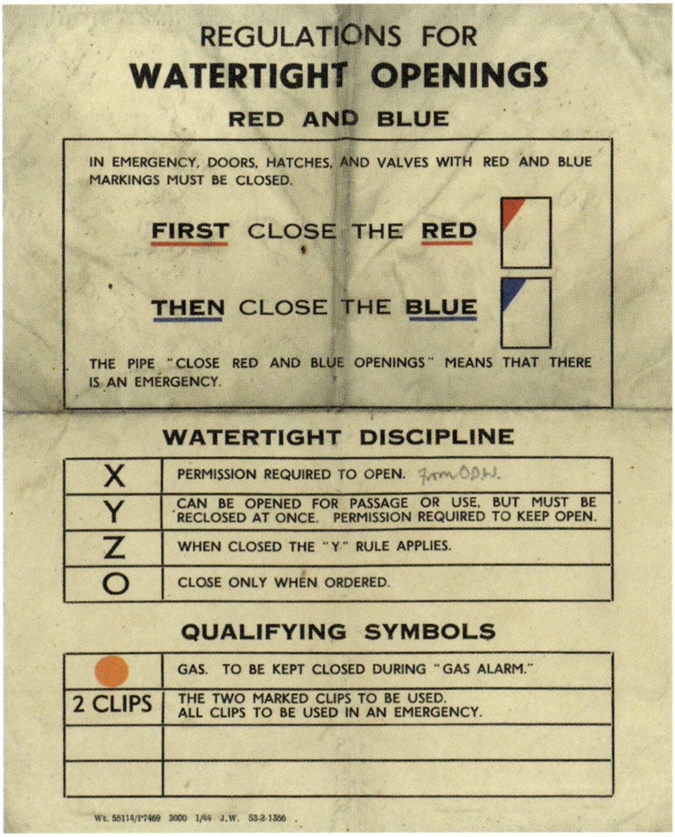

REGULATIONS FOR
WATERTIGHT OPENINGS
RED AND BLUE

IN EMERGENCY, DOORS, HATCHES, AND VALVES WITH RED AND BLUE MARKINGS MUST BE CLOSED.

FIRST CLOSE THE **RED**

THEN CLOSE THE **BLUE**

THE PIPE "CLOSE RED AND BLUE OPENINGS" MEANS THAT THERE IS AN EMERGENCY.

WATERTIGHT DISCIPLINE

X	PERMISSION REQUIRED TO OPEN.
Y	CAN BE OPENED FOR PASSAGE OR USE, BUT MUST BE RECLOSED AT ONCE. PERMISSION REQUIRED TO KEEP OPEN.
Z	WHEN CLOSED THE "Y" RULE APPLIES.
O	CLOSE ONLY WHEN ORDERED.

QUALIFYING SYMBOLS

●	GAS. TO BE KEPT CLOSED DURING "GAS ALARM."
2 CLIPS	THE TWO MARKED CLIPS TO BE USED. ALL CLIPS TO BE USED IN AN EMERGENCY.

Wt. 55114/P7469 3000 1/44 J.W. 53-2-1356

Mackrill kept these instructions with the notes which he took during his training.
(Mackrill family collection)

ship-handling manoeuvres using elementary signals, and boat-work at anchor. In their last week afloat, trainees worked as crew members on 6-inch guns and 20mm Oerlikons, firing live ammunition at targets.

Mackrill wrote to Robertson in May 1944 whilst on leave in Yorkshire pending officer training:

> I left the *Dauntless* a short time ago and am at present spending a very short seven days at home, after which I am going to *King Alfred*. While I was on board, I met a Lieutenant Salmon RN who lives in Winchester and said he knew you. He was just going on leave when I left and told me he would probably see you, and all this may be stale news… .
>
> I met Robin Lewin when I was last in London, which was about two months ago – he seems to be getting on pretty well, and has risen to a Lieutenant in the 60th.[20]

* * *

Like Mackie, Richardson was in Ceylon in April, but on May 5th he set sail on HMS *Illustrious* – elder sister to his old friend *Victorious*. The mission, code-named Operation Transom, was a raid on the Japanese-held port of Surabaya on Java. Sailing from Ceylon, the British Eastern Fleet – in company with another old friend, USS *Saratoga* – refuelled in Western Australia before heading for Java. On the morning of May 17th, American and British aircraft took off from the two carriers, formed up, and at 0720hrs headed north towards their targets. Two FAA Avengers crashed on take-off, but their crews were rescued.

An Avenger prepares for launch from HMS Illustrious *as the sun rises.* (IWM A24254)

When the Allied aircraft arrived over Surabaya at 0830hrs they took the defenders completely by surprise. Force A – nine Avengers from *Illustrious,* twelve Dauntless dive-bombers from *Saratoga,* and an escort of eight Corsair fighters – flew in from the south to bomb industrial complexes, with the Avengers hitting the Braat Engineering Works, and the Dauntlesses bombing an oil refinery at Wonokromo. The larger Force B, swinging round to attack from the north, focused on the port and shipping, with twenty-one Avengers, six more Dauntlesses, another eight Corsairs and twelve Hellcats. The defenders managed to shoot down an American Avenger, the crew being taken prisoner, but were otherwise largely ineffective. The elated Allied aircrew returned boasting of having flattened both the Braat works and the oil refinery, destroyed sixteen aircraft on a local airfield, and damaged ten ships. Japanese sources do not suggest that the damage was that severe.

Above: the raid on Surabaya, May 17th 1944. (US Navy photograph, public domain)

Below: an Avenger lands back on HMS Illustrious. (IWM A24270)

Crews of the Avengers from HMS Illustrious *after the Surabaya raid; gunners form the front row, observers the middle row, & the pilots the rear row.* (IWM A24258)

Saratoga carried on towards the Pacific afterwards, whilst *Illustrious* returned to Ceylon, arriving on May 27th. At that point, 832 Squadron transferred to the smaller HMS *Begum*.

* * *

May 29th
Letter from Brucie telling me that … Doug Nicoll has been killed – oh God, what a bloody war.[21]

Avengers (& two Corsairs) aboard HMS Illustrious, *May 1944.* (IWM A24272; edited by dansteele.net)

XVI

'Being bombed in harbour at night; a most unpleasant experience'

Cassino to the Gothic Line, March 15th–September 4th 1944

When you look round the mountains, through the mud and rain,
You'll find the scattered crosses, some which bear no name.
Heartbreak and toil and suffering gone,
The boys beneath them slumber on.
They were the D-Day Dodgers, who'll stay in Italy.
(Song of Allied troops in Italy, to the tune of *Lili Marlene*)

In May 1944 the Allies launched Operation Diadem, their fourth and final attempt to break the Gustav Line. The fighting in front of Cassino all this while had been bloody and uncomfortable. Disbelieving German assurances that they were not using the Monastery as an observation post, in February 1944 the Allies took the decision – hotly debated ever since – to bomb the building into rubble. On February 15th a huge artillery and aerial bombardment smashed the Monastery to pieces, but succeeded only in making it even harder to winkle out the German defenders. The Germans moved into the ruined buildings immediately after the raid, and from the rubble gained a panoramic view of the Allied positions below.

Balked of success when they bombed the Monastery in February, the Allies then meted out the same treatment to the town of Cassino itself, at the foot of Monastery Hill. On March 15th their guns and aircraft obliterated Cassino, reducing the town to an earthly Hell. But some of the American aircraft involved dropped their bombs miles short of the town (just as they had in February). Bombs which fell four miles to the south hit the Command Post of 100 Battery, 74 Medium Regiment RA, killing two officers, four signallers and six other men. The Battery Commander was one of the two officers killed: he was Major Philip ('Pip') Sturt, a Hopperite aged twenty-nine.[1]

* * *

Among the units waiting to be let off the leash were XII Royal Lancers (12RL), an armoured reconnaissance regiment without proper employment given the static nature of the front line. They were deployed as infantry near Castel di Sangro on the edge of the Abruzzi, north of Cassino. Middleditch described the waiting in a letter to Robertson:

> I was extremely bored with doing nothing for so long and thoroughly sick of North Africa, so I was very glad to move and am enjoying seeing a new country extremely. I'm also trying to learn Italian, so far without conspicuous success. At the moment we are living very comfortably in a large house decorated in the most bogus style imaginable: hideous oil paintings and murals, marble busts, a gold fish-pond in the ante room, and a number of marble benches. This astonishing edifice is in the middle of a very squalid slum. The poverty here is appalling, and people fight for the food in the swill tubs left from the troops' meals. If it's bad here, I can't think what it's like in occupied Europe.[2]

Middleditch.

12RL were posted on the south-east bank of the River Sangro, whilst the Germans were in the mountains on the north-west side. Although there were many features in the local area over 1,000 metres, some still topped with snow, the Germans held Point 1883, which gave them unrivalled views across the whole valley. Movement, therefore, was by night; by day, a line of observation posts looked out for the enemy. Boredom was alleviated by vigorous patrolling by night from the OPs; this was intended to dominate the valley and deter Germans patrols from attacking. Middleditch, in 'A' Squadron, was billeted in Capracotta – whose name means 'cooked goat'.

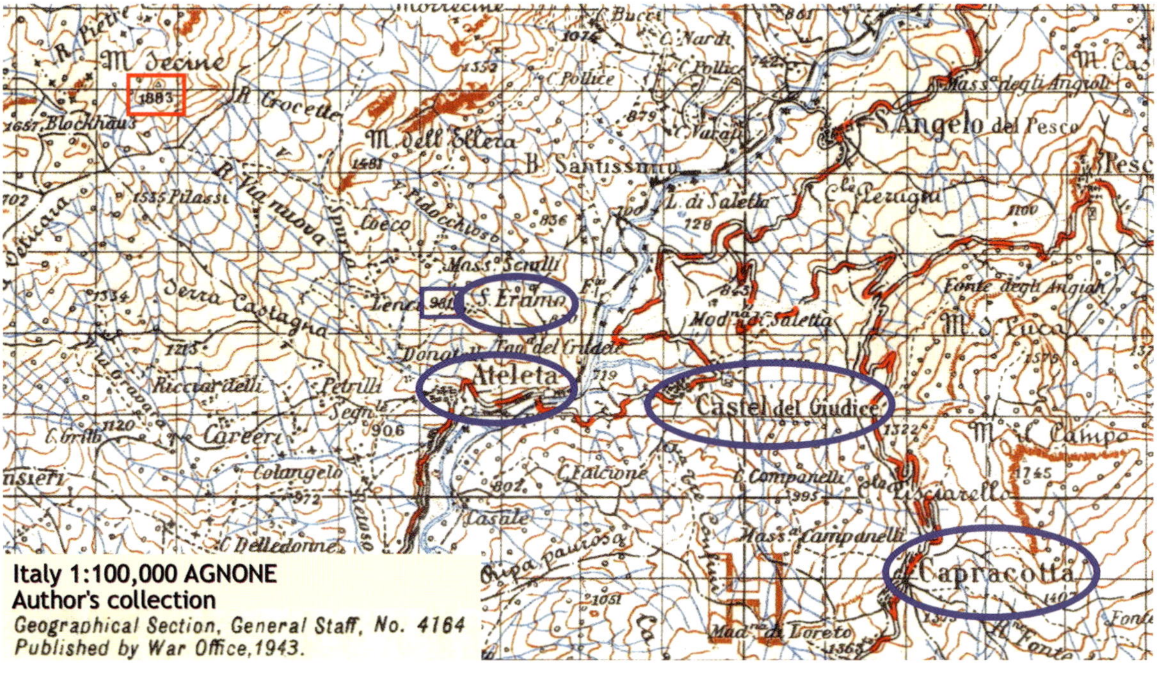

Italy 1:100,000 AGNONE
Author's collection
Geographical Section, General Staff, No. 4164
Published by War Office, 1943.

On the night of April 30th, a fortnight after writing the above letter, Middleditch led five of his men out to find a suitable location for a forward patrol base on the far side of the Sangro.[3] Their route took them through Castel del Giudice across the river to Ateleta, followed by a stiff climb to Point 981 before descending to S Eramo.

* * *

For his part, Peter Walker was nearing the end of his training at Sandhurst. He wrote to Robertson on May 1st:[4]

Walker.

May-day! – And what a glorious day. So glorious that I feel supremely happy. We have a 'sports afternoon' which means we play some sort of a game and have from 1400hrs to 1700hrs free and start work again afterwards. Consequently I have an hour free in which to write down some of the thoughts that have been whirling around in my head this last week-end and I can think of no better outlet than to address them to you, as I feel you'll understand them better than anyone. These short periods when exuberance and good spirits, happiness and pure *joie-de-vivre,* take hold of one are opportunities not to be missed, so here I start.

First, let me tell you why I feel so supremely happy, and then I'll try to be more serious. I suppose this glorious weather at one of the most beautiful times of the year has much to do with it. Anyway I seem to be one of the luckiest men alive – to be as happy as this at a time when the rest of the world stinks with unhappiness. I managed to get a day off yesterday and arrived home with Daniel [Awdry] in time for a late Sunday breakfast.[5] The little railway line that takes me home is a very small one, rather like the Winchester–Newbury line, and the trains stop at every station – one or two people get off and one or two people get on – for the most part country people, a few soldiers possibly, but anyway a different sort of person to those who travel on the main lines. Anyway, I knew I was set for a good day – it was a beautiful day and when I arrived home the beech trees were just out and the grass was beautifully green, the lilac and wistaria almost out, and it was really lovely. We played tennis; Keith and I sang 'Watchman'! – and it was just a day away from all that reminded one of misery and poverty, hatred and cruelty and all the rest. And I couldn't help feeling how unfortunate so many people were who couldn't get pleasure from seeing flowers and trees all coming out and couldn't appreciate the beauty and innocence of farmyards and fields. And I felt strangely sorry not only for those who never have a chance of seeing them, but also for those who see them and yet still can't appreciate it and love it all.

I have had a wonderful time since I've been here. I have five weeks more to go and in the spare time that I have had in the last twenty-one I have read, played games, made friends, gone to parties, listened to gramophone recitals, and generally had a lovely time. I know it's probably wrong, and even if it isn't I don't deserve it, and many a time I've imagined you saying 'you just don't know what war is' and I've thought of you and your generation in the last war who would have given anything for 1/20 of the breaks and leave I have had, but believe me I haven't just dismissed it and said 'Well, this isn't 1914' – still my thoughts are running away with me and I meant to talk about that later.

I have had dinner and lunch with the Sinclairs … . I thought the Sinclairs quite the most charming and worthy (in its broadest sense) people I have ever met, and we talked of John, and I was able to tell her of the days when he was Senior Prefect and I looked after his clothes as a one-year man, and she showed me photographs and talked with a frankness and sincerity and a brave understanding which I couldn't help admiring terribly …

We work hard, especially these last six weeks: I have a regular soldier (Captain Walker in the Buffs) for my Troop officer for this final course – the tactics. We go out continually on schemes, but last Thursday, on being attacked in the middle of the night, sent up parachute flares which started a terrific forest fire … around Hartford Bridge Flats, and this soon proved quite out of our control and firemen from the aerodrome, National Fire Service, and literally a regiment of soldiers – or, rather, a battalion – came out to help put it out. At about 0300hrs the wind dropped and by a stroke of luck we put it out – nevertheless, quite an experience. We patrolled all the rest of the night in case it broke out again, as of course the place was covered with embers.

It so happened that the following night was a passing-out dinner for one of the troops in the Squadron. At 0100hrs this time, they decided to let off three 4-inch smoke-generators in our building. Dan [Awdry] and I woke up coughing our heads off, grabbed our respirators, and got out of it! Our room was more full of smoke than most as both doors and windows were open. We managed to wake up everybody. It was a very stupid thing to do and three of the Cadets were kept back (all of them Guards), though of course there were others equally responsible, and as we now get no leave on being commissioned, they will have had to report to their units (Pirbright, I suppose) with a rather damaged reputation – one of them a Belt winner too!

I can't tell you how good this place has been. It has combined the discipline of Winchester with occasionally the laxity of Oxford, which as a way of life is ideal and as practical experience – first class training. As regards the future I can only say that although I may not have generalship in the sense of a good tactical brain, I have the confidence and the enthusiasm which I trust will see me through. To one like me, who has seen in nearly twenty years more fun, more happiness, more lovable things than one in thousands are privileged to see in a life-time, there is not the slightest excuse why I should not put every ounce of energy and sense of duty that I can possibly build up. I can only hope that I have an opportunity to put it all into practice.

* * *

On May 11th, 12RL were briefed on wider operations which had begun that day. Their own role was to keep the Germans on the Sangro under pressure so that they could not be moved to support other sectors of the line. And so at noon on May 12th, Middleditch and his colleague Lieutenant Wise led a platoon-sized force across the Sangro to Petrilli, where they set up a forward patrol base. The plan was to have two bases (Petrilli and Coeco), with two OPs (Points 1213 and 1481):

The 12RL war diary reported with satisfaction that the enemy were definitely still present and had increased their shelling of British positions in response to the aggression in the sector. On May 15th, Middleditch and the troops north of the Sangro moved back to the 'friendly' side of the river, their diversionary aims achieved.

* * *

Operation Diadem not only planned to break the Gustav Line, but also the fortified Hitler Line which lay ten miles behind it. Diadem involved four Army Corps, each of a different nationality. Furthest west, the American II Corps was to advance up the coast along Route 7; to its east, the French Corps was to break out of its bridgehead across the Garigliano and push through the Aurunci Mountains; the British XIII Corps was to force a crossing of the Rapido River, and then attack up the Liri Valley; meanwhile, II Polish Corps, on the eastern flank, was to outflank the monastery on Monte Cassino and try to link up with XIII Corps. I Canadian Corps would then pursue the enemy up the Liri Valley. If Diadem succeeded, and the Allied troops in the Anzio beach-head to the north broke out westwards, there was a good chance that the German Tenth Army could be trapped and destroyed.

The offensive began on May 11th with a huge artillery bombardment, as XIII Corps tried to batter its way across the Rapido, but did not develop quite as planned. Although XIII Corps was successful, sucking in the German reserves and making the tasks of the other formations easier, it was the spectacular success of the French in the Aurunci Mountains which broke the Gustav Line on May 14th; their mountain troops, the infamous Goumiers, achieved an advance which no one (Germans or Allies) had thought possible.

* * *

Brooke.

There were many Wykehamists in front of Cassino in May 1944 – too many to do them justice – and the difficulty of crossing the rivers barring the entrance to the Liri Valley led to numerous acts of courage. Our subjects must stand as examples of what the troops experienced.

In the forefront of the advance were the Sherman tanks of 16th/5th Lancers (16th/5th), who, as we have seen, had landed at Naples in January, spent a good while in defence at Minturno, and late in February had moved to be ready for an advance which had not occurred. This time, in support of 78th Infantry Division, they were to cross 'Oxford' and 'Congo' bridges and advance westwards to cut Route 6 and join up with Polish troops.

On the night of May 11th-12th, the Royal Engineers attempted to erect bridges to allow Allied armour to get across to the German bank. However, the infantry encountered strong opposition, a smoke screen mixing with heavy mist in the valley to make it hard to tell what was happening. Two of the three bridging sites came under sustained machine-gun fire, preventing any work on them; the third, 'Amazon' bridge, suffered intense sniper and mortar fire, which made progress very difficult. It was not until 0415hrs on May 13th that Amazon bridge was completed, after heroic efforts by the Sappers.

As they crossed the river early on May 14th, 16th/5th were held up at 'Oxford', which had the fortuitous outcome that they missed a German counter-attack which came in at 0830hrs. By the time that Brooke crossed, at around 0940hrs, the Germans were running

The triangle on the turret of this Sherman tank of 16th/5th Lancers shows that it is from 'A' Squadron; the photograph was taken in the front line in May 1944. In the foreground is a 17-pounder anti-tank gun, with a Bren gun for close protection. (Copyright holder unknown; edited by dansteele.net)

out of steam, and by noon 'B' Squadron had come into the line, which remained static for the rest of the day.

Enemy mortar and *Nebelwerfer* fire was fairly heavy by day and sporadic through the night. Troops who had experienced both said that German shell-fire, mortar-fire, and *Nebelwerfer* projectiles were far worse than what they had encountered in Africa or

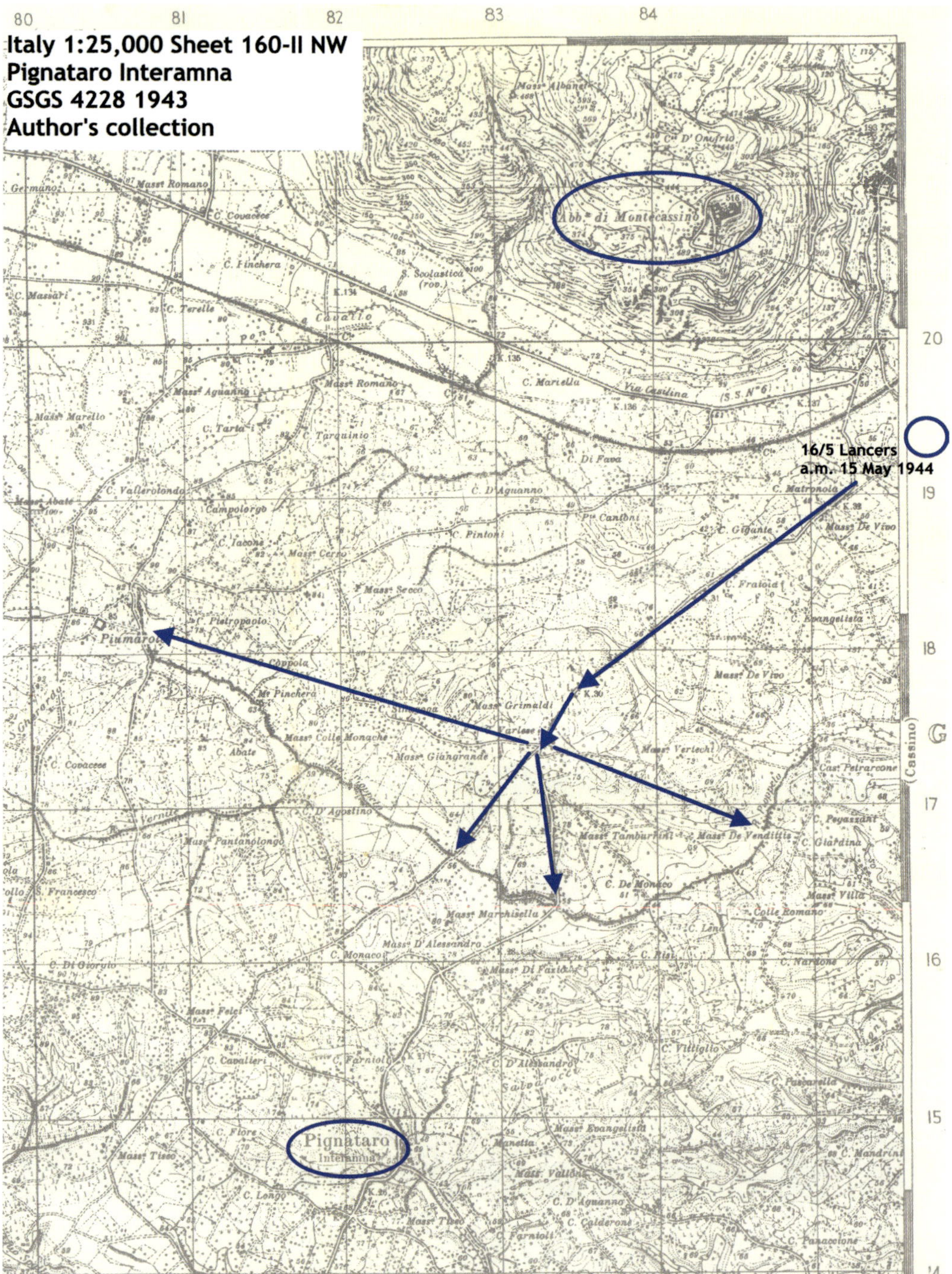

Sicily. The following morning – May 15th – found the Regiment about 200 metres east of what is now the Commonwealth War Graves Commission's Cassino War Cemetery.

16th/5th then pushed south-west, and by early afternoon were nearly up to the line of the road from Cassino to Pignataro, code-named 'Grafton'. At 1515hrs, the advance encountered anti-tank guns, and Brooke's commanding officer – a Wykehamist, Lieutenant Colonel John Loveday[6] – paused to confer with Lieutenant Colonel Goff, the OC of the accompanying 2nd London Irish Rifles. Lieutenant Nicholas Mosley – son of the notorious Wykehamist Sir Oswald Ernald Mosley[7] – was with 2LIR, and explained in his memoirs what happened next:[8]

> The day after our crossing of the Rapido, we were on stand-by all day to take the lead in the big push to the north. The starting time for this kept being, as usual, postponed. There were said to be not enough tanks yet across the river; the blocking-off of the monastery by smoke had to be renewed. When we had been crossing the river, the smoke had often enveloped us like a low-lying fog; now, in the clearer morning air, the monastery floated like a celestial city above a fitful low-lying cloud. During the day we moved closer to our leading positions, but even with the smoke clearing it was difficult to make out anything of the larger picture. The Liri river was a tributary of the Rapido, running into it from the north; the landscape of the valley was a pleasant one of low undulations and clumps of trees. All we knew of the battle was from what we heard, and endured, from what seemed to be the random violence of exploding shells and the wailing of the *Nebelwerfers,* which we had christened Moaning Minnies. We learned that our commanding officer, Colonel Goff, had been killed by a shell from one of these while trying to see what lay ahead; also killed with him was the commanding officer of the tank regiment appointed to work with us.

Brooke wrote to Robertson that 'our Colonel John Loveday was killed the first day across the Rapido, which was a terrible blow as he was a most charming man and a very good soldier.'[9]

The countryside was very 'close' and this made it hard to see what was ahead; tanks and infantry had to co-operate in concert or risk disaster. Brooke showed real quality that day:

> On May 15th, his was one of the leading troops. The action was a difficult one and necessitated several changes of direction and the careful use of ground. He manoeuvred his Troop so well that not only did all his men reach the objective, but they succeeded in putting the infantry on to the objective, inflicting many casualties on the enemy. Later in the day, when one of Lieutenant Brooke's tanks went up on a minefield, he inspired the tank commander to such an extent that he remained in his tank firing and observing during the rest of the day.[10]

By nightfall, after heavy concentrations of artillery fire on enemy positions, 'Grafton' had largely been secured.

The following morning, the advance continued under cover of a barrage towards objective 'Pytchley', 16th/5th again on the left. A few German tanks and self-propelled guns (SPGs) were encountered, and several were knocked out. By 1040hrs the day's first objective was reached and by noon 16th/5th had reached 'Pytchley' – but its accompanying infantry had been held up short of the objective by heavy machine-gun fire from the left flank. As German infantry, SPGs, and anti-tank weapons were encountered, they were engaged and destroyed, despite heavy fire from mortars and *Nebelwerfers*:

> On May 16th, Lieutenant Brooke's troop was in reserve on the left flank of the advance, but by his careful observation he was able to spot one anti-tank gun and a half-tracked vehicle, both of which he was able to knock out and so enable the advance to proceed on the left.[11]

As evening drew in, a counter-attack developed on both flanks. It was repelled, but the advance was painfully slow and Monte Cassino was still in enemy hands.

At first light on May 17th, 16th/5th were to push west and north, with 'B' Squadron leading on the left of the advance. Care had to be taken, since enemy anti-tank guns were known to be in the village of Piumarola to the west. Thick mist slowed the approach to the start line, but the attacks eventually went in successfully behind another artillery barrage and by 0855hrs the initial objectives were secure.

> On May 17th, the Squadron was again supporting the infantry, this time on to two objectives, both of which meant going through very thick country, entirely unsuitable for tanks, and strongly defended. With great calmness, Lieutenant Brooke led his Troop, which was again leading, so well that the infantry gained both their objectives exactly to plan, with extremely few casualties to the infantry and none to his Troop. The attacks started at 0800hrs and 1200hrs, approximately, and the objectives were reached at 0930hrs and 1400hrs, approximately – the whole advance covering 2½ hours.[12]

At midday 'A' Squadron was warned to prepare to attack Piumarola, which was a threat to the left flank of the advance, whilst 'B' Squadron pushed on to clear a ridge which had been holding up other units. But at 1410hrs they reported tanks to their front – at least one 'Tiger' had allegedly been spotted, although there were in fact no Tigers south of Anzio at the time. Nevertheless, elements of 'A' Squadron moved cautiously forwards to the '*wadi*' which lay between them and Piumarola; by 1930hrs the whole Squadron was across and under heavy shell-fire in the village. 'A' Squadron withdrew when relieved by M-10 tank destroyers.

It was in the fighting of these three days – May 15th to 17th – that Brooke earned a Military Cross.

> The Military Cross
> Lieutenant Henry Arthur Gunning Brooke.
> 16th/5th Lancers, Royal Armoured Corps.
> Italy – 1944
> During the fighting on the 15th, 16th, and 17th May, Lieutenant BROOKE's handling of his troop was beyond praise… During these three days, Lieutenant Brooke's Troop knocked out two Mark IV tanks, three anti-tank guns, one half-tracked vehicle, and

two mortars, as well as inflicting heavy casualties among enemy infantry. The success of these attacks was very largely due to the magnificent way in which Lieutenant Brooke led his troop. He was a great inspiration to all.[13]

The letters which Brooke's father and mother wrote to Robertson when they heard the news show the pride and sense of achievement which was the other side of the coin to the misery of loss:[14]

My dear Bobber,
I am sure you will be pleased and interested to hear that Henry got the MC. I don't know definitely what for, but one of his brother subalterns wrote to Essex and said he had done 'magnificently'. It has not been in the papers yet. One thing I never had any qualms [about] for Henry [was] on the score of 'guts'.

Dear Bobber,
Thank you so much for your very nice letter. I knew you would be pleased about Henry getting the MC. We are very proud of him. I am enclosing you a copy of the citation we got from the War Office, which will tell you what he did. I don't want it back. I think he must have done a good job. I had an awfully nice letter from his Colonel, who said he had done consistently well and in his opinion he had got a very well deserved award. We heard from him last week; they are out of the line there and having a well earned rest – but I doubt them being left there long.[15]

All that Brooke himself said to Robertson of this period was:

We weren't launched until May 14th, when we passed through Sant'Angelo, and then had some pretty heavy fighting for about a week, which included being bombed in harbour at night; a most unpleasant experience.[16]

* * *

In Germany, meanwhile, Simpkin could only wait for the longed-for day when he would see Barbara again. He sent Robertson a postcard on May 17th:

Simpkin.

Things go on much the same here; I'm plugging frantically at my languages, trying to work up a second string if Army prospects aren't too good after the war. I have been hearing from Barbara regularly; she seems quite well, but I gather rather over-working.[17]

* * *

By contrast with the grinding fight of May 17th, the Liri battle changed for the better the following day. The freshest squadron of 16th/5th – 'C' Squadron – attacked north at 0945hrs, but encountered no opposition. At 1110hrs came the news that Monte Cassino had fallen to the Poles, and that the Germans were attempting to break contact and retire to their next set of defences, the Hitler Line, between Aquino and Pontecorvo. (The Germans hurriedly re-christened it the Senger Line when they realized what an ill omen its fall might be). 16th/5th were left in reserve as the advance sped towards Aquino.

After bitter fighting, the Hitler Line was smashed open by the Canadians at Pontecorvo on May 23rd, just as the troops at Anzio began their break-out. Had it not been for General Mark Clark's controversial decision to direct his advance on Rome, instead of against the retreating German Tenth Army as he had been ordered, the war in Italy might have been shortened considerably. As it was, the Germans managed to extricate their forces from the trap, and were able to retreat by stages.

* * *

Kemp and 7RB had landed in Italy on May 4th, a year since the end of the Battalion's operations in Tunisia, but it was to be another month before they found themselves in action. Kemp later explained in a letter to Robertson what he had been up to since their last meeting:

Kemp.

> After meeting you at Charles Duffin's wedding, I sailed for the Middle East, arriving in three weeks, after a very pleasant passage through the Med. We were attacked twice from the air, and after the first attack, in which a ship was sunk, I had to line the boat deck with a squad of my Riflemen whenever action stations was sounded. We never got a shoot, though, as the planes came in too high the second time.
>
> I was lucky enough to get a posting in a matter of days to 7RB – no easy thing as all the battalions were full, but the Adjutant and one of the Company Commanders were old friends whom I had known in England. Quite naturally I had to drop my third pip as I was almost the only officer in the Battalion who hadn't seen action in the desert or Tunis. I commanded a Motor Platoon in 'A' Company with Dick Adams (of 'F') as 2i/c of the Company.[18] Johnny Persse was the only other Wykehamist, though Bill Adams joined us a little later.[19]
>
> We spent an enjoyable and useful five months in the Delta area training for 'close warfare' … I spent a most enjoyable leave at the beginning of April, when I 'hitched' with a fellow officer from near Suez to Beirut and thence on to Bechare,[20] a little village in the hills above Tripoli some thousand feet below the Cedars, Lebanon, where the Army has a ski school. Strictly, the Cedars slopes are out of bounds to all except official students, but nobody objected to our using the lower slopes provided that we kept well out of the light. We got in some three days' skiing, before having to hitch back. The journey itself was not interesting and the whole leave thoroughly worth while.
>
> After that the Battalion lent a hand in quelling the Greek Troubles around Alex. From the looks of the news at the moment these troubles seem to be starting all over again in Athens …
>
> We weren't sorry to leave the country for Italy in May. Quite apart from the hot season, which was just starting, the constant parties of Alex and Cairo were beginning to make holes in most people's bank balances.[21]

One such occasion became family legend:

> One evening David and several friends went to Cairo to find a bar. They settled on one and sat at a table and ordered fourteen Kimmel (the local fire-water). After a while they were getting impatient. David saw the waiter again and said 'Where are my fourteen Kimmel?' Still nothing happened.
>
> By then some of the soldiers were drifting away to another bar. David saw the waiter again and again asked for his fourteen Kimmel.
>
> Quite a few of the group had drifted away by the time that forty-two Kimmel turned up at the table. Well, being under-paid soldiers, the few who were left decided to drink everything. By the time that they had finished the drinks it was getting late, so they had to rush to catch the last truck back to base. David was running for the truck, which was just leaving. He missed his step, fell off the back of the truck, and rolled to the side of the road in a drunken stupor. In those times it was not unknown for soldiers to be robbed and even killed, so David was lucky that the MPs found him. They took him back to base, where he slept the rest of the night in the guard house.
>
> The next day was an inter-regimental football match. This was not pleasant in the heat, with a raging hangover.[22]

It was clear that infantry were more useful than armour in the broken terrain of Italy, and units like 7RB – trained and equipped to operate alongside tanks in mobile warfare – were now reorganized on more conventional lines. Kemp explained the implications in his letter to Robertson:

> On the boat over to Italy we had an uneventful voyage, during which I played a lot of bridge and enjoyed fantastic luck. We hadn't been out here long before we said goodbye to most of our transport and became transformed from a Motor Battalion to Lorried Infantry.

By May 28th 7RB were ready to move into the front line. From now on, the Battalion was closely supported by 'I' Battery, 2RHA, whose Forward Observation Officer often accompanied the Battalion: he was another Wykehamist, Captain Christopher Seton-Watson.[23]

7RB spearheaded the advance through Alatri, on the northern flank of the Liri valley, and around half-way between Cassino and Rome. As they set out on June 3rd, almost at once their scouts were engaged by two 88mm guns and German infantry, which led to a running battle to secure a T-junction five miles to the north. Kemp was a Platoon Commander in 'A' Company, which hooked around the left flank of the enemy position, taking fourteen prisoners; 'B' Company then fought through, before 'A' Company took over again and finished the enemy off. Further advances that day were forestalled when the Germans blew up a bridge just as the advance elements arrived. Two officers had been killed, with casualties of around twenty in all; the capture of three enemy guns and over thirty prisoners was small consolation. This set the pattern for the campaign in general: each day, probing forwards until enemy delaying parties were encountered – which inevitably meant casualties.

* * *

The last Wykehamist to land at Anzio had been Holtby. He had been commissioned in November 1943, 'strings' having been pulled to get him into the Black Watch. In August, Jack Parr, in charge of the Winchester College OTC, wrote to the most important Wykehamist (and Black Watch officer) then living, Viscount Wavell, who was in the process of becoming Viceroy of India. On leave in Scotland, Wavell was also putting the finishing touches to his successful anthology of poetry, *Other Men's Flowers*, but still took the time to deal with Parr's request. Wavell's reply found its way into Robertson's papers:

> Dear Parr,
> Have sent your letter about Holtby to the Colonel of the Black Watch, General Wauchope. He will do anything he can.
> Yours in haste
> Wavell[24]

Holtby.

Wauchope was a great friend of Wavell, and the result was that Holtby joined the Black Watch.[25] However, when he went out to Italy he was transferred to the Seaforth Highlanders. Although his Battalion – 6 Seaforth – had landed at Anzio in March, Holtby had still not joined them when he wrote to Robertson in the middle of May:[26]

> I've moved again but I'm still waiting until someone wants me and by the look of things it won't be long. There is not much doing with me and life goes on much the same as ever ... There was a Symphony Concert on in Naples conducted by Flight Lieutenant James Robertson, no doubt your nephew, but unfortunately I had no chance of seeing him as I couldn't get to Naples that particular weekend.
>
> It is a most depressing part of the country I am in just now, all heat and dust complete with very dirty and smelly Italians. I'm afraid I cannot feel sorry for them, for they have ample opportunity for keeping themselves and their dwellings clean but they simply do not avail themselves of it – too lazy no doubt. I think I told you that I met Sydney Middleditch in Naples and I have also come across Stowe (College) who is in the same Battalion as me. It is very pleasant to hear all the news of Wykehamists both old and present. However I have been very anxious to have word of old McArthur, so when you have time to write again please let me know anything you have heard ...
>
> I don't know whether you have heard of PPA [Popski's Private Army, a 'special forces' unit]? Of course I can't tell you about it, but at any rate I am endeavouring to wheedle my way into it; a very good job, but most exclusive and consequently very hard to get into. However, we shall see!

6 Seaforth were involved in the breakout from Anzio which formed a key part of the Allied plan. Holtby, however, only joined the Battalion on June 3rd, having been promoted Lieutenant on May 20th.[27] After the war, he told his family that he arrived in the Anzio pocket in the morning, met his Platoon at lunch-time, and led them into battle in the afternoon. His battle was short; at 1600hrs on June 4th his Battalion came out of the line, and did not see action again until the following year.

Also on June 4th, Peter Walker was commissioned into the Royal Wiltshire Yeomanry as a 2nd Lieutenant.[28] The date was of wider significance, as on that day Rome at last fell to the Allies – though Elliott-Binns was unimpressed:

> I heard that the Americans had taken Rome, the final goal of our months of fighting. It didn't excite me much. Rome, Milan, Vienna, Berlin – what were they to me? We had captured what I was interested in: the little villages and farms, and *wadis,* which I had watched and fired on for so long, places which we had won and lost again and bled for. Those places are hallowed to me – Carroceto, Pantoni, the Factory, Dead End Road, the Railway Bed, and Buonriposo. Buonriposo in particular. 'After life's fitful fevers they sleep well.'

Two days later, the news about Rome was eclipsed by that of the invasion of North-West Europe: D-Day.

XVII

'The man behind me ... was hit in the head by an 88mm solid shot, and just fell down headless, which rather shook me – but I soon got over it'

Normandy, June 1944

Whilst fighting had raged across the world, large numbers of troops had been training in England for the long-awaited return to France, the liberation of North-West Europe, and an attack on Germany itself. Offensive operations had been carried out by air for several years, but only the infantry can seize and hold ground. The last eleven months of the war against Germany would involve many more of Robertson's boys: from our photograph alone, Boyd, Clerk-Rattray, Duffin, Holtby, Kennedy, Lewin, Martyn, McArthur, and the Somervilles. For most of them, the last year of the war was the exciting and dangerous part, and many of them therefore recorded their experiences in some detail. Although final victory was not in doubt, there was always the uncertainty of whether or not one would live to see it. Not all of them did.

Unlike the war in Italy, constrained by the narrow peninsula and the relatively small size of the forces involved, the Allied liberation of occupied Europe was a vast affair beyond easy summary. Even to relate the actions of the British component – which of course included divisions of Canadians and Poles – is far beyond the scope of this work. We can only look at details from the picture, individual pieces in a complex mosaic, and hope that these small fragments of personal history illuminate and make human these dark and inhuman events.

* * *

Late in 1943, units which were needed for the battles to come in Normandy were withdrawn from Italy and the Middle East and returned home. It was hoped that their experience of action and campaigning would provide a useful leavening. One such was Hirst's Regiment, the Yorkshire Hussars, who had arrived back in Britain on December 12th:

Hirst.

> We had a long train journey to Brandon in Norfolk. There was snow on the ground and we were freezing, but the unit which had prepared the camp for us had itself just returned from the Middle

East and realised what a shock to the system the change of climate was. To our delight, a hot meal was ready, the stoves in the Nissen huts were nearly red-hot, and the beds were all made up with blankets.

In Norfolk we were converted from a tank unit to a reconnaissance regiment. This involved a big change in our role, the learning of new infantry skills, and our re-equipment with different vehicles – Bren-gun carriers and armoured scout cars. We became the recce regiment of 50th (Northumbrian) Infantry Division, a Division with a very fine record, which was preparing for the invasion of Europe.

During one night 'scheme' a stove exploded in a 3-ton truck while the cooks were cooking on the move. One man was badly burned, and I took him to hospital in Ipswich in a scout car, very cramped and uncomfortable for an injured man. It was the middle of the night, and I had great difficulty in finding the hospital in a strange town. When I eventually found it and roused the Sister who was on duty, I was furious that she insisted in writing down all his particulars before she gave any first aid to the man, who was obviously in great pain.

Meanwhile, Sim Feversham,[1] who resented going from tanks to Bren-gun carriers (and, horror of horrors, even being liable to fight on foot!), intrigued to get our tanks back. The result? Monty heard of it, said 'I will have no strings pulled in my Army', and we stayed as a recce regiment and were transferred to 61st Division. This was a second line division, unlikely to go into action. Although we were fed up with this, many of us were probably lucky, as a recce unit leading the way in the landing would have had heavy casualties.

So we moved down south to Shorncliffe, near Dover. It was an old garrison town – we were in barracks which probably dated from Napoleonic times. This was nearly the last time the Regiment was together before I left for India, as we were soon split up. 'A' Squadron were lucky, as we had a mobile defence role in case of counter-attack by the Germans. The other squadrons had the unenviable job of setting up and running the camps for the troops taking part in D-Day.

* * *

Dan Somerville.

D-Day did not stand alone, but came as a pivotal moment in a long series of connected actions. Preparations had been going on for years, and valuable experience had been gained in Operations Husky (Sicily), Avalanche (Salerno), and Shingle (Anzio) in the Mediterranean. Deception had been attempted before Husky, and the cost of poor security paid during Avalanche. For the Normandy landings, great efforts were made to conceal the Allies' intentions. Dan Somerville was rightly proud to have been involved in this important part of the plan, even though he did not reach the continent himself.

Operation Fortitude South was intended to convince the Germans – who were very good at signals interception – that the (fictional) First United States Army Group (FUSAG) would land in the Pas de Calais from South-East England several weeks after a smaller diversionary landing in Normandy. Somerville was involved in a sub-operation – Quicksilver II – a radio deception plan which tried to give the impression that large numbers of units had moved into the South-East.

> I played a part in the D-Day deception – Operation Fortitude – which saved many lives. We wanted the Germans to think that the attack in Normandy was only a diversion, and that the main assault was going to come across to the Channel Ports in the direction of Calais and Boulogne. The Channel is narrower there. To that end we dispatched a skeleton force, of which I was one. We went out into the countryside opposite Calais with vans and radios, and we pretended to be whole units, in my case an artillery regiment because I knew about guns. Others did infantry brigades and things. This was all to try and make the Germans think that the radio traffic they were hearing was being produced by an army which was in fact not there at all. It seems to have worked. Hitler was firmly convinced, even after D-Day had taken place. Even a week later, the Germans were still not certain whether it was the main attack or simply a diversion.[2]

Fortitude was so effective that the Germans kept fifteen divisions in position, in case D-Day was just a distraction ahead of a real invasion at Calais. Somerville could rightly speak of having saved many lives, perhaps including that of his own brother.

* * *

Another of those whose work in the background contributed to the success of D-Day was Horace Barlow. On coming down from Cambridge, he began work for the National Institute for Medical Research at the Mount Vernon Hospital in Hampstead. Barlow later explained the problem which he had worked on there, delaying his arrival at Harvard (via an Atlantic crossing on the *Queen Mary*), by a year:

> [They] had a unit there doing research on diving for the Naval Personnel Research Committee. It was a few months before D-Day, actually, and they were concerned with harbour clearance and one-man submarines and that kind of thing. So it was improving diving gear. The chief problem that we were working on was oxygen poisoning, which is what happens if you breathe oxygen at more than one or two atmospheres pressure, and particularly if you're in a diving suit ... ; you get convulsions and things like that ... We thought that some cases were mis-diagnosed as oxygen poisoning and were actually caused by carbon dioxide accumulation, because the diving gear they had – the shallow water diving gear they used – was just a submarine escape apparatus, which had a small canister for absorbing CO2, and we reckoned that when people were working hard, they just produced more CO2 than it could absorb.[3]

* * *

Mackrill.

In the First World War, the British had made it a priority to 'dominate' no-man's-land by aggressive patrolling. In the Second, for long periods between June 1940 and June 1944, no-man's-land was the English Channel. This had become the preserve of the Motor Torpedo Boats and Motor Gun Boats of Coastal Forces: flotillas of tiny, fast, heavily-armed, plywood boats tasked with interdicting enemy convoys and preventing the enemy from doing the same to British coastal traffic. One of their most famous officers was naturalist Peter Scott, and at least one Wykehamist – son of Robertson's colleague and friend F.W. Goddard – was killed in action with them. A full history of their war has yet to be written.[4]

The boats of Coastal Forces were for the most part manned by officers and ratings of the Royal Naval Volunteer Reserve; by the end of the war, 80 per cent of Royal Naval officers were 'Wavy Navy'. RNVR officer training was concentrated at a single training centre, HMS *King Alfred*, at Hove Marina; the first batch of new recruits arrived in late September 1939. The standard training course was to last three months. As space began to run out at the original HMS *King Alfred*, sub-stations were opened in schools evacuated because of the threat of invasion: Mowden School became *King Alfred (M)* and Lancing College, *King Alfred (L)*.

On May 23rd 1944, Mackrill wrote to his parents from Mowden.

> We spend our entire time here doing Field Training (arms drill, etc.), Signals (morse, semaphore, and flags), and Passive Defence (gas and bombs, etc.). We do all our work in Mowden School, which once used to be a girls' prep school, and everyone – including officers – live out in billets. We eat and sleep out – in fact, we merely use it as a day school.
>
> I have met still another OW, Guy Rendel, in 'G' House, a great friend of mine. He was in practically every Div. with me all the way up the school. We spent the weekend together and had a real beano.[5]

After assessment at Mowden, the next stage of officer training was a six-week course at Lancing, where the Cadet Ratings learned seamanship, navigation, and signals. Mackrill would have found the dormitory accommodation at Lancing very reminiscent of Sunnyside, though the spectacular views from Lancing are wholly different from Winchester. Navigation training was the most important part of the syllabus at Lancing, and part of this involved pedalling around the cricket pitches on tricycles, steering a compass course, and signalling with small flags. Hazards representing lighthouses, buoys, and headlands were set in the trainees' paths, around which they had to steer successfully.

In June 1944, Mackrill and his fellow members of Jellicoe Division posed for a graduation photograph – Mackrill labelled himself 'Sub-Lieutenant Sunshine' on his copy.

Having passed at Lancing, Mackrill moved down to *King Alfred* proper, at Hove Marina, for the last four weeks of his training. There he and his peers were accommodated in a converted underground car park. As commissioning loomed, the Cadet Ratings were fitted for uniforms at one of the naval tailors which had opened up shop nearby; if all went well, and they passed their final examinations, they paid for the uniforms and wore them at their passing-out parade. On successful completion of the course, recruits were commissioned as Midshipmen if aged under nineteen-and-a-half, and as Sub-Lieutenants if over that age.

King Alfred turned out one hundred RNVR officers a week: fifteen of the top twenty were sent to Coastal Forces. One 'perk' of this was being sent for two weeks to the Royal Naval College in Greenwich for what was termed the 'knife and fork' course. After that, those allocated to Coastal Forces spent three weeks at Whale Island (gunnery) and Roedean (torpedoes) before being sent to HMS *St Christopher*, the Coastal Forces training base at Fort William.

* * *

McArthur.

Experience in Madagascar, Dieppe, and the Mediterranean had refined the Allies' techniques for ensuring that landing beaches were organized and controlled so that the troops put ashore could achieve their objectives efficiently. In 1942, the Royal Naval Beach Commandos were formed – sailors in battledress who would be amongst the very first ashore in any assault landing. A beach would be controlled by the Principal Beachmaster, supported by a Beachmaster and a group of Sub-Lieutenants acting as Assistant Beachmasters. On the beach itself, the Beachmasters temporarily outranked any Army officer, and each Beach Commando was responsible for the landing of the personnel, vehicles, and stores of an entire brigade – around 5,000 men. For this task a Beach Commando deployed ten officers and sixty-six other ranks. Since a brigade consisted of three battalions, these personnel were also sub-divided into three: and thus in September 1943 John McArthur became a member of Royal Naval Beach Commando 'Tare 3' (Naval Party 1510).

The RNBCs had selected Loch Long for their training, and had purchased a forestry camp and Glenfinart House at Ardentinny on the Firth of Clyde. The camp was named HMS *Armadillo* – allegedly because one of its founders had promised to donate his stuffed armadillo to the Wardroom. One of McArthur's ratings described a typical day's *Armadillo* training, which the officers and men conducted together:[6]

> Each day at 0700hrs the men collected on the parade ground at the flag. Then breakfast; then an assault course up the river. We ran up the path; the whistle blew twice. We had to jump in the river fully clothed. Then over the assault course, including scaling walls,

> through broken tyres. There was one large rope between two large trees. Each man had a toggle rope (a six-foot length of rope with a toggle at one end and an eye at the other) which was used to slide down between the two trees. After that, we ran through the camp to the jetty, dived in, and swam back to the beach. At midnight there were speed marches: march a mile and run a mile. After about seven miles we returned to camp for cups of cocoa.

The instructors often enlivened these runs by hurling thunderflashes towards the trainees. McArthur and his comrades were trained to use explosives to demolish beach obstacles, and to deal with the plentiful barbed wire with which German defences were liberally festooned. Their simple, but effective, technique was for one man to throw himself flat on to the wire (with his arms protecting his face) and for the rest of the group to run over his back. That was not all; members of RNBCs were expected to be able to exit a lorry travelling at 30mph, land safely, and be ready to fight with PIAT, rifle, sub-machine gun, or pistol. No wonder that in December 1943 McArthur signed his Christmas card to Robertson as follows:[7]

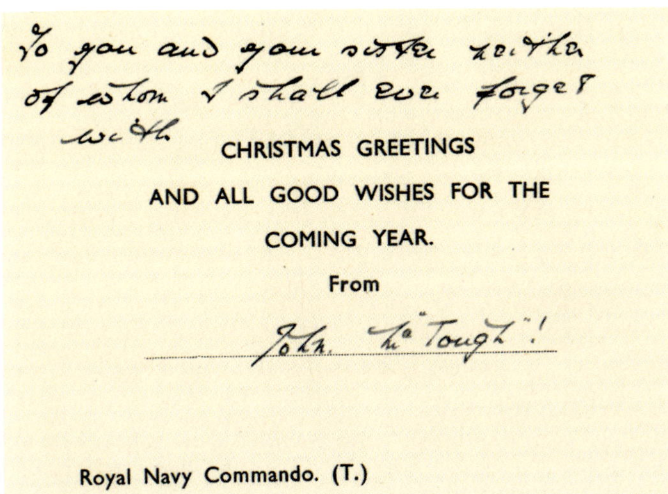
CHRISTMAS GREETINGS
AND ALL GOOD WISHES FOR THE
COMING YEAR.
From
John "Mc Tough"!
Royal Navy Commando. (T.)

McArthur's official confidential report, covering the period September 31st 1943 to March 31st 1944, summarized his performance at *Armadillo*:

Capacity in which employed:	Beachmaster.
General Conduct:	Satisfactory.
Of temperate habit?	Yes.
Professional Ability:	7.
Personal Qualities:	8.
Leadership:	7.
Intellectual Ability:	7.

General opinion of Officer: An outstanding young officer with a charming personality and presence. He should do well under all circumstances. An able administrator, a fine athlete, and a good messmate who should develop into an excellent officer.

Whether recommended for promotion: Accelerated.[8]

A later report on him, when he was acting as Administration Officer for Tare Commando in April 1945, described McArthur as

> very efficient in his present appointment, and shows tact and intelligence in dealing with all with whom he comes in contact. Thinks sanely and clearly, and can be relied upon to reach sound conclusions. Possesses a charming personality and is popular with his fellow officers. A high sense of humour and can mix in any company … Plays a good game of Rugby and Association Football; of good physique. Also a keen cricketer and Squash player.[9]

McArthur honed his military skills in exercises at Gailes and Inverary on Loch Fyne, and in February 1944 Tare settled at Inverary for assault training with 50th (Northumbrian) Infantry Division. Amongst the Wykehamists in this division were Hopperites Lieutenant Colonel Humphrey Woods DSO, MC* (commanding 9th Durham Light Infantry, in 151 Infantry Brigade)[10] and Lieutenant Nick Somerville (2nd South Wales Borderers, in 56 Infantry Brigade), both of whom landed on D-Day in the follow-up waves.

Robertson was very fond of Woods, who became one of the finest battalion commanders produced by Winchester in the war. Woods had an astonishing wartime record. From the outbreak of war until March 1943 he served in 1KRRC, at first as a subaltern and later as 'D' Company Commander. Four times wounded and twice mentioned in dispatches, Woods was awarded a bar to his MC in 1942, and the DSO came early in 1943. He then joined 2KRRC as Second-in-Command, but had already been selected, at the age of twenty-seven, for command of a battalion. The call came quickly; on July 23rd 1943, in Sicily, 9DLI's commanding officer was killed in action by mortar fire; he was a Wykehamist, Lieutenant Colonel Andrew Board Stephenson Clarke DSO.[11] Woods was told of his new posting on July 26th, but did not manage to reach the Battalion for four days. The radio broadcaster Lewis Hastings described a perilous journey in a Jeep down a torrent-bed with 'this young new CO, a soft-speaking, friendly, smiling person, but obviously possessed of tremendous drive'. Woods' letters show that he became proud of his Durham men, and they of him.

Woods had returned to England with 9DLI late in 1943, after nearly eight years of overseas service – but he was only able to give his many Winchester friends a few hours, when he had tea with Robertson shortly before D-Day.

RNBC Tare returned to *Armadillo* before moving on March 28th to Portland. For D-Day, they had been assigned to No.9 Beach Group, which was responsible for the 'King' sector of Gold Beach, at the eastern end between Le Hamel and La Rivière; Tare were to land at La Rivière.

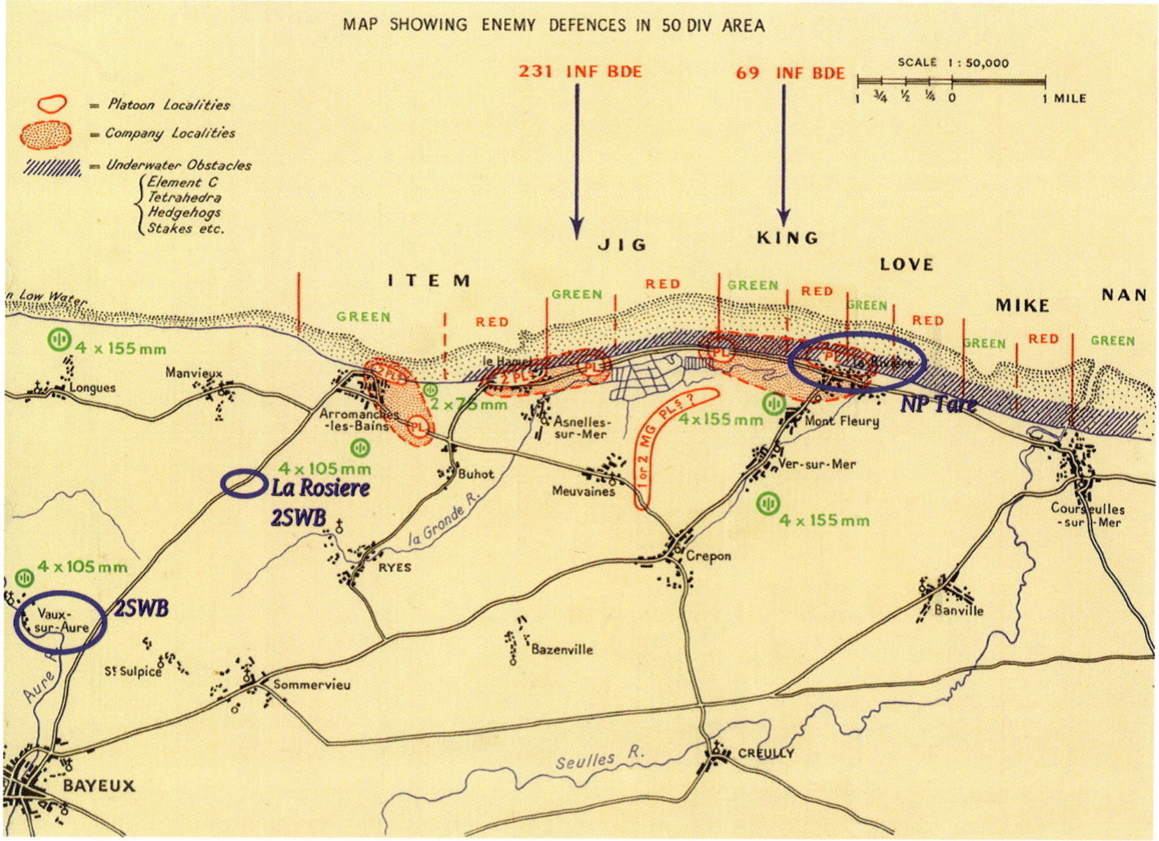

As D-Day neared, they assembled at HMS *Squid* II – a grandiose name for the Westcliff Hall Hotel in Hythe – and landed on Gold Beach on June 6th. There they would remain until the middle of July.[12] It had not been a pleasant crossing. Tare Commando's Principal Beachmaster recalled that breakfast that morning was liver and onions,

> a horrible mixture to offer at 0200hrs to men who would be eating their last decent meal for days, if not for ever. After breakfast we mustered alongside our landing craft, the RN Commando being split up among several of these. It was a dark silent night except for the drone of aircraft overhead. Far to the eastward silent gun flashes flickered along the horizon. The LSIs anchored about seven miles off the Normandy coast and the assault waves embarked in their landing craft. As each man went over the side, he was handed anti-seasick pills and a vomit bag, which seemed a curious contradiction. But the planner responsible obviously knew his pills, because the bags were in constant use during our slow wet passage through a choppy sea which was rougher than it had looked from the high decks of a large ship.

One of the few surviving official documents relating to Tare describes their D-Day very briefly: 'Despite the fact that some of its officers and men had to land before H-Hour on the AVRE tanks to help establish signal links, no casualties were sustained, though one officer and one rating were in an LCT(A) which sank on the way across.'[13]

The official history of the British campaign in Normandy described the RNBCs on Gold Beach that day as

> men whose task it was to resolve the confusion which was inevitable at first, when craft of every sort were arriving minute by minute to discharge men and vehicles hurriedly on beaches which the rising tide was narrowing rapidly, and from which an adequate number of exits were not yet cleared. They were the naval Assistant Beachmasters with small advance parties … The first task of these reconnaissance elements of naval and military beach organisation was to make a rapid survey of local hazards, both off-shore and on land, and to decide the precise location of beach exits to be cleared; to begin marking positions for ammunition and supply dumps for the guidance of incoming craft and of vehicle drivers; and at the earliest possible moment to set up signal stations … This work of beach organisation began while beaches were still under enemy fire and in some cases men engaged in it joined in fighting to overcome near-by enemy posts which were hindering progress. Like others employed on the beaches in this early stage they had a full share of casualties.[14]

We are fortunate that McArthur's commanding officer and one of his fellow Sub-Lieutenants left vivid recollections of the landings:

> A number of badly wounded were clinging weakly to beach obstacles against which the flood tide was brutally battering them. Closer inshore, several dead men were lying in the shallows, their bodies rolling back and forth as the waves advanced and receded over them. Higher up the beach, little mounds, which from a distance looked like piles of sand, proved to be khaki-clad casualties of the initial assault. Of the living there was no sign. The several hundred men who had just landed had vanished into the dunes as if the sand had swallowed them. Only the rattle of small-arms fire gave them away.
>
> It was shortly after 0730hrs when we waded ashore. Mitchell, the Beachmaster [of Tare 3, McArthur's group], turned left and I turned east to ensure that the Commandos were acting according to plan. I ran along the half-tide mark, looking for runnels and other obstructions. To my right, the battle among the dunes was still continuing, although it was barely audible amid the general noise of aircraft, naval guns, landing-craft engines, and shouting men. With the Commandos now ashore, the tides immediately became a problem again. Although the approach of high water meant that the obstacles which had not been destroyed were now out of harm's way in deep water, the plain fact was that … the sea was filled with hundreds of landing craft which were heading into Gold, and they needed to off-load their vehicles and men before the tide started to go out again.
>
> More than four hundred vehicles were now ashore or wading towards it. But, owing to casualties among the assault vehicles, only a few exits had been cleared, and the planned flow of tanks, guns, and trucks into the open countryside had dwindled to a mere trickle. Conditions off-shore were just as bad, and the shallows were now blocked by wrecks and empty craft trying to back off the beach in the teeth of a strong westerly wind. Prudence clearly demanded that the third wave of vehicle carriers must defer beaching for a time.
>
> 'Tell the Flotilla to wait offshore for ten minutes,' I told the Yeoman. Signals were semaphored, lamps flashed, and the R/T chattered. But they might have been sending

their message to the moon for all the good it did, and the third wave of LCTs bulldozed their way through the flotsam and discharged another two hundred vehicles – which came to a grinding halt behind the waiting queue …

It seemed only prudent to dig in the control post, so we borrowed pick and shovels. One of the Commandos swung his pick into the ground. Immediately there followed a blinding flash, and my brain went blank until I found myself lying on the ground among the gruesome bits and pieces which had once been a human being …

Some time after midnight, after confirming that the wounded were now being smoothly evacuated, I scraped a hole in the mud. During the past twenty-two hours I had been in and out of the water, and had eaten only a bar of chocolate. So I was cold, wet and hungry, and badly in need of alcoholic refreshment. But, having none, I lay shivering in my foxhole.[15]

I remember the lack of enemy aircraft on D-Day, but at dusk they came over and strafed the beach. When they appeared, the whole invasion fleet opened up with tracer fire, so there were fireworks everywhere.[16]

McArthur was a hopeless correspondent from a researcher's point of view, in that he did not date his letters from Normandy (annoyingly, the GPO did not frank them with a date). However, the following clearly dates from June 1944:[17]

I'm sorry I haven't written sooner, but all in all it was impossible. All I can say now is that I'm in France, which you probably guessed. And after some rather unpleasant experiences we have at last got pretty well organised. I live at the moment in a shell-shattered house with Jack Wyllie, Paddy Gallagher, and Keith Andrews. It was originally some German officers' mess; what is left of it is quite comfortable. Little did I think I should have to drink Vichy Water again, let alone bath in it, which I've been doing lately. About anything else you will know more than I do. We don't get all the news here, only the main points. I believe they call this beach the "Death or Glory" beach. Little do they know.

The weather, thank God, is really marvellous. And some of the country around here is beautiful. You probably know it. And I have an egg for breakfast every morning. That is on private enterprise. I have a French girl friend in the village who swops me eggs for cigs!

But despite all this fun, I'd rather be in England, and to see a pint right now would send me mad. The food is good but very monotonous. Sleep is patchy and at night rather noisy.

McArthur's immediate superior, Lieutenant J.E.M. Mitchell RNVR, wrote of him on their return from France:

An intelligent officer who acts on his own initiative. Has a keen sense of responsibility. His loyalty to his superior officers is an example to officers and men of the Commando. He works well and has a good sense of foresight. Is a keen sportsman. Phyical fitness, Class 'A'.

A little forgetful at times.

Was an asset on the beaches of Normandy.[18]

At 1020hrs on D-Day, Humphrey Woods and 9DLI disembarked on King sector of Gold Beach, wading through five feet of water carrying all their kit. One wonders whether Woods and McArthur recognized one another from their practice exercises.

* * *

As well as McArthur, two more of our subjects landed in Normandy on June 6th. Nick Somerville's unit – 2nd Battalion, South Wales Borderers (2SWB) – was in 56 Brigade, which was a follow-up Brigade landing on Gold Beach to the west of McArthur's sector. John Boyd – Adjutant of 1st King's Own Scottish Borderers (1KOSB) – was heading for a different beach: Sword. Somerville left several accounts of his experiences of D-Day, but on August 4th 1944 he sat down in Normandy to write to his Hopper's contemporary and dear friend Peter Walker.[19] This letter was never revised, and so is perhaps the most immediate account of those which Somerville left.

Nick Somerville.

My dear Peter,
I don't know where or when this will ever reach you, but I am writing it in order to try and make contact again. It seems years since I last saw you, so I thought perhaps you might like to know how I was getting on, as I should certainly like to hear your news.

It seems a long time since a fortnight before D-Day, when we were all sealed up, terribly hush-hush, in a ghastly forest camp, where we never saw the light of day, and the food consisted of lukewarm rissole and cold chips every day. We had been doing invasion exercises and in this gloomy atmosphere settled down to briefing for the 'Pukka' job. We went over in American LCIs and had a concert party on board followed by a short service before we left. As we steamed out of a port which you and I know pretty well, in line ahead, we looked a grand sight. We must have passed hundreds of ships, and as we sailed by, the Navy manned all their yards and gave us three cheers, which was a bloody good show. The whole thing was really an inspiration. Most of us had our own thoughts that night, and next morning when we awoke we all rushed on deck to see if we could see the land, but there was nothing to see except our own string of LCIs and escorting destroyers. However, the air was full of aeroplanes and we arrived off the beaches. We hung about there for a time and at last received the word to go in. I think everybody felt a little tug inside somewhere when they said that we were off over the ships's blower.

Boyd also left an unpublished account of his time in Normandy, which consists of a vivid series of disjointed impressions and memories. It begins with his journey across to Sword Beach:

Steaming out through the great crowd of shipping in the Solent, past Southsea, the measured mile, and Calshot; seeing the Isle of Wight disappearing into the distance behind us, and wondering if this time we were really going, and if this was to be my last sight of England.

Boyd.

> Waking up (only once!) on my stretcher on the deck of the LCT on the night of D-1 and hearing the engines racing and the roar of aircraft overhead. The unforgettable morning of D-Day with the mass of shipping, the long coastline stretching away to Le Havre behind us on the left. Destroyers racing about, and a big ship firing at some target well inland. The white, dusty, houses behind the beach with the mortar fire coming down on them. The one gun from near Deauville which fired at us. The first whistle of a shell, and the rattle of splinters on the deck.

Although Somerville complained about the long wait before 2SWB landed, his letter to Walker makes it clear that the Battalion was hot on the heels of the assault wave.

> We were unlucky in hitting an underwater obstacle going in and so had to land into eight feet of water. This was not easy with a full pack, etc., on, as everybody was out of their depth and we had to get bicycles ashore as well. We were lucky to have only two drowned, as the waves were quite powerful and kept hitting one on the back of the head and bowling one forward. They were fighting about two hundred yards off the beaches when we landed, and there was one particularly offensive MG post, which was silenced by a PIAT pretty quickly. It was a bit difficult trying to organise oneself in a hurry; however, it all turned out all right after an hour's rather confused fighting, each man for himself.

Somerville's diary gives more detail, including his close brush with death as he left the beach:

> The congestion on the beach exit was terrific, but luckily the enemy was not shelling it – though why I simply can't imagine. We passed some German dead and one of our Casualty Clearing Stations, which gave us our first glimpse of war. Also on the way inland we passed numbers of our own dead, as 231 Brigade had had a fair number of casualties. On the way up to the Assembly Area we had twelve casualties from mortar fire and a couple from snipers. Snipers seemed to be everywhere. The man behind me, riding a bicycle, was hit in the head by an 88mm solid shot, and just fell down headless, which rather shook me – but I soon got over it.

Boyd came ashore on Queen White sector of Sword Beach at around midday:

> Wading through the water up to the beach; seeing the first casualties come back; hearing for the first time the loud crack of the mortar and the typewriter rattle of the Spandau. Meeting the Battalion in the Assembly Area; hearing that Arthur Onions had been killed and Jim Cunningham and most of his staff wounded.

2SWB did well that first day, advancing some six miles inland and seizing their first objective, a bridge at Vaux-sur-Aure, just north of Bayeux, as Somerville recorded:

> We reached our assembly area at about 1500hrs. It had been shelled and bombed previously and there were six very dead and rather disgusting horses and cows slap in

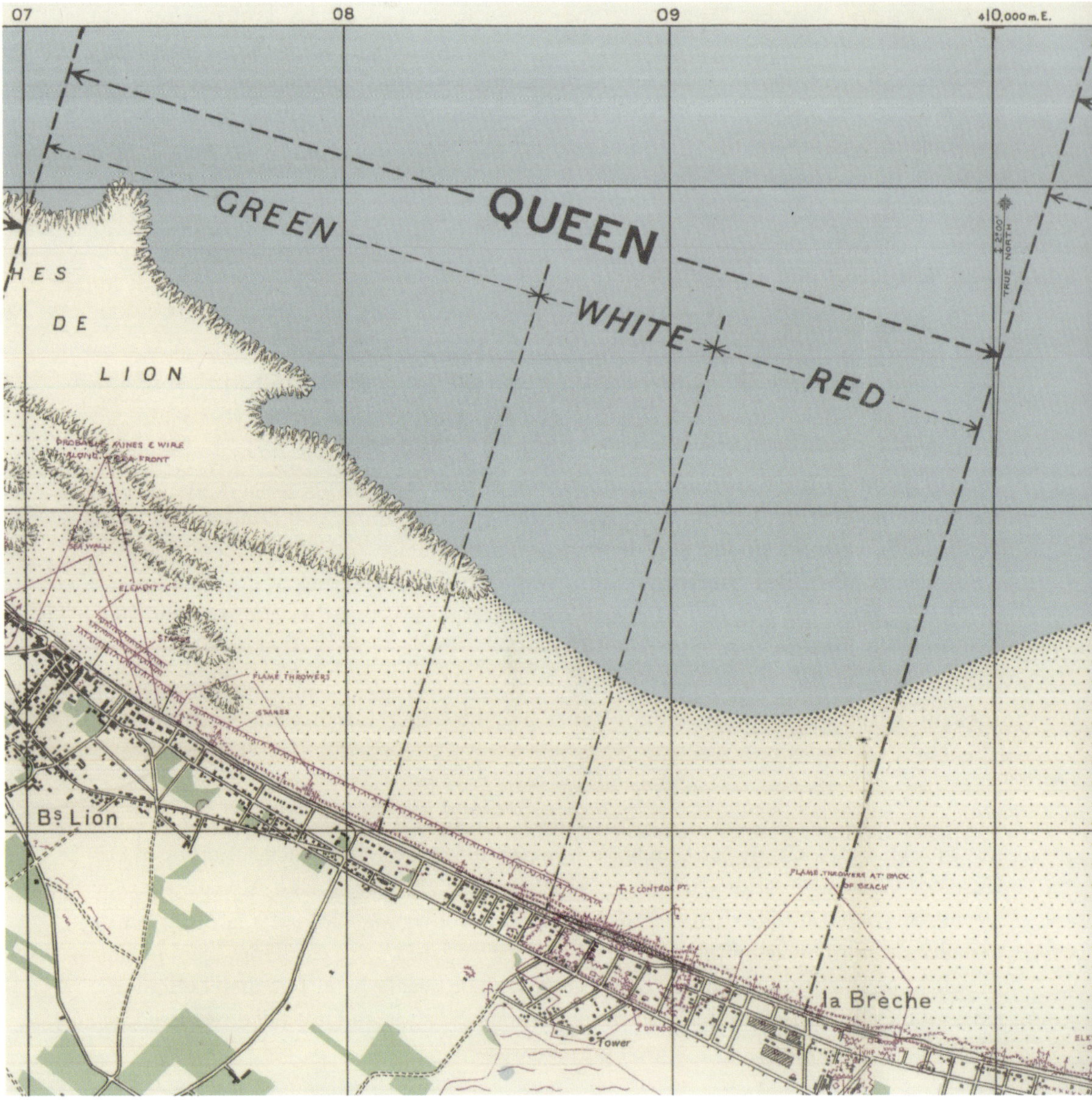

the middle of it – the smell was appalling. We waited there until 1600hrs for our carriers to come up. They had landed at the same time in LCTs, and we were very fortunate to see them so soon.

At 1630hrs the forward body set off on bicycles, commanded by Major Barlow, with the Carrier Platoon and 'D' Company commanded by Major Martin. I was travelling in Major Barlow's carrier, and we did not meet any enemy for some time …. Just beyond La Rosiere the carriers ran into an enemy LMG; Captain Wickert stood up in his carrier to fire a burst of Bren at it and knocked it out in one. This was first blood. We then contacted the enemy at an RDF [radar] station about a mile down the road. This necessitated a company attack by 'D' Company. The enemy managed to burn the place and get out before our bayonets could reach him. The road was mined outside the RDF station, and one of our carriers was blown up. The FOO's tank ran on to a mine on the verges, and unfortunately Major Martin happened to be standing by at the time and was wounded in the stomach.

By now it was getting dark, and the RDF station was exploding Hun ammunition left, right, and centre. However, we pushed on and reached the bridge at Vaux-sur-Aure by about 2300hrs. We managed to get the Battalion firm-based on this bridge by midnight and at last felt fairly secure. During the night several enemy patrols bumped into our position and we had several clashes in the darkness. That day we took about twenty prisoners. It was about 0200hrs before I was able to lie down on a cold floor of a farmhouse and sleep until 0400hrs. Our clothes were still damp from the landing, but nobody seemed to mind much.

1KOSB had a less stressful afternoon, as Boyd recalled:

Marching inland, seeing some pretty girls in a convent in Hermanville-sur-Mer. The first night at St Aubin d'Arquenay, when the gliders came over, black against the sunset, and the many-coloured parachutes dropped from the darkening sky. Trying to

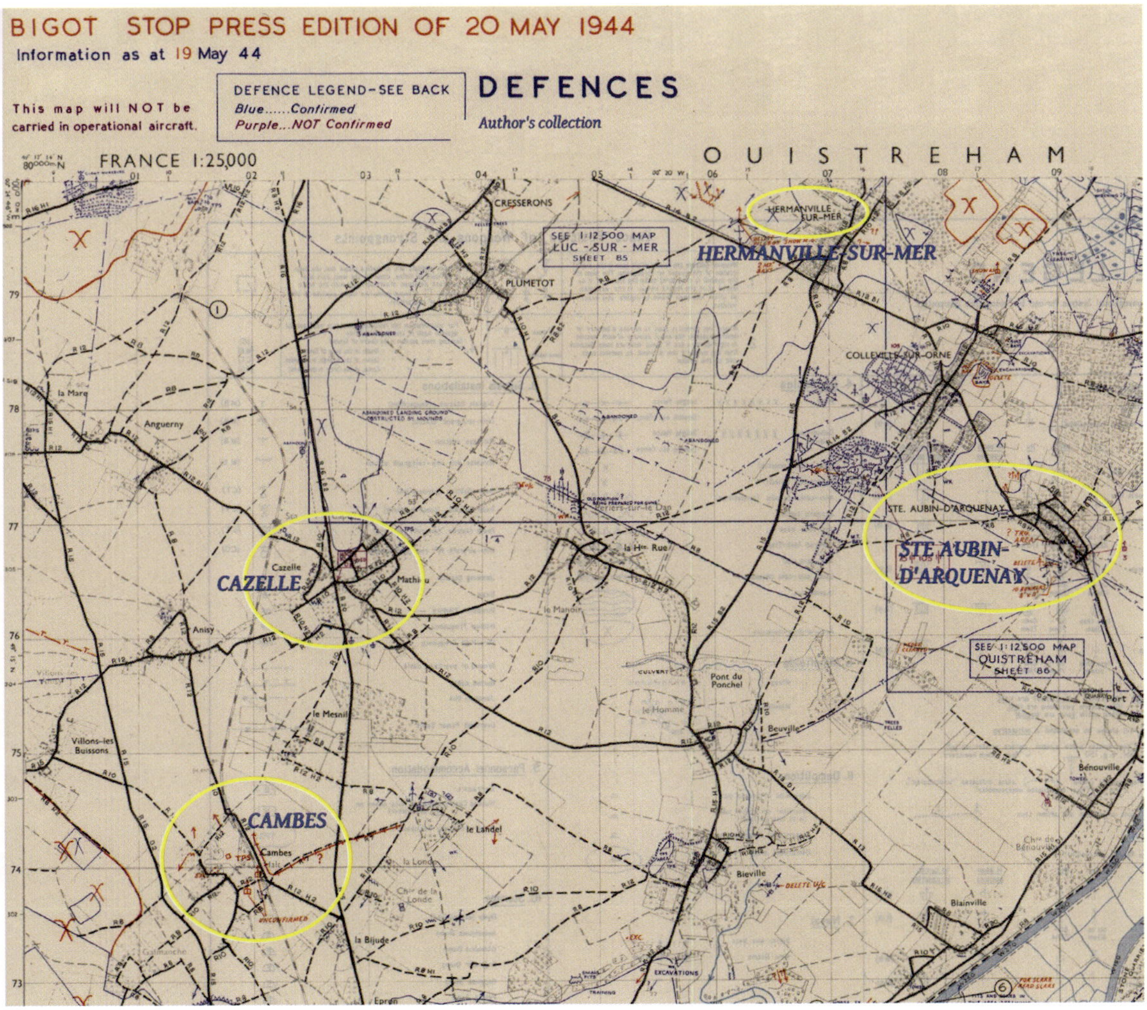

> cook and eat my 24-hour rations without much success, and eventually falling back on self-heating cocoa.

From June 7th onwards, the Allies tried to consolidate their beach-head, pouring in troops and equipment under the cover of naval gunfire support. As they attempted to form a defensible perimeter, the Germans probed for weaknesses and rushed forces to the area – though not as many as they might have done had Operation Fortitude not been so successful. Boyd and 1KOSB moved west from their overnight bivouac near the Caen Canal and River Orne, cycling towards Cambes via Cazelle. It was here that Boyd nearly fell victim to 'friendly fire':

> The long cycle-ride up through Cazelle; the first sight of a dead man cut up like meat in a butcher's shop on the road. Mortar fire in the big wood, and the first of our own wounded going back. The awful moments when our own tanks stood off and BESA'ed us in the wood, thinking there were snipers there; standing up and shouting to people to stop firing, and the sharp smack of a bullet grazing the back of my neck.

June 7th also saw 2SWB push westwards across the Aure River towards Sully, where control of a bridge would allow the British and American beach-heads to link up.

> At 0400hrs we got ready to push on and moved at 0430hrs to get on to the high ground north-west of Bayeux. We arrived to find the whole area full of snipers in the orchards. They were very well camouflaged, and most of them were up trees. The result was that once we had got into a defensive position based on Le Parquet, the battle developed into Section stalks in the orchards trying to get these snipers … Meanwhile 'A' Company … ran into pretty stiff opposition, and withdrew to the Battalion area to report that Sully was held in strength. Meanwhile, civilians kept pouring out of Bayeux, some with Resistance arm bands, and I had a job to interrogate them and send them back to Division. We stayed put that day and brought in a dozen more snipers in the evening. Patrols contacted the enemy at Sully that night.

The next day's unsuccessful attack on Sully nearly cost Somerville his life. His diary account of his first major action is worth quoting at length:

> No accurate information was available as to the force holding Sully, but it was thought that it was in the nature of a hundred men. Civilians reported that they had been forced to dig fortifications round the Chateau at Sully, and that they were very extensive. That morning the attack was planned with 'A' and 'B' Companies, two Field Regiments, one 6″ cruiser, and a squadron of tanks. Unfortunately the FOO couldn't find an accurate OP and so the cruiser was unable to fire.
>
> The attack was launched at 1230hrs, and in the initial stages our troops advanced too close to the guns and we had a few shrapnel casualties. However, 'B' Company pressed on into Sully and just by sheer guts shot itself in. One Corporal dashed forward throwing a grenade and shooting his Sten gun, thus killing the crew of an 88mm which was blocking the road. Captain Thomson was conspicuous in this fighting and

was responsible for getting the two leading platoons inside the village and clearing it properly. Unfortunately he was wounded in the stomach, and went away on a stretcher smiling and smoking a pipe.

'B' Company were able to push on over the bridge, where 'A' Company joined them. Phase One of the battle, therefore, was successfully dealt with. There was then a pause while 'A' Company formed up for the attack on the Chateau and the gunners strafed the place pretty severely. Then 'A' Company went in. We discovered afterwards that the Chateau had cellars fourteen feet deep, with tunnels running out from them to a circular ring of little dug-outs or pill-boxes. The whole Chateau was surrounded by close orchards with large fences. We discovered afterwards from prisoners that it had been a regimental headquarters and was held by about 250 men.

'A' Company got right forward into the orchards, where a very close battle soon developed. All the trees had snipers in them, and there were also two 88mm guns to scare the tanks away. The dug-outs had machine-guns in them. 'A' Company fought magnificently, platoons getting right up to the dug-outs, but all that happened was that the Germans went to ground and then lobbed grenades out as fast as they could go. 'A' Company attacked three times, but still couldn't get in. They were then given a platoon of 'B' Company and a troop of tanks. These succeeded in knocking out the crew of an 88mm gun, and the men got right up to the Chateau; Jerry then set the thing on fire and got out into the woods behind it.

The fighting now got very confused, with platoons and sections having their own little fights in the orchards. During this the CO was hit in the shoulder, and I had to dress it for him. He refused to be evacuated until the battle was over. At this stage the Brigadier arrived, and he definitely inspired the men by his presence – and the next

German Strong Point in the Château de Sully, near Bayeux, by Anthony Gross. (Art.IWM ART LD 4462)

attack had everything behind it. Unfortunately, at this time an enemy SPG got round behind us and was covering the only way out over the bridge. It knocked out three of our carriers, one anti-tank gun, and a brigade Jeep. Unfortunately, a Firefly was able to fire the first shot at it but missed, and the SPG got the Firefly instead. On account of this threat, the Brigadier ordered us to get out. So we called for smoke from the gunners and then proceeded to get out.

We put the Brigadier in a tank and the 2i/c and myself were the last out. The road was being shelled like Hell as we rushed down it. Five shells landed within twenty yards of our carrier as we were getting out. I was extraordinarily lucky, as I was lying on top of Major Barlow and a shell splinter hit my tin hat and went on to snap the barrel off a Bren gun immediately above my head. I felt a little stunned and could see blood dripping from my head on to the back of Major Barlow's tunic. My tin hat had been knocked off my head and was on the floor of the carrier, and I could see a gash in it about four inches by two. The result of all this was that I wondered how long I would go on thinking for. But luckily it was all right and I only had a cut about ¼-inch deep, which healed in about a week. The only thing was that I had to go about like a tonsured monk for a long time afterwards.

The amazing thing was that we had no casualties getting out, except for the FOO's tank which overturned on the bridge coming out, and the FOO was drowned. After that the battle quietened down a bit and 'C' Company came out to hold the village north-east of the river. The other two companies and the tanks then withdrew to the Battalion area. The tanks had found it extraordinarily difficult country to fight in, but had been able to put a few rounds of HE into the dug-outs and to shoot our men forward with BESAs. I learnt afterwards of a man in the 'B' Company platoon which went to support 'A' Company, who performed a particularly brave act. The Platoon Commander had got across a gap and the next two to follow were both killed by a machine-gun. This man jumped into the gap, knelt down, and fired the whole of his Bren magazine at the machine-gun post, thus covering the whole of his Platoon across. He was slightly wounded during this, but carried on.

That evening 'C' Company patrolled into the Chateau and reported it empty, and next morning they were able to take possession of it.

On June 9th it was Boyd's turn, as 1KOSB went into the attack at Cambes. The overriding impression is of disorientation:

The dusty confusion before the attack on Cambes. The hurried, excited preparations; the advance through the growing corn with tracer zipping head-high and bullets whistling through the corn-stalks. The deathly silence of Cambes Wood; the mingled smell of dead bodies and high explosive; the ghostly white of the empty, ruined Chateau in the half light through the broken trees. The sudden roar of the mortars when I was on the road; lying down on the road not daring to move, and for the first time feeling really frightened. Going back to look for the wireless set and getting lost in the wood. Walking alone through the deserted village; Sam Freeman hopping out of a house and asking me to take him to the RAP. Escorting him to 'B' Company with an Ulsterman whilst the mortars started again. Meeting Bones [Captain Roynon-Jones] with part of 'B' Company, also lost, but digging in. Finding the carrier and the nightmare drive round Cambes in the dark with two wounded men in the back; ditching the carrier but finding Battalion HQ at last and getting the wounded off.

The Battalion would spend the next month in and out of Cambes, surrounded by dense woodland. The terrain of Normandy made life very hard for an attacker, with thick foliage everywhere and high hedges restricting fields of view and of fire. Contact with the enemy could come at very close range and as a surprise to both sides. The advance stalled at Cambes, and Boyd later confided in Robertson that 1KOSB's time there reminded him of accounts of trench warfare in the Great War:[20]

> I am allowed to give you some account of our activities provided, as the authorities say, that fourteen days have elapsed since they took place. We landed as reserve brigade on D-Day – I came ashore at about mid-day and there was still a certain amount of stuff flying about the beaches. However, we got quickly inshore and were off our mark fairly briskly on the way to our objective. We never quite got there, as an SS *Panzer* Division came up on the same day and we met about two thousand yards short of our objective. We pushed them out of the first place, and then proceeded to sit down for about a month or even longer in the same place. We got down to what must, I imagine, have been very like last-war soldiering: slit trenches, dug-outs, patrols, constant shelling, and the occasional raid. It was an annoying period and rather took the edge off our fitness – especially the feet!

Like his former housemaster, Boyd witnessed the steady attrition of friends and comrades of all ranks, as well as hearing of the deaths of friends in other units.

> The long weeks in Cambes, going round companies in the early mornings and wondering when the shelling would start again. Getting organised into the daily routine of trench warfare; seeing Bones going out on the patrol from which he never returned;[21] hearing of Edmund Passy's death.[22] Life in the crowded German dug-out which was our HQ. Creeping along one day on the shell-scarred avenue towards La Bijude. The Communion service I attended in the cellar of the Chateau. Watching from OPs and seeing the Germans a little way off in their tanks. Our own guns coming down like a roll of gigantic drums on Galmanche, Epron, or St Contest.

* * *

June 11th 1944 was Christopher Pringle's twenty-first birthday. He claimed later that he spent it darning his socks on the roof of a Nissen hut in Greenland. His brother Michael had gone ashore in Normandy on D+3 with the RASC and would spend the rest of the war supporting the advance into France and beyond.

Pringle.

* * *

Lewin.

Next to land in Normandy was Robin Lewin, a Platoon Commander in 'A' Company, 2KRRC, the infantry component of 4 Armoured Brigade. The '2nd 60th', travelling in American M3 half-tracked carriers, disembarked on Mike sector of Gold Beach between June 7th and 12th. Lewin's Company was ready to go ashore at 1500hrs on June 9th, but their LST ran aground and disembarkation did not begin until 2100hrs, being completed at 0100hrs.

'A' Company were allocated as infantry support to 3rd County of London Yeomanry (Sharpshooters). But there was little call on the armour at this point, and by June 26th 2KRRC had still not gone into action. Allied plans had been disrupted by bad weather in the English Channel; a major storm raged from June 19th to 22nd, almost completely preventing any further build-up of personnel or supplies. Of the two artificial 'Mulberry' harbours which had been constructed, that at Arromanches survived, but the harbour off Omaha Beach was destroyed.

Among 2KRRC's 39 officers and 896 other ranks were several other Wykehamists, one of them a Hopperite who had left Robertson's care in 1936. Lewin wrote to Robertson on June 23rd:

> I thought I'd just let you know where I've got to; we've been out here some time now, and it could have been a lot worse. I can't say I like it, but then I wouldn't have missed it for the world.
>
> The other Wykehamists out with us are the two Stows – Sandy[23] and Jimmy[24] – David Fletcher, and myself. David is commanding 'B' Company; he was all through Africa and Italy and is very good. Jimmy is Signals, Sandy and I ordinary platoons.
>
> The weather has not been too bright of late, but it's better today again. I can't tell you my locality or what we are doing but it could be so much worse; I'm not complaining. We've got first class men and equipment and amongst charming officers.[25]

The following day, 4 Armoured Brigade – whose Brigadier had been fatally wounded by a shell – welcomed a new commanding officer, a Wykehamist, the brilliant Brigadier R.M.P. Carver DSO, MC, later a Field Marshal;[26] Carver was only twenty-nine when he took over. 4 Armoured Brigade did not form part of any specific division but was attached to whatever formation needed its services; this meant that it would increasingly be in the thick of the action.

* * *

As Lewin and 2KRRC awaited orders to move, other infantry were involved in brutal combats all along the British front. One such took place south of Bayeux on June 13th and 14th, near Tilly-sur-Seulles. Nick Somerville and 2SWB were in the front line at Bucéels in the run-up to this attack:

June 12th
Battalion was ordered to withdraw to Jerusalem for a period of organised rest. This was badly needed and I slept in the sun from 0830–1330hrs and just woke up in time to have a magnificent lunch of chicken, new potatoes, and green peas. They all came from the cookhouse somehow and nobody asked any questions. We lay about all afternoon and that evening moved up to Bucéels again. We patrolled during the night and bumped enemy in the Tilly area.

Jerusalem Crossroads, June 13th 1944, by Anthony Gross. (Art.IWM ART LD 4467)

June 13th
The DLI attacked through our position, the line Tilly–Verrières. This had been dive-bombed and shot up by rocket Typhoons during the morning, and had had the whole of the Corps artillery on it for an hour before the attack went in. The attack got right up onto the objective but they couldn't get beyond it. At Verrières the Essex attacked a wood and came in for some counter-attacks with Tigers and flame-throwers, which were nasty. During the DLI attack, the Battalion area and particularly Battalion HQ came in for some very nasty mortaring. I was in the bottom of the slit trench with three others, and three wounded crawled in on top as well. I did not realise it at the time, but the SAA [small arms ammunition] truck was standing just by us and a bomb landed ten yards from it. We were between the bomb and the truck. There was a direct hit on the Regimental Aid Post which killed the Doctor and wounded the Padre. The HQ Company cooks and CQMS were extraordinarily good in evacuating the wounded, and the stretcher-bearers, after they had recovered from the shock of the RAP bomb, did wonders. The cooks had hot tea round five minutes after the bombing had finished.

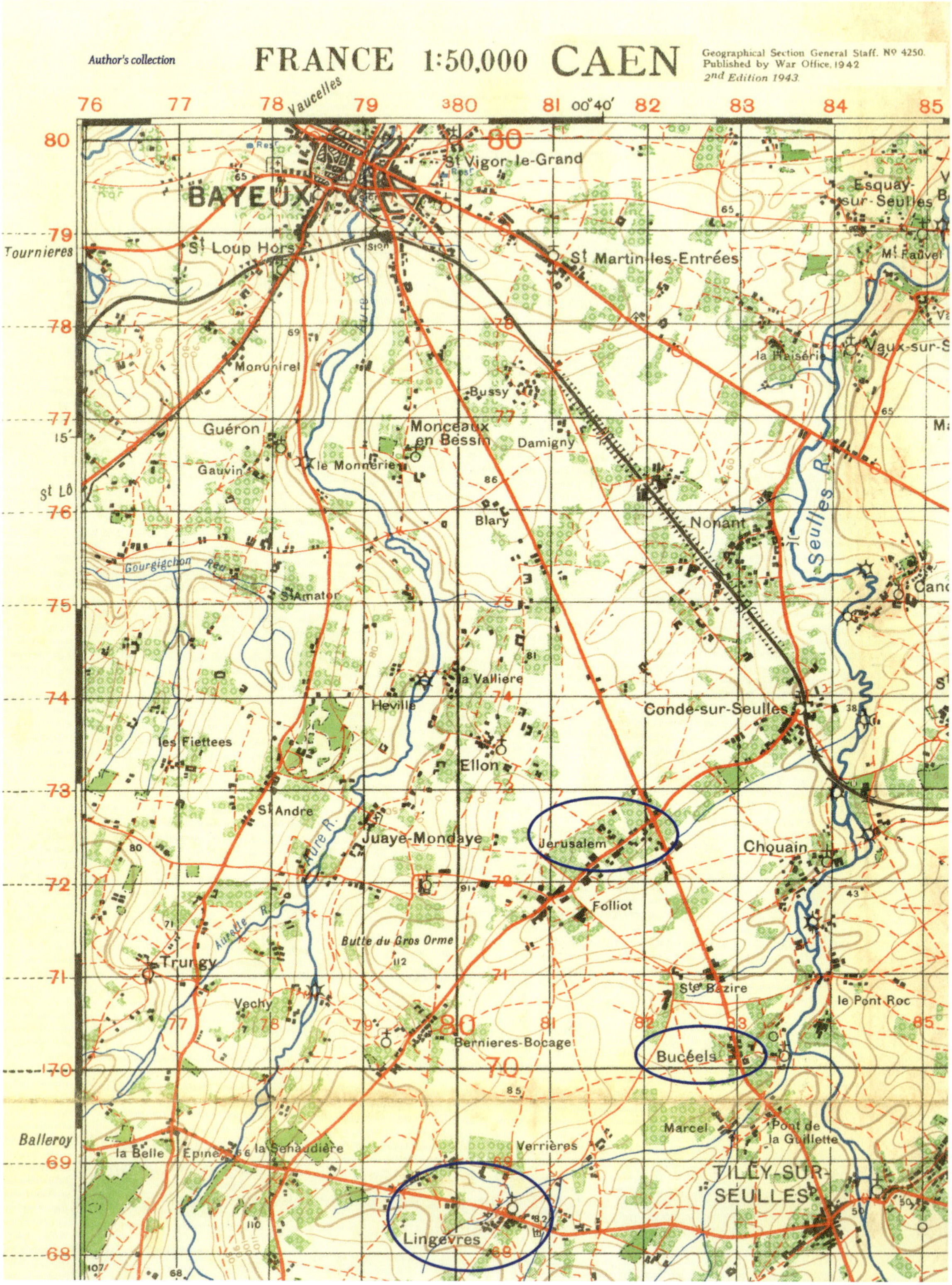
Author's collection
FRANCE 1:50,000 CAEN
Geographical Section General Staff. Nº 4250.
Published by War Office, 1942
2nd Edition 1943.
Vaucelles
BAYEUX
St Vigor-le-Grand
St Loup Hors
St Martin-les-Entrées
Esquay-sur-Seulles
Mt Fauvel
Tournieres
Monunirel
Bussy
la Hoiserie
Vaux-sur-S
Guéron
Monceaux en Bessin
Damigny
Gauvin
le Monnerie
Blary
Nonant
St Lô
Seulles R.
Aure R.
Gourgiechon Rau
St Amator
la Valliere
Heville
Conde-sur-Seulles
les Fiettees
Ellon
St Andre
Juaye-Mondaye
Jerusalem
Chouain
Folliot
Butte du Gros Orme
Aurette R.
Trungy
Ste Bazire
le Pont Roc
Vechy
Bernieres-Bocage
Bucéels
Balleroy
la Belle Epine
la Senaudière
Verrières
Marcel
Pont de la Guillette
TILLY-SUR-SEULLES
Lingevres

> This certainly taught Battalion HQ to dig, and now wherever we go we find that the Battalion is always dug in straight away.
>
> The DLI could not hold their ground and had to withdraw through our positions that night. The Intelligence truck had a number of bits of shrapnel in it. Private Poet was asleep in the front of it when the first bomb landed. A piece of shrapnel went between his back and the back of the seat and through the 18 Set; a second went past his head and through the roof; and a third hit the gear lever. He woke up all right and was soon in a slit trench perfectly all right. One of the tyres was punctured and had to be changed. The Signaller at the 14 Set was killed at his post.[27] We patrolled again all that night and found the enemy still in Tilly.

Humphrey Woods and 9DLI made a reconnaissance in force towards the German positions around Lingèvres on that day, though it became clear that this would be a tough nut to crack and that resistance would be stubborn. Woods planned his attack very carefully, and intended to be in the thick of the action:

> The attack on the 14th was under the direction of Colonel Woods himself. He had a full call on a battery of 25-pounders, Typhoon fighters, a section of 4.2″ mortars and a section of heavy machine-guns, the latter two weapons being our share of the Brigade Support Battalion …
>
> The Colonel's intention was to take the village in a two-phase attack, the first objective being the wood opposing the axis of advance. It was to be a two company attack … The idea was to subject the wood to a concentration of 25-pounders; then the Typhoons were to strafe and bomb; then the infantry were to 'crash' it – tactics which were successful on the first few days; but Jerry learns quickly.
>
> Early on the morning, Colonel Woods sent for me [Lieutenant John Williams] and told me I would accompany him on the attack, in my own carrier, with two men of my Platoon, to give him protection in the field and to give him a tank-hunting unit once the wood was ours.[28]

The attack was preceded by a massive bombardment, described by one eye-witness as 'like something from the First World War: a mass of bursting shells, trees being thrown into the air; there were tanks on fire all over the place and planes dive-bombing; a real Hell on Earth. It was hard to imagine that anything could survive such an onslaught.'[29]

However, the defenders were very much alive, and as 9DLI advanced through standing corn, first machine-guns and snipers, and then mortars and tanks opened fire on them. 'A' Company lost all its officers, but the remains of the Company, together with 'C' Company, managed to get into the wood. There they found machine-guns sited in depth, making any advance perilous. Within five minutes, the only officers left were Woods and his Intelligence Officer. Woods ordered his other two companies into the trees, but 'B' Company were decimated straight away, all but one of the officers being hit. It was clear that German marksmen were deliberately targeting anyone who looked like a leader. The attack was only an hour old, but 9DLI had suffered enormously, and Woods ordered his men to consolidate their positions rather than continue the advance.

However, it is always unwise to remain on an objective which one has taken, since the enemy knows exactly where it is. Shells began to fall, hitting Woods' bodyguards first, as Sergeant Charles Eagles later recalled:[30]

> A few minutes later the carriers were hit by mortar fire. Our driver, a young ginger-headed lad, was in a terrible state, but he was dead – killed immediately. We ran over to the other carrier, which had been hit, and pulled the Corporal clear. He was screaming in agony, as his leg and arm had been blown off. There were dead and dying all around us, and gruesome screams filled the air, mingled with the sound of gun-fire, which was so intense it was cutting the corn like a scythe.
>
> Jack [Williams] screamed at me 'This way' as he ran towards Colonel Woods' carrier, where the Colonel, who was standing beside another officer, turned and shouted some order to Jack, who turned and started to run towards me. Then he started to stagger until he fell at my feet, blood pouring from his thighs. Jack gasped, 'Take a look, Eagles – if they've shot my balls off, shoot me.' I pretended to look and said, 'You're OK', then somehow I managed to get him across my shoulders and, how I'll never understand, carried him fifty yards, or maybe one hundred and fifty yards, I don't know, until I spotted a medic and dropped Jack at his feet. Then back I went.

As well as his bodyguards, Woods' Tactical HQ personnel had been devastated. He remained, however, in contact with his Second-in-Command, who was on the right flank with 'C' Company. Woods told him to advance on Lingèvres with 'C' and 'D' Companies, while he himself extricated 'A' and 'B' and brought them up in support. By now, Sergeant Eagles was on his way back:

> We had re-grouped into a pack of perhaps twenty or so in the apex of the cornfield, and I noticed the Colonel at the head. We scrambled through the hedgerow, into a chaotic scene. We tried to gather our composure and wits about us as the Colonel shouted, 'This way, lads.' We were bunched together when we noticed the turret of a tank behind a copse of trees, and we scattered in all directions and flung ourselves down for cover, except for Colonel Woods, who stood there watching, and ordered, 'Get that tank.'

Woods then returned to his carrier, and sat down in a ditch to speak to HQ on his radio set. Three minutes later, a mortar bomb scored a direct hit on his vehicle. In the carrier was the Intelligence Officer, whose survival with only light wounds was a miracle. He turned round after the blast, to see Woods looking at him and smiling; Woods then suddenly slumped over to his left. Eagles was on the scene soon afterwards:

> By this time I was about six to eight feet away from Colonel Woods, and crawled over to him. His eyes were open wide as he muttered his last words: 'Surely they haven't hit me?' Then he died. He had terrible wounds – about the worst I had seen – he was virtually cut in half.

* * *

(IWM B 7321, edited by dansteele.net)

Woods' death struck Robertson, Hopperites, and the wider Winchester community with uncommon force. Montgomery was so affected by the news that he asked for photographs of Woods' field grave. Robertson heard the news from Woods' father, who wrote to him on June 22nd:[31]

> My dear Bobber,
> I feel I must write and tell you the awful news that we have heard poor Humphrey was killed on June 14th in a battle somewhere south of Bayeux. I heard it, thank God, from a brother officer over there and so far have had no official (War Office) notification, so when that comes we shall now be prepared.
>
> It is too awful to contemplate the future without him and we both feel there is now no future for us – all was pinned and planned on and for Humphrey.

Reggy Woods wrote again on July 4th:

> My dear Bobber,
> We thank you ever so much for your very kind letters of condolence in this our awful grief – and for the very nice 'appreciation' that you wrote in the paper, two copies of

which reached us yesterday. We thank you from the bottom of our broken hearts. Poor Ivy was on the verge of a breakdown from excessive household duties which she has done – including all the cooking – for the past three months, and when this sad news came I hardly dared break it to her. Then she collapsed – her circulation, brain, eyes, and hearing all weak, and the Doctor was really rather worried. She is better today, thank God, but I have had an anxious time since 24th June. She can just scribble a few lines in pencil and will write you later. I know you will understand. We have had over two hundred letters already and to answer them all as we shall do eventually will take her a long time at any rate, so please don't expect one for a few days from her. All his brother officers and past as well as present officers of the 60th and several RAs with him in the North African campaign have all written such charming letters. We never knew a quarter of half the stories they tell of his bravery and all the wonderful charm he showed and possessed.

Our future outlook is a poor one, seeing that we naturally relied on Humphrey to have everything and kept all for him, but he is happy now, we realise, and that thought helps us. I did not know one could have such a knock-out blow and yet exist.

Ivy did not really grasp it when ill and not till two days ago did she really cry properly – her brain was so stunned by this illness. Luckily we have a treasure of a gardener's wife who has been able to do the cooking for us and all goes well enough at present. We do so look forward to the time when we can meet all Humphrey's friends and hear more about his Army life – we have seen so little of him since 1937, as you know.

I have asked for details of how he was killed, but one former officer today in a letter says 'I see in the papers that he was alone fighting ten Germans' – I have wired to him for the paper. Did you hear of anything in any paper? We only have *The Times* and *Daily Mail.*

All our love to you both,
Yours ever,
Reggy[32]

Walker wrote to Robertson immediately on hearing the news, to which Robertson replied sadly on July 5th:

My dear Peter,
Thanks very much for your sympathy about Humphrey Woods; yes, it is a very sad blow to us, and shattering to his parents (another only child, and always such an unspoilt one – a great credit to them).[33]

Robertson of course passed on the news to his extensive contacts. The Bishop of Durham (Woods' former Headmaster at Winchester) replied on July 8th:

I remember him well and what a capital boy he was: I will write to his people. I'm almost surprised now when I find anyone I knew not gone; the Winchester generations of my time and the Christ Church too have been terribly thinned.[34]

* * *

Nick Somerville and 2SWB were pulled out of the Tilly area two days after Woods' death.

> June 16th
> Battalion went into Bayeux for baths. We found the town absolutely packed with troops. de Gaulle had just been there and all the civilians were out in the streets. Le Lion d'Or was going strong and I managed to get a bath and a marvellous dinner. Beef-steak and chips, with a bottle of Sauternes et Medoc. What a relief to wear shoes again and change your clothes. We had a War Correspondent representing the Welsh papers down here and we gave him our story. This grand weather is making new men out of the Battalion.
>
> June 17th
> Another meal in Bayeux and more sleep …
>
> June 18th
> Went with the CO down to Caumont to recce the ground over which we hope to break through. Went into 1/6th Queens area to get an OP. Their CO was twenty-six with a DSO and MC. They had been attacked three times by a *Panzer Grenadier* battalion and were feeling pretty tired. Had a good look at the ground, which was very close.

One of the officers in 1/6th Queen's was Wykehamist Hugh Sperling Morshead, who would be killed in action in January 1945. Somerville did not record whether they met. It was a busy time for an Intelligence Officer, as Somerville discovered on June 25th:

> Went on recce with Company Commanders. A pretty daring one. We took a patrol with us and managed to get within 250 yards of the first objective without being seen. Left the patrol there and I took 2i/cs of companies out there again afterwards. It meant a fair amount of crawling, but we did get a look at the ground. We have never been able to do this before.
>
> Forward companies still being shelled, and some were landing as we came in from the recce. Nasty as we couldn't hear them coming because of the Jeep engines.
>
> June 26th
> Rained like hell all day, which didn't help matters at all. Everybody got soaking wet.
>
> Conference in the morning. Took a trip to Brigade in the afternoon and nearly knocked an MP. Missed him by inches. Took another Jeep to Brigade in the evening and the bloody thing broke down coming back. Petrol feed jammed. Cleared that and then she wouldn't go, so went to the ignition. Took adhesive tape off the high tension lead to the distributor to take it down, and found she was sparking OK; got a tow in. What actually happened was first petrol, then water, on the points. This dried out when we were being towed.

* * *

Boyd and 1KOSB came out of the line at Cambes on June 21st, but even as they did so German shelling took its toll of the Battalion:

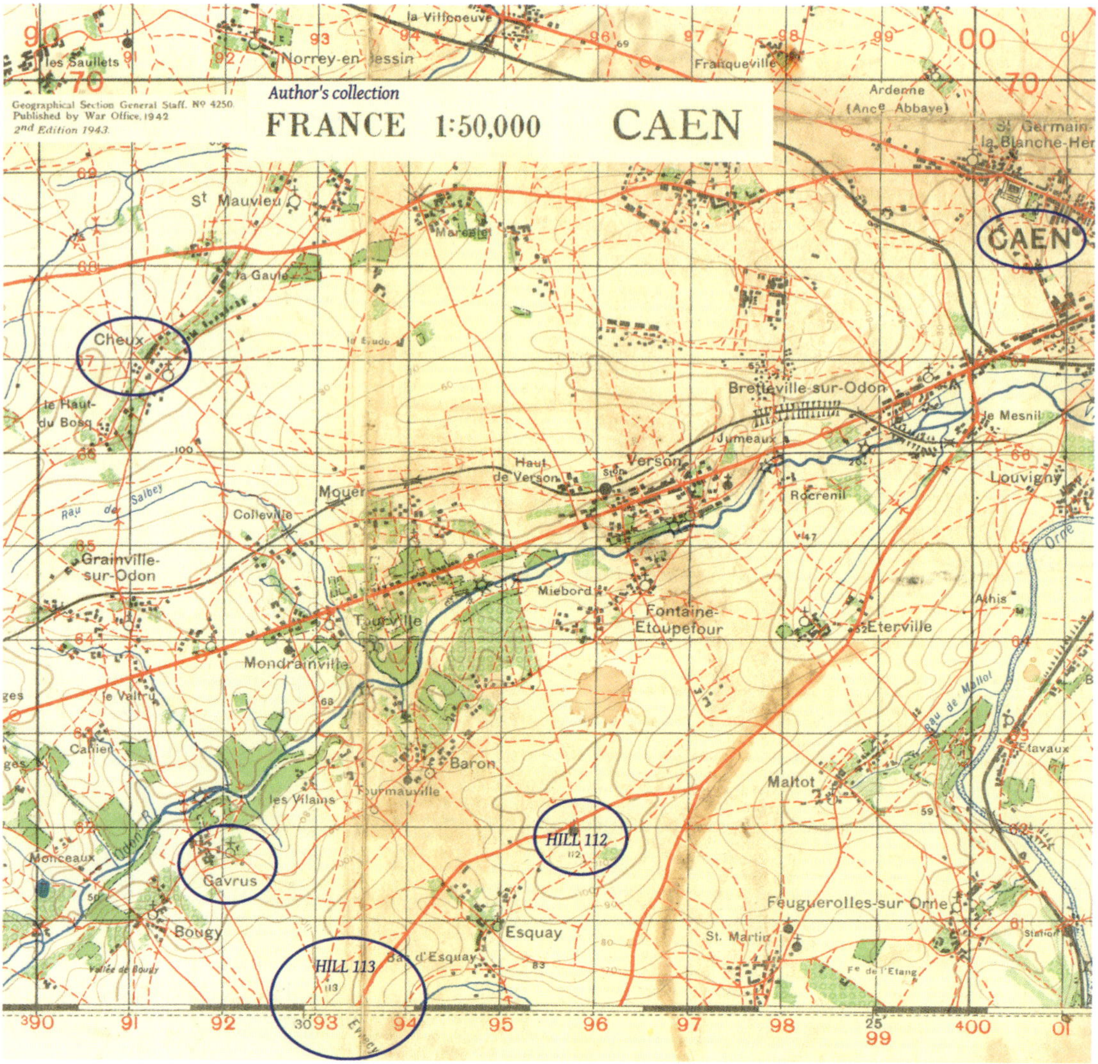

Our first relief, and the sudden concentration of shells at Le Mesnil when Atkinson was killed and my batman Hall was wounded. The Chateau there almost undamaged; picking redcurrants in the garden and wearing a rose every day to keep my spirits up!

* * *

The main focus in the British sector was to advance on Caen. Montgomery unleashed Operation Epsom to the west of Caen on June 26th, but it had only limited success; bad weather restricted air support, and although British troops crossed the River Odon and reached the vital Hill 112, between Evrecy and Maltot, they failed to secure it. Hill 112 was a critical observation point, and it was said that whoever controlled Hill 112 controlled Normandy. The Germans were determined to hold it.

On June 29th, as part of Operation Epsom, 44 RTR and 'B' Company 2KRRC – commanded by Lewin's fellow Hopperite Fletcher – pushed south towards Evrecy, west of Hill 112. However, as they reached the summit of Hill 113, enemy fire rained upon them, thirteen tanks being lost in the ferocious fighting which followed. Fletcher's signed report on this action survives in the Battalion war diary:

On 25 June '44 "B" Coy., 2/KRRC came under command 44 RTR
in area SECQUEVILLE-EN- BESSIN 9274.
During the afternoon the column moved down and took up posn
in area 9067 N.W. of CHEUX to protect flank of 29 Armd Bde.
"B" Coy took up a posn at night covering the leaguer, but
was not engaged.

2. During this period, 44 RTR xxxxxxxx accounted for 4 Panther
tanks. On the afternoon of 27 June column moved to 9166
South of CHEUX. "B" Coy again employed in protective role
at night.

3. Soon after 1st light on 28 June 6 Pl commanded by Lieut
Elgar pushed fwd supported by "B" Sqn 44 RTR through thick
country with the intention of clearing woods 903649.
This operation was stopped as it entailed crossing the Corps
boundary and 6 Pl was employed in clearing the woods
immediately in front of "B" Sqn.

4. Column moved during afternoon 28 June directed on high ground
between GAVRUS 9161 and EVRECY 9259. "B" Coy moving at tail
of column being heavily shelled and engaged by isolated
spandau posns. Three men killed and four men wounded.
One spandau posn believed destroyed. One sniper wounded
and captured. At night "B" Coy took up a protective posn
925614.

5. During day 29 June 44 RTR moved South in direction of EVRECY.
"B" Coy maintained standing patrols commanded by Lieut
Strachan in GAVRUS. During day one German captured,
four abandoned 88 m.m. guns destroyed by R.Es on patrol with
Lieut Radclyffe.

6. At 1600hrs German tank counter attack from West. "B" Coy
withdrawn under very heavy fire and rallied behind 44RTR
in area 935627. Lieut Strachan and three men wounded.
One man missing. Two vehicles destroyed by A.P. fire.

7. Night 29/30 June armoured regts South of River ODON withdrawn
and "B" Coy returns under command 2/KRRC.

=====================================

J.F. Fletcher
Major,
The King's Royal Rifle Corps,
7.7.44. O.C. "B" Company, 2nd. Bn.

Boyd and 1KOSB were also back in the front line:

> Back to Cambes again. The smell of dead cattle; the high pitched whine and roar of the *Nebelwerfers;* hearing the guns of the rest of the Second Army creeping daily closer to Caen on our right. Seeing raids go out, and wondering who would come back.

However, on June 29th they were relieved:

> Back to rest at last for the first time; clean pyjamas; sleeping above ground; and hearing the pipe band playing. The first visit to civilisation in Bayeux. Seeing the columns of troops and vehicles pouring in off the beaches. The nightly red streamers of AA fire over the beaches against the deep blue of the June sky.

Among the vehicles which Boyd saw coming off the beaches were the Sherman tanks of David Martyn's unit – 1st (Armoured) Battalion, Coldstream Guards – which disembarked near Arromanches on July 1st. Martyn had by now risen to the rank of Lieutenant, serving as a Troop Commander in 1 Squadron. He was regarded as a most capable and promising young officer, who inspired his men with confidence from his arrival. Martyn's Squadron Commander was Wykehamist Reggie Batt;[35] another Wykehamist, Lieutenant Thomas Miles Courtenay Bodley,[36] was in 3 Squadron. All three would be dead before the end of 1944.

Martyn.

* * *

The day that Martyn landed, Somerville was moving into La Butte, on the high ground west of Lingèvres, where the front line marked the western flank of the British positions in Normandy. The British knew the area as Granville, though it is now known as Crauville, and it was dense *bocage*, encompassing a large wood called the Bois de Saint Germain. The many mines which the Germans had laid had taken their toll of the local cattle, which created its own problems:

> A great number were killed, and gave off an appalling stench as they lay in the summer sun, swollen like toy balloons with their legs thrust out stiffly. As a result the area was full of flies and bluebottles.[37]

According to intelligence, there were no Germans in the Bois de St Germain. However, extensive patrolling by the British infantry in the line established that this was far from correct, as Somerville – 2SWB's Intelligence Officer – was well aware:

> Night patrols confirm enemy in north-west corner of Bois de St Germain. Half-tracks heard at night. We have 2 *Panzer* Division Recce opposite us … Patrols gradually building up a picture of the enemy. Shelling and rain as usual.

Such patrols were intensely wearing, and 2SWB were by now exhausted. Somerville commented in his diary that 'the men are getting a bit tired of this sort of warfare, and the mortaring is not good for one's nerves … We are wondering when we are going to attack again, as this sitting about getting mortared is no fun.'

Somerville was to get his wish all too soon.

XVIII

'Longing to share some of the misery, the pain, and the discomfort'

Italy, June 1944

Right, now I understand people think you're the Forgotten Army on the Forgotten Front. I've come here to tell you you're quite wrong. You're not the Forgotten Army on the Forgotten Front. No, make no mistake about it. Nobody's ever heard *of you.*
(Louis Mountbatten, Supreme Allied Commander, South-East Asia, 1943)

The troops in Burma called themselves the 'Forgotten Army'; those in Italy called themselves, ironically, the 'D-Day Dodgers', after an unfortunate remark by Lady Astor. From June 1944 onwards, the British public focused on the events closest to home: the Normandy landings; the liberation of Paris, Brussels, and Antwerp. After the euphoria of the liberation of France and Belgium, in late 1944 these successes were followed by the unsuccessful Arnhem operation and Hitler's Ardennes offensive. But meanwhile, whether the public were interested or not, the killing went on in Italy with the same bitter intensity. The liberation of Rome on June 4th had changed very little; the Germans continued to retreat with a dogged determination to make the Allies pay in blood for every advance.

The difficulties faced by the Allies were increased by the refusal of the Americans to treat the Italian campaign as anything other than a sideshow. Churchill saw things differently; with his eye on the post-war future of Europe, he wanted to smash through to Austria and Hungary to forestall any Russian advance. But in the summer of 1944, some seven divisions-worth of American and French troops were taken from Italy and sent to France; only one division, from Brazil, was sent to replace them. After the fall of Rome, the Allies advanced on Florence and the German Gothic Line, which ran from the coast north of Pisa, through the Apennines around Florence and Bologna, to the Adriatic south of Rimini. The Allies' first task was to push up to this line and to secure their rear; then, late in August, they tried to break through the Gothic Line. But although they pierced it in places, they could not break it, and thus the troops were condemned to a second winter in the Italian mountains. Brooke, Edmunds, Elliott-Binns, Kemp, Middleditch, Murray, and Walker were among the Hopperites still involved in this hard slog up the Italian peninsula.

Michael Finch, by contrast, was by now safely in German prisoner-of-war camp *Stalag* VIIA, as he explained to Robertson on a postcard sent in June but not received until after Christmas.[1] In fact, Robertson received more detail from Finch's father three months before the postcard arrived:

Finch.

My dear Bobber,
Michael is at *Stalag* VIIA. His POW number is 128919. The full address we have is *Kriegsgefangenenpost* POW 128919 2/Lt M.H.A. FINCH, *Stalag* VIIA, Germany. This is a transitional camp for which the British Red Cross will accept no personal parcels.

We have had six postcards and two letters, the last of the latter dated July 31st. The previous post-card was dated May 15th. What has happened to the intervening ones I don't know.

On July 25th he received four letters from us, the first since he left England on January 3rd, though of course we've each written each week. He is well, uninjured, and he says in rags – but we can get nothing through to him. At any rate, thank God he is well – young Lascelles [is] at the same camp badly wounded but recovering.

According to the British Red Cross map the camp is at Mussburg between Munich and Nuremberg. I must have motored through the district six times. It is in the Bavarian Highlands, beautiful scenery but cold in winter. It is a nuisance I cannot get any books, clothes, etc., out to him. Sir Richard Livingstone sent me a list of books which the Bodleian have, but the British Red Cross will not accept them or anything for transitional camps. I should think he'll be there for the rest of the war.

He asked me if I had let you know and sent his kind regards to you both. I want him to do Bodley there so that he'll get a chance of some post-graduate work at Oxford later. I do hope they'll let these youngsters off fairly soft when they were interrupted in their University career. However, we must wait. Thank you both for your enquiries and kindness.

Yours,
Ernest Finch[2]

* * *

Kemp.

The day after Rome fell, Kemp's battalion drove through the night and camped two miles east of the city limits. The newly-formed 61 Brigade was about to advance, with 7RB leading, followed by 2RB (commanded by John Sinclair's Hopperite brother, Lieutenant Colonel Chris Sinclair).[3] The aim was to push up through Monterotondo and Montopoli di Sabina, advances measured in tens of miles instead of the tortoise-like progress near Cassino. But at around 0800hrs on June 10th, when 7RB reached Cantalupo in Sabina, they came under heavy fire from mortars and artillery. All day they sat there, unable to advance or to escape the enemy shell-fire, which lasted until the small hours of the following morning. Fifty Riflemen were killed or wounded. 7RB then pushed on, delayed the while by German demolitions, before resting in Narni for the day on June 14th. The following morning, they received orders to capture Todi, seventeen miles north as the

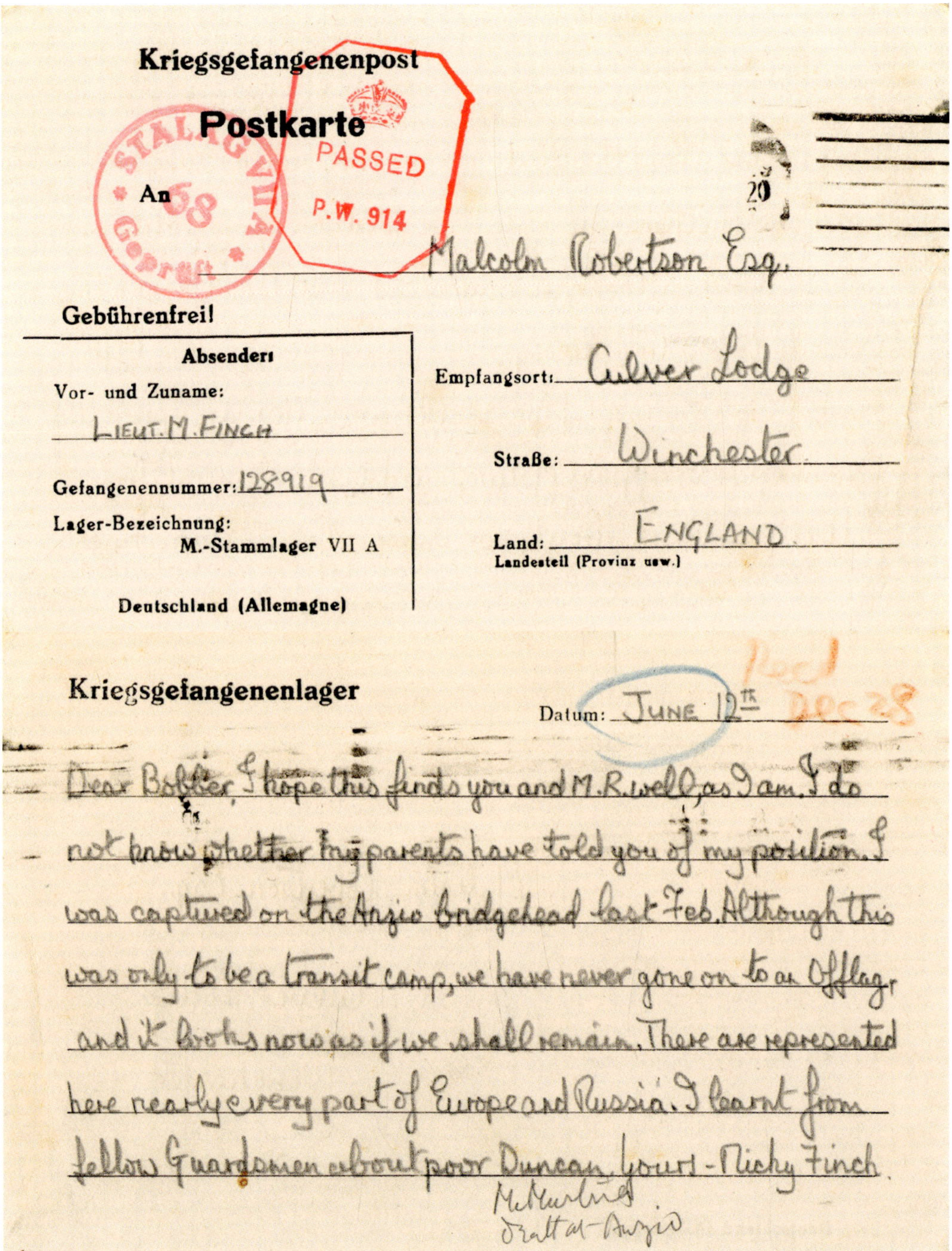

Kriegsgefangenenpost

PASSED
P.W. 914

STALAG VII A
68
Geprüft

Postkarte

An Malcolm Robertson Esq.

Gebührenfrei!

Empfangsort: Culver Lodge

Straße: Winchester

Land: ENGLAND
Landesteil (Provinz usw.)

Absender:
Vor- und Zuname: LIEUT. M. FINCH

Gefangenennummer: 128919

Lager-Bezeichnung:
M.-Stammlager VII A

Deutschland (Allemagne)

Kriegsgefangenenlager

Datum: JUNE 12th

Recd DEC 28

Dear Bobber, I hope this finds you and M.R. well, as I am. I do not know whether my parents have told you of my position. I was captured on the Anzio bridgehead last Feb. Although this was only to be a transit camp, we have never gone on to an Offlag, and it looks now as if we shall remain. There are represented here nearly every part of Europe and Russia. I learnt from fellow Guardsmen about poor Duncan. Yours - Micky Finch

[illegible]
[illegible] at Anzio

crow flies – though in those hills the route on the ground was often nearly twice as long. Nevertheless, 7RB reached Todi by mid-afternoon, occupying it without opposition and pushing on to a bridge three miles north, which they captured intact. But on the evening of June 16th, Kemp's company was heavily shelled again, Dick Adams being wounded.

* * *

Middleditch.

On May 29th, Middleditch and his colleagues in 12RL had received the welcome news that they were to revert to being an armoured car regiment, and take their rightful place in the vanguard of the advance. Rather surprisingly, the Regiment had formed a new Troop equipped with the most old-fashioned of transport; what they called the Cavalry Troop. The Troop consisted of four mounted men, commanded by Captain Carson, Middleditch at his side; with them was Sergeant Green, a former member of the Scots Greys, who was Middleditch's Troop Sergeant in 5 Troop. The Cavalry Troop joined 'A' Squadron near Carsoli on June 12th and patrolled forwards to Pietrasecchа, finding no enemy. On June 14th, Green took the horses forwards to Pescorocchiano, whilst Middleditch went back to armoured cars as 12RL probed for undemolished roads leading north and east. By June 18th they had reached Assisi, but as the British spearhead units approached Perugia, German resistance was noticeably stronger. The official history of 7RB describes the difficulties ahead for Kemp and Middleditch:

> We were now in the mountains: the ground favoured the defenders more than ever, and it was evident that resistance was stiffening. There were signs that here the Germans would make their next determined stand to hold us as long as possible, to inflict casualties and prepare yet more demolitions and booby-traps, to lay mines and plan ambushes … Despite the summer sunlight, showing Italian beauty at its best, the capture of these mountains was not an inviting prospect.[4]

One of those caught up in a German delaying action was Middleditch, at the forefront of battle in his armoured car:

> 'A' Squadron, meanwhile, had been engaged in some severe fighting on its sector. On June 19th it had captured the bridge held by the enemy on the road running north-east from Assisi, but in pushing on Lieutenant Middleditch had run into trouble, his armoured car being brewed-up by a mortar and both he and his gunner wounded. Despite the fact that Perugia fell to the 8th Indian Division on the 20th, resistance in this area continued to strengthen.[5]

The war diary supplies the detail that the mortar-bomb scored a direct hit on his armoured car. In his own copy of the Regimental history, Middleditch added many annotations in pencil; he noted here that his wounded companion was Trooper Alibone. He later made light of his wound when writing to Robertson:

> As regards the wounds that my mother mentioned, they were nothing very serious. The first was a few fragments of mortar shell which landed in my side in June. I spent about five very pleasant days in hospital having them out and then went back to the Regiment.[6]

The actions in the hills to the west of Perugia involved 61 Brigade in four successive night attacks, the preferred method of these battle-hardened infantrymen, as Wykehamist Jim Wilson – serving in 10RB – explained:[7]

> At this time the Rifle Brigade technique was to advance at night and aim to be installed at first light on our objective. Usually these attacks were 'silent'; artillery support would only be called for when the attack encountered opposition. In all these battles there was little chance of reconnaissance and no time for patrolling. Our tactics required a high standard of map-reading and cross-country navigation; on a dark night the attackers had no exact idea of their whereabouts. Often it was a night compass march, hoping somehow one would end up in the right place.

7RB headed for Monte Malbe, a commanding feature 2,139ft high but without an obvious peak. Seton-Watson, supporting the Battalion with his guns, described what was to become the scene of a fierce action:

> [Monte Malbe was a] steep hill rising over a thousand feet above Route 75, the main road running west from Perugia to Lake Trasimene. The first three hundred feet were cultivated, but immediately above the small village and palatial villa of Fontana, dense woods began, intersected with ravines which gave excellent cover for snipers and made very hard going for the infantry. After Fontana, the road degenerated into a rough cart track with sharp corners and bad gradients, impassable to wheeled vehicles larger than a Jeep. At La Trinità the woods stopped, and the summit was rocky and bare. La Trinità itself consisted of a red farm-house and a large yard behind, with the small chapel which gave it its name in one corner.[8]

7RB had orders to attack on the night of June 19th, and there was time before darkness fell for a quick reconnaissance of at least some of the feature.

> The Battalion was called up and left its vehicles at Pila. By this time it was, even in mid-summer, after dark, and a little time was needed to rest the Riflemen and to get orders down to platoon and section commanders. A silent attack was to be made, starting at 0100hrs. It was hoped to capture the objective in the dark and repel the inevitable counter-attack in the morning light. There were, of course, advantages to us in moving in the dark, but this particular night, pitch-black with rain, tried the attackers to the utmost.[9]

After a five-mile approach march, 'A' Company took up positions at L'Olmo, whilst 'B' Company advanced a mile further to take the village of Fontana (where it captured three prisoners).

'D' Company reached La Trinità without being detected, and eliminated a German post in the red-roofed farm-house there (killing two and capturing three). 'C' Company, paralleling 'D' on the western slopes, captured a 150mm gun and its crew of twelve *en route*. 'C' then dug in at the farm-housc, and 'D' descended to Fontana. It had been a textbook operation.

However, the ground was rocky, and apart from two rows of trees to the north of the farm-house, La Trinità was devoid of cover. Although Malbe was not much use as an observation post, the hills to the north being higher, it was a vital stepping-stone, and it was clear that the Germans would counter-attack. At 0730hrs on June 20th their artillery

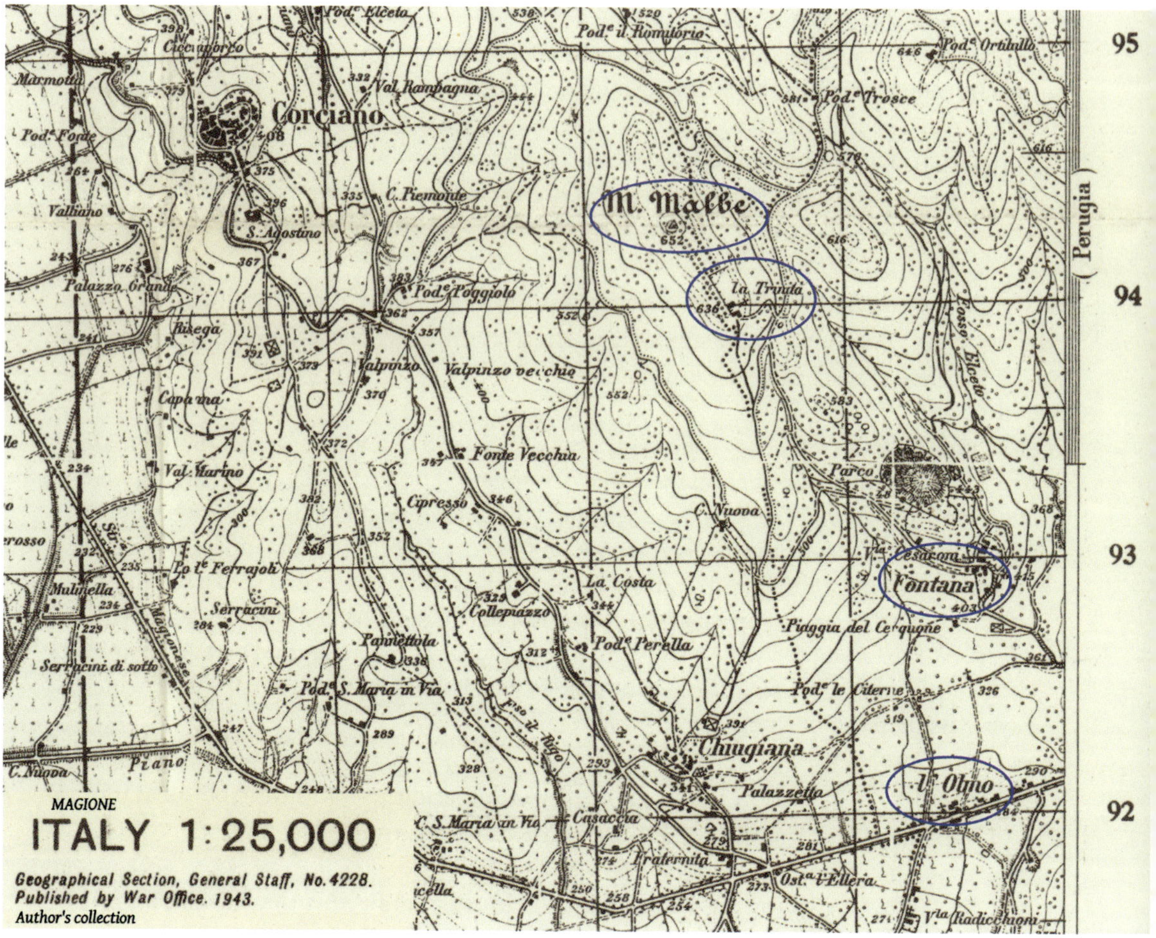

Author's collection

and mortars began to pound the hill. At 1000hrs infantry attacks came in from the north-west, and although these were initially held off, mist and rain cut visibility and enabled the Germans to get closer – indeed, at one point they were driven off from 'C' Company HQ by men unaccustomed to handling rifles. 2RHA provided valuable supporting fire, sometimes as close as fifty yards to 'C' Company's positions, as Seton-Watson recalled:

> Spandaus on the flanks made movement on the summit impossible ... The view from La Trinità was extremely limited, and it was possible for enemy infantry to lie unobserved within less than a hundred yards of Company HQ ...
>
> 'I' Battery moved during the morning, with great difficulty owing to the rain-soaked fields and tracks, past Perugia station and into action north of Route 75 at L'Olmo. While it had been moving, the enemy had counter-attacked ... For twenty minutes 'H' and 'L' batteries were firing almost continuously. The Riflemen held their ground and about 1330hrs the enemy withdrew.
>
> At 1715hrs came a second counter-attack, even more determined than the first. The enemy very nearly succeeded in recapturing La Trinità, and for fifteen minutes it was touch and go ... [We] called for concentration after concentration on to Trig Point 652, the summit of Monte Malbe, and its reverse slopes ... Ammunition supplies sank very

low, but when the situation was really serious, two loaded three-tonners arrived, amid cheers from the whole gun position. The Colonel set to with everyone else to hump the boxes from the road over the muddy field to the guns. The mediums also joined in with, as we learned later, devastating effect.

['C' Company] kept howling for more and more fire, and sent over the air the most bold and alarming corrections: 'Drop two hundred.' 'Drop four hundred, right three hundred.' 'Drop two hundred.' I edited these orders before passing them on, and usually halved the corrections. The only possible explanation seemed to be that the infantry were bringing the rounds down upon themselves. This, in fact, proved to be the case, and it probably saved the day. The price was two Riflemen killed and three wounded by our own shells, and a gaping hole in the side of the Red House caused by a direct hit from a medium shell.[10]

To everyone's surprise, a tank of 17th/21st Lancers eventually made it up to La Trinità. Its arrival was too much for the attackers, who gave up and never tried to attack again. By 7RB's estimate, they had left behind at least thirty dead and thirty-four prisoners – but Seton-Watson counted fifty corpses, one of them only 35 yards from the Red House.

After 1800hrs, the battle died down, and the enemy retreated to lick his wounds. So ended the battle of Monte Malbe ... The day had proved one thing – the value of teamwork and mutual understanding based on personal contact between gunners and infantry. The battle quickly passed into legend. Already, in the middle of July, I heard a Rifleman describing to the rest of his section how a thousand German corpses had been found in a wood behind Malbe after one of our stonks. When I tried to interrupt, I was accused of false modesty and howled down.[11]

But the hill had been held at a cost. Among 7RB's many casualties that day, Wykehamist Johnnie Persse[12] had been killed by mortar-fire while going out to the help of a wounded Rifleman in Fontana.

* * *

The British manpower shortage in front-line units would become acute as the year went on, and especially so at junior officer level; many British units had 'CanLoan' officers, seconded from the Canadian Army. Nevertheless, some of our subjects were still in England awaiting their call – among them Peter Walker, with his great Winchester friend Dan Awdry. They were at Barnard Castle with 61st Training Regiment, RAC, pending posting to the Wiltshire Yeomanry in Italy. News of the fall of Rome and the Normandy landings frustrated Walker, as he explained to his father late in June:

Walker.

A letter which has been put off from day to day because every time I settled down to write I began to feel very miserable and I loathe writing to either of you when I'm miserable.

Things are still no brighter, and it's an awful strain trying to think of something unusual to make one forget the dismal outlook that awaits us as we wake up each morning. Three of us went on embarkation leave yesterday, and I do so hope ours will come through soon. They say that only those with family connections are going, and yet Dan hasn't gone yet.

The real problem is not to find something which will occupy one's mind, because that's quite easy. I can read books, ride, go for walks, go to the cinemas, drink, write, and so on – the point is that it's impossible to want to do anything except win the war, and when you read the papers you can't help feeling how terribly out of it one is. And it's funny that I didn't always feel like that and in my worse moments still don't, even now. I used to face the matter logically, saying that whether I fought or not was not going to make any difference, as I'm a very indifferent soldier. My one consolation, when thinking like that, was that to be in action would strengthen one's character. There was no sort of patriotism, just a faint longing to become more of a man.

Now, when I think a bit deeper, I realise how terribly self-centred and priggish that outlook was, and I now feel in my better moments a longing to share some of the misery, the pain, and the discomfort that thousands have already felt in the past five years. As it is, I waste my time here from day to day. Dan is no help; gets far more depressed than I do.

How cruel life is.

Your dejectedly,

Pete[13]

XIX

'That was some game, tho' parts of it I don't want to remember'

Normandy, July 1944

A 6-pounder anti-tank gun of 1KOSB on Rue Montoir Poissonnerie, Caen, July 10th 1944; Canadian Sherman tanks are in the background. In April, British troops had been issued with the Mark III steel helmet – sometimes referred to as a 'turtle' – seen here, instead of the more familiar Mark II 'Brodie' design. (IWM B6924, colourized by Doug @colour_history)

On July 8th, Operation Charnwood opened, with British and Canadian troops attacking Caen from the north. To pave their way, over four hundred heavy bombers of the RAF bombed the city, causing huge damage. Boyd and 1KOSB were involved, in their case entering Caen itself.

July 7th
The earth-shaking hour of the bombardment of Caen; sleeping through it, but being aware of the roar of many wings above my head and shaking of the slit trench. The night march up towards Bieville with Caen burning in the sky in front of us.

Boyd.

July 8th
Then Lebisy and the mortars, the burned-out vehicles, and British and German dead.

July 9th
Being left behind when the Battalion went forward to Caen … Rushing up to Caen with the vehicles; getting jammed in a street with no exit and full of bomb craters …

The Church of St Jean among the Ruins of Caen, Normandy, 1944, by Anthony Gross. (Tate N05697)

> Being shelled there – a near one – then the entry into Caen, picking and eating cherries on our way ... The smell of burning houses and dead flesh ... The deserted streets; the few white-helmeted *Maquis* who did such gallant work to help us ... HQ in a café with an unexploded bomb underneath ... Morning in Caen, and the full realisation of the shattering effect of air bombardment ... The visit to the school where the refugees were crowded.

* * *

On the western flank, 2SWB also attacked on July 8th. They received a day's notice, which was not really enough for such a major undertaking. Somerville wrote:

> We are to attack tomorrow. Conferences, maps, air-photos, patrol information are all put on view and we have a terrific conference with all supporting arms. The plan is made and we are all set for tomorrow. June 8th was Sully; I wonder whether July 8th will be so sticky.

2SWB were to attack from La Butte astride the 'Granville' road, press on to the main road from Hottot to Caumont, and occupy the ridge at La Chapelle. To their left, 2nd Essex would move round the 'empty' Bois de St Germain to cut the main road at La Croix-des-Landes. Armoured bulldozers were supplied to break through the *bocage* hedges, and huge support was provided:

> The Battalion, supported by British and American artillery on a pre-arranged programme, a platoon of 4.2-inch mortars, two MMG platoons, a squadron of the 4/7 Dragoon Guards, one M10 troop and one 17-pounder troop, a troop of Flails, a section of RE, a troop of AVREs, and a troop of Crocodiles, attacked down the road from La Butte-Granville-La Chapelle with a start line just south of La Butte, and the objective as the southern edge of the orchard at La Chapelle.

There were weapons here to deal with any eventuality: over a dozen Sherman tanks; M10 tank-destroyers, armed with the superb 17-pounder gun, which could also, as here, be used in a towed form; Sherman 'Flails' fitted with revolving drums which battered the ground ahead with chains, thus detonating most mines; Churchill 'Crocodile' tanks fitted with devastating flame-throwers; Churchill AVREs, fitted with a 290mm 'spigot mortar', which fired a 'flying dustbin' capable of demolishing most fortifications. MMGs were the famous tripod-mounted Vickers medium machine-guns, capable of being used in an indirect fire mode to rain bullets on a specific area; and 4.2-inch mortars were heavy mortars which would supplement 2SWB's own 3-inch versions.

Unfortunately for the attackers, the Germans were also intending to attack that day, and ahead of 2SWB lay their 277 Regiment – three infantry battalions – supported by tanks from 2nd *Panzer* Division. Somerville describes July 8th in detail:

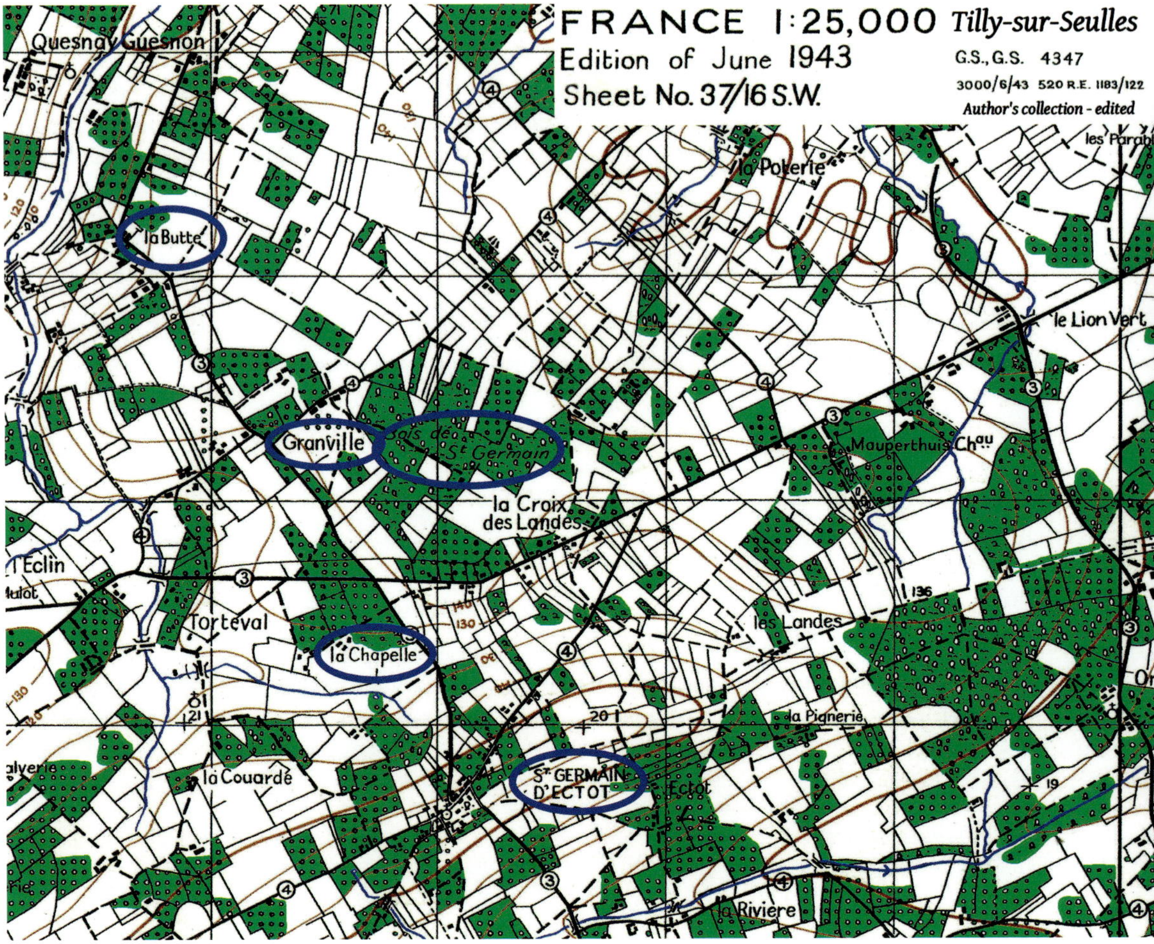

The attack was launched at 0800hrs, with 'C' Company on the right of the road and 'A' Company on the left of the road, a squadron of 4/7 DGs supporting both companies. 'C' Company reached the lateral road through Granville under cover of the barrage and found no opposition. 'A' Company were held up by the enemy in a farm on the left of the road just before reaching Granville. These they dealt with, but on reaching the lateral road through Granville, they ran into the enemy's mortar DFs [DF tasks are pre-registered targets on to which defenders can call down intense and accurate fire at a moment's notice] and were at the same time held up by an enemy strong-point in the north-east corner of the Bois de St Germain. The tanks could not come up with them owing to a minefield. A Flail was sent up to deal with the mines, and three AVREs followed to try and blast out the strong point. They succeeded in blowing to bits two very obnoxious houses.

By now, however, the enemy mortar fire was very heavy indeed, and 'A' Company were ordered to fall back, as they had suffered heavy casualties and were unable to cross the road. Meanwhile 'C' Company, the Company Commander having been wounded … continued to advance under heavy mortar and artillery fire, and fought their way to the final objective at La Chapelle. This advance was costly, as the enemy had his mortar DFs all the way along the road, and particularly on the final objective. As soon as it was known that 'C' Company were on their objective, 'D' Company were sent up to their right rear in order to make the position more tenable. Meanwhile 'B' Company formed up behind 'C' Company in order to attack the south-west corner of the Bois de St Germain.

While these operations were taking place, 'C' Company were counter-attacked by enemy infantry supported by tanks. The preliminary mortaring caused casualties in 'C' and 'B' companies, the latter being caught in their follow-up. Owing to a misunderstanding, the troop of M10s withdrew from 'C' Company's area, and the tanks moved back in order to support the Company better. This left what was remaining of 'C' Company to withstand the brunt of the attack. Having immobilised two enemy tanks, they were forced to withdraw and firm-base themselves with 'B' and 'D' companies a little further back. These three companies succeeded in beating off the counter-attack, so that by nightfall 'C' Company were able to withdraw and come into reserve. They had only about twenty-four men left.

During the day the Regimental Aid Post had dealt with about 150 cases, great bravery being shown by the Stretcher Bearers in evacuating casualties by Jeep under heavy mortar fire. 'B' and 'D' companies were cut off from the rest of the Battalion during the night, and it was impossible to get food up to them.

July 9th
'D' and 'B' companies were counter-attacked in the early morning, and the left-hand platoon was over-run. Two enemy tanks were covering an open gap between this platoon and the rest of the company, and this made a counter-attack on the platoon position impossible. Food was taken out to the forward companies by a tank during the morning. Shelling and mortaring continued during the day.

July 10th
Contact established with forward companies. Usual shelling and mortaring.

* * *

Lewin.

2KRRC and the rest of 4 Armoured Brigade had spent a week in reserve before British forces attacked again. Then, as part of Operation Jupiter, they joined the attack on Hill 112. Control of this key ground see-sawed back and forth, with many casualties on both sides. 2KRRC crossed the Odon at 0500hrs on July 10th with orders to follow up an infantry attack between Hill 112 and Maltot. As they waited in a ruined chateau, under sporadic shell-fire and mortaring, they realized that the attack was floundering, and although Lewin and 'A' Company moved up to join their armoured regiment, from 2000hrs they endured a nasty hour-long artillery bombardment. As the war diary explained, chaos reigned:

> Part of the infantry ahead began to move back through them, and the situation was, to put it mildly, confused. In the midst of this *melée,* a Tiger tank sneaked up over a

ridge ahead and started a direct shoot on to our vehicles. Finally the situation cleared somewhat and a most uncomfortable night was spent by both companies …

Three officers had been killed and three wounded, for no gain. The next day was less bloody: 'At 1730hrs Battalion Tactical HQ was shelled sharply, the only casualty being a can of "tinned fruit" – a most regrettable incident.'

* * *

As 2KRRC's tinned fruit met its Waterloo, Boyd was 'marching out of Caen with the pipes playing, and back for a few days' rest'. However, the initiative was passing to the Allies, and 1KOSB were soon on the move again:

July 16th
Across the Orne to the mosquito-infested country round Breville; meeting Alastair [Thorburn] and his Commando … The feeling of great things in the air.

Nick Somerville's diary records that on July 16th he 'went for a day's holiday to the sea and bathed with Sam Weaver. It was a wonderful break, but I got very sunburnt.' This seems likely to be the occasion on which he visited McArthur, who was still working on Gold Beach:

Nick Somerville.

John McArthur was on the same beach that we landed on, as an RN Commando, but unfortunately I didn't see him. However, he saw SWB on the men's shoulder tabs and asked one of our chaps to tell me he was there. I was able to get down to the beaches later on when we got our three days' rest and found him with an enormous red beard. We had a long chat and he produced a loaf of bread, which we had not heard of, let alone seen.[1]

McArthur referred to the same strange meeting in a letter addressed simply FRANCE, which must have been written some time after July 3rd:

McArthur.

Dearest Mum, Dad, and Louie,
Have just received your letter posted on July 3rd. Not too bad, but it seems you still haven't heard from me. Believe me, Mum and Dad, your son does think of you and he has been writing; this is his ninth or tenth letter to you. I know you worry. Please try not to; there's no need to. I'm on this business for you, and believe me when I honestly say I'd do it a thousand times again for you people, because you're so worth it. So please don't think that I've forgotten you or just haven't bothered to write. It's this damn postal business of the GPO. It's the worst bit of organisation I've come across.

Well, Louie, how did the party go? I should have loved to have been there. Fresh faces would be a big change. We don't come in contact with the French much.

Of all people, Nick Somerville rolled up the other day from the front to see me. He was in great form. Landed near me. Some day I'll tell you what happened on D-Day. That was some game, tho' parts of it I don't want to remember. I'm Beachmaster again nowadays; another fellow has taken on my old job. It's good to be in charge of all these things again… .

Must go. Love to all and God bless you.

'J' x x x[2]

A Beachmaster's control station on Mike sector of Gold Beach, June 13th 1944 – not McArthur's, but very like it. (IWM A2409; edited by dansteele.net)

* * *

Martyn.

After two weeks spent visiting the battlefield, attending lectures, bathing, and shooting, Martyn and his comrades in 1st Coldstream assembled at 1200hrs on July 16th for an address by the Commanding Officer. The attritional battles around Caen were now sucking in armoured units. Montgomery launched Operation Goodwood on July 18th, the intention being to pour three armoured divisions – 7th, 11th, and Guards – through a narrow sector on the eastern flank of the British perimeter. 11th Armoured (arguably the best British armoured division) was to lead, with the Guards Armoured Division following. Almost 2,000 Allied bombers were allocated as support. The threat of all this British armour meant that the Germans did not dare shift forces westwards to oppose the Americans; the British and Canadians faced three times as many German tanks. This made the American break-out south of Saint-Lô – Operation Cobra, which began on July 25th – much, much easier. But the cost to the British armoured divisions was high. Goodwood soon went awry, with severe opposition forcing 11th Armoured to bypass the fortified village of Cagny and leave it to the Guards.

> Every advantage lay with the defenders: the ground haze was thickened by the dust churned up by the armour, and thick hedges and belts of tall trees limited the vision of the tank commanders as they peered through their field-glasses, trying to pick out the enemy guns in the corn and root fields.[3]

Although the Guards Armoured Division was ready for action, 5 Guards Armoured Brigade had expected no move before 1000hrs on July 18th.[4] But as Martyn and his companions in 1st Coldstream sat down for breakfast at 0800hrs they received orders to move at once, and their Shermans sped off for the Orne Bridge, 1 Squadron in the lead. The Battalion deployed, and then became embroiled in the battle for Cagny, as the official history explains:

> Cautiously, Major Batt took 1 Squadron up on the left of [2nd] Grenadiers [with which two Wykehamists were serving], with Lieutenant Lock and Lieutenant Loyd in the lead. A shot from a Panther carried Lieutenant Lock's aerial away; he jumped from his tank, ran to his 'Firefly' [each troop contained one up-gunned Sherman, nicknamed the Firefly, which carried the only effective anti-tank weapon available to Sherman units], and holed the Panther with his first shot. Major Anstruther-Gray, with 2 Squadron, was feeling his way round to the right of Cagny … The Squadron came up to the line of the Paris–Caen railway, which ran obliquely across its front, and paused …
>
> [Lieutenant Boscawen, of 2 Squadron, wrote:] 'Beyond the railway the horizon was covered with blazing Shermans; I could see nearly a whole squadron burning in one field alone. More were hidden behind the black smoke of others brewing up, while yet others were still being hit and bursting into flames.'[5]

At least two of those blazing tanks contained Wykehamists.

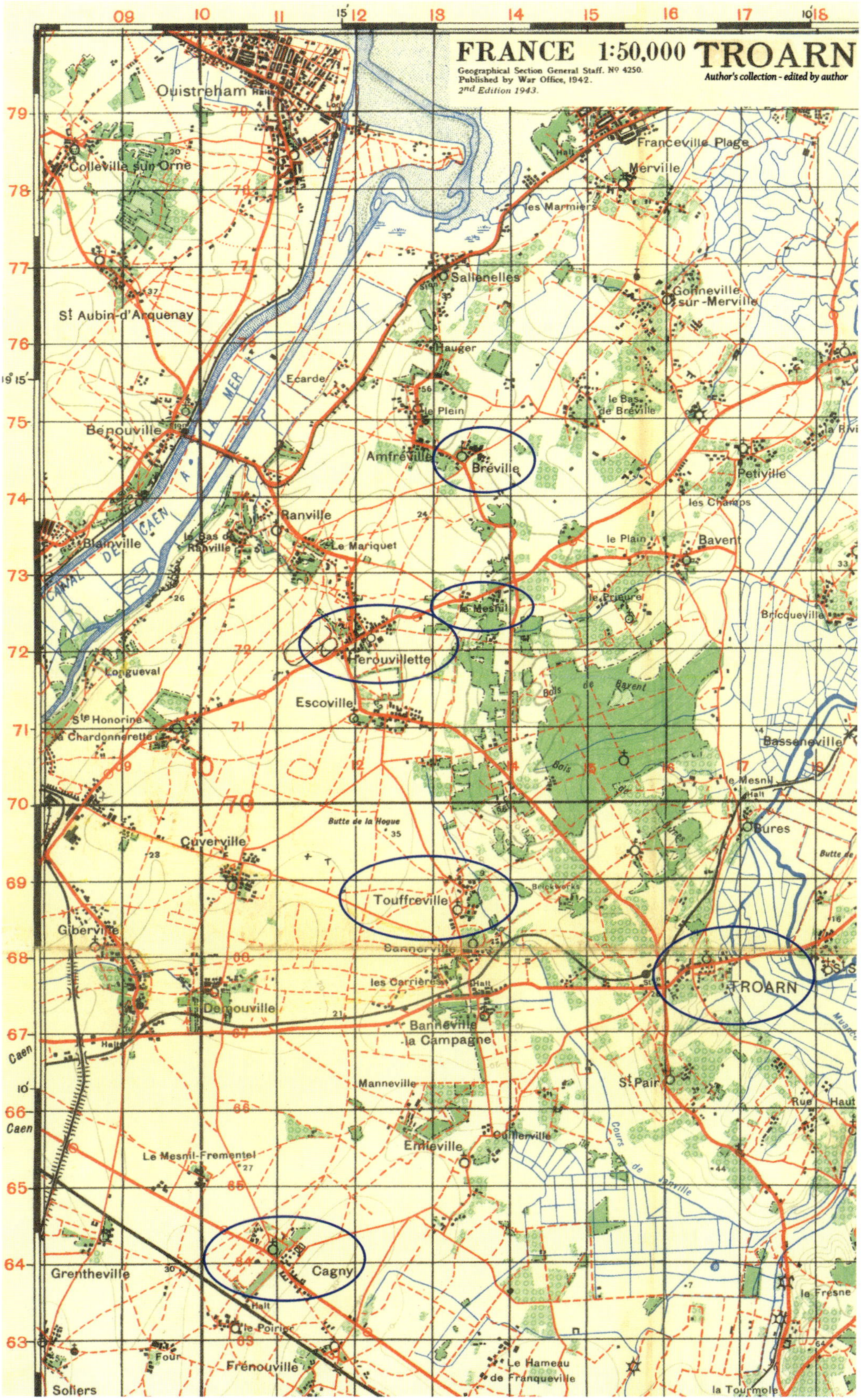
FRANCE 1:50,000 TROARN
Geographical Section General Staff. Nº 4250.
Published by War Office, 1942.
2nd Edition 1943.
Author's collection - edited by author
Ouistreham
Colleville sur Orne
St Aubin-d'Arquenay
Franceville Plage
Merville
les Marmiers
Sallenelles
Gonneville sur-Merville
Hauger
Ecarde
le Plein
le Bas de Bréville
Bénouville
Amfréville
Bréville
Petiville
Ranville
le Bas de Ranville
Le Mariquet
Blainville
les Champs
le Plain
Bavent
CANAL DE CAEN A LA MER
le Mesnil
le Prieuré
Bricqueville
Hérouvillette
Longueval
Escoville
Bois de Bavent
Ste Honorine
Chardonnerette
Basseneville
le Mesnil
Bures
Cuverville
Butte de la Hogue
Touffreville
Brickworks
Giberville
Sannerville
les Carrières
TROARN
Demouville
Banneville la Campagne
Manneville
St Pair
Emiéville
Cuillerville
Cours de Janville
Le Mesnil-Frementel
Grentheville
Cagny
le Fresne
le Poirier
Four
Frénouville
Le Hameau de Franqueville
Soliers
la Tourmole
Caen

It was clearly impossible to proceed, and so 1st Coldstream halted for the night a mile north of Cagny, though still under fire. The Battalion spent the next two days in reserve, sheltering in its tanks from the rain, German shells, and rifle-fire, before retiring from the battlefield on July 21st.

1KOSB were also in the thick of the action on July 18th, slightly to the north-east of Cagny. From Bréville, they moved south to Le Mesnil, then on through Herouvillette and Toufreville. While they advanced, often across country, they came under fire, and Boyd had to dress his commanding officer's wounds:

> The long advance through the armour along the hot, dusty tracks towards Sannerville ... Seeing dead Germans cut into small pieces and in batches of ten and twenty, killed by our anti-personnel bombs ... The *Nebelwerfer* on the road down; putting a field dressing on Douglas Renny while the Battalion marched by.

As 1KOSB approached Sannerville, enemy machine-guns opened fire, and it became clear that there were strong defences ahead. The heat, dust, and the damage caused by Allied bombing had made the Battalion's advance that day a difficult one.

> The bomb craters at Sannerville, and the struggle to get the transport through the hedges and ditches up to the Battalion ... The confusion when darkness fell and we were unable to reach them ... Hurriedly trying to organise a local defence out of the carrier crews, machine-gunners, and anti-tank gunners who were there ... My overpowering thirst after the long, hot, dusty day ... Suddenly finding that Battalion HQ had moved back and were within a hundred yards of me ... Lying down exhausted and sleeping for an hour on the ground.

1KOSB went into the attack the following morning, trying to break through to Troarn. But despite tank support the attack failed, and when 1KOSB withdrew to their start line they came under accurate shell-fire, some of it 'friendly'.

> The next day's attack; the short artillery fire; the sudden silence and then the rattle of machine-guns; wounded coming back... Going up to the CO to find out what was happening; climbing on to a tank and trying to get some sense out of a very frightened commander; the tank in front being knocked out ... Further advance being hopeless, and sitting down where we were ... Finding out who was left ...

The Battalion had lost twelve officers and 140 Other Ranks killed or wounded in the space of two days. July 20th and 21st were most uncomfortable – 'forty-eight hours of rain making the men wet, filthy and miserable'.

* * *

At the opposite end of the British lines, 2SWB launched another attack on July 20th. After their partially successful but costly advance on July 8th, they were inclined to be cautious. On July 18th their patrols reported to Somerville that La Chapelle, Granville, and most of the Bois de St Germain were unoccupied by the enemy. A meeting was held to discuss moving forward, and the advance was named Operation Pursuit. As it turned out, it took until the end of the month to achieve their objectives.

On the morning of July 19th, Somerville recorded in his diary:

> Lieutenant Reynolds and ten men of 'C' Company managed to get into La Chapelle orchard under cover of artillery. They found themselves surrounded by six Spandaus, but managed to get away, capturing one prisoner. Later on, another patrol got up to the orchard and found it empty, but were heavily mortared as soon as they got there. It was decided to make a plan to capture the La Chapelle high ground and the Bois-de-St Germain on the next day.

The main problem which faced 2SWB now was not so much German troops as the mines with which they had liberally sown the static front line; we have already seen how terrifying these weapons were to the troops in North Africa and Italy. Among those encountered were anti-tank Teller mines and anti-personnel 'Mustard Pots'. The latter were small metal cylinders filled with explosive, which could be set off by a pressure of just 16kg. Easy to disarm, the *Behelfs-Schützenmine* S.150 was nevertheless a dangerous nuisance. As 'C' Company dug in at La Chapelle on July 20th, Major Coles trod on one and was evacuated. 'A' Company found the Bois de St Germain clear, apart from booby-traps. Although there was incoming mortar fire, 2SWB were largely undisturbed that day, enabling the RE to help them to lift no fewer than 150 Teller mines and 128 Mustard Pots. Patrolling forwards, 2SWB found that there were Germans in the next village, St Germain d'Ectot. The next two days were spent burying the German dead and lifting more mines: 322 Tellers and 158 Mustard Pots.

* * *

Duffin.

Duffin, a Troop Commander in Left Flank Squadron of 3rd (Armoured) Battalion, Scots Guards, sailed for Jig Sector of Gold Beach on July 20th. It was a rough crossing in the face of the storm which was soaking 1KOSB, and it was not until 0530hrs on July 21st that the first shipload disembarked. Duffin was not the only Wykehamist with the Battalion; commanding 'S' Squadron was another of Robertson's former charges, Captain (Acting Major) 89506 William Whitelaw; the Signals Officer with HQ Squadron was Lieutenant Harold Llewellyn Smith;[6] and with Duffin in Left Flank Squadron was fellow Troop Commander Henry Marshall.[7] Like Duffin, Marshall was a married man, despite being only twenty-one.

3SG moved their Churchill tanks to an assembly area just east of Bayeux, at Esquay-sur-Seulles, before transferring on July 29th to St Honorine de Ducy, preparatory to an attack. British forces had been moved to the west of Caen for a major attack called

Jig Sector, Gold Beach, looking towards Le Hamel, June 7th 1944, by Anthony Gross. (Art.IWM ART LD 4461)

Operation Bluecoat. Their objective was to be Mont Pinçon, the highest point in Normandy, in the hope that this threat would prevent the Germans from interfering with the developing American breakthrough.

1KOSB were still in the line during this period, and Boyd recorded a local ceasefire on July 23rd, as well as being lucky to escape serious injury:

> The truce one morning when the Germans came down to let us bury our dead and to bury their own between the lines … Walking out between the lines with a feeling of some uncertainty, and seeing the field-grey figures in their slit trenches … When the shells came over, the hectic propping-up of the door of our little Boche dugout which faced the wrong way … Sitting in there with Terry, drinking gin and reading the *Tatler* … The whistle and roar of the *Nebelwerfer* and my arm swinging round when a small piece hit it.

A new commanding officer took over three days later, which made for a busy day for Boyd, as Adjutant:

John Macdonald arriving, and frenzies of reorganisation ... The burst of shelling which unkindly shattered his first conference.

However, the next day – July 27th – was quiet enough for Boyd to be able to write to Robertson:

I have been meaning to write to you for some time, but we have been in action practically continually since D-Day and I have not had an awful lot of time. I am still Adjutant of this Battalion, and expect I shall be for a bit yet – unless either something hits me or I get sacked! I am quite happy in the job, but rather long to go to a Rifle Company and get some proper soldiering!

We were very glad when we got mobile again and went into the big attack. After that we had a short – very short! – rest and then started off again, so, taken all in all, I think we have had a fair amount of action.

We found the French people in the country areas a bit apathetic, but in the only big town in which we've been they were absolutely magnificent. They rescued our wounded under fire, acted as guides, and some even fought most gallantly beside our forward troops. It did a tremendous amount of good, as it did more than anything else to make the men realise that they were really doing a worthwhile job of work.

I have met one or two people you would know. Tom Howarth[8], who was a Don just before the war, is GSO3 at our Brigade and is very good. He needs to be, as we now have a shocking bad Brigade Major. I met Alastair Thorburn who is, as you know, in the Commandos, the other day. His lot were with us on D-Day and did very well. He was in very good form, but very browned off with sitting still.

I am sorry to have seen a good many Wykehamist casualties including Humphrey Woods – have you any news of anyone else?

I must stop now and do some work.[9]

* * *

Somerville and 2SWB were meanwhile still edging their way south in the dense *bocage* around the ridge at La Chapelle. First, they inched their line forwards to the road which ran through La Chapelle. The following day (July 24th) saw more patrolling:

Day patrol under Lieutenant Pope. This officer shot three Germans dead with two magazines of his Sten, and managed to extricate his patrol with distinction. A concentration of enemy vehicles in the area of St Germain-d'Ectot was strafed pretty heavily by our artillery during the night.

But the job of mine clearance went on, not always with total success. In 'D' Company's area, a scout car set off a mine which killed two men from 2SWB and wounded two more. The score was evened on July 26th, when a fighting patrol went forwards with orders to bring in a prisoner so as to confirm the identity of the opposing unit. When a machine-gun opened fire at close range,

> Sergeant Edwards immediately took the Bren guns over to the flank, under fire, re-crossed again to a different direction, and shouted 'Charge' to deceive the enemy as to the direction from which the attack was coming. He himself was first into the enemy position. He found three wounded Germans and one live one, whom he hit on the head, slung over his shoulder, and carried away up to the north end of the orchard. He then fired a Green Verey light and the artillery came down on a pre-arranged plan, enabling the patrol to withdraw. Unfortunately the prisoner died before he could be interrogated, but his identification proved that 326th Division had taken over from 2nd *Panzer* Division.

All this activity had been preparation for an attack on St Germain d'Ectot, which went in at 0530hrs on July 31st. 2SWB advanced on La Couarde with 'C' Company in the lead, supported by a troop of tanks. The infantry ran into ten mutually-supporting machine-gun positions, which proved a formidable obstacle to progress, even when the tanks attempted to help. Three times 'C' Company tried to get forward, without success.

> 'B' Company was put in round the right flank and got on the high ground in this area. Mines were encountered and the Flails succeeded in clearing a path up to 'B' Company's position. This enabled 'D' Company to form up in 'B' Company's area, supported by the flame-throwers which were now in action … 'D' Company attacked the enemy positions just this side of the village, and they followed so close on the Crocodiles that they attacked treading in the flames. This attack was so fearsome that the enemy withdrew. In the morning, 'D' Company, supported by the flame-throwers, attacked St Germain d'Ectot village and secured it, firm-basing themselves on the southern side of the village. 'A' Company, following up patrols, established themselves on the bridge at Candon. The day was spent in clearing up the mines. Battalion HQ moved forward to La Couarde. We found a very valuable artillery OP of the enemy and captured some very valuable documents. There was a fair number of enemy dead in the St Germain d'Ectot area who had to be buried.

On August 4th, 2SWB moved to a rest area at Chouain, 'an awfully nice undamaged village'.

* * *

Bluecoat had begun on July 30th, and Duffin's Battalion experienced a scorching baptism of fire south of Caumont. Llewellyn Smith later compiled an account of 3SG's campaigns which includes the Caumont battle.[10] In addition, a very full account of the action was appended to the war diary, which in itself gives a clear, terse narrative of the day's fighting. What follows is compiled from all three.

In support of 2nd Argyll and Sutherland Highlanders, 3SG had been ordered to advance southwards from Caumont for six miles, to break through the German lines and pave the way for a major advance by the rest of the British armour. The Germans had thinned out their defences to reinforce their line to the west against the Americans, but the advantages of the terrain lay with them. Duffin and the other officers spent the day before the attack meeting their infantry counterparts, and looking out from the

Caumont ridge at the area to be attacked. The Battalion's objective was Point 309. It was not an attractive prospect:

> Although our front line in this area had been static for a considerable period, information about the enemy was very scanty. It was known that they were in some strength in Lutain Wood, but it was impossible to identify positions in the 'Bocage' country in the valley. Their strength was believed to be one Field Division (361st), with two regiments up and one in reserve.

A German regiment was the equivalent of an Allied infantry brigade, with three battalions and supporting troops. In fact, the German 735 Infantry Regiment lay right in front of 3SG's planned axis of advance.

> 2nd *Panzer* Division, together with a self-propelled anti-tank battalion, were said to be within easy reach. A minefield was suspected in the Le Bourg area, and anti-tank defences on all roads and tracks.
>
> The ground as viewed from the Observation Post at Le Repas was extremely enclosed, and consisted of small fields surrounded by 3–4 foot earth banks with 14–20 foot hedges on top of them; there were no roads forward anywhere in the Battalion axis of attack, and no vehicles, except Churchills, could possibly get across the country. A good many of the fields contained cider-apple orchards.

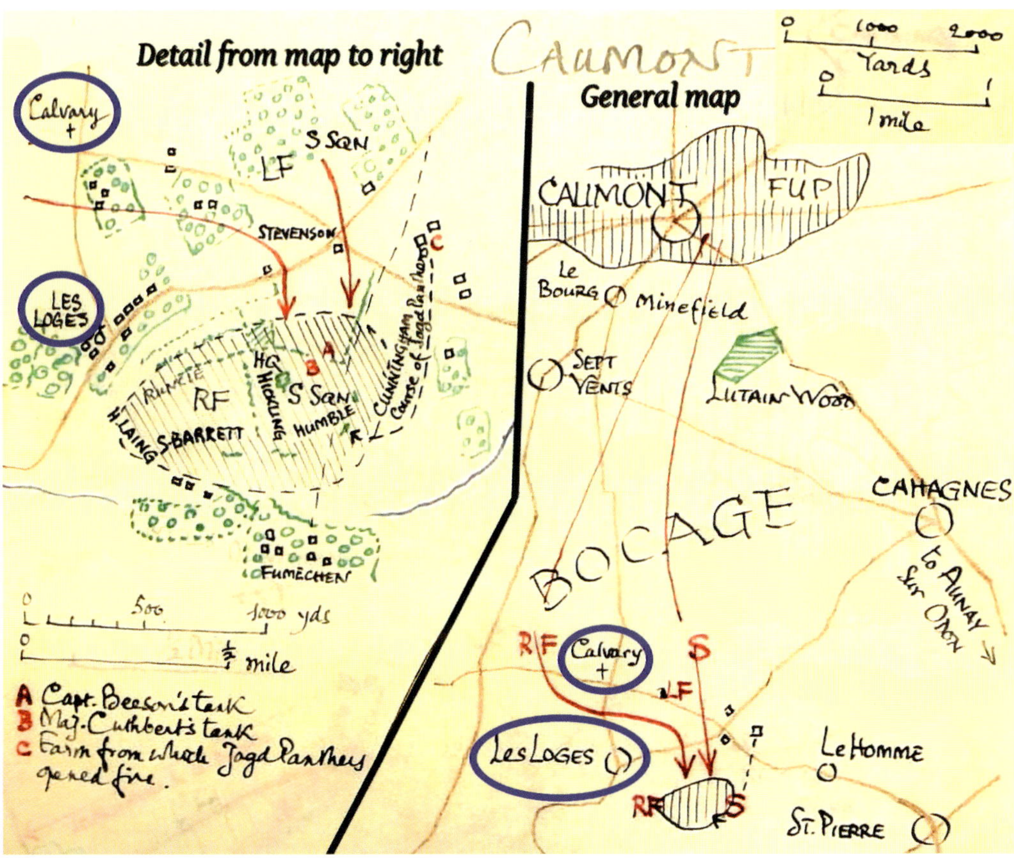

At approximately 0630hrs on July 30th the preliminary attack to take Lutain Wood went in; owing to the strength of the enemy defences, this was a slow business, and it was nearly 0715hrs before 3SG crossed their Start Line and began to descend the forward slope of the ridge. They advanced with Right Flank Squadron on the right, 'S' Squadron on the left, and Left Flank following Whitelaw's 'S' Squadron. Whitelaw earned an 'immediate' Military Cross that day. His citation stated:

> The course of the attack led for some six thousand yards through country in which it was rarely possible to see more than two hundred yards. The fields were small, surrounded by high banks with hedges on top. Nevertheless, Major Whitelaw kept perfect control and direction of his Squadron throughout the whole of this long advance, in spite of minefield diversions and considerable resistance from enemy infantry and snipers.[11]

Llewellyn Smith continues the narrative, which can be followed on the sketch map in his account:

> We encountered heavy fire from 150mm guns and 120mm mortars. For the next quarter of a mile the strength of the enemy positions between Le Bourg and Lutain Wood made fast progress impossible … At 0930hrs we were still fighting in that area and it became clear that unless we hurried the pace we should miss the barrage for the main attack. The Commanding Officer therefore ordered the tanks to move forward as fast as possible in spite of the opposition. This they did, dealing successfully with numerous enemy pockets on the way; heavy casualties were inflicted on the enemy, 735 Infantry Regiment suffering in particular. A minefield, however, was encountered and two tanks were immobilised before avoiding action could be taken.
>
> By 1215hrs we had advanced well over a mile, killing many Germans with Besa and HE fire and causing a considerable number to surrender. But the result was that we outstripped the Argylls, who were unable to keep up over the rough ground. We were now so far ahead of the Argylls that we were ordered to halt and wait for them to catch up.
>
> During this halt, 'S' Squadron were worried by sniping from various cottages, but Lieutenants Humble and Cunningham silenced this with HE, and later a number of corpses were found in the buildings. By 1315hrs it was apparent that the infantry were so far behind that if we waited longer for them the chance of benefiting from the barrage and gaining the ridge without undue opposition would be gone. The Commanding Officer therefore obtained permission for us to push on with all speed alone. Moving with remarkable rapidity, 'S' Squadron reached the left slope of the feature, which has been described as forming a separate summit, at 1430hrs. Right Flank, unable to pass through the village of Les Loges without infantry support, were forced to turn left and follow them.

Whitelaw's leadership was proving crucial:

> When ordered to push on with the utmost boldness to secure the objective before the effects of the barrage had passed, he speeded up the momentum of the attack in a remarkable manner and was successful in reaching the objective up to time.[12]

Tank crewman J.E. Davies recalled:

> Willie Whitelaw, with head and shoulders out of the turret hatch, came plunging over the hedge leading his 'S' Squadron. He angrily shouted something at me that was incomprehensible in the din, and not lip-readable either. But I think he was annoyed that we had got in the way of his cavalry charge.

The position was consolidated by 1430hrs, with Right Flank on the right, 'S' Squadron on the left, and Left Flank in support. Llewellyn Smith's account goes on as follows:

> We were now ready to go on to Point 309 – the final objective – but permission to do so was refused ... Meanwhile, the point which we occupied was a full four miles as the crow flies into enemy territory. If it was lost, the door which had been opened towards St Martin-des-Besaces would be closed again. An immediate German counter-attack, with armour, was therefore to be expected, and until such time as the infantry could get up with some anti-tank guns there was no question of our being able to withdraw. Unfortunately the position was so exposed to shell and mortar fire that the Argylls were reluctant to come up further than the village of Les Loges; so there was nothing to be done but remain where we were.
>
> About 1800hrs, just when the BBC news of the battle was coming over the air, the Germans put down a very heavy 'stonk', hitting Captain Beeson's tank twice – the second time killing him as he got out to rescue his wounded hull gunner. Five minutes later the long-awaited counter-attack arrived – but from an entirely unexpected direction. It began with a hail of armour-piercing shot from the depths of a thick wood some three hundred yards to the left rear – an area which according to the plan should by now have been cleared by 43rd Division. They were, alas, far behind.

The German counter-attack only involved three vehicles, but they were handled very well, coming at 3SG's rear and avoiding the notice of Left Flank Squadron by using the cover of a cottage and hedges.

> The force consisted of three enormous self-propelled guns – Germany's latest and most formidable, the *Jagdpanther*, until then never seen by the British in action. Their first three shots knocked out the whole of Lieutenant Cunningham's Troop, the guardians of that flank, thus clearing a path for the enemy attack. Two of these monsters, covered by a third, charged through the gap into the centre of 'S' Squadron and then slipped out of sight over the ridge to the left front, leaving eight more flaming hulks in their wake. Though over in perhaps five minutes, this counter-blow was a heavy one; the more so since Major Cuthbert, the Second-in-Command, had chosen that moment to move over to look at the left flank. He must have met the enemy head-on, his tank being penetrated through its heaviest frontal armour, the ammunition exploding, and the turret leaping clean off.

The war diary recorded four officers and forty other ranks killed, missing, or wounded; some twenty-five of those were in fact dead, almost all of them in Whitelaw's 'S' Squadron. A lesser man would have folded under that pressure and shock – not Whitelaw:

> When a strong enemy armoured counter-attack developed from thickly wooded ground to the left rear, causing considerable tank casualties to his squadron in an extremely short time, he dealt with a very awkward situation with outstanding coolness, quickly reorganising the remainder and continuing the action, with the result that the enemy withdrew. Major Whitelaw's outstanding leadership and cool courage contributed greatly to the successful capture and retention of an important objective.[13]

It was 3SG's first day in action, and its heaviest losses in the entire war. Hard to bear was the fact that they had not had time to react decisively against the *Jagdpanthers*:

> They were engaged going over the hill, and not without effect: for some time later, two of them were found, a few hundred yards away, their tracks leading back to the scene of the action. The hit on one, which was burnt out, approximated closely to a claim by Lieutenant Bankes' tank.

The burnt-out vehicle had been abandoned and destroyed by its crew when it shed a track; the second had been abandoned because Bankes' shot had broken its track.[14] It was perhaps more consolation to 3SG that the German 735 Infantry Regiment had been wholly destroyed by the Churchills' advance.

> At about 1930hrs our own self-propelled guns were at last got into position and at about 2200hrs we were able to withdraw from the ridge to a 'Forward Rally' near a burning cottage at the eastern extremity of Les Loges. We had been for nearly seven hours upon the ridge after a long and bloody attack following two almost sleepless nights. As we moved back in the dark to find a harbour area, we fell in by good luck with Major Sir Charles Maclean and 'A' Echelon, and turned aside into the nearest field. The cooks had a hot meal ready for us as soon as we had filled up with petrol, but most men were too tired to eat.
>
> The lessons that can be drawn from this action would appear to be:
>
> 1. That the cross-country capacity of the Churchill tank completely surprised the Germans, who considered the ground crossed by them to be tank-proof and had therefore concentrated their anti-tank defences on the roads and tracks.
> 2. That the properly co-ordinated fire-power of a Churchill squadron is so tremendous that it will completely demoralise infantry unsupported by anti-tank weapons. They subsequently offered little or no opposition to the infantry following up.
> 3. That it is very necessary to have some form of reconnaissance vehicle that can keep up with the Churchill over bad going.
>
> The following appointments were made as a result of casualties incurred during 30 July:
> Major W.S.I. WHITELAW – Second-in-Command.

* * *

As Whitelaw stepped into a dead colleague's boots, 1KOSB's own ordeal in the front line ended, Boyd recording

the exhausted struggle back over the Orne when we were eventually relieved.

August 1st
Minden Day, with the pipe band playing and roses in our hats. Thinking of the last one at Inverary, and the many who celebrated that day so gaily and who were no longer with us.

August 2nd
Next day, the quick transport move across the bridge-head, past Bayeux, and towards the right where the break-through was taking place. Unscarred country again with green fields, pleasant farm-houses, and an exercise atmosphere after our battered little bridge-head.

* * *

Hirst.

Back in England, the bombardment of London and the Channel ports with V-1 flying bombs launched from the Pas-de-Calais – Operation *Eisbär* – had begun on June 12th. Nine were fired that day, but none reached England; on June 13th four landed, one of them in London, where it killed eight civilians. From then on the pace accelerated, 144 V-1s reaching these shores on the night of 15/16th June alone.[15] It was not until the Allies broke out of Normandy that the Germans paused the V-1 attacks, on August 29th. Hirst, therefore, was in a different front line:

The Squadron had many moves round Kent and Sussex, mainly being based in some country house, which was very pleasant. Some of the places where we were stationed included Maresfield, Lewes, and Romney Marsh. It was just after the invasion that the first flying bomb, the V-1 (or 'Doodle Bug'), passed over us. We had no idea what it was; we thought it might have been one of the new jet planes, and were puzzled when the engine cut out, which it always did before plunging to earth to explode. When we were at New Romney, on the Marsh, we were right under their fixed course, which made them quite easy to shoot down, and we were probably in most danger from bombs shot down by our own gunners. Along the sea-front at New Romney the AA guns, rockets, even .5 Brownings mounted on tanks, were practically wheel-to-wheel, and very few got past them. Those that did were either shot down or tipped over by the fighters with their wing-tips. But of course they still exploded, either in the air, or (hopefully) in an open field, but we had a few near-misses in the town where we were billeted. I remember the Sergeants' Mess ringing up the Officers' Mess to see whether we were still alive!

I went away on a couple of courses, one to Eastbourne on Bren-gun carrier driving and maintenance, which, after tanks, was a piece of cake. We spent a lot of time, aided and abetted by our instructor, tooling around seeing how few cylinders the V8 engine in the carrier would run on. Coming down Beachy Head one day flat-out, a carrier hit a bump, and 'bucked', as they did, throwing my Troop Sergeant into the air. He landed on the edge of the armour plating, and was quite badly hurt.

The other course was to the Small Arms School at Hythe, learning all about infantry weapons: rifles, Bren-guns, mortars, and so on. I did not do too well; the result was a terse note from the Divisional Commander asking 'Is this officer fit to be in my Division?' As we did not think much of his Division anyhow, I am glad to say this report was not taken very seriously by my seniors.

As the danger of a German counter-attack receded and the D-Day camps were closed, the Regiment got together again. Our trained tank crews began to be taken as replacements for casualties in Europe, and soon we were solely on a care-and-maintenance basis. All our time was spent maintaining the vehicles we still possessed with fewer and fewer men.

* * *

Nick Somerville's letter to Walker dated August 4th was written in a rare period of rest for him and his Battalion, near Chouain.[16]

We have been in the line continuously since 'D' Day except for a break of two days, and considering that that is nearly two months ago, it is no wonder that we are a little tired. However, we have now come out for another few days' rest, which is simply marvellous. George Formby gave us a show last night which went down very well with the men. Everybody today is fast asleep without a care in the world …

The weather has been perfectly foul until recently, when it cleared up, and it is now boiling hot and we are getting very sunburnt.

I spent an afternoon going round Bayeux Cathedral, which was a very good experience. It was an astonishing thing to come out of a world of dust and traffic and destruction, smell, and hate, into the cool, unmoved, vastness of the cathedral. Being of course Catholic, it had an atmosphere of reverence and sincerity which was almost overpowering. There were Catholic peasants calmly praying in front of their accustomed altars while Americans and British walked past a little self-consciously. I listened to the evening service, and enjoyed the singing, which was wonderful.

Do write and let me know where you are and news of everybody. I am completely out of touch.

Elsewhere, however, the battle continued, and that same day one of Somerville's Hopper's contemporaries was killed in action at St Charles de Percy, some 28 miles to the south.

XX

'Quite the most unpleasant day of my life'

Italy, July 1944

Kemp.

By the end of June, 7RB, with Kemp, were in reserve five miles south of Lake Trasimene, where they spent some days resting before advancing again on July 3rd, operating in concert with the tanks of 16th/5th Lancers – including Brooke.

The first stage of the advance, in pursuit of the retreating Germans, was along the Chiana Valley towards Arezzo; they caught up with the enemy five miles south of Arezzo on the evening of July 4th, in torrential rain. To continue the advance, however, required three features to be cleared: Monte Maggio,[1] Monte Lignano, and Monte Camurcino. All three were covered in scrub and without clear peaks, but they gave the Germans good fields of view, which led to heavy shelling of 7RB and its accompanying tanks.

Yet another Wykehamist – Dick Fyffe[2] – took over command of 7RB on July 5th, just in time to plan the Battalion's assault on Maggio the following night.

> 'C' Company of 7RB reached the top [Point 756] at 0300hrs [on July 7th] and took two prisoners of 194 Artillery Regiment (the artillery observation post), but the enemy were dug in on the reverse slopes, some of them within hand-grenade range, and a sharp exchange took place. The essential was to get dug in before first light, and while a covering party continued this duel the remainder dug positions thirty yards down on our side, with 'A' Company on the right and 'C' Company on the left.
>
> This action had caused some improvement in the situation, as the enemy had lost his observation post; but the position was still in the nature of a stalemate, with the enemy and ourselves on the respective reverse slopes on both features, and the enemy probably still having observation from Lignano.[3]

The night of July 7th was to be spent conducting fighting patrols to probe German positions on Maggio and Lignano. The enemy, however, refused to cooperate, and launched a strong counter-attack on both features. Civilians had given warning of the German attack on Lignano, and this was repulsed without loss, but 7RB on Maggio were less fortunate when the attack came in at 2215hrs:

> In the dark before the moon rose the enemy came round both sides of the summit, as 7RB was just preparing to send two strong fighting patrols in the opposite direction.

Owing to these preparations, and the darkness, the enemy got to within fifty yards of our positions before being spotted. Confused hand-to-hand fighting (in places quite literally) took place, and after receiving and inflicting a number of casualties the two companies withdrew five hundred yards.[4]

Seton-Watson was with 7RB that night:

[The Germans] were over the ridge and in among our platoon positions almost before anyone realized what was happening. The forward positions immediately became untenable, and as the two companies withdrew in the dark down the steep hill, all their communications failed. I withdrew with them in some haste. The help we could give was limited, and in one area our own and the enemy's troops were so hopelessly mixed up that our shells were undoubtedly responsible for a few casualties among the Riflemen. At first it seemed that the casualties had been extremely heavy, but all through the night stragglers came in, some of them after lying up for hours in the enemy's lines. Fortunately, he did not press his attack home.[5]

7RB withdrew for a rest in the small hours of July 10th.

* * *

Middleditch.

The situation around Assisi was very fluid, without a clear front line. The Germans had carried out demolitions on most of the roads which snaked through the hills and mountains, making it difficult to follow them up or to establish their whereabouts. In some areas, only 12RL's Cavalry Troop or patrols mounted in unarmoured Jeeps could make any progress at all. On July 11th, the Regiment decided to push along the road leading north-east from Assisi to Gualdo Tadino, even though it had been demolished in two places; they hoped that the Sappers would be able to repair the route. Three squadrons attempted to advance north-eastwards, but progress was slow, although by July 13th it was clear that the Germans were beginning to thin out their forces for a withdrawal. That day, Middleditch led a Jeep-borne patrol to see whether the enemy were still in Gualdo Tadino. He took his vehicles through Annifo and Nocera before making a dash north towards his objective. It was a risky move: the landscape was rugged, the roads winding. and the Jeeps helpless against any determined opposition. Fortunately, the Germans had already pulled out of the area.

The Jeeps continued their exploration on the following day. Despite the German withdrawal, conditions were far from enjoyable, as the Regimental history recounts:

This was perhaps the most unpleasant period experienced by the 12th Lancers – all white roads and fraught with lurking ambushes. And it was just as unpleasant when, as July opened, the enemy began deliberately to withdraw. The patrols of the Regiment moved after him.

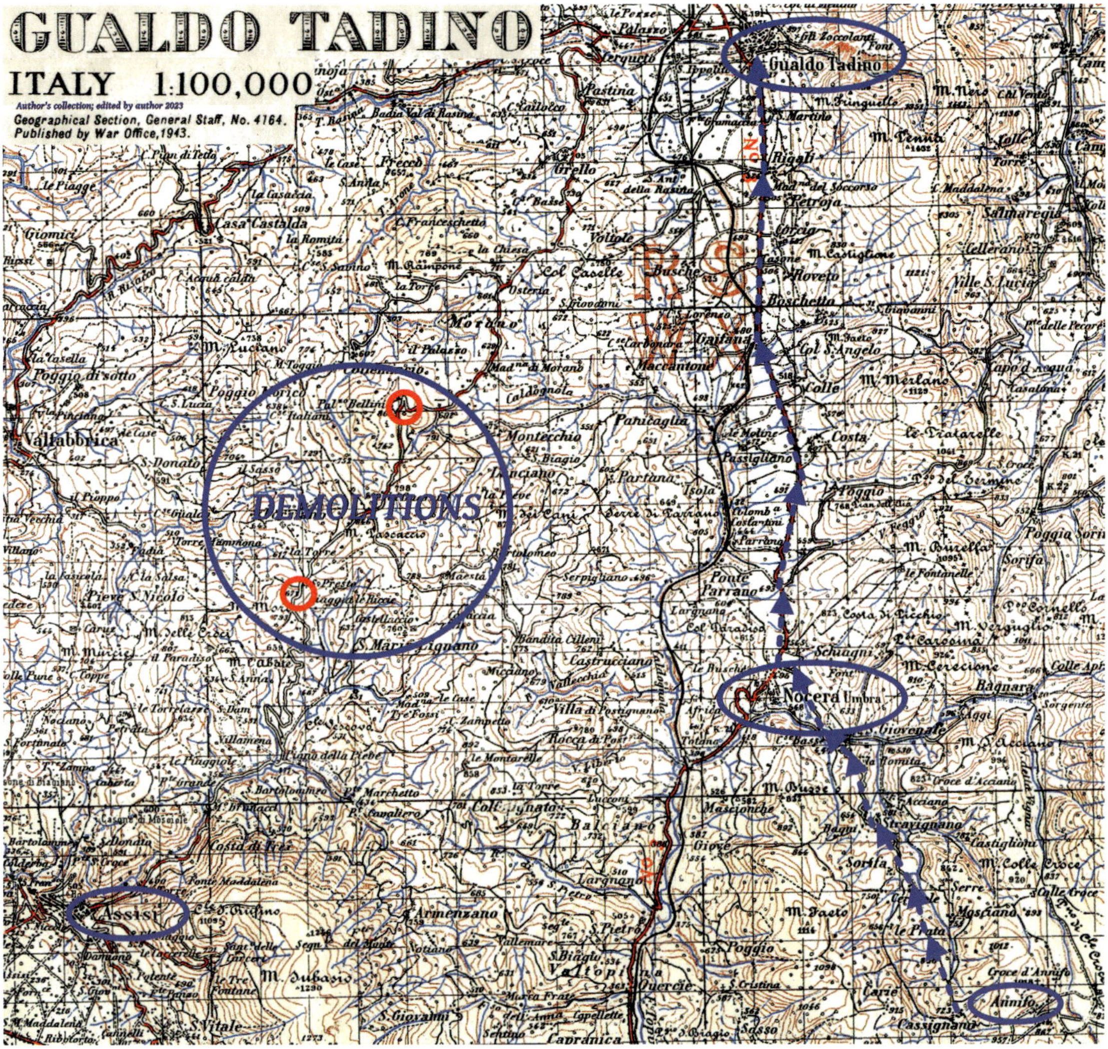

'The greenness of the country', wrote an officer, 'made it almost impossible to spot enemy, and the information of the locals was usually inflamed and exaggerated … We had to be prepared to be attacked, as 'C' Squadron was, in leaguer by infantry. It made matters more complicated and moves more deliberate. Ahead, one or two troops nosed warily forward, frequently dismounting to patrol on foot, frequently being unaccountably sniped, finding mines, blows in the road, and signs of recent enemy retreat. Their nerves were kept taut. They could never relax completely, even for a brew. Indeed a lot of the conversation on the air was taken up with requests for permission to "stop and brew". But even then one might be being observed from some unsuspected angle and suddenly be shelled … Every day someone was having a miraculous escape, and Squadron Leaders bore a heavy responsibility in human life.'

This sense of strain, this unremitting attention, was the human reality behind the unvarnished sitreps, the unemotional reports of the War Diary, and the chinagraph markings on the maps.

* * *

On the morning of July 17th 61 Brigade crossed the Arno, but found it hard to make progress. Kemp and his comrades in 7RB prepared for yet another night attack, this time on Castiglion Fibbocchi. The march was at first uneventful, but at 0230hrs the peace of the night was suddenly shattered as 7RB came under fire from five or six Spandaus. They had been carefully positioned to make any advance suicidal, and in the dark it proved impossible to locate them. 7RB had no choice but to fall back, take up a defensive position and dig in to await daylight. Seton-Watson reached the position at around 0400hrs and joined in the digging:

> Daylight on July 18th found the Battalion on a slight slope among crops and vines, with a view of not more than fifty yards to the front. It was overlooked by high hills not more than two thousand yards away, and it was impossible to move without being observed. The road back to Quarata was particularly bare and conspicuous. Moreover, it was soon obvious that the enemy knew exactly where we were, and about 0630hrs the shelling and mortaring began – which were to continue, with very few quiet periods, for the whole day. Fortunately most of the shelling was by 75s, though 88s and 105s joined in from time to time. One shell fell on the very edge of my slit trench: I felt it penetrate the earth touching my right shoulder, but miraculously it was a dud and didn't explode. It proved impossible to locate the enemy guns, and all that we gunners could do was to stonk Castiglion and the likely valleys where there was a chance that the mortars might be.[6]

'A' Company tried to work round the left flank of the enemy position, supported by the tanks of 16th/5th Lancers. They managed to reach a position, Point 262, which gave them observation into Castiglion Fibocchi, but were fired upon heavily and counter-attacked before they could dig in; this immediate shelling and counter-attack was typical of the German response whenever they felt threatened. 'A' Company rejoined the Battalion and remained under constant artillery and Spandau fire all day. The war diary records that one shell knocked out the radio on the Commanding Officer's Jeep, but whilst this inconvenient fact was being digested, another shell landed nearby and shook the radio back into life. Seton-Watson graphically describes the privations and discomforts of July 18th 1944:

> It was a day of great strain and discomfort for the whole Battalion. Casualties had not been light, and the men were tired and dispirited by not being able to hit back. They were also so thirsty in the hot sun that in spite of the certainty that it would be observed, a Jeep had to be sent up loaded with water. When orders came over the air that the Battalion was to hold its position overnight, everyone was reduced to something near despair. Major Meldrum protested so energetically, however, that these orders were cancelled and we were told to pull back to the bridge at last light. Every man undoubtedly shared my feelings of relief at getting away from a position where I had spent quite the most unpleasant day of my life.[7]

* * *

Hill.

The last of our subjects to make it into the armed forces during the war was Crispin Hill. He had gone up to Brasenose College, Oxford, in 1942, and came down after taking his shortened Physics Finals in 1944. On July 24th 1944 he was commissioned as a Probationary Temporary Midshipman (Special Branch) (Sc) in the RNVR. The letters (Sc) against the name of an officer denoted that he was employed on scientific duties, but had not received any training of an executive nature – in other words, he was a specialist in his subject but not trained for command. This explains why Hill's service record does not include any mention of attending HMS *King Alfred* or any sea time as Mackrill had experienced months before; instead, on August 21st 1944 he started a radio technical course at HMS *Mercury,* the appropriate name for the Royal Navy Signals School at Leydene House in East Meon, Hampshire.

* * *

The unpleasantness of the war in Italy was deepening daily. There were many discomforts. Any movement forwards in daylight was made at a crawl: the roads were so dusty that speeds over 5 or 10mph raised clouds which the enemy immediately shelled. As the Allied advance continued north-west along the Arno valley towards Florence, units encountered road demolitions and felled trees blocking every route forwards. The Germans were not resisting in strength, but covered every obstacle with machine-gun and artillery fire to prevent the British troops from clearing it too quickly. Whilst small delaying forces harassed the advance, the main German units fortified strong defensive lines at which they would make a stand before melting away when pressure became too great.

As 7RB leapfrogged forwards on July 29th, pushing along the Arno and its tributaries, they encountered enemy strongpoints along the Resco, and although they patrolled aggressively, looking for a weak spot, the enemy positions and the crossing of the Resco were stiff with Spandaus and horrible little 'Schu-mines', the infantryman's nightmare. These were little wooden boxes – invisible to a standard mine-detector – containing 200gm of TNT. When triggered, the blast was enough to blow a man's foot off – as happened to one of our subjects. The Germans were also patrolling and sneaking small parties into the British positions; indeed, Dick Fyffe was almost captured by enemy infiltrators on the morning of July 30th. Shelling and mortaring, as well as projectiles from the infamous *Nebelwerfers,* caused 7RB twenty-six casualties that day, and they lost a Platoon Commander to a sniper, an ever-present danger for officers. By noon, however, the Battalion had pushed on and taken the forward slopes of the ridge from which the Germans had been observing them and spraying them with Spandau fire.

Shortly afterwards, it was decided that the depleted 61 Brigade needed at least a fortnight's rest, and its units were therefore ordered to patrol vigorously but to keep as many personnel as possible out of the line and resting. 7RB made the most of their break from offensive operations. Their three weeks out of the front line were blissful after what the Battalion's history describes as 'one of the most unpleasant spells of fighting in the whole campaign, eight days of great heat and hard fighting which had little to show for it'.[8]

The patrolling which they were now conducting up to Vallombrosa was not that dangerous, and 7RB had a fairly restful time: the weather was lovely; their patrols were largely unopposed; there was little shelling; and those not on patrol could rest in Faella or in a rest camp on the shores of Lake Trasimene. The days in Faella were a golden time in the memory:

> It was, for Italy, a clean little place, whose inhabitants gave the Riflemen an overwhelming welcome. It was a time of the year when fruit was plentiful, and many people who may remember little else of the campaign will not forget the peaches showered on them by the villagers. There was a rest of several days in this area, and then, after a short spell in the line near Regello ... the Battalion had almost three weeks of comparative inactivity.[9]

On August 1st the men watched a screening of the George Formby film *Bell Bottom George* – though the war diary recorded that the show was interrupted 'several times by the annoying presence of suspicious aircraft'. On August 6th the Battalion held a dance in the village cinema in Faella, the first of several such occasions. On the regimental birthday, August 25th, the rifle companies set up stalls on the village green, with various fairground activities, followed later in the afternoon by a series of comic performances, one by each company, on a stage erected by the Italian inhabitants. 'These, in spite of the fact that there had been so little time to prepare them, were very good indeed, and intensely amusing. This was run on a competitive basis, and 'D' Company were the ultimate victors.'[10]

Afterwards there was a beauty contest for the 'belles of Faella', with prizes for the 'three best lookers' and one for the 'Rifleman who escorted the winner'. The proceedings were rounded off by a party in the Sergeants' Mess and dancing on the village green late into the night.

XXI

'We buried him that same evening – he had a very nice burial'

Normandy, August 1944

Martyn.

Martyn and 1st Coldstream had returned to Bayeux for a rest on July 30th, only to be thrown into Operation Bluecoat on August 1st. For the first day of their part in the Bluecoat offensive, 1st Coldstream split up: 1 Squadron went to support 3rd Irish Guards; 2 Squadron remained in Brigade reserve; and 3 Squadron assisted 1st Welsh Guards. In the difficult terrain of Normandy, the close *bocage* countryside often constricted advances to a nerve-racking crawl:

> The weather was perfect; a spell had set in of brilliant, unclouded sunshine, which was to last for sixteen days. The country through which the column passed was very different … The hedges were thick, planted along high banks and studded with tall, ivy-covered trees; the fields measured only a hundred yards from end to end, and were knee-deep in sweet-smelling grass. Often the lanes were merely dark tunnels between the fields, and they so twisted and rose and fell, through woods, over hills, and down innumerable valleys, that advance along them could at best be measured in hundreds of yards. In such country, a Tiger tank could easily lie hidden, and for the sniper it was paradise.[1]

As a result, infantry and tanks depended on one another to a huge extent, as had been clearly shown by 3SG's experiences at Caumont. Battle-groups of a tank squadron in support of an infantry battalion were now standard practice, as in Italy. In 2KRRC, for example, Fletcher's 'B' Company was affiliated as supporting infantry to 44 RTR, a Sherman tank unit. Nick Somerville's diary records the drill which 2SWB arranged with their own supporting armour from 1RTR:

> Discussed the drill for infantry working with tanks. Finally agreed on the following. Infantry advance down hedgerows while tanks cover them forward. As soon as the infantry reach the next lateral hedge they show a green flag. This is confirmed by 38 Set working to the tank. The tanks then go forward to the next hedge, and the infantry then go on again. The leading infantryman carries a small yellow flag to show where the leading troops are. If the infantry encounter opposition, they fire a round of tracer at it and the tank engages it with fire. If they spot an anti-tank gun they fire a low green

Verey light followed by tracer, and then stalk it themselves. This drill was evolved to deal with the difficulties of the *bocage* close country.[2]

On August 1st, however, 1st Coldstream advanced eight miles through the *bocage* without contacting the enemy.

On August 2nd, Batt's Shermans of 1 Squadron passed through the village of St Charles de Percy, but were held up at Courteil to the east, and so leaguered back at St Charles.

A scene which Martyn witnessed on August 2nd 1944: a Sherman Firefly, M10 tank-destroyers, Jeeps, motorcycles, & trucks in St Charles de Percy. (IWM B 8487; edited by dansteele.net)

At dawn on August 3rd, 1 Squadron helped to repel an attack on 3rd Irish Guards by firing their Browning machine-guns through the hedges. However, the action came at a cost, as a fellow Coldstream officer recalled:

> We heard in the evening that Reggie Batt had been killed by a sniper while getting in his tank. He commanded No.1 Squadron, an able and brave officer; he was our first senior casualty. A sniper jumped up on a bank in a narrow lane and at a few yards range shot him in the head.[3]

Martyn did not long outlive his Squadron Commander. The advance resumed on August 4th, and later that day Martyn and his radio-operator were killed instantly by a direct hit on their tank turret, while guarding a threatened flank at Point 176, near Beaulieu.

> Late in the evening news came that No.1 Squadron were having a sticky battle, so we stood by to help them, but they did not need us. David Martyn was killed when his tank was hit by a Panther around Point 176, and No.1 Squadron lost another knocked out.[4]

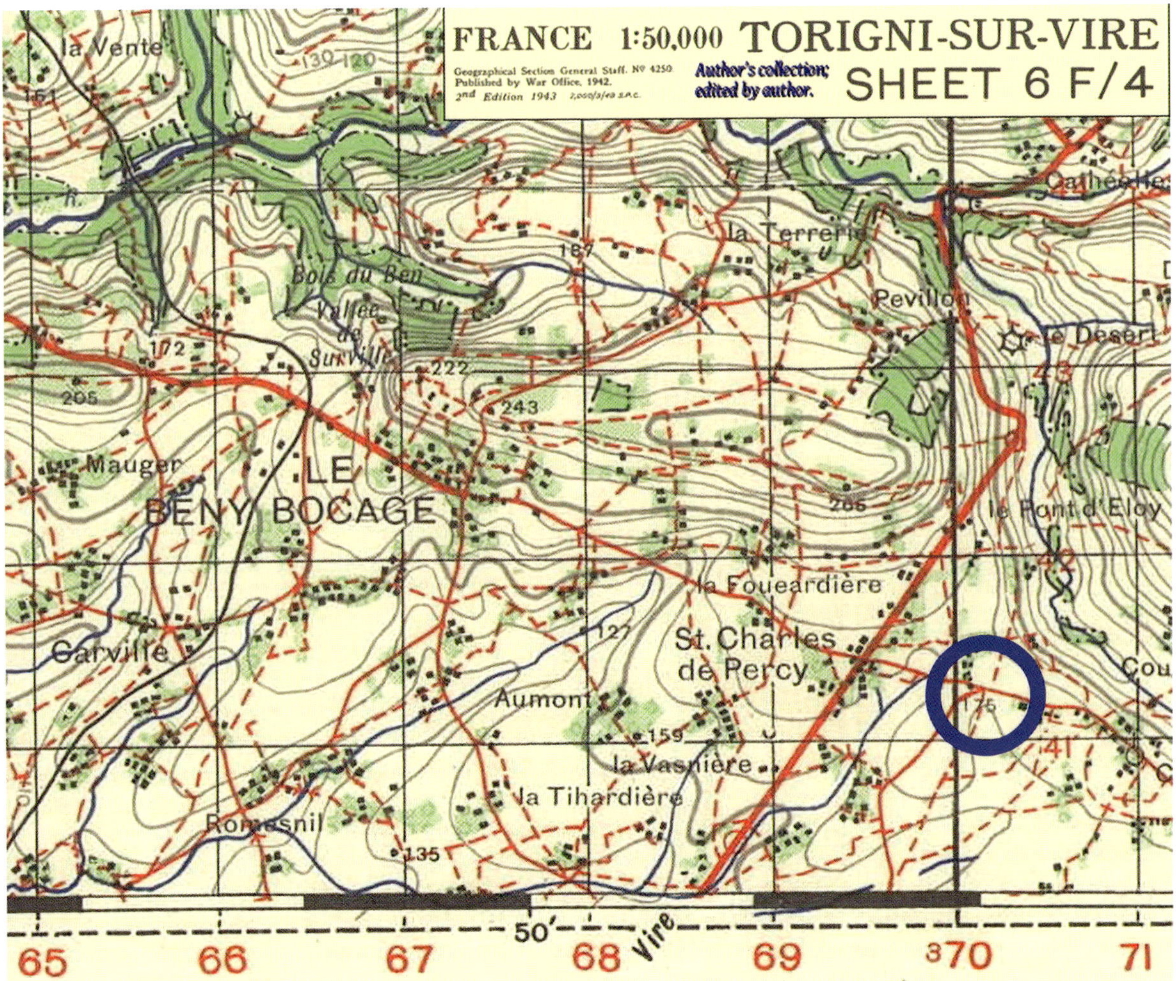

Captain J.F. Priestley was only yards away when Martyn's Sherman was hit:

> We set off under Reggie Batt to hunt some Panthers and also to relieve some friends of ours who looked like being surrounded. Reggie, who was brilliant, was killed shortly after the start by a sniper. David was leading at the time, and we were trapped in a sunken lane, being fired at by a Panther and some infantry. I went up and spoke to David, who was very calm, and we decided to push on in spite of some unpleasant reports of enemy tanks ahead of us – we reached our objective without further casualties. Later on in the afternoon we got a report that one of our flanks was in danger of attack. David was ordered to go to the threatened flank and he led the way himself to a thick hedge, which was to be his protection. Due to the dust, which is inevitable out here, he was spotted by a Panther hidden six hundred yards away. I was within fifteen yards of him at the time and he was killed instantly by a shell which entered his heart. I can only say he knew nothing whatever about it. The action ended in the loss of four enemy tanks and four of our own, and the defeat of the enemy.[5]

One of Martyn's best friends in the Battalion – Lieutenant P.W. Loyd – also described the incident:

> I have been meaning to write to you to tell you the circumstances of David's death, and, as you probably know, we are not allowed to write for a fortnight and today is the first opportunity I have had.
>
> His tank was shot at by an enemy tank from a range of approximately five hundred yards, and the shot pierced the turret of David's tank, killing him and his operator instantly. We buried him that same evening – he had a very nice burial.[6]

Martyn, who was just twenty, is now buried in joint grave V.C.7 of the St Charles de Percy War Cemetery. With him lies his radio-operator, Guardsman 2664943 John William Peart, who was twenty-two years old when he and Martyn were killed.

* * *

By August 6th, Operations Bluecoat and Cobra had crippled German forces in Normandy, and the campaign was beginning to open up; within a fortnight, rapid open warfare would begin, ending in Holland and Belgium in mid-September. But there was still tough fighting to be done. On August 4th, 1KOSB moved to just north of the Forêt l'Évêque and began to prepare for action, having received orders to capture Montisanger – north-east of Vire – on the 6th. They moved out to their assembly area at 0500hrs, and attacked at 0845hrs. Unexpectedly, they took Montisanger without a fight, but then received instructions to cross the river south of Le Pissot and attack positions there. The orders arrived at 1700hrs; the attack was to be made at 1800hrs; the bridges over the river had been blown and so no armoured support was at first available.

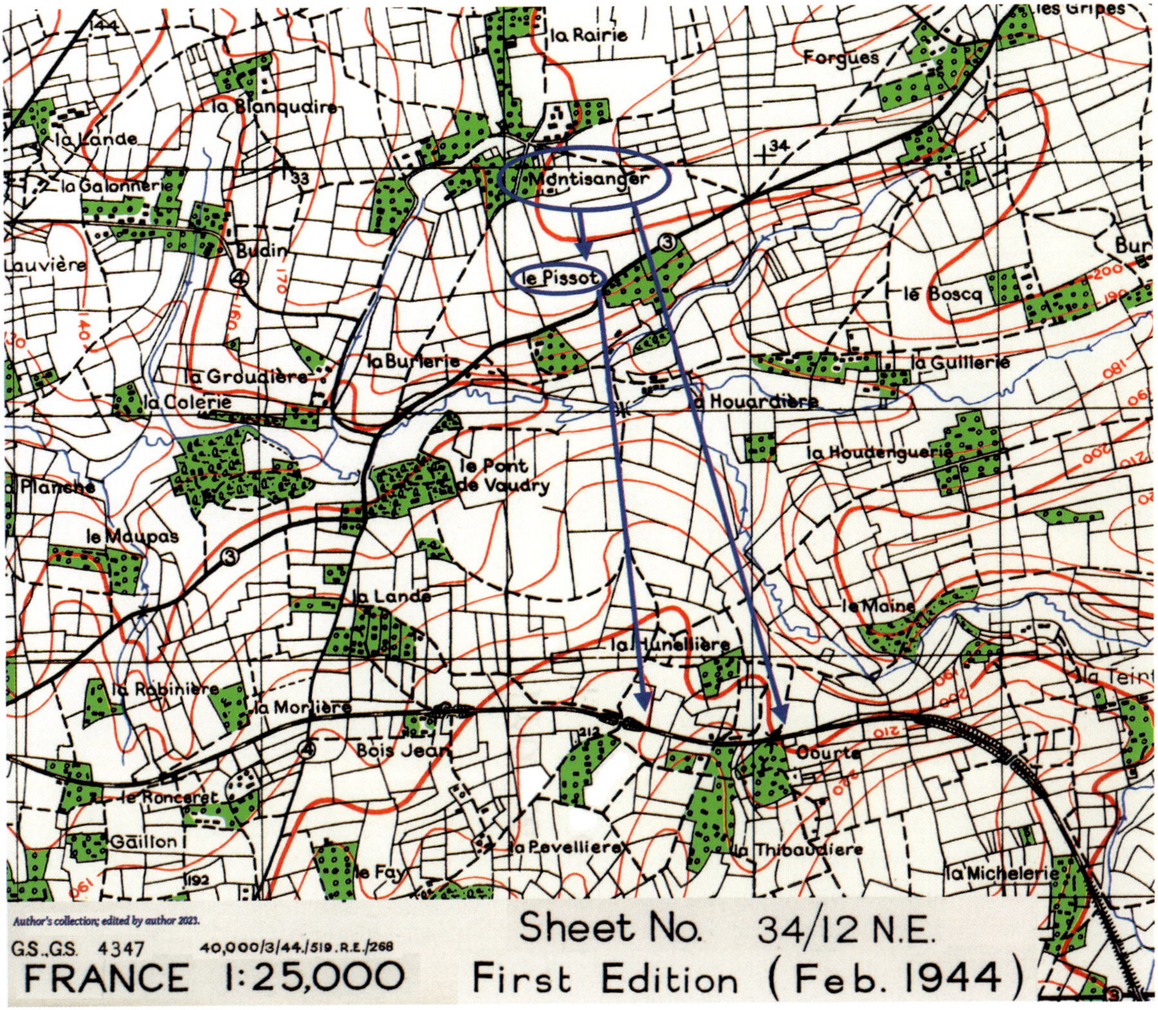

> Later the same day the hurried unprepared attack down to the railway line. Seeing Jim Wise standing on his tank watching the battle through field glasses like someone at a race meeting, except that shells were bursting all round him. Then down the steep, narrow track into the 'Dead Horse' Valley and finding the Colonel. The runner coming back from 'A' Company to say they and 'C' were on the railway line and in contact, but that both had lost a lot of men. The conference by candle-light in the barn when the two forward companies were ordered to withdraw again.

Despite the lack of artillery support, the two attacking companies had reached their first objective, but as they pressed on towards the railway line had became pinned down by German machine-gun fire from their flanks. Their situation had become increasingly precarious, but fortunately a troop of tanks had made it across the river and launched a timely counter-attack. By the next morning it was clear that one complete platoon of 'A' Company was missing, and that casualties had been numerous.

Food coming up at last in the early morning ... The long, hot day in the valley while the dead horse smelt worse and worse, with the mortars always landing well away from us on the far side.

* * *

Duffin.

After their experiences at Caumont, 3SG had been alternately resting and helping infantry to advance southwards; Whitelaw's 'S' Squadron was off the board, re-forming. On August 6th Duffin was in action again, as Left Flank Company pushed ahead with 10th Highland Light Infantry, aiming to seize the village of Estry, at which point Duffin and his comrades would pass through to take Le Theil, a mile or so to the south-east. However, around Estry some of the best German troops – *Panzergrenadiers* and Panther tanks from 9th SS *Panzer* Division – were in position and determined not to give way. Nothing went according to plan.

Left Flank moved off at about 1130hrs. As the Churchills drove up the southern side of the road they encountered the troops who were supposed to have taken Estry, still fighting their way up a sunken lane. Llewellyn Smith's account makes clear how closely the battle that day involved Duffin (14 Troop) and Marshall (12 Troop).

Captain Balfour's tank was ditched in the sunken lane, so Lieutenant Marshall's Troop remained to cover the ditched tank while efforts were made to recover it. These were unsuccessful, and owing to snipers it was decided to leave it. [The] attack on Estry down the sunken lane failed, and they withdrew back under cover. This delayed 10 HLI with Left Flank, who had halted along the road and were now coming under heavy mortar and shell-fire. It was decided therefore to deploy and get a firm base round the area where the sunken lane met the Estry–La Caverie road. During this operation, some enemy machine-gun nests were mopped up and Lieutenant Duffin's tank was attacked by a 'bazooka' patrol, which was beaten off by a round of HE, completely disintegrating one man. Left Flank then remained there under intermittent shell fire till about 1900hrs in support of 10 HLI.

At 1915hrs a further attempt was made to reach the crossroads in Estry, following an artillery bombardment. On each side of the road a company of 10 HLI was supported as closely as possible by two troops of Churchills. The artillery fire was not forthcoming, but Left Flank attacked nonetheless.

No opposition was met on the right of the road, and two companies, supported by Lieutenant Marshall's and Lieutenant Duffin's Troops, reached the objective. Lieutenant Marshall's tank went up on a mine as soon as he came on to the road, and his co-driver, Guardsman Finch, was killed. The reserve Troop and Squadron HQ then moved up to join them, and Captain Balfour, who had been ordered to find a way across the cross-roads, had his tank blown up on a mine.

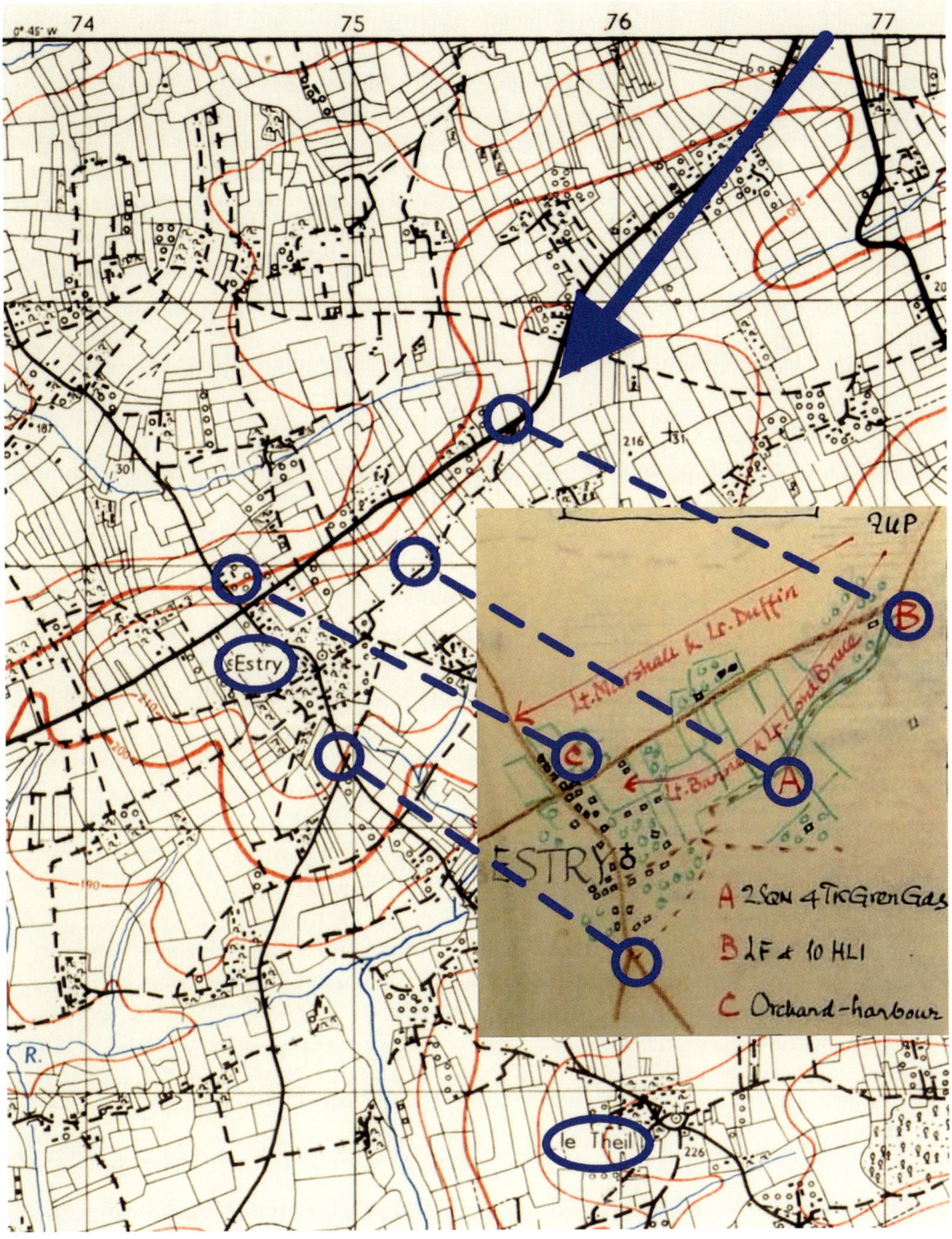

A contemporary map of the Estry area, with, as an inset, a map trace from Llewellyn Smith's account of 3SG's operations. The evening advance of the two Wykehamist Troop Commanders – Marshall and Duffin – can be clearly seen to the north ('right') of the main road. (Image edited by author)

The rest of Left Flank had a tough time south of the road; one officer was approached by Germans calling on him to surrender, but he shot the leader with his revolver. The enemy must have been very close. By 2200hrs Left Flank had rallied just north of the cross-roads, and as darkness fell, the Churchills formed a tight 'hedgehog' to protect the infantry. There they stayed until 1500hrs on August 7th, under constant mortar and machine-gun fire. They were then pulled out, since the assault on Estry had clearly failed. The cost to the infantry had been incredibly high, despite 3SG's best efforts.

Meanwhile, yet another Wykehamist had joined 3SG: Lieutenant J.M. Gow arrived from a replacement unit to command the tanks of Battalion HQ.[7]

* * *

The news of their son's death reached Rendel and Nancye Martyn a week afterwards, on the evening of Friday August 11th. As usual, as soon as they found out, they informed Robertson. Their letter makes it clear that Robertson had seen David Martyn more recently than they had.

> My dear Robertson,
> David has gone, and we are broken hearted; we received a telegram on Friday evening to say he had been killed in action on August 4th.
>
> I thought I would like you and your sister to know before you saw the sad story in *The Times*. We have had no details yet but if I get any news I will let you know; I hear Reggie Batt his Squadron Commander was also killed.
>
> I won't enlarge on how great a blow it is to us as I am sure you fully realise what an immense loss we have suffered; his very short time in the Regiment was enough for him to have made his presence felt and I continually heard from all sides how well he was doing and how good he was with his troops.
>
> Both of you deserve our very best thanks for the great assistance you gave us in the moulding of his character, and this will never be forgotten. I know his many friends will miss him.
>
> Poor Peter is completely shattered; they were very attached to each other. Would you tell Marcus Hampton, Harry, and Budge – also the Headmaster, as I don't want to write too many letters just yet.
>
> Last time Nancye spoke to him was when he telephoned from Winchester and was thrilled he had managed to get over and had seen you before crossing over to France.
>
> Though the blow is great, we must rise above it, as we realise we are not half so badly hit as many others have been.
>
> Our love to your sister.
>
> Yours ever,
>
> R. Martyn[8]

One consolation to the family was, of course, the abundant testimony from fellow officers that Martyn had borne himself with coolness and courage:

> Up to the time of his death, David had done extremely well. His men had the greatest confidence in him, and, as you know, he was one of my greatest friends, which makes it all that harder to write this letter. Reggie Batt, as you doubtless know, was killed by a sniper the day before, and I know he had the highest opinion of David's capabilities. He will be greatly missed by everyone here, as his cheerfulness and wit were never lacking.[9]

> May I please write you a line to tell you of my great admiration for David. It was my lot to be in command of the half-Squadron when David was killed, and I should like to pay tribute to the splendid example he displayed up to the time of his death … We all loved David so much, and I have some idea of what he must have been to you and Mrs Martyn.[10]

* * *

Lewin.

On July 28th, 4 Armoured Brigade had come under Canadian command as preparations began for an offensive to the south of Caen, aiming for Falaise in the hope of encircling German forces before they could withdraw from Normandy. With the addition of British and Polish units, and supported by heavy bombers and tactical air support, First Canadian Army launched Operation Totalize (August 8th–10th) followed by Operation Tractable (August 14th–15th). Brigadier Carver had requested that 4 Armoured should lead the advance to cut the road between Falaise and Conde, helping to seal off the Falaise Pocket. Thus Lewin was to be in at the kill.

* * *

Duffin went into action again on August 11th, not far to the south-west of Estry. Marshall and 12 Troop, however, appear to have been among the troop from each squadron which was left out of battle. This time the objective was Chenedolle. Having learned the value of tight tank-infantry co-operation in Estry, each troop of Churchills was accompanied by one platoon of infantry. As they formed up slightly north of Le Bas-Perrier at 0700hrs, the tanks were completely invisible – even to each other – in a thick ground mist. The infantry, already under sniper fire, requested a delay, and were rewarded when the sun came out at 0730hrs and cleared the mist. As Left Flank advanced, they encountered fierce machine-gun fire from a German platoon in two houses, which were destroyed by fire from the Churchills. Resistance and the terrain became worse the further that Duffin and his comrades advanced. But by 0900hrs they were in possession of their objective, which they held until 1530hrs, withdrawing to a Forward Rally position close to their start point. It had been a successful day, the attack having seized the commanding Point 242 as intended. And that, as it turned out, was that; 3SG did not see action in Normandy again.

* * *

Somerville and 2SWB were also back at the tip of the spear, this time north-east of Thury-Harcourt. On August 10th Somerville helped with the move southwards across the River Orne:

Nick Somerville.

The whole bridge-head area was under considerable shell-fire, and it was not very comfortable riding up and down the main axis on a motorbike. The Battalion moved on and was concentrated by 1400hrs. During the night 'A' and 'C' Companies moved forward with Sappers to capture the Courts-Genets feature, and 'B' and 'D' Companies the high ground to the right of this. Battalion HQ moved up to Forge-à-Cambraye. All these moves were completed by 0530hrs.

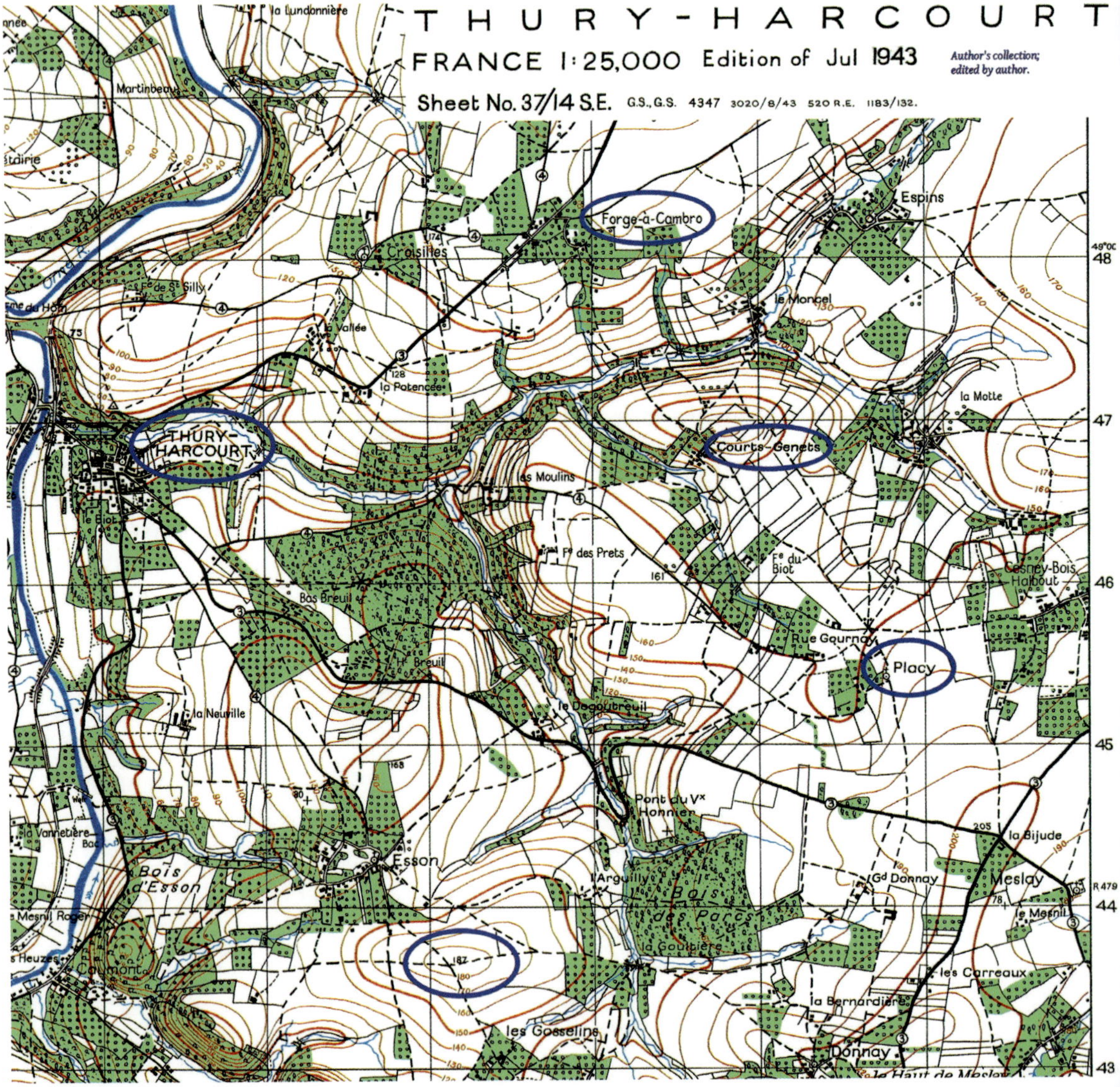

Author's collection; edited by author.

The following morning, movement of a tank unit on the hill above Courts-Genets brought down artillery and *Nebelwerfer* fire on 'A' and 'C' companies, as well as on Somerville's own position in Forge-à-Cambraye ('Forge-à-Cambro' on the wartime map). The

Germans were putting up strong resistance in an attempt to prevent the encirclement of their forces at Falaise.

> Forge-à-Cambraye came in for a belting that morning from Moaning Minnies [*Nebelwerfers*], and Battalion HQ was exceedingly hot. We spent most of the time lying under the 14 Set with a pair of headphones. Battalion HQ moved back in the afternoon. Went down to 'A' and 'C' companies with the CO in a Jeep in the afternoon. Had to go through Forge-à-Cambraye and down a very open forward slope in order to get there. Had a very nasty journey down, driving at 45mph downhill on a very narrow and bumpy track as the enemy was shelling any movement on the very open road. Arrived to find 'A' Company HQ with a direct hit and ten casualties. Company Commander OK. 'A' and 'C' companies' area pretty hot at the time, and I was glad we didn't stay long. All movement by daylight on 'A' Company's road now banned except for ambulance Jeeps. Fifty casualties through RAP today from Jerry's stonking.

2SWB captured a German *Nebelwerfer* observer the next day, and as Intelligence Officer it fell to Somerville to interrogate him:

> He confirmed that we had the entire 7th *Werfer* Brigade on our front, and was rash enough to say that Forge-à-Cambraye had been one of his targets.

That night, 2SWB moved south to the village of Placy and occupied it without opposition. From there, on the morning of August 14th, they pressed south-westwards to occupy commanding ground overlooking Esson, where Somerville had another narrow escape.

> The forward body formed up at 1000hrs with orders to advance and capture Pt 187. We were lucky to find this unoccupied and it was a trifle nerve-racking to have to advance down a forward slope in full view of the objective … I was just putting the screen in position when Jerry started stonking the crest like hell. It was really most uncomfortable, as there was no cover there at all. Bombs and shells seemed to be landing everywhere, but somehow I managed to work my way along the road to the wireless carrier. I had just nipped behind this when there was a terrific explosion, and a shell burst just where I had been lying in the road – and it pretty well blew me round the carrier. It actually ripped open a roll of blankets that was fastened on the back of the carrier, and so I was lucky. I was able from then on to stay by the wireless set and let people know more or less what was happening. It was fortunate that I was not in the CO's carrier, as it blew up on a mine and then received a direct hit from a shell, which wounded the Signaller and killed the gunner Battery Commander. Luckily the CO was not in the carrier at the time. Battalion dug in on the reverse slope for the night.

* * *

August 14th and 15th also saw 2KRRC advance, in their case through dense *bocage* country towards Falaise. Lewin's superior in 'A' Company, Major Hereward Wake, wrote:

> The country was damnably thick and close, and anything but suitable for tanks. The German infantry are well-armed with bazookas, and enjoy knocking out our tanks from ten yards range from thick hedge-rows, orchards, lanes, etc., and our tanks can do nothing about it. Real infantry country, and so 'A' Company led the advance all day, giving the tanks [of 3rd/4th County of London Yeomanry] close protection, combing the thick bits, and detecting and picking up mines in the lanes. A slow business indeed.[11]

'Sandy' Stow's Platoon were active in patrolling and mine clearance that day, and 'A' Company captured fifty Germans of 271st Infantry Division near Treprel. Lewin was in his element, as his Company Commander recorded:

> No.2 Platoon, under Robin Lewin, did wonderfully. I put him under command of 'B' Squadron of the Yeomanry to help them … 'B' Squadron came to the village of Treprel on the right, which was full of determined Huns. Robin, with his thirty men, was ordered to clear it, because it lay on the road down which Brigade HQ behind us intended moving.
>
> Robin was thoroughly enjoying himself. He had already taken one German officer prisoner, who said there were fifty more in the village, and well could I believe it. They kept on potting at us from every house and orchard, and you could not see them. In spite of civilians, we got Hugh Barrow RHA to fairly shell the place. Civilians were running about between trying to salvage stuff out of their burning houses.
>
> There were mines about, but one splendid tank came up the road to help us. He was missed by bazookas which landed quite near me, and I thought it was a mine going off at first.
>
> One Boche, sniping from behind an apple tree, gave himself up, and Colonel Ronnie [Littledale] seized his rifle and fairly pumped him for information, in what I thought was an unhealthy place. However, they were such rotten shots or they would have hit us. I think they were rather shaken.[12]

Wake and Littledale were clearly commanders who believed in leading from the front. When one of Lewin's men was wounded, they took him into a house in which some French civilians were sheltering:

> It didn't seem real, in a fight, to be drinking wine out of a wine-glass with people who, in spite of the fact that our shelling had thoroughly knocked about their house, didn't seem to realise there was a war on.
>
> I left Robin tackling an immense German tank, and got Peter Gosse, my second-in-command, to help him … Robin ended by taking thirty-eight prisoners, the remainder escaping to the south. The Germans then shelled the village very heavily.[13]

By nightfall, 44 RTR had cut the Conde–Falaise road south of Treprel. Carver's brigade was heavily mortared, and it poured with rain. Carver received orders to take his formation on towards Argentan the next day to complete the envelopment of German forces.

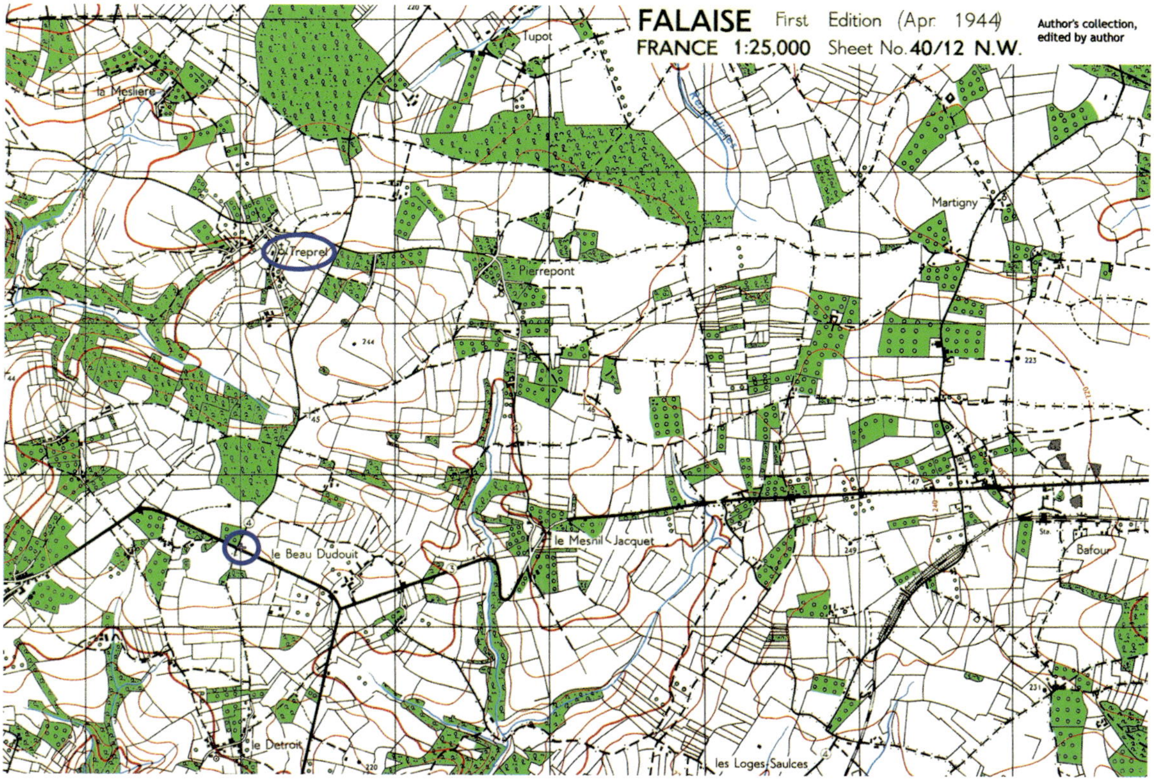

Fletcher's 'B' Company took the lead, first clearing an orchard of the German infantry company which was defending it. 'B' moved on and cleared the next orchard, but as Fletcher paused at a crossroads, mortar shells fell, killing him and Lieutenant Wyndham. Soon afterwards, 'B' drove off a German counter-attack by a single platoon, which left behind it six prisoners, one wounded, and two dead. By now 'B' Company had suffered four killed and twenty wounded. Fletcher, a veteran of El Alamein but still aged only twenty-six, was buried by his own armoured car's crew. His brother, then on the staff of 79th Armoured Division, visited his grave soon afterwards. It was clear that Fletcher had developed great qualities; his Commanding Officer wrote:

> He was a great leader in battle, and his determination was a big asset, especially when things seemed to be not going very well.

Brother officers commented that

> anyone who wanted cheering up used to go to his 'B' Company Mess, where they were immediately given a new lease of life … David was brave beyond the ordinary, very efficient, and much loved by his Company: their esteem was shown by the way they went on fighting after his death.

He now rests in grave IX.D.25 of the Ranville War Cemetery.

* * *

The day after Fletcher's death, 2SWB moved just west of Falaise, occupying Point 231 that night. At 0100hrs, fighting patrols encountered German troops in Fourneaux-le-Val wood, and by daylight these defenders – probably around company-strength – were causing what Somerville referred to as 'considerable trouble'. Despite a bombardment at 1300hrs an attack failed to dislodge the German troops, and therefore

> it was decided that the whole of the Corps artillery would be used on the wood in an effort to shift them; and so at 2200hrs it came down for ten hours. The noise and destruction was terrific. You could hear the shells crunching through the trees.

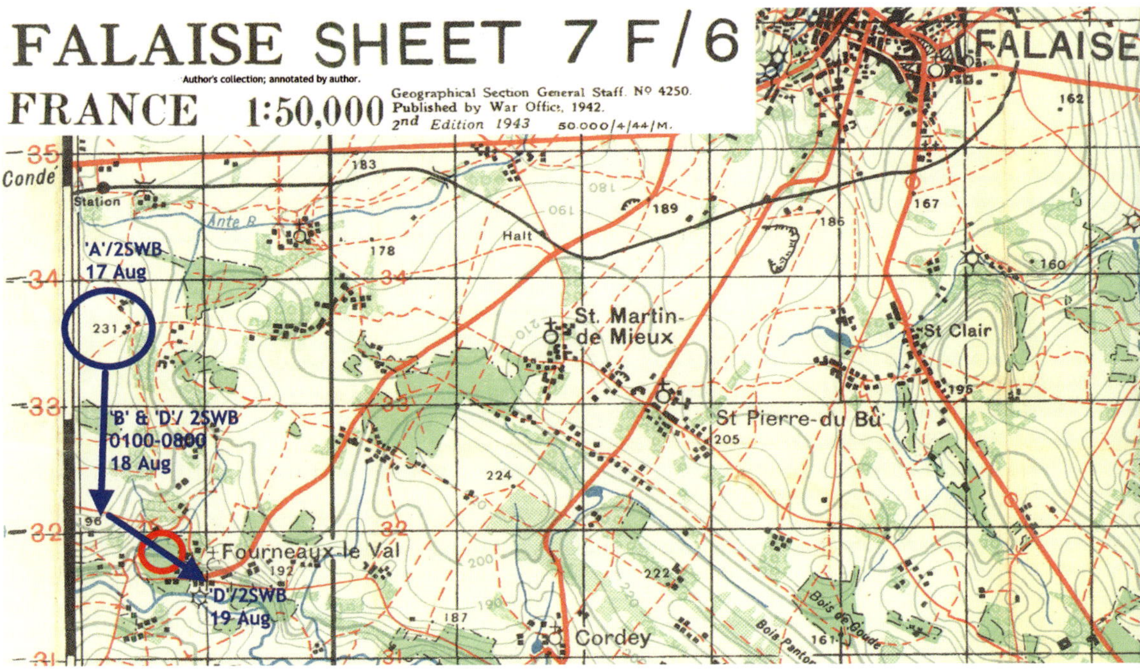

Author's collection; annotated by author.

Still the enemy refused to give way, and so on August 19th another bombardment was followed by a three-company attack. The German defenders broke, and 2SWB took thirty-three prisoners as 'D' Company moved into Fourneaux itself. In the evening the Battalion drove through Falaise,

> which was in the most terrible state. Not a house standing, and many still burning, the whole place littered with bomb craters, dead horses, Germans, and civilians. It made one wonder just how long it was going to take to clear up this terrible battlefield with its fires and dysentery and the terrible smell of death and destruction. Only a Crucifix and William the Conqueror remained unchanged.
>
> August 21st
> A wonderful bath, and a quick visit to Caen in a Jeep. It was a terrible sight. One mass of wreckage. Bridges, trains, railway lines, all thrown together in a pile of rubbish and dust. The streets all black where the great fires had been. I remember in particular the railway

> station, which was a mass of twisted girders and engines with their boilers wrenched into the most fantastic contortions. Over everything was a thick layer of the terrible Normandy dust, which was something that everybody who fought there will remember.

Disease was becoming a problem:

> The mosquitoes in Pedouze are terrible. There are quantities of them, and everybody is bitten. The Army have provided anti-bite cream, but it is not so good. The doctor has a hundred cases of dysentery. It comes from the flies that these Huns leave behind.
>
> August 22nd
> Recce party went off, but the Battalion is not moving until tomorrow, and so they came back again with reports of quantities of beautiful French girls in Bonnebosq.

Somerville was now appointed Adjutant, and was as a result too busy to keep up his diary. However, he later wrote an outline of the Battalion's subsequent exploits, as we shall see.

German transport along the Gace–Trun road, destroyed by rockets fired from Typhoon ground-attack aircraft, by Anthony Gross. (IWM ART LD 4489)

The closing of the Falaise Gap led to the charnel house of the Falaise Pocket. 2KRRC were now allocated to mopping-up operations, and on August 22nd the war diary recorded

> 0200hrs
> 'B' Company shelled by Canadian artillery until stopped by Higher Formation. Most annoying – it was raining, too.
>
> 0600hrs
> The Battalion were in the centre of the killing ground. By daylight it was possible to see the fantastic destruction which had taken place. The Battalion never saw anything like this in Italy or the Middle East.
>
> 1300hrs
> Prisoners of war came in all morning in batches; impossible to record numbers.

Six days later, Lewin crossed the Seine.

XXII

'I passed through Rome, which unfortunately is intact.'

Africa & Italy, August 1944

In August 1944, Huggins – by now a Flight Lieutenant – was instructing in Southern Rhodesia, taking trainee pilots through the same course which he himself had followed years before. No.20 Service Flying Training School operated from RAF Cranborne, in the suburbs of Salisbury (now Harare); its aircraft were Harvards and (for multi-engine training) Airspeed Oxfords.

> Now that I have got down to work again I have modified my views on the non-combatant nature of the flying out here. As a matter of fact it is becoming more and more interesting as it goes along. There is also this about it; until one has had to learn how to instruct others in the art of flying, it is hard to realize just how little one really knows about it all, even if in operations one has done well. Other pilots on the course who have as much as two thousand hours to their credit all agree that it is amazing how little they know about pure flying when not aimed at combat conditions. There is also the point that after doing a course of this nature it is much simpler to get a really good

job when this one is over. All the pilots I know who went through a phase of instructing got more or less what they wanted when back on operations.

Toby Kidd has just had a letter from you and will no doubt be dropping you a line in a few days.

Kidd did so,[1] enclosing a photograph of himself, Huggins, and John Matthews.[2]

Kidd is very well, and we get together sometimes and have a game of squash. Our standards are much the same, and so some rather good games ensue. Next week I shall be starting lectures and will then pass judgement on him as a teacher of navigation! So long as he does not put me on to 'compass swinging' when I want to go out for the afternoon we shall probably get on amicably! John Matthews is a course ahead of me, so I do not see very much of him outside the Mess, as our timetables differ. He seems to be getting on all right in his work. His exams are drawing nigh …

It is grand the way the war is progressing so well these days. The Russians are certainly knocking hell out of the Hun. One cannot help wondering how much this will influence their attitude at the Peace Table. There is the consolation that they were very busy constructing a new Russia when the trouble did start, and so after all the destruction that has occurred in their land they should have their hands full putting their own house in order. America, on the other hand, will not have that to consider, and will probably try to maintain her current monopoly of the export trade. Whether we, with all our other commitments, can rise up to her standards and compete, is a matter of conjecture. Meanwhile they seem to be pulling their weight in the Western offensive and we have no cause to belittle them in military matters …

I still hanker after England, but that looks less possible as time goes on. Did I mention to you my interest in journalism? I have often thought of it and now that has become more concrete and I am actually studying the subject in my spare time. Whether anything will come of it I do not know. But that applies to anything when the individual is placed like myself – no real training, and not too keen to spend a long time before becoming qualified to hold down a reasonable job.[3]

* * *

Middleditch.

Middleditch's Regiment was still holding the Allied flank north of Perugia as August began, but the dry weather of July vanished, and on August 4th torrential rains began to affect operations. Locals reported that S. Giustino and Sansepolcro had been abandoned by the enemy, so 'A' Squadron got back into their Daimler armoured cars and on August 5th set out to investigate. By 1445hrs 3 Troop and the Commanding Officer were in Sansepolcro, whilst Middleditch and 5 Troop had dealt with some tricky demolitions in their path to reach Galliano. The following day, RHQ began to move to S. Giustino, but as they did so enemy were reported to have reoccupied Selci and S. Giustino. RHQ hurriedly went into all-round defence at Pistrino, whilst 'A' Squadron moved cautiously to have a dekko. Middleditch was in the forefront, entering S. Giustino with 5 Troop at 1325hrs, whilst another troop managed to reach Celalba but was then halted by a large demolition.

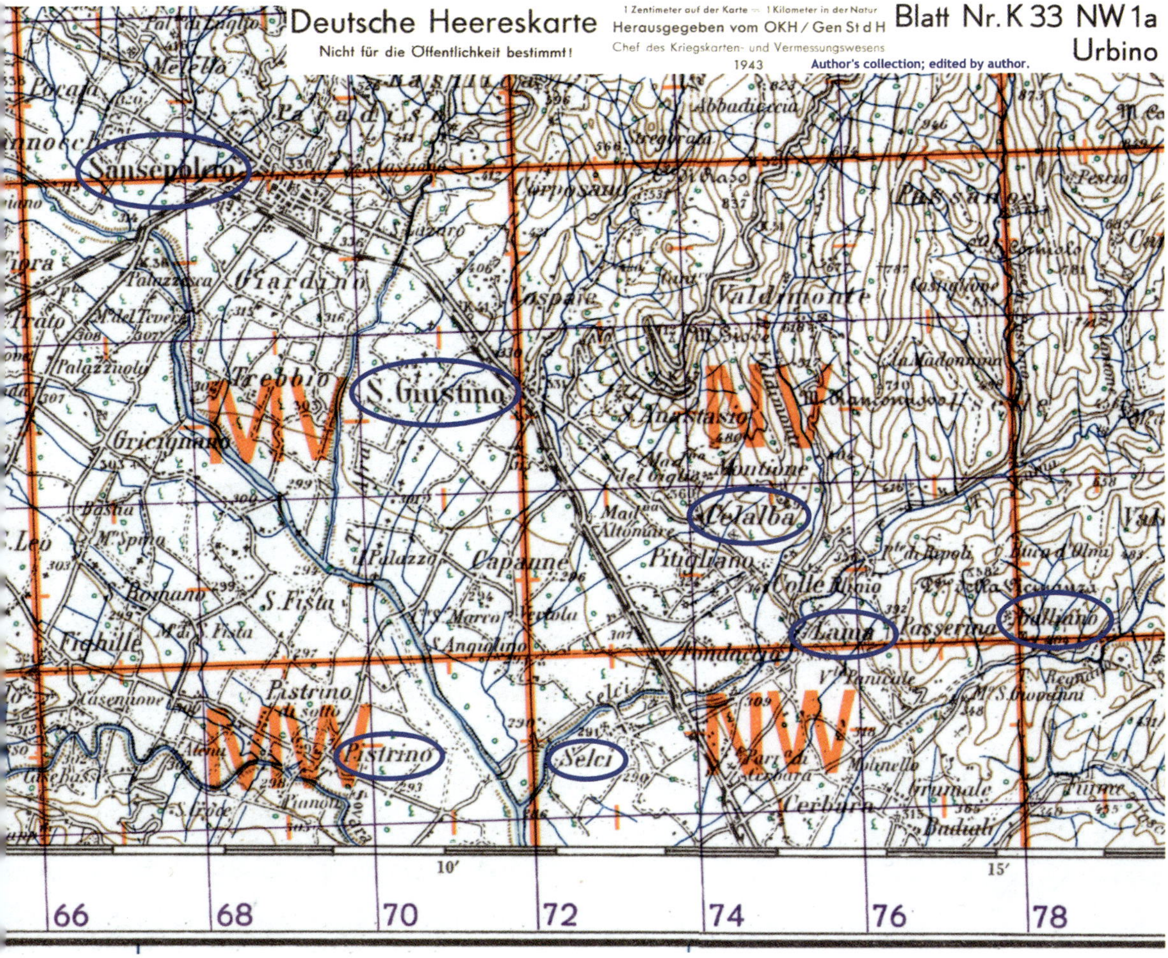

Author's collection; edited by author.

Middleditch and 12RL's second-in-command then decided to split up; whilst the Major directed an artillery shoot, Middleditch took his men up the twisting road leading north-east, only to be halted by yet another large breach in the road. 'A' Squadron pulled back in the late afternoon.

It was apparent that the Germans had blown up all the roads leading towards the hills, and were now on the high ground north and east of Sansepolcro, from which they were patrolling forwards into 12RL's area – the war diary reported that 'the enemy are becoming more and more insolent'. Middleditch's Troop approached Lama on the morning of August 7th and reported mines in the area; on the 10th, they slithered forwards through hazardous mud – there had been heavy rain in the night – to a point a mile south of S. Giustino, from where Middleditch reported enemy shelling visible. The following day, 'A' Squadron came out of the line and into reserve at Citta di Castello. The war diary reported a near-miss for RHQ that afternoon:

> The great event of the day, due entirely to the intuition of the CO, was the discovery of a time-bomb, ticking merrily away in the cellar of RHQ. It was nestling comfortably

> on a huge heap of Dynamite, sufficient in quantity to blow not only the house, RHQ, and all the vehicles several miles high, but half the mountain-side as well. A clue to this dastardly plot was found written on the shutters of the CO's room, thus: A/B 21/7/44 HD 13/14. The clock was set for nineteen days, nineteen hours, and if the bomb was laid on July 21st then RHQ had a very fortunate escape from complete destruction. RHQ moved …[4]

Middleditch and the rest of 'A' Squadron relieved 'D' Squadron in the front line on the morning of August 22nd, but within the week the whole Regiment had stood down for some hard-earned rest in Citta di Castello. Some officers escaped to Rome, whilst the men mainly attended a rest camp on the shores of Lake Trasimene.

* * *

Murray.

The Lovat Scouts had at long last reached the war, and Charles Murray had disembarked in Naples from HMT *Queen of Bermuda* on July 29th. The Regiment headed north a few days later, going into the front line in the mountains north-east of Arezzo on August 8th. A German shell wounded an officer almost immediately. The Scouts began patrolling the hills on August 11th and were soon in contact with the enemy's own patrols, losing their first man killed that same day. Murray was with RHQ:

> We came out here almost at once on our return from Canada, a change quite definitely for the worse, but it has taken a long time for us to get embroiled in things. Not that I'm very actively so, as I'm at HQ at moment. I'm doing very little… It really is a large detachment. Most interesting as I know just what is going on. Apart from a couple or so nights at the wrong end of a mortar or something, I've had no excitements at all. As a country, I dislike Italy as well as its inhabitants, who are filthy. I passed through Rome, which unfortunately is intact. I say unfortunately for two reasons. These people there started this thing and have not really been affected by it, while the peasants and small towns are in the hell of a mess. Also the Romans are quite apathetic to us and our winning. I saw Cassino, which is past belief. Just a heap of stones. I see a lot of refugees coming through the lines; in fact, I'm sick of the sight of them. They have the mistaken idea that we like to see them and will do everything for them. As I said before, they started it, so why should we worry! There are a lot of amazing stories about them. The best that I've heard was about one who came to us and said that he was a Colonel in the Italian Army and would we give him time to get his best uniform before we sent him back. As he was in tears on the subject, he was allowed to.
>
> The news these days is great and another few months should see it all finished in Europe. And then, I suppose, Burma![5]

* * *

By this stage of the war, British troops everywhere were extremely cautious and keen to avoid unnecessary casualties; their commanders felt the same, given the shortage of infantry soldiers available after so many years of war. In Italy, the Germans always retreated gradually, and would not stand if they came under pressure; so the orders from higher command were to 'lean on' the enemy, not allowing them time to prepare an elaborate defence, but not pursuing so closely that the Germans were forced to turn and give their pursuers a bloody nose. All the advantages lay with the defenders – a few men with machine-guns and mines could hold up the advance of an army. The usual pattern was that the Germans would pull out during the night; there was no point in incurring casualties simply in order to knock out a couple of Spandaus and their crews. Any determined German counter-attacks or defences could usually be crushed by the British superiority in artillery; the Germans had a healthy respect for the British 25-pounder guns, which they considered worse than anything which they experienced on the Russian Front. One of those directing the 'fearful thunder-roar of red-breathed cannon'[6] was Elliott-Binns.

Allied troops were by now coming up to the German Gothic Line, another fortified position, running for some 200 miles from Pesaro on the Adriatic to Massa Carrara on the Tyrrhenian sea. It was a tough proposition, designed to prevent the Allies from breaking through the Apennines into the valley of the River Po. It was laced with Panther tank gun-turrets, steel shelters, rock tunnels, over 2,000 machine-gun posts, some 500 anti-tank guns, anti-tank ditches, 100 miles of barbed wire, and extensive minefields. Troops who breached the line then faced a 'Security Line' and, twelve miles beyond, a second 'Gothic' Line. The attempt to breach it involved over a million men, and a giant pincer manoeuvre by the British Eighth Army on the Adriatic and the American Fifth Army in the Apennines. It was a vital moment for the Allied advance in Italy, as General Oliver Leese (Commander of Eighth Army) stated in his Order of the Day on August 25th:

> Now we begin the last lap. Swiftly and secretly we have moved an army of immense strength and striking power to break the Gothic Line. Victory in coming battles means the beginning of the end for the German Armies in Italy.

* * *

Elliott-Binns had served at Anzio with 19 Field Regiment throughout, but after the Allies had broken out of the beach-head and captured Rome, 1st Infantry Division had been taken out of the line to rest and refit. Elliott-Binns had spent the whole of July away from his Regiment, on a course, but was back in time to join them when they returned to the offensive.

Elliott-Binns.

> We went into action again in August looking down at Florence. In this campaign, which began before Florence and ended in the mountains above the Po valley, my exaltation and intensity of feeling were dissipated, though not entirely lost.

Elliott-Binns' Regiment was involved in the battle for the Gothic Line between August 25th and September 22nd. From August 21st, 19 Field fired at targets on the slopes north-east of Florence, moving slightly forwards on the 26th. Fighting continued in the area until the Germans withdrew and 19 Field moved up across the Arno on August 31st to take up position in the very areas which they had been shelling.

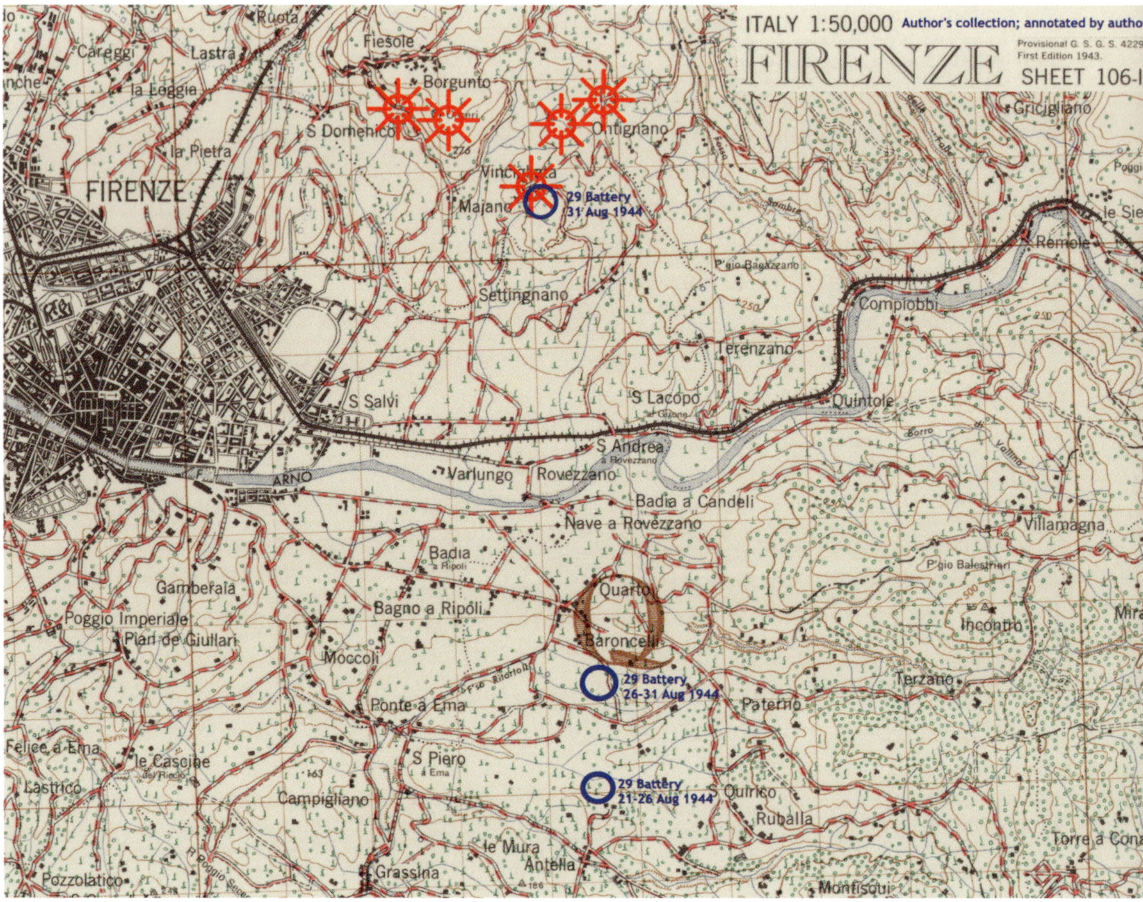

* * *

Peter Walker was also making a crossing, though somewhat longer; on August 20th he embarked at Southampton aboard his transport to the Mediterranean. His excitement shone through in his letters home:

Walker.

> Life on a troop-ship is something quite new to me. My first impression was one of great excitement after the rather drab atmosphere of the last days in England … Of the journey here I can say nothing, except we saw Hills and said goodbye to the finest city in England, which Dan and I thought a bit tough!
>
> On board we are a pretty mixed crowd, which makes it all so much more interesting. I haven't anything so luxurious as a cabin, but I have managed to find a bunk near what

little ventilation there is at night on a blacked-out ship, which was a stroke of luck. Of course we are pretty crowded and it's all very different from peacetime, but conditions could be a lot worse … The food is unbelievably good and I should imagine not far removed from peacetime days, including white bread! We have little to do; we have conferences where the OC Ship tells us more and more of the routine on the ship for the rest of our time. We walk on the decks, leaning over the rails looking at all the many things there always are to look at on board ship, even if it's only the sea and the sun and seagulls.

There are several of my Sandhurst friends on board, and so I am not at a loss for someone to talk to – and anyway there is always someone or something to watch. After the excitement of embarkation leave it's good to be able to sleep to one's heart's content, and by the end of the voyage I should feel pretty refreshed!

I'm at the moment gloriously contented with my lot and eagerly looking forward to what lies ahead. Most of the moments of regret are gone – I suppose everyone hates leaving England, but of course I should also have hated staying behind. Sometimes it all feels like a complete dream, and I can't really believe I am where I am and on the way whither I'm going – I suppose it is partly due to the war news being so good and peace feeling so near. Not until one gets into action I suppose will one's dream really be shattered.[7]

He disembarked in Italy on September 4th and started to make the tortuous journey to join what, in the end, turned out to be a different regiment entirely.

XXIII

'Every day I feel more and more glad I am not in the infantry'

India & Burma, June–December 1944

Metcalfe.

By the middle of May, 45th Cavalry had begun to reassemble in the Dimapur/Kohima area, with HQ Squadron moving by rail up from Ranchi. On June 1st, Metcalfe and 'B' Squadron received orders for Dimapur. It was an intricate operation. The Squadron was split into two parties, the first to travel by road in twelve trucks; its departure was slated for 0630hrs on June 6th, and the journey time was estimated at twelve days (in fact, the party arrived a day early, on June 17th). The other party was to travel by rail with the Squadron's armoured vehicles: sixteen Stuart light tanks, two carriers, and one scout car. It would depart at 1200hrs on June 6th, but arrive on June 10th, ahead of the road party – in fact, however, the rail party reached Dimapur late, on June 13th. Metcalfe was assigned the extra duty of loading and checking the rail party's 'second line ammunition', as well as making sure that it was trans-shipped whenever the party changed transport. By June 25th, the entire unit was in camp at Merema, to the north of Kohima.

* * *

Richardson.

After their attack on Surabaya and return to Ceylon, 832 Squadron had flown off HMS *Illustrious* on May 26th on to the much smaller escort carrier HMS *Begum*. The Ruler-class carrier had been earmarked for anti-submarine operations in the Indian Ocean, where both Japanese and German submarines were operational. These raiders tended to avoid attacks on convoys and concentrated on lone vessels, so instead of escort work, carriers conducted hunter-killer operations.

832 Squadron formed *Begum*'s entire air wing, with twelve Avengers and four Wildcats. *Begum* had not operated aircraft since

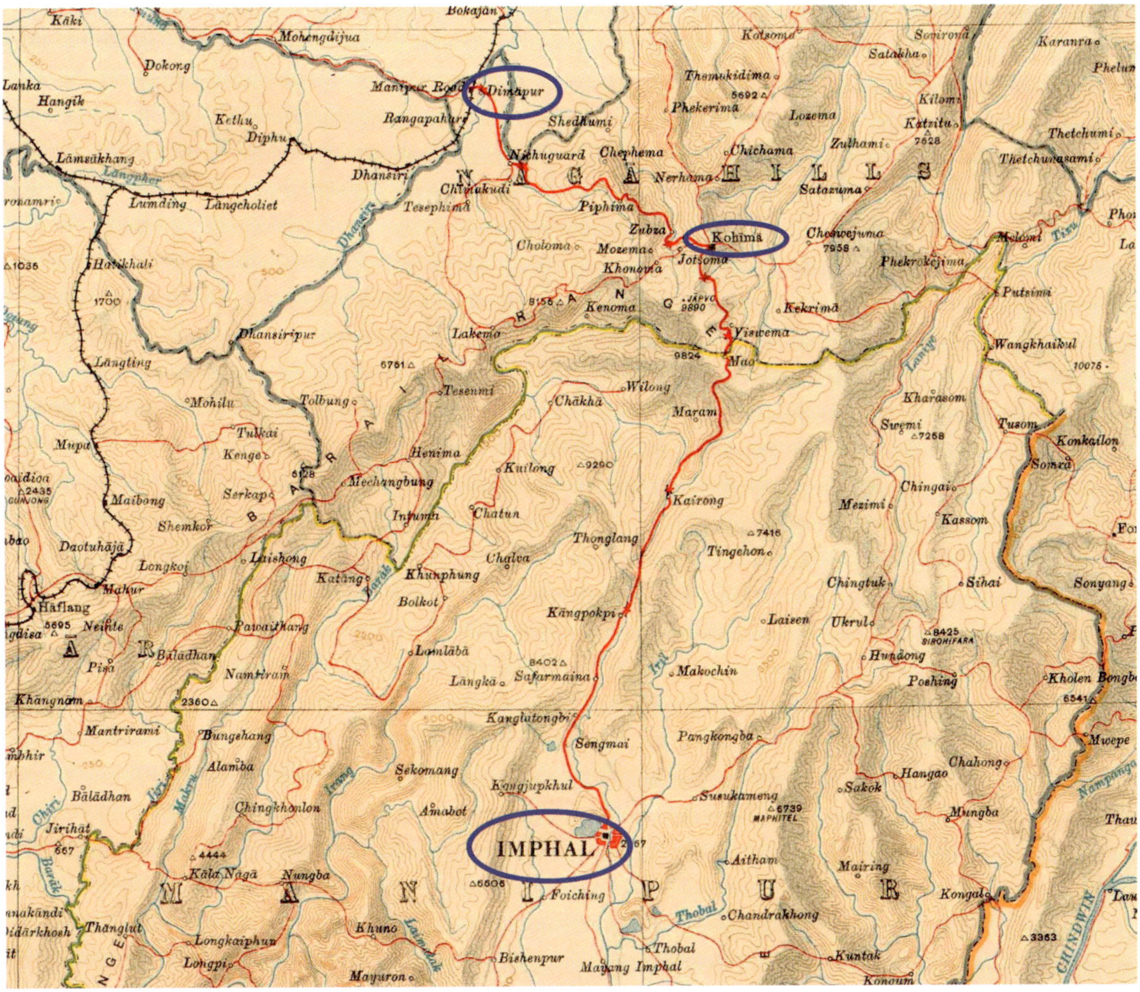

commissioning, and it was a steep learning curve for all involved, since none of 832's operations had been conducted from a postage-stamp sized deck before. It is no surprise, then, that there were frequent accidents at first. Indeed, on June 1st no fewer than three aircraft suffered accidents, writing off two of them, fortunately without fatalities.[1] Whether Richardson was aboard either of the Avengers involved is not yet known.

When *Begum* sailed for operations on June 11th, 832 were not aboard, landing on three days later. This inaugural anti-submarine sweep covered the Bay of Bengal and took three weeks; it was marred only by the ditching of Avenger '4B' on June 22nd after it suffered a catastrophic loss of oil pressure, though the crew were rescued.[2] At the end of the operation, on July 2nd, 832 flew ashore to HMS *Bherunda* (Colombo race-course).

* * *

On June 15th, Rigby wrote to fill Robertson in on what he was up to:[3]

Above: Avenger JZ231 '4Q' takes the barrier aboard HMS Begum, *June 1st 1944.* (Richardson family collection)

Below: Avenger 4P made a heavy landing aboard HMS Begum *on June 1st 1944, resulting in a broken tail-wheel.* (Richardson family collection)

Having spent a most pleasant winter with my Squadron on detachment in the NWFP – a most enthralling country – I was sent to Ahmednagar, seventy miles from Poona, for a three months' course, dealing with the mechanics and maintenance of every different kind of tank and soft vehicle that one is likely to come across out here. A very interesting course; I feel a fairly competent general mechanic as a result of it.

Rigby.

We went for one week to a large lake in the mountains about ninety miles from here, and did repairs in the open in field conditions. The scenery there was magnificent and swimming in the lake at all hours of the day and night. I was doing a guard there one night when a panther approached to within about twenty yards of me. Fortunately he winded the camp and sheared off; it was rather disturbing because I was unarmed and there was no cover within thirty yards.

I had just come to the last week of my course when I got a violent bout of malaria. So I have been and still am in hospital. I hope to be up in three or four days. They give you fourteen days' treatment, which is supposed to be a positive cure. But I am afraid it will recur – not a pleasant malady. All this means I won't get back to 'Pindi until the beginning of July, and then with any luck I may get fourteen days in the hills. My Regiment (18th Cavalry) being stationed in 'Pindi is very conveniently situated for anyone wanting to get up to Srinagar in Kashmir.

I think that Pat Metcalfe will have been in action on the eastern front for some time now. I believe they're doing quite well… .

Great news from Normandy. I hope they manage to keep the battle fluid …

I hope your sister has been keeping well. It will be a great day when I come to visit you at Culver Lodge. I hope not very far off.

* * *

Late in June 1944, Walker sent Robertson a press photograph of Wavell which appeared to show Fortune in his role as ADC. Robertson commented:

Thanks, too, for photo of ADC, which I too, and anyone I showed it to till today, accepted as Bruce. The joke is that today some Black Watch pipers are here, and the Pipe Major and two others swear the figure in foreground is not Bruce but a Captain Mervine-Austin, with a Captain Swannel behind him. I see now there is a less obtrusive figure, looking down, in the background, and perhaps that is all the time the one you meant. All of us accepted the other. Very odd, but the last photo of him his mother gave me, with moustache etc., was hardly recognisable as the old Bruce![4]

Fortune.

Despite every obstacle, Fortune and Susan managed to arrange their leaves to coincide, and Susan flew back to Delhi on Monday June 26th – ostensibly to do a few days' duty for Mountbatten, but in fact to ensure that when her leave began she was with Fortune.

> We landed and I jumped out into an oven – the searing heat hit me in the face – it was 111 degrees! A second later I spotted the crested VR car coming across the airfield. It drove right up to the plane and Brucie jumped out, looking so wonderful and handsome – he was in his kilt. It was quite heart-stopping.

On Thursday, June 29th Fortune, Susan, and Joan Spens (daughter-in-law of Sir Patrick Spens, Chief Justice of India) set out by train for Ranikhet, a cantonment (army town) commanding extensive views of the Himalayas and standing at 6,000ft. They were accompanied by Fortune's bearer, Rhamet. On arrival, the couple stayed in the Spens' bungalow, five miles from the cantonment. Up early most mornings, they walked before breakfast, rode in the mornings, visited the pub for a few beers at lunch time, had lunch, and rested in the afternoon. A walk with Joan and her children preceded baths and a change into either evening dress (if going out to party) or dressing-gowns (if staying in for dinner). On the final day of their fortnight's leave, the clouds which had been obscuring the mountains lifted, and Fortune and Susan went for their last walk after breakfast:

> We climbed up to the great flat overhanging rock half-way up the hill, and had a world of pine trees and shaded valley before us, and we lay in the sun exulting in what we had seen. We wanted to remember this moment, so Brucie set the camera and rushed to be beside me so's he could be in the shot as well.

The couple treasured the photograph, which they referred to as the 'Woodland Idyll'.[5]

On arriving in Delhi, Susan was ordered to depart immediately on Mountbatten's own luxuriously-equipped Dakota, FL510 'Sister Ann'. She arrived at the airport at 0530hrs:

> Just before we were getting ready to take off … a Viceregal car came rushing up – and my Brucie hopped out. I was so happy that he had come, and it was with a lightened heart that I left, as I knew he was coming down to Ceylon next month. Last time I left Delhi I thought I might never see him again. He stood on the runway as we took off.

* * *

At Merema, 45th Cavalry were warned early in July that they might be redeployed to the Imphal plain. Instead, they spent the rest of the month concentrating at Dimapur. Where they might go next was anyone's guess.

* * *

On July 13th Fortune accompanied Wavell to Simla, where they remained until July 24th. Wavell's main concerns at the time were Gandhi's attempts 'to raise a political turmoil if he can'.[6] Fortune took the opportunity to write to Robertson on the 17th:[7]

> This job is always full of surprises – can be very interesting, but has such stretches of unmitigated boredom that sometimes one wonders is it worth while. However I know that it has been – for I have seen most of India, in absolute luxury, though it has all been so quick I have found it difficult to digest the greater part. And also the peacetime atmosphere doesn't agree with me, and I have discovered all the more that my place is in the field, and not in the armchair! However perhaps next year, God being willing, and the doctors, I will be back with the boys!
>
> I was sorry to see John Sinclair's death, also McMurtrie – who was surely distressingly young. But the fine records of all these Wykehamists, especially Hopperites, I notice, shows that none of them die in vain.
>
> We had a huge OW dinner the other day *'chez nous'*, which you will have seen in the *Wykehamist*. It was a great success … .
>
> I saw David Wilson in Delhi the other day, and heard from Guy Dodgson – but on the whole all the OWs in India are so ancient that I know very few of them. As someone once said, 'If you find any grit in the cogs of the Government of India, you can be sure it is caused by some Old Wykehamist', which although not quite true, has a semblance of truth! I saw Michael Scott, late of Beloe's, when we were in Bombay – and stayed with B.J. Gould in Sikkim when we were up there. It was a wonderful spot – we trekked to the Tibetan border – reached there in a heavy hailstorm, so had to take refuge in a cave, with a bandit and a bottle of brandy. The latter very welcome, the former rather tough. Will write again soon. My love to Sheila. I always remember you both in spite of the silence.

That same day, Rigby's father died suddenly from a duodenal haemorrhage. Working on the other side of the globe, his son was unable to attend the funeral – yet another of the small personal sadnesses which the war left in its wake.

* * *

Begum's second patrol had lasted only a week (July 23rd to 30th), since she was being redeployed as part of Task Force 66, a hunter-killer group tasked with protecting shipping in the northern Indian Ocean. The heart of the force was the sister carriers *Begum* and *Shah,* escorted by four frigates and two sloops. On August 3rd, 832 flew on and the hunt began for the Type IXD2 U-198. On August 6th the U-boat sank MV *Empire City,* and on August 7th MV *Empire Day.* A Wildcat (JV507) was written off when it hit the barrier on August 9th, but the next day *Shah*'s aircraft spotted U-198 near the Seychelles, and Avengers from *Shah* and *Begum* attacked on August 12th. Although they reported no success, they vectored two of the escorts to the U-boat's location, and had the satisfaction of hearing that she had been sunk. Her entire crew of sixty-five went down with her, as well as Robert Courteney Selfe, the first Officer of *Empire Day,* who had been taken prisoner five days before. 832 had lost one Avenger (FN926) when it took the barrier after missing the wires. Three days later, Avenger FN923 did the same thing.

On August 21st, during a stop-over in Kilindini in Kenya for refuelling and replenishment, Richardson wrote to Sheila Robertson:

> You and your Brother seem to have that perfect gift of writing just the news that really counts. I could not have wished for a more delightful survey of our friends and our little corner of England.
>
> I am afraid I am a bit of a black sheep as regards school sporting activities as I have now become a rugger addict. We have quite a respectable Squadron team, and with a complete disregard for modesty we challenge all comers wherever we go. It's tremendous fun and we often find ourselves embroiled with very formidable teams. We are playing one of these the day after tomorrow. I am defaulting again tomorrow by playing hockey.
>
> It would probably amuse your Brother to know that I have now taken over the duties of Squadron Staff Officer and spend my days engulfed in piles of paper. I now regard my flying as a few hours' holiday from official wordiness. I am afraid that the rather abrupt style that I adopt does not always please my superiors, but it usually gets results, which is the main thing. I hope they don't see through me and realise that it is really because I never got above SP3.
>
> I have been having a great time this evening trying to repair one of my suits. It is rather an uncomfortable proceeding as it is tough stuff and I always seem to leave one of my fingers where the needle wants to go. One of the boys in the Squadron has put us all to shame by making a pair of khaki shorts. They are really good ones, so just for the principle of the thing I shall have to persevere with my own stitchery.
>
> Please apologise to Major Robertson for my scrappy airgraph. I will write him one of these things when I get some more news.

An official verdict on his performance in his new role came in the Captain's assessment of him on August 14th:

> General conduct: satisfactory.
> Of temperate habit.
> Professional ability: above average.

> Zeal and energy: above average.
> Power of command: above average.
> Judgment: above average.
> Reliability: above average.
> SCORE 6.2.
> A capable and hard-working officer and an efficient observer. As Squadron Staff Officer, he has shown keenness and ability, and exerts a good influence at all times. Recommended for promotion to Temporary Lieutenant (A) RNVR. Captain J.E. Broome

Task Force 66 set out on August 27th as escort to convoy KM5, en route for Aden. The perils of operating from the *Begum* were once again made clear when Avenger '4Q' (JZ231) took off the next day; she stalled, and plunged into the Indian Ocean. Once again, however, prompt action saved her crew.

* * *

By August 13th, 45th Cavalry were browned off. They had received no information; their commanding officer had been posted to the staff; and then orders had arrived to hand in their vehicles. The acting commanding officer set off to HQ Fourteenth Army to ask what was going on. The following day, the Regiment received orders to move to Poona by road and rail, taking their tanks with them, and the first party left on August 16th. The war diary stated that

> during the journey by rail across India, the men who travelled on this [Main Personnel] train were given most hearty and prolonged welcomes at nearly all stations where they halted.[8]

On arrival, the Regiment concentrated in camp at Chattarsinghi. Metcalfe and his comrades still had no idea what their future held.

* * *

Fortune's thoughts were in Ceylon, where he arrived by air on August 17th. Susan had come down to Colombo to meet him, and they travelled back to Kandy by train.

> The next three days, when I wasn't working, we did nothing but walk and talk and see all our friends … As we were all working overtime, Brucie went up to Udapussellawa on August 21st to stay with his cousin Daphne Cathcart, who lives on a tea plantation in the hills. I didn't ask for leave, as I had just had some, but Heather[9] sent me off – and gave me five days to be with him. She also told me to go and settle my life and if I wanted to marry Bruce, she and Micky[10] would do everything they could to help me. The Wren officer in charge of Rear HQ Signal Office in Delhi was leaving the Wrens, as she was having a baby and wanted to be with her husband – and I could be sent to replace her. I was completely staggered.

When Susan set off on August 29th to join Fortune on the Cathcarts' plantation, it was with an end in view for them both. At some stage in those five days Fortune proposed to her, and she accepted. She kept the news as quiet as she could, but confirmation of her posting to take charge of the Signals Office at Rear HQ in Delhi came on September 18th. Five days later, Susan was at Mountbatten's official residence, King's Palace, socializing with Prince Philip of Greece ('he is very handsome and unaffected, fair-haired, and has a very ready laugh – we had an amusing time chatting away').

> Arthur came bursting in to say that Lord Mountbatten was coming down to congratulate me on my engagement himself. I was a bit taken aback, and anyway I was an awful mess. However, he was awfully sweet: 'What's this I hear, Susan? Another engagement in my HQ?'
>
> I felt very shy and didn't know quite what to say, as my engagement wasn't public property – yet. Heather Hayes came to see me later and told me that Lord Mountbatten had announced it at the party!
>
> After the Supremo's effort at broadcasting the fact that I was engaged, [General] Wedemeyer tackled me on the subject. I told him that it was not yet public. He said, in his wonderful drawl, 'I promise you I won't tell more than a dozen people.'

Susan's belongings were packaged off and sent by train to Colombo to be airlifted to Delhi. Despite going missing for five days, the luggage was safely stowed on board 'Hapgift', another of Mountbatten's personal Dakotas, this one a present from the American General Hap Arnold. Susan was allowed to send an official signal to her fiancé:

FROM:	SACSEA	030541 Z OCT
TO:	REAR SACSEA	
RESTRICTED	KAN 1568	
	For MASON	

Please pass the following to FORTUNE VICEROY'S HOUSE
From MACKIE
Luggage awaiting collection WILLINGDON AIRPORT ex HAPGIFT
TOO 030541 Z OCT
(DSO)
Copy to DSO only

She flew to Delhi in 'Sister Ann' on October 9th, and Fortune turned up to meet her at the airport. A new chapter in his life was beginning. He and Susan would be together for the next fifty years, until his death did them part.

* * *

In Poona, Metcalfe had a new commanding officer, Arthur Goring, who had been promoted from within the unit. He wrote a charming letter to Metcalfe's mother on September 24th:[11]

My Dear Lady Metcalfe,
You will not recollect me, for, although I have had the pleasure of meeting you several times during the past eighteen years in India, I have always been very small fry in the Indian Cavalry Ocean.

However, I am now taking the liberty of writing to you, because I am sure you will be glad to know how extremely well your son Pat is both doing and looking. I have been lucky enough to get command of the 45th Cavalry, which Jerry Priolean raised from nothing to its present proud position of second to none in the Indian Armoured Corps; and I should like you to know that Pat is one of the cardinal pillars which support the Regiment.

To begin with, he is as fit as a fiddle, and plays a magnificent game of football. Next, he has got complete command of his men, who just love him. With his enormous sense of humour, a real sense of duty and obedience, and a most persuasive manner, he is always cool and quiet, but completely inflexible when he knows himself to be in the right.

He is doing so well that I have specially selected him to command my own Regimental HQ Troop of tanks, which is double the size of any other troop, and a most tricky command withal, as the CO's tank must never go wrong.

There happens to be no vacancy at the moment for another Captain; but as soon as there is one, I intend to promote Pat – but you mustn't tell him that!

Lastly, and perhaps to me most important of all, he is a most charming companion, quite fearless, and exquisitely politely frank. I am most grateful to you and Sir Aubrey for giving the 45th Cavalry a son so worthy of it.

If there is anything you want to know about him, do please write to me. I promise you that I am taking great care of him, but I know that he will never give me a moment's more anxiety than he has ever given you.

Yours sincerely,
Arthur Goring

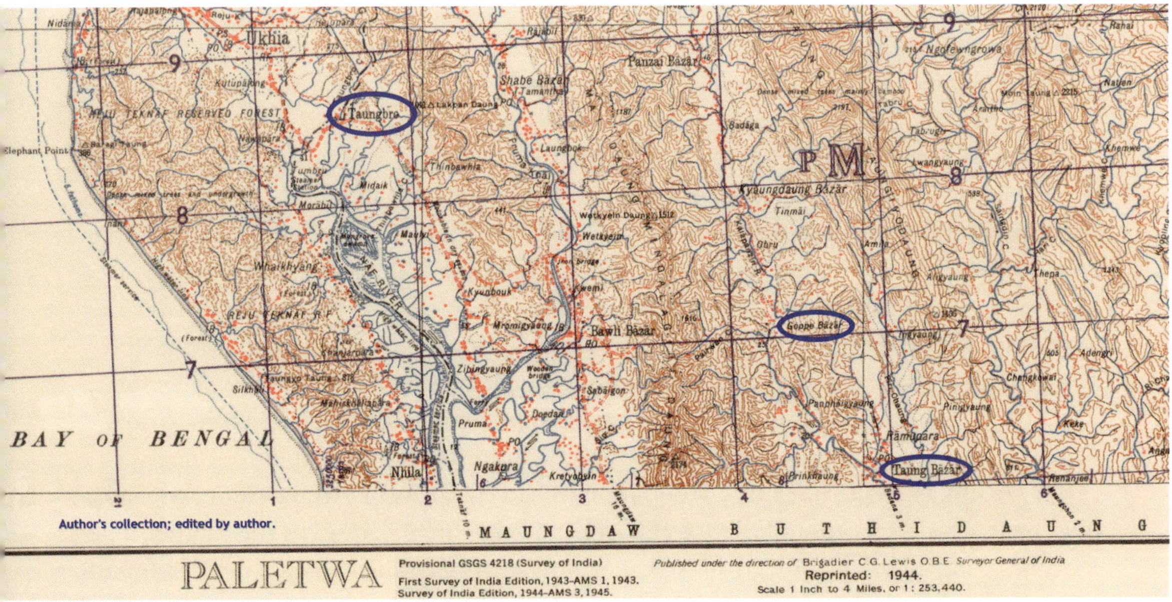

Author's collection; edited by author.

A week later, the 45th were on the move, as they sent their tanks and Bren-gun carriers to Chittagong in eastern Bengal; they were bound for the Arakan. During a pause at Dohazari, they received orders to set out for Taungbro on November 3rd. As they prepared to move, Goring delivered on his promise, making Metcalfe an acting Captain with effect from October 28th.

Orders arrived on November 6th:

> Regiment to be prepared to send at short notice one Squadron to TAUNG BAZAR in support of 2 West African Brigade to operate in the general area long ridge 5259 TAUNG BAZAR GOPPE BAZAR 422705. Regiment ordered to carry out recces in consultation with 2 West African Brigade of routes crossing over *chaungs* [water-courses] on both sides of the KALAPANZIN river and construct ferries where necessary to enable tanks to cross the river. The presence of tanks in the area must NOT be disclosed and black berets are NOT to be worn.[12]

At 0730hrs on November 9th Goring and Metcalfe set out for Goppe Bazar, returning the same day after a recce; by now they were aware that a Japanese attack was expected on the area, and so their role was to launch a counter-attack if necessary. Nothing happened for the rest of the month, and the Regiment was soon split up in various locations. By December 10th Metcalfe was in Wabyin, from where he wrote to Robertson.[13]

> A very Merry Xmas to you and Miss Bobber, and thank you very much for yours of November 17th. It was the first letter of mine in which I had presumed to call myself Captain! Tho' I have not risen to the heights of Adjutant like Roger [Rigby] and Nick [Somerville]! However, we are having quite a nice little party down here on our own. Every day I feel more and more glad I am not in the infantry. They really do get all the 'blood, sweat, toil, and tears' in this jungle business, whereas we only appear at the best time of year, when it is comparatively dry, and by virtue of looking large and impressive manage to smuggle in sufficient kit to make ourselves quite comfortable. I really do admire the 'feet' who have to live and fight in these conditions the whole year round.

However, on December 14th a new Allied offensive began, with attacks down both sides of the Mayu. On the eastern side, near Goppe Bazar, Metcalfe and RHQ Squadron were active in the valley of the Kalapanzin river. Their first move was to Goppe Keep on the 14th, harbouring overnight before crossing the Kalapanzin the following morning. On December 17th Goring and Metcalfe went forwards to look at the crossings over the next water obstacle, the Myaw Chaung; the next day Metcalfe took the tanks of his HQ Troop to inspect a feature known as the Funnel, a passage between two nearby features. The Stuarts crossed the Myaw Chaung over a bridge laid by a specialist Valentine bridge-layer, but the recce was called off because no one quite knew where the front line was.

On December 19th, Metcalfe's Troop supported a company of 9th Battalion, Nigerian Regiment, on a recce from the south end of the Long Ridge feature to the Funnel. The accompanying Royal Engineers cleared not only anti-personnel mines but also found an improvised explosive device which could have ruined everyone's day:

> I gather Arthur Goring has told you the RHQ Troop has been into "battle". What a battle it was! We moved along a valley on a reconnaissance and then came back, and it was not until we were very safely back that the Sappers, who were with us, told us that Arthur Goring's tank had only missed a mine by ten yards! It was rather a big mine too, consisting of two 500-pound bombs (ours, which had not gone off) and half-a-dozen mortar bombs all tied up together! It would have made a very nice bang, if he had gone over it. However, not knowing this at the time, it was all rather dull.[14]

Metcalfe returned to Bawli on December 21st, to decide on a harbour location for RHQ, and by the end of December 26th the Regiment was back across the Kalapanzin.

* * *

Begum had returned to Ceylon in October, 832 flying off on October 12th and returning on the 21st after the carrier had returned to sea. But on October 28th *Begum*'s catapult failed, preventing her from launching aircraft, and she returned to port. One of her Wildcats crashed into the sea four days later, killing the pilot.[15]

Task Force 66 now went on the offensive looking for a Japanese submarine – RO113 – which had sunk SS *Marion Moller* on November 5th, but no trace was found. As the focus of Britain's war began to shift to the Far East, the Eastern Fleet to which *Begum* had belonged was split into the East Indies Fleet and the British Pacific Fleet. *Begum* stayed with the East Indies Fleet, but conducted her final patrol just before Christmas 1944. Thus Richardson and his comrades spent the last Christmas of the war in Ceylon.

Stuart tanks cross the Kalapanzin on December 18th 1944. (IWM SE 1348)

Begum's orders for 1945 were to carry the personnel and aircraft of 832 Squadron back to England, where she would be converted into an aircraft ferry ship.

* * *

On December 7th Fortune left Delhi again with the Viceroy, this time to visit Bombay, Hyderabad, Calcutta, and Imphal. Fortune hated Hyderabad, as he told Susan on December 13th:

On December 16th 1944, at Imphal, Wavell knighted Bill Slim, amongst others. Fortune is visible beside the table to the left of the kneeling Slim. (IWM SE 2815; edited by dansteele.net)

We were all glad to leave the territory of that terrible Nizam. Yesterday evening we all had dinner with him in his private Palace, and it could never have been more spooky. Wretched, depressed, and haggard women lurked everywhere, and one was brought for special exhibition. She sat on a sofa and shivered and shrank with fear – that such feudalism should be in operation today made me feel rather sick. In absolute contrast to these wretches, whom he called his daughters, were the two Princesses [Niloufer and the Princess of Berar], who were noble of bearing and 'wondrous fair'. They are of Turkish origin and quite European to look at, and wear the most beautiful saris.[16]

* * *

To the Editor of the Wykehamist.

Dear Sir,—On December 31st, 1944, an Old Wykehamist Reunion was held in Japanese Prisoner of War Camp, Group IV (Tha Muang), Thailand. There were present :

Lieut. H. G. D. Lewin (F, 1930-34), Straits Settlements Volunteer Force.
Captain G. Rickman (I, 1933-38), 5th Northumberland Fusiliers.
Gunner S. W. Clayton (I, 1931-36), unfortunately continent.

There was consumed :—

Doughnuts (*licet*).
Banana beer (strictly *non-licet*).

The toast of "Stet fortuna Domus" was honoured, but "Domum" could not be sung owing to the objections of the authorities. A hot was not possible—no opposition!

Yours sincerely,
Henry Lewin.

Given everything which he had been through, it is not surprising that Clayton was unwell ('Continent').

* * *

By the autumn of 1944 Hirst had become fed up with the dead-end of the Yorkshire Hussars, tinkering with Bren-gun carriers on the south coast of England. He and his fellow officers started applying for postings elsewhere, and when there was a call for personnel to transfer to the Armoured Corps in India, he applied.

I was very happy in the end that I went, as I loved being with Indian troops and it was the happiest period of my service. After the usual delays we (Draft RWZYA) sailed from Tilbury in London docks. We had Christmas Day 1944 at sea; turkey, plum pudding, and a bottle of beer.[17]

XXIV

‘Don’t bother to sympathise. We are quite sensible people and nothing does real good.’

Italy, September–December 1944

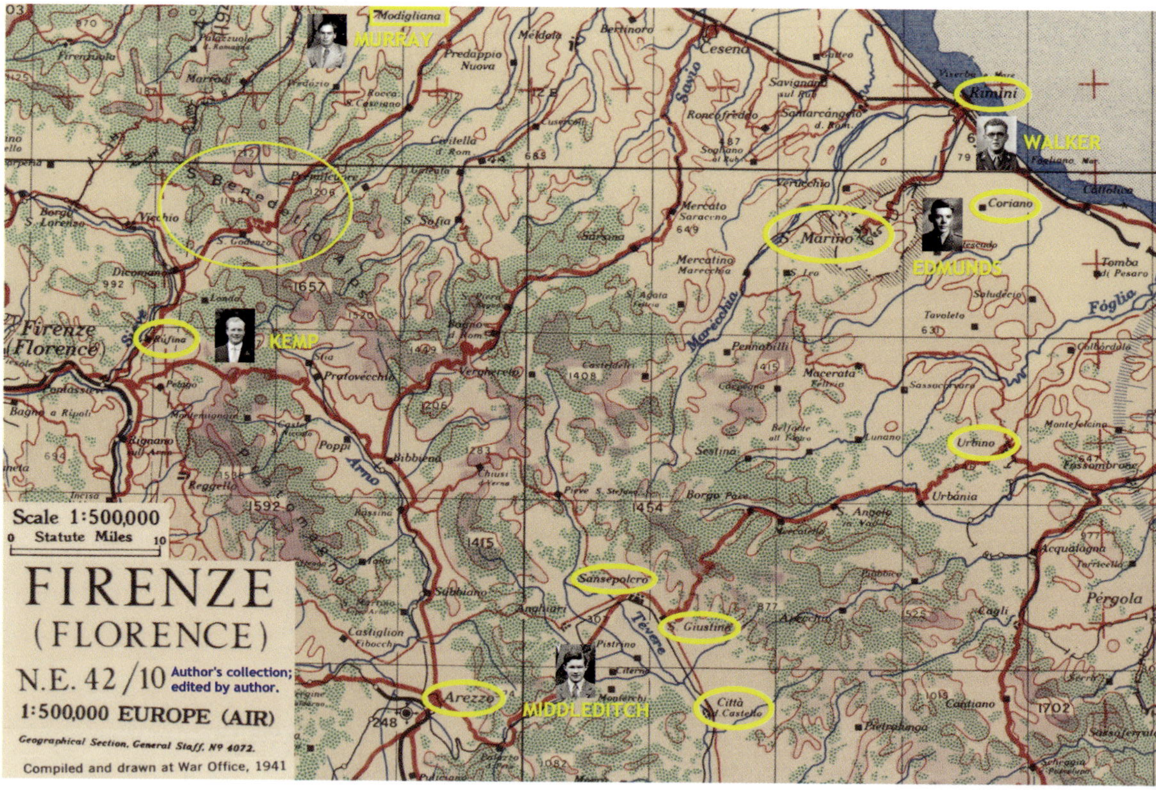

The hot summer was coming to an end, and amid the torrential rains and storms of September there would be clear hints of the bitter winter weather to come. But there were compensations. 7RB went into the front line at Rufina on the evening of September 5th, and Kemp preserved the memory for the rest of his life:

> If we ever went to an Italian restaurant with David, he would check the wine list for Chianti from Rufina. He had to buy it, as he was with the Rifle Brigade when they liberated Rufina in the war.[1]

Kemp.

Walker, meanwhile, was near Naples at the RAC Training Depot:

Walker.

> I do not expect to be at the above address long … Life is taking on an entirely new complexion. When you next see me I shall be completely altered. I have changed already. There has been so much of interest and there is so much to tell you. I will attempt it later. At the moment I am wildly excited, overwhelmingly bewildered at all that is new, and ecstatically happy. Life is one terrific adventure. Had I known what it was going to be like before I left, I should have been even more impatient than I was. Dan is the best friend in the world and we do everything together. My only fear is lest we should not reach the Regiment before all is over. That will be an enormous disappointment. Dan and I have great schemes. I hope to go to Naples tomorrow and possibly meet some friends. The country is superb, but there is much to make one realise the chaos and filth of the whole business. Food here is good. I share a tent with Dan and another. Bad mosquito country and malaria precautions are strict. Wine is plentiful, and most things – if you are careful – are bought quite cheap.[2]

* * *

7RB's 'A' Company broke the German hold on Rugiano on September 7th under cover of an immense artillery barrage; the attackers suffered no casualties and took eleven prisoners. It is typical that the number of enemy encountered seems to have been in the tens rather than the hundreds. During the night there was a terrific thunderstorm, which made tracks up to front-line companies impassable for anything but porters, and washed away a Bailey bridge close behind the Battalion. According to the war diary, 'The remainder of the night was a chaos of carrying, cable-laying, and recovery parties.'[3]

As the fighting moved past, 7RB were able to rest for a short while. As always, the Allies took the morale of their men very seriously. 7RB were in the front line on September 10th; the following day, a mobile cinema reached them and they watched *Millions Like Us*, a war romance starring Patricia Roc and set in an American factory producing aircraft parts.[4] How strange it must have seemed to be watching a film such as this in a mountain village in Italy, where only the day before the men had been patrolling in contact with the enemy. A week later they watched *The Wagons Roll at Night*, starring Humphrey Bogart as a circus owner.

* * *

Having been wounded on the Garigliano in January, Edmunds had rejoined 7OBLI as it re-formed after Anzio. The old Battalion had died there, coming out only 180-men strong, and late in March had been sent to Egypt, where new drafts of men and officers had joined. The task of rebuilding was no easy one, as the Regimental *Chronicle* reported:[5]

> Of those left, most were exhausted, and the shock of battle had left some with a natural loss of enthusiasm for battle. Others who had had more nerve-racking experiences

Edmunds.

> required strong stimulation to enable them to carry out the daily toil. How could this Regiment, having lost the best of its members and its inspiring and admired commander, rise again to the high standards of the past? In this state of battle exhaustion loyalties were liable to weaken, eyes dwelt on the past, and thoughts dwelt on home and family. Some felt shame, others jealousy. Those left out of battle might be looked upon with suspicion, while some who had been to battle exaggerated their ability and values. However, amongst all the natural human weaknesses was an intense pride in the Regiment. Its strength was almost unbelievable, and, based on that sure and sound foundation, the work of reconstruction started, leading to still greater success.
>
> The task was not only to recognize and train the Regiment but also to bind together as a team the old and the new, and to infuse into it a spirit of enthusiasm and determination to be ready for battle after only a short break. Inevitably some old members had to be left out of the team and found more restful work.

7OBLI left Egypt on July 11th and landed at Taranto on the 17th. On September 2nd, they moved to a concentration area in the Foglia valley, surrounded by German minefields.

At 0130hrs on September 4th 'A', 'C' and 'B' companies crossed their start lines, covered by 'D', for an attack by 167 Brigade on Montefiore Conca. It was slow going, but by 0550hrs they had contacted the enemy. From then on, the fighting was intense. 167 Brigade then moved north-west in the direction of Croce, but their route was commanded by the hilltop village of Gemmano, which had been heavily bombed and shelled that day. The troops were ordered to by-pass the position, 7OBLI being left behind to clear the

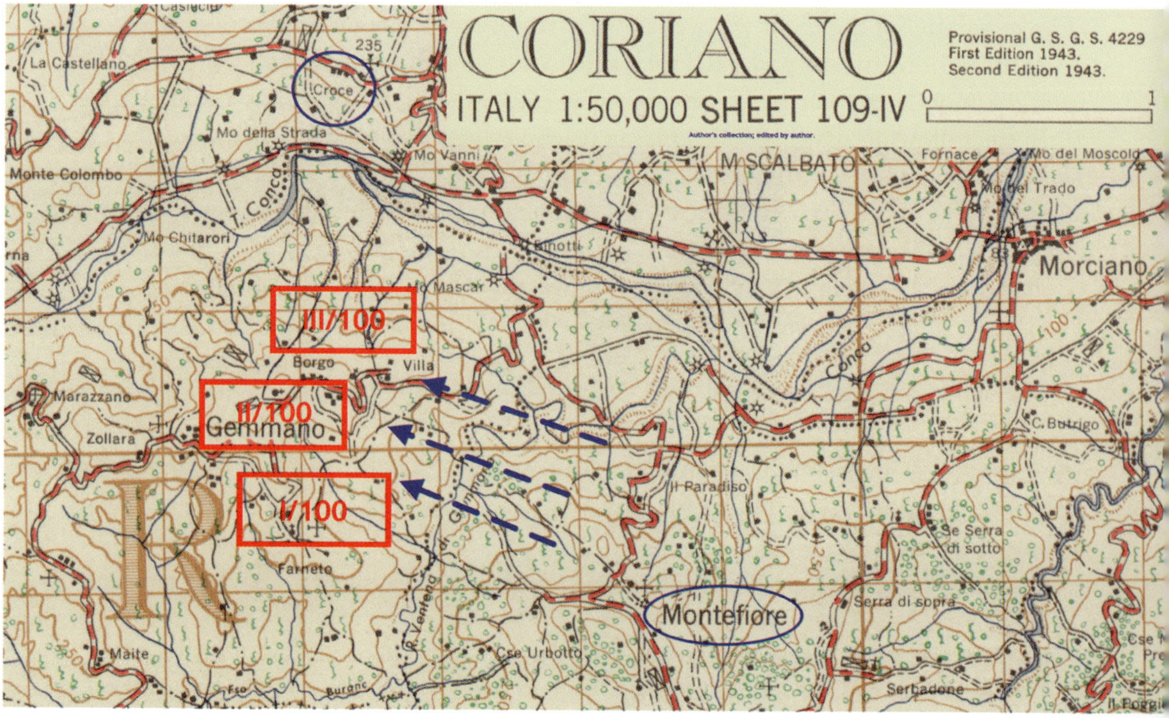

village of any stray Germans who might be there. In fact, Gemmano was the Germans' anchor for their whole defensive line, and the three battalions of 100 *Gebirgs* Regiment, well-trained and with high morale, clung to it tenaciously.

As Edmunds' Battalion moved on the dominating feature from the east they came under heavy fire. Although troops of 7OBLI managed to reach the hamlet known as 'The Villa', the Battalion was driven back repeatedly. It was the same story on the following day, September 5th, except that by now it was raining heavily and the plentiful dust had become mud. The fighting see-sawed across the slopes around 'The Villa', with 7OBLI unable to make progress and the *Gebirgsjäger* unable to push them off the mountainside.

The ruins of Gemmano as seen from 'The Villa', on September 14th 1944. The difficulty of any assault up these bare slopes can be appreciated – no wonder that Gemmano has been described as 'The Cassino of the Adriatic'. (IWM NA18623)

Divisional command had by now appreciated the danger which Gemmano represented to the flanks of the main advance, and on September 6th ordered 44th Reconnaissance Regiment to get a squadron of tanks into Gemmano. However, the defenders let the Shermans come nearly to the summit before opening fire with *Panzerschreck* rocket-launchers and SPGs hidden in the ruins. Within a short time, fourteen tanks had been destroyed.

Taken on September 6th 1944 outside Gemmano, this photograph shows three young Platoon Commanders of 7OBLI being briefed for the attack, probably by their Company Commander. (IWM NA18394; edited by dansteele.net)

As the rain tipped down, 7OBLI tried again, under cover of a tremendous bombardment which pulverized Gemmano, church and all. Although they managed to get up close to the village, German counter-attacks in the small hours drove them back again. The battle raged throughout September 7th; 7OBLI captured Gemmano, Borgo, and Point 449 four times, and four times they were driven out. Exhausted and depleted, the Battalion was pulled out of the line that night, being replaced by the three battalions of 169 Brigade.

Gemmano was not finally cleared until September 15th, when 100 *Gebirgs* Regiment withdrew, having been outflanked by developments further north. The battle deserves to be better known, as it was one of the hardest of the campaign. The military rule-of-thumb which suggests that attackers should outnumber defenders three to one had been reversed, yet 7OBLI had almost succeeded in storming one of the strongest positions in the Gothic Line. Indeed, afterwards the Battalion received the following message:

> From Eighth Army commander.
> Personal to Lieutenant-Colonel Houchin, Commanding 7 Oxf Bucks.
> My congratulations to you and all ranks of your Battalion on your hard fighting at Gemmano. The Regiment may be proud of its part in a great and hard-fought victory. With my thanks and best wishes to you all.

By now, the toll being taken of junior officers in the British Army had reached terrible levels, proportionately worse than in the First World War. Anyone who thinks that officers led a pampered and sheltered existence whilst their men faced all the danger need only look at the statistics to see how wrong this assumption is; officer casualties were disproportionately high, and mostly fell upon young Platoon Commanders. Furthermore, battle fatigue caused many men to fail to play their full part in battle, and the officers had to lead by example. Some officers, however, were called upon again and again to take the full burden of command in action. Up to this point, Edmunds had been the Intelligence Officer with Battalion HQ, recording events for the war diary amongst his other tasks. Now, since casualties among his more experienced colleagues were seriously weakening 7OBLI's ability to fight, he took over as second-in-command of 'A' Company. It was a fateful appointment.

* * *

12RL were on the move on September 8th, heading for Urbino. This was only sixty miles away from their existing location, but Middleditch and his comrades could not take a direct route, since 'the torrential rain on 6th and 7th September had washed away a great many bridges and made any diversions impassable, as a result of which our route was an extremely roundabout one, totalling some 250 miles in all.'[6]

Middleditch.

Over three days, the Regiment drove via Arezzo, Foligno, and Fano to their destination, arriving on September 10th.

* * *

Walker's journey towards the perils of the front line had stalled outside Naples. On September 12th he wrote:

Walker.

> I have been to Naples twice since I arrived here. Dan and I made friends with some American pilots who flew us over in a Liberator and I came back the next day in a Fortress – quite fun! The normal means of travelling is the old hitch-hike. Lifts are plentiful and it isn't difficult to travel long distances in quite a short time. It is surprising when I think of the large-scale preparations and trouble that precede a journey to Frinton, whereas here a journey of a hundred miles or so is a very ordinary proposition. At night it is not so easy and we took 5½ hours last Saturday, travelling on the backs of lorries in company with drunken soldiers, driven by

half-crazy Wops, passing through the ruins of many towns, and picking up an Italian whose truck had overturned by the roadside and made quite an unpleasant mess of him ... My other activities during the comparatively short time I have been here amount to generally seeing, eating, and drinking as much of Italy as I can before we really get down to the business with the Regiment.

The sights one sees are of course quite appalling – everywhere shows signs of the battles and nowhere have I seen a village or town which is not half in ruins and crawling with unimaginable filth and squalor. Most people treat the Italians like dirt, which they probably deserve, but I am not sure that it does much good. But it is all absorbingly interesting.[7]

Our last weekend in Naples was most pleasant. We drove out along the coast to Sorrento with Jacobine [Hichens][8] and two of the other girls, and of course lunch and dinner at the club, which is always wonderful. Food in all the big places is wonderful and of course drink flows everywhere. I can't tell you how much pleasure we have had knowing Jacobine. Dan and I – both of us, which is surprising – like her so much, and I think she tolerates us pretty well! I hope one day you'll be able to meet her.[9]

On the night of September 15th, Walker went to hear a concert conducted at the San Carlo Opera House in Naples by Robertson's Wykehamist nephew, James Robertson.[10] His move, when it came the next day, was as sudden as it was welcome:

We are really quite lucky to be getting away so quickly, as life in a backwater such as this is soon liable to make you very dissipated and slack through its inactivity and remoteness from anything approaching action or excitement. One's feelings, however, are always mixed on such occasions, and it does seem rather futile to be pouring men into the Italian campaign with the war so nearly over and the Italian battle having little bearing on the final situation compared with the gigantic advances through the Siegfried Line – but still, that's neither here nor there. Dan and I have got what we wanted, and if we see a bit of action we shall be so measurably more confident and older that one cannot regret the opportunity. On the other hand we may not see action, which will be disappointing but probably more of a relief for you.[11]

* * *

In mid-September Elliott-Binns had two weeks' leave,[12] and his next letter to Robertson tells us how he spent it:[13]

As you can see I am still in Italy, where I have remained faithfully ever since I landed, nearly a year ago. . . . I have managed to see quite a lot of Italy; most of the big towns which we have captured. I had a leave in Rome and saw quite a bit of it. I am ashamed to say that I was more interested in the mediaeval than the classical side. I have seen too much of ruins to be really interested in them. All the same I have seen a lot of the ruins of Rome, and also Pompeii, and Ostia, which in my opinion is much the more interesting and pleasant to look at of the two.

Elliott-Binns.

The rest of his letter found him in nostalgic mood, and as usual McMurtrie was never far from his thoughts.

I am still in the same Troop as when I last wrote, and the same job, Gun Position Officer, though in spite of that I have been to more OPs than any other officer in my Battery, though I would not mention it before our Captains. I really feel quite an experienced soldier, and am very superior and fatherly to the rookies who come out, and sneer like anything at base wallahs.

This is dull campaigning compared to Anzio, just a steady advance over bad ground in appalling weather at times. It is much the same as the fighting between Anzio and Cassino, but now I have my own guns to look after …

I want to hear how things are with you and Winchester and all those I knew. I suppose a great many are in Holland now and probably you have some bad news for me.

I don't know if I told you, but I found out where Duncan's grave is. It is just outside Anzio looking down onto the sea. The sea being there makes him seem nearer home. I managed to get down there a couple of times, when I had a day off after being up with the infantry. I enjoyed the walk through the spring woods after being cooped up in an OP.

It really does seem nearly over now. Having seen a bit of foreign countries I have made a resolution to see my own, the bits I know and the bits I don't, when I get back. Winchester is certainly one of the first places I must go to. I think of it quite a lot now that things are fairly leisurely. It makes me realise what a lot I have to be thankful for.

I am afraid this is a very meandering letter. It is written late at night between firing.

* * *

Walker's 'rather futile' offensive was now concentrating on the coastal plain towards Rimini, but before that could happen, the area around Coriano had to be secured. On the afternoon of September 13th, still reeling from the fighting at Gemmano, 7OBLI were warned to prepare for a night attack on the Sensoli Ridge. From just east of Morciano they forded the Conca before marching to Cevolabbate, from where the suggested route was a steep track leading through a mine-riddled jumble of paths, covered by heavy German fire. 7OBLI declined that option, and halted east of Cevolabbate before moving up two miles to the cemetery of San Savino, their start line for the attack. It was 1900hrs before the Company Commanders got a glimpse of the ground which they were to cross to their objective, 2¼ miles to the west. From the San Savino ridge they would have to cross two more before reaching the Sensoli Ridge – in the dark, and moving on a compass bearing of 291°. Edmunds' 'A' Company would be one of two companies in the lead, in a compact extended line, with the Intelligence Section steering from the middle and the other two companies following in file formation behind Battalion HQ. On each ridge the Battalion would halt to reorganize. At the final road junction, 'A' Company were to push towards Sensoli and Point 164. It was a difficult task, and 7OBLI were an hour late in starting. When they moved out at 2300hrs, 'A' and 'B' companies made only slow progress, and on reaching the first ridge at 0300hrs on September 14th discovered that they had lost 'C' and 'D'. Stretcher-bearers who had been the 'link' party had fallen asleep during a halt. Luckily, no opposition was encountered, and by 0615hrs 'A' Company had taken some fifty prisoners and were firm on their objective at Sensoli. However, 'B' Company fired

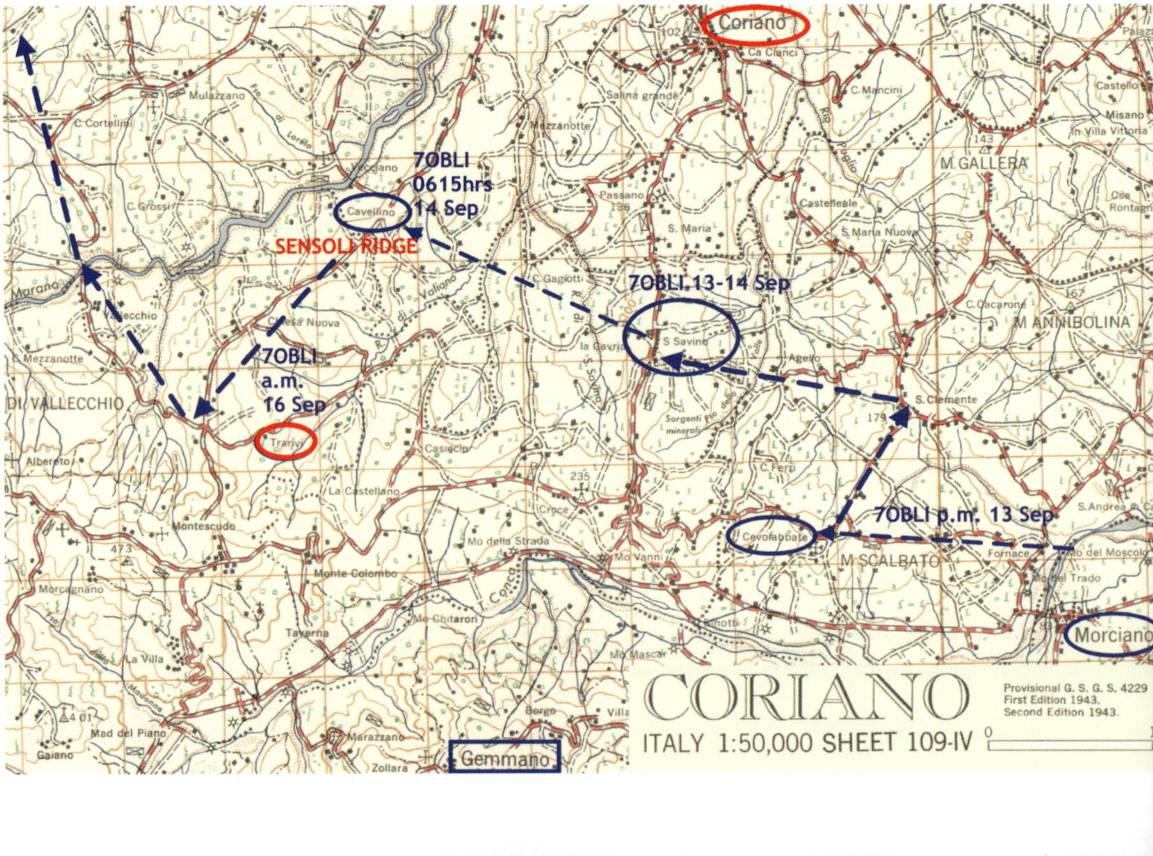

a flare to signal their own success, which brought down the wrath of the Germans in the form of a counter-attack supported by tanks. 'B' Company were driven back, but by now tanks and support weapons were coming up. Very heavy fire from snipers, artillery, mortars, and tanks poured down on to 7OBLI's positions, though 'B' Company re-took their objective by 1300hrs. Three hundred prisoners, a lorry, a 75mm anti-tank gun, and nine 81mm mortars testified to the success of the operation. It was impossible to go any further, however.

The next day's phase was to push across the River Marano, Mulazzano on the far side being captured that night. 7OBLI followed on September 16th, advancing some four miles to Monte Olivo, but a commanding enemy position at Trarivi on the left flank threatened their route forwards through Vallecchio. As soon as 7OBLI set out in the darkness before dawn, heavy fire lashed 'C' Company, reducing it to a pitiful forty men, with only a single officer. 7OBLI were unable to make progress until Trarivi had been cleared by other troops.

The following day was spent resting. 7OBLI were in a parlous state, as the Battalion's own history makes clear: 'Companies were now commanded by inexperienced officers, and had not the backing of experienced NCOs. They were very reduced in numbers, and everyone was in need of a good rest.'

As a result, instead of forming the tip of the spear, 7OBLI now found themselves relegated to flank protection. Edmunds and 'A' Company moved forwards at 1500hrs on September 18th in Bren-gun carriers, heading for dominating ground near Ceriano, the last ridge before the Po Valley. The rest of the Battalion was ferried forwards in trucks. Their advance was halted by shell-fire near Vecciano, and on reporting to HQ 7 Armoured Brigade for orders, 7OBLI were blithely assured that all they needed to do the next day was to follow the tanks, which would do all the fighting.

* * *

Walker's journey to the front continued. On September 18th he spent the night in Orvieto:

> This is the nicest place I have yet been to. In peace time it was famous for its white wine, cathedral, and general antiquity. I spent last night listening to the piano in an Italian house which belonged to quite well-to-do Italians. I was very warmly received, and the daughter played Scarlatti, Bach, Brahms, and Chopin superbly. It was an incredible performance, as Scarlatti is very difficult and she played it faultlessly. Then we drank *vino* with ice and talked of music and war and the Americans. Her mother and a British Sergeant Major were the remainder of the party. The house, though unlike British houses in decoration, was filled with little ornaments, cushions, and portraits of musicians and friends and flowers and china – all in extremely good taste. I thought myself very lucky to have spent such an entertaining evening. I met James Robertson in Naples and had lunch yesterday in Rome. Rome is magnificent.[14]

* * *

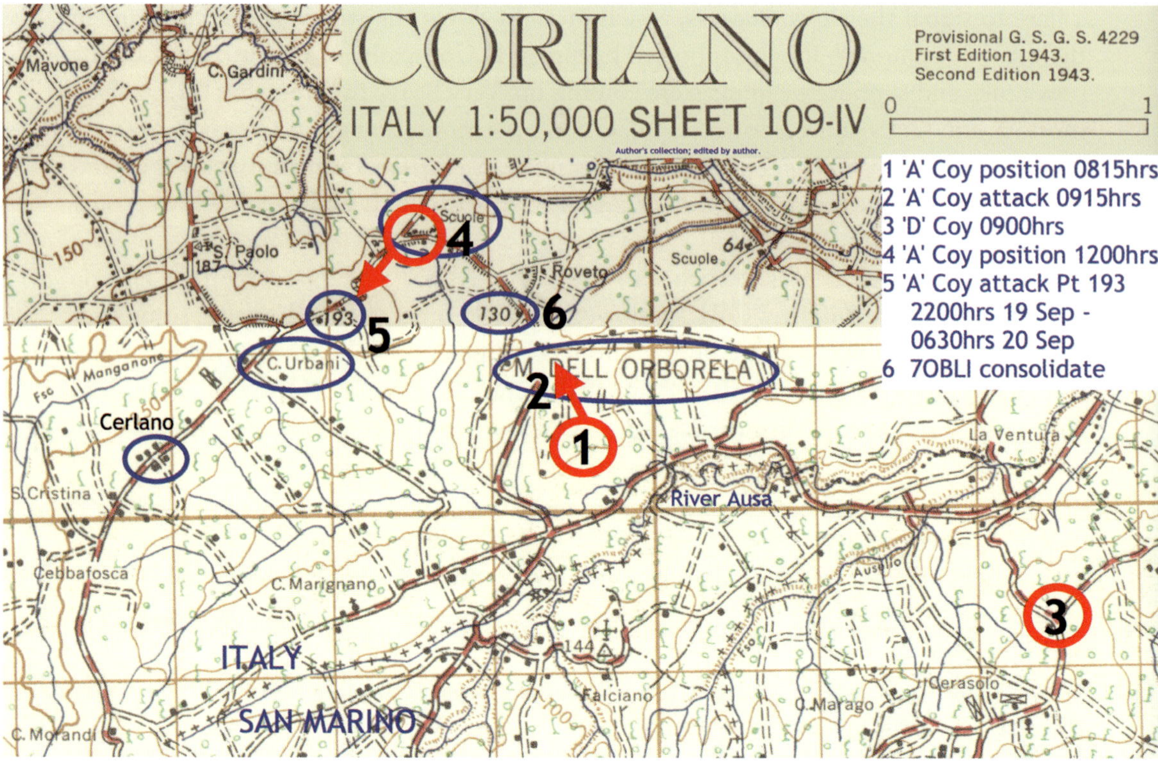

At 0215hrs on September 19th, Edmunds and the men of 'A' Company received instructions to go forwards under command of a squadron of 8RTR, who were up ahead on the River Ausa. Although chaos ensued owing to the *laissez-faire* attitude of the Brigadier, by 0815hrs 'A' Company were at their rendezvous. But so vague were their instructions and so poor the communications that the 'A' Company Commander left Edmunds in charge whilst he rushed back to Battalion HQ in search of more information. Of course, at that very moment his Company received orders to advance at 0845hrs.

The Brigadier now appeared, and started trying to run the battle for the 8RTR/7OBLI battle-group. As at Homs eighteen months before, such interference was unwelcome and potentially dangerous.

> He suggested that an advance be made across the Ausa up to Scuole (7891) – a road junction north-east of C. Urbani (7790) – followed by a move south-west to Cerlano (7690). He asked the Commanding Officer if he considered such an advance practicable. This was difficult to answer, as the attack was an armoured one, no reconnaissance could be made, and the enemy dispositions were unknown. The move south-west up to Cerlano did not appear to be a sound proposition, as it was across the enemy's front. It was quite obvious that the tank commander wanted to be left alone to fight his own battle in accordance with the development of the situation, and not be influenced by his Brigade Commander. The enemy could view the whole area of action from the high hills to the west, particularly from the independent state of San Marino, where rocky pinnacles rose up like some castle in fairyland. A fantastic suggestion was made that

all this ground be smoked by use of the whole Corps artillery. This was resisted, and the artillery used in close support in the battle.

Enemy shell-fire was becoming a real problem, and fresh German troops were coming into the line; speed was of the essence. 'A' Company crossed their line of departure at 0915hrs and, with the support of 8RTR, captured Point 140 (Monte Dell Orborela). The Brigadier ordered them to push on to Scuole – not, in fact, a place-name, but a primary school at a junction – whilst 'D' Company and another 8RTR squadron were to move up to Point 140. 7OBLI protested that it would take time to bring 'D' Company up, as they were on foot and being heavily shelled.

> Brigadier Prior-Palmer, speaking on the wireless from his HQ in rear, refused to accept any delay. He stated that the Cerlano Ridge was unoccupied, no enemy could be seen from the air, and ordered both companies to go forward riding on top of the tanks of their respective squadrons. Not only did this lead to immediate friction and disagreement between the Brigadier and the Commanding Officer, but the order was impossible to execute. The Brigadier did not appear to appreciate the time a company takes to walk across country.

By 0900hrs, in fact, 'D' had halted at a cross-roads a kilometre short of the Ausa. Ignoring the Brigadier, 7OBLI and 8RTR agreed to delay the attack until 1130hrs, but 'D' Company only reached 'A' at 1055hrs and were left behind when their tank squadron moved out. 'A' Company, meanwhile, had obeyed the Brigadier's orders to the letter, riding forwards on tanks. They reached Scuole at 1200hrs, badly disorganized, and then all Hell broke loose as the enemy concentrated its fire on the leading squadron of tanks, and 'the area was soon a tank graveyard.'

It took 'A' Company two hours to consolidate their position, by which time the situation was fouled up beyond recognition; the tankers' chatter on the radios drowned out any attempts by 7OBLI to contact its own units; 'D' Company were out of touch; casualties were flooding in from both tanks and infantry, but 8RTR's medical arrangements had broken down and 7OBLI had to do its best to help; under shell-fire, the tanks battened down their hatches, rendering them safe but vulnerable to German infantry – those which had gone forwards without infantry support were now begging for it, but the tanks were drawing fire and the infantry trying to help them suffered badly in doing so. By 1700hrs, even in the rear, 'C' Company had been reduced to eighteen men (still with one officer), and 'B' Company to thirty-five men with only three surviving officers; they were combined into one under-strength rifle company.

'D' Company were located and finally went forwards at around 1400hrs to support 'A' near Cerlano. They made contact with the left flank of 'A', but at that point a tank unit from the neighbouring 1st Armoured Division moved up behind 'A' and opened fire on 'D' Company: 'This was, to say the least of it, a most unfortunate accident.'

The combined 'B/C' Company moved forwards to assist at 1715hrs, but the Company Commander was wounded and the unit withdrew by 1900hrs. As heavy rain and German shells continued to fall, and communications remained confused, 8RTR pulled back to form a tight leaguer, as had been standard practice in the desert but was wholly unsuited to the terrain. The tanks asked 'A' and 'D' Companies for close protection, but when the Commanding Officer of 7OBLI found out he put his men back into a proper defensive line. As it turned out, this was a wise decision.

Later that night, a probe forwards by 'A' and 'D' companies towards Point 193 encountered stiff opposition and the units returned to Scuole. At first light the following day, at the northernmost point which Eighth Army had then reached, a heavy enemy counter-attack fell on 'A' and 'D' companies, forcing the two weak units back.

> The situation was now so critical that the Commanding Officer went forward with the Battery Commander to restore the situation. It was soon apparent that the Regiment was too weak to re-take the ground lost. 'A' Company was only twenty strong. 'B' Company was therefore ordered to occupy a defensive position about Point 130. It was in this action that Lieutenant M.C. Edmunds, commanding a platoon of 'A' Company, was killed.

On September 22nd, the shattered 7OBLI was broken up to provide reinforcements for other Battalions.

> TOPSEC.
> Personal to Lieutenant-Colonel HOUCHIN, commanding 7 OXF BUCKS, from LEESE. I much regret the reduction of your Battalion to a cadre on account of the reinforcement situation. Your Battalion has a distinguished record in this war. Its battles include ENFIDAVILLE, SALERNO, the VOLTURNO, CAMINO and GARIGLIANO, ANZIO, and recently MONTEFIORE, GEMMANO, SENSOLI, and the CERIANO ridge. My thanks and best wishes to you all.

* * *

> Dear Bobber,
> You are one of the few people whom we do not want the papers only to inform that Michael was killed in Italy on September 23rd.[15] We know no details of course. From what I have heard, 'I' House has had more than its share …
>
> Don't bother to sympathise. We are quite sensible people and nothing does real good.
>
> I am just off to Northern Ireland to give up my job and bring everything home. There is no emergency there now and I can be of more use here.
>
> Yours ever
> Maurice Edmunds
> Regards to both from us both.[16]

> My dear Bobber,
> I have delayed answering your letter until I knew something. The Colonel's letter took a month to arrive, and the Padre's only came on Friday. Your kind note was much appreciated by us both. My own wish was to say 'no letters' in *The Times*, and yet it is strange how much they help, as certainly we have had shoals and all answered! They are most from Evie's and my friends, for Mi had no young life and was only known

at Winchester and to the young people in North Oxon. His was as you say a case of 'gifts and promise' more than achievement. My wife is marvellous, and though she and I were prepared and had been for some time, the blow is wickedly hard. He and I were intimate friends, a happy thing for father and son to be.

After being gazetted Mi served at the Depot and then the 70th (Young Soldier's) Battalion of the Regiment in Northern Ireland, where I was able to see a lot of him. From there he went to 2nd Battalion – airborne – but didn't take to glider work and asked to go, whence he was posted to 7th Battalion, which proved to be the outstanding fighting battalion of the Ox and Bucks. He was in India, Persia, and Iraq, and Egypt, then North Africa, followed by Sicily and Italy. There the Battalion was cut up in, I think, the Anzio business, and Mi was wounded. The Battalion was made up again in Egypt, where they had a good time and Mi was subjected to the attentions of Paget and other old friends of mine; a bit hard for a young boy!

Then back to Italy, this time to Eighth Army. Mi had by then reverted from Captain second-in-command of a Company to become Intelligence Officer, obviously his bent – but up on the Adriatic he was left out as second-in-command the reinforcement company ('5%ed' as we used to call it last time).

The Battalion's attack succeeded and reached the furthest point Eighth Army had got beyond Rimini, but the Boche 'reacted' and reinforcements were called up covered by tanks. The Boche put a heavy barrage on the reinforcements and Mi was killed instantaneously. He was buried on the spot, and will be re-buried at San Marino. I understand the Battalion was reduced to five officers and sixty men, and is out again for reconstruction.

This is a purely factual account and is for an ex-soldier to understand. Don't bother to write again, as nothing now can be done and I expect there are other cases to deplore.

I came back rather reluctantly from Northern Ireland on Thursday and am now to be County Commandant of Cadets! What next?

With all regards to your sister and yourself.

Yours sincerely

Maurice Edmunds[17]

* * *

7OBLI was not the only unit being disbanded. The Army was implementing the PYTHON scheme, whereby all personnel with over 4½ years' service overseas were repatriated. Since Walker's unit – the Royal Wiltshire Yeomanry – had been overseas since February 1940, over 80 per cent of its personnel were due to go home. After personal intervention by Churchill, the core of the Regiment returned to England, but the remainder were dispersed to other units. So when Walker reached his Regiment on September 26th, it was but a fleeting visit:

I have moved … a good deal nearer the fun and games and well within earshot of the guns.

Yesterday Daniel and I took a day off to visit the Regiment proper [at Jesi], which we hadn't done before – the RWY. We arrived at the Mess during dinner, wet through and very dirty. We were, however, treated like Generals – one on each side of the Colonel, surrounded by the Second in Command and Squadron Leaders, who wouldn't let our glasses fall below the half-way mark. We then listened away the evening while they all reminisced in true bufferish, blimpish, Yeoman style, making us laugh till we ached, and the old *vino* jug went round and round the whole time. The next morning I had my first hot-water shave since I left England, and after a wonderful breakfast returned here … We use a small and draughty garret in one of the few houses left habitable in this part, while the Italian family living in the other room try and stop the baby's perpetual screaming or mend the tiles on the roof.

I hope to move to a Regiment shortly – probably 10th Hussars – and then life will become more interesting. That we have not and can not join our own Regiment, and the reasons, I expect are now clear to you; but if you do feel you haven't much of a clue, Dan's father will explain. It is a great pity and a disappointment, as what we saw of the Regiment we both liked so much and would have felt at home so easily. The 10th too is a good Regiment, but being regulars obviously different, and it may take us a little longer to find our feet – but we hope to go with two other RWY officers who we both like immensely, so things should be all right.[18]

Walker's diary recorded his reception by 10th Hussars:[19]

Thursday September 28th
Daniel and I had an interview with the Colonel of 10th Hussars yesterday, and we expect to go to the Regiment sometime today. Quite what happens then we don't know … I feel comparatively confident. A boy called Gordon Scott is going with us to the 10th. Only 21, he has been with the Regiment two years and is exceptionally easy to get on with and very interesting, modest, and comforting to talk to.

Dying is the one subject nobody seems to talk about. I suppose it is better that way. Thirty minutes later; we go to the 10th this afternoon.

Friday September 29th
Written in a cow shed … about seven [miles] north of Coriano or three north-west to Rimini. I am now in the 10th Royal Hussars. We (Dan, Gordon Scott, and myself) arrived last night having travelled in an open truck … taking four hours over the five mile journey. We were, however, well received by the Adjutant, warmed with rum produced by the MO, and served with a good plateful of the traditional 'M and V'. Everyone in the RHQ Mess was exceptionally good to us, and about 2100hrs we were left to ourselves for the night, the Mess Tent precariously positioned above us with definite signs of its coming to grief in the near future – which it undoubtedly did. At 0300hrs the crisis came. Gordon on his bed, Dan on a table, and myself on two benches were all drenched (except me) and there was a threatening bulge in the middle of the roof which must have held many gallons of water. After the most unenviable manoeuvre – everything wet and covered with mud – we eventually clambered into bed …

This morning we were taken to our respective Squadrons; Dan to 'C', Gordon and myself to 'A'. Our Mess had just finished breakfast, and after the usual introductions we joined in the general moan about the unbearable dampness and wet that had spoiled everyone's night's sleep. The rest of the day has been spent meeting all the new people here, eating and drinking, and trying to find somewhere to sleep tonight – inspecting pig-sties and similar hovels as prospective sites!

It is all intensely interesting and the greatest fun, full of new, exciting, experiences. I love it, and I am looking forward to recording the many new impressions which are bound to come along – meantime, goodnight to you and the candle!

* * *

Faced with mountains 6,500ft high as they tried to break their way through the Apennines, the British had been forced to abandon motorized transport and to begin once again to make use of mules. On September 24th Lieutenant Colonel Darling, Kemp's commanding officer in 7RB, took a calculated risk, setting out on foot along Route 67 with a platoon-sized escort. Nine miles later, at San Benedetto in Alpe, Darling found two bridges intact, which 7RB successfully protected that night when the Germans sent a patrol with a mule-load of explosives to destroy them. But beyond the bridges, the road had been blown, and whilst engineers laboured to repair the breaches, intense shell-fire made any advance impossible.

Further along the road stood Bocconi, beyond which was yet another demolition, covered by yet another German outpost. The Germans were only in platoon strength, but all the advantages of the terrain lay with them. 7RB studied the ground with care, and decided that only a flanking movement had any chance of success. However, this would not be easy, as the Battalion's official historian explained:

> The only approach was by a long detour to the left, involving a march along a narrow and precipitous mountain ledge, finally coming in on the position from the rear. To protect this route … 7RB had first to capture Monte Freddo.[20]

As well as Monte Freddo – 'Cold Mountain', which would live up to its name – Monte Fuso ('The Spindle') had also to be secured. 'C' Company were sent up Fuso on September 28th, but when Darling visited them there on the following morning he found that one man had died of exposure in the night and that the other Riflemen were in 'very poor physical condition'. He pulled his men off the summit forthwith and into the shelter of houses: none too soon, as the Germans shelled Fuso immediately afterwards.

From the high peaks amidst which 7RB were operating, Ravenna could be seen fifty miles away – on a clear day. But there were few clear days: the weather was conspiring against the British. 'General Winter', which had saved the Russians in 1941, now helped to stave off the inevitable defeat of the German forces in Italy.

* * *

Given that there were so many Wykehamists in Italy at the time – for example, Walker's Squadron Commander was Geoff Ford North MC,[21] and in 'A' Squadron there was a different Henry Brooke[22] – it should not surprise us that Walker and Middleditch met on Saturday September 30th:

> After a glorious night, considering the smell of cows, pigs, dogs, cats, and bad wine and grape husks, I woke to a wonderful breakfast at 0930hrs with two eggs and bacon. This afternoon Gordon, Campbell, and myself took the Jeep into Morciano intending to get kit at the officers' shop. This proved fruitless, as they refused to serve our Division, but I met David Middleditch (Hopper's) and Douglas Rae (son of Reigate Bank Manager) … A plane came over and dropped a few bombs this evening, quite near. The Bofors opened up and it looked like a fireworks display.[23]

Middleditch and his Regiment had been sitting in the rain for some days, awaiting the call to join the advance. The area in which they were operating had been totally wrecked by war, and there were few buildings standing in which to shelter. Two weeks later, they were still waiting.

The fighting had now reached its climax for the year. The Gothic Line had been breached, Rimini captured, and the German defences in the Apennines outflanked. The German commander, Kesselring, faced a real possibility of being surrounded and twice begged Hitler for permission to withdraw from Italy entirely. But it would take until May 1945 to drive the Germans out.

* * *

7RB kept up their attempts to clear Fuso and Freddo. On October 1st their observation post on Fuso was shelled; below, Sappers and Riflemen were hacking out a Jeep track to lessen the distance over which mules had to be used – but the weather closed in again and stopped work in the small hours of October 2nd. A platoon made it on to the summit of Freddo the following day, but when two sections went forwards over the crest they were immediately spotted by the Germans, who rained heavy machine-gun and mortar fire on them. The Riflemen were pinned down, unable to retreat for a time, and took heavy casualties: of about twenty men, four were killed and seven wounded.

The plans for the assault on the German outpost beyond Bocconi were therefore changed; instead of crossing Freddo, the attackers would skirt the feature and work down to the road beyond the demolition. 'A' Company were to make the attack. As the operation proceeded in the morning darkness of October 4th, communications broke down, but by 0615hrs the men were in position, having taken no casualties but having killed one German and captured four. The Germans had guessed what was happening, and had withdrawn, leaving behind only an infantry section as rearguard. One can only admire the strenuous efforts which the Riflemen made, and commiserate with the frustration which they felt when after all their hard work and suffering they found the enemy had, once more, slipped away. Worse still, the Germans shelled the breach in the road mercilessly for the next three days and nights, preventing the engineers from completing a new bridge until dawn on October 7th.

Apart from patrol work, there was little for the men of 7RB to do; as a diversion from their privations, on the evening of the 7th there were three screenings of Orson Welles' version of *Jane Eyre.* The Battalion would hold its ground for the next ten days, but on October 16th 7RB were withdrawn. For the next five months the front line remained almost entirely static, with only local limited advances. The Riflemen of 2RB, 7RB, and 10RB engaged mostly in static defence and aggressive patrolling. Wykehamist Jim Wilson described life over the winter as follows:

> Our opponents, 715th Division, included a fair proportion of Poles and Alsatians, neither of whom had their heart in the conflict. Patrol clashes consistently went our way, and during the next month 61 Brigade inflicted seventy casualties on the enemy – including the capture of thirty-seven prisoners of war – without losing a single prisoner ourselves. Life, despite heavy rain, might well have been worse; nearly everyone had a *casa* as a base. We became used to the tempo of mule supply, while the routine of fourteen days at the sharp end followed by a week at the Battalion's base, Grassina, south of Florence, provided variety.[24]

* * *

Holtby, meanwhile, was in Palestine, and thoroughly fed up. After the break-out from Anzio early in June, he and four other officers had been sent to the 5th Division Tactical School, and when 6th Seaforths had left for the Middle East in July, he had been left behind as part of the 'Rear Party'. But he had caught them up, and wrote to Robertson from Palestine on October 10th:

Holtby.

Many thanks for your letter and all the news, it was a great pleasure to get it, although I'm sorry to hear about David Martyn. I'm very out of touch here and it's the first I've heard of how anyone from Winchester has fared in France.

[James Robertson's] concert in Naples was a great success and I had the pleasure of taking Phillippa out to dinner and once again before I left for the Middle East. She is really most excellent company, and I thoroughly enjoyed both evenings. It is most refreshing to be able to have dinner with anyone like that; the company of the Mess gets very trying after a time, although really they are a very good set on the whole (even if none of them are Wykehamists!) …

I'm glad John McArthur is still going strong. I'm sure Sheila and you enjoyed your spell down there; they are a very pleasant family.

I'm very fit, for myself, but even more bored; I wish we would either go home or back into action. This sitting about is very trying.[25]

* * *

Murray.

Murray and the Lovat Scouts had been conducting a vicious little war of patrols in the mountains since August, until at the end of October they withdrew and went for a rest in Arezzo. For the first week of November they did absolutely nothing other than send leave parties to Florence. However, on November 8th the Regiment rushed into the Apennines to relieve a Polish unit, taking up positions near Monte Sacco, almost exactly half-way between Florence and Ravenna. Settlements were few and far between in this rugged landscape, and patrolling focused on the village of Modigliana, south of Faenza; as Intelligence Officer, Murray was busy co-ordinating the reports of these patrols, identifying enemy units, and interrogating prisoners. On November 15th the Lovat Scouts were the first troops into Modigliana after the Germans pulled out.

* * *

With 16th/5th Lancers, Brooke finally had leisure in the second week of November to write to Robertson again:

Brooke.

Since [May] we have had a pretty easy time except for the odd day or so. The only trouble is that we've never really been out of the line until now. But looking back on it one can't help thinking that if the Germans had made a really determined stand we'd never have got as far as here. It's not so bad for us but it's absolute Hell for the poor infantry who have to climb all these mountains and live up there. All the Italians say that they have never seen such rain as we have had in the last few weeks. Rivers rose fifteen to twenty feet and washed away even the normal bridges. Still, I am extremely glad I'm not in Burma …

I have really very little news of OWs except that John Persse was killed near Perugia and our Colonel John Loveday was killed the first day across the Rapido … Also John Bodley in the Rifle Brigade.

I am very glad Nick [Somerville] is doing so well. I always thought he'd make a good soldier. I rather fear that wave of optimism for an early finish to the war was very wrong. The Germans seem to be fighting as hard as ever … I hope these V2 rockets won't cause as much damage as the flying bombs as I don't like the thought of Mummy being in London. Please excuse this peculiar colour in ink [red].[26]

* * *

In late October, after orders, counter-orders, and cancellations, 12RL had at long last followed the Allied advance north of the Apennines to Forlimpopoli, near Forli on the ancient Via Emilia which connected Rimini and Bologna. On October 26th to 27th, the Regiment – including Middleditch, who appears to have switched to command 3 Troop at around this time – took over a three-mile stretch of the banks of the River Ronco, which formed the front line on the right flank of 4th Infantry Division. There they stayed until the advance continued in November.

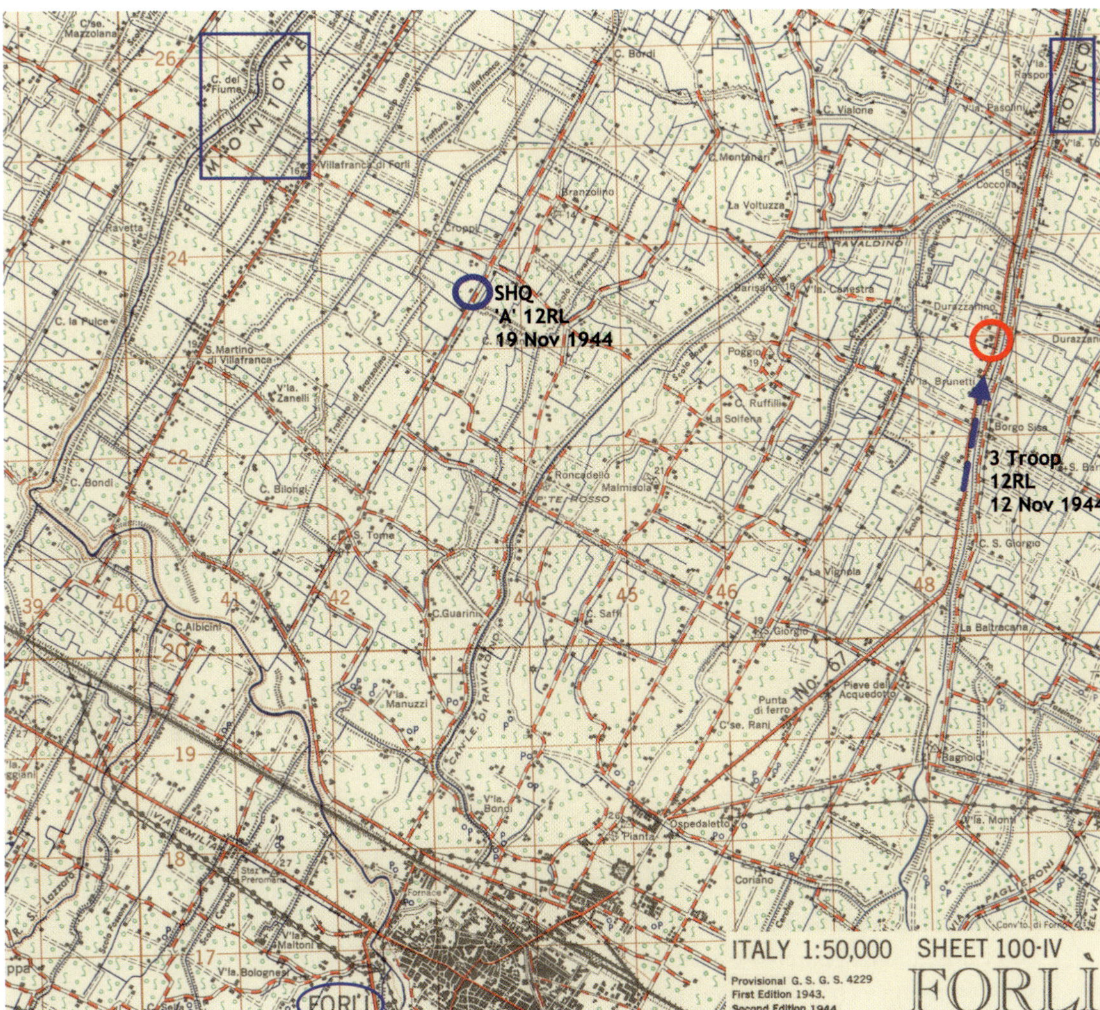

As the advance continued north-west from Forli on November 12th, 12RL provided flank protection along the Ronco, with 'A' Squadron closest to the river. Middleditch's 3 Troop were hard up against the river itself, and therefore were the easternmost unit in the whole attack. By noon all troops were in contact with the enemy, who had a number of positions in houses looking eastwards over the river. Middleditch came under fire at V'la Brunetti, the German position being in a house just to the north. 7 Troop sent a section of armoured cars round to attack from behind, but the Germans reacted with intense mortar-fire and the British were forced to withdraw. That day and the next were frustrating; although the main advance was going well, 12RL could not keep up, their progress hampered by demolitions, mines, and sudden, sharp contacts at close quarters with small parties of German soldiers hiding in houses. Without supporting infantry, 'A' Squadron patrols often had to dismount all their personnel, leave the drivers with the vehicles, and go in on foot.

* * *

Walker was always pleased when his former housemaster wrote: 'Good letters today including a peach from the Bobber bringing sad news of Michael Sinclair's death as a POW – as he said, unspeakably sad – also, he said, Dan Meinertzhagen.'[27]

So eager to see action, Walker finally got his chance in the middle of November, as he recorded in his diary:

> November 14th
> Today we moved up to a small farm. Just beyond – tomorrow or some time – we split the Squadron and go up the line and this time there is no getting out of it! We are pretty near the Germans, and I should think we might easily expect the odd shell tonight.
>
> Up here everything is chaos. I saw my first dead German today – the first dead man, in fact, I have ever seen. The house where our HQ now are is just typical of war and fighting. Everything smells, and it is all so horribly ugly. I talked to one woman tonight. She was dressed in black. She told me her brother had been killed by one of our rifle shots. They had placed him in one corner of the room while the Germans ate, drank, sang, and danced in the same room. She had rather a wonderful restraint about it, which only made it all the more horrible. She must have detested the Germans. Mussolini had brought it all on them, she said …
>
> I myself am in good spirits. I don't feel very brave, nor am I yet too afraid. It all seems somehow quite natural. Tomorrow I am James' rear link, as we are now fighting in half-squadrons. It has now started to rain, which doesn't help.
>
> November 18th
> Well I had my two days so-called battling, which – since I was in HQ – proved no more than a glorified wireless scheme. We were relieved by 'A' Squadron the second evening, and came back that night to the original area … No shell landed nearer than 100 yards, and there were no casualties in the Squadron. 'A' Squadron were not so lucky, and yesterday both Hector Graham and Eric Clarke were hit.

I have now taken over 3rd Troop … They are known as the 'Dead End Kids', and are renowned to be the toughest group in the Regiment – two members of the Troop having a three-year sentence to serve after the war. They are, however, reputed to be extremely efficient.

Walker seated (centre) among the men of No.3 Troop, 10th Hussars, February 1945. (Walker family collection; edited by dansteele.net)

Walker kept a school exercise book with notes on all of his men. From it we learn that they were from a variety of locations and backgrounds:

556774 Sergeant R. 'Barney' Ross – first name not recorded (a motor driver in civilian life back in Southport).
7901540 Lance Sergeant James O'Neill (a baker and pastry cook, from Barnoldswick in Lancashire).
814039 Corporal Charles Arthur Jones (a driller from Birmingham).
320516 Lance Corporal Stanley Jefferson Tate (a fitter from Bristol).
7916109 Trooper Roland Newton Beale (a former transport driver in Worcester).
7901778 Trooper Edmund Clark (a lorry driver from Hanworth).
7899221 Trooper Philip Edward Farr (a tiler from New Milton).
14252830 Trooper Harold Garforth (a Dewsbury mill worker).
4616195 Trooper Russel Hatton (a paper maker from Oldham).

7951682 Trooper Gordon Eric James (listed as a teacher and Apprenticed Aircraft Mechanic, from Hounslow).
4544852 Trooper Harold Newell (a mechanical labourer from Leeds).
321946 Trooper John O'Connor (formerly a butcher in Hull).
7939154 Trooper George Pateman (a civil servant in London).
317060 Trooper Ernest Weaire (a postman from Stoke Newington).
320431 Trooper George Brown (an Apprenticed Electrical Engineer from Newfield in County Durham, who had reverted from Corporal to Trooper in March at his own request).

All were Church of England except Brown (Presbyterian), James (Wesleyan), and O'Connor (Roman Catholic); Beale, Brown, Jones, Ross, Tate, and Weaire were married men, and every member of the Troop was older than Walker, the oldest being fourteen years his senior – even the baby of the Troop, Garforth, was a year older than his commander. Seven of the men had joined the Regiment before the war, the earliest in 1931; the most recent arrivals were Garforth and Hatton, who had joined from other units in January 1944. Despite his youth and inexperience, it was Walker's responsibility to see that they all made it back from the war alive. He felt the responsibility keenly, and formed a strong bond with his Troop. He later discussed the subject in a letter home:

> There is a peculiar, in fact a unique companionship in this sort of life – a common sharing of everything pleasant and unpleasant added to real responsibility – for which at Winchester and later one has been trained and which is now being given a real test. In many ways I find the men far easier to like than the officers. The men are so simple – or, rather, naive – and officers are all so well educated, complicated, and intelligent people, and, I find, rather hidebound – most of them (not the younger ones) living in their own little world; very pleasant, but I should imagine rather boring.
>
> None of us will be sorry when it's all over. I have seen so little of the really tragic side of the war, and my short experiences have been far more like a game – rather like small-game hunting, if there is such a thing – than such as to make me loathe it as much as I ought.[28]

* * *

By November 19th, 12RL were a little further north than before, but still near Forli. 'A' Squadron had taken up positions along the river Montone, with their SHQ almost due west of where Middleditch had been in action the week before. He suffered his second wound of the campaign that day when another mortar-bomb injured him slightly. It was not serious enough to take him away from his unit, as he later told Robertson:

> As regards the wounds that my mother mentioned, they were nothing very serious.... The second was in November [1944] when I got a very small shell splinter in the shoulder and merely spent a few days with the transport before rejoining my Squadron. I gather that my mother was officially notified or I wouldn't have bothered to tell her.[29]

* * *

Walker had his first 'proper' taste of action on November 23rd, when he was very lucky not to lose his friend Dan Awdry:

> After a day of hanging around doing nothing while old Dan was feeling a bit uncomfortable up the sharp end, I went to sleep with a plan all laid on to cross the Cosina at first light and meet the infantry, who were supposed by this time to have captured their objective. At 0200hrs I was woken up, and Geoff told me to go off to Battalion HQ and make another crossing, as things hadn't gone too well. This I did, and met Dan, who was roughly doing the same thing. There was shelling almost all the time, and every haystack on both sides of the river seemed to be brewing (all quite exciting). After eventually having found out what I had to do, I returned to Geoff, told him the form, back to the Troop, and off we went around 0500hrs. I then went off in my tank, saw the Company Commander, had a miraculous brew of tea, and adjusted my steel helmet with a certain amount of apprehension as to what the day would bring.
>
> As it was, Dan had already crossed the river on the left and Tony [Overy] at the same place as I was going. Unfortunately, Sergeant Ross got bogged, thereby blocking the road. It was close by a minefield; the crew of the recovery vehicle had all been wounded by a stonk which fell quite close; and things looked none too promising. In the end, after hopping backwards and forwards several times to the infantry over the river, an Ark[30] came along and we got over. More delay over wireless sets, and we eventually moved on to what turned out to be an unoccupied house. The next objective was held, however, and here I first heard Spandau whistling overhead. I shot up the house and two Germans came out with a white flag. Spandaus on both sides were still holding us up, but eventually the infantry got in and nothing unusual happened. Then we shot up more houses; there was more stonking, mostly from our guns; and we set one bomb blazing beautifully, and that was really that. [We] returned the next evening, having inspected at close quarters the damage we had caused the day before. I suppose at the time I was a bit scared.
>
> Dan, however, did terribly well. Sergeant Moore got a Mark IV, and Dan himself was brewed up, losing all his kit.[31]

* * *

Looking back on the previous six months, Kemp wrote to Robertson on December 4th:

> We had quite a good run up Italy from Cassino to Lake Trasimene, taking part in a number of encounter battles and one heavier engagement north of Perugia. It was here on Monte Malbe that Johnny Persse was killed. Just after this I went down to Rome to defend some people on a court martial. When I got back I took over as 2i/c of 'A' Company and Dick Adams commanded. From Trasimene on the going was much more sticky and we haven't really had any decent sun.
>
> At the moment we have still got a number of hills between us and the fabulous plains of Lombardy, but it's possible to see the plains from neighbouring hills on a clear day.
>
> I myself am in the best of health and any tendencies that I might have had towards rotundity have been checked by miles and miles of walking with mule trains up and

down muddy mountain paths. We have had our first fall of snow and ample rain, but recently the weather has improved, and long may it hold.

There are a number of other Wykehamists about. Bill Adams commands a platoon in our Battalion but is sick at the moment with a form of meningitis; Dick's a Major commanding 'B' Company; John Eggar has just joined us and is 2i/c of 'D' Company. Antony Sturt is at Brigade. Jim Wilson and Tony Pawson are commanding companies in 10RB. Robert Hone is Signal Officer in 2RB. Dick Fyffe commands 10RB and Chris Sinclair, of course, 2RB. Still, I expect that the latter has given most of this sort of news.

You mention in your letter our brigade villa in Florence. It's really delightful and I have been lucky enough to have two spells of leave there.

Have you any news of Guy Richardson, Bruce Fortune, or Charles Duffin? They are the OWs in whom I am most interested, but any news and if possible the address of any of my contemporaries would be very welcome.

Apart from occasional bits of bloodiness when we have to spend a few days in slits at the top of some desolate hill in the rain and mud, or try to coax stubborn mules to go where they don't want to, we really have not at all a bad time. We usually get hold of some farm in which to establish ourselves, and when not actually in action live very well. At the moment we are reserve company and my activities are being directed to procuring a good supply of pigs and turkeys for our Christmas dinner. The Company is starting a small farm back with the rear echelon of the Battalion, and any wandering livestock get whipped up and sent back.[32]

According to Kemp's obituary in 2003 in the *Daily Telegraph*,

he was given the nickname 'Il Capitano Robusto', although he insisted that any reputation which he enjoyed was entirely due to his donkey train's success in liberating the contents of enemy wine cellars and stores, and feeding his company and the local population.[33]

Tracing Kemp's movements is difficult because the 7RB war diary, although superbly detailed and entertainingly written, contains almost no mentions of any personnel by name or appointment; the official history of the Rifle Brigade in the war also has few names below company commander level. Kemp's December letter is the last which we possess. We will therefore leave Kemp and 7RB until the run-up to the final offensive in April 1945.

* * *

Walker had just enjoyed a rather special leave, as he recorded on December 2nd:[34]

I have come to the end of four glorious days of leave in Rome … Tuesday night we decided to spend at a small fourth-class hotel off the Corso Umberto. After a wash and shave I went off to the Eden, and after a late lunch sat down to organise the next four days. I rang up Jacobine and arranged to go to Naples on Thursday, and that afternoon managed to do a little odd shopping. John Powles, who had come with me to Rome, knew some WVS girls, and in the evening we had dinner at the Eden with Marjorie

Farrant, Pop Ealy, and a Bays subaltern. Later Colonel Rodzianko[35] joined us. He was superb and he sat and entertained us for the rest of the evening, beaming perpetually over his four rows of ribbons. Everyone in the Regiment apparently knows him, and as I hadn't met him before, it was as I say superb. We then drank brandy in the lounge while the orchestra played to order.

[Rodzianko] told us he had a private audience with the Pope the next morning, and insisted on trying to take us along with him, which he did. So at 1200hrs on Wednesday he called for us. We drove to St Peter's. Swiss guards would stop us at every courtyard and archway, passes were flashed through the window, and through we went, until eventually we arrived at the Pope Paul residence. We climbed up the great staircases, and by now the place was swarming with guards, all dressed in their original mediaeval costumes designed by Michelangelo. Through ante-room, closet, state rooms, reception rooms we went, where stood sentries and officers of the Vatican Guard, shining with epaulettes and medals, swords, spurs, and heaven knows what.

At last we arrived in one room where we waited for the Pope. He came in, dressed in cream-coloured robes, and as he entered it was really rather beautiful with the red plush carpets, pictures, curtains, and candelabras. We knelt down and kissed his ring, and then stood up and he talked to us in rather broken English with how pleased he was to meet English people and where we lived and what we were doing and how young we were. He seemed so simple and unassuming and unpretentious and reminded me much of Spencer Leeson. Then he blessed us, gave us a small picture of himself, and a little medallion. It was all most impressive.

We then lunched with the Colonel at the Flora; more shopping, tea and a bath at the Eden, and then to dinner with Marjorie and Mary MacSweeney in the black market. This was disappointing, as the dinner was poor and cost too much, but it was made up for by the Columbia Club, where we went to dance and drank champagne while a girl played the xylophone. It is a club run by the ACC, and at first we were refused to go in. The Colonel then arrived and gave the American in charge as good a rocket as ever I've heard, and anyway that was soon settled. It was a very enjoyable evening, and I thought both the girls were charming.

Thursday morning I set off in a TCV [Troop Carrying Vehicle: a lorry] for Naples. It was a dreadful journey and rained hard, with the tarpaulin leaking in every possible place. I met Jacobine. We wandered around the shops, eating hot chestnuts, and after tea drove in her General's staff car to the Orange Grove, where we dined and· danced. Unfortunately I had one too many gins and felt a bit queer. Jacobine too had been suffering from a party the night before, but on the whole the evening was a success and I enjoyed meeting her again.

That night I got a lift in a black American lorry back to Rome, where I arrived at three in the morning. With very treacherous roads through very treacherous country, I was rather frightened, but managed to sleep. After a lift from the Tiber I got a room in the Boston, where I slept until 0830hrs – breakfast, a bath, and then off to the gift shop in the Alexander Club. We went to the girls' flat and had a drink; Marjorie packed my parcels, and I took Mary to lunch. That afternoon I explored St Peter's, was most impressed, and climbed to the very highest dome where only four people can get in at once. Tea at the flat, with a wonderful chocolate cake, and after tea but who should walk in but Michael Wilson, who the Bobber had told me to look out for.[36] Very refreshing and very lucky.

That night we were to spend at Nicolo's family's house in the Via Mercadente. I had called there on Wednesday to arrange it, and these last two nights have really made our leave. They have a most beautiful house with beautiful furniture and everything to remind one of home. To dinner came the Colonel, Bianca Corsi and Brita (two Italian girls, both very sweet), and after dinner Brita's step-mother. We had a beautiful dinner, with white-gloved waiters, wine, and glorious food. Then we sat by a log fire and talked. I loved it. I then arranged to take Brita to the pictures in the Palazzo Venezia and then to lunch the next day. I woke up – breakfast was brought to me in bed – trousers were whipped away to be pressed, shoes to be polished. I had a bath, and the Marquesa told me Brita had phoned to say she had to sell at a fair and would I go and see her there? I then picked up her Mother in the 3-tonner, arranged to pick up Brita for lunch, and then we went round Rome. We saw much that I wanted to see, though there is much more yet. She showed me palaces, monuments, churches with glorious mosaics and frescoes, and a particularly beautiful one – San Clemente – where an Irish monk showed us round. It was glorious, and she was very good to me. Then lunch with Brita on the terrace of the Trocadero. We ate ice-cream and talked of how she had travelled, of Italy and her friends. I thought she was sweet and delightful and altogether it was new and refreshing. Met Colonel Todhunter there, who lent us his Jeep for the afternoon. Down to the opera to book tickets for tonight and then to the picture gallery, which, although I know little of it, I thought wonderful – Brita as my guide. Back to the Clarellis' for a late tea of toasted scones, and then on in a taxi, picked up Mary, and on to the opera. This too was magnificent. We met Ronald Perrill and all went to the Grand for dinner – the best dinner in Rome at £2.00 a head. Still, a fitting end to one's leave and I didn't mind.

* * *

From the sunnier climes of Southern Rhodesia, Huggins wrote to Robertson from the Officers' Mess at RAF Cranborne on December 6th:[37]

I sincerely hope that for all of you at home, this will be the last Christmas under wartime conditions. There are indications that our hopes will come true. I have not heard from anyone in England for some weeks and do not know any news from there. Judging by the paper you are not being blitzed overmuch by the V-2, but then you know what the Press is like. I see that your rations are to be improved – I should think they could import fruit from South Africa and California.

Huggins.

Here in Rhodesia we live a pleasant enough existence. Life as an instructor has its points and I am only 3½ miles from home and cycling is no trouble in these flat regions. I get five gallons a month for a small Austin and that saves taxi fares over the weekends. Out here with no hardships and no war it is only too easy to forget what is going on in Europe. Thank goodness we have the wireless to keep us alive to things. At this distance the morning paper does not maintain one's interest.

Toby Kidd is still teaching navigation at an instructors' school. He is not exactly keen on his job and his ability is not used at all. But then that is so typical of the Services. I expect you have had the photograph of Kidd, Matthews, and myself. Three Twerps!!

My interests at the moment are in civil aviation. In the next two months or so I shall know if they will accept me when all this business is over.

* * *

10th Hussars were by December assisting 56th Infantry Division on the left flank of V Corps. The advance there had stalled in the face of harsh winter weather, determined German resistance, mines, demolished infrastructure, and waterlogged terrain criss-crossed by rivers and canals. Walker was getting to grips with the trials of troop command:

Saturday December 9th
Well, I came back, and like the first day of term it wasn't so bad as I expected. There have been many changes while I was away … 3 Troop still seem in good spirits – and I still like the idea of having to command. Yesterday, Corporal Jones and I went out to fire a Browning. Thank God I'm not worrying these days what impression I am making or how I'm getting on. I am getting better, I hope, or I'm trying at any rate to make up my mind and banish what anyone else thinks about it …

I have a new servant, who at the moment strikes me as rather wet, though efficient nevertheless. I now have two pips, which is comforting but nothing out of the ordinary...

A bit more duffying would be good for me, but maybe it won't be long.

Tuesday December 12th
Pateman came up to me yesterday and asked if he could change crews. I saw Sergeant Ross, who was most helpful and told me not to take any notice and he'd deal with him. So today all seems to be settled, though I must see Pateman myself tomorrow.

December 19th
Midnight. I feel rather superb tonight. We move early tomorrow with the prospect of Christmas in the line – the only squadron. However, here, drinking hot *bianco* punch, I feel indescribably happy. Sergeant Ross was wonderful tonight and it's all – once again I say it – terribly encouraging.

* * *

Meanwhile, Middleditch had bumped into Henry Brooke and other Wykehamists of 16th/5th Lancers:

I recently met Henry Brooke and Christopher Foot (G),[38] when I got away for a day's leave. Henry now bears the MC and Africa Star on his very ample chest. He is even redder and stouter than he used to be, and seems to have done very well. Christopher is Intelligence Officer to the same regiment. Gray of Kenny's has left us; I felt sorry for him as he really was keen and tried very hard, but he seemed to have a genius for doing the wrong thing.[39] Kate Savill and I remain the only two OWs in the Regiment.

I hope that you spent a very pleasant Christmas and have been able to have a good holiday. I expect Chapel is filled with Wykehamists back on leave from Western Europe;

I only wish I was one of them! I heard from Henry that Nick Somerville is Adjutant of his battalion, which is a very good effort if true.[40]

* * *

Fighting continued, however, and Christmas 1944 was far from peaceful as far as Walker was concerned.

We moved up early next morning [December 20th] to Faenza, and by midday had arrived at an O-group of the Royal Fusiliers in a *casa* near the river east of Faenza. That afternoon nothing exciting occurred, and the next day [December 21st] we didn't start till late-ish and little happened except that Sergeant O'Neill got a piece of shrapnel in his eye, and I had to dodge the odd shell myself. We spent that night in another house and had a lovely chicken stew.

The next day [December 22nd] was more eventful. We started by brewing up the odd house, and Sergeant Ross had a good shoot at some Teds [Germans, after the Italian 'Tedeschi'] trying to cross the road. We then advanced quietly until about 1500hrs. We arrived at a small village called Pieve del Castra – after the previous activity we met quite a considerable hail of fire, and Sergeant Ross was firing everything in all directions when I joined him. However, after ditching my tank and generally feeling rather frightened we returned for the night to another house, where 3 Troop were liberally entertained by the young girls who lived there.

The next morning [December 23rd] we played around once again and got stonked quite heavily. That night we got back later than usual after I had imagined us all getting stuck with flat batteries! This time we came to what had been a school at the village mentioned in yesterday's entry; four officers had been expected to dine and as they hadn't arrived we sat down to pasta soup, roast rabbit, cold ham and beef, grapes, wine, and what-not. This was excellent, and we came back to this same house every night after that.

The next day [December 24th] we went down on the right of the Battalion axis and 1 Troop … had come up to help support the left. That day we received the biggest stonk I or even Sergeant Ross or Sergeant O'Neill had ever been in, and certainly the biggest Sergeant O'Neill or I had ever seen. However, we had no direct hit, though they seemed to be all around us. One of the Royal Fusiliers pioneers was killed, which was a pity, as it turned out that the mines he was lifting were unimportant.

Christmas Day began mildly. Sergeant Ross and myself examined the crossing and decided it wasn't on … In the afternoon we supported another attack, and I unfortunately went up on a mine, but got into Sergeant Ross' tank and got quite a good shoot, though the infantry had heavy casualties.

In a letter home written on New Year's Day, Walker gave a little more detail of December 25th:

Christmas Day was spent in different surroundings, though we had our photographs in the morning and hope one day you will be able to see it – me and my Troop all looking quite warlike but full of the 12-o'clock-on-Christmas-morning Wray Mill spirit. That afternoon I went up on a mine, which wasn't much of a present, but no one was hurt and that evening we were able to share a bottle of whisky I had saved up for the occasion![41]

When his parents wrote back to express their concern at their son's experience of being mined, Walker replied with the not-entirely-reassuring 'You needn't have been at all worried about my Christmas Day effort, as I can assure you there are many, many worse things that can happen to you in a tank.'[42]

The next day, with only two tanks, we attacked from a different direction and saved the lives of several infantrymen who were pinned down by Spandau positions. Here again they lost a lot of chaps and it was all rather horrible.

Christmas cards to The Bobber from Middleditch, Murray, and Elliott-Binns.

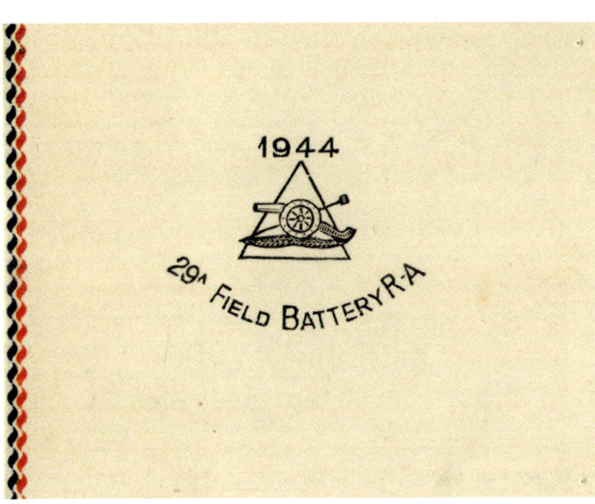

The next morning we were fairly inactive, and in the afternoon, after being relieved by 'A' Squadron, returned to Forli in good spirits, though the billets were somewhat disappointing. Looking back, it doesn't appear as exciting or as strenuous as I seem to remember it was, but one thing that does stand clear is the terrific *esprit de corps* that was present the whole time. Every man in the Troop has so many good points, and it's a wonderful job to be their Troop leader.[43]

Recent experiences have brought new joys, very hard to put on paper – maybe one day I'll try. So much is expected of one, and it's awful yet at the same time rather splendid. When one lives with these chaps one feels very proud. So far it's all been jam – none of my friends have been killed – that's when it must be horrid. Still, no need to be depressing at the moment; I am gloriously happy, so don't worry.[44]

XXV

'I ought to get cracking properly soon'

North-West Europe, August 20th–October 31st 1944

By the middle of August 1944 Allied forces were bursting out of Normandy across a wide front. American troops reached the River Seine on August 19th, but from August 25th Canadian and then British troops made it across this last natural barrier. Somerville, now Adjutant of 2SWB, was in the force tasked with advancing along the coast, crossing the Seine, and taking the port of Le Havre. Such an advance required five river crossings before the Seine, and Somerville stated that 'the Sappers were really magnificent. They were erecting 40ft Bailey bridges – in pitch darkness, over bridges that already had been destroyed – in just under four hours, generally under shell-fire.'

* * *

Boyd.

After their final battles in Normandy, on August 20th Boyd and 1KOSB settled in to La Chapelle-au-Moine. The speed of the advance meant that when they next moved, on September 3rd, their unopposed journey was 147 miles long and ended in Hacqueville, south-west of Rouen. Their war diary noted that 'the country in this area shows very little sign of battle, and the enemy has shown very little or no opposition in his quick withdrawal.'[1]

There 1KOSB rested until September 16th.

* * *

Nick Somerville.

On August 24th 56 Brigade began its own eastwards advance, crossing two rivers as it covered the fourteen miles to the town of Cormeilles. That town fell easily, but as the spearhead troops reached Épaignes five miles further on they met fierce resistance. 2SWB and Somerville were not involved until the 26th. Somerville's diary and memoirs record events:

> We fought the usual pursuit battle and got across four of the rivers with only rather stiffish rearguard actions by the enemy supported by a lot of mortars. When we reached Pont Audemer, however, we found it much stiffer than usual.

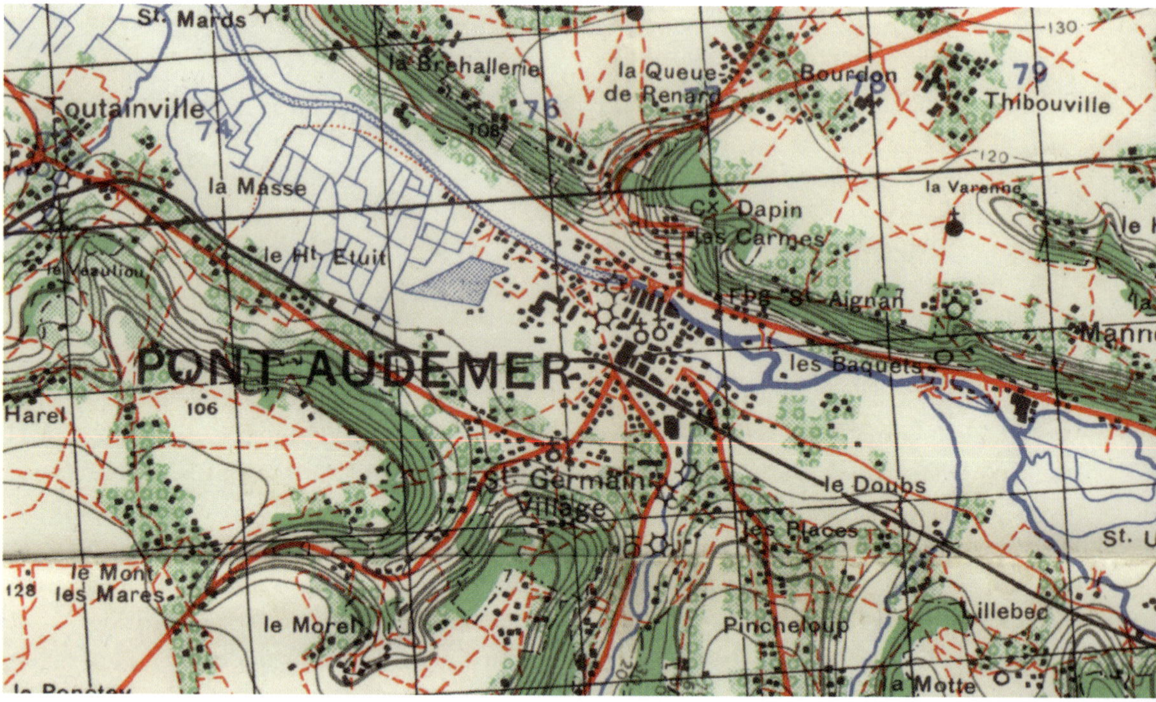

The River Risle was a significant obstacle, in a steep-sided valley thick with trees, and the Germans had of course blown the bridges and positioned mortars, artillery, and machine-guns to cover the approaches. It was the sort of fighting which had been going on in Italy for some time. 2SWB showed great initiative in crossing the river in the centre of the town and pushing on to the dominating heights beyond.

> It was impossible to do anything by daylight, and so two companies, led by a Resistance man, managed to work their way through the town, wade through the river up to their necks, and establish themselves on the high ground behind the town. They laid a signal cable as they went, and during the next day we heard how they were shooting up the unsuspecting Huns as they tried to evacuate the town. During the whole of this operation the town was shelled and mortared, and a number of rockets fell as well, so that at Tac HQ (which was in a house in the town) we had a rather unpleasant night. After two days all the houses had been cleared and only a few odd snipers still remained, so that the Sappers were able to build a bridge that night, and we and the tanks passed over next morning.

Beyond Pont Audemer lay the Seine, which, as it approached the sea, meandered back and forth in great loops. It was so wide that there were no bridges, only ferries, which the Germans were using to get their forces back across the river and on to the high ground to the north, which commanded the flat ground south of the river. In one loop lay the dense Forêt de Brotonne, a main road running through the middle towards the ferry at La Mailleraye-sur-Seine.

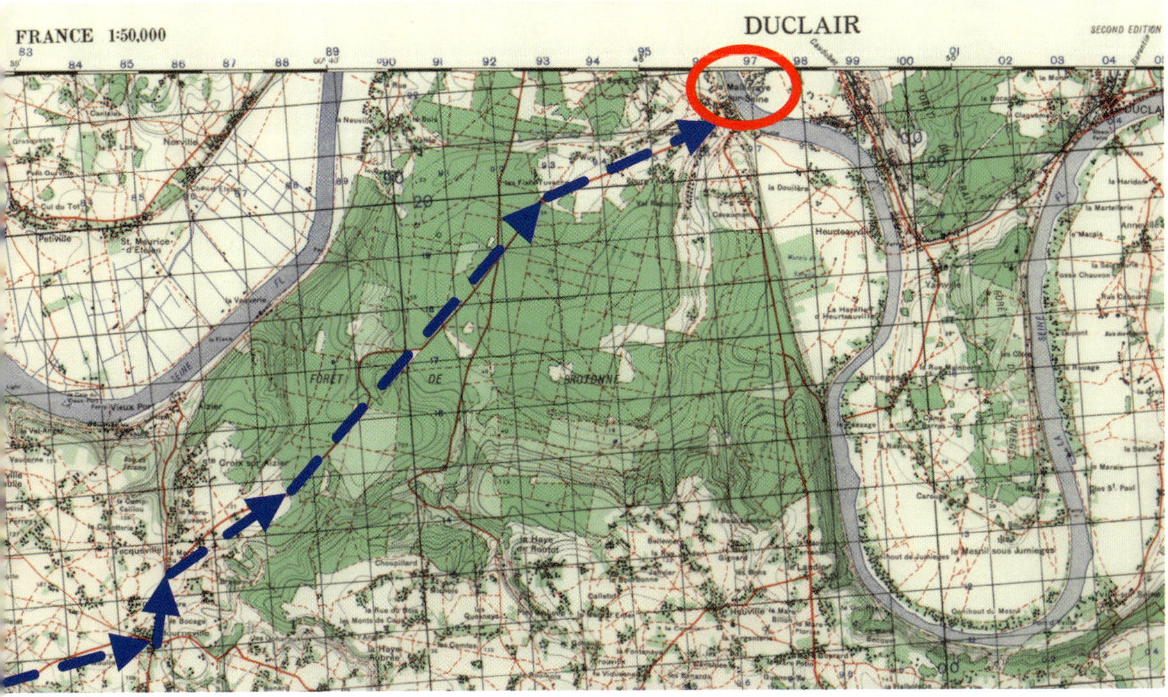

The plan was that the Battalion, with a troop of tanks, would make a dash straight down the main road through the forest and capture La Mailleraye, which was the main ferry that the Boche was using. This plan was adopted because it was thought that the enemy were disorganised and just hiding up in the forest. Accordingly we set out, expecting to be ambushed at every turning, but were lucky to get through going at about thirty miles an hour and captured La Mailleraye just as it was getting dark. We took it with about six hundred prisoners, to the credit of the Battalion, and only a few casualties.

All the banks of the Seine were littered with burnt-out vehicles of all descriptions: *Nebelwerfers,* mortars, 88s, field guns – everything you can think of, all packed together. There were over three hundred vehicles at La Mailleraye alone. All along the river it was exactly the same. The fields were full of hundreds of horses which had been used to pull away all the transport. They all looked absolutely finished; heads hanging, and bones sticking out in all directions. However, you could see that they were at last happy.

If Falaise had been a charnel-house, then the Forêt de Brotonne was the breakers' yard of the German Seventh Army. 2SWB's war diary recorded that the entire forest had been used as a vehicle park, the rides filled with trucks and guns, all waiting their turn to cross, all now burnt-out and abandoned.

* * *

2KRRC pushed across the Seine on August 28th and headed north. By September 1st they were coming up on the Somme, between Abbeville and Amiens. By now, Allied forces were racing across France far more quickly than the Germans had in 1940; the

British referred to their advance as 'The Great Swan' (as in 'swanning about'). As they surged forwards they left enemy forces behind to their flanks who then desperately tried to retreat either in parallel or across the Allied axis of advance. The result was a series of clashes, none of them large in scale but all brutal for those involved.

Lewin.

Lewin had clearly not been very communicative, as a letter from his parents to Robertson shows:

> Dear Bobber,
> How nice of you to write about Robin. We had been a bit worried ourselves as we hadn't heard for nearly a month. But we have had a lovely long letter from him today, dated August 26th. He seems to think they are doing fairly well and his Platoon have taken more than their fair share of prisoners. He went over either on D-Day or the day after – we are not sure which – and his Battalion have been attached to an independent armoured brigade.
>
> We are down here for a week with Jane to give her a rest from the flying bombs – not that she seems to need one much. She seems very well in spite of hard work, long hours, and flying bombs. I am delighted to get away from cooking, so we are all thoroughly enjoying our holiday – Do come.[2]

As 2KRRC advanced to set up blocking positions at Airaines, the beloved Battalion Commander, Lieutenant Colonel Ronnie Littledale, raced ahead in his scout car – only to be engaged at close range by a German anti-tank gun, which killed him instantly. 'A' Company and a squadron of the CLY were sent to take the village and exact revenge. The Germans resisted with determination as the British troops came at them from the north-east, finding the enemy well dug-in on the high ground and in the village houses. Although one platoon alone killed or captured fifty-two Germans for little loss, 'A' Company was unable to break in. Lieutenant 'Dwin' Bramall – later Field Marshal Bramall, Baron Bramall KG, GCB, OBE, MC, JP, DL – was wounded (but survived, and was present many years later at Lewin's funeral). Lewin himself, according to the Battalion history, 'narrowly missed being killed'.[3]

One wishes that this remark were not so cryptic.

* * *

Somerville continued to record events involving 2SWB:

> We spent three days in La Mailleraye, sending patrols over the river in boats, one of which found a German U-boat that had been destroyed in its pen. Our patrols reported that the enemy had withdrawn from the further bank and had retreated to Le Havre. Accordingly, it was decided to cross the river by ferry. The men were to cross by one type of ferry, and the rest of the Battalion went all the way up to Rouen and over the bridge.

2SWB moved to Caudebec for the crossing. 'D' Company crossed safely, but the swiftness of the river and the turn of the tide then caused problems:

> One of 'A' Company's rafts overturned, drowning fourteen men. All rafting was then stopped immediately. This meant that only half the Battalion was over the water, and both the CO and the Second-in-Command were left behind. I therefore had to take over command of what was left, and was able to hand over to Major Dauncey when he arrived with the remainder of 'A' Company.

It was September 3rd 1944. The war was five years old. 2SWB now swung west and headed for Le Havre.

> All the towns and villages that we passed through on our journey to Le Havre gave us the most tremendous welcome, and although we had got up to Le Havre pretty quickly we had had time to stop and crack open a bottle of champagne or *vin rouge*. The next day we were sitting outside the defences.

* * *

2KRRC crossed Robertson's battlefields of the Somme and Ypres at a pace which must have shocked those who had fought across this ground yard by yard in the previous war, and given great satisfaction to those who had retreated across it in 1940. Warlus (east of Amiens) on September 1st; Ligny-sur-Conche on the 4th; *eighty-five miles* on September 5th alone, by-passing resonant names such as Bethune, Givenchy, Festubert, La Bassée, Neuve-Chapelle, Aubers, Armentières, Ypres, Zillebeke, and on towards Ghent. They would have moved faster but for the Belgians:

> While the French had been most welcoming in their reception of the Allies, the Belgians were positively ecstatic. Cheering crowds, flowers, kisses, and even champagne greeted our columns at every village.[4]

Lewin and 'A' Company reached Oudenaarde that evening, but the west flank was very exposed, and the next day 2KRRC faced west along the Lys–Escaut Canal – close to where Rickman and the BEF had defended the opposite bank in 1940 – as trapped German units tried to move eastwards. On September 6th, 'A' Company took a German convoy and 100 men prisoner.

* * *

As 2SWB reached Le Havre, the much bigger and better port of Antwerp fell to the Allies. This was a victory crying out to be exploited; the port facilities were essentially intact, but the approach to Antwerp up the Scheldt estuary was dominated by German forces on the north bank, so the port could not be used. At the same time, just as Antwerp fell, the retreating German troops began to form a defensive crust in front of the Allied advance. They had traded space for time, and succeeded in throwing hastily cobbled-together formations into the line at a moment when the Allied supply routes had become stretched to breaking-point (back in Normandy, 3SG had been stripped of its transport vehicles to help to support 3rd Infantry Division). Among the troops thrown into the German defence were 65,000 men of their Fifteenth Army, who had been trapped on the south bank of the Scheldt, west of Antwerp, but had been allowed to escape across the estuary. The German genius for improvisation saved them from the total collapse which the Allied command believed to be imminent.

* * *

2KRRC moved to Dendermonde, due east of Ghent, on September 8th, and then on to Sint-Niklaas near Antwerp.

> The sight which greeted the Battalion at St Nicholas was indescribable. The whole population of some 60,000 was cheering in a seething mass in the square; so dense was the crowd that it was impossible to move. Every tank and every truck had about twenty Belgians on it, with bunches of flowers, baskets of fruit, and wine, and every good thing for 'Les Tommies'.

The crowd had to disperse when two German vehicles approached from the north-east, though these were promptly brewed up by 'D' Company.

* * *

The Allied plan had called for the capture of Le Havre by D+90; the attack in fact began on the evening of September 10th (D+98). Part of the delay was actually due to Somerville, who came into possession of highly secret German documents stolen from the German headquarters, which enabled the plan of attack to be changed and improved:

> It took a week to plan the battle of Le Havre, and not a single detail was missed. In the middle of the planning a Maquis brought in a file of drawings which he had captured, showing all the defences of the town. I got hold of it at 0200hrs and Division had it by 0245hrs, which shows how important it was. The men spent days practising with tanks and AVREs and flame-throwers and Flails, and eventually we were all ready for the attack. The plan was roughly that 56 Brigade should assault the outer defences from the north, and having made a hole the two other brigades should pass through and clear the town.

Over the preceding week, heavy air raids by Allied bombers had killed some 2,000 civilians whilst trying to degrade the German defences. Many Allied soldiers were shocked by the damage to the town, and in a later interview Somerville confessed to having been appalled to see the damage and civilian casualties caused by the bombing. It was different, however, when the bombing was directed at German front-line positions:

> The attack was preceded by a terrific air bombardment. It really was wonderful to watch. We were only about a mile away. The first aircraft over was a Pathfinder who dropped

> a basketful of little green incendiary bombs. He was followed by wave after wave of Lancasters, all of which dropped their cookies dead on our objectives.
>
> We attacked in the afternoon and, supported by tanks and flame-throwers, we pushed through the gaps that the Flails had made in the minefield, crossed the anti-tank ditch over the bridges that the AVREs were carrying, and went into the objective behind six Crocodiles, actually treading in the flame. 'D' Company … took their objective, which was the first one, but 'A' Company – who were to pass through them – came under concentrated 88mm fire from the right flank and suffered very heavy casualties on their start line. Eventually only ten men of 'A' Company managed to reach their objective. OC 'B' Company, who was waiting to pass through 'A' Company's objective on to the third objective, realised that all was not well, and so assaulted 'A' Coy's position, finding some enemy and the ten men of 'A' Company having a hand-to-hand fight. Having mopped these up, he proceeded to assault and capture the third objective.
>
> Next day … instead of pushing the two other brigades through into the town, the General decided on one of his famous bold strokes – and 56 Brigade, with the infantry riding on the back of the tanks that had shot them on to their original objectives, advanced in three columns straight into the heart of the city with the crowd roaring its applause. It got dark just after we had entered the city, and so we leaguered up for the night in the main street, and next morning proceeded our procession to the dock area, where the trouble started. The place was full of snipers and there were a few strong-points still holding out. A tank ran over the door of the prison and took two hundred prisoners straight away. 'D' Company, down in the docks, had trouble with a 20mm anti-aircraft gun mounted on a mole, which was firing tracer at point-blank range. CSM Cude got a Bren gun on top of a pill-box and, under concentrated fire, fired off four magazines, thereby silencing the gun and getting an MM.
>
> The day was spent in rounding up the prisoners. The Battalion took 1100 and the Brigade total was 2900.

The garrison of Le Havre had been 11,000, so these were impressive statistics. However, in the aftermath of the bombing of the town centre, the liberators were not universally popular:

> The town had been badly bombed, and the civilians were none too friendly, so they pulled us out of Le Havre and sent us to Lillebone, which was a lovely little village where we had a week's good rest, which everybody enjoyed. We felt we had come to the end of the Normandy journey, and everybody felt grand to have the enemy about two hundred miles away. There had been a lot of German booty from Le Havre, including a large percentage of champagne and brandy. This we soon managed to drink in about three really good parties.

* * *

To the north, Kennedy was finally getting the action which he had craved for so long. He had joined 248 Squadron, a Coastal Command Mosquito-equipped unit, which started flying in September from Banff in Scotland to attack shipping off the Norwegian coast. It was hazardous but exciting work.[5] His first combat mission appears to have been on

John Kennedy (at right) & his navigator, Flying Officer 153491 Francis Walter Rolls, in front of one of the Mosquito FB.VIs in which they flew missions over Norway in the last three months of 1944. (Kennedy family collection; coloured by dansteele.net)

September 14th. Kennedy took off at the controls of Mosquito VI DM-U, accompanied by navigator Flying Officer 153491 Francis Walter Rolls. Theirs was one of ten Mosquito VIs and four Mosquito XVIIIs which took off between 1432 and 1451. The FB.VI Mosquito was armed with four 20mm cannon and four .303 machine-guns in the nose, and could carry in addition bombs, depth-charges, and unguided rocket projectiles, making it a potent attacker. The FB.XVIIIs – nicknamed 'Tsetses' – carried a self-loading 57mm gun for attacks on shipping. The mission was an 'armed reconnaissance' – going out looking for trouble.[6] On this occasion, they found it.

The Squadron's diary recorded:

> In formation on armed recce from Eigerøy 1719 to Store Torungen Light on Norwegian coast. Wing Commander D.G. Sise leading 248 Squadron formation in J/248 with twelve Beaufighters of 404 Squadron armed with rocket projectiles, and seven Beaufighters

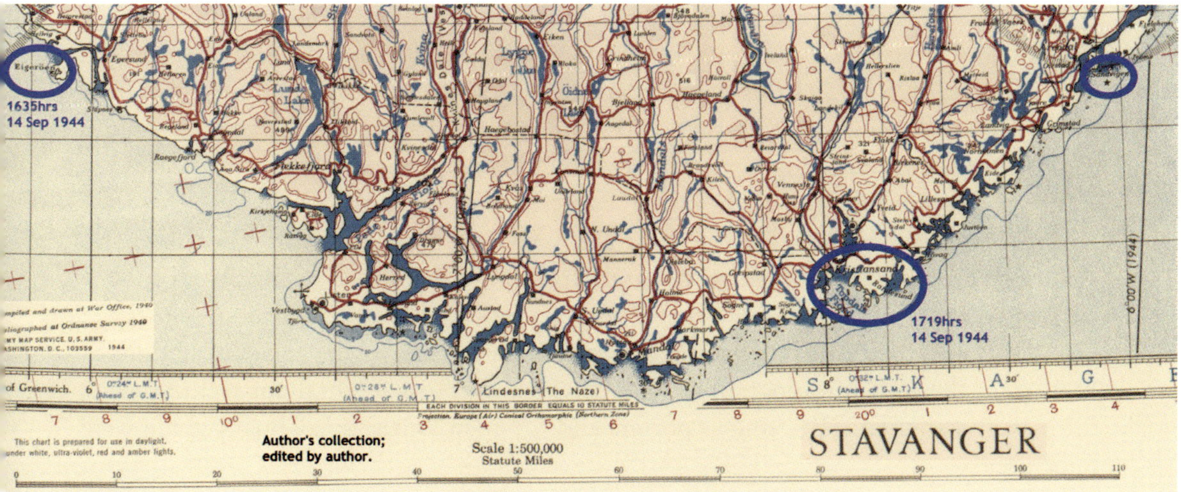

of 144 Squadron armed with torpedoes, and eleven Mosquitos of 235 Squadron; S/Ldr Schoales in L/404 leading Strike Force. At 1512 B/248 landed base owing to air pressure failure, and at 1635hrs landfall was made at Eigerøy. Three Swedish merchant vessels were sighted at 1653hrs. At 1712hrs L, O, E, H/248 left the formation, as they had then reached prudent limit of endurance, and set course for base.

At 1719hrs, just south of Cristiansand, the formation sighted and attacked a north-bound convoy comprising following vessels: two merchant vessels of 3000 tons and 2500 tons, and two Trawler Type Auxiliaries and one merchant vessel 1000 tons on starboard side of convoy, and one merchant vessel of 1500 tons in rear of convoy. Attacks were made by the formation with torpedoes, rocket projectiles, cannon, and machine-gun. Strikes were claimed by aircraft of 248 on all vessels attacked, which were seen to be on fire and smoking – while the leading TTA blew up.[7] Heavy and light Flak experienced from all ships, which was quickly silenced as the anti-Flak aircraft attacked. The leading TTA and first merchant vessel fired parachute-and-cable, and heavy predicted Flak was experienced from the shore between Rostad and Cristiansand – which was accurate for height but short for range.

Three days later, Kennedy was once again in the air over the Norwegian coast, this time hunting the U-Boats which transited the area on their way into the North Atlantic. The U-Boats travelled on the surface as much as possible and so were vulnerable to air attack. The first of five Mosquitoes took off from Banff at 1441hrs, Kennedy this time flying DM-V, Walter Rolls again at his side.[8]

In formation on anti U-Boat sweep from 60.25N to Florø with two aircraft of 235 Squadron: S/Ldr J. Maurice in C/248 leading formation. At 1612hrs were at Yyelterone and swept to west of leads owing to cloud base and visibility. At 1632hrs formation were off patrol, having seen nothing, and set course for base.

The strain of flying at low level over the sea in poor visibility for over three hours was immense; the Mosquito had two very reliable engines, but a moment's inattention on Kennedy's part could have been disastrous.

* * *

After their rest near Rouen, 1KOSB were swiftly on the move to the border between Belgium and Holland, east of Antwerp. The Germans were holding the north bank of the Meuse–Escaut Canal, and this line needed to be broken so that Montgomery's narrow thrust towards Eindhoven, Nijmegen, and Arnhem – Operation Market Garden – could begin. 3rd Infantry Division were tasked with effecting a crossing of the canal.

The move up to the front crossed the battlefields of the First World War, bypassed Brussels, and took 1KOSB through Louvain, 'which, to those few of the Battalion who were serving with the original 1st Battalion during the campaign in 1940, brought back memories'.

1KOSB and the rest of 9 Infantry Brigade arrived south of the canal, near Lille St Hubert, in the early afternoon of September 17th. Two other battalions were to make the assault, with 1KOSB acting as porters and oarsmen for the small boats which were to be used.

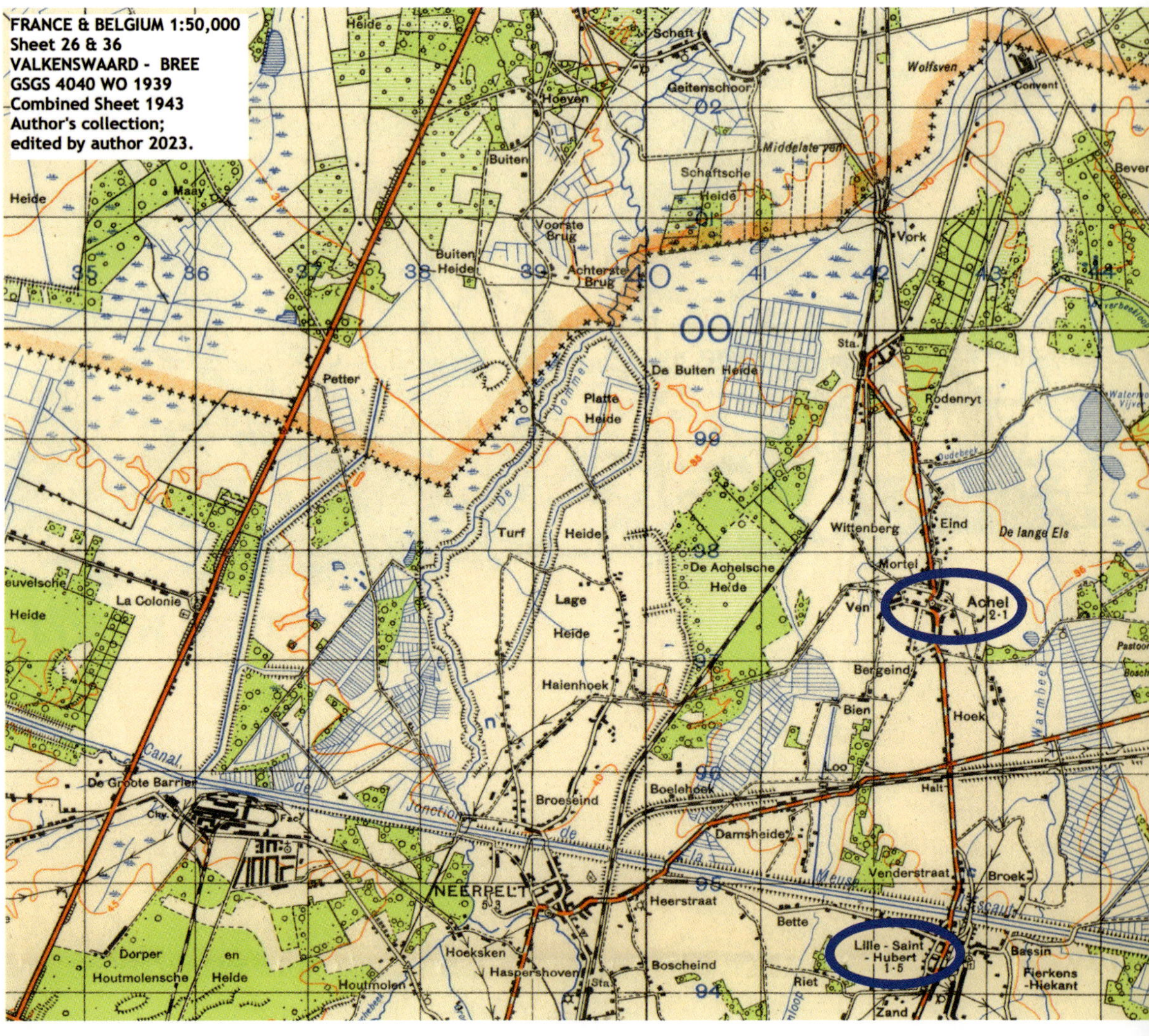

When the attack began at midnight on September 18th, 1KOSB took some casualties in its work parties, but the entire Battalion started to cross at 0430hrs under cover of heavy mist. Their first objective was the railway line, which would then become their firm base for a push on Achel. By 0900hrs on the 20th 1KOSB were established in Achel, at which point 11th Armoured Division began streaming through northwards into Holland.

* * *

On September 19th, Kennedy and Rolls took a third Mosquito (DM-Q, HR632) out on a 'Rover' patrol seeking German shipping and U-Boats. The twelve-aircraft formation was in the air by 1235hrs and landed by 1533hrs.[9]

> In formation with one aircraft of 333 Squadron on Rover from Blonv [?] to Strolshaven [?][10] through leads to Selbjørnsfjord. Captain Johanneson, leading formation in K/333 aircraft, covered Selbjørnsfjord, Bjørnafjord, and Korsfjord up to Hjeltefjord. At 1355hrs the formation turned southwards and at 1400hrs set course for base. Weather conditions were 10/10 cloud from 500 feet to sea level – but with good visibility in the leads.

The above photograph was taken during an attack by Mosquitoes elsewhere off Norway on September 19th 1944, & shows the sort of scene which Kennedy would have witnessed during sorties which encountered enemy shipping. (IWM C 4835)

* * *

1KOSB stepped east across the frontier to Budel, where they received a warm welcome from the inhabitants, and began patrolling the canal lines in relative calm. Indeed, on September 29th the war diary reported that 'to our intense relief the Bath Unit eventually arrived and the whole Battalion felt clean again for the first time since Étrépagny [which they had left on September 16th]. Clean laundry was also provided.' That day, Boyd wrote to his family:[11]

> I just got Father's letter written from Whiterigg … I wish I was there with you. I am sorry to hear about the harvest; the weather has been filthy here too, but thank heavens we are not forced to live in our slit-trenches as we were in the early days when the Boche had plenty of guns and mortars.
>
> The Battle at Arnhem must have been a magnificent show, and I hope it will remind people at home that the war in the west is by no means over yet, although the German army has had the most tremendous defeat in its history. It is a great thing that this time, the people of Europe have seen the German army retreating through their countries ragged, dirty, disorganised, and closely pursued by the British and Americans. Last time they were able to march through Europe with their weapons and in formation; even so, we find notices chalked on the walls saying 'We shall be back', and some of the SS even think that they will push us out again next spring! They're a bit optimistic.
>
> We are getting a great welcome from the Dutch. I had never been in Holland or Belgium, but was very impressed with the cleanness of the houses and the enthusiasm of the people in both countries – more so I think in Holland than in Belgium. Holland really lives up to its pictures with all the people walking about in clogs and full skirts or patched trousers (as the case may be); the country as flat as your hand, with hundreds of canals behind which the Boche sits with his machine-guns. You get the most wonderful views over the country from the tops of church towers. Four of us were up one the other day when the Boche started sniping us with a couple of 88 millimeters! We descended rapidly!

* * *

Duffin.

Duffin and 3SG had crossed the Seine on September 12th, but then paused. Left Flank enjoyed a dance at Les Andelys on September 17th – as Allied troops were parachuting in near Arnhem – and sight-seeing excursions to Rouen began on the following day. On September 19th, Duffin was transferred from 14 Troop on his appointment to Battalion HQ as Intelligence Officer. He had a gentle introduction to the role, since 3SG did not move again until their tanks were shipped off to the front on September 26th. The tank transporters took the Churchills past Cambrai, through Brussels, and unloaded at the Albert Canal, the tanks making their own way on to Geldrop, near Eindhoven, where they arrived at 2100hrs on September 29th.

The initial drive into Holland – the famous Operation Market Garden, which was just petering out – had established a long, narrow salient, whose tip lay on

'The Island', a damp muddy patch between the Waal and the Neder Rhine beyond Nijmegen. This salient – effectively just one road – was very vulnerable to attack, and with plans to bounce the Rhine now at an end, the corridor had to be widened. To the west, it would be an advantage to capture the road which led from Nijmegen to Antwerp by way of 's-Hertogenbosch and Tilburg. To the east lay a large area of boggy heathland called the Peel. 3SG spent some time guarding the Geldrop area from counter-attack, but would see fighting in both directions in due course.

* * *

After Le Havre and the parties in Lillebone, Somerville and 2SWB moved to Lille by way of Dieppe.

> One could not help noticing how thin and undernourished the people of Lille looked. There were swarms of thin, pale-faced, rickety-looking little boys, all tugging at one's sleeve and shouting 'Cigarette pour Papa' and then smoking them themselves.
>
> Next day we crossed the Belgian border and, driving through Brussels, finished up in a charming little village called Iteghem which lay about fifteen miles south of the Antwerp–Turnhout Canal. Here the people welcomed us with open arms, and the Battalion spent four of the best days of rest that they had had since D-Day. One could not help marvelling at the quantities of fruit, tomatoes, and pears in this part of the country. All along the line of march we had been showered with fruit, and there was as much as one could eat of lovely juicy pears just for the asking.
>
> During our stay there the local priest organised the first processional thanksgiving that they had held since the Germans first came five years before. Some of our RCs were invited to carry the canopy in the procession. Of course, during this carnival

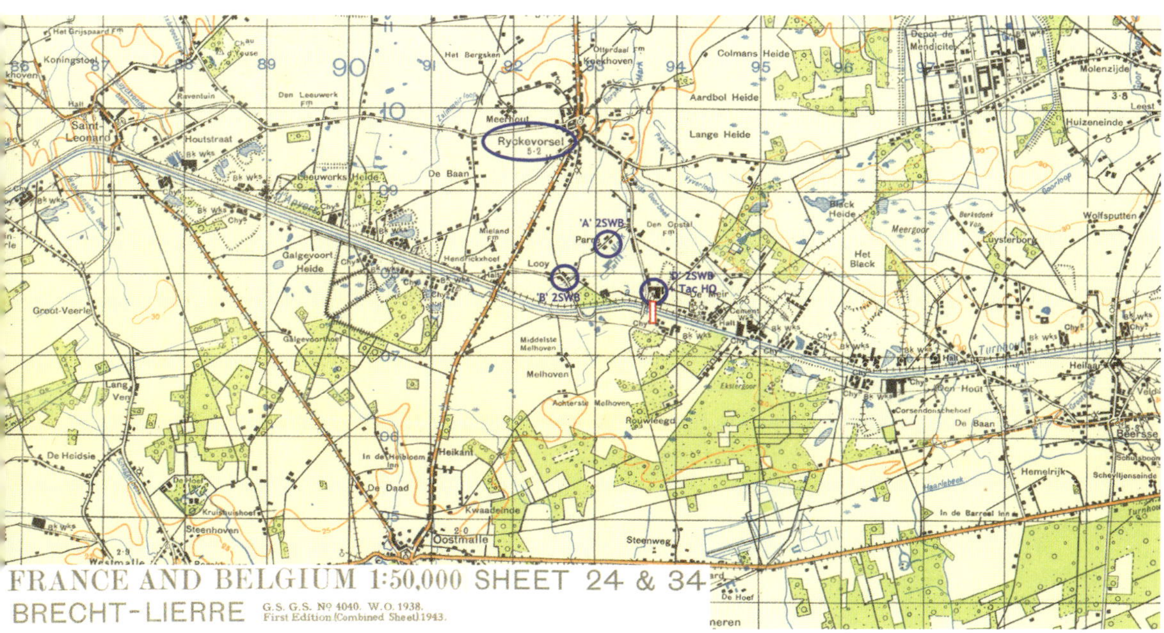

> week everybody went completely mad, and it was with deep regret that we moved out on 25th September to our next action. By this time the Battalion was extremely fresh again, having had a good rest.

The first British troops crossed the Antwerp–Turnhout Canal south-east of Rijkevorsel on the night of September 24th, and managed to defend their gains long enough for a Bailey bridge to be erected over the Sint Jozef lock, north of Rouwleegd. The Germans had repelled attacks at other points, and spent the next three days focusing on this single bridgehead.

Somerville arrived on September 25th:

> They had been badly shelled and counter-attacked, and so we went over the canal at dusk into un-reconnoitred positions on the left flank in order to strengthen the perimeter. Everything went well until the early morning, about 0200hrs, when the Germans attacked in fair strength. 'B' Company was cut off and had to fight hard to prevent being over-run. About 150 Germans penetrated as far as 'D' Company, whom they attacked, shouting like devils as they came, and a fair proportion of them talking in English. They succeeded in over-running one of 'D' Company's platoons and got within 150 yards of Battalion HQ. However in about ¾ of an hour, by some good fighting patrols, we were able to use up a lot of grenades and oust him out of it, so that by dawn we were back in our original positions. At that time we were only working with three companies, and it showed how valuable a fourth would have been in a counter-attack role.
>
> That morning after first light the Boche attacked again, this time concentrating his efforts on 'B' Company. One platoon in a café, commanded by Lieutenant Crane, was cut off from the rest of the Company by fire and had to hold out against about fifty or sixty Boche. This they proceeded to do with admirable coolness and determination. Some amazing feats of gallantry were performed by this platoon, including the mortar man, who dashed out under a hail of fire to fire six bombs 'crash action' low angle at a hedge only twenty-five yards in front of him. When the attack had been beaten off, no fewer than forty dead bodies were found behind a hedge which ran only fifty yards in front of the platoon position.
>
> All throughout the day the enemy counter-attacked the left flank, losing an incredible number of casualties, as we had a troop of tanks, which just swanned about mowing them all down like flies. By the end of the day the Battalion had accounted for nearly 250 German casualties. During these counter-attacks the whole bridge-head had been mercilessly shelled, including a direct hit on Battalion HQ which killed two and wounded five.
>
> Next day the bridge-head was extended to include Rijkevorsel, and the Battalion advanced accordingly. Rijkevorsel was one of the most continuously and accurately 'stonked' areas that the Battalion had ever been in, and it was unfortunate that we should have to sit there for a fortnight. During this time we patrolled a lot and did one diversionary attack which cost us a fair number of casualties and didn't get anybody anywhere.

* * *

Kennedy, however, was more productively engaged. He and his regular partner, Rolls, were allocated yet another Mosquito (DM-S) and took off with six others shortly before 1300hrs on September 24th.

The Mosquito FB.VI DM-S flown by Kennedy & Rolls on their mission on 24th September 1944. (Kennedy family collection; edited by dansteele.net)

Their mission was to look for U-Boats between the lighthouses at Utvaer (north of Bergen) and Marstein (south of Bergen). They did not find any submarines, but did encounter the enemy:[12]

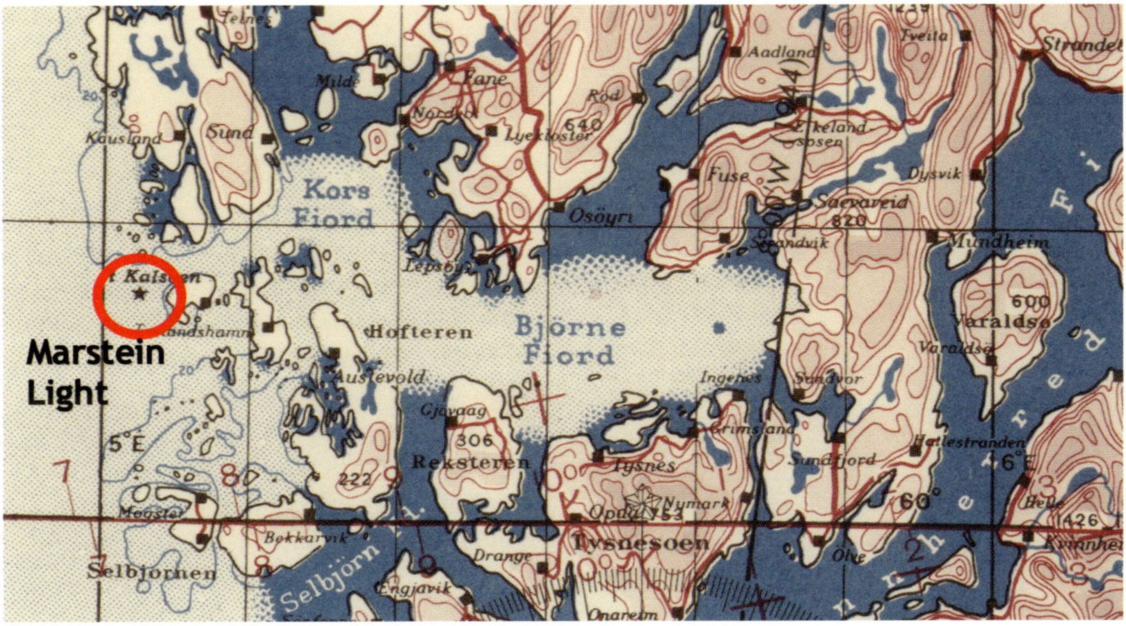

> At 1443hrs, off Marstein Light, sighted one coaster type of merchant vessel of 300 tons which fired light Flak and 'parachute and cables'. At 1507hrs sighted two enemy vessels, one heading north-east, one north-west; one TTA of 500 tons, and vessel resembling old type of minesweeper of 400 tons. At 1510hrs aircraft attacked with cannon and 6-pounder cannon. The TTA was seen well on fire with smoke and flames, and the minesweeper was seen to be smoking heavily – accurate medium and light Flak was experienced from both vessels. Medium and heavy accurate Flak also from shore positions during attack. X/248 had fire extinguishers set off by Flak during attack, and was escorted back to base by E/248. I, B, and G were hit in wings and fuselage, but all aircraft returned safely to base [by 1640hrs].

The TTA left 'well on fire' was probably the German *Vorpostenboot* V5502 *Biber*, which was sunk that day, one of its eight crew being killed.

* * *

Mike Sinclair.

Far away, in *Oflag* IVC (Colditz), Mike Sinclair was brooding. Captured at Calais in May 1940, along with his friends Gris Davies-Scourfield (a fellow Wykehamist) and Ronnie Littledale – later to become Lewin's commanding officer in 2KRRC – Sinclair had become one of the most prolific escapers of the war. He, Davies-Scourfield and Littledale had escaped from Stalag XXI-D at Poznan in northern Poland on May 28th 1941. After months in hiding, Sinclair and Littledale had been recaptured in Bulgaria in November, but while being returned to Germany in January 1942 had leapt from the train. Sinclair had been recaptured quickly, but Littledale managed to stay at large until being arrested near Prague on May 29th – a year and a day since their initial escape.

Littledale and Sinclair had reached Colditz in July 1942, and Sinclair escaped again almost immediately, whilst in Leipzig for a court martial. He was on the run for a few days before being recaptured in Cologne. His ardour for escape was undimmed. On May 19th 1943 he attempted to take over the guard positions on the east terrace of the castle, disguised as one of the guard commanders, *Stabsfeldwebel* Rothenberger; this would have allowed a brief window of around three minutes in which as many prisoners as possible were to escape. However, one of the real guards refused to budge, the real Rotherberger appeared, and in the resulting confusion Sinclair was shot. For ten minutes he lay on the ground, many of the prisoners thinking that he was dead. However, he recovered – physically, but not mentally.

By the time of Sinclair's next escape attempt, in September 1944, his brother John had been killed at Anzio; furthermore, Ronnie Littledale had escaped from Colditz on October 15th 1942, travelled by way of Switzerland, France and Spain, and had reached Gibraltar on March 25th 1943. Awarded the DSO for his escape, Littledale had returned to active service and, as we have seen, been killed in action at Airaines on September 1st

1944. These two blows must have added force to Sinclair's conviction that he should be doing more; as he had written to Robertson in March, 'We must carry on and do what little we can.'

On September 25th, Sinclair tried a bold daylight escape which involved climbing a barbed-wire fence and running across an open park. It had already been done once, successfully, so the guards were alert to it as a possibility. Some have suggested that Sinclair was in effect committing suicide. Reports suggest that the guards were very restrained, initially shooting to miss, but eventually a bullet hit his arm and ricocheted into his heart. He was buried with full military honours, and after the war received a posthumous DSO for his devotion to his duty to escape. Lieutenants did not usually receive DSOs, and the medal was not usually awarded posthumously. But Albert Michael Sinclair had been exceptional, and Robertson mourned his loss with especial force.

* * *

September 26th saw Lewin and 2KRRC – still mourning Littledale – move to Weert, just inside Holland, where the Battalion took over the defence of a huge sector facing east along the Wessem-Nederweert Canal, 'A' Company's area being roughly central in the zone, east of Zwartbroek. Over the next fortnight KRRC became embroiled in a scrappy little war against enemy patrols across the canal, both sides attempting to dominate the other. The Germans were *Kampfgruppe Graßmehl* of 20 *Fallschirmjäger* Regiment, formidable opponents.

> October 1st
> 1430hrs Battalion HQ area shelled for ten minutes. A direct hit on the RAP caused casualties. The Adjutant was bathing.
>
> October 3rd
> 0900hrs Strong patrolling by enemy; we claim six killed and one prisoner-of-war.
>
> October 7th
> 1500hrs A day patrol caught while tank-hunting. We killed one and wounded four. Rifleman Fairman sniped three enemy during the day … .[13]

American troops relieved 2KRRC on October 8th. After a brief rest, the Battalion prepared to go up into the line again.

* * *

On September 27th, in DM-Q again, Rolls and Kennedy came under heavy and accurate anti-aircraft fire as part of a five-aircraft formation patrolling between Christiansand and South Lister. Although they sighted a good deal of shipping at Christiansand, Tregde, and Farsund, they returned to Banff at around 1530hrs, having been in the air since 1200hrs.

But it was the following day, September 28th, that the pair scored their first significant success. Once again they were on an anti U-Boat patrol, this time of six Mosquitoes. The Squadron's records explain what happened after take-off at 1453hrs:

> In formation on anti U-Boat patrol, Lister to Christiansand south, Flight Lieutenant L.R. Bacon leading in S/248. At 1614hrs aircraft were at Lister and on patrol. At 1626hrs, in position 57.58N 07.31E, the formation sighted and attacked one ex-Norwegian torpedo boat with cannon and 6-pounder cannon, and depth-charges from Q/248 and K/248. Concentrated hits were seen on torpedo boat from all aircraft, and the depth-charges exploded under and near the vessel's starboard side amidships. The result of these attacks was a large explosion with black smoke 100 feet high, the torpedo boat then being covered in grey smoke, and was seen to sink on an even keel. No wreckage or survivors were seen after sinking.

The aircraft straggled slightly on return, landing between 1841hrs and 1902hrs. Four hours in the air, with a battle in the middle, must have been emotionally and physically draining for the crews. But they had been correct in their identification of their victim: the 28-year-old torpedo boat *Kjell* had been captured by the Germans in 1940. Rebuilt as minesweeper NK 02, she took the name *Dragoner.* Seven of her crew were killed when she was sunk.

A week later, in Mosquito DM-V for a second combat sortie, Kennedy and Rolls took part in a much larger operation, as twelve aircraft of 248 Squadron set out on an anti-U-Boat patrol, escorted by an additional six Mosquitoes of 235 Squadron. The patrol took off at 1435hrs, but apart from heavy anti-aircraft fire from Lister, and the sight of some moored merchant shipping in Kristiansand, there was little to report for their four hours in the air.

* * *

On October 11th, Boyd left his post as Adjutant 1KOSB and went to 'A' Company as second-in-command. He was just in time for the front-line role he had long wished for, as the Battalion moved at 0930hrs the following day for operations near Overloon in Holland. By lunch time 'A' Company was just south-west of St Anthonis. October 13th involved an early reveille, the troops setting off on foot at 0530hrs southwards to a small wood, from which they moved up to their Assembly Area at 1030hrs. The commanding officer delivered his briefing – the 'O' Group – at 1220hrs, just forty minutes before the scheduled start of the attack on a nearby wood, which actually went in at 1320hrs. 1KOSB followed a squadron of Churchill tanks and another of Sherman 'flails', with flame-throwers in support. After the first wave secured the northern edge of the wood, 'A' and 'C' Companies moved through them, advancing 300 yards before halting and letting the first wave past. Leapfrogging in this way, they cleared the wood and set up positions two hundred yards short of the southern edge. Apart from isolated machine-gun fire, there was no real opposition on the ground, but heavy fire from mortars, *Nebelwerfers*,

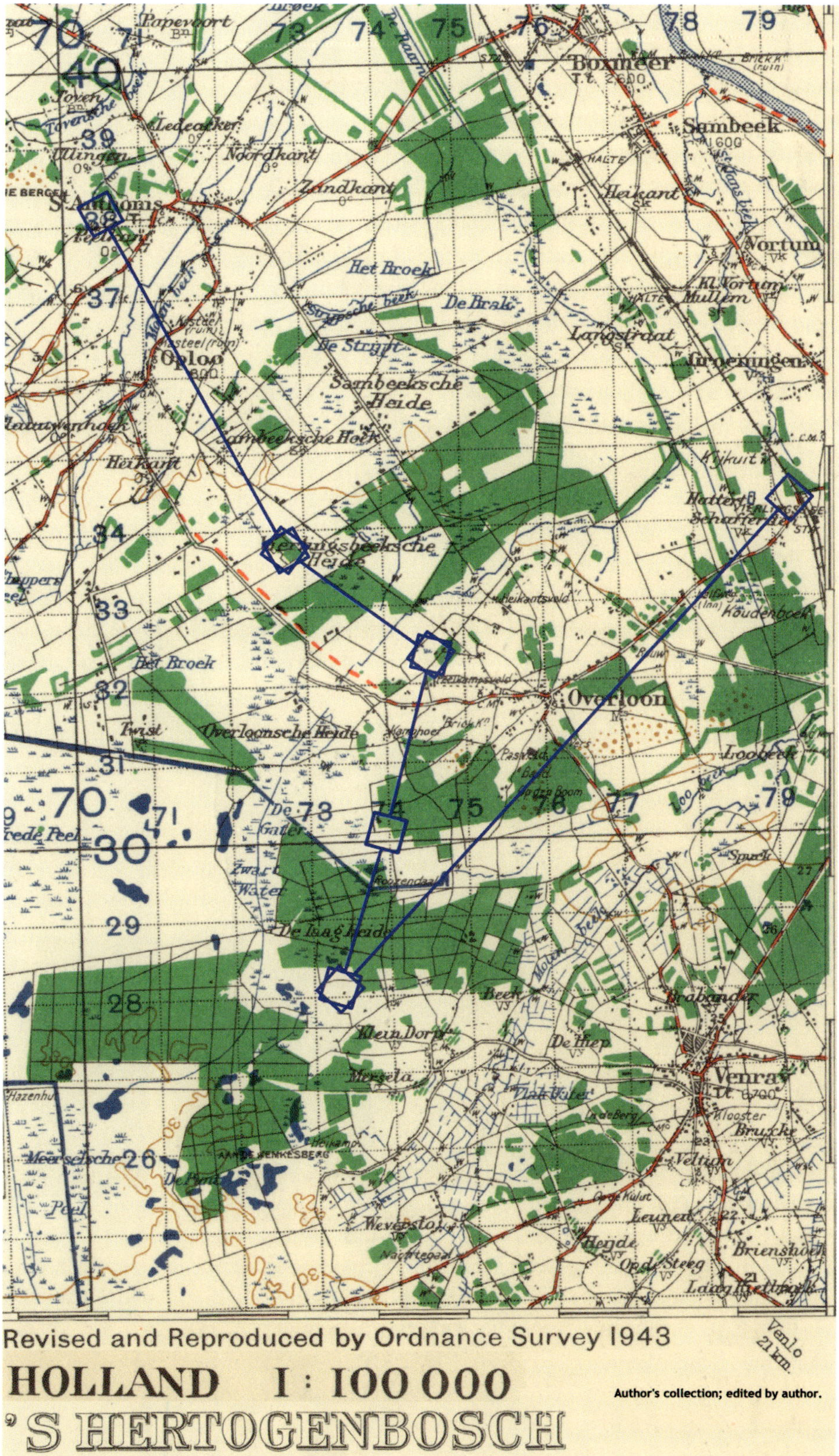

Author's collection; edited by author.

and artillery. 'A' Company ended the 13th in the south-west of the wood, and one of its patrols heard the enemy digging in to the south.

After a quiet night, another battalion launched an attack on another wood to the south of 1KOSB. Heavy German shell-fire and machine-gunning put paid to that, but a stronger effort at 1400hrs scraped home. Boyd's Company pushed the line forwards to the edge of their wood, and sent out a recce patrol which brought back valuable information about the next day's objectives. The enemy withdrew during the night of October 14th, however, and although the advance continued on the 16th, 1KOSB was rushed to the far side of Overloon to take up positions near Smakt. The hurried move started close to dusk and the Battalion did not arrive until after dark, occupying invisible and 'as yet not very habitable'[14] slit trenches under fire ('during the takeover the *Nebelwerfers* were busy').

And so it went on. From their static positions, 1KOSB sent out patrol after patrol, whilst under constant mortar, *Nebelwerfer*, and shell-fire; 'the worst', states the war diary, 'the Battalion has experienced so far'. There they stayed until relieved on November 4th.

* * *

Lewin was transferred to the X.ii List by 2KRRC on October 13th, signifying that he had been evacuated on medical grounds beyond the Regimental First Aid Post.[15] The war diary does not state what was wrong with him, but he did not return to the Battalion until November 4th, and his parents soon afterwards informed Robertson that he had spent three weeks in hospital in Brussels suffering from pleurisy, an inflammation around the lungs most probably caused by an infection such as influenza or pneumonia. The Germans were not the only enemy.

* * *

Off Norway, a patrol on October 23rd netted better results than 248 Squadron had achieved previously. In DM-W this time, Kennedy and Rolls took off at 1145hrs as part of a formation of twenty-one Mosquitoes from two squadrons. The mission was once again armed reconnaissance, from Marstein lighthouse northwards to Ålesund. Shortly after making landfall, at 1319hrs, the formation encountered anchored shipping in Hjeltefjorden, just six miles from Bergen:

> Four vessels in anchorage: a merchant vessel 2000 tons, one large TTA alongside, one TTA lying off quay, one tug-type vessel; also a small coaster under way. At 1321 the formation attacked with cannon and machine-guns, bombs, and 6-pounder cannon. All vessels were raked with cannon and machine-gun fire, and were later seen on fire with clouds of grey and black smoke. Near misses with bombs were claimed on the TTA alongside the quay by aircraft B/248, other bombs from 'V' not being observed owing to the smoke from the vessel attacked. Light Flak came from the merchant vessel and TTA alongside, and accurate light and inaccurate heavy Flak from the shore batteries.[16]

The TTA which was alongside the merchant vessel was another *Voorpostenboot,* V5506 *Zick.* This was another converted Norwegian vessel; as the *Trygg,* she had been sunk by a German bomb in April 1940 but raised and repaired. She was escorting a convoy of three other vessels when she came under attack that day. Her crew of thirty-three had a 3-inch gun, two 20mm anti-aircraft guns, two machine-guns and two torpedo tubes as armament, and they made efficient use of all except the torpedoes as they came under attack. Mosquito E/235 came away with a large hole in its fin and a shell through its nose; S/248 suffered damage to her port wing. But the *Zick* paid a price for her resistance; she capsized, and three of her crew went down with her. All the other ships in the convoy were damaged.

* * *

Further to the south, the Germans were determined to stop the Allies from opening the port of Antwerp and therefore had to hold the South Beveland peninsula and island of Walcheren, whilst preventing British and Canadian forces from advancing north from Antwerp and cutting the base of the peninsula. Somerville's Battalion were involved in the advance north-east, which bogged down about half-way between Turnhout (in Belgium) and Tilburg (in Holland), at a small Belgian village called Poppel.

> We started out from Turnhout in great form, but were finally stuck good and hard at the village of Poppel. From here onwards the ground was all in the enemy's favour, and he had far more men than was at first anticipated. It began by a strong counter-attack on the Lincolns lasting for two days, and extremely heavy shelling of Poppel. Accordingly we were rushed up to meet the situation. We took over from the hard-pressed Lincolns, and managed to hold on to our gains so far. Patrolling discovered the enemy defences in considerable strength ... We sat in Poppel for three weeks, being shelled pretty regularly, but once in a while getting a bath in Turnhout.

The baths were much-needed. Every veteran who served at Poppel that month remembered the ceaseless rain, the water and mud ankle-deep – at least – in the trenches, the incessant shelling and mortaring, the constant patrolling and vigilance as the Germans tried to infiltrate, and the impossibility of moving in daylight. For sheer misery, it sounds like our vision of Passchendaele in 1917. Towards the end of October, therefore, 2SWB were delighted to move westwards, closer to Antwerp, where they joined Operation Rebound, a drive north past Bergen-op-Zoom. From Esschen, just inside the Belgian border, they were tasked with the capture of Roosendaal, three miles to the north in Holland, and to establish themselves on the Maas at Wilhelmstaadt.

> Jerry had about thirty SPGs in the area and a large stock of ammunition which he was intent on using before his eventual retreat over the Maas. He shelled Esschen all day and night, which made movement of any sort extremely difficult. One shell was unlucky for our Battalion, as it knocked out thirteen good men, killing the Doctor and MT Sergeant, and wounding the Medical Sergeant. All the casualties were specialists of some sort.

They advanced from Esschen towards Nispen on the night of October 25th:

> We were to start the ball rolling with a night attack by 'D' Company on to a wood which we knew was occupied by the enemy. It was a difficult task, and our own 'artificial moonlight' had to be switched off before we could get a platoon on to the objective. That day the Brigade advanced, capturing the village of Nispen and letting the armour through.

* * *

At some point in October, Duffin had rushed home on compassionate leave. He explained why in a letter written to Robertson in December:[17]

> I was home for a week in October, as you have heard, as my Ann was very ill, but luckily she took a turn for the better the day I arrived (strangely enough) and I had a much more pleasant time than I ever expected. I didn't have time to see anybody, as I should have liked to – the days went by so quickly that it only seemed a moment before I was outward-bound again …

On October 24th 3SG finally got moving from Eindhoven, advancing west towards Moergestel. Llewellyn-Smith's account of operations includes a description of their arrival at the Moergestels Broek, which had something of a festival atmosphere:

> Here we found the bridge blown; but instead of the anti-tank guns and defended crossing which reconnaissance reports had indicated, the opposite bank was crowded with the whole population of the village, who gave Lieutenant Fletcher's Troop one of the most enthusiastic receptions of the whole campaign. People waded across and jumped on to the tanks with food and drink. Orange flags appeared from nowhere. One woman with two small twins clinging to her skirts whisked them away and produced them within five minutes clad in orange blouses and blue trousers.
>
> But the pressing question was how to get the tanks across, and the leading tank commander was busy inspecting the river bed. When the civilians saw our need, led by a priest from the monastery nearby they began rolling boulders, throwing stones, and heaving anything on which they could lay their hands down into the stream. All took part – priests, nuns, elderly women, and tiny children. To stand on the opposite bank became quite dangerous under the volley! Soon Lieutenant Fletcher, deciding that it was time to make a bid to reach the other bank, drove his tank down on the reinforced river-bed but just failed to make the further side – 'Montrose' finally slithering back to sink in the mud – a pitiful picture as the waters lapped against its side.
>
> Meanwhile things had been set moving further back, and it was only five minutes later that the bridge-laying tank came up with a reconnaissance party of Sappers. A spot was chosen for lowering the bridge and as the operation began a silence of wonder descended on the jubilant crowd. When, however, the bridge was being balanced in mid-air and began slowly to come to earth, the whole crowd broke into the Dutch national anthem, which was sung with great fervour.

Remarkably, a photograph exists in the archives of the very moment described by Llewellyn-Smith; Fletcher's tank 'Montrose' can be seen at right, & the helpful priest is visible on the bank below the right-hand end of the bridge. (IWM B11364; edited by dansteele.net)

By half-past three in the afternoon the whole Battalion was across, rolling on to liberate Tilburg. But just as 3SG prepared to enter the town on October 27th they were rushed back eastwards to block a German counter-attack towards Helmond. Nothing much happened, though for the next few weeks the Battalion was involved in small actions across the front.

* * *

As we have seen, training for Coastal Forces was conducted at HMS *St Christopher* in Fort William, from which Mackrill wrote to Robertson on October 25th (on note-paper which he had clearly 'liberated' from HMS *King Alfred*).[18]

Mackrill.

> At present I am finishing a Coastal Forces Course and with any luck I should soon be sent to an operational flotilla. We have been in Fort William where it does nothing but rain. However, last Saturday we managed to find a fine day to go up the Ben – I say 'we' because David

> Savill and I and quite a party went up together. However we were unlucky because when we got to the top, the clouds came down and we could not see anything. I must say, it nearly killed us – but it was well worth it; there were eighteen inches of snow at the top.
>
> I was terribly sorry to see in 'The Times' the other day that Professor Gleadowe was dead. It seems only a short time ago that I was doing drawing up to him. I saw also that poor David Martyn and Daniel Meinertzhagen had been killed. It makes me feel I ought to get cracking properly soon; I seem to have been such ages on my course, but even so it is short compared to some of the Army ones.

* * *

Somerville, meanwhile, was outside Roosendaal,

> a strongly-defended town surrounded by a large anti-tank ditch. Unfortunately the momentum of the attack was slowed up on the line of the anti-tank ditch by the concentrated fire of thirty SPGs. We sat down outside the defences to think it out. We whistled up heavy and light anti-aircraft regiments, who fired air-bursts at roof-top height over Roosendaal all day, and also got the Typhoons cracking. Next day we found that Jerry had pulled out.

It was October 30th 1944.[19] That afternoon, Kennedy conducted an uneventful patrol over the Norwegian coast,[20] whilst Rigby's mother, in a long and chatty letter to Robertson, signed off with the remark, 'I am very sorry about Michael Sinclair. I think to die as a Prisoner of War is one of the hardest trials, and very sad for relatives and friends to think of.'[21]

XXVI

'I am now back in England, unfortunately minus my left leg'

North-West Europe, November 1st–December 31st 1944

When Roosendaal fell on October 30th, the Maas lay only ten miles to the north, but those ten miles took 2SWB until November 6th to cover, owing to what Somerville described as

Nick Somerville.

> an entirely new problem: floods. From Oudcastel to Wilhelmstaadt, on the south bank of the Maas, is about seven miles. In this area the dykes had been blown and all the fields were under water; some to a depth of two feet, others to a depth of eight feet. The only movement possible was along the roads, many of which were under two feet of water themselves. Digging was, of course, out of the question, and one had to use houses as the only means of protection.

Every move had to be at night, which made the advance slow and cautious. One strange feature of this period was that on November 4th – just before the capture of Wilhelmstaadt – the unpopular Brigade Commander, Brigadier Ekins, apparently shot himself in the head in his car outside his headquarters. The circumstances remain shrouded in mystery.

The final approach to the Maas showed the dangers which 56 Brigade faced in pressing on along narrow routes in the face of determined delaying tactics.

> Eventually all was set for the battle of Wilhelmstaadt. The plan was that the Lincolns – who had worked their way up to the Maas – should assault the fort (as it was) from the east, crossing the moat by assault boats. We were to capture a similar fort and village to the south-west of Wilhelmstaadt and cause a diversion from that side. Owing to a time programme 'D' Company had to attack the village at first light, and the plan for the fort would be made after this, probably as a night operation.
>
> Unfortunately the entrance to the village was over a bridge, which every single man had to cross. Just before the attack was due to start, we had a message over the air to say that some of the Lincolns were already in the village and that we were to send an officer forward to contact them and get 'D' Company up as quickly as possible to take over. As it happened, the Lincolns were *not* in the village, and the officer drove straight into the enemy, being killed and his Jeep captured. 'D' Company, marching up the road by sections, had got one platoon over the bridge when the enemy opened up with well-

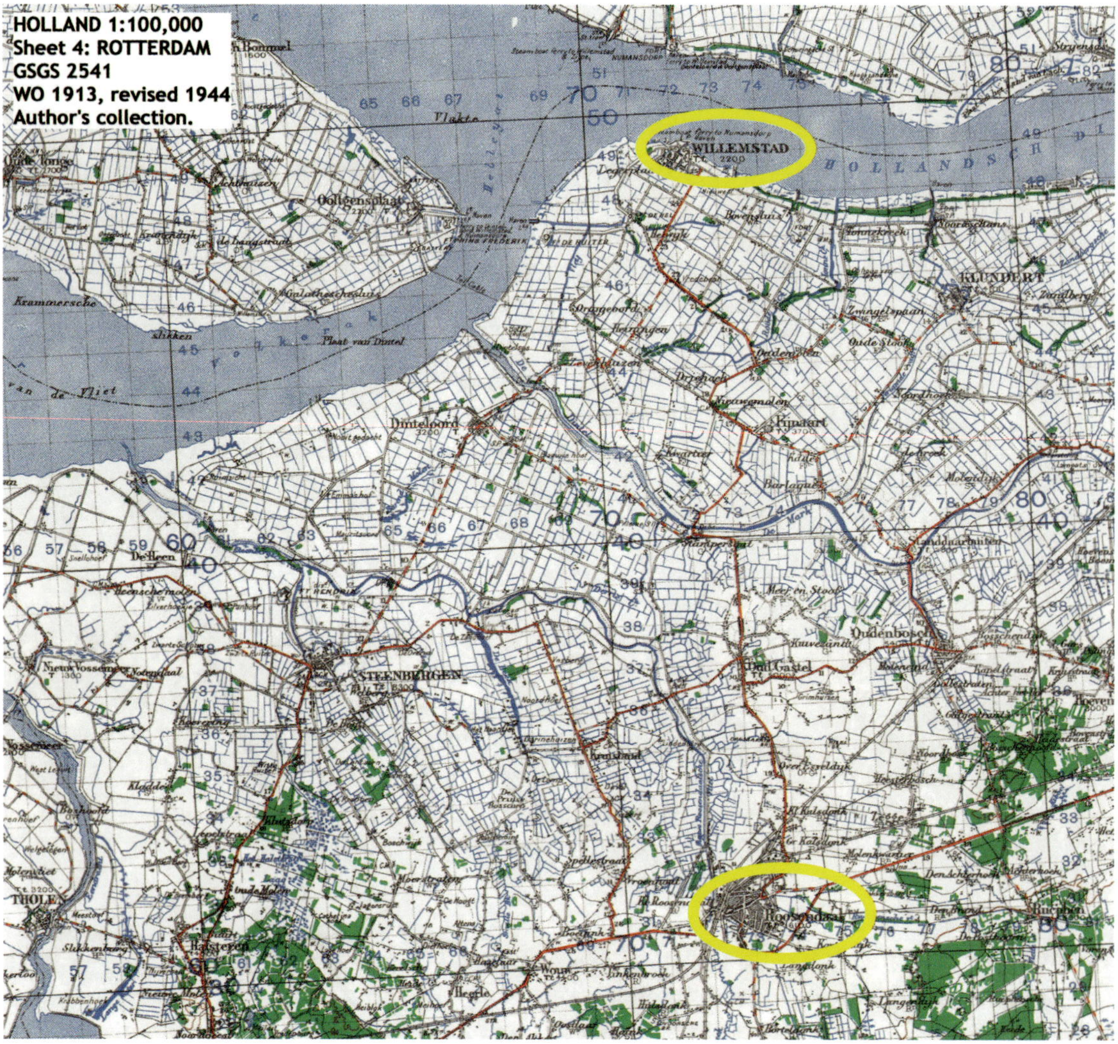

concealed Spandaus at twenty yards, writing off the leading section and pinning the first platoon on the wrong side of the bridge. We tried to get them out under artillery and smoke, but Jerry had a fixed line on the bridge which made it impossible. Therefore they had to stay there all day, within about twenty yards of the Germans, who were pretty strong with about eight Spandaus. We managed in the end to get them out at dusk.

Meanwhile, a Maquisard had arrived saying that the fort was only occupied by a hundred Dutch civilians and that he knew a way through the floods to get there. Accordingly a strong platoon of 'A' Company moved off and occupied the fort. That night, after the 'D' Company platoon had been extricated, a terrific barrage (much too large) was put on to the village, and 'B' Company attacked the place, rushing the bridge and clearing the village completely.

They then passed through a patrol of 'A' Company, who went up to the west of Wilhelmstaadt and fired tracer at it from different places. During the night the Lincolns got into the place, thus clearing for once and ever all resistance up to the Maas.

* * *

2KRRC, meanwhile, spent the first week of November resting:

4 No change. Maintenance and baths. No evening stand-to, as the danger of an attack is now considered less. Lieut. R.O. Lewin rejoins "A" Coy from hospital and Lt. R.H. Burton joins Bn. and goes to "B" Coy.

Later that month, Lewin's mother replied to a letter from Robertson:

> My dear Bobber,
> It was very nice to hear from you. Robin's address is the same: 'A' Company – 2nd Battalion KRRC, BLA. We hear from him very seldom, but got a nice lot of letters from him when he was in hospital for three weeks with pleurisy. He was in Brussels at that time; he didn't go to a convalescent home or have any leave – straight back from hospital to his Battalion: three weeks seemed a very short time to be fit to fight off his pleurisy.
> It was tragic about Michael Sinclair. I always thought he was the nicest boy I knew – just everything one could want – and after five years of prison it seems just too cruel. Poor Iris and Sandy.
> Amy[1]

* * *

Boyd.

1KOSB also came out of the line on November 4th, moving into comfortable billets at St Anthonis. The standard routine for units in that area – who remained at three hours' notice to move in an emergency – was two days resting and sleeping, and three days getting weapons, ammunition, and stores back into good order. For those seeking a change of scene or company, there was a cinema in Mill, the 'Stage Door Canteen' in Oploo, and the Divisional Club in Helmond. On November 6th, as 2SWB finished their operation at Wilhelmstaadt, a party from 1KOSB set off for a two-day city break in Brussels. Boyd was not one of them; he took over 'A' Company on November 7th. As he later told Robertson, 'I gave up being Adjutant just after I last wrote to you and went to a Rifle Company for about three weeks as second in command, and then took over command. I have never been so happy in my life as when I was commanding the Company. I think it's the best possible job for a junior soldier.'[2]

* * *

Kennedy and Rolls were by now an experienced crew, with nearly two months of combat operations under their belts, and fresh from some leave. Their next mission took place on November 3rd, but in a taste of things to come, the appalling weather called an early halt. The sixteen Mosquitoes of 248 and 235 Squadrons which took to the air at 1012hrs were meant to be looking for U-Boats, but forty minutes later ran into weather so bad

Kennedy.

that the patrol was abandoned at 1108hrs. Within an hour all the aircraft were back down again at Banff.

Nothing daunted, they tried again the following day, this time aboard DM-Q, one of nine 248 Squadron aircraft launched at 1130hrs on November 4th; with them were seven from 235 Squadron. Patrolling from Bremanger to Utvaer, and flying at a comfortable 6,000ft, two hours after take-off they spotted a 2,000-ton merchant vessel under way off Kinn, and another of similar size moored to a jetty. Kennedy was one of four pilots who were sent in to attack using cannon and machine-guns. The vessel in fact turned out to be a trawler-type auxiliary, which the attack left smoking, and by 1550hrs the formation had landed safely.

DM-S gave the crew their next ride across the North Sea on anti-submarine patrol, on November 9th.

> Time Up: 1105hrs-1108hrs
> Time down: 1457hrs-1503hrs
> In formation with six aircraft 235 Squadron, Wing Commander Atkinson leading in X/235. B/248 landed base 1306hrs, petrol feed unserviceable. 1345hrs X1, H, F/248 lost main formation in bad weather and returned to base. Landed 1416hrs-1418hrs. Patrol Utvaer-Kimmkelou completed; low cloud and fog obscured fiords. Landed base, nothing to report.[3]

Kennedy did not fly an operation again until November 21st; during the lull, on November 12th, he wrote to Robertson:[4]

> I have now been on operations 2½ months and am thoroughly enjoying it. I am in Coastal Command and am flying one of the fastest aircraft of the day. I find it far more fun than a good day's shooting. On the whole the rest of the Squadron are a very decent crowd and we have an A1 CO, a New Zealander.
>
> I have got as much shooting locally on my hands as I can deal with. As I only get one day off a week I cannot take full advantage of it all. I have my own dog up here, a blue roan cocker spaniel, and also have my car, which is a great asset.
>
> The CO of the station here is the Hon. Max Aitken, Lord Beaverbrook's son, and also a fighter ace. We had a big party in the Mess here last night and had the Coastal Command band playing. Sir Sholto Douglas was up here for it.
>
> I was home on leave two weeks ago. By some good management both my sisters were home at the same time. So we had an amusing time.

* * *

Mackrill had joined an operational flotilla at Great Yarmouth (HMS *Midge*) on Monday November 6th; he was now assigned to 16th MGB Flotilla. The unit's mission was essentially the same as 248 Squadron's, but over shorter distances.

> When I arrived on Monday I was put on an MTB, but forty-eight hours later I was moved to an MGB as temporary First Lieutenant. There are only two officers aboard, and I am responsible to the Captain for the boat. I must say for the first day or so I was completely at sea, but now things are running smoothly …

> Yarmouth is not much of a place, I'm afraid, and as yet I know very few people, which makes going ashore very dull.
>
> Since I have been here the weather has been shocking. It has rained practically every day – just as bad as Scotland. As you will probably [know], the 'weather in the Straits of Dover' is of great importance to me now.[5]

Mackrill's MTB had been a Fairmile 'D' – a 'Dog Boat' – MTB 761, commanded by RNVR Lieutenant W.J. Kempner. But the MGB was the older MGB 325, a Fairmile 'C' class boat which, amazingly enough, still survives in use as an office at Hayling Island. Mackrill's Captain was Lieutenant A.C. Shearer. At 110ft long, and with a crew of sixteen, the MGB was heavily armed but one of only twenty-four of its type built. It carried a formidable armament: two quick-firing 40mm guns, two twin .5-inch Vickers machine-guns, and two twin .303 Vickers.

On November 24th, Mackrill recorded: 'I had a super messy postcard from Bobber yesterday, written on both sides and rather messed up in the post. It took me at least ten minutes to read!'[6]

* * *

2SWB's parent formation – 49th Division – had successfully completed its task, and was therefore reassigned to other operations. On November 15th, according to Somerville, the Battalion

> concentrated in the area of Lille-St Hubert, preparatory to an advance towards Venlo. This was an extremely difficult piece of country. There was only one road in the whole area, and everything else was a mud track about two feet deep in mud. The result was that progress was very slow. There was a great deal of work for the Sappers. Countless bridges had to be built over the many canals and waterways in the area. The enemy had laid countless numbers of mines of all sorts. All this, together with the weather (which was appalling) made progress very slow.
>
> After a lot of waiting the Battalion was at last committed to attack. We had to attack a series of woods, beastly things, with an axis that was a forest track about four feet deep in mud. No ordinary vehicle could get up and maintenance was done by Kangaroo. We were unfortunate in having more casualties from mines than anything else, mainly 'R' and *Schu.* The attack was successful, but the companies were very heavily mortared on the objective and digging-in in four feet of mud is not easy.
>
> At last we reached the defences of Venlo – almost a frontier town, on the Maas – which was heavily defended with four belts of wire and an anti-tank ditch (20 feet x 15 feet) all round it. Jerry had a lot of artillery the other side of the Maas, which was pretty active. We went into reserve at Sevenum preparatory to the attack on Venlo. It took five days with a sand model to plan the attack, and then the day before it was due they called it off.

* * *

Boyd had taken 'A' Company 1KOSB into the same sector of the line at Overloon on November 9th. The weather was very wet, but the usual patrolling and occasional shifts of position were conducted, without the same level of shelling as on their last stay. By November 21st they were preparing for an attack at Veulen, which went in on the 23rd. It was unopposed, and the Battalion's main concern was how wet and muddy they were getting; first they crossed open boggy ground covered with water-filled ditches; there was rain on and off all morning, but it then set in solidly all afternoon. The author of the war diary complained:

> Everyone was soaked through. Although everyone was under cover, there was little chance of drying clothing during the night.

They were near Venraij, only three or so miles and the Maas from the German border. Despite the miserable conditions, Boyd took his Company on a patrol on November 24th:

> In the morning, 'A' Company went out to inspect the Molenbeek and its bridges in the area of Tienraij 8523. The Company set out at 0900hrs, reporting Kastenraij 8122 clear of enemy at 0930hrs. From Kleinoorloo 8223, reported clear at 0945hrs, then moved by tracks to the wood at 850233.

On the way towards this wood, a local accosted one of 'A' Company's stretcher-bearers and asked him to come to give first aid to another wounded civilian who was in a farm nearby. The bearer, Private Cope, did as he was asked, but whilst he was giving treatment he was taken prisoner by a German patrol. It had not been a trap, and the civilians rushed to Boyd to tell him what had happened. He instantly decided to send a patrol of his own to try to cut off the Germans before they could get Cope back to their own lines. Unfortunately, it was too late, and Cope 'went into the bag'. Boyd's men continued into the wood and came under ineffective fire from a concrete works nearby; they found the Molenbeek swollen and its bridge blown before they returned to the rest of the Battalion.

Duffin.

By one of those quirks of the war, Duffin and 3SG were also near Tienraij at this time, and occupied the town without opposition on the 25th whilst 1KOSB rested. The Guards then endured a night of heavy artillery fire, and at 0800hrs on November 26th shells rained down on Left Flank Squadron to the north of the town, killing Duffin's fellow Wykehamist Marshall, along with two of his tank crew. Despite this blow, 3SG advanced north towards the Maas, and after a few skirmishes were released to billets in Helmond on November 29th.

* * *

Meanwhile, on November 21st Kennedy and Rolls flew their next combat sortie, in Mosquito DM-R. It was a huge operation; not only were there eight Mosquito FB.VI and six FB.XVIII 'Tsetses' from 248 Squadron, but twelve Mosquitoes from 235, six from 143, and twelve from 404 Squadron RCAF. And then there were the Beaufighters: thirteen from 144, one from 333 (Norwegian) Squadron, eleven from 455 Squadron RAAF, and six from 489 Squadron RNZAF. As though this was not enough, additionally twelve Mustangs provided 'top cover' against enemy fighters. The multinational formation of eighty-seven combat aircraft was led by Kennedy's commanding officer – New Zealander Wing Commander G.D. 'Bill' Sise DSO, DFC – in N/248, and its objective was the shipping in the Norwegian port of Ålesund. It must have been a huge anticlimax when they found no targets in the water there. After five hours in the air, they all touched down safe, but deflated.

But soon enough, mere disappointment would have seemed a blessing. December 1944 was a miserable month for 248 Squadron. It started promisingly, with the Squadron stood down for the first four days. But on December 5th, 248 participated in another large operation, a 35-aircraft anti-shipping patrol to Ytterone. Rolls and Kennedy were again in DM-R when the first aircraft got airborne at 1148hrs. There were eight from 235 Squadron, twelve from 143, and fourteen from 248. The thirty-fifth aircraft was from 138 (Photographic) Wing and recorded the mission on camera from start to finish. The resulting film is in the Imperial War Museum archives and available to watch;[7] although it is not possible to identify DM-R, it is stunning footage which gives the viewer a vivid sense of the missions which Kennedy flew.

By 1340hrs the Mosquitoes were over Nordgulen at heights of between 3,000 and 5,000ft, and within minutes had spotted an enemy convoy (BE-1075-AL) at anchor; the Mosquitoes assessed it as four merchant vessels of between 2,500 and 4,000 tons, two TTAs, and a large tug-boat. The surrounding hills forced the attacking aircraft to make steep diving attacks; two Tsetses were sent in, which scored two hits on one merchant vessel and three on the largest. There was intense anti-aircraft fire from the shore, so Sise decided to move on to investigate other targets. At 1358hrs they noted three small vessels in Orsfjord, and in Straumhaven a 6,000-ton cargo vessel at anchor, but in such a position that attack was not possible. So back to Nordgulen they went, where the northbound convoy had been joined by a southbound one. The attack commenced at

1410hrs, with devastating effect; damage was inflicted on at least six of the enemy ships, of which two were left burning.[8]

But the price was high. The shore-based anti-aircraft guns were positioned on the mountain slopes and so able to fire at the attacking aircraft as they dived past, and the three escorts of the first convoy[9] had been reinforced by three more *Vorpostenboote*,[10] together with three more merchant vessels, all with anti-aircraft guns. Mosquito P/143 limped home on one engine and crash-landed at Sumburgh, killing the pilot; three more aircraft each came back on a single engine, including M/248, damaged in its port engine. A further four Mosquitoes sustained battle damage, with N/248 being hit in the tail. Worse still, when G/248 (HR120) was hit by anti-aircraft fire, its starboard engine caught fire. The pilot nevertheless pressed home his attack on the tug *Aasenfjord*, but the Mosquito was again hit and crashed into the sea at 1415hrs. There were no survivors.[11]

Worse was to follow. On December 7th a formation of sixty-five aircraft from both the Banff and Dallachy strike wings – with an escort of twelve Mustangs – headed out to attack Ålesund again. By 1330hrs the force was north of its objective when news arrived that there were good targets in the harbour. However, as the formation made landfall near Gossen at 1412hrs, it was bounced by some twenty enemy fighters – Bf109s and FW190s of III *Gruppe*, *Jagdgeschwader* 5 *'Eismeer'* – and forced to scatter. The formation commander transmitted terse order to his crews:

'Bandits ahead.'

'Turn out to sea.'

'Seek cloud cover. Engage bandits if in position to do so, but withdraw to sea.'

'Formation check petrol; divert if necessary.'

Two of 248 Squadron's Mosquitoes were amongst those lost: DM-O (NT224) and DM-Z (PZ346). One aircraft had been reported with an engine in flames, and another had been seen to plunge into the sea. All four crew-members were posted missing.[12]

Luckily for Kennedy and Rolls, they had not been on this mission. But as the weather worsened and the days grew ever shorter, the task before them could only become more dangerous.

* * *

At around this time, General Fortune suffered a stroke, as his wife informed Robertson in early December:[13]

> Dear Bobber,
> It's too tragic; I had word from the War Office yesterday that Victor was being seriously ill. Apparently he has had high blood pressure which resulted in a cerebral haemorrhage and paralysis down his right side. It's too sad after all he has done. I rushed up yesterday but they knew nothing more. They are trying to get him back but the trouble is we have no one of this rank in the country (they have all been sent to America) …
>
> I was so sorry about Michael Sinclair. Awful. Poor parents.

However, General Fortune refused offers of repatriation, telling the Germans that he had brought his men out and that he would go back with them. When he was finally liberated in April 1945 he was decorated in recognition of his selfless work in captivity. But his health had suffered, and he had only four years left to live.

* * *

By December 5th 1944, 1KOSB were manning various positions east of Venraij, right up against the Maas around Wanssum. Boyd and 'A' Company had been in reserve in Zandhoek, further from the river, but moved that day into Wanssum itself. It was a quiet sector; the Germans were on the east bank – much of which was flooded – and the state of the river was such that crossings by small boats were impossible, so the Germans could not send patrols across. They seemed to be in a very peaceable mood, and the 1KOSB war diary does not even report any shelling during this period. Or, at least, none until December 9th, when two mortar bombs landed in Wanssum.

On the following day, Boyd wrote to his father and his sister, Elisabeth, who was always known as 'Mickey':[14]

> Just a line to let you that I have been wounded and am now in hospital, and that you are **NOT** to worry as it's only a flesh wound through the left calf, and no bones broken or anything.
>
> I shall be being moved on from this hospital before very long, so no good my asking you to send letters here – I'll send you a more permanent address as soon as I get one.
>
> I've told Bus [his mother] **DON'T** worry.

Those two chance mortar bombs had fallen only two yards from him; in later life, Boyd claimed that the shiny cap-badge on his Glengarry must have given away his position to the enemy. His commanding officer wrote to Boyd's father within days:[15]

> I have no doubt that you have heard from John by now, and he has told you that he has been wounded in both knees. We were all very distressed when it happened, especially as he came through so much safely and then got hit at a comparatively quiet period. However, in some respects he was lucky, as the mortar bomb which hit him landed only about two yards away, and really it is miraculous that he escaped with his life.
>
> I haven't been able to find out how serious his wound is; I gather that no bones are broken, but that he has no feeling in one knee – the other one, I think, is not too bad. I do hope he makes a speedy recovery.
>
> He is a great loss to us. He did sterling work as Adjutant and was making a first-class Company Commander. I don't know whether he will be repatriated to England, but hope for your sake he is, as I am sure you would welcome the chance of his convalescing at home.
>
> He was exceedingly plucky when he was hit – as, for that matter, he was at all times. In fact, I can say with no exaggeration that there is no officer in the Battalion who showed less signs of fear, under the most trying circumstances, than John. For that reason alone he commanded great respect from his men.

I hope he gets fit again soon enough to come and rejoin us, for I shall be very glad to have him back. In the meanwhile I am sure there is no cause for you to worry about him, as the medical services are quite first-class, and he is sure to be well looked-after.
Yours sincerely,
R.C. Macdonald

However, it turned out that Boyd's injuries were more serious than his own letter and that from his commanding officer had suggested. He did end up convalescing in England, but – as he told Robertson in a letter from Leicester Royal Infirmary[16] – his wound had actually been what we would now call 'a life-changing injury':

As you see, I am now back in England, unfortunately minus my left leg. My luck eventually gave out on December 9th and two mortar bombs exploded very near to me as I was going round my Company positions. I was hit in both legs (and very lucky to get away with that). The right one is all right again, but they had to take the left off through the knee before I left Holland …

I shall have to give up all idea of being a regular soldier now, although I had just been accepted for a regular commission with the KOSB. I am rather undecided what to do when I am able to get about again, which won't be for some time yet. I thought either of the legal profession or of trying to get a job in some branch of the Foreign Office – it sounds very vague, I'm afraid, but I really know nothing about either. The main drawback to the former is that it would require such a long period of training and I don't want to go on being dependent on my parents for any longer than I have to – really it's rather like starting out at twenty-four instead of eighteen!

I hope you don't mind my bothering you with all this – but I wonder if you have any suggestions to make. I don't think there is any frightful hurry at the moment, as they are still waiting for my leg to clear up a bit before re-amputating in order to fit an artificial one. However, I don't want to waste any time when I am able to get about again.

Have you news of any of my contemporaries, I wonder? I have been rather out of touch with Wykehamical matters since Tom Howarth left our Brigade HQ to go to Division (where I believe he was very unhappy).

Please excuse this very bad writing, but it's a bit difficult lying flat on your back in bed!

Robertson wasted no time in complying with Boyd's request for job suggestions – giving advice, solicited or otherwise, was one of the Bobber's defining characteristics. Equally in character, soon after receiving the news, he wrote to Commander Boyd, who replied:

My dear Robertson,
Very many thanks for your very kind letter; as you say, it is very bad luck on John, but when I heard what hit him (a mortar bomb two yards away) I'm only thankful that he is alive at all.

I saw him while he was at Leicester recently and he was very cheerful; he told me, however, that they would require to do a re-amputation above the knee in order to get his leg suitable for fitting an artificial limb. This will take longer than we all expected, and I heard yesterday that he will not be ready for the operation before six months, which is a long time to wait for it.

> It is very good of you to have taken so much trouble to find out about suitable occupations for him. I don't suppose he will be able to continue in the Regular Army, which is very bad luck on him as he was very keen on it and was very pleased when he was informed that he'd been gazetted. I did not see it in the paper myself.[17]

* * *

As I write these words, it is December 16th 2022, seventy-eight years to the day since the events which I am about to describe. In North-West Europe it was the opening day of the German offensive in the Ardennes – the 'Battle of the Bulge'. Further north, in Norway, German coastal shipping crept through the leads and fjords, hoping to avoid the attentions of the Banff strike wing. Today is very cold, and snow and ice lie on the ground; but it is as nothing, nothing, to the cold that day over Norway.

Kennedy and Rolls took off from Banff at around 0950hrs on December 16th in Mosquito DM-R (HR156). There were twenty-one other aircraft with them (from 248, 235, and 143 Squadrons), though DM-L suffered an engine problem on take-off and crashed on making a forced landing back at Banff minutes later. Her crew survived, but it was an inauspicious start. The anti-shipping patrol headed for Utvaer, with the usual outrider Mosquito from 333 (Norwegian) Squadron ahead of them. The formation

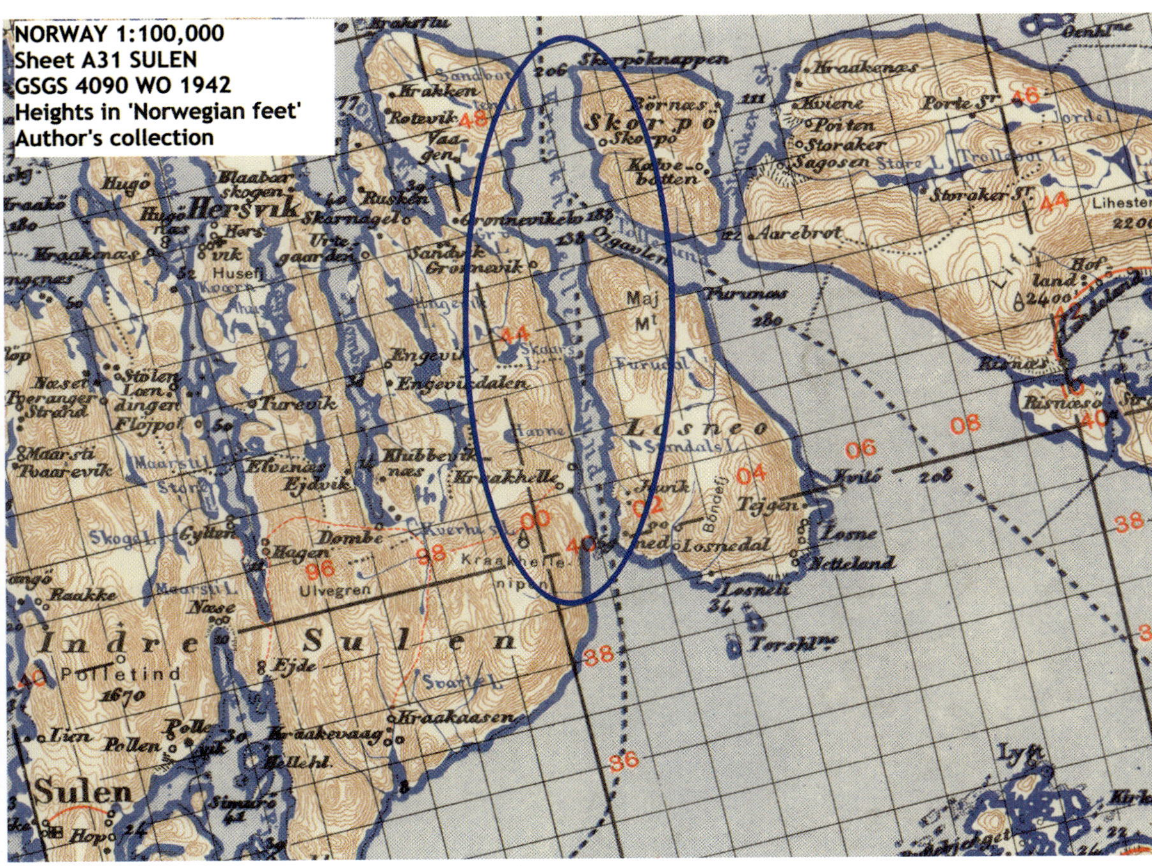

had intelligence that a large merchantman, *Ferndale* (4,300 tons), had run aground in Krakhellesund, about seventy miles north of Bergen. Because of the threat from the air, German convoys tended to sail at night and anchor by day. Obviously, the knock-on effect was that more vessels ran aground. Thus it was with *Ferndale,* built in Germany in 1925 and 380ft long. Laden with a cargo of potatoes from Poland, on the night of December 14th/15th she had drifted on to the Seglstenen rocks as she crossed a narrow point in

Parat & Ferndale burning, December 16th 1944. (Copyright holder unknown)

A Mosquito climbs away from the blazing Parat & Ferndale, *December 16th 1944.* (IWM C4901)

Sognesjøen. Other ships in the convoy were *Wilhelms* and a tug-boat, *Fairplay X. Wilhelms* continued to Ålesund with two of the convoy's escorts, leaving *Ferndale* stranded. It soon became clear that divers would be needed to get her off, and so the 100ft salvage vessel *Parat* was summoned; meanwhile, *Fairplay X* and *Vorpostenboot* V-5305 *Jäger* (formerly the Norwegian *Hval VI)* remained on the scene.

At 1144hrs on December 16th the Norwegian Mosquito confirmed *Ferndale*'s presence, and the formation prepared to attack. As the aircraft roared in at mast-head height along the length of the waterway – the only avenue of approach between the steep hillsides – *Jäger* hid herself in shadow against the western side. *Fairplay X* remained in the main fairway, whilst *Parat* lay alongside *Ferndale.* The attack lasted only a couple of minutes, but at the end of it *Parat* and *Ferndale* were in flames. Casualties are unclear – one source states eight killed, one seriously wounded and four slightly wounded aboard *Ferndale* – but at least three of the dead were anti-aircraft gunners.[18]

Forty-five minutes later, another six Mosquitoes attacked, having been attracted by the smoke, but S/235 was shot down by the *Jäger.* By a quirk of fate, its pilot was an Australian whose mother was Scottish and father Norwegian.[19] But this second attack delivered the *coup de grâce*; *Parat* sank first, settling in around thirty fathoms; *Ferndale* cracked in half, as can be clearly seen in this photograph.

Ferndale, *soon after December 16th 1944.* (Copyright holder unknown)

Four hours after *Parat* sank, *Ferndale*'s stern hit the sea bed a matter of feet from the smaller vessel. The surviving section of *Ferndale* was still full of potatoes, however, and no sooner had the wreck cooled than German troops and local civilians began to plunder the upper decks – a sort of poor man's *Whisky Galore.*

The Parat *& stern of the* Ferndale *still lie where they sank in Krakhellesund, a popular diving attraction.*[18]

Although this had been by any standard a successful strike, 248 Squadron had again been unfortunate. As Kennedy piloted DM-R to strafe *Ferndale* and *Parat* he reported that he had taken a hit to his port engine. He turned the Mosquito away out to sea, with flames pouring from the engine and swiftly losing altitude. It was clear that Kennedy and Rolls would have to ditch the aircraft. Rolls fired a red flare to mark their position, and at 1203hrs Kennedy successfully landed the Mosquito on the sea.

The Mosquito FB.VI was equipped with a rubber dinghy stowed in the upper fuselage behind the cockpit canopy. This was inflated automatically by an immersion switch, though a manual system was also fitted behind the pilot in the cabin roof. As two other Mosquitoes watched, Kennedy and Rolls were seen to leave their aircraft and clamber aboard their dinghy. DM-R floated for a few minutes, then slipped beneath the waves. A fix was taken on the position – 60.59N/04.09E, some fifty miles south-west of Krakhellesund – before shortage of fuel forced the circling Mosquitoes to leave. Kennedy and Rolls were alone on the North Sea, wet, cold, and uncertain of their fate. There were only six hours of daylight at that time of year, and although aircrew had survived in dinghies for as long as five days, realistically they had at most twenty-four hours.

By now, the RAF's air-sea rescue organisation and procedures had been honed by years of practice. Warwick aircraft – bigger and better developments of the Wellington – shadowed the Banff strike wing whenever it set out on a mission. That day, Warwick

Warwick 'B' of 282 Squadron, RAF, carrying an airborne lifeboat beneath its belly. 279 Squadron's Warwicks were of the same configuration. (IWM MH5337; edited by dansteele.net)

RL-F of 279 Squadron had taken off at 0939hrs and followed the faster Mosquitoes across the North Sea. At 1157hrs the call came from the formation leader that DM-R was in trouble. The crew spotted Kennedy and Rolls almost as soon as they ditched, and at 1206hrs – only three minutes after DM-R had gone down – an Airborne Lifeboat was dropped.

The Airborne Lifeboat had been designed by the distinguished sailor Uffa Fox in 1943. Fitted beneath an aircraft like the Warwick, it would be dropped from 700ft, parachutes slowing its descent. It was self-righting, and when it reached the water the parachutes would detach whilst rockets in the bow and stern fired lines 100 yards, so that aircrew within reach could drag themselves to the lifeboat or pull it to them. The lifeboats contained survival equipment such as food, first aid kits, a radio, and waterproof clothing. They were fitted with two small engines, a mast, and sails, so that rescued men were able to start making their way to safety at a rate of around six knots – but 'unfortunately, the parachutes fell off in mid-air and the lifeboat sank on striking the water.'[21]

The pilot who dropped it, Flying Officer O'Reilly, would have been fuming; Warwicks only carried one Airborne Lifeboat. However, they were also able to drop two sets of Lindholme Gear. This consisted of five containers, connected by a floating rope, which held a large rubber dinghy (which automatically inflated on hitting the water), as well as other emergency supplies. The gear would be dropped upwind of the men in the water, in the hope that at least some of the spread would float to them, enabling the rest to be gathered in. At 1223hrs O'Reilly dropped a set of this equipment, and he and his crew were delighted to see one of the two soaked and freezing airmen clamber into the Lindholme's dinghy.

The second survivor remained in the small dinghy from the Mosquito, and at 1228hrs F/279 came in for another drop of Lindholme Gear. To O'Reilly's dismay, this landed downwind and out of the airman's reach. RL-F had run out of resources, and the crew watched the survivor as he paddled across to the wreckage of the Airborne Lifeboat and fastened his dinghy to it. All that O'Reilly could do was continue to circle and to drop sea-markers until a relief aircraft could arrive. Just the sight and sound of the Warwick must have given hope to Rolls and Kennedy, now in separate craft, as alone as they had ever been in their lives.

O'Reilly's crew summoned a second Warwick to take over; perhaps, with a fresh Airborne Lifeboat, the Mosquito crew would have a chance of surviving the night. Warwick P/279, flown by Warrant Officer Bolton, took off from RAF Wick at 1336hrs and arrived overhead at 1455hrs, spotting the two survivors. At 1512hrs Bolton made his approach at 700ft to drop the Airborne Lifeboat. Amazingly, a photograph exists which shows this moment; it was taken by one of O'Reilly's crew, Wireless Operator/ Air Gunner Don Mabey.[22]

The lifeboat landed 100 yards from Kennedy and Rolls – a good drop – but this time the parachutes failed to detach; the lifeboat capsized, and the parachutes filled with wind, dragging the lifeboat fully a mile away.

Bolton still had Lindholmes, of course, and he tried to drop both, but the sea was becoming increasingly rough, and the survivors were unable to reach the rescue gear. RL-P, like its predecessor, summoned a relief and orbited anxiously.

Warwick RL-U took off at 1820hrs, piloted by Flying Officer Garven, and when it arrived the crew saw a marker in the sea and P/279 circling. Garven dropped more markers, but at 2156hrs

> an unidentified enemy aircraft was seen approaching from the east at 500 feet, showing a headlight. This enemy aircraft immediately extinguished its headlight and closed range to about seven hundred yards. Evasive action was taken by 'U' and the enemy aircraft was not seen again.

Unfortunately, this incident had caused the Warwick to lose contact with Kennedy and Rolls. Garven dropped another marker and headed back, landing at Sumburgh at 2333hrs.

* * *

Despite the start of the German Ardennes offensive the day before, Montgomery had time to write to Robertson on December 17th, enclosing a copy of his Christmas message to his troops.

B. L. Montgomery
Field-Marshal

21 ARMY GROUP

PERSONAL CHRISTMAS MESSAGE FROM THE C-IN-C

(*To be read out to all troops*)

1. The forces of the British Empire in western Europe spend Christmas 1944 in the field. But what a change has come over the scene since last Christmas.

The supreme Battle of Normandy carried with it the liberation of France and Belgium.

Last Christmas we were in England, expectant and full of hope; this Christmas we are fighting in Germany.

The conquest of Germany remains.

2. It would have needed a brave man to say on D day, 6 June, that in three months we would be in Brussels and Antwerp: having liberated nearly the whole of France and Belgium; and in six months we would be fighting in Germany: having driven the enemy back across his own frontiers.

But this is what has happened.

And we must not fail to give the praise and honour where it is due:

"*This was the Lord's doing, and it is marvellous in our eyes.*"

3. At Christmas time, whether in our homes or fighting in the field, we like to sing the carols we learnt as children; and in truth, this is indeed a link between us and our families and friends in the home country: since they are singing the same verses. The old words express exactly what we all feel today:

"*Glory to God in the highest, and on earth peace, good will toward men.*"

That is what we are fighting for, that is what we desire: on earth peace, good will toward men.

4. And so today we sing the Christmas hymns, full of hope, and steadfast in our belief that soon we shall achieve our hearts' desire.

Therefore, with faith in God, and with enthusiasm for our cause and for the day of battle, let us continue the contest with stout hearts and with determination to conquer.

5. And at this time I send to each one of you my best wishes and my Christmas greetings.

Wherever you may be, fighting in the front line, or working on the lines of communication or in the ports, I wish all of you good luck and a happy 1945. We are all one great team; together, you and I, we have achieved much; and together, we will see the thing through to the end.

6. Good luck to you all.

B. L. Montgomery
Field-Marshal
C-in-C 21 Army Group.

Belgium.
Xmas. 1944

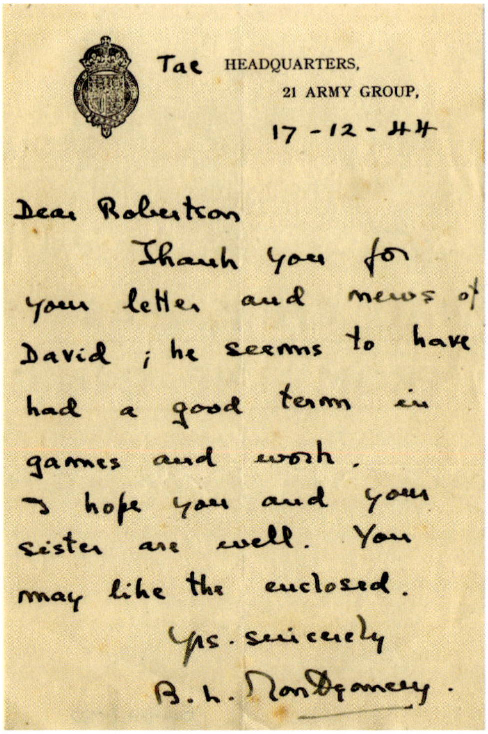

Tac HEADQUARTERS,
21 ARMY GROUP,
17-12-44

Dear Robertson

Thank you for your letter and news of David; he seems to have had a good term in games and work.

I hope you and your sister are well. You may like the enclosed.

Yrs. sincerely

B. L. Montgomery.

* * *

The efforts to rescue the crew of DM-R resumed as soon as light made a search possible on December 17th. Two Warwicks were allocated to it: RL-E (piloted by Flying Officer Grimston) took off at 0913hrs, and RL-C followed at 1034hrs, Flying Officer Richards at the controls. At 1120hrs, two of 248 Squadron's Mosquitoes (DM-V and DM-S) flew off to provide fighter cover for the Warwicks and to help with the search. Grimston was first on the scene, drawn there by the sight of Mosquito K/235 circling the dinghies, which 'were found in position 61.05N 03.53E … A body was seen in one of the dinghies, but there was no sign of life or movement.'[23]

The Warwicks left the scene. No one could fault the efforts which 279 Squadron had made to rescue Kennedy and Rolls, but the best air-sea rescue technology of the time had simply been unable to cope with the weather conditions, as well as being too prone to equipment failure. A message was transmitted to the Germans in the hope that they might succeed where the RAF had failed, but nothing was ever seen again of Kennedy or Rolls. They are commemorated, like so many, on the Runnymede Memorial.[24]

When Kennedy's half-brother Geoffrey Gwyer had been killed in action in March 1943, Kennedy had told Robertson that 'I am afraid my mother will have taken it very hard as she lost a husband, two brothers, and a brother-in-law in the last war, and I think that is anyone's share of the nightmares of war – let alone this, on top of it all.'

Constance Kennedy's nightmare was about to increase still further. Sise had sent her a telegram on December 16th to tell her that John was missing. Three days later, Sise sat down to write a particularly hard letter, for it gave news not of his death, but the presumption of it.

Dear Mrs Kennedy,
It is with the greatest regret that I have to write and confirm my telegram (of the 16th) that your son is missing from an operational trip on December 16th. I have delayed writing to you because there was every possible hope until today that he would be successfully rescued. Now I am afraid that hope is remote.

Your son was flying as Pilot in an aircraft in a formation detailed to attack a target on the Norwegian coast. The attack was successfully completed, but during the action your son's aircraft was hit. With great skill he successfully carried out a 'ditching' about twenty-five miles from the enemy coast and both your son and his navigator got into the aircraft's dinghy. Air Sea Rescue operations were immediately begun and further dinghies dropped. Bad weather hampered rescue operations, which were carried on for three days, but no rescue could be made. Your son and his navigator became separated, and were last seen in two different dinghies still about twenty-five miles from the enemy coast. You may rest assured that no effort was spared to rescue them. Now our only hope is that your son may have been picked up by the enemy at sea, or drifted to the coast.

During the time John was with this Squadron he greatly impressed me with his skill in the air and his efficiency on the ground. He had completed many sorties, and always did his job with skill and determination. In the Mess he was perpetually cheerful and always prepared to do all he could. He was an asset to the Squadron and we will all miss him very much.

G.D. Sise[25]

* * *

After Kennedy's loss was announced, Robertson received a Christmas card from him, containing a brief message:[26]

To you both & hoping you are very well.

My promotion came through about three weeks ago dated from October 9th.

WITH BEST WISHES
FOR
CHRISTMAS AND THE NEW YEAR
FROM

John Kennedy

No.248 SQUADRON
ROYAL AIR FORCE
BANFF
SCOTLAND

When Constance Kennedy eventually wrote to Robertson, the misery of it all came pouring forth.[27]

> Dear Major Robertson,
> It was so kind of you writing me that nice letter about John. It has been a terrible blow and very difficult to think of any future with those two beloved boys gone. I think perhaps you, more than most people, realized how much they meant to me – I don't know why you should have, but somehow I have felt that you did.
>
> I had guarded and tried to guide Geoffrey all his life and he was such a joy to me and repaid it all a thousand times when he grew up – and John was just so sweet to me – I doubt if anyone ever had two such grand sons – and all the future seemed to have been built up for them – it's difficult to think of it without them …
>
> Yours very sincerely,
> Constance F. Kennedy

* * *

The day after Sise wrote to Kennedy's mother, Duffin and 3SG left Helmond for Maastricht, in response to the German attack in the Ardennes; it was possible that British troops might need to attack the northern flank of 'The Bulge'. The Battalion arrived on the 22nd, and Duffin took the opportunity to pen a letter to Robertson:[28]

> This in reply to your postcard, for which many thanks. I'm afraid I've been rather long in replying, but have been fairly busy of late.
>
> So the Boche has still got a kick in him, it seems. I must say one has got to admire him in some ways, for scraping together an offensive weapon out of remnants – however, I think it'll be to our good in the end, if it's only to wake some people out of their "end of the war relaxation" attitude, which is a very easy thing to get a hold of one and difficult to shake off – unless it is done forcibly for one.
>
> I suppose you heard that we lost Willy Marshall ('A') some time ago. A very unlucky shell indeed killed him outright. I feel very sorry for his young wife – they'd only been married for a few months and together for not more than a fortnight.
>
> I get occasional news of Win.Coll., chiefly through Harold Smith's *Wykehamist*, which arrives regularly and is read by all … I see Marcus Hampton has had a son and heir – any other families on the way? It's about time J.D'E.E.F. added to his country's birth-rate, I feel.[29] I in return can promise no contribution as yet!
>
> My pressure lamp is on the wane, so I shall close before it goes out entirely, wishing you both a very Happy New Year, with lots of old friends available once again to come and see you, in fairly small numbers at a time, of course!

The result of the move was that instead of being converted into infantry and guarding the banks of the Maas, as expected, Duffin and his comrades spent a cosy Christmas in Valkenburg. The seemingly incessant rain gave way to sunshine and frost; the Dutch inhabitants were enthusiastically hospitable; and the attack proved unnecessary.

* * *

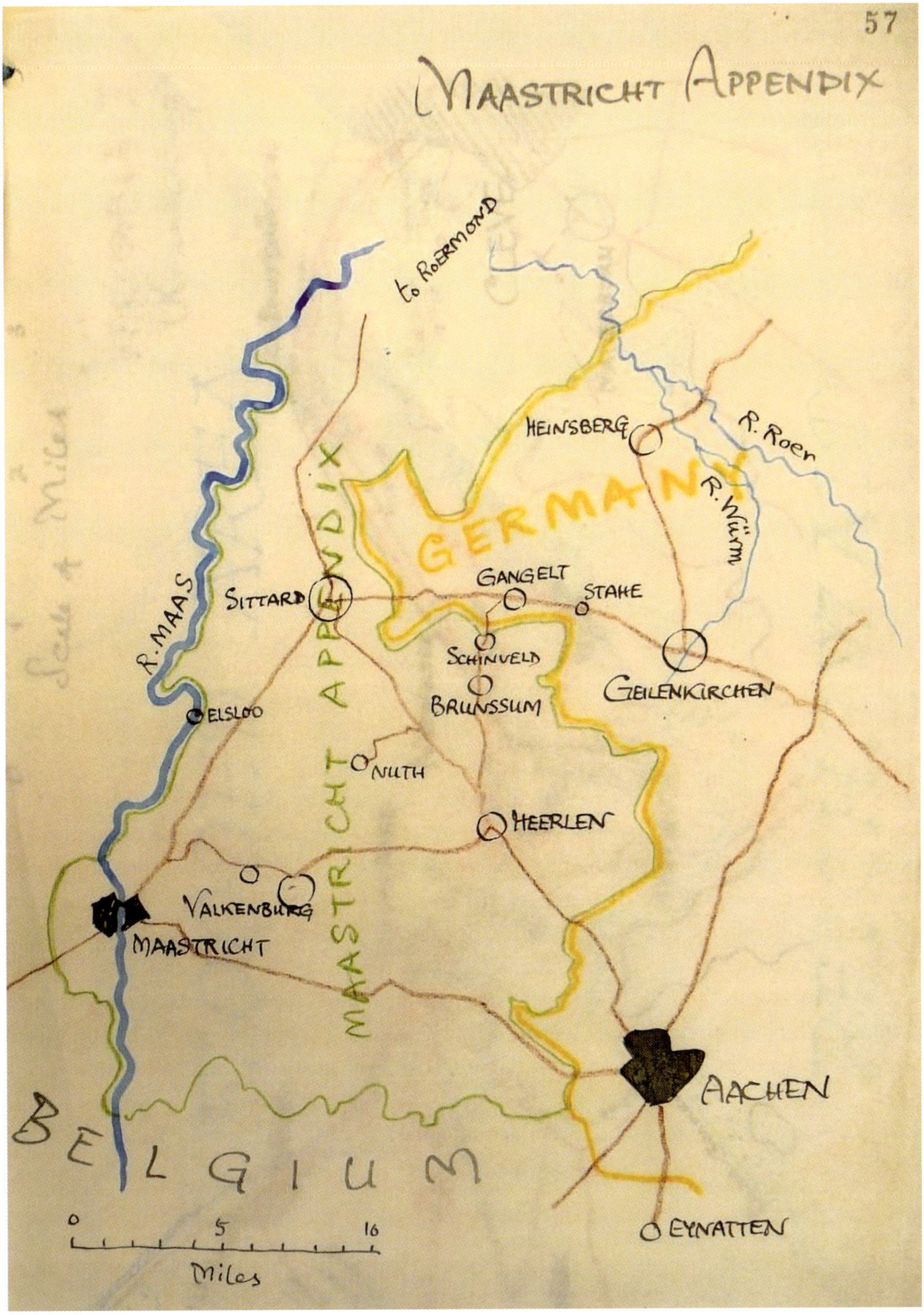

Map trace of 3SG's area of operations, Christmas 1944. (National Archives CAB 106/1029: Account of Operations of 3rd Tank Battalion Scots Guards 1944 July 20–1945 May 8)

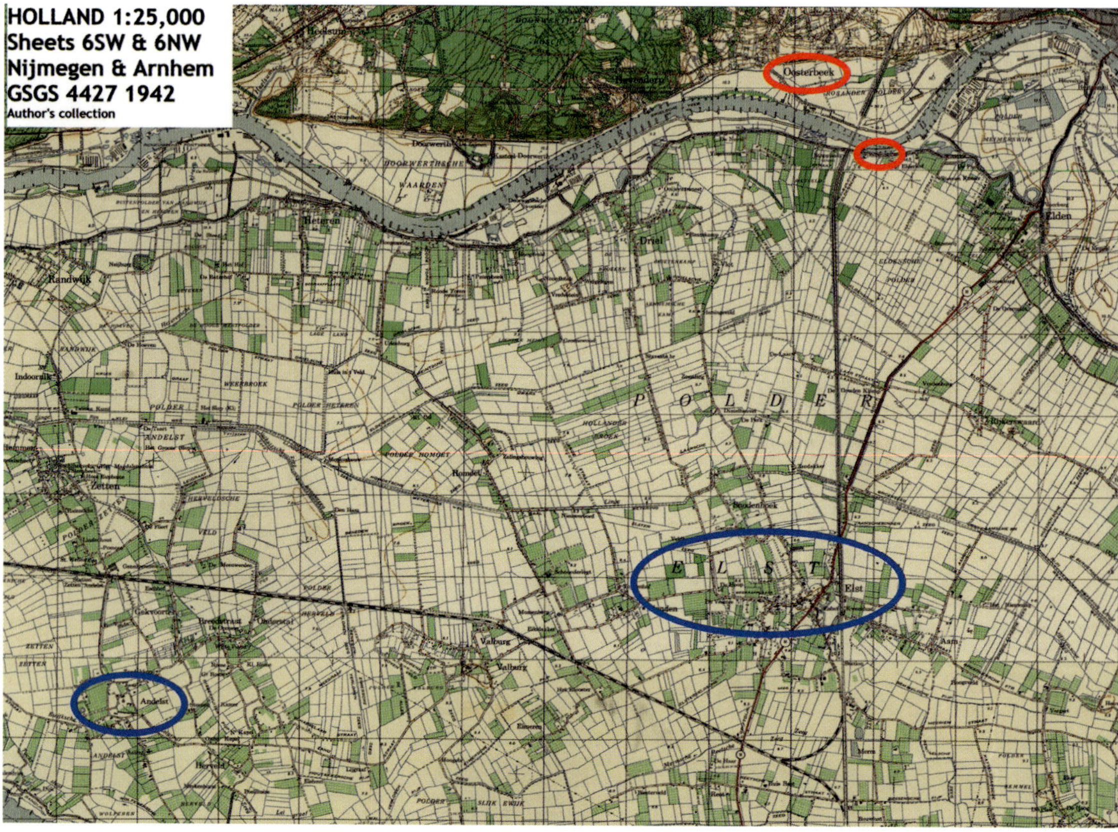

When Montgomery's land forces had failed to reach the paratroops at Arnhem in September, they had nevertheless made it across the Waal at Nijmegen and reached the Neder Rijn eight miles to the north. This left them with a salient running roughly south-north, with major rivers at its northern tip and at its base. The patch of land between the rivers – liberally sprinkled with mines, unexploded ordnance, burnt-out vehicles, and the graves of those killed in September's fighting – became known to the Allied troops who occupied it as 'The Island'. It was completely overlooked by high ground behind Arnhem, which was held by the Germans. The whole tract lay below the level of the rivers and was protected by dykes. Access to The Island was across the half-collapsed bridge at Nijmegen, and Elst, the centre of the British positions, was in ruins. Conditions grew worse when, on December 2nd, the Germans blew a hole in the dyke holding back the Neder Rijn just south-east of Oosterbeek.

Somerville was not impressed:

> Life on The Island was not very pleasant. It consisted of doing nothing by day, sitting in houses and patrolling, and being shelled at night. After we had arrived on The Island, Jerry blew the dykes and the whole Island flooded, which caused a great deal of alarm and despondency. All our positions had to be changed because of these floods, and gum-boots appeared, as well as Ducks and Weasels and other aquatic eccentricities. Life became better on The Island when we learned to make ourselves comfortable. It

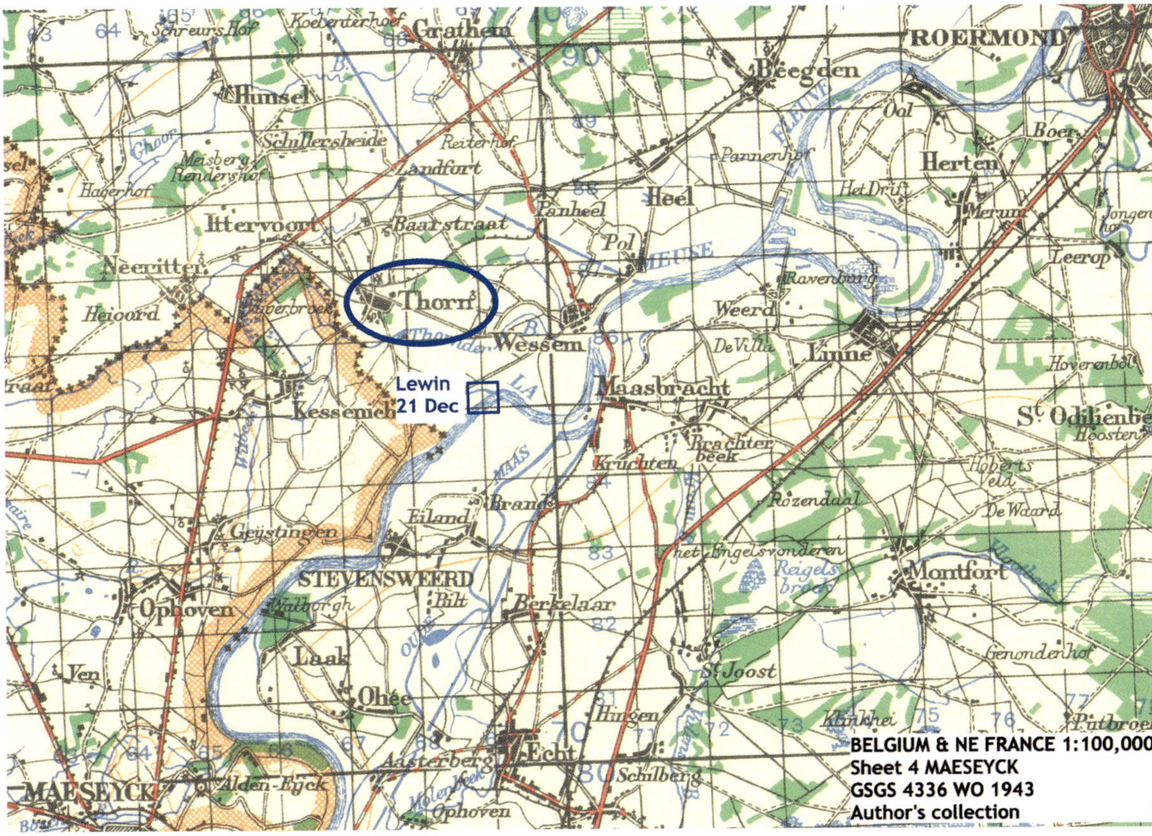

developed into a large patrollable No Man's Land, with neither side being very active except for one attack.

The only compensation for the misery was that Nijmegen lay just across the Waal, and so units or personnel could be rotated out of the line for a rest.

Christmas was spent in the Andelst area, with two companies more or less in reserve and able to have a magnificent dinner and general celebration. The other two had their dinners on the 27th, having had a swap round.

* * *

After a long period of inactivity, 2KRRC were by the second week of December in the line in Thorn, south-west of Roermond, hard up against the Belgian border. To their east lay the Maas; to their north, the Wessem–Nederweert Canal. Across the water, in Maasbracht, was a German garrison, and there was vigorous patrolling on both sides of the river.

At 1700hrs on December 21st, Lewin took a patrol of five men out towards the Maas opposite Maasbracht. Visibility was poor, but all seemed quiet. But by the small hours, the war diary recorded, things had taken a turn for the worse:

0045hrs
'A' Company patrol at 690852 surprised. Lieutenant Lewin and one Rifleman report several wounded.

0115hrs
Two more of patrol back; one wounded, at least one of remaining two wounded. One German believed killed, one known to be wounded. Colonel says nobody to go out searching, as enemy will probably be waiting in ambush.

The visibility had become even poorer by the time that a search-party was sent out:

1000hrs
Patrol to 690852 to pick up one of missing men, wounded. No signs of the other.

1440hrs
No signs of missing man found by patrol sent to look for him.

'With the best wishes to you & Sheila. I'm afraid we'll have to wait another year for Lenzerheide. Robin.'[30]

* * *

Robertson, as we know, looked after not only his boys but also their loved ones. A Christmas card to Barbara Simpkin elicited this response as 1944 shaded into the last year of the war:

Dear Major Robertson,
Very many thanks for your card and good wishes. This is just to give you the latest news of Richard. I heard last just before Christmas (a wonderful present!) and he wrote cheerfully as usual, but of course he has had many severe disappointments during the year – as indeed they all must have experienced. He does look forward to your letters. I am most thankful to have been moved to London (am working at Broadcasting House now) as it has given me a chance to try and get a home ready for him to come back

to. I've taken a flat here and got our furniture up as it would be so miserable for him to come home and find his things in store. I hope the rockets keep off! It's been hard work as the only one I could get was in a dilapidated condition, but getting something ready for him made it all seem not so bad! Please give my love to Miss Robertson. I shall never forget how kind she was to me.

Yours sincerely,
Barbara[31]

Barbara's reference to 'many disappointments' conceals a bigger, depressing saga. Life in *Oflag* IXA/Z was dull and slow-moving, unchanging almost, punctuated by trivial highlights: the arrival, in March 1944, of parcels which Barbara had posted to her husband in July 1942; language examinations in April; a delivery of books in May; two days' work outside the camp on a construction project; a recital of German sacred music; the funeral of one of the inmates; a failed escape tunnel; a letter from Sheila Robertson in July; a Mass with the intention for Barbara on her birthday (July 8th); losing weight, down to ten stone four pounds by August.

But of course, back in England, 'real' life went on, and relatives had to decide how much to tell the prisoners. Barbara was working for the BBC as an engineer in the wireless monitoring station at Tatsfield, south of London. There the BBC monitored not content (that was done at Caversham Park) but which frequencies were in use and from where. In July 1944, the danger from V-1 flying bombs led to the staff being evacuated to Crowsley Park near Reading. On August 28th Barbara wrote to Simpkin describing

Simpkin (left) *with other inmates of Oflag IXA/Z, 1944.* (Simpkin family collection; edited by author)

Simpkin in Oflag IXA/Z, 1944. (Simpkin family collection; edited by dansteele.net)

the sexual harassment she was suffering from her line manager; she treated it lightly, calling it an 'amusing complication'. The sequel was far from amusing. It seems that the harassment was more serious than Barbara let on, since she requested a transfer into London; despite having to take a demotion, she was at Broadcasting House by the end of September. Her spurned suitor then wrote to Simpkin's mother alleging that what he had desired had actually transpired. On October 11th Simpkin wrote to Barbara to tell her that his mother Evelyn had sent him a letter relaying the allegations – which he said he did not believe. A month later, he wrote to tell his wife that Evelyn – who was now living with 'Occy' Coller – had also convinced Occy that Barbara had been unfaithful. Evelyn seems to have been intercepting Simpkin's letters to his grandmother, as he wrote regularly but her own letters to him always complained that she never heard from him. The effect of all this on Simpkin's mental health cannot have been positive.

One problem was that delays in letters meant that Barbara was not aware of these allegations until December; as soon as she found out about them she wrote – on December 17th – explaining that her former boss must have been behind it all. Her letter had still not reached Simpkin when he wrote his final letter of 1944 on New Year's Eve. He directed his energies into studying for his examinations and staying warm in the biting cold of his *Oflag*.

XXVII

'I very stupidly trod on a German mine'

World War, January–February 1945

At the beginning of 1945, our subjects were in contact with the enemy in Italy, North-West Europe, Burma, and at sea. VE Day would be celebrated on May 8th, but less well known is that German forces in Italy surrendered on April 29th, with hostilities south of the Alps coming to a formal end on May 2nd. That same day in Burma, as the monsoon began, the great prize of Rangoon fell to a seaborne attack. The two events brought to an end offensive operations for the year. The first five months of 1945, then, were the end-game for most of our subjects. However, there was still suffering and brutal fighting enough for all.

In Italy with 10th Hussars, Peter Walker was still unsure of himself and feeling his way with 3 Troop, as he confided to his diary on January 1st:

> 3rd Troop in good fettle, though tomorrow I hold a personal arms inspection. I like it all more than I can say, though I feel I ought to take stock of my position more often. None of this overdoing motherly touch, nor yet the familiar slack attitude. Sergeant Ross a bit cold recently, but he's not been too well anyway – probably my imagination.[1]

* * *

In Stobs, near Hawick, 2SG were gearing up for their return to the front line. Clerk-Rattray was still with the Battalion, which had been stripped of personnel in March 1944 to bring 1SG up to strength after its evisceration at Anzio. 201 Guards Brigade had also gone into limbo, meaning that Clerk-Rattray had left Brigade HQ and returned to his Battalion. In April 1944, 2SG had returned to Britain, though it was not until 1945 that Clerk-Rattray got round to writing to Robertson:

Clerk-Rattray.

> I must apologise most humbly for not having written ever since I left Winchester, but all I can is that my silence does not signify lack of interest!
>
> Since I last saw you, I have travelled a long way, and seen many a sight that was both amazing and of interest. As you know I went abroad in 1942, and therefore did the long sea voyage round the Cape. We were lucky enough to have three weeks in Durban, which after war-time England we enjoyed immensely.

When we reached the Middle East, we were sent up to Damascus, which was a great piece of luck. Apart from Christmas, Hanuka, and getting to know Damascus itself, we also went on a motor-tour round Syria. I only completed half this trip, because I had to go on a course, but during the time I was on it, I had the chance of seeing Baalbek, Aleppo, and eastwards from there as far as the Euphrates.

Later on in the winter I fell off a motor bicycle while crossing the Sinai Desert, and on being given some sick leave went to Luxor.

I enjoyed the Middle East very much, and although so squalid, nevertheless it has a great attraction. It is remarkable that a country should have progressed so little in such a long period of time, but judging from the paintings on the walls in the tombs at Luxor, life cannot have been very different in those days.

We saw the completion of the campaign in Africa, and came home from Italy in April last year.[2]

It is typical of letters home from the war that Clerk-Rattray focused on the travel rather than his experience of, say, Monte Camino. All the evidence suggests that he was profoundly affected by his front-line service.

* * *

Lewin was on patrol again on January 2nd 1945. It had been a quiet day in Thorn, and late that afternoon he set out with one of his men to cross the Maas and investigate what was going on at Eiland. Lewin's typewritten patrol report survives in the National Archives and shows the stresses involved in such work.[3]

Lewin.

1. (a) Unit:	2/60th
(b) Formation:	4 Armd Bde
2. Date:	2 Jan 45
3. Patrol Leader:	Lt Lewin
4. Composition of patrol:	1 Off and 1 OR
5. Object of patrol:	To recce road junction area 687833
6. Route:	690860 – 689854 – 679844 – 685845 – 690853 – 690860
7. (a) Time out:	1610hrs
(b) Time in:	1900hrs

Information gained or results achieved

8. On the way down, movement was seen through glasses at 685844. Patrol embarked at 679844. Intention was to land at 685844. On the way across, movement was heard at 685844 which more or less coincided with the movement seen on the way down. Comd decided not to land here, but to continue to 689849. On arrival here, two Germans were definitely seen near the crane, silhouetted above bank; there were possibly more; Patrol Comd decided to continue further downstream, but was carried across the river to the north bank at 693853. The alternatives were to land at the bulge 694852 or to come home. If he landed so far downstream, he would

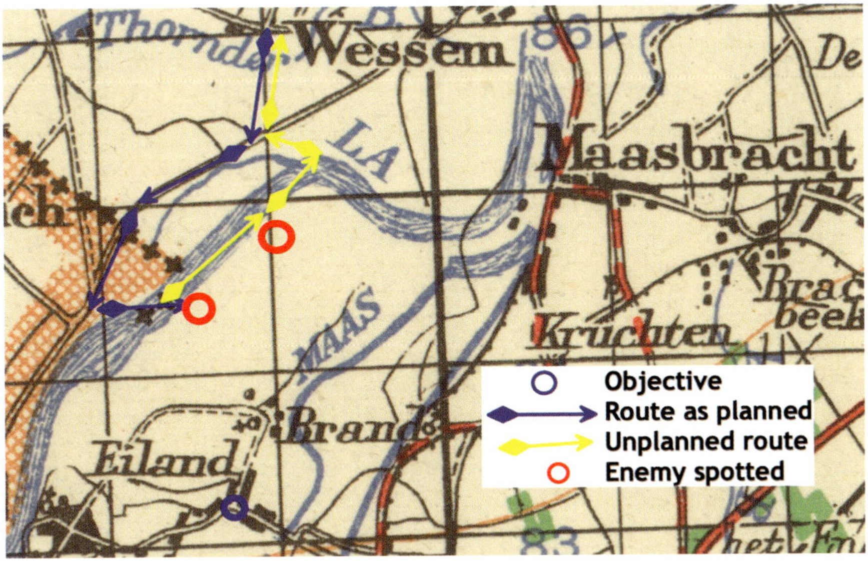

have too far to go to complete his mission before moon came up, and a long way to go over very open country. Also, on his return journey, he would have to pass Maasbracht. He therefore decided to come home.

9. Deductions:		Movement has been heard in the area of the crane before. They will be harassed night 3-4 Jan.
10. Identifications obtained:		Nil
11. Casualties	- enemy	Nil
	- own tps	Nil

* * *

Middleditch.

January 1st 1945 had seen 'A' Squadron of 12RL move up to Mezzano, just west of Ravenna. The terrain was similar to that encountered in Holland by Somerville, Duffin, Lewin, and Boyd: flat, and traversed by drainage ditches, dikes, rivers, and canals; by January 4th some of these had frozen over. It was an active sector of the line with aggressive patrolling; 1KRRC were holding an outpost in a house at Fossatone which came under attack on New Year's Day by twenty enemy troops armed with machine-guns and *Panzerfäuste*; the house collapsed, and its defenders suffered nine wounded and two missing.

'A' Squadron of 12RL were to cover the left flank of an attack the next morning by Canadian troops, whose first objective was Conventello. The attack was a success, and in its aftermath, on January 3rd, 'A' Squadron began to take over the forward positions from 1KRRC. According to the war diary,[4] at 'last light 'A' Squadron, under command 1KRRC, were holding a part of the line, area 4746.'

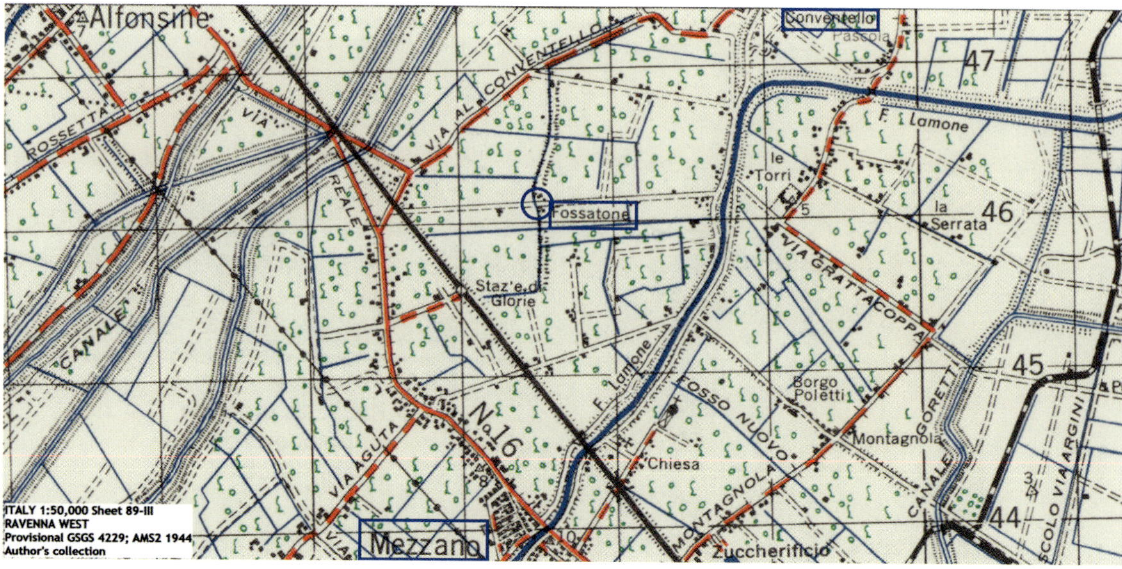

This is the same area as the action on January 1st, and so it seems that Middleditch's men were taking over the same post at Fossatone. Soon afterwards, 'whilst on a night patrol, Lieutenant Middleditch trod on a Schu mine, as a result of which he lost his left foot. Lieutenant Folkard and Serjeant Syms were also slightly wounded by the explosion and had to be evacuated.'

When Middleditch wrote to Robertson about the incident, he stated with great insouciance: 'My military career has suffered a slight check … I very stupidly trod on a German mine and have lost my left leg about six inches below the knee.'

At 0515hrs on January 4th, as Middleditch was being passed back down the casualty evacuation chain, a counter-attack was made by three companies of *SS Panzer-Aufklärungsabteilung 16,* the recce battalion of 16th SS *Panzergrenadier* Division '*Reichsführer SS*'. 16th SS Division was responsible for many war crimes in Italy, its recce battalion being the most vicious sub-unit in the Division. In one week in late September and early October 1944, in the village of Marzabotto south of Bologna, its Austrian commanding officer, *Sturmbannführer* Walter Reder, had overseen the execution of over 700 Italian civilians, the largest mass shooting in Italian history.[5] It is therefore pleasing to note that the forty men of 'A' Squadron in the outpost – including Middleditch's Troop – held fast and inflicted heavy casualties on their attackers; 120 prisoners were taken that day in the sector, a courtesy which these SS troops had not extended to their Italian victims.

* * *

About 18 miles due west, near Faenza, 10th Hussars mounted a local attack to clear a pocket of the enemy between the Naviglio Canal and the River Senio. Starting about three miles north of Faenza on the morning of January 4th, they advanced with 2RTR on their left and four battalions of infantry following in Kangaroos – an early form of armoured personnel carrier. The Canadians had created these by removing the turrets from hundreds of redundant Ram tanks (a Canadian-built derivative of the American M3 medium tank); they were also converted from Sherman tanks or from unfrocked 'Priest' 105mm self-propelled guns.

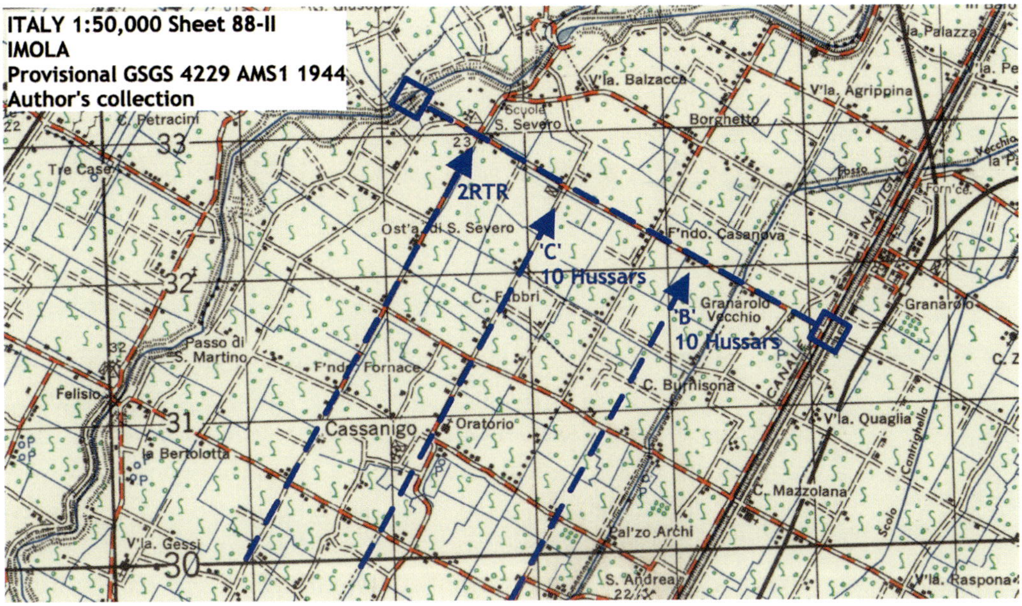

Walker's 3 Troop of 'C' Squadron took part in the advance, which went very well, with all objectives – on a road running from S. Severo to the canal – reached by nightfall, 140 prisoners taken, and only four men lightly wounded. Walker was content:

Walker.

> We had another duffy in the form of an armoured swan – quite fun and apparently successful. 3rd Troop suffered no casualties, and everyone was, as usual, superb. I do hope Sergeant Ross's award comes through. We found ourselves in a wonderful *casa* only a thousand yards from the Senio, and here we installed ourselves, complete with telephones, in the maximum of luxury. The most generous and kind Italian family I have yet met. Once again roast rabbit was prepared for us, and for the next four days we were waited on hand and foot, even to the extent of having our boots cleaned, beds made, and the Brownings cleaned. They had sheltered six escaping prisoners, and showed us photos and addresses.[6]

* * *

The winter of 1944-1945 was bitterly cold, like that of 1939-1940 but worse; some sources suggest that Europe experienced its coldest January and February of the entire twentieth century. The New Year was marked by heavy snow-falls in Belgium, Holland, and Germany, particularly bad on January 8th-9th. The British Liberation Army now shivered as had their predecessors in the British Expeditionary Force. The task had changed, however; whilst the BEF had been waiting for the Germans to attack, the BLA was planning to advance into Germany. German air superiority in 1940 had given way to Allied air supremacy in 1945.

In Italy the cold was equally bitter, and Walker was lucky to be indoors in his luxurious *casa.* On January 7th the weather was described in his Regiment's war diary as 'atrocious', and by the next day there was 'a good six inches of snow on the ground'. The bad news was that the Regiment had been earmarked to switch to an infantry role; it was not the best weather in which to be giving up their vehicles, but the infantry battalions were exhausted and had to rest. With the front static, armour would not be needed until the spring.

* * *

Murray.

In the mountains above Faenza, Murray and the Lovat Scouts continued their war of patrols in the area of Monte Mauro, east of Tossignano along the striking Vena del Gesso feature. It is very hard to trace their movements – even on a detailed map – as the place-names to which the war diary refers are often no more than individual farmhouses, and the diary itself is essentially a laconic list of patrol destinations and outcomes – all, however, recorded in Murray's neat handwriting. We know, for example, that 'A' Squadron sent a patrol forwards into Rivola on January 15th, which was engaged by enemy fire from the north (the grid reference suggests that it came from an enemy-occupied building), but little else. The Regiment came out of the line on January 17th.

* * *

Duffin.

From January 12th onwards, Duffin and 3SG held the line of the road between Gangelt and Geilenkirchen, just inside Germany. Left Flank Squadron – Duffin's – were in the ruins of Geilenkirchen itself, and the rest of the Battalion moved in to join them five days later. As the Churchills were camouflaged with bed-sheets, parachutes and whitewash, plans were being made for an attack north-east to the River Roer.

* * *

Dodgson was by now serving with Support Company, Special Force, from which he wrote to Robertson on January 15th to let his former housemaster know his news:[7]

> I spent a day in Delhi a week or two ago and went and had lunch with Bruce [Fortune], had a bath, and then tea. The bath was especially welcome as I was in the middle of a

Dodgson.

long train journey. He seemed in very good fettle – but I'm afraid over a year in Delhi has turned him back into a normal civilized human – I felt positively uncouth, as in addition to everything else I had eczema on the face!!

I have noted all the other news too with much interest – one seems to pick up awfully little out here. Bruce gave me some recent *Wykehamists* – my family seem to have been a bit lax the last month or two. They seem to have had a reasonable Christmas … Out here I fear for most people it was a drunken orgy – it's a shocking hole. I myself am Mess Secretary so was sober all the time – guarding the bar!

I dropped my third pip … and probably could have got it back, but volunteered for this company, which has entailed plenty of new training to me with a good run for one's money. Being a volunteer company, there's bags of spirit and keenness. I feel the more experiences one can have at the Army's expense the better – and anything to get out of all that marching I did last year. I feel we shall capture Rangoon before very long now – and might even beat Japan before Germany goes down, but for China – where things aren't quite so rosy.

We've a most amusing OC, a war substantive Lieutenant-Colonel – acting Major. Was a peacetime Naval officer. Bought himself out and started a chain of filling stations, joined the Irish Fusiliers as a Private on the outbreak of war, was commissioned, commanded the Special Service Company that went in with Wingate. Drinks like a fish – my main responsibility as Mess Secretary is to maintain a good bar.

I found my bearer wearing an Old Wykehamist scarf the other day – but couldn't find out its origin. At the moment we're near a large town and have such luxuries also plenty of excellent beer – which everyone enjoys …

Thank you both so much for your new year wishes – I only hope I'll be home for the next and able to see you.

* * *

Middleditch also wrote to Robertson on the 15th. Having described his 'stupidity' in treading on the mine, he went on to say:

I've also received a number of flesh wounds in my right leg, but these are healing up well and I can move it about again pretty well now. I gather that I shall be brought back to England to be fitted up with an artificial limb. They are supposed to be very good if one's knee is all right, and although I probably wouldn't be a strong competitor in senior Steeplechase nowadays I expect I shall be pretty nimble in a few months! Anyway, it will be very pleasant to come back to England again and I'm looking forward to seeing you both this summer. I shall miss the Regiment very much indeed and it was particularly annoying that a few hours after I was wounded my Troop had their most successful action of the campaign and that I wasn't with them for the first time since we landed out here.

Please thank Miss Robertson for the letter which she very kindly wrote me. I will reply shortly but it's a bit difficult to write on one's back. I hope it won't be long before I see her again.

In hospital with me is an Etonian brother of Brooke of 'F', who left I think early in the war at an early age. He tells me that the OW Brooke has just got the MC. He is in 10th Hussars and I remember meeting him some time ago in Africa.[8]

* * *

Begum received orders to sail for the UK on January 16th 1945. She was to carry passengers for the journey, including the aircrew and maintenance personnel of 832 Squadron, who flew in the day before departure. That day, *Begum*'s Captain penned his final assessment on Richardson:

Richardson.

General conduct: satisfactory.
Of temperate habit.
Professional ability: above average.
Zeal & energy: above average.
Power of command: above average.
Judgment: above average.
Reliability: above average. SCORE 6.9.
A very capable officer who has worked extremely well over a period of two years in the Squadron, first as Safety Equipment Officer and later as Staff Officer. Has recently become Senior Observer of the Squadron. He demands a high standard and exerts a good influence at all times. Good at most sports, particularly swimming, rugby, soccer, and tennis.
Recommended for Squadron Command.
Captain J.E. Broome.

It was to be 832 Squadron's final voyage. When *Begum* arrived in the Clyde on February 20th, 832 flew ashore; the following day, the Squadron was permanently disbanded. A month later, Richardson rejoined HMS *Condor*, where he had attended Observer training in 1942, but this time as an instructor. It would be another year before he was released from the Navy. His final appraisals from *Condor* noted that his reliability had fallen to 'below average', but that he was

> a good officer who has a good influence on his pupils. He uses his initiative and has some sound ideas. He is always smartly turned-out and he has a good bearing. General officer-like qualities above the average. Recommended for extended service in the RN.

In the Richardson family collection are two photographs of him which at first sight seem to show him on a carrier during the war. The only problem is that in the second, a picture on the wall is of an American Shooting Star, an early jet fighter, and that picture would appear to date from 1947.

* * *

FLEET STATE
SURFACE RAID

The day after Dodgson and Middleditch wrote their letters and Richardson embarked for the journey home, Nick Somerville celebrated his twenty-first birthday. It is a sobering thought that by such a young age he had already become a Captain and Adjutant of 2SWB. But he had come to the conclusion that he could not continue in the role. The commanding officer with whom he had been working – Lieutenant Colonel Barlow – had become unwell enough to require surgery, and agreed to it on condition that he would return to 2SWB afterwards.

Nick Somerville.

> Imagine therefore our dismay when he was replaced without explanation by Lieutenant Colonel Douglas Wilson from the Lincolnshire Regiment. This was a dirty trick by our Brigadier Ekins, for whom none of us had any respect. I found it difficult as Adjutant to serve Wilson, particularly when I found him using his batman to loot silver from civilian houses. Furthermore, he had established a most unsuitable relationship with his batman.

Somerville sought advice from an old family friend in 2SWB, Henry Gillespie, who had been his own father's Adjutant. Gillespie advised him to resign, and Somerville was transferred to 'C' Company as second-in-command. No one else could be found from within 2SWB willing to take on the role of Adjutant – which is a sure indication that Somerville was not alone in his disapproval of Wilson – and so an outsider was drafted in.

> I was thankful to get away from the difficult atmosphere in Battalion HQ. I went to 'C' Company during the first week in January. Every six weeks or so, the Battalion came out of the line to civilian billets in Nijmegen, where they had a good time for seven days.
>
> January 16th 1945
> This is my twenty-first birthday. I have a party laid on for tonight and we are lucky to be at rest in Nijmegen. Routine hot drinks etc this morning. A wonderful party, and Geoffrey produced a bottle of champagne. Harry Reid and Sam in good form on the piano. Everybody very merry; broke up at 0200hrs.
>
> January 17th
> Breakfast a mug of tea at 1000hrs with the pillow over my head.

* * *

Holtby, meanwhile, was still with 6th Seaforths in Palestine, whence he wrote to Robertson on January 18th. Holtby's letters were always full of restlessness – he kept making plans and applications for other units which seemed more exciting than his own.

Holtby.

> Life here goes on much the same as ever with everyone wishing they were home and doing as little work as possible. But one can't expect anything else really. Personally I have put in an application for a transfer to the Airborne Forces in the Far East and I'm awaiting an interview. I

have been waiting six weeks now and doubtless it will be another six weeks before I hear anything. Strange though it may seem to you, Bobber, with your previous experience of me, I hate inaction and even more do I hate trying to look as if I were doing something when there is nothing to do. Of course there is sport – football teams to be organized, tug-o'-war to be got going, and a certain amount of training – but it seems an awful waste of time when we might be doing something that really has to be done. Hence my decision to 'go east'. I'm too young a soldier to enjoy this.

I was unfortunate over Christmas in not being able to go to Jerusalem and Bethlehem; there was an expedition arranged and they tell me it was a good show even though it was rather like Wembley at a cup final! We have managed to procure some horses and I go riding when I can. They are young Arab ponies and make a very exciting ride and excellent exercise. I thoroughly enjoy it.

My Platoon were well in the running for the Divisional drill competition when it was stopped for some reason or other, but they were doing very well. I had to drill them myself and I think we all enjoyed it. I always maintain that you can't have too much drill; it's the best thing in the world for smartening up your men.

There are no Wykehamists in this part of the world and I feel rather out of touch.... If I succeed in getting a posting to the Far East I should get a home leave first so I will come down and see you if I may.[9]

* * *

Fortune.

Fortune, meanwhile, spent January 14th to 19th with Wavell in Nepal, where they were guests of the Nepalese government. The then Prime Minister – Field Marshal Sri Sri Sri Maharaja Sir Juddha Shumsher Jung Bahadur Rana GCB, GCSI, GCIE[10] – followed his dynasty's tradition of huge, almost industrial, shooting expeditions involving the slaughter of tigers and rhinoceroses. Archduke Franz Ferdinand of Austria, King Edward VII, and King George V had all taken part in such shoots before the First World War. Fortune's description attempts to strike a light-hearted note, but one can tell that he was somewhat disgusted by the whole affair.

The shooting is rather overdone, I am afraid. We have already bagged ten tigers and five rhinos, and my sporting instinct is rather shattered by the whole proceedings. Here they ring the tiger (or rhino) with elephants, and stretch round a white ring of cloth over which it can't jump. Then with three to four tuskers they proceed to beat it out of cover. When it breaks cover, no matter how bad a shot you are you have ample opportunity to riddle it with bullets ... There were three rhinos which alternately charged us, and one felt there was an element of danger and that one was shooting in self-defence ... Peter [Coates] shot a tiger in the leg. The tiger, resenting this, leaped out of the ring and made off ... The elephant tribe ... made another ring round where they thought the tiger would be. It resented its encirclement and promptly charged Peter on his elephant and caught the elephant in its hind quarters, causing the beast to stampede ... A certain Nepalese General, who was with Peter, however, saved the situation, and, leaning over the back, and using his rifle as a pistol, shot the tiger dead in its tracks.

Wavell also felt that it was all very unsporting; Fortune later told Susan that Wavell turned to him, handed over his rifle, and said, 'I've had enough.'

* * *

By the beginning of January 1945 it was so cold on The Island that British troops had to add paraffin to their rifle oil to stop it from freezing. The front was wholly static, with the result that 49th Division were being mockingly referred to as the 'Nijmegen Home Guard'. 2SWB had some advanced positions around 200 yards from a moated manor house – formerly a castle – in Hemmen, north-east of Zetten. Intelligence suggested that German parachute troops were planning to attack from Hemmen, though Zetten, to Nijmegen. When a platoon went out to clear the manor – known to 2SWB as 'The Castle' – it found determined German defenders in strength, from *Fallschirmjäger-Regiment* 7. To rescue the patrol, which was pinned down and had taken casualties, the Pioneer Platoon sent three Wasps (Bren-gun carriers fitted with flame-throwers) up the road, which rattled across the moat and rained liquid fire upon the main building. A 6-pounder anti-tank gun was also brought up to engage the manor at point-blank range. The Germans continued to defend the building and to attempt counter-attacks from the north. A troop of Sherman tanks then put 120 main gun rounds into the house, and once 2SWB's platoon had been extricated that evening, an additional 2,000 mortar bombs and 1,500 artillery shells fell on The Castle and its defenders. 2SWB then had smoke bombs

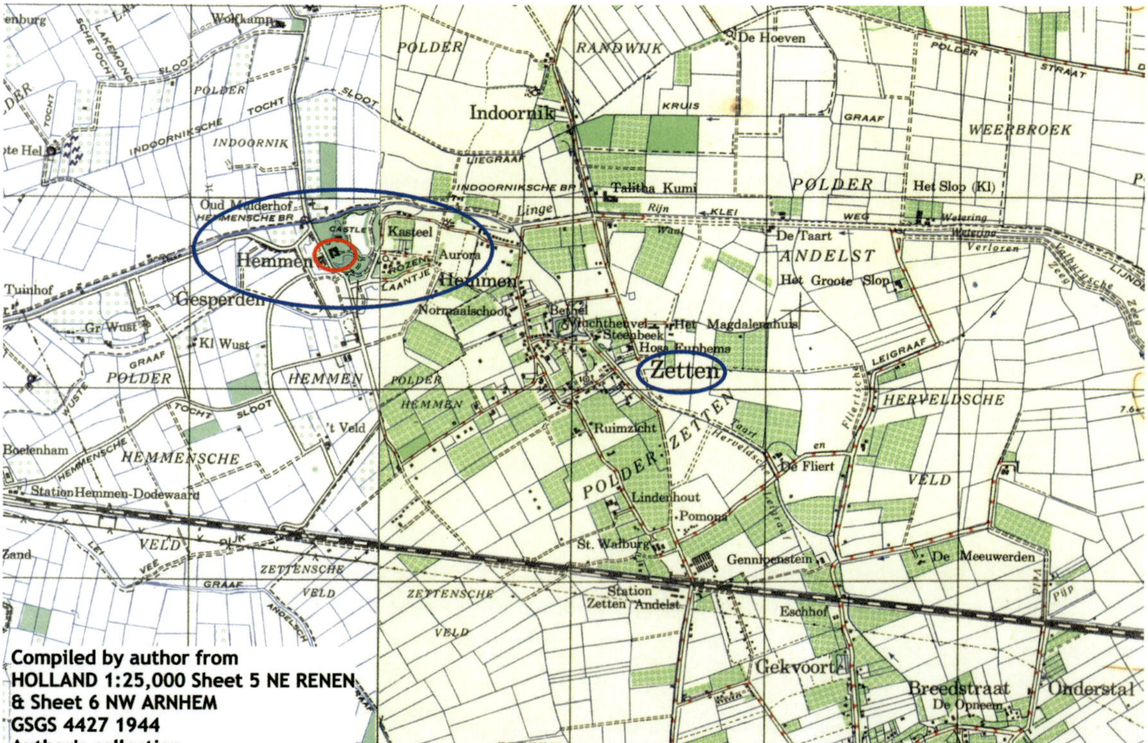

Compiled by author from
HOLLAND 1:25,000 Sheet 5 NE RENEN
& Sheet 6 NW ARNHEM
GSGS 4427 1944
Author's collection

fired into the building from 4.2-inch mortars; these contained white phosphorus, and soon The Castle was well ablaze. Still more German troops advanced from north of the Neder Rijn, but were successfully engaged by artillery. 2SWB admired their handiwork, but left Hemmen to the Germans.

It was clear that the German plan to attack from Hemmen was nearly ready, and 2SWB prepared to counter-attack if the Germans struck – which they did on January 18th, making inroads south of Zetten. Somerville prepared 'C' Company to move:

> January 19th
> Quick move back on to The Island and concentration for a counter-attack. The Leicesters in Andelst have had forward company surrounded by a number of Jerry. Battalion dance for tonight cancelled, unfortunately. Brigade attack tomorrow by us and 2nd Essex. 2nd Glosters already committed. My first attack with a company. 'C' Company are to start the ball rolling.

2SWB's objective was The Castle, and to reach it the Battalion planned for 'C' Company to attack, supported by 'D'; after this, 'B' Company would pass through and secure the start line for 'A' Company, which would assault the moated manor itself, supported by two troops of Canadian Shermans. Heavy snow fell as Somerville led 'C' Company forwards on January 20th.

> Up early. Move off at 0630hrs and reach assembly area. Move off down railway to start line. An unlucky shell gets seven men in 13 Platoon, only twenty-five yards behind me. Company attack goes in. A bloody bit of open country. About a dozen Jerries in houses with a Spandau, Schmeissers, etc. Platoons work very well. Close fighting in about ten different houses. Burst of Bren wounded one of them. A narrow squeak crossing the road from a burst of Schmeisser. Idiot with the PIAT has dropped his bombs in the dyke. We've got these chaps taped now. Some 77 smoke[11] to get the section forward. Section have cleared the enemy house. Jerry must have bolted out of the back door when smoke was down. 14 and 15 Platoons push through to their objectives.
>
> 'B' Company go through us, and the twelve Jerries surrender to them just down the road – but we claim them as ours. We have thirteen casualties, and one lucky. Chaps fought well. 'B' Company on objective no trouble. 'A' Company pass through to attack Castle with tanks. 'A' Company held up. Strong opposition from Castle. Fighting all afternoon. One platoon in stables. Fighting stops at dusk. Platoon in stables forced to withdraw at dawn. Forty enemy surrounded it and shot bazookas into stables. 'A' Company now only forty men left on ground.
>
> January 21st
> Tanks form up with 'D' Company and attack Castle. Castle taken and 121 prisoners taken. More prisoners came in later. Total for Battalion: 208. Quantities of German dead and wounded in Castle grounds. German commander shot himself. Two companies – 'A' and 'D' – in Castle area for night.

January 22nd
Glosters and Essex clean up in Zetten and Hemmen. Whole area is now quite quiet. Return to Nijmegen to continue rest. A great welcome from the civilians for everybody.

* * *

Lewin and 'A' Company 2KRRC finally crossed the Maas on January 19th, after other units had secured the far bank. They were all over the river by 1600hrs and took up residence in Stevensweert. Their patrols found that any Germans who had been nearby had retreated. By the morning of January 23rd, enemy troops finally vacated Maasbracht – 'in a hurry', as the 2KRRC war diary put it,

> and the first Commando patrols, and also Captain Gosse, Lieutenant Lewin, and some Riflemen had entered the village. They found some civilians, who had just infiltrated through the German lines, already in possession. During the day steady progress was made by our troops, and, as it was obvious that our sector was by now several miles behind the front line, several officers crossed to Stevensweert and joined 'A' Company in a duck-shoot.[12]

The Battalion had been left behind by the British advance, and so 2KRRC settled down to training and typhus inoculations, moving to Tilburg on February 17th. By now experienced veterans, Lewin and his contemporary 'Dwin' Bramall would attend interviews for Regular (permanent) commissions on February 11th. Meanwhile, 4 Armoured Brigade's intelligence staff continued to pass on information vital to the next phase of operations, as this Intelligence Summary appended to 2KRRC's war diary shows:

Appendix "A" to 4 Armd
Bde Int Summary No.41.

WINES OF THE RHINELAND.

Virtually all German wines are grown on the banks of the RHINE or one or other of its tributaries. Though there is no country where the wine is more lovingly and scientifically tended, Germany grows comparatively little wine - a shrinking acreage of 70,000 hectanes (175,000 acres) has an av annual production of under 2,250,000 hecto litres - because away from the sun-traps of the sheltered river valleys either climate or soil is unsuitable for viticulture. Yet the fact that the little is almost wholly white, and also almost wholly the juice of a single variety of grape, the Riesling gives Germany a unique posn among the wine-growing nations. Now the Riesling is what the French term a "plant noble" - i.e. a vine of quality, not quantity, so it is only in the natural order of things that the very choicest growths of what our ancestors called, generically, "Rhenish" should be the most costly wines in the world. But if the august " Spitzennamen" of the Rheingau seem fabulously expensive(a Schloss Johannisberger Cabinet, 1921, costs double a Chareau Yquem, 1921), the connoisseur knows that while these are well worth their price,there is the widest choice of others from 75 pf to 17½Mk. A bottle to tempt every purse and palate. Nor will the wise traveller despise the "offen Weine", the lighter draught wines that are served in decanters holding fractions of a litre. These are nearly always good, and more often excellent. Try them both with and without meals; or as a prelude to "something better" in one of the graceful, long-necked, amber-brown or grass-green bottles which so perfectly embody the clear, sun-gold colour and meadow fragrance implicit in these cool, gently gurgling names, Hock and Moselle.

* * *

In Great Yarmouth, Mackrill was still with MGB 325, but bemoaning the lack of action: 'We haven't been out much either, as the boat has been "crocked" up; however, we are working again now. It is a foul day now, blowing and raining like mad.'[13]

Mackrill.

When his boat did go out, he was able to take photographs which show a Fairmile 'C' MGB in fairly typical seas. It is not known what the pennant number of this MGB is, but it is unlikely to be MGB 325, as that is presumably where Mackrill stood when he took the pictures. Note the four depth-charges installed aft, giving the MGB an anti-submarine and anti-surface-vessel capability (depth charges released close alongside an enemy vessel would explode beneath it, breaking its back or stoving in hull-plates).

Mackrill would stay with the same boat for the rest of the war, and although it appears that he saw no action, he clearly had an affection for MGB325, because when she was decommissioned in August 1945, he took the boat's carved wooden badge, which still bears traces of grey paint from where it was screwed to the cockpit. One hopes that one day the badge might be reunited, if only for a day, with its former home, now moored in Hayling Island.

* * *

(Mackrill family collection; edited by dansteele.net)

On January 20th, Clerk-Rattray's mother replied to a letter of congratulation from Robertson:

> Dear Malcolm,
> So many thanks for your most welcome postcard, which was the first news I had had that James has been mentioned in Despatches. I am glad, and have written to ask whose Despatch it was – if in Tunisia, where I was told privately that he had done well, or in Italy. He is, I fear, a very bad correspondent even to his Ma, and those letters I have are certainly unilluminating! No Censor could take any exception to any word. It is very bad, as he has seen so much of interest and Grizel and Persis and Elizabeth[14] (at home) write so very well. James has come out wonderfully, and I am proud of him, but what he has seen has affected him and he does not want to talk about it. I fear they are still in the north, and are due elsewhere any time now, and will go straight out. Had he been south, I know that he was hoping to see you and Sheila. They are at Stobs Camp Hawick, which is a most miserable spot.
> Love to you both.
> Ferelith C-R.[15]

* * *

3SG's next taste of action was what the Allies referred to as a 'pepperpot shoot'; essentially, any weapon available was used to bombard an enemy target. Tank guns, field artillery, anti-aircraft weapons, machine-guns, mortars – anything capable of doing damage was unleashed in a lethal *feu de joie*. Destruction was to be visited upon the villages of Putt, Waldenrath, and Straeten. On January 21st the Churchills ground their way to high ground north-west of Geilenkirchen and prepared for action, but the operation was postponed until dawn the following day. After a miserable night in the snow, the tanks opened fire at around 0730hrs and kept it up until 1100hrs. Having returned to Geilenkirchen, 3SG received a message that the infantry attack due to sweep in on the targets from the west had become bogged down by mines, and that another pepperpot was required immediately. As they turned themselves around, four Allied aircraft strafed and bombed the tanks – luckily, they missed. An afternoon's firing on the three unfortunate German communities followed, but the infantry were still not in a position to attack, and so 3SG stayed out on the hilltops until dawn the next day and then pounded Straeten for a third time. After two hours they ran out of ammunition, having fired by their calculations 12,000 rounds of main-gun ammunition, amounting to 28 tons of munitions. Soon afterwards, Allied forces reached the Roer.

3SG were now needed up near Nijmegen for the planned offensive through the Reichswald Forest, on to the Siegfried Line, Cleve, and the Rhine. The Battalion started its move on January 27th, and its history states that 'two days later the tanks slithered somehow to Waterscheide in Belgium, where they loaded on to transporters for the long march north to Tilburg.'

* * *

The Lovat Scouts moved to the small village of Paganica, near L'Aquila in the mountains 80 miles east of Rome, on January 23rd. After settling in, they began to practise a skill in which they had become adept but which had become rusty with disuse: downhill skiing. The region is now full of ski resorts. The war diary for January 25th reports that skiing conditions were only moderate, owing to the wetness of the snow, but for the rest of the month states nothing more than, 'Training continued. All ranks getting used to skiing again.' On February 6th, Murray recorded in the war diary his own attachment as an instructor in mountain warfare to 7th Mountain Regiment RA, with whom the Lovat Scouts had worked in the front line. Ski instructor was probably not one of the jobs which Murray had expected to add to his portfolio when he went to war.

* * *

Walker was also away from his unit on January 23rd and, like Murray, up in the snow-covered Apennines, about halfway between L'Aquila and Rome – though his diary makes it clear that he resented it hugely:

> I was sent on this intolerable tank Observation Post course at Rieti, where I now am. Had such a thing turned up two months ago, I should probably have welcomed it in my heart of hearts, while pretending that I much preferred to stay, and that it was better for me, and all that sort of poppycock. This time I could honestly say, in all sincerity, [that] I could have imagined nothing more disagreeable. I was furious, just as 3rd Troop and I had begun to click. To make it worse, John Warren, who took over from me, is apparently none too popular, and it was horribly awkward when he came in and no-one said anything. All very embarrassing.
>
> I share a room here ... We've both been feeling ill most of the time, but get on very well and hopefully can get some skiing in the mountains.
>
> Sunday, January 28th
> Up in the mountains miles from anywhere (I believe there is a village called Monteleone somewhere near). The first afternoon we attempted to ski – since then through the snow and rain visibility has been too fine for much firing. Consequently we have spent most of our time sitting in an intolerably stuffy room reading and writing letters. Today I read *Kipps* and rather imagined that married life owning a small bookshop would be far from unpleasant.
>
> The news is good and I am unjustifiably optimistic. I hope to have a few days in Rome before returning to the Regiment.
>
> Tuesday, January 30th
> Tonight life is wearing a less brilliant cloak. I am aching – probably through smoking too much. I lost at poker, and worst of all I am beginning to appreciate how very stupidly I behave. Thank God the course is nearly over, and soon I shall be back – though with all these infantry rumours life may be none too pleasant.
>
> Today the weather was glorious – the snow was beautifully crisp and the sky beautifully blue.

* * *

Elliott-Binns.

Elliott-Binns' war had ground to a halt in the Apennines above Bologna, and he later wrote his only poem of the Italian campaign about this dangerous experience.

Silence returns. Our gun-flashes no more
Make the horizon dance. Machine-guns cease
Tapping their lunatic morse. Only the breeze
Blows up its whispered memories of peace.

Shadow this hill-top with your hand. Forbid
Shells' shrieked crescendo, burst of searing light.
Keep far the stealthy footsteps of patrols.
My courage drains. Save me at least to-night.

Like giants' fingers, white and fossilised,
Stretch the thin barren ridges from my hill,
Pointing across the dark to those whom we
By mutual contract are compelled to kill.

Save us from hate, and safely guide our feet
Past pit-falls of war's inessential slime.
Only our love can partially redress
These unredeemed and pitiable times.

They through whom widows weep and men become
Bare scaffolding of bones like winter trees,
Somewhere toward the Pole and Cassiopaea
Beyond my range irrelevantly sleep.

Within this valley's amphitheatre stand
Press-ganged the bloody-handed sons of Cain.
Around the white-mantillaed mountains wait
Either with inattention or disdain.

Invisible between us stretch the wires,
The complex net-work of man's common sin.
Relayed each slight electric shock, proclaims
That we are joined by closer bond than kin.

Ceaselessly our owed and guilty blood
Is draining quietly through indifferent ground.
A giant's strength and giant's suffering
Brood a perpetual shadow all around.

The amputation of our gangrened limb
Is necessary evil. May we gain
The surgeon's steady hand and gentleness,
The patient's taut endurance against pain.

But his war ended, to all intents and purposes, on January 27th – he just did not know it yet. This was the day on which 19 Field Regiment left Italy *en route* for Palestine. They arrived on February 2nd, and that was where they remained.

* * *

After a miserable journey down to Tilbury from Stobs (a Transit Camp at Purfleet was 'universally condemned as a military crime'), 2SG crossed the Channel in two main parties between January 29th and 31st. Clerk-Rattray was in 'F' Company, which boarded SS *Longford* – an Irish Sea packet – at 1630hrs on January 28th, spent the night at sea off Southend, and disembarked at 1300hrs in Ostend the next day. They sat down in No.111 Transit Camp shortly afterwards for their first hot meal in several days. The Camp was efficient and comfortable, occupying a former *Kriegsmarine* barracks, and gradually the rest of the Battalion trickled in and contact was established with 32 Guards Brigade, part of the Guards Armoured Division.

* * *

On January 31st, Walker wrote:

> We returned to Rieti this evening and found a note from Geoff telling me to return at once to the Regiment. This I shall do tomorrow morning. Corporal Rush has come to collect me; he says 3rd Troop still have their tanks, Sergeant Ross acting as Troop leader. I hate to doubt it, but am hoping I shall still be with them when I return … Tonight I have a splitting headache, so rum and aspirin is 'just the caper', as the Kiwis would say. I was trying not to be sentimental as we came back tonight. The sun was giving the snow-capped mountains a glorious dying ember colour, but I couldn't help feeling what a wonderful crowd 3rd Troop were and how much I'd look forward to being back with them. I reached Villanova that evening after a swiftish journey in which I drove part of the way, clipping the odd lorry here and there! Still, no casualties.

When he awoke on February 1st, not far to the south of where Middleditch had stepped on his mine, Walker discovered that he had got his wish and was still in charge of 3 Troop, which was at the time equipped with two Shermans fitted with 105mm howitzers in place of the 75mm main gun, and one Sherman Firefly. However, his joy was short-lived, since the Regiment had centralized its 105mms into one 'Battery', and the Firefly (his personal tank) had been attached to Squadron HQ. As a result, Walker was sent to act as Gun Position Officer with the Sherman 105s, lodging with the officers of 'A' Squadron in Villanova.

> Most of these I find at times shits, and I shall not be displeased when Geoff decides that one of the forward Troop Leaders deserves relieving.
>
> I am at the moment on an extremely safe job, shooting the guns whenever anyone asks for them. Apart from having to get up sometimes in the middle of the night, it

has few disadvantages except for the monotony and being away from the Squadron and especially, of course, my Troop.[16]

* * *

In yet another re-shuffle, 16th/5th Lancers had been informed that they, too, would be deployed as infantry in order to give the 'real' infantry a break from the front line. So for Brooke it was back from Ancona to Florence, which they reached on the evening of January 24th. There they learned that they would be taking over from 10RB in the mountains around Casola Valsenio, with their rear headquarters at Antella. The Regiment moved in on the night of February 2nd, 'B' Squadron being the first to man the front-line positions. These were four houses, referred to as Point 388, Casa Grande, and Casa Monte (where there were two houses). Each was manned by a troop, with Squadron HQ at Point 388. The reserve squadron was at Casola Valsenio itself, whilst the third squadron was resting miles back in Antella, the other side of the Arno. Each squadron spent a week or so in the front line.

Brooke.

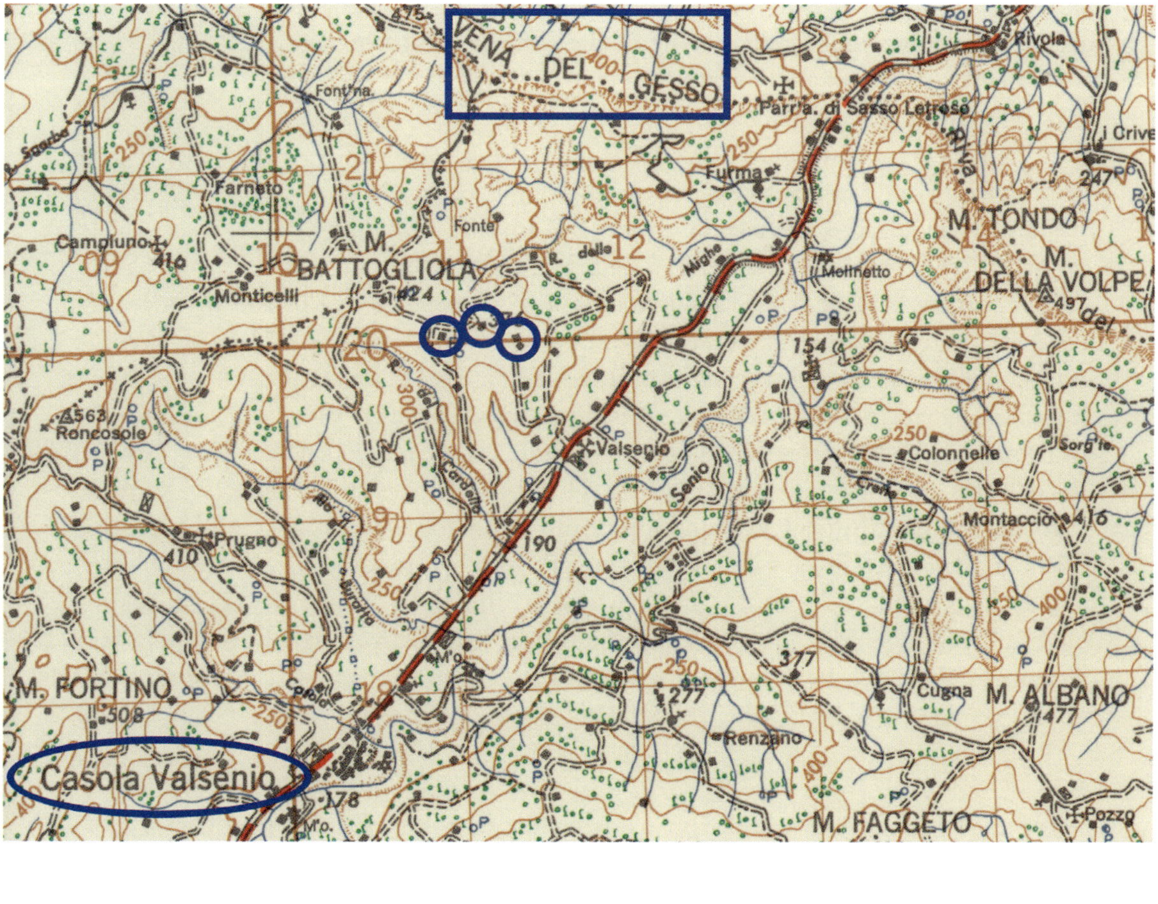

There was a great deal of snow, meaning that even Jeeps could not make it up to the British positions; instead, over 200 mules and their Indian handlers were required. The journey from the 'Mule Head' took an hour and a half each way. Despite the snow, 'B' Squadron conducted an active defence, patrolling constantly to stop German infiltration from their higher positions about 500 yards away.

The dangers were very real. There was a lot of shelling, which caused few casualties but, during 'B' Squadron's first few days, damaged one of the houses. Serjeant Shuttleworth decided to explore a nearby house, thus far unused, as an alternative. It was booby-trapped, and he died that night (February 8th).[17] Two days later, after an artillery 'stonk' which demolished the front wall of another house, 'B' Squadron left the position, which was taken over by 'C' Squadron. With great pleasure, they returned to Antella.

16th/5th spent only a brief time as foot-sloggers; they came out of the mountains a month after they arrived, on the night of March 2nd. Spring was coming, and with it the time for a war of movement in which tanks would play a vital role.

* * *

Simpkin.

Simpkin was by 1945 running the *Oflag* IXA/Z news service – culling and digesting snippets from newspapers, German gossip, and (when available) clandestine wireless sets tuned to the BBC. In his last surviving letter from captivity, written on January 31st, he told Barbara that 'if I manage to get them back, you'll be tickled to see my attempts to present news to the camp – it's really great fun, tho' often very irritating, especially as many seem to expect the gift of prophecy.'

He had taken more language examinations in January, though it is unclear whether his papers made it back to the Royal Society for the Encouragement of Arts, Manufactures, and Commerce in London for marking. He had already, however, gained certificates for papers which he sat in 1944: Written Advanced German Class 1; Written Advanced Italian Class 2; Commercial Examinations Intermediate Stage Italian Class 1. A Certificate of Proficiency in German from the University of London states that in June 1944, Simpkin had passed English Essay, German Essay, Translation from and into German, Dictation, Phonetics and Spoken German.

In the aftermath of his examinations, Simpkin enjoyed ice-skating and exploring German literature, but was saddened by the split with his grandmother. To cheer himself up, he thought aloud about the future when writing to Barbara: 'All sorts of exciting ideas … among which, I must admit, the peace-time Army does not occupy a very prominent place.'[18]

* * *

With the Fourteenth Army in Burma, Metcalfe and 45th Cavalry had begun 1945 around Taungmaw in the Arakan region. A week later, they began to move back to Wabyin, where the Regiment was concentrated by January 10th. And there their active

Metcalfe.

Fourteenth Army.

war came to an end. The Regiment was slated to exchange its battered old Stuarts for bigger, more powerful Shermans, and at the end of January the officers began courses on gunnery, driving, and maintenance of these new vehicles. But Wabyin was not suitable for a full regimental conversion to the type, and so on February 16th the 45th retraced its steps to Dohazari, before embarking on two ships at Chittagong; the remaining vehicles and their essential personnel were on HMT *Salween*, whilst the other 422 officers and other ranks travelled separately. Their destination was Madras, whence, at the end of the month, they set out by train to Poona. There is no war diary for March, but Metcalfe took over as Adjutant on the 12th; most people were away on leave or on courses.

* * *

Dan Somerville.

'Dan' Somerville was on his way to the front line at last, being posted to the Far East in January:

> I never got to France, unlike my brother, and when it was quite clear that the Nazi empire was over and the Germans were tottering they had other plans for people like me. We were still in the UK and not doing anything very much, so they sent us out to the Far East on a troop-ship in January 1945; as a Lieutenant, I was officer in charge of a draft of thirty men …
>
> We had a marvellous journey out. It took us something like three weeks to get to the Suez Canal because we had to dodge about in the North Atlantic to get away from the U-Boats, which were still active. We were in convoy at first, but after we got into the Mediterranean we were on our own. We ended up in Bombay. As soon as we arrived in India, I was sent to sit in a base camp north of Bombay called Deolali, which the troops referred to as Doolally. 'Doolally' became a synonym for a mental illness, which was really boredom; most of us sat around in Deolali whilst the Army deliberated what to do with us all. I had to collect a draft of Indian soldiers from what soon became Pakistan, up through the desert and Delhi all the way to Deolali. We went down through the Indus valley and into Karachi, which was then a small town of half a million people – very pleasant. I little knew that I would later be spending three years there.
>
> We were ordered to Burma and to go up-country to the regiments to which we were appointed. We were all given Mills hand-grenades and rifles just in case the Japanese tried to attack. Everybody said they would have been very sorry to go anywhere near me when I was loaded up with grenades and things, as I might not have known what to do with them. I was thankful to get rid of them, at any rate.[19]

* * *

In letters to his parents, Walker passed on news of former schoolmates: 'David Middleditch (Hoppers '36–'41) had his leg blown off by a *schu*-mine the other day. Rotten luck.'[20]

* * *

Rigby.

When Dan Somerville went up to Karachi, he was closer than he realized to his school-mate Rigby, still on the North-West Frontier, from where he wrote to Robertson in early February:[21]

> I have just got your letter of January 19th. As always, it has given me a great moral leg up. I like being reminded of people who one knew so well, but had forgotten through meeting so many others; and those who one will never meet again.
>
> I am thoroughly enjoying the few, cold mountains that the Indian climate affords. Every day one can enjoy a clear, cold sun; and ever changing panoramas of snow-covered Himalayan foothills.
>
> I went to Peshawar last week for the first time. The bleakness of the weather tended to accentuate the austere militarism of this frontier capital. But it's a clean, well-planned cantonment and definitely has character. An immense Sikh fort – much larger than anything I can remember in the UK – stands just outside the town's defences, and on the other side is the entrance to the Khyber, clearly visible and very near. The shops are full of skins, rugs, and Russian china, and would definitely merit an afternon's shopping with a very fat purse; prices are absurdly high, although no American has yet been within five hundred miles of here.
>
> The Viceroy presented VCs and new colours to Gurkhas and Rajputs here about two weeks back. An impressive ceremony, and the march-past was something not to be forgotten. I was disappointed not to see Bruce Fortune as ADC. Presumably he has re-joined his unit. A rather sissy Grenadier was in his place.
>
> We're still many miles from the jungle and the war; one can but hope.

* * *

Hirst.

Hirst was at last in India, and now began his journey through the Indian Armoured Corps training which had been set up by Rigby and Metcalfe at Babina and Ahmadnagar.

> We arrived in Bombay early in January 1945 and went to the infamous transit camp at Deolali, near Nasik, about 120 miles north-east of Bombay.
>
> I only stayed there a few days, then went to the Indian Armoured Corps Tank School at Babina Cantonment, near Jhansi in the United Provinces in central India. We had a fairly rough journey; two nights and a day on a troop train, with wooden seats and wooden shelves which you could let down to sleep on. It gets cold in central and northern India in winter, and we only had one blanket. We played Solo continuously, and got good meals at the station restaurants.[22]

Before he could be posted to an Indian unit, Hirst had first to become able to communicate with the personnel who would be under his command.

> Our first task was to learn Urdu. We had a *munshi* (Indian teacher) – a dear old, very high caste, gentleman. As RAC, attached IAC, we got an extra fifty rupees a month,

total monthly pay 579 rupees (£43), compared with the £20 I got in the UK. (When I had started at Blackdown I got sixpence a day, from which barrack room damages were deducted!). In Jhansi, I was very pleased to get, as well as an Urdu grammar, Salim Ali's book of Indian birds.

We now had a bearer between the five of us, at eighteen rupees a month each. He cleaned our boots and tidied our room, took our clothes to the *dhobi* (washerman), and saw that the *bahisti* (water-carrier) filled the bath tub in the *gussul khana* (bathroom). After we had two suits of white cotton made for him, he waited on us in Mess. At training schools your bearer always waited on you. I was really enjoying the curries!

The Urdu lessons were quite intensive, 0800–0900hrs six days a week, and 1700-1800hrs four days, as well as homework. For the first time in the Army I had an office job, checking vehicle log-books; very boring. We had half days on Wednesday and Saturday, and all Sunday, so of course I used to go birding. The village tanks (dams) were full of bird life.

However, we soon had a break, as we were sent off as umpires on a three-day scheme in Gwalior State. I was attached to the East African Regiment, formerly recruited from white settlers, but now Africanised as a recce regiment. They had tanks with the turret removed to act as armoured troop carriers. The tank commanders were British Sergeants, in contrast to the Indian Army, as the Africans were not considered bright enough. The drivers had the habit of driving through the thorn bushes which covered the tops of Indian wells, and falling in. Unfortunately, a British Sergeant was killed that way while I was there. The Africans climbed out grinning.

I saw two or three buck and a couple of jackals in the jungle there, but only heard a tiger, thank God![23]

It was then Hirst's turn to spend some time at Ahmadnagar, like Metcalfe before him.

We got back from the scheme at 1400hrs on February 21st 1945 and had to get on the train to Ahmadnagar (about a hundred miles south-east of Deolali) at 2300hrs. After a 48-hour journey we arrived at the Fighting Vehicle School at 0200hrs. The School was the chief training establishment for the Armoured Corps in India, and was very efficient. They had a hot meal laid on for us when we arrived in the middle of the night.

I now had my own room and bathroom-cum-lavatory; a chamber pot emptied by the *mihtar* (sweeper) who was on the very bottom rung of the caste ladder. I had a bearer, Babu, who of course was not allowed by the caste system to perform such works. Babu was from southern India and was very dark – in fact, the other bearers called him 'Negro-walla'. He was pleasant, but not very efficient. Fourteen of us were asked by him and his friends to visit a school for Untouchables (low-caste Hindus). I suppose as we were all new to India we were looked on as a 'soft touch', but we responded to the appeal by the schoolmaster for funds for the school, and were duly garlanded.

We resumed normal tank training, I passed my Urdu exam, and we visited the Club and the cinema.[24]

* * *

In early February 1945, Nijmegen was heaving with British troops and their vehicles as they prepared for their push south-east to the Rhine, Operation Veritable. The going was awful; the hills of the Reichswald Forest turned to mud very easily, and the plain in front of the Rhine had been allowed to flood, making movement off the few roads all but impossible. Indeed, German high command had assessed that the area was impassable and that the attack would come further north. The road east from Nijmegen to Cleve ran between the forest and the plain, in the course of twenty miles passing through Wyler, Kranenburg, and Nutterden. Between the latter two communities lay the fortifications of the northern end of the Siegfried Line.

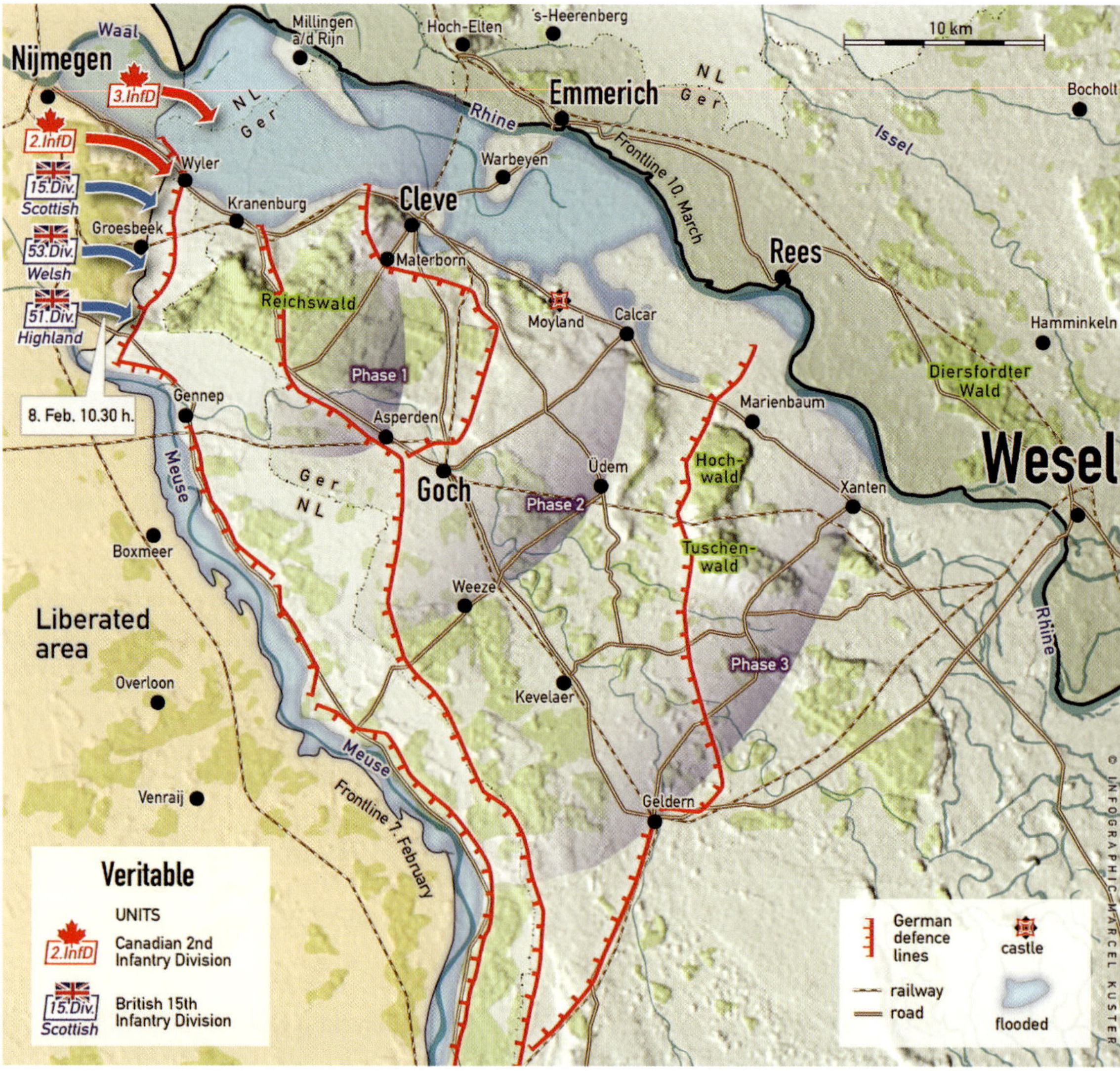

Operation Veritable, February 1945. (©TracesofWar.com)

3SG were to support 227 Infantry Brigade of 15th (Scottish) Division in a push straight down the road as far as Kranenburg, with Canadian troops to their left on the flood-plain, and other British units clearing the forest on their right.

3SG set out at 0500hrs on February 8th along the road to Wyler, but branched off southwards at Berg-en-Dal until they reached their assembly area in the Nederijksche Woods at 0730hrs. It was already clear that the main road was far too narrow and flimsy for the amount of traffic which would be using it, and 3SG pinned their hopes on the legendary mobility of their Churchills. As they advanced eastwards at 0915hrs, 3SG had some initial trouble with mine-fields, but a troop of Churchills pushed along a narrow track which turned out only to have *Schu* mines on it; these exploded under the pressure of the tanks' tracks, and the infantry and 'S' Squadron pushed on, with Right Flank hot on their heels. Next stop was Kranenburg, where fire from Right Flank helped the infantry to gain a foothold. The advance had been so rapid that the main road bridge into the town was intact – though eight Churchills bogged down as they approached it. Some of the tanks which bogged down were impossible to recover, and 3SG never saw them again. But Kranenburg fell without much opposition, and as the day's objectives had been reached, 3SG pulled back about a mile west for the night.

However, Duffin and Left Flank Squadron had had a less successful day. The infantry whom they were supporting – 2nd Gordon Highlanders – had failed to make it through the German mine-field, and one of the Churchills hit a mine which had apparently been attached to an unexploded bomb. The Churchill exploded, killing its commander, Lieutenant Campbell. Left Flank had been tasked with pushing on beyond Kranenburg on the evening of February 8th, but instead moved up that night to launch their attack the following day. Ahead lay the Siegfried Line, fronted by an anti-tank ditch at Tutheese.

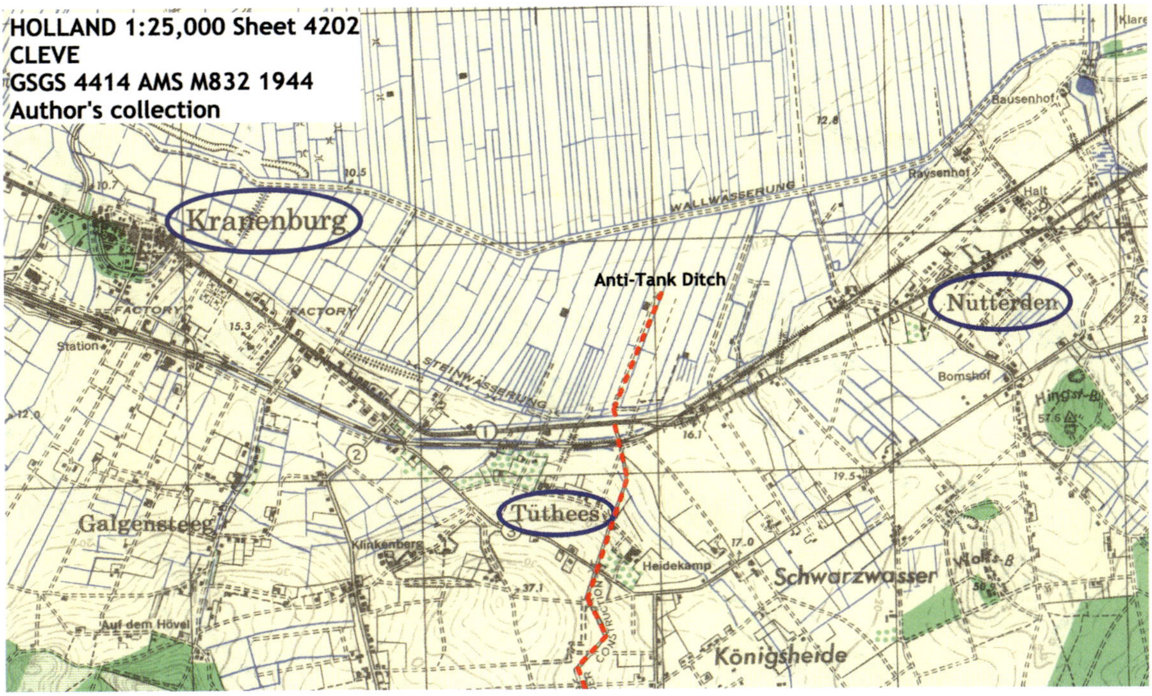

Left Flank attacked straight along the road at 0800hrs on February 9th. Things went much better; the anti-tank ditch presented no difficulties, they reached Nutterden with little trouble, and they lost no tanks. They had also become the first British tanks to pass through the Siegfried Line. By the end of the day, they had added 200 prisoners to the 300 taken by the other squadrons the day before.

February 10th was supposed to be the day Cleve fell, but events conspired against 3SG. First, although Left Flank and 'S' Squadrons were ready to move off at 0800hrs, they found 43rd (Wessex) Division blocking the road. Just as the Churchills reached a narrow strip of woodland running north from the Reichswald, they received orders to halt. The Recce Troop took its Stuart 'Honey' tanks forwards to secure the Forming-Up Point, a lookout tower on the western outskirts of Cleve, but came under fire and lost two tanks to *Panzerfäuste*. As a result, Left Flank returned to Nutterden for the night, determined to have another go the next day.

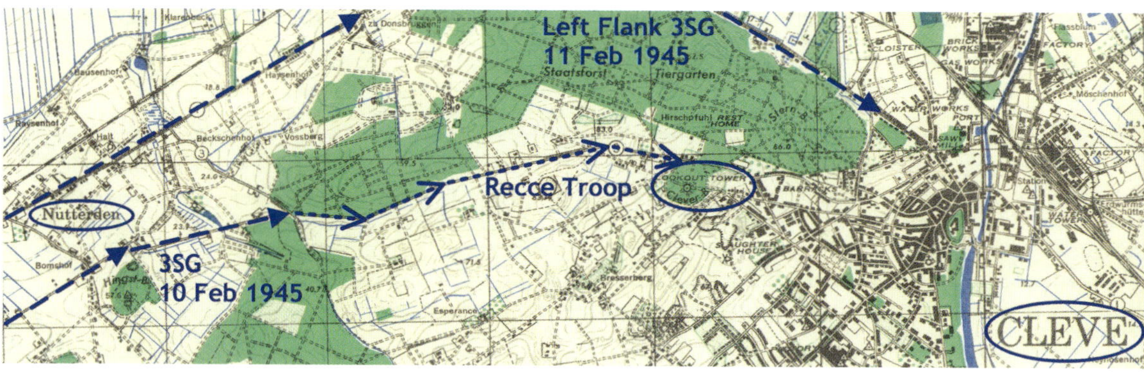

3SG took a more northerly route on February 11th, hooking round behind the *Staatsforst*. There was some trouble from Germans equipped with *Panzerfäuste* to begin with – the defenders had good cover in the trees to the south of the road – but Left Flank sent in a troop of Churchills to silence them before stopping at a crossroads near the waterworks and allowing Right Flank to roll into Cleve, which fell that evening.

But 3SG now halted. The flood waters had been rising quickly, not only inundating the land to the north but even submerging the Nijmegen–Cleve road under three feet of water. The bogged Churchills at Kranenburg disappeared under the rising tide, though their crews were able to use Weasel amphibious jeeps to retrieve their belongings before they were swamped. The only way for the front-line units to receive supplies or send back casualties was by DUKW, the famous swimming lorries which still operate sightseeing tours in London. Many tough actions followed as the advance continued, biting off small chunks of territory against resistance alternately bitter and half-hearted, and by the end of February 3SG had reached Udem, about ten miles west of Xanten and the Rhine. Within the month, they would be across the last great barrier between them and Berlin.

* * *

Men of 2nd Gordon Highlanders, with whom 3SG frequently operated, search a 16-year-old German prisoner in Cleve on February 11th 1945. A Churchill of 3SG is at left. (IWM B 14610, coloured by Doug @colour_history)

Clerk-Rattray and 2SG were waiting for the moment when the Guards Armoured Division would be let off the leash, which had been put on hold until Cleve was captured. Their war diary is one of the best – full of detail, names and appendices, all delivered in a wry tone which brings it alive even after so many years.[25]

February 3rd
After lunch, officers and senior NCOs attended a demonstration by a Squadron of 2nd Battalion Welsh Guards and 'X' Company Scots Guards who showed us how to co-operate with tanks. The demonstration was a success, and filled in a gap in our training which everyone felt badly; though training to become an infantry battalion in the Guards Armoured Division at Stobs, we had never co-operated with or even seen a single tank.

During the night 3rd–4th February, Lieutenant A.N.J. Gordon was shot through the shoulder by an Irish Guards sentry; his remarks to the sentry after the incident are unprintable.

February 8th
The whole Battalion, less Left Flank, who are in Tilburg, are billeted in a Trappist Monastery just outside the town.

February 15th
A wreath and a letter of condolence were sent to the monks of the Monastery to mark our respect for the Abbot, who died yesterday. Efforts are being made to increase our billeting area. The Monastery affords little space for the Battalion less one Company … The quarters are too cramped and therefore unhygienic … Originally the intention was for the Battalion to be here for not more than two days, but in view of the progress of the battle, our billet can no longer be regarded as merely a concentration area where one expects to be crowded up.

February 17th
In the evening permission was given by Division for Right Flank to move into new billets in Tilburg. Captain H.L.St. V. Rose made a reconnaissance of the new area and discovered that another unit had the same idea, whereupon it was resolved to move in early the next morning and so forestall this other unit.

February 18th
During the morning Right Flank moved out into their new billets and took them over with no opposition, thereby allowing the remainder of the Battalion to disperse itself more comfortably in the Monastery.

February 19th
1000hrs A memorial service was held in the Chapel for the Abbot who died a few days ago. Many top-hatted notables arrived from Tilburg, and the Battalion was much honoured by being asked to send representatives.

February 21st
In the morning the Battalion moved off and by 1100hrs had taken over the Irish Guards' billets in Hommersum [west of Goch, itself west of Udem]. The Irish Guards, being in reserve, were not in tactical positions, and all companies except 'F' Company were close together in the village, which had suffered through shell-fire in no small way.

Most of the Battalion found itself in Germany, but Battalion HQ was about twenty-five yards over the frontier in Holland. The Irish Guards moved out and attacked at

> 1300hrs with initial success, but later they ran into heavy opposition and were compelled to withdraw having had fairly heavy casualties. The night was spent in being as hospitable as possible to the Irish Guards who trickled into Hommersum, lighted by 'F' Company HQ, which was conveniently set on fire (NOT by enemy action).

It is highly likely that it was on this day that Clerk-Rattray wrote his long-overdue letter to Robertson:

> Now we are sitting in Germany, where the whole battle will go very slowly till the whole terrain becomes firmer. It is very curious going from Holland to Germany; there is hardly any difference in atmosphere, and the countryside consists of small towns surrounded by fertile country, and farms of eighty to a hundred acres.
>
> Everybody is very optimistic out here that this war will end soon, but I don't see that it is possible to come to any accurate conclusion as to when the Germans will give in, till one knows the extent of the reserves they are holding east of the Rhine.[26]

* * *

Herbert.

Back in Catterick, Herbert had spent the middle of January on leave, returning to find Scotton Lake frozen solid enough for skating, which he enjoyed almost every day until a thaw set in on Tuesday 30th. His diary for the start of February records Mess dances, shooting matches, 'tea with Penny', and country dancing, as well as a day as Duty Officer. But his days at Catterick were numbered. He relinquished his instructor role on February 10th, after just over a year in post. He was permitted to retain his rank of Captain (probably, knowing the Army, unpaid, but now 'temporary' rather than 'acting'). His posting was to 47th (Reserve) Division Signals in Norwich, but this was presumably for administrative convenience; having arrived on the evening of Sunday 11th, he was sent on leave at 1300hrs on the Monday. When he returned, on February 26th, he discovered that he was being transferred to Draft ROZYH pending transport overseas.

* * *

Fortune, meanwhile, had taken Susan on holiday. On February 9th the couple headed off to Jaipur, there to stay as guests of Maharaja Sawai Man Singh II GCSI, GCIE – known as 'Jai' to his friends. Jai had been adopted by the previous Maharaja and had acceded to the throne in 1922 at the age of ten; he was still only thirty-three. Jai had three wives, the third Maharani being Gayatri Devi, later a member of the Indian Parliament, with whom Susan got on very well. The Maharaja was a great Anglophile (he died in 1970 in Cirencester after a polo accident), and made the couple very welcome, even opening his palace at Ramgarh for them, as Susan recorded:

> Ramgarh is a paradise overlooking an enormous lake with hundreds of deep creeks and backed by hills. At one end, Jai has built what he calls a 'weekend bungalow'. It is huge, and the inside is like a modern London store show-room ... The decor was too lush for words. The large entrance hall had a gaming table and cocktail bar ... My eyes were, as they continued to do the whole week, popping out of my head with amazement.[27]

* * *

Perhaps the nastiest place on The Island was the shattered village of Haalderen, north-east of Nijmegen. The two sides, sometimes separated by only a hundred yards, lived a troglodytic existence in fortified rubble. Snipers and mortar bombs caused a steady trickle of casualties. The only consolation was that a thaw set in on February 4th and by the following day the snow had gone – though, of course, the sequel was increased flooding. 2SWB went into this little corner of Hell on February 15th, and within a week they had had enough. So they brought up an anti-tank gun which, over the course of February 22nd and 23rd, systematically flattened every house in the area which was suspected of being used by the Germans.

* * *

Curiously enough, in Italy Walker was living exactly the same sort of existence as Somerville, in very similar terrain – watercourses everywhere across flat countryside – and living in similarly ruined buildings. The following letter could have been written by either, though one suspects that the Italian experience was marginally the less miserable:

> This is written in rather uncomfortable surroundings, but nevertheless rather unusual and interesting.
>
> It is midnight. As I expect you have guessed, we are in the line, and since I last wrote I have a more active job. I took over this Troop some days ago, thirty-one men in all. We live in a very dilapidated house, of which two rooms only are habitable. Here we are about a thousand yards away from the Germans, but very amply protected. There has been a lot of work to be done in fortifying the place: building dug-outs and machine-gun positions, blocking windows and entrances, and in general trying to get as much work as possible out of the men who, with the long hours they have had to do at night with guards and the hard unaccustomed work during the day, are getting very tired. Of course, this is all a quite different life to what we usually lead, and a good deal more strenuous.
>
> I love it. The back of the work has been broken and I have been wonderfully busy organising all the defence systems – getting parties on to this and that job, and so on. At the moment I am on telephone watch, which is spread throughout the night between me and the two Sergeants. Quite strenuous, with the added possibility of a flap stand-to just as you think you are getting off to sleep.
>
> What a dirty stuffy room it is, with the old peasant fireplace, the floor covered with mud we bring in on our boots from outside – for the mud is now worse, far worse than it's ever been.

On the hard floor sleep fifteen men packed like sardines (my servant miraculously having found me a thin mattress) – rifles and equipment hang on the walls, three or four chairs with some magazines, the now empty cocoa dixie, and dirty boots placed by the fire to dry – dirty, wet socks too, and on the table all the rations for the next two days. Looking at it in that way, one could hardly imagine anything more uncomfortable. And yet everyone is cheerful. They laugh perpetually. The meals are cooked and everybody eats like lions.

Funny how enjoyment doesn't come from comfort necessarily.

I luckily have brought my own cellar: gin, some orange juice, cherry brandy, beer, and ordinary brandy.

Picture me if you can – gum boots and long socks (both indescribably muddy), my corduroys camouflaged in mud and full of holes where I've got caught up in the barbed wire in the dark. My golf jacket – now very dirty – over my sheepskin waistcoat, and scarf to hide my dirty shirt collar!

Well, it's time for me to be relieved so I must finish off. A very quiet night, so should get five or six hours.[28]

* * *

2SG moved from their billets in Hommersum into the front line on February 22nd, taking over trenches from 5th Coldstream Guards. After improving these positions, 2SG got down to the serious business of patrolling. They found no enemy to their front, and within a couple of days the battle had moved on. Just as at Tilburg, in quick succession, the Battalion received orders to be ready to move, to relax as no move was planned, and to move instantly. But by the end of the month they were still in Hommersum.

* * *

Further to the east, however, Lewin and 2KRRC were on the move. 4 Armoured Brigade had been attached to 11th Armoured Division, and assigned to an attack south of Udem. On February 23rd, in Tilburg,

> the Battalion prepared for the move and tried to disengage itself from the thousands of children … The Battalion left Tilburg at 0300hrs [February 24th] and moved to the Reichswald south of Cleve … By 1300hrs the whole Battalion was reported in, and the Battalion settled down to make the best of a very wet area.[29]

The attack on Udem commenced on February 26th, but 2KRRC were not committed until the following morning. Their objective was Gochfort z B, south-east of Udem itself.[30] Pushing through the woods to the west of Udem, in support of 44 RTR, Lewin's Battalion set off at 0600hrs. The war diary records that there was tough fighting along the way to the objective:

'B' Company and 'B' Squadron moved along the woods to the south in area Udem 9740, and dealt with many Bazooka parties, capturing about twenty prisoners-of-war. Later, 'A' Company moved up through the woods in support of 'B' Company, and many small actions were fought throughout the day. The Battalion worked its way forward, and, assisted by an attack by 159 Infantry Brigade from Udem, managed to get forward to the objective which it had been given. All companies consolidated in the area of the objective (000401), while the vehicles moved up through Udem to join them.

Throughout the day, the Battalion had taken about 100 prisoners of war, but had been subjected to very heavy shelling and mortaring in the woods. It had been continuously attacking for twenty-four hours, and had to make many small attacks to clear the enemy from the axis from 9742 to 9940.

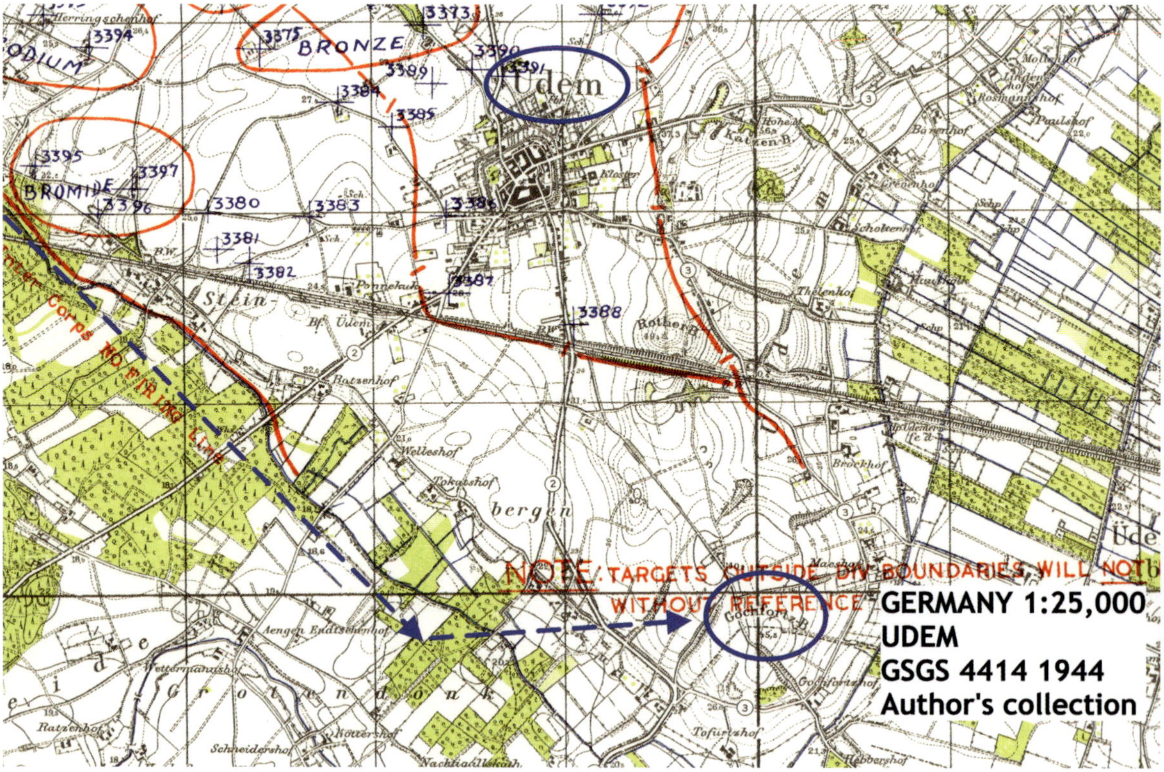

* * *

Hill had successfully completed his course at HMS *Mercury* on February 24th, and was promoted Temporary Acting Sub Lieutenant (Special Branch) (Sc). He was proud of his service, and kept not only his Midshipman tabs but also his Sub Lieutenant epaulettes. On March 6th he was detailed for further training, this time at HMS *Mercury* II, the experimental wing of the Royal Navy Signal School, located in Haslemere.

Hill.

* * *

As February 1945 drew to a close, Walker was still not able to call 3 Troop his own, though his relationship with them was still close, as his diary entry for February 28th shows:

> Today news of Sergeant Ross's MM came through, and that was the high spot of the day – in fact it was the best news that has come through for a long time, and everyone was extremely pleased … Sergeant Ross told me yesterday how the general undercurrent flowed … Matters had not been improved by the arrival of 'X' in the Squadron … All very upsetting. Corporal Jones told me yesterday that if I didn't come back to 3rd Troop they were all going to apply for transfers – encouraging as they are, these sort of things are acutely embarrassing. I shall never forget the night when Corporal Tate, O'Connor, and Clark had returned from a night patrol with more than usual excitement. I had told them to come round to me afterwards and I would give them something to warm them up, intending actually the odd thimbleful of cognac. They got talking, and the long and short of it was that not only the thimbleful but the whole bottle was empty, and of course the three of them well and truly sozzled! Now, when people get drunk they say a lot of things they'd never dream of saying when sober (so take it with a pinch of salt!). Anyway, I feel honoured to have command of such a wonderful lot of men – anxious slightly about living up to it! Sergeant Ross's MM was wonderful news, and somehow it shows the spirit that does seem to exist (how I hope I'm not rather blind and all this is not just a bucket of eye wash!). 3rd Troop's merit lies in their possessing, in spite of all their foul mouths (not all of them!), an innate and childishly simple good nature and sense of humour.
>
> I now have a new servant, Weaire. An unimaginable improvement on 'Y'. I took Weaire out of 3rd Troop, where he didn't after a time seem to click – and he is quite the most wonderful servant, and I like him. I think he has rather a wretched time one way and another.

* * *

Allied victory was drawing closer, but the 270,000 American and Commonwealth prisoners of war in Germany were anxious about their fate. Instead of awaiting the advancing Allied forces, many found themselves being forced to march away from the front lines into the heart of Germany. Some feared that they were being transferred to concentration camps for liquidation; others believed that Hitler would use them as hostages to force the Allies to the negotiating table. Perhaps their fears were justified – Hitler's death and the refusal of some of his subordinates to put his scorched earth orders into action make it unclear exactly what the *Führer* had planned. But certainly huge numbers of the half-starved inmates were marched west (away from the Russians) or east (away from the Americans), often in terrible weather conditions – not to mention the risk of attack by the Allies' own roving fighter-bombers. The marches probably caused the deaths of around 3,000 prisoners of war, but some Germans accused of war crimes later argued that they actually had a duty under the Geneva Convention to move the prisoners away from the dangers of the front line, and that Allied bombing had made it impossible to use trains. Simpkin was one of those caught up in the great migration.

Finch.

Finch was in a different camp to Simpkin: *Offizierslager (Oflag)* 79 in Waggum, a northern suburb of Braunschweig (Brunswick). Adjacent to the camp was a Luftwaffe airfield and wind-tunnel test facility (the wonderfully-named *Luftfahrtforschungsanstalt Hermann Göring*), which had led to an accidental attack on *Oflag* 79 by Allied bombers on August 24th 1944; three prisoners had been killed and fourteen badly wounded. *Oflag* 79 was based around a three-storey brick barracks built for parachute troops, but by April 1945 it contained 1,957 officers and 412 other ranks, most of them British.

Finch had been moved to Brunswick in August 1944 from *Stalag* VIIA Moosburg, the largest German prison camp of all. His arrival has not yet been precisely dated, but it may well have been before the unfortunate attack. With him was Pat Metcalfe's older brother John, who wrote to Robertson on Christmas Eve 1944:[31]

Kriegsgefangenenpost

OFLAG 79 Geprüft 13

Postkarte

RECOVERED P.O.W. MAIL
FROM EUROPE
RECENTLY RECEIVED
BY BRITISH P.O.

An Malcolm Robertson Esq

Gebührenfrei!

Absender:
Vor- und Zuname: LT. JOHN METCALFE
Gefangenennummer: 1043/VIIA F
Lager-Bezeichnung: OFLAG 79
3 Coy
Deutschland (Allemagne)

Empfangsort: CULVER LODGE
Straße: WINCHESTER
Land: HANTS
Landesteil (Provinz usw.)
GREAT BRITAIN

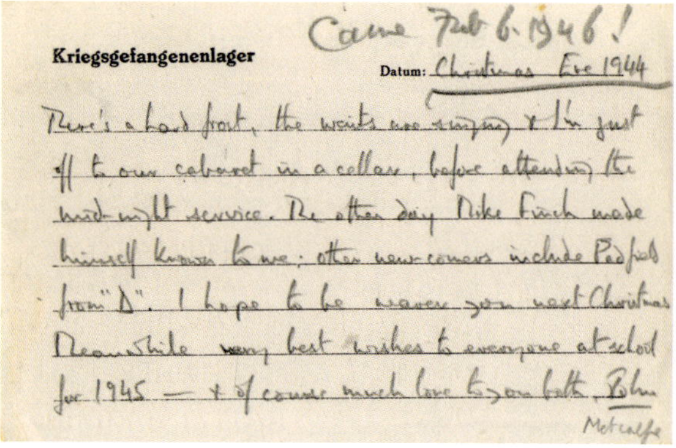

Came Feb 6. 1946!

Kriegsgefangenenlager

Datum: Christmas Eve 1944

There's a hard frost, the waits are singing & I'm just off to our cabaret in a cellar, before attending the mid-night service. The other day Mike Finch made himself known to me; other new-comers include Padfield from "D". I hope to be nearer you next Christmas. Meanwhile very best wishes to everyone at school for 1945 — & of course much love to you both. John Metcalfe

Apart from Metcalfe, Finch, and Padfield,[32] Wykehamist inmates included Captain Alistair 'Robin' Savage of 7 Commando, who had been captured on Crete in 1941.[33] Also in the camp was Simpkin's friend from 4RTR, 'Pip' Gardner VC, MC.

New inmates' initial impressions of Brunswick on arrival in the autumn of 1944 had been that it was uncomfortable, but not unbearably so. Despite the bombing, morale was high, and Red Cross food parcels arrived regularly. However, all that had changed in the bitter winter of 1944. Allied bombing had so badly dislocated the German railway network

Another prisoner in Oflag 79 was Lieutenant W.G. Anderson, an Army photographer who took surreptitious photographs at Moosburg & Brunswick whilst an inmate. This photograph, taken secretly on March 31st 1945, shows prisoners walking in one of the Oflag 79 compounds; from behind the trees smoke rises as the Germans demolish facilities at the airfield. (IWM BU 5986)

that the parcels stopped arriving; the Germans were unable to keep the heating going; the accommodation was falling apart. Morale, by some accounts, collapsed. But it was because of this that Brunswick became a very special camp indeed. Lieutenant Colonel James Dunhill realized that the boredom, hunger, and cold were doing to the prisoners what similar conditions did to so many impoverished children back in Britain. He called a meeting on February 14th 1945 at which he proposed that the inmates of *Oflag* 79 should raise funds to open a Boys' Club after the war; this would give the prisoners a purpose in their lives, as well as bringing some good out of the war. A Parachute Regiment Private captured at Arnhem then delivered a passionate speech about the transformative effect on his life of the Eton Manor Boys' Club at Hackney Wick. He tipped the balance; fund-raising began, with promises of donations and annual subscriptions, as well as events and raffles for such prizes as Isle of Man kippers or a weekend for two at the Savoy Hotel. By the end of March 1945, £13,000 had been raised (equivalent to around £460,000 today), with promises of annual standing orders of £700 (around £25,000) for running costs. And so the Brunswick Boys' Clubs in London, Liverpool, and Glasgow were born. They survive to this day.

XXVIII

'He has grown a moustache & shepherds His Excellency everywhere.'

World War, March 1945

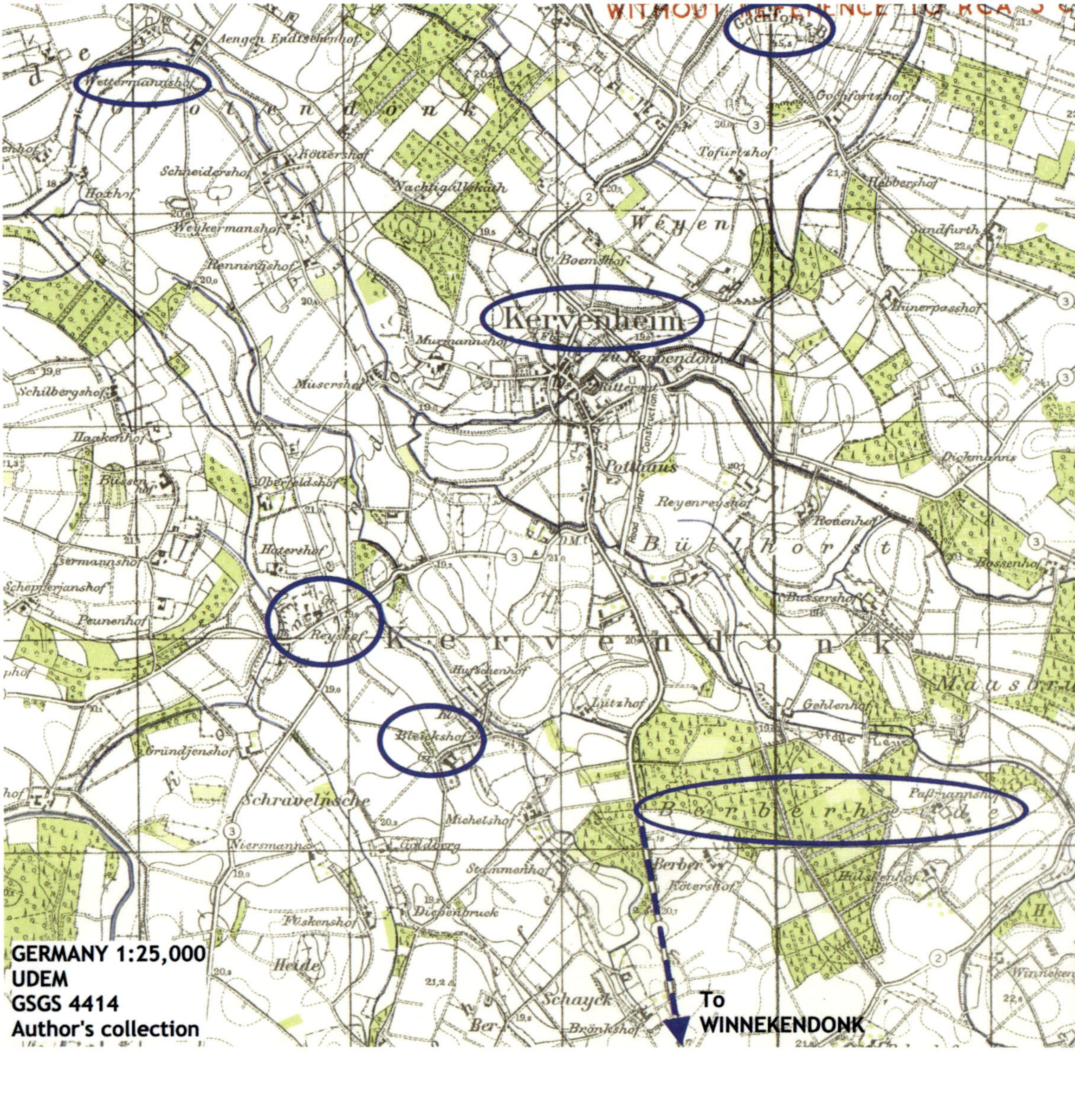

Duffin.

As Operation Veritable plodded on through the mud, the Germans improvised defensive positions on the line of the Muhlen-Fleuth between Weeze and Kervenheim, just south of Gochfort z B, where Lewin and 2KRRC had attacked on February 27th. Duffin and 3SG received orders to smash through these defences, outflank Kervenheim by taking Berberh Wood, and press on to capture Winnekendonk to the south-east.

Infantry seized a crossing over the Muhlen-Fleuth at Wettermannshoff on March 1st, and the following morning, despite every tank bogging down, 'S' Squadron crossed, together with infantry from Boyd's old unit, 1KOSB. They faced determined opposition at the Reyshof crossroads, but by 0900hrs were on that objective. Now Left Flank Squadron came through, with infantry of 2RUR, who were supposed to be riding in Kangaroo armoured personnel carriers but ended up going in on foot. Left Flank met fierce resistance in Bleickshof, west of Berberh Wood, and also had the misfortune to be on the receiving end of 'overs' from Typhoons strafing the wood from the east. The west end of Berberh Wood was taken by 1400hrs, at which point 'S' Squadron passed through. The decision was taken to push on astride the road south and take Winnekendonk, but immediately south of Bronkshof all hell broke loose.

Anti-tank weapons opened fire from both flanks and ahead, whilst shells landed all around. All three tanks in the leading troop were hit, and the artillery FOO's tank exploded. The right-hand troop following behind was commanded by Lieutenant Robert Runcie – later the Archbishop of Canterbury – who took his tanks forward on to the open ground and destroyed two 75mm SPGs and an 88mm anti-tank gun. Though Runcie's previous tank had been brewed up only the day before, his courage saved 3SG from a sticky situation, and he was awarded an immediate MC.[1] Llewellyn-Smith's account of the fight runs as follows:

> It was now quite dark. Very close hand-to-hand fighting took place with a large number of paratroops in the streets and houses. Lieutenant MacDonald-Buchanan's Troop, though several times bazooka'd and grenaded, shot the infantry right up to the back end of the town and stayed with them there. One tank fell into a bomb crater, and had to be abandoned. The crew were making their way back when it was discovered that the Slidex Card [cipher key] had been left behind, and MacDonald-Buchanan and Guardsman Hunt went back through the enemy-infested town to retrieve it. The crew then returned to the forward rally on the other tank of the Troop: on the way they were bazooka'd and sniped and fought hand-to-hand in the narrow streets. By 2100hrs the situation was under control and the Squadron was able to concentrate for the night … in the houses near the road junction north of the town.
>
> All through the night and the next morning prisoners continued to be brought in, the final count being 250, all from the Para Lehr Regiment. They had fought fanatically and then suddenly given up. But it was not until the next day that the strength of the position was fully realised. In addition to the two 88mm and two SPGs knocked out, tracks of other SPGs were discerned, and six dug-in 50mm anti-tank guns were found; two more 88mms were captured at the back of the town, and the haul of Spandaus

> and infantry weapons of all kinds was very large. For it appears that one battalion of the Para Lehr Regiment and a Fortress Battery had been holding the place, and that it was regarded as a key point in the German defence scheme. Indeed, so open was the approach, so strong the anti-tank screen, and so well dug-in the infantry, that it was hard to believe that one infantry battalion and a squadron of tanks could have captured it against the pick of German troops, success which will surely rank as one of the finest small-scale tank/infantry battles ever executed.

The next morning, Left Flank cleared a large wood south of Winnekendonk without opposition. 3SG had spent the past twenty-four days in the front line and fought fifteen significant actions. It was time to rest. There was a Rhine to cross.

* * *

Lewin.

2KRRC were also due a rest, although on February 28th they had been delighted to become armoured infantry, transported in Kangaroos. 2KRRC set off in these vehicles at 1000hrs on March 1st to breach the German Schlieffen Line, which ran north-south through the Hochwald forest east of Udem. There was plenty of shelling, but the new armoured protection prevented casualties. As 'C' Company and 'C' Squadron 44RTR moved up to an anti-tank ditch, they encountered determined resistance from 1223 *Grenadier* Regiment, and 'A' Company moved up in support. The following morning, 'B' Company forced a crossing through four feet of water, losing their Company Commander in doing so, and held the bridge-head until relieved by Canadian troops that night. 2KRRC had suffered fifty casualties in the preceding five days – 'Going had been hard, but it had been proved again that an armoured regiment and an infantry battalion, when properly co-ordinated, take some holding.'[2]

By March 9th the Battalion was back at a rest area at Bourg Léopold, where 4 Armoured Brigade had concentrated. The following day, a strength return of officers in the war diary does not list Lewin; it appears that the strain of operations and vile weather had caused him to need hospitalization again. He would miss the Rhine crossing.

* * *

Clerk-Rattray.

As March began, 2SG's war diary bridled with irritation. On the morning of March 1st the Battalion received orders to be at one hour's notice to move: 'In view of the previous instruction saying that we were unlikely to move for forty-eight hours, this change of plan caused considerable pandemonium.'

The Commanding Officer's instructions were to move the Battalion forwards to Winkel, to an area which was clear of friendly forces. But when he went forwards to recce the area,

> the ground was found thick with troops, including two Battalion HQs who had no idea that the Battalion had been ordered to move in. Company Commanders had a swift look at their company areas, and a skeleton 'O' Group was held on the side of the road. Plans were made for the move tomorrow, but it was decided that unless the troops at present in the area moved before the Battalion arrived, it would be impossible to accommodate the companies or the Battalion HQ.

Brigade HQ promised that the area would be clear by the morning of March 2nd. But when advance parties set off to the new area at 0830hrs, they found that no one had moved out and that no one knew anything about orders to move. And so, just as the Battalion was about to leave Hommersum, the men instead returned to their billets. Even when genuine orders to move at last arrived on March 5th,

> progress was slow, and after passing the Brigade Signals Post in Goch became agonising. The road in front consisted of one mass of tanks and transport jammed together nose to tail, and we moved in short sharp jerks through Weeze to Kevelaer, arriving at about 1100hrs.

It was fortunate that the Luftwaffe was a spent force.

It is possible that Clerk-Rattray and Duffin met that evening, since officers from 3SG were invited to dinner with 2SG. The party, however, broke up early when orders arrived for 2SG to launch an attack in the morning. It was to be their first action in Germany.

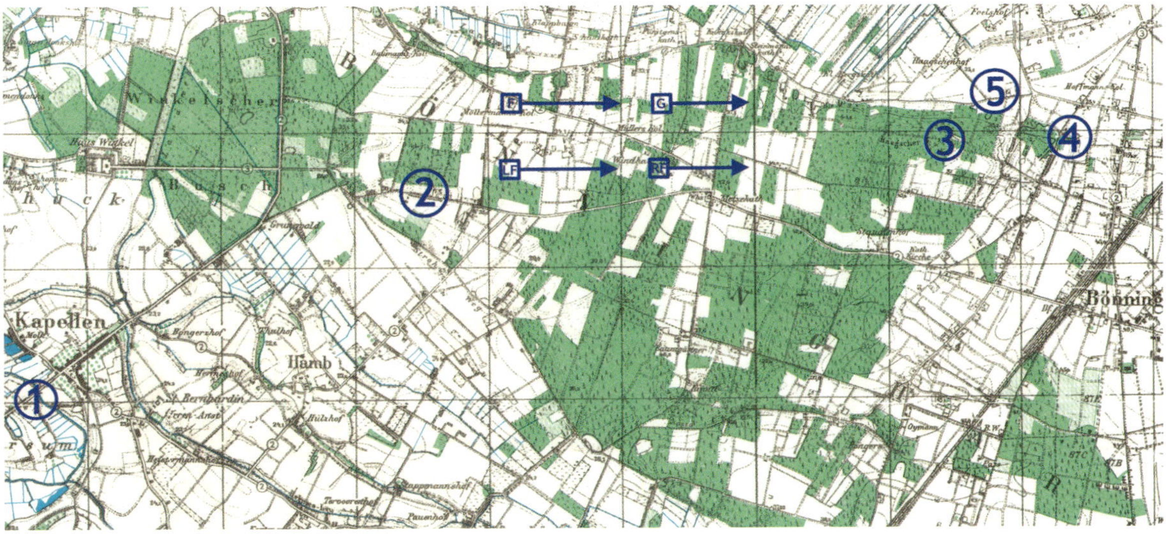

The attack, scheduled for 1100hrs on March 6th, was to assault and secure the eastern end of a low wooded hill overlooking Bönninghardt. 2SG would move in from the west, starting at Kapellen, with 1st Welsh Guards to their south. At 0730hrs 2SG de-bussed south-west of Kapellen (1) and moved to their assembly area, which was in the area of a house (2) where the final briefing for Company Commanders was held. From there, at 1015hrs, the companies moved off to their forming-up point. This procedure is still standard today; what was lacking on March 6th 1944 was any time for reconnaissance of the routes to the objective, Haagscher Wood (3). There was also no opportunity for the Platoon Commanders to brief their men effectively. This could have been a recipe for disaster, especially given the difficult terrain and the fact that the unit had not fought a battle in over a year.

At 1100hrs the preliminary bombardment began – with Right Flank not quite ready – and 2SG followed close behind it. Right Flank found the going easy and started to take prisoners, despite delays caused by fallen trees and the fact that their axis was mined. But the woods were thicker in front of 'G' Company, and the opposition more determined. 'G' bypassed one enemy position, which was cleared up by 'F', who then passed through the Haagscher objective and at 1415hrs pressed on to a secondary objective, an isolated wood (4). It did not help when British 25-pounders started to drop shells on to them, killing the Company Sergeant Major, but they reached their goal. 2SG had taken over 150 prisoners from the German 1062 *Grenadier* Regiment, for the loss of eight men killed and twenty-six wounded.

The leading companies now began to dig in as fast as they could, which was relatively easy in the soft ground. That was no bad thing, since the Germans had plenty of artillery nearby and seemingly limitless ammunition. 'F' Company – Clerk-Rattray's – had the worst of it in their exposed forward position; the enemy kept them under machine-gun fire throughout the night of March 6th, and the shelling was so heavy that they were unable to move out until the evening of March 7th. Although they had to maintain a low profile during the day, 'F' did send out a patrol to a group of houses to the north (5); the patrol brought back thirteen prisoners.

* * *

Holtby.

Holtby was no longer bored in Palestine; his Battalion had been summoned for the campaign in North-West Europe, and on March 3rd 6th Seaforths left their accommodation near Naples to embark on the final stage of their journey by sea; they disembarked in Marseilles on March 6th and within the week were in Belgium. But there they stayed for another month.

* * *

After a brief rest, Clerk-Rattray and 2SG now prepared to attack again, and were fortunate in having most of March 8th in which to plan. North-east of Bönninghardt, two railway lines enclosed a triangular area which needed to be cleared so that other units could use it as a jumping-off point to push forwards to the Rhine. This involved getting over the small River Romer – which could be crossed at a bridge nicknamed 'Nigel', if the Germans had not demolished it.

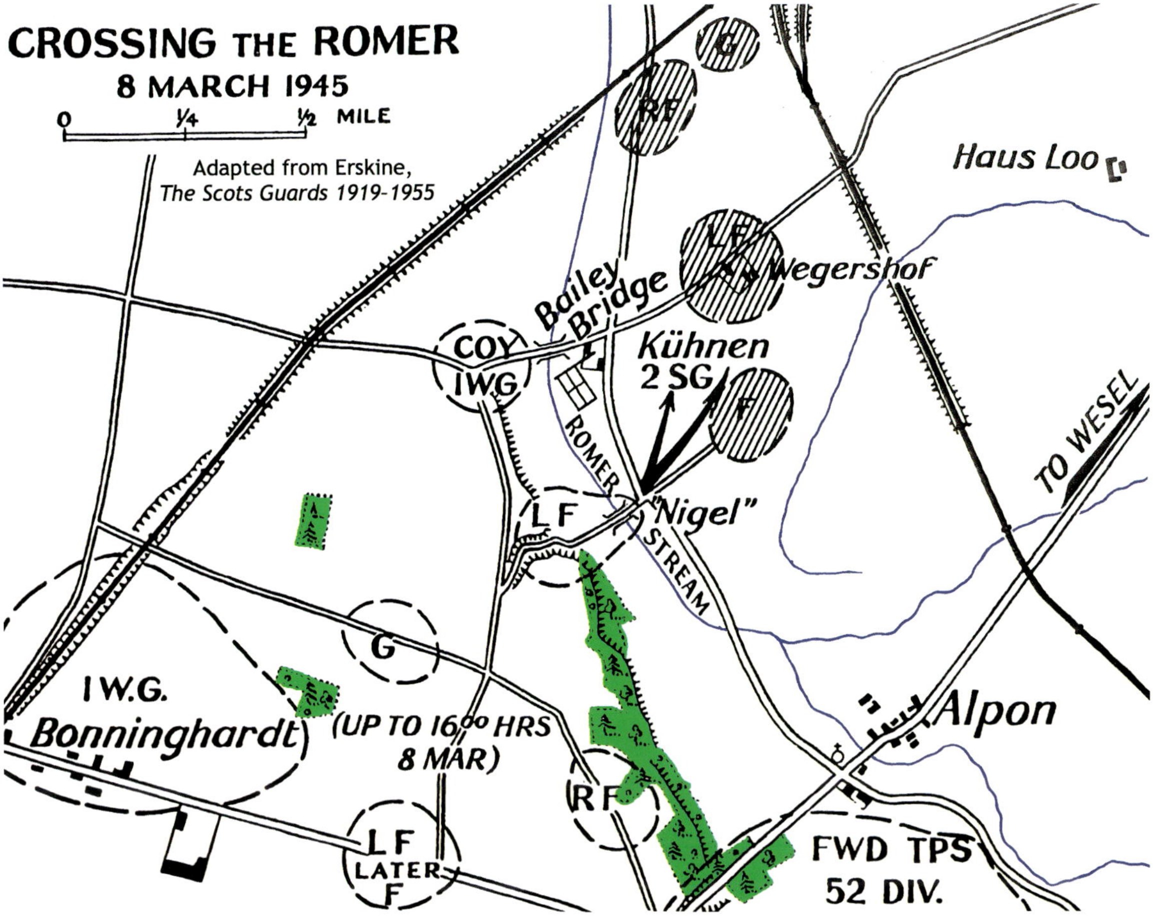

Reconnaissance revealed that NIGEL was still standing, and so Left Flank secured it on the night of March 7th. NIGEL was strong enough to take tanks, but the approaches from the south-west were very difficult and under German shell-fire. Around 1630hrs Left Flank rushed NIGEL, followed by Right Flank, 'G', and finally 'F'. Tanks then followed until the message was broadcast that 'NIGEL is crumbling'. 2SG held their ground, picking off any Germans incautious enough to poke up their heads from the railway embankment, until the evening of March 9th. Again, 'F' Company bore the brunt of the misery; from their positions they could see German SPGs firing at them from near Alpon, but because troops from 52nd Division were in the vicinity, 'F' could not call in fire to silence the enemy – 'Anything that moved in 'F' Company and Left Flank localities was shot at.'[3]

There had been losses: six officers and forty-one other ranks killed or wounded. In three days of fighting the Battalion had taken eighty casualties, nearly a company's worth. The following morning, it became clear that the Germans had withdrawn behind the Rhine. 2SG returned to billets in Heumen: 'All ranks were badly in need of sleep, and soon the Battalion was snoring peacefully for the first time since March 5th.'[4]

* * *

At Viceroy's House in Delhi, Fortune continued to serve Wavell as ADC. In early March, Officer Cadet Michael Ryall – another of Robertson's boys, who had left Sunnyside in 1944 – was in Delhi and reported back to his old housemaster in a letter written on the 8th:

Fortune.

> We have had a hell of a time here. We went to the big VC presentation and saw the 'Auk' [Auchinleck] from a distance and also the Viceroy and Captain Fortune. Last night we were invited to drinks at a Colonel Curry's. There I was actually introduced to Bruce Fortune!! He is engaged, I believe, to a Wren, but I did not see her. He has grown a moustache and shepherds His Excellency everywhere. He wished to be remembered to you and Sheila, and hopes you are managing OK back in England.[5]

At some point that month, Fortune took his fiancée to see the Taj Mahal by moonlight. They had the whole place to themselves.

* * *

In the somewhat less romantic Huddersfield, Herbert entrained for Liverpool at 0430hrs, where he boarded HMS *Durban Castle*, a former liner of the Union Castle Line which had been converted into a Landing Ship, Infantry, in 1943, serving at Salerno and Anzio. There was, of course, no castle at Durban, but the Line had run out of British castles and so began naming its vessels after fictional South African ones. The ship was anchored in the Mersey when Herbert embarked, and his diary records that they were fog-bound on March 9th, setting sail the following day. He reported that Sunday 11th was 'Rough. Squeamish all day'.[6]

The Monday was better, and he watched an ENSA production of *Much Ado about Nothing* (in modern dress), which he thought very good. He then made himself useful for the rest of the voyage setting up microphones and lighting for concerts and productions on board. It was a rapid passage, passing Gibraltar on March 16th, Bone on the 18th, Port Said on the 21st, Suez on the 22nd, Aden on the 26th, and Bombay on March 31st. A new chapter was beginning.

* * *

Brooke.

On March 8th, 16th/5th Lancers, with Brooke, quitted Antella for the final time, moving to the seaside town of Pesaro. There they got to work preparing new-model Sherman tanks for battle; they had first received these tanks in late September, but no sooner had they begun adapting them for use than they had been made to hand them back to store. Now they received Shermans with 76mm main guns, though each Squadron also had one Troop completely equipped with Fireflies, and in each HQ Troop there were two heavy-support Shermans armed with 105mm guns.

One question was how to deal with the *Panzerfaust* threat. The *Panzerfaust* used a shaped-charge warhead – devastating if it detonated in contact with armour, but ineffective if it exploded even an inch from the surface. Thus the tank crews began to festoon their Shermans with spare track-links or even chicken-wire mesh to explode warheads at a distance from the tank itself. The best protection, however, was infantry who could cover the blind spots around a tank and prevent a German tank-hunter from getting close enough to use his *Panzerfaust*.

* * *

Nick Somerville.

March saw Somerville and his men of 'C' Company 2SWB still immobile on The Island, though it seemed that the Germans were beginning slowly to abandon the area. Somerville was tasked to occupy three farmhouses, well forward of the main line of defence, to keep an eye open for movement. One of his Platoon Commanders recalled that their instructions were to remain completely hidden, with no movement by day. Each platoon would occupy its position for up to a week, food being brought up at night. When one platoon reached the barn in which it was to lie up, the men found a dead horse lying at the middle of the floor. They dug a huge hole beside the corpse, dragged it in, filled in the hole, and stayed in position.

Plans were, however, afoot for something more exciting. The British were going to have a second go at capturing Arnhem.

* * *

Walker.

10th Hussars came out of the similarly miserable front line near Ravenna in the first week of March, occupying more comfortable accommodation near Forli and re-equipping with tanks after their brief experience of infanteering. Walker was once again happy:[7]

> Our present location [is] well back in a good area and free from any apparent damage. All the billets are clean, the people well dressed, and with the present glorious weather one could wish for little more.
>
> We celebrated Sergeant Ross's MM a few nights ago in true 3rd Troop style, and the Sergeant Major and myself went along after dinner, about 2130hrs. By then, of course, there was nobody left sober. We had a few speeches and everybody sang a song, and everyone made drunken contributions – much to everyone's amusement – and then, of course, everyone had to be put to bed!

However, it all turned sour very quickly.

Tuesday, March 13th
Corporal Jones and Pateman handed me two suspicious little notes with applications for an interview to change troops. As usual they had had an orgy the night before – somebody had thumped somebody else, tipped them out of bed, and all the rest of the usual story. I rather tended towards letting Corporal Jones go, good gunner though he is – talked to Sergeant Ross who thought the whole thing was childish, but agreed that if they persisted to let the thing go through. I saw Pateman again, who decided to let the matter drop, and Corporal Jones too, after Sergeant Ross had seen him. Corporal Jones goes on leave tomorrow, which may make him feel better. I can't help sympathising as well as criticizing him … The Mess is becoming rather intolerable, 3rd Troop an all-too-scorching furnace – what a life!

Saturday, March 17th
Tonight, for a change, I am beginning to hate the Army. I love the idea of being with 3rd Troop but being with 'Z' etc., is too bloody for words. I am beginning to appreciate 3rd Troop so much – I shall have to write some short character studies. I see now how far easier it is to be a good officer in the Army when there is no bullshit and we are fighting – static life is pretty grim.

March 27th
The Troop, I hope, in good form as ever, and one of the few comforts in an otherwise monotonous and boring existence.

March 28th
Since yesterday my mental gloom has been somewhat cleared. I had been unusually depressed, feeling how difficult it was to be a good troop officer in times like the present than in action. I still maintain that I would far sooner know any seven men from 3rd Troop than our own noble seven officers in 'C' Squadron. I do sincerely feel it is possible without losing one's self respect … I am far and away happier when with them than when listening to the people in the Mess.

* * *

On March 11th 3SG, together with the rest of 6 Guards Tank Brigade, reached Kevelaer, only a short distance from Winnekendonk. The weather had improved at long last, with bright sunshine creating a much more cheerful mood. On March 20th, Duffin and Clerk-Rattray almost certainly met, since the officers of 2SG once again dined with 3SG in Kevelaer that evening.

In Montgomery's usual methodical way, plans for the crossing of the Rhine were at an advanced stage, and on March 22nd Duffin and the other officers were briefed on their intended role when Operation Varsity-Plunder began. The concept of operations was that an assault crossing would be made in the Xanten/Rees sector, at which point 6th Airborne Division would land on the other side of the Rhine to swamp the defences and prevent a counter-attack. On the evening of March 25th, Left Flank were to cross, link up with the airborne troops, and prepare for the break-out.

D-Day for the crossing was Saturday March 24th. The sky was blue and cloud-free as 6th Airborne Division flew in, and the following day, Left Flank moved to its assembly area at Point 185 near Wardt. In the darkness of that Sunday night, the Squadron crossed the Rhine, its tanks on rafts. Duffin, therefore, became the first of our subjects to cross the Rhine voluntarily.

Left Flank met up as planned with the British airborne forces, but a planned joint operation was aborted when the Allies realized just how weak and disorganized resistance was. Instead, an improvised Anglo-American battle-group was pointed up the Wesel–Munster road and told to get going. At 1500hrs on March 27th, 3SG fell in behind 3rd Reconnaissance Regiment and moved off from Peddenberg, American parachute infantrymen riding on every tank to deal with any *Panzerfaust*-wielding diehards. At Damm the Recce troops encountered opposition and 3SG moved through them, 'S' Squadron in the lead. Almost immediately they were engaged by German self-propelled guns and lost a Churchill. Rather than press on in the gathering darkness, 3SG halted.

But orders soon arrived demanding that Dorsten be captured without delay, with its bridges over the River Lippe intact if possible. At 0045hrs on March 28th, 3SG set out again, Left Flank at the rear; there was fog, and the American tank-riders had to stay alert despite the darkness. At Schermbeck a roadblock forced 3SG off the road and across boggy ground, but by 0345hrs they were back on the road and pressing on for Dorsten. By 0700hrs, 3SG were in control of the town, despite sniping, though the bridges were down.

Three hours later, Left Flank received orders to move east towards Hervest to support the American paratroopers capture the bridge over the Lippe Canal. However, the woods

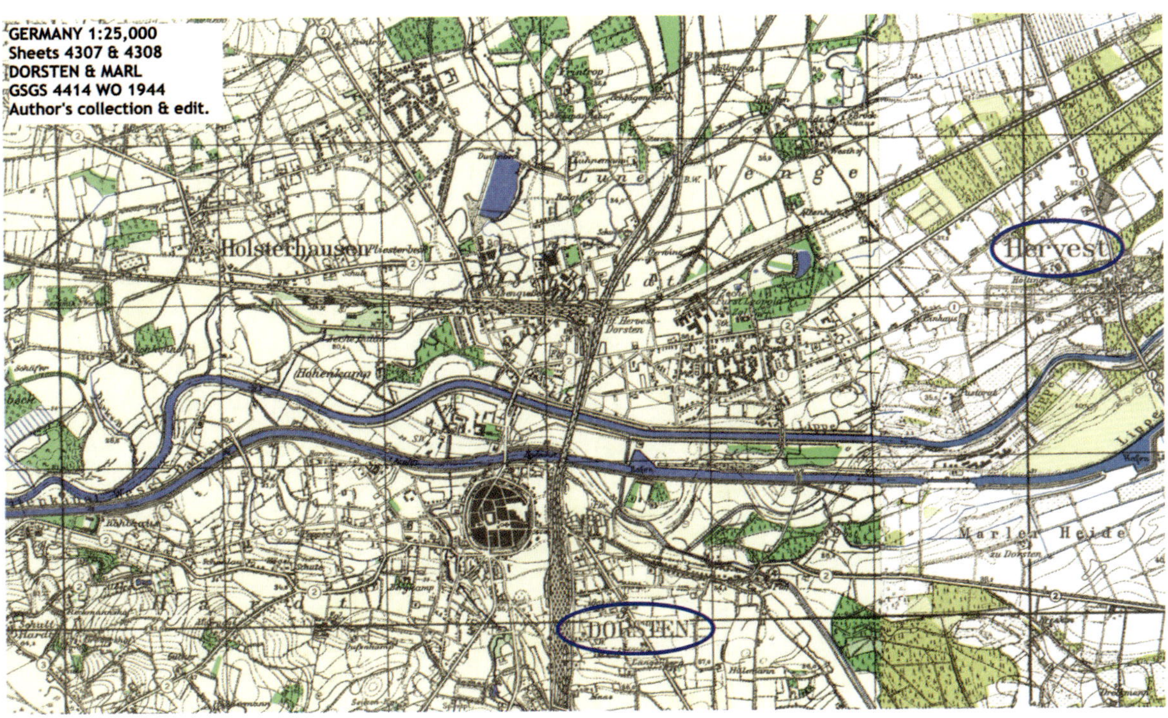

were full of German troops, liberally equipped with *Panzerfäuste*, and they put up such fierce resistance that at 1300hrs the Churchills withdrew.

* * *

Simpkin.

On March 27th, the inmates of *Oflag* IXA/H and *Oflag* IXA/Z were informed that they should get ready to move out of their camps. *Oflag* IXA/H (the 'H' stands for *Hauptlager*, 'main camp'), on two sites in Spangenberg bei Kassel, had opened in 1939. In June 1940, a sub-camp (*Zweiglager*) had been opened a short distance away in the Jacob Grimm girls' school at Rotenburg an der Fulda. There were Wykehamists in both camps. In Spangenberg there were at least two: one was Lieutenant Colonel Edward Lillingston, 4th Hussars;[8] the other was Major Maurice Wilson, 1st Battalion, Queen's Own Cameron Highlanders, a prisoner of war since 1940.[9]

In June 1943, Rotenburg had witnessed the suicide of a prominent Wykehamist officer, Brigadier Claude Nicholson, hero of the defence of Calais in May 1940. By March 1945, its '*kriegies*' included Bruce Shand, father of Queen Camilla. There were also three Wykehamists: Major the Hon. George Milne RA;[10] Lieutenant John R.K. Sinclair, 1st Battalion, Queen's Own Cameron Highlanders;[11] and Richard Simpkin.

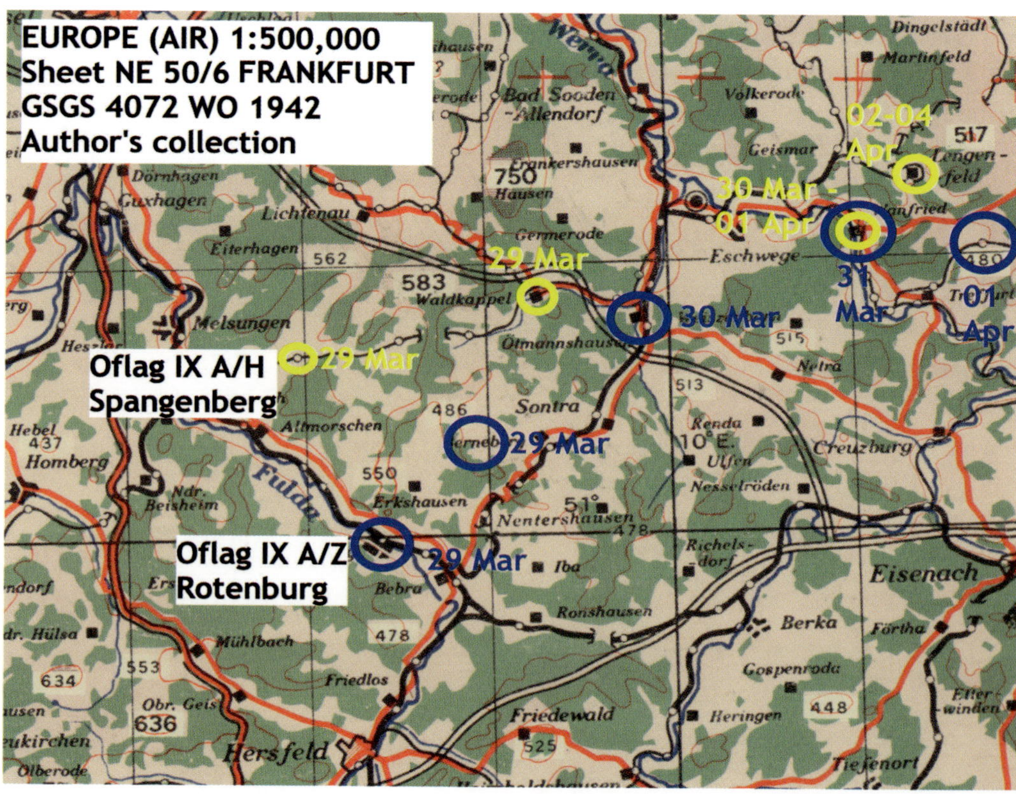

March 29th saw the beginning of the prisoners' pointless march eastwards.[12] Their captors knew that there were American troops advancing eastwards to the north and to the south, and tried to keep their prisoners moving along the corridor between those two thrusts. But the situation was very fluid, and so the prisoners found themselves halting or moving first north, then south, without any clear sense of for how long or how far they would be driven until rescued. Simpkin and the others from Rotenburg were moving more north-eastwards than the Spangenbergers, with the result that their paths merged on March 31st in the Eschwege area.

* * *

3SG stayed where they were in Dorsten until the afternoon of March 29th, and then pushed north-east through Haltern to Dulmen, covering nineteen miles in one day. Continuing the following morning towards Munster, the Battalion encountered opposition near Horst, but by nightfall Left Flank were safely harboured in a farm. Soon after noon the next day, 3SG began to move towards Roxel, a few miles west of Munster itself. With Left Flank in the lead, by nightfall the Churchills had reached Boesensell, where they halted rather than press on through difficult terrain in the darkness.

* * *

Kemp.

Early in March, 7RB had moved to Cattolica, on the Adriatic coast south of Rimini, to prepare for the April offensive. Life at Cattolica was pleasant, Wykehamist Jim Wilson describing it as being 'on a suburban and semi-detached basis in groups of villas by the sea'.[13] 7RB enjoyed sailing competitions in dinghies which had been donated to the Battalion, played basketball and hockey, and visited the cinemas, which showed films such as *You Were Never Lovelier* (with Fred Astaire), *The Woman of the Town* (with Claire Trevor), and *Babes on Broadway* (starring Mickey Rooney and Judy Garland). A symphony orchestra performed Rossini, and an ENSA variety troupe put on a daily show called *Listen to This*.

We are apt to forget that as the war had gone on, the British Army had matured into the finest infantry in the world, the roots from which the modern British Army sprang, never forgetting the lessons learned in six years of bitter experience. Wilson was well aware of this:

> We embarked on a training period which proved the best I can remember anywhere. We practised our techniques, regained lost skills and confidence with our weapons, and developed sensible methods for operating in the Po valley, where Eighth Army's offensive would be launched … The weather was lovely.[14]

In preparation for the attack, 7RB were paired with 17th/21st Lancers; each infantry company would be operating with a squadron of tanks, just as we have seen in Normandy, Belgium, Holland, and Germany.

On March 31st, as Herbert landed in India, Kemp was admitted to 66 British General Hospital in Rimini, although he was discharged on April 4th. He had just a month of war left.

* * *

Clerk-Rattray crossed the Rhine by way of 'London' bridge, at Rees, at around 2000hrs on March 30th. The battlefield on to which they were moving was fluid, and as the Allied forces probed forwards they changed their plans constantly depending on whether they met stiff opposition or none. 2SG had been slated to move in the direction of Hamburg, but on the following morning were allocated a different axis of advance on the left flank of the main thrust, heading along the Dutch-German border. Each company had been married up with a squadron of 2nd (Armoured) Battalion, Welsh Guards. To start with, at least, their progress would be more of a triumphal procession than a battle.

XXIX

'Back in England, arriving home tomorrow'

World War, April 1945

Metcalfe.

Easter Sunday 1945 fell on April 1st. At Ahmednagar, 45th Cavalry formally stood up as a Sherman tank unit, though virtually no one was there at the time to mark the event. Even Metcalfe, the Adjutant, did not return from leave until April 9th, along with the commanding officer; three days later, 121 other ranks came back, on the 18th another 104, and 118 more on April 26th. The 45th even then only had thirteen Shermans, meaning that the Regiment was far from operational. However, its likely employment was becoming clearer. Major amphibious operations were in prospect: the Arakan had been cleared by landings along its coast during December and January; troops were scheduled to land at Rangoon early in May (Operation Dracula); and planning was also afoot for landings in Malaya (Operation Zipper). 45th Cavalry could see where their future lay.

* * *

Outside Ravenna, Walker celebrated Easter properly.

Walker.

> To church early this morning: my first visit for a long time. It was a beautiful morning and I listened to the Messiah 'He was despised' (even now, as I write this, the church bells in the village are ringing). Then a conference over yesterday's scheme, and lunch with the landlord's family: salami, some form of pasta, steak, and then English trifle and cake – what a meal. I had to sleep it off for four hours this afternoon!
>
> Moving is definitely in the air. Yesterday I had to pack all my surplus kit – what is going to happen? Everything seems very mysterious and momentous. Where will it all lead to? Maybe we are about to have a really big battle; maybe not … I am tonight feeling quite contented and prepared, though as usual frightened, I suppose. However, if one can control it once, one can do it again, though maybe it is not going to be all jam this time.
>
> Tonight I heard that Farr's name had been drawn out of the hat for leave to England. I was glad. He deserves it as much as anyone, and I went and congratulated him tonight. I shall be very sorry to lose him all the same.

'A' Squadron have just moved out, which would appear most unpoetic and uninspiring. It is however a lovely time of the year. The corn-fields and fruit blossoms are all beginning to look beautiful – everything is fresh and lovely. I know we have churned up the fields and half-destroyed the roads, and the coming battle is by now in most people's minds. Yet one catches a glimpse occasionally – something simple like a bird singing, a rising moon, or a little girl in her cool little white dress – which is terribly peaceful, innocent, and refreshing. Then one can think of all that is lovely and beautiful in England. 'Leave Out' days at Winchester in the spring-time; visits to Juniper Hill and Water Meads. How lovely it was. 'Toll 2' round Trench on a cold November afternoon; the swans' nest by Dalma, Sunday walks to St Cross – evening Chapel on Saturdays, the Close, and the peaches for tea with the Bishop, Domum nights, the birds, lines with Francis King on I think Thursday mornings – we had them by Meads Wall where the irises grow in summer, and then the ground was always so wet with the dew. What a glorious country it is. Then the orange-blossom girls, and the parties, and the day with June on the river at Oxford. I've had a glorious life, seeing all that is lovely and fresh and good and beautiful. Nowadays life is really far from beautiful; how glorious it will be when it's all over.[1]

* * *

Clerk-Rattray.

Clerk-Rattray's advance on April 1st with 2SG took him north-east along the Dutch side of the Dutch-German border, and thus they were seen as liberators. Their war diary recorded that they passed 'through villages newly liberated, and lined with rejoicing Dutchmen, who seemed genuinely pleased to see us … In the afternoon, we passed through the Coldstream, losing our way in Enschede, where we received a great welcome.'[2]

However, to the north of Enschede lay a large airfield, and as the advance guard neared it they came under anti-tank gun-fire, which brewed up two tanks. Rather than launch an attack in the gathering darkness, 2SG and 2WG waited until 0700hrs on April 2nd – but when 'F' Company attacked it found the defenders gone, though they had left behind three anti-tank guns in the woods east of the airfield. The rest of the day would involve greater excitement. As 2SG pushed north through Oldenzaal towards the German border, the Household Cavalry blazed the trail ahead, until they came up against a blown bridge and an active German SPG just on the border. 2SG were told that it was essential to capture Nordhorn, the first town in Germany, and to push on the twelve miles to Lingen on the River Ems. The importance of the task was such, 2SG were told, that if the armour could not get through, they would have to advance on foot in the darkness to accomplish the task.

And so it was that the 'Mad Night Dash to the Ems' was set in motion.

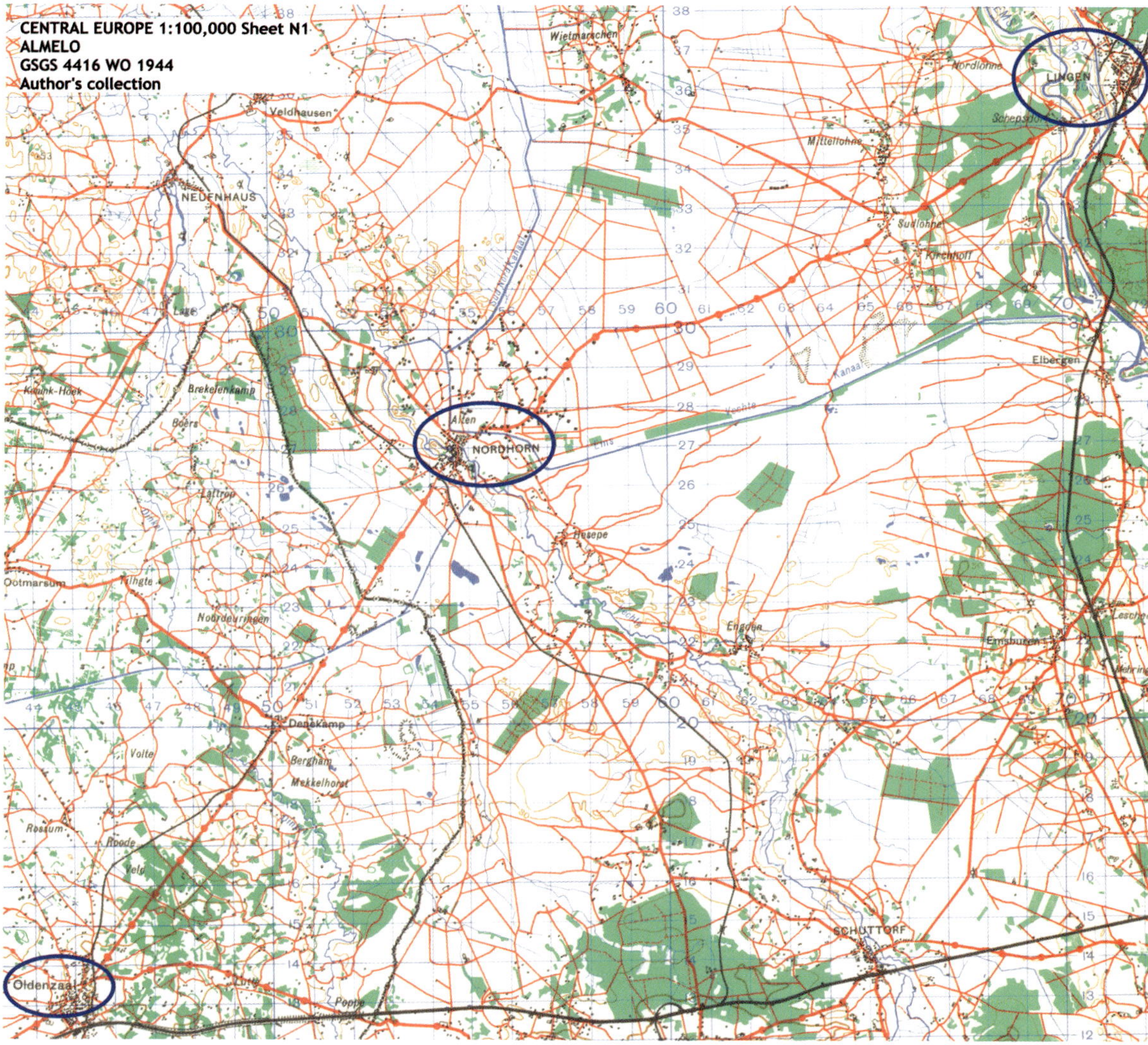

On April 7th, the *Daily Mail* ran a story as follows:[3]

TANKS LEAD BIG BREAK-THROUGH
MIDNIGHT 15-MILE 'MAD' DASH BY GUARDS

It was midnight, a pitch-black night under the cold, distant stars over Germany, and forward elements of the Guards Armoured Division halted for orders. Eager, hushed voices echoed in the still of the night. Lumbering tanks stopped with grating squeals of protest. The orders came, short, curt, and definite. 'Get going – and go fast', they said.

The Guards got going. Huge Cromwell tanks and every kind of armoured vehicle, blurred and shapeless in the inky blackness, moved off. Their lightning advance against every kind of opposition opened up the road for streams of British armour to pour on to the plains of North-West Germany.

In the van were a battle-group of Scots Guards riding on Welsh Guards tanks. They travelled at top speed, without lights, in an attempt to force the Ems River and

> the Dortmund–Ems Canal. Battle was joined at Nordhorn, where the Guards group fought their way to the bridges in the town, which was blazing fiercely. The bridges blew up in their faces.

In fact, there were more bridges and fewer detonations. When the Household Cavalry had met the hold-up on the border they had quickly found another bridge, over which Right Flank passed, riding on a squadron of tanks. They rushed the first bridge in Nordhorn and took it intact. The next bridge in the town was partially blown, and the third completely down and covered by German fire. The Household Cavalry again found an alternative bridge intact to the north; leaving 'G' Company to garrison Nordhorn, 2SG formed up, riding on their tanks, with Right Flank leading, then Left Flank, and then Clerk-Rattray with 'F' Company. At 2300hrs, their headlights on full to help them to thread their way through Nordhorn, they set off for Lingen.

> Then came a long, thrilling fifteen-miles dash. As the leading tank squadron, with its supporting infantry company, raced into the black night, they met groups of bewildered Germans walking or driving down the road towards them. Motor-cycles, carts, and lorries laden with equipment were knocked off the road and fired on by the racing wreckers. But they did not slow down. A German officer captured in Nordhorn said he was on leave, and declared that his comrades would be taken absolutely by surprise. They had no conception such an advance could be made.
>
> For eight miles the tanks roared on, and the burnt shells of enemy vehicles by the roadside next morning showed how their daring charge had succeeded. Then the leading tank ran into the back of two self-propelled guns, and a captured Sherman camouflaged by the Germans, which were also moving towards Lingen. Seventeen-pounder shells put paid to these.
>
> 'I could only see a blur of a target through my sights, but I let them have all we had got,' the gunner of the leading tank said.
>
> These guns blocked the road and the column was halted in a murderous blaze of bazooka and Spandau fire. The two leading tanks were disabled. A German motor-cyclist raced past and threw a bomb on to one of the tanks. The crew were blinded by smoke and fumes, but their machine-gunner squared the account with a sharp burst.
>
> The night was lit by red tracer from British and German machine-guns, and explosions of 75mm and bazooka shells. Resistance broke after a short but hectic battle. Another troop took the lead, and a detour was made through fields adjoining the road, where the headlong charge continued. More German trucks travelling from and towards Lingen were shot up and left blazing in the ditches.
>
> On went the Guards to Sudlohne, a village on the west bank of the river opposite Lingen. Here more bazookas were encountered, but the Scotsmen leapt from the tanks to dash ahead with the leading troop of tanks. Two sections raced across the bridge. When the tracks of the first tank were only three yards away, it was blown by the Nazis on the far bank.
>
> As soon as the bridge was blown, the Germans sent a hail of Spandau and 20mm fire across the Ems river and the nearby canal. The leading tank was hit and ditched; the second tank was hit twice, but managed to reach cover. Infantry sections, cut off

and under fire, swam back across the river, with some losses, to dig in on the near side and hold the bridge approaches until relieved in the morning.

Lieutenant W.A. Elliott MC, of Right Flank Company, followed the route the following morning:

> As we neared Lingen the road was lined with charred bodies (like burnt wood) at the side of gutted vehicles. Horses and limbers littered the roadside in ghastly confusion. There were some knocked-out 88s on trailers, and I thought it must be the work of rocket-firing Typhoons, till I saw the fresh blood of the horses and that the trucks were still smouldering, showing it to be the work of the previous night.[4]

Remarkably, 2SG's losses that night were two men killed in action and one died of wounds.

Despite a sleepless but exhilarating night, 'F' Company went into action again on the afternoon of April 3rd, being sent from Sudlohne to clear the woods south of Schepsdorf, but they encountered no enemy and returned to their company area. They had earned a rest.

* * *

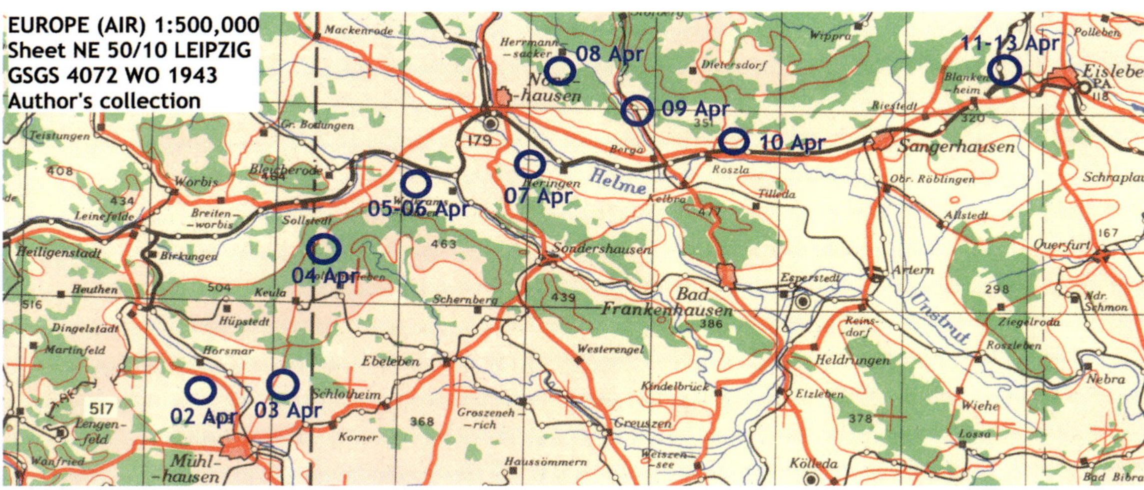

Simpkin.

There was no rest for Simpkin, however, and the other inmates of *Oflag* IX A/Z from Rotenburg, who continued to plod north-eastwards, heading into the forests and steep slopes of the Holzthalbener Wald: from Wanfried to Diedorf on April 1st; to Lengefeld on April 2nd; Windeberg on April 3rd; Friedrichsrode on April 4th; and Nohra on April 5th, with a rest day there. A remarkable series of images of the march exists in the Imperial War Museum archives, taken by a clandestine photographer, inmate Leighton McLeod Hill.[5]

Prisoners on the march, outside Windeberg, April 3rd 1945. (IWM HU 109911)

But the German guards were now in something of a quandary; they wanted to head north, but north lay through the infamous town of Nordhausen. This was where the Germans had moved production of V-2 rockets after Allied air attacks in August 1943. The Kohnstein hill, north-west of the town itself, had already been riddled with tunnels used to store fuel and poison gas, and the Germans had begun to expand this network into a vast factory. Labour had been provided by the inmates of Dora-Mittelbau concentration camp. Originally these had been political prisoners, transferred from Buchenwald. They were worked horrifically hard, living and dying in the tunnels which they were digging. When the war on the Eastern Front started to go badly, the Germans had evacuated tens of thousands of prisoners from Auschwitz, increasing the proportion of Jews, women, and children at Nordhausen. The Auschwitz staff also moved to the site, bringing with them their merciless cruelty. It is estimated that, in all, 60,000 victims passed through Dora-Mittelbau and its satellite camps, of whom 20,000 died. As 1945 began, the production lines were still in operation, and between January and April they constructed at least 6,000 V-1s and 1,700 V-2s, even though these weapons had no chance of changing the course of the war. Inmates who were too sick to work were transferred to the Boelcke Kaserne, a barracks at Nordhausen itself, where they were kept indoors in concrete bunkers and hangars and left to die. When the Americans arrived they would find some sheds containing hundreds of unburied corpses and one or two survivors.

Tunnel 'B' under the Kohnstein hill north of Nordhausen, shortly after its capture in April 1945. The outer skins of V-2 rockets can be seen, in the process of being lined with glass wool by the inmates of Dora-Mittelbau. (©Ceges/Soma, Brussels.)

As Simpkin and his companions walked closer to Nordhausen on April 3rd and 4th, over 240 Lancaster bombers launched daylight raids on the town, something unthinkable a year before. The town of Nordhausen was almost completely destroyed, nearly 9,000 people being killed out of a population of 40,000 – as well some 1,500 of the dying prisoners in the Boelcke Kaserne. With the Americans only a few miles away, the concentration camp staff decided to move the inmates out. On April 6th, at a time when the Germans had very little fuel for transport of any sort, they wasted precious railway resources shipping these slave labourers by train to Belsen, Ravensbrück, and Sachsenhausen. More ominously for the Allied prisoners of war who skirted Nordhausen to the east on April 7th and 8th, they were moving in the same direction as columns of concentration camp inmates being force-marched by the SS. Those who could not keep up were murdered; at Gardelegen, a thousand prisoners from Mittelbau were placed in a barn – like those in which the Allied personnel were sleeping – which was then set on fire. Anyone who survived the flames was shot. Was this to be the fate of the Allied prisoners as well?

* * *

Murray.

By April 5th, the Lovat Scouts, with Murray, were back almost exactly where they had been in January: patrolling the mountainous front line around Monte Mauro, on the Vena del Gesso, and the valley of the Senio as it flowed down to Faenza. There they remained for some weeks, suffering heavy casualties (four killed and twenty-two wounded) to mines whilst trying to force their way on to the Vena del Gesso during the night of the 12th. On April 17th it became clear that the Germans were conducting large-scale demolitions preparatory to falling back to the north, and on April 23rd, the Lovat Scouts came down to rest in Brisighella, about six miles south-west of Faenza.

* * *

By now, there was no predicting whether the Allied advance into Germany would meet any resistance. In some places whole communities festooned their homes with white sheets, praying that the invaders would not blast the houses with artillery or bombs.

American parachute infantrymen of 17th Airborne Division ride into Munster on a 3SG Churchill, April 3rd 1945. (Copyright holder & editor unknown)

Elsewhere, Nazi true believers forced their town to fight, hanging or shooting anyone who showed signs of defeatism. From Berlin, Hitler issued repeated orders to fight for every inch, to scorch the earth ahead of the Allies, all in the vain hope of giving the Western Allies so bloody a nose that they would agree to peace talks. And across Germany, civilians who had been bombed out of the towns or had fled the Russians, unwanted slave-workers from all over the continent, and impatient Allied prisoners of war, streamed in whichever direction seemed to them best. If they were lucky they had belongings which they carried on hand-carts, bicycles, or even in prams. Huge columns of Allied vehicles poured eastwards whilst German prisoners of war marched west.

Duffin.

On April 3rd the 3SG battle-group took Munster, the largest German town so far to fall to British forces. 3SG pushed north-east through the human debris without opposition, past Osnabruck and on. On April 7th they motored 54 miles, stopping for a rest at Sapelloh, a few miles north of Minden. There they stayed until April 10th, when they moved forwards ready for their next task, the capture of Celle, at the edge of Lüneburg Heath, where Montgomery would accept the German surrender less than a month later. Celle had survived the war thus far almost intact, having first been bombed only on April 8th. One victim of this bombing was a train carrying 4,000 people to the Belsen concentration camp, which lay nearby – perhaps some of the passengers were from Nordhausen. The bombing killed many of those on the train, but also allowed several hundred more to escape. The SS and local residents then hunted the escapees down, killing hundreds by April 10th.

Duffin was about to experience one of his most intense days of combat in the campaign. At 0715hrs on April 11th – just too late to help the victims of the SS's pointless savagery

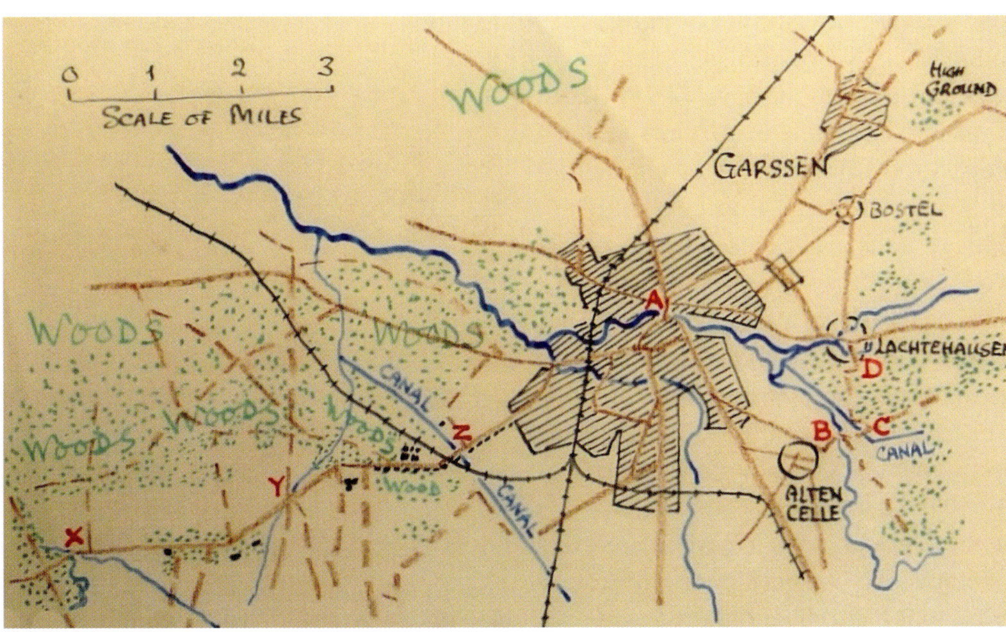

– 3SG set off, covering fifteen miles before a blown bridge forced them to detour. Then, at around 1300hrs, they came to another bridge demolition, which is labelled 'X' on the above map trace from Llewellyn Smith's account of 3SG's war.[6]

The demolition was protected by German infantry, some of them with the ubiquitous *Panzerfäuste*. One Churchill was hit and damaged, wounding the crew, and a German shell struck an accompanying Churchill bridge-layer, killing one man.

Despite these casualties, Duffin took his Troop forwards to the bridge, and his support enabled some infantry to cross. This in turn allowed the bridge-layer to throw its span across the gap. Left Flank pushed across and engaged the German troops in the thick woods on either side. Meanwhile, engineers filled the gap in the bridge, and then the entire column was able to press on for Celle.

Three miles later, another bridge was down ('Y' on the trace), this time covered not only by German small-arms but even by 20mm Flak guns to the south. Duffin's Troop engaged the defenders and managed to cross the stream-bed without bogging down. As darkness fell, 3SG halted, went into all-round defence, and refuelled and rearmed. But as they did so, orders arrived telling them to continue to advance overnight. At midnight, Duffin's Troop led the artillery OP tank and two companies of Gordon Highlanders to the next bridge ('Z') where the road crossed a canal. There Duffin was expected to halt, at which point Right Flank were to push through and take Celle.

Duffin did not in fact stop until his force reached the centre of Celle; the Germans had decided not to defend the town. By nightfall on April 12th 3SG had advanced a couple of miles beyond the town limits.

* * *

April 6th saw 2SG set off once again, with Clerk-Rattray still second-in-command of 'F' Company, who led the advance riding on the tanks of 2WG. They left Sudlohne at 0700hrs and crossed the Ems at 0830hrs, aiming to head east along Route 'CLUB' through Fürstenau to reach the River Hase. But, as the saying goes, no plan survives first contact with the enemy.

British troops passing through Lingen on April 6th 1945, three days after the 'Mad Dash'. (IWM BU 3164)[7]

At 0900hrs, that first contact was made by 'F' Company, when their tanks encountered mines covered by fire from an SPG. The contact lasted until 0930hrs, at which point the crew of the German vehicle surrendered. The advance was resumed, only to grind to a halt only a hundred yards on at a mined road-block. Sappers were summoned, but meanwhile another SPG and infantry in the woods either side of the road engaged 'F' Company. Clerk-Rattray's Company Commander, Major Kemble MC, was killed by machine-gun fire. With a month to go until the end of the war, Clerk-Rattray now found himself in charge of an infantry company, already committed to action and under pressure. As 'F' Company attempted to break contact, Right Flank Company listened to the *Nebelwerfer* rockets screaming in on 'F' and the rattle of small-arms fire lasting some two hours. They passed the time looting the shops where they had halted. Infantrymen took small articles; tank crews had room to acquire larger items like typewriters.

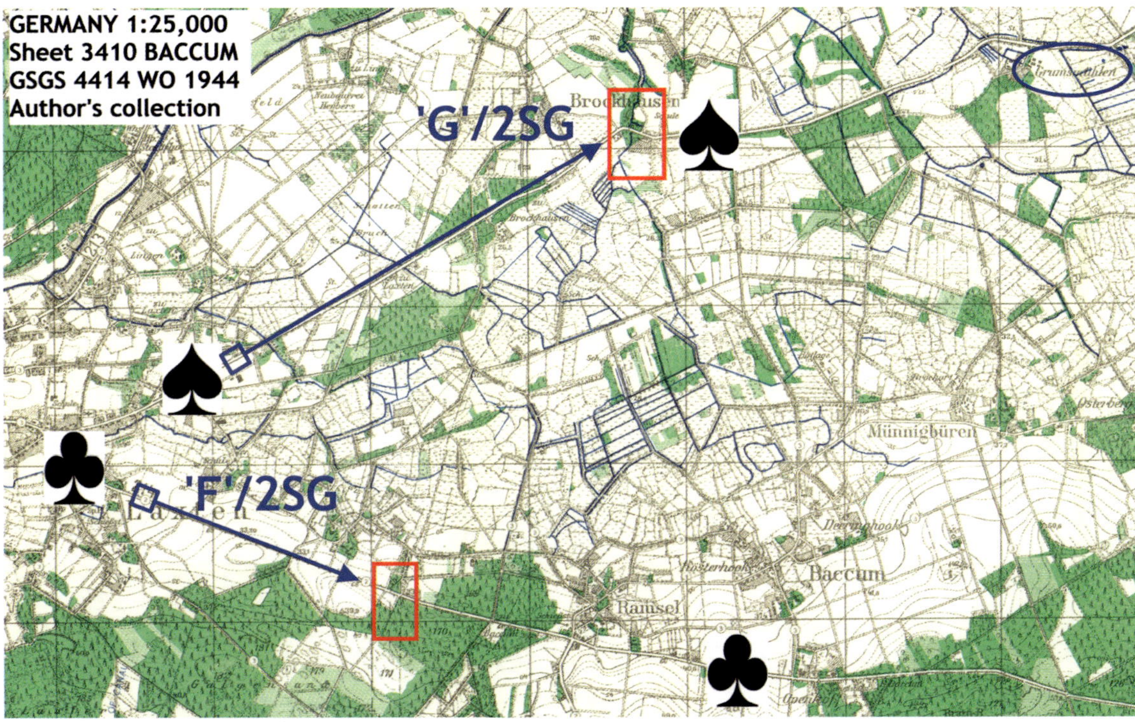

The axis of advance switched to the more northerly Route 'SPADE', with 'G' Company taking over the lead. Again, the Germans had laid on entertainment in the form of another SPG and infantry at Brockhausen. By the time that Right Flank had been brought up to launch an attack, the defenders had melted away, leaving only mines behind them. The Household Cavalry passed through at 1700hrs but were unable to get far, owing to fire from four 88mm anti-tank guns; by the time that 2WG had accounted for these it was too late to continue, and 2SG halted for the night at Grummsmuhlen.

The following afternoon at 1515hrs, an attack was made on the village of Lengerich, preceded by bombardment from artillery, mortars, and Typhoon ground-attack aircraft. 'G' Company went in first, and Clerk-Rattray took 'F' Company through them to the second objective. The enemy had melted away because of the preliminary pounding, and 2SG stayed in the ruins until they moved to new positions on the evening of April 8th. From then on for the next few days their advance was halting, with occasional brutal brushes with thc enemy, but nothing affecting 'F' Company deeply. On April 10th, having taken the village of Menslage and destroyed most of it in the process, the officers of 2SG and 2WG sat down for a celebratory dinner in a large farmhouse. Since they had been stood down for the evening, much champagne was consumed by the light of large candelabra.

* * *

East of Nordhausen, in the village of Dittichenrode, the prisoners from Rotenburg thought that their ordeal was almost over. They had halted there on April 10th, and been told that the 11th would be a rest day. They had been witnessing American air attacks which suggested that ground forces could not be far away – in fact, they were within six miles of the prisoners of war. But on the morning of April 11th, the prisoners heard that they were moving by lorry that evening to Wimmelburg, twenty miles to the east. How this had been arranged, and why the trucks were being diverted to this pointless move when Germany's survival was at stake, are questions not easily answered. The trucks took their human cargo to Wimmelburg overnight, having postponed the inevitable liberation by perhaps a day.

* * *

The US Ninth Army, meanwhile, was also speeding through Germany; on April 11th, their 2nd Armored Division covered fifty-two miles to reach the River Elbe near

Allied prisoners at the moment of Oflag 79's liberation on April 12th 1945. (IWM BU 5985)

Magdeburg; on April 12th, as Duffin and 3SG fought their way through Celle, three more American divisions reached the same river. It had taken them only nineteen days to cover the 226 miles from the Rhine and, with Berlin only sixty miles away, Ninth Army were confident that they could easily reach the city before the Soviets. It was not to be, but in their headlong advance they had captured Hannover, Hildesheim – and Brunswick, thirty-five miles south-west of Celle. Finch's former camp – *Stalag* VII A at Moosburg – would not be liberated until April 29th; but on April 12th, an American Jeep rolled unopposed up to the gates of *Oflag* 79. Anderson's camera captured the moment from inside the camp, and the aftermath.

An American soldier photographs the inmates. (IWM BU 5992)

* * *

Walker's musings on Easter Sunday had taken place as the Eighth Army began to stir from its winter misery. When the final Allied offensive in Italy began in the second week of April 1945, few of those involved dared imagine that the war in Europe had less than a month to run. Although in North-West Europe the Allies had crossed the Rhine and were thrusting across Germany, they expected that Hitler would abandon Berlin and make his last stand in southern Germany, in what they termed his 'Alpine Redoubt'. It was a phantasm, but they did not know that.[8]

The Allied plan on the Italian front was to deliver a knock-out blow to the German army in the Po valley. The Eighth Army was to push in two directions around areas flooded by the Germans: west along Highway 9 towards Bologna, and north-west between the floods and Lake Comacchio, through what the Allies knew as the Argenta Gap.

A variety of clothing & nationalities, but all delighted to have been liberated. (Copyright holder unknown)

Whichever attack went best would become the main effort. Meanwhile, the American-led Fifth Army would launch an encircling move from the Apennines. 6th Armoured Division formed the British mobile reserve, ready to be launched into any gap which appeared in the German lines. The Germans were by now very weak in transport – the German Army, for all its vaunted mobility, remained largely horse-drawn until the end of the war – and vulnerable to attack from the air. If their lines were broken, they lacked the agility to extricate themselves from encircling movements. Allied forces in Italy now had the opportunity to carry out every general's dream, a double envelopment manoeuvre, whereby one turns both flanks of the enemy and thus surrounds them. The two Allied armies were to meet up near Bologna, thus trapping the best remaining German troops, I Parachute Corps, south of the River Po, a substantial obstacle over 1,200ft wide. The Allies had hoped to bring off just such a coup after breaking through at Cassino, but had been thwarted by General Clark's fixation on Rome.

If the encircling movement failed, and sufficient German forces managed to escape north of the Po with their heavy equipment, they would be able to use the line of the river to hold up the Allies once again, buying time for the fortification of the Alps and the mythical southern German redoubt. In North-West Europe, Allied forces had crossed the Rhine with the help of a major airborne operation; in Italy, the poor relation of the European war, there were no airborne forces. The Po would have to be crossed the old-fashioned way.

When they launched their offensive on April 9th, it surpassed all their expectations.

* * *

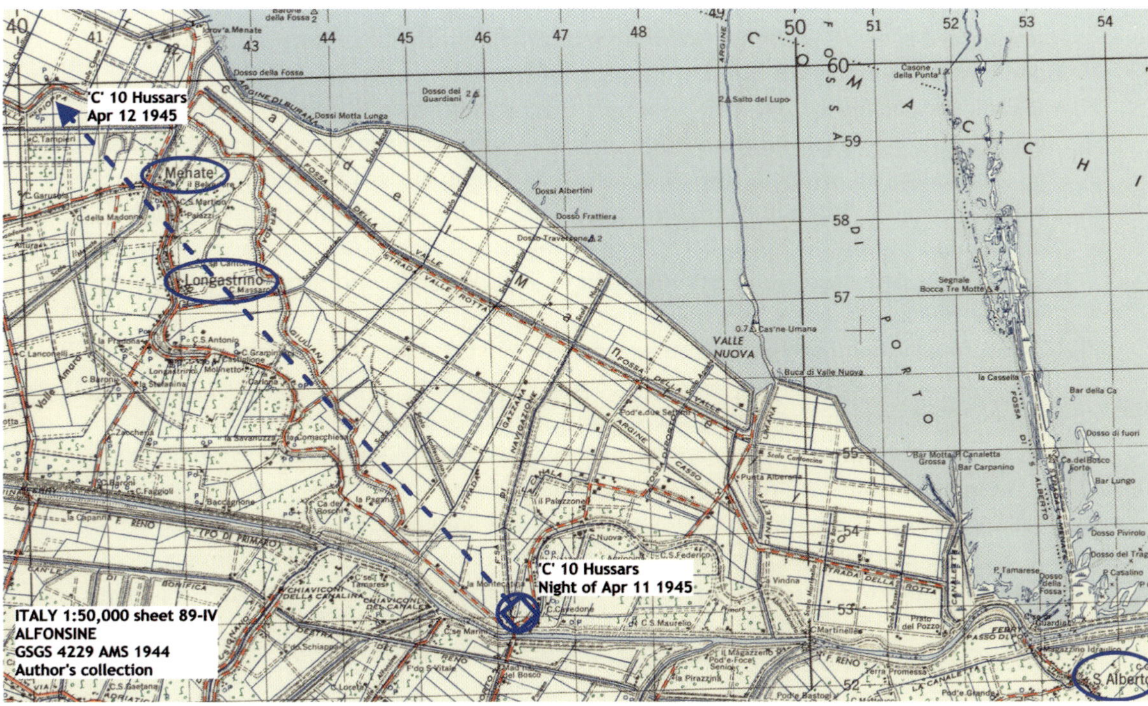

At 1800hrs on April 11th, 'C' Squadron of 10th Hussars moved out of S. Alberto, on the shores of Lake Comacchio, and prepared for their role in an attack by 169 Infantry Brigade on Longastrino and Menate. They were only a few miles from where Middleditch had lost his argument with a mine back in January. The following morning they commenced their attack. There were losses in 'B' Squadron – one tank to an enemy SPG, another to a mine – but 'C' Squadron had pushed on past its objectives by nightfall. However, Walker was not with them by then, as he explained in his diary in June.

> It is indeed a long, long, time since I last wrote – nearly two months. The blankest, dullest, and most uneventful two months I have ever spent.
>
> It was early on April 12th when I was called half-way through breakfast to Frank's tank, and was told that 3rd Troop would go up and contact a 'B' Squadron tank somewhere near Longastrino. With Corporal Lindsay and Robin Smith and a Honey-full of Sappers it seemed quite like old times, and I think I was fairly confident. There was a muddle over the route. We came to a blown bridge and as I was standing on Sergeant

Lindsay's Honey, a passing lorry sandwiched me and bruised me a bit. Newell made some facetious remark. My hat blew off and Sergeant Ross nearly ran over it! So far things hadn't gone too well.

At last we found a route and managed to contact 2/5th Queens in Menate. Menate, taken the day before, we managed to reach quite quickly, and I found the Colonel waiting for me and anxious to begin. I stuffed down some tinned salmon and biscuit he offered me, trying to rearrange my map, understand what he wanted me to do, and look at air photographs – all at the same time! I gave him Sergeant Lindsay and the Honey, and all seemed in order. I vaguely saw what I would have to do, and I moved off to look for the company I was to support, I hope quite confidently in spite of the great hurry I was in – or, rather, had been put in. I found the Company Commander in good spirits and pretty keen, and he asked me if I would mind carrying a platoon on the tank, the idea being that we would support this platoon when the leading platoon met any opposition. We moved from house to house without a sign of anything German, and I had stopped at one house as the Platoon Commander (a Sergeant) asked if I minded having his platoon a bit closer together – when suddenly there was a bang – I felt a pain in my jaw, saw blood come out onto my golf jacket, made a stupid gurgling noise as I lost my balance, and half-slumped to the floor of the turret. Something rather unexpected had obviously happened!

Corporal Jones quietly asked Pateman for the First Aid kit, and I climbed out of the tank into the house. Here I was made a complete fuss of by the Troop as they gathered round while I was bandaged up. I was too surprised to be really angry – an infantryman had let his rifle off – and not [*sic*] feeling very weak settled down after everybody had been terribly helpful and they all said good luck.

After that it was the usual succession of Jeeps and ambulances – a lovely hot day – to CCSs, FDS, and hospital. Beginning to feel a bit sleepy, longing for some orange juice – Dan around being terribly sympathetic – operation – more hospital – trains – a pretty nurse in a room to myself for two days at Jesi [near Ancona] – two days in Rome, and then to Naples where I have been for seven weeks.[9]

Walker had been incredibly fortunate. The negligent discharge of a .303-inch bullet (or .45-inch; Walker blames two different weapons) at point-blank range could so easily have been fatal. The bullet had hit his elbow and then his jaw, breaking the latter. Sergeant Ross wrote to him about the incident soon afterwards:

The whole of the Troop are pleased to hear you are getting along fine, and are hoping to see you very soon. As you say, it was all very unfortunate and, like you, I would have given anything for it not to have happened. But I suppose it's all the luck of the game.[10]

Walker wrote to his parents on April 16th and 23rd about the accident and its aftermath:

As you may have heard by now either from Dan or even 'official sources', I did last Thursday 'stop a packet' as they say. In other words, just as we were about to charge into battle some rather stupid man belonging to the infantry who we were giving a lift to let off his Tommy Gun by mistake, and my head happened to be in the light. (Actually it went through my elbow and stuck in my jaw.) Well, you must agree it was pretty lucky as well as unlucky if you see what I mean.

At the minute I am looking a far deal worse than I feel, which is all to the good as I'm made a terrific fuss of. It's a very interesting chain of events that takes place when you are wounded. First you are given first aid and put on a stretcher by your crew; then you get to the Regimental Aid Post; then an Advanced Dressing Station where they clean you up a bit; then to a similar place a bit further back where they started giving me plasma; then to a Divisional Casualty Clearing Station; and then to a Field Dressing Station; and eventually, at midnight, I found myself in Rimini, having just finished my fifth bottle of blood!

The next morning I was operated on, and two days later, even further back to Jesi where I now am, though tomorrow I believe I go to Rome where they have a special department to deal with faces.

The hole in my elbow luckily didn't break a bone, though my jaw was not quite so easy. Anyway, they took the bullet out and wired up my jaw, with the inevitable result that it is extremely difficult to get many words out of my mouth, and quite impossible to get any food into it. I therefore live on delicious 'nutritious fluids' (actually, my only saving factor is where I chipped my front tooth, as it does leave a tiny hole through which I can just manage to put a piece of soaked bread!) (No, I'm really doing quite well, so don't worry.)

This hospital is heaven, and I shall be desperately miserable to leave it. It was built by the Fascists for tubercular babies, and the wards have lovely frescoes of little Dutch boys and girls – something like the old nursery ones. I have a room all to myself (the only one in the building, which is usually reserved for Colonels and above!) and added to that I have a sweet little nurse who couldn't be more sympathetic and kind. She came in to talk to me this evening and I was asleep. I haven't forgiven myself.

Another bulletin from your stupid son, who reports good progress. Since I last wrote I was sent to Rome, where they were under the impression that the face specialists were – or, to be professional, a 'Maxillo-Facial team'. Actually, of course, they had made a mistake, and after two days there – spent very comfortably in spite of one afternoon in the theatre – I was dispatched by ambulance to Naples to the above hospital [65th British General Hospital] where I suppose I shall be for some time. Today my dentist re-wired my jaw, and I had some drain tubes taken out of the wound. It looks pretty healthy and neither that nor the elbow should take long to heal up, I hope!

This hospital is far from being a paradise for sick soldiers. It is right in the middle of Naples, in quite the filthiest part. I have been, I'm afraid, more miserable than I thought possible. I intolerantly and illogically find fault with everything: the dirt, the noise, the beastly greasy Italians, the stupid nurses, the wretched detached atmosphere of the place. All that I do find consolation in is the undoubtedly first-class medical attention – but God, how I hate everybody.

All this is very childish I know but the whole thing on looking back is quite the most horrible thing that could possibly have happened. You've no idea what I have missed (but don't worry, I shall feel better when I can get out of this place).

Julian Brooke, who left the regiment about two months ago, is visiting tomorrow. His brother Henry (son of the Ulster PM and a new man to Chawker's in the same

> Half as me) was killed just after I left the Regiment. Other than that I have no news, which is upsetting also …
>
> From the most miserable boy in the world.

* * *

'Pretty lucky as well as unlucky' – had Walker not been accidentally shot on April 12th he might well have been in his tank the following day when the Germans hit it. But Sergeant O'Neill was now its commander. A letter from a fellow officer ('Brian'), written on April 17th, explained what happened on April 13th:

> Oh dear, what a bloody business all this is. I'm afraid poor old 3 Troop rather bought it after you'd gone, though they did the hell of a lot of good work beforehand. Sgt Ross assumed command with accustomed ease and went on down the road until there was a check at 'Walker', and at about this time Sgt O'Neill's tank broke a clutch going down a very steep slope to get on to the bottom, and so they went on with only two tanks, Sgt Jones in yours and Sgt Ross commanding in the 'powerful' thruster. At 'Whitbread' there was also a check and a partisan came up to them and said there was an SPG just down the road – in fact, he pointed out where it was and Sgt Ross managed to manoeuvre into position for a shot. I gather that they could see nothing, it was so well camouflaged, and I also gather that the first round was successful as that's all they asked for on the admin replenishment that night! Anyway, there was that satisfying black cloud of smoke and the whole thing, including crew, brewed. Well done Hatton!
>
> Next day Tony [Overy] took over the Troop in his own tank; Sgt O'Neill left his broken one and commanded yours, and Sgt Ross continued as usual in his. Towards the late afternoon they went off to the right with a company and managed to work forward about level with Sidney, who was still on the road and almost up to 'Parrot'. Everything was going well, and it looked as if 'Parrot' would fall, for your Troop had got over the lateral road like this.

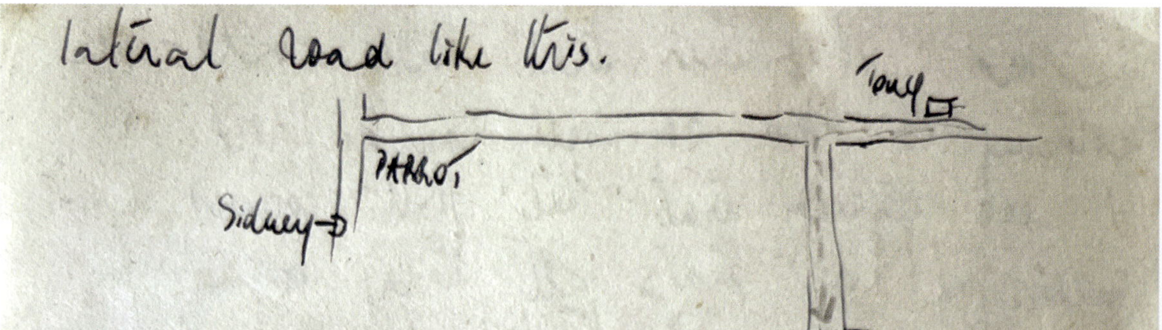

> Suddenly an SPG opened up on the farm where I've shown Tony [Overy] and with whom Robin [Welsh] was. There was not enough cover, and they were forced to withdraw to the other farm marked. Sgt O'Neill's tank was hit through the turret on its way back. Sgt O'Neill and Pateman were killed, I think outright; L/Cpl Tait and

> Newell got out OK, and then under fire L/Cpl Tait got into the turret and rescued Cpl Jones, who was wounded fairly lightly in the head and shoulder. Robin stood by and took the whole lot back on his tank. Meanwhile Sgt Ross was unlucky enough, when he got back to the other farm, to go up on a very sizeable mine, which made a mess of the tank, but all the crew were OK. All very nasty, Peter, I'm afraid, and it shook us all a lot. I saw them buried today with Hotchkiss, who was killed the next day when Sgt Moore had a similar experience … Although it was bloody at times, we did advance really quite a long way and now we're sleeping it all off … Fuckin' roll on, tell the girls hullo for me, and look after yourself.[11]

Walker noted in his diary: 'Horribly sad when it was all so nearly over'.[12]

Sergeant Ross was saddened by the loss, but very fortunate not to have been killed himself shortly afterwards:

> We ran into it next day under the brilliant leadership of Mr Overy, and I expect by now you know we lost Sgt O'Neill and Pateman killed, and Cpl Jones wounded. The Troop as one man swear that it would never have happened if 'Syd' (excuse the name, Sir)[13] had been there, so you can draw your own conclusions about the Troop Leader. About five minutes after Sgt O'Neill's tank 'brewed up', mine went up on what must have been 5,000lbs of TNT – anyway, it blew off the sprocket, a couple of bogie assemblies, eight feet of track, and split the hull underneath and up the side, and also split the gear box and differential. Needless to say, it's been written off. But we were very lucky, and apart from O'Connor being blind for half an hour, and me getting a knock on the side of the face which I thought had broken my jaw, we got away OK. We had to 'bale out' and I came round about three hundred yards down the track being helped by Hatton; O'Connor was also being helped by Crawford.[14]

The only light relief amid the Regiment's fourteen casualties on April 13th was provided by a 'B' Squadron Sherman which, whilst driving through a sugar factory, fell into a shell-crater invisible under a sea of treacle – surely the only tank in the history of warfare to have been written off in this fashion.

Despite his own plight, Walker wrote letters of sympathy to the families of all the casualties in 3 Troop. He also received many, for example this one from his soldier-servant, Weaire:

> Dear Mr Walker,
> The accompanying parcel contains a few items of your kit that you may possibly need. At the suggestion of Mr Awdry, I have retained your private papers and diary etc., until you return or write requesting it. In the little green bag you will find a cap-badge, which may not be obtainable where you are. The fountain pen you may be able to get repaired before you return, as all the kit that you had on the tank with you has been destroyed.
>
> I was very relieved to hear from Mr Awdry that your condition is now satisfactory, and sincerely trust that your recovery will be speedy and pleasant. Awaiting your return,
>
> I am yours sincerely,
> Weaire[15]

The Sherman which came to a sticky end. (IWM NA 24123; edited by dansteele.net)

On this letter, Walker's wife later noted: 'Everything destroyed. Makes me cry.'[16] It was the second time that Walker's belongings had been destroyed; one set drowned in Naples harbour, and now a second set immolated on the pyre of his Sherman.

* * *

Back in Holland, The Island had been cleared of German forces by April 2nd, but the long-overdue liberation of Arnhem was postponed repeatedly until April 12th. There was not much left to liberate, especially since the Germans had driven the population out after the September battles. The Allies left nothing to chance for their assault this time.

Nick Somerville.

They wrong-footed the defenders by attacking from the south-east, across the River Issel from Westervoort; they took the troops across in tracked, lightly-armoured 'Buffalo' vehicles; massive air attacks preceded the advance; torrential shell-fire drenched the defenders; and a pre-fabricated Bailey Bridge capable of taking tanks was floated downstream and put into position as soon as a bridge-head had been secured. The first troops landed at 2315hrs, followed at 0200hrs by 2SWB, with Somerville, who then pushed on into the town despite heavy shell-fire as they crossed the Issel. There was some tough fighting – 2SWB faltered when a counter-attack hit them near a railway junction – but with armoured support 'C' Company had reached the city centre by the end of April 13th. It took three more days before the street-fighting was over.

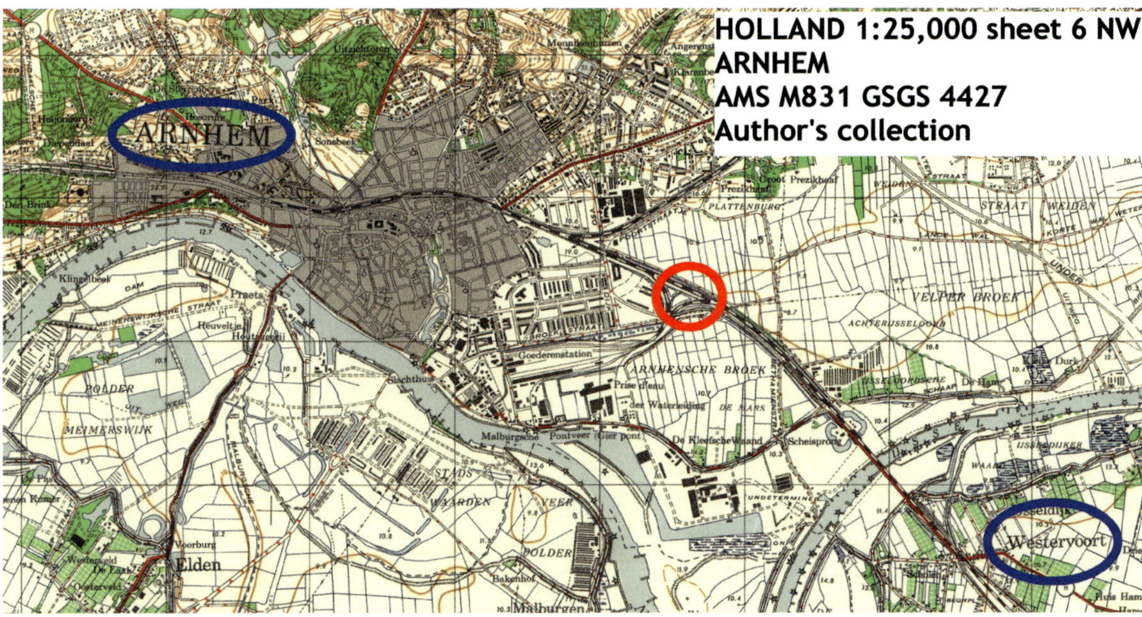

* * *

At Wimmelburg, Simpkin and his friends were still waiting. The German guard commander insisted that they would be moving on eastwards; the Senior British Officer refused; and at 2200hrs on April 12th most of the guard force marched off into the darkness, leaving the refugees from *Oflag* IX A/Z to listen to the sounds of heavy artillery fire falling in the area. They immediately began to take control of their own destiny, posting sentries and observers to give warning of the approach of any German units bent on revenge. But it was the Americans of 3rd Armored Division, Combat Command B, who reached them on Friday, April 13th. Grown men cried, and the American soldiers, fresh from the horrors of Nordhausen, were overjoyed to see the Commonwealth prisoners of war safe and well. Simpkin described his liberation to his grandmother; she passed the description on to Robertson, and despite the distortion which undoubtedly crept in, it appears that Simpkin had been part of a sub-group which had separated from the main party:

> Dear Major Robertson,
> Thank you very much for your kind letter – I was indeed thankful to have Richard back safe – he came up to see us for one night as soon as he got back – he looks so fit and well – and had a most exciting escape – a hundred of them, he fears the older men have not got away – some Poles told them the American lorries were in a certain place – they got to them.[17]

Supplies of fuel and lubricants were reaching the advancing armour by Dakota aircraft, and on April 16th the aircraft made the return journey not empty, but crammed with jubilant – though airsick – former prisoners of war. The following day, the inmates of Rotenburg reached Brussels, travelling in twenty-four hours a distance which it had taken their liberators seven months to traverse. Simpkin filled in his official liberation questionnaire in Brussels on April 17th, and the next day flew back to England.

> The Americans got them to the planes, and he thinks they landed them in Buckinghamshire!!! You know how vague Richard is! – He certainly has learnt a lot of German and Italian and he summed up as 'It was not too bad' – he must have been lucky – he is just the same; not changed a bit, 'happy go lucky' – you and Sheila were the first people he asked for.[18]

Simpkin sent a telegram to Barbara: 'Back in England, arriving home tomorrow.'

From the flat which Barbara had furnished in the hope of his safe return, Simpkin wrote to Robertson within the week:[19]

> Just a line to tell you that I've got back safely and am now on six weeks leave. You can imagine what it feels like to be back again. We now have a flat here as a temporary base. I'm hoping very much that we shall be able to get down and see you and your sister in the not too distant future. Barbara has luckily been able to get leave, but we have not yet made any definite plans. I want to catch the Mayfly, perhaps on the Meon, but it's very inaccessible these days. (The Meon I mean; the Mayfly always was).
>
> I've no definite news of anyone you know who was a prisoner-of-war in Germany, but I see they've got some Colditz people out, so I hope Mike Sinclair may be safe.

How many disappointments and sadnesses those who survived must have experienced as they caught up on what they had missed. But there were joys too; nine months after this letter, in February 1946, Barbara gave birth to their son Michael.

XXX

'I was awakened by gunfire and awful screams'

World War, April 1945

For Simpkin, the war was over; for Hirst, it was in some ways just beginning. He had been in transit and training for years, but was now about to reach his Regiment and the front line. It was an exciting time to be joining the Burma campaign, since Slim's forces were racing against the onset of the monsoon to recapture Rangoon. Fourteenth Army wanted the satisfaction of revenge for their defeat in 1942. By now, Fourteenth Army was one of the largest formations of its type in the world, Slim commanding about a million men. His was certainly the largest army in the Commonwealth, comprising troops from the British Army, Indian Army, and Africa. However, this huge force was being channelled by the landscape to essentially one road's width on each of its axes of advance – like the road to Arnhem, but on a vastly longer route. Slim was worried that the Japanese would stage a defiant last stand in Rangoon, a sort of Burmese Berlin, and that this would leave his forces stretched down the Irrawaddy and Sittang valleys without the means to supply themselves, since they had become so dependent on air supply, which would be difficult during the monsoon. Slim had therefore requested that plans for an amphibious attack on Rangoon – Operation Dracula – be dusted off and put into effect as quickly as possible.

Hirst.

The constricted topography of the Sittang and Irrawaddy corridors meant that the foremost elements of Fourteenth Army were small – just an all-arms battle-group – and Hirst was to find himself at the very point of Fourteenth Army's sword.

In mid-March my posting came through to the 7th Light Cavalry IAC in Burma. I arrived in Calcutta on March 28th after a train journey of three nights and two days, during which we again played Solo continuously.

After a brief stay in a hotel in Calcutta (very dirty), we went by train, Ganges river ferry, and truck to Comilla in East Bengal, the jumping-off base for Burma. There I saw my cousin, Elizabeth Fisher, who was a physiotherapist at 74th Indian General Hospital. We left on April 12th and flew in a Dakota transport plane to Myotha, between Mandalay and Meiktila. There had been a big tank battle at Meiktila after Fourteenth Army crossed the Chindwin River … We saw Jap bodies still lying about from this battle as we made our way by truck and tank transporter to the reinforcement camp at Meiktila. You often had to find your own means of transport in a war zone.

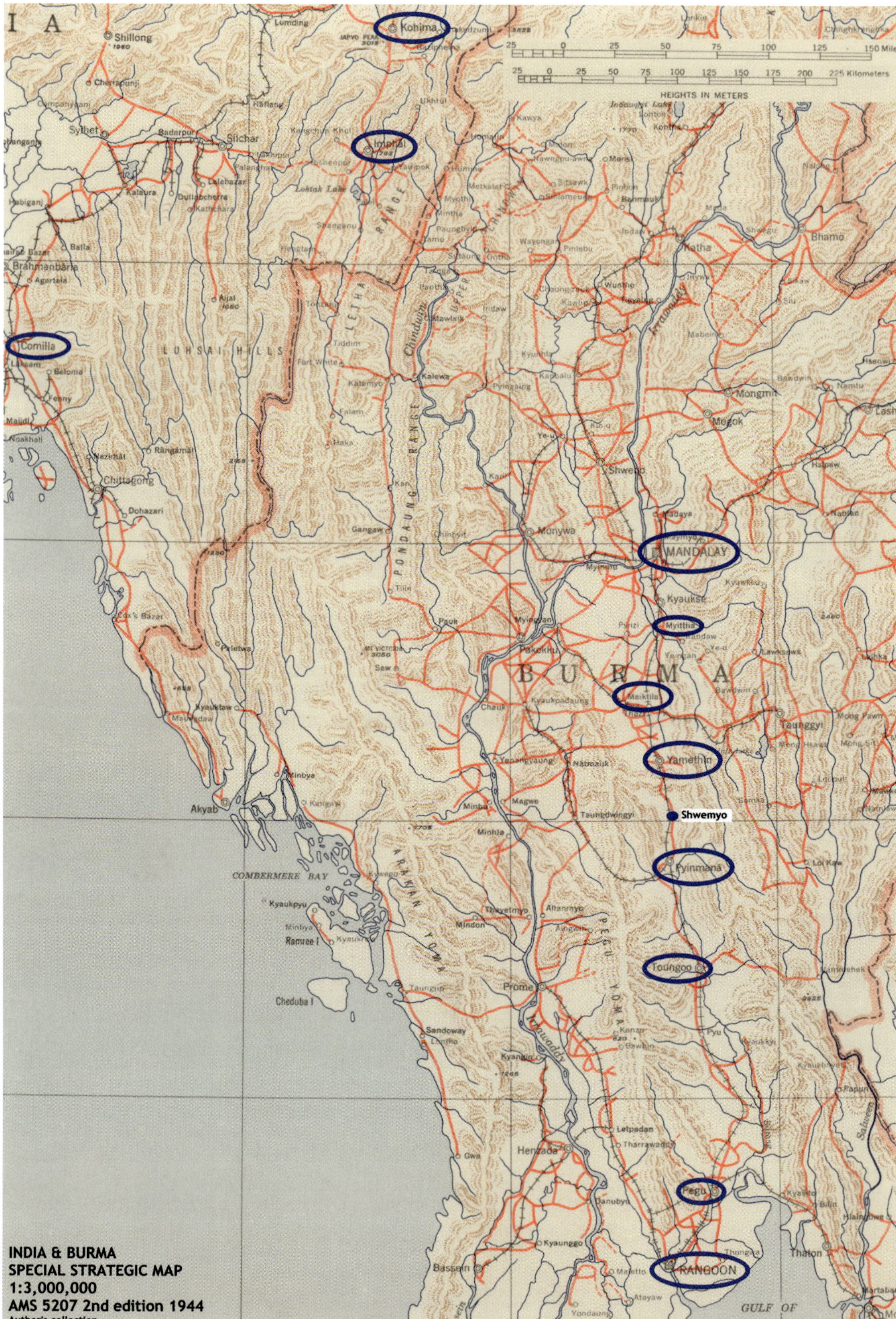

INDIA & BURMA
SPECIAL STRATEGIC MAP
1:3,000,000
AMS 5207 2nd edition 1944
Author's collection

After a couple of days we were flown forward in L5s, light ambulance planes. Their pilots were old Yankee civilians, Tom Mix characters[1] with ivory-handled pistols, and a law unto themselves. Only one passenger per plane, but as the pilots were not concerned about weight regulations, I took my 'swag' (valise). Another irregular band of Americans were the ambulance Jeep drivers; we had one with us. They were Quakers – conscientious objectors and non-combatants – but very, very brave, evacuating the wounded under fire in their unprotected Jeeps.

We were headed for Pyawbwe, but there was a dust storm and we could not land, so returned to Meiktila, as did several others. I was fairly frightened on the flight, as when we banked my valise tended to fall out, dragging me with it. So on the next attempt I left a lot of my gear behind and we landed safely at Yamethin, where I found that 7th Cavalry were several miles down the road. It was not safe to go down the road alone, but I fell in with a unit which was to work with them the next day and eventually caught up at Sinthe Chaung ('chaung' means 'creek'), just north of Shwemyo.[2]

This must have been on April 16th, since 7th Cavalry's war diary recorded Shwemyo as their final position the night before.

Hirst explained the mission of his force – code-named BARCOL:

Two squadrons of 7th Cavalry were part of a mixed force being rushed down the road ahead of the main Fourteenth Army to try to capture Rangoon before the monsoon rains made mobile operations impossible. The column ('Barcol') was commanded by our Colonel, Lieutenant Colonel Jack Barlow: a great character, very forceful, and a fire-eater who won the DSO and Bar and the MC. His command tank was unique, an old Stuart minus the turret which had been abandoned on the banks of the Chindwin by 7th Hussars during the retreat from Burma and repaired by our workshop. It was named the 'Curse of Scotland'.[3]

Barcol consisted of two halves, which leap-frogged past each other. The column was not in direct physical contact with the rest of Fourteenth Army, and was completely supplied by air. Our portion consisted of 'B' Squadron 7th Cavalry (in Stuart light tanks), 'A' Squadron 16th Cavalry (armoured cars), 'A' Squadron 3rd Carabiniers (Sherman medium tanks), a company of infantry (Bombay Grenadiers), artillery, and so on. The other half of Barcol had a similar composition, the 7th Cavalry component being 'A' Squadron.

This poor-quality image shows Barlow's cut-down Stuart tank, 'Curse of Scotland', the only vehicle known to have participated in both the 1942 & 1945 campaigns. Note the improvised grenade-cage over the former turret-ring. (Copyright holder unknown)

In the Indian Armoured Corps we were very much over-officered. On joining 7th Cavalry, therefore, I was at once lent to 16th Cavalry, as they were short of officers, while 7th Cavalry had received half a dozen new officers. I got on very well with their 'A' Squadron Commander, Jimmy Bowen.[4]

* * *

Duffin.

By April 13th, Allied formations in Germany were making plans for advances of tens of miles a day. 3SG were no exception, despite the low top speed of a Churchill tank. Their next objective after Celle was to be Uelzen, over thirty miles to the north-east. Duffin had a quieter day, as Left Flank were the rearmost squadron. Despite the repeated obstacles which 3SG encountered – craters in the roads, demolished bridges, delayed-action explosive charges, trees felled across forest rides – they made twenty miles before halting for the night. They set off again before first light on the 14th, continuing along the forest rides in order to avoid German demolitions. It was a risk – the close country provided perfect opportunities for *Panzerfaust* teams, and navigation was a nightmare. But it paid off; 3SG were rampaging through areas where the enemy were not expecting them, and at a time of the night when the human spirit is at its lowest ebb. Over the course of the day the British troops took 900 prisoners.

Churchills of 3SG pass a crater in the forest between Celle & Uelzen, April 14th 1945. The lip of the crater has been reinforced by a Churchill bridge-laying tank. (IWM BU3420)

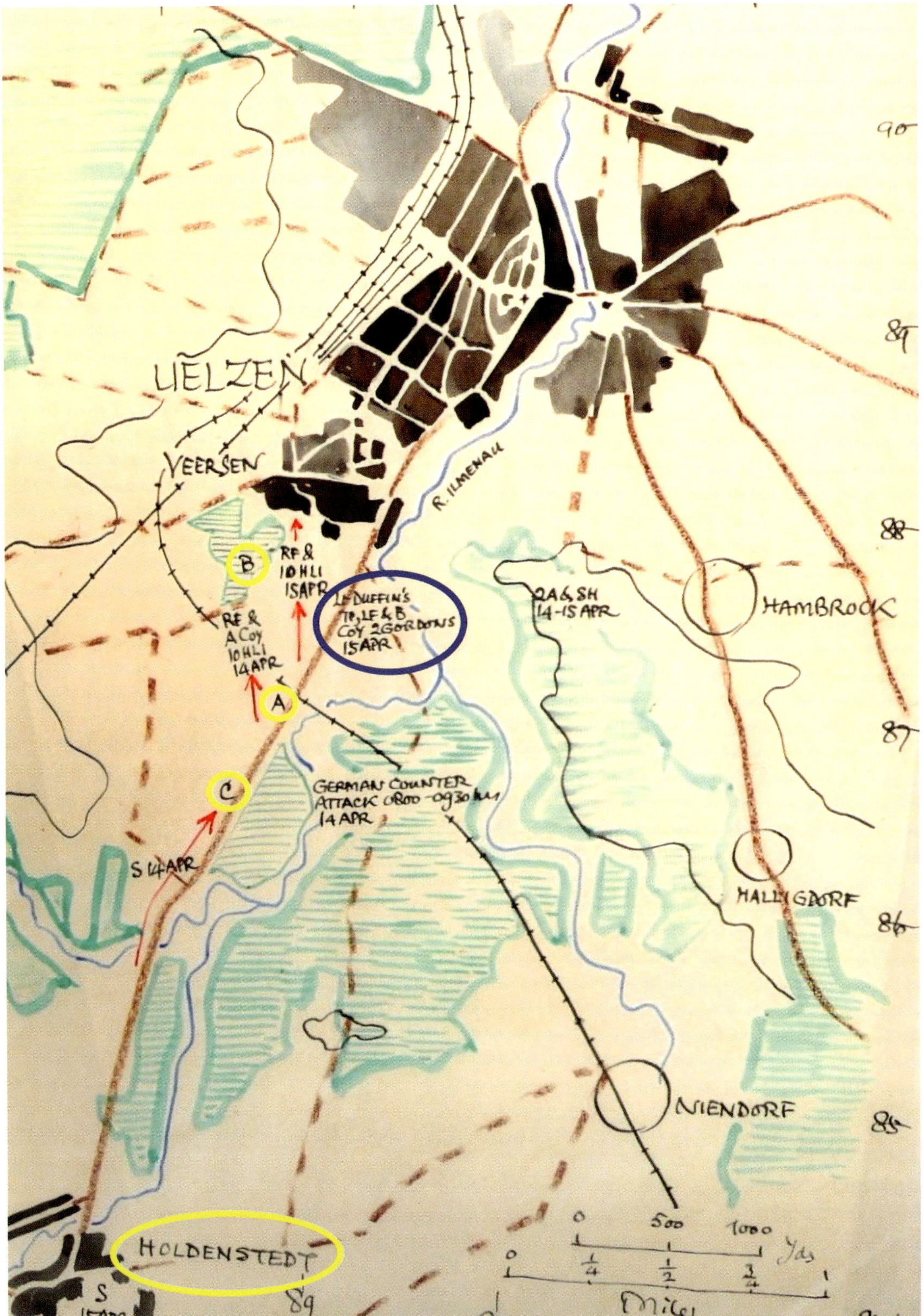
UELZEN
VEERSEN
R. ILMENAU
B
RF &
10 HLI
15 APR
Lt DUFFIN'S
TP, LF & B
COY 2 GORDONS
15 APR
2A&SH
14-15 APR
HAMBROCK
RF &
A Coy
10 HLI
14 APR
A
C
GERMAN COUNTER
ATTACK 0800-0930 hrs
14 APR
S 14 APR
HALLIGDORF
NIENDORF
HOLDENSTEDT
S
15 APR
0 500 1000 Yds
0 1/4 1/2 3/4 1
Miles
90
89
88
87
86
85
84
89
90
91

It was not until first light that the Germans fired red flares to alert Uelzen to its peril, by which time 3SG were within three miles of their objective. As the Battalion swung on to the main road at Holdenstedt they found enemy vehicles parked along it ('C' on the above map trace). These were shot up, but one of them (at 'A', near the level-crossing) proved to be full of ammunition, and the resulting explosions rendered the road impassable even for tanks. With the growing light came increased danger; German Flak guns now opened fire from the west, and in the east the woods were full of enemy infantry. A sharp action developed, during which Right Flank pushed west to destroy the enemy guns.

To maintain momentum, the battle-group tried an advance via Veersen, west of the main road, but the woodland ('B') was heavily defended, and although infantry broke in around 0715hrs they were forced to withdraw. It was clear that – unlike at Celle – the Germans were determined to defend the town. Indeed, at 0800hrs they counter-attacked from the east with infantry and armoured cars. Although this did not succeed, it was enough to stop the advance, and by 1300hrs the British troops had gone firm where they were. Right Flank withdrew and Left Flank came up to replace them. Plans were made to attack that night; at 2300hrs infantry would seize high ground between Veersen and Hambrock, after which Left Flank would attack up the main road into Uelzen itself.

On the morning of April 15th, Left Flank ran into fierce opposition near the level-crossing, the German defence comprising infantry with the usual machine-guns and *Panzerfäuste,* as well as SPGs, which brewed up the leading Churchill. To the west, an assault on Veersen descended into a brutal house-to-house fight between Right Flank and the defenders – to the extent that the tank crews had to dismount and stalk the German SPGs with PIATs.

Although Left Flank had stalled before reaching Uelzen, Duffin now led his Troop into the town in style, accompanied by infantry of the Gordon Highlanders. The situation on the ground was so confused that as Duffin approached the town around 1200hrs, a German staff car drove out of the town and straight down the main road towards him. The four officers found inside its blazing remains had clearly had no idea that the British were so close. However, Duffin and his men were engaged by snipers and so had to batten down their hatches and hope for the best.

German counter-attacks further back down the main road forced 3SG to look to its rear, so further advances were ruled out. The action had been so frenetic and the opportunities for sleep so few that Left Flank were withdrawn that night – but Duffin and his Troop stayed in place until 0500hrs on April 16th. They had been in action for seventy-two hours without a moment's rest.

* * *

After all his travels, waiting, and training for armoured warfare, Hirst found himself in an unexpectedly mundane role alongside the Humber armoured cars of 'A' Squadron, 16th Cavalry:

I looked after their transport, which trailed at the tail of the column. In spite of being trained at great expense in gunnery, wireless, map reading, tactics, and so on, all I had to do was to follow the road to Milestone xyz for each night's rendezvous (RV). I had neither wireless, maps, nor binoculars – just a Jeep and driver …

At night the column used to harbour; that is, stop in a box formation, with the tanks and armoured cars on the perimeter, with guns pointing out, the soft (transport) vehicles in the middle, and the infantry in slit-trenches in front of the armoured vehicles, but behind the wire. The Stuart tanks, having come all the way through Burma, were in a bad way, and it was only through the dedicated work of the LAD (Light Aid or Workshop Detachment) that they kept going at all. In the morning the ones that would start on their own towed the others till they too got going. The trucks were in a similar state. The first night after I joined, we were shelled in harbour, but not badly and no casualties.

* * *

Clerk-Rattray.

During the late afternoon of April 17th, 2SG had occupied positions around Walsrode, south-east of Bremen, preparatory to swinging round on the city from the east. The area was one which would become the British Army's playground for decades to come: familiar names such as Soltau and Fallingbostel jump from the map. Clerk-Rattray's 'F' Company took up post on the road north out of Walsrode, very conscious that there were numerous and determined German forces preparing to defend Bremen. When a report reached them from 11th Hussars that an SS battalion was approaching from the north, 'F' Company requested support, and 'G' Company turned out of its billets to assist. Nothing materialized, but it is understandable that at this stage of the war no one wanted to take any chances.

'F' led the advance towards Visselhövede at 0700hrs on April 18th, riding as usual on tanks. The leading troop of tanks usually did not carry infantry, to save casualties when opposition was encountered; the tanks meanwhile used their BESA 7.92mm machine-guns to hose down any buildings along the way, in order to deter snipers. Since the belts of ammunition were laced liberally with tracer rounds, the result was that the British advanced along corridors of burning farm-houses and out-buildings. As usual, before the objective could be reached, 'F' Company came into contact with the enemy, when they were ambushed by infantry with *Panzerfäuste* at a junction south of Kettenburg. The opposition from 2nd *Marine Infanterie* Division was stiffer than what 2SG had become used to in recent weeks; the Division had been formed in March, and had been declared operational only at the start of April. Its 13,000 men were not elite marines as the name might suggest, but a hodge-podge of shipless *Kriegsmarine* personnel, Hitler Youth, SS, and Hungarians.

Attempts to outflank the block by way of Ottingen and Riepholm failed, and it became necessary to launch a set-piece attack on Kettenburg. It was a tough fight for Clerk-Rattray's men, and one of his platoons, on the left flank, had to fight through and destroy a German unit which refused to surrender. Some 250 prisoners were taken, but 2SG lost another seven killed and twenty-eight wounded, including one of Clerk-Rattray's Platoon Commanders. By now some of 2SG's companies were down to fifty men, all of them exhausted, and by the time that darkness fell the battle-group had gone firm in Kettenburg. When Clerk-Rattray arrived at the spot which he had chosen as his Company HQ he had to evict a unit of German soldiers who had decided to sleep there.

The next day would be harder still.

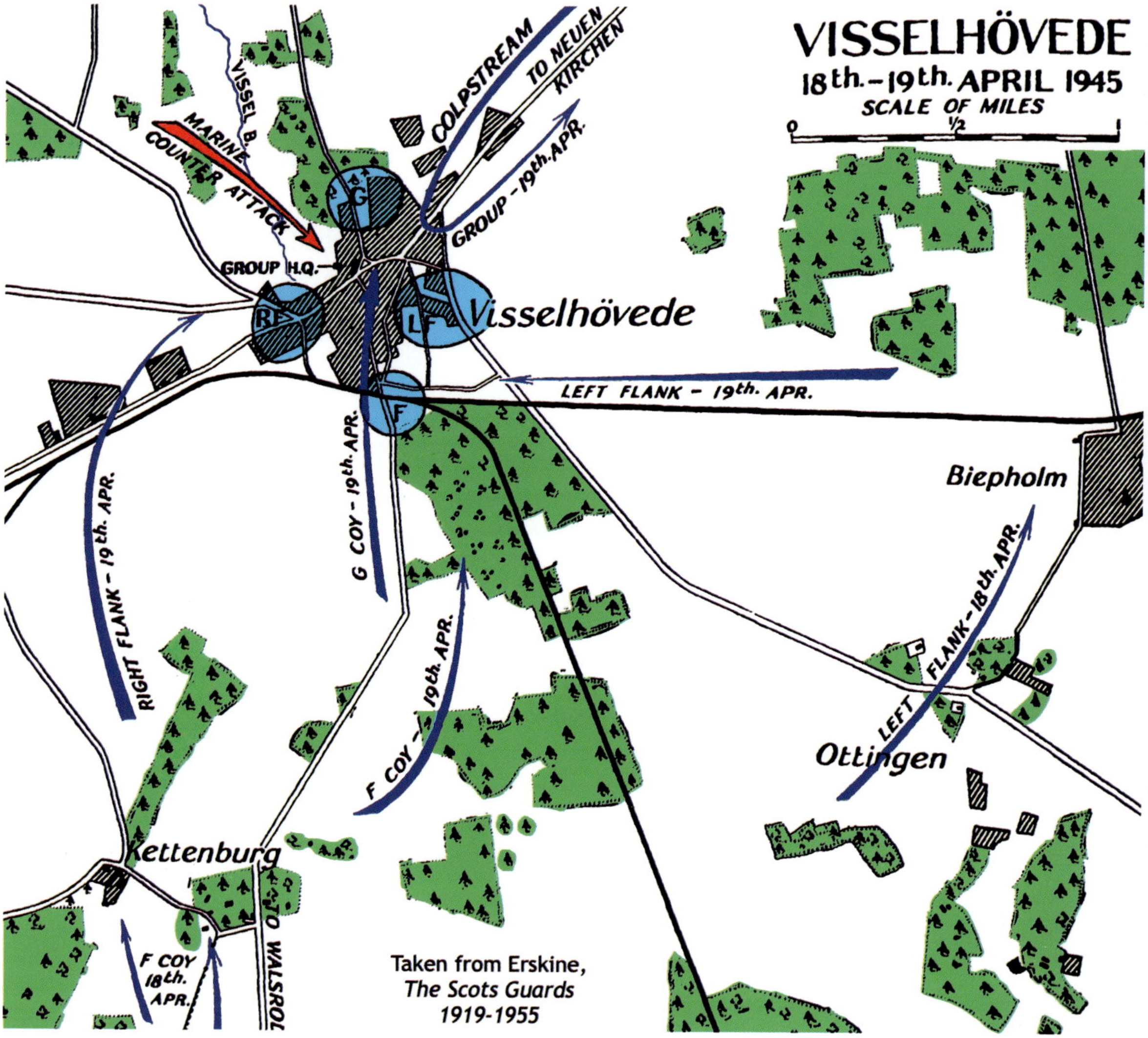

Taken from Erskine, *The Scots Guards 1919-1955*

Just before midday on April 19th, 2SG and its accompanying armour pushed north from Kettenburg towards Visselhövede. On the centre-line, 'G' Company took casualties from the tree lines to the east of the road, and 'F' Company began the task of clearing these woods. Without tank support, they found themselves embroiled in bitter fighting in which no mercy was shown by either side.

By the time that Battalion HQ moved into the centre of town, a company/squadron group was positioned at each of the cardinal points of the compass, 'F' Company to the south. But then the Germans counter-attacked in their usual fashion, sending in 1st Battalion, 7 *Marine Grenadier* Regiment, from the north-west. Battalion HQ itself came under fierce attack (the Intelligence Officer was killed by machine-gun fire) and had to be rescued by parties detached from the rifle companies – by the time that this help arrived, the HQ personnel were firing revolvers from the windows. Despite this desperate fighting, and the loss of another fourteen dead, 2SG had taken 400 prisoners that day, including the commanding officer and HQ staff of 5 *Marine Grenadier* Regiment.

2SG pushed on after their bloody nose at Visselhövede, but the going was sticky, and despite the capture of hundreds of prisoners they took two days to reach a position from which they could make an attempt on Rotenburg (not the one in which Simpkin had been incarcerated). However, 'F' Company 'added to the bag that night when an absent-minded party of six Germans with a handcart, under a disgruntled and booted and spurred artillery officer (he had been turned into an infantryman that morning) walked into their position.'[5]

When the attack was launched on April 22nd, 'F' Company encountered little opposition – 2nd *Marine Infanterie* Division had been reduced to no more than 3,000 men by this stage. 2SG were then withdrawn for a badly-needed rest.

* * *

In Burma, Hirst followed 'A' Squadron as it led the advance south towards Pyinmana on April 19th.

> We advanced down the main Rangoon road, parallel to the railway. At Pyinmana we had to make a diversion round the town, which was heavily held by the Japs. It did not fall for several days to the troops following us. We regained the road a few miles to the south of the town and harboured on the road that night.[6]

On the night of the 18th, Hirst and his comrades had leaguered at Milestone 258; twenty-four hours later they were at MS 240, eighteen miles closer to Rangoon.

> Several Jap lorries drove into the harbour, not realising that we were there, and were shot up. That night south of Pyinmana was spectacular with tracer bullets and Jap trucks going up in flames when they blundered into our harbour.[7]

Barcol's rapid progress continued on April 20th, as they overran an airfield (now Nay Pyi Taw International Airport) and sent a troop of armoured cars forwards as far as MS 216. The road was reported clear, and the force harboured there for the night. At 1800hrs, 'A' Squadron spotted Japanese troops in boats near the far shore of the river, and shot them up successfully.

* * *

Duffin.

After a three-day pause in Holdenstedt near Uelzen, at 0900hrs on April 19th Duffin and 3SG moved off northwards towards Lüneburg, beyond which lay the Elbe. They were all wondering what to expect. In fact, their advance turned out to be something of an anti-climax. At 0130hrs on April 21st, 3SG were in position to attack Artlenburg on the Elbe south-east of Hamburg. Left Flank fired their last shots of the war in support of the infantry as they moved in on Avendorf and Artlenburg, which fell without much of a fight. By the end of the day, 3SG had moved back twenty miles to the south to Bevensen, with seemingly nowhere left to go; Eisenhower had ordered a halt on the Elbe, leaving Berlin to the Soviets.

But news had reached 3SG of what they had missed near Celle, and personnel travelled back the forty-odd miles to confirm that their comrades had died in a worthy cause.

> During our stay at Bevensen, a few officers took the opportunity of visiting Belsen concentration camp and witnessing its unspeakable horrors, taking with them a Jeep-load of chocolate and sweets for the unfortunate children there.[8]

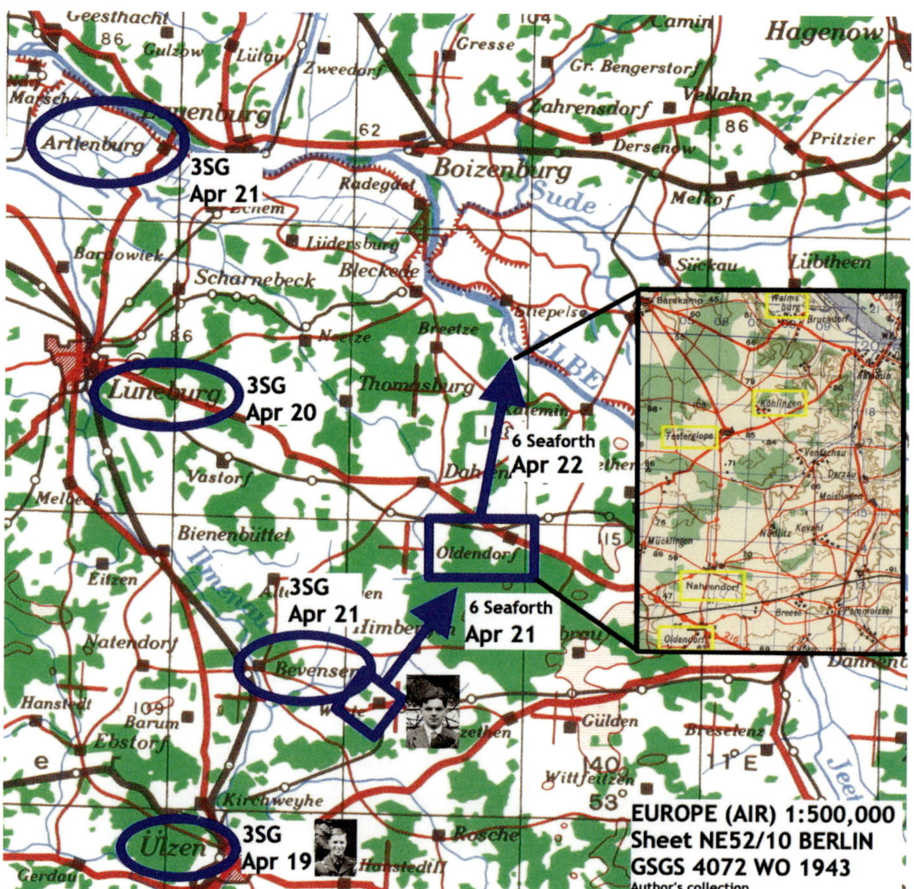

* * *

Hill.

Hill was at last on his way to the war. In preparation for the defeat of Japan by conventional means, the Royal Navy was assembling its most powerful fleet to date, bigger by far than the entire Royal Navy today. The British Pacific fleet, based in Australia, was intended to support Operation Downfall, the planned invasion of the Japanese home islands. On April 20th 1945 – Hitler's fifty-sixth (and last) birthday – the young naval officer embarked on the vessel which was to take him across the globe to HMS *Golden Hind* in Australia. This was the Royal Navy's headquarters in Australia, at Hargrave Park in Liverpool, Sydney. A vast camp of tents occupied the centre of the nearby Warwick Farm racecourse, where all Royal Naval personnel arriving for duty with the British Pacific Fleet were first accommodated.

* * *

Holtby.

Holtby and 6th Seaforths re-entered the war on April 21st at Oitzendorf, only around three miles south-east of Bevensen. Their advance was to take them north-east towards the Elbe, further south than where Duffin had reached it. During the course of the day they encountered small parties of the enemy at various locations, but there was little in the way of actual fighting. The Battalion reached Oldendorf by the evening, suffering its first fatality as it fought its way in.

Holtby advanced again on April 22nd at 0600hrs; the Battalion was on a one-company frontage in the order 'C' – 'D' – 'B' – 'A'. The war diary unhelpfully gives most locations with reference to points named after London streets such as Whitehall and Regent Street, making it hard to pinpoint where they were on the map. However, we can trace the Battalion's progress to an extent. During the morning Battalion HQ moved twice, first to Nahrendorf, then to Tosterglope. To that point there had been little action. But at 1050hrs 'C' Company, advancing from Tosterglope, encountered stiff opposition and called for mortar support, just as patrols from another unit reported strong enemy forces in Barskamp and its surrounding woods. By 1245hrs 'C' Company had killed and wounded many of the enemy and was fighting its way on in the direction of Köhlingen, supported by 'D'. There was heavy fighting, but at 1430hrs 'C' Company was entering Walmsburg under SPG fire.

The rest of April passed quietly, though with some shelling. It seemed that 6th Seaforths' war in Germany was going to be incredibly brief. This doubtless pleased Holtby's mother, who wrote to Robertson on April 24th:

> It is such an anxious time with all three boys in the fighting – David in Italy, Ronald and Robert both with the BLA. Robert is delighted to be at the finale with his 6th Seaforths. He got very tired of Palestine, but I was glad to have him out of the line![9]

* * *

Kemp.

Kemp had made it out of hospital on April 4th, and as he re-joined 7RB, 61 Brigade formed up at Forlimpopoli, 7RB making up a regimental group with its allotted armour, 17th/21st Lancers. In December, Kemp had been second-in-command of 'A' Company, and, absent indications of a move, we shall follow that sub-unit.

Although 61 Brigade's objective was clear – to exploit any breach in the German defences and reach the Po north-west of Ferrara – it was uncertain just where Eighth Army would make its breakthrough and thus where they would begin their advance. As the battle raged, German reserves were sucked in to Eighth Army's front and destroyed; when the Americans began their advance from the mountains of central Italy further west on April 14th, they found the going easier as a result. The fighting in the Argenta Gap beside Lake Comacchio continued to be bitter, however, and around noon on April 17th, as 'A' Squadron of 10th Hussars pushed forwards, Wykehamist Lieutenant Henry Alan Brooke MC was killed.[10]

> Just to end this tale of woe, I must tell you that poor old Henry Brooke was killed today, having been brewed up only two days before and had a miraculous escape.[11]

But by the following day, Eighth Army had broken through the Argenta Gap. The town of Argenta was cleared, from where Route 16 ran north-west to Ferrara. The area was criss-crossed by canals and rivers, any of which might provide obstacles to a swift advance if the bridges were blown. Speed was now crucial.

* * *

Brooke.

Had 16th/5th Lancers still been horsed cavalry, their mounts would have been champing at their bits. The Regiment had spent April 10th, 11th, and 12th fitting extensions to their tank tracks; these were known as 'Platypus Grousers' and widened the tracks to decrease the ground-pressure exerted by the 30-ton vehicles. Their use was a double-edged sword; although they permitted the Shermans to cross muddy ground with less risk of bogging down, the grousers chewed up road surfaces and damaged the tanks' suspension. To fit the system to the tracks of just one Sherman involved the separate fitting of 180 grousers, all done by hand. 16th/5th had then waited in Lugo from April 14th, each squadron paired with the matching-lettered Rifle Company of 1KRRC; from Lugo they could move north or south as the outcome of the battle demanded.

The breakthrough at Argenta determined their next move – north. In fact, they were to be the first unit through the Argenta Gap. At 0800hrs on April 19th they began to advance through the streams of traffic moving in the same direction. Although Brooke did not know it, his active part in the Second World War had just five days to run.

Having paused outside Boccaleone, by 1400hrs 16th/5th were on the move again, tasked with taking two crossings over a wonderfully-named tributary of the River Reno: the Po

Morto di Primaro. The southern crossing was at Traghetto (aptly, the name means 'The Crossing'), whilst half a mile north there was another bridge; 'B' Squadron's objective was the northern bridge, whilst 'A' would make for Traghetto itself. The Shermans would launch their attack from a Forming-Up Point in olive groves west of Il Trombone. As they moved forwards, the vehicles of 1KRRC bogged down where the tanks' grousers destroyed the surfaces, and so the infantry instead boarded the Shermans, and the advance continued.

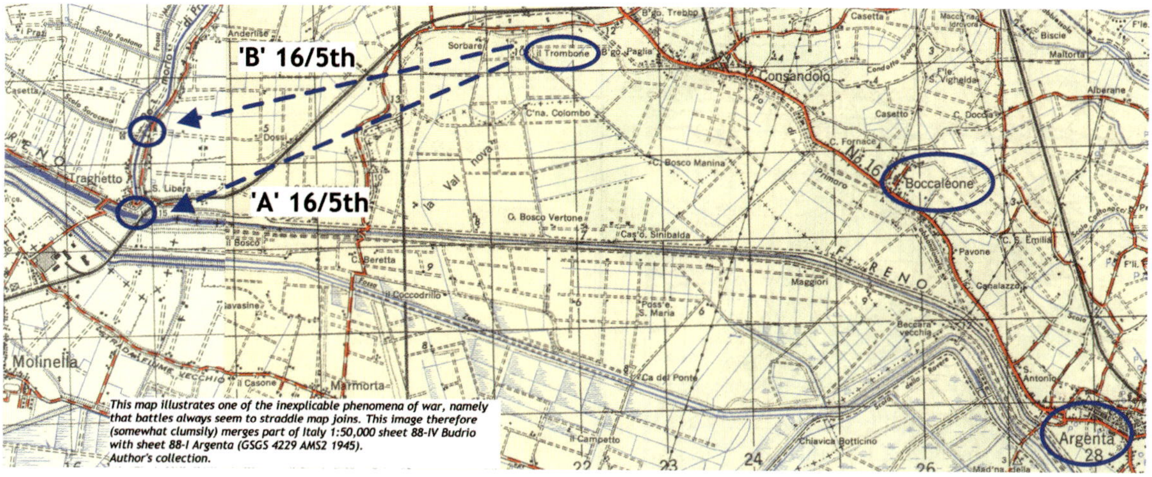

This map illustrates one of the inexplicable phenomena of war, namely that battles always seem to straddle map joins. This image therefore (somewhat clumsily) merges part of Italy 1:50,000 sheet 88-IV Budrio with sheet 88-I Argenta (GSGS 4229 AMS2 1945). Author's collection.

No plan survives first contact with the enemy; reconnaissance revealed that there were enemy positions in houses on the intended start line, and that beyond them the Germans were holding the lines of several watercourses. Time was slipping away, as a preliminary air-strike and artillery bombardment of Traghetto were due at 1600hrs. With three and a half miles still to go, the infantry disembarked and proceeded on foot with the leading tanks. Within minutes it became clear that they were not going to get to Traghetto by 1600hrs; there were numerous lines of mature olive trees, and dykes between 8ft and 12ft wide running across the axis of advance. German small-arms fire forced the infantry to seek cover and the Shermans to close their hatches, limiting their field of view.

1600hrs: three miles still to go. The air-strike went in, but the artillery were asked to drench the area in front of the tanks instead of firing on Traghetto. As so often, the 25-pounders proved decisive, and by dusk 'B' Squadron were just one mile short of their bridge. Overnight, the decision was taken to make 'B' Squadron's bridge the main effort in the morning; if 'B' could get across, it would be possible to outflank the strong defences in Traghetto. Meanwhile, 'A' would lean on these defences to distract the Germans, and 'C' Squadron would seek another crossing of the Po Morto di Primaro, further to the north.

When 'B' Squadron reached their bridge at 0830hrs on April 20th, it had – not unexpectedly – been demolished. The Po Morto di Primaro was not fordable at that point, and the Germans had troops dug in on the raised banks on both the near and far sides. Something had to be done if the attack was to succeed – and it was Brooke who did it. He ordered his Troop up on to the near bank, from where his tanks could pour fire on to the defenders on both sides. This enabled the accompanying infantry of 'B' Company, 1KRRC, to obtain a foothold on the far side. All that remained was to get a bridge-layer up to the crossing point. At 0930hrs 'A' Squadron broke in to Traghetto, whose defenders had probably realized what was likely to happen if they stayed put.

Past Traghetto, 17th/21st Lancers and 7RB took over the advance north-west along the Reno towards where the Fossa Cembalina joined the river, whilst 16th/5th turned north for Marrara, at the other end of the Fossa. But the flat ground left the tall Shermans exposed, and as 'B' Squadron pushed on, German SPGs hidden in barns opened fire. Five of 'B' Squadron's tanks were knocked out in minutes and others damaged.

One of the leading tanks was Brooke's – and it had been knocked out at extremely close range. He and his crew were fortunate not to be killed or seriously injured (one crewman in an adjacent tank had been decapitated by a German armour-piercing shell); they abandoned ship in a hurry. On this flat ground there was nothing to hide behind, so they took cover in a ditch, but whenever they tried to escape, the Germans opened fire on them. However, Brooke's wireless operator, Trooper 'Reg' Robinson, decided to do something about their predicament, as his citation for an immediate Military Medal explains:

> In the advance after crossing the river Po Morto di Primaro, Trooper Robinson was the Operator in the Troop Leader's tank of the leading troop of 'B' Squadron. After advancing some two or three miles against considerable enemy opposition, his tank was knocked out by an enemy self-propelled anti-tank gun at a range of approximately one hundred yards. Trooper Robinson was himself wounded in the knee, but although the remainder of the crew baled out, Trooper Robinson, realising that other tanks of the Troop were exposed to armour-piercing fire from the same gun, stayed at his post for a sufficient length of time to lay a smoke-screen with his 2-inch smoke discharger, thus enabling the remainder of the Squadron to manoeuvre into fire positions and engage the enemy SPG.
>
> Trooper Robinson's high courage and extremely cool action at a very critical moment not only saved further losses in tanks, but materially assisted in the continuation of the advance.[12]

From the 'cab-rank' of ground-attack aircraft on call nearby, a strike was called in, and the rockets which were fired obliterated the enemy position. As night fell, 'B' Squadron licked its wounds, and Brooke must have reflected on his narrow escape. Three days of war remained for him.

* * *

The Riflemen of 7RB had also been waiting for their moment. For the first time since Tunisia the troops were able to advance with clear fields of fire and views on all sides – though, as Brooke had discovered, this was not a wholly unmixed blessing. Kemp and the rest of his Battalion set off at 0400hrs on April 21st, and quickly reached the Fossa Cembalina at Segni, finding the bridge there blown but forty bemused Germans on the far side happy to surrender.

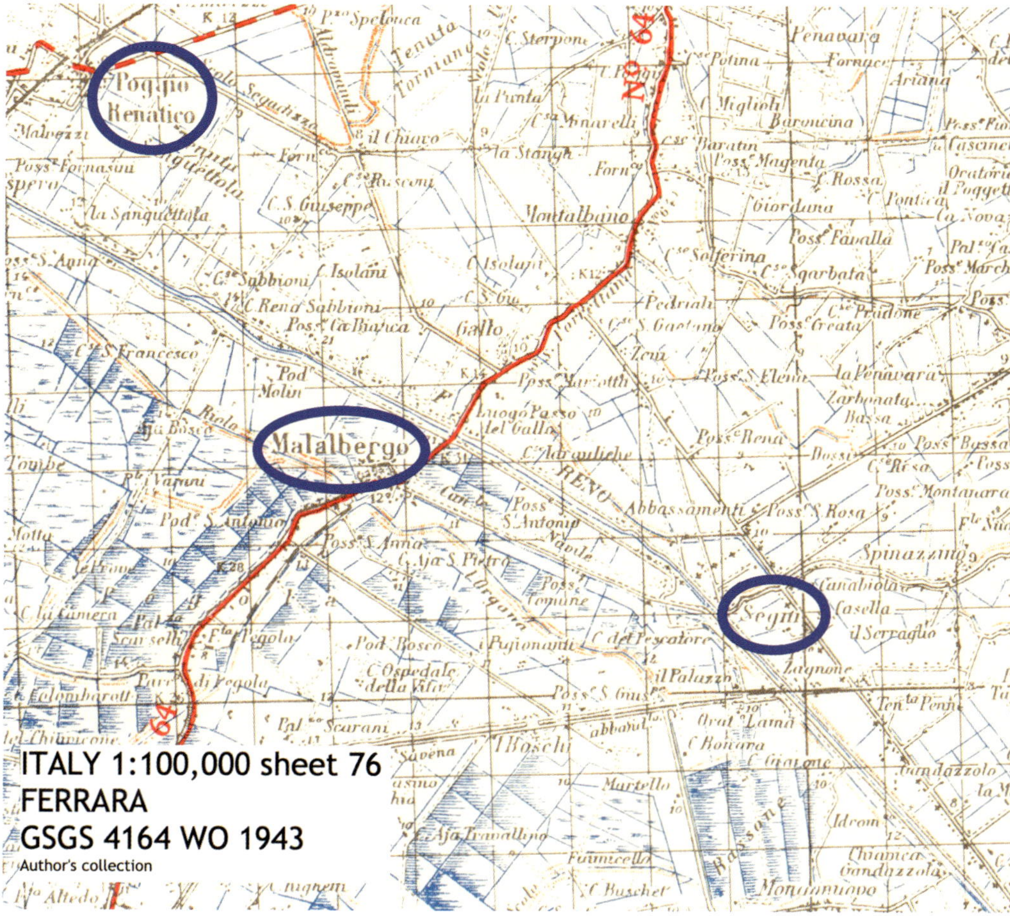

But from here north-west two watercourses constrained the advance into a narrow corridor, which led towards Route 64, the road between Ferrara and Bologna. At 1400 'A' and 'C' companies advanced slowly behind a barrage, until suddenly, at 1700hrs, the tanks of 17th/21st Lancers announced that they had captured the bridge carrying Route 64 across the northern canal. The advance turned into a mad scramble to secure this bridge and to push north-west into the town of Poggio Renatico, thereby cutting the enemy's line of retreat from Bologna. Two squadrons of the Lancers led the way as fast as the tanks would go, with 7RB's Bren-gun carriers rattling along in their wake, the men of 'A' Company clinging on for dear life.

As the troops hurtled on towards Poggio Renatico they overtook the Germans, but did not stop:

> The leading tanks, moving at great speed, over-ran an enemy horse-drawn transport column, which took to the ditch. The German crews baled out and took refuge in the farm-houses lining the road, from which they attempted to snipe at the column. Those houses that were not brewed up by the tanks were sprayed by the medium machine-gun Platoon, who fired their guns from their carriers.[13]

By dusk the leading elements of 7RB were in the south-eastern outskirts of the town, where resistance was beginning to stiffen. A German 150mm gun was knocked out, but there were many infantry around who began to stalk the tanks with *Panzerfäuste*. A German Flak battery equipped with the deadly 88mm guns sent armour-piercing shot hurtling along the streets, which made the tank crews increasingly nervous. It was nevertheless decided to drive the enemy out, and the Lancers remarked somewhat perplexedly in their official account that 7RB's Colonel Darling 'appeared quite enthusiastic about clearing some twenty houses with only about fifty men in pitch darkness.'[14]

But there were problems identifying targets (one tank crew destroyed what they thought was an 88mm gun, but turned out to be a cowshed); Darling therefore decided to wait for the rest of his Battalion. During the night three hundred prisoners of war were taken, some two hundred of whom drifted out of the town. The war diary commented amusedly that 'at last light a German motor-cyclist, completely unaware of the situation, rode straight into the 'A' Company road-block. He joined his three hundred comrades in the ever-expanding prisoner-of-war cage forthwith.'[15]

7RB's attack went in at 0400hrs on April 22nd and succeeded brilliantly, forty prisoners being taken by a detachment of 'B' Company alone (including a German staff officer who was 'almost crippled and had to be helped to a chair'). There was some trouble with snipers, who killed an NCO in 'A' Company, but when the rest of 7RB arrived the town fell rapidly, and by 0900hrs the Riflemen had taken Poggio Renatico. The Lancers added fifty more prisoners to the 'bag' when a single lorry packed with fleeing Germans was induced to stop by one of their tanks.

* * *

April 21st was a hard day for Barcol. Five miles south of their night-time leaguer, they came to a *chaung* crossing at MS 211 which they found to be heavily mined. One armoured car hit a mine on the road, though it only suffered minor damage to its front near-side wheel. As the engineers worked to clear the mines, Japanese snipers harassed them. One troop of armoured cars pressed on into the next village, but the Japanese set off an explosive charge to greet them, luckily causing no damage. In all, 'A' Squadron estimated that they had killed some forty Japanese that day, though this did not slow the advance down; they were at MS 189 by nightfall.

> One very nervous night we got into a harbour late, which was astride the railway line, and the tanks had difficulty crossing the rails, which could damage the tracks. Eventually we harboured in complete chaos, with the tanks in the middle and the soft vehicles on the outside. Luckily the Japs were not aware of our predicament, and we were not attacked.
>
> Another night was very frightening at the time, but very funny, except for one participant, in retrospect. We slept under mosquito nets when we could. They were dyed green for camouflage, but, being a new chum, mine was white and very conspicuous. I was awakened by gunfire and awful screams. Not knowing what was going on, but thinking that the Japs had got into the harbour, I rolled out of my swag, and took shelter behind my pillow, with pistol drawn, determined to sell my life dearly. At last things

settled down and we found out what had happened. One of the infantry, sleeping in a slit-trench, had a nightmare, screamed, and rolled over, touching his mate alongside. *He* thought that he was being attacked, and let off his Tommy gun, shooting his *Naik* (Corporal) in the bottom. Then a Sikh cook seized *his* rifle, climbed on top of a truck, and started shooting outwards from the middle of the harbour. He, not the Japs, was our greatest danger.

We did another diversion, coming back on to the road at Thawatti, where we captured the airstrip. We then kept straight on till we reached Toungoo. I was going to go out in an armoured car with one of the troop leaders, but when we reached Toungoo the other half of the column passed through.

The following day was relatively peaceful, the lead being taken by other units who occupied Toungoo; however, 'A' Squadron pulled back from the town that evening to harbour on the nearby airfield.

* * *

As Kemp and 7RB fought their way into Poggio Renatico on April 22nd, Brooke and 16th/5th Lancers were again on the move, with the Riflemen of 1KRRC riding on their tanks. Their axis of advance took them to the north of Poggio Renatico, closer to Ferrara, and by sticking to the roads they made eight miles in short order, entering Coronella just after the Germans had left. It was a race, now, to cut the enemy off from the Po. On the Regiment drove, by-passing a crater in the road which had been mined, and encountering enemy troops who knocked out a tank from 'A' Squadron with a *Panzerfaust.* Information came in suggesting that Mirabello was strongly held and must be cleared. Resistance proved very stubborn, however, and 'A' Squadron was unable to break in. Despite this setback, the Regiment had taken over 450 prisoners since 0430hrs.

April 23rd involved another early start, this time with 'B' Squadron in the lead. The day's objective was the village of Finale, but only a mile short of the village 16th/5th met

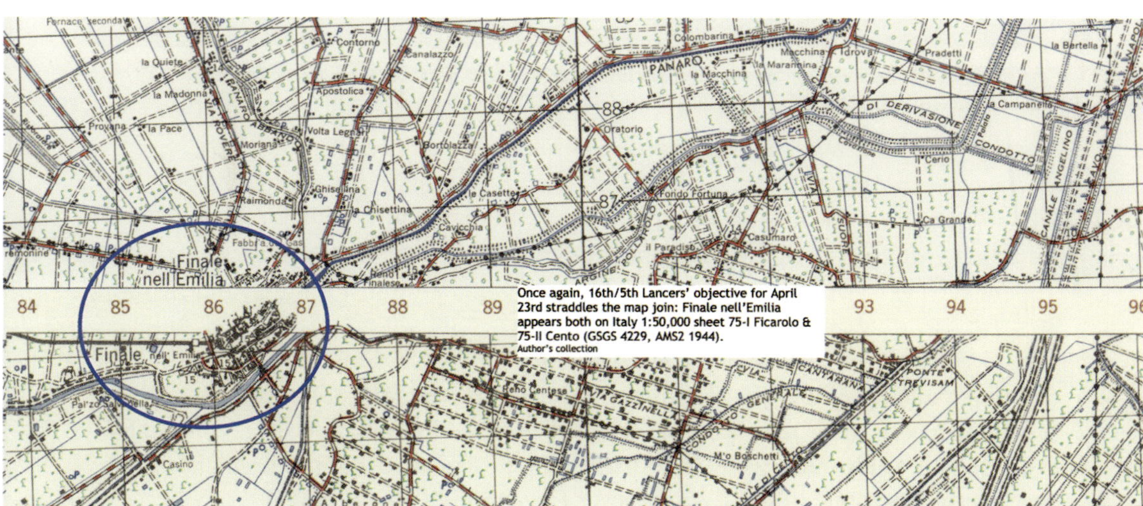

Once again, 16th/5th Lancers' objective for April 23rd straddles the map join: Finale nell'Emilia appears both on Italy 1:50,000 sheet 75-I Ficarolo & 75-II Cento (GSGS 4229, AMS2 1944).
Author's collection

opposition from two light tanks and two assault guns, which were destroyed. These proved to have been a rearguard screening a retreating convoy of lorries. 'B' Squadron's Shermans made short work of these unarmoured vehicles and pushed on into Finale. There they met head-on a German convoy which was trying to escape 11 South African Armoured Brigade. The result was chaos and slaughter, as the soft-skinned German vehicles came to a halt, densely packed in the streets of Finale, and 'B' Squadron laid about them with every weapon to hand. The hundreds of Germans in the convoy scattered for cover.

By the end of St George's Day, 16th/5th Lancers put their daily haul at 987 prisoners, at least seventy-three enemy dead, 161 lorries, seven half-tracks, four Flak guns, thirty-two artillery pieces, four tanks, fifteen *Panzerschreck* shoulder-fired anti-tank rocket launchers, four *Nebelwerfer* mortars, four 120mm mortars, and small arms too numerous to count. It had been a good day, and a fitting finale to the Regiment's war.

The difference a war makes. Brooke on commissioning in 1943 (left) and shortly after the war in 1945 (right). (Brooke family collection)

* * *

After an advance of over eighty miles in six days, Barcol's pace now slackened. April 23rd was spent resting at MS 185, if rest includes maintenance, gun-cleaning, and re-supply.

> We stayed some days in Toungoo. We were supplied by air-drop, and I was sent with the supply trucks to Thawatti airstrip, to pick up our share of the drop. Any stores likely to be damaged, such as jerry-cans of fuel, were dropped by parachute; but unbreakable articles such as clothing were 'free dropped' – just pushed out of the plane. They were pretty lethal missiles, and I will never forget a little Royal Indian Army Service

> Corps Sepoy running like Hell while everyone was shouting '*Upar dekho*!' ('Look up!'). Unfortunately, he was not looking up, and ran so fast that he tripped over a bale of boots as it hit the ground. If he had been a split second faster, he would have been concertina-ed, but his luck was in.

The only excitement on April 24th was when four Japanese 'Oscar' fighters carried out a rare strafing run on the harbour first thing in the morning.

* * *

In Bicknoller, on the edge of the Quantocks in Somerset, Robertson was enjoying a holiday with friends. He took April 21st as a day off from relaxation and wrote several letters, one to Peter Walker in Italy, in which he talked about the loss of his former pupils:[16]

> I finished seven more obituary notices before I came away, for the next *Wykehamist* supplement, which no doubt Keith will send you. Pip Sturt, John Kennedy, and Michael Sinclair. It's terribly hard to get even facts right and to steer a course between adulation and bald statement. It breaks my heart to think of them all – H. Woods and Michael Sinclair in particular – and John Kennedy, so young and so keen …
>
> What price the Germany news and the concentration camps? Good for those MPs to have to go and see (and smell) them. No wonder one Labour man went sick before starting. Very sorry to see death of your (not 'our') Henry Brooke. He, like Julian, was once in my English Div. B, and I let him state the Ulster case, which he did with much vigour. They were likely to make 'bonny fighters'. Victor Fortune's rescue and return – and his KCB for help to prisoners, in yesterday's *Times* – are a great satisfaction to us. Hope Bruce may now get home to see him. I saw also last week Edward Lillingston – prisoner-of-war for three years since Greece, father of Nigel[17] – just home from Germany, where he and 450 others in last stages of exhaustion were rescued by Yanks – a wonderful story.
>
> And now I see your lot are well on the move, which will be a satisfaction after your enforced marking time.

The letter caught up with Walker in 65 British General Hospital, after his close approach to becoming the subject of another of Robertson's obituaries. As he lay there, Polish troops entered Bologna, and American troops reached the Po beyond the city. On April 23rd, units of Eighth Army also reached the Po.

* * *

In the small hours of April 23rd, 7RB had a regrettable clash with unidentified troops who tried to cross the River Reno from the south: it was not until one of the approaching soldiers had been killed that the defenders discovered that the newcomers were New Zealanders.

As 7RB pushed westwards to San Agostino they acquired 250 further prisoners and some sizeable loot: two 150mm guns, a 'monstrous half-track of huge dimensions', an

Opel 3-ton truck, a Ford 30-cwt truck, two armoured personnel carriers, one Volkswagen *Schwimmwagen* (amphibious Jeep), and two cars. By now it had been confirmed that the jaws of the trap had closed, and that German forces in Bologna had been cut off from the Po. 7RB were able to rest for the remainder of the day, basking in the delightfully hot sunshine, before moving to Ferrara on April 24th to join the rest of 61 Brigade.

* * *

Lewin.

Lewin was on his way back to the war. The war diary for 2KRRC reveals that on April 24th he rejoined the Battalion after a period in hospital – how long, where, and for what is unclear. It was a strange time to be reaching the front line again, but it gave Lewin the opportunity to be among his men and messmates as they finally crossed the line between war and peace.

He had been very fortunate to miss a series of vicious little actions in which 2KRRC had taken casualties but given much worse than they had received. By the time that Lewin returned, the Battalion was in Baden, around six miles east of Bremen; two days after he arrived, 2KRRC moved to Mahndorf in the suburbs. There they remained, 'in theory in an operational role, in practice with no real commitments against an enemy who had abandoned the very precarious salient on that side of Bremen'.[18]

* * *

3 Troop's Sergeant Ross wrote to Walker on April 25th.

Walker.

Dear Sir,
Very glad to receive your letter late last night. We had just come out after a very hard day, but as usual the old Troop was well up the 'sharp end' … Yesterday was pretty tough; 3rd Troop was very lucky and stuck it out till last light, and this morning the push was on and 'Ted' was finished this side of the Po. But I would have liked you to have been there and received the congratulations instead of me. The whole operation 'Patton' went very well, the final check being about forty 'Teds' and an 88mm self-propelled gun, knocked out at three hundred yards by Corporal Jones in my 17-pounder …

Anyway, today I can look out of the tank and see the Po; can't say it gives me a thrill, but here we are, and I don't think I had better tell you the plans for the future in a letter, I mean for the next couple of days …

Hurry up and get back – that comes from all the Troop and myself included. I can't say don't worry and keep your chin up – I expect that's a very sore point at the moment – but no one will take your place in the Troop; we will see to that. So here is wishing you all the best.

Sgt Ross

P.S. O'Connor says 'Hurry up and get back on the road with your barrow.'[19]

It was not possible; although the elbow healed well, Walker required two more operations to scrape out small areas of dead bone from his jaw, and another to reduce scarring.

* * *

2SG were by now almost exactly midway between Bremen (25 miles south-west) and Hamburg (the same distance to the north-east). The experiences which they underwent in this last fortnight of war would have been enough for a lifetime.

They attacked south-west from Zeven at 0600hrs on April 26th, as usual in concert with the tanks of 2WG, making contact west of the town shortly afterwards. A road junction had been blocked, and German infantry were as usual covering the obstacle from the woods. They had a light gun with them which was knocked out, but an SPG also engaged the British from further away along the road leading north-west. All this opposition cost time – as the defenders intended – and the Guards were suitably cautious in clearing the woodland. Despite their care, there were casualties in 2SG, one Platoon Commander being killed by machine-gun fire. It was a lottery; 'G' Company and its tanks had taken a different road out of Zeven, brushed aside light opposition, and taken Oldendorf and thirty prisoners.

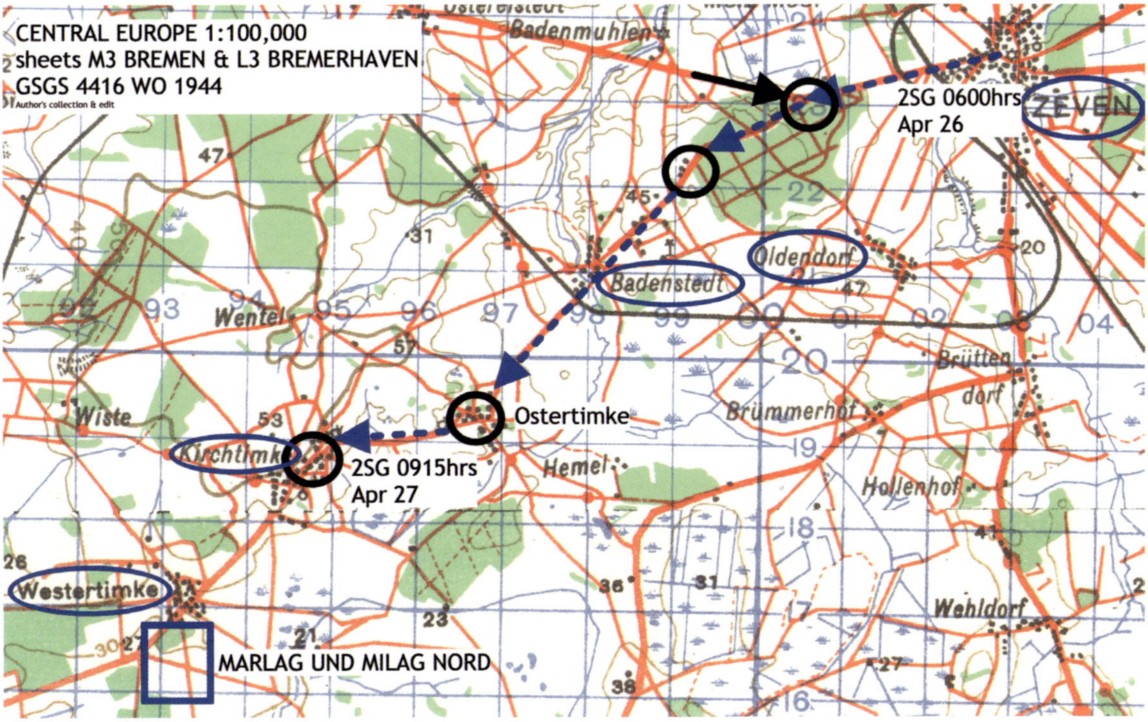

Once the woods had been cleared, the main thrust continued towards Badenstedt, but beyond the village the road bridge had been blown, and a railway bridge gave up the ghost after only 'F' Company had crossed. As the rest waited in Badenstedt for engineers to build a new bridge, and 'F' entered Ostertimke, the Germans shelled both areas heavily.

The German unit facing the Guards – *Generalleutnant* Eberhard Rodt's battle-hardened 15th *Panzergrenadier* Division – noted in its war diary that poor signals security by the Guards provided the intelligence needed to make such an effective defence:

> We learn constantly from wireless intercepts about positions of enemy spearheads, successes of our artillery, and planning and preparations for coming attacks ... Today brings a crisis for the Division. It is only because of the superb work of our wireless intercept unit that we are able to prevent a breakthrough at several points, and to build up again and again new centres of resistance wherever the enemy tries to break through our lines.[20]

Beyond Kirchtimke to the south-west lay the village of Westertimke. There stood a complex of prison camps known collectively as *Marlag und Milag Nord*, which held, amongst others, some 5,000 Allied merchant seamen. These men were supposed to be interned rather than treated as prisoners, but neither side respected this. Protests from the Red Cross had led the Germans to separate merchant seaman from prisoners of war in July 1941, and they had been transferred to the new *Marineinterniertenlager (Milag)*, completed in February 1942. *Marlag (Marinelager)* was a separate facility, completed in July 1942; *Marlag* 'O' housed Royal Navy officers, and *Marlag* 'M' was for Royal Navy NCOs. The *Kriegsmarine* had also moved its transit camp – *Durchgangslager (Dulag)* – to Westertimke in March 1942 after bombing raids had made Wilhelmshaven too dangerous. The last camp to be constructed – *Milag Inder*, or *Inderlager* – had opened in September 1943 and housed over 600 Burmese, Chinese, Indian, and Middle Eastern merchant seamen. Conditions had worsened late in 1944 as inmates of other camps were moved, and early in February 1945 3,000 former denizens of *Stalag Luft* III had taken over *Marlag* 'M', the Royal Navy NCOs then moving into *Marlag* 'O'.

At the beginning of April a detachment of SS *Feldgendarmerie* had removed 3,000 inmates and begun to march them eastwards. A fair number were killed by Allied air attacks along the march, which ended at Lübeck on April 28th. Meanwhile, the 8,000 overcrowded residents of the Westertimke camps awaited liberation. Their guards were replaced by older men on April 9th, as every able-bodied combatant was enlisted for the defence of Bremen. Ten days later, *Generalleutnant* Rodt deployed his tanks and artillery around the camps, facing eastwards in the direction from which the Guards Armoured Division was approaching.

On the afternoon of April 26th, the Commandant of the Westertimke camps and a *Kriegsmarine* Lieutenant approached 2SG under a flag of truce, with a letter from Rodt suggesting that a ten-hour truce be declared so that the British could evacuate all the prisoners. The Battalion promptly shuffled the problem up the chain of command and got on with its advance, while 15th *Panzergrenadier* Division monitored their delegation thanks to the Guards' lax security:

> We follow, by wireless intercepts, their progress, as each enemy unit reports the arrival of these officers. We discover by this means that the General commanding the Guards

> Armoured Division decided to detain these two officers as prisoners, and that he ordered an attack by all available tanks for 1800hrs to break through to Westertimke. As the Bailey bridge north of Badenstadt was finished by 1700hrs, the order to attack was in fact given at 1730hrs. As soon as we found out about this attack, all available units – especially anti-tank units – were regrouped. The Division considers it a matter of honour that this attack on Westertimke should not be allowed to succeed, and that the camp should not be reached today by the enemy. We had wanted to hand over the camp by way of our envoys. The Guards Armoured Division may have considered the sending of these two officers to parley as a sign of our weakness. Divisional HQ moves into the area west of Kirchtimke.[21]

It is interesting that at this stage the Germans were still talking of honour, as well as taking what little comfort they could from delaying the inevitable and giving ground on their own terms. British troops in the same position would probably have done exactly the same.

Rodt's delaying actions were successful; by the time that all of 2SG reached Ostertimke it was dark, and 'F' Company were forced back by SPG-fire when they tried to get on to Kirchtimke. The ferocious shelling had caused no fewer than fifty casualties in an already depleted battalion. However, the presence of the inmates of *Marlag und Milag Nord* meant that the Scots Guards/Welsh Guards battle-group was honour-bound to attack the next morning, just as 15th *Panzergrenadier* Division felt honour-bound to resist.

2SG's attack on Kirchtimke began at 0915hrs on April 27th; preceded by a heavy bombardment from artillery and 4.2-inch mortars, 'F' Company advanced across the fields to the south of the road, whilst Left Flank did the same to the north. The two weak units made good progress, but German shell-fire was also very heavy and Left Flank lost yet another officer. Clerk-Rattray and his Left Flank counterpart had stayed back with Battalion HQ, but when they tried to proceed down the road to join their companies, it turned out that the road was mined. For the time being, Clerk-Rattray was cut off from his men, who were by 1100hrs fighting through the village with just one officer left in each company, one of them wounded. 'F' Company had a Platoon Commander standing, the only other officer having been wounded in the advance. Only two tanks had made it through, but with their help the men of 2SG flushed out the ubiquitous snipers and destroyed three SPGs – one with the much-maligned PIAT. Clerk-Rattray walked forwards across the fields to take over his Company, but found matters well in hand on arrival. Behind him, the Sappers announced that the road was clear of mines, but the leading tank went up on one after only a hundred yards.

> The Royal Engineers reported that the mines on the road were laid very deep and that their detectors could not reach them owing to the magnetic quality of the cobble stones; also that the leading tanks could easily go over a mine, packing down the earth on top of it so that a later tank touched it off. As a result the road was never reported 100% clear and vehicles continued to get blown up as we took the risk of continuing. Eventually the whole group got into the village … 'G' Company and 3 Squadron 2WG pushed through the village with orders to capture Westertimke, where thirty-five prisoners-

> of-war from 104 *Panzergrenadier* Regiment were taken … Contact was made with the prisoner-of-war camp during the night.[22]

The Germans had pulled back during the day, and so the following morning 2SG had a rest, while 'the prisoner-of-war camp was visited by a large number of people. The prisoners, some of whom had been prisoners-of-war for five years, were overjoyed to see us.'[23]

But there were bitter pills to swallow, too – such as a decision taken on April 28th:

> SPECIAL ORDER OF THE DAY
> Owing to the high rate of casualties among all ranks of the Battalion in the last few weeks, and to the lack of reinforcements, it has been found necessary to reform the Battalion on a three Company basis. I have therefore decided temporarily to disband 'F' Company, and to re-form this Company again as soon as the reinforcement situation permits.
>
> In the meantime, I wish to congratulate 'F' Company on the magnificent example they have set throughout many weeks of hard fighting, and to thank all ranks for their gallant and untiring efforts.
>
> H.N. Clowes
> Commanding, 2nd Battalion Scots Guards
> British Liberation Army[24]

* * *

Hirst's section of Barcol had salvaged the Humber armoured car which had run over a mine on April 21st, but left it behind for repair when they set out again on April 27th, reaching MS 144, just north of Pyu, by nightfall. The next day saw them cover another good stretch, as far as MS 95, beyond Nyaunglebin. But there they halted for two days.

* * *

2SWB must have thought that their active part in the campaigns was over, and that their war would end in Holland. However, on April 26th they discovered that they were leaving 49th Division and moving to 53rd (Welsh) Division. One of the infantry battalions in 158 Infantry Brigade – 7th Royal Welch Fusiliers – had suffered so many casualties that it was easier to replace it than to bring it back up to strength. Since 53rd Division was on its way to Hamburg, 2SWB's presence was urgently needed. So they scurried across the Rhine and caught up with their new formation as quickly as they could. Although organized resistance in Germany was rapidly coming to an end, the defenders of Hamburg were not prepared to give up without a fight. On April 26th, SS troops even launched a counter-attack at Vahrendorf. Once that had been successfully dealt with, the British forces moved in for the kill. But it was hard going. In woods south of the city 53rd Division encountered over 2,000 enemy troops – SPGs, Hungarian SS, and numerous infantry armed with the ubiquitous *Panzerfäuste*. On the outskirts of Hamburg itself, the defenders turned all the anti-aircraft defences to a ground role; the German forces called themselves First Parachute Army but were in fact a rag-tag of *Fallschirmjäger*, *Waffen* SS, *Wehrmacht*, *Kriegsmarine*, *Volkssturm* (the German equivalent of the Home Guard), Hitler Youth, police, and firemen. All they could do was delay the inevitable. As British shells began to fall amid the rubble of the city on April 28th, a white flag was seen; the following day, a delegation of the city authorities entered into surrender negotiations, but these were still going on when, on April 30th, Lewin and 2KRRC prepared to join the attack on Hamburg. Somerville, Lewin, and their comrades in 2KRRC and 2SWB had orders not to enter the city while the discussions went on – and so they were left with the worry of whether they would be called upon to attack one last time. No one wanted to be the last man to die.

* * *

Eighth Army had crossed the Po on April 25th and thrust for Venice and Trieste, whilst the American-led Fifth Army drove towards Milan and Austria; on the west coast, an American infantry division captured Genoa; and the Brazilian Division made a lightning advance on Turin, causing the collapse of German and Fascist Italian forces in that area. All along the line, the Germans were in disarray and headlong retreat, the Alps at their backs. It was like the end in Tunisia all over again, but this time not just the end of a phase, but the end of a war.

The German high command in Italy had by now recognized that further resistance was useless, and on April 29th *Generaloberst* von Vietinghoff's representative signed a formal surrender of all German forces south of the Alps. The document stated that all hostilities would cease on May 2nd – but it was hard for the Germans to get word of this surrender to all their units, and the Allies wanted to take as much ground as possible, especially wishing to reach Trieste before it could be occupied by Tito's Yugoslav forces. On April 29th, therefore, as German resistance disintegrated and their commanders discussed surrender, 7RB moved swiftly northwards across the River Adige.

7RB reached Padua in the small hours of April 30th, under orders to co-operate with the armoured cars of 27th Lancers and to advance on Treviso, just north of Venice; they passed through Treviso by mid-morning. However, on taking the direct eastwards route in the vanguard of Eighth Army, they found the Piave bridges down. Darling turned his Battalion round, sped back through Treviso, and motored on to Oderzo. There 7RB received a rapturous welcome from the locals. They encountered no resistance that day, and left their hundreds of German prisoners in the hands of the ubiquitous Italian partisans.

In Berlin, Hitler shot himself.

XXXI

'The whole thing has been such a ghastly waste of life'

War & Peace, May 1945

As dawn broke on May 1st, the leading elements of 7RB, Kemp among them, entered S. Vito al Tagliamento, just west of the river Tagliamento:

Kemp.

> The welcome was more elaborate than on any previous occasion, and crowds lined the streets and streamers fluttered down from the church steeple while martial music from loud-speakers was played interspersed with proclamations and speeches of welcome made by the local big-shots ... Local inhabitants indulged in breaking up bust of Mussolini in main square, amidst much applause.[1]

The locals reported that there were large numbers of Germans nearby, so 7RB's Scout Platoon went to investigate. The war diary records the sequel:

> 0805hrs
> Scout Platoon reported one hundred prisoners of war.
>
> 0810hrs
> Scout Platoon reported two hundred and fifty prisoners of war.[2]

7RB were far in front of the rest of the army, out of radio contact and off the edge of their issued maps, and any determined opposition could have hurt them badly; as it was, a short skirmish on the river line later that morning left them in possession of several *Panzer* III tanks. 7RB then sped at 40mph along the main road to Udine, which they entered amidst the cheers of the civilians and celebratory volleys of the partisans. But their war was not over; the ceasefire in Italy had yet to come into effect; and north of Udine German tanks were reported to be advancing southwards. 'B' Company, commanded by Wykehamist Dick Adams, with support from anti-tank guns and the armoured cars of 27th Lancers, went to block Route 13, which led into Udine from the north. They took up positions at Salt.

It was clear that the Germans were divided; some of them wanted to surrender, but others did not. As evening approached, 'B' Company misjudged the mood of one German tank unit. When a Platoon Commander approached the Germans to discuss their surrender, he was shot and severely wounded by one of the German tank commanders, then taken prisoner, along with a Rifleman; a Corporal was killed.[3] The Germans, who had two Panther tanks and two Fiat Ansaldo M13/40s, also began to shoot up 7RB's White scout cars, and three carriers had to be abandoned. 7RB did not hesitate to take their revenge, bringing up their anti-tank guns and brewing up one of the enemy tanks. It had all been a futile waste of human life at this late stage of the war – and it was the last action which 7RB was to fight.

German prisoners confirmed that two men had been taken captive and were receiving medical treatment, and at first light on May 2nd 'B' Company recovered its missing men.

* * *

In Delhi, Fortune and Susan went shooting on May 1st. The heat was intense, and as Susan relaxed with the newspaper in a stand of trees, Fortune went off to try to bag a blackbuck.

Fortune.

> I learned more about the San Francisco Conference than I'll ever want to know – got tired of that and went on to the German atrocities – and was revolted – so lay back and snoozed ... And there was Brucie, looking for all the world as if he'd just been fighting in the desert, complete with rifle. The salt was caked hard on his lips and he was filthy – but he'd had a wonderful time. The salt on his lips was awfully difficult to remove.[4]

* * *

On the same day, Hirst continued to advance towards Rangoon. His memoirs and the unit war diary tell the story.

Hirst.

> Towards the end, the leading armoured cars had to cope with suicide squads of Japs, sitting in the ditch beside aerial bombs, ready to give the nose fuse a bang when a tank or armoured car passed. A few Jap prisoners were taken; unusual, but a sign that they were cracking up. I also witnessed a large band of Jiffs surrendering. They were Indian troops captured in Singapore who had been forced to fight for the Japs. They were very emotional and greeted our men with open arms, though this was not reciprocated.

> 1700hrs May 1st 1945
> Arrived at harbour MS 74.

> 1100hrs May 2nd 1945
> Arrived at harbour MS 58.

Fourteenth Army.

The 1945 monsoon broke on the afternoon of May 2nd, just as Rangoon was falling – not, as had originally been planned, to troops advancing through the Arakan, nor to those coming down the Irrawaddy valley, nor to the thrust along the Sittang – the one in which Hirst had been involved – but to assault from the sea.

> May 3rd 1945
> Rest. Maintenance and gun-cleaning.
>
> May 4th 1945
> Rest. Maintenance and gun-cleaning.
>
> 1200hrs May 5th 1945
> Squadron arrived harbour PEGU MS 50.

> I enjoyed my short stay with 16th Cavalry. The squadron that I was with were Punjabi Mussulmans. They had at least one other officer beside Jimmy Bowen – a very dashing Indian troop leader and armoured car commander.
>
> I remember our mess cook, Imam Ali, who cheerfully made good meals out of very little. Curried salmon was his *specialité de la maison* – tinned, of course, but he also made a delicious curry of some Yabbies [crayfish] we got out of a canal. It was here that I first met Australian 'anagram jam' in our rations: melon and lemon. While I was with them, in open country, with the Japs on the run, the tanks looked like menageries, with chooks tied on the back by one leg (and even a goat!). They were let down to feed and lay eggs at night.
>
> By the time that we settled down at Pegu, I had returned to 7th Cavalry, reluctantly at first because I had so liked 16th Cavalry; but I found 7th Cavalry a very good mob and had no regrets. The rains had started, and we were glad that we were living in houses and not in the bush. The insects were terrible, and one night when we were having pears I thought that they were a bit sweet but suddenly found that there was a stink beetle in them. Another form of wildlife were weaver birds, who made a pair of nests on a wire on our verandah and successfully hatched out.

* * *

Although the surrender of German forces in Italy came into effect on May 2nd, Murray and the Lovat Scouts, being in a rest area, were completely in the dark about what was going on. The war diary for May 2nd to 4th recorded that 'the war in Italy seems to be rushing ahead and extremely difficult to follow owing to lack of information in rear areas.'

As the German forces in Italy crashed out of the war, they became the least of 7RB's worries. Udine was filling with mutually hostile groups of Yugoslavs: partisans loyal to Tito, and some 20,000 retreating Chetniks (Yugoslavs who had collaborated with the Germans). As 7RB's war diary explained,

> if these two rival armies were to get at each others' throats, a bloody battle would ensue. So steps were taken to try and prevent any such disaster occurring. At this time the Chetniks, about three Divisions strong under General Damyanevic, had reached the Cormons area, where they had occupied all the houses, but were behaving tolerably well.

Tito's troops had reached Gorizia in much greater strength and were preparing, in spite of numerous parleys to try and dissuade them, to cross the river Isonzo … In view of a possibility of a clash between Tito's troops and the Chetniks already mentioned, it was decided to form a firm barrier between the two until the latter could be got away and disarmed. They appeared to be quite willing to be subjected to this.[5]

On May 4th, Finch contacted Robertson with some good news:

Just a short note to tell you I am back home on six weeks' leave. In fact, I arrived a week ago, and I found all well at home. All seems very much the same, only I find myself very out of touch with politics, education, art, etc., and subjects of general interest.[6]

On May 5th the news of the cessation of hostilities in Italy reached the Lovat Scouts. 'Considerable jubilation all round', Murray recorded, in his usual economic style.

* * *

Holtby.

Nick Somerville.

Lewin.

Holtby and 6th Seaforths had been rushed forwards towards Lübeck in the final week of April, and it was there that they ended the war. Meanwhile, in Hamburg, the commander of German forces – General Wolz – drove out of the city to negotiate a surrender on May 1st. As he emerged, Lewin and 2KRRC were moving in, occupying Ammelinghausen in the outskirts, ready for the assault. Wolz reached those authorized to treat with him the following day, and the formal surrender took effect on May 3rd. 2KRRC's war diary noted that 'the German was beginning to crumble completely now.'[7]

British troops entered the city immediately, and 2SWB followed on the next day. They took no chances, advancing cautiously for ten miles with tanks covering their every move. For Nick Somerville, too, the war was over – bringing with it a whole new set of problems.

We marched into Hamburg with our feet sounding on the cobbled streets. The whole town had been destroyed by bombing and a terrible fire-storm. A layer of dust and rubble covered the streets and the houses, and few windows had any glass. There were no civilians on the street, for they were all taking refuge in their cellars. We marched in eerie silence for nearly two hours until we reached our battalion and company areas, which had been selected arbitrarily beforehand and drawn on our town maps in chinagraph pencil. On arrival, I set up my Company HQ in a cigarette factory which

> was not severely damaged, and then chose various buildings for my three platoons. I then found the nearest German police station, and located a senior police officer who seemed very willing to assume responsibility and provide me with an interpreter.
>
> I immediately toured the area and found urgent problems. The first was a smoked fish factory containing a pile some thirty feet high of rotting fish, attracting rats, and likely to spread disease. Then I discovered two prisoner-of-war camps, one in a park for about five thousand Russians, and the other, in a building, for over a hundred Italian officer prisoners. The prisoners were starving and needed feeding immediately. Our Quartermaster managed to get hold of a three-ton lorry with a quantity of German bread and a number of jars of honey. It required soldiers with fixed bayonets to control the issue of this food to so many Russians. The Italians were delighted to gobble up the bread, but to our amazement they put the honey on their hair, spruced up their uniforms, combed their locks, put on their hats with feathers in them, and walked up and down arm-in-arm with the flies buzzing all around them.
>
> The fish factory problem was solved by the German police officer. I had arranged for him to report to me at 0800hrs every morning, and the first order I gave him was to remove the rotten pile of fish. He replied 'Jawohl' with a click of his heels, and left. He stopped every adult in the street and ordered him or her to get a shovel and report to the factory straight away. He also stopped every horse and cart and ordered them to the factory, firstly to move all the fish to a dump, I think in the park, and then to collect white lime from somewhere and cover the factory location and the dump in the park with lime. The whole operation was completed in forty-eight hours.

And so the Allied occupation of a defeated Germany began.

* * *

Unlike the planners of the 2003 invasion of Iraq, the Allies had a complete plan – Operation Eclipse – in place for the immediate aftermath of their victory. Orders for Eclipse had been formulated as far back as November 1944.[8] Nevertheless, the scale of the problems faced is clear from 2KRRC's war diary entries for May 4th to 8th:[9]

> At once the problem became one of rounding up German stragglers, DPs [displaced persons], and generally assisting a rather harassed and very overworked Military Government Staff. In the morning came the wonderful official news that all German forces in Denmark, northern Germany, and the islands all round the Danish coast, including the forces in northern Holland, had surrendered to Field Marshal Montgomery. The war, as far as 21st Army Group were concerned, was over. The Battalion celebrated in an appropriate manner.
>
> The Battalion settled in Bergedorf and set about the vast problem of controlling all the thousands of stragglers. Two check-posts were set up to control the thousands of German Army stragglers and convert them into prisoners of war. Measures were carried out to control and organize the great multitude of foreign workers now moving aimlessly about. The whole German nation was on the move, and the first job was to stop the whole process: arrest the soldiers, organize the DPs in camps, and prevent the

civilians from moving. Throughout, of course, the Intelligence blacklist problem was big, for war criminals both large and small were also on the move.

German movement on the streets became less and less till it nearly ceased. The Russian 'slave workers' and prisoner-of-war camps provided a little trouble, but by the evening it was more or less under control … The 'Eclipse' instructions were put into force in all the details relating to transport, DPs, and German troops detached from their formations …

The Prime Minister announced VE Day, and the end of the war in Europe. Once again, the Battalion paused from its 'Eclipse' operations to have a short-lived celebration in honour of the occasion.[10]

The Lovat Scouts were delighted to hear on the BBC that the German war was over: 'Regimental V celebrations took place in the evening, and large quantities of Vino consumed.'

When Robertson had written to Walker in April he had not been aware that Walker had been wounded. He remedied the omission by writing again on May 9th, with news of how Winchester College had celebrated VE Day:

When I got back here Keith told me of your most unlucky and unpleasant wound, from which I hope you are now beginning to recover. It was maddening to get hit just before the advance for which you had so long fought and waited, and to be separated from your men in the hour of triumph … Since that, the end has come in Germany, and now tonight we hear that Goering is himself in the bag (and Goebbels, poisonous to the end, himself died some days ago). I don't myself believe Hitler is dead, and have hopes the Russians will round him up or find his beastly body at least. I saw Victor Fortune, safe home, a week ago at Fleet with his daughter, who lives there, and we hear Finch, Simpkin, and others are home – not yet R. Wood, Blades and J. Metcalfe, as far as we know, but there has been no post today, and I think they really must be back. We had a whole day off (VE Day) yesterday, and another (Ascension) tomorrow, but worked today, tho' one hour went west for a lecture by the Viceroy, who had a great reception.[11]

* * *

In Delhi, news of VE Day was also welcomed by Fortune and Susan – though in her elation she seems to have forgotten about the Japanese:

It is difficult to believe it is all over; how wonderful it is for all of you at home – how I wish I were there. Bruce had to go with HE to Broadcasting House this evening, as he was talking just after the Prime Minister. I listened to it from his room, and when they played 'Pomp and Circumstance' I could have howled. The whole thing has been such a ghastly waste of life. The attitude 'Why not be glad now it's all over' – when so much has happened and so many have paid the price – won't help anybody, but it sobers one up and makes one think. But I do thank God it is over and that Brucie has recovered so much, and do realise – and am thankful – that we are two of the lucky ones. We have heard that Brucie's father has at last come home after five long years as a POW,

> which is wonderful. After he had a stroke, some months ago, the Germans were going to repatriate him – but he refused, saying that he came in with the 51st and that he would go out with them. He must be a wonderful man.[12]

* * *

But the war was not over – not by a long chalk – although for most of our subjects the end of the war in Europe left them expecting to be sent to the Far East. Not to Burma, since that campaign was all but won, but to Malaya and Singapore and Hong Kong. Hirst was in Pegu when he heard the news of the end of the European war:

> It was amazing how little impression it made on us; we were more interested in our own little war, and the fact that we got a beer issue, the first grog I had since February.[13]

Slim had defeated the Japanese in Burma decisively. With the fall of Rangoon, the Japanese had been pushed out of central Burma eastwards across the Sittang River. There, in February 1942, the battle of the Sittang Bridge had been the decisive defeat which had lost the British the country. The British commander had been forced to blow the main bridge across the Sittang, leaving most of 17th Indian Infantry Division trapped on the east bank, with 600 yards of water between them and escape. In 1945 the Sittang was to prove an equal obstacle to larger numbers of Japanese as they retreated eastwards – and 17th Indian Infantry Division was there to take its revenge. The speed of Fourteenth Army's advance had left 20,000 Japanese troops trapped in the Pegu Yomas hills between the Irrawaddy and Sittang Rivers. Although the Allies now had to consolidate their gains and eliminate these Japanese troops, and the monsoon meant that further advances were problematic, their eastern flank was relatively secure on the Sittang River and the hills to its east.

> Before we left, tank patrols were sent to the Sittang River to cut off Japs trying to cross over and escape into Siam (Thailand). This was part of a bigger operation to destroy the Japanese forces which had been cut off in the Pegu Yomas mountains. All along the road which we had followed, posts had been set up to kill them as they tried to cross.[14]

What followed was, essentially, a massacre, as the emaciated and disorganized Japanese tried to cross the main north-south road held by Fourteenth Army. No one will ever know how many died.

XXXII

'It was not a happy time, but I survived. A lot did not'

Worldwide, VE to VJ, 1945

For most of our subjects, the period between VE and VJ days was one of waiting, wondering whether they would be called upon again to go into action or – in many cases – whether they would ever see action at all. It was a time for reflection, for beginning to plan an adult life which had been postponed by years of war, and it was marked by a surge in letter-writing.

* * *

In Palestine, Elliott-Binns had received notice of when he was likely to be demobbed: 1947.

Elliott-Binns.

> Things are very different from the time when I last wrote. If my memory serves me correctly – those days seem about ninety years ago – either the term would have just started or just not on VE Day. I am sorry; I should have said 'half'. Anyway I suppose nobody did any work for several days, and celebrated in a very noisy manner. It is very pleasant to think that all danger is over for England and I am very glad that Winchester has been almost untouched – that is, presuming you have not had any damage since last I heard. Cambridge and Winchester will be at least two links with the past which will be almost unaltered.
>
> I would be glad if you would write to me fairly soon and tell me any news, particularly bad news as I suppose nothing so good as that can have happened without some sacrifice.
>
> About myself there is little to say. I spent the last few months of the war sitting on my behind doing nothing in Palestine, where I still am. It has been very irritating just at the time when fighting would have been almost pleasant. I have done a lot of fairly hard training and a bit of sight-seeing. I had a very pleasant leave in Alexandria just after arriving and I am afraid I was more concerned with the flesh-pots than Classical or Egyptian history. I have not been able to get to Jerusalem yet, but I have seen a lot of Galilee, been over Nazareth, seen the Sea of Galilee and the Jordan. I have dropped in on Syria and seen Damascus and Baalbek. A lot of these places you visited with my father, didn't you? Tomorrow I leave for Cairo and a course. I reckon that with North Africa and Italy I have got to know the Mediterranean quite well.

All the same I am very bored. Everybody seems to be just waiting to get out and I have the shocking age group of 47, almost the highest in the Battery. So that means either twiddling my thumbs for a couple of years or volunteering to go out East, as in a month's time my service abroad will stop me being sent. The immediate future looks rather bleak.

My spider seems to be running out.[1]

* * *

In the Far East, Hirst and 7th Cavalry left Burma in June and began to prepare for Operation Zipper, the amphibious landings planned to re-take Malaya.

Hirst.

We embarked for Madras on June 9th and had a short but rather rough voyage. I was now in charge of HQ Squadron vehicles, and I cured my fitters of sea-sickness by pouring their illegal palm toddy over the side. They were mostly Sikhs; very good bush mechanics, but they liked their grog, like Australians. From Madras we went by train to Ahmednagar, where we were to convert to Sherman tanks in preparation for the invasion of Malaya. We attended courses at the AFV School (where I had studied before), but lived with the Regiment, which was only a few miles away. I found it pretty boring, especially having to learn the workings of the internal combustion engine from scratch for the seventh time! The Regiment was in 'bashas', comfortable wooden huts with roofs thatched with brushwood.

7th Cavalry had three squadrons, plus HQ Squadron, in which I served as Technical Officer and Troop Leader of the only armoured vehicles in the Squadron, which also served as command vehicles for the CO. The men all came from the Punjab province of north-west India, but each squadron consisted of men from a different religion, with HQ containing all three.

'A' Squadron consisted of Jats, who were Hindus; fairly stolid and reliable, rather than brilliant. They had their heads shaven, with one lock left so that they could be pulled up to heaven.

'B' Squadron contained Punjabi Musselmans ('PMs'), Mahomedans who were rather volatile. Traditionally they wore their hair in long, rather greasy, locks, though the more modern ones had conventional haircuts.

'C' was the Sikh Squadron, though it contained a few Rajputs, as Sikhs were in short supply by this stage of the war ... The Sikhs were clever and inclined to be 'bush lawyers'. They never cut their hair, but wore it in a bun under their turban, while the other religions wore the Armoured Corps beret. (Sikh dandies wore two hairnets at night, one for their beard and one for their hair). They were forbidden to smoke, but liked their grog. They had to wear the five Ks: *kris* (their hair), *kanghi* (the comb they wore in it), *kirpan* (the sword, usually a miniature stuck in the hair), *kals* (iron bangles on their wrists), and *kacha* (the underpants which they always wore, even when bathing).

Each religion had their own taboos about food: the Hindus ate no beef, and the higher-caste ones were vegetarian; the PMs ate no pork; and the Sikhs ate no beef, though they could eat mutton. So each Squadron had its own *langar* (cookhouse), and if we were away from the main Regiment, poor old HQ had to have three! The mixture of religions in the same unit was the result of the Indian Mutiny, a case of divide and rule. We never had any inter-religious trouble, but had to be very careful to be even-handed in everything: promotion, leave, amenities. They had a much stronger attachment to their religions than any British or, I suspect, Australian soldier.[2]

* * *

Next to write to Robertson was Herbert, in June, from Calcutta, where he was based in an office in Fort William:[3]

Herbert.

I fear I have neglected my letter-writing rather, as I see I have not written to you since March, which is really very remiss … Very little has happened in that time. I had a very pleasant voyage over, and was quite sorry when we arrived! Our draft was at first quartered in a Transit Camp at Kalyan, near Bombay. Like most transit camps it was rather a depressing spot. Lots of red dust, isolated, and with very little to do. Two redeeming points about the place; it had two cinemas, and you could get into Bombay for the day periodically, so that I saw round Bombay and spent some happy times in the Cricket Club there, swimming.

After a short time there we moved up to Mhow, in Central India, [on April 13th 1945] and stayed there awaiting posting. This was a much more reasonable place, being a peace-time station, with decent buildings and so on. I was there about six weeks before being posted, and got rather bored, having nothing to do.

One of the nothings with which Herbert bored himself was learning Urdu every afternoon. His incarceration at Mhow ended on May 18th, when he set out for Calcutta:

I was posted in the end across India to a job as second-in-command of a Signal Company of Eastern Command Signals.

Herbert's diary records that his new unit as from Wednesday May 23rd was 2 Company, Eastern Command Signals – but not for long: his posting to 303 Lines of Communication in Calcutta's Fort William came into effect on Wednesday 30th.

I was sent to be tried as GIII (Lines) on a CSO's Staff, to replace a fellow going on two months' English leave…. We have quite a nice little mess there in the Old Fort of this place. The office and Mess are next to each other, and are equipped with all 'mod. cons'. In the Mess there is the CSO (a full Colonel), a GII, who is going on leave soon, a GIII (Admin), and a GIII (Lines), and that is all. They are all nice chaps, and I think life should be quite enjoyable. It is very hot here at present, and the humidity is very high, so that one sweats a lot; otherwise, life is tolerable!

I haven't run into the Viceroy or any other OWs yet, but am on the look out!

He began to get to grips with his new job, visiting sub-units such as Fault Control, but on the Sunday he began to feel unwell, and on Tuesday 5th June reported sick to 21 British General Hospital:

> After a week I got jaundice and am now in hospital, having been here a fortnight! However I am getting better, and hope to be out soon, and then, after fourteen days 'sick leave', I return to the CSO's Staff, from which I gather that my brief trial was satisfactory!
>
> Well I think that concludes my news. You at Winchester will be preparing for Eton Match, I suppose, and perhaps beginning to do some work after the distracting influences of V-E day, the Viceroy's lecture, and Ascension Day in close sequence!

On discharge from hospital on June 26th, Herbert was sent to the Army's rest camp at Lebong, close to Darjeeling. He arrived on the 28th, and apart from catching glimpses of the Himalaya when the rain cleared, spent most of his time doing physical exercise and playing volleyball until July 18th, when he set off back to Fort William.

* * *

In Winchester, Robertson not only received letters from his former pupils, but also welcomed visits from those who were back from their wars, as he told Walker's father early in July:[4]

> My dear Norman,
> I too was sorry to miss you. I saw little cricket and was nearly all the time concentrating on our special guests, several POWs and their people, and two poor one-legged boys Peter'll know: David Middleditch and John Boyd. This is mainly to send my love to Peter when you next write. I've had to knock off letters to such as him lately.

* * *

The Allies warned Japan on July 26th – by way of the Potsdam Proclamation Defining Terms for Japanese Surrender – that she faced 'prompt and utter destruction' if she did not surrender immediately. If she did surrender, the declaration went on, 'we do not intend that the Japanese shall be enslaved as a race or destroyed as a nation, but stern justice shall be meted out to all war criminals, including those who have visited cruelties upon our prisoners.' The surrender was to be unconditional, its terms not negotiable: 'We will not deviate from them. There are no alternatives. We shall brook no delay.'

On August 6th, an American B-29 Superfortress dropped the first atomic weapon to be used in anger, over the city of Hiroshima.

* * *

Fortune wrote to Robertson only two days later, with no mention of the Hiroshima bombing – perhaps because his mind was on other things:[5]

Fortune.

Thank you so much for your letter with all the news of the school and (more important) of yourselves. The flow of Wykehamists through here seems to be as steady as usual. Guy Dodgson came to visit us one day on his way to become 'airborne' [joining 12 Parachute Squadron, Royal Engineers] and I heard news of Roger Rigby at the same place.

A Lieutenant-Colonel Sparrow – a Coldstreamer, and College about 1925 I think – came to stay here. Rather a 'jig', as Robin Ridgway put it. He was out here on some welfare job and was bold enough to take off his badges of rank and travel out on the troop-deck in order to get a first-hand knowledge of conditions. I gather it was revealing.

Robin is a constant clearing house of all old Wykehamists who come through here, and they seem to treat him as a sort of agency.

We have just finished the Simla fiasco which, although not a success, was not a complete failure. HE had the opportunity of meeting with all the (so-called) leaders, which he would otherwise not have done – and having tried, he has certainly revealed that the cause of deadlock is not with the British. I wish you could have seen the bunch of senile delegates who between them claimed to be the heads of political India. Some were so old they could scarcely walk, and some were so doddering they couldn't talk audibly. And this was the new India, crying out to be released from bondage and with nothing but destructive criticism in their knapsacks and nothing constructive to offer at all. Still, it gave HE a chance of meeting face to face his critics, be they many, and of adding that personal touch, which in so many cases changed that attitude of criticism so often adopted automatically by Indians. This is a 'funny' country.

What do you think of the result of the elections? Rather a devastating majority. Still, one must pity any Government that has the misfortune to be given the task of running the country in postwar years!

I am so glad you saw my father. He writes quite cheerfully, but is obviously disappointed that he can't do more. Now that he has got up to Scotland he seems to be ten times more at ease. I think that all that dashing about in the South was very bad for him and for my mother who, God bless her, tries hard enough to assist him in all things.

Yes, Bobber I have got engaged! Many people had their gravest suspicions at first (my age, etc.) but I have found such a 'topper' that I am sure I am right! I will take your advice and, as you say, hold on to her, and I know I shall never regret it. She comes from good Scottish blood, and is intelligent, attractive, and has common sense, which is lacking in most lassies these days!

I hope Sheila is well. She and you were the two kindest people one could hope for to guide one into the world of today – (or should I say yesterday) and it is significant that all of us who call ourselves 'old Hopperites' look upon our days at Sunnyside as the happiest of our life. Thank you for all you did for us. It bears fruit now.

The following day, August 9th, the Allies used a second atomic weapon over Nagasaki, and the Soviet Union declared war on Japan. With, as they believed, national extinction staring them in the face, the Japanese government told the Allies on August 10th that they would surrender as soon as they were able, on the stated terms.

* * *

Hill.

Hill had travelled to Australia to join the British Pacific Fleet (BPF) as it readied itself for the final attack on Japan. By the end of the war, the BPF comprised over two hundred surface vessels and submarines. There were four battleships, eleven cruisers, thirty-five destroyers, fourteen frigates, forty-four other warships, thirty-one submarines, and fifty-four large support ships; 750 aircraft operated from six fleet aircraft carriers, four light carriers, and nine escort carriers, and were cared for aboard two dedicated maintenance carriers. The fleet carriers proved much more resilient than their American equivalents, and one USN officer commented that whilst a *kamikaze* hit on a US carrier would put it out of action for six months, the same hit on a British carrier just required a large sweeping detail.

But in other respects the BPF was at a disadvantage; because the Royal Navy had always planned to operate within reach of shore bases, its ships had smaller stores and tanks for fuel than American ones, and it soon became apparent that British resources in shipping would be hard-pressed to provide the number of supply vessels required for the Fleet Train to make the BPF self-sufficient, as the British had promised. This had delayed the deployment of the BPF to Australia until February 1945. American commanders did not want the British to take any credit for the defeat of Japan, and so sidelined the BPF as much as they could – though those lower down the chain of command had a much more sympathetic view, telling the Fleet Train's commander that they would give him anything he wanted as long as Fleet Admiral King, the American Chief of Naval Operations, did not find out.

An integral part of the BPF's Fleet Train was a group of four *Beachy Head* class maintenance ships, which had been ordered from a Canadian shipyard in the spring of 1944. One of them was HMS *Flamborough Head,* and one of its officers was Hill.

HMS Flamborough Head. *After the war she served in the Royal Canadian Navy, eventually being sunk as an artificial reef in the 1990s.* (IWM A30467)

On August 14th he wrote a long letter to Robertson from the BPF's forward base at Manus in the Admiralty Islands (Papua New Guinea):[6]

> I have now joined my ship and am getting down to a practical job, which is good after a long time of waiting. I enjoyed that time very much all the same. I think I was on board the liner coming over when I last wrote.
>
> We arrived at Sydney in the middle of June, and although I had no official leave, I had plenty of time to explore the city, while waiting for my ship. I had a magnificent time there, and will always remember it. Sydney itself is just another large city, dominated of course by the Bridge, which certainly lives up to its reputation. It is absolutely vast. The harbour is extraordinarily beautiful. Large ships can anchor close into the shore, and it is a strange sight to see enormous aircraft carriers etc. dwarfed by the steep sides of the harbour, in many places built over.
>
> I was sent to Brisbane after leaving Sydney, where they were able to tell me when and where I was to join this ship. Through the Australian Comforts Fund, I was put in touch with some people who had volunteered to put up service people on leave, and went to their farm for the inside of a week. They were amazingly kind, and although we were five miles from the nearest town, Roma, I had a wonderful time. Roma is a grape and orange-growing town, apart from general farming, and is famous for its wines. It is 350 miles west of Brisbane (no distance for that part of the world). The population is very scattered and the roads are just tracks. The farm I was on covered 2,000 acres – and is considered small. The people are all friendly and I enjoyed myself thoroughly.
>
> We are now at a very hot but censored place. I flew up here, which was a great experience (only twice before, and a long time ago). The tropics are perfectly bearable on board ship because there is nearly always a breeze and there are plenty of fans, etc. Tropical deluges refresh everything quite often. The jungle ashore is impenetrable. I walked along a road through it one day. The thickness of the undergrowth and the profusion of trees and creepers is almost unbelievable. There are the most wonderful blue butterflies, bigger than anything you ever see in England. We bathe a lot. There do not seem to be any sharks about. I have seen quite a bit of coral, which is extraordinarily interesting.
>
> I have come to the right ship. The Captain (Commander John Frederick Denman RN)[7] is an Old Wykehamist. He says he remembers being in your Div. just before the last war, and asks to be remembered to you. We are comfortable on board. This is a new ship with every modern convenience, an 'Escort Maintenance Ship'. This should give you some idea of our job.
>
> What do you think of the Atomic Bomb? The prospect of its use in the future seems appalling. It is grand to think that the war is nearly over, though we had great celebrations on Friday night when the Jap surrender offer was announced. The war is not yet actually over, though.
>
> The other officers are all friendly and we get on extremely well. The only thing is that they are nearly all pretty old. I am the youngest, easily.
>
> I am sorry to have rambled on so ungrammatically for so long about myself. I hope I have not bored you.

* * *

On August 15th (14th in the United States), the Japanese Emperor announced his country's surrender over the wireless, though the actual document of surrender was not signed until September 2nd. For the British, August 15th remains VJ Day. Hirst remembered it well, especially since Operations Zipper and Downfall would not be going ahead, and so 7th Cavalry would be going to Japan not as attackers but as occupiers:

> We celebrated V-J Day with much more enthusiasm than V-E Day, it being our lives that were on the line. This also caused a change in plan. 7th Cavalry had been selected to represent the Indian Armoured Corps in the occupation of Japan, and thoroughly deserved it for their record in Burma, especially in the siege of Imphal. We now had to start a new course on Daimler armoured cars. They were chosen because none of the roads in the area to which we were going in Japan were wide enough to take a tank; also they were British, not American, like the Shermans. Incidentally, when we got to Japan, we found that there were only ten miles of road that would take the armoured cars.[8]

* * *

Rigby only heard about the Japanese surrender by accident – his letter to Robertson on August 18th quite appropriately mentions the matter only *en passant*:[9]

Rigby.

> Having spent most of the spring in Peshawar and the neighbouring part of the North West Frontier Province, we moved to a very different part of India, where there is unvarying jungle. The change on the whole was a pleasant one; camp life and rough rations, a reasonably cool climate, and a complete absence of unnecessary paper-work were all welcome changes. But now that the war is over jungle training will presumably cease and we shall either revert to the Frontier or be used for internal security purposes in some recaptured territory. Whatever it is, it will not affect me for very much longer, as I have now completed a tour of 3¼ years overseas and am eligible for repatriation to the UK.
>
> At the moment I am enjoying twenty-eight days' leave. With two others I am trekking in the part of Kashmir which borders the Gilgit Agency on the south and Ladakh on the west. We have been out for a week now. Today, owing to continuous heavy rain, we are staying in camp in the valley of Gurais. Our tents are pitched on the bank of the Kishanganga river, which is a very fast-flowing stream of icy snow-water, having its origin in the glaciers that come down from the Nanga Panbhat range, which is only some thirty miles as the crow flies from here. All around the mountains tower up for six thousand feet or more, and their gullies are still full of snow, even as late in the year as this. To get here we had to cross a twelve thousand foot pass, where we had some very long views of the higher mountains to the north and across the vale of Kashmir to the Pir Paiyal range in the south. Cloud at this time of the year tends to spoil some of the best views, but this is the best time to take leave as the plains are unpleasantly hot and sticky just now and malarial incidence is high.
>
> Unfortunately I forgot to bring any water-colours. I managed some quite interesting pictures on a similar trip last year. Flowers are magnificent just now, and the walnuts

and apples just ripe. We have passed several other camps, mostly of fishermen. All the streams are full of snow trout, and the huge ones hold *mahseer* (which corresponds to the salmon). We have two cameras between us and sufficient films; I should be able to bring home some really good snaps.

This sort of holiday is much more fun than the usual small life of the average Indian hill station, and of course makes one tremendously fit and sunburnt and gives one a prodigious appetite and about nine hours sleep a night …

I hope to stop in Delhi for a day or two and meet my brother, on the way back to RHQ. He is being demobilised at the end of the year and proposes to marry shortly after returning home. I hope I manage to be at the wedding.

All this is about myself up till now. It's rather difficult to think of anything outside the vicinity of these hills. We only heard of the Japanese capitulation from two other walkers who passed us a day or so back, so our victory holidays were over before we could celebrate. I should like to know how it will affect things at home. I imagine rationing will continue for at least eighteen months on the present scale.

I have met or heard of singularly few OWs. I saw Robin Ridgway in Peshawar several months ago when he came there with the 'Auk', but he was too taken up with brass hats for me to get a word in.

* * *

Dan Somerville – by now a Captain in Burma – commented in his memoirs on what the cessation of hostilities meant to him:

'Dan' Somerville.

I didn't have a dangerous war; the only time when I might have attacked was when I arrived in Rangoon in Burma. The Japanese were on the high ground beyond the vast great river to the east of us, and we were due to assault, but the atom bomb put paid to that. I'm afraid that I always regarded the atom bomb as having saved my life.

I went to be rail transport officer in Toungoo in Central Burma before I was demobilised over a year later.

From Toungoo, Somerville wrote to Robertson early in September, signing himself 'Charlie':

As you can see, now that the war is over, I and a good many others have been put on administrative jobs. It's a good thing really, because here I am actually of some use, while there will be no further use for guns, I should imagine. I don't, however, think I got the job for my organizing ability, but simply because I was the latest-joined officer and therefore the easiest missed.

As you say, it's been a dullish war for me. There was nothing much happening, and the only Battery we had in action spent most of its time and did most of its shooting on pie-dogs with a .303. We had thought there would be a new push, but of course it came to nothing.

The people here are a pleasant lot; very courteous and clean – a great change from India. They seem glad to see British rule restored, and do us a number of small kindnesses quite unsolicited. There have been a few dacoities [incidents of brigandry], and I think these will increase. About one man in twelve has got a firearm of some sort, Jap or British, and I foresee trouble. The Burma National Army has got most of them. The local Magistrate (late Subedar Major, Burma Rifles), with whom I talked for some time, thinks that all arms will be handed in peacefully, but I doubt it. The Magistrate is an amazing old fellow, rather short and quite enormous round the middle. His English is peculiar, and a bit difficult to follow, but as he talks all the time this doesn't matter much. His quotations, verbatim, in his peculiar accent, of the rockets he received from officers of the Burma Rifles, are worth hearing.

The sun is coming out a bit more now, and it is getting hot and steamy. The monsoon should be over in about a month and then we should get a month of frightful damp

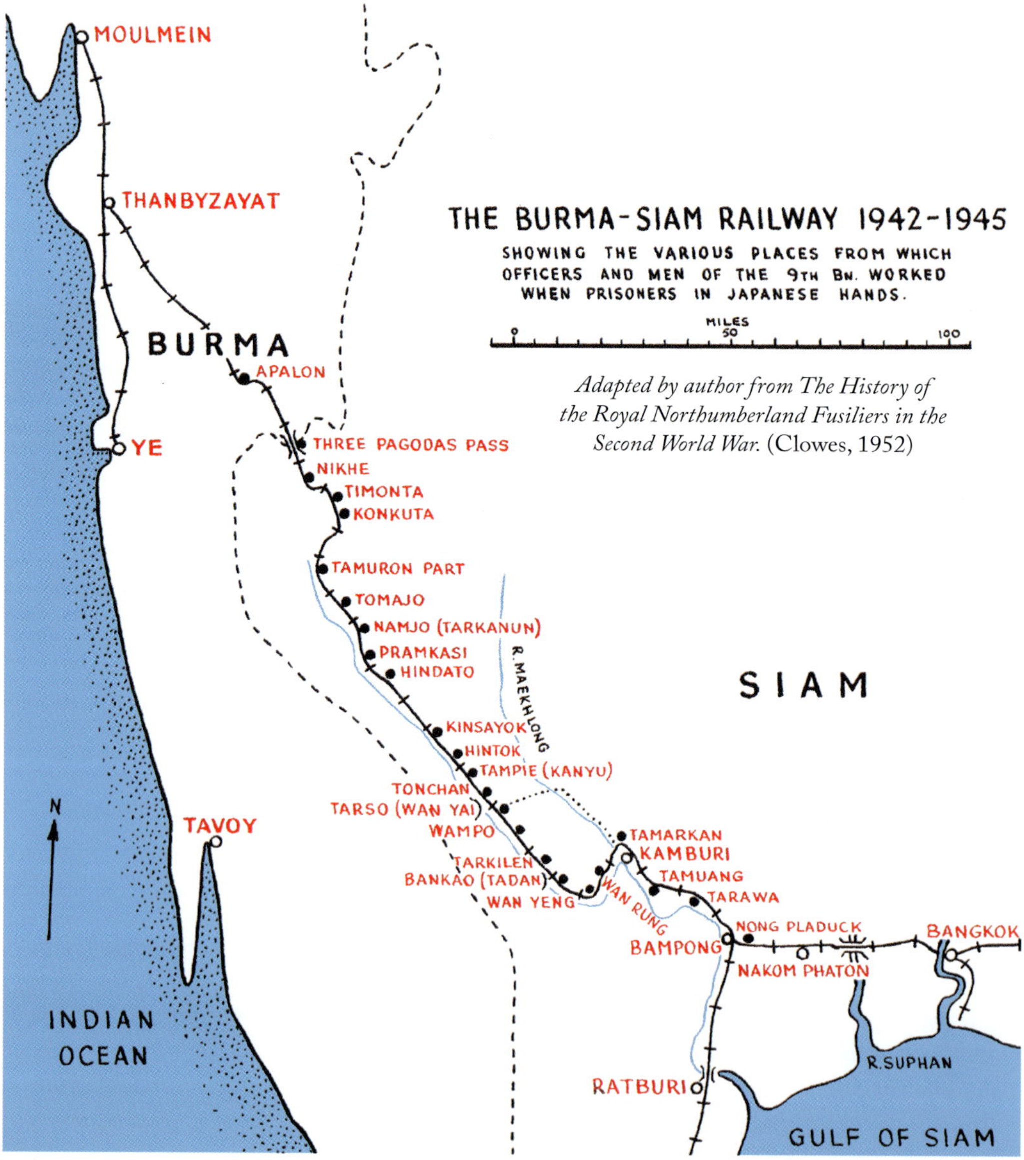

Adapted by author from The History of the Royal Northumberland Fusiliers in the Second World War. (Clowes, 1952)

heat, followed by some decent weather, for a change. This monsoon is very over-rated, but you do get a lot of water coming down in a very short time, with fine intervals.

We have some Indian Other Ranks next door who are in the middle of Ramazan or something and so deprived of grub and booze; they are trying to keep their spirits up by singing the same interminable phrase over and over again. The thing is unending and goes round and round like a rat in a cage. They have now added as a final touch a bamboo flute as accompaniment. If they go on I shall have to get up and shriek at them.

* * *

Rickman.

There was, of course, one of our subjects to whom Japan's surrender was of more than academic interest. Rickman had been in Japanese captivity since February 1942, and as the war had turned against Japan it had become clear that the Japanese were preparing to murder all their prisoners. In January 1945 the biggest remaining body of 9RNF – some seventeen officers and 130 other ranks – had been at Tamuang, but the Japanese had decided to separate all officer prisoners from the rest, and most officers were transferred to Kanburi. Conditions had hardly been pleasant before, but the Japanese (and their Korean minions who made up most of the guard force) knew that they were losing the war and took it out on their captives. There were more beatings, and a crackdown on anything which might help with a rising of the prisoners in concert with the Thais; even walking-sticks and pencils were banned.

For three and a half long years we lived on this knife-edge, interspersed with the frequent beatings and punishments dished out by our Japanese and Korean guards on the slightest pretext and often on fabricated and trumped-up charges. If no excuse arose, they simply invented one. It was little wonder that men's souls were stretched to breaking point. Their companions in misery were 'utter despair', 'infernal boredom', and a 'solitary loneliness'. In spite of all this, discipline held and morale did not crack. When things got extra tough, that extraordinary sense of humour and of the ridiculous won the day for the British and Australians (not so for the Dutch).[10]

Rickman and his comrades did not hear about the defeat of Germany until June at the earliest, and there were only rumours of how badly things were going for the Japanese in Burma.

We always held strongly to the belief that eventual victory would be ours. This belief was based on the fact that we had occasional access to news from an illicitly-operated radio, run very bravely by two of our colleagues. Had they been discovered, they would have been shot (as were others).[11]

But their joy at the news was tempered by the fear that the Japanese would kill them all if the Allies attacked:

> The Japs told us that if our own troops ever over-ran the camp and attempted to rescue us, they (the Japs) would shoot the lot of us – and we knew they would have done so.[12]

The Allies had set up groups of Special Forces who were to parachute in and help defend the prisoners if need be. For the final months of the war, teams from Force 136 of SOE were operating with the Thai underground movement – which had heroically provided money and medicines for the prisoners at many camps – to assist the prisoners in any way they could. The Thai Army, which had smarted at its humiliating docility under what was effectively Japanese occupation, also became increasingly active in assisting the prisoners.

The news of the Japanese surrender came mostly from secret radio sets operated in the camps, though a group of 9RNF officers at Nakom Nayok found out from the Japanese camp commandant. As Rickman told his granddaughter,

> We were, in fact, released thanks to the Americans dropping the atomic bombs on Japan. Had it not been for those bombs, I might well not have survived. If I had not survived, then neither your mother nor your sisters or you would ever have been born. So there was some good arising from 'the bomb'.

Most camps knew by August 17th, and the transformation in their lives was immediate. Allied flags were hoisted and national anthems sung. A central HQ for the prisoners was established in Bangkok, and the first prisoners were flown out on September 1st. Rickman was one of the last of his Battalion to be evacuated, on September 4th.

A measure of the brutality of the conditions which he and his comrades had undergone can be gained from the statistic that of the 830 personnel of 9RNF who had sailed from Liverpool on October 30th 1941, 151 had died in Japanese captivity – compared to the mere twenty-two who had died in action at Singapore.

On September 5th, from the comfort of a real bed in Rangoon, Rickman wrote to his old Headmaster, who passed it on to Robertson:[13]

> Dear Mr Leeson,
> Freed at last after 3½ years hellish existence! Flew from Bangkok yesterday to Mingaladon airfield by Douglas Dakota plane. Now reposing between white sheets in British General Hospital Rangoon, surrounded by delightful QAIMNS Nursing Sisters, and female RAMC Doctors – in our element! Smoking Players and eating European food for first time since Xmas '41 – wonderful! Terrific mental reaction has set in, not to be wondered at after being treated worse than cattle for so long. Hope to return by ship some time around November. Trust I shan't smell like an Asiatic, as I haven't had a hot bath for 3½ years!
>
> Win.Coll. has been ever in our thoughts; besides myself there are to my certain knowledge the following Old Woks alive and kicking:
>
> Captain Henry Lewin ('F') FMSVF.
> Captain Tomkinson ('D') Worcs.
> Captain David Nunneley ('K') Gordons.
> Sgt Sam Clayton ('I') FMSVF.

We've had several sort of Domum Dinners, consisting of Hot Rice Coffee, Rice Bread, and Rice Cakes. What I can't tell you about Rice, Bamboo, Jungle, Bugs, Lice, and other vermin is hardly worth knowing. I'll come along as soon as I'm back as there's so much Old Wok news I want to hear. Please remember me to your wife and family, The Bobber, and any who may remember me.

Yours ever

Gerry Rickman

Rickman might have been forgiven for nursing an abiding dislike of the Japanese, but in his memoirs he wrote:

After the war, one had to cease hating our captors. To continue hatred for them could only have harmed oneself – that would have been stupid. One cannot, however, forget the experience. It was not a happy time, but I survived. A lot did not.[14]

* * *

On October 23rd 1945 – the third anniversary of Hugh Rose's death at El Alamein – Fortune married Susan Mackie in the Cathedral in Delhi. The Wavells were there and signed the register; the wedding reception was held at the Viceroy's House. It comes as no surprise that Fortune wrote to tell Robertson all about it:[15]

How very nice to get your letter wishing Susan and myself so many nice things. How ironical, also, that you should end up by saying 'keep away from Java and Palestine and any of those places', because Java is just where I am!

We had a wonderful wedding. I wish you and Sheila could have been there. Two Black Watch pipers piped us in and out of the Church and then we adjourned to the Viceroy's House for an enormous reception – there seemed to be plenty of food and drink and everyone had a great time.

We honeymooned in Mussourie – very cold and peaceful – with a bungalow to ourselves, given to us by HH Maharaja of Rampur. Then we went to Bombay to stay with the Colvilles at Government House, where we also had a very peaceful rest by the sea.

I returned to Delhi only for a week, and then had to abandon poor Susan and come on here.

(Fortune family collection; edited by dansteele.net)

Life in Batavia isn't too bad. It is a lovely place with tree-lined avenues – and wide roads, but still has an atmosphere of drabness caused by Jap occupation. The Dutch are very trigger-conscious and the Indonesians have a standard of brutality unsurpassed by the Amazons! The situation is very tricky – as we are not trusted by either the Dutch or the Indonesians, although I might say we are respected by both. However, in spite of all lies issued by the extremely immoral press around here, and the fifth columnists such as Lady Louis Mountbatten, the British and Indian troops are in great heart and think nothing of killing fifty extremists before lunch!

The restraint shown by the troops is marvellous, and as long as they know that they are protecting women and children they don't mind whom they shoot. There is a lot of trouble coming from India, however, when crooked politicians rave about Indian soldiers fighting against the would-be free Indonesians – a 'would-be' free people fighting against a 'would-be' free people – and all that nonsense! And this is bound to have a certain effect on the troops in time. The press, needless to say, encourages it!

The country of Java itself is near starvation point – there is no labour and consequently no rice. Most of the white civilian population is fed off Army rations! The British are the only people who are attempting to do anything about it. We have taken over the railways and local transport and are trying to organise labour and put the people in a position where they can stave off starvation.

Underneath, of course, are the Japs – slowly and methodically stirring up the Indonesians, cultivating them, as they have done for the last three years, to hate and despise the Dutch. Openly the Japs are repentant and obeisant – but underneath they are the same double-crossing wretches they ever were!

And so it goes on – there are so many issues at stake and so many compromises to be arrived at. It calls for great astuteness and understanding, not only from those on the spot – but also from those behind us in England, India, and Malaya, who never cease to change their minds and their policies! Such are the tribulations of the soldier in a foreign country, raging with revolution, and in the first year of peace!

I hope we may be coming home some time next year and will bring my Susan to see you. She is at present remaining in Delhi until I see what is happening in this place! I am very lucky, as she really is an absolute winner!

Incidentally, my job here is Military Secretary to General Christison – and is very interesting. I was very lucky to get it.

* * *

We last saw Walker convalescing after his accidental shooting just before the end of the war in Europe. On November 11th 1945[16] he wrote to Robertson, explaining what life was like as a member of the occupation forces in Italy and Austria:

Walker.

I re-joined the Regiment at the beginning of August after a very monotonous four months of hospitals and convalescent homes, never feeling ill and nearly always feeling bored.

I found the Regiment in a small village on the banks of the Isonzo. Sagrado was about twenty miles from Trieste and a very delightful place. All the country north of the Po is so refreshing after the barren dry soil and hot dusty olive trees of the south. It was wonderful to see rivers and meadows again, and I felt better at once (I found jaundice pulled me down a bit.) We had glorious bathing and sailing, riding (we have some twenty to thirty horses), mountaineering, and fishing parties to Austria – and always the more artificial attractions of Trieste. Daniel [Awdry] was there for a short while before going to be ADC to General Whitfield of 56th Division. He had found a really delightful Italian girl of whom he grew very fond, but on the whole we don't think much of the Wops. This girl, however, was an exception, and we had some very pleasant evenings, taking them to the opera, etc. Apart from that it gave us ample opportunities to learn the language, which we did with some success. There was little or no work to be done; leave was priority one and sports priority two. I took over signals and sports from Dan when he went to be ADC– a good job, making one responsible to no one except the Colonel, who I like immensely. In addition I was officer in charge of Mess accounts, which took up more time than anything else.

As I say, there was ample opportunity to enjoy oneself, and one did that to the full. We had plenty of time to study the obstreperous 'Jugs', especially when for our last two months we moved into the hills overlooking Trieste, where all the inhabitants were Slav-speaking. Apart from their processions and flags, they would occasionally beat up one of the men returning late at night to barracks, and they were continually cutting our telephone lines. On the whole, a very unattractive people, though up in Austria where we are now they seem harmless compared with the Russians.

On the whole, though, we were not sorry when we had to move up to Austria. 56th Division were far better people to work with than the 46th, with whom we now are, but the cost of living in Trieste was very high and here it is practically nil. We are split up in to squadrons again, all dotted around Graz. I motored up from Trieste for a couple of days before the main party came, and I have never in my life seen such beautiful country. The autumn colours were just at their best – all the houses different shapes and styles, different colours – it was really perfectly heavenly. We have now been here about three weeks and today the first snow has begun to fall. I gather it will continue to fall for some time.

They have the winter sports well organized, and it should be great fun if only we stay here. Unfortunately, we are to move to Germany quite soon, which I feel will not be nearly so pleasant. I hope we stay here: I have a wonderful billet with a glorious view of the hills and an old Austrian family to look after me. I took the son, an ex-regular of the Austrian army, and his Czech wife to a concert in Graz this week. They had not been to a concert for two years and I have seldom seen anyone quite so happy as they were to be taken to the concert in a car instead of catching a train at 4 o'clock in the morning. The old mother in her long dress and embroidered bodice (they always wear their national dress) kept on saying '*Das ist fein, das ist wunderbar, Herr Oberleutnant*'!!

All is not quite so rosy and not all the inhabitants so friendly. Coming here after the Russians is a mixed blessing. One could write pages about the Russians, but I expect you hear enough. One certainly feels ashamed to be called their allies, at any rate. Our fore-runners in this particular village, not a very good regiment, apparently did all the wrong things. They went about with all the wives of leading Nazis who were in gaol, and took no steps against the underground current of Nazism which still remains in the country places. Consequently we have been doing all the work they have undone, and the local gaol has been quite full recently of local bad-hats, and ex-SS men hiding in the hills! Still, as I say it is a good life, and I hope I am getting some benefit from it all.

I am so looking forward to seeing Win.Coll. again and talking over the future. It looks so bad – though I refuse to agree with the pig-headed General who commands this Division that there is bound to be another war. Why did we fight this one? However bad it looks, I regard it as tragic to regard another one as inevitable.[17]

* * *

Metcalfe was also looking to the future, and asked Robertson for a favour from his new station in Risalpur:

Metcalfe.

> We were pushed off the Malaya show – most annoying, as having spent a whole month in Bombay attending a conference to plan the show, and having learned practically everything that was possible to know about the place from maps and intelligence summaries, I very much wanted to see how it compared in actual fact. However, when the Japs collapsed, they not unnaturally decided that heavy tanks were rather expensive toys to use in a simple occupation force, so they put railway engines on instead.
>
> We then sat around outside Bombay for a month not hearing a word about our future, and then suddenly the most frightful excitement started on a Saturday evening, when a Colonel from GHQ suddenly arrived and began demanding lists of deficiencies. The next morning, the doors of the Ordnance Depot swung open to us and the most incredible collection of useful and useless gear came tumbling out. In reply to discreet questions as to what it was all about, we got,
>
> 'Well we don't *really* know, but it's frightfully hush-hush, and we *think* you are sailing for Tokyo at the end of the week!'
>
> This continued throughout Sunday, until at mid-day on Monday we suddenly got a wire telling us to come up here. All the Ordnance Depot shut immediately! Units in North-West Army are on peace-time scales, and aren't allowed anything. However, we did not mind; we had already drawn everything we wanted and quite a few other things besides, and it had all been done in such a hurry that no-one in the Ordnance Depot knew what we had got. So now, by the kindness of some high-up in GHQ who mis-read a telegram, we are the best-equipped unit on the frontier.
>
> We got up here about six weeks ago and have so far done little more than settle ourselves into peace-time bungalows – and very comfortable they are too – and do a few recces. We are spending a lot of time preparing for demobilisation and 'educating' the men for their return to civil life. The men don't help at all. One day one tells them of the advantages of release – the fifty-six days' release leave, the gratuities, etc., and they all rise in a body and demand immediate discharge; the next day one points out that civilian life won't be all that attractive in the immediate post-war period, and that they are drawing far more money now than they would be squatting in their villages, and they all want to stay.
>
> This letter is becoming much too long and I still have not got down to what I really wanted to say – my own release and resettlement. I have decided to have a shot at the Colonial Service, and have put down yours and Spencer Leeson's names on my application as House- and Head-master respectively. They seem to want to know what everybody I have ever met thinks of me, so you may hear from the Colonial Office sometime asking if I was a good boy at school. Would you please warn the Headmaster too, and, if they do write, be as merciful as possible? I apologise for this, but hope it won't be too much trouble.[18]

* * *

David Middleditch had been awarded a Mention in Dispatches, though he did not know about it until Robertson told him in December. By now he had returned to active service and was ADC to Lieutenant General Sir Brian Robertson, the Deputy Military Governor of Occupied Germany. Middleditch sat down and wrote to The Bobber on December 21st.

Middleditch.

> The somewhat ponderous address above will give you an idea of my whereabouts. The DMG is General Sir Brian Robertson, son of the Field Marshal of the last war and, I think, a very good man. I've had this job for rather over a month and have never regretted taking it altho' in a way it's rather marking time. However, one has a ringside seat for a good deal that goes on over here, and meets a lot of interesting people and lives in considerable comfort.
>
> My duties are mainly domestic, and I am becoming a very considerable housekeeper, though there are moments when I'd value Miss Robertson's advice! However, although I don't deal directly with matters of state very much, I hear them discussed a good deal, which is interesting.
>
> The leg continues to be a great success and stood up well to quite a long afternoon's shooting last weekend. I can also ride, run, and dance on it, so I'm almost as good as new again.
>
> Give my regards to Roger Rigby if he has not already been over. I've quite lost touch of him since he went to India and have no idea of his regiment, rank, or what he has done in the war. My mother tells me that John Boyd now has a job at the War Office and has been staying at our flat while looking for somewhere to live. We saw a lot of each other while on sick leave.
>
> I hope this reaches you in time to wish you both a very happy Christmas. I shan't get home for it myself but I anticipate quite a good one out here.[19]

Miss Bobber never gave Middleditch that advice, nor did she and the Bobber have a happy Christmas – ten days before Middleditch wrote this letter, Sheila Robertson had suffered a sudden heart attack and died, at the age of sixty-four, in the Winchester home which she shared with her brother.

XXXIII

'I hope I have done something of use'

The Bobber, 1945–1956

Sheila Robertson's memorial service was held in the Chapel of Winchester College on December 17th 1945. The Headmaster, Canon Spencer Leeson, officiated, and as many of Sheila's siblings as could make it were there: her unmarried sister Gerda and her brothers Ainslie, Malcolm, and Dennis attended – but Colin was in Africa. Their father had clearly spread his bets, since the four brothers had attended Winchester (Ainslie), Marlborough (Malcolm), Rugby (Colin), and Eton (Dennis). There were many present, but prominent among the list of the congregation were ten Hopperites – including Rickman, Rigby, and Pinney. The Bobber sent others – including the Mackrills – a copy of the report in the *Hampshire Chronicle.* Colonel and Mrs Sinclair attended as well – their sons Michael and John would doubtless have been there if they could.

* * *

The Hopperites of the 1938 photograph stayed connected for the rest of their rich, full lives. To tell their stories – the scientific genius of Horace Barlow, for example – would be a lifetime's work in itself. We can only skim the surface of the connections between them. Dodgson and Rickman, for example, were cousins, since their mothers Eveline and Muriel were daughters of Robert Fulton; the Sinclairs and Martyn had been similarly related. But some connections were forged after the war; Richardson's daughter Sarah writes as follows:

> David [Kemp] and my father first met my mother [Diana] when in Switzerland skiing. She had fallen and broken her ankle. David, who was an Olympic skier, gallantly carried her down the mountain on his back to the hospital, where my father visited her every day. David was Best Man at their wedding in August 1948, two days after my father had rowed in the Olympic Games, winning a Silver medal. David was also my godfather.[1]

Kemp was later Richardson's executor, whilst Charles Murray was the family solicitor.

> David Kemp and Charles Murray were both very good friends of my father's all his life, and continued to be supportive of our family after his death.[2]

Diana Richardson was the daughter of a Royal Naval officer – Captain Tufnell DSC – and her sister Patricia married Roger Rigby in 1957, making Richardson and Rigby brothers-in-law. Richardson's daughters were the bridesmaids.

Holtby and Mackrill, who had been at preparatory school and Hopper's together, remained friends after the war, as both were farming in the same area of Yorkshire. Mackrill became godfather to Holtby's eldest son, David, whilst Walker's daughter Nicola is godmother to Mackrill's granddaughter. Mackrill's daughter Henrietta writes:

> The Bobber certainly had a huge influence on all of them for a lifetime, and Dad often made mention of his time at Hopper's. I remember many of the 'Notions' included in our lives; although we were not 'sweaty Tollsters' (runners) we were very much 'sweaty Boglers' (bicycle riders!) … 'Dock the Giz' (turn out the light) was a frequent call in our house.[3]

* * *

The Bobber kept in touch with as many of his former charges as possible; he was unable to attend Mackrill's wedding in 1950, but did send a long letter, a book as a wedding present, and a photograph of his sister Sheila taken when she was thirteen. What sustained him in his loneliness was his crowning achievement, the *Wykehamist War Service Record and Roll of Honour.* Winchester had produced two publications in the aftermath of the First World War: a summary of the wartime careers of all boys and staff (the *Wykehamist War Service Roll*) and four memorial volumes containing obituaries and photographs of all those who had died (*Wykehamists Who Died in the War 1914–1918*).

Robertson was asked – along with Evelyn Rockley Wilson, another Winchester fixture – to compile a similar volume for the Second World War, building upon the obituaries which he had written for supplements to *The Wykehamist* during the conflict. In March 1954, Robertson sent a copy of the resulting volume – the *Wykehamist War Service Record and Roll of Honour* (1947) – to the headmaster-elect of Winchester, Mr Lee, and by a happy chance the copy has survived, together with Robertson's autograph letter, addressed from the Hampshire Club, enclosing the book, on March 20th:

D. Lee
Headmaster Elect
March 1954
With all good wishes from its main author & compiler with E.R.W.
M.R.

> Though it will (I hope!) be only one more thing for you to bring (back) to Winchester, I send you now this copy, the last spare one at my disposal, of the War Record, the compilation of which was my last big job for Winchester (and cost me my left eye!). Perhaps you would find time to read now just the introductions, and the notices towards the end of two of the best boys I ever had in the house, who were near-sons to my sister and myself (M. Sinclair and H. Woods).
>
> The whole thing might have been much better done, but dear old Rockley Wilson (whom you'll get to know) was dippy and difficult to work with (no telephone, and half a mile uphill to get to …) and in the end I did nine-tenths of the job.
>
> I think you may be glad to have it for reference later on …[4]

The job of doing justice to his boys must have been of huge importance to Robertson in the aftermath of Sheila's death and, as he explained in a typewritten letter to all his correspondents in November 1953, the numerous blows which fortune had delivered after that.[5]

> My only chance, I think, of sending some Christmas or New Year good wishes, or acknowledging others, is to write a circular letter, to which I may or may not add a few words, if we have not recently been in touch. To some of you, my main news will be stale. I left Culver Lodge in September, when John Manisty took over Fearon's ('D'), and I was lucky enough to get one big room here, warm and convenient, and looking over into the beautiful (new) Hampshire Regiment Memorial Garden, where I can take a stroll after meals! I stopped teaching in July 1946, six rather miserable months after Sheila's death: then for seven years Manisty and a very efficient housekeeper looked after me. My main job for most of that time was War Memorial work of two or three kinds, generously acknowledged in a letter from the Secretary in the last *Wykehamist* (No. 1002). That work cost me, I think, my left eye, which has now been blind for five years.
>
> I had built up a new home to retire to with my sister Gerda in a nice big flat near Lord's. From January 1950 I spent many weeks there, and on November 16th that year some twenty-five Hopperites in London rallied there and heard Dick Wood and Peter Walker sing 'Watchman' again. In October 1951 Gerda was killed on a Belisha crossing. We had to break up and get rid of the flat in a fortnight, and a fortnight later, after coping with hundreds of letters, I cracked and for the first time in my life was two or three weeks in bed, and my second eye was affected too. Neither my sight nor my memory is what it was and, having for forty years known almost every Wykehamist at least by sight, I minded more and more not knowing most of the School, and not recognising those I did as they passed and re-passed Culver Lodge. I have, however, had much kindness from Dons old and young, and much enjoy lunching up to various Houses from time to time, and being introduced to sons of those I knew, many of whom come and talk to me in New Field or elsewhere. But I cannot entertain them at the Club, though I have some older guests much more easily at lunch or tea, except on Sundays. So look me up here, if you have time!
>
> A few things you may like to know. I did not ask for such fame, but I am told that the Electric Light I asked for about 1926 on the tree outside War Cloister, when I had broken my shins several times in the dark on Chitty's seat, is still known to many of the School (in spite of six years war-darkness) as 'Bobber's Giz'. Secondly, when Havergal decided last year to have a second competition for House Choirs (Schuster Cup, which we won seven times in our twenty-two years, being kept for quartets), I was asked to give another Cup. I offered the nice silver Sports Cup, won four times by my Cadet Company at Pirbright in 1917–1918, and never by any other. It was given to me with my name on in 1919, when I took up from Winchester to stay in my old Mess the Bisley VIII, which won by one point. On the other side is now inscribed just 'In Mem. S.M.R. and Sunnyside' – both gone now! I also gave to Marcus and his Bridget the fine pair of silver napkin-rings presented to Sheila and me from the House in 1930 by outgoing (Dick Wood) and incoming (Fred Hollins) senior prefects. They are inscribed 'A notable decade', and as Marcus has completed the same I have asked him to add their initials and date, and pass them perhaps to his successor if he lives to

see one complete that period (or to his two boys, which I have not got!). Dick Wood much approved of this (I hope to attend his parents' golden wedding party in London on December 7th and I hope you will!).

I gave to Fellows' Library (with the family's approval) my most valuable book, a first edition of 'Gilbert White' given to me by the Ferguson family, and wrote on a spare sheet in it the record of their brother Alan ('G' 1914) and Maurice Savory ('I' 1913) and the other two Wykehamists who joined 'the Duke's' with me in 1914. I gave to Mob. Lib. Whymper's book about the first ascent of the Matterhorn, which he gave to my father, who helped (in 1865) to find, and buried, the bodies of those who fell. Budge Firth kindly accepted several things of interest for his 'Wiccamica' collection, John Dancy many of my classical books to take to HQ at Lancing, and most of the rest of my library went in armfuls to young dons who would carry them away, to Marlborough, or to 'Hopper's' for House Library, or individuals who had varying luck about what reached them. I have kept here a small nucleus of reference and local books, and a selection of 'old friends' among poets and novelists, and childhood books with which I could not bear to part.

Enough! But let me end with this. I shall not again write such a letter, nor, as I used to, try to thank for every Christmas card. But as long as I can see as well as I do now, I shall like to get news of you, and try to answer, at least by one of my famous illegible and overloaded postcards, anything in the way of a letter. I had six parties, three laid on for, and three by, me last (1952) November when I reached the Psalmist's limit. The future must be uncertain, but I feel I have had thirty-seven years of bonus life since the July 1st when the 'Somme' started, and I hope I have done something of use, as well as had much happiness and made many friends, since that.

Goodbye for now.
Yours ever,
Bobber.[6]

THE YORKSHIRE OBSERVER, TUESDAY, MARCH 27, 1956

Leaves £100 to "batman and friend"

A FRIENDSHIP developed in the trenches in the 1914-18 war between an officer and his batman was one which only death severed early this year.

That was not the final severing of the link, for the officer has left £100 in his £44,366 will "to my batman and friend."

The Batman, Mr. Wilson Turnbull—now an overlooker—of 19, Colenso Grive, Keighley, was left the money by Major Malcolm Robertson, formerly of Winchester College.

KNOWN TO MANY

Mr. Turnbull said last night that Major Robertson would be known to a number of 1914-18 war veterans in the Keighley and Bingley district for he was in command of 'D' Company of the Duke of Wellington's West Riding Regt. when it was raised early in the war.

"We kept in touch with one another after the war and attended re-unions, mostly held in Bradford. My wife and I visited him when he was a housemaster at Winchester and he stayed with us for a few days about four years ago," he said.

Mr. Turnbull said of the friendship: "I got used to his ways and he got used to depending on me, and we always got on well together."

Glossary

ABDACOM	American-British-Dutch-Australian Command.
ACV	Armoured Command Vehicle.
ADC	*Aide de Camp;* a junior officer acting as a dogsbody for a senior commander.
Adjutant	Junior officer assistant to a unit commander.
Army	A group of several corps & their supporting units.
Association XI	Winchester College soccer 1st XI.
ATS	Auxiliary Territorial Service; the female branch of the Territorial Army, formed on September 9th 1938.
Battalion	Infantry unit of some six hundred men, made up of four infantry ('rifle') companies with headquarters & support elements. It would be commanded by a Lieutenant Colonel.
Battle-group	Balanced force of infantry, armour, & supporting arms, formed from several separate units for a specific operation.
BEF	British Expeditionary Force.
Bisley VIII	Winchester College shooting team.
BLA	British Liberation Army.
BNAF	British North Africa Forces.
Brigade	An infantry brigade was usually made up of three infantry battalions. An armoured brigade would usually contain three tank battalions & one motorized infantry battalion. A brigade was commanded by a Brigadier. Note that 'Rifle Brigade' was the name of an infantry regiment and not, confusingly, that of a brigade.
CMF	Central Mediterranean Forces.
CO	Commanding Officer.
College XV or VI	Winchester College Football *(not* soccer) teams drawn exclusively from the Scholars in College.
Commoner XV or VI	Winchester College Football *(not* soccer) teams drawn from the Commoners' tribe of houses.
Company	Infantry unit of around a hundred men, usually commanded by a Major, & made up of three platoons. Companies were usually designated A-D.
Corps	An administrative body controlling several divisions & their supporting units.

CSM	Company Sergeant Major.
CSO	Chief Signals Officer.
cwt	Hundredweight (112lbs, or one-twentieth of a ton).
DFC	Distinguished Flying Cross.
Division	An infantry division would contain three infantry brigades, a reconnaissance battalion in armoured cars, several batteries of artillery, a unit of engineers, & other supporting arms, making it a balanced force. An armoured division would usually comprise two armoured brigades & one infantry brigade, with their supporting arms. The commander of such a formation would be a Major General.
DSO	Distinguished Service Order.
ENSA	Entertainments National Service Association.
FB	Fighter-Bomber.
Flight	RAF squadrons were usually divided into smaller sub-units called flights.
FMSVF	Federated Malay States Volunteer Force.
FOO	Forward Observation Officer; a spotter for the artillery working closely with a front-line unit.
GOC	General Officer Commanding.
GSO	General Staff Officer; officer assigned to assist in the running of a brigade or higher formation. GSO3 was a Captain's post; GSO2 a Major's post; and GSO1 a Lieutenant Colonel's post.
HAC	Honourable Artillery Company.
IAC	Indian Armoured Corps.
LDV	Local Defence Volunteers (the Home Guard).
Lords	Winchester College cricket 1st XI.
M-13	An Italian tank.
MC	Military Cross.
MEF	Mediterranean Expeditionary Force.
MM	Military Medal.
MT	Motorized Transport (i.e. lorries).
MTB	*(Army)* Motor Training Battalion, a training unit to teach motorized infantry their specialized role in support of tanks. *(Navy)* Motor Torpedo Boat, a small high-speed boat armed with guns & torpedoes for coastal patrolling.
NAAFI	Navy, Army, & Air Force Institutes.
NCO	Non-commissioned officer; soldier with some authority over his juniors, having been promoted from the ranks. The lowest NCO rank was Lance Corporal, the highest Sergeant Major.

OBE	Order of the British Empire.
OC	Officer Commanding.
OCTU	Officer Cadet Training Unit.
OP	Observation Post.
OR	Other Ranks; non-officer personnel.
OTC	Officer Training Corps.
OTH XV or VI	Winchester College Football *(not* soccer) teams drawn from the Old Tutors' Houses tribe.
OTU	Operational Training Unit; an RAF formation which trained aircrew to operate the types which they would fly on operations.
P14	The .303-inch Pattern 1914 Enfield rifle was a technically advanced British design, an alternative to the more famous Lee-Enfield. It was heavier, but more accurate & robust, though its 5-round magazine was too small for rapid fire, & it was largely relegated to training & Home Guard use in the Second World War
Panzer	A German tank; short for *Panzerkampfwagen.* These progressed from the *Panzer* III (standard in 1940-1941), *Panzer* IV (standard 1941-1945), *Panzer* V 'Panther', & *Panzer* VI 'Tiger' (both from 1943)
Platoon	Infantry unit of around thirty men, usually commanded by a Lieutenant or Second Lieutenant. Platoons were usually numbered 1-16.
PR	Photographic Reconnaissance.
Princes	Winchester College 1st rackets pair.
QAIMNS	Queen Alexandra's Imperial Military Nursing Service.
QMS	Quartermaster Sergeant.
RAC	Royal Armoured Corps (the umbrella for all armoured units, both RTR & the former cavalry).
RAF	Royal Air Force.
RAFVR	Royal Air Force Volunteer Reserve.
RAMC	Royal Army Medical Corps.
RB	The Rifle Brigade 2RB = 2nd Battalion, the Rifle Brigade 7RB = 7th Battalion, the Rifle Brigade 10RB = 10th Battalion, the Rifle Brigade
RE	Royal Engineers

Regiment	Infantry battalions of the British army were grouped into regiments of the same name, differing in the battalion number but sharing traditions and often a geographical affiliation; personnel would often move between battalions of the same regiment. Artillery regiments were composed usually of three batteries of guns, sub-divided into two troops (each of four guns). Thus a Field Regiment would have twenty-four 25-pounders. Cavalry regiments were the equivalent of an infantry battalion; the numbering of these regiments was consecutive but they were separate regiments, some formed by mergers of two antecedent regiments, & some regiments being part of the Indian Army, not the British. So, for example, 10th Hussars, 11th Hussars, 12th (Royal) Lancers, 13th/18th (Royal) Hussars, 14th/20th (King's) Hussars, 15th/19th Hussars, 16th/5th Lancers, 17th/21st Lancers, 18th Cavalry, 22nd Dragoons, 23rd Hussars.
RHA	Royal Horse Artillery; mobile artillery units atttached to British armoured formations. 3RHA = 3rd Regiment, Royal Horse Artillery. 11RHA = 11th Regiment, Royal Horse Artillery.
RMA	Royal Military Academy, Woolwich.
RMC	Royal Military College, Sandhurst.
RN	Royal Navy.
RNF	Royal Northumberland Fusiliers. 2RNF = 2nd Battalion, Royal Northumberland Fusiliers. 9RNF = 9th Battalion, Royal Northumberland Fusiliers.
RNVR	Royal Naval Volunteer Reserve (hostilities-only branch of Royal Navy).
RSM	Regimental Sergeant Major; the senior NCO in an infantry battalion or tank regiment, tasked with maintaining discipline & efficiency.
RTR	Royal Tank Regiment. 2RTR = 2nd Tanks = 2nd Battalion, Royal Tank Regiment. 4RTR = 4th Tanks = 4th Battalion, Royal Tank Regiment.
Sappers	Nickname of the Royal Engineers.
School IV or VIII	Winchester College 1st rowing teams.
Section	An infantry section consisted of eight or so men, & was commanded by a Corporal.
SMLE	The 'Short, Magazine, Lee-Enfield' .303-inch rifle, the standard British rifle of the First World War & early Second World War.

SPG	Self-propelled gun. Essentially turretless tanks fitted with a gun with limited elevation & traverse, they could be produced more cheaply & quickly than tanks with rotating turrets. The Germans produced them in large quantities when they went on to the defensive, for which SPGs were well suited.
Squadron	*(Army)* In an armoured battalion or regiment, a squadron was a unit of three troops, with some twelve tanks or armoured cars, & a headquarters detachment. It would be commanded by a Major. *(RAF)* A unit of some twelve aircraft, their aircrew, & ground staff to service & maintain them.
Subaltern	An army officer below the rank of Captain.
TD	Territorial Decoration.
TEWT	Tactical Exercise Without Troops.
Troop	An armoured troop usually consisted of four vehicles, commanded by a Lieutenant or Second Lieutenant.

Winchester College Houses:

Letter:	**Name:**	**Nickname:**
A	Chernocke	Furley's
B	Moberly's	Toye's
C	Du Boulay's	Cook's
D	Fearon's	Kenny's
E	Morshead's	Freddie's
F	Hawkins'	Chawker's
G	Sergeant's	Phil's
H	Bramston's	Trant's
I	Turner's	Hopper's
K	Kingsgate	Beloe's
X	College	Coll.

Army Ranks (in increasing order of seniority)

Other Ranks:	Private/ Gunner/ Sapper/ Rifleman / Trooper
	Lance-Corporal
	Corporal
	Sergeant
	Sergeant Major
Officers:	Second Lieutenant
	Lieutenant
	Captain

	Major
	Lieutenant Colonel
	Brigadier
	Major General
	Lieutenant General
	Field Marshal

RAF Aircrew Ranks (in increasing order of seniority)

NCOs:	Sergeant Pilot	Sgt
	Flight Sergeant	FS
	Warrant Officer	WO
Officers:	Pilot Officer	PO
	Flying Officer	FO
	Flight Lieutenant	Flt/Lt
	Squadron Leader	Sqn/Ldr
	Wing Commander	Wg/Cdr

Notes

Introduction

1. Elliott-Binns, M., *Finding Through War: Poems of Fifty Years Ago* (William Sessions, 1995).
2. *Somerville family collection:* Somerville, C., unpublished memoirs, typescript, undated.
3. Craig, N., *The Broken Plume: a Platoon Commander's Story 1940–1945* (IWM, 1982).
4. Born November 16th 1882, Robertson was the son of the Revd James Robertson, Head Master of Haileybury College from 1884 to 1890, & then Vicar of Whittlesford; his mother was Constance Elizabeth *(née* Wilson). He was a Scholar & later Senior Prefect at Marlborough, & then a Scholar of Oriel College, Oxford, from which he went straight into teaching at Winchester College after taking his Classics degree in 1905; the Winchester connection was that his older brother Ainslie John Robertson had joined Chernocke House ('A') in 1893. Between June & September 1906 Robertson was on leave, studying in Germany, after which he returned to take Middle Part II, to be a house tutor in 'A', & to take up a commission in the Officer Training Corps. A second leave of absence in 1913 & early 1914 saw him teach in two South African schools: Michaelhouse (Natal) & St Andrew's College (Grahamstown). He took over as the third House Don of Sunnyside/Hopper's/'I' in 1920 (the house had been founded in 1869); he would remain in post until 1943, & a Don until 1946. He was the editor of the *Wykehamist College War Service Record & Roll of Honour.* His death on February 14th 1956 merited a headline obituary in *The Wykehamist* (1030, March 13th 1956).
5. *The Wykehamist* (1030, March 13th 1956).
6. Somerville J.N., *Memories of my Life: The Memoirs of D-Day Veteran Brigadier Sir Nicholas Somerville CBE* (privately published, 2014).
7. David Ashton McIntyre Kemp ('I' 1935–1940), born October 14th 1921, was the only son of Sir Kenneth McIntyre Kemp & Margaret Caroline Clare, daughter of Colonel Ashton Street. As Somerville states, he was an Exhibitioner; he won awards for Latin Prose, Verse, & Speech, & was President of Boat Club.
8. Somerville J.N., *Memories of my Life: The Memoirs of D-Day Veteran Brigadier Sir Nicholas Somerville CBE* (privately published, 2014).
9. Whitelaw, W.S.I., *The Whitelaw Memoirs* (Aurum, 1989).
10. *Mackrill family collection:* postcard from MR to Graham Mackrill, dated March 14th 1938; addressed 'Sunnyside'.
11. **An Apology to Purists**

    For ease of reading, in quotations from primary material I have removed spelling errors & emended punctuation (I am a teacher, after all). I have also adopted the regrettable modern practice of giving abbreviations without full stops; thus RAF instead of R.A.F. In a still more arbitrary fashion, I have changed all times to the more military 24-hour clock system, & the format of dates to Month-Day-(Year). Please rest assured that the original documents remain pristine.

    Almost all the letters from our subjects to Robertson began 'Dear Bobber' or 'My Dear Bobber', & ended with best wishes to 'Miss Bobber', 'Miss Robertson' or, daringly, 'Sheila'. For reasons of space these have been omitted in transcripts, but the deep affection should be understood throughout.

I

1. *The Wykehamist* (534, October 1914).
2. Lieutenant Colonel Frederick Arthur Hayden DSO, OBE (College 1873–1879), born in 1861, was commissioned as a Lieutenant into the Duke of Wellington's (West Riding) Regiment in

1880. His DSO came in the Boer War in 1900, along with a mention in dispatches; as OC 9DWR 1914–1916, he added his OBE & three more 'mentions'.

3. Robertson was well known for the strength of his friendships, & Miller became a lifelong friend, Robertson standing godfather to Miller's elder son. To Robertson, friendship meant the offering of advice, whether or not such advice was sought. One former Warden stated that 'there were indeed few matters on which his counsel was not asked; there were none on which it was not given.' Nevertheless, his obituary in *The Wykehamist* recorded that 'he was a shrewd critic, & his comments, often mordant, sometimes outrageous, tended to let in daylight & to dispel the merely sentimental or bogus. His advice was usually worth having, nor was it hard to obtain … No one ever hesitated to take his trouble to Bobber, & few indeed can have failed to find comfort in his sympathy, & a clearer vision from his analysis of the issues.'
4. *WinColl E3/5/97*: letter from Captain Thomas Weatherby to the Revd John Trant Bramston, undated but probably November 1914; addressed from '9th Battalion, Duke of Wellington's Regiment, The Club, Wimborne'.
5. Lieutenant Walter Evelyn Parke (born July 27th 1891; 'B' 1905-1909) was the second son of Lieutenant Colonel Laurence Parke ('H' 1874-1877). His younger brother Lieutenant John A. Parke ('B' 1906-1911, Durham Light Infantry), was also killed in action, in September 1915. A brilliant cricketer & shot, he joined the Army in 1909 &, after Sandhurst, was commissioned into 2nd Battalion, Durham Light Infantry – his father's Regiment – as a Second Lieutenant in August 1911. 2DLI proceeded to France on September 7th 1914. At 1400hrs on October 13th, in misty, damp conditions, 2DLI attacked from the area of Vieux Berquin. 2DLI lost two officers and eleven other ranks killed, with sixty-one wounded. Parke was one of the dead. He had been twenty-three years old when he fell, & was buried at the Vieux Berquin crossroads by Sergeant-Major J. Watson. In the same attack, another Wykehamist, Lieutenant Anthony George Atwood Morris ('I' 1900-1903, 1st Battalion, King's Own Royal Lancaster Regiment), was also killed. Parke now lies in grave I.E.10 of Outtersteene Communal Cemetery Extension, Bailleul. He was mentioned in despatches after his death.
6. Robert Douglas Baird ('H' 1907–1913) served in the Rifle Brigade 1914–1918, being awarded an MC.
7. *The Iron Duke,* June 1935 (report on the reunion dinner at the Rawson Hotel, Bradford, on Saturday February 23rd 1935: '134 sat down to dinner, & late arrivals brought up the number to about 200.')
8. *The Iron Duke,* November 1925, in a letter from Robertson giving news of former officers of 9DWR.
9. *The Iron Duke,* June 1930 (recording the reunion dinner for Old Comrades of 9DWR held on February 22nd 1930 at the Osborne Hotel, Bradford. Robertson sent his apologies for being absent, which was unusual).
10. *The Iron Duke,* June 1931 (recording the 9DWR reunion dinner held in the Market Tavern, Bradford on Saturday February 28th 1931).
11. *The London Gazette,* October 13th 1914.
12. *WinColl E3/5/24/6:* letter from Alan Ferguson to the Revd John Trant Bramston, undated but almost certainly May 1915; addressed from '9th Duke of Wellington's, Bovington Camp, nr Wareham'.
13. *The Wykehamist* (541, May 1915): 'We regret to announce the death … from spotted fever, of Capt. T. Weatherby, West Riding Regt., 9th Battn. ('H', 1907–1913)'. Weatherby rests in grave 1480 of the Lindfield Rural (Walstead) Cemetery in Haywards Heath. The *Mid Sussex Times* of Tuesday 18 May 1915 reported as follows: 'CAPTAIN WEATHERBY'S FUNERAL AT LINDFIELD. MILITARY HONOURS RENDERED. The interment of the remains of Captain Thomas Weatherby, of Barrington House, Lindfield, whose death was announced in our last issue, took place on Tuesday afternoon … The gallant young officer was a popular member of 'B' Company, 9th Battalion Duke of Wellington's (West Riding) Regiment, & was 20 years of age. The only son of Mrs Weatherby & the late Mr C.T. Weatherby, of Barrington House, he was educated at Crowborough & Winchester College, being much esteemed at both schools … The mourners included … Mr M. Rendall (Headmaster of Winchester College) … From the deceased's regiment

came Lieutenant Colonel Hayden DSO, Captain Rodgers ('B' Company), Captain Robertson, Captain Berrisford, Lieutenant Cullinan, Lieutenant Savory, Lieutenant Benjamin, & Second Lieutenant Ferguson; also Company-Sergeant-Major Coxon, a Sergeant, & a Private ... Upon the coffin rested the deceased's sword & service cap, & several of his fellow officers – some of whom are Old Wykehamists – acted as supporters of that most glorious of palls – the Union Jack.'

14. *The Iron Duke*, October 1927: *Selections from the Diary & Letters of the late Lt. J. W. Russell, an Officer of 'C' Company, 9th Battalion, by Major M. Robertson OBE, MC, TD.*
15. Robertson continues: 'No officer of the 9th Duke's was better loved by all ranks, or did his duty more manfully, & those who remember his fine physique, cheery smile, & infectious good spirits, will like to read some of his own impressions & descriptions. He was at school at Oundle (where he learnt his 'Rugger'), had just been elected a scholar of University College, Oxford, when he joined us in January 1915, at Wimborne, & was only twenty when he was killed after just a year in the trenches.'
16. *WinColl E3/5/20/1:* letter from Fred Cullinan to the Revd John Trant Bramston, dated September 8th 1915; addressed from 'In Trenches, Flanders'.
17. *The Wykehamist* (546, November 1915).
18. *The Iron Duke*, November 1925: *HMS Iron Duke & the 9th Battalion*, by M. Robertson.
19. *The Iron Duke*, March 1926: *Christmas at Ypres, 1915*, by F.A. Potts.
20. *The Grantham Journal,* Saturday January 22nd 1916.
21. *The Iron Duke*, March 1926: *Christmas at Ypres, 1915*, by F.A. Potts.
22. *The Wykehamist* (560, January 1917): *Christmas Cards. An Experience. 'BEF, January 1917'.* The article is not credited, but the style is Robertson's.
23. *Yorkshire Evening Post*, Saturday January 29th 1916.
24. *WinColl E3/5/20/9:* letter from Fred Cullinan to the Revd John Trant Bramston, undated but almost certainly January 1916; addressed from 'BEF'.
25. *The Iron Duke,* June 1928: *The Bluff*, by F.A. Potts.
26. National Archives WO 95/2009: War Diary, 52 Infantry Brigade.
27. *The Iron Duke*, June 1928: *The Bluff*, by F.A. Potts
28. Arthur Sunley, *Diary of a Battalion Orderly 1914–1918, 15th July 1915 to 18th July 1918.*
29. *The Wykehamist* (551, April 1916).
30. *The [St Helens] Examiner*, May 13th 1916: 'Private Ireland was 39 years of age, and leaves a widow and seven children. He also was an old soldier, having served in the Boer War. He was not a Reservist, however, but enlisted of his own accord in September 1914. He was formerly employed by Mr J. Starkey, metal dealer, Mersey Street, as a carter. It is only five weeks ago since he returned to the Front, after a well earned furlough.' Ireland was, however, soon afterwards confirmed as a prisoner of war; the May 27th edition of the paper stated that 'the post brought the unhappy woman a letter from her "dead" husband.'
31. *WinColl E3/5/20/19:* letter from Fred Cullinan to the Revd John Trant Bramston, dated June 8th [1916]; addressed from 'BEF'.
32. Brigadier General J.L.J. Clarke, OC 52 Brigade, quoted in Michael Renshaw, *Mametz Wood* (Pen & Sword, 1999).
33. Lieutenant Alan Ferguson's obituary appeared in *The Wykehamist* (555, August 1916). Born in Weybridge on February 3rd 1896, he was the elder son of George Ferguson, of Dunwood Manor, Romsey, Hampshire, & Mary Fanny Ferguson (daughter of Thomas Oakley). He was the brother of Ronald Ferguson ('G' 1911–1916). Ferguson was distinguished as a sportsman & became a Commoner Prefect in 1914; in the same year he won Senior Steeplechase, & was a member of 2nd XI Soccer. A keen naturalist, he served on the committee of the Natural History Society, before which he read several papers. Killed in action on July 4th 1916, aged twenty, he is buried in grave II.B.13 of the Mericourt-L'Abbé Communal Cemetery Extension.
34. The QAMH, opened in July 1905, still stands just north of what is now Tate Britain but was then known as the National Gallery of British Art.

35. *WinColl E3/5/20/16:* letter from Fred Cullinan to the Revd John Trant Bramston, dated July 10th [1916]; addressed 'QAM Millbank'.
36. *WinColl E42/28.* The board was presented to the Winchester College Archives in June 2014 by Hugh Hill, a Maths don, who had found the board in a skip about twenty years previously when the Contingent Commander of the CCF was clearing Armoury of accumulated *bric-a-brac.*
37. *WinColl E3/5/20/2:* letter from Fred Cullinan to the Revd John Trant Bramston, dated November 13th 1916; addressed from 'Corps Rest Station, BEF'.
38. *The Wykehamist* (562, April 1917).
39. Captain Maurice Jeffery Savory died in either 34th or 2/2nd London Casualty Clearing Station, both of which dealt with casualties from the Somme area & fed the cemetery in which Savory is buried. He was twenty-two years old, & lies in grave I.A.12 of Grove Town Cemetery, Meaulte. His obituary appeared in *The Wykehamist* (562, April 1917). Born on October 2nd 1894, Savory was the eldest son of Ernest Jeffery Charles Savory ('I' 1875–1879) & Madeline Savory *(née* May), of 'The Red Lodge', Brooklyn Road, Woking, Surrey. He came to Hopper's in 1908, was a House Prefect in 1913, & reached Sixth Book, devoting himself with special interest to scientific work; he also shot at Bisley for the Cadet Pair in 1911 & for his last two years was in the Bisley VIII. On leaving school in 1912, he entered upon the study of the law, but in September 1914 obtained his commission in 9DWR.
40. National Archives WO 95/2014: War Diary, 9th Battalion, Duke of Wellington's (West Riding Regiment).
41. National Archives WO 95/2010: War Diary, 52 Infantry Brigade.
42. *The Wykehamist* (561, March 1917): 'MENTIONED IN DESPATCHES ... Capt. M. Robertson, The Staff, Duke of Wellington's Regt.'
43. *The London Gazette* (June 1st 1917): 'His Majesty the King has been graciously pleased to approve of the mentioned rewards for distinguished service in the field ... Military Cross ... Captain (Temporary Major) Malcolm Robertson, General List, formerly West Riding Regiment.'
44. *The Wykehamist* (584, July 1919): 'We wish Major Robertson every success on taking over Command.'
45. As reported in *The Iron Duke*, Robertson sent his apologies when he was unable to attend. One absence was in 1936 *(The Iron Duke,* June 1936): 'We were glad to see so many of the old officers, especially those who, with many other old comrades, were present for the first time. Two notable absentees were Major Robertson (T'Owd Bobber) & Capt. Kingston (Numero Neuf), both regrettably from ill-health. The former's unfathomable store of humorous reminiscence was sadly missed; may they soon be fit again.' The report on the 1937 dinner stated that 'Major Robertson proposed the "Guests" with his usual genial and discursive bonhomie.'
46. *The Wykehamist* (638, October 1923): 'Frederick John Fitz-James Cullinan ('E' 1909–1914). Fred Cullinan was Irish on both sides of his family, and was brought up in Dublin, his father, Sir Frederick Cullinan, being head of the Financial Division of the Chief Secretary's Office for nearly thirty years. Like his brothers, Max & George, he came to Winchester from Horris Hill. All three were Morsheadites & head of that House. He took what is now Junior Part I, and reached Sixth Book, & not one of his removes was got without hard work. He was not a natural athlete, but he had plenty of "guts". He was in Commoner Six in 1913, & ran in the winning team in Senior Steeplechase his last two years. His greatest contribution to cricket was to get together a British side at Kobe, stimulating their enthusiasm by articles in the local Press, & by having a dozen selected bats sent out by Simons.

    His father died in the winter of 1913, & instead of going to Cambridge, he left Winchester at Easter & had just passed the entrance examinations for Trinity College, Dublin, when War broke out. With the 9th Duke of Wellington's Regiment he went through three years' severe fighting on the Western Front. He won the MC at the Bluff in March 1916, was wounded at Fricourt in July 1916, & was back at the Front in the autumn. In the retreat necessitated by the breaking of the British Front in March 1918, after four days' continuous fighting, he was carried out of the line, against his will, by his Colonel's orders, & was operated on for appendicitis, just in time, directly he reached London. He was given a regular commission in the King's Liverpool Regiment after the War & went with it to Egypt. In January 1920 he resigned his commission, & a few days after his return to England was engaged by the Asiatic Petroleum Co. & sent out to Japan. There he travelled about, trying to beat the agents of the Standard Oil Co. at selling oil. For some time his headquarters were at Kobe; last Christmas he was given charge of a branch of the business at Yokohama. His last letter spoke of a strenuous tour he was to make in August in the extreme north of Japan, with a return to Yokohama on August 31st. He was found dead there after the earthquake on September 1st.

Fred Cullinan inherited a tradition of public service & a love of reading. He did a great deal to educate himself. He did not learn easily; he was sensitive, very independent, subject to fits of gloom over a check or failure, not an easy member of a Division or a Company. But with him disappointment never meant relaxation of effort, & he was at once responsive to a friend who refused to be put off by a temporary dourness of manner. His "travellings" in Japan are amusingly described in "Notes from the Diary of a Bagman in Japan", which he contributed to the "Pipe Line". A postcard written at dawn on Fujiyama betrays an inherited love of high places. He was liked as well as respected by both British & Japanese, though he himself could never get over his dislike of the type of Japanese with whom he came in contact. Fred was no Puritan & his religion was far below the surface, but his standard of morality was exceptionally high. The desire to carve out a career for himself, to avoid the risk of being a charge on others, sent him, as it has sent others, to the East. He earned his living by commending oil; by his industry, by his loyalty to those he served, & to the faith that was in him, he commended much besides.'

II

1. Hugh Rose ('I' 1935–1940) was born on November 26th 1921, the only son of Lieutenant Colonel Hugh Rose CMG & Ruth Antoinette Rose, of Kilravock Castle, Gollanfield, Inverness-shire, where the family had been established over 600 years before.
2. *John & Joanna Baird collection:* letter from Hugh Rose to Lieutenant Colonel & Mrs Rose, dated September 25th 1938; addressed from 'Sunnyside, Winchester'.
3. Winchester records state that James Sylvester Burn-Clerk-Rattray ('I' 1933–1938) was variously later known as J.S.B. Rattray or Craighall-Rattray. However, he was known in the Scots Guards as J.S.B. Clerk–Rattray and will be referred to by that name in this account. He was born on August 13th 1919, the only son of Colonel Paul Robert Burn-Clerk-Rattray CBE, JP, DL & Ferelith, sister of Wykehamist Lieutenant Sir Nigel Neis Ramsay ('E' 1889–1894), 'B' Company, 2nd Battalion, Black Watch (Royal Highlanders), who had been killed in action in South Africa on December 11th 1899.
4. Angus Ivor Grant (born March 21st 1920; 'I' 1933–1938) was the second son of Wykehamist Colonel John Peter Grant CB, MC, TD, DL ('A' 1899–1904), of Rothiemurchus, Aviemore, Inverness-shire. His mother was Gertrude Margaret Grant (daughter of the Reverend W.H.A. Truell), & his older brother was John Peter Grant, junior ('I' 1928–1933).
5. Gerald ('Gerry') Rickman (born December 6th 1919; 'I' 1933–1938) was the third son of Wykehamist Colonel Arthur Wilmot Rickman DSO* ('I' 1888–1890) & Muriel Joicey Rickman, daughter of Robert Squarey Fulton. He was the cousin of fellow Hopperite Guy Dodgson. Gerry's father died in an accident at home on October 16th 1925, aged only fifty-one; Muriel Rickman then re-married, becoming Muriel Philbrick.
6. Hew Francis Caryer Tompson (born February 19th 1920; 'I' 1933–1938) was the only son of Wykehamist Major General Reginald Henry Dalrymple Tompson CB, CMG, DSO ('I' 1893–1897), a distinguished gunner & staff officer, of Bay Tree Cottage, Bentley, Hampshire. His mother – Bridget Dorothea Tompson – was the daughter of the Venerable F.N. Thicknesse ('C' 1871-1877).
7. Whitelaw, W.S.I., *The Whitelaw Memoirs* (Aurum, 1989).
8. Guy Henley Dodgson (born March 9th 1920; 'I' 1934–1938) was the elder son of Philip Henley Dodgson MC ('B' 1905) & Eveline Joicey Dodgson, daughter of Robert Squarey Fulton. He was therefore Gerry Rickman's cousin.

9. John Brooke Boyd (born in Portsmouth on Trafalgar Day, October 21st, 1920; 'I' 1934–1939) was the only son of Commander John Gordon Boyd RN & Violet Constance Sophia 'Bus' Boyd, daughter of J. Stuart Brooke. Between the wars, Boyd's father was stationed in Alexandria, training Egyptian recruits in navigation. His son spent a solitary childhood in Whiterigg near Melrose in Roxburghshire, being looked after by his grandparents, whilst his sister Elisabeth ('Mickey') remained with their parents in Egypt. By the Second World War 'Bus' easily outranked her husband, as she became Officer Commanding WRNS.
10. Charles Kenneth Murray (born April 17th 1920; 'I' 1934–1939), was the only son of Wykehamist Sir Kenneth Murray WS ('G' 1905-1910) & Edith Maud 'Betty' Tustin, daughter of W. J. Tustin.
11. John Pinney (born 22 June 1920; 'I', 1934–1939), was the youngest of three Hopperite sons of Wykehamist Major General Sir Reginald John Pinney KCB, JP, DL ('B' 1877-1881) & Hester, daughter of Henry Head, Shoreham, Sussex. His brother Bernard was killed in action in North Africa in 1941 & recommended for a posthumous VC; Robert Pinney served with the New Zealand Cavalry in North Africa. At Winchester, John Pinney played Winchester College Football at VIs level, achieved his Running Colours in 1938, & played for the Soccer XI in 1939. Not just a sportsman, he also edited *The Wykehamist.*
12. Richard Evelyn 'Dick' Simpkin ('I' 1935–1939) was born on April 25th 1921. He was the only son of Sir Oswald Richard Arthur Simpkin KCB, CBE & Evelyn Mary Isobel, daughter of George Arthur Coller of Twyford, Hamsphire. Documents in the family's archives tell a complicated & in many ways unhappy story, of which only the barest outlines will be included in this narrative.
13. John Henry Lund Sinclair (born November 9th 1920; 'I' 1934–1939) was the third son of Colonel Thomas Charles Sinclair CBE, RA, of Winchester, & of Lucy Iris Sinclair, the sister of Lieutenant General Sir Otto Marling Lund KCB, DSO ('I' 1905–1909). His two elder brothers were Christopher ('I' 1929–1934) – who later commanded a battalion of the Rifle Brigade, & won two MCs in 1941, one at Beda Fomm & one at Sidi Rezegh – & Michael ('I' 1931–1936), who was killed trying to escape from Colditz.
14. *London Gazette*, July 4th 1939: 'The undermentioned Gentlemen Cadets from the Royal Military College, to be 2nd Lts. 3rd July 1939.'
15. *London Gazette*, March 10th 1939.
16. Michael Melville, *The Story of the Lovat Scouts.* Lord Lovat had raised two companies of scouts in 1899 to gather intelligence about the Boers. His main recruits were stalkers, ghillies, & shepherds from the northern Highlands of Scotland.
17. Alfred Holt & Co.
18. Supplement to the *London Gazette,* September 19th 1939: '4th Bn. Seaforth – Charles Kenneth MURRAY (88754) (late Cadet Corporal, Winchester College Contingent, Junior Division, OTC) to be 2nd Lieutenant April 26th 1939.' Supplement to the *London Gazette,* January 9th 1940: 'SCOUTS. 2nd Lieutenant C.K. Murray (88754), from Seaforth, to be 2nd Lieutenant January 10th 1940.'
19. Supplement to the *London Gazette,* January 13th 1939: 'YEOMANRY. Scottish H. — James Silvester BURN–CLERK–RATTRAY (late Cadet Lance-Serjeant, Winchester College Contingent, Junior Division, OTC) to be 2nd Lieutenant January 14th 1939.' Supplement to the *London Gazette,* February 28th 1939: 'Scottish Horse — The Christian names of 2nd Lieutenant James Sylvester Burn–Clerk–Rattray are as now described & not as notified in the Gazette of January 13th 1939.' Supplement to the *London Gazette,* May 10th 1940: 'Transferred from Scouts' as 2nd Lieutenant 79648 J.S. Burn-Clerk-Rattray.
20. One of Boyd's closest friends at Winchester was Alastair Thorburn, who became godfather to Boyd's eldest son. Boyd was always immensely proud of Winchester & in particular its reputation for being far more intellectual than Eton – where he nevertheless sent his sons Simon & James.
21. Sir Oswald Richard Arthur Simpkin KCB CBE (College, 1892–1898) proceeded to New College, Oxford, as a Scholar in 1898, & took a double first in Literae Humaniores. He then went into the law, & during the First World War was the Director of the Blockade Section, War Trade Intelligence Department, gaining the OBE in 1917; from 1919–1934 he was a Public Trustee, &

picked up his CBE in 1920, CB in 1922, & KCB in 1928. In 1919 he became a Fellow (governor) of Winchester College. His marriage on April 20th 1920 to Evelyn Mary Isobel, daughter of G. Arthur Coller, produced only one child. Sir Oswald was elected Warden on October 1st 1932, & resigned on February 15th 1936; he died on May 31st that year, & there is a commemorative tablet in Cloisters.

22. *Simpkin family collection.*
23. *Simpkin family collection:* letter from MR to Richard Simpkin, dated May 31st 1936.
24. *Simpkin family collection:* letter from Sheila Robertson to Richard Simpkin, dated May 31st 1936.
25. During his residence at Trinity, from October 1939 to June 1940, Simpkin gained a Class 1 pass in the first of three examinations for a Certificate of Proficiency in Engineering Studies. His papers were Applied Mechanics I, Engineering, Physics, Properties & Testing of Materials, & Mathematics.
26. The Simpkin family collection contains his Winchester College OTC 'Certificate A' (dated November 9th 1937); a medical certificate from No.6 Reception Unit, Cambridge, confirming Simpkin's Grade 1 fitness (dated September 27th 1939); his Cambridge University OTC 'Certificate B (Infantry) (provisional)' (August 4th 1940); & a statement by Major H.M. Taylor (Adjutant, CUOTC) that 'R.E. Simpkin has served in the Local Defence Volunteer Unit of this contingent for six months to September 14th 1940. It should be noted that the CUOTC Unit of the LDV has been engaged in whole–time service attached to regular units of HM Forces.' A handwritten addendum says, 'During the period between September 14th 1940 & his date of calling up for military service, may he be transferred to his home unit, please.'
27. Duncan Gilbert Scott McMurtrie ('I' 1937–1941), born on December 16th 1923, was the elder son of Donald Scott Anderson McMurtrie, of St Ibbs Bush, Hitchin, Hertfordshire, & Margaret Isobel Stratton McMurtrie (the daughter of Major H.G.M. Amos DSO). His brothers, Peter & Anthony, were not Wykehamists.
28. Anthony McMurtrie, interview with author, 2021.
29. Christopher Somerville ('I' 1935–1940), born on July 11th 1921, was the elder son of Brigadier Desmond Henry Sykes Somerville CBE, MC ('I' 1903-1908). His mother was Moira Burke Somerville, daughter of the Hon. A.C.B. Roche, of Fermoy, County Cork. His own son, John Henry Somerville, joined Hopper's in 1969.
30. *Somerville family collection:* Christopher Somerville, unpublished memoirs.
31. Horace Basil Barlow FRS, MD, MB, B.Chir., MA, was born on December 8th 1921, the younger son of civil servant Sir James Alan Barlow, Bt. & Emma Nora Barlow, daughter of Sir Horace Darwin KBE; his brother Thomas Erasmus Barlow had also been in Hopper's ('I' 1927–1932). Barlow's achievements in a lifetime of research are too numerous to do justice here, but an indication of his breadth of interests is that on his return to Cambridge after the war he was a founder member – the youngest – of the Ratio Club, a society debating the future of computing & robotics, amongst whose members was Alan Turing. He became a Fellow of Trinity in 1950, & Fellow & Professor of Physiology at King's College, Cambridge (1954-1964), after which he took up the post of Professor of Physiology at Berkeley (1964–1973). He was elected FRS in 1969 (Royal Medal 1993); his research into mechanisms of visual perception earned him the 1993 Australia Prize; & in 2009 the Society for Neuroscience awarded him the Swartz Prize for Theoretical & Computational Neuroscience. Barlow received the inaugural Ken Nakayama Prize from the Vision Sciences Society in 2016. He was married twice: from 1954 until their divorce in 1970, to Ruthala Salaman, with whom he had four daughters (Rebecca, Natasha, Naomi, & Emily). In 1980 he married Miranda Weston-Smith; they had a son, Oscar, and two daughters, Ida & Pepita. His children had given him thirteen grandchildren by the time of his death, at the age of ninety-eight, on July 5th 2020.
32. Guy Colquhoun Richardson ('I' 1935–1939) was three months older than Barlow, having been born on September 8th 1921. He was the younger son of Major General Alexander Whitmore Colquhoun Richardson CB, DSO, & Agnes Mackay Richardson, daughter of Alexander Thackeray JP. General Richardson had earned his DSO with the Bedfordshire Regiment during the First

World War, & in 1924 was a member of the silver medal-winning bobsled team at the Winter Olympics. He rose to command 4th Battalion, RTC by the time of his retirement in 1931, but was recalled to service in 1938 & served as OC 26 Armoured Brigade, Director-General Armoured Fighting Vehicles, Brigadier General Staff Second Army (1942), Chief of Staff Eighteenth Army Group (Tunisia 1943), & Chief of Staff Fifteenth Army Group, Italy.

33. Major 66188 James Alexander Colquhoun 'Jim' Richardson DSO (born October 21st 1916) came to Winchester College ('I' 1929–1933) from Tom Pellatt's school, played soccer & cricket for the House, & as an oar got into 2nd IV, coaching a winning Hewett Cup boat. He was a very efficient NCO at school & a strict disciplinarian as a prefect. He won Recruit Cup as Lance Corporal in the OTC, & was a Sergeant at RMC Sandhurst, whence he passed out very well in 1935 to 2RTR, of which when war broke out he was Adjutant.
34. *The Wykehamist* 861, October 10th 1939.
35. For example, Professor Reginald Gleadowe, the art master who had designed the lettering in Winchester's glorious War Memorial Cloister, had been called to the Admiralty, where he would work until his death in October 1944. Amongst his achievements there would be the design of the Stalingrad Sword, presented by Churchill to Stalin at the Teheran Conference in 1943; for this Gleadowe would be awarded the CVO. Colonel Cowland, former commander of the OTC, had been posted to the Directorate of Military Training at the War Office, & would die in London in March 1942. The head of the Modern Languages department, William Ridgway, had gone off to be an intelligence officer – he would return after the war with an OBE, after a prolific correspondence with Robertson. Another linguist, George Hamilton, had also joined the Intelligence Corps, rising to the rank of Colonel with Fourteenth Army in Burma; he too would come back with an OBE after the war. Geoffrey Hodges from the Physical Education department had gone into the RN, where he would win a George Medal for bomb disposal work, ending the war as a Lieutenant Commander. Humphrey Wright – an old boy of Sherborne – had become a meteorological officer, but was killed when HMS *Neptune* struck a mine off Libya in December 1941.
36. Somerville J.N., *Memories of my Life: The Memoirs of D-Day Veteran Brigadier Sir Nicholas Somerville CBE* (privately published, 2014).
37. Major 12994 Henry Johnston ('Harry') Younger ('I' 1912–1916; born January 16th 1899) of the 1st Lothians & Border Horse, was the elder son of Lieutenant Colonel William Johnston Younger ('C' 1881-1886). After service in the First World War, Harry Younger took his degree at Emmanuel College, Cambridge, in 1921; he then settled down in the family business in Edinburgh & became Director of Wm. Younger and Co., Wm. McEwan and Co., & Scottish Brewers Ltd. But he had also a wide range of other interests: archaeology, curling, history, books, pictures, shooting, fishing, farming, & forestry. In 1939 he acquired the farm of Baro on the slopes of the Lammermuirs, where he was building a house, planning a garden, & planting woods. Out of a strong sense of public duty, typical of him, he joined the Lothians & Border Horse, a Yeomanry unit, & after commanding a Squadron for some time, found himself Lieutenant Colonel in command of the now mechanized regiment when it went to France in January 1940. However, he willingly took a step back to become second-in-command to a Regular CO before the heavy fighting near the Somme in May. 'The philosophical way he accepted the position was typical of him, as also was his utter hatred of war, so freely expressed in his recent letters. He refused to write details of the war, but dwelt in his letters on happy memories of the past & the days of peace to come when he could return to his charming family, to whom he was entirely devoted.' He had four children, the eldest of whom, Gavin William Younger ('I' 1940–1944), went on to join the Scots Guards in 1945. Gavin's brothers were also Hopperites – Simon Gerard Younger ('I' 1944–1949) & Roland Nicholas Younger ('I' 1948–1953). Harry's brother – Lieutenant Colonel Lawrence Richardson Younger ('I' 1915–1920) – was killed in action in 1943 whilst in command of the Ayrshire Yeomanry.
38. *WinColl E42/25/1:* letter from Harry Younger to MR, dated January 13th 1940.
39. John Bruce Forrester Fortune ('I' 1934–1940), born July 19th 1921, was the only son of Major General Sir Victor Morven Fortune & Eleanor Fortune *(née* Steel).

40. Major General Sir Victor Morven Fortune KBE, CB, DSO, DL was born in Aberdeenshire on August 21st 1883, the only son of John 'Jack' Fortune, a farmer's boy who had attended St Andrews University before making his fortune as an East India merchant. With his money he bought a country estate (Bengairn, Castle Douglas in Kirkcudbrightshire), & was granted a coat of arms in 1903. He married Julia Catherine, daughter of James John Kinloch DL of Keir.

    Victor Fortune attended Winchester College ('D' 1897–1901), playing cricket for Lords (the 1st XI) in his final year. He then went on to RMC Sandhurst, being gazetted a 2nd Lieutenant in 1st Battalion, Black Watch, in 1903. His coeval & Winchester contemporary Archibald Wavell was commissioned into the Black Watch two years ahead of him.

    On August 22nd 1912 – still only a Lieutenant – Fortune married Eleanor, daughter of Arthur Jackson Steel, of Kirkwood, Lockerbie. Two years later, he went to war.

    The First World War accelerated his promotion; in 1914 he was a Lieutenant in 'A' Company, but after the Retreat from Mons & the Battle of the Aisne, he was promoted Captain in September 1914 when his Company Commander was killed in action. He commanded 'A' Company during First Ypres – being one of the few officers to survive 'Black Watch Corner' – before becoming Adjutant on November 11th; he was in that role at Givenchy, Cuinchy, Neuve Chapelle, & Aubers Ridge. His luck held for the rest of the war; he was mentioned in dispatches three times in 1915, & on September 30th he was appointed Brigade Major of 1 Infantry Brigade, seeing action at Loos. In 1916 he earned two more 'mentions' & in June was awarded a DSO. From September 16th 1916, as a Brevet Major (Acting Lieutenant Colonel), he commanded 1BW on the Somme & at Passchendaele, earning another 'mention' in 1917. In January 1918 he took over Fourth Army Musketry School, but then commanded 46 Infantry Brigade – still only a substantive Captain, but a Brevet Major & Temporary Brigadier General. He survived the war with a DSO, *Légion d'honneur*, Greek Order of the Phoenix, & six mentions in dispatches.

    Although peacetime slowed the frantic pace, Fortune continued to be trusted with command appointments: after Staff College in 1920–1921, he became a Company Commander at Sandhurst. In 1923 he was posted to the Small Arms School, Hythe, as Assistant Commandant. Command of 1st Battalion, Seaforth Highlanders followed in 1927; GSO1 5th Division in 1930; promotion to Brigadier of 5 Infantry Brigade in 1932; Major General GOC 52nd (Lowland) Infantry Division in 1935; CB in 1936; & GOC 51st (Highland) Infantry Division in 1937. He took the latter division to war in 1939, & his steadfast support of his French allies earned him the admiration of de Gaulle, who stated that 'the comradeship of arms, sealed on the battlefield of Abbeville in May & June 1940, between the French armoured division which I had the honour to command, & the gallant 51st Division under General Fortune, played its part in the decision which I made to continue the fight at the side of the Allies, to the end, come what may.'

    Fortune died on January 2nd 1949, at the age of sixty–five. His life had a value far greater than its length.
41. John Kennedy was born on April 23rd 1923 & came to Winchester in 1936 ('I' 1936–1940).
42. Peter Stoddart, interview with author, 2009.
43. Patrick Delaforce, personal communication to author, 2009.
44. Morgan ('K' 1930–1935) is commemorated on panel 35 of the Tower Hill Memorial in London.
45. Patrick Delaforce, personal communication to author, 2009.
46. Pawson, A., *Indelible Memories* (Foxbury Press, 2004).
47. Michael 'Mi' Charles Edmunds ('I' 1935-1940) was the son of Brevet Colonel Maurice William Edmunds OBE, TD, DL ('I' 1900-1905), of Stone House, Banbury, & Evelyn Gertrude Edmunds, the daughter of the Vicar of Bodicote, the Revd Hugh Newell Fowler (College 1864-1871). He was born on September 21st 1921 in Bodicote & baptized in Bodicote Church on October 30th 1921. His father was a director of brewers Hunt Edmunds. Although he was an only son, Michael had a sister, Mary Christine Edmunds.
48. John Somerville, personal communication to author, 2022: 'He didn't like the name Christopher; he said that he didn't like it being abbreviated to Chris. 'Charlie' perhaps originated at Winchester; it has the same initial, of course, but I never heard him called Charlie. As long as my mother

(and I) knew him he was always Dan. I think that his parents had disagreed on his name, but settled on Christopher and the Dan got left out. I recall that my grandfather joked that he wouldn't have let him be called C.D. Somerville! In the army he was known as 'Slim' (after the American actor Slim Somerville, I presume).'

49. *Somerville family collection:* Christopher Somerville, unpublished memoirs.
50. *WinColl E42/21/86:* letter to MR, dated November 9th 1942; addressed from 'Magdalene College, Cambridge'.
51. National Archives WO 167/798: War Diary, 2nd Battalion, Royal Northumberland Fusiliers.
52. *WinColl E42/15/12:* letter from Colonel Charles F. Kennedy to MR, dated May 16th 1940; addressed from 'Welburn Manor, Kirbymoorside'.
53. Major 17921 Jack Charles Algernon Battye ('I' 1913–1917) was thirty-nine years old when he died. He now rests in Grave 2.B.4 of the Karachi War Cemetery, Pakistan.
54. National Archives WO 167/798: War Diary, 2nd Battalion, Royal Northumberland Fusiliers.
55. National Archives WO 166/1401: War Diary, Lovat Scouts.
56. *The Wykehamist* (866, June 4th 1940). Born on March 24th 1922, David John Eccles was the only son of Mr & Mrs Joseph Eccles of Halston Hall, Oswestry, & had come to Winchester from Twyford in September 1935.
57. *Metcalfe family collection*: letter from Patrick Metcalfe to Sir Aubrey & Lady Metcalfe, dated May 28th 1940; addressed from 'Sunnyside, Winchester'.
58. National Archives WO 167/798: War Diary, 2nd Battalion, Royal Northumberland Fusiliers.
59. National Archives WO 167/798: War Diary, 2nd Battalion, Royal Northumberland Fusiliers.
60. Major 6859 James Patrick Arthur Gore 'Jimmy' Graham (born January 6th 1902, 'I' 1915–1920), of 4th Battalion, Oxford & Bucks Light Infantry, was killed in action during the retreat from Cassel on May 30th 1940. In 1925 he ran for England against France in the 1500 metres. He could run the Mile in 4.21, & was easily the best miler Winchester had then produced. He was also well known as one of the best point-to-point jockeys of the day; he could afford good horses & loved riding them. Graham, a capital cricketer, also won prizes at Bisley for rifle & revolver shooting. Men in the Regiment testified to his gallantry, concern for others, & coolness in the hour of danger. He was mentioned in dispatches after his death, & is commemorated on column 91 of the Dunkirk Memorial. A cup for athletics was established in his memory.
61. Captain 67092 Geoffrey Charles Francis Gwyer (born February 12th 1916) entered Hopper's as a 'War Commoner' ('I' 1930–1934). Robertson recorded that 'Geoffrey was not easy to handle in his early days at school, but intensely loyal to those who helped him. He left as a prefect, having made his mark as a good naturalist, a plucky cross–country runner, & a good swimmer. He passed well into & out of RMC Sandhurst, gaining Colours for running there, & on joining his father's old battalion, 2nd Grenadier Guards, at Alexandria in 1936 became Sports Officer & did effective work.' After a period of service at the Tower of London, he went out to France in 1939. Despite his wounds at Dunkirk, by the middle of 1942 he was out in North Africa, & soon commanding a company in 6th Battalion, Grenadier Guards.
62. *Wykehamist War Service Record & Roll of Honour.*
63. Captain 41788 John Graeme Middleditch ('E' 1920–1926) was promoted Major after Dunkirk & went overseas as second-in-command of a battalion of the Green Howards. He died in Cyprus on March 26th 1942, & is buried in grave 3.C.7 of the Nicosia War Cemetery.
64. Major 26994 Bernard Pinney (born May 14th 1903) was the eldest son of Major General Sir Reginald John Pinney KCB, JP, DL ('B' 1877–1881) and Lady Pinney (Hester Pinney, daughter of Henry Head of Buckingham, Shoreham). He had two brothers, Robert ('I' 1920–1925) & John. The family home, Racedown, in Bridport, Dorset, had once been lent by the Pinney family rent-free to the poet Wordsworth & his sister. Pinney inherited from his father & from this home the best traditions of soldiering, public service, & sportsmanship, according to his obituary in *The Times:* 'Fox-hunting in his native Dorset, riding in point-to-point races, fishing wherever he found water, pig-sticking in India, shooting in Asia & Africa – whatever he undertook, it was with joy & thoroughness in its doing ... Bernard took all that is good & clean out of life, & gave nothing

bad in return. He came of the very best type bred in the English country, & can ill be spared as a leader of men.' Pinney came to Winchester from Copthorne ('I' 1916–1921), played against Eton in Claude Ashton's winning Lords XI in 1920 & again in 1921, & was in the soccer XI in the same years. After RMA Woolwich, he joined the RA, serving in Egypt & India. From 1933 Pinney did two tours of duty with the Sudan Defence Force on the Abyssinian border, which he much enjoyed, although his second tour in the Sudan was professionally a mistake, as it precluded his going to the Staff College. *The Times* noted the positive impact which he had everywhere he went: 'What he did, he did well. With these great qualities he had a quiet, modest manner, a slow and deliberate way of speech, & a sense of humour that helped him wherever he met men. From Generals to Gunners, Gonds of the Indian jungle, & his beloved Fuzzy Wuzzies in the Sudan, he had a way with them that brought affection. He had his family's gift of drawing, & was a good Arabic scholar.' He was serving at home as a Captain in the RHA by 1938, & went abroad as a Major with the BEF in September 1939, gaining an MC at Dunkirk. Almost immediately after his return, on June 17th 1940, he married Rosemary Segrave, the only daughter of Vice-Admiral John Roderick Segrave CB; they lived at first in Chetnole, Dorset, but by the time of Pinney's death his wife was living at Hartley Court, Three Mile Cross, near Reading. His daughter – Elizabeth Ann Pinney – was born in June 1941, but Pinney never saw her, as he was in the Middle East by then. He was wounded in Syria in June 1941, & in October given command of 'J' Battery, 3RHA. In Egypt he met his brother Robert, a Corporal in the New Zealand Cavalry, after a separation which had lasted ten years. Pinney's obituary notice in *The Times* called him a 'deeply loved & loving husband'.

65. National Archives WO 373/15/98: Recommendation for Award for Pinney, B.
66. The official casualties totalled 66,426: 11,014 killed or died of wounds; 14,074 wounded; & 41,338 missing or captured.
67. National Archives AIR 50/62: Combat Reports, 145 Squadron.
68 *Hansard*, volume 361, chapter 796: House of Commons Debate, June 4th 1940.
69. *Metcalfe family collection:* letter from Patrick Metcalfe to Sir Aubrey & Lady Metcalfe, dated June 4th 1940; addressed from 'Sunnyside, Winchester'.
70. 1st Lothians effectively ceased to exist with the fall of France in June. Only three officers & seventeen other ranks succeeded in avoiding capture after the final stand of 51st Highland Division at St Valery-en-Caux. *The Times* stated that 'the recent news of Major H.J. Younger's death came with a terrible shock to his wide circle of friends, who had been hoping ever since he was missing at St Valery that he might be a prisoner … His unconquerable cheerfulness in the most depressing circumstances will be widely missed by all those who had the privilege of his close friendship. He was of the salt of the earth.' Aged forty-one when he died on June 12th 1940, he rests in grave D.17 of the St Valery-en-Caux Franco-British Cemetery.

III

1. Winchester College archives, College Record Book.
2. National Archives AIR 50/62: Combat Reports, 145 Squadron.
3. Deletions made in the original.
4. National Archives AIR 50/62: Combat Reports, 145 Squadron.
5. Somerville J.N., *Memories of my Life: The Memoirs of D-Day Veteran Brigadier Sir Nicholas Somerville CBE* (privately published, 2014).
6. Christopher William Sheepshanks (born February 20th 1922) came to Hopper's ('I' 1935–1940) from Pinewood School, Farnborough. Sheepshanks was good enough at cricket to earn his 'flannels', & good enough at music to play in a winning Palmer Cup side. He was the elder son of Sir Thomas Herbert Sheepshanks KCB, KBE (College 1908–1913) of Broom House, Horsell, Woking, Surrey, & Lady Sheepshanks (*née* Elizabeth Creemer Calvert, daughter of James Calvert). On his father's side, Sheepshanks was the grandson of the Right Revd John Sheepshanks, Bishop of Norwich 1893–1909. Bishop Sheepshanks sent four sons to Winchester, although there were fourteen Sheepshanks children in all, including Mary (a prominent Suffragette & peace

campaigner), Richard (College 1885–1890), Edward (College 1897–1903), & 2nd Lieutenant William Sheepshanks 2KRRC, who died of wounds as a prisoner of war on July 10th 1917.

7. Roger Macbeth Rigby ('I' 1936–1940) had been born on June 7th 1922, the second son of Sir Hugh Rigby, Bt., KCVO, FRCS, & Flora, daughter of Norman Macbeth, Woldingham. His elder brother John did not attend Winchester; he also had a sister, Margaret. He won the Art Prize in 1940.
8. *Rigby family collection:* Rigby, R.M., *Old Risalawallah Goes Walkabout,* typescript, 2003.
9. *WinColl E42/21/33:* letter from Cadet Rigby to MR, dated December 14th 1941; addressed from '102 RAC OCTU, Alma Barracks, Blackdown'.
10. National Archives AIR 50/62: Combat Reports, 145 Squadron.
11. Pilot Officer L.A. Sears, in Hurricane P2955, was last seen in combat with Bf109s at 0905hrs; Sergeant E.D. Baker, in Hurricane P3381, was last seen in combat with Ju87s & Bf110s at 0915hrs.
12. From 145, three more pilots had failed to return: Pilot Officer Wakeham, in Hurricane P2957, was last seen in combat with Ju87s & Bf110s at 1640hrs; Flying Officer Lord Kay-Shuttleworth, in Hurricane P3163, was last seen alive at 1640hrs; a Fleet Air Arm pilot on loan to the RAF, Sub-Lieutenant Smith, in Hurricane P3545, appears to have been shot down whilst attacking Ju87s at 1645hrs, but may possibly have been hit by fire from an escorting Bf109.
13. *WinColl E42/11/29:* letter from Bruce Fortune to MR, dated August 13th 1940; addressed from 'Bengairn, Castle-Douglas, Kirkcudbrightshire'.
14. *WinColl E42/11/17:* letter from Miss Jean Fortune to MR, dated 'Thursday'; addressed from '71 Eaton Place, SW1'.
15. *WinColl E42/11/16:* letter from Julia Fortune to MR, dated November 15th 1940; addressed from 'Aberdalgie House, Perth'.
16. *WinColl E42/25/5:* letter from Anna Younger to MR, dated September 18th 1940; addressed from 'Baro, Haddington'.
17. *WinColl E42/11/16:* letter from Julia Fortune to MR, dated October 25th 1940; addressed from 'Aberdalgie House, Perth'.
18. *WinColl E42/15/01:* letter from David Kemp to MR, dated September 16th 1940; addressed from 'The Country House Hotel, Crowborough, Sussex'.
19. John Willoughby 'Jack' Parr was the real deal: a Wykehamist, a soldier, & a teacher. He was a pupil from 1904 to 1910 ('A'), & then went up to New College, Oxford. He signed up at the outbreak of war as a Seaman in the Royal Naval Division, but transferred to the Highland Light Infantry as a Lieutenant. Wounded in Palestine in 1917, he went out to France in 1918, where he was wounded & captured. He returned to Winchester College as an Assistant Master in 1919, & stayed (with only a term's break, in 1951) until 1954, including an eighteen-year stint as a housemaster ('G' 1933–1951). From 1919 until 1947 he served with the Winchester OTC, commanding the unit from 1939 until 1947; during the war he was also OC 31 Platoon of the Winchester Home Guard.
20. Supplement to the *London Gazette,* May 9th 1941.
21. Leading Aircraftman 938476 Arthur Hugh Townsend RAFVR (born February 26th 1916) was the third & youngest son of Charles Lucas Townsend, a solicitor, of Norton House, Elton, Stockton-on-Tees. His mother, Ivy Townsend, was the daughter of William Kirk. He came to Winchester ('I' 1929–1934) from Horris Hill in September 1929, following his brothers Peter Norton Townsend ('E' 1923–1928) & David Charles Humphrey Townsend ('I' 1925–1931). He was in the final stage of his training as a pilot when he was killed, at the age of twenty-four, whilst flying Harvard I N7165 of No.15 SFTS (Service Flying Training School); his aircraft crashed whilst on approach to Kidlington airfield (National Archives AIR 81/3532). His instructor, Flying Officer R.K. Cassels, was injured in the crash. Townsend is buried in Woodstock Cemetery (grave I.2).
22. Flying Officer 73593 Archibald Nigel Charles Weir DFC, RAFVR, was the elder son of Wing Commander Archibald Graham Weir of Pensbury House, Shaftesbury, who was lost at sea in April 1941. His mother was Mary Evelyn Oldfeld Weir, the daughter of Canon Charles Oldfield Bartlett, Canon of Gloucester. His younger brother – Major Adrian John Anthony Weir MC ('B' 1933–1939) – was killed at Anzio in Italy in February 1944. The family had paid a devastating price

in the space of four years. Nigel Weir had been born on June 2nd 1919, & his story is sketched out in the introduction to his posthumously published *Verses of a Fighter Pilot* (Faber & Faber, 1941): 'As a small child he was taken out to Egypt, where his father was stationed; & this early experience stimulated his later passion for the East, & particularly his love for the Arabian deserts as shown in 'Sand Lover'. When Nigel was three, the family returned to England, & soon after settled in the country home near Andover, where they were to spend the greater part of the next ten years. Here, with his brother & his two sisters, he led a free & active life: in the woods bordering on their land the children learned that love of wild life, & especially of birds, which became a notable trait of Nigel's character. At this period also appeared his passion for aeroplanes & flying, which became more marked later when his father was sent to Oxford as the founder adjutant of the newly-formed University Air Squadron. When he was nearly nine, he & his brother were sent to Abberley Hall, Worcestershire, where he was able to continue to indulge his love of freedom & of wild life & animals.' He was a keen linguist, spent some time in Europe (sometimes with bicycle or caravan), & began Arabic as a hobby: 'He had spent many of his school holidays in Switzerland, France, & Austria: in consequence, he learned to speak French & German fluently. He also, in his spare time, studied Arabic with great enthusiasm, hoping always to be able to return to the East.' Arriving at Sunnyside, Weir played most games for his house, but his special interest was fencing: he was Captain of the school side, & later fenced for Oxford, where he studied at Christ Church: 'He kept up his fencing at Oxford, & got his half-blue during his first term: at the outbreak of war he was Captain-elect of the University team.' After a year at Oxford, he turned from modern Greats to Medicine, a progession which appealed to his sensitive & sympathetic nature: 'His passion for flying did not seem likely to be gratified by a career in the Air Force, as he was handicapped by a slight defect of eyesight: so he had been educated with a view to the Diplomatic Service. After his first year at Christ Church, he decided that he was not fitted to become a civil servant: he was much too individual, & was eager to use his own initiative. He turned his mind to medicine, and set himself with immense energy to make up for lost time, spending two or three vacations in London, in study & in doing voluntary work in the poorer districts.' Despite the problems with his eyesight, he had nevertheless joined the UAS: 'He was also an enthusiastic member of the University Air Squadron ... In the early summer of 1939 he learned that his defective vision might be sufficiently improved by exercises to qualify him for the RAF. He worked hard at these exercises, with such good result that he was pronounced fit to apply for a commission at the next board meeting, which was to take place in March 1940 ... & was granted a commission in the Volunteer Reserve in June 1939 ... The sudden realization of his dearest ambition made him exceedingly happy. But meanwhile war had broken out; so instead of returning to Oxford, he started his training as a pilot ... In spite of his adventurousness & love of flying, Nigel was not by temperament a fighter, but rather a thinker, reformer, & idealist. Even when he was a small boy, it was observed of him that his opinions were always carefully weighed, & his questions intelligent and searching. He strove to find his true ideals & then to put them into practice; he sought for truth & was never content with appearances. His chief fault perhaps (which time would doubtless have corrected) was intolerance of those who fell conspicuously below his own standards, intolerance especially of insincerity & of slackness: but his standards were as rigid for himself as for others. On the other hand, he was a person of wide sympathies & great understanding, with a gift for making friends of the most diverse people. He was acutely sensitive to the sufferings of others, & ready with sympathy for all who suffered from disability or injustice. In all his undertakings, he was careful, methodical, & thorough: having once embarked upon any enterprise, he would see it through to the end. These qualities revealed themselves conspicuously in any crisis, when he could always be relied upon to act with coolness & swift decision. With these gifts, he had also great charm of manner, & the quiet dignity, the courteousness, & the consideration for others that come from complete unselfishness. His life, though so short, was crowded with variety, & he had a great capacity for extracting the fullest value from every experience.'

23. *WinColl E42/08/33*: letter from Bill Cliff Hodges to MR, dated December 18th [1940]; addressed from 'Ardenlee, Falkirk'.

24. *The Wykehamist* (880, February 1942).
25. Tim J.M. Corsellis ('C' 1934–1938).
26. *WinColl E42/11/30:* letter from Officer Cadet Bruce Fortune to MR, dated December 9th 1940; addressed from ' 'C' Company, 165 OCTU, Dunbar'.
27. *WinColl E42/7/75:* letter from Officer Cadet John Boyd to MR, dated December 10th 1940; addressed from 'No.5 Platoon, 'B' Company, 165 OCTU, Dunbar'; written in the Cadets' Club, Beach Hotel, Dunbar.
28. Lieutenant Colonel Philip Thomas Flower MBE ('H' 1926–1931) was commissioned as a 2nd Lieutenant into the Rifle Brigade in 1940, & served with the 2nd Battalion in North Africa from 1941 to 1943 (Captain & Adjutant 1942–1943); in 1943 he joined HQ Eighth Army Staff, first as Major GSO2 & later Lieutenant Colonel GSO1, in both Italy and Austria.
29. *WinColl E42/12/33:* letter from Angus Grant to MR, dated December 10th 1940; addressed from 'Lovat Scouts, APO 400.'

IV

1. Charles John Riddell Duffin (born 20 July 1922; 'I' 1935–1940) was the only son of Major Charles Grimshaw Duffin MC, of Dunmurry, & Eva Margaret Maude Duffin (daughter of Colonel James Clarkson of the Indian Medical Service). Duffin's son, Simon Charles Hugh Duffin, would later follow his father into Hopper's ('I' 1964-1969).
2. Michael Julian Hirst (born less than a week after Duffin, on 25th July 1922; 'I' 1936–1940) was also the only son of a decorated veteran; his father was Colonel Charles Julius Hirst MC, TD, & his mother was Phyllis Mary Hirst *(née* Secretan).
3. John Godfrey Huggins (born October 26th 1922; 'I' 1936–1940) was the son of Godfrey Huggins & Blanche Elizabeth Huggins, the daughter of James Slatter of Pietermaritzburg; his grandfather, also Godfrey Huggins, had been an early Hopperite ('I' 1870-1875). His younger brother, the Hon. Martin James Huggins, was born in 1928.
4. Godfrey Martin Huggins, 1st Viscount Malvern, PC, CH, KCMG, FRCS was a doctor who became the fourth Prime Minister of Southern Rhodesia in 1933. He held that office until 1953, at which point he became the first Prime Minister of the newly-formed Federation of Rhodesia & Nyasaland. At the end of his premiership, in October 1956, he entered the record books as the longest-serving Prime Minister in the history of the Commonwealth. His hereditary peerage ('Viscount Malvern, of Rhodesia & of Bexley in the County of Kent') was created in March 1955. He held the title until his death in 1971, at which point John Huggins inherited the title as 2nd Viscount Malvern. Since 1978, the title has been held by his grandson, the 3rd Viscount.
5. *WinColl E42/15/03:* letter from John Kennedy to MR, dated March 6th 1941; addressed from 'Welburn Manor, Kirby Moorside, Yorks'.
6. *WinColl E42/17/16:* letter from Sir Kenneth Murray to MR, dated January 19th 1941; addressed from 'New Club, Edinburgh'.
7. Out of a total of 133,298 men, 420 tanks, & 845 guns taken during the advance as a whole. No wonder that Winchester is proud of Wavell.
8. 'Combeforce' was made up of detachments from 11th Hussars, 4RHA, & 106 RHA – the latter including two Wykehamists, Lieutenant Barry Domvile ('C' 1930–1935) & Captain John Colpoys Haughton ('F' 1926–1932). The infantry component of Combeforce – 2nd Battalion, Rifle Brigade – contained three Wykehamists: Christopher Sinclair ('I' 1929–1934), John Davies-Scourfield ('B' 1929–1934), & David Orme Wilson ('A' 1926–1932).
9. Farran, R., *Winged Dagger* (Collins, 1948).
10. *Richardson family collection:* letter from MR to Mrs Richardson, dated Sunday May 11th 1941; addressed from 'Sunnyside, Winchester'.
11. Somerville J.N., *Memories of my Life: The Memoirs of D-Day Veteran Brigadier Sir Nicholas Somerville CBE* (privately published, 2014).
12. Francis Arthur Burlton ('I' 1898–1902), born on March 30th 1884, was the elder son of Edward Richard Hughes Burlton, of Sunning Hill, Epsom, & Edith Mary Burlton, sister of the famous explorer Ewart Grogan DSO ('D' 1888–1891). He left Hopper's young in 1902, an able boy &

promising cricketer who would have made his mark. He went up to Exeter College, Oxford, but did not take his degree, instead going into business with the firm of Elder & Fyffes, fruit importers, in Bow Street. An excellent rider, he held a commission before the First World War in the Hertfordshire Yeomanry, with whom he went to the Middle East in 1915, but did not serve with them at Gallipoli, being left behind in Egypt & rejoining them on Imbros on November 16th. He then transferred to the Machine Gun Corps (Cavalry), with which he served until 1919, being wounded. He was killed when on ARP duty at his firm's Bow Street offices, aged fifty-six. The night of January 11th 1941 is particularly remembered for a direct hit on Bank Underground Station, which blew out the windows of two trains, wrecked the escalators, & collapsed the road into the station. The bomb left a crater over 100ft across & killed fifty-six people, injuring another sixty-nine. Burlton left a widow, Edith Clarissa Burlton, of 33 Vicarage Road, East Sheen. He is commemorated in the City of Westminster Roll of Honour & on the civilian 1939–1945 memorial in the City of Westminster (Hanwell) Cemetery, which the author has visited several times.

13. Account of Mrs Young, *née* Bowen, available on the BBC *People's War* website (*https://www.bbc.co.uk/history/ww2peopleswar/user/38/ u536638.shtml,* last accessed April 21st 2022).
14. *Somerville family collection:* Christopher Somerville, unpublished memoirs.
15. *WinColl E42/15/03:* letter from John Kennedy to MR, dated March 6th 1941; addressed from 'Welburn Manor, Kirby Moorside, Yorks'.
16. Henry Wagstaffe Thomson BA, CMG ('I' 1888–1893) was the son of Henry John Phipps Thomson – Secretary of the Great Indian Peninsula Railway – & Sarah Thomson *(née* Wagstaffe). He was born on February 22nd 1874 in Byculla, Bombay, & after Winchester attended Trinity College, Oxford, gaining an Exhibition in 1894. In 1896 he joined the Federated Malay States Civil Service as a Cadet, holding various posts in Selangor between 1898 & 1900. He became District Officer in Kuantan, Pahang, in 1900, & in 1903 was seconded for service with the Siamese Government, as Assistant Adviser to His Highness the Raja of Kelantan. For his services he was awarded the Royal Siamese Order of the Crown (4th Class) in 1905; he formally resigned from the FMSCS the following year to join the Siamese Civil Service in Bangkok. In 1907 his father died, & he married Yvonne Mary Winn in Portsmouth. By 1921 he was British Adviser in Kelantan. On his retirement, he settled in his wife's Southsea home, 33 Nettlecombe Avenue.
17 *https://www.mirrorpix.com/id/01016294.*
18. Letter from the Revd Charles Mason to the school magazine of King's College, Taunton (*The Aluredian* XVII.1, Lent 1942, p.36). Harry's niece & nephew who died with him at Mixbury, in Lower Warberry Road, were Elizabeth & Thomas Windeatt. Elizabeth was six years old; Thomas was fourteen. The maid was 25-year-old Marjorie Turner.
19. Henry Graham Mackrill ('I' 1938–1943) was born on February 1st 1925, the second son of Henry Whittick Mackrill of Sutton-on-Hull & Marjorie Doris, daughter of Charles Hellyer JP. His brothers were Ian Rollo Mackrill ('I' 1932–1937) & David Mackrill ('I' 1941–1945).
20. In 1944 Ian Mackrill was active in Normandy &, attached to Tactical HQ 12 US Army Group, received the American Bronze Star. By the end of the war he commanded 3rd GHQ Liaison Regiment. He died in 2013.
21. *WinColl E42/17/07:* letter from Mr H.W. Mackrill to MR, dated May 7th 1941; addressed from 'Lamwath Hall, Sutton-on-Hull, East Yorkshire'.
22. The following account is partially quoted & partially distilled from information supplied by Mike Simpkin, son of Richard & Barbara Simpkin. Their story would fill a book on its own, but much of the detail is too deeply personal. The author would like to express his gratitude to Mike Simpkin for supplying so much information, which has been vital in understanding the context of Dick Simpkin's wartime career.
23. As war loomed in 1938, London County Council had augmented the London Ambulance Service with the London Auxiliary Ambulance Service. By September 1939, 5,000 people had volunteered, half of them women; when the Blitz started on September 7th 1940, they manned 112 auxiliary ambulance stations, with 900 ambulances & 700 ambulance cars. Simpkin family archives contain Barbara Grant Johnson's LCC Mobilisation Certificate, dated September 1939, appointing her

for wartime service at Ambulance Station 44, Dolphin Square Garage: Dolphin Square was a relatively new development, constructed in 1935–1937; its parking was underground, & its gym had been converted into a First Aid post. Barbara recorded that on March 7th 1940 she was sent to Worcester Street to help with ten casualties there; the following day she received her National Civil Defence Safe Driving Award. Then, just as the Blitz began, she wrote, 'First meeting [with Richard] during an Alert'.

24. Barbara Simpkin *(née* Johnson) was the granddaughter of Major James Grant, founder of the Glen Grant distillery. Her mother, Hilda, left her first husband & daughter Rose in 1912 (Major Grant disinherited her as a result), & Barbara was born in London on July 8th 1913. After being deserted by her second husband (Noel Johnson), Hilda moved south with Barbara & converted to Catholicism. At the age of nineteen, Barbara started writing articles about the nature of faith for the *Catholic Gazette.* In 1933 she & her mother visited Rome to receive a Papal Blessing, but two years later – aged only fifty-two – Hilda died of double pneumonia on the Isle of Wight. Barbara was with her when she died. In 1936 Barbara moved from Hatfield to London & became Secretary of the Westminster Legion of Mary, a lay Catholic organisation whose members give voluntary service to the Church. In December 1936, Barbara wrote an article for the *Clergy Review* on the subject of *'Women & Catholic Action',* arguing that the role of women in the home is key to producing the Catholics of the future, but emphasising the need for women also to participate in all parts of society, from work to entertainment, in order to promote & model Catholicism. Barbara made annual pilgrimages to Walsingham, & in 1937 to Lourdes; she also spoke on behalf of the Catholic Evidence Guild at Speakers' Corner in Hyde Park. In later life she would go on to be a founder member of Amnesty International.
25. It was also, until they married, unconsummated – not surprisingly, given that Barbara was a practising Catholic. Evidence comes from the couple's own letters to one another, & from hotel receipts making it clear that even when travelling together they stayed in separate rooms.
26. *Simpkin family collection:* 'INSTRUCTIONS TO CANDIDATES FOR COMMISSIONS ATTESTED THROUGH RECEPTION UNITS … 7900313 Simpkin R.E. has voluntarily enlisted at a Reception Unit for general service in the Armed Forces & is therefore not liable for National Service'.
27. *Simpkin family collection:* letter from Richard Simpkin to Barbara Johnson, December 1940.
28. *Simpkin family collection:* letter from Richard Simpkin to Lady Evelyn Simpkin, December 1940.
29. Patrick Ross Metcalfe ('I' 1936–1941) was born on December 30th 1922, the younger son of Sir Herbert Aubrey Francis Metcalfe KCIE, CSI, & Elinor Joyce Metcalfe (the sister of R.W. Potter, 'I' 1900-1906).
30. John Alan Metcalfe ('I' 1932–1937), born on July 6th 1919, rose to be Sen:Co:Prae., and won English Speech, Latin Speech, & the Reading prize. In 1938 he started work with the wine merchants Portal, Dingwall, & Norris, though in 1940 he was commissioned as a 2nd Lieutenant in the Coldstream Guards. He joined the fighting in Libya in 1941, but was captured (along with Simpkin) at the fall of Tobruk in June 1942 & spent the rest of the war as a prisoner in Italy & Germany.
31. His officer training was complete by May 1942, & his commission as a 2nd Lieutenant was dated May 6th 1942.
32. *WinColl E42/11/18:* letter from Lady Fortune to MR, dated April 24th 1941; addressed from 'Aberdalgie House, Perth'.
33. *Simpkin family collection:* letter from Ethel Coller to MR, dated April 9th 1941; addressed from 'Wildwood'.
34. *Simpkin family collection:* letter from Richard Simpkin to Barbara Simpkin, June 1941.
35. *WinColl E42/22/22:* letter from Ethel Coller to MR, dated June 19th 1941; addressed from 'Kettlewell'.
36. Supplement to *The London Gazette,* February 28th 1941.
37. A Bren-gun carrier was a lightly-armoured tracked vehicle (likened by American troops to a sardine can on tracks) which was originally intended to bring mobile firepower to bear on the enemy. In

practice, the vehicles were used for reconnaissance, towing anti-tank guns, transporting supplies & ammunition, & any one of a multitude of tasks for which their mobility suited them. By the end of the war some had even been fitted with flame-throwers. Not without reason was its other name the 'Universal' Carrier.

The Bren which the carrier carried was the standard light machine-gun of the British Army, issued one per infantry section of eight men to give covering fire in the attack & volume of fire in the defence. It was immensely reliable and accurate – perhaps too accurate for a weapon intended to rain bullets over a wide area – & had the great disadvantage that it was fed from a thirty-round magazine, thus requiring constant pauses to change the magazine in action. It was still in use by the Royal Marines in the 1982 Falklands War.

38. *WinColl E42/11/31:* letter from Bruce Fortune to MR, dated May 7th 1941; addressed from 'Aberdalgie, Perth'.
39. Alastair Murray Thorburn ('A' 1933-1938) attended RMC Sandhurst in 1939 & was commissioned into the KOSB as a 2nd Lieutenant. He served with them in the BEF in 1940, before transferring to No.4 Commando in 1942. By 1943 he was a Captain, & went ashore with his unit on D-Day, fighting through North-West Europe until the war's end. Along the way he was wounded & picked up a *Croix de Guerre.* After the war he remained in the Army, seeing service in Aden & Korea and commanding 1KOSB from 1962.
40. Captain 89502 William Harold Cliff Hodges ('I' 1932–1937) was serving with 78 (Lowland) Field Regiment RA when he was killed in action in Italy on January 16th 1944.
41. Major James Gilbert Sydney Gammell MBE ('G' 1933–1938) went to Clare College, Cambridge, with a scholarship in 1938, but joined the Grenadier Guards in 1939. Commissioned as a 2nd Lieutenant in 1940, he served in the BEF before becoming Captain & Adjutant of his battalion in 1942. He then joined the staff, crossing to Normandy in June 1944, & by the end of the war was a Major in Moscow with a mention in dispatches to his credit.
42. *WinColl E42/7/76:* letter from 2nd Lieutenant John Boyd to MR, dated May 7th 1941; addressed from '1st Battalion, The King's Own Scottish Borderers, attached V Corps School, Home Forces'.

V

1. Simpkin's correspondence is largely intact in the family archives, & I am indebted to Mike Simpkin for excerpts & summaries of the key documents. The correspondence includes airgraphs & cables; letters were fairly regular, with a slight gap during the Tobruk breakout in November–December 1941, & continued until the last airgraph in May 1942.The first printed card notification from captivity is dated June 27th 1942. After a couple of short notes, the first letter from Italy is dated August 31st 1942 & the last July 20th 1943. The next note comes from Germany & is dated September 20th 1943; the letters continue until April 15th 1945. Few letters from Barbara are extant, since they were with Simpkin's possessions which were destroyed by enemy action while being returned to the UK in 1942. However, some of her letters were returned undelivered to Barbara after Simpkin was taken prisoner.
2. Convoy WS9A formed off Oversay on June 3rd 1941, with vessels assembling from Avonmouth and Liverpool. It was made up of the ships *Aagtekerk*, *Capetown Castle*, *Durban Castle*, *Eastern Prince*, *Empire Condor*, *Empire Curlew*, *Empire Egret*, *Empire Widgeon*, *Empress of Japan*, *Franconia*, *Highland Brigade*, *Llangibby Castle*, *Mendoza*, *Mooltan*, *Orbita*, & *Samaria.*
3. *WinColl E42/22/21:* letter from Simpkin to MR, dated June 10th 1941; addressed 'Cunard-White Star'.
4. Abbassia Barracks was a huge garrison complex on the edge of Cairo. Within it was the RAC Training Depot – also known as the RAC Base Depot – where troops were brought to combat readiness on armoured vehicles & equipment; the Depot also trialled new equipment & devised procedures for operations & maintenance.
5. Christopher Beney Pringle ('I' 1936–1941) was the youngest son of John Pringle MD, DPH, a medical practitioner first in Rochdale & then Manchester. He was born on born on June 11th 1923 to Dorothy Emily Pringle, daughter of W.A. Beney of Beckenham; his brothers were John William Sutton Pringle (College, 1926–1931), Alexander Patrick Pringle ('I' 1931–1936), & A.M.

Pringle (who went to Rugby). Christopher Pringle was an excellent shot, & joined the RNVR in 1942.

6. Born on August 18th 1923, David Seton Middleditch ('I' 1936–1941) was the only son of Major Robert Henry Middleditch ('I' 1908-1912) & Dorothea Elizabeth Middleditch *(née* von Schenk). Whilst serving with 2nd Battalion, Yorkshire Regiment, in 1914, Robert Middleditch had been severely wounded & taken prisoner (he was shot in the thigh by a sniper on October 30th, & captured as he was being carried away on a stretcher; his four stretcher-bearers were shot on the spot by his captors). He was subsequently interned in Switzerland, whence he was repatriated in 1918, having been officer-in-charge of British officers in that country. He married Dorothea von Schenk in August 1917 in Berne. Although he rose to the rank of Major after the war, he was invalided out in 1934, & died on February 19th 1937.
7. Professor Patrick William Duff (College, 1914–1919) was elected a Fellow of Winchester College in December 1947 & appointed Warden in 1959. In the following year he also became Vice-Master of Trinity.
8. *WinColl E42/9/15:* letter from Patrick W. Duff to MR, dated February 19th 1941; addressed from 'Trinity College, Cambridge'.
9. Michael Ferrers Elliott-Binns ('I' 1937–1941; born August 17th 1923) was the second son of the Revd Canon Leonard E. Elliott-Binns DD, Vicar of North Cadbury, Somerset, & Anna Scott Kilner, daughter of Dr Charles Kilner, Bury St Edmunds. His son, J.R. Elliott-Binns, came to Winchester, but not to Hopper's ('G' 1964-1968).
10. Elliott-Binns, M., *Finding through War: Poems of Fifty Years Ago* (William Sessions, 1995).
11. A Royal Artillery Field Regiment of the period had a strength of twenty-four guns divided into three eight-gun batteries. The 25-pounder was the best all-round artillery piece of the war, capable of firing up to eight rounds a minute to a distance of over 13,000 yards. So heavy was the weight of fire which the weapon could lay down that many Germans believed the British had developed an automatic version: in fact, the weapon was hand-loaded by its crew of six.
12. John Lionel Frederick 'Slogger' Armitage (College 1933–1937) won prizes for Greek Verse, Greek Prose, & Spanish, & went up to Oriel College, Oxford, as a Scholar in 1937. He fenced for the university. In 1939 he joined the Royal Artillery as a 2nd Lieutenant, becoming an instructor at 121 OCTU in 1940 before setting out for the Middle East with 11RHA.
13. *WinColl E42/23/21:* letter from Tompson to MR, dated June 16th 1941; addressed from '11th (HAC) Regiment, RHA, Chilton Foliat, Hungerford, Berkshire'.
14. Supplement to *The London Gazette,* August 5th 1941.
15. *WinColl G317, from Pike collection*: letter from Tompson to MR, dated August 10th 1941; addressed from '11th (HAC) Regiment, RHA, Chilton Foliat, Hungerford'.
16. At this point in the war, British armoured divisions fielded two armoured brigades (each with three regiments of tanks & one battalion of infantry), assisted by a Support Group which provided resources for the armoured brigades: a field artillery regiment, an anti-aircraft regiment, an anti-tank regiment, & an infantry battalion. Divisional troops included Royal Engineers.
17. *WinColl G317, from Pike collection*: letter from Tompson to Mrs Tompson, dated September 22nd 1941; addressed from '11th (HAC) Regiment, RHA'.
18. *WinColl G317, from Pike collection*: letter from Tompson to Mrs Tompson, dated September 27th 1941; addressed from '11th (HAC) Regt, RHA c/o Army Post Office 1515'.
19. *Mackrill family collection*: letter from MR to Graham Mackrill, dated September 14th 1941; addressed from 'Sunnyside, Winchester'.
20. Edmond Holtby ('I' 1903–1907) was the father of Robert Holtby, & stepfather of David Welsh ('I' 1921–1926).
21. *WinColl G317, from Pike collection*: letter from Tompson to Mrs Tompson, dated September 29th 1941; addressed from 'Cunard White Star'.
22. Convoy WS12 included the vessels *Almanzora, City of Paris, Clan Campbell, Clan Lamont, Dominion Monarch, Duchess of Richmond, Empire Pride, Empire Trust, Empress of Canada, Empress of Russia, Franconia, Highland Brigade, Highland Princess, HMS Prince Baudouin, HMS Royal Ulsterman, Leopoldville, Mendoza, Narkunda, Ormonde, Perseus, Perthshire, Samaria, Sarpedon,* & *Strathaird.*

23. *WinColl G317, from Pike collection*: letter from Tompson to Mrs Tompson, dated October 2nd 1941; addressed from 'Cunard White Star'.
24. Tompson did not use this word in a modern, offensive, sense, but in the casual slang of his times. He intended no offence & so none should be taken. His comments in a later letter show that he was no racist.
25. *WinColl G317, from Pike collection:* letter from Tompson to Mrs Tompson, dated October 24th 1941; addressed from '11th (HAC) Regiment, RHA, c/o Army Post Office 1515'.
26. National Archives ADM199/402, South Africa War Diary: 'Monday, 3rd November 1941: *Derbyshire,* escorting Durban portion of Convoy WS 12 (*Franconia, Clan Campbell, Clan Lamont, Almanzora, City of Paris, Duchess of Richmond, Empress of Russia, Highland Brigade, Perseus, Ormonde, Samaria*) arrived Durban from Freetown 0944GMT.'
27. *WinColl G317, from Pike collection*: letter from Tompson to Mrs Tompson, dated November 16th 1941; addressed from '11th (HAC) Regiment, RHA, c/o Army Post Office 1515'.
28. *The Wykehamist* 880, February 1942.
29. After a remarkably successful wartime career, the aircraft carrier HMS *Ark Royal* had been torpedoed on November 13th 1941 by *U-81,* & sank early the following morning. Only one of her 1,488 crew was killed.

VI

1. *WinColl E42/20/12:* letter from Bernard Pinney to MR, dated September 3rd 1941; addressed from ' 'J' Battery, 3rd Regiment RHA, MEF'.
2. Simpkin, R., *Men against Tanks,* in *The Mechanized Battlefield: A Tactical Analysis* (Pergamon-Brassey's, 1985).
3. National Archives WO 373/18/59: Recommendation for Award for Simpkin, Richard Evelyn.
4. Hastings, R.H.W.S., *The Rifle Brigade in the Second World War 1939–1945* (Gale & Polden, 1950).
5. 'E' 1932–1936.
6. Hastings, R.H.W.S., *The Rifle Brigade in the Second World War 1939–1945* (Gale & Polden, 1950).
7. Quoted in Dey, J.H., *Cairo to Berlin: the 3rd Regiment, Royal Horse Artillery 1939–1945* (Arcturus Press, 2005).
8. Hastings R.H.W.S., *The Rifle Brigade in the Second World War 1939–1945* (Gale & Polden, 1950).
9. *Ibid.*
10. Dey, J.H., *Cairo to Berlin: the 3rd Regiment, Royal Horse Artillery 1939-1945* (Arcturus Press, 2005).
11. National Archives WO 169/1439: War Diary, 'J' Battery, 3 Regiment RHA.

    Pinney's grave was lost after the fighting, & he is commemorated in Column 1 of the Alamein Memorial. Those who had played cricket with Pinney for Winchester or Dorset, or rode with him at home or in India, long remembered him as a lover of peace & the most modest & unselfish of men. After the war, Pinney's beloved 'J' Battery was officially renamed 'Sidi Rezegh 'J' Battery', because of its conspicuous role in the battle. But perhaps the finest testament to Pinney's bravery came from General G.L. Verney. In 1945 there was a huge victory parade in Berlin, in which 7th Armoured Division participated. After it, looking back across the war as a whole, Verney wrote: 'What thoughts must have passed through the minds of the veterans as they saluted their great war leader *[Churchill]*. Of that first venture through the wire of the Egyptian frontier & the overwhelming victory of Beda Fomm & Sidi Saleh; of Sidi Rezegh in November 1941 & the desperate fighting in that same area a few months later. Alam Halfa & Alamein; Tripoli & Tunis; the crossing of the Volturno … So many scenes, good times & bad, savage heat & extreme cold, sand storms & snow, rain & sunshine, & perhaps too so many names – O'Connor & Creagh, the first architects of victory; Gott & Campbell; Pinney, Ward Gunn, & Beeley; Halliman & Wainman & all those others whose names have no written records but who gave their whole endeavours to their comrades & their Regiments & who died in battle.'
12. *WinColl E42/20/13:* letter from Lady Pinney to MR, dated December 26th 1941; addressed from 'Racedown, Bridport, Dorset'.
13. National Archives WO 373/18/59: Recommendation for Award for Simpkin, Richard Evelyn.

14. *Ibid.*
15. *WinColl E42/12/34:* letter from Angus Grant to MR, dated December 7th 1941; addressed from ''A' Squadron, Lovat Scouts, Faroe Island Force'.
16. *WinColl G317, from Pike collection*: letter from Tompson to Mrs Tompson, dated December 7th 1941; addressed from '11th (HAC) Regiment, RHA, MIDDLE EAST FORCES'.
17. *John & Joanna Baird collection*: letter from Officer Cadet Hugh Rose to his sisters Elizabeth & Madeleinc, dated December 9th 1941; addressed from ''C' Company, 165OCTU, Dunbar'.
18. *WinColl E42/11/32:* letter from Bruce Fortune to MR, dated December 10th 1941; addressed from 'Raigmore Hospital, Inverness'.
19. Anthony McMurtrie, interview with author, 2021.
20. Michael Henry Ainsworth Finch was the only son of Sir Ernest Frederick Finch FRCS, of Sheffield, & Mary Finch *(née* Ainsworth). Born on June 28th 1923, he attended Hopper's from 1937 to 1941. He returned to university after the war to complete his BA & MA.
21. Born in London on September 17th 1923, Henry Arthur Gunning Brooke ('I' 1936–1941) was the only son of Major Basil Gerald Brooke ('H' 1908-1911) & Essex Vere Brooke, daughter of Brigadier General Sir Charles Vere Gunning Bt, CB, CMG.
22. Arthur Herbert ('I' 1937–1941), born on December 9th 1923, was the only son of Arthur Stanley Herbert, of Woldingham. His mother was Marjorie Herbert, the sister of Alan Ferguson ('G' 1910-1914).
23. *WinColl E42/21/33:* letter from Cadet Rigby to MR, dated December 14th 1941; addressed from '102 RAC OCTU, Alma Barracks, Blackdown'.
24. Supplement to the *London Gazette,* April 1st 1941.
25. *WinColl E42/20/14:* letter from John Pinney to his parents, dated January 11th 1942; addressed from 'Machakos, Kenya'.

VII

1. National Archives WO 169/4577: War Diary, 11 (HAC) Field Regiment, RHA. 'BARON Column formed under command Lt/Col W.A. Ebbels MC RHA. Composition – RHQ 11 (HAC) Regt RHA. 'A' Bty HAC. 237 A/Tk Bty (76 A/Tk Regt RA), less 1 Tp. 'A' & 'C' Tps 43 Lt AA Bty (61 Lt AA Regt RA). 'C' & 'D' Coys, 2 KRRC. ROGER detachment also formed, consisting of – 'E' Bty HAC, less 1 T ('H'). 1 Tp 237 A/Tk Bty 1 Tp 239 A/Tk Bty'.
2. James Column consisted of elements of 1RB, B/11RHA, & similar anti-tank & anti-aircraft units to the above. Its commander, later Brigadier Thomas James Bolle Bosvile CBE, DSO & Bar, MC, Legion of Honour, *Croix de Guerre,* Legion of Merit (USA) ('G' 1910–1914) had been a Prize Cadet at Sandhurst before taking his commission in the Rifle Brigade in 1915. He served in France, earning an MC & a Mention in Dispatches. By 1940 he was a Lieutenant Colonel commanding 1RB, which he led into action in North Africa. Subsequently he joined the War Office (1943) & SHAEF (1944), but died in London in July 1945.
3. National Archives WO 169/4577: War Diary, 11 (HAC) Field Regiment, RHA.
4. *WinColl E42/23/22:* letter from Mrs Tompson to MR, dated February 9th 1942; addressed from 'Bay Tree Cottage, Bentley, Nr Farnham'.
5. The nickname for RMA Woolwich.
6. *WinColl E42/23/23:* letter from Mrs Tompson to MR, dated February 15th 1942; addressed from 'Bay Tree Cottage, Bentley, Nr Farnham'.
7. National Archives WO 169/4577: War Diary, 11 (HAC) Field Regiment, RHA.
8. *John & Joanna Baird collection*: letter from Officer Cadet Hugh Rose to Madeleine Rose, dated January 28th 1941; addressed from ''C' Company, 165 OCTU, Dunbar'.
9. *WinColl G317, from Pike collection:* letter from Major Benson to Mrs Tompson, dated February 18th 1942; addressed from '11th (HAC) Regiment RHA, Middle East Force'.
10. *WinColl G317, from Pike collection:* letter from Lieutenant Colonel W.A. Ebbels RHA to Mrs Tompson, dated February 22nd 1942; addressed from '11th (HAC) Regt RHA, MEF'.

11. *WinColl E42/23/24:* letter from Mrs Tompson to Mr Spencer Leeson, dated February 25th 1942; addressed from 'Bay Tree Cottage, Bentley, Nr Farnham'.
12. *WinColl G317, from Pike collection:* letter from Mrs Tompson to Lieutenant Colonel William Pike, dated February 28th 1942; addressed from 'Bay Tree Cottage, Bentley, Nr Farnham'.
13. *WinColl E42/23/25:* letter from Mrs Tompson to MR, dated October 14th 1942; addressed from 'Bay Tree Cottage, Bentley, Nr Farnham'.
14. *WinColl E42/17/80:* letter from Officer Cadet P.R. Metcalfe to MR, dated February 8th 1942; addressed from 'Cadet Wing, Fighting Vehicles School, Ahmednagar'.
15. *Rigby family collection*: Rigby, R.M., 'My War with the Duke of Aosta'.
16. *Rickman family collection:* Rickman, G., 'Agro's 1989 thoughts of nearly fifty years ago'.
17. *Ibid.*
18. National Archives WO344/398/3: Liberation questionnaire completed by Rickman, 1945.
19. *WinColl E42/21/22:* letter from Mrs Muriel Philbrick to MR, dated April 12th 1942; addressed 'as from Bartley Lodge, Cadham, Southampton'.
20. Supplement to the *London Gazette,* February 24th 1942.
21. After Beda Fomm, Jim Richardson had been attached to GHQ in Cairo until September 1941, & after a spell at the local Staff College in Haifa, he was temporarily an acting Lieutenant Colonel & an instructor, but gained release to be a GSO2 in 7th Armoured Division.
22. *WinColl E42/22/24:* letter from 2nd Lieutenant R.E. Simpkin to MR, dated February 24th 1942; addressed from ' 'A' Sqn., 4th RTR, MEF'.
23. *WinColl E42/7/81:* letter from 7948724 Trooper Brooke to MR, dated Sunday February 22nd; addressed from '21B Troop, 'C' Squadron, 58th Training Regiment RAC, Bovington Camp, Wareham, Dorset'.
24. Christopher Robert Foot ('G' 1936–1941) joined the Army in 1941, & in the following year was commissioned as a 2nd Lieutenant in 16/5th Lancers. He served in North Africa & Italy (where he became Intelligence Officer). By the end of the war he was a Captain & in Austria.
25. In Hopper's there was a stuffed sandgrouse, next to which were placed any cups or trophies.
26. *WinColl E42/12/37:* letter from Iain Grant to MR, dated March 18th 1942; no address stated.
27. Melville, M.I.L., *The Story of the Lovat Scouts 1900–1980* (Saint Andrew Press, 1981).
28. Ellen Marie 'Ellemi' Rubeksen was born on the Faroes on April 6th 1921, & died in Guisborough on September 19th 1978. She was the daughter of Rubek & Rasmina Rubeksen, & sister to Olivia Johannesen, Mourits Rubeksen, & Harry Rubeksen. She married Kenneth Cecil Fuggle, with whom she had two children.
29. Nororagøta, often referred to as Gøta, is a village on Eysturoy.
30. *Fuggle family collection*: letter from Angus Grant to Ellemi Rubeksen, dated Wednesday April 23rd 1941; addressed from 'Lovat Scouts, Fuglefjord'.
31. *Fuggle family collection*: letter from Angus Grant to Ellemi Rubeksen, dated June 25th 1941; addressed from 'Vensil Petersen's'.
32. *Fuggle family collection*: letter from Angus Grant to Ellemi Rubeksen, dated December 24th 1941; addressed from 'Gote'.)
33. *Fuggle family collection*: letter from Angus Grant to Ellemi Rubeksen, undated; not addressed.
34. Grant is also commemorated on the family memorial in Rothiemurchus graveyard, to the south of Aviemore; an inscription thereon reads IN MEMORY OF ANGUS IVOR GRANT / LIEUTENANT IN THE LOVAT SCOUTS / YOUNGER SON OF TWELFTH LAIRD / BORN 21ST MARCH 1920 / DIED ON ACTIVE SERVICE 18TH MARCH 1942.
35. *WinColl E42/17/162:* letter from Charles Murray to MR, dated March 23rd 1942; addressed from "C' Squadron, The Lovat Scouts, The Faroe Islands Force'.
36. John Connock McArthur (born August 5th 1923; 'I' 1937-1942), was the only son of Valentine Goold McArthur MC ('I' 1897-1901), & Monica Augusta, daughter of William Nicholas Connock Marshall JP ('A' 1860-1865).
37. Supplement to the *London Gazette,* May 5th 1942. Rigby himself states in his memoirs that his commissioning date was April 16th 1942.

38. *Rigby family collection:* Rigby, R.M. 'Old Risalawallah Goes Walkabout'.
39. *WinColl E42/21/35:* letter from Roger Rigby to MR, undated but certainly May 1942; addressed from '23rd Hussars, 'C' Squadron, Plumpton Race Course, Sussex'.
40. *WinColl E42/21/36:* letter from Margaret Rigby to MR, dated May 15th 1942; addressed from 'Military Hospital, Kinmel Hall, Abergele, North Wales'.
41. Born on May 11th 1911, 70317 Squadron Leader Frederick Undecimus 'Fred' Hollins AFC was the eleventh child of William Hollins JP & Mary Hollins. The couple's seventh son, Fred was one of six Hopperite brothers who (with a break of one term) spanned twenty-two years (1909–1930) between them. His eldest brother William Humphrey Hollins ('I' 1909–1914) was killed in action in 1915; the others were John Charles Hollins ('I' 1913–1917), Henry Hollins ('I' 1918–1922), Frank Hollins ('I' 1920–1926), & Charles Hollins ('I' 1923–1928). He went to Trinity College, Cambridge, but left after two years for the Air Training School at Hamble, from which in 1934 he moved to Imperial Airways, mostly in Africa. He returned to Hamble as an instructor in 1938, & married Daphne Jackson there on July 29th 1939; she brought him much happiness & one daughter. His arduous work as an instructor in navigation was rewarded in July 1941 by the Air Force Cross, & that December by promotion to Squadron Leader. At about 1420hrs on Monday May 4th 1942, near Lochboisdale on the Scottish island of South Uist, Sunderland II T9084 of 228 Squadron RAF crashed whilst coming in to moor. As soon as the Sunderland disappeared behind Gasay Island, rescue efforts were immediately put in hand, & the first boats reached the scene within six minutes. Twelve of the crew were found – most of them injured, wet, cold, & in shock – clinging to the wreckage or to nearby rocks. They were taken ashore rapidly. When the tide went out, two bodies were recovered from the Sunderland: Hollins, and 67616 Pilot Officer Ronald Jones. Hollins was buried in grave I.27 of Pennyfuir Cemetery, Oban. He was thirty years old when he died.
42. *WinColl E42/13/60:* letter from Patrick Duff to MR, dated September 3rd 1942; addressed from 'Trinity College, Cambridge'.
43. The quotation is a line from William Ernest Henley's poem *In Hospital: Apparition.*
44. *WinColl E42/13/57:* letter from Mrs Daphne Hollins to MR, dated 'Sunday' but endorsed '1945' by MR; addressed from 'Corner Cottage, Liss, Hants'.
45. *Rickman family collection:* Rickman, G., 'Agro's 1989 thoughts of nearly fifty years ago'.
46. https://www.cofepow.org.uk/armed-forces-stories-list/the-9th-battalion-royal-northumberland-fusiliers (accessed December 23rd 2020).
47. *Walker family collection:* letter from 4209970 Fusilier J.N. Somerville to Peter Walker, dated Sunday May 24th 1942; addressed from 'No.6 Platoon, 'D' Company, 21st ITC, Dering Lines, Brecon, South Wales'.
48. *WinColl E42/9/17:* letter from Charles Duffin to MR, undated, but internal evidence suggests late May/early June 1942; addressed from 'Royal Military College, Camberley, Surrey, 'A' Squadron, RAC Wing, 101 OCTU'.
49. National Archives WO169/4507: War Diary, 4th Battalion, Royal Tank Regiment.
50. *WinColl E42/22/25:* letter from 2nd Lieutenant R.E. Simpkin to MR, dated May 21st 1942; addressed from 'BHQ 4 RTR, MEF'.
51. Peter Vaux, quoted in Forty, G., *Desert Rats at War: North Africa, Italy, Northwest Europe* (Air Sea Media Services, 2014). Captain Donald Graham Russell Reid had been a member of 'C' house (1930–1934).
52. Lieutenant General Sir Frank Walter Messervy CB, DSO (1893 –1974) was nicknamed 'The Bearded Man' because he often did not bother to shave when in the field.
53. Farran, R., *Winged Dagger* (Collins, 1948).
54. *Rigby family collection:* Rigby, R.M., 'Old Risalawallah Goes Walkabout'.
55. *WinColl E42/21/33:* letter from Roger Rigby to MR, dated May 28th 1942; addressed from 'Long Durford, Petersfield, Hants'.
56. *WinColl E42/21/34:* letter from Roger Rigby to MR, undated but early June 1942; addressed from 'Long Durford, Petersfield, Hants'.

57. At least four other Wykehamists were captured at Tobruk: Anthony Haig ('A' 1925–1930), Herbert Wake Bowell (College 1931–1936), Lionel Sackville-West ('K' 1926–1931) and Donny Mackenzie ('B' 1928–1933).
58. National Archives WO 344/288/1, PoW Interview Report, dated April 17th 1945.
59. Simpkin's companions in the attempted evasion were Major I.D. Banks and Lieutenant M.W. Sykes.
60. Fortune, V.M., in Foreword to Prittie, T.C.F. & Edwards, W.E., *Escape to Freedom* (Hutchinson, 1946)
61. Philpot, O., *Stolen Journey* (Hodder & Stoughton, 1950).
62. *WinColl E42/11/19:* letter from Lady Fortune to MR, dated June 20 1942; addressed from 'Aberdalgie House, Perth'.
63. Prittie, T.C.F. & Edwards, W.E., *Escape to Freedom* (Hutchinson, 1946).
64. Montgomery, D. & Horne, A., *The Lonely Leader: Monty 1944–45* (Macmillan, 1994).
65. David Bernard Montgomery, 2nd Viscount Montgomery of Alamein CMG, CBE (born August 18th 1928; 'I' 1942–1946), was the only son of Field Marshal Viscount Montgomery of Alamein KG, GCB, DSO, & Elizabeth Ada Noel 'Betty' Hobart, daughter of Robert Thompson Hobart, who already had two sons from her first marriage – her husband had been killed at Gallipoli. However, Betty died in 1937; whilst holidaying in Burnham-on-Sea, she was bitten by an insect; the bite became infected, & her leg was amputated. The septicaemia, however, killed her. After that, David spent his holidays with Major Thomas Reynolds (headmaster of his preparatory school), & Jocelyn Carver, wife of his half-brother John.

    Whilst at Winchester, he was Captain of Running; he then attended the RAC OCTU in 1947, where he won the Belt of Honour (which was presented to him by his father); commissioned into the RTR as a 2nd Lieutenant, he went up to Trinity College, Cambridge, in 1948, taking his Mechanical Science BA in 1950. In 1951 he began work for Shell International Petroleum, moving to Yardley International Ltd in 1962. He was married twice: in February 1953 to Mary Connell, & after his divorce in 1967 to Tessa de Zulueta, daughter of General Sir Frederick Browning & Daphne du Maurier. He died on January 8th 2020.
66. Wykehamists should take great pride in the fact that a former pupil – 281240 Lieutenant Lawrence Lawson Boyd ('G' 1923-1928) – was one of the four men of 'E' Troop, 83/85 Battery, 11RHA decorated for their part in the desperate stand which prevented the Germans from breaking the Alamein line. Just how desperate it was can be gauged from the fact that a fifth gunner, Bombardier Johnson, after his left arm had been blown off, continued to act as No.1 of his 25-pounder, aiming & firing it. He refused all aid, died two days later, & received no recognition. Boyd had only just assumed command of 'E' Troop's five guns, which were manned by personnel from four different Regiments. Boyd's citation for the immediate MC which he earned that day *(National Archives WO373/21/55)* runs: 'On 2 July during the attack on his column near the RUWEISAT RIDGE this officer showed most conspicuous courage & devotion to duty. He fought his Troop with success all day, largely contributing to driving off an attack by infantry. When it was attacked by Mk III & IV tanks, & heavily machine-gunned & shelled, he set a splendid example to all ranks by his complete disregard of danger. Although himself twice wounded, he took command of a gun when the Number 1 was killed. He continued to fight his guns until two of them were put out of action & all his ammunition was expended.' After the war, Boyd became a sales executive with the British Steel Corporation in Yorkshire.
67. National Archives WO 169/4509: War Diary, 6th Battalion, Royal Tank Regiment.
68. Seton-Watson (College 1931–1937) was later a distinguished historian.
69. Seton-Watson, C., *Dunkirk – Alamein – Bologna* (Buckland, 1993). Richardson rests in grave XVII.G.23 of the El Alamein War Cemetery.
70. *Supplement to the London Gazette,* June 29th 1943; McMurtrie's commission was dated December 4th 1942.
71. *Supplement to the London Gazette,* July 28th 1942.
72. *WinColl E42/9/16:* postcard from 2nd Lieutenant Charles Duffin to MR, postmarked July 31st 1942; addressed from 'Pirbright Camp, Woking'.

73. *WinColl E42/9/18:* letter from 2nd Lieutenant Charles Duffin (signed 'Duff') to MR, undated but late 1942; addressed from 'Guards Club, Brook Street W1'.
74. *Walker family collection:* letter from 4209970 Lance Corporal J.N. Somerville to Peter Walker, dated July 18th 1942; addressed from 'NCOs Cadre, 21st ITC, The Barracks, Brecon, South Wales'.
75. *Richardson collection:* letter from Miss Sheila Robertson to Mrs Agnes Richardson, dated July 21st 1942; addressed from 'Sunnyside, Winchester'.
76. *Richardson collection:* letter from MR to Mrs Agnes Richardson, dated July 21st 1942; addressed from 'Sunnyside, Winchester'.
77. *Wincoll E42/21/30:* letter from Mrs Agnes Richardson to MR, dated July 22nd 1942; addressed from 'The Lodge, Guildford Road, Fleet, Hants'.)
78. *WinColl E42/21/31:* letter from General Alec Richardson to MR, dated January 1st 1943; addressed from 'DAFV, The War Office'.

VIII

1. Crispin Hill ('I' 1937–1942) was the elder son of Frederick Ernest Hill, Headmaster of Aldro School near Godalming, & Audrey Blanche Hill, daughter of the Revd Francis Atkinson. He was born on January 14th 1924.
2. Robin Ord Lewin (born March 4th 1924; 'I' 1937–1942) was the only son of Major General Ernest Ord Lewin CB, CMG, DSO ('E' 1892-1897) & Anne Elizabeth Henderson Lewin, daughter of Robert Slack, of Keswick; his own son, Nicholas Ord Lewin, would later attend Winchester ('F' 1969-1973).
3. David Vivian Martyn ('I' 1937–1942), born on December 11th 1923, was the elder son of Major Rendel Vivian Martyn (Coldstream Guards) of 20 Queen's Gate Gardens, Kensington, London, & Florence Nancye Martyn. His maternal uncle was Lieutenant General Sir Otto Lund KCB ('I' 1905–1909). Like his Sinclair cousins & his younger brother, he came to Winchester from the Revd P.C. Underhill's school (Wellington House, at Westgate). After leaving Hopper's, he joined the Army & ended his career as Lieutenant 278662 D.V. Martyn, 1 Squadron, 1st (Armoured) Battalion, Coldstream Guards.
4. Peter Marshall Walker ('I' 1937–1942), who was born on June 16th 1924, was the elder son of Norman M. Walker JP of Reigate & Winifred Mary Walker, daughter of J.E. Whitton. His brother was K.P. Walker. His sons would become Wykehamists in their turn: Patrick N.C. Walker ('I' 1965–1970), Richard M. Walker ('I' 1969–1974), & Michael B.P. Walker ('I' 1972–1977).
5. 'A' 1939–1943.
6. *WinColl E42/17/144:* letter from Lieutenant General B.L. Montgomery to MR, dated August 8th 1942; addressed from 'Headquarters, South Eastern Command, Home Forces'.
7. Supplement to the *London Gazette,* March 31st 1942.
8. *WinColl E42/11/19:* letter from Lady Fortune to MR, dated June 20th 1942; addressed from 'Aberdalgie House, Perth'.
9. *WinColl E42/21/81:* letter from 2nd Lieutenant Hugh Rose to MR, dated September 23rd 1942; addressed from ' 'B' Company, 1st Battalion, The Black Watch RHR, Middle East Forces'.
10. Captain (Adjutant) Nigel Griffith Amedroz Noble ('E' 1933–1937) ended the war a Major, with an MC & two MiDs – one award for each of his three wounds. He went on to command 1BW from 1961 and retired from the Army in 1970 as a Brigadier.
11. *WinColl E42/21/81:* letter from 2nd Lieutenant Hugh Rose to MR, dated September 23rd 1942; addressed from ' 'B' Company, 1st Battalion, The Black Watch RHR, Middle East Forces'.
12. *WinColl E42/11/33:* letter from Lieutenant J. Bruce Fortune to MR, dated September 20th 1942; addressed from '1st Battalion, The Black Watch RHR, Middle East Forces'.
13. *WinColl E42/17/48:* letter from 2665309 Guardsman Recruit Martyn, L/Sgt. Brassington's Squad, 14th Company, Grenadier Guards, Guards Depot, Caterham, Surrey, to MR, dated September 20th 1942; addressed from '20 Queen's Gate Gardens SW7'.
14. The answer, of course, is Wavell. *WinColl E42/21/81:* letter from 2nd Lieutenant Hugh Rose to MR, dated September 23rd 1942; addressed from ' 'B' Company, 1st Battalion, The Black Watch RHR, Middle East Forces'.

15. *WinColl E42/21/81:* letter from 2nd Lieutenant Hugh Rose to MR, dated September 23rd 1942; addressed from ' 'B' Company, 1st Battalion, The Black Watch RHR, Middle East Forces'.
16. *Ibid.*
17. *Ibid.*
18. 52576 Major The Hon. Henry George Angus Browne ('I' 1925–1929), was the younger son of John Edward Deane Browne, 5th Baron Kilmaine, of Bexhill, Sussex, &, on his mother Lady Kilmaine's side, grandson of the Third Marquess of Ailsa (she was born Aline Kennedy). Born on October 9th 1911, 'he came to Winchester from Horris Hill four years after his brother John Francis Archibald Browne ('I' 1916–1921) had helped as Senior Prefect to start a new regime in the boarding house. Browne was a fine shot & helped to win Mackenzie Cup (twice) & House Cup, but cricket – he was a useful bowler & got his Flannels – kept him from Bisley. He went to RMC Sandhurst early in 1930, & in October 1931 joined the Rifle Brigade at Devonport, going to Malta two years later. Standing six feet six inches, & with good looks, Browne was always a striking figure. He enjoyed the polo & social life there & was on leave playing in Greenjacket Week in 1934 & again in 1936. Some sterner soldiering then seemed indicated, & he went early next year to Transjordania, where he was promoted Captain, & became Adjutant of the Frontier Force as well as being mentioned in despatches. He was acting Major when at the Staff College in Haifa at Christmas 1941, & afterwards was GSO2 in Transjordania. However, he pressed to go back to his Regiment in Egypt. He was posted to 1st Battalion, which had been re-formed after being destroyed at Calais in May 1940 (where it had been commanded by a fellow Wykehamist). He joined the Battalion as second-in-command in June 1942, in time for the grim fighting of the headlong retreat from Gazala to the El Alamein line. The desert bronzed & hardened Browne, & made him, by all accounts, a fine soldier & leader of men: he was expected shortly to get command of a battalion. On September 8th he was killed at El Alamein, aged thirty, by enemy action from the air.' He is buried in grave XXVII.H.25 of the El Alamein War Cemetery.
19. *WinColl E42/21/81:* letter from 2nd Lieutenant Hugh Rose to MR, dated September 23rd 1942; addressed from ' 'B' Company, 1st Battalion, The Black Watch RHR, Middle East Forces'.
20. *WinColl E42/21/80:* letter card from Hugh Rose to MR, dated October 17th 1942; no sender's address.
21. Quoted in *Winchester War Service Record & Roll of Honour.* 'The 42nd' were the Black Watch; many regiments liked to refer to themselves by their old number in the regimental system; for example, the King's Royal Rifle Corps often called themselves 'The 60th'.
22. For this & other memories which Fortune shared with his family, the author is indebted to summaries compiled & forwarded by Jack Fortune. To avoid distortion, these have often been incorporated verbatim into the text.
23. *WinColl E42/21/82.*
24. *WinColl E42/11/20:* letter from Lady Fortune to MR, dated November 7th 1942; addressed from 'Aberdalgie House, Perth'.
25. *WinColl E42/21/84:* letter from Bruce Fortune to MR, dated November 24th 1942; addressed from '1st Battalion, The Black Watch RHR, MEF'.
26. *WinColl E42/21/97:* letter from 14497437 Officer Cadet Michael James Ryall ('I' 1939–1944) to MR, dated March 8th 1945; addressed 'c/o Major General R.A.B. Freeland MC, Cecil Hotel, Delhi'.
27. Fergusson, B., *The Black Watch & the King's Enemies* (Collins, 1950).
28. 228632 Lieutenant Hugh Rose lies in grave XXVI.F.7 of the El Alamein War Cemetery.
29. *WinColl E42/21/83:* letter from Donald Dundas Scott ('B' 1937–1942) to MR, dated 'Thursday morning'; addressed from '69 Kingsgate Street, Winchester'.
30. *WinColl E42/21/85:* letter from 12 Platoon, 'B' Company, 1BW, to Colonel Hugh Rose CMG.
31. *WinColl E42/21/84:* letter from Bruce Fortune to MR, dated November 24th 1942; addressed from '1st Battalion, The Black Watch RHR, MEF'.
32. Supplement to the *London Gazette,* June 29th 1943.
33. *WinColl E42/17/18:* letter from Duncan McMurtrie to MR, undated but probably December 1942; addressed from 'St Ibbs Bush, Hitchin, Herts'.
34. *WinColl E42/13/82:* letter from Lieutenant Colonel Edmond Holtby OBE, MC ('I' 1903-1907) to MR, dated November 16th 1940; addressed from 'Dowthorpe Hall, Skirlaugh, Hull'. Robert

Leslie Holtby ('I' 1938–1942), his only son, was born on December 4th 1924. Holtby's mother was Alexandra Mary Bell (Smith), of Ecclefechan; he was half-brother to David Welsh & eventually father of John Holtby ('I' 1970-1975). His grandson was in Hopper's when this author was a house tutor there.

35. *WinColl E42/13/83:* letter from Lieutenant Colonel Holtby to MR, dated October 6th 1942; addressed from 'Dowthorpe Hall, Skirlaugh, Hull'.
36. *The Wykehamist (*887, December 1942).
37. William Marcus Hampton (1903–1964).
38. Captain Thomas Cloud Hampton was commanding the anti-aircraft cruiser HMS *Carlisle* when, during the battle for Crete, she was damaged by enemy aircraft on May 22nd 1941; he was killed by a direct hit. The *Carlisle* nevertheless continued to engage the enemy convoy which she had been attacking.
39. *WinColl G317, from Pike collection*: letter from MR to Mrs Tompson, dated December 18th 1942; addressed from 'Sunnyside, Winchester'.

IX

1. *Somerville family collection:* Somerville, C. unpublished memoirs, typescript, undated.
2. *WinColl E42/22/49:* letter from 'Dan' Somerville to MR, dated November 25th 1941; addressed from 'Potential Officers Training Squad, 'D' Battery, 4th Field Training Regiment RA, Bulford Camp, Wiltshire'.
3. *WinColl E42/22/54:* letter from Brigadier D.H.S. Somerville to MR, dated 'Xmas Day '41'; addressed from 'HQ 72 Infantry Brigade, Home Forces'.
4. *London Gazette,* April 14th 1942: 'Sgts: 2nd Jan. 1942. 778275 John Godfrey HUGGINS (80269).'
5. *WinColl E42/13/95:* letter from Godfrey Huggins to MR, dated January 4th 1942; addressed from 'Salisbury, Southern Rhodesia'.
6. *WinColl E42/13/96:* letter from Pilot Officer J.G. Huggins to MR, dated January 10th 1942; addressed from 'The Hotel Edward, Marine Parade, Durban, PO Box 105, Durban'.
7. Antony Hanbury ('K' 1936–1940) trained in Rhodesia, was commissioned in 1942, & by 1945 had seen service as a pilot in Syria, the Western Desert, & Italy. Along the way he had reached the rank of Flight Lieutenant & had been wounded.
8. Boys at Winchester were organized not according to their age & year of joining, but instead began in the form which seemed to the school best to reflect their standard on arrival, & were promoted ('removed') to the next form when their teachers felt that they were ready. The eccentric system of naming for forms still survives in part, but in the 1930s the progression was: Junior Part 2, Junior Part 1; Middle Part 3, 2, Science, & 1; Senior Part Science III, 3, 2, Science II, Science I, & 1; & Sixth Book 2, Science, 1b & 1a.
9. *WinColl E42/21/26:* letter from Guy Richardson to MR, dated December 14th 1941; addressed from '76 Hut, HMS *Goshawk*, c/o GPO London'.
10. *WinColl E42/17/81:* letter from Pat Metcalfe to MR, dated June 21st 1942; addressed from '45th Cavalry, Nira, near Poona, India'.
11. *Rigby family collection:* Rigby, R.M., 'Old Risalawallah Goes Walkabout'.
12. *Ibid.*
13. *WinColl E42/21/38:* letter from Roger Rigby to MR, dated December 6th 1942; addressed 'c/o Lloyd's Bank, Bombay'.
14. *Rigby family collection:* Rigby, R.M., 'Old Risalawallah Goes Walkabout'.
15. Supplement to the *London Gazette,* July 17th 1942, p.3142.
16. The Territorial units of 61st Infantry Division were responsible for the defence of Northern Ireland from June 1940, but returned to England in February 1943. Stationed in Essex, the Division was downgraded to home service only, training replacement soldiers for units on active service, & acting as enemy in major training exercises. Its only 'active' role was in Operation Fortitude in 1944.
17. Colin George Champion Rae MC ('B' 1934–1939) was commissioned into the Royal Artillery in 1940 but by 1944 was a Captain in No.3 Commando, which whom he served in Normandy & Germany. He was wounded in the process.

18. Edward Peter Blake Frewen ('E' 1935–1940) attended New College, Oxford, in 1940 but was commissioned as a 2nd Lieutenant into 10RB in 1941. With them he served in Tunisia, where he was killed in April 1943. He bequeathed to Winchester College a Father Smith Chamber Organ & a sum of money.
19. *WinColl E42/22/50:* letter from 2nd Lieutenant C. Somerville to MR, dated November 1st 1942; addressed from '396 Field Battery RA, c/o 7th Glosters, Home Forces'.
20. National Archives WO 361/2123, Prisoners of War, Far East: 9th Battalion, Royal Northumberland Fusiliers; nominal roll 01 Jan 1943 – 31 Dec 1945.
21. *https://www.cofepow.org.uk/armed-forces-stories-list/the-9th-battalion-royal-northumberland-fusiliers* (accessed December 23rd 2020).
22. *WinColl E42/21/23:* letter from Mrs Muriel Philbrick to MR, dated June 7th 1943; addressed from 'Appleshaw House, Compton, near Winchester'.
23. *WinColl E42/08/27:* letter from Sam Clayton to MR, dated October 27th 1945; addressed from 'Hampton Court Palace, Middlesex'.
24. Supplement to the *London Gazette,* September 2nd 1941: commission dated August 23rd 1941.
25. A Royal Engineers Field Park Company provided the heavy equipment, workshop and stores for the Sappers in an infantry division (in an armoured division it was called a Field Park Squadron). Commanded by a Major, with a Captain as second-in-command, it contained three platoons.
26. *WinColl E42/09/09:* letter from Lieutenant G.H. Dodgson RE to MR, dated December 29th 1942; addressed from '219 Field Park Company RE, c/o Army Base Post Office, India'.
27. du Boulay, interview with author, 2010.
28. Details taken from White, E.G., *Nightfighter Navigator* (published online).
29. *WinColl E42/15/4:* letter from 1247078 Kennedy J. LAC to MR, dated February 18th 1942; addressed from 'ON ACTIVE SERVICE, ARNOLD/ALLAY c/o RCAF, Ottowa, Canada'.
30. 74 Operational Training Unit (OTU) had formed at Ismailia in Egypt in September 1941, but had immediately moved to Gordon's Tree in Sudan. The following month, it had again relocated, this time to Aqir in Palestine.
31. Z4025 was built by the Gloster Aircraft Company between July 1940 & August 1941. She suffered an accident whilst taxiing at 74 OTU on June 12th 1942, with 2nd Lieutenant Black at the controls.
32. *The Times,* October 21st 1941: 'The Student at War'.
33. *WinColl E42/15/05:* letter from 1247078 Kennedy J. to MR, dated April 20th 1942; addressed from 'RAF, US Army Air Corps, Training Detachment, Class 421, Alabama Institute of Aeronautics, Hargrove Van De Graaff Field, Tuscaloosa, Alabama'.
34. The American Dorothy Celene Thompson (1893–1961) was an influential journalist & broadcaster who had been expelled from Nazi Germany in 1934 because of her contempt for Hitler. At the time Kennedy heard her, she was an outspoken supporter of Zionism.
35. This & many other details concerning Huggins' time with 237 are taken from National Archives AIR 27/1450/35, the unit's Operations Record Book
36. *WinColl E42/13/97:* letter from Pilot Officer J.G. Huggins to MR, dated May 2th 1942; addressed from '237 Squadron RAF, MEF'.
37. *WinColl E42/22/43:* postcard from Lieutenant A.M. Sinclair to MR, dated Sunday June 21st 1942; addressed from 'Oflag IVC/E, Germany'.
38. *WinColl E42/13/98:* letter from Blanche E. Huggins to MR, dated October 13th 1942; addressed from 'Cathedral Peak Hotel, PO Winterton, Natal'.
39. *WinColl E42/15/10:* letter from Mrs Constance Kennedy to MR, dated July 26th 1942; addressed from 'Welburn Manor, Kirbymoorside, Yorkshire'.
40. Supplement to the *London Gazette,* December 1st 1942: 'LAC (Ldg Acm) … 09 Oct 1942 … 1247078 John Kennedy (131030).'
41. Supplement to the *London Gazette,* March 12th 1941.
42. *WinColl E42/10/01:* airgraph letter from Lieutenant M.C. Edmunds to MR, dated November 17th 1942; addressed from '7th Oxford & Bucks Light Infantry, PAIFORCE'.

43. *WinColl E42/22/44:* postcard from Lieutenant A.M. Sinclair to MR, dated December 31st 1942; addressed from 'Oflag IVC/E, Germany'.
44. *WinColl E42/17/02:* letter from Mrs Monica Augusta McArthur to MR, dated January 11th 1943; addressed from 'Combe End, Alcombe, Minehead, Somerset'.
45. Form S.206, dated May 1943.
46. Form S.206, dated July 1943.
47. *Mackrill family collection:* letter from Graham Mackrill to Mr & Mrs H.W. Mackrill, dated Monday March 15th 1943; addressed from 'Sunnyside, Winchester'.
48. *Mackrill family collection:* H.G. Mackrill, Diary, 1943.
49. *WinColl E42/13/99:* letter from Flying Officer J.G. Huggins to MR, dated January 30th 1943; addressed from '237 Squadron RAF, Persia & Iraq Forces'.
50. National Archives AIR 27/1450/35, 237 Squadron Operations Record Book, entry for February 9th 1943: 'F/O Huggins posted to 2 PRU'.

X

1. For this and other memories which Fortune shared with his family, the author is indebted to summaries compiled and forwarded by Johnnie Fortune. To avoid distortion, these have often been incorporated verbatim into the text.
2. National Archives WO 179/1971: War Diary, 1 Black Watch, 1943.
3. *Ibid.*
4. Fortune, S.M., *Time to Remember* (privately published, 2002). Their son states that Fortune in fact used the words 'by doing something *bloody* stupid!'
5. 92nd General Hospital was located in Kantara, Egypt, from November 1942 until October 1943.
6. *WinColl E42/11/22:* letter from Lady Fortune to MR, dated March 16th 1943; addressed from 'Balgray, Lockerbie'.
7. *WinColl E42/11/34:* letter from Lieuenant J.B. Fortune MC to MR, dated March 18th 1943; addressed from '1st Black Watch RHR, c/o 92nd General Hospital, MEF'.
8. Captain Gilbert Seymour Wyndham Talbot ('A' 1935–1940) served in 1st Battalion, Rifle Brigade, from 1941, seeing action in North Africa, Italy, & Normandy until his death in action near Bayeux on June 20th 1944. He had twice been wounded, & served for a time as ADC to Sir Maitland Wilson in Cairo.
9. National Archives WO 373/24/194: Recommendation for Award for Fortune, John Bruce Forrester.
10. *WinColl E42/17/102:* letter from 6107070 Officer Cadet Middleditch D.S. to MR, dated November 1st 1942; addressed from '18 Troop, 'C' Squadron, RAC OCTU, Camberley'.
11. *Wincoll E42/07/32:* letter from Michael Elliott-Binns to MR, undated but probably February 1943; addressed from 'Newton St Cyres Vicarage, Exeter'.
12. *WinColl E42/17/101:* letter from 6107070 Officer Cadet Middleditch D.S. to MR, misdated February 7th 1942 for 1943; addressed from '18 Troop, HAC Squadron, RAC OCTU, Camberley, Surrey'.
13. *WinColl E42/21/39:* letter from 2nd Lieutenant R.M. Rigby to MR, dated January 29th 1943; addressed 'c/o Lloyd's Bank, Bombay'.
14. *WinColl E42/17/82:* letter from Lieutenant P.R. Metcalfe to MR, dated February 13th 1943; addressed from '45th Cavalry, c/o No21 Advanced Base Post Office, India'.
15. Lieutenant Colonel William Robin Palmer Ridgway OBE, TD, joined the staff at Winchester in 1926, having seen brief service in the Royal Garrison Artillery in 1918. On the outbreak of war he became a staff officer, serving in Norway in 1940. His promotion was rapid; by 1942 he was a Lieutenant Colonel GSO1 in GHQ India, & he became Private Secretary to the Commander-in-Chief India from 1943, Field Marshal Sir Claude Auchinleck. He returned to Winchester in 1946 & remained on the staff until 1953.
16. *WinColl E42/15/6:* letter from P/O J. Kennedy to MR, dated February 13th 1943; addressed from 'GAFS, Greenville, Mississippi'.
17. Campbell Crichton-Miller ('I' 1929–1934) was killed in action when Halifax DK123 was shot down by flak over Distré, near Saumur in France, on February 19th 1943. He is buried in Grave 3 Row 1 of the Military Plot in the Saumur Communal Cemetery.

18. Supplement to the *London Gazette,* April 2nd 1943.
19. *Hirst family collection:* Hirst, M.J., 'M.J.H.'s War Service', typescript, 29 pages, undated.
20. Supplement to the *London Gazette,* March 3rd 1942, & Supplement to the *London Gazette,* April 3rd 1942.
21. Major Kenneth Beauchamp Hicks ('K' 1914–1918) had joined the Rifle Brigade in 1920 & risen to Major by 1938. He was second-in-command of 7th Battalion in Tunisia from 1942 (where he was wounded), & posted as Lieutenant Colonel commanding 44th Reconnaissance Regiment in 1943. He served in Italy & Greece, became a full Colonel in 1944, & was awarded the OBE in 1945.
22. Lieutenant Richard Borlase Adams ('F' 1934–1939).
23. 2nd Lieutenant William Mercer Adams ('F' 1937–1941).
24. Denis James Purdon ('A' 1914–1918) was commissioned into the Rifle Brigade in 1920, & by 1941 had risen to Lieutenant Colonel commanding 9RB. He served in North Africa & Italy until 1944, was twice mentioned in dispatches, & received the US Legion of Merit in 1946.
25. Hew Dacres George Butler ('E' 1935–1940) was commissioned into the Rifle Brigade in 1941 & served with 7RB in Tunisia from 1942 until his wounding & capture in 1943.
26. More of Cliff Hodges later.
27. Sheepshanks is not exaggerating; his was the worst handwriting of any of the 1938 cohort. *WinColl E42/22/12:* letter from 226413 Lt C.W. Sheepshanks to MR, dated February 1st 1943; addressed from '7th Battalion, The Rifle Brigade, MEF'.
28. Anthony Napier Sturt ('I' 1925–1930) took a commission in the Rifle Brigade in 1940 & served with 7RB in Tunisia & Italy from 1942 to 1945. He was wounded, & reached the rank of Captain.
29. Again, Sheepshanks is spot-on in his assessment. *WinColl E42/22/13:* letter from 226413 Lt C.W. Sheepshanks to MR, dated March 9th 1943; addressed from '7th Battalion, The Rifle Brigade, MEF'.
30. 6th Grenadier Guards suffered terrible losses on the Mareth Line, where Gwyer was killed in action on March 17th 1943. He rests in grave XIII.D.8 of the Sfax War Cemetery, Tunisia. A memorial to the Battalion – the Mareth Cross – was rescued from the battlefield & now stands outside the Guards Chapel in Wellington Barracks.
31. *WinColl E42/15/07:* letter from Pilot Officer J. Kennedy to MR, dated April 24th 1943; addressed from 'Royal Air Force, GAFS, Greenville, Mississippi'.
32. *Ibid.*
33. Supplement to the *London Gazette,* May 28th 1943.
34. Hastings, R.H.W.S., *The Rifle Brigade in the Second World War 1939-1945* (Gale & Polden, 1950).
35. *Ibid.*
36. National Archives WO 169/10287: War Diary, 7RB.
37. The Rifle Brigade traditionally referred to bayonets as swords.
38. Hastings, R.H.W.S., *The Rifle Brigade in the Second World War 1939-1945* (Gale & Polden, 1950).
39. Hastings, R.H.W.S., *The Rifle Brigade in the Second World War 1939-1945* (Gale & Polden, 1950).
40. Sheepshanks lies in grave XI.C.19 of Sfax War Cemetery.
41. *WinColl E42/22/14:* letter from Sir Thomas Sheepshanks to MR, dated April 14th 1943; addressed from 'Broom House'.
42. Douglas Lyle Darling, an Etonian, retired as a Major General in 1978. His daughter Christine married a Wykehamist, Major Robin N.H. Alers-Hankey ('F' 1949–1954), who in September 1971 was fatally wounded by an IRA sniper in Londonderry whilst serving as OC 'C' Company, 2nd Battalion, Royal Green Jackets. He died of his wounds in hospital in London on January 30th 1972. At the Bloody Sunday inquiry, it was alleged that the terrorist who shot him was a certain Martin McGuinness.
43. εὐκλεὴς μὲν ἁ τύχα, καλὸς δ'ὁ πότμος, βωμὸς δ'ὁ τάφος, πρὸγόων δὲ μνᾶστις, ὁδ' οἶκτος ἔπαινος.
44. *WinColl E42/22/51:* letter from Lieutenant C. Somerville to MR, dated March 28th 1943; addressed from 'HQ 183 Infantry Brigade, Home Forces'.
45. Lieutenant Colonel Kenneth Edward 'Kate' Savill DSO ('K' 1920–1924). For the last five years of his life he was the 'Sen Man', the oldest surviving Wykehamist. According to his obituary in the

Hampshire Chronicle (March 20th 2008), 'He took a lively interest in local and family affairs, & had many friends of different generations, whose lives he greatly enhanced with his humour & generous nature – none more than his two daughters, five grandchildren, & eight great-grandchildren, with whom he was playing hide & seek on the day he died.' He was 101 years old.

46. *WinColl E42/17/103:* letter from 2nd Lieutenant D.S. Middleditch to MR, dated May 1st 1943; addressed from 'Officers' Mess, 27th Lancers, Kirkby Stephen, Nr Penryth, Westmorland (until May 9th)'.
47. 26346 Lieutenant Colonel Lawrence Richardson Younger ('I' 1915–1920) was killed in action by shell-fire on April 26th 1943 near Djebel Kournine, Tunisia. He rests in grave 16.H.1 of the Medjez-el-Bab War Cemetery.
48. Since Worm's Head is in Wales, Mackrill's postcard was presumably an image of that place. The limestone peninsula forms the westernmost tip of the Gower Peninsula. Far from being named by a biologist, the promontory's name came from Old English for a sea-serpent, which the rocky formation could be said to resemble.
49. *Mackrill family collection*: letter from MR to Graham Mackrill, dated April 26th 1943 '(SMR's birthday tomorrow!)'; addressed from 'Culver Lodge, Winchester'.
50. 69381 Lieutenant Colonel Guy Gervers Holmes Wilson ('I' 1918–1922), Royal Artillery, was the CRA of 3rd Infantry Division. He is buried in grave B.B.101 of the Windlesham Additional Burial Ground in Surrey.
51. *WinColl E42/11/35:* letter from Lieutenant J.B. Fortune BW to MR, dated May 9th 1943; addressed from '13th General Hospital, MEF'. 13th British General Hospital was located in Suez at this time.
52. Lieutenant Christopher Robert Foot ('G' 1936–1941).
53. Paul Annesley Gore ('A' 1934–1939).
54. *WinColl E42/7/82:* letter from from Lieutenant H.A.G. Brooke to MR, undated but probably July 1943; addressed from '16th/5th Lancers, BNAF'.
55. Knowles, S.W., *Soldier On: The Personal Experiences of a Tank Crewman in the 16th/5th Lancers during the Second World War* (Leonaur, 2016).

XI

1. 850 Squadron, established in January 1943, was disbanded at the end of the same month.
2. The Grumman TBF-1 Avenger entered service in January 1942 & first saw action at the Battle of Midway in June that year. Able to carry a torpedo or 2,000lbs of bombs out to a radius of 500 miles, the Avenger had a crew of three (or four), a rear defensive turret, & a top speed of around 260mph. By the end of 1943 over two thousand had entered service with the USN & FAA.
3. *WinColl E41/21/32:* letter from Mrs Nan Richardson to MR, dated March 18th 1943.
4. John Fay, quoted in Smith, M., *Voices in Flight: The Fleet Air Arm: Recollections from Formation to Cold War* (Pen & Sword, 2013).
5. The three airmen who suffered fatal injuries were buried at sea & are commemorated on the Lee-on-Solent Memorial. Temporary Lieutenant (A) Harold Eyre, the Pilot, was twenty-six. He left a widow called Margaret. Behind him sat Temporary Sub Lieutenant (A) William Hugh Gillespie Browne, the Observer, aged twenty-three, who was also married; his widow was Catherine. In the aft turret was P/LD/X 5299 Temporary Leading Airman William Frederick Lovell (Telegraphist Air Gunner 3rd Class), aged twenty-five, from Peckham. Almost exactly a year before, he had been mentioned in dispatches; he also left a widow, Gladys.
6. *WinColl E41/21/27:* letter from Sub Lieutenant G. Richardson (A) RNVR to MR, dated March 15th 1943; addressed from '[XXXXXX]'.
7. This crash, on April 8th, killed Temporary Sub Lieutenant (A) Kenneth Roberts Smith (Pilot) & Temporary Sub Lieutenant (A) Reginald Edgar Highland (Observer). Both rest in the Oahu Cemetery, Honolulu (Plot 163A, Section 2).

XII

1. Supplement to the *London Gazette*, July 13th 1943.
2. *WinColl E42/17/49:* letter from David Martyn to MR, dated June 10th 1943; addressed from 'St Enodoc Golf Hotel, Rock, Nr. Wadebridge, Cornwall'.
3. National Archives WO 166/11295: War Diary, 145th Field Regiment RA.
4. Bart Stevens (stepson of David Kemp), personal communication to author, February 28th 2022.
5. Supplement to the *London Gazette*, July 2nd 1943: 'Cdts to 2nd Lt: KRRC Robin Ord LEWIN (277430).' On the same KRRC list was an Etonian, Dwin Bramall, later Field Marshal Edwin Noel Westby Bramall, Baron Bramall KG, GCB, OBE, MC, JP, DL. Bramall served alongside Lewin in 2KRRC in Normandy & beyond, & their friendship was lifelong. Bramall (1923–2019) rose to become Chief of the General Staff (the professional head of the British Army) from 1979 to 1982, & Chief of the Defence Staff (head of the entire British armed forces) 1982–1985.
6. *WinColl E42/16/31:* letter from Major General Ernest Ord Lewin CB, CMG, DSO to MR, dated October 25th 1943; addressed from 'The Manor, Bourton on the Water'.
7. The KRRC were often known as 'The Sixtieth' as this was the Regiment's original number in the order of precedence.
8. *The Wykehamist* (890, June 2nd 1943).
9. 'Old Wykehamists send best wishes to The Bobber and his most outstanding sister. Captured Wykehamists greet you, Bobber, in ranks, and neither distance nor any shackles prevent it. Your *protegés* are sad because you are stepping down from your post, but nevertheless, because you are held close to their hearts, they calm their grieving spirits. Soon now Almighty God will decide to give you the best of things and welcome rest.'
10. Monday May 24th 1943.
11. Henrietta Fenton *(née* Mackrill), personal communication to author, January 18th 2022.
12. 140305 Lieutenant Paul Hugh Gearing's MC was gazetted in the same issue as Simpkins' (Supplement to the *London Gazette,* February 24th 1942); as well as the action for which he won the medal, he had been in the tank which accompanied Pip Gardner on his VC-winning rescue mission. He was awarded a bar to his MC in 1945.
13. *WinColl E42/22/28:* letter from Mrs Ethel Coller to MR, dated November 24th 1942; addressed 'Kettlewell'.
14. National Archives WO 344/288/1: Prisoner of War Interview Report, dated April 17th 1945.
15. *Simpkin family collection:* R.E. Simpkin to Barbara Simpkin, November 3rd 1942.
16. *Rigby family collection:* Rigby, R.M., 'Old Risalawallah Goes Walkabout'.
17. The Himalayan Red Bear *(Ursus arctos isabellinus)* is also referred to as the Isabelline Bear or Himalayan Brown Bear. Essentially a local sub-species of Brown Bear, it may be the origin of the myth of the Yeti.
18. *Rigby family collection:* Rigby, R.M., 'Old Risalawallah Goes Walkabout'.
19. The *Batory* had a varied wartime career. In 1940 alone, she ferried British troops to Norway & collected others from Dunkirk; she transported Polish treasures & some £40,000,000 of Britain's gold reserves to Canada; & she delivered nearly 500 evacuated children to Australia. In April 1942 she took Roald Dahl across the Atlantic, before assisting with Allied landings in Algeria (Operation Torch, November 1942), Sicily (Operation Husky, July 1943), & southern France (Operation Dragoon, August 1944). She survived several enemy attacks & was nicknamed the 'Lucky Ship' (as well as the 'Singing Ship' after her voyage with the children).
20. As part of Operation Husky, the *Batory* & nineteen other ships sailed as convoy KMF 18 from the Clyde on June 28th 1943, arriving off Sicily on July 10th 1943.
21. The same information is given in *WinColl E42/13/47,* a letter from 264517 2nd Lieutenant Hirst M.J. to MR, dated July 15th 1943, & addressed from 'RAC, No.2 CRU, BNAF'. The letter adds no detail to this later account, and is thus not quoted here.
22. *Walker family collection:* letter from 2nd Lieutenant J.N. Somerville to Peter Walker, dated August 28th 1943; addressed from '24th Regiment, 21 ITC, Dering Lines, Brecon'.
23. *Ibid.*

24. *WinColl E42/17/106:* letter form from Lieutenant D.S. Middleditch to MR, dated October 26th 1943; addressed from ''A' Squadron, XII Royal Lancers, BNAF'.
25. National Archives WO 166/11295: War Diary, 145th Field Regiment RA.
26. *WinColl E42/17/14:* letter from 253912 2nd Lieutenant D.G.S. McMurtrie, Scots Guards, to MR, undated but clearly summer 1943; addressed from ''E' Company, 3rd Battalion, 1st IRTD, BNAF'.
27. *WinColl E42/17/17:* three airgraphs from 253912 Lieutenant D.G.S. McMurtrie to MR, dated October 31st 1943; addressed from '1st Battalion Scots Guards, BNAF'. *WinColl E42/17/16:* one airgraph from 253912 Lieutenant D.G.S. McMurtrie to SMR, dated October 31st 1943; addressed from '1st Battalion Scots Guards, BNAF'.
28. *WinColl E42/12/47:* letter from Major General Geoffrey Hind to MR, dated September 30th 1943.
29. *WinColl E42/21/40:* letter from Roger Rigby to MR, dated November 17th 1943; addressed 'c/o Lloyd's Bank, Bombay'.
30. An *aide-de-camp*'s role has varied over time & with different national customs, but essentially it was that of a personal assistant to a senior officer. In battle, an ADC might convey written or oral orders to subordinate commanders; more usually, an ADC would help to organize his officer's social calendar, household affairs, & ceremonial.
31. Column 17: infantry from 2nd Battalion, Royal Leicestershire Regiment.
    Column 21: infantry from 2nd Battalion, Queen's Royal Regiment (West Surrey).
    Column 22: infantry from 2nd Battalion, Queen's Royal Regiment (West Surrey).
    Column 45: infantry from 45th Reconnaissance Regiment.
    Column 51: infantry from 51 Field Regiment, Royal Artillery.
    Column 54: infantry from 45th Reconnaissance Regiment.
    Column 69: infantry from 69 Field Regiment, Royal Artillery.
    Column 71: infantry from 2nd Battalion, Royal Leicestershire Regiment.
    Column 99: HQ column.
    Most of these Column numbers relate to the identity of their core unit; for example, 17 Column was formed from the historic 17th Regiment of Foot, with 71 Column being the reverse of 17. The Queen's West Surreys were the second most senior Regiment in the British Army, so the two Column numbers represent 2-1 and 2-2.
32. *WinColl E42/21/40:* letter from Roger Rigby to MR, dated November 17th 1943; addressed 'c/o Lloyd's Bank, Bombay'.
33. *Rigby family collection:* Rigby, R.M., 'My War with the Duke of Aosta'.
34. *Ibid.*
35. *Ibid.*
36. Supplement to the *London Gazette,* May 25th 1943.
37. *WinColl E42/13/27:* letter from Acting Captain Arthur Herbert to MR, dated December 12th 1943; addressed from 'HQ Mess, School of Signals, Catterick Camp, Yorkshire'.
38. *Rigby family collection:* Rigby, R.M., 'My War with the Duke of Aosta'.
39. Daughter of Charles James Mackie.
40. Fortune, S.M., *Time to Remember* (privately published, 2002).

XIII

1. Imperial War Museum AYY 375/3.
2. National Archives AIR 27/2197/9: Operations Record Book, 680 Squadron. Spitfire BS363 was a PR.IV, which had left the factory in September 1942 & survived to be scrapped at the war's end.
3. National Archives AIR 27/2197/9: Operations Record Book, 680 Squadron:
   June 11th 1943: 'LG219 1815-1835 F/O J.G. HUGGINS air tested Spitfire BR430, but returned after twenty minutes as the oil temperature was over 90°C. Time: .20.' Spitfire BR430 was a PR.IV which had left the factory in May 1942; she failed to return from a PR mission over Crete & Greece on February 14th 1944, Flight Sergeant V.A. McCarthy, RAAF, being posted missing.
   June 12th 1943: 'LG219 1750-1815 F/O J.G. HUGGINS air tested Spitfire BR654. Time: .45.' BR654 was another PR.IV, which had her first flight on July 8th 1942; she was scrapped at the war's end.

June 12th 1943: 'LG219 1830-1900 F/O J.G. HUGGINS air tested Spitfire BR427. Time: .30.' Spitfire PR.IV BR427 first flew on May 24th 1942; she seems to have remained with 680 Squadron until struck off charge on May 31st 1945.

4. National Archives AIR 27/2197/9: Operations Record Book, 680 Squadron. Spitfire AB310, another PR.IV, first flew on December 16th 1941; she would crash on landing on September 4th 1943.
5. National Archives AIR 27/2917/9: Operations Record Book, 680 Squadron:
   June 16th 1943: 'LG 219 1055-1155 F/O J.G. HUGGINS air tested Spitfire EN254. Time: 1.00.' Spitfire IX EN254 had only recently arrived in the Middle East; she was transferred to the Royal Hellenic Air Force in 1947.
   June 16th 1943: 'LG219 1245-1645 F/O J.G. HUGGINS air tested Spitfire BP908. Time: 4.00.' BP908 was a Spitfire PR.IV, which survived the war only to be scrapped in 1946.
   June 18th 1943: 'LG219 1130-1200 F/O J.G. HUGGINS air tested Spitfire BP908. Time: .30.'
6. Spitfire PR.IV BR644 first flew on June 20th 1942; she force-landed in Turkey on a PR mission over the Aegean on September 26th 1943.
7. National Archives AIR 27/2917/9: Operations Record Book, 680 Squadron:
   June 22nd 1942: 'LG219 1125-1215 F/O J.G. HUGGINS air tested Spitfire BP908. Time: .50.'
   June 24th 1942: 'LG219 1115-1215 F/O J.G. HUGGINS air tested Spitfire BP908. Time: 1.00.'
   June 25th 1942: 'LG219 1755-1805 F/O J.G. HUGGINS air tested Spitfire BR652, returning early with windscreen covered in oil. Time: .10.' Spitfire PR.IV BR652 had first flown on on July 4th 1942, & was struck off charge in May 1945.
   June 26th 1942: '1150-0800 F/O J.G. HUGGINS flew to Derna in Spitfire BR644 & from there carried out a successful PR of ARGOS & HASSANI returning to Matruh. The Pilot stayed the night & returned to base the following morning. Time 5.25.'
8. National Archives AIR 27/2917/9: Summary for June 1943 by Wing Commander J.R. WHELAN DFC, OC 680 Squadron: 'This month's weather was good & work unlimited, being connected with the Sicilian preparations, & the Crete raid. 53 sorties were carried out, 5 being unsuccessful, none through weather ... 'C' Flight completed their second cover of Rhodes & Dodecanese Islands & are carrying on their third. Preparations were made to detach 'B' Flight at Derna, so that no operations are carried out from base [LG 219] now. 'A' Flight becomes the communications flight & tests flight. Three ferry pilots & three Hurricanes have been attached to maintain communications with detachments.'
9. National Archives AIR 27/2917/11: Operations Record Book, 680 Squadron.
10. Image sources:
    https://i.pinimg.com/originals/a7/65/95/a765954efbcf8606f84b8b9c9871741a.jpg
    https://www.facebook.com/The-Photo-Reconnaissance-Spitfire-Page-2171517989742300/photos/PR.IV-br416-with-mascot-carrying-an-interesting-camo-pattern/2195067440720688.
11. National Archives AIR 27/2917/11 & 13: Operations Record Book, 680 Squadron:
    July 17th 1943: 'Nicosia 1035 F/O HUGGINS, Spitfire PR.IV BR416, air test, landed 1120.'
    July 20th 1943: 'Nicosia 0730 F/O HUGGINS, Spitfire PR.IV BS493, took off on a PR of Simi island, complete cover, & Rhodes, coastal strips & Maritza aerodrome, with 36-inch camera. Landed 1110. Ops: Hrs: 3.40.' Spitfire PR.IV BS493's first flight had been in October 1942. She was struck off charge in September 1945.
    July 23rd 1943: 'Nicosia 0740 F/O HUGGINS, Spitfire PR.IV BR416, took off on a PR of Rhodes with one 36-inch camera. Rhodes harbour & coast south to Cape Ladiko were covered. Landed 1040. Ops: Hrs: 3.00.' Spitfire PR.IV BP904 was one of the oldest on 680 Squadron, having first flown in February 1942. In January 1945, at RAF Qastina in Palestine, her engine cut out on landing; she belly-landed & overturned.
    July 28th 1943: 'Nicosia 0730 F/O HUGGINS, Spitfire PR.IV BP904, took off on a PR of aerodromes on Scarpanto & Rhodes with split 20-inch cameras. Effialti (Scarpanto), Kattavia, & Calato (Rhodes) were covered. Landed 1100. Ops: Hrs: 3.30.'

August 3rd 1943: 'Nicosia 07.40 F/O J. HUGGINS, Spitfire PR.IV BR644 to LG219. Landed 10.10 … 14.55 F/O J. HUGGINS, Spitfire PR.IV BR644, to Nicosia. Landed 17.10.'
August 4th 1943: 'Nicosia 08.30 F/O J. HUGGINS, Spitfire PR.IV BP904, split 20-inch cameras, took off on a PR of Scarpanto & Rhodes. At Scarpanto, Effialti aerodrome was covered. At Rhodes, Kattavia & Calato aerodromes were covered. Also runs inland on north of island. Landed 1205. Ops: Hrs: 3.35.'
August 9th 1943: 'Nicosia 1215 F/O J. HUGGINS, Spitfire PR.IV BR645, two 20-inch cameras, took off on a PR of Rhodes. Returned unsuccessful. Glycol trouble. Landed 1530. Ops: Hrs: 3.05.' Spitfire PR.IV BR645, which first flew in June 1942, did not have long to live; she crashed near Berka whilst returning from a sortie on September 26th.
August 12th 1943: 'Nicosia 0735 F/O J. HUGGINS, Spitfire PR.IV BP920, two 20-inch cameras, took off on PR of Scarpanto, covering Effialti aerodrome, & Rhodes, covering Kattavia & Calato aerodromes. Landed 1040. Ops: Hrs:3.05.' Three months older than BR645, BP920 was also a Spitfire PR.IV. She survived until April 3rd 1945 when, serving with 74 OTU, she taxied into Harvard EZ340 at Petah Tiqva. She was struck off charge the following month.

12. National Archives AIR 27/2917/13: Operations Record Book, 680 Squadron:
August 12th 1943: 'Nicosia 0730 F/O J. Huggins in Spitfire PR.IV BR645 took off on a PR of Rhodes. After two runs, one of the two cameras developed trouble. Op hours: 3.10.'
August 22nd 1943: 'Nicosia F/O D.W. BARBOUR arrived to relieve F/O HUGGINS.'
13. National Archives AIR 27/2917/13, 14, & 15: Operations Record Book, 680 Squadron:
August 26th 1943: 'LG219 1000-1235 F/O J. Huggins flew Spitfire BS360 to Derna. 2.35.' Spitfire PR.IV BS360 was later transferred to 74 OTU, but her engine caught fire & she was abandoned near Petah Tiqva in February 1944.
August 28th 1943: 'LG219 1000–1245 F/O J. Huggins returned from Derna in Spitfire BR428. 2.45.'
August 30th 1943: 'BR432 Spitfire F/O J. Huggins. Comm Flight. 0900–1140 Derna to Tocra.' Spitfire PR.IV BR432 swung on landing & tipped over at Petah Tiqva in January 1945.
August 31st 1943: 'BR432 Spitfire F/O Huggins. Comm Flight. 1000–1045 Kilo 8 *[LG219]* to Derna.'
September 3rd 1943: 'Tocra 0755 F/O Huggins took off *[in Spitfire PR.IV BP905]* for Greece & covered roads & railways in the northern Peloponnese. Landed at 1210hrs after an uneventful trip.'
14. National Archives AIR 27/2917/13: Operations Record Book, 680 Squadron.
15. For an admirable modern overview of this cruel period of Italy's history, readers are recommended to consult the excellent *Italy's Sorrow* by James Holland.
16. *Simpkin family collection:* letter from Major Basil Carey to Barbara Simpkin, dated October 30th 1943.
17. *WinColl E42/22/31:* post-card from R.E. Simpkin to MR, dated October 31st 1943; addressed from 'Oflag IX A/Z'.
18. National Archives AIR 27/2917/16: Operations Record Book, 680 Squadron:
September 6th 1943: 'AA789 Spitfire F/O Huggins Camera Test 1000–1100 Engine rough. No camera test.'
September 7th 1943: 'AA789 Spitfire F/O Huggins Camera Test 1005–1135 Duty carried out. Engine still rough.'
19. National Archives AIR 27/2917/15 & 16: Operations Record Book, 680 Squadron:
September 13th 1943: 'Tocra EN388 Spitfire; F/O Huggins. A/C Test. 0930–1040. Duty carried out.'
September 15th 1943: 'BR432 Spitfire. F/O Huggins. Comm Flight. Tocra to Derna & return. Duty carried out.'
September 16th 1943: 'F/O Huggins. Comm Flight. 0900–1200 Tocra to Kilo 8.'
September 17th 1943: 'BR414 Spitfire. F/O Huggins. Comm Flight. 1410–1705 Kilo 8 to Tocra.' PR.IV BR414 flew into a hill near Bodrum in Turkey on October 24th 1943.
September 18th 1943: 'BR421 F/O Huggins. Air test. 1430–1500 Duty carried out.'
September 19th 1943: 'BR432 Spitfire. F/O Huggins. Camera test. 1015–1115 Duty carried out.'

20. Lieutenant 186926 Roderick Campbell McLeod ('G' 1935–1940) died at the age of twenty-one, & was originally posted missing in action. Confirmation of his death came very rapidly, & he is buried in grave II.A.36 of the Salerno War Cemetery. A correspondent to *The Times* wrote as follows: 'His one fear was that the war would be over while he was still too young to play his part. At the earliest possible moment he left school & in due course received his commission in the Scots Guards… . Full of life and gaiety, he made friends wherever he went. His fearless and gallant spirit will always be remembered by those who were privileged to know and love him.'
21. *WinColl E42/13/100:* letter from F/O J.G. Huggins to MR, dated September 20th 1943; addressed from '680 Squadron RAF, Middle East'.
22. Flight Lieutenant 41946 Leonard Charles Murch was twenty-two years old when he died. He rests in the Benghazi War Cemetery in Libya, in grave 3.D.23, on which his parents (Charles Thomas Murch and Ethel Esther Murch, of Plymstock, Devon) requested the following inscription: TO LIVE IN HEARTS WE LEAVE BEHIND IS NOT TO DIE. HIS SORROWING MUM AND DAD. The author visited his grave in 2007.
23. National Archives AIR 27/2917/15 & 16: Operations Record Book, 680 Squadron. Huggins' flight from Tocra in Spitfire PR.IV EN388 lasted from 0900hrs to 1315hrs; a colleague took off at the same time for Crete.
24. National Archives AIR 27/2917/15 & 16: Operations Record Book, 680 Squadron. Huggins' mount was Spitfire BP905.
25. National Archives AIR 27/2917/15 & 16: Operations Record Book, 680 Squadron:
    September 25th 1943: Spitfire BR421 'F/O J. Huggins. PR 0740–1200 Athens area & Piraeus.'
    September 27th 1943: Spitfire EN388 'F/O J. Huggins. Air test. 0930–1000 Duty carried out … F/O J. Huggins. PR 1225–1630 Larissa – Navarino – visual.'
    September 28th 1943: Spitfire EN388 'F/O J. Huggins. PR 0800–1110 Crete – Run on Maleme aerodrome. Run on Kastelli.'
26. National Archives AIR 27/2917/17: Operations Record Book, 680 Squadron.
27. National Archives AIR 27/2917/18: Operations Record Book, 680 Squadron:
    October 1st 1943: 'Spitfire PR.IV BP905. F/O J. HUGGINS. PR 0810–1210 Megara, Eleusis, Tatoi, Hassani & Piraeus.'
    October 2nd 1943: 'Spitfire PR.IV BR664. F/O J. HUGGINS. PR 0845–1145 Kandia, Heraklion & Kastelli Pediata.'
    October 3rd 1943: 'Spitfire PR.IV AB421. F/O J. HUGGINS. Camera Test. 09.55–10.30 Duty carried out … Spitfire PR.IV AB421. F/O J. HUGGINS. PR 1440–1900 Yanina, Paramythia, Agrinion, Araxos & Patras.'
    October 4th 1943: 'Spitfire PR.IV EN388. F/O J. HUGGINS. PR 0710–1055 Piraeus area.'
    October 5th 1943: 'Spitfire PR.IV BR654. F/O J. HUGGINS. PR 1430–1820 Argos & Piraeus.' First flown on July 8th 1942, Spitfire PR.IV BR654 served in the Middle East from April 1943, & was eventually struck off charge on September 14th 1945.
    October 6th 1943: 'Spitfire PR.IV BR654. F/O J. HUGGINS. PR 1430–1800 Piraeus, Argos & Syros. Unsuccessful sortie due to cloud.'
    October 8th 1943: 'Spitfire PR.IV BR654. F/O J. HUGGINS. PR 0755–1230 Crete & shipping sweep.'
    October 9th 1943: 'Spitfire PR.IV BP904. F/O J. HUGGINS. PR 0805–1255 Crete & Syros.'
    October 10th 1943: 'Spitfire PR.IV BS366. F/O J. HUGGINS. PR 1410–1825 Piraeus & Salamis.' BS366 was a PR.IV & had first taken to the air exactly two years previously. She was finally struck off charge on May 31st 1945.
    October 10th 1943: 'Spitfire PR.IV BS366. F/O J. HUGGINS. PR 1355–1840 Piraeus, Tanagra, Salamis, central Athens, Marathon.'
28. *Mackrill family collection:* letter from B.L. Montgomery to H.G. Mackrill, dated September 29th 1943; addressed from 'HQ Eighth Army, CMF, Italy' – but post-marked London, October 5th 1943.
29. National Archives WO 169/8985: War Diary, HQ 201 Guards Brigade.
30. National Archives AIR 27/2917/19: Operations Record Book, 680 Squadron:

October 16th 1943: 'Spitfire PR.IV EN388. F/O J. HUGGINS. PR 0930–1410 Crete & shipping in the Kyklades.'
October 17th 1943: 'Spitfire EN155. F/O J. HUGGINS. PR 1400–1830 Piraeus & Kyklades.' EN155 was yet another Spitfire PR.IV. Having first flown in December 1942, she was struck off strength on May 31st 1945.
October 19th 1943: 'Spitfire PR.IV. E.N. E.N.388. F/O J. HUGGINS. PR 08.40–13.10 Crete & Kyklades islands.'

31. National Archives AIR 27/2917/21: Operations Record Book, 680 Squadron, December 31st 1943: 'Matarya. Personnel Movements. Posted Out 80269 F/O J.G. Huggins to AHQ, ADEM Non effective sick wef 29.11.43.'
32. National Archives WO 169/10170: War Diary, 2nd Battalion, Scots Guards.
33. National Archives WO 169/8985: War Diary, HQ 201 Guards Brigade.
34. *Ibid.*
35. National Archives WO 169/10170: War Diary, 2nd Battalion, Scots Guards.
36. Born on February 27th 1918, Squadron Leader 72030 Philip Michael Hermann 'Mike' Thomas ('I' 1931–1936) shot as a cadet at Bisley in 1934, in the VIII in 1935, & (as captain) in 1936. Robertson described him as follows: 'He was also a prefect & a keen member of the Hopper's band which helped to win Palmer Cup. Though sometimes obstinate, he was singularly straightforward & courageous. He had considerable ability, & though he did not always use it on the main job in hand, he left in Sixth Book & took a third in Mechanical Science at Trinity College, Cambridge, in 1939. Whilst there he spent a lot of his time flying (he was the first Hopperite to come down for a weekend by air, & he served as a Pilot Officer in the Cambridge University Air Squadron from 1938). He was one of a number of enthusiastic gliders whose experience proved invaluable in the war. His friends remembered him as a quick thinker & mover, & as a loyal and efficient comrade.

    In 1939 he was just starting a career with Messrs Mather & Platt but at once joined the RAFVR as a Flying Officer, & a number of responsible jobs, in which he won golden opinion from his superiors & subordinates, brought him rapid promotion. Despite his parents' doubts, he was married on June 8th 1940 to Daphne Gertrude Bryant (daughter of George William Bryant, of the Malayan Civil Service, who fell into Japanese hands in 1942). It was a brave venture at the age of twenty-two, but brought him great happiness & an incentive to hard work. He first served with Bomber Command, being promoted to Flight Lieutenant in 1941, & then transferred to the Technical Branch, becoming a Squadron Leader in 1943.'

    On December 5th 1943, Sunderland III W6013 '2-B' was carrying out a non-operational transit flight to Stranraer from Castle Archdale. Its normal crew was ten, but the Sunderland had more than that on board, probably sixteen (some sources state twelve, but sixteen names are recorded). The second leg of the trip was from Lough Foyle to Rathlin Island, & the RAF accident report stated: 'The Captain & the Navigator were flying by Dead Reckoning Navigation alone, and they were assumed to be crossing the coast line & on track from Limavady to Rathlin island. The DR navigation was inaccurate, & no use was made by the crew of the ASR (air-to-surface radar), nor was any use made of other radio aids to establish the correct position of the aircraft.' Knocklayd was shrouded in cloud & the visibility was poor. The RAF investigation concluded that the accident was caused by a premature descent in marginal weather conditions & low visibility.

    According to his Winchester obituary, Thomas was a passenger on the Sunderland. Although some sources state that Thomas was the aircraft Captain (& therefore held overall responsibility for its safe operation), other sources make it clear that the Captain was Flying Officer Russell, RCAF. Russell survived the crash, though he was seriously injured. Pieces of the aircraft were still visible in 2004, according to walkers. Thomas rests in grave 2.36 of Irvinestown Church of Ireland Churchyard.
37. Henrietta Fenton *(née* Mackrill), personal communication to author, January 18th 2022.
38. *Mackrill family collection:* letter from Ordinary Seaman H.G. Mackrill to Mr & Mrs H.W. Mackrill, dated December 16th 1943; addressed from 'Jellicoe Annexe, HMS *Ganges*'.

39. *Mackrill family collection:* letter from Ordinary Seaman H.G. Mackrill to Mr & Mrs H.W. Mackrill, postmarked December 23rd 1943; addressed from 'Jellicoe Annexe'.
40. Elliott-Binns had been gazetted 2nd Lieutenant 261567 on February 6th 1943. (Supplement to the *London Gazette* March 9th 1943.)
41. Elliott-Binns, M., *Finding through War: Poems of Fifty Years Ago* (William Sessions, 1995).

XIV

1. *WinColl E42/22/32:* letter from R.E. Simpkin to MR, dated January 12th 1944; addressed from '*Oflag* IXA/Z'.
2. He was treated with 'M&B' (May & Baker 693), a first-generation sulphonamide antibiotic. It could cure pneumonia, as well as treat gangrene & other bacterial blood infections. Patients could take it as tablets, or a powdered form could be sprinkled on wounds. Invented in 1938, it saved countless lives in the war.
3. On December 18th 1939, for example, he wrote from Godalming whilst awaiting call-up (*WinColl E42/08/34):* 'I have also been up to Cambridge for two separate weeks & seen something of Michael, John 'calf, & Pat D.' Then from Falkirk, on December 18th 1940 *(WinColl E42/08/33):* 'After our weekend in France we travelled round England for a month or so ... We've now had fourteen moves!' On January 4th 1942, writing from Dunblane, he apologised for the lateness of his usual letter *(WinColl E42/08/35):* 'During the summer I saw .... in Edinburgh Bruce Fortune, John Kidd, John Boyd, Gow (Coll), who's instructing at a gas school, Ensor (Coll), & Charles Murray.' His letter of December 26th 1942 *(WinColl E42/08/36)* was as insouciant as always: 'I'm afraid it's some time since I last wrote, but thank goodness it is not from Scotland this time! Another winter there with all the dull routine work would have broken me .... I had fully intended writing some time ago, but I've been looking at a yellow face when I shave in the morning since December 10th & had not been feeling too good for a week before that. However, I'm well on the mend now, after a journey of ten days back to Hospital, which I'm due to leave for a convalescent home in a day of so. Saw Michael Barstow in the ship coming back. We have managed to get off a lot of ammunition since our arrival & have had some quite exciting moments .... I should think that a hospital is as good a place as any to spend Xmas out here. They did us extremely well. Lady Lampson's Xmas bar was an astonishingly good show.'
4. *WinColl E42/08/37:* airgraph letter from 89502 Lt. W.H. Cliff Hodges to MR, dated May 30th 1943; addressed from 'No.9 General Hospital, MEF'.
5. *WinColl E42/08/38:* airgraph letter from Capt. W.H. Cliff Hodges to MR, date illegible; addressed from '309/78th Field Regiment RA, CMF'.
6. *The Times,* 1944.
7. *WinColl E42/7/84:* airgraph letter from Henry Brooke to MR, dated February 6th 1944; addressed from 16/5 Lancers, CMF.
8. Pawson, H.A., *Indelible Memories* (Foxbury Press, 2004).
9. Major 97136 John Herbert Leslie BROWNRIGG ('D' 1922–1927), 1st Battalion, Loyal North Lancashire Regiment.
   Lieutenant Peter Cecil BULL ('I' 1925–1929), RNVR, commanding Landing Craft Flak 16.
   Lieutenant 261567 Michael ELLIOTT-BINNS ('I' 1936–1941), 29 Battery, 19 Field Regiment, Royal Artillery.
   2nd Lieutenant 292998 Michael Henry Ainsworth FINCH ('I' 1937–1941), 'A' Company, 2/7th Battalion, Queen's Own Royal Regiment (West Surrey).
   Lieutenant Colonel 39334 Anthony Edmond Hubert HAMILTON OBE ('D' 1921–1926), OC 19 Field Regiment, Royal Artillery.
   Lieutenant 253912 Duncan McMURTRIE ('I' 1937–1941), 1st Battalion, Scots Guards.
   Lieutenant Colonel 53684 the Hon. David SCRYMGEOUR-WEDDERBURN DSO ('K' 1925–1930), OC 1st Battalion, Scots Guards.
   Major 109756 John Gervase Kensington SHELDON ('D' 1927–1932), Royal Artillery.

Captain 176764 John Henry Lund SINCLAIR ('I' 1934–1939), Right Flank Company, 1st Battalion, Scots Guards.
Lieutenant 256126 Walter Raleigh TREVELYAN ('E' 1937–1942), Rifle Brigade, attached 1st Battalion, The Green Howards (Alexandra, Princess of Wales' Own Yorkshire Regiment).
Captain 165050 Anthony Favill TUKE ('H' 1934–1939), OC Anti-Tank Platoon, 1st Battalion, Scots Guards.
Major 176758 Adrian John Anthony WEIR MC ('B' 1933–1939), OC Right Flank Company, 1st Battalion, Scots Guards.
At least two more served off-shore: Midshipman John Selwyn HERBERT ('C' 1938–1942), aboard HMS *Grenville*, & Lieutenant Commander Robert Fortescue PHILLIMORE ('E' 1925–1930). Winchester's records incorrectly state that another of our subjects, Lieutenant Mi Edmunds, was also at Anzio, with 7OBLI; this is not the case, & stems from a mis-reading of a letter from his father to MR. In fact, Edmunds had been wounded on the Gustav Line between January 16th & 24th, & had only rejoined his Battalion in mid March, after they had been withdrawn from Anzio, having suffered crippling casualties.

10. *WinColl E42/22/45:* postcard from Lieutenant A.M. Sinclair to MR, dated January 29th 1944; addressed from 'Oflag IVC'.
11. Extracts compiled from Elliott-Binns, M. *Realisation* (Mendip, 1993) & *Finding through War: Poems of Fifty Years Ago* (Sessions, 1995).
12. *WinColl E42/20/27:* letter from John Pinney to MR, dated February 2nd 1944; addressed 'c/o Secretariat, Nairobi'.
13. 2nd Lieutenant 253912 Duncan Gilbert Scott McMurtrie, 'B' Company, 1st Battalion, Scots Guards, rests in grave IV.G.6 of the Anzio War Cemetery. He is also commemorated on the Memorial Cross situated in the churchyard of St Ippolyts Parish Church, near Hitchin in Hertfordshire, as well as on the choir stalls erected in his memory by his family.
14. *WinColl E42/17/19:* letter from Captain Eustace Balfour to Mrs McMurtrie, dated February 8th 1944; addressed from '1 Battalion Scots Guards, CMF'.
15. *WinColl E42/17/19:* letter from Mr Donald McMurtrie to MR, dated February 26th 1944; unaddressed.
16. *WinColl E42/17/20:* letter from Anthony McMurtrie to MR, dated February 29th 1944; addressed 'Field House, Marlboro College, Wilts'.
17. *WinColl E42/17/21:* letter from Mrs Margaret McMurtrie to MR, dated March 1st 1944; unaddressed.
18. National Archives WO 170/1352: War Diary, 1st Battalion, Scots Guards. Captain 176764 John Henry Lund Sinclair, 1st Battalion, Scots Guards, had gained his commission in March 1941, coincidentally in the same cohort as John Weir, who would go on to be his Company Commander at Anzio (Supplement to the *London Gazette,* March 28th 1941). John, like his brothers, was reported on as a quite first-rate officer who took great pride in his Platoon. Having been promoted Captain two days before his death, he was still only twenty-three. He rests in grave XX.D.12 of the Beach Head War Cemetery, Anzio. A Colonel Thorburn wrote *(WinColl E42/22/41):* 'Poor John Sinclair was killed while leading a patrol which did valuable work in rounding up a number of Bosche who were in a position threatening the main position held by his Regiment. The CO is a delightful chap, David Wedderburn, and he was very pleased with the patrol action, and the action of the whole Regiment in that particular situation was commented on by General Penney.'
19. *WinColl E42/22/41:* letter from Guardsman 2697903 Raeburn R. to Mr & Mrs McMurtrie, dated February 9th 1944; addressed from 'Right Flank Company, 1st Battalion, Scots Guards, CMF'.
20. *WinColl E42/22/32:* letter from Mrs Ethel Coller to MR, dated February 24th 1944; addressed from 'The Lodge, Kettlewell'.
21. *WinColl E42/7/85:* airgraph letter from Henry Brooke to MR, dated November 10th 1944; addressed from '16/5 Lancers, CMF'.
22. *WinColl E42/17/163:* letter from Mr Ken Murray to MR, dated February 13th 1944; addressed from '4 Lennox Street, Edinburgh'.

23. Field Marshal Harold Rupert Leofric George Alexander, 1st Earl Alexander of Tunis, KG, GCB, OM, GCMG, CSI, DSO, MC, CD, PC (Canada), PC, (1891–1969) was at the time in charge of Allied ground forces in Italy (Fifteenth Army Group). Given that the original Anzio idea had been his, one hopes that Alexander showed a little humility on this occasion.
24. Major 97136 John Herbert Leslie Brownrigg ('D' 1922–1927) was the elder son of Charles Edward Brownrigg, Headmaster of Magdalen College School, Oxford. His Winchester obituary states that 'Brownrigg came to 'D' as Honorary Exhibitioner in Short Half 1922. Without achieving any notable distinction, except for persistent cheerfulness & good citizenship, he won a firm place in the affection of many & the respect of all. There was often a certain whimiscal nonchalance in his outward bearing, which belied the more enduring & practical qualities of his character. In the field, he loved "the game beyond the prize"; never afraid of odds, nor dismayed by defeat; & as an opening batsman he was more concerned with proving a problem to dislodge than with his own contribution to the score. After taking an Honours Degree from Corpus Christi College, Oxford, in 1931, he entered the service of the Burma Oil Company, & remained with them till the outbreak of war. He then took a commission in the Devonshire Regiment, was promoted to Captain in 1941, & then to Major in 1943.' He was serving on attachment with 1st Battalion, Loyal North Lancashire Regiment, when he was killed, at the age of thirty-five. He left a widow, Muriel Christabel Fraser Brownrigg, & is buried in Anzio War Cemetery IV.N.2.
25. *History of the First Division: Anzio Campaign January–June 1944* (Ahva Press, Jerusalem, 1944).
26. Officer Cadet 6107407 M.H.A. Finch was gazetted as 2nd Lieutenant 292998 into the Suffolks on September 11th 1943. (Supplement to the *London Gazette*, November 19th 1943.)
27. National Archives WO 170/1467: War Diary, 2/7th Battalion, The Queen's Royal Regiment.
28. Bullen, R., *History of the 2/7th Battalion The Queen's Royal Regiment 1939-1946* (Besley & Copp, 1958).
29. *WinColl E42/11/09:* letter from Sir Ernest Frederick Finch FRCS to MR, dated Tuesday March 7th 1944; addressed from '442 Glossop Road, Sheffield'.
30. *WinColl E42/11/10:* letter from Sir Ernest Frederick Finch FRCS to MR, dated Wednesday March 22nd 1944; addressed from '70 Upper Hanover Street, Sheffield'.
31. Lieutenant Colonel 39334 Anthony Edmond Hubert Hamilton OBE, nicknamed 'Puggins', was born on February 12th 1908 to Madeleine Tocas Hamilton (daughter of Fernand Toucas Massillon), a native of Paris. His father, Major Harry Austen Hamilton RFA ('I' 1893–1897), was killed in January 1916 at Poperinghe. Tragedy stalked the family; his younger brother, Archibald George Arthur Hamilton ('D' 1923–1928), was killed in a flying accident in 1934. 'Small of stature, but tough and undefeatable in spirit, Hamilton won early distinction in fields where pluck and steadiness are as necessary as skill. In his second year he represented his house ('D' 1921–1926) in Richardson Shield, scoring second highest marks in the whole competition, and the highest in the winning side of 1924. In the same spirit he proved a most reliable shot in the Bisley teams of 1925–1926, helping also to win Mackenzie Cup in his last Short Half, & the Country Life Cup in 1926. No record of 'Puggins' could be complete without some witness both to his own charming nature, & to his love of bird & beast. Of these he was a most skilful hunter, but his only weapon was a camera; & his inseparable socius [ally] was Roddie Casement ('D' 1920–1925). Many others of their time owed a new & undying interest in nature to these two, a not insignificant service for any boy to render to his own generation at school.

    In 1926 he entered RMA Woolwich as a King's Cadet, passing out first two years later, taking the King's & Pollock Medals, the Tombs Memorial Prize, & an Army Scholarship. He went to India in 1928 as a subaltern in the RA, but resigned in 1931 & became the editor & publisher of sporting books, & subsequently a wine merchant. He was married to Pamela Hamilton.

    In 1936 he took a commission in the Territorial Army, & served as a Captain with the BEF in 1940, being promoted Major that same year. In 1942 he went out to serve in the Middle East, & was promoted to Lieutenant Colonel in 1943. He was reported wounded in July 1943, & in September of the same year received the OBE (Military) for his services in North Africa with 1st

Infantry Division. He was also mentioned in despatches.' Aged thirty-six when he died, he rests in grave I.J.11 of Anzio War Cemetery.

32. Major 176758 Adrian John Anthony Weir MC (born August 22nd 1920; 'B' 1933–1939) was still only twenty-three years old when he became OC Right Flank Company, 1SG. Having done superbly well in 2SG, in January 1944 Weir was transferred to 1SG. His school-friend Tony Pawson wrote that 'the timing & manner of his death made it the more distressing ... His battalion had just been moved to a rest area to await being shipped away from Anzio and re-organized after its multiple casualties. As a long-serving officer, John qualified for return to England, & an eagerly-awaited marriage ... The Scots Guards history records how good an officer Weir had been: "probably the best Company Commander in the Brigade". But the final judgement on an officer is what his men think of him. When he was killed their comments to his family were equally effusive. One wrote: "Right Flank Company mourned John's death to a man. Many have I heard – old soldiers too – say that he was the best Company Commander they ever had." His Sergeant's letter was in the same vein: "Many of the Platoon spoke to me of how they admired & liked your son's firm, but friendly, manner in the way he treated officer, or NCO, or Guardsman alike." His Winchester obituary stated that "it may be seen how quickly he proved himself as a soldier, as indeed might be expected of one possessed of his brains, decision, & nerve." *The Times*' obituarist added "that he should have been killed by a chance shell at Anzio is a tragedy for his many friends & for the Regiment. But there is another side of him without which the picture is incomplete – his pursuit of shooting on the Solway, in Syria, & even in the marshes of the Garigliano; his love of the country & especially of Pensbury, to which so many of his letters referred; his love of his many friends of very different types; his devotion to his family.... John has followed worthily in the footsteps of his father & brother, leaving behind him many proud hearts."' Weir rests in grave V.H.3 of the Beach Head War Cemetery, Anzio.

33. Lieutenant Colonel 53684 the Hon. David Scrymgeour-Wedderburn DSO was the second son of Lieutenant Colonel Henry Scrymgeour-Wedderburn (10th Earl of Dundee) & his wife Edith (daughter of John Moffat). His older brother was Henry James Scrymgeour-Wedderburn MP ('K' 1916–1921, 11th Earl). Born at Kingennie, Forfar, on April 2nd 1912, he came to Kingsgate House from Ardvreck, Crieff, in September 1925 ('K' 1925–1930). 'His progress up the school was slow, but he contributed much to life, not merely with his high character & consistent good temper, which made him an excellent prefect, but also through his unfailing humour & brilliant power of mimicry: voice, gestures, & even facial expression were at his command, without a touch of malice, to the delight of his friends. He was a brilliant pianist, & those who heard his solo performance at his last concert long remembered its enthusiastic reception. He was a good friend to all at the school. He entered RMC Sandhurst in January 1931; his interests had lain always in soldiering, & from his earliest days of service he showed a remarkable gift of leadership. Thereafter he developed rapidly, becoming a Junior Under-Officer before gaining his commission in the Scots Guards. After some years of regimental service he was appointed as an equerry to the household of HRH the Duke of Gloucester. At the outbreak of war he rejoined his regiment, & served as a Captain in Norway in 1940, at first with Right Flank Company, & from May 19th as Adjutant (his predecessor having been taken ill with jaundice).'

On September 9th 1940 he married Patricia Katharine Faulkner, daughter of Colonel Lord Herbert Montagu-Douglas-Scott & the widow of Walter Douglas Faulkner, who had been killed in action on May 14th 1940 at Bodo in Norway. They had two daughters: Janet Mary Scrymgeour-Wedderburn, born on August 14th 1941, & Elizabeth Scrymgeour-Wedderburn, born on October 5th 1943.

Having been promoted to Major in 1941, Scrymgeour-Wedderburn served with 1SG in Italy & took over as commanding officer on January 8th, just before their landing in the first wave at Anzio. For his work once ashore he was posthumously awarded the DSO – an unusual honour. When he died he was only thirty-one years old. He is buried in grave VI.H.1 of the Beach Head Cemetery, Anzio, Italy.

His wife Patricia – now twice widowed, having lost two husbands to the war – remarried on October 30th 1946; her third husband was David's older brother, Henry. Close to Balmerino Abbey, North Fife, stands a block of houses built by Henry in David's memory: the David Scrymgeour Wedderburn Memorial Square. The houses stand in a beautifully formal square surrounding a lawn & facing the Tay.

34. *Walker family collection:* letter from MR to Lieutenant Peter Walker, dated February 28th 1944; addressed from 'Culver Lodge'.
35. *Walker family collection:* letter from Mrs Margaret McMurtrie to Lieutenant Peter Walker, dated February 28th 1944; addressed from 'St Ibbs Bush, Hitchin, Herts'.
36. *Walker family collection:* letter from Mr D.S.A. McMurtrie to Lieutenant Peter Walker, dated February 28th 1944; addressed from 'St Ibbs Bush, Hitchin, Herts'.)
37. *WinColl E42/17/164:* letter from Lieutenant C.K. Murray to MR, dated March 13th 1944; addressed from 'MPO 1314 c/o Base Post Office, Ottowa, Canada'.
38. *WinColl E42/22/46:* postcard from Lieutenant A.M. Sinclair to MR, dated March 31st 1944; addressed from 'Oflag IVC'.
39. *WinColl E42/22/35:* postcard from R.E. Simpkin to MR, dated March 30th 1944; addressed from 'Oflag IXA/Z'.

XV

1. Wavell, A.P., *The Viceroy's Journal* (OUP, 1973).
2. Sir Maurice Hallett (College 1896-1902). Wavell opined in his journal that 'The U.P. is well run. Maurice Hallett, in spite of his rather vague demeanour, is a first-class administrator & a firm one, & gets things done without fuss or friction or eyewash'.
3. Michael Scott ('K' 1930–1936) was the son of Sir Basil Scott, Chief Justice of the Bombay High Court. He took part in the Oxford University Expedition to Western Greenland in 1938. Whilst a 2nd Lieutenant with the Coldstream Guards in 1940, he was severely injured whilst on duty, & then served as ADC to the Governor of Bombay 1943–1945.
4. *WinColl E42/22/07*: letter from Michael Scott to MR, dated January 29th 1944; addressed from 'Bombay Governor's Camp'.
5. du Boulay, interview with author, 2010.
6. Fergusson, B., *The Wild Green Earth* (Collins, 1946).
7. *Pollard family collection: My History Project with Guy Dodgson*, by William Jackson 4X, 2003.
8. Fergusson, B., *The Wild Green Earth* (Collins, 1946).
9. *Ibid.*
10. *Ibid.*
11. Sir Cecil Walter Hardy Beaton CBE (1904–1980) was a British photographer of fashion, portraits, & the war. He also excelled as a painter, interior designer, & an Oscar-winning costume designer for film and theatre.
12. Beaton, C., *Cecil Beaton's Diaries: 1939–1944 The Years Between* (Weidenfeld & Nicolson, 1965).
13. National Archives WO 172/4592: War Diary, 45 Reconnaissance Regiment.
14. *WinColl E42/09/10:* letter from Captain G.H. Dodgson to MR, dated May 17th 1944; addressed from '2nd Field Company RE, India Command'.
15. Lieutenant 165794 Douglas Leonard Nicoll, 2nd Battalion, Black Watch, was killed in action in Burma on May 8th 1944, aged twenty-three. He rests in grave 13.A.8 of the Taukkyan War Cemetery.
16. *The Wykehamist* (898, June 7th 1944).
17. *Rigby family collection*: Rigby, R.M., 'My War with the Duke of Aosta'.
18. Letter from Bruce Fortune to Susan Mackie, dated May 1944; quoted in Fortune, S.M., *Time to Remember.*
19. *Dauntless,* a light cruiser of the *Danaë* class, had been launched in April 1918 & missed the First World War by eleven days.

20. *WinColl E42/17/08:* letter from Graham Mackrill to MR, dated May 12th 1944; addressed from Lamwath Hall, Sutton on Hull.
21. Fortune, S.M., *Time to Remember* (privately published, 2002).

XVI

1. Major Philip Charles Napier Sturt ('I' 1927–1932) is buried in grave II.E.3 of the Cassino War Cemetery. The author first visited Sturt's grave with pupils of Winchester College in October 2006. The inscription chosen by his family is *qui procul hinc, qui ante diem periit, sed miles, sed pro patria* ('He died far from home; he died before his time; but as a soldier, and for his country'). The quotation is from Henry Newbolt's poem, *Clifton Chapel.*
2. *WinColl E42/17/105:* letter from Lieutenant D.S. Middleditch to MR, dated April 17th 1944; addressed from ' 'A' Squadron, XII Royal Lancers, CMF'.
3. What *Blackadder* devotees would call 'Sausage Side'.
4. *WinColl E42/24/02:* letter from 6108073 Officer Cadet Walker P.M. to MR, dated May 1st 1944; addressed from '126 Troop, 'E' Squadron, 100 (Sandhurst) OCTU, RAC, Camberley, Surrey'.
5. Daniel Edmund Awdry ('B' 1937–1942) won a Belt of Honour at the RAC OCTU, was commissioned into the Royal Wiltshire Yeomanry (his family regiment), & then transferred to 10th Hussars. He became Conservative MP for Chippenham in 1962, serving until 1979. He died in October 2008.
6. Lieutenant Colonel 45364 John Noel Ronald Loveday (born March 22nd 1911; 'H' 1924–1929) was the younger son of Arthur Frederic Loveday OBE & Mary Cornelia Loveday, the sister of Sidney Eric Backus ('C' 1904–1908). His elder brother, George Arthur Loveday, also came to Winchester ('H' 1923–1928). Loveday slowly but surely won his way to leadership & was both a House & a School Prefect. From 1929 to 1932 he studied Law at Hertford College, Oxford, gaining Second Class Honours, a triumph of industry. On leaving university he joined 16th/5th Lancers, distinguishing himself by his horsemanship & playing polo for his Regiment. In 1936 he gained his Captaincy, being at the time the youngest Captain in the Army; he then served as Adjutant of the Regiment. In 1938 he went out to India, but by 1939 he was serving in the United Kingdom as a GSO3. On June 23rd 1940 he married Miss Nancy Buxton (daughter of Ivor Buxton), of Ware, Hertfordshire; he left a daughter when he died. After his unit was mechanized in 1940, he was promoted Major, & attended Staff College in 1941. He was attached to 27th Lancers in 1942, & in 1943 served as Brigade Major of 21 Armoured Brigade in Libya & Tunisia. When taken prisoner in Tunisia & lined up against a wall to be shot, he fell, feigning death, & made good his escape. He then returned to 16th/5th Lancers as second-in-command, before being promoted Lieutenant Colonel & going to Italy in November 1943, on the HQ Staff of 46th Division. After a spell as OC 48RTR in 1944, he finally went on to command his parent regiment. Posthumously mentioned in dispatches, he was described as 'amongst the most brilliant of our young soldiers … for whom every man in the Regiment was ready to do anything … His simplicity and modesty, coupled with an intense fidelity and great youthful charm, left an imperishable memory with all who knew him.' Loveday is buried in grave XI.E.4 of Cassino War Cemetery. The inscription which his family chose to add to the gravestone is: R.I.P. 'These are the souls/To whom great valour/Gave glory undying.'
7. 'H' 1909–1912.
8. Mosley, N., *Time at War* (Weidenfeld & Nicolson, 2006).
9. *WinColl E42/7/85:* airgraph letter from Henry Brooke to MR, dated November 10th 1944; addressed from '16th/5th Lancers, CMF'.

10 National Archives WO373/08/24: Recommendation for Award for Brooke, H.

11. *Ibid.*
12. *Ibid.*
13. *Ibid.*
14. *WinColl E42/7/87:* letter from Basil Brooke to MR, dated October 19th 1944; addressed from '114 General Hospital, High Street, Oxford'.

15. *Wincoll E42/7/88:* letter from Essex Brooke to MR, dated December 4th 1944; addressed from '23 Halsey Street, SW3'.
16. *WinColl E42/7/85:* airgraph letter from Henry Brooke to MR, dated November 10th 1944; addressed from '16th/5th Lancers, CMF'.
17. *WinColl E42/22/34:* postcard from R.E. Simpkin to MR, dated May 17th 1944; addressed from 'Oflag IXA/Z'.
18. Richard Borlase Adams ('F' 1935–1939) served with 7RB right through from November 1942 in Tunisia to Austria in 1945. He rose to the rank of Major, was mentioned in dispatches, & was wounded three times. He later became Chairman of P&O.
19. William Mercer Adams ('F' 1937–1941) studied at Trinity College, Oxford, before joining the Rifle Brigade in 1943. He served alongside his elder brother in 7RB, ending the war as a Captain.
20. Bsharri – which has many different spellings – lies some 80 miles from Beirut on the slopes of the highest peak in the Lebanon, Qurnat as Sawda (3088m). It is the site of the Lebanon's oldest ski resort & the centre of a Maronite Christian enclave with thirty-seven churches, the Saint Saba Cathedral, & many ancient Christian monastic communities.
21. *WinColl E42/15/02:* letter from Captain D. Kemp to MR, dated December 4th 1944; addressed from '7RB, CMF'.
22. Mr Bart Stephens (stepson of David Kemp), personal communication to author, February 28th 2022.
23. Christopher Ivan William Seton-Watson was the son of a distinguished historian (R.W. Seton-Watson), & was born in London in August 1918. A Scholar (College 1931–1937), he went on to New College, Oxford, where he read PPE. He served with 2RHA throughout the war, rising to the rank of Major & winning the MC & bar. His first MC came during a rearguard action at Ptolemais in Greece in 1941. At Ruweisat Ridge in 1942 the tank from which he was observing was hit by enemy fire, killing three men & wounding Seton-Watson. In Italy, from April 1944 until the end of the war, he commanded 'I' Battery; the bar to his MC came for his actions at Monte Malbe & for his courage at Castiglione near Arezzo, where a German shell landed in his slit-trench but failed to explode, after which he calmly went on directing his Battery's fire. He celebrated VE-Day by firing his flare-pistol into a petrol-soaked bonfire topped with a portrait of Mussolini. After the war Seton-Watson became a distinguished historian & expert on nineteenth-century Italian politics. He was soon elected Fellow in Modern History & Politics at Oriel College, Oxford, despite the fact that he had technically not finished his undergraduate degree. He was honoured by the Italian government in 1984 by being appointed a *Commendatore* of the Order of Merit. His obituary in the *Daily Telegraph* recorded, *inter alia,* that he helped to recruit students for the Security Services, & when his advice was not followed threatened to 'send them his Burgesses & Macleans'; that at Princeton he had regularly shared a taxi with Einstein, but never mentioned the fact until 1983; & that he was an expert builder of sand-castles.
24. *WinColl E42/24/03:* letter from Viscount Wavell to Jack Parr, dated August 12th 1943; addressed from 'Dalmeny House, Edinburgh'.
25. Supplement to the *London Gazette,* February 29th 1944.
26. *WinColl E42/13/77:* letter from Lieutenant R.L. Holtby to MR, dated May 13th 1944; addressed from 'Seaforth Highlanders, 'D' Company, 6 Battalion, No1 IRTD, CMF'.)
27. National Archives WO 170/1474: War Diary, 6th Battalion, Seaforth Highlanders: 'Officers Joined: 300365 Lt R.L. Holtby, Seaforth, posted to this unit from No1 Reception Camp June 3rd 44.'
28. Supplement to the *London Gazette,* July 4th 1944.

XVII

1. Charles William Slingsby 'Sim' Duncombe, 3rd Earl of Feversham, DSO, was a Conservative politician, & brother-in-law to Anthony Eden, the Foreign Secretary.
2. *Somerville family collection:* Somerville, C., unpublished memoirs, typescript, undated.
3. The Physiological Society, interview with Horace Barlow, conducted by Ann Silver, David Tolhurst, & Martin Rosenberg, May 21st 2010; published March 2015.

4. One of the best works on the Coastal Forces is MTB veteran Leonard Reynolds' *Dog Boats at War: Royal Navy D Class MTBs & MGBs 1939–1945* (Sutton, 1998). In a review of this work published in the *Naval War College Review* in 2001, retired US Navy Captain Carl Otis Schuster summed up the work of Coastal Forces better than I have seen it done anywhere else: 'Serving in small plywood craft much like the more famous American PT boats, the Coastal Forces wreaked havoc with Axis forces in British & foreign waters. Operating from small harbours & primitive forward bases, theirs was a war of small, close-knit crews & close action with the enemy. They did it all, from convoy escort to shipping interdiction, clandestine landings to reconnaissance operations, & finally, distant screening for invasion forces... It took a special kind of sailor to man a plywood boat filled with five thousand gallons of highly volatile aviation gasoline. The Royal Navy found their early crews among the yachtsmen, racing enthusiasts, & fishermen who populated Britain's coastal towns & villages. These early recruits shaped the force that followed. The Dog Boats went to war with small crews of thirty to thirty-two men commanded by young Royal Navy Volunteer Reserve officers, many drawn from the Commonwealth. The commanding officers were generally in their twenties, & most had at least two years of experience in fast-attack craft. The crews were also either reservists or "wartime only" ratings. The average age of the crewmen was between eighteen & nineteen, with perhaps one career regular Petty Officer on board to provide experience. The result was a tightly knit, young, & aggressive crew – ideally suited to the unconventional fighting that characterized warfare in fast-attack craft. Survival depended on the commander's judgment & the crew's teamwork. It was a successful formula that served the boats well from Norway to the eastern Mediterranean.'
5. *Mackrill family collection*: letter from OS H.G. Mackrill CJX 656091 to Mr & Mrs H.W. Mackrill, post-marked May 23rd 1944; addressed 'c/o Muswood, The Cottage, Barrowfield Drive, Hove'.
6. Able Seaman Fred Simpson (Tare Commando), quoted in Lee, D., *Beachhead Assault: The Story of the Royal Naval Commandos in World War II* (Pen & Sword, 2017).
7. *WinColl E42/17/01.*
8. Form S.206 (Amended), dated March 31st 1944, signed by Commander G.A. Davis RN; countersigned April 19th 1944 by Rear Admiral (Retired) H.E. Horan DSC, Commanding Combined Operational Bases, Western Approaches Command.
9. Form S.206 (Amended), dated April 1st 1945; signed by Lieutenant Commander Neaves RNVR.
10. Lieutenant Colonel 67184 Humphrey Reginald Woods DSO, MC* ('I' 1929-1934) was born on September 23rd 1915, the son of a commanding officer of 1KRRC, Lieutenant Colonel Reginald Herbert Woods OBE, MC. Robertson said of him that although slow at some forms of book-work, he saw & knew a lot which cleverer people missed, & combined a disarming charm with very shrewd common sense. He was a House Prefect, Twelfth Man for the soccer XI, & a keen cricketer. He went to RMC Sandhurst in September 1934, and on being gazetted to his father's regiment joined 2KRRC at Aldershot in January 1936. He then spent two years with 1KRRC in Burma, where he entered with zest into the life of an officer and a gentleman in a British colony. 1KRRC then moved to Egypt, where Woods spent a year before getting his first leave in time for Green Jacket Week in the summer of 1939, during which he & Michael Sinclair played cricket together for their Regiment.
11. 'H' 1920–1924.
12. Tare returned from Normandy to HMS *Armadillo,* moving to HMS *Dundonald* (Troon) in the middle of September. In January 1945 Naval Party 1510 was renumbered NP 4008 and moved to HMS *Mylodon* in Lowestoft, where it was eventually disbanded in November 1945.
13. *National Archives DEFE 2/987.*
14. Ellis, L.F., *Victory in the West: Volume I: The Battle of Normandy* (HMSO, 1962).
15. Captain W.F.N. Gregory-Smith DSO*, DSC*, OC Tare Commando; quoted in Lee, *op.cit.*
16. Sub-Lieutenant Keith Andrews RNVR, Assistant Beachmaster, Tare Commando; quoted in Lee, op.cit.
17. *McArthur family collection:* letter from Sub-Lieutenant McArthur J.C. to Major & Mrs V.G. McArthur, undated; addressed from 'NP 1510, c/o GPO, London'; franked MARITIME.

18. Form S.206 (Amended), dated August 8th 1944, signed by Lieutenant J.E.M. Mitchell RNVR.
19. *Walker family collection:* letter from J.N. Somerville to Peter Walker, dated August 4th 1944; addressed from '2nd Battalion, The South Wales Borderers, BLA'.
20. *WinColl E42/7/77:* letter from Captain J.B. Boyd to MR, dated July 27th 1944; addressed from '1KOSB, BLA'.
21. Captain 129983 James Roynon-Jones and two Other Ranks failed to return from a patrol on the night of June 10th 1944. Aged twenty-five, 'Bones' was the son of Captain Edward Roynon-Jones RN, & Anne Harley Roynon-Jones, of Edinburgh. He rests in grave III.H.4 of the Ryes War Cemetery at Bazenville.
22. Major 73166 Edmund Lancelot Gerald Passy, 2nd Battalion, Middlesex Regiment, was twenty-six when he was killed on June 9th 1944. He rests in grave J.7 of the Cambes-en-Plaine War Cemetery.
23. Alexander Douglas 'Sandy' Stow ('D' 1935–1941) was severely wounded in 1944 & invalided out of the Army in 1946. He went up to Trinity College, Oxford, that year, & in 1957 became joint Headmaster of Horris Hill Preparatory School.
24. Montague James Lindsay 'Jimmy' Stow ('D' 1934–1939) ended the war as a GSO3 with a mention in dispatches; like his brother Sandy, he went up to Trinity College, Oxford, in 1946. He became a teacher at Horris Hill in 1948, & in 1965 took over as Headmaster.
25. *WinColl E42/16/32*: letter from Lieutenant R.O. Lewin to MR, dated June 23rd 1944; addressed from ' 'A' Company, 2 KRRC, AEF'.
26. 'G' 1928–1933.
27. British military radios were known by numerical designations. Wireless Set No.14 was a mobile transmitter/receiver for short-range voice communications between a group of vehicles less than one mile apart.
28. Lieutenant John Williams, OC Assault Pioneer Platoon, 'S' Company, 9 DLI, quoted in Moses, H., *The Gateshead Gurkhas* (County Durham Books, 2001).
29. Sergeant Jim Ratcliffe, 9DLI; retrieved on October 14th 2022 from https://www.bbc.co.uk/history/ww2peopleswar/stories/19/a2494019.shtml.
30. Sergeant Charles Eagles, 9DLI, quoted in Moses, H., *The Gateshead Gurkhas* (County Durham Books, 2001).
31. *WinColl E42/24/59:* letter from Lieutenant Colonel Reginald Herbert Woods OBE, MC, to MR, dated June 22nd 1944; addressed from 'Woodfield House, Stevenage, Hertfordshire'.
32. *WinColl E42/24/63:* letter from Lieutenant Colonel Reginald Herbert Woods OBE, MC, to MR, dated July 4th 1944; addressed from 'Woodfield House, Stevenage'.
33. *Walker family collection*: letter from MR to 2nd Lieutenant P.M. Walker, dated July 5th 1944; addressed from 'Culver Lodge'.
34. *WinColl E42/24/32:* letter from the Rev Alwyn Terrell Petre Williams DD, MA, to MR, dated July 8th 1944; addressed from 'Auckland Castle, Bishop Auckland, County Durham'.
35. 'E' 1922–1927.
36. 'F' 1934–1939.
37. Boon, T., *History of the South Wales Borderers & the Monmouthshire Regiment.* Part II *The 2nd Battalion, The South Wales Borderers, D-Day 1944 to 1945* (Griffin Press, 1955).

XVIII

1. *WinColl E42/11/05: Kriegsgefangenenpost Postkarte. Absender: Vor- und Zuname: Lieut. M. Finch Gefangenennummer 128919* to MR, *datum June 12th [1944];* addressed from '*Lager-Bezeichnung: M.-Stammlager VII A*'.
2. *WinColl E42/11/11:* letter from Mr Ernest Finch to MR, dated September 23rd 1944; addressed from '70 Upper Hanover Street, Sheffield, 3'.
3. 'I' 1929–1934.
4. Hastings, R.H.W.S., *The Rifle Brigade in the Second World War 1939-1945* (Gale & Polden, 1950).
5. Stewart, P.F., *History of the XII Royal Lancers (Prince Of Wales's)* (OUP, 1950).

6. *WinColl E42/17/104:* letter from Lieutenant D.S. Middleditch to MR, dated January 15th 1945; addressed from '66 British General Hospital, CMF'.
7. Wilson, A.J., *Unusual Undertakings (Pen & Sword, 2002).*
8. Seton-Watson, C., *Dunkirk – Alamein – Bologna* (Regency, 1995).
9. Hastings, *op.cit.*
10. Seton-Watson, *op.cit.*
11. *Ibid.*
12. Lieutenant 232598 John Henry Persse ('H' 1935–1940) rests in grave VII.A.4 of the Assisi War Cemetery.
13. *Walker family collection*: letter from Peter Walker to Mr Norman Walker, dated June 25th 1944; addressed from 'Officers' Mess, 61st Training Regiment, RAC, Streatlam Camp, Barnard Castle, County Durham'.

XIX

1. *Walker family collection:* letter from J.N. Somerville to Peter Walker, dated August 4th 1944; addressed from '2nd Battalion, The South Wales Borderers, BLA'.
2. *McArthur family collection:* letter from J.C. McArthur to Major & Mrs V.G. McArthur, undated; addressed simply 'FRANCE'.
3. Nicolson, N. & Forbes, P., *The Grenadier Guards in the War of 1939–1945,* Volume I (Gale & Polden, 1949).
4. 5 Guards Armoured Brigade was one of three brigades in the Guards Armoured Division (the others being 6 Guards Armoured Brigade & 32 Guards Infantry Brigade). 5 Brigade comprised three tank battalions (2nd Grenadier Guards, 1st Coldstream Guards, & 2nd Irish Guards), & the motorized infantry of 1st Battalion, Grenadier Guards.
5. Howard, M. & Sparrow, J., *The Coldstream Guards 1920–1946* (OUP, 1951).
6. Captain H.W. Llewellyn Smith MC, MiD ('D' 1920–1925) compiled the 'Account of Operations of 3rd Tank Battalion Scots Guards 1944 July 20–1945 May 8' (*National Archives CAB 106/1029*), from which many excerpts have been taken, including sketch maps.
7. Lieutenant Henry William Somerville Marshall ('A' 1936–1941) was born on February 23rd 1923 in Hampstead. No athlete, according to Robertson, he was however an enthusiastic & exceptionally well-qualified Secretary of Archaeological Society; his tastes for the ancient & the beautiful were catholic, but as a numismatist he was outstanding. The owner of a valuable collection, bequeathed in his will to the Royal Numismatic Society, he had a knowledge of coins far beyond his years & would undoubtedly have attained the highest distinction in this province. By no means 'military' by nature, William became a keen & efficient soldier, & on a fleeting visit to Winchester on the evening before he sailed it was clear that he had fully found himself. In France he persistently made the best of both worlds; he would read *The Connoisseur* in a slit-trench, argue any subject in the Mess, & seize every chance he got of seeing what war had left of Norman culture; but his Squadron Commander testified to his unwavering coolness, sound judgement, & equanimity in battle. He married Sylvia Mary Hasell, of Penrith, Cumberland on June 7th 1944, only six weeks before he went overseas. Marshall was killed on November 26th at Tienray in the 'Venlo Pocket', aged twenty-one, & is buried in grave VI.E.9 of the Venray War Cemetery.
8. Major Thomas Edward Brodie Howarth MC became a liaison officer to Montgomery in 1945; he was a Don at Winchester from 1938 to 1948, returning as Second Master in 1952. He left Winchester to become High Master of St Paul's in 1962.
9. *WinColl E42/7/77:* letter from Captain J.B. Boyd to MR, dated July 27th 1944; addressed from '1KOSB, BLA'.
10. National Archives CAB 106/1029: 'Account of Operations of 3rd Tank Battalion Scots Guards 1944 July 20–1945 May 8'.
11. National Archives WO 373/49, & *London Gazette*, 21 December 1944.)
12. *Ibid.*
13. *Ibid.*

14. A party from 3SG visited the site of the action on August 28th, & observed the following: 'The [*Jagdpanther*] which came up through the position had withdrawn to an orchard about half a mile to the east. In this orchard were a number of tank tracks, which led to the supposition that it might have been a harbour area for the Germans. Tracks led from this orchard on to the main road running east from Les Loges. About a mile down this road a *Jagdpanther* was found. It had apparently pulled off the road into a field on the right. Here it had lost a track, & apparently been set on fire by its own crew. There was no sign of a hit on it, but the whole inside was burnt out & one side ripped open by exploding ammunition. None of those officers who saw this *Jagdpanther* now had seen one, either in the flesh or on a recognition chart, before. It was a stupendous equipment. A very long 88mm gun stuck out from a very heavily armoured sloping front-plate. Long sloping sides extended for three-quarters of the length of the vehicle. The gun appeared to have about 20 degrees of traverse. On the top were two exit hatches for the crew. All round was a length of wire on which camouflage could be hung – camouflage which would not interfere with the rotation of the turret, as on a tank.

    Later, another *Jagdpanther* was found ... This one was fairly intact ... It had been found about half a mile beyond the burn-out one ... The only apparent damage, apart from two small holes in the side and the roof, which did not in any way affect the working of the tank, was two missing teeth in the left front sprocket. These must have broken the left track. Two new links were found in it, showing where it had first been repaired, & it was again broken when found. The crew had obviously then given up hope of repairing it, & therefore abandoned it.'
15. Of these, seventy-three landed in London & fifty-three in Southampton and Portsmouth.
16. *Walker family collection:* letter from J.N. Somerville to Peter Walker, dated August 4th 1944; addressed from '2nd Battalion, The South Wales Borderers, BLA'.

XX

1. Properly Monte Castiglion Maggio.
2. Richard Alan 'Dick' Fyffe ('G' 1925–1930) was a great soldier, trusted & liked by his subordinates & superiors. He entered RMC Sandhurst in 1931 & swept the board, being a Cadet Scholar, Prize Cadet, & winner of the Sword of Honour. Commissioned into the Rifle Brigade in 1932, by 1935 he was a Lieutenant. In 1939 he was seconded to IV (Army Co-operation) Squadron RAF as an acting Flight Lieutenant, operating Westland Lysander observation aircraft until March 1940. He then served as a Staff Captain at the War Office before taking a staff course. From 1942 until 1944 he was a Major with 10RB in North Africa & Italy, first as a Company Commander & then as Second-in-Command of the Battalion. Promoted Lieutenant Colonel, he commanded in succession 6th Battalion Royal West Kents, 7RB, & 10RB in Italy & Austria. Along the way he picked up an MC & a DSO.
3. Hastings, R.H.W.S., *The Rifle Brigade in the Second World War 1939-1945* (Gale & Polden, 1950).
4. *Ibid.*
5. Seton-Watson, C., *Dunkirk – Alamein – Bologna* (Regency, 1995)
6. *Ibid.*
7. *Ibid.*
8. Durand A.T.M., & Hastings, R.H.W.S., *The London Rifle Brigade 1919 to 1950* (Gale & Polden, 1952).
9. *Ibid.*
10. National Archives WO 170/1469: War Diary, 7th Battalion, The Rifle Brigade.

XXI

1. Howard, M., & Sparrow, J., *The Coldstream Guards 1920–1946* (OUP, 1951).
2. Somerville, diary for June 29th 1944.
3. Boscawen, R., *Armoured Guardsmen* (Pen & Sword, 2001).
4. *Ibid.*

5. *WinColl E42/17/51:* letter from Captain J.F. Priestley to Major R.V. Martyn, dated August 21st 1944; no address given.
6. *WinColl E42/17/51:* letter from Lieutenant P.W. Loyd to Major R.V. Martyn, dated August 22nd 1944; no address given.
7. Lieutenant James Michael Gow ('C' 1937–1942), who arrived at 3SG from 261 Forward Delivery Squadron, Royal Armoured Corps, had gained his commission in June 1943, despite being told during training that he looked like a bag of manure tied with pink string. Having survived Normandy, he was wounded so severely in Belgium in October that he did not return to 3SG for six months, at which point he became one of the first British officers to enter Belsen in April 1945. He rose to become General Sir James Michael Gow GCB, & in a rich career commanded the British Army of the Rhine at the height of the Cold War. He died in 2013.
8. *WinColl E42/17/50:* letter from Major R.V. Martyn to MR, dated August 13th 1944; addressed from '20 Queen's Gate Gardens, SW7'.
9. *WinColl E42/17/51:* letter from Lieutenant P.W. Loyd to Major R.V. Martyn, dated August 22nd 1944; no address given.
10. *WinColl E42/17/51:* letter from Captain J.F. Priestley to Major R.V. Martyn, dated August 21st 1944; no address given.
11. Major H. Wake, OC 'A' Company 2KRRC, quoted in Mills, G., *The Annals of the King's Royal Rifle Corps,* Volume VII (Celer et Audax Club, 1979).
12. *Ibid.*
13. *Ibid.*

XXII

1. *WinColl E42/15/21:* letter from Flight Lieutenant Gordon Kidd ('I' 1931–1935) to MR, dated August 31st 1944. Kidd had joined the RAFVR in 1940 after reading Mechanical Science at Trinity College, Cambridge; he did his flying training in South Africa before joining Coastal Command in the United Kingdom in 1942. In 1944 he was posted to Southern Rhodesia as a flying instructor.
2. John Richard Cawthorne Matthews ('D' 1938–1942) was commissioned into the RAFVR in 1944, having joined in 1942. He was posted as a Flying Officer to Southern Rhodesia for instructional duties, & by the end of the war was a Flight Lieutenant with a mention in dispatches.
3. *WinColl E42/13/101:* letter from John Huggins to MR, dated August 8th 1944; addressed from 'Officers' Mess, Royal Air Force Norton, Southern Rhodesia'.
4. National Archives WO 170/824: War Diary, 12 Royal Lancers.
5. *WinColl E42/17/165:* letter from Charles Murray to MR, dated September 4th 1944; addressed from 'HQ Squadron, The Lovat Scouts, CMF'.
6. From the poem *Lookout Mountain* by George Dennison Prentice (1802–1870).
7. *Walker family collection:* letter from Peter Walker to Mr & Mrs Norman Walker, date removed by censor but clearly between August 20th 1944 & September 4th 1944; addressed 'Royal Wiltshire Yeomanry'.

XXIII

1. Lieutenant F.K.A. Low broke the back of Avenger '4A' when he hit the round-down (stern end of the flight deck); Sub-Lieutenant J.E. Randall missed the arrester cables & so Avenger '4Q' (JZ231) hit the barrier; & then New Zealand Sub-Lieutenant G.O. Smith also smacked his aircraft (Wildcat JV585) into the round-down & it went over the side into the sea. Luckily, he was rescued.
2 Avenger '4B' JZI80 was being flown by Sub-Lieutenant J. Swift.
3. *WinColl E42/21/41:* letter from Roger Rigby to MR, dated Thursday June 15th 1944; addressed 'c/o Lloyd's Bombay'.
4. *Walker family collection:* letter from MR to 2nd Lieutenant P.M. Walker, dated July 5th 1944; addressed from Culver Lodge.

5 Edited by author.
6. Wavell, *Viceroy's Journal*, July 14th 1944.
7. *WinColl E42/11/36:* letter from Bruce Fortune to MR, dated July 17th 1944; addressed from 'Viceroy's House, New Delhi'.
8. National Archives WO 172/4613: War Diary, 45th Cavalry, entry for August 27th 1944.
9. First Officer Heather Hayes WRNS, Susan Mackie's superior at SACSEA.
10. Captain Michael Hodges RN, Signals Officer at SACSEA.
11. *WinColl E42/17/83:* letter from Lieutenant Colonel Arthur Goring to Lady Metcalfe, dated September 24th 1944; addressed from '45 Cavalry, c/o Lloyds Bank, Bombay'.
12. National Archives WO 172/4613: War Diary, 45th Cavalry, entry for November 6th 1944.
13. *WinColl E42/17/84:* letter from Metcalfe to MR, dated December 10th 1944; addressed from '45th Cavalry, SEAC'.
14. Letter from Metcalfe to Sir Aubrey & Lady Metcalfe, dated January 22nd 1945; addressed from 45th Cavalry, SEAC *(Metcalfe family collection).*
15. Sub-Lieutenant (A) Ronald Ernest Pritchard RNVR was lost in Wildcat JV592.
16. Letter from Bruce Fortune to Susan Mackie, dated December 13th 1944; addressed from Government House, Calcutta (quoted in Mackie, *Time to Remember).*
17. *Hirst family collection:* Hirst, M.J., 'MJH's War Service'.

XXIV

1. Bart Stephens (stepson of David Kemp), personal communication to author, February 28th 2022.
2. *Walker family collection:* letter from Peter Walker to Mr Walker, dated September 5th 1944; addressed from 'RACTD – CMF'.
3. National Archives WO170/1469: War Diary, 7th Battalion, Rifle Brigade.
4. Despite its obvious propaganda elements, it is one of the best of its kind.
5. Neville J.E.H., *War Chronicle of the Oxfordshire & Buckinghamshire Light Infantry, Volume III: 1942-1944* (Gale & Polden, 1951).
6. National Archives WO170/824: War Diary, 12th Royal Lancers.
7. *Walker family collection:* letter from Peter Walker to Mr & Mrs Norman Walker, dated September 12th 1944; addressed from 'RWY, RACTD, CMF'.
8. Jacobine Hichens, *née* Menzies-Wilson, was the older sister of a Wykehamist (William N. Menzies-Wilson, 'A' 1940–1945) & widow of another (John Hichens, 'H' 1933–1939). After the war, she married yet another Wykehamist, Captain Lionel Bertrand Sackville-West ('K' 1926–1931), who had been captured at Tobruk in June 1942 with the Coldstream Guards & remained a prisoner of war until 1945. Their marriage produced five daughters – but no heir to the Knole estate, to which they moved in 1960. Jacobine's life there as chatelaine was sadly cut short by cancer in 1971.
9. *Walker family collection:* letter from Peter Walker to Mr & Mrs Norman Walker, dated September 21st 1944; addressed from 'RWY, 1st ARR, CMF'.
10. Wykehamist James Robertson CBE ('A' & College 1926–1931) studied at Trinity College, Cambridge, the Leipzig Conservatory, & the Royal College of Music. In 1937 he started work at Glyndebourne before moving in 1938 to the Carl Rosa Opera (a touring company in Britain). He joined the Royal Air Force during the war but continued his conducting as an entertainer to the armed forces. His career in opera after the war was long & distinguished.
11. *Walker family collection:* letter from Peter Walker to Mr & Mrs Norman Walker, dated September 27th 1944; addressed from 'RWY, 278 Field Delivery Squadron, CMF'.
12. The War Diary shows him as absent from his Regiment on September 9th & 16th, but back by the 23rd.
13. *WinColl E42/07/30:* letter from Lieutenant Elliott-Binns to MR, undated but late 1944; addressed from '29 Field Battery, 19th Field Regiment, CMF'.
14. *Walker family collection:* letter from Peter Walker to Mr & Mrs Norman Walker, dated September 19th 1944; addressed from '1st ARR, CMF'.

15. Edmunds was twenty-two years old when he died, & lies in grave XVIII.B.7 of the Coriano Ridge War Cemetery.
16. *WinColl E42/10/02:* letter from Maurice Edmunds to MR, dated October 1st 1944; addressed from 'The Stone House, Banbury'.
17. *WinColl E42/10/04*: letter from Maurice Edmunds to MR, dated October 29th 1944; addressed from 'The Stone House, Banbury'.
18. *Walker family collection:* letter from Peter Walker to Mr & Mrs Norman Walker, dated September 27th 1944; addressed from 'RWY, 278 Field Delivery Squadron, CMF'.
19. *Walker family collection:* extract from diary by Peter Walker: 'Observations and Reflections of a Very Inexperienced Soldier, supposedly On Active Service. Transferred from a rather dirty notebook into this beautiful sixty lira worth manuscript bought in Perugia. Observations continued (their predecessors missing believed drowned in Naples Bay)'.
20. Hastings, R.H.W.S., *The Rifle Brigade in the Second World War 1939–1945* (Gale & Polden, 1950).
21. Major Geoffrey Edward Ford North MC ('K' 1930–1934) had transferred from the Royal Wiltshire Yeomanry to 10th Hussars in 1940; he served in North Africa, earning a Commander-in-Chief's Commendation for Gallantry & a mention in dispatches in 1942 as well as his MC. Wounded twice, he was promoted Major in 1943 & then served as a GSO2 at HQ Eighth Army until 1945, at which point he returned to become second-in-command of 10th Hussars.
22. 259934 Lieutenant Henry Alan Brooke MC ('F' 1937-1939), 'A' Squadron, 10th Royal Hussars. More of him later.
23. *Walker family collection:* Walker, 'Observations and Reflections of a Very Inexperienced Soldier'.
24. Wilson, *op.cit.*
25. *WinColl E42/13/78:* letter from Lieutenant R.L. Holtby, dated October 10th 1944; addressed from ' 'S' Company, 6th Battalion, The Seaforth Highlanders, MEF'.
26. *WinColl E42/7/85:* air letter from Henry Brooke to MR, dated November 10th 1944; addressed from '16th/5th Lancers, CMF'.
27. *Walker family collection:* Walker, 'Observations and Reflections of a Very Inexperienced Soldier'.
28. *Walker family collection:* letter from Lieutenant Peter Walker to Mr & Mrs Norman Walker, dated February 3rd 1945; addressed from 'Xth Royal Hussars, CMF'.
29. *WinColl E42/17/104:* letter from Lieutenant David S. Middleditch to MR, dated January 15th 1944 (in error for 1945); addressed from '66 British General Hospital, CMF'.
30. An Ark was a Churchill tank converted to serve as a bridge across deep trenches; the tank would be driven into the obstacle (a stream, a crater, or such like) & lower ramps from its front & rear (hence its official title, an Armoured Ramp Carrier). The upper surface of the tank then formed the central span of the roadway bridge thus created.
31. *Walker family collection:* Walker, 'Observations and Reflections of a Very Inexperienced Soldier'.
32. *WinColl E42/15/02:* letter from Captain David Kemp to MR, dated December 4th 1944; addressed from '7RB, CMF'.
33. *Daily Telegraph*, August 21st 2003.
34. *Walker family collection:* Walker, 'Observations and Reflections of a Very Inexperienced Soldier'.
35. Colonel Paul Rodzianko CMG, 1880–1965.
36. Michael Wilson ('I' 1926–1932) had taken Holy Orders in 1938 & served as a Chaplain to the Forces from 1941 to 1946.
37. *WinColl E42/13/102:* letter from Flight Lieutenant J.G. Huggins to MR, dated December 6th 1944; addressed from 'Officers' Mess, RAF Cranborne, Southern Rhodesia'.
38. Christopher Robert Foot ('G' 1936–1941) joined the Army in 1941 & served with 16th/5th Lancers from 1941, rising to the rank of Captain by demobilization in 1946.
39. John David Gresham Gray ('D' 1937–1941) had joined the RAF in 1942, but was commissioned into 12th Lancers in 1944. He was wounded in Italy, transferred to the RTR, sent to Greece with the Royal Fusiliers in 1945, & then became an instructor at the Middle East School of Infantry in 1946. Demobilized on December 13th 1947, he died four days later whilst climbing Ben Nevis.

40. *WinColl E42/17/107:* letter from Lieutenant David Middleditch to MR, dated December 14th 1944; addressed from ' 'A' Squadron, XII Royal Lancers, CMF'.
41. *Walker family collection:* letter from Lieutenant Peter Walker to 'Dearest Madajak', dated January 1st 1945; addressed from 'Xth Royal Hussars, CMF'.
42. *Walker family collection:* letter from Lieutenant Peter Walker to Mr & Mrs Norman Walker, dated February 7th 1945; addressed from 'Xth Royal Hussars, CMF'.
43. *Walker family collection:* Walker, 'Observations and Reflections of a Very Inexperienced Soldier'.
44. *Walker family collection:* letter from Lieutenant Peter Walker to 'Dearest Madajak', dated January 1st 1945; addressed from 'Xth Royal Hussars, CMF'.

XXV

1. National Archives WO 171/1318: War Diary, 1st Battalion, KOSB.
2. *WinColl E42/16/35:* letter from Mr & Mrs Lewin to MR, dated August 30th 1944; addressed from 'Grenville Hotel, Bude, Cornwall'.
3. Mills, G., *The Annals of the King's Royal Rifle Corps,* Volume VII (Celer et Audax Club, 1979).
4. *Ibid.*
5. The full story of the Banff Strike Wing can be found in Andrew D. Bird's outstanding *A Separate Little War* (Grub Street, 2003).
6. National Archives AIR 27/1497/18: Operational Record Book, 248 Squadron RAF.
7. The vessel which exploded was *Vorpostenboot* (patrol craft) V-1608 *Sülldorf.*
8. National Archives AIR 27/1497/18: Operational Record Book, 248 Squadron RAF.
9. *Ibid.*
10. The spelling of Norwegian place-names in the 248 Squadron Operational Record Book is sometimes so idiosyncratic as to be impossible to pin down on a map.
11. *Boyd family collection:* letter from Captain J.B. Boyd to Commander John Gordon Boyd, dated September 29th 1944; addressed from '1KOSB, BLA'.
12. National Archives AIR 27/1497/18: Operational Record Book, 248 Squadron RAF.
13. National Archives WO 171/1327: War Diary, 2nd Battalion, KRRC.
14. National Archives WO 171/1318: War Diary, 1st Battalion, KOSB.
15. National Archives WO 171/1327: War Diary, 2nd Battalion, KRRC.
16. National Archives AIR 27/1497/18: Operational Record Book, 248 Squadron RAF.
17. *WinColl E42/9/19:* letter from Charles Duffin to MR, dated December 22nd 1944; addressed from '3rd Battalion Scots Guards, BLA'.
18. *WinColl E42/17/09:* letter from Graham Mackrill to MR, dated October 25th 1944; addressed from 'Grand Hotel, Fort William, Inverness-shire'.
19. There is a monument in the town to the 49th (Polar Bear) Division for their role in the liberation.
20. National Archives AIR 27/1497/18: Operational Record Book, 248 Squadron RAF, states that eight Mosquitos took off 1258-1301hrs for an Offensive Patrol from Ytteroneyia anchorages to Utvaer with another seven aircraft from 235 Squadron. Mosquito FB.VI W/248 was crewed by F/O J. Kennedy & F/O W. Rolls. At 1439hrs the formation reached Vaer & commenced its patrol, continuing north to Ytteroene lighthouse, but at 1449hrs Wing Commander Sise abandoned the mission & set course for Banff, owing to adverse weather conditions. The aircraft had all landed by 1640hrs.
21. *WinColl E42/21/43:* letter from Lady Rigby to MR, dated October 30th 1944; addressed from 'Long Durford, Petersfield, Hants'.

XXVI

1. *WinColl E42/16/33:* letter from Mrs Amy Lewin to MR, dated November 24th 1944; addressed from 'The Manor, Bourton-on-the-Water, Gloucestershire'.
2. *WinColl E42/7/79:* letter from Captain J.B. Boyd to MR, dated January 6th 1945; addressed from 'Royal Infirmary, Leicester'.
3. National Archives AIR 27/1497/18: Operational Record Book, 248 Squadron RAF.

4. *Wincoll E42/15/08:* letter from Flight Lieutenant John Kennedy to MR, dated November 12th 1944; addressed from 'Officers' Mess, RAF Station Banff, Banffshire'.
5. *Mackrill family collection*: letter from Graham Mackrill to Mr H.W. Mackrill, dated November 11th 1944; addressed from Box 138, Fleet Mail Office, Great Yarmouth.
6. *Mackrill family collection*: letter from Graham Mackrill to Mr & Mrs H.W. Mackrill, dated November 24th 1944; addressed from Box 138, Fleet Mail Office, Great Yarmouth.
7. For example, at http://www.aparchive.com/metadata/youtube/b32c6d1b3ef04a3f9d506a253354ef63
8. The vessels attacked included the 5,273-ton *Ostland*, which was hit, though no casualties were suffered; she was under tow by two tugs, *Fairplay* & *Aasenfjord. Aasenfjord* took hits to her superstructure, including the bridge, which killed one & wounded two; the *Tucuman* (4,621 tons) was struck by a rocket projectile, which knocked out her quad 20mm *Flakvierling* 38 mount; the *Magdalena*, of 3,283 tons, caught fire after a hit amidships; & the *Helene Russ*, a 993-ton ammunition transport, was lucky only to suffer damage to her deck.
9. *Vorpostenboote* V-5102 *Orkan* (156 tons), V-5305 *Schnepfe*, & V-5306 (name unknown).
10. *Vorpostenboote*V-5109, V-5308 *O.B. Rogge*, & V-5310 *Seewolf.*
11. The two crew killed were the pilot, Flight Lieutenant 129254 Leslie Norman Collins RAFVR, & his navigator, Flying Officer 153223 Robert Henry Hurn RAFVR, who was twenty-four. Collins was three years older, & married; he left a widow – Joan Dorothy Collins – in Southampton. Both airmen are commemorated on the Runnymede Memorial.
12. All four are commemorated on the Runnymede Memorial. The pilots were: Flying Officer J/23429 Kenneth Cecil Wing RCAF, a 23-year-old from Saskatchewan & Flying Officer J/23397 William Nathan Cosman DFC, RCAF. Their navigators were Flying Officer 152972 Leslie Morris Freedman RAFVR & Pilot Officer 428055 Vernon Rippon Shield RAAF; he left a widow, Lynne Boyd Shield, in Tasmania, & was twenty-eight when he died.
13. *WinColl E42/11/23:* letter from Lady Fortune to MR, dated December 7th 1944; no address.
14. *Boyd family collection:* Captain J.B. Boyd to Captain John G. Boyd RN & Miss E. Boyd, dated December 10th 1944; no address.
15. *Boyd family collection:* letter from Lieutenant Colonel R.C. Macdonald to Captain John G. Boyd RN, dated December 15th 1944; addressed from '1st Bn KOSB, BLA'.
16. *WinColl E42/7/79:* letter from Captain J.B. Boyd to MR, dated January 6th 1945; addressed from 'Royal Infirmary, Leicester'.
17. *WinColl E42/7/78:* letter from Captain John G. Boyd RN to MR, dated January 30th 1945; addressed from 'Captain of Dockyard's Office, HM Dockyard, Rosyth'.
18. According to one source, they were *Matrosenobergefreite* (Seamen 1st Class) Walter Kutscher, Artur Spandehra, & Konrad Watzlawik.
19. The crew of this Mosquito are buried in British Plot B.9 & B.1 of Sola churchyard. The pilot was Flight Lieutenant 410034 Kenneth Cupples Beruldsen RAAF, whose parents were Einar Bjorn & Helen Yeats Beruldsen, of Traralgon, Victoria. He was just twenty-two, whilst his navigator was only twenty one: he was Pilot Officer 185410 Tom Damas Seller Rabbitts RAFVR, from Farlington in Hampshire.
20. Copyright holder unknown; retrieved December 16th 2022 from https://www.redd.it-ww2-shipwrecks-cargo-ship-m-s-ferndale-and-tug-boat-parat-v0-jie5n9hh6jy91.jpg.
21. National Archives AIR 27/1610/24: Operational Record Book, 279 Squadron RAF.
22. Photograph reproduced from Docherty, T., *Dinghy Drop: 279 Squadron at War 1941-1946* (Pen & Sword, 2007).
23. National Archives AIR 27/1610/24: Operational Record Book, 279 Squadron RAF.
24. Kennedy is commemorated on Panel 202 of the Runnymede Memorial; Flying Officer 153491 Francis Walter Rolls is commemorated on Panel 209. Rolls, the son of Francis Albert Edwards Rolls & Margaret Rolls, from Reading, was only twenty-two when he died.
25. *WinColl E42/15/09:* letter from Wing Commander G.D. Sise DSO, DFC, to Mrs Constance Kennedy, dated December 19th 1944; addressed from 'RAF Banff'.

26. *WinColl E42/15/13.*
27. *WinColl E42/15/11:* letter from Mrs Constance Kennedy to MR, dated September 8th 1945; addressed from 'Welburn Manor'.
28. *WinColl E42/9/19:* letter from Charles Duffin to MR, dated December 22nd 1944; addressed from '3rd Battalion Scots Guards, BLA'.
29. The Revd Canon John D'Ewes Evelyn Firth (College 1912–1918, staff 1922–1954) was a housemaster at Winchester at the time, & had married in 1939. He was an excellent cricketer (he took 10 for 41 off Eton in 1917) & enjoyed the nickname 'Budge' at the College.
30. *WinColl E42/16/34.* Lenzerheide is a ski resort in Switzerland.
31. *WinColl E42/22/36:* letter from Mrs Barbara Simpkin to MR, undated but probably just before January 1st 1945; addressed from '68 Cornwall Gardens SW7'.

XXVII

1. *Walker family collection:* Walker, 'Observations and Reflections of a Very Inexperienced Soldier'.
2. *WinColl E42/8/31:* letter from Captain J.S.B. Clerk Rattray to MR, undated but probably around February 21st 1945; addressed from '2nd Battalion, Scots Guards, BLA'.
3. National Archives WO 171/5212: War Diary, 2nd Battalion, King's Royal Rifle Corps.
4. National Archives WO 170/4626: War Diary, 12th Royal Lancers.
5. Reder reported that he & his men had executed 728 'bandits' – partisans, those suspected of aiding partisans, & the local populace in general. The actual figure seems to have been 770, though some estimates have put it as high at 1,800. Of the confirmed victims (454 male, 316 female), 155 were children under ten years old; 95 were aged between ten & sixteen; a further 142 were over sixty. Five priests were among those executed. The massacre was the subject of a 2009 film, *L'uomo Che Verrà*, & at least one book: Ortner, C., *Marzabotto: The Crimes of Walter Reder – SS-Sturmbannführer* (Vienna, 1985). Reder was arrested in Salzburg after the war by British troops & extradited to Italy, where he was tried in 1951 & given a life sentence. He was released in 1985 & died in 1991.
6. *Walker family collection:* Walker, 'Observations and Reflections of a Very Inexperienced Soldier'.
7. *WinColl E42/09/11:* letter from Lieutenant Guy H. Dodgson to MR, dated January 15th 1945; addressed from 'Support Company, Special Force, India Command'.
8. *WinColl E42/17/104:* letter from Lieutenant David S. Middleditch to MR, dated January 15th 1944 (in error for 1945); addressed from '66 British General Hospital, CMF'.
9. *WinColl E42/13/79:* letter from Lieutenant Robert L. Holtby to MR, dated January 18th 1945; addressed from ' 'C' Company, 6th Battalion, The Seaforth Highlanders, MEF'.
10. In full, actually 'His Highness Field Marshal Supradipta-Manyabara Svasti Sri Madati Prachandra Bhujadandyetyadi Projjwala-Nepala Taradhisha Sri Sri Sri Maharaja Sir Juddha Shumsher Jung Bahadur Rana GCB, GCSI, GCIE, Prime Minister of Nepal, Maharajah of Lamjang and Kaski'.
11. The No.77 Mark 1 smoke grenade was highly effective, being filled with white phosphorus to generate an intense screen of smoke. Its contents also made it a deadly anti-personnel weapon, especially in confined spaces.
12. National Archives WO 171/5212: War Diary, 2nd Battalion, King's Royal Rifle Corps.
13. *Mackrill family collection*: letter from Graham Mackrill to Mr & Mrs H.W. Mackrill, endorsed 'received January 20th 1945'; addressed from 'MGB 325, c/o GPO, London'.
14. Senior Commander 196306 Charlotte Elizabeth Burn-Clerk-Rattray (August 1st 1911–March 1st 1945) died on active service with the ATS. Formerly in the Women's Transport Service (FANY), she was at the time of her death attached to 145(M) HAA Regiment, Royal Artillery. Before the war, she had been awarded the Royal Scottish Geographical Society's Silver Medal, & she was a Bronze Medallist of Edinburgh University. She is buried in Rattray Parish Churchyard, Perthshire.
15. *WinColl E42/8/32:* letter from Mrs Ferelith Clerk-Rattray to MR, dated January 20th 1945; not addressed.
16. *Walker family collection:* letter from Lieutenant Peter Walker to Mr & Mrs Walker, dated February 7th 1945; addressed from 'Xth Royal Hussars, CMF'.

17. 7905330 Serjeant James Shuttleworth was twenty-five years old when he died, & rests in grave V.E.7 of the Faenza War Cemetery on the plains beyond the Apennines. From Astley Bridge, in Bolton, he left a widow & two sons, as is recorded on his headstone: 'James, the Beloved Husband of Edna, & Darling Daddy of Jeffrey & Barry'.
18. *Simpkin family collection:* letter from R.E. Simpkin to Mrs Barbara Simpkin, dated January 31st 1945; addressed from '*Oflag* IXA/Z'.
19. *Somerville family collection:* Somerville, C., unpublished memoirs, typescript, undated.
20. *Walker family collection:* letter from Lieutenant Peter Walker to Mr & Mrs Walker, dated February 3rd 1945; addressed from 'Xth Royal Hussars, CMF'.
21. *WinColl E42/21/44:* letter from R.M. Rigby to MR, dated February 4th 1945; no sender's address.
22. *Hirst family collection:* Hirst, M.J., *M.J.H.'s War Service,* typescript, 29 pages, undated.
23. *Ibid.*
24. *Ibid.*
25. National Archives WO 171/5149: War Diary, 2nd Battalion, Scots Guards.
26. *WinColl E42/8/31:* letter from Captain J.S.B. Clerk Rattray to MR, undated but probably around February 21st 1945; addressed from '2nd Battalion, Scots Guards, BLA'.
27. Fortune, S.M., *Time to Remember* (privately published, 2002).
28. *Walker family collection:* letter from Lieutenant Peter Walker to Mr & Mrs Walker, dated February 12th 1945; addressed from 'Xth Royal Hussars, CMF'.
29. National Archives WO 171/5212: War Diary, 2nd Battalion, King's Royal Rifle Corps.
30. The grid references given in the typescript version of the 2KRRC war diary for this action are very confused, one assumes through misreading of a pencilled draft: for example, Gochfort z B is stated to be at 000898, which should read 000398; a nearby position is later given as 090401 (actually 000401). Woods south of Udem are stated to be at 0740, which should read 9740.
31. *WinColl E42/17/97: Kriegsgefangenenpost Postkarte to MR. Absender: Vor- und Zuname: Lieut. John Metcalfe. Gefangenennummer: 1043/VMF. Datum: Christmas Eve 1944.* Addressed from *Lager-Bezeichnung: OFLAG 79, 3 Coy, Kriegsgefangenlager.*
32. Lieutenant 268995 Henry Kenyon Padfield ('D' 1937–1941) had been commissioned into the Welsh Guards in 1943 & served with 2nd (Armoured) Battalion in North-West Europe in 1944 until his capture in September. Between September 8th & 12th, 2WG were involved in severe fighting around Hechtel, & Padfield had been wounded & posted missing in Helchteren.
33. Captain 63567 Alistair Carpendale McEwan 'Robin' Savage, of No.7 Commando, was reported wounded & missing on June 2nd 1941 in Crete. He was held & mistreated in an Italian civilian prison – *Carcere Penale* Badia – before being transferred to Brunswick. Born in 1914, he died in July 2000.

XXVIII

1. In later years, the author's grandmother claimed that Archbishop Runcie kindly rubbed sun cream on to her during a cruise.
2. National Archives WO 171/5212: War Diary, 2nd Battalion, King's Royal Rifle Corps.
3. *Ibid.*
4. *Ibid.*
5. *WinColl E42/21/97:* letter from Officer Cadet 14497437 Michael James Ryall ('I' 1939–1944) to MR, dated March 8th 1945; addressed 'c/o Major-General R.A.B. Freeland MC, Cecil Hotel, Delhi'. Ryall was the son of J.E. Ryall OBE, Chief Constable of Somerset. He joined the Somerset Light Infantry on leaving Winchester, & attended the Mhow OCTU before being commissioned later in 1945.
6. *Herbert family collection:* Herbert, A., diary for Sunday March 11th 1945.
7. *Walker family collection:* Walker, P.M., *Observations and Reflections of a Very Inexperienced Soldier.*
8. Lieutenant Colonel Edward George Grey Lillingston ('K' 1906–1911) had served with 4th Dragoon Guards in France & Belgium from 1914 until the war's end, being mentioned in dispatches, but was still only a Lieutenant in 1918. He acceded to the command of 4th Hussars in 1939, & led

the Regiment into battle in Egypt and Greece in 1940-1941. He was captured whilst defending the Corinth Canal in April 1941, & spent the rest of the war in captivity in Germany. His services were rewarded in 1945 with a DSO.

9. Major Maurice James Hartley Wilson OBE ('H' 1912–1916) had been commissioned into 3rd Battalion, Cameron Highlanders, in 1917, & by 1919 was a Captain. In 1938 he was promoted Major & the following year went out to France as Second-in-Command of 1st Battalion. There he was captured, remaining in German hands until 1945.
10. Major the Hon. George Douglass Milne ('F' 1922–1927) was a 2nd Lieutenant in the Royal Artillery (Territorial Force) in 1939, & the following year served in Norway as a Captain. He went to Crete as a Major with 51 Heavy AA Regiment, where he was wounded & captured in May 1941. He was mentioned in dispatches, but was a prisoner of war in Germany for the next four years.
11. 2nd Lieutenant John Robert Kilgour Sinclair ('A' 1932–1938) had been serving with the Cameron Highlanders in France & Belgium when he was taken prisoner in 1940. He spent the rest of the European war as a prisoner. He was mentioned in dispatches.
12. This journey has been documented in superb detail by Peter Green – son of one of the prisoners – in his book *The March East, 1945: The Final Days of OFLAG IX A/H & A/Z* (Spellmount, 2012).
13. Wilson, A.J., 'The Apennines to the Alps, 1945' in *The Rifle Brigade 1939–1945,* Volume 2.
14. *Ibid.*

XXIX

1. *Walker family collection:* Walker, P.M., 'Observations and Reflections of a Very Inexperienced Soldier'.
2. National Archives WO 171/5212: War Diary, 2nd Battalion, Scots Guards.
3. Copy appended to National Archives WO 171/5212: War Diary, 2nd Battalion, Scots Guards.
4. Elliott, W.A., *Esprit de Corps: A Scots Guards Officer on Active Service 1943–1945* (Michael Russell, 1996).
5. The whole sequence of photographs – catalogued as 'The Prisoner of War Photographs of Leighton 'Lee' Mcleod Hill, March from *Oflag* IX A/Z, March-April 1945' – can be viewed on the IWM website: https://www.iwm.org.uk/collections/search?filters%5BmakerString%5D%5BHill%2C%20Leighton%20McLeod%5D=on&style=image
6. National Archives CAB 106/1029: 'Account of Operations of 3rd Tank Battalion Scots Guards 1944 July 20–1945 May 8'.
7. Retrieved from *@rgpoulussen*; posted at 0656hrs, April 6th 2018. RG's posts on the platform formerly known as Twitter are one of the few things which make social media worth while.
8. For a superb recent summary of this period of the war, look no further than Peter Caddick-Adams' *1945: Victory in the West* (Hutchinson Heinemann, 2022).
9. *Walker family collection:* Walker, P.M., 'Observations and Reflections of a Very Inexperienced Soldier'.
10. *Walker family collection:* letter from 556774 Sergeant R. Ross to Lieutenant P.M. Walker, dated April 25th 1945; addressed from ' 'C' Squadron, 10th Royal Hussars, CMF'.
11. *Walker family collection:* letter from 'Brian' to Lieutenant P.M. Walker, dated April 17th 1945; not addressed.
12. *Walker family collection:* Walker, P.M., 'Observations and Reflections of a Very Inexperienced Soldier'.
13. Walker's nick-name was derived from the British comic actor Syd Walker, who had died of appendicitis on January 13th 1945, aged 58. A veteran of music hall, he had performed as part of Fred Karno's troupe, which had been so famous for its chaotic comedy that in the First World War the phrase 'Fred Karno's Army' was used for any shambolic situation. Syd Walker regularly appeared on the BBC radio show 'Band Waggon', as a rag-&-bone man; his catch-phrase was 'What would you do, chums?' He then had his own programme, 'Mr Walker Wants to Know'.
14. *Walker family collection:* letter from 556774 Sergeant R. Ross to Lieutenant P.M. Walker, dated April 25th 1945; addressed from ' 'C' Squadron, 10th Royal Hussars, CMF'.
15. *Walker family collection:* letter from 317060 Trooper E. Weaire to Lieutenant P.M. Walker, dated April 16th 1945; addressed from ' 'C' Squadron, 10th Royal Hussars, CMF'.

16. *Walker family collection*: handwritten note by Margaret Walker on letter from 317060 Trooper E. Weaire to Lieutenant P.M. Walker, dated April 16th 1945; addressed from 'C' Squadron, 10th Royal Hussars, CMF'.
17. *WinColl E42/22/37:* letter from Mrs Ethel Coller to MR, dated May 2nd 1945; addressed from 'Wood Close, Grasmere'.
18. *Ibid.*
19. *WinColl E42/22/38:* letter from R.E. Simpkin to MR, dated April 22nd 1945; addressed from '68 Cornwall Gardens, London, SW7'.

XXX

1. Tom Mix was an American film star active in Westerns between 1909 & 1935.
2. *Hirst family collection:* Hirst, M.J., 'MJH's War Service'.
3. *Ibid.*
4. *Ibid.*
5. Erskine, D., *The Scots Guards 1919–1955* (Clowes, 1956).
6. *Hirst family collection:* Hirst, M.J., 'MJH's War Service'.
7. *Ibid.*
8. *National Archives CAB 106/1029:* Captain H.W. Llewellyn Smith, 'Account of Operations of 3rd Tank Battalion Scots Guards 1944 July 20–1945 May 8'.
9. *WinColl E42/13/81:* letter from Mrs Edmond Holtby to MR, dated April 24th 1945.
10. Lieutenant 259934 Henry Alan Brooke MC ('F' 1937–1939) was the third & youngest son of Captain the Right Hon. Sir Basil Stanlake Brooke KG, CBE, MC, Croix de Guerre, PC, DL, MP, 5th Baronet, 1st Viscount Brookeborough, Prime Minister of Northern Ireland 1943–1963 ('D' 1901–1905). His brother, Lieutenant Basil J.D. Brooke ('F' 1933–1938), of the Grenadier Guards, was killed in Tunisia in 1943. Their great-uncle was Lord Alanbrooke, Chief of the Imperial General Staff, & on October 2nd 1942 Henry & his mother dined with Alanbrooke in his London flat. Brooke was promoted to Lieutenant in 1943 & served in North Africa & Italy, winning the MC in December 1944. He made a splendid officer, & everybody testified to his dash & fearlessness. When news of his death reached Alanbrooke on the evening of April 17th (passed on by General Alexander), he wrote in his diary: 'Poor old Basil and Cynthia!' Brooke is buried in grave I.C.29 of the Ravenna War Cemetery.
11. *Walker family collection:* letter from 'Brian' to Lieutenant P.M. Walker, dated April 17th 1945; not addressed.
12. National Archives WO 373/13/392: recommendation for award for 14292418 Trooper Reginald Arthur Robinson.
13. National Archives WO 170/5063: War Diary, 7th Battalion, The Rifle Brigade.
14. Quoted in Hastings, *The Rifle Brigade 1939–1945.*
15. National Archives WO 170/5063: War Diary, 7th Battalion, The Rifle Brigade.
16. *Walker family collection:* Walker, P.M., 'Observations and Reflections of a Very Inexperienced Soldier'.
17. Nigel William Lillingston ('K' 1938–1942) had been commissioned into the Royal Scots Greys in 1944 but had then been severely wounded in Normandy.
18. National Archives WO 171/5212: War Diary, 2nd Battalion, King's Royal Rifle Corps.
19. *Walker family collection:* letter from 556774 Sergeant R. Ross to Lieutenant P.M. Walker, dated April 25th 1945; addressed from ' 'C' Squadron, 10th Royal Hussars, CMF'. The reference to the barrow is probably an allusion to Walker's nick-name, 'Syd', since the comedian Syd Walker's most memorable character had been a rag-&-bone man.
20. Quoted in Erskine, D., *The Scots Guards 1919–1955* (Clowes, 1956).
21. *Ibid.*
22. National Archives WO 171/5212: War Diary, 2nd Battalion, King's Royal Rifle Corps.
23. *Ibid.*
24. *Ibid.*

XXXI

1. National Archives WO 170/5063: War Diary, 7th Battalion, The Rifle Brigade.
2. National Archives WO 170/5063: War Diary, 7th Battalion, The Rifle Brigade.
3. Corporal 6970245 Edwin Albert Tyler was the son of Thomas Edward Tyler & Ada Jane Louise Tyler, of Poplar in London. He was twenty-two years old when he died, & now rests in grave II.C.15 of the Udine War Cemetery.
4. Fortune, S.M., *Time to Remember* (privately published, 2002).
5. National Archives WO 170/5063: War Diary, 7th Battalion, The Rifle Brigade.
6. *WinColl E42/11/06:* postcard from Michael Finch to MR, postmarked May 4th 1945; addressed from '442 Glossop Road, Sheffield 10'.
7. National Archives WO 171/5212: War Diary, 2nd Battalion, King's Royal Rifle Corps.
8. A flavour of this astonishing documentation can be found at: https://www.ibiblio.org/hyperwar/ETO/Surrender/ECLIPSE/index.html
9. National Archives WO 171/5212: War Diary, 2nd Battalion, King's Royal Rifle Corps.
10. An excellent sense of the chaos which pertained can be gained from Keith Lowe's *Savage Continent: Europe in the Aftermath of World War II* (Viking, 2012).
11. *Walker family collection:* letter from MR to 2nd Lieutenant P.M. Walker, dated May 10th 1945; addressed from 'Culver Lodge, Winchester'.
12. Fortune, S.M., *Time to Remember* (privately published, 2002).
13. *Hirst family collection:* Hirst, M.J., 'MJH's War Service'.
14. *Ibid.*

XXXII

1. *Wincoll E42/07/29:* letter from Lieutenant Elliott-Binns to MR, post-marked FPO316, May 28th 1945; addressed from '29 Field Battery, 19 Field Regiment, MEF'.
2. *Hirst family collection:* Hirst, M.J., 'MJH's War Service'.
3. *WinColl E42/13/38:* letter from Captain A. Herbert to MR, dated June 18th 1945; addressed from 'Chief Signals Officer's Branch, 303 Lines of Communication Area, c/o 12 ABPO, India Command'.
4. *Walker family collection:* letter from MR to Mr Norman M. Walker, dated July 3rd 1945; addressed from 'Culver Lodge, Winchester'.
5. *WinColl E42/11/37:* letter from Captain J.B. Fortune to MR, dated August 8th 1945; addressed from 'The Viceroy's House, New Delhi'.
6. *WinColl E42/13/32:* letter from Crispin Hill to MR, dated August 14th 1945; addressed from 'HMS *Flamborough Head,* c/o GPO'.
7. John Frederick Denman ('K' 1910–1914).
8. *Hirst family collection:* Hirst, M.J., 'MJH's War Service'.
9. *WinColl E42/21/45:* letter from R.M. Rigby to MR, dated August 18th 1945; addressed 'c/o Lloyd's, Bombay'.
10. *Rickman family collection:* Rickman, G., 'Agro's 1989 thoughts of nearly fifty years ago'.
11. *Ibid.*
12. *Ibid.*
13. *WinColl E42/21/21:* letter from Gerry Rickman to Mr Spencer Leeson, dated September 5th 1945; addressed 'c/o Recovered POW Mail Centre, India Command, Bombay'.
14. *Rickman family collection:* Rickman, G., 'Agro's 1989 thoughts of nearly fifty years ago'.
15. *WinColl E42/11/38:* letter from Major J.B. Fortune, DAMS, to MR, dated December 12th 1945; addressed from 'HQ ALFNEI, SEAC'.
16. The day that this author's father was born.
17. *WinColl E42/24/65:* letter from Peter Walker to MR, dated November 11th 1945; addressed from 'Xth Royal Hussars, British Troops in Austria, CMF'.
18. *WinColl E42/17/85:* letter from Patrick Metcalfe to MR, dated November 17th 1945; addressed from '45th Cavalry, Risalpur Cantonment, North-West Frontier Province, India'.

19. *WinColl E42/17/109:* letter from Captain D.S. Middleditch (ADC to DMG) to MR, dated December 21st 1945; addressed from 'Main Headquarters Control Commission, Lubeck, Westphalia, British Army of the Rhine'.

XXXIII

1. Sarah Richardson, personal communication to author, 2022.
2. *Ibid.*
3. Henrietta Fenton *(née* Mackrill) , personal communication to author, 2022.
4. *Winchester College collection:* discovered in 2022 by former Winchester Don, Lieutenant Colonel Michael Wallis.
5. *Winchester College collection:* letter from MR to all correspondents, dated November 30th 1953; addressed from 'The Hampshire Club, Winchester'.
6. When Robertson died on February 14th 1956, his obituary in *The Wykehamist* (1030, March 1956) stated that 'his war service meant a great deal to him, as it did to many of his contemporaries … The war widened his horizons and gave him the self-confidence that comes from having proved oneself in the face of death and endured what at times seemed almost unendurable. To the young he sometimes seemed to be exaggerating or sentimentalising it all, but those of them who in later life had similar experiences in the Second War will have come to understand him better.'

Sources

Primary Sources – Published

Beaton, C., *Cecil Beaton's Diaries: 1939–44 The Years Between* (Weidenfeld & Nicolson, 1965)
Boscawen, R., *Armoured Guardsmen* (Pen & Sword, 2001)
Elliott-Binns, M., *Finding through War: Poems of Fifty Years Ago* (William Sessions, 1995)
Elliott-Binns, M., *Realisation* (Mendip Publishing, 1993)
Fortune, S.M., *Time to Remember* (privately published, 2002)
Knowles, S.W., *Soldier On: The Personal Experiences of a Tank Crewman in the 16th/5th Lancers during the Second World War* (Leonaur, 2016)
Pawson, H.A., *Indelible Memories* (Foxbury Press, 2004)
Seton-Watson, C., *Dunkirk – Alamein – Bologna* (Regency, 1995)
Simpkin, R.E., *Men Against Tanks,* in *The Mechanized Battlefield: A Tactical Analysis* (Pergamon-Brassey's, 1985)
Somerville, J.N., *Memories of My Life* (privately published, 2014)
Wavell, A.P., *The Viceroy's Journal* (OUP, 1973)
Whitelaw, W.S.I., *The Whitelaw Memoirs* (Aurum, 1989)
Wilson, A.J., *Unusual Undertakings* (Pen & Sword, 2002)
WW2 People's War is a valuable online archive of wartime memories contributed by members of the public & gathered by the BBC. The archive can be found at *bbc.co.uk/ww2peopleswar.*

Primary Sources – Unpublished

Herbert, A., diary, 1945.
Hirst, M.J., *MJH's War Service,* typescript, 29 pages, undated.
Rickman, G., *"Agro's" 1989 thoughts of nearly fifty years ago; being the recollections of a prisoner-of-war of the Japanese in World War II from 1942 to 1945,* typescript, 1989.
Rigby, R.M., *Old Risalawallah Goes Walkabout* & *My War with the Duke of Aosta,* typescripts, Ansty Plum, May 2003.
Somerville, C., unpublished memoirs, typescript, undated.
Somerville, J.N., *Recollections of D-Day,* typescript, 36 pages, undated.
Walker, P.M., *Observations and Reflections of a Very Inexperienced Soldier, supposedly On Active Service. Transferred from a rather dirty notebook into this beautiful sixty lira worth manuscript bought in Perugia . Observations continued (their predecessors missing believed drowned in Naples Bay),* typescript, undated.

Select Bibliography

Anon., *History of the First Division: Anzio Campaign January-June 1944* (Ahva Press, Jerusalem, 1944)
Bird, A.D., *A Separate Little War* (Grub Street, 2003)
Blackwell, I., *Battleground Europe: Anzio* (Pen & Sword, 2006)
Bowlby, A., *Countdown to Cassino: the Battle of Mignano Gap, 1943* (Leo Cooper, 1995)
Buckingham, W.F., *Tobruk* (History Press, 2008)

Bullen, R., *History of the 2/7th Battalion The Queen's Royal Regiment 1939-1946* (Besley & Copp, 1958)
Caddick-Adams, P., *1945: Victory in the West* (Hutchinson Heinemann, 2022)
Clark, L., *Anzio: The Friction of War* (Headline Review, 2006)
Delaforce, P., *Battles with Panzers* (Sutton, 2003)
Dey, J. H., *Cairo to Berlin: The 3rd Regiment, Royal Horse Artillery 1939-1945* (Arcturus, 2005)
Durand A.T.M., & Hastings, R.H.W.S., *The London Rifle Brigade 1919 to 1950* (Gale & Polden, 1952)
Ellis, L.F., *Victory in the West: Volume I: The Battle of Normandy* (HMSO, 1962)
Erskine, D., *The Scots Guards 1919-1955* (Clowes, 1956)
Farran, R., *Winged Dagger* (Collins, 1948)
Fergusson, B., *The Black Watch & the King's Enemies* (Collins, 1950)
Fergusson, B., *The Wild Green Earth* (Collins, 1946)
Forty, G., *Desert Rats at War: North Africa, Italy, Northwest Europe* (Air Sea Media Services, 2014)
Green, P., *The March East: the Final Days of OFLAG IXA/H & A/Z* (Spellmount, 2012)
Hastings, R.H.W.S., *The Rifle Brigade in the Second World War 1939-1945* (Gale & Polden, 1950)
Holborn, A., *The 56th Infantry Brigade & D-Day* (Continuum, 2010)
Howard, M., & Sparrow, J., *The Coldstream Guards 1920–1946* (OUP, 1951)
Jephson, F.R., & Jephson, C., *The Day Rommel Was Stopped: The Battle of Ruweisat Ridge 2 July 1942* (Casemate, 2017)
Lee, D., *Beachhead Assault: The Story of the Royal Naval Commandos in World War II* (Greenhill, 2004)
Lowe, K., *Savage Continent: Europe in the Aftermath of World War II* (Viking, 2012)
MacArthur, B., *Surviving the Sword* (Time Warner, 2005)
Melville, M.I.L., *The Story of the Lovat Scouts 1900-1980* (Saint Andrew Press, 1981)
Mills, G., *The Annals of the King's Royal Rifle Corps,* Volume VII (Celer et Audax Club, 1979)
Montgomery, D., & Horne, A., *The Lonely Leader: Monty 1944-45* (Macmillan, 1994)
Morgan, H., *By the Seat of Your Pants: Basic Training of RAF Pilots in Rhodesia, Canada, South Africa & USA during WW2* (Newton, 1990)
Neville J.E.H., *War Chronicle of the Oxfordshire & Buckinghamshire Light Infantry,* Volume III: 1942-1944 (Gale & Polden, 1951)
Nicolson, N., & Forbes, P., *The Grenadier Guards in the War of 1939–1945,* Volume I (Gale & Polden, 1949)
Perret, B., *Tank Tracks to Rangoon* (Pen & Sword, 1978)
Philpot, O., *Stolen Journey* (Hodder & Stoughton, 1950)
Pike, H., *From the Front Line* (Pen & Sword, 2008)
Prittie, T.C.F., & Edwards, W.E., *Escape to Freedom* (Hutchinson, 1946)
Smith, M., *Voices in Flight: The Fleet Air Arm: Recollections from Formation to Cold War* (Pen & Sword, 2013)
Stewart, P.F., *History of the XII Royal Lancers (Prince Of Wales's)* (OUP, 1950)
Woods, R., *One Man's Desert: the Story of Captain Philip Gardner VC, MC* (William Kimber, 1986)

The following relatives kindly supplied documents or information for this project (with apologies to anyone whose name has been inadvertently omitted):
John and Joanna Baird (ref. Rose), Miranda Barlow, John Binns, Simon Boyd, Mary Butler (née Hirst), John Chatfeild-Roberts (ref. Brooke), Susanna Dodgson, Simon and Kate Duffin, Henrietta Fenton (née Mackrill), John Fortune, Sarah and Rupert Foster (ref.

Kennedy), Norman Fuggle (ref. Grant), Philippa Goddard (née Hirst), Johnnie Grant, Simon Herbert, Christine Hill, John Holtby, Mike Huggins, Josephine Jackson (ref. Dodgson), Nicholas Lewin, Tanya Lole (née Rigby), Brigid Lomax (née Metcalfe), Rory MacColl (ref. Rickman), Charlotte McArthur, Anthony McMurtrie (since deceased), Julian Metcalfe, Matthew Middleditch, Tom Murray, Richard Perkins (ref. Richardson), Hew Pike (ref. Tompson), Mark Pinney, Nigel Pringle, Lachlan Rattray, Haoli Rein (née Huggins), Rebecca Rickman Brecher, Harriet Roupell (née Middleditch), Sarah Russell (née Richardson), Mike Simpkin, Andrew Sinclair, John Somerville, Robin Somerville, Bart Stevens (ref. Kemp), Richard Walker, Melissa Wills (née Rigby), Belinda Wollen (née Rickman)

Index

Winchester Men & Dons

Weapons & Equipment

General

Places Mentioned in the Text